DISABILITY CIVIL RIGHTS LAW AND POLICY

CASES AND MATERIALS

Third Edition

■ ■ ■

by

Peter Blanck
University Professor
Chairman, Burton Blatt Institute
Syracuse University

Michael Waterstone
Associate Dean and Professor of Law
Loyola Law School, Los Angeles

William N. Myhill
Director of Legal Research & Writing
Burton Blatt Institute
Syracuse University

Charles D. Siegal
Partner
Munger, Tolles & Olson LLP

AMERICAN CASEBOOK SERIES®

WEST ACADEMIC PUBLISHING

Mat #41236052

American Casebook Series is a trademark registered in the U.S. Patent and Trademark Office.

© West, a Thomson business, 2005
© 2009 Thomson Reuters
© 2014 LEG, Inc. d/b/a West Academic
    444 Cedar Street, Suite 700
    St. Paul, MN 55101
    1-877-888-1330

West, West Academic Publishing, and West Academic are trademarks of West Publishing Corporation, used under license.

Printed in the United States of America

ISBN: 978–0–314–27976–7

Dedication

We dedicate this third edition of our casebook to our
late friend, colleague, and coauthor,
Charles "Chuck" Siegal. May his memory be a
blessing and constantly inspire us to make the world
a better place.

PB, MW, WM

Preface

Since this casebook was first published, there have been even more dramatic legal and policy developments, and strong academic and practical interest, in the area of American and international disability civil rights law. This third edition of this casebook presents a comprehensive examination of the development of disability rights law and policy in the United States, with additional commentary on international disability law. We have edited significantly from previous editions, resulting in a shorter and we hope more usable book.

The material in this casebook is placed in the context of disability civil rights law in general, and the law of the Americans with Disabilities Act (ADA) of 1990 in particular.

We begin the casebook in Part 1 with an examination of the basis of discrimination against people with disabilities, including the history of such discrimination and a review of studies that explore why people engage in this sort of discrimination. The casebook progresses through an examination of the federal laws that culminated in the passage of the ADA.

The definition of "disability" under the ADA and other laws, and the identification of those who have a covered disability are, to say the least, critical to any discussion of ADA law and policy. In Part 2, we explore the threshold question of how the ADA's definition of disability has been explained, interpreted, and amended through the ADA Amendments Act of 2008.

In Part 3, the casebook presents extensive coverage of ADA employment discrimination issues and case law (Title I of the Act). The analysis includes review of issues associated with pre-employment interviews, job qualifications, medical examinations, and the constellation of issues associated with reasonable accommodations. We provide an extensive review of the remedies available for the Title I claims and the procedures required to pursue them, including alternative dispute resolution.

We proceed in Part 4 to address the ADA's requirements applicable to governmental entities (Title II of the Act), including issues related to the integration of people with disabilities into communities. We discuss, among other topics, the issue of whether Congress validly abrogated the states' sovereign immunity under Title II. We highlight several pressing Title II issues, such as access to voting and transportation. We conclude with a discussion of Title II's remedial scheme and enforcement procedures.

We next turn in Part 5 to the law's requirements applicable to places of public accommodation under Title III of the statute. We review the scope of Title III coverage, prohibited conduct, effective communication, and the nature of reasonable modifications needed to achieve access to private businesses. We also address accessibility of buildings and other facilities. Finally, we address the remedies available under Title III.

Part 6 addresses discrimination in education, and specifically the operation of the Individuals with Disabilities Education Act (IDEA) – the law's principles, coverage, procedure and remedies.

Part 7 discusses discrimination in housing against people with disabilities, focusing primarily on the 1988 Amendments to the Fair Housing Act.

Part 8 gives more in depth treatment to an array of policy issues impacting the lives of people with disabilities. We examine the applicability of the ADA to employment, welfare, and health care policy – examining the ADA and the Workforce Investment Act, the Ticket to Work and Work Incentives Improvement Act, Medicaid and health insurance law, and genetic discrimination. We explore research seeking to understand the Act's real-world consequences. We also discuss the applicability of the ADA to technology law and policy, examining issues such as the relation of ADA accessibility requirements to the operation of private Internet sites, as well as the technology accessibility requirements of section 508 of the Rehabilitation Act. In this Part, we also examine the effect of federal and state tax policies on access for people with disabilities.

Finally, Part 9 looks beyond the United States to examine other countries' approaches to disability civil rights. We discuss how some states expand on the civil rights ideas at the heart of the ADA, while others adhere to a more paternalistic view and attempt to elicit a critical discussion of the two approaches. We focus on the United Nations' 2008 Convention on the Rights of Persons with Disabilities, perhaps the most significant recent international initiative.

We have tried throughout to intersperse questions among the cases that will provoke thought. None of us believes a casebook's success is a function of how well it hides the ball. Still, the bodies of law we address are evolving rapidly. Every week has brought us new and often significant cases. Readers should bear in mind the evolving nature of the law when drawing on our analysis and the cases we cite. Our questions are designed to make the reader think more deeply about both law and policy.

We have tried to reflect our respective perspectives as law teachers and lawyers, social science researchers, non-profit legal advocates and policymakers, and practitioners working in the area of disability civil rights and labor law. The casebook has benefited greatly from input from many colleagues, leaders in the disability advocacy community, and others. As always, any errors are ours.

P. B.

M. W.

W. M.

Acknowledgments

We open the third edition of our casebook with a heavy heart, as we mourn the loss of our dear friend and coauthor Charles "Chuck" Siegal. Chuck influenced all of our lives, and his imprint is and will continue to be on every page of this book. A compilation of Chuck's accomplishments can be found at http://www.mto.com/lawyers/Charles-D-Siegal. Although too short, his was a life well lived, both personally and professionally.

Chuck's firm, Munger, Tolles, & Olson, was incredibly generous in continuing to support this project even after Chuck's passing. We give special thanks to Ron Olson and Sandra Seville-Jones. Puneet Sandhu offered valuable advice and assistance. And as always, we again single out Brenda Shurtleff, who imposed word-processing order on our chaos.

Eve Hill, now the Deputy Assistant Attorney General for the Civil Rights Division of the U.S. Department of Justice, contributed immeasurably to the first two editions of this book. We are proud of the work she is now doing enforcing the civil rights of people with disabilities.

This project could not have been accomplished without the generous contributions of many individuals. Our editor, Louis Higgins, had the foresight and perseverance to support our work as West Publishing's first major treatment of disability civil rights law. Many of our colleagues read various drafts of the casebook and provided most helpful feedback.

Throughout the project, many members of the staffs at the Burton Blatt Institute at Syracuse University (BBI), Loyola Law School, and Munger, Tolles & Olson, LLP provided outstanding editorial and technical assistance. BBI Senior Vice President Janet Lord helped immensely on the international and comparative law section. Other helpful BBI staff in Syracuse included Kelly Bunch, Dana Mele, Robert Borrelle, Ryan Elliott, Stephanie Woodward, Alessandra Baldini, Jenna Furman, Kate Battoe, Susan Schneider, Douglas Curwin, Dani Morrison, and Josh Tumen. In Los Angeles, Suhagey Sandoval led us through the Brazilian law and made sure our international citations were current. Throughout various editions, extensive help in organizing, cite checking and proof reading the materials was provided by David Chon, Jeff Mitchell, Dave Splaingard, Amy Jenkins, Jennifer Finch, Brandi Tolbert, Hyde Carby, Ann Wilichowski, Daniel Kresowik, Molly Sutter, Haven Claytor, Todd Schmidt, and Terry Sanchez.

The work on the casebook was funded in part by grants to Peter Blanck from the U.S. Department of Education, National Institute on Disability and Rehabilitation Research (NIDRR); see http://bbi.syr.edu for project details. Michael Waterstone's work on this casebook was supported in part by Loyola Law School.

The views herein, of course, reflect only those of the authors and not any funding agency, university, law school or law firm.

Summary of Contents

                                                                   Page
Dedication v
Preface... vii
Acknowledgments.. xi
Summary of Contents.. xiii
Table of Contents.. xix
Table of Cases xxx
Table of Other Authorities lxix

**Part 1   HISTORICAL AND CONCEPTUAL
               FOUNDATIONS** 1
Chapter 1   INTRODUCTION..1
    § 1.1   Overview 1
    § 1.2   American Conceptions Of Discrimination On The
               Basis Of Disability..2
    § 1.3   The Limits Of Constitutional Protection 8
    § 1.4   ADA Precursors 24
Chapter 2   THE ADA'S HISTORY AND PHILOSOPHY.................43
    § 2.1   A Brief Guide To The ADA 43
    § 2.2   ADA Background And Fundamentals....................45
    § 2.3   The History, Theory And Economics Of The
               Accommodation Principle.................................55
Part 2   DEFINITIONAL ISSUES 69

Chapter 3   DISABILITY..69
    § 3.1   Overview 69
    § 3.2   Actual Disability...71
    § 3.3   Record Of A Disability.....................................99
    § 3.4   Regarded As Having A Disability.......................100
Chapter 4   OTHER PROTECTIONS 110
    § 4.1   Association 110
    § 4.2   Retaliation..111
    § 4.3   Harassment...117
Chapter 5   QUALIFIED 119
    § 5.1   Prerequisites 119
    § 5.2   Essential Requirements 125
    § 5.3   Estoppel..129

**Part 3   EMPLOYMENT DISCRIMINATION: ADA
               TITLE I** 137
Chapter 6   OBJECTS OF TITLE I...138
    § 6.1   Overview 138
    § 6.2   Covered Entities 139
    § 6.3   Hiring, Discipline And Benefits.........................190

Summary of Contents

		Page
Chapter 7	**EXAMINATIONS AND INQUIRIES**	**194**
§ 7.1	Permissible Scope Of Inquiries And Examinations	195
§ 7.2	Confidentiality Of Information	205
§ 7.3	Rights Of People Without Disabilities To Bring Inquiry/Examination Claims – Standing	206
Chapter 8	**REASONABLE ACCOMMODATION**	**209**
§ 8.1	Overview And Illustrations	209
§ 8.2	The Process	243
§ 8.3	Undue Hardship	247
§ 8.4	Burdens Of Production And Proof	250
Chapter 9	**TITLE I DEFENSES BASED ON QUALIFICATIONS STANDARDS**	**260**
§ 9.1	Direct Threat Defense To Others And To Self	261
Chapter 10	**TITLE I ENFORCEMENT AND REMEDIES**	**280**
§ 10.1	Introduction To Remedies	280
§ 10.2	Title I Remedial Procedure	281
§ 10.3	Title I Remedies	298
§ 10.4	Statute Of Limitations	308
§ 10.5	Attorneys' Fees	308
§ 10.6	A Note On The Taxability Of Attorneys' Fee Awards	321
Chapter 11	**ALTERNATIVE DISPUTE RESOLUTION**	**324**
§ 11.1	Mediation Of Disability Rights Disputes	324
§ 11.2	Arbitration Of Disability Rights Disputes	325
Part 4	**ACCESS TO PUBLIC SERVICES: ADA TITLE II**	**331**
Chapter 12	**STATUTORY BACKGROUND**	**331**
§ 12.1	Statutory And Regulatory Scheme	332
§ 12.2	Constitutionality	334
Chapter 13	**COVERAGE**	**359**
§ 13.1	Introduction	359
§ 13.2	Elements Of Title II Claim	370
§ 13.3	"Qualified Person With A Disability"	370
§ 13.4	Not Excluding, Denying, Or Discriminating – Affirmative Responsibilities Of Public Entities	376
§ 13.5	By Reason Of Disability – Intentional Discrimination Versus Disparate Impact	432
Chapter 14	**Remedies And Enforcement**	**437**
§ 14.1	Introduction	437
§ 14.2	Procedure	438
§ 14.3	Remedies	441

Summary of Contents

		Page
Part 5	**ACCESS TO PUBLIC ACCOMMODATIONS: ADA TITLE III**..	**449**
Chapter 15	**COVERED ENTITIES**..	**449**
§ 15.1	Places Of Public Accommodation And Commercial Facilities..	450
§ 15.2	Examinations And Courses..................................	487
§ 15.3	Exempt Entities...	489
§ 15.4	Relationship To Title II..	489
§ 15.5	Geographic Limits..	490
Chapter 16	**PROHIBITED CONDUCT**...	**509**
§ 16.1	General..	509
§ 16.2	Reasonable Modifications	510
§ 16.3	Effective Communication.....................................	536
§ 16.4	Architectural Barriers..	550
§ 16.5	The Complexity Of Compliance	597
Chapter 17	**ENFORCEMENT AND REMEDIES**............................	**600**
§ 17.1	Procedures...	601
§ 17.2	Remedies	604
Part 6	**SPECIAL EDUCATION: INDIVIDUALS WITH DISABILITIES EDUCATION ACT**..............................	**655**
Chapter 18	**BACKGROUND**..	**655**
§ 18.1	Precursors To IDEA	655
§ 18.2	General Statutory Requirements Of IDEA..........	657
Chapter 19	**PERSONS PROTECTED**...	**661**
§ 19.1	General..	661
§ 19.2	Infants And Toddlers With Disability..................	662
§ 19.3	Specific Learning Disability.................................	662
§ 19.4	Other Health Impairment.....................................	663
§ 19.5	Eligibility, Child Find, And Re-Evaluations.........	663
Chapter 20	**FREE APPROPRIATE PUBLIC EDUCATION**	**668**
§ 20.1	FAPE Standard...	669
§ 20.2	FAPE Applications...	686
Chapter 21	**LEAST RESTRICTIVE ENVIRONMENT**	**689**
Chapter 22	**RELATED SERVICES**	**699**
§ 22.1	Health Services..	699
§ 22.2	Speech / Language Services..................................	705
§ 22.3	Extended School Year (ESY) Services..................	705
Chapter 23	**SPECIAL SITUATIONS**	**708**
§ 23.1	Discipline, Behavior And Restraint......................	708
§ 23.2	Residential Placement, Private School Placement, And Juvenile Justice Issues...................................	718
§ 23.3	Distance Learning	721

Summary of Contents

		Page
Chapter 24	**PROCEDURAL SAFEGUARDS, EXHAUSTION AND REMEDIES**	**724**
§ 24.1	Special Education Process	724
§ 24.2	Exhaustion Of Administrative Remedies	738
§ 24.3	Civil Action	739
§ 24.4	Pro Se Representation In Federal Court	740
§ 24.5	Remedies	752
Part 7	**DISCRIMINATION IN HOUSING**	**769**
Chapter 25	**FAIR HOUSING ACT**	**769**
§ 25.1	Overview	769
Chapter 26	**COVERAGE**	**771**
§ 26.1	Single-Family House And Living Quarters Exemption	771
§ 26.2	Maximum Occupancy Exemptions	779
Chapter 27	**DISCRIMINATION**	**783**
§ 27.1	Failure To Allow Reasonable Modifications To Premises Or To Make Reasonable Accommodations To Rules, Policies, Practices, Or Services	783
§ 27.2	Proving Discrimination	820
§ 27.3	Design And Construction Of Dwellings	822
Chapter 28	**ENFORCEMENT AND REMEDIES**	**834**
Part 8	**RELATED POLICY ISSUES: EMPLOYMENT, WELFARE, HEALTH CARE, TECHNOLOGY AND TAX**	**835**
Chapter 29	**INTRODUCTION**	**836**
§ 29.1	Overview	836
Chapter 30	**DISABILITY AND EMPLOYMENT POLICY**	**838**
§ 30.1	Workforce Investment Act (WIA)	839
§ 30.2	Ticket To Work And Work Incentives Improvement Act (TWWIIA)	841
Chapter 31	**DISABILITY AND WELFARE POLICY**	**847**
§ 31.1	Social Security Disability Insurance (SSDI)	847
§ 31.2	Temporary Assistance For Needy Families (TANF) Programs	848
Chapter 32	**DISABILITY AND HEALTH CARE POLICY**	**858**
§ 32.1	Medicare And Medicaid	859
§ 32.2	Patient Protection And Affordable Care Act (PPACA)	863
§ 32.3	Genetic Discrimination	867
Chapter 33	**DISABILITY AND THE INTERNET**	**874**
§ 33.1	Overview	874
§ 33.2	Internet Accessibility And Access To Data	875
§ 33.3	Applications Of The ADA: Title II	877
§ 33.4	Applications Of The ADA: Title III	885

Summary of Contents

		Page
§ 33.5	Applications Of Section 504 Of The Rehabilitation Act	905
§ 33.6	Applications Of Section 508 Of The Rehabilitation Act	906
§ 33.7	Twenty-First Century Communications And Video Accessibility Act Of 2010	909
§ 33.8	Other Policy Issues	911
§ 33.9	Commentary / Web Equality	913
Chapter 34	**DISABILITY AND TAX POLICY**	**917**
§ 34.1	Overview: Tax Policy And Persons With Disabilities	917
§ 34.2	Tax Policies And Economic Security For Americans With Disabilities	917
§ 34.3	Tax Policies And The ADA	920
Part 9	**INTRODUCTION TO COMPARATIVE AND INTERNATIONAL DISABILITY RIGHTS LAW**	**933**
Chapter 35	**OVERVIEW**	**933**
§ 35.1	Statistics On People With Disabilities	934
§ 35.2	Legal Approaches Toward Disability Issues	938
Chapter 36	**OTHER STATES' APPROACHES TO DISABILITY RIGHTS**	**940**
§ 36.1	Welfare/Medical Model Versus Rights-Based Social Model	940
§ 36.2	States Following A Rights Model	945
§ 36.3	States Following A Welfare/Medical Model: France	953
Chapter 37	**INTERNATIONAL HUMAN RIGHTS LAW BASICS**	**960**
Chapter 38	**UNITED NATIONS**	**962**
§ 38.1	United Nations Initiatives Prior To 2001	962
§ 38.2	Convention On The Rights Of Persons With Disabilities	968

Table of Contents

                                                                    Page
Dedication v
Preface..vii
Acknowledgments...xi
Summary of Contents.. xiii
Table of Contents...xix
Table of Cases xxx
Table of Other Authorities lxix

Part 1   HISTORICAL AND CONCEPTUAL
              FOUNDATIONS 1
Chapter 1   INTRODUCTION...1
    § 1.1   Overview 1
    § 1.2   American Conceptions Of Discrimination On The
              Basis Of Disability..2
              A. Evolution Of Models For Societal Treatment Of
                  Disability 3
              B. A Note On The Evolution Of Ideas About
                  Disability In America After The Civil War And
                  Their Relevance Today 4
              C. The Modern Disability Rights Model............5
    § 1.3   The Limits Of Constitutional Protection 8
    § 1.4   ADA Precursors 24
              A. Vocational Rehabilitation And Benefits 24
              B. Early Disability Civil Rights Statutes (1968-88) 25
                  1. Architectural Barriers Act of 1968 26
                  2. Rehabilitation Act of 1973 26
                  3. Individuals With Disabilities Education Act
                      (Education For All Handicapped Children
                      Act of 1975) 26
                  4. Voting Accessibility For The Elderly And
                      Handicapped Act of 1984 27
                  5. Air Carrier Access Act of 1986..............28
                  6. Fair Housing Amendments Act of 1988................28
              C. Interpretation Of The Rehabilitation Act.....................30
Chapter 2   THE ADA'S HISTORY AND PHILOSOPHY.................43
    § 2.1   A Brief Guide To The ADA 43
    § 2.2   ADA Background And Fundamentals...................45
              A. The Story Of The Passage Of The ADA......................45
              B. Key Legislative Trade-Offs............................49
              C. Constitutional Basis.....................................52
              D. Role Of Federal Agencies................................52
                  1. Regulations 52
                  2. Enforcement...52

Table of Contents

		Page
§ 2.3	The History, Theory And Economics Of The Accommodation Principle	55
	A. The Evolution And Legislative History Of The Reasonable Accommodation Requirement	56
	B. Theory And Economics Of The Reasonable Accommodation Requirement	64
Part 2	**DEFINITIONAL ISSUES**	**69**
Chapter 3	**DISABILITY**	**69**
§ 3.1	Overview	69
§ 3.2	Actual Disability	71
	A. Physical Or Mental Impairment	71
	B. Substantially Limits	72
	1. Individualized inquiry	82
	2. Mitigation	82
	3. Substantiality	85
	C. Major Life Activity	87
§ 3.3	Record Of A Disability	99
§ 3.4	Regarded As Having A Disability	100
Chapter 4	**OTHER PROTECTIONS**	**110**
§ 4.1	Association	110
§ 4.2	Retaliation	111
§ 4.3	Harassment	117
Chapter 5	**QUALIFIED**	**119**
§ 5.1	Prerequisites	119
§ 5.2	Essential Requirements	125
§ 5.3	Estoppel	129
Part 3	**EMPLOYMENT DISCRIMINATION: ADA TITLE I**	**137**
Chapter 6	**OBJECTS OF TITLE I**	**138**
§ 6.1	Overview	138
§ 6.2	Covered Entities	139
	A. Definition Of Employer	139
	B. Definition Of Employee	140
	C. Jurisdictional Versus Merits Analysis Of Covered Entity	147
	D. States As Employers	148
	E. Title I Covered Employers: Illustrations	168
	1. Temporary employment agencies and staffing firms	168
	2. Single and multiple employers	169
	3. Extraterritorial application of Title I	170
	4. Religious entities as employers	171

Table of Contents

Page

5. Employers under Section 504 of the Rehabilitation Act.............................184
6. Indirect employment relationships 185
7. Supervisors and other employees.........................187
8. Labor organizations...188
9. Federal employers and contractors 189

§ 6.3 Hiring, Discipline And Benefits...................................190
A. Hiring...190
B. Discipline 191
C. Benefits And Privileges Of Employment.....................191

Chapter 7 EXAMINATIONS AND INQUIRIES.............. 194
§ 7.1 Permissible Scope Of Inquiries And Examinations 195
A. Pre-Employment 195
1. No known disability or requested accommodation 195
2. Known disability or requested accommodation 198
B. Post-Conditional Offer 199
1. What constitutes a "job offer"?.............................199
2. Post-offer medical examinations and inquiries 200
C. Course Of Employment...201
D. Return To Work...203
§ 7.2 Confidentiality Of Information...205
§ 7.3 Rights Of People Without Disabilities To Bring
Inquiry/Examination Claims – Standing.........................206

Chapter 8 REASONABLE ACCOMMODATION.......................... 209
§ 8.1 Overview And Illustrations..209
A. Statutory Definitions 209
B. EEOC Regulations 210
C. Failure To Accommodate Claim: Summary 211
D. Accommodation Illustrations 212
1. Workplace attendance, schedule modifications..213
2. Home work 214
3. Job reassignment – generally 215
4. Job reassignment – collective bargaining or seniority agreement..216
5. Company policies, discipline and termination......226
6. Job rotation 233
7. "Light duty" positions...234
8. Equipment modifications/computer technology/accessible materials..........................234

Table of Contents

9. Provision of services such as interpreters and job coaches 235

10. Leave of absence 243

§ 8.2 The Process 243
A. The Request 243
B. Interactive Process 245
C. Accommodation For "Regarded As" Disability 246

§ 8.3 Undue Hardship 247
A. Statutory Definition 248
B. EEOC Regulations 249

§ 8.4 Burdens Of Production And Proof 250
A. Reasonable Accommodation And Undue Hardship 250
B. Disparate Treatment – Application Of McDonnell Douglas Corp. And Price Waterhouse 254
C. Disparate Impact – ADA Title I Class Actions 257

Chapter 9 TITLE I DEFENSES BASED ON QUALIFICATIONS STANDARDS.............................. 260
§ 9.1 Direct Threat Defense To Others And To Self 261

Chapter 10 TITLE I ENFORCEMENT AND REMEDIES............. 280
§ 10.1 Introduction To Remedies 280
§ 10.2 Title I Remedial Procedure 281
A. Administrative Exhaustion 281
B. Administrative Limitations Periods - Accrual 283
1. Violations outside the limitations period 285
2. Equitable grounds for relief from a delayed filing 288
C. Statute Of Limitations 288
D. Role Of The EEOC 289
1. EEOC's authority 289
2. EEOC procedures – administrative exhaustion 296
§ 10.3 Title I Remedies...298
A. Equitable Remedies 299
1. Injunctive relief – reinstatement.........................299
2. Back pay; front pay...300
a. Back pay 300
b. Front pay 300
c. Limitations on back and front pay – mitigation and collateral sources...................301
d. Limitations on back and front pay – collateral payments...................................302
B. Compensatory Damages 303
C. Punitive Damages 307

Table of Contents

		Page
§ 10.4	Statute Of Limitations	308
§ 10.5	Attorneys' Fees	308
	A. Prevailing Party	309
	B. Reasonableness Of Fees	312
§ 10.6	A Note On The Taxability Of Attorneys' Fee Awards	321

Chapter 11 ALTERNATIVE DISPUTE RESOLUTION ... 324
§ 11.1	Mediation Of Disability Rights Disputes	324
§ 11.2	Arbitration Of Disability Rights Disputes	325
	A. Arbitrability Of ADA Disputes	325
	B. Enforceability Of The Arbitration Agreement: Procedural And Substantive Unconscionability	328

Part 4 ACCESS TO PUBLIC SERVICES: ADA TITLE II ... 331

Chapter 12 STATUTORY BACKGROUND ... 331
§ 12.1	Statutory And Regulatory Scheme	332
§ 12.2	Constitutionality	334
	A. Did Congress Validly Abrogate The States' Sovereign Immunity?	334
	B. Other Constitutional Issues.	355

Chapter 13 COVERAGE ... 359
§ 13.1	Introduction	359
	A. "Public Entity"	359
	B. Service, Program, Or Activity	362
	1. The general rule – broad construction	362
	2. Employment under Title II	369
§ 13.2	Elements Of Title II Claim	370
§ 13.3	"Qualified Person With A Disability"	370
§ 13.4	Not Excluding, Denying, Or Discriminating – Affirmative Responsibilities Of Public Entities	376
	A. Reasonable Modifications To Policies, Practices, And Procedures	378
	B. Opportunity For Equal Benefit	389
	C. Integration	395
	D. Facilities Modification	406
	1. Existing facilities	407
	2. New or modified facilities	412
	E. Effective Communication	418
	F. Transportation	426
	1. Pre-ADA statutes and regulations	427
	2. ADA transportation provisions	427
	a. Subpart I – trains, cabs, buses, and other paratransit	427
	i. Fixed route systems	428

Table of Contents

		Page
ii.	Demand responsive systems	429
iii.	Transportation facilities	430
b.	Subpart II – intercity and commuter rail	430

§ 13.5 **By Reason Of Disability – Intentional Discrimination Versus Disparate Impact** **432**

Chapter 14 REMEDIES AND ENFORCEMENT **437**
§ 14.1 Introduction 437
§ 14.2 Procedure 438
§ 14.3 Remedies 441
   A. Private Rights Of Action...............................441
   B. Available Types Of Relief 442
   C. Attorneys' Fees And Statute Of Limitations..............447

Part 5 **ACCESS TO PUBLIC ACCOMMODATIONS: ADA TITLE III** **449**
Chapter 15 COVERED ENTITIES **449**
§ 15.1 Places Of Public Accommodation And Commercial Facilities 450
   A. General 450
   B. Responsible Parties..................................452
   C. Covered Areas 459
   D. Physical Structures..................................461
§ 15.2 Examinations And Courses............................487
§ 15.3 Exempt Entities.....................................489
§ 15.4 Relationship To Title II 489
§ 15.5 Geographic Limits 490
Chapter 16 PROHIBITED CONDUCT **509**
§ 16.1 General...509
§ 16.2 Reasonable Modifications 510
   A. Burdens Of Proof....................................511
   B. Reasonableness/Fundamental Alteration 519
§ 16.3 Effective Communication............................536
   A. General 536
   B. Distance Education 549
§ 16.4 Architectural Barriers.............................550
   A. Existing Facilities 551
      1. Barrier removal 551
   B. Alterations 580
      1. Path of travel 582
      2. Technically infeasible 582
   C. New Construction...................................583
      1. ADAAG 583
§ 16.5 The Complexity Of Compliance 597

Table of Contents

Page

Chapter 17 ENFORCEMENT AND REMEDIES.......................... **600**
§ 17.1 Procedures..601
    A. Notice 601
    B. Statute Of Limitations...................................603
    C. Alternative Dispute Resolution....................603
§ 17.2 Remedies 604
    A. Injunctive Relief 604
        1. Consequences of lack of damages 604
        2. Standing...605
        3. Examples of injunctive relief 613
    B. Enforcement By The Attorney General –
       Compensatory Damages And Civil Penalties.............615
    C. Attorneys' Fees..620
        1. Prevailing Party 621
        2. Reasonableness Of Fees 644

**Part 6 SPECIAL EDUCATION: INDIVIDUALS WITH
DISABILITIES EDUCATION ACT**.............................. **655**
Chapter 18 BACKGROUND **655**
§ 18.1 Precursors To IDEA 655
§ 18.2 General Statutory Requirements Of IDEA......................657
Chapter 19 PERSONS PROTECTED.............................. **661**
§ 19.1 General..661
§ 19.2 Infants And Toddlers With Disability.......................662
§ 19.3 Specific Learning Disability................................662
§ 19.4 Other Health Impairment....................................663
§ 19.5 Eligibility, Child Find, And Re-Evaluations...................663
Chapter 20 FREE APPROPRIATE PUBLIC EDUCATION **668**
§ 20.1 FAPE Standard..669
§ 20.2 FAPE Applications 686
Chapter 21 LEAST RESTRICTIVE ENVIRONMENT **689**
Chapter 22 RELATED SERVICES **699**
§ 22.1 Health Services...699
§ 22.2 Speech / Language Services 705
§ 22.3 Extended School Year (ESY) Services...........................705
Chapter 23 SPECIAL SITUATIONS **708**
§ 23.1 Discipline, Behavior And Restraint..............................708
§ 23.2 Residential Placement, Private School Placement,
       And Juvenile Justice Issues.................................718
§ 23.3 Distance Learning 721
**Chapter 24 PROCEDURAL SAFEGUARDS, EXHAUSTION
AND REMEDIES**.. **724**
§ 24.1 Special Education Process 724
§ 24.2 Exhaustion Of Administrative Remedies 738

Table of Contents

		Page
§ 24.3	Civil Action	739
§ 24.4	Pro Se Representation In Federal Court	740
§ 24.5	Remedies	752

Part 7 Discrimination In Housing — **769**
Chapter 25 FAIR HOUSING ACT — **769**
| § 25.1 | Overview | 769 |

Chapter 26 COVERAGE — **771**
| § 26.1 | Single-Family House And Living Quarters Exemption | 771 |
| § 26.2 | Maximum Occupancy Exemptions | 779 |

Chapter 27 DISCRIMINATION — **783**
§ 27.1	Failure To Allow Reasonable Modifications To Premises Or To Make Reasonable Accommodations To Rules, Policies, Practices, Or Services	783
§ 27.2	Proving Discrimination	820
§ 27.3	Design And Construction Of Dwellings	822

Chapter 28 ENFORCEMENT AND REMEDIES — **834**

Part 8 Related Policy Issues: Employment, Welfare, Health Care, Technology And Tax — **835**
Chapter 29 INTRODUCTION — **836**
| § 29.1 | Overview | 836 |

Chapter 30 DISABILITY AND EMPLOYMENT POLICY — **838**
§ 30.1	Workforce Investment Act (WIA)	839
	A. Overview	839
	B. Applicability Of The ADA To WIA	840
§ 30.2	Ticket To Work And Work Incentives Improvement Act (TWWIIA)	841
	A. Overview	841
	B. Applicability Of The ADA To TWWIIA's Employment Networks (ENs)	843

Chapter 31 DISABILITY AND WELFARE POLICY — **847**
§ 31.1	Social Security Disability Insurance (SSDI)	847
	A. Overview	847
	B. Interaction Of The ADA And SSDI	847
§ 31.2	Temporary Assistance For Needy Families (TANF) Programs	848
	A. Overview	848
	B. Applicability Of The ADA To TANF	849

Chapter 32 DISABILITY AND HEALTH CARE POLICY — **858**
§ 32.1	Medicare And Medicaid	859
	A. Overview	859
	B. Compliance And Litigation	862
§ 32.2	Patient Protection And Affordable Care Act (PPACA)	863

Table of Contents

			Page
	A.	Provisions In Effect	863
	B.	Provisions Taking Effect 2013-14	865
§ 32.3		Genetic Discrimination	867
	A.	Genetic Information Nondiscrimination Act (GINA)	867
	B.	Asymptomatic Genetic Traits Under The ADA	869

Chapter 33 DISABILITY AND THE INTERNET   874

§ 33.1		Overview	874
§ 33.2		Internet Accessibility And Access To Data	875
§ 33.3		Applications Of The ADA: Title II	877
§ 33.4		Applications Of The ADA: Title III	885
	A.	The "Place" Requirement	885
	B.	Effective Communication	902
	C.	First Amendment Issues	904
§ 33.5		Applications Of Section 504 Of The Rehabilitation Act	905
§ 33.6		Applications Of Section 508 Of The Rehabilitation Act	906
§ 33.7		Twenty-First Century Communications And Video Accessibility Act Of 2010	909
§ 33.8		Other Policy Issues	911
§ 33.9		Commentary / Web Equality	913

Chapter 34 DISABILITY AND TAX POLICY 917

§ 34.1		Overview: Tax Policy And Persons With Disabilities	917
§ 34.2		Tax Policies And Economic Security For Americans With Disabilities	917
§ 34.3		Tax Policies And The ADA	920
	A.	Disabled Access Credit	920
	B.	Tax Deduction For Removal Of Architectural And Transportation Barriers	930
	C.	Work Opportunity Credit	931

Part 9   INTRODUCTION TO COMPARATIVE AND INTERNATIONAL DISABILITY RIGHTS LAW 933

Chapter 35 OVERVIEW 933

§ 35.1		Statistics On People With Disabilities	934
§ 35.2		Legal Approaches Toward Disability Issues	938

Chapter 36 OTHER STATES' APPROACHES TO DISABILITY RIGHTS.. 940

§ 36.1		Welfare/Medical Model Versus Rights-Based Social Model	940
§ 36.2		States Following A Rights Model	945
	A.	Canada	945
	B.	South Africa	949

Table of Contents

		Page
§ 36.3	States Following A Welfare/Medical Model: France	953
Chapter 37	**INTERNATIONAL HUMAN RIGHTS LAW BASICS**	**960**
Chapter 38	**UNITED NATIONS**	**962**
§ 38.1	United Nations Initiatives Prior To 2001	962
§ 38.2	Convention On The Rights Of Persons With Disabilities	968
	A. Background	968
	B. The Convention	969
	C. Impact	977

Table of Cases

A

A.E. v. Indep. Sch. Dist. No. 25, 936 F.2d 472 (10th Cir. 1991)—**666**

A.R. v. Kogan, 964 F.Supp. 269 (N.D. Ill. 1997)—**604**

A.W. v. Jersey City Pub. Sch., 486 F.3d 791 (3d Cir. 2007)—**754**

A.W. v. Jersey City Pub. Schs., 341 F.3d 234 (3d Cir. 2003)—**358**

A.W. v. Nw. R-1 Sch. Dist., 813 F.2d 158 (8th Cir. 1987)—**695**

Abbott v. Bragdon, 163 F.3d 87 (1st Cir. 1998)—**98**

Ability Ctr. of Greater Toledo v. City of Sandusky, 385 F.3d 901 (6th Cir. 2004)—**368, 377**

Access 4 All, Inc. v. Ramos-Mejia, Inc., No. 02-60733-Civ-Dimitrouleas (S.D. Fla. Sept. 22, 2003)—**648**

Access Now, Inc. v. Claire's Stores, Inc., No. 00-14017-CIV, 2002 WL 1162422 (S.D. Fla. May 7, 2002)—**485**

Access Now, Inc. v. S. Fla. Stadium Corp., 161 F.Supp.2d 1357 (S.D. Fla. 2001)—**602, 611**

Access Now, Inc. v. Sw. Airlines Co., 385 F.3d 1324 (11th Cir. 2004)—**486, 645, 893**

Access Now, Inc. v. Sw. Airlines, Co., 227 F.Supp.2d 1312 (S.D. Fla. 2002)—**478-486, 893**

ACLU of Georgia v. Barnes, 168 F.3d 423 (11th Cir. 1999)—**646**

Adkins v. Briggs & Stratton Corp., 159 F.3d 306 (7th Cir. 1998)—**310-311**

Agranoff v. Law Sch. Admission Council, 97 F.Supp.2d 86 (D. Mass. 1999)—**488**

Aikins v. St. Helena Hosp., 843 F.Supp. 1329 (N.D. Cal. 1994)—**459, 537-546**

Aka v. Wash. Hosp. Ctr., 156 F.3d 1284 (D.C. Cir. 1998)—**226**

Alaska Dep't of Envtl Conservation v. EPA, 540 U.S. 461 (2004)—**730, 733**

Albertson's, Inc. v. Kirkingburg, 527 U.S. 555 (1999)—**86, 119-124, 260**

Alcazar v. Corp. of Catholic Archbishop of Seattle, 627 F.3d 1288 (2010)—**183**

Alden v. Maine, 527 U.S. 706 (1999)—**158**

Alexander v. Choate, 469 U.S. 287 (1985)—**42, 59, 103, 128, 383, 391-392, 394, 433-434, 795, 880**

Alexander v. Gardner-Denver Co., 415 U.S. 36 (1974)—**326**

Alexander v. Internal Revenue Serv., 72 F.3d 938 (1st Cir. 1995)—**321, 323**

Alexander v. Sandoval, 532 U.S. 275 (2001)—**441, 443**

Alford v. City of Cannon Beach, No. CV-00-303-HU, 2002 WL 31439173 (D. Or. Jan. 15, 2002)—**579-580**

Allen v. A.G. Thomas, 161 F.3d 667 (11th Cir. 1998)—**483**

Allen v. Wright, 468 U.S. 737 (1984)—**399**

Alvarez v. Fountainhead, Inc., 55 F.Supp.2d 1048 (N.D. Cal. 1999)—**614**

Alvarez v. N.Y.C. Health & Hosps. Corp., No. 99 Civ. 3215(RCC), 2002 WL 1585637 (S.D.N.Y. July 17, 2002)—**547**

Table of Cases

Alyeska Pipeline Serv. Co. v.
Wilderness Soc'y, 421 U.S. 240
(1975)—**318, 622, 627, 635**

Am. Ass'n of People with
Disabilities v. Harris, 647 F.3d
1093 (11th Cir. 2011)—**386, 418,
58**1

Am. Ass'n of People with
Disabilities v. Shelley, 324
F.Supp.2d 1120 (C.D. Cal.
2004)—**386**

Am. Bus Ass'n v. Slater, 231 F.3d 1
(D.C. Cir. 2000)—**604**

Am. Disability Ass'n v. Chmielarz,
289 F.3d 1315 (11th Cir. 2002)—
641

Am. Fed. of State, Cnty. & Mun.
Employees v. Cnty. of Nassau,
96 F.3d 644 (2d Cir. 1996)—**320**

Amadio v. Ford Motor Co., 238
F.3d 919 (7th Cir. 2001)—**213,
245**

Ams. Disabled for Accessible Pub.
Transp. v. Skinner, 881 F.2d
1184 (3d Cir. 1989)—**427, 431**

Andersen v. District of Columbia,
877 F.2d 1018 (D.C. Cir. 1989)—
725

Anderson v. City of Bessemer, 470
U.S. 564 (1985)—**794**

Anderson v. Little League
Baseball, Inc., 794 F.Supp. 342
(D. Ariz. 1992)—**274**

Anderson v. Ross Stores, Inc., No.
C 99-4056 CRB, 2000 WL
1585269 (N.D. Cal. Oct. 10,
2000)—**511**

Arbaugh v. Y&H Corp., 546 U.S.
500 (2006)—**148**

Argen v. N.Y. State Bd. of Law
Exam'rs, 860 F.Supp. 84
(W.D.N.Y. 1994)—**488**

Argenyi v. Creighton Univ., 703
F.3d 441 (8th Cir. 2013)—**488-
489**

Arizona v. Harkins Amusement
Enters., Inc., 603 F.3d 666 (9th
Cir. 2010)—**548**

Arline v. Sch. Bd. of Nassau Cnty.,
692 F.Supp. 1286 (M.D. Fla.
1988)—**108**

Arlington Cent. Sch. Dist. Bd. of
Educ. v. Murphy, 548 U.S. 291
(2006)—**748, 755-768**

Arlington Cent. Sch. Dist. v.
Murphy, 402 F.3d 332 (2d Cir.
2005), 74 U.S.L.W. 3379 (U.S.
Jan. 6, 2006) (No. 05-18)—**755**

Armendariz v. Found. Psychcare
Servs., Inc., 24 Cal.4th 83
(2000)—**325, 329**

Armstrong v. Schwarzenegger, 622
F.3d 1058 (9th Cir. 2010)—**361**

Armstrong v. Turner Indus., Ltd.,
141 F.3d 554 (5th Cir. 1998)—
207, 234

Armstrong v. Turner Indus., Ltd.,
950 F.Supp. 162 (M.D. La.
1996)—**207-208**

Armstrong v. Wilson, 124 F.3d
1019 (9th Cir. 1997)—**356**

Arnold v. City of Appleton, Wis., 97
F.Supp.2d 937 (E.D. Wis.
2000)—**86**

Arnold v. United Parcel Serv., Inc.,
136 F.3d 854 (1st Cir. 1998)—
368

Ass'n for Disabled Ams. v. North
Beach Hotel, Inc., 97-133-Civ-
Highsmith (S.D. Fla. June 21,
1998)—**651**

Ass'n for Disabled Ams., Inc. v.
City of Orlando, 153 F.Supp.2d
1310 (M.D. Fla. 2001)—**406**

Table of Cases

Ass'n for Disabled Ams., Inc. v. Concorde Gaming Corp., 158 F.Supp.2d 1353 (S.D. Fla. 2001)—**602**

Ass'n for Disabled Ams., Inc. v. Fla. Int'l Univ., No. 02-10360, 2005 WL 768129 (11th Cir. Apr. 6, 2005)—**349**

Ass'n for Disabled Ams., Inc. v. Key Largo Bay Beach, LLC, 407 F.Supp.2d 1321 (S.D. Fla. 2005)—**579**

Astrowsky v. First Portland Mortgage Corp., 887 F.Supp. 332 (D. Me. 1995)—**169**

Aswegan v. Bruhl, 113 F.3d 109 (8th Cir. 1997)—**369**

AT&T Corp. v. Iowa Utils. Bd., 525 U.S. 366 (1999)—**737**

Atascadero State Hosp. v. Scanlon, 473 U.S. 234 (1985)—**499**

Aughe v. Shalala, 885 F.Supp. 1428 (1995)—**851-857**

B

Babicz v. Sch. Bd. of Broward Cnty., 135 F.3d 1420 (11th Cir. 1998)—**440**

Bacon v. City of Richmond, Virginia, 475 F.3d 633 (4th Cir. 2007)—**411**

Baird ex rel. Baird v. Rose, 192 F.3d 462 (4th Cir. 1999)—**257**

Baird v. Rose, 192 F.3d 462 (4th Cir. 1999)—**305**

Ball v. Abbott Advertising, Inc., 864 F.2d 419 (6th Cir. 1988)—**289, 308**

Ball v. AMC Entm't, Inc., 246 F.Supp.2d 17 (D.D.C. 2003)—**548-549, 614**

Ballard v. Rubin, 284 F.3d 957 (8th Cir. 2002)—**251**

Banaitis v. Comm'r of Internal Revenue, 340 F.3d 1074 (9th Cir. 2003)—**321**

Bangerter v. Orem City Corp., 46 F.3d 1491 (10th Cir. 1995)—**814, 821**

Barden v. City of Sacramento, 292 F.3d 1073 (9th Cir. 2002)—**257, 364-368, 406**

Barker v. Int'l Paper Co., 993 F.Supp. 10 (D. Me. 1998)—**115, 247**

Barnard v. ADM Milling Co., 987 F.Supp. 1337 (D. Kan. 1997)—**234**

Barnes v. Cochran, 944 F.Supp. 897 (S.D. Fla. 1996)—**197, 201**

Barnes v. Gorman, 536 U.S. 181 (2002)—**438, 442-445, 447, 754, 764-765**

Barnett v. Memphis City Schs., 113 F. App'x 124 (6th Cir. 2004)—**753**

Barnett v. U.S. Airways, Inc., 228 F.3d 1105 (9th Cir. 2000)—**220, 244-246, 252-253**

Barnhart v. Walton, 535 U.S. 212 (2002)—**736**

Barrios v. Cal. Interscholastic Fed., 277 F.3d 1128 (9th Cir. 2002)—**640**

Barth v. Gelb, 2 F.3d 1180 (D.C. Cir. 1993)—**220-221, 252**

Bartlett v. N.Y. State Bd. of Law Exam'rs, 226 F.3d 69 (2d Cir. 2000)—**891-892**

Bates v. Dura Automotive Systems, Inc., 625 F.3d 283 (6th Cir. 2010)—**207-208**

Bates v. United Parcel Service, Inc., 511 F.3d 974 (9th Cir. 2007)—**247**

Battle v. Pennsylvania, 629 F.2d 269 (3d Cir. 1980)—**707**

Table of Cases

Bauer v. Muscular Dystrophy Ass'n., Inc., 268 F.Supp.2d 1281 (D. Kan. 2003)—**460**

Bay Area Addiction Research Treatment, Inc. v. City of Antioch, 179 F.3d 725 (9th Cir. 1999)—**361, 367, 369**

Bay Area Laundry & Dry Cleaning Pension Tr. Fund v. Ferbar Corp. of Cal., 522 U.S. 192 (1997)—**829**

Bd. of Ed. of Hendrick Hudson Cent. Sch. Dist. v. Rowley, 458 U.S. 176 (1982)—**727, 730-731, 736, 738, 756**

Bd. of Educ. of the City Sch. Dist. of N.Y. v. Tom F., 127 S.Ct. 1393 (2007)—**720**

Bd. of Educ. of the City Sch. Dist. of N.Y. v. Tom F., 128 S. Ct. 1 (2007)—**720**

Bd. of Educ. of the City Sch. Dist. of the City of N.Y. v. Tom F., 193 Fed. App'x 26 (2d Cir. 2006)—**720**

Bd. of Educ. of the City Sch. Dist. of the City of N.Y. v. Tom F., No. 01 Civ. 6845 (GBD), 2005 WL 22866 (S.D.N.Y. Jan. 4, 2005)—**719, 720**

Bd. of Educ. of the City Sch. Dist. of the City of New York v. Tom F., No. 06-637 (Nov. 3, 2006)—**720**

Bd. of Educ. v. Rowley, 458 U.S. 176 (1982)—**670-684, 756**

Bd. of Trs. of the Univ. of Ala. v. Garrett, 531 U.S. 356 (2001)—**24, 148-167, 335, 337, 339, 342-346, 348, 357, 754**

Beck v. Univ. of Wis. Bd. of Regents, 75 F.3d 1130 (7th Cir. 1996)—**203-204, 250**

Bell v. Hood, 327 U.S. 678 (1946)—**445-446**

Bell v. New Jersey, 461 U.S. 773 (1983)—**761, 764**

Bennett v. Ky. Dep't of Educ., 470 U.S. 656 (1985)—**444, 764**

Benson v. Nw. Airlines, Inc., 62 F.3d 1108 (8th Cir. 1995)—**252**

Bentley v. Peace & Quiet Reality 2 LLC, 367 F.Supp.2d 341 (E.D.N.Y. 2005)—**798**

Benz v. Compania Naviera Hidalgo, S. A., 353 U.S. 138 (1957)—**492**

Berard v. Wal-Mart, 2011 WL 4632062 (M.D. Fla. 2011)—**109**

Bercovitch v. Baldwin Sch., Inc., 133 F.3d 141 (1st Cir. 1998)—**327-328**

Bercovitch v. Baldwin Sch., Inc., 191 F.3d 8 (1st Cir. 1999)—**311, 643**

Berry v. Board of Sup's of L.S.U., 715 F.2d 971 (5th Cir. 1983)—**286**

Bertrand v. City of Mackinac Island, 662 N.W.2d 77, 81-88 (Mich. Ct. App. 2003)—**445-446**

Best v. Shell Oil Co., 4 F.Supp.2d 770 (N.D. Ill. 1998)—**300**

Betancourt v. Federated Dep't Stores, 732 F.Supp.2d 693 (W.D. Tex. 2010)—**605**

Beth B. v. Van Clay, 211 F.Supp.2d 1020 (N.D. Ill. 2001)—**698**

Biank v. Nat'l Bd. of Med. Exam'rs, 130 F.Supp.2d 986 (N.D. Ill. 2000)—**488**

Bill M. ex rel. William M. v. Neb. Dep't of Health & Human Servs., Fin. & Support, 408 F.3d 1096 (8th Cir. 2005)—**349**

Table of Cases

Bingham v. Or. Sch. Activities Ass'n, 24 F.Supp.2d 1110 (D. Or. 1998)—**554-555**

Bircoll v. Miami-Dade Cnty., 480 F.3d 1072 (11th Cir. 2007)—**385, 425**

Blackman v. District of Columbia, 633 F.3d 1088 (D.C. Cir. 2010)—**768**

Bledsoe v. Palm Beach Cnty. Soil & Water Conservation Dist., 133 F.3d 816 (11th Cir. 1998)—**369, 460**

Bloom v. Bexar, 130 F.3d 722 (5th Cir. 1997)—**186**

Blue Chip Stamps v. Manor Drug Stores, 421 U.S. 723 (1975)—**36**

Blum v. Bacon, 457 U.S. 132 (1982)—**701**

Blum v. Stenson, 465 U.S. 886 (1984)—**646**

Boddie v. Connecticut, 401 U.S. 371 (1971)—**337, 341, 343**

Boise Cascade Corp. v. U.S. EPA, 942 F.2d 1408 (9th Cir. 1991)—**830**

Bolker v. Comm'r, 760 F.2d 1039 (9th Cir. 1985)—**276**

Bollard v. Cal. Province of Soc. of Jesus, 196 F.3d 940 (9th Cir. 1999)—**179**

Bolmer v. Oliveira, 594 F.3d 134 (2d Cir. 2010)—**355**

Bonilla v. Muebles J.J. Alvarez, Inc., 194 F.3d 275 (1st Cir. 1999)—**53**

Boose v. Tri-Cnty. Metro. Transp. Dist. of Oregon, 587 F.3d 997 (9th Cir. 2009)—**427**

Borden's Farm Prods. Co. v. Baldwin, 293 U.S. 194 (1934)—**162-163**

Borkowski v. Valley Cent. Sch. Dist., 63 F.3d 131 (2d Cir. 1995)—**220-221, 252, 382, 803**

Botosan v. Paul McNally Realty, 216 F.3d 827 (9th Cir. 2000)—**458, 601-602**

Bowen v. Am. Hosp. Ass'n, 476 U.S. 610 (1986)—**544**

Bowers v. Nat'l Collegiate Athletic Ass'n, 475 F.3d 524 (3d Cir. 2007)—**355**

Bowers v. Nat'l Collegiate Athletic Ass'n, 9 F.Supp.2d 460 (D. N.J. 1998)—**361**

Boyd v. U.S. Postal Serv., 752 F.2d 410 (9th Cir. 1985)—**441**

Bradley v. Pizzaco, 7 F.3d 795 (8th Cir. 1993)—**458**

Bradwell v. Illinois, 83 U.S. (16 Wall.) 130 (1873)—**19**

Bragdon v. Abbott, 524 U.S. 624 (1998)—**75, 77, 88-98, 269-270, 274-275, 398, 870**

Brandt v. Vill. of Chebanse, Illinois, 82 F.3d 172 (7th Cir. 1996)—**812**

Breece v. AmeriCare Living Ctrs., No. IP 01-0997-C-K/T, 2002 WL 31132308 (S.D. Ind. Sept. 25, 2002)—**170**

Brian S. v. Vance, 86 F.Supp.2d 538 (2000)—**728**

Briggs v. Bd. of Educ. of Conn., 882 F.2d 688 (2d Cir. 1989)—**685**

British Columbia (Public Service Emp. Relations Comm'n) v. B.C.G.E.U., [1999] 3 S.C.R. 3 Can.—**949**

Brockett v. Spokane Arcades, Inc., 472 U.S. 491 (1985)—**15**

Bronk v. Ineichen, 54 F.3d 425 (7th Cir. 1995)—**805, 812**

Table of Cases

Brookhart v. Ill. State Bd. of Educ., 697 F.2d 179 (7th Cir. 1983)—**685**

Brown v. Bd. of Educ. of Topeka, 347 U.S. 483 (1954)—**19, 656**

Brown v. Bd. of Trs. of LaGrange Indep. Sch. Dist., 187 F.2d 20 (5th Cir. 1951)—**879**

Brown v. City of Los Angeles, 521 F.3d 1238 (9th Cir. 2008)—**436**

Brown v. J. Kaz, Inc., 581 F.3d 175 (3d Cir. 2009)—**257**

Bruggeman ex rel. Bruggeman v. Blagojevich, 324 F.3d 906 (7th Cir. 2003)—**356**

Brumley v. Pena, 62 F.3d 277 (8th Cir. 1995)—**199**

Brunke v. Goodyear Tire & Rubber Co., 344 F.3d 819 (8th Cir. 2003)—**86**

Bryant v. Madigan, 84 F.3d 246 (7th Cir. 1996)—**369**

Bryant Woods Inn, Inc. v. Howard Cnty., 124 F.3d 597 (4th Cir. 1997)—**802-803, 805-806, 811**

Bryce v. Episcopal Church in the Diocese of Colorado, 289 F.3d 648 (10th Cir. 2004)—**179**

Buchanan v. City of San Antonio, 85 F.3d 196 (5th Cir. 1996)—**256**

Buchanan v. Maine, 469 F.3d 158 (1st Cir. 2006)—**386**

Buck v. Bell, 274 U.S. 200 (1927)—**8, 9**

Buckhannon Bd. & Care Home, Inc. v. W. Va. Dep't of Health & Human Res., 530 U.S. 1304 (2000)—**622**

Buckhannon Bd. & Care Home, Inc. v. W. Va. Dep't of Health & Human Res., 532 U.S. 598 (2001)—**309, 441, 621-639, 641-642, 645**

Bullard v. Sercon Corp., 846 F.2d 463 (7th Cir. 1988)—**288**

Bultemeyer v. Fort Wayne Cmty. Schs., 100 F.3d 1281 (7th Cir. 1996)—**211, 244**

Burfield v. Brown, Moore & Flint, Inc., 51 F.3d 583 (5th Cir. 1995)—**456**

Burkhart v. Asean Shopping Ctr., Inc., 55 F.Supp.2d 1013 (D. Ariz. 1999)—**601**

Burkhart v. Wash. Metro. Area Transit Auth., 112 F.3d 1207 (D.C. Cir. 1997)—**879**

Burlington v. Dague, 505 U.S. 557 (1992)—**626**

Burns v. Coca-Cola Enters., 222 F.3d 247 (6th Cir. 2000)—**226**

Burrell v. City of Kankakee, 815 F.2d 1127 (7th Cir. 1987)—**777**

Burriola v. Greater Toledo YMCA, 133 F.Supp.2d 1034 (N.D. Ohio 2001)—**511**

C

Cada v. Baxter Healthcare Corp., 920 F.2d 446 (7th Cir. 1990)—**830**

Camenisch v. Univ. of Tex., 616 F.2d 127 (5th Cir. 1980)—**440**

Camenisch v. Univ. of Tex., 616 F.2d 127 (5th Cir. 1980)—**60**

Cannon v. Univ. of Chi., 441 U.S. 677 (1979)—**438, 440-441, 443-444**

Cantrell v. Nissan N. Am., Inc., No. 3:03-0082, 2006 WL 724549 (M.D. Tenn. Mar. 21, 2006)—**306**

Carlson v. Liberty Mut. Ins. Co., 237 F. App'x 446 (11th Cir. 2007)—**86**

Table of Cases

Carparts Distr. Ctr., Inc. v. Automotive Wholesaler's Ass'n of New England, Inc., 37 F.3d 12 (1st Cir. 1994)—**185-186, 454, 461-465, 472-473, 483, 886**

Carr v. Fort Morgan Sch. Dist., 4 F.Supp.2d 989 (D. Colo. 1998)—**301**

Carroll v. Blinken, 105 F.3d 79 (2d Cir. 1997)—**320, 654**

Carten v. Kent State Univ., 282 F.3d 391 (6th Cir. 2002)—**446**

Carter v. Carter Coal Co., 298 U.S. 238 (1936)—**166**

Caruso v. Blockbuster-Sony Music Entm't Ctr., 193 F.3d 730 (3d Cir. 1999)—**584-596**

Caruso v. Blockbuster-Sony Music Entm't Ctr., 968 F.Supp. 210 (D.N.J. 1997)—**595**

Cason v. Rochester Hous. Auth., 748 F.Supp. 1002 (W.D.N.Y 1990)—**821**

Cassimy v. Bd. of Educ. of Rockford Pub. Schs., 461 F.3d 932 (7th Cir. 2006)—**86**

Castaneda v. Burger King, 597 F.Supp.2d 1035 (N.D. Cal. 2009)—**606**

Castellano v. City of N.Y., 142 F.3d 58 (2d Cir. 1998)—**128**

Castle v. Sangamo Weston, Inc., 837 F.2d 1550 (11th Cir. 1988)—**302**

Cavanaugh v. Cardinal Local Sch. Dist., 409 F.3d 753 (2005)—**741-742**

Cedar Rapids Cmty. Sch. Dist. v. Garret F., 526 U.S. 66 (1999)—**703, 736, 747, 764-765**

Celotex Corp. v. Catrett, 477 U.S. 317 (1986)—**134**

Chabner v. United of Omaha Life Ins. Co., 225 F.3d 1042 (9th Cir. 2000)—**897**

Chaffin v. Kan. State Fair Bd., 348 F.3d 850 (10th Cir. 2003)—**356, 377, 441**

Chaffin v. Kansas, No. 01-1110-JTM, 2005 WL 387654 (D. Kan. Feb. 17, 2005)—**652**

Chandler v. City of Dallas, 2 F.3d 1385 (5th Cir. 1993)—**258**

Chao v. Conocophillips Co., No. Civ. A. 03-MC-0136, 2003 WL 22794705 (E.D. Pa. Nov. 5, 2003)—**267**

Charlie F. v. Bd. of Educ. of Skokie Sch. Dist. 68, 98 F.3d 989 (7th Cir. 1996)—**754**

Che v. Mass. Bay Transp. Auth., 342 F.3d 31 (1st Cir. 2003)—**301**

Chedwick v. UPMC, 2007 WL 4390327 20 A.D. Cases 677 (W.D. Pa. 2007)—**285**

Chenoweth v. Hillsborough Cnty., 250 F.3d 1328 (11th Cir. 2001)—**86-87**

Chesler v. Conroy, 2008 WL 4543031 (N.D. Ill. 2008)—**782**

Chevron U.S.A., Inc. v. Echazabal, 536 U.S. 73 (2002)—**262-269, 275, 870**

Chevron U.S.A., Inc. v. Natural Res. Def. Council, Inc., 467 U.S. 837 (1984)—**41, 94, 265, 398, 737, 796**

Christiansburg Garment Co. v. EEOC, 434 U.S. 412 (1978)—**320, 638, 643**

Christopher P. v. Marcus, 915 F.2d 794 (2d Cir. 1990)—**642**

Christopher S. v. Stanislaus Cnty. Office of Educ., 384 F.3d 1205 (9th Cir. 2004)—**739**

Table of Cases

City of Boerne v. Flores, 521 U.S. 507 (1997)—**151, 154-155, 164-165, 334, 338, 341-346, 354**

City of Burlington v. Dague, 505 U.S. 557 (1992)—**317**

City of Canton v. Harris, 489 U.S. 378 (1989)—**447**

City of Cleburne v. Cleburne Living Ctr., 473 U.S. 432 (1985)—**9-23, 152-153, 158-163, 335, 337-338, 778, 821, 943, 948**

City of Edmonds v. Oxford House, Inc., 514 U.S. 725 (1995)—**771, 779-782**

City of Rome v. United States, 446 U.S. 156 (1980)—**164, 166**

Civic Ass'n of the Deaf of N.Y. City, Inc. v. Giuliani, 970 F.Supp. 352 (S.D.N.Y. 1997)—**418**

Civic Ass'n of the Deaf of N.Y.C. v. Giuliani, 970 F.Supp. 352 (S.D.N.Y. 1997)—**581**

Clackamas Gastroenterology Assocs., P.C. v. Wells, 538 U.S. 440 (2003)—**140, 141-147**

Clark v. Cal. Dep't of Corr., 123 F.3d 1267 (9th Cir. 1997)—**358**

Clark v. Martinez, 543 U.S. 371 (2005)—**500-501, 506**

Clark v. Peco, Inc., No. 97-737-HU, 1999 WL 398012 (D. Or. April 16, 1999)—**652**

Clarkson v. Coughlin, 145 F.R.D. 339 (S.D.N.Y. 1993)—**422**

Cleburne Living Ctr., Inc. v. City of Cleburne, 726 F.2d 191 (5th Cir. 1984)—**10**

Cleveland v. Pol'y Mgmt. Sys. Corp., 526 U.S. 795 (1999)—**129-135, 729, 847**

Clevinger v. Intel Corp., 254 F. App'x 615 (9th Cir. 2007)—**99**

Cmty. for Creative Non-Violence v. Reid, 490 U.S. 730 (1989)—**142, 147**

Cmtys. Actively Living Indep. & Free v. City of Los Angeles, CV 09-0287 CBM RZX, 2011 WL 4595993 (C.D. Cal. Feb. 10, 2011)—**387**

Coady v. Comm'r, 213 F.3d 1187 (9th Cir. 2000)—**321**

Coalition of Montanans Concerned with Disabilities, Inc. v. Gallatin Airport Auth., 957 F.Supp. 1166 (D. Mont. 1997)—**615**

Cohon v. New Mexico Dep't of Health, 646 F.3d 717 (10th Cir. 2011)—**404**

Coleman v. Zatechka, 824 F.Supp. 1360 (D. Neb. 1993)—**361**

Coll. Sav. Bank v. Fla. Prepaid Postsecondary Ed. Expense Bd., 527 U.S. 666 (1999)—**150, 166-167, 288, 357**

Collins v. Raytheon Aircraft Co., No. 01-1415-JTM, 2003 WL 192553 (D. Kan. Jan. 16, 2003)—**268**

Collins v. United Air Lines, Inc., 514 F.2d 594 (9th Cir. 1975)—**828**

Collinsgru v. Palmyra Bd. of Educ., 161 F.3d 225 (3d Cir. 1998)—**746, 751**

Colo. Cross Disability Coalition v. Hermanson Family Ltd. P'ship I, 264 F.3d 999 (10th Cir. 2001)—**552-562**

Colo. Cross-Disability Coalition v. Taco Bell Corp., 184 F.R.D. 354 (D. Colo. 1999)—**257**

Comm'r of Internal Revenue v. Schleier, 515 U.S. 323 (1995)—**321**

Table of Cases

Comm'r v. Banks, 543 U.S. 426 (2005)—**321-322**

Comm'r v. Culbertson, 337 U.S. 733 (1949)—**322**

Comm'r v. Glenshaw Glass Co., 348 U.S. 426 (1955)—**322**

Comm'r v. Jacobson, 336 U.S. 28 (1949)—**322**

Concerned Parents to Save Dreher Park Ctr. v. City of W. Palm Beach, 846 F.Supp. 986 (S.D. Fla. 1994)—**127**

Concerned Parents to Save Dreher Park Ctr. v. City of West Palm Beach, 846 F.Supp. 986 (S.D. Fla. 1994)—**376, 393**

Conn. Nat. Bank v. Germain, 503 U.S. 249 (1992)—**757**

Conneen v. MBNA Am. Bank, N.A., 334 F.3d 318 (3d Cir. 2003)—**214**

Conrad v. Bd. of Johnson Cnty. Comm'rs, 237 F.Supp.2d 1204 (D. Kan. 2002)—**204**

Conroy v. N.Y. State Dep't of Corr. Servs., 333 F.3d 88 (2d Cir. 2003)—**201-203, 207**

Consolidated Rail Corp. v. Darrone, 465 U.S. 624 (1984)—**103**

Constantine v. Rectors & Visitors of George Mason Univ., 411 F.3d 474 (4th Cir. 2005)—**349**

Cook v. U.S. Dep't of Labor, 688 F.2d 669 (9th Cir. 1982)—**275**

Cooper v. Olin Corp., 246 F.3d 1083 (8th Cir. 2001)—**86**

Corbett v. Nat'l Prods., No. 94-2652, 1995 WL 284248 (E.D. Pa. May 9, 1995)—**652**

Corder v. Lucent Techs., Inc., 162 F.3d 924 (7th Cir. 1998)—**213**

Corey v. HUD, 719 F.3d 322 (4th Cir. 2013)—**806**

Cornilles v. Regal Cinemas, Inc., No. Civ. 00-173-AS, 2002 WL 31440885 (D. Or. Jan. 3, 2002)—**548**

Cornilles v. Regal Cinemas, Inc., No. Civ. 00-173-AS, 2002 WL 31469787 (D. Or. Mar. 19, 2002)—**614**

Corp. of Presiding Bishop of Church of Jesus Christ of Latter-day Saints v. Amos, 483 U.S. 327 (1987)—**181**

Cossette v. Minn. Power & Light, 188 F.3d 964 (8th Cir. 1999)—**207**

Covelli v. Nat'l Fuel Gas Dist., 49 F. App'x 356, 2002 WL 31422862 (2d Cir. Oct. 29, 2002)—**202**

Craig v. Boren, 429 U.S. 190 (1976)—**21**

Cravens v. Blue Cross & Blue Shield of Kan. City, 214 F.3d 1011 (8th Cir. 2000)—**226**

Crawford Fitting Co. v. J. T. Gibbons, Inc., 482 U.S. 437 (1987)—**759-760, 762, 766**

Crocker v. Tenn. Secondary Sch. Athletic Ass'n, 980 F.2d 382 (6th Cir. 1992)—**754**

Crowder v. Kitagawa, 81 F.3d 1480 (9th Cir. 1996)—**392-394**

Cruz ex rel. Cruz v. Pa. Interscholastic Athletic Ass'n, Inc., 157 F.Supp.2d 485 (E.D. Pa. 2001)—**361**

Cunard S.S. Co. v. Mellon, 262 U.S. 100 (1923)—**494**

Cupolo v. Bay Area Rapid Transit, 5 F.Supp.2d 1078 (N.D. Cal. 1997)—**882, 883**

Curtis v. Loether, 415 U.S. 189 (1974)—**829**

Cutter v. Wilkinson, 544 U.S. 709 (2005)—**174-175**

Table of Cases

D

D'Amico v. N.Y. State Bd. of Law Exam'rs, 813 F.Supp. 217 (W.D.N.Y. 1993)—**793**

D'Angelo v. ConAgra Foods, Inc., 422 F.3d 1220 (11th Cir. 2005)—**247**

Dadian v. Vill. of Wilmette, 269 F.3d 831 (7th Cir. 2001)—**811-812**

Daggitt v. United Food & Commercial Workers Int'l Union, Local 304A, 245 F.3d 981 (8th Cir. 2001)—**320**

Daggitt v. United Food & Commercial Workers Int'l Union, Local 304A, 245 F.3d 981 (8th Cir. 2001)—**654**

Dahlberg v. Avis Rent A Car Sys., Inc., 92 F.Supp.2d 1091 (D. Colo. 2000)—**554**

Daigle v. Friendly Ice Cream Corp., 957 F.Supp. 8 (D.N.H. 1997)—**601**

Dalton v. Subaru-Isuzu Auto., Inc., 141 F.3d 667 (7th Cir. 1998)—**234**

Daniel R.R. v. State Bd. of Educ., 874 F.2d 1036 (5th Cir. 1989)—**695, 697-698**

Dao v. Auchan Hypermarket, 96 F.3d 787 (5th Cir. 1996)—**297**

Dare v. Wal-Mart Stores, Inc., 267 F.Supp.2d 987 (D. Minn. 2003)—**257**

Darian v. Univ. of Mass. Boston, 980 F.Supp. 77 (D. Mass. 1997)—**361**

Dasgupta v. Univ. of Wis. Bd. of Regents, 121 F.3d 1138 (7th Cir.1997)—**285**

Daugherty v. City of El Paso, 56 F.3d 695 (5th Cir. 1995)—**226-227**

Davidson v. Am. Online, Inc., 337 F.3d 1179 (10th Cir. 2003)—**255**

Davis v. Monroe Cnty. Bd. of Ed., 526 U.S. 629 (1999)—**443-445**

Davis v. N.C. Dep't of Corr., 48 F.3d 134 (4th Cir. 1995)—**288**

Davis v. Southeastern Comm. Coll., 424 F.Supp. 1341 (E.D.N.C. 1976)—**35, 39**

Davis v. Southeastern Comm. Coll., 574 F.2d 1158 (4th Cir. 1978)—**35-36**

Davoll v. Webb, 160 F.R.D. 142 (D. Colo 1995)—**258**

Davoll v. Webb, 194 F.3d 1116 (10th Cir. 1999)—**251, 301, 440**

Deal v. Hamilton Cnty. Bd. of Educ., 392 F.3d 840 (6th Cir. 2004)—**734**

Debra P. v. Turlington, 730 F.2d 1405 (11th Cir. 1984)—**685**

Deck v. Am. Hawaiian Cruises, Inc., 121 F.Supp.2d 1292 (D. Haw. 2000)—**605, 610**

Dehne v. Med. Shoppe Int'l, Inc., 261 F.Supp.2d 1142 (E.D. Mo. 2003)—**309, 642**

Dekalb Cnty. Sch. Dist. v. M.T.V. ex rel. C.E.V., 413 F.Supp.2d 1322 (N.D. Ga. 2005)—**704**

Delaware State College v. Ricks, 449 U.S. 250 (1980)—**284**

DeLong v. Brumbaugh, 703 F.Supp. 399 (W.D. Pa. 1989)—**422**

Den Hartog v. Wasatch Acad., 129 F.3d 1076 (10th Cir. 1997)—**247**

Dentice v. Farmers Ins., 2012 WL 2504046 (E.D. Wis. 2012)—**109**

Dep't of Agric. v. Moreno, 413 U.S. 528 (1973)—**161**

Dep't of Educ. v. Katherine D., 727 F.2d 809 (9th Cir. 1983)—**695, 703**

Table of Cases

Desert Palace, Inc. v. Costa, 539 U.S. 90 (2003)—**255-256**

Design & Prod., Inc. v. United States, 20 Cl.Ct. 207 (Cl. Ct. 1990)—**647**

Detz v. Greiner Indus., Inc., 346 F.3d 109 (3d Cir. 2003)—**135**

Devine v. Indian River Cty. Sch. Bd., 121 F.3d 576 (11th Cir. 1997)—**751**

DeVinney v. Me. Med. Ctr., No. Civ. 97-276-P-C, 1998 WL 271495 (D. Me. May 18, 1998)—**619-620**

Devries v. Fairfax Cnty. Sch. Bd., 882 F.2d 876 (4th Cir. 1989)—**695**

DeWyer v. Temple Univ., No. CIV.A.00-CV-1665, 2001 WL 115461 (E.D. Pa. Feb. 5, 2001)—**460**

Dia Navigation Co. v. Pomeroy, 34 F.3d 1255 (3d Cir. 1994)—**590-591**

Dilley v. SuperValu, Inc., 296 F.3d 958 (10th Cir. 2002)—**215-216, 226, 299, 307-308**

Dir., Office of Workers' Comp. Programs v. Greenwich Collieries, 512 U.S. 267 (1994)—**729**

Disabled in Action of Pennsylvania v. Se. Pennsylvania Transp. Auth., 635 F.3d 87 (3d Cir. 2011)—**411, 418**

Doane v. City of Omaha, 115 F.3d 624 (9th Cir. 1997)—**256**

Dobard v. S.F. Bay Area Rapid Transit Dist., No. C-92-3563-DLJ, 1993 WL 372256 (N.D. Cal. Sept. 7, 1993)—**425-426, 542**

Doctor's Assocs., Inc. v. Casarotto, 517 U.S. 681 (1996)—**328**

Doe v. Bd. of Educ. of Baltimore Cty., 165 F.3d 260 (4th Cir. 1998)—**745**

Doe v. Belleville Pub. Sch. Dist., 672 F.Supp. 342 (S.D. Ill. 1987)—**666**

Doe v. Brookline Sch. Comm., 722 F.2d 910 (1st Cir. 1983)—**714**

Doe v. Deer Mountain Day Camp, 682 F.Supp.2d 324 (S.D.N.Y. 2010)—**536**

Doe v. Judicial Nominating Comm'n, 906 F.Supp. 1534 (S.D. Fla. 1995)—**361**

Doe v. Maher, 793 F.2d 1470 (1986)—**711**

Doe v. Mut. of Omaha Ins. Co., 179 F.3d 557 (7th Cir. 1999)—**528, 886**

Doe v. Nat'l Bd. of Med. Exam'rs, 199 F.3d 146 (3d Cir. 1999)—**488**

Doe v. Pfrommer, 148 F.3d 73 (2d Cir. 1998)—**383**

Doe v. U.S. Postal Serv., 317 F.3d 339 (D.C. Cir. 2003)—**206**

Donnell C. v. Ill. State Bd. of Educ., 829 F.Supp. 1016 (N.D. Ill. 1993)—**721**

Donofrio v. N.Y. Times, No. 99CV1576RCCJCF, 2001 WL 1663314 (S.D.N.Y. Aug. 24, 2001)—**204**

Dopico v. Goldschmidt, 687 F.2d 644 (2d Cir. 1982)—**795**

Doran v. Salem Inn, Inc., 422 U.S. 922 (1975)—**729**

Drinker v. Colonial Sch. Dist., 78 F.3d 859 (3d Cir. 1996)—**725**

Dudley v. Hannaford Bros. Co., 146 F.Supp.2d 82 (D. Me. 2001)—**609, 611**

Dudley v. Hannaford Bros. Co., 190 F.Supp.2d 69 (D. Me. 2002)—**511, 604**

Table of Cases

Duffy v. Riveland, 98 F.3d 447 (9th Cir. 1996)—**419-424**

Dumas v. Hurley Med. Ctr., 837 F.Supp.2d 655 (E.D. Mich. 2011)—**869**

Duncan v. Walker, 533 U.S. 167 (2001)—**767**

Dunn v. Blumstein, 405 U.S. 330 (1972)—**346**

Durrenberger v. Tex. Dep't of Criminal Justice, 757 F.Supp.2d 640 (S.D. Tex. 2010)—**109**

Duvall v. Cnty. of Kitsap, 260 F.3d 1124 (9th Cir. 2001)—**446-447**

Dvorak v. Mostardi Platt Associates, Inc., 289 F.3d 479 (7th Cir. 2002)—**284**

E

E.R.K. v. State of Hawaii Dep't of Educ., 728 F.3d 982 (9th Cir. 2013)—**660**

Easley in re Easley v. Snider, 36 F.3d 297 (3d Cir. 1994)—**404-405**

Ebbert v. Daimler Chrysler Corp., 319 F.3d 103 (3d Cir. 2003)—**53, 289, 298, 308**

Echazabal v. Chevron USA, Inc., 226 F.3d 1063 (9th Cir. 2000)—**262-263**

Echazabal v. Chevron USA, Inc., 336 F.3d 1023 (9th Cir. 2003)—**268-278**

Edison v. Douberly, 604 F.3d 1307 (11th Cir. 2010)—**361**

Edwards v. Brookhaven Science Assocs., LLC, 390 F.Supp.2d 225 (E.D.N.Y. 2005)—**306**

EEOC v. AIC Sec. Investigations, Ltd., 55 F.3d 1276 (7th Cir. 1995)—**140**

EEOC v. Amboy Bus Co., 96-CV-5451 (ARR) (Aug. 19, 1998)—**186**

EEOC v. Arabian Am. Oil Co., 499 U.S. 244 (1991)—**170**

EEOC v. Arabian Am. Oil Co., 499 U.S. 244 (1991)—**499, 507**

EEOC v. Aramark Corp., Inc., 208 F.3d 266 (D.C. Cir. 2000)—**192**

EEOC v. Argo Distribution, LLC, 55 F.3d 462 (5th Cir. 2009)—**296**

EEOC v. Catholic Univ., 83 F.3d 455 (1996)—**183**

EEOC v. CNA Ins. Cos., 96 F.3d 1039 (7th Cir. 1996)—**128**

EEOC v. CNA Ins. Cos., 96 F.3d 1039 (7th Cir. 1996)—**192**

EEOC v. Dillon Co., Inc., 310 F.3d 1271 (10th Cir. 2002)—**298**

EEOC v. Dollar Gen. Corp., 252 F.Supp.2d 277 (M.D.N.C. 2003)—**242**

EEOC v. Dowd & Dowd, Ltd., 736 F.2d 1177 (1984)—**140-141, 147**

EEOC v. E. I. DuPont de Nemours & Co., No. 03-1605, 2004 WL 2347570 (E.D. La. Oct. 15, 2004)—**277-278**

EEOC v. E.I. DuPont de Nemours & Co., 406 F.Supp.2d 645 (E.D. La. 2005)—**129**

EEOC v. E.I. DuPont de Nemours & Co., 480 F.3d 724 (5th Cir. 2007)—**129**

EEOC v. Federal Exp. Corp., 558 F.3d 842 (9th Cir. 2009)—**298**

EEOC v. Founders Pavilion, Inc., 6:13-cv-06250 (W.D.N.Y. May 16, 2013)—**869**

EEOC v. Hertz Corp., No. 96-72421, 1998 WL 5694 (E.D. Mich. Jan. 6, 1998)—**236-242**

EEOC v. Home Depot, USA Inc., No. 03 Civ. 4860 (E.D.N.Y. Sept. 24, 2003)—**242**

Table of Cases

EEOC v. Hosanna-Tabor Evangelical Lutheran Church & Sch., 582 F.Supp.2d 881 (E.D. Mich. 2008)—**172-183**

EEOC v. Hussey Copper Ltd., 696 F.Supp.2d 505 (W.D. Pa. March 12, 2010)—**279**

EEOC v. Lee's Log Cabin, 546 F.3d. 438 (7th Cir. 2008)—**98**

EEOC v. Prevo's Family Mkt., Inc., 135 F.3d 1089 (6th Cir. 1998)—**202**

EEOC v. Sara Lee Corp., 237 F.3d 349 (4th Cir. 2001)—**226**

EEOC v. St. Francis Xavier Parochial Sch., 117 F.3d 621 (D.C. Cir. 1997)—**148**

EEOC v. Sw. Baptist Theological Seminary, 651 F.2d 277 (1981)—**182**

EEOC v. Thrivent Fin. for Lutherans, 700 F.3d 1044 (7th Cir. 2012)—**206**

EEOC v. United Airlines, Inc., 693 F.3d 760 (7th Cir. 2012)—**215**

EEOC v. W & O, Inc., 213 F.3d 600 (11th Cir. 2000)—**304**

EEOC v. Waffle House, Inc., 193 F.3d 805 (4th Cir. 1999)—**292**

EEOC v. Waffle House, Inc., 534 U.S. 279 (2002)—**290-295, 328**

EEOC v. Woodbridge Corp, 263 F.3d 812 (8th Cir. 2001)—**871**

EEOC v. Yellow Freight Sys. Inc., 253 F.3d 943 (7th Cir. 2001)—**245**

Eichman v. Linden & Sons, Inc., 752 F.2d 1246 (7th Cir. 1985)—**310**

Eiland v. Westinghouse Elec. Corp., 58 F.3d 176 (5th Cir. 1995—**306**

Elderhaven, Inc. v. City of Lubbock, 98 F.3d 175 (5th Cir. 1996)—**803, 806, 811, 816-819**

Eldridge v. British Columbia, [1997] 151 D.L.R. (4th) 577, 3 S.C.R. 624—**948**

Ellen S. v. Fla. Bd. of Bar Exam'rs, 859 F.Supp. 1489 (S.D. Fla. 1994)—**488**

Elvig v. Calvin Presbyterian Church, 375 F.3d 951 (9th Cir. 2004)—**183**

Elwell v. Oklahoma ex rel. Bd. of Regents of Univ. of Okla., 693 F.3d 1303 (10th Cir. 2012)—**369-370**

Emerick v. Kahala L & L, Inc., No. Civ. 97-01174 FIY, 2000 WL 687662 (D. Haw. May 16, 2000)—**458**

Emerson v. N. States Power Co., 256 F.3d 506 (7th Cir. 2001)—**250**

Emery v. Caravan of Dreams, Inc., 879 F.Supp. 640 (N.D. Tex. 1995)—**903**

Emery v. Roanoke City Sch. Bd., 432 F.3d 294 (4th Cir. 2005)—**751**

Employment Div., Dep't of Human Res. of Ore. v. Smith, 494 U.S. 872 (1990)—**176-177**

Ennis v. Nat'l Ass'n of Bus. & Educ. Radio, Inc., 53 F.3d 55 (4th Cir. 1995)—**113**

Equal Rights Ctr. v. Post Properties, Inc., 633 F.3d 1136 (D.C. Cir. 2011)—**833**

Erdman v. City of Ft. Atkinson, 84 F.3d 960 (7th Cir. 1996)—**811-812**

Espino v. Besteiro, 520 F.Supp. 905 (S.D. Tex. 1981)—**697**

Table of Cases

Evans v. Jeff D., 475 U.S. 717 (1986)—**626**

Eversley v. Mbank Dallas, 843 F.2d 172 (5th Cir. 1988)—**794, 796**

Ex parte Virginia, 100 U.S. 339 (1879)—**165-166, 352**

Ex Parte Young, 209 U.S. 123 (1908)—**355, 446**

Exeter-West Greenwich Reg'l Sch. Dist. v. Pontarelli, 788 F.2d 47, 51 (1st Cir. 1986)—**637**

F

Faibisch v. Univ. of Minn., 304 F.3d 797 (8th Cir. 2002)—**298**

Fair Housing Council Inc. v. Vill. of Olde St. Andrews, 210 F. App'x 469 (6th Cir. 2006)—**832**

Fan v. Comm'r, 117 T.C. 32 (T.C. 2001)—**924-930**

Faretta v. California, 422 U.S. 806 (1975)—**337, 343**

Farrar v. Hobby, 506 U.S. 103 (1992)—**320, 624, 631, 640, 654**

FCC v. Beach Commc's, Inc., 508 U.S. 307 (1993)—**152, 163**

Feist v. Louisiana, 730 F.3d 450 (5th Cir. 2013)—**210**

Feldman v. Pro Football Inc., 419 F. App'x 381 (4th Cir. 2011)—**549**

Ferguson v. City of Phoenix, 157 F.3d 668 (9th Cir. 1998)—**435, 446, 891**

Fernandes v. Costa Bros. Masonry, Inc., 199 F.3d 572 (1st Cir. 1999)—**256**

Ferren C. v. Sch. Dist. of Philadelphia, 612 F.3d 712 (3d Cir. 2010)—**686**

Fialka-Feldman v. Oakland Univ. Bd. of Trustees, 678 F.Supp.2d 576 (E.D. Mich. 2009)—**385**

First Options of Chi., Inc. v. Kaplan, 514 U.S. 938 (1995)—**328**

First Step, Inc. v. City of New London, 247 F.Supp.2d 135 (D. Conn. 2003)—**445**

Fischer v. SJB-P.D. Inc., 214 F.3d 1115 (9th Cir. 2000)—**318, 640, 642, 653**

Fisher v. Okla. Health Care Auth., 335 F.3d 1175 (10th Cir. 2003)—**404**

Fisher v. Sup. Ct., 223 Cal.Rptr 203 (Cal. Ct. App. 1986)—**60**

Fitch v. Solipsys Corp., 94 F.Supp.2d 670 (D. Md. 2000)—**116**

Fitzpatrick v. Bitzer, 427 U.S. 445 (1976)—**151, 166, 352**

Fitzpatrick v. City of Atlanta, 2 F.3d 1112 (11th Cir. 1993)—**202**

Fjellestad v. Pizza Hut of Am., Inc., 188 F.3d 944 (8th Cir. 1999)—**252, 820**

Fla. Prepaid Postsecondary Educ. Expense Bd. v. Coll. Sav. Bank, 527 U.S. 627 (1999)—**153, 165, 334-335, 338, 344-346**

Flannery v. Recording Indus. Ass'n Of America, 354 F.3d 632 (7th Cir. 2004)—**283-284**

Fleck v. Wilmac, 2012 WL 1033472 (E.D. Pa. 2012)—**109**

Fletcher v. Tufts Univ., 367 F.Supp.2d 99 (D. Mass. 2005)—**478**

Florence Cnty. Sch. Dist. Four v. Carter, 510 U.S. 7 (1993)—**718**

Flowers v. Komatsu Mining Sys., Inc., 165 F.3d 554 (7th Cir. 1999)—**300, 302**

Fogleman v. Mercy Hosp., Inc., 283 F.3d 561 (3d Cir. 2002)—**117**

Table of Cases

Folkerts v. City of Waverly, Iowa, 707 F.3d 975 (8th Cir. 2013)—**425**

Ford Motor Co. v. EEOC, 458 U.S. 219 (1982)—**301**

Ford v. Long Beach Unified Sch. Dist., 461 F.3d 1087 (9th Cir. 2006)—**754-755**

Ford v. Schering-Plough Corp., 145 F.3d 601 (3d Cir. 1998)—**128, 478, 885**

Foster v. Arthur Anderson, LLP, 168 F.3d 1029 (7th Cir. 1999)—**256**

Fountain v. N.Y. State Dep't of Corr. Servs., 190 F.Supp.2d 335 (N.D.N.Y. 2002)—**201, 203, 208**

Fox v. Gen. Motors Corp., 247 F.3d 169 (4th Cir. 2001)—**117, 305**

Frame v. City of Arlington, 575 F.3d 432 (5th Cir. 2009)—**832**

Frame v. City of Arlington, 657 F.3d 215 (5th Cir. 2012)—**368-369, 832**

Frank G. v. Bd. of Educ. of Hyde Park, 459 F.3d 356 (2d Cir. 2006)—**720**

Franklin v. Gwinnett Cnty. Pub. Schs., 503 U.S. 60 (1992)—**443-444, 446**

Frazier v. Fairhaven Sch. Comm., 276 F.3d 52 (1st Cir. 2002)—**739**

Frazier v. Simmons, 254 F.3d 1247 (10th Cir. 2001)—**251**

Fredenburg v. Contra Costa Cnty. Dep't of Health Servs., 172 F.3d 1176 (9th Cir. 1999)—**207**

Frederick L. v. Dep't of Pub. Welfare, No. Civ. A 00-4510, 2004 WL 1945565 (E.D. Pa. Sept. 1, 2004)—**403**

Frederick L. v. Dep't of Public Welfare, 422 F.3d 151 (3d Cir. 2005)—**403**

Freed v. Consolidated Rail Corp., 201 F.3d 188 (3d Cir. 2000)—**905**

Freilich v. Upper Chesapeake Health, Inc., 313 F.3d 205 (4th Cir. 2002)—**110, 112-117**

Fresnius Med. Care Cardiovascular Res., Inc. v. Puerto Rico, 322 F.3d 56 (1st Cir. 2003)—**362**

Friends of Earth, Inc. v. Laidlaw Envtl. Servs. (TOC), Inc., 528 U.S. 167 (2000)—**626, 637**

Friendship Edison Pub. Charter Sch. Collegiate Campus v. Nesbitt, 669 F.Supp.2d 80 (D.D.C. 2009)—**768**

Frontiero v. Richardson, 411 U.S. 677 (1973)—**11, 20, 943**

Fry v. Saenz, 98 Cal.App.4th 256 (Cal. App. 2002)—**857**

FTC v. Morton Salt Co., 334 U.S. 37 (1948)—**730**

Fuller v. Phipps, 67 F.3d 1137 (4th Cir. 1995)—**256**

Furnish v. SVI Sys., Inc., 270 F.3d 445 (7th Cir. 2001)—**86**

G

G.J. ex rel. E.J. v. Muscogee Cnty. Sch. Dist., 704 F.Supp.2d 1299 (M.D. Ga. 2010)—**665**

G.J. v. Muscogee Cnty. Sch. Dist., 668 F.3d 1258 (11th Cir. 2012)—**665**

Gagliardo v. Arlington Cent. Sch. Dist., 489 F.3d 105 (2d Cir. 2007)—**720**

Gagliardo v. Connaught Lab., Inc., 311 F.3d 565 (3d Cir. 2002)—**305, 307**

Gallo v. Bd. of Regents of Univ. of Cal., 916 F.Supp. 1005 (S.D. Cal. 1995)—**187**

Galloway v. Sup. Ct. of D.C., 816 F.Supp. 12 (D.D.C. 1993)—**361**

Table of Cases

Galyen v. Comm'r, 2006 WL 416404 (Tax Ct. 2006)—**930**

Garcia v. Brockway, 526 F.3d 456 (9th Cir. 2008)—**827-832**

Garcia-Ayala v. Lederle Parenterals, Inc., 212 F.3d 638 (1st Cir. 2000)—**218**

Garret v. Univ. of Alabama, 507 F.3d 1306 (11th Cir. 2007)—**86, 99**

Garrett v. Bd. of Trs. of the Univ. of Ala., 354 F.Supp.2d 1244 (N.D. Ala. 2005)—**167**

Garrett v. Bd. of Trs. of Univ. of Ala., 989 F.Supp. 1409 (N.D. Ala. 1998)—**149-150**

Garrett v. Univ. of Ala., 344 F.3d 1288 (11th Cir. 2003)—**167**

Garrison v. Baker Hughes Oil Field Operations, Inc., 287 F.3d 955 (10th Cir. 2002)—**200, 206-207**

Gary B. v. Cronin, 542 F.Supp. 102 (N.D. Ill. 1980)—**905**

Gately v. Commonwealth of Massachusetts, 2 F.3d 1221 (1st Cir. 1993)—**305**

Gates v. Rowland, 39 F.3d 1439 (9th Cir. 1994)—**360-361**

Gathright-Dietrich v. Atlanta Landmarks, Inc., No. 05-14229, 2006 WL 1716751 (11th Cir. June 23, 2006)—**580**

Gaworski v. ITT Commercial Fin. Corp., 17 F.3d 1104 (8th Cir. 1994)—**302**

Gebser v. Lago Vista Indep. Sch. Dist., 524 U.S. 274 (1998)—**443-445**

Gen. Tel. Co. of Northwest v. EEOC, 446 U.S. 318 (1980)—**291-292, 295**

George v. N.J. Bd. of Veterinary Med. Exam'rs, 635 F.Supp. 953 (D.N.J. 1985)—**187**

Gibson v. Firestone, 741 F.2d 1268 (11th Cir. 1984)—**879**

Gibson v. Neighborhood Health Clinics, Inc., 121 F.3d 1126 (7th Cir. 1997)—**328**

Gilbert v. Frank, 949 F.2d 637 (2d Cir. 1991)—**234, 241**

Giles v. Gen. Elec. Co., 245 F.3d 474, 493-95 (5th Cir. 2001)—**303-304, 306, 318-319, 652-653**

Gillen v. Fallon Ambulance Serv., Inc., 283 F.3d 11 (1st Cir. 2001)—**191, 197, 200**

Gillespie v. Dimensions Health Corp., 369 F.Supp.2d 636 (D. Md. 2005)—**546**

Gilmer v. Interstate/Johnson Lane Corp., 500 U.S. 20 (1991)—**325-326, 328**

Gold Coast Publ'ns, Inc. v. Corrigan, 42 F.3d 1336 (11th Cir. 1994)—**878**

Goodwin v. C.N.J., Inc., 436 F.3d 44 (1st Cir. 2006)—**600**

Gorman v. Bartch, 152 F.3d 907 (8th Cir. 1998)—**361, 446**

Gotthardt v. Nat'l R.R. Passenger Corp., 191 F.3d 1148 (9th Cir. 1999)—**302, 304**

Graham v. Richardson, 403 U.S. 365 (1971)—**11**

Granovsky v. Minister of Emp. & Immigration [2000] 1 S.C.R. 703—**948**

Greater L.A. Council on Deafness, Inc. v. Cmty. Television of S. Cal., 719 F.2d 1017 (9th Cir. 1983)—**440**

Green v. Mansour, 474 U.S. 64 (1985)—**356**

Table of Cases

Greenberg v. Bellsouth Commc'ns, Inc., 498 F.3d 1258 (11th Cir. 2007)—**86**

Greenier v. Pace, Local No. 1188, 245 F.Supp.2d 247 (D. Me. 2003)—**311, 643**

Greenlaw v. Garrett, 59 F.3d 994 (9th Cir. 1995)—**187**

Greenleaf's Lessee v. Birth, 31 U.S. 302 (1832)—**731**

Greenway v. Buffalo Hilton Hotel, 951 F.Supp. 1039 (W.D.N.Y. 1997)—**319** § 6:59

Greer v. Richardson Indep. Sch. Dist., 472 F. App'x 287 (5th Cir. 2012)—**408-411**

Greer v. Rome City Sch. Dist., 950 F.2d 688 (11th Cir. 1991)—**695**

Gregory v. Ashcroft, 501 U.S. 452 (1991)—**359-360**

Grenier v. Cyanimid Plastics, Inc., 70 F.3d 667 (1st Cir. 1995)—**196, 199, 203, 245**

Greyhound Corp. v. Mt. Hood Stages, Inc., 437 U.S. 322 (1978)—**36**

Griffin v. Steeltek, Inc., 160 F.3d 591 (10th Cir. 1998)—**196, 206-208**

Griggs v. Duke Power Co., 401 U.S. 424 (1971)—**56-57, 164**

Groner v. Golden Gate Gardens Apartments, 250 F.3d 1039 (6th Cir. 2001)—**799-805**

Grutter v. Bollinger, 539 U.S. 306 (2003)—**129**

Guardians Ass'n v. Civil Serv. Comm'n of N.Y. City, 463 U.S. 582 (1983)—**443, 446**

Gunther v. Lin, 144 Cal.App.4th 223, 50 Cal.Rptr.3d 317 (2007)—**898-899**

Guttman v. Khalsa, 669 F.3d 1101 (10th Cir. 2012)—**349**

Guzman v. Denny's, Inc., 40 F.Supp.2d 930 (S.D. Ohio 1999)—**579**

H

Hafer v. Melo, 502 U.S. 21 (1991)—**355**

Hainze v. Richards, 207 F.3d 795 (5th Cir. 2000)—**386**

Hamlin v. Charter Twp. of Flint, 165 F.3d 426 (6th Cir. 1999)—**303, 319, 653**

Hankins v. El Torito Restaurants, Inc., 63 Cal.App.4th 510, 74 Cal.Rptr.2d 684 (1998)—**899**

Hanrahan v. Hampton, 446 U.S. 754 (1980)—**623-625**

Hans v. Louisiana, 134 U.S. 1 (1890)—**150**

Hansen v. Deercreek Plaza, LLC., 420 F.Supp.2d 1346 (S.D. Fla. 2006)—**644-652**

Harding v. Cianbro Corp., 473 F.Supp.2d 89 (D. Me. 2007)—**302**

Hardwick v. Curtis Trailers Inc., 896 F.Supp. 1037 (D. Or. 1995)—**187**

Hardy v. S. F. Phosphates Ltd. Co., 185 F.3d 1076 (10th Cir. 1999)—**254**

Harlow v. Fitzgerald, 457 U.S. 800 (1982)—**356**

Harris v. Capital Growth Investors XIV, 52 Cal.3d 1142 (Cal. 1991)—**898**

Harris v. Harris & Hart, Inc., 206 F.3d 838 (9th Cir. 2000)—**194, 203**

Harris v. Wilters, 596 F.2d 678 (5th Cir. 1979)—**879**

Hartford Fire Ins. Co. v. California, 509 U.S. 764 (1993)—**502**

Hartog v. Wasatch Acad., 129 F.3d 1076 (10th Cir. 1997)—**111**

Table of Cases

Hason v. Med. Bd., 279 F.3d 1167 (9th Cir. 2002)—**367-368**

Haugh v. Sec'y of Dep't of HHS, No. 90-3128V, 1999 WL 525539 (Fed. Cl. June 30, 1999)—**647**

Havens Realty Corp. v. Coleman, 455 U.S. 363 (1982)—**827-828**

Hazen Paper Co. v. Biggins, 507 U.S. 604 (1993)—**232**

Hedberg v. Ind. Bell Tel. Co., 47 F.3d 928 (7th Cir. 1995)—**310**

Heidemann v. Rother, 84 F.3d 1021 (8th Cir. 1996)—**754**

Helen L. v. DiDario, 46 F.3d 325 (3d Cir. 1995)—**433, 572, 880**

Helen L. v. DiDario, No. 94-1243 (3d Cir. 1994)—**397**

Heller v. Doe, 509 U.S. 312 (1993)—**24, 152, 159, 164**

Hendricks-Robinson v. Excel Corp., 154 F.3d 685 (7th Cir. 1998)—**218, 234**

Hendricks-Robinson v. Excel Corp., 164 F.R.D. 667 (C.D. Ill. 1996)—**258**

Hennigan v. Ouachita Parish Sch. Bd., 749 F.2d 1148 (5th Cir. 1985)—**634**

Henrietta D. v. Bloomberg, 331 F.3d 261 (2d Cir. 2003)—**356, 378-385, 435**

Henrietta D. v. Giuliani, 119 F.Supp.2d 181 (E.D.N.Y. 2000)—**380-384, 434**

Henrietta D. v. Giuliani, 81 F.Supp.2d 425 (E.D.N.Y. 2000)—**384**

Henrietta D. v. Giuliani, No. 95 Civ. 0641, 1996 WL 633382 (E.D.N.Y. Oct. 25, 1996)—**381**

Hensley v. Eckerhart, 461 U.S. 424 (1983)—**316, 319, 621, 623, 626, 645-647, 653**

Hernandez v. Hughes Missile Sys. Co., 298 F.3d 1030 (9th Cir. 2002)—**228, 231-233**

Herr v. City of Chi., 447 F.Supp.2d 915 (N.D. Ill. 2006)—**285**

Hetz v. Aurora Med. Ctr. of Minitowoc Cty., 2007 WL 1753428 (E.D. Wis. 2007)—**460**

Hewitt v. Helms, 482 U.S. 755 (1987)—**623-625, 630, 634, 639**

Higgins v. New Balance Athletic Shoe, Inc., 194 F.3d 252 (1st Cir. 1999)—**211**

Hiler v. Brown, 177 F.3d 542 (6th Cir. 1999)—**184**

Hoeft v. Tuscon Unified Sch. Dist., 967 F.2d 1298 (9th Cir, 1992)—**705**

Hogan v. Bangor & Aroostook R. Co., 61 F.3d 1034 (1st Cir. 1995)—**301, 305-306**

Hogar Agua y Vida en el Desierto, Inc. v. Suarez-Medina, 36 F.3d 177 (1st Cir. 1993)—**778**

Holbrook v. City of Alpharetta, 112 F.3d 1522 (11th Cir. 1997)—**880**

Hollins v. Methodist Helathcare, Inc., 474 F.3d 223 (6th Cir. 2012)—**179**

Holmes v. Sec. Investor Protection Corp., 503 U.S. 258 (1992)—**433**

Honig v. Doe, 484 U.S. 305 (1988)—**708-716**

Hooper v. Demco, Inc., 37 F.3d 287 (7th Cir. 1994)—**638**

Horgan v. Simmons, 704 F.Supp.2d 814 (N.D. Ill. 2010)—**201**

Hornsby v. U.S. Postal Serv., 787 F.2d 87 (3d Cir. 1986)—**308**

Hornstine v. Township of Moorestown, 263 F.Supp.2d 887 (D.N.J. 2003)—**703**

Table of Cases

Lochner v. New York, 198 U.S. 45 (1905)—**21**

Lonberg v. Sanborn Theaters Inc., 259 F.3d 1029 (9th Cir. 2001)—**451**

Long Island Care at Home v. Coke, 551 U.S. 158 (2007)—**862**

Longshoremen v. Ariadne Shipping Co., 397 U.S. 195 (1970)—**495, 499**

Louisiana ex rel. Francis v. Resweber, 329 U.S. 459 (1947)—**352**

Love v. Pullman Co., 404 U.S. 522 (1972)—**282**

Lovejoy-Wilson v. NOCO Motor Fuel, Inc., 263 F.3d 208 (2d Cir. 2001)—**245, 247-248**

Lovell v. Chandler, 303 F.3d 1039 (9th Cir. 2002)—**395, 447, 651**

Lowe v. Ala. Power Co., 244 F.3d 1305 (11th Cir. 2001)—**269**

Lowe v. Indep. Sch. Dist. No. 1, 363 F. App'x 548 (10th Cir. 2010)—**246**

Loye v. Cnty. of Dakota, 625 F.3d 494 (8th Cir. 2010)—**424-425**

Lucas v. Earl, 281 U.S. 111 (1930)—**322**

Lucas v. W.W. Grainger, Inc., 257 F.3d 1249 (11th Cir. 2001)—**251**

Lujan v. Defenders of Wildlife, 504 U.S. 555 (1992)—**206-207, 605, 609, 729**

Lund v. J.C. Penny Outlet, 911 F.Supp. 442 (D. Nev. 1996)—**187**

Lussier v. Runyon, 50 F.3d 1103 (1st Cir. 1995)—**303**

Lyons v. Lower Merrion Sch. Dist., No. 09-5576, 2010 WL 8913276 (E.D. Pa. Dec. 14, 2010)—**663**

Lyons v. Smith, 829 F.Supp. 414 (D.D.C. 1993)—**666**

M

M.C. v. Dep't of Children & Families, 750 So.2d 705 (Fla.Dist.Ct.App. 2000)—**364**

M.L. v. El Paso Indep. Sch. Dist., 369 F. App'x 573 (5th Cir. 2010)—**705**

M.L. v. Fed. Way Sch. Dist., 341 F.3d 1052 (9th Cir. 2003)—**698**

M.L. v. Fed. Way Sch. Dist., 387 F.3d 1101 (9th Cir. 2004)—**739**

M.L.B. v. S.L.J., 519 U.S. 102 (1996)—**337**

M.R. v. Dreyfus, 697 F.3d 706 (9th Cir. 2012)—**405**

M'Culloch v. Maryland, 17 U.S. 316 (1819)—**165**

Mack v. Great Dane Trailers, 308 F.3d 776 (7th Cir. 2002)—**247**

Maher v. Gagne, 448 U.S. 122 (1980)—**624-625, 630, 632, 639**

Majocha v. Turner, 166 F.Supp.2d 316 (W.D. Pa. 2001)—**546**

Malowney v. Fed. Collection Deposit Group, 193 F.3d 1342 (11th Cir. 1999)—**610**

Mancini v. Union Pac. R.R. Co., 98 F. App'x 589 (9th Cir. 2004)—**86**

Mannick v. Kaiser Found. Health Plan, Inc., No. 03-5905, 2006 WL 2168877 (N.D. Cal. July 31, 2006)—**900**

Mansfield, C. & L.M.R. Co. v. Swan, 111 U.S. 379 (1884)—**627, 633, 635**

Mantolete v. Bolger, 767 F.2d 1416 (9th Cir. 1985)—**274**

Marbrunak, Inc. v. City of Stow, 974 F.2d 43 (6th Cir. 1992)—**776, 818**

Marek v. Chesny, 473 U.S. 1 (1985)—**623, 626, 763**

Table of Cases

Maroni v. Pemi-Baker Reg'l Sch. Dist., 346 F.3d 247 (1st Cir. 2003)—**742**

Marr v. Rife, 503 F.2d 735 (6th Cir. 1974)—**776**

Martin v. Kansas, 190 F.3d 1120 (10th Cir. 1999)—**204**

Martin v. Metro. Atlanta Rapid Transit Auth., 225 F.Supp.2d 1362 (N.D. Ga. 2002)—**447, 484, 878-883**

Martin v. PGA Tour, 994 F.Supp. 1242 (D. Or. 1998)—**526**

Martini v. Fed. Nat'l Mortgage Ass'n, 178 F.3d 1336 (D.C. Cir. 1999)—**304**

Mary Jo C. v. New York State & Local Ret. Sys., 707 F.3d 144 (2d Cir. 2013)—**376**

Mass. Bd. of Retirement v. Murgia, 427 U.S. 307 (1976)—**11, 153**

Mathews v. Eldridge, 424 U.S. 319 (1976)—**730**

Matthews v. Jefferson, 29 F.Supp.2d 525 (W.D. Ark. 1998)—**446**

Matthews v. Nat'l Collegiate Athletic Ass'n, 179 F.Supp.2d 1209 (E.D. Wash. 2001)—**511**

May v. Sheahan, 226 F.3d 876 (7th Cir. 2000)—**354**

Mayberry v. Von Valtier, 843 F.Supp. 1160 (E.D. Mich. 1994)—**554**

Mayes v. Allison, 983 F.Supp. 923 (D. Nev. 1997)—**601**

Mayes v. Whitlock Packaging Corp., 2010 WL 1754200 (E.D. Okla. Apr. 29, 2010)—**279**

Mays v. Principi, 301 F.3d 866 (7th Cir. 2002)—**250-251**

McCarthy v. Hawkins, 381 F.3d 407 (5th Cir. 2003)—**356**

McClure v. Salvation Army, 460 F.2d 553 (5th Cir. 1972)—**180**

McCormick v. Waukegan Sch. Dist. No. 60, 374 F.3d 564 (7th Cir. 2004)—**739**

McCulloch v. Sociedad Nacional de Marineros de Honduras, 372 U.S. 10 (1963)—**492, 504, 507**

McDonnell Douglas Corp. v. Green, 411 U.S. 792 (1973)—**231, 254**

McGary v. City of Portland, 386 F.3d 1259 (9th Cir. 2004)—**798**

McGregor v. La. State Univ. Bd. of Supervisors, 3 F.3d 850 (5th Cir. 1993)—**818**

McGregor v. Nat'l R.R. Passenger Corp., 187 F.3d 1113 (9th Cir. 1999)—**269**

McKnight v. Gen. Motors Corp., 973 F.2d 1366 (7th Cir. 1992)—**300**

McLaughlin v. Florida, 379 U.S. 184 (1964)—**11**

McPherson v. Fed. Express Corp., 241 F. App'x 277 (6th Cir. 2006)—**86**

McPherson v. Mich. High Sch. Athletic Ass'n, 119 F.3d 453 (6th Cir. 1997)—**376**

Meagley v. City of Little Rock, 639 F.3d 384 (8th Cir. 2011)—**446**

Medlock v. Ortho Biotech, Inc., 164 F.3d 545 (10th Cir. 1999)—**304**

Mengine v. Runyon, 114 F.3d 415 (3d Cir. 1997)—**245**

Menkowitz v. Pottstown Mem'l Med. Ctr., 154 F.3d 113 (3d Cir. 1998)—**460**

Meyer v. Nebraska, 262 U.S. 390 (1923)—**17, 746**

Miami Univ. v. Ohio Civil Rights Comm'n, 726 N.E.2d 1032 (Ohio Ct. App., 1999)—**242**

Table of Cases

Mich. Protection & Advocacy Serv., Inc. v. Peggy Babin, 18 F.3d 337 (6th Cir. 1994)—**772-778**

Midgett v. Tri-Cnty. Metro. Dist. of Or., 74 F.Supp.2d 1008 (D. Or. 1999)—**879**

Midgett v. Tri-Cnty. Metro. Transp. Dist., 254 F.3d 846 (9th Cir. 2001)—**428**

Miener v. State of Missouri, 800 F.2d 749 (8th Cir. 1986)—**753**

Miles v. State, 320 F.3d 986 (9th Cir. 2003)—**309**

Miller v. Abilene Christian Univ. of Dallas, 517 F.Supp. 437 (D.C. Tex. 1981)—**905**

Miller v. Cal. Speedway, 536 F.3d 1020 (9th Cir. 2008)—**596**

Miller v. Cigna Corp., 47 F.3d 586 (3d Cir. 1995)—**256**

Miller v. King, 384 F.3d 1248 (11th Cir. 2004)—**351, 353, 356**

Miller v. Maxwell's Int'l, Inc., 991 F.2d 583 (9th Cir. 1993)—**140, 187**

Miller v. Pub. Storage Mgmt., Inc., 121 F.3d 215 (5th Cir. 1997)—**328**

Miller v. Tx. Tech Univ. Health Scis. Ctr., 421 F.3d 342 (5th Cir. 2005)—**358**

Mills v. Bd. of Educ. of D.C., 348 F.Supp. 866 (D.D.C. 1972)—**656-657, 675-677, 724, 730**

Mills v. Habluetzel, 456 U.S. 91 (1982)—**18**

Milton v. Scrivner, Inc., 53 F.3d 1118 (10th Cir. 1995)—**216**

Miranda B. v. Kitzhaber, 328 F.3d 1181 (9th Cir. 2003)—**357-358**

Miss. Univ. for Women v. Hogan, 458 U.S. 718 (1982)—**18**

Mitsubishi Motors Corp. v. Soler Chrysler-Plymouth, Inc., 473 U.S. 614 (1985)—**294, 326**

Mobile v. Bolden, 446 U.S. 55 (1980)—**164**

Mohr v. Dustrol, Inc., 306 F.3d 636 (8th Cir. 2002)—**256**

Molloy v. Metro. Trans. Auth., 94 F.3d 808 (2d Cir. 1996)—**418, 581**

Molski v. Evergreen Dynasty Corp., 500 F.3d 1047 (9th Cir. 2007)—**460-461**

Molski v. Foley Estates Vineyard & Winery, LLC, 531 F.3d 1043 (9th Cir. 2008)—**562**

Molski v. M.J. Cable, Inc., 481 F.3d 724 (9th Cir. 2007)—**460, 897**

Monette v. Elec. Data Sys. Corp., 90 F.3d 1173 (6th Cir. 1996)—**240, 253, 802**

Mont. Fair Hous., Inc. v. Am. Capital Dev., Inc., 81 F.Supp.2d 1057 (D. Mont. 1999)—**825**

Moor v. Cnty. of Alameda, 411 U.S. 693 (1973)—**160**

Moreno v. G&M Oil Co., 88 F.Supp.2d 1116 (C.D. Cal. 2000)—**583, 609-610**

Morgan v. Hilti, Inc., 108 F.3d 1319 (10th Cir. 1995)—**254-255**

Morissette v. United States, 342 U.S. 246 (1952)—**629**

Morrison v. Circuit City Stores, Inc., 317 F.3d 646 (6th Cir. 2003)—**328**

Morrison v. Nat'l Australia Bank Ltd., 561 U.S. ___ (2010)—**179-180**

Morton v. United Parcel Serv., Inc., 272 F.3d 1249 (9th Cir. 2001)—**247**

Table of Cases

Mosely v. Bd. of Educ. of Chicago, 434 F.3d 527 (7th Cir. 2006)—**751**

Moskowitz v. Trs. of Purdue Univ., 5 F.3d 279 (7th Cir. 1993)—**285**

Motzkin v. Boston Univ., 938 F.Supp. 983 (D. Mass. 1996)—**460**

Moysis v. DTG Datanet, 278 F.3d 819 (8th Cir. 2002)—**302**

Ms. K. v. City of So. Portland, 407 F.Supp.2d 290 (D. Me. 2006)—**447**

Mt. Healthy City Bd. of Educ. v. Doyle, 429 U.S. 274 (1977)—**729**

Muller v. Costello, No. 94-CV-842 (FJS), 1996 WL 191977 (N.D.N.Y. Apr. 16, 1996)—**870**

N

N. Kitsap Sch. Dist. v. K.W., 123 P.3d 469 (Wash. Ct. App. 2005)—**725**

N.M. Ass'n for Retarded Citizens v. New Mexico, 678 F.2d 847 (10th Cir. 1982)—**903**

N.Y. Trust Co. v. Eisner, 256 U.S. 345 (1921)—**22**

NAACP v. Button, 371 U.S. 415 (1963)—**15**

Nat'l Ass'n of the Deaf v. Netflix, Inc., 869 F.Supp.2d 196 (D. Mass. 2012)—**877, 886, 913**

Nat'l Fed. of the Blind v. Target Corp., 582 F.Supp.2d 1185 (N.D. Cal. 2007)—**893-902, 913**

Nat'l Fed'n of Indep. Bus. v. Sebelius, 132 S. Ct. 2566 (2012)—**865**

Natal v. Christian & Missionary Alliance, 878 F.2d 1575 (1989)—**179**

Nathanson v. Med. Coll. of Pa., 926 F.2d 1368 (3d Cir. 1991)—**243**

National Railroad Passenger Corp. v. Morgan, 536 U.S. 101 (2002)—**285**

NationsBank of N. C., N. A. v. Variable Annuity Life Ins. Co., 513 U.S. 251 (1995)—**737**

Nationwide Mut. Ins. Co. v. Darden, 503 U.S. 318 (1992)—**140, 142-145, 147**

Ne. Fla. Chapter of Ass'n of Gen. Contractors of Am. v. Jacksonville, Fla., 896 F.2d 1283 (11th Cir. 1990)—**878**

Neely v. PSGE Tex., 2013 WL 5942233 (5th Cir. 2013)—**109**

Neff v. Am. Dairy Queen Corp., F.3d 1063 (5th Cir. 1995)—**453-458**

Neitzke v. Williams, 490 U.S. 319 (1989)—**312, 643**

Nev. Dep't of Human Res. v. Hibbs, 538 U.S. 721 (2003)—**335, 339, 341-343, 345**

New Orleans v. Dukes, 427 U.S. 297 (1976)—**152, 164**

Newberry v. E. Tex. State Univ., 161 F.3d 276 (5th Cir 1998)—**247**

Newhouse v. McCormick & Co., Inc., 110 F.3d 635 (8th Cir. 1997)—**300**

Newman v. Piggie Park Enters., Inc., 390 U.S. 400 (1968)—**545, 604, 635, 645**

Niece v. Fitzner, 922 F.Supp. 1208 (E.D. Mich. 1996)—**369, 446**

Nieves-Marquez v. Puerto Rico, 353 F.3d 108 (1st Cir. 2003)—**440, 754**

No Barriers, Inc., v. Brinker Chili's Tex., Inc., 262 F.3d 496 (5th Cir. 2001)—**319, 653**

Table of Cases

Noel v. N.Y.C. Taxi & Limousine Comm'n, 687 F.3d 63 (2d Cir. 2012)—**369, 430**

Noel v. N.Y.C. Taxi & Limousine Comm'n, 837 F.Supp.2d 268 (S.D.N.Y. 2011)—**430**

Nolley v. Cnty. of Erie, 776 F.Supp. 715 (W.D.N.Y. 1991)—**354**

Nordlinger v. Hahn, 505 U.S. 1 (1992)—**152**

Norman v. Hous. Auth. of City of Montgomery, 836 F.2d 1292 (11th Cir. 1988)—**646-648**

Norman-Bloodsaw v. Lawrence Berkeley Lab., 135 F.3d 1260 (9th Cir. 1998)—**200**

Nowak v. St. Rita High Sch., 142 F.3d 999 (7th Cir. 1998)—**213**

Nunes v. Wal-Mart Stores, Inc., 164 F.3d 1243 (9th Cir. 1999)—**269, 274-275**

O

O'Gilvie v. United States, 519 U.S. 79 (1996)—**321**

O'Neal v. McAninch, 513 U.S. 432 (1995)—**735**

O'Shea v. Littleton, 414 U.S. 488 (1974)—**610**

Oberti v. Bd. of Educ., 995 F.2d 1204 (3d Cir. 1993)—**695, 697, 733**

Occidental Life Ins. Co. of Cal. v. EEOC, 432 U.S. 355 (1977)—**292**

Oconomowoc Residential Programs, Inc. v. City of Milwaukee, 300 F.3d 775 (7th Cir. 2002)—**807-815, 819**

Ohio Pub. Emps. Ret. Sys. v. Betts, 492 U.S. 158 (1989)—**467, 472**

Olinger v. U.S. Golf Ass'n, 205 F.3d 1001 (7th Cir. 2000)—**522**

Oliveras-Sifre v. P.R. Dep't of Health, 214 F.3d 23 (1st Cir. 2000)—**115, 117**

Olmstead v. Zimring, 527 U.S. 581 (1999)—**382, 385, 396-403, 433-434**

Or. Paralyzed Veterans of Am. v. Regal Cinemas, Inc., 339 F.3d 1126 (9th Cir. 2003)—**597, 614**

Oregon v. Mitchell, 400 U.S. 112 (1970)—**163**

Orr v. Wal-Mart Stores, Inc., 297 F.3d 720 (8th Cir. 2002)—**267**

Ostrach v. Regents of the Univ. of Cal., 957 F.Supp. 196 (E.D. Cal. 1997)—**187**

Overley v. Covenant Transp., Inc., 178 F. App'x 488 (6th Cir. 2006)—**111**

Owusu-Ansah v. Coca-Cola Co., 715 F.3d 1306 (11th Cir. 2013)—**207**

Oxford House, Inc. v. Township of Cherry Hill, 799 F.Supp. 450 (D.N.J. 1992)—**786**

Oxford House-C v. City of St. Louis, 77 F.3d 249 (8th Cir. 1996)—**821**

Ozlowski v. Henderson, 237 F.3d 837 (7th Cir. 2001)—**250**

P

Pa. Ass'n for Retarded Children v. Pennsylvania, 334 F.Supp. 1257 (E.D. Pa. 1971)—**656, 675-677, 730**

Pa. Ass'n for Retarded Children v. Pennsylvania, 343 F.Supp. 279 (E.D. Pa. 1972)—**675, 713**

Pa. Dep't of Corr. v. Yeskey, 524 U.S. 206 (1998)—**352, 359-360, 526**

Pac. States Box & Basket Co. v. White, 296 U.S. 176 (1935)—**162**

Padilla v. Sch. Dist. No. 1, Denver, 233 F.3d 1268 (10th Cir. 2000)—**739, 754**

Table of Cases

Pallozzi v. Allstate Life Ins. Co., 198 F.3d 28 (2d Cir. 2000)—**487, 886**

Pals v. Schepel Buick & GMC Truck, Inc., 220 F.3d 495 (7th Cir. 2000)—**304**

Pantazes v. Jackson, 366 F.Supp.2d 57 (D.D.C. 2005)—**908**

Papa v. Katy Indus., Inc., 166 F.3d 937 (7th Cir. 1999)—**146, 148, 170**

Paralyzed Veterans of Am. v. D.C. Arena L.P., 117 F.3d 579 (D.C. Cir. 1997)—**591, 596**

Parents of Student W. v. Puyallup Sch. Dist. No. 3, 31 F.3d 1489 (9th Cir. 1994)—**768**

Parham v. Sw. Bell Tel. Co., 433 F.2d 421 (8th Cir. 1970)—**625, 629, 637**

Parker v. Metro. Life Ins. Co., 121 F.3d 1006 (6th Cir. 1997)—**465-478, 486, 885**

Parker v. Metro. Life Ins. Co., 99 F.3d 181 (6th Cir. 1996)—**474**

Parker v. Universidad de P.R., 225 F.3d 1 (1st Cir. 2000)—**406**

Parks v. Potter, No. 01A12128, EEOC DOC 1A12128, 2002 WL 31232213 (EEOC Sept. 27, 2002)—**268**

Parr v. L & L Drive-Inn Rest., 96 F.Supp.2d 1065 (D. Haw. 2000)—**555, 579-580, 611-612, 615**

Parsons v. First Quality Retail Servs., 2012 WL 174829 (M.D. Ga. Jan. 20, 2012)—**201**

Pascuiti v. N.Y. Yankees, No. 98 CIV. 8186(SAS), 1999 WL 1102748 (S.D.N.Y. Dec. 6, 1999)—**553, 555, 560**

Pashby v. Delia, 709 F.3d 307 (4th Cir. 2013)—**404**

Pazer v. N.Y. State Bd. of Law Exam'rs, 849 F.Supp. 284 (S.D.N.Y. 1994)—**488**

Pedigo v. P.A.M. Transp., Inc., 60 F.3d 1300 (8th Cir. 1995)—**256, 309, 642**

Pedigo v. P.A.M. Transp., Inc., 98 F.3d 396 (8th Cir. 1996)—**309, 642**

Pennhurst State Sch. & Hosp. v. Halderman, 451 U.S. 1 (1981)—**398, 443-444, 748, 756, 761**

Pennsylvania v. Del. Valley Citizens' Council for Clean Air, 478 U.S. 546 (1986)—**318, 653**

People ex rel. Spitzer v. Cnty. of Del., 82 F.Supp.2d 12 (N.D.N.Y. 2000)—**447**

People v. Caldwell, 603 N.Y.S.2d 713 (N.Y. City Crim. Ct. 1993)—**361**

Perrin v. United States, 444 U.S. 37 (1979)—**634**

Petersen v. Hastings Pub. Schs., 31 F.3d 705 (8th Cir. 1994)—**425**

Petersen v. Univ. of Wis. Bd. of Regents, 818 F.Supp. 1276 (W.D. Wis. 1993)—**440**

Petit v. U.S. Dept. of Educ., 675 F.3d 769 (D.C. Cir. 2012)—**688**

Petition of Rubenstein, 637 A.2d 1131 (Del. 1994)—**361**

Petruska v. Gannon Univ., 462 F.3d 294 (2006)—**179**

PGA Tour Inc., v. Martin, 532 U.S. 661 (2001)—**459, 519-532, 613**

Phillip C. ex. Rel. A.C. v. Jefferson Bd. of Educ., 701 F.3d 691 (11th Cir. 2012)—**663**

Phillips v. W. Co. of N. Am., 953 F.2d 923 (5th Cir. 1992)—**303**

Table of Cases

Pickern v. Holiday Quality Foods Inc., 293 F.3d 1133 (9th Cir. 2002)—**604, 606-611**

Pierce v. Cnty. of Orange, 526 F.3d 1190 (9th Cir. 2008)—**361**

Pierce v. Soc'y of Sisters, 268 U.S. 510 (1925)—**745**

Pino v. Locasio, 101 F.3d 235 (2d Cir. 1996)—**320, 654**

Pioneer Inv. Servs. Co. v. Brunswick Assocs. Ltd. P'ship, 507 U.S. 380 (1993)—**629, 632, 634**

Piquard v. City of E. Peoria, 887 F.Supp. 1106 (C.D. Ill. 1995)—**361**

Plessy v. Ferguson, 163 U.S. 537 (1896)—**19**

Plumo ex rel. Doe v. Bell, 754 N.Y.S.2d 846 (N.Y. Sup. Ct. 2003)—**278**

Plyler v. Doe, 457 U.S. 202 (1982)—**10, 17-18, 20**

Poff v. Prudential Ins. Co. of Am., 882 F.Supp. 1534 (E.D. Pa. 1995)—**169**

Polera v. Bd. of Educ. of Newburgh, 288 F.3d 478 (2d Cir. 2002)—**739**

Polera v. Bd. of Educ. of the Newburgh Enlarged City Sch. Dist., 288 F.3d 478 (2d Cir. 2002)—**753**

Pollard v. E.I. du Pont de Nemours & Co., 532 U.S. 843 (2001)—**300**

Pollard v. E.I. DuPont de Nemours & Co., 213 F.3d 933 (6th Cir. 2000)—**304**

Pona v. Cecil Shitaker's, Inc., 155 F.3d 1034 (8th Cir. 1998)—**458-459**

Pool v. Riverside Health Serv., Inc., No. 94-1430-PFK, 1995 WL 519129 (D. Kan. Aug. 25, 1995)—**519**

Poore v. Peterbilt of Bristol, L.L.C., 852 F.Supp.2d 727 (W.D. Va. 2012)—**869**

Posadas v. Pool Depot, Inc., 858 So.2d 611 (La. App. 2003)—**328**

Pottgen v. Mo. State High Sch. Activities Ass'n, 40 F.3d 926 (8th Cir. 1994)—**371-375, 853-856**

Pottgen v. Mo. State High Sch. Activities Ass'n, 857 F.Supp. 654 (E.D. Mo. 1994)—**372, 375, 853**

Powers v. Ohio, 499 U.S. 400 (1991)—**114**

Preiser v. Rodriguez, 411 U.S. 475 (1973)—**359**

Press-Enter. Co. v. Super. Ct. of Cal., 478 U.S. 1 (1986)—**338, 343**

Presta v. Peninsula Corridor Joint Powers Bd., 16 F.Supp.2d 1134 (N.D. Cal. 1998)—**899**

Price Waterhouse v. Hopkins, 490 U.S. 228 (1989)—**255**

Procunier v. Martinez, 416 U.S. 396 (1974)—**359**

Pulcinella v. Ridley Twp., 822 F.Supp. 204 (E.D. Pa. 1993)—**779**

Pulley v. United Health Group Inc., No. 4:11CV00634 KGB, ___ F.Supp.2d ___, 2013 WL 1947552 (E.D. Ark. 2013)—**869**

Purvis v. Williams, 73 P.3d 740 (Kan. 2003)—**358**

Pushkin v. Regents of Univ. of Colo., 658 F.2d 1372 (10th Cir. 1981)—**440, 793**

Pyles v. Kamka, 491 F.Supp. 204 (D. Md. 1980)—**422**

Table of Cases

Q

Quackenbush v. Johnson City Sch. Dist., 716 F.2d 141 (2d Cir. 1983)—**754**

Quad Enters. Co., LLC v. Town of Southold, 369 F. App'x 202 (2010)—**821**

Québec (Comm'n des Droits de la Personne & des Droits de la Jeunesse) v. Montréal (Ville), [2000] 1 S.C.R. 665, 185 D.L.R. (4th) 385, 2000 CarswellQue 650 (2000)—**947**

R

Radaszewski ex rel. Radaszewski v. Maram, 383 F.3d 599 (7th Cir. 2004)—**403-404**

Ramirez v. City of San Antonio, 312 F.3d 178 (5th Cir. 2002)—**284**

Rauen v. U.S. Tobacco Mfg., 319 F.3d 891 (7th Cir. 2003)—**214**

Rayburn v. Gen. Conference of Seventh-Day Adventists, 772 F.2d 1164 (1985)—**182**

Raygor v. Regents of Univ. of Minn., 534 U.S. 533 (2002)—**500**

Raytheon Co. v. Hernandez, 540 U.S. 44 (2003)—**228-233**

Red Cloud-Owen v. Albany Steel, Inc., 958 F.Supp. 94 (N.D.N.Y. 1997)—**320, 654**

Reed v. LePage Bakeries, Inc., 244 F.3d 254 (1st Cir. 2001)—**220, 221, 227, 243, 250, 252, 253, 254**

Reed v. Reed, 404 U.S. 71 (1971)—**19**

Regal Cinemas, Inc. v. Stewmon, 124 S.Ct. 2903 (2004)—**597**

Regents of Univ. of Cal. v. Doe, 519 U.S. 425 (1997)—**160**

Rehling v. City of Chicago, 207 F.3d 1009 (7th Cir. 2000)—**246**

Reichmann v. Cutler-Hammer, Inc., 95 F.Supp.2d 1171 (D. Kan. 2001)—**204**

Reickenbacker v. Foster, 274 F.3d 974 (5th Cir. 2001)—**357**

Reid v. District of Columbia, 401 F.3d 516 (D.C. Cir. 2005)—**768**

Reigel v. Kaiser Found. Health Plan of N.C., 859 F.Supp. 963 (E.D.N.C. 1994)—**237, 241**

Rendine v. Pantzer, 661 A.2d 1202 (N.J. 1995)—**315-317**

Rendon v. Valleycrest Prods., Ltd., 294 F.3d 1279 (11th Cir. 2002)—**481-892**

Reno v. Am. Civil Liberties Union, 521 U.S. 844 (1997)—**166**

Resnick v. Magical Cruise Co., Ltd., 148 F.Supp.2d 1298 (M.D. Fla. 2001)—**610**

Rettig v. Kent City Sch. Dist., 788 F.2d 328 (6th Cir. 1986)—**686**

Reusch v. Fountain, 872 F.Supp. 1421 (D. Md. 1994)—**706-707**

Reyes-Gaona v. N.C. Growers Ass'n, 250 F.3d 861 (4th Cir. 2001)—**171**

Rhoads v. FDIC, 257 F.3d 373 (4th Cir. 2001)—**86, 116**

Rhoads v. FDIC, No. CCB-94-1548, 2002 WL 31755427 (D. Md. Nov. 7, 2002)—**306**

Rhodes v. Stewart, 488 U.S. 1 (1988)—**624**

Richard S. v. Dep't of Developmental Servs., 317 F.3d 1080 (9th Cir. 2003)—**641-642**

Richards v. CH2M Hill, 111 Cal.Rptr.2d 87 (Cal. 2001)—**286**

Richmond v. J.A. Croson Co., 488 U.S. 469 (1989)—**160**

Ricks v. Xerox Corp., 877 F.Supp. 1468 (D. Kan. 1995)—**241**

Table of Cases

Riel v. Elec. Data Sys. Corp., 99 F.3d 678 (5th Cir. 1996)—**253, 513-514**

Ringwood Bd. of Educ. v. K.H.J., 469 F.Supp.2d 267 (3d Cir. 2006)—**725**

Rizzo v. Goode, 423 U.S. 362 (1976)—**878, 881-882**

Robb v. Bethel Sch. Dist. No. 403, 308 F.3d 1047 (9th Cir. 2002)—**739**

Robb v. Horizon Credit Union, 66 F.Supp.2d 913 (C.D. Ill. 1999)—**86**

Robert v. Bd. of Cnty. Comm'rs of Brown Cnty., 691 F.3d 1211 (10th Cir. 2012)—**213**

Roberts v. U.S. Jaycees, 468 U.S. 609 (1984)—**18**

Roberts v. United States Jaycees, 468 U.S. 609 (1984)—**176**

Robins v. Scholastic Book Fairs, 928 F.Supp. 1027 (D. Or. 1996)—**652**

Robinson v. Kansas, 295 F.3d 1183 (10th Cir. 2002)—**358**

Robinson v. Shell Oil Co., 519 U.S. 337 (1997)—**128**

Rodde v. Bonta, 357 F.3d 988 (9th Cir. 2004)—**389-395**

Rode v. Dellarciprete, 892 F.2d 1177 (3d Cir. 1990)—**313-315**

Rodriguez v. 551 W. 157th Street Owners Corp., 992 F.Supp. 385 (S.D.N.Y. 1998)—**784-786**

Roe v. Cheyenne Mountain Conference Resort, Inc., 124 F.3d 1221 (10th Cir. 1997)—**196, 203, 207**

Roe v. Cheyenne Mountain Conference Resort, Inc., 920 F.Supp. 1153 (D. Colo. 1996)—**196, 203**

Roland M. v. Concord Sch. Comm., 910 F.2d 983 (1st Cir. 1990)—**695**

Roland v. Cellucci, 106 F.Supp.2d 128 (D. Mass. 2000)—**319, 653**

Roncker v. Walker, 700 F.2d 1058 (6th Cir. 1983)—**690, 695, 698, 740**

Ross v. Commc's Satellite Corp., 759 F.2d 355 (4th Cir. 1985)—**116**

Ross v. Ryanair Ltd, 1 W.L.R. 2447 (C.A. 2005)—**944**

Rothschild v. Grottenthaler, 907 F.2d 286 (2d Cir. 1990)—**543-545**

Rowley v. Bd. of Educ. of Hendrick Hudson Cent. Sch. Dist., 632 F.2d 945 (2d Cir. 1980)—**673**

Rush v. Nat'l Bd. of Med. Exam'rs, 268 F.Supp.2d 673 (N.D. Tex. 2003)—**615**

Rutledge v. United States, 517 U.S. 292 (1996)—**634**

S

S.F. v. McKinney Indep. Sch. Dist., No. 4:10-CV-323-RAS-DDB, 2012 WL 718589 (E.D. Tex. Mar. 6, 2012)—**663**

S.-Suburban Hous. Ctr. v. Greater S.-Suburban Bd. of Realtors, 935 F.2d 868 (7th Cir. 1991)—**776**

S-1 & S-2 v. State Bd. of Ed. of N.C., 21 F.3d 49 (4th Cir. 1994)—**622**

Sacramento City Unified Sch. Dist. v. Rachel H., 14 F.3d 1398 (9th Cir. 1994)—**690-698**

Saladin v. Turner, 936 F.Supp. 1571 (N.D. Okla. 1996)—**301**

Salitros v. Chrysler Corp., 306 F.3d 562 (8th Cir. 2002)—**299-300, 303, 307**

Table of Cases

Salute v. Greens, 918 F.Supp. 660 (E.D.N.Y. 1996)—**785-786**

San Antonio Indep. Sch. Dist. v. Rodriguez, 411 U.S. 1 (1973)—**18, 22**

Sanchez v. Johnson, 416 F.3d 1051 (9th Cir. 2005)—**403**

Sanders v. City of Minneapolis, 474 F.3d 523 (8th Cir. 2007)—**385**

Sandison v. Mich. High Sch. Athletic Ass'n, 64 F.3d 1026 (6th Cir. 1995)—**375, 435**

Sandison v. Mich. High Sch. Athletic Ass'n, Inc., 863 F. Supp. 483 (D. Mich. 1994)—**905**

Santa Fe Indus., Inc. v. Green, 430 U.S. 462 (1977)—**36**

Santa Maria v. Pac. Bell, 202 F.3d 1170 (9th Cir. 2000)—**830**

Santana v. Lehigh Valley Hosp. & Health Network, No. Civ.A.05-CV-01496, 2005 WL 1941654 (E.D. Pa. Aug. 11, 2005)—**306**

Satterfield v. Tennessee, 295 F.3d 611 (6th Cir. 2002)—**187**

Savage v. City Place Ltd. P'ship, No. 240306, 2004 WL 3045404 (Md. Cir. Ct. Dec. 20, 2004)—**511**

Save Our Summers v. Wash. State Dep't of Ecology, 132 F.Supp.2d 896 (E.D. Wash. 1999)—**369**

Scelta v. Delicatessen Support Servs., Inc., 203 F.Supp.2d 1328 (M.D. Fla. 2002)—**650**

Sch. Bd. of Nassau Cty, Fla. v. Arline, 480 U.S. 273 (1987)—**71, 78-79, 101-107, 268, 373, 378, 400, 854, 855**

Sch. Comm. of Burlington v. Dep't of Ed. of Mass., 471 U.S. 359 (1985)—**714, 731, 740, 753, 764**

Schaffer v. Bd. of Educ. of Montgomery Cnty., 554 F.3d 470 (4th Cir. 2009)—**738**

Schaffer v. Weast, 126 S.Ct. 528 (2005)—**726-737, 743**

Scheerer v. Potter, 443 F.3d 916 (7th Cir. 2006)—**86**

Scherr v. Mariott Int'l Inc., 703 F.3d 1069 (7th Cir. 2013)—**606**

Schorr v. Borough of Lemoyne, 243 F.Supp.2d 232 (M.D. Pa. 2003)—**385**

Schrader v. Ray, 296 F.3d 968 (10th Cir. 2002)—**184**

Schultz v. Potter, 142 F. App'x 598 (3d Cir. 2005)—**86**

Schutts v. Bently Nev. Corp., 966 F.Supp. 1549 (D. Nev. 1997)—**312, 643**

Schwarz v. City of Treasure Island, 544 F.3d 1201 (11th Cir. 2008)—**782, 820, 821**

Scoggins v. Lee's Crossing Homeowners Ass'n, 718 F.3d 262 (2013)—**806**

Se. Cmty. Coll. v. Davis, 442 U.S. 397 (1979)—**34-41, 59, 103, 127, 788, 794-795, 854**

Se. Cmty. Coll. v. Davis, 480 U.S. 273 (1987)—**378**

Se. Cmty. Coll. v. Davis, 439 U.S. 1065 (1979)—**36**

Seattle Sch. Dist. No. 1 v. B.S., 82 F.3d 1493 (9th Cir. 1996)—**718**

Sedima, S.P.R.L. v. Imrex Co., 473 U.S. 479 (1985)—**360**

Sellers v. Sch. Bd. of City of Manassas, 141 F.3d 524 (4th Cir. 1998)—**754**

Seminole Tribe of Fla. v. Florida, 517 U.S. 44 (1996)—**150-151, 167, 356**

Table of Cases

Serbian E. Orthodox Diocese for United States & Canada v. Milivojevich, 426 U.S. 696 (1976)—**175**

Seremeth v. Bd. of Cnty. Com'rs Frederick Cnty., 673 F.3d 333 (4th Cir. 2012)—**425**

Serwatka v. Rockwell, 591 F.3d 957 (7th Cir. 2010)—**257**

Shapiro v. Cadman Towers Inc., 844 F.Supp. 116 (E.D.N.Y. 1994)—**792-793**

Shapiro v. Cadman Towers, Inc., 51 F.3d 328 (2d Cir. 1995)—**785, 790-797**

Shapiro v. Thompson, 394 U.S. 618 (1969)—**11, 346**

Shapiro v. Twp. of Lakewood, 292 F.3d 356 (3d Cir. 2002)—**250-251**

Sharp v. United Airlines, Inc., 236 F.3d 368 (7th Cir. 2001)—**283**

Shaw-Campbell v. Runyon, 888 F.Supp. 1111 (M.D. Ala. 1995)—**189**

Shea v. Tisch, 870 F.2d 786 (1st Cir. 1989)—**299**

Shearson/Am. Express, Inc. v. McMahon, 482 U.S. 220 (1987)—**326**

Shekoyan v. Sibley Int'l Corp., 217 F.Supp.2d 59 (D.D.C. 2002)—**170**

Shellenberger v. Summit Bancorp, 318 F.3d 183 (3d Cir. 2003)—**112**

Shepard v. Honda of Am. Mfg., Inc., 160 F.Supp.2d 860 (S.D. Ohio 2001)—**651**

Shore Reg'l High Sch. Bd. of Educ. v. P.S., 381 F.3d 194 (3d Cir. 2004)—**697**

Shotz v. Cates, 256 F.3d 1077 (11th Cir. 2001)—**610**

Shotz v. City of Plantation, Fla., 344 F.3d 1161 (11th Cir. 2003)—**117, 356**

Silk v. City of Chicago, 194 F.3d 788 (7th Cir. 1999)—**118**

Singh v. George Washington Univ. Sch. of Med., 508 F.3d 1097 (D.C. Cir. 2007)—**87**

Singleton v. Wulff, 428 U.S. 106 (1976)—**114**

Sizova v. Nat'l Inst. of Standards & Tech., 282 F.3d 1320 (10th Cir. 2002)—**288**

Skidmore v. Swift & Co., 323 U.S. 134 (1944)—**398**

Skinner v. Oklahoma ex rel. Williamson, 316 U.S. 535 (1942)—**11, 346**

Skomsky v. Speedway Superamerica, LLC, 267 F.Supp.2d 995 (D. Minn. 2003)—**254**

Smith & Lee Assocs., Inc. v. City of Taylor, 102 F.3d 781 (6th Cir. 1996)—**802, 812**

Smith v. Barton, 914 F.2d 1330 (9th Cir. 1990)—**440**

Smith v. Donahoe, 917 F.Supp.2d 562 (E.D. Va. 2013)—**869**

Smith v. Midland Brake, Inc., 180 F.3d 1154 (10th Cir. 1999)—**250**

Smith v. Robinson, 468 U.S. 992 (1984)—**713, 761, 764**

Snyder v. San Diego Flowers, 21 F.Supp.2d 1207 (S.D. Cal. 1998)—**601-602**

Soto v. City of Newark, 72 F.Supp.2d 489 (D.N.J. 1999)—**361, 369, 424**

South Carolina v. Katzenbach, 383 U.S. 301 (1966)—**156, 165**

South Carolina v. Katzenbach, 383 U.S. 301 (1966)—**338, 345**

South Dakota v. Dole, 483 U.S. 203 (1987)—**756**

Spades v. City of Walnut Ridge, 186 F.3d 897 (8th Cir. 1999)—**86**

Speciner v. Nationsbank, N.A., 215 F.Supp.2d 622 (D. Md. 2002)—**583**

Spector v. Norwegian Cruise Line Ltd., 356 F.3d 641 (5th Cir. 2004), cert. granted, 72 U.S.L.W. 3644 (U.S. Sept. 28, 2004) (No. 03-1388)—**490-492**

Spector v. Norwegian Cruise Line Ltd., 427 F.3d 285 (5th Cir. 2005)—**508**

Spector v. Norwegian Cruise Line Ltd., 545 U.S. 119 (2005)—**486, 490-507**

Spence v. Straw, 54 F.3d 196 (3d Cir. 1995)—**441**

Sporn v. Ocean Colony Condo. Ass'n, 173 F.Supp.2d 244 (D.N.J. 2001)—**798**

Sprogis v. United Air Lines, Inc., 444 F.2d 1194 (7th Cir. 1971)—**399**

Spurlock v. Simmons, 88 F.Supp.2d 1189 (D. Kan. 2000)—**424**

St. Mary's Honor Ctr. v. Hicks, 509 U.S. 502 (1993)—**729**

State ex rel. Okla. Bar Ass'n v. Busch, 919 P.2d 1114 (Okla. 1996)—**361**

Staton v. Boeing Co., 327 F.3d 938 (9th Cir. 2003)—**318, 652**

Steger v. Franco, Inc., 228 F.3d 889 (8th Cir. 2000)—**609-610**

Stepney v. Naperville School Dist. 203, 392 F.3d 236 (7th 2004)—**285**

Stern v. Cal. State Archives, 982 F.Supp. 690 (E.D. Cal. 1997)—**188**

Stevens v. Premier Cruises, Inc., 215 F.3d 1237 (11th Cir. 2000)—**482, 491**

Stone v. City of Indianapolis Pub. Utils. Div., 281 F.3d 640 (7th Cir. 2002)—**112**

Stoutenborough v. Nat'l Football League, Inc., 59 F.3d 580 (6th Cir. 1995)—**469, 473, 485, 890-891**

Support Ministries for Persons with AIDS, Inc. v. Vill. of Waterford, N.Y., 808 F.Supp. 120 (N.D.N.Y. 1992)—**806**

Sutton v. Piper, 244 F. App'x 101, 103 (6th Cir. 2009)—**798**

Sutton v. United Air Lines, Inc., 527 U.S. 471 (1999)—**70, 72-83, 80, 101, 634**

Suzuki Motor Corp. v. Consumers Union of U.S., Inc., 330 F.3d 1110 (9th Cir. 2003)—**276**

Svoboda v. Comm'r, No. 3176-04, 2006 WL 12952 (Tax Ct. Jan. 3, 2006)—**930**

Swallows v. Barnes & Noble Book Stores, Inc., 128 F.3d 990 (6th Cir. 1997)—**169**

Swanson v. Allstate Ins. Co., 102 F.Supp.2d 949 (N.D. Ill. 2000)—**204**

Swanson v. Univ. of Cincinnati, 268 F.3d 307 (6th Cir. 2001)—**86**

T

T.B. ex rel. W.B. v. St. Joseph Sch. Dist., 677 F.3d 844 (8th Cir. 2012)—**686-687**

Tandy v. City of Wichita, 380 F.3d 1277 (10th Cir. 2004)—**428**

Taylor v. Books A Million, Inc., 296 F.3d 376 (5th Cir. 2002)—**297-298**

Taylor v. Louisiana, 419 U.S. 522 (1975)—**338, 343**

Table of Cases

Taylor v. Onorato, 428 F.Supp.2d 384 (W.D. Pa. 2006)—**387**

Taylor v. Phoenixville Sch. Dist., 174 F.3d 142 (3d Cir. 1999)—**251**

Taylor v. Rice, No. 05-5257, 2006 WL 1736199 (D.C. Cir. June 27, 2006)—**267**

Taylor v. Vermont Dep't of Educ., 313 F.d 768 (2d Cir. 2002)—**752**

Teamsters v. Daniel, 439 U.S. 551 (1979)—**40**

Teamsters v. United States, 431 U.S. 324 (1977)—**231, 607-608**

Temple v. Gunsalus, No. 95-3175, 1996 WL 536710 (6th Cir. Sept. 20, 1996)—**804**

Tenbrink v. Fed. Home Loan Bank, 920 F.Supp. 1156 (D. Kan. 1996)—**192**

Tennessee v. Lane, 315 F.3d 680 (6th Cir. 2003)—**167**

Tennessee v. Lane, 541 U.S. 509 (2004)—**336-348, 352-354, 357**

Tex. Dep't of Cmty. Affairs v. Burdine, 450 U.S. 248 (1981)—**232**

Tex. State Teachers Ass'n v. Garland Indep. Sch. Dist., 489 U.S. 782 (1989)—**621, 624-626, 645**

Thao v. City of St. Paul, 481 F.3d 565 (8th Cir. 2007)—**386**

The Baltimore, 75 U.S. (8 Wall.) 377 (1869)—**627**

Thelen v. Marc's Big Boy Corp., 64 F.3d 264 (7th Cir. 1995)—**283**

Thomas Jefferson Univ. v. Shalala, 512 U.S. 504 (1994)—**592**

Thomas v. Honeybrook Mines, Inc., 428 F.2d 981 (3d Cir. 1970)—**636**

Thompson v. Borg-Warner Protective Servs. Corp., No. C-94-4015 MHP, 1996 WL 162990 (N.D. Cal. Mar. 11, 1996)—**197**

Thompson v. Davis, 282 F.3d 780 (9th Cir. 2002)—**367**

Thompson v. Pharmacy Corp. of Am., 334 F.3d 1242 (11th Cir. 2003)—**646**

Thornburgh v. Abbott, 490 U.S. 401 (1989)—**359**

Three Rivers Ctr. for Indep. Living v. Hous. Auth. of the City of Pittsburgh, 382 F.3d 412 (3d Cir. 2004)—**826**

Tice v. Cent. Area Transp. Auth., 247 F.3d 506 (3d Cir. 2001)—**202, 205-206**

Tilton v. Richardson, 403 U.S. 672 (1971)—**175**

Timothy W. v. Rochester Sch. Dist., 875 F.2d 954 (1st Cir. 1989)—**662**

Tipton-Whittingham v. City of Los Angeles, 34 Cal.4th 604 (Cal. 2004)—**642**

Todd v. Am. Multi-Cinema, Inc., No. Civ. A. H-02-1944, 2004 WL 1764686 (S.D. Tex. Aug. 5, 2004)—**548**

Toledo v. Sanchez, 454 F.3d 24 (1st Cir. 2006)—**355**

Tomic v. Catholic Diocese of Peoria, 442 F.3d 1036 (7th Cir. 2006)—**179**

Torres v. AT&T Broadband, LLC, 158 F.Supp.2d 1035 (N.D. Cal. 2001)—**451, 485**

Torrico v. IBM, Corp., 213 F.Supp.2d 390 (S.D.N.Y. 2002)—**171**

Town of Burlington v. Dep't of Educ. of Mass., 736 F.2d 773 (1st Cir. 1984)—**740**

Toyota Motor Mfg., Ky., Inc. v. Williams, 534 U.S. 184 (2002)—**70-71**

Table of Cases

Trafficante v. Metro. Life Ins. Co., 409 U.S. 205 (1972)—**780, 787, 796, 832**

Trans World Airlines, Inc. v. Hardison, 432 U.S. 63 (1977)—**57-58, 64, 794, 796-797**

Trotter v. Bd. of Tr. Univ. of Ala., 91 F.3d 1449 (11th Cir. 1996)—**256**

Trovato v. City of Manchester, N.H., 992 F.Supp. 493 (D.N.H. 1997)—**798**

Tuck v. HCA Health Servs., 7 F.3d 465 (6th Cir. 1993)—**440**

Tugg v. Towey, 864 F.Supp. 1201 (S.D. Fla. 1994)—**883**

Turner v. Hershey Chocolate USA, 440 F.3d 604 (3d Cir. 2006)—**129, 135**

Tyler v. City of Manhattan, 118 F.3d 1400 (10th Cir. 1997)—**438**

Tyler v. Corner Constr. Corp., 167 F.3d 1202 (8th Cir. 1999)—**638**

Tyndall v. Nat'l Educ. Ctrs., Inc., 31 F.3d 209 (4th Cir. 1994)—**214, 905**

U

U.S. Airways, Inc. v. Barnett, 535 U.S. 391 (2002)—**212, 216-227, 245**

U.S. Dep't of Agric. v. Moreno, 413 U.S. 528 (1973)—**15**

United Airlines, Inc. v. E.E.O.C., 133 S.Ct. 2734 (2013)—**216**

United Food & Commercial Workers Union Local 751 v. Brown Group, Inc., 517 U.S. 544 (1996)—**613**

United States v. Adkinson, 256 F.Supp.2d 1297 (N.D. Fla. 2003)—**652**

United States v. Am. Multi-Cinema, Inc., 232 F.Supp.2d 1092 (C.D. Cal. 2002)—**597**

United States v. AMC Entm't, Inc., 549 F.3d 760 (9th Cir. 2008)—**597**

United States v. Basye, 410 U.S. 441 (1973)—**322**

United States v. Cal. Mobile Home Park Mgmt. Co., 29 F.3d 1413 (9th Cir. 1994)—**787-789, 794, 801-802**

United States v. Carolene Prods. Co., 304 U.S. 144 (1938)—**21-22**

United States v. City & Cnty. of Denver, 927 F.Supp. 1396 (D. Colo. 1996)—**445**

United States v. Darby, 312 U.S. 100 (1941)—**166**

United States v. Edward Rose & Sons, 384 F.3d 258 (6th Cir. 2004)—**823-825**

United States v. Freer, 864 F.Supp. 324 (W.D.N.Y. 1994)—**786**

United States v. Gambone Bros. Dev. Co., No. 06-1386, 2008 WL 4410093 (E.D. Pa. Sept. 25, 2008)—**827**

United States v. Georgia 126 S.Ct. 877 (2006)—**350-355**

United States v. Grace, 461 U.S. 171 (1983)—**15**

United States v. Hoyts Cinemas Corp., 380 F.3d 558 (1st Cir. 2004)—**597**

United States v. Inc. Vill. Of Island Park, 791 F.Supp. 354 (E.D.N.Y. 1992)—**833**

United States v. Kubrick, 444 U.S. 111 (1979)—**829-830**

United States v. Lopez, 514 U.S. 549 (1995)—**356**

United States v. Morrison, 529 U.S. 598 (2000)—**356**

Table of Cases

United States v. N.Y. State Dep't of Motor Vehicles, 82 F.Supp.2d 42 (E.D.N.Y. 2000)—**186-187**

United States v. Neb. Dept. of Health & Human Servs. Finance & Support, 547 U.S. 1067 (2006)—**349**

United States v. New York, New Haven & Hartford R.R. Co., 355 U.S. 253 (1957)—**731**

United States v. Raines, 362 U.S. 17 (1960)—**340, 347**

United States v. Rodgers, 466 U.S. 475 (1984)—**629, 632**

United States v. Venture Stores, Inc., No. 92 C 6677, 1994 WL 86068 (N.D. Ill. 1994)—**511**

United States v. Vill. of Marshall, 787 F.Supp. 872 (W.D. Wis. 1991)—**796**

United States v. Virginia, 518 U.S. 515 (1996)—**166**

United States v. York Obstetrics & Gynecology, No. 00-8-P-DMC, 2001 WL 80082 (D. Me. Jan. 30, 2001)—**615, 617-619**

Univ. Interscholastic League v. Buchanan, 848 S.W.2d 298 (Tex. Ct. App. 1993)—**853**

Uravic v. F. Jarka Co., 282 U.S. 234 (1931)—**494**

Urhausen v. Longs Drug Stores of Ca., Inc., No. A113937, 2007 WL 2092927 (Cal. Ct. App. Sept. 18, 2007)—**901**

US Airways, Inc. v. Barnett, 535 U.S. 391 (2002)—**67, 811**

V

Vande Zande v. State of Wis. Dept. of Admin., 44 F.3d 538 (7th Cir. 1995)—**211, 213-214, 239, 253, 811**

Vandermolen v. City of Roosevelt Park, No. 1:97CV 200, 1997 WL 853505 (W.D. Mich. Oct. 28, 1997)—**612**

Varnagis v. City of Chi., No. 96 C 6304, 1997 WL 361150 (N.D. Ill. June 20, 1997)—**197**

Vaughn G. v. Mayor & City Council of Baltimore, No. MJG-84-1911, slip op., 2005 WL 1949688 (D.C. Md. Aug. 12, 2005)—**738**

Vinson v. Thomas, 288 F.3d 1145 (9th Cir. 2002)—**245, 820**

Vinson v. Thomas, No. CIV 97-00091 HG, 2000 WL 33313071 (D. Haw. Feb. 28, 2000)—**820**

Visco v. Sch. Dist. of Pittsburgh, 684 F.Supp. 1310 (W.D. Pa. 1988)—**685**

Vitek v. Jones, 445 U.S. 480, 100 S.Ct. 1254, 63 L.Ed.2d 552 (1980)—**354**

Volt Info. Scis., Inc. v. Bd. of Trs. of Leland Stanford Junior Univ., 489 U.S. 468 (1989)—**294**

Voyeur Dorm, L.C. v. City of Tampa, 265 F.3d 1232 (11th Cir. 2001)—**485**

W

W. Chester Area Sch. Dist. v. Bruce C., 194 F.Supp.2d 417 (E.D. Pa. 2002)—**666**

W.V. Univ. Hosps, Inc. v. Casey, 499 U.S. 83 (1991)—**759-760, 762, 766**

Wade v. Knoxville Utils. Bd., 259 F.3d 452 (6th Cir. 2001)—**205**

Waggoner v. Olin Corp., 169 F.3d 481 (7th Cir. 1999)—**213**

Wal-Mart Stores, Inc. v. Dukes, 131 S.Ct. 2541 (2011)—**259**

Table of Cases

Walton v. Mental Health Ass'n, 168 F.3d 661 (3d Cir. 1999)—**252, 815**

Ward ex rel. Carter v. Prince George's Cnty. Pub. Schs., 23 F.Supp.2d 585 (D. Md. 1998)—**666**

Ward v. Caulk, 650 F.2d 1144 (9th Cir. 1981)—**828**

Ward v. Mass. Health Research Inst., Inc., 209 F.3d 29 (1st Cir. 2000)—**214**

Ward v. Tipton Cnty. Sheriff Dep't, 937 F.Supp. 791, 797 (S.D. Ind. 1996)—**302**

Ware v. Wyo. Bd. of Law Exam's, 973 F.Supp. 1339 (D. Wyo. 1997)—**361**

Warth v. Seldin, 422 U.S. 490 (1975)—**114**

Wash. State Commc'n Access Project v. Regal Cinemas, 293 P.3d 413 (Wash Ct. App., Jan. 28, 2013)—**915**

Washington v. Davis, 426 U.S. 229 (1976)—**156, 158, 163-164**

Washington v. Ind. High Sch. Athletic Ass'n, 181 F.3d 840 (7th Cir. 1999)—**376, 434**

Watson v. Cnty. of Riverside, 300 F.3d 1092 (9th Cir. 2002)—**642**

Watson v. Lithonia Lighting, 304 F.3d 749 (7th Cir. 2002)—**233**

Weast v. Schaffer ex rel. Schaffer, 377 F.3d 449 (4th Cir. 2004)—**728, 730, 733-735**

Weber v. Strippit, 186 F.3d 907 (8th Cir. 1999)—**247**

Wein v. Am. Huts, Inc., 313 F.Supp.2d 1356 (S.D. Fla. 2004)—**613**

Weinreich v. Los Angeles Cnty. MTA, 114 F.3d 976, 978 (9th Cir. 1997)—**391**

Weissman v. Dawn Joy Fashions, Inc., 214 F.3d 224 (2d Cir. 2000)—**116-117**

Wells v. Clackamas Gastroenterology Assocs., P.C., 271 F.3d 903 (2001)—**141-142**

Wenger v. Canastota Cent. Sch. Dist., 146 F.3d 123 (C.A.2 1998)—**751**

Wernick v. Fed. Reserve Bank of N.Y., 91 F.3d 379 (2d Cir. 1996)—**383**

Wexler v. Westfield Bd. of Educ., 784 F.2d 176 (3d Cir. 1986)—**739-740**

Weyer v. Twentieth Century Fox Film Corp., 196 F.3d 1092 (9th Cir. 1999)—**192**

Weyer v. Twentieth Century Fox Film Corp., 198 F.3d 1104 (9th Cir. 2000)—**128, 460, 478**

Wharf (Holdings) Ltd. v. United Int'l Holdings, Inc., 532 U.S. 588 (2001)—**729**

Wheeler v. Hurdman, 825 F.2d 257 (10th Cir. 1987)—**458**

White v. City of Boston, 7 Mass. L. Rptr. 232, 1997 WL 416586 (Mass. Super. 1997)—**203**

White v. York Int'l Corp., 45 F.3d 357 (10th Cir. 1995)—**250, 252, 820**

Whitney v. Greenberg, Rosenblatt, Kull & Bitsoli, PC, 258 F.3d 30 (1st Cir. 2001)—**86**

Wildenhus's Case, 120 U.S. 1 (1887)—**494**

Williams v. Alioto, 625 F.2d 845 (Cal. 1980)—**642**

Williams v. Banning, 72 F.3d 552 (7th Cir. 1995)—**140**

Williams v. Little Rock Mun. Water Works, 21 F.3d 218 (8th Cir. 1994)—**298**

Table of Cases

Williams v. Owens-Ill., Inc., 665 F.2d 918 (9th Cir. 1982)—**285**

Willis v. Conopco, Inc., 108 F.3d 282 (11th Cir. 1997)—**250, 253**

Wilson v. Haria & Gogri Corp., 479 F.Supp.2d 1127 (E.D.Cal. 2007)—**899**

Wilson v. Marana Unified Sch. Dist., 735 F.2d 1178 (9th Cir. 1984)—**696**

Wilson v. Murillo, 163 Cal. Rptr. 3d 214 (Cal. Ct. App. 2008)—**510**

Wilson v. MVM, Inc., 475 F.3d 166 (3d Cir. 2007)—**86, 288**

Wilson v. Pa. State Police Dep't, No. CIV. A. 94-CV-6547, 1995 WL 422750 (E.D. Pa. July 17, 1995)—**258**

Winkelman v. Parma City Sch. Dist., 550 U.S. 516 (2007)—**740-752**

Winters v. Pasadena Sch. Dist., 124 F. App'x 822 (5th Cir. 2005)—**86, 99**

Wis. Cmty. Servs., Inc. v. City of Milwaukee, 465 F.3d 737 (7th Cir. 2006)—**361, 435-436**

Wis. Dep't of Health & Family Servs. v. Blumer, 534 U.S. 473 (2002)—**737**

Wojewski v. Rapid City Reg'l Hosp., Inc., 394 F.Supp.2d 1134 (D.S.D. 2005)—**460**

Wojewski v. Rapid City Reg'l Hosp., Inc., 450 F.3d 338 (8th Cir. 2006)—**460**

Wong v. Regents of Univ. of Cal., 379 F.3d 1097 (9th Cir. 2004)—**87**

Wood v. Green, 323 F.3d 1309 (11th Cir. 2003)—**243**

Wooden v. Bd. of Regents of Univ. Sys. of Ga., 247 F.3d 1262 (11th Cir. 2001)—**610**

Woodman v. Runyon, 132 F.3d 1330 (10th Cir. 1997)—**803**

Workman v. Frito-Lay, Inc., 165 F.3d 460 (6th Cir. 1999)—**247**

Worth v. Tyer, 276 F.3d 249 (7th Cir. 2001)—**170**

Wray v. Nat'l R.R. Passenger Corp., 10 F.Supp.2d 1036 (E.D. Wis. 1998)—**431**

Wright v. Universal Mar. Serv. Corp., 525 U.S. 70 (1998)—**326**

Wurzel v. Whirlpool Corp., 2010 WL 1495197 (N.D. Ohio Apr. 14, 2010)—**279**

Wurzel v. Whirlpool Corp., No. 10-3629, 2012 WL 1449683 (6th Cir. Apr. 27, 2012)—**268**

Wynne v. Tufts Univ. Sch. of Med., 976 F.2d 791 (1st Cir. 1992)—**128-129, 243**

Y

Yaris v. Special Sch. Dist., 558 F.Supp. 545 (E.D. Mo. 1983), aff'd 728 F.2d 1055 (8th Cir. 1984)—**707**

Yeiter v. Sec'y of Health & Human Servs., 818 F.2d 8 (6th Cir. 1987)—**24**

Yeskey v. Pa. Dep't of Corr., 118 F.3d 168 (3d Cir. 1997)—**352, 367**

Young v. Comm'r, 240 F.3d 369 (4th Cir. 2001)—**321**

Youngberg v. Romeo, 457 U.S. 307 (1982)—**338, 402**

Z

Zadvydas v. Davis, 533 U.S. 678 (2001)—**500**

Zardui-Quintana v. Richard, 768 F.2d 1213 (11th Cir. 1985)—**878**

Zelman v. Simmons-Harris, 536 U.S. 639 (2002)—**718**

Zervos v. Verizon N.Y., Inc., 252 F.3d 163 (2d Cir. 2001)—**367**

Table of Cases

Zillyette v. Capital One Fin. Corp., 179 F.3d 1337 (11th Cir. 1999)—**308**

Zimmerman v. Or. Dep't of Justice, 170 F.3d 1169 (9th Cir. 1999)—**369, 440, 460**

Zimring v. Olmstead, 138 F.3d 893 (11th Cir. 1998)—**397, 401**

Zingher v. Yacavone, 30 F.Supp.2d 446 (D. Vt. 1997)—**362**

Zipes v. Trans World Airlines, Inc., 455 U.S. 385 (1982)—**288**

Zivkovic v. S. Cal. Edison Co., 302 F.3d 1080 (9th Cir. 2002)—**245**

Zobel v. Williams, 457 U.S. 55 (1982)—**15**

Zobrest v. Catalina Foothills Sch. Dist., 509 U.S. 1 (1993)—**718**

Zukle v. Regents of Univ. of Cal., 166 F.3d 1041 (9th Cir. 1999)—**129**

Zulauf v. Ky. Educ. Television, 28 F.Supp.2d 1022 (E.D. Ky. 1998)—**440**

Table of Other Authorities

2 Legislative History of the Americans with Disabilities Act (Leg. Hist.) (Committee Print compiled for the House Committee on Education and Labor), Ser. No. 102-B (1990)—**161-162**

2 McCormick, J. Strong, on Evidence (5th ed. 1999)—**729-731, 733**

2006 Election Administration and Voting Survey 26 (2006)—**387**

9 Wigmore, J., Evidence (J. Chadbourn rev. ed. 1981)—**733**

A

Abrar, Ali & Dingle, Kerry J., From Madness to Method: The Americans with Disabilities Act Meets the Internet, 44 Harv. C.R.-C.L. L. Rev. 133 (2009)—**875, 904**

Access Board, Proposed Accessibility Standards for Medical Diagnostic Equipment (Feb. 8, 2012)—**866**

Ad Hoc Comm., United Nations, Ad Hoc Committee Documents (2003-2004)—**969**

Ad Hoc Comm., United Nations, Enable, Meeting of the Ad Hoc Committee 29 July-9 August 2002 United Nations, New York—**969**

Ad Hoc Comm., United Nations, Enable, Regional and Interregional Workshops and Seminars Organized in Relation to the Proposed Convention (2003-2004)—**969**

ADA Best Practices Tool Kit for State and Local Governments, Chapter 5, "Website Accessibility Under Title II of the ADA—**884**

ADA Notification Act, Hearing on H.R. 3590 Before Subcomm. on the Constitution of the House Comm. on the Judiciary, 106th Cong. (2000)—**598**

Afflerbach, Thorsten & Garabagiu, Angela, Council of Europe Actions to Promote Human Rights and Full Participation of People with Disabilities: Improving the Quality of Life of People with Disabilities in Europe, 34 Syracuse J. Int'l Law & Comm. 463 (2007)—**939**

Agreement Between Complainants and AOL (July 26, 2000)—**876**

Allen, Kathryn G., GAO, Nursing Homes: Efforts to Strengthen Federal Enforcement Have Not Deterred Some Homes from Repeatedly Harming Residents 24 (May 2007)—**862**

Alston, Philip, Making Space for New Human Rights: The Case of the Right to Development, 1 Harv. Hum. Rts. Y.B. 3 (1988)—**976**

Am. Pub. Health Ass'n: The Supreme Court's ACA Decision & Its Implications for Medicaid 1 (July 27, 2012)—**865**

Amir Paz-Fuchs, Behind the Contract for Welfare Reform: Antecedent Themes in Welfare to Work Programs, 29 Berkeley J. Emp. & Lab. L. 405 (2008)—**849**

Table of Other Authorities

Anderson, Cheryl L., Damages for Intentional Discrimination by Public Entities Under Title II of the Americans with Disabilities Act: A Rose by Any Other Name, but Are the Remedies the Same?, 9 BYU J. Pub. L. 235 (1995)—**437**

Anderson, Michael P., Ensuring Equal Access to the Internet for the Elderly: The Need to Amend Title III of the ADA, 19 Elder L.J. 159 (2011)—**904**

Applicability of the Americans with Disabilities Act (ADA) to Private Internet Sites: Hearing Before the Subcomm. on the Constitution of the House Judiciary Comm., 106th Cong. (2000)—**876, 903-904, 909**

Application of Section 504 of the Rehabilitation Act to HIV-Infected Individuals, 12 Op. Off. Legal Counsel 264 (Sept. 27, 1988)—**93**

Architectural Barriers Act Accessibility Guidelines; Outdoor Developed Areas, 78 Fed. Reg. 59476-01 (Sept. 26, 2013)—**584**

Arnold, Mitylene, & Lassmann, Marie E., Overrepresentation of Minority Students in Special Education, 124 Educ. 230 (2003)—**665**

Aron, Lester, Too Much or Not Enough: How Have the Circuit Courts Defined a Free and Appropriate Public Education After Rowley, 39 Suffolk U. L. Rev. 1 (2005)—**686**

Aspects of Disability Law in Africa (Pretoria University Press 2012)—**934**

Auvergnon, Philippe, L'Obligation d'Emploi des Handicapes [The Obligation to Employ Persons with Disabilities], Droit Social 596 (Juillet-Août 1991)—**957**

Azinger, Natalie R., Too Healthy to Sue Under the ADA? The Controversy Over Pre-Offer Medical Inquiries and Tests, 25 Iowa J. Corp. L. 193 (1999)—**208**

B

Bagenstos, Samuel, The Structural Turn and the Limits of Antidiscrimination Law, 94 Cal. L. Rev. 1 (2006)—**836**

Baker, Paul M.A., et al., Municipal WiFi and Policy Implications for People with Disabilities 1 (2008)—**874-875**

Baker, Paul M.A., et al., The Promise of Municipal WiFi and Failed Policies of Inclusion: The Disability Divide, 14 Info. Polity (forthcoming 2009)—**913**

Ball, Carlos A., Preferential Treatment and Reasonable Accommodation Under the Americans with Disabilities Act, 55 Ala. L. Rev. 951 (2004)—**226**

Bazelon Center for Mental Health Law, The Supreme Court's Decision on the ACA (2012)—**865**

Befort, Stephen F., Reasonable Accommodation and Reassignment Under the Americans with Disabilities Act: Answers, Questions and Suggested Solutions After U.S. Airways, Inc. v. Barnett, 45 Ariz. L. Rev. 931 (2003)—**226**

Table of Other Authorities

Berson, M.D., Frank C., Kuperwaser, M.D., Mark C., Aiello, M.D., Lloyd Paul, and Rosenberg, M.D., James W., "Visual Requirements and Commercial Drivers" (Oct. 16, 1998)—**125**

Berven, Heidi M., & Blanck, Peter, Assistive Technology Patenting Trends and the Americans with Disabilities Act, 17 Behav. Sci. & L. 47 (1999)—**909**

Berven, Heidi M., & Blanck, Peter, The Economics of the Americans with Disabilities Act Part II – Patents and Innovations in Assistive Technology, 12 Notre Dame J.L. Ethics & Pub. Pol'y 9 (1998)—**909**

Besner, Eric, Employment Legislation for Disabled Individuals: What Can France Learn from the Americans with Disabilities Act? 16 Comp. Lab. L.J. 399 (1995)—**941, 954**

Bickenbach, Jerome, Disability Human Rights. Law, and Policy, in Handbook of Disability Studies (2001)—**938-939**

Blanck, Peter & Pransky, Glen, Workers with Disabilities, 14 Occupational Med. 581 (1999)—**260**

Blanck, Peter et al., Employment of People with Disabilities: Twenty-Five Years Back and Ahead, 25 Law & Ineq. 323 (2007)—**838, 867**

Blanck, Peter, "The Right to Live in the World": Disability Yesterday, Today, and Tomorrow, 2008 Jacobus tenBroek Disability Law Symposium, Tex. J. Civ. Lib. & Civ. Rights, 13 (2008)—**4**

Blanck, Peter, Closing: Special Issue on Disability Policy and Law, Flattening the (In-Accessible) Cyber World for People with Disabilities, Assistive Technology Journal, 20 (2008)—**486**

Blanck, Peter, eQuality: Web Rights, Human Flourishing and Persons with Cognitive Disabilities (forthcoming 2014)—**191, 235, 450, 478, 550, 913, 916**

Blanck, Peter, et al., AIDS-Related Benefits Equation: Soaring Costs Times Soaring Needs Divided by Federal Law, in 2 Mealey's Litigation Reports: Americans with Disabilities Act 21 (1994)—**185**

Blanck, Peter, et al., Calibrating the Impact of the ADA's Employment Provisions, 14 Stan. L. & Pol'y Rev. 267 (2003)—**235, 249, 875**

Blanck, Peter, et al., Disability Civil Rights Law & Policy (2004)—**427**

Blanck, Peter, et al., Disability Civil Rights Law & Policy: Accessible Courtrom Technology, 12 Wm. & Mary Bill Rts. J. 825 (2004)—**884**

Blanck, Peter, et al., Disability Civil Rights Law and Policy: Cases and Materials 1251 (2005)—**726**

Table of Other Authorities

Blanck, Peter, et al., Legal Rights of Persons with Disabilities: An Analysis of Federal Law (2d ed. 2013)—**877**

Blanck, Peter, Flattening the (Inaccessible) Cyberworld for People with Disabilities, 20 Assistive Technology: The Official Journal of RESNA 50, 51 (2008)—**907**

Blanck, Peter, Keynote Address: Justice for All? Stories about Americans with Disabilities and Their Civil Rights, 8 J. Gender Race & Just. 1 (2004)—**721**

Blanck, Peter, The Americans with Disabilities Act and the Emerging Workforce: Employment of People with Mental Retardation 46 (1998)—**235**

Blanck, Peter, The Economics of the Employment Provisions of the Americans with Disabilities Act, in Employment, Disability, and the Americans with Disabilities Act 201 (Peter Blanck, ed., Nw. Univ. Press 2000)—**212-213**

Breathwaite, Jeanine & Mott, Daniel Disability and Poverty: A Survey of World Bank Poverty Assessments and Implications (2008)—**936**

Brief for Defendant-Appellant, Greater Los Angeles Agency of Deafness, Inc. v. Cable News Network, Inc. (9th Cir. Sept. 12, 2012)—**905**

Bruyère, Suzanne, A Comparison of the Implementation of the Employment Provisions of the Americans with Disabilities Act of 1990 (ADA) in the United States and the Disability Discrimination Act 1995 (DDA) in the United Kingdom (Cornell Univ. Program on Emp. & Disability Sch. of Indus. & Lab. Relations 1999)—**944**

Buhai, Sande & Golden, Nina, Adding Insult to Injury: Discriminatory Intent As a Prerequisite to Damages Under the ADA, 52 Rutgers L. Rev. 1121 (2000)—**437**

Bureau of Democracy, Human Rights, & Lab., U.S. Dep't of State, Country Reports on Human Rights Practices for 1999 (Feb. 2, 2000)—**938**

Burgdorf Jr., Robert L., Restoring the ADA and Beyond: Disability in the 21st Century, 13 Tex. J. C.L. & C.R. 241 (2008)—**876**

Burgdorf, Jr., Robert L., 'Substantially Limited' Protection from Disability Discrimination: The Special Treatment Model and Misconstructions of the Definition of Disability, 42 Vill. L. Rev. 409 (1997)—**66, 68**

Burris, Scott & Moss, Kathryn, The Employment Discrimination Provisions of the Americans with Disabilities Act: Implementation and Impact, 25 Hofstra Lab. & Emp. L.J. 1, 3 (2007)—**838-839**

Table of Other Authorities

C

Callegary, Ellen A., The IDEA's Promise Unfulfilled: A Second Look at Special Education & Related Services for Children with Mental Health Needs After Garret F., 5 J. Health Care L. & Pol'y 164 (2002)—**703**

Castaneda, Ruben, Disabled Commuters Settle Suit, Wash. Post, Dec. 28, 2005—**432**

CERMI, Human Rights and Disability: Alternative Report Spain 2010—**979**

Chambers, J., Harr, J., & Dhanani, A., Department of Education, What Are We Spending on Procedural Safeguards in Special Education 1999-2000 (May 2003)—**731**

Chirikos, Thomas N., The Economics of Employment, 69 Milbank Q. 150 (1991)—**65**

Chirikos, Thomas N., Will the Costs of Accommodating Workers with Disabilities Remain Low?, 17 Behav. Sci. & L. 93 (1999)—**65**

Chollet, Deborah & Bernstein, Jill, How Will the ACA Affect Community Rehabilitation Programs?, Final Report, Mathematica Pol'y Res., Inc. (Apr. 2012)—**863-866**

Coleman, III, John J. & Debruge, Marcel L., A Practitioner's Introduction to ADA Title II, 45 Ala. L. Rev. 55 (1993)—**437**

Colker, Ruth, ADA Title III: A Fragile Compromise, 21 Berkeley J. Emp. & Lab. L. 377 (2000)—**599-600, 604**

Colker, Ruth, The Mythic 43 Million Americans with Disabilities, 49 Wm. & Mary L. Rev. 1 (2007)—**84-85**

Collignon, Frederick C., The Role of Reasonable Accommodation in Employing Disabled Persons in Private Industry, in Disability and the Labor Market: Economic Problems, Policies, and Programs (Monroe Berkowitz & M. Anne Hill, eds. 1986)—**65**

Community Support for Disabled and Elderly, Before the Senate Comm. on Health, Education, Labor & Pensions, 2007 WL 1986363 (F.D.C.H.) (July 10, 2007)—**861**

Concluding Observations of the Committee on the Rights of Persons with Disabilities, Sixth Session – Spain (Oct. 19, 2011)—**980**

Cros-Courtial, Marie-Louise, Les Obligations Patronales à l'Égard des Handicapés Après la Loi du 10 Juillet 1987 [Protective Obligations Toward Handicapped People Following the Law of July 10, 1987], Droit Social (Juillet-Août 1988)—**955-958**

Ctr. for an Accessible Soc'y, Employers Know Little about Tax Credits, Says Study (Apr. 29, 2003)—**551**

Ctrs. for Medicare & Medicaid Servs., Medicare Program – General Information: Overview—**859**

Table of Other Authorities

Cummins, Jim, Bilingualism and Special Education: Issues in Assessment and Pedagogy 1-2 (1984)—**665**

D

Davies, Jackie, A Cuckoo in the Nest? A 'Range of Reasonable Responses', Justification and the Disability Discrimination Act 1995, 32 Indus. L.J. 164 (2003)—**944**

Davis, Martha F., Learning to Work: A Functional Approach to Welfare and Higher Education, 58 Buff. L. Rev. 147 (2010)—**840**

Dayton, John, Special Education Disability Law, 163 West's Educ. L. Rep. 17 (2002)—**716**

De Vise, Daniel, Special-Ed Racial Imbalance Spurs Sanctions: Number of Black Students in Montgomery, Arundel Programs Seen as Too High, Washington Post, Aug. 2, 2005—**665**

Degener, Theresia & Quinn, Gerard, A Survey of International, Comparative and Regional Disability Law Reform (Oct. 22-26, 2000)—**941-942**

Degener, Theresia & Quinn, Gerard, The Current Use and Future Potential of United Nations Human Rights Instruments in the Context of Disability (2002)—**962**

Degener, Theresia, Disabled Persons and Human Rights: The Legal Framework, in Human Rights and Disabled Persons (Theresia Degener & Yolan Koster-Dreese, eds. 1995)—**965**

Dep't of Econ. & Soc. Affairs, United Nations, Enable: Report of the U.N. Consultative Expert Group Meeting on International Norms and Standards Relating to Disability (2003-2004)—**968**

Dep't of Int'l Econ. & Soc. Affairs, United Nations Disability Statistics Compendium, Statistics on Special Population Groups, Series Y, No. 4 (1990)—**935-937**

Dep'ts of Labor, Health, & Human Servs., Educ. & Related Agency Appropriations for 2002, Hearing Before the U.S. House Appropriations Subcomm., 107th Cong. 2nd Sess. (2002)—**6**

DePaul Univ. & Ill. Dep't of Commerce & Econ. Opportunity, Exploring the Bottom Line: A Study of the Costs and Benefits of Workers with Disabilities (Oct. 2007)—**56**

Despouy, Leandro, Human Rights and Disabled Persons, Human Rights Series No. 6 (1988)—**935, 965-967**

Deval, Patrick, Core Letter #149, U.S. Dep't of Justice, Civil Rights Div.—**534-535**

Deval, Patrick, Core Letter #172, U.S. Dep't of Justice, Civil Rights Div.—**535**

Dhanda, Amita, Legal Capacity in the Disability Rights Convention: Stranglehold of the Past or Lodestar for the Future? 34 Syr. J. of Int'l L. & Com. 429 (2007)—**973**

Table of Other Authorities

Disability and Self-Directed Employment: Business Development Models (Alfred H. Neufeldt & Alison L. Albright, eds. 1998)—**937**

Disability Rights Section, U.S. Dep't of Justice, Accessible Stadiums 2—**596**

Donlin, Johanna M., Moving Ahead with Olmstead: To Comply with the Americans with Disabilities Act, States Are Working Hard to Find Community Placements for People with Disabilities, 29 State Legislatures 28 (Mar. 1, 2003)—**405**

Donohue, III, John J., Employment Discrimination Law in Perspective: Three Concepts of Equality, 92 Mich. L. Rev. 2583 (1994)—**64, 66**

Drimmer, Jonathan C., Cripples, Overcomers, and Civil Rights: Tracing the Evolution of Federal Legislation and Social Policy for People with Disabilities, 40 UCLA L. Rev. 1341 (1993)—**32**

E

EEOC Policy Guidance on Executive Order 13145: To Prohibit Discrimination in Federal Employment Based on Genetic Information (July 26, 2000)—**873**

EEOC, ADA Enforcement Guidance: Preemployment Disability-Related Questions and Medical Examinations—**200**

EEOC, ADA Technical Assistance Manual Addendum—**212**

EEOC, Americans with Disabilities Act of 1990 (ADA) Charges FY 1997-FY 2012—**289, 297**

EEOC, Enforcement Guidance on Disability-Related Inquiries and Medical Examinations of Employees Under the Americans with Disabilities Act—**194-195, 197-199, 227**

EEOC, Enforcement Guidance on the Americans with Disabilities Act and Psychiatric Disabilities—**191, 228**

EEOC, Enforcement Guidance: Application of EEOC Laws to Contingent Workers Placed by Temporary Employment Agencies and Other Staffing Firms (Notice No. 915,002), 8 FEP Man. (BNA) 405: 7551 (Dec. 3, 1997)—**168-169, 198-199, 244**

EEOC, Enforcement Guidances and Related Documents—**205**

EEOC, History of EEOC Mediation Program—**324**

EEOC, Mediation—**324**

EEOC, Press Release, EEOC and BNSF Settle Genetic Testing Case Under Americans with Disabilities Act (May 8, 2002)—**871**

EEOC, Press Release, Sears, Roebuck to Pay $6.2 Million for Disability Bias (Sept. 9, 2009)—**306**

EEOC, Questions & Answers About Persons with Intellectual Disabilities in the Workplace and the Americans with Disabilities Act—**205**

EEOC, Reasonable Accommodation and Undue Hardship Under the ADA, 8 Fair Emp. Prac. Man. (BNA) 405: 7601 (Oct. 17, 2002)—**211, 215, 243-244**

Table of Other Authorities

EEOC, Technical Assistance Manual: Title I of the ADA § 2.2(b) (Jan. 1992)—**72**

EEOC, The Americans with Disabilities Act: A Primer for Small Business—**212, 246**

EEOC, The Americans with Disabilities Act: Applying Performance and Conduct Standards to Employees with Disabilities—**191**

EEOC, Title I Technical Assistance Manual (EEOC-M-1A) No. 24 (1992)—**215**

Elwan, Ann, Poverty and Disability – A Survey of the Literature No. 9932 (Soc. Protection Unit, World Bank Dec. 1999)—**935, 938**

Ely, J., Democracy and Distrust 150 (1980)—**13**

Enforcement Guidance on Pre-employment Inquiries Under the Americans with Disabilities Act, 8 Fair Emp. Prac. Man. (BNA) 405: 7191, 7193-94 (1995)—**245**

Enforcment Activities, United States Department of Justice Civil Rights Division (Nov. 2013)—**615**

Equal Employment Opportunity for Individuals With Disabilities, 56 Fed. Reg. 35734 (1991)—**275**

Esteves, Anne M. & Joseph, Beth S., Public Accommodations Under The Americans With Disabilities Act Compliance and Litigation Manual (2006)—**930**

F

Feldblum, Chai R., Medical Examinations and Inquiries Under the Americans with Disabilities Act: A View from the Inside, 64 Temp. L. Rev. 521 (1991)—**202-203, 280**

Feldblum, Chai, Definition of Disability Under the Federal Anti-Discrimination Law: What Happened? Why? And What Can We Do About It?, 21 Berkeley J. Emp. & Lab. L. 91 (2000)—**70, 82, 84**

Feldblum, Chai, The (R)evolution of Physical Disability Antidiscrimination Law, 20 Mental & Physical Disability L. Rep. 613 (1996)—**62**

Fembek, Michael et al., Zero Project Report 2012: International Study on the Implementation of the UN Convention on the Rights of Persons with Disabilities (Nov. 2011)—**980**

Fotopulos, M. Christine, Civil Rights Across Borders: Extraterritorial Application of Information Technology Requirements Under Section 508 of the Rehabilitation Act, 36 Pub. Contract L. J. 95, 113-14 (2006)—**908**

Fourth Disability High Level Group Report on the Implementation of the UN Convention on the Rights of Persons With Disabilities (May 2011)—**975**

Fox, Susannah, E-patients with a Disability or Chronic Disease (Oct. 9, 2007)—**875**

Table of Other Authorities

French, Phillip & Kayess, Rosemary, Deadly Currents Beneath Calm Waters: Persons with Disability and the Right to Life in Australia, University of New South Wales Faculty of Law Research Series (2008)—**971-972, 975**

Frieden, Lex, When the Americans with Disabilities Act Goes Online: Application of the Americans with Disabilities Act to the Internet and Worldwide Web (July 10, 2003)—**903**

G

Gallie, Beth, & Smith, Deirdre M., Representing Deaf Clients: What Every Lawyer Should Know, 15 Me. B.J. 128 (Apr. 2000)—**920**

Gimm, Gilbert W., et al., Working with Disability: Who Are the Top Earners in the Medicaid Buy-In Program?, Working with Disability, No. 3 (Mar. 2007)—**846**

Glendinning, Caroline & Baldwin, Sally, The Costs of Disability, in Money Matters, Income, Wealth and Financial Welfare (Robert Walker & Gillian Parker, eds. 1988)—**937**

Global Universal Design Comm'n, Inc., Welcome (2008)—**535**

Gooding, Caroline, The Application of the ECHR in British Courts in Relation to Disability Issues (DRC, 2003)—**944**

Gostin, Lawrence O., Health Information Privacy, 80 Cornell L. Rev. 451 (1995)—**872**

Greenhouse, Steven, Justices to Hear Case on Wages of Home Aides, N.Y. Times (Mar. 25, 2007)—**863**

Gurbai, Sandor Case Study from Hungary – Systematic Revision of Legislation in Contradiction—**975**

H

H.H.S., Medicare Beneficiary Savings and the Affordable Care Act (Feb. 2012)—**864**

H.H.S., The Affordable Care Act for Americans with Disabilities—**865**

Hahn, Harlan, Accommodations and the ADA: Unreasonable Bias or Biased Reasoning?, 21 Berkeley J. Emp. & Lab. L. 166 (2000)—**3**

Hahn, Harlan, Equality and the Environment: The Interpretation of "Reasonable Accommodations" in the Americans with Disabilities Act, 17 J. Rehab. Admin. 101 (1993)—**6, 61, 68**

Hall, Jean P., Fox, Michael H., & Fall, Emily, The Kansas Medicaid Buy-In: Factors Influencing Enrollment and Health Care Utilization, Disability & Health Journal, No. 3 (Apr. 2010)—**861**

Harris, Seth D., Re-Thinking the Economics of Discrimination: U.S. Airways v. Barnett, the ADA, and the Application of Internal Labor Market Theory, 89 Iowa L. Rev. 123 (2003)—**226**

Table of Other Authorities

Haveman, Robert H. et al., Public Policy Toward Disabled Workers: Cross-National Analyses of Economic Impacts (1984)—**937**

Hawke, Constance S. & Jannarone, Anne L., Emerging Issues of Web Accessibility: Implications for Higher Education, 160 Educ. L. Rep. 715 (2002)—**907**

Helander, Einer, Prejudice and Dignity: An Introduction to Community-Based Rehabilitation (U.N. Dev. Programme Report 1992)—**935**

Hendricks, D.J., et al., Cost and Effectiveness of Accommodations in the Workplace: Preliminary Results of a Nationwide Study, 25 Disability Stud. Q. (Fall 2005)—**249**

Henig, Allison, Employment Aid for Youth Aging Out of Foster Care: Extending One-Stop Career Centers to Include A Division for Foster Care Youth, 47 Fam. Ct. Rev. 570 (2009)—**839**

Hernandez, Robert D., Reducing Bias in the Assessment of Culturally and Linguistically Diverse Populations, 14 J. Educ'l Issues Language Minority Students 269 (1994)—**663**

Heyer, Katharina C., From Special Needs to Equal Rights: Japanese Disability Law, 1 Asian-Pac. L. & Pol'y J. 7 (2000)—**953**

Heyer, Katharina C., The ADA on the Road: Disability Rights in Germany, 27 Law & Soc. Inquiry 723 (2002)—**953**

Hill, Eve L. & Blanck, Peter, Future of Disability Rights: Parte Three Statutes of Limitations in the Americans with Disabilites Act "Design and Construction Cases," 60 Syracuse L. Rev. 125 (2009)—**580, 583, 603, 832**

Hoffman, Sharona, Settling the Matter: Does Title I of the ADA Work?, 59 Ala. L. Rev. 305 (2008)—**838**

Hughes, Molly, Title III of the ADA: More Than an Employment Statute, S.C. Law. (Jan./Feb. 2001)—**600**

I

Incentives to Help You Return to Work, SSA Publication No. 05-10060, ICN 463261 (Aug. 2012)—**841**

Inge, Katherine, et al., Survey Results from a National Survey of Community Rehabilitation Providers Holding Special Wage Certificates, Journal of Vocational Rehabilitation 30 (2009)—**841**

Initial Reports Submitted by States parties in Accordance with Article 35 of the Convention – Spain (May 3, 2010)—**977**

International Disability Rights Monitor, Regional Report on Europe, Executive Summary (2007)—**934-935**

International Disability Rights Monitor, Report on the Americas (2004)—**936-937**

IRS Publication 915, "Social Security and Equivalent Railroad Retirement Benefits" (2008)—**919**

Table of Other Authorities

J

Jacquart, D., Rapport du Projet de Loi au Nom de la Commission des Affaires Culturelles, Familiales et Sociales de l'Assemblée Nationale [Report of the Legal Project in the Name of the Commission of Cultural, Domestic, and Social Affairs of the National Assembly] (1987)—**957**

Jimenez, Rodrigo, The Americans with Disabilities Act and Its Impact on International and Latin American Law, 52 Ala. L. Rev. 419 (2000)—**943**

Johnson, David R., et al., Diploma Options for Students with Disabilities, Information Brief (Nat'l Ctr. on Secondary Educ. & Transition Feb. 2005)—**685**

Jolls, Christine, Accommodation Mandates, 53 Stan. L. Rev. 223 (2000)—**66-67**

K

Karlen, Pamela S., & Rutherglen, George, Disabilities, Discrimination, and Reasonable Accommodation, 46 Duke L.J. 1 (1996)—**65-66**

Katz, Marsha Rose, et al., Aspects of Disability Decision Making: Data and Materials, 1 & 2 (Feb. 2012)—**847**

Kauff, Jacqueline, Mathematica Pol'y Research, Inc., Assisting TANF Recipients Living with Disabilities to Obtain and Maintain Employment Final Report (Feb. 2008)—**850**

Kaye, H. Stephen, Improved Employment Opportunities for People with Disabilities (Disability Statistics Report 17, 2003)—**838**

Kayess, Rosemary & French, Phillip, Out of Darkness Into Light? Introducing the Convention on the Rights of Persons With Disabilities, 8 Hum. Rts. L. Rev. 1 (2008)—**941, 981**

Kelman, Mark, Market Discrimination and Groups, 53 Stan. L. Rev. 833 (2001)—**67**

Klein, David, et al., Electronic Doors to Education: Study of High School Website Accessibility in Iowa, 21 Behav. Sci. & L. 27 (2003)—**234, 874**

Krenek, S. A., Beyond Reasonable Accommodation, 72 Tex. L. Rev. 1969 (1994)—**66**

Kruse, Doug & Krueger, Alan, Nat'l Bureau of Econ. Research, Labor Market Effects of Spinal Cord Injuries in the Dawn of the Computer Age (Working Paper No. 5302 Oct. 1995)—**235**

Kruse, Doug, et al., Computer Use, Computer Training, and Employment Outcomes Among People with Spinal Cord Injuries, 21 Spine 891 (1996)—**235**

Kruse, Douglas, & Schur, Lisa, Employment of People with Disabilities Following the ADA, 42 Indus. Relations 31 (2003)—**838**

Kuczynski, Christopher, Core Letter #127, U.S. Dep't of Justice, Civil Rights Div.—**534**

Table of Other Authorities

L

Labropoulou, Koula & Suomeli, Eva, Workers with Disabilities: Law, Bargaining and the Social Partners (2001)—**953**

LaCheen, Cary, Using Title II of the Americans with Disabilities Act on Behalf of Clients in TANF Programs, 8 Geo. J. on Poverty L. & Pol'y 1 (2001)—**850-851**

LaCheen, Cary, Welfare Law Ctr., Using the Americans with Disabilities Act to Protect the Rights of Individuals with Disabilities in TANF Programs: A Manual for Non-Litigation Advocacy (2004)—**851**

Law, Janice Y. Comment, Changing Welfare "As We Know It" One More Time: Assuring Basic Skills and Postsecondary Education Access for TANF Recipients, 48 Santa Clara L. Rev. 243 (2008)—**848**

LawGuru.com Legal News, Congress Weighs 90-Day Delay for All Litigation Under ADA (June 16, 2000)—**602**

Lawson, Anna, The United Nations Convention on the Rights of Persons with Disabilities: New Era or False Dawn, 34 Syr. J. Int'l L. & Com. 563 (2007)—**970-971**

Letter from Deval Patrick, Assistant Attorney General, Civil Rights Division, U.S. Dep't Justice, to Tom Harkin, U.S. Senate (Sept. 9, 1996)—**902**

Letter to Dr. James Rosser, President of Cal. St. Univ. at L.A., from Adriana Cardenas, Team Leader, Office for Civil Rights, U.S. Dept. of Educ. (April 7, 1997)—**883-884**

Lewis, Jr., Harold S. & Norman, Elizabeth J., Employment Discrimination Law and Practice 115 (West Group 2001)—**254**

Lewis, Oliver, The Expressive, Educational and Proactive Roles of Human Rights: An Analysis of the United Nations Convention on the Rights of Persons with Disabililties, in Rethinking Rights-based Mental Health Laws (Bernadette McSherry & Penelope Weller eds., 2010)—**941**

Lewyn, Michael, "Thou Shalt Not Put a Stumbling Block Before the Blind": The Americans with Disabilities Act and Public Transportation for the Disabled, 52 Hastings L. J. 1037 (2001)—**431-432**

Liu, Su, & Weathers, Bob, Do Participants Increase Their Earnings After Enrolling in the Medicaid Buy-In Program?, Working with Disability, No. 4 (May 2007)—**861**

Livermore, Gina A., et al., Center for Studying Disability Policy, Mathematica Pol'y Res., Inc., Ticket to Work Participant Characteristics and Outcomes Under the Revised Regulations (Sept. 24, 2012)—**845**

Table of Other Authorities

Loeb, Mitchell E. et al., Approaching the Measurement of Disability Prevalence: The Case of Zambia, 2 Euro. J. Disability Research 32 (2008)—**934**

Logue, Larry M. & Blanck, Peter, Race, Ethnicity, and Disability: Veterans and Benefits in Post-Civil War America (2010)—**4-5**

Long, Alex, Introducing the New and Improved Americans with Disabilities Act: Assessing the ADA Amendments Act of 2008, 103 Nw. U. L. Rev. Colloquy 217 (2008)—**108**

Loprest, Pamela & Maag, Elaine, The Urban Institute, Disabilities Among TANF Recipients: Evidence from the NHIS (May 2009)—**849**

Lord, Janet E. & Stein, Michael Ashley, The Domestic Incorporation of Human Rights Law and the United Nations Convention on the Rights of Persons with Disabilities, 83 U. Wash. L. Rev. 449 (2008)—**941**

Losen, Daniel J. & Gillespie, Jonathan, Opportunities Suspended: The Disparate Impact of Disciplinary Exclusion from School 16 (Aug. 2012)—**717**

M

Mantel, Ruth, Housing Discrimination Complaints Hit Record with Disability, Race as Leading Reasons, MarketWatch, Apr. 4, 2007—**834**

Martin, Mark, Accommodating the Handicapped: The Meaning of Discrimination Under Section 504 of the Rehabilitation Act, 55 N.Y.U. L. Rev. 881 (1980)—**60**

McDevitt, William J., Esq., I Dream of GINA: Understanding the Employment Provisions of the Genetic Information Nondiscrimination Act of 2008, 54 Vill. L. Rev. 91 (2009)—**867, 869**

McDonough, Molly, Job Coach a 'Reasonable Accommodation': Home Depot Agrees to Consultations on Developmentally Disabled Workers, ABA J. Rep., Nov. 4, 2005—**242-243**

Melvin II, Daniel H., The Desegregation of Children with Disabilities, 44 DePaul L. Rev. 599 (1995)—**655, 660**

Mendelsohn, Steven, et al., Tax Subsidization of Personal Assistance Services, 5 Disability & Health J. 75 (2012)—**919**

Mendelsohn, Steven, et al., Tax Subsidization of Personal Assistance Services, Disability & Health J., 5 (2012).—**909**

Mendelsohn, Steven, Federal Income Tax Law: A Tool for Increasing Employment Opportunities for Americans with Disabilities, Report to the Presidential Task Force on Employment of Adults with Disabilities (2002)—**917**

Mendelsohn, Steven, Role of the Tax Code in Asset Development for People with Disabilities, 26 Disability Studies Quarterly 1 (Winter 2006)—**918**

Table of Other Authorities

Metts, R. L. & Oleson, T., Assisting Disabled Entrepreneurs in Kenya: Implications for Developed Countries, in Partners for Independence: Models that Work (1993)—**937-938**

Michailakis, Dimitris, Government Action on Disability Policy: A Global Survey (1997)—**968**

Mikochik, Stephen, The Constitution and the Americans with Disabilities Act: Some First Impressions, 64 Temp. L. Rev. 619 (1991)—**24**

Milani, Adam A., Go Ahead. Make My 90 Days: Should Plaintiffs Be Required to Provide Notice to Defendants Before Filing Suit Under Title III of the Americans with Disabilities Act?, 2001 Wis. L. Rev. 107 (2001)—**601**

Miller, Paul Steven, Is There a Pink Slip in My Genes? Genetic Discrimination in the Workplace, 3 J. Health Care L. & Pol'y 225 (2000)—**98**

Miller, Paul Steven, Thinking About Discrimination in the Genetic Age, 35 J. L. Med. & Ethics 47 (2007)—**867**

Minow, Martha, Learning to Live with the Dilemma of Difference: Bilingual and Special Education, Law & Contemp. Probs., Winter 1985—**689**

Moberly, Richard E., The Americans with Disabilities Act in Cyberspace: Applying the "Nexus" Approach to Private Internet Websites, 55 Mercer L. Rev. 963 (2004)—**892**

Moisides, Yoanna X., I Just Need Help . . . TANF, the Deficit Reduction Act, and the New "Work-Eligible Individual", 11 J. Gender Race & Just. 17 (2007)—**848**

Montgomery, Patricia A., Workplace Drug Testing: Are There Limits?, Tenn. Bar J., Mar./Apr. 1996—**871**

Mueller, C. & Kirkpatrick, L., Evidence §3.1 (3d ed. 2003)—**729**

Müller, Eve & Markowitz, Joy, Project Forum, Synthesis Brief: English Language Learners with Disabilities 2 (2004)—**665**

Myhill, William N., et al., Developing Accessible Cyberinfrastructure-Enabled Knowledge Communities in the National Disability Community: Theory, Practice, and Policy, 20 Assistive Tech. 157 (2008)—**722, 874, 906**

Myhill, William N., et al., Developing the Capacity of Teacher-Librarians to Meet the Diverse Needs of All School Children: Project ENABLE, J. Research Spec. Educ'l Needs, 12 (2012)—**875, 906**

Myhill, William N., et al., Distance Education Initiatives and Their 21st Century Role in the Lives of People with Disabilities, in Focus on Distance Education Developments (E.P. Bailey, ed., 2007)—**549-550, 688, 721-723, 875, 904-905, 907**

Table of Other Authorities

Myhill, William N., Law and Policy Challenges for Achieving an Accessible eSociety: Lessons from the United States, in 2 Euro. Yrbk. of Disability Law 103 (2010)—**659, 874, 907**

Myhill, William N., Note, No FAPE for Children with Disabilities in the Milwaukee Parental Choice Program: Time to Redefine a Free Appropriate Public Education, 89 Iowa. L. Rev. 1051 (2004)—**685, 719, 738**

Myhill, William N., The State of Public Education and the Needs of English Language Learners in the Era of 'No Child Left Behind,' 8 J. Gender Race & Just. 393 (2004)—**666**

N

Nagase, Osamu, Difference, Equality and Disabled People: Disability Rights and Disability Culture (1995)—**954**

Nat'l Conference of State Legislatures: Ass'n of Assistive Tech. Act Programs, Summary of Assistive Technology Act of 1998, As Amended Public Law 108-364—**912**

Nat'l Consortium for Health Sys. Dev., At a Glance: The Final Ticket to Work Regulations 1 (June 1, 2009)—**845**

Nat'l Council on Disability, Achieving Independence: The Challenge for the 21st Century: A Decade of Progress in Disability Policy Setting an Agenda for the Future (July 26, 1996)—**6**

Nat'l Council on Disability, Implementation of the Americans with Disabilities Act: Challenges, Best Practices, and New Opportunities for Success 169-79 (July 26, 2007)—**597-599, 858-859**

Nat'l Council on Disability, National Disability Policy: A Progress Report (Oct. 2011)—**839, 863, 866**

Nat'l Council on Disability, National Disability Policy: A Progress Report December 2001-December 2002, at 101 (July 26, 2003)—**920**

Nat'l Council on Disability, On the Threshold of Independence (1988)—**48**

Nat'l Council on Disability, Over the Horizon: Potential Impact of Emerging Trends in Information and Communication Technology on Disability Policy and Practice (Dec. 26, 2006)—**885, 912**

Nat'l Council on Disability, TANF and Disability – Importance of Supports for Families with Disabilities in Welfare Reform (Mar. 14, 2003)—**849**

Nat'l Council on Disability, The Americans with Disabilities Act: Ensuring Equal Access to the American Dream (Jan. 26, 1995)—**49**

Nat'l Council on Disability, The Current State of Health Care for People with Disabilities (2009)—**7**

Table of Other Authorities

Nat'l Council on Disability, The Impact of the Americans with Disabilities Act: Assessing the Progress Toward Achieving the Goals of the ADA (July 26, 2007)—**550-551, 859-860**

Nat'l Council on Disability, The State of 21st Century Financial Incentives for Americans with Disabilities 105 (Aug. 8, 2008)—**917-919**

Nat'l Council on Disability, When the Americans with Disabilities Act Goes Online: Application of the ADA to the Internet and the Worldwide Web (July 10, 2003)—**912**

Nat'l Disability Rights Network, All Aboard (Except People with Disabilities): Amtrak's 23 Years of ADA Compliance Failure (Oct. 2013)—**411, 431**

Nat'l Fed'n of the Blind v. Am. Online, Inc., No. 99CV12303EFH (D. Mass. filed Nov. 4, 1999), reprinted in 6 Am. Disabilities Pract. & Compliance Man. § 6:59 (West 2004)—**876**

Nat'l Org. on Disability, 2004 National Organization on Disability/Harris Survey of Americans with Disabilities (2004)—**550-551**

Nat'l P'ship for Women & Families, Faces of Genetic Discrimination: How Genetic Discrimination Affects Real People 3 (2004)—**871**

Nat'l Spinal Cord Injury Ass'n, Impact of Health Care Reform on People with Disabilities (Apr. 27, 2010)—**863-864, 866**

National Council on Disability, Finding the Gaps: A Comparative Analysis of Disability Laws in the United States to the United Nations Convention on the Rights of Persons with Disabilities (CRPD) (May 12, 2008)—**975**

National Council on Disability, Towards the Full Inclusion of People with Disabilities: Examining the Accessibility of Overseas Facilities and Programs (2013)—**977**

Natowicz, Marvin R., et al., Genetic Discrimination and the Law, 50 Am. J. Hum. Genetics 465 (1992)—**871-872**

Norwalk, Leslie V., Letter to Acting Administrator of the Centers for Medicare and Medicaid Services, to Kathryn G. Allen, G.A.O. Healthcare Director (Feb. 20, 2007)—**862**

O

Occupational Safety & Health Admin., U.S. Dep't of Labor, Recommendations for Workplace Violence Prevention Programs in Late-Night Retail Establishments OSHA 3153-12R-2009 6 (2009)—**870**

Odem, Nathan & Blanck, Peter, Physician-shareholder Practice Groups and ADA Compliance, 28 Spine 3, 309 (2003)—**147**

Office of Family Assistance, U.S. Dep't of Health & Hum. Servs. Caseload Data 2011 (Apr. 3. 2012)—**849**

Office of the Attorney Gen., Tax Incentives Packet on the Americans with Disabilities Act—**920**

Table of Other Authorities

Olenick, Donald, Accommodating the Handicapped: Rehabilitation Section 504 After Southeastern, 80 Colum. L. Rev. 171 (1980)—**60**

Oneglia, Stuart, Core Letter #116, U.S. Dep't of Justice, Civil Rights Div.—**534**

Orford, Anne, Globalization and the Right to Development, in People's Rights (Philip Alston ed., 2001)—**976**

Org. for Econ. Co-Operation & Dev., Labour Market and Social Policy, Occasional Papers, Employment Policies for People with Disabilities, Occasional Papers No. 8, OCDE/GD(92)7 (1992)—**953**

Orslene, Louis, et al. Job Accommodation Network (JAN), Personal Assistance Services (PAS) in the Workplace (Aug. 23, 2006)—**243**

Osborne, Jr., Allan G., Discipline of Special-Education Students Under the Individuals with Disabilities Act, 29 Fordham Urb. L.J. 513 (2001)—**717**

Oversight Hearing on H.R. 4468 before the House Subcommittee on Select Education of the Committee on Education and Labor, 100th Cong., 2d Sess., 40-41 (1988)—**339**

P

Paul, James C. N., The Human Right to Development: Its Meaning and Importance, 25 J. Marshall L. Rev. 235 (1992)—**976**

Pavetti, Ladonna, et al., Mathematica Pol'y Research, Inc., Conducting In-Depth Assessments (Feb. 2008)—**849, 851**

Payne, Jr., Perry W., Genetic Information Nondiscrimination Act of 2008: The Federal Answer for Genetic Discrimination, 5 J. Health & Biomedical L. 33 (2009)—**867**

Pear, Robert, Oversight of Nursing Homes is Criticized, N.Y. Times, Apr. 22, 2007—**862**

Pendo, Elizabeth A., The Politics of Infertility: Recognizing Coverage Exclusions as Discrimination, 11 Conn. Ins. L. J. 293 (2005)—**478**

Perdue, Abigail Lauren, Justifying GINA, 78 Tenn. L. Rev. 1051 (2011)—**870**

Perez, Thomas E., Letter from Assistant Attorney General, U.S. Department of Justice, to Hon. Haley R. Barbour, Governor of the State of Mississippi (Dec. 22, 2011)—**406**

Perritt, Jr., Henry H., 1 Americans with Disabilities Act Handbook § 2.3 (3d ed. 1997)—**50**

Positively Minn., Dep't of Emp. & Econ. Dev., Workforce Investment Act (WIA)—**839**

Post, Robert & Siegel, Reva, Equal Protection by Law: Federal Antidiscrimination Legislation After Morrison and Kimel, 110 Yale L.J. 441 (2000)—**166**

Pothier, Dianne & Devlin, Richard, Critical Disability Theory (2007)—**946**

Table of Other Authorities

President's Comm'n on Excellence in Special Educ., A New Era: Revitalizing Special Education for Children and their Families, 31 (July 2002)—**660**

Press Release, Attorney Gen. of Mass., Monster.com First in Industry to make Website Accessible to Blind Users (Jan. 30, 2013)—**877**

Press Release, Conn. Attorney General's Office, National Federation of Blind Applaud On-Line Tax Filing Services for Agreeing to Make Sites Blind-Accessible for 2000 Tax Season (Apr. 17, 2000)—**911**

Press Release, Nat'l Fed'n of the Blind, Amazon.com and National Federation of the Blind Join Forces to Develop and Promote Web Accessibility (Mar. 28, 2007)—**877**

Q

Quinn, Gerard, Resisting the 'Temptation of Elegance': Can the Convention on the Rights of Persons with Disabilities Socialise States in Rights Behaviour?, in The UN Convention on the Rights of Persons with Disabilities: European and Scandinavian Perspectives (Oddný Mjöll Arnardóttir & Gerard Quinn eds., 2009)—**941**

R

Registry of Interpreters for the Deaf, NAD-RID Code of Professional Conduct (2005)—**548**

Relton, Joy, The Assistive Technology Act of 2004, Access World, 6(1)—**911**

Rengel, Katherine, The Americans with Disabilities Act and Internet Accessibility for the Blind, 25 J. Marshall J. Computer & Info. L. 543 (2008)—**892**

Report of the Ad Hoc Committee on a Comprehensive and Integral International Convention on Protection and Promotion of the Rights and Dignity of Persons with Disabilities, U.N. Doc. A/58/118, 3 July 2003—**969**

Respuestas de España. (July 4, 2011)—**979**

Ritchie, Heather & Blanck, Peter, The Promise of the Internet for Disability: A Study of Online Services and Web Site Accessibility of Centers for Independent Living Web Sites, 20 Behav. Sci. & L. 5 (2003)—**234**

Roberts, Jessica L., Preempting Discrimination: Lessons from the Genetic Information Nondiscrimination Act, 63 Vand. L. Rev. 439 (2010)—**867, 872**

Rothstein, Mark A., Genetic Discrimination in Employment and the Americans with Disabilities Act, 29 Hous. L. Rev. 23 (1992)—**871**

Rothstein, Mark A., GINA, the ADA, and Genetic Discrimination in Employment, 36 J.L. Med. & Ethics 837 (2008)—**873**

Rozycki, Carla J. & Haase, David K., Do WebSites Need to be Accessible to the Blind?, Law.com (Jan. 10, 2007)—**875**

Table of Other Authorities

S

Sager, Lara & Cohen, Stephen, How the Income Tax Undermines Civil Rights Law, 73 S. Cal. L. Rev. 1075 (2000)—**323**

Sandler, Leonard A., & Blanck, Peter, The Quest to Make Accessibility a Corporate Article of Faith at Microsoft: Case Study of Corporate Culture and Human Resource Dimensions, 23 Behav. Sci. & L. 39 (2005)—**909**

Schartz, Helen, et al., Workplace Accommodations: Empirical Study of Current Employees, 75 Miss. L. J. 917 (2006)—**213, 250**

Schartz, Helen, et al., Workplace Accommodations: Evidence-Based Outcomes, 27 Work 345 (2006)—**58, 213, 250**

Schartz, Kevin, et al., Employment of Persons with Disabilities in Information Technology Jobs: for Individuals with Disabilities: Literature Review for "IT Works," 20 Behav. Sci. & L. 637 (2002)—**234**

Schimmel, Jody, et al., How Do Buy-In Participants Compare with Other Medicaid Enrollees with Disabilities?, Working with Disability, No. 5 (June 2007)—**860**

Schlein, Daniel, New Frontiers for Genetic Privacy Law: The Genetic Information Nondiscrimination Act of 2008, 19 Geo. Mason U. Civ. Rts. L.J. 311 (2009)—**870**

Schmeling, James, et al., The New Disability Law and Policy Framework: Implications for Case Managers 26 (2004)—**851**

Schriner, Kay & Batavia, Andrew, The Americans with Disabilities Act: Does It Secure the Fundamental Right to Vote?, 29 Pol'y Stud. J. 663 (2001)—**386**

Schur, Lisa A., Dead End Jobs or a Path to Economic Well-Being? The Consequences of Non-Standard Work Among People with Disabilities, 20 Behav. Scis. & L. 601 (2002)—**859**

Schur, Lisa, et al., Corporate Culture and the Employment of Persons with Disabilities, Behav. Sci. & L. 3 (2005)—**68**

Schur, Lisa, et al., Is Disability Disabling in All Workplaces?: Disability, Workplace Disparities, and Corporate Culture, 48 Indus. Relations 381 (2009)—**68**

Schwemm, Robert G., Barriers to Accessible Housing: Enforcement Issues in "Design and Construction" Cases Under the Fair Housing Act, 40 U. Rich. L. Rev. 753 (2006)—**826**

Secunda, Paul M., At the Crossroads of Title IX and a New "IDEA": Why Bullying Need Not Be "A Normal Part of Growing Up" for Special Education Children, 12 Duke J. Gender L. & Pol'y 1 (2005)—**697**

Seligmann, Terry Jean, Not as Simple as ABC: Disciplining Children with Disabilities Under the 1997 IDEA Amendments, 42 Ariz. L. Rev. 77 (2000)—**714, 717**

Sengupta, Arjun, The Right to Development as a Human Right (2000)—**976**

Table of Other Authorities

Seto, Theodore P., & Buhai, Sande L., Tax and Disability: Ability to Pay and the Taxation of Difference, 154 U. Pa. L. Rev. 1053, 1053 (2006)—**917-919**

Settlement Agreement Between the United States and the City of Davenport, Iowa Under the Americans with Disabilities Act DJ 204-28-57 (Aug. 5, 2004)—**885**

Settlement Agreement between U.S. DOJ and City of Shreveport, Louisiana—**884**

Settlement Agreement Between United States of America and Nat'l Bd. of Med. Exam's, DJ#202-16-181 (Feb. 23, 2011)—**605**

Shapiro, Joseph P., No Pity: People with Disabilities Forging a New Civil Rights Movement (1993)—**6, 31**

Shapiro, Joseph P., No Pity: People with Disabilities Forging a New Civil Rights Movement (Times Books 1994)—**689, 697**

Siegal, Charles, Fifty Years of Disability Law: The Relevance of the Universal Declaration, 5 ILSA J. Int'l & Comp. L. 267 (1999)—**939, 961**

Smetanka, Stella L., The Disabled in Debt to Social Security: Can Fairness Be Guaranteed?, 35 Wm. Mitchell L. Rev. 1084 (2009)—**841**

Smith, Scott, et al., Genetic Privacy Laws: 50 State Survey, 5 J. Health & Life Scis. L. 75 (2011)—**872**

Soc. Sec. Admin., Annual Statistical Supplement to the Social Security Bulletin, 2011 (Feb. 2012)—**860**

Social Development Division, United Nations, Hidden Sisters: Women and Girls with Disabilities in the Asian and Pacific Region, UN Doc. ST/ESCAP/1548 (1995)—**935, 938**

Stapleton, David, Mathematica Pol'y Research, Ticket to Work at the Crossroads: A Solid Foundation with an Uncertain Future (Sept. 2008)—**846**

Statement of the Managers to Accompany the Americans with Disabilities Act Amendments Act of 2008, Cong. Rec. S8840, S8842 (Sept. 16, 2008)—**82, 87**

Stead, Jonathan, Toward True Equality of Educational Opportunity: Unlocking the Potential of Assistive Technology Through Professional Development, 35 Rutgers Computer & Tech. L.J. (2009)—**874**

Stein, Jacob A., Stein on Personal Injury Damages, § 5: 9 (3d ed. 1997)—**281**

Stein, Michael A. & Lord, Janet E., Monitoring the Committee on the Rights of Persons with Disabilities: Innovations, Lost Opportunities, and Future Potential' 31 Human Rights Q. 689 (2010)—**977**

Stein, Michael A. & Waterstone, Michael, 56 Duke L.R. 861 (2006)—**259**

Table of Other Authorities

Stein, Michael A., and Waterstone, Michael, Disabling Prejudice, 102 Northwestern Univ. L. Rev. 1351 (2008)—**118**

Stein, Michael A., Disability Human Rights, 95 Cal. L. Rev. 75 (2007)—**941, 976**

Steiner, Henry J., Social Rights and Economic Development: Converging Discourses?, 4 Buff. Hum. Rts. L. Rev. 25 (1998)—**976**

Suter, Sonia M., The Allure and Peril of Genetics Exceptionalism: Do We Need Special Genetics Legislation?, 79 Wash. U. L.Q. 669 (2001)—**872**

Swedish Int'l. Dev. Auth., Poverty and Disability: A Position Paper 2 (Apr. 1995)—**938**

T

Takamine, Yutaka, Disability Issues in East Asia: Review and Ways Forward (July 2003)—**936**

Task Force on the Rights and Empowerment of Americans with Disabilities, From ADA to Empowerment (Oct. 12, 1990)—**339**

Taylor, Paul, The Americans with Disabilities Act and the Internet, 7 B.U. J. Sci. & Tech. L. 26 (2001)—**904**

The Genetic Information Nondiscrimination Act of 2008 (GINA), Pub. L. 110-233 (2008)—**98**

Thornton, Craig, et al., Mathematica Pol'y Res., Inc. & Cornell Univ. Inst. Pol'y Res., Evaluation of the Ticket to Work Program: Assessments of Post-Rollout Implementation and Early Impacts, Volume 1 (May 2007)—**842, 845**

Thornton, Patricia & Lunt, Neil, Employment Policies for Disabled People in Eighteen Countries: A Review (1997)—**954-956**

Thornycroft, Peta, Beating the Drum, Johannesburg Mail and Guardian, July 27, 2001, reprinted in Peta Thornycroft, Disabled Take Struggle to Parliament, The Braille Monitor, Dec. 2001—**953**

Ticket to Work and Work Incentives Advisory Panel, Testimony 35-37 (May 3, 2002)—**844-845**

Townsend, Peter, Employment and Disability, in Disability in Britain: A Manifesto of Rights (Alan Walker & Peter Townsend, eds. 1981)—**937**

Travis, Michelle, Impairment as Protected Status: A New Universality for Disability Rights, 46 Ga. L. Rev. 937 (2012)—**100**

Tucker, Bonnie P., Insurance and the ADA, 46 DePaul L. Rev. 915 (1997)—**192**

Tucker, Bonnie Poitras, The ADA's Revolving Door: Inherent Flaws in the Civil Rights Paradigm, 62 Ohio St. L.J. 335 (2001)—**605**

Turner, James, Core Letter #132, U.S. Dep't of Justice, Civil Rights Div.—**534**

Table of Other Authorities

U

U.S. Civil Rights Commission, Accommodating the Spectrum of Individual Abilities 39 (1983)—**339**

U.S. Comm'n on Civil Rights, Accommodating the Spectrum of Individual Abilities (1983)—**60, 65**

U.S. Dep't of Health & Human Servs. Office of Civil Rights, Summary of Policy Guidance, Prohibition Against Discrimination on the Basis of Disability in the Administration of TANF—**850**

U.S. Dep't of Hous. & Urban Dev., Fair Housing Act Design Manual: A Manual to Assist Designers and Builders in Meeting the Accessibility Requirements of the Fair Housing Act 22 (1998)—**828**

U.S. Dep't of Justice Title II Technical Assistance Manual § 2.3000 (1993)—**72, 127**

U.S. Dep't of Justice Title III Technical Assistance Manual § 2.3000 (Nov. 1993)—**72, 110**

U.S. Dep't of Justice, 2010 ADA Standards for Accessible Design, (Sept. 15, 2010)—**581**

U.S. Dep't of Justice, ADA Enforcement Cases 2006 - Present: Title III—**579**

U.S. Dep't of Justice, ADA Mediation Program—**324**

U.S. Dep't of Justice, Addressing Police Misconduct—**905-906**

U.S. Dep't of Justice, Administrative Complaints (June 14, 2004)—**907**

U.S. Dep't of Justice, Enforcing the ADA: A Status Report from the Department of Justice (April-June 2008)—**603, 616**

U.S. Dep't of Justice, Enforcing the ADA: Looking Back on a Decade of Progress (July 2000)—**603**

U.S. Dep't of Justice, Nondiscrimination on the Basis of Disability in State and Local Government Services (Sep. 15, 2010)—**877**

U.S. Dep't of Justice, Press Release, Justice Department Settles with National Board of Medical Examiners Over Refusal to Provide Testing Accommodations to Yale Medical School Student (Feb. 22, 2011)—**605**

U.S. Dep't of Justice, Project Civic Access—**884**

U.S. Dep't of Justice, Title III Technical Assistance Manual (Nov. 1993)—**451-452, 534, 547, 580-581**

U.S. Dep't of Labor, A Study of Accommodations Provided to Handicapped Employees by Federal Contractors: Final Report (1982)—**65**

U.S. Dep't of Labor, Persons with a Disability: Labor Force Characteristics Summary (2011)—**838-839**

U.S. Dep't of Labor/Employment & Training Admin., Work Opportunity Tax Credit—**931**

U.S. Dep't of State, Country Reports on Human Rights Practices: South Africa (Mar. 31, 2003)—**952**

Table of Other Authorities

U.S. Dep't of Justice, Title III Technical Assistance Manual (1994 Supplement)—**587**

U.S. Election Assistance Comm'n, A Summary of the 2004 Election Day Survey: Access to Voting for the Disabled 14-4 (2005)—**387**

U.S. General Accounting Office, "Business Tax Incentives: Incentives to Employ Workers with Disabilities Receive Limited Use and Have an Uncertain Impact GAO-03-39 (Dec. 2002)—**920**

U.S. Gov't Accountability Office, GAO-10-812SP, Highlights of a Forum: Actions That Could Increase Work Participation for Adults with Disabilities 11 (July 2010)—**861**

UN, Washington Group on Disability Statistics (Mar. 5, 2013)—**934**

V

Vasichek, Laurie A., Genetic Discrimination in the Workplace: Lessons from the Past and Concerns for the Future, 3 St. Louis U.J. Health L. & Pol'y 13 (2009)—**871**

Vetter, Gregory R., Comment, Is a Personality Test a Pre-Job-Offer Medical Examination Under the ADA?, 93 Nw. U. L. Rev. 597 (1999)—**197**

"Victory for Pistorius Gives Paralympians Hope," Int'l. Herald Trib., 2008 WLNR 9430943 (May 19, 2008)—**84**

W

W3C, Web Content Accessibility Guidelines 1.0 (May 5, 1999)—**893**

Waddell, Cynthia D., The Growing Digital Divide in Access for People with Disabilities: Overcoming Barriers to Participation in the Digital Economy, Remarks at Understanding the Digital Economy Conference, Washington, D.C. (May 25-26, 1999)—**902**

Waddington, Lisa, Future Prospects for EU Equality Law. Lessons to be Learnt from the Proposed Equal Treatment Directive, 36 Euro. L. Rev. 163 (2011)—**934**

Waddington, Lisa, Reassessing the Employment of People with Disabilities in Europe: From Quotas to Anti-Discrimination Laws, 18 Comp. Lab. L.J. 62 (1996)—**941**

Waddington, Lisa, The European Union and the United Nations Convention on the Rights of Persons with Disabilities: A Story of Exclusive and Shared Competences, 18 Maastricht J. Euro. & Comp. L. 431 (2011)—**934**

Wagner, M., Marder, C., Blackorby, J., & Cardoso, D., The Children We Serve: The Demographic Characteristics of Elementary and Middle School Students with Disabilities and their Households (Sept. 2002)—**735**

Waterstone, Michael E., Constitutional and Statutory Voting Rights for People with Disabilities, 14 Stan. L. & Pol'y Rev. 353 (2003)—**27**

Table of Other Authorities

Waterstone, Michael E., Let's Be Reasonable Here: Why the ADA Will Not Ruin Professional Sports, 00 BYU L. Rev. 1489 (2000)—**532**

Waterstone, Michael E., The Untold Story of the Rest of the Americans with Disabilities Act, 58 Vand. L. Rev. 1807 (2005)—**604**

Waterstone, Michael, A New Vision of Public Enforcement, 92 Minn. L. Rev. 434 (2007)—**441**

Waterstone, Michael, Constitutional and Statutory Voting Rights for People with Disabilities, 14 Stan. L. & Pol'y Rev. 353 (2003)—**386**

Waterstone, Michael, Disability Constitutional Law, __ Emory L. J. __ (forthcoming 2013)—**24**

Waterstone, Michael, Lane, Fundamental Rights, & Voting, 56 Ala. L. Rev. 793 (2005)—**349**

Waterstone, Michael, Returning Veterans and Disability Law, 85 Notre Dame L. Rev. 1081 (2009-2010)—**5**

Weber, Mark C., Beyond the Americans with Disabilities Act: A National Employment Policy for People with Disabilities, 46 Buff. L. Rev. 123 (1998)—**954**

Weber, Mark C., Disability Discrimination by State and Local Government: The Relationship Between Section 504 of the Rehabilitation Act and Title II of the Americans with Disabilities Act, 36 Wm. & Mary L. Rev. 1089 (1995)—**437**

Weber, Mark C., Reciprocal Lessons of the ADA and European Disability Law, 93 Am. Soc'y Int'l L. Proc. 338 (1999)—**954**

Weber, Mark, Disability Harassment (2007)—**118**

Weicker, Jr., Lowell, Historical Background of the Americans with Disabilities Act, 64 Temp. L. Rev. 387 (1991)—**49**

White, T., The Making of the President 1960 (1961)—**634**

Wickard, William D., The New Americans Without a Disability Act: The Surprisingly Successful Plight of the Non-Disabled Plaintiff Under the ADA, 61 U. Pitt. L. Rev. 1023 (2000)—**208**

Wiley, David T., If You Can't Fight 'Em, Join 'Em: Class Actions Under Title I of the Americans With Disabilities Act, 13 Lab. Law. 197 (1997)—**258**

Williams, John M., Clint Eastwood Explains His Beef with the ADA, Business Week online (May 17, 2000)—**601**

Wodatch, John, Core Letter #159, U.S. Dep't of Justice, Civil Rights Div.—**534**

Wood, Robert, et al., Mathematica Pol'y Research, Inc., Social Service Review , Vol. 82, No. 1 (March 2008)—**849**

Work World, Ticket to Work Regulation Changes – 2008—**842, 845**

Working Methods of the Committee on the Rights of Persons with Disabilities Adopted at its Fifth Session (11-15 April 2011)—**977**

Table of Other Authorities

World Health Org., Disability Prevention and Rehabilitation, Technical Report Series No. 668 (1981)—**935**

World Health Organization & World Bank, Summary 2011 World Report on Disability (2011)—**935-936**

World Health Organization, Monitoring of United Nations Standard Rules on the Equalization of Opportunities for Persons with Disabilities: Government Responses to the Implementation of the Rules on Medical Care, Rehabilitation, Support Services and Personnel Training: Summary, vol. I (WHO/DAR/01.1) (2001)—**967**

World Health Organization, Monitoring of United Nations Standard Rules on the Equalization of Opportunities for Persons with Disabilities: Government Responses to the Implementation of the Rules on Medical Care, Rehabilitation, Support Services and Personnel Training: Main Report, vol. II (WHO/DAR/01.2) (2001)—**967**

Wright, Peter W.D., U.S. Supreme Court Hears Oral Arguments in Arlington v. Murphy, Wrightslaw, Apr. 24, 2006—**767**

Y

Yukins, Christopher R., Making Federal Information Technology Accessible: A Case Study in Social Policy and Procurement, 33 Pub. Cont. L.J. 667 (2004)—**908**

Z

Zedlewski, Sheila R., et al., Hard-to-Employ Parents: A Review of Their Characteristics and the Programs Designed to Serve Their Needs (June 2007)—**850**

DISABILITY CIVIL RIGHTS LAW AND POLICY

CASES AND MATERIALS

Third Edition

Part 1

Historical And Conceptual Foundations
Analysis

Chapter 1   INTRODUCTION
§ 1.1   Overview
§ 1.2   American Conceptions Of Discrimination On The Basis Of
        Disability
        A. Evolution Of Models For Societal Treatment Of Disability
        B. A Note On The Evolution Of Ideas About Disability In
            America After The Civil War And Their Relevance Today
        C. The Modern Disability Rights Model
§ 1.3   The Limits Of Constitutional Protection
§ 1.4   ADA Precursors
        A. Vocational Rehabilitation And Benefits
        B. Early Disability Civil Rights Statutes (1968-88)
        C. Interpretation Of The Rehabilitation Act
Chapter 2   THE ADA'S HISTORY AND PHILOSOPHY
§ 2.1   A Brief Guide To The ADA
§ 2.2   ADA Background And Fundamentals
        A. The Story Of The Passage Of The ADA
        B. Key Legislative Trade-Offs
        C. Constitutional Basis
        D. Role Of Federal Agencies
§ 2.3   The History, Theory And Economics Of The Accommodation
        Principle
        A. The Evolution And Legislative History Of The Reasonable
            Accommodation Requirement
        B. Theory And Economics Of The Reasonable Accommodation
            Requirement

Chapter 1 INTRODUCTION

§ 1.1 Overview

OPENING QUESTIONS

1.   What does it mean to have a disability for purposes of United States law, both historically and today?   Does the meaning differ depending on whether the question is asked by a governmental official or a private employer?   By a school board or the owner of a theater?   What about under the law of other countries?

2.   What are the place of and the rights of people with disabilities in society?   Should the government attempt to eliminate barriers to

participation? Which barriers? Should the government affirmatively assist people with disabilities to participate in society? Why? How?

3. Should private entities – employers and store-owners and e-commerce businesses – be required by law to employ or open their facilities and websites to people with disabilities? Under what conditions and at what costs?

4. If the federal or state governments address disability issues, what models are available for understanding those issues and what legal framework should apply to them? Should we treat disability like race, like gender, like age?

5. If the legislature decides to intervene, what is the most effective or most efficient way to do so?

In this casebook, the authors – three academics who also are disability rights advocates, and who have litigated on both sides of disability cases – ask you to think about these and other questions. We do so via a tour of the civil rights laws and policies affecting persons with disabilities, with primary focus on the Americans with Disabilities Act (ADA) of 1990, and the Americans with Disabilities Amendments Act (ADAAA) of 2008. Along the way, we examine the history of the ADA and look at what other countries and international organizations are doing about disability issues.

"Disability law" is almost wholly statutory, that is, guided by federal and state laws. But, the courts also have interpreted and shaped the statutes, giving them a broad scope here, a narrower one there. Throughout this book, we explore the ways in which courts have responded to disability legislation. On the federal level, Congress has assigned various executive agencies, especially the Equal Employment Opportunity Commission (EEOC), a prominent role in interpreting and enforcing disability policy, and the courts have had to come to terms with that role. Disability law evolves within these interacting institutions.

We begin with a telescoped view of disability policy and then move to the direct progenitor of the ADA, the Rehabilitation Act of 1973. As we move along, we will encounter the forces – political, economic, social, and attitudinal factors regarding conceptions of disability – that shape law and policy.

§ 1.2 American Conceptions Of Discrimination On The Basis Of Disability

The answer to the question "What is a disability?" seems straightforward – an inability to see, to hear, to walk, to think and the like. But in a legal context, the reason for the question may shape the response. Is the question asked to form a legislative response to high unemployment rates among injured veterans? Is it asked to provide an answer to parents who want to be able to send their children who use wheelchairs to their neighborhood school? Is it asked to explain why people with limited hearing cannot go to the movies? Any one of these perspectives might shape the answer. The next sections describe the two primary ways such questions are usually answered.

A more subtle way of asking the question is whether certain impairments would be disabilities at all if the "built environment" – courthouses or museums with stairs, public events without signers for people with hearing-impairments, television broadcasts and webcasts without close captioning – were different? The answer to that question may not only define disability, but also suggest ways for erasing artificially created barriers between people with disabilities and others.

A. *Evolution Of Models For Societal Treatment Of Disability*

In the past thirty years, disability laws and policies have attracted widespread attention from policymakers, courts, legal academics, researchers, employers, and disability advocates. The magnitude and tenor of the debate is not surprising. Since its passage in 1990, the ADA has become America's prominent national policy statement affecting the lives of persons with disabilities. Yet, to a remarkable degree, contemporary employment, health care, and governmental and rehabilitation programs for persons with disabilities still are modeled on outmoded and medicalized stereotypes about disabilities. These longstanding views date back to the birth of the Civil War pension system, which first linked the definition of disability to an inability to work and established physicians as the medical gatekeepers of disability benefits. The medical model focused on the individual, whose disability was conceived as an infirmity that precluded full participation in the economy and society.

Historically, the medical model cast people with disabilities in a subordinate role in their encounters with doctors, rehabilitation professionals, governmental bureaucrats, and social workers who aimed to "help them" adjust to a society structured around the convenience and interests of people without disabilities. The medical model never questioned the physical and social environment in which people with disabilities were forced to function. It countenanced their segregation and economic marginalization. For a review, *see* Harlan Hahn, Accommodations and the ADA: Unreasonable Bias or Biased Reasoning?, 21 Berkeley J. Emp. & Lab. L. 166 (2000).

Because the medical model aimed to address the "needs" of people with disabilities rather than recognize their civil rights, it led to government policies that viewed assistance for people with disabilities as a form of either charity or welfare.

3

B.   *A Note On The Evolution Of Ideas About Disability In America After The Civil War And Their Relevance Today*

The Civil War changed how Americans thought about disability. Attitudes were shaped about and by veterans returning with disabilities and their families as they engaged the Civil War pension system. There were some 860,000 survivors with disabilities from the nearly 2.5 million members of the Union Army. The pension scheme for Union veterans with disabilities became, up to that time, this nation's largest and most medicalized welfare scheme, albeit for a select group.

As part of a larger investigation, Professor Blanck and his colleagues examine the lives of a large sample of Union Army veterans and emerging conceptions of disability in American society after the Civil War. The information was created by Nobel Laureate and economist, Robert Fogel, and his colleagues at the Center for Population Economics at the University of Chicago. *See generally* Peter Blanck, "The Right to Live in the World": Disability Yesterday, Today, and Tomorrow, 2008 Jacobus tenBroek Disability Law Symposium, Tex. J. Civ. Lib. & Civ. Rights, 13, 367 (2008); Larry M. Logue & Peter Blanck, Race, Ethnicity, and Disability: Veterans and Benefits in Post-Civil War America (2010).

We find that during the pension system stigmatized and less understood disabilities, mostly mental and infectious conditions, were harshly criticized. The rhetoric became detached from the actual workings of the law, and indeed from the behavior of disabled with disabilities themselves. Despite evidence to the contrary, veterans with disabilities were portrayed as scamming the system, bilking the public treasury and trust. In complex ways then, the identity and definition of disability was tied in the public's mind to the character and moral fiber of veterans. Veterans with severe, physical disabilities were seen as particularly worthy beneficiaries, as compared to those with mental disabilities; for instance, those with "nervous" disorders or what we label today as post-traumatic stress disorder (PTSD). Logue & Blanck, *supra.*

What may we learn from this period in history that is relevant today? Of particular importance is unearthing deep ideas about disability and worthiness, dependency and malingering, acceptable and abnormal mental disability, and disability advocacy versus frivolous litigation. At the core of each of these dimensions of tension, many of which are discussed in this case book, are ideas about disability, civil rights, and identity.

Not surprisingly, the studies of Civil War disability pensions show discrimination on the basis of race. All else equal, black veterans were much less likely as white veterans to be approved for pensions. The end result of this discrimination was that, compared to whites, lower pension payments were linked to a shorter life expectancy for African-American veterans with disabilities. Veterans fortunate enough to receive pensions had their lives extended. Logue & Blanck, *supra*, at 41-83.

Study of evolving attitudes about contemporary disability laws and policies thus may be enhanced by an appreciation of the experiences of Americans with disabilities historically. The Civil War pension scheme evolved within a unique system of attitudes about disability combined with partisan, economic, and social forces that in many ways parallel challenges and tensions in the world today. Stigma and discrimination against disability affected pensions even when the law was drafted as neutral. Political advantage made the people with disabilities an easy target in calls for social reform. Lawyers, physicians, and bureaucrats often distorted the operation of the system, sometimes for personal gain. Logue & Blanck, *supra*, at 111-127.

All this occurred at a time when social norms about disability had not developed and advocacy for disability rights and social justice was non-existent. Yet, this also was a time of new group affiliation and identity for people with disabilities that in many ways transcended ethnicity, race, and socioeconomic status. This birth of collective action occurred not just for veterans, but also for others with disabilities and their families – through new schools for the deaf, the blind, and in other settings. Still evident, however, was segregation and discrimination.

With this unprecedented array of factors, it is not surprising a political and social backlash to the pension system occurred that affected notions of disability worthiness and advocacy for decades to come, indeed perhaps until the beginnings of the modern rights-based approach embodied in the ADA. But it must not be overlooked that tens of thousands of Civil War veterans with disabilities – white and black, immigrants and natives, across the spectrum of physical and mental disability – and their families fought for their newfound right to participate and to live in the world. For the first time in U.S. history, disability was linked to the right to participate in our democracy.

Today's children and young adults, many who are veterans, are the first generation who will not know a world without the ADA. Will the stubborn legacies of disability and exclusion, unworthiness, and incapacity continue, or will this generation develop values toward equal rights and inclusion? *See* Michael Waterstone, Returning Veterans and Disability Law, 85 Notre Dame L. Rev. 1081 (2009-2010). Either way, disability is no longer invisible to the world's political, social and economic process.

C.   *The Modern Disability Rights Model*

The modern disability civil rights model began to influence government policy in the 1970s. The model conceptualized persons with disabilities as a minority group entitled to the same hard-won legal protections for equality that emerged from the struggles of African Americans and women. Proposing that disability is a social and cultural construct, the civil rights model focuses on the laws and practices that subordinate persons with disabilities. It insists that government secure the equality of persons with disabilities by eliminating the legal, physical, economic, and social barriers that preclude their equal involvement in society.

The civil rights model conceptualizes barriers to full citizenship as being socially created, and therefore assigns society with some of the cost and responsibility of removing them. The emphasis is not on giving any group special treatment; rather, the issue involves balancing the scales. One commentator suggests:

> [T]he configurations of the existing environment confer enormous advantages on nondisabled persons. Machines have been designed to fit hands that can easily grip these objects, steps have been built for legs that bend at the knee . . . . Everything has been standardized for a model human being whose life is untouched by disability. All aspects of the built environment, including work sites, have been adapted for *someone*; the problem is that they have been adapted exclusively for the nondisabled majority.

Harlan Hahn, Equality and the Environment: The Interpretation of "Reasonable Accommodations" in the Americans with Disabilities Act, 17 J. Rehab. Admin. 101, 103 (1993).

Although, until recently, federal policy continued to conceptualize disability from a medical perspective, people with disabilities as individuals and in organized groups began to challenge these stereotypes. Beginning in the 1970s, individuals with disabilities asserted their right to be independent in pursuing education and housing. *See* Joseph P. Shapiro, No Pity: People with Disabilities Forging a New Civil Rights Movement (1993) (reviewing the history of modern disability rights movement). In New York, for example, an advocacy group for the rights of individuals with disabilities was formed in 1971 called "Disabled in Action." For a review of the disability civil rights movement, *see* Nat'l Council on Disability, Achieving Independence: The Challenge for the 21st Century: A Decade of Progress in Disability Policy Setting an Agenda for the Future (July 26, 1996), http://www.ncd.gov/publications/1996_Publications/July1996.

During this period, national disability policy began to integrate the concepts of the independent living philosophy. Title VII of the Rehabilitation Act of 1973 initiated funding for Centers for Independent Living (CILs). Not only did the CILs provide services *for* individuals with disabilities, but also they were required to be operated *by* individuals with disabilities. *See* Dep'ts of Labor, Health, & Human Servs., Education, and Related Agency Appropriations for 2002, Hearing Before the U.S. House Appropriations Subcomm., 107th Cong. 2nd Sess. at 192 (2002) (statement of Kelly Buckland regarding reauthorization of the Rehabilitation Act of 1973).

The National Council on Disability (NCD), however, finds that even with heightened national awareness, "people with disabilities experience . . . specific problems in gaining access to appropriate health care." Nat'l Council on Disability, The Current State of Health Care for People with Disabilities 9 (2009), *available at* http://www.ncd.gov/raw media_repository/0d7c848f_3d97_43b3_bea5_36e1d97f973d?document.pdf. Specifically, the NCD finds that people with disabilities "frequently lack either health insurance or coverage for necessary services such as specialty care, long-term care, care coordination, prescription medications, durable medical equipment, and assistive technologies." *Id.* Despite various attempts to address these barriers, "significant problems remain." *Id.*

The need to focus on disability rights is unlikely to abate. Several factors are contributing to a significant increase in the number of persons with disabilities in the United States, such as the aging population, adults with disabilities living with aging parents who will no longer be able to care for them, and persons currently institutionalized who have the desire and the ability to live in an inclusive society. Todd Zwillich, U.S. Unready for Rise in Disabled, Web MD (Apr. 2007), http://www.cbsnews.com/ stories/2007/04/24/health/webmd/main2724291.shtml. Seventeen states have identified 25,000 individuals with disabilities who in the next few years will move out of institutional settings and into the community.

The evolving policy of inclusion proceeded to foster federal and state laws from accessibility to voting and air travel, to independence in education and housing, culminating with passage of the ADA in 1990. In the ADA as originally enacted, Congress expressly recognized the minority status of people with disabilities, finding that:

> historically, society has tended to isolate and segregate individuals with disabilities, and, despite some improvements, such forms of discrimination against individuals with disabilities continue to be a serious and pervasive social problem; . . . individuals with disabilities are a discrete and insular minority who have been faced with restrictions and limitations, subjected to a history of purposeful unequal treatment, and relegated to a position of political powerlessness in our society. . . .

42 U.S.C. § 12101(a) (2006).

Notes & Questions

1. Do you agree with Professor Hahn's thesis about the barriers that the environment creates? What would you do about them?

2.   Should the U.S. Constitution protect people with disabilities at all? Why?

3.   If there are constitutional protections, should disabilities be treated by the law using the same civil rights model used for racial distinctions? There is a difference between that model and the one used for gender. Is the latter more appropriate? The response by the United States Supreme Court has been a resounding rejection of heightened scrutiny as applied to state or private action that discriminates against persons with disabilities.   Do you think that is a useful distinction between disabilities and other categories?

4.   We will observe in Part 9 that other nations have adopted a broader view of disability rights than that taken by the U.S. Supreme Court. Why might that be the case? Is the "human rights" model of other nations different from the multi-tiered "civil rights" model followed by U.S. courts?

5.   Is disability today even a civil rights issue? Why or why not?

§ 1.3   The Limits Of Constitutional Protection

In several cases, the Supreme Court has indicated an unwillingness to treat people with disabilities as a group deserving of special, or "heightened" protection under the Equal Protection Clause of the Fourteenth Amendment.

The Supreme Court first addressed the protection afforded to people with disabilities under the Equal Protection Clause in 1927. In *Buck v. Bell*, the plaintiff challenged the constitutionality of a Virginia law requiring compulsory sterilization of people with intellectual disabilities at the age of 18. 274 U.S. 200, 205 (1927). Although the Court held that the Virginia statute did not violate the Equal Protection Clause, it did not analyze the constitutional standard of review for disability-based discrimination. *Id.* at 207.

The *Buck* Court relied on the view, as articulated by Justice Oliver Wendell Holmes, of the limited societal, or perhaps moral, responsibility for people with disabilities:

> We have seen more than once that the public welfare may call upon the best citizens for their lives. It would be strange if it could not call upon those who already sap the strength of the state for these lesser sacrifices, often not felt to be such by those concerned, in order to prevent our being swamped with incompetence. It is better for all the world, if instead of waiting to execute degenerate offspring for crime, or to let them starve for their imbecility, society can prevent those who are manifestly unfit from continuing

their kind. The principle that sustains compulsory vaccination is broad enough to cover cutting the Fallopian tubes . . . . Three generations of imbeciles are enough.

Id. Whatever the standard, the Court considered the state's interest in preventing the birth of people with disabilities to be a significant or compelling reason to satisfy it.

A life-time later, in 1985, the Court conducted a different analysis of the constitutional standard of review as applied to persons with disabilities, in the case *City of Cleburne v. Cleburne Living Center.*

&

CITY OF CLEBURNE, TEXAS v. CLEBURNE LIVING CENTER

Supreme Court of the United States, 1985
473 U.S. 432

Justice WHITE delivered the opinion of the Court.

A Texas city denied a special use permit for the operation of a group home for the mentally retarded,[1] acting pursuant to a municipal zoning ordinance requiring permits for such homes. The Court of Appeals for the Fifth Circuit held that mental retardation is a "quasi-suspect" classification and that the ordinance violated the Equal Protection Clause because it did not substantially further an important governmental purpose. We hold that a lesser standard of scrutiny is appropriate, but conclude that under that standard the ordinance is invalid as applied in this case.

I

[U]nder the zoning regulations applicable to the site, a special use permit, renewable annually, was required for the construction of "[h]ospitals for the insane or feeble-minded, or alcoholic [sic] or drug addicts, or penal or correctional institutions." The city had determined that the proposed group home should be classified as a "hospital for the feebleminded." * * *

CLC [(Cleburne Living Center)] then filed suit in Federal District Court against the city and a number of its officials, alleging, inter alia, that the zoning ordinance was invalid on its face and as applied because it discriminated against the mentally retarded in violation of the equal protection rights of CLC and its potential residents. The District Court found that "[i]f the potential residents of the Featherston Street home

---

[1] Prior to 2010, courts often used the term "mentally retarded" because federal law used that term extensively. Congress passed Rosa's Law in 2010 which replaced all uses and variations of the term "retardation" in federal law with the term "intellectual disability." Pub. L. 111-256, 124 Stat. 2643 (Oct. 5, 2010).

were not mentally retarded, but the home was the same in all other respects, its use would be permitted under the city's zoning ordinance," and that the City Counsel's decision "was motivated primarily by the fact that the residents of the home would be persons who are mentally retarded." App. 93, 94. Even so, the District Court held the ordinance and its application constitutional. Concluding that no fundamental right was implicated and that mental retardation was neither a suspect nor a quasi-suspect classification, the court employed the minimum level of judicial scrutiny applicable to equal protection claims. The court deemed the ordinance, as written and applied, to be rationally related to the city's legitimate interests in "the legal responsibility of CLC and its residents, * * * the safety and fears of residents in the adjoining neighborhood," and the number of people to be housed in the home. * * * Id. at 103.

The Court of Appeals for the Fifth Circuit reversed, determining that mental retardation was a quasi-suspect classification and that it should assess the validity of the ordinance under intermediate-level scrutiny. 726 F.2d 191 (1984). * * * Without group homes, the court stated, the retarded could never hope to integrate themselves into the community. * * * Applying the test that it considered appropriate, the court held that the ordinance was invalid on its face because it did not substantially further any important governmental interests. The Court of Appeals went on to hold that the ordinance was also invalid as applied. * * * Rehearing en banc was denied with six judges dissenting in an opinion urging en banc consideration of the panel's adoption of a heightened standard of review. * * *

* * *

II

The Equal Protection Clause of the Fourteenth Amendment commands that no State shall "deny to any person within its jurisdiction the equal protection of the laws," which is essentially a direction that all persons similarly situated should be treated alike. *Plyler v. Doe*, 457 U.S. 202, 216 (1982). Section 5 of the Amendment empowers Congress to enforce this mandate, but absent controlling congressional direction, the courts have themselves devised standards for determining the validity of state legislation or other official action that is challenged as denying equal protection. The general rule is that legislation is presumed to be valid and will be sustained if the classification drawn by the statute is rationally related to a legitimate state interest. * * * When social or economic legislation is at issue, the Equal Protection Clause allows the States wide latitude, * * * and the Constitution presumes that even improvident decisions will eventually be rectified by the democratic processes.

The general rule gives way, however, when a statute classifies by race, alienage, or national origin. These factors are so seldom relevant to the achievement of any legitimate state interest that laws grounded in such considerations are deemed to reflect prejudice and antipathy – a view that those in the burdened class are not as worthy or deserving as others. For these reasons and because such discrimination is unlikely to be soon rectified by legislative means, these laws are subjected to strict scrutiny and will be sustained only if they are suitably tailored to serve a compelling state interest. *McLaughlin v. Florida*, 379 U.S. 184, 192 (1964); *Graham v. Richardson*, 403 U.S. 365 (1971). Similar oversight by the courts is due when state laws impinge on personal rights protected by the Constitution. *Kramer v. Union Free School District No. 15*, 395 U.S. 621 (1969); *Shapiro v. Thompson*, 394 U.S. 618 (1969); *Skinner v. Oklahoma ex rel. Williamson*, 316 U.S. 535 (1942).

Legislative classifications based on gender also call for a heightened standard of review. That factor generally provides no sensible ground for differential treatment. "[W]hat differentiates sex from such nonsuspect statuses as intelligence or physical disability . . . is that the sex characteristic frequently bears no relation to ability to perform or contribute to society." *Frontiero v. Richardson*, 411 U.S. 677, 686 (1973) (plurality opinion). Rather than resting on meaningful considerations, statutes distributing benefits and burdens between the sexes in different ways very likely reflect outmoded notions of the relative capabilities of men and women. A gender classification fails unless it is substantially related to a sufficiently important governmental interest. * * * Because illegitimacy is beyond the individual's control and bears "no relation to the individual's ability to participate in and contribute to society," * * * official discriminations resting on that characteristic are also subject to somewhat heightened review. Those restrictions "will survive equal protection scrutiny to the extent they are substantially related to a legitimate state interest." * * *

We have declined, however, to extend heightened review to differential treatment based on age:

> "While the treatment of the aged in this Nation has not been wholly free of discrimination, such persons, unlike, say, those who have been discriminated against on the basis of race or national origin, have not experienced a 'history of purposeful unequal treatment' or been subjected to unique disabilities on the basis of stereotyped characteristics not truly indicative of their abilities." *Massachusetts Board of Retirement v. Murgia*, 427 U.S. 307, 313 (1976).

The lesson of Murgia is that where individuals in the group affected by a law have distinguishing characteristics relevant to interests the State has the authority to implement, the courts have been very reluctant, as they should be in our federal system and with our respect for the separation of powers, to closely scrutinize legislative choices as to whether, how, and to what extent those interests should be pursued. In such cases, the Equal Protection Clause requires only a rational means to serve a legitimate end.

III

Against this background, we conclude for several reasons that the Court of Appeals erred in holding mental retardation a quasi-suspect classification calling for a more exacting standard of judicial review than is normally accorded economic and social legislation. First, it is undeniable, and it is not argued otherwise here, that those who are mentally retarded have a reduced ability to cope with and function in the everyday world. Nor are they all cut from the same pattern: as the testimony in this record indicates, they range from those whose disability is not immediately evident to those who must be constantly cared for.[9] They are thus different, immutably so, in relevant respects, and the States' interest in dealing with and providing for them is plainly a legitimate one.[10] How this large and diversified group is to be treated

---

[9]   Mentally retarded individuals fall into four distinct categories. The vast majority – approximately 89% – are classified as "mildly" retarded, meaning that their IQ is between 50 and 70. Approximately 6% are "moderately" retarded, with IQs between 35 and 50. The remaining two categories are "severe" (IQs of 20 to 35) and "profound" (IQs below 20). These last two categories together account for about 5% of the mentally retarded population. App. 39 (testimony of Dr. Philip Roos).

Mental retardation is not defined by reference to intelligence or IQ alone, however. The American Association on Mental Deficiency (AAMD) has defined mental retardation as "'significantly subaverage general intellectual functioning existing concurrently with deficits in adaptive behavior and manifested during the developmental period.'" Brief for AAMD et al. as *Amici Curiae* 3 (quoting AAMD, Classification in Mental Retardation 1 (H. Grosman ed. 1983)). "Deficits in adaptive behavior" are limitations on general ability to meet the standards of maturation, learning, personal independence, and social responsibility expected for an individual's age level and cultural group. Brief for AAMD et al. as *Amici Curiae* 4, n.1. Mental retardation is caused by a variety of factors, some genetic, some environmental, and some unknown. Id. at 4.

[10]   As Dean Ely has observed:

Surely one has to feel sorry for a person disabled by something he or she can't do anything about, but I'm not aware of any reason to suppose that elected officials are unusually unlikely to share that feeling. Moreover, classifications based on physical disability and intelligence are typically accepted as legitimate, even by judges and commentators who assert that immutability is relevant. The explanation, when one is given, is that those characteristics (unlike the one the commentator is trying to render suspect) are often relevant to legitimate

12

under the law is a difficult and often a technical matter, very much a task for legislators guided by qualified professionals and not by the perhaps ill-informed opinions of the judiciary. Heightened scrutiny inevitably involves substantive judgments about legislative decisions, and we doubt that the predicate for such judicial oversight is present where the classification deals with mental retardation.

Second, the distinctive legislative response, both national and state, to the plight of those who are mentally retarded demonstrates not only that they have unique problems, but also that the lawmakers have been addressing their difficulties in a manner that belies a continuing antipathy or prejudice and a corresponding need for more intrusive oversight by the judiciary. Thus, the Federal Government has not only outlawed discrimination against the mentally retarded in federally funded programs, see § 504 of the Rehabilitation Act of 1973, 29 U.S.C. § 794, but it has also provided the retarded with the right to receive "appropriate treatment, services, and habilitation" in a setting that is "least restrictive of [their] personal liberty." Developmental Disabilities Assistance and Bill of Rights Act, 42 U.S.C. §§ 6010(1), (2). In addition, the Government has conditioned federal education funds on a State's assurance that retarded children will enjoy an education that, "to the maximum extent appropriate," is integrated with that of nonmentally retarded children. Education of the Handicapped Act, 20 U.S.C. § 1412(5)(B). The Government has also facilitated the hiring of the mentally retarded into the federal civil service by exempting them from the requirement of competitive examination. See 5 C.F.R. § 213.3102(t) (1984). The State of Texas has similarly enacted legislation that acknowledges the special status of the mentally retarded by conferring certain rights upon them, such as "the right to live in the least restrictive setting appropriate to [their] individual needs and abilities," including "the right to live . . . in a group home." Mentally Retarded Persons Act of 1977, Tex. Rev. Civ. Stat. Ann., Art. 5547-300, § 7 (Vernon Supp. 1985). * * *

Such legislation thus singling out the retarded for special treatment reflects the real and undeniable differences between the retarded and others. That a civilized and decent society expects and approves such legislation indicates that governmental consideration of those differences in the vast majority of situations is not only legitimate but also desirable. It may be, as CLC contends, that legislation designed to benefit, rather than disadvantage, the retarded would generally withstand examination under a test of heightened scrutiny. See Brief for Respondents 38-41. The relevant inquiry, however, is whether heightened

---

purposes. At that point there's not much left of the immutability theory, is there?

J. Ely, Democracy and Distrust 150 (1980) (footnote omitted). See also id. at 154-155.

scrutiny is constitutionally mandated in the first instance. Even assuming that many of these laws could be shown to be substantially related to an important governmental purpose, merely requiring the legislature to justify its efforts in these terms may lead it to refrain from acting at all. Much recent legislation intended to benefit the retarded also assumes the need for measures that might be perceived to disadvantage them. The Education of the Handicapped Act, for example, requires an "appropriate" education, not one that is equal in all respects to the education of nonretarded children; clearly, admission to a class that exceeded the abilities of a retarded child would not be appropriate. * * * Similarly, the Developmental Disabilities Assistance Act and the Texas Act give the retarded the right to live only in the "least restrictive setting" appropriate to their abilities, implicitly assuming the need for at least some restrictions that would not be imposed on others. * * * Especially given the wide variation in the abilities and needs of the retarded themselves, governmental bodies must have a certain amount of flexibility and freedom from judicial oversight in shaping and limiting their remedial efforts.

Third, the legislative response, which could hardly have occurred and survived without public support, negates any claim that the mentally retarded are politically powerless in the sense that they have no ability to attract the attention of the lawmakers. Any minority can be said to be powerless to assert direct control over the legislature, but if that were a criterion for higher level scrutiny by the courts, much economic and social legislation would now be suspect.

Fourth, if the large and amorphous class of the mentally retarded were deemed quasi-suspect for the reasons given by the Court of Appeals, it would be difficult to find a principled way to distinguish a variety of other groups who have perhaps immutable disabilities setting them off from others, who cannot themselves mandate the desired legislative responses, and who can claim some degree of prejudice from at least part of the public at large. One need mention in this respect only the aging, the disabled, the mentally ill, and the infirm. We are reluctant to set out on that course, and we decline to do so.

Doubtless, there have been and there will continue to be instances of discrimination against the retarded that are in fact invidious, and that are properly subject to judicial correction under constitutional norms. But the appropriate method of reaching such instances is not to create a new quasi-suspect classification and subject all governmental action based on that classification to more searching evaluation. Rather, we should look to the likelihood that governmental action premised on a particular classification is valid as a general matter, not merely to the specifics of the case before us. Because mental retardation is a characteristic that the government may legitimately take into account in a wide range of decisions, and because both State and Federal Governments have recently committed themselves to assisting the retarded, we will not presume that

14

any given legislative action, even one that disadvantages retarded individuals, is rooted in considerations that the Constitution will not tolerate.

Our refusal to recognize the retarded as a quasi-suspect class does not leave them entirely unprotected from invidious discrimination. To withstand equal protection review, legislation that distinguishes between the mentally retarded and others must be rationally related to a legitimate governmental purpose. This standard, we believe, affords government the latitude necessary both to pursue policies designed to assist the retarded in realizing their full potential, and to freely and efficiently engage in activities that burden the retarded in what is essentially an incidental manner. The State may not rely on a classification whose relationship to an asserted goal is so attenuated as to render the distinction arbitrary or irrational. See *Zobel v. Williams*, 457 U.S. 55, 61-63 (1982); *United States Dept. of Agriculture v. Moreno*, 413 U.S. 528, 535 (1973). Furthermore, some objectives – such as "a bare ... desire to harm a politically unpopular group," id. at 534, 93 S.Ct. at 2826 – are not legitimate state interests. See also *Zobel, supra*, 457 U.S. at 63. Beyond that, the mentally retarded, like others, have and retain their substantive constitutional rights in addition to the right to be treated equally by the law.

IV

We turn to the issue of the validity of the zoning ordinance insofar as it requires a special use permit for homes for the mentally retarded. * * * We inquire first whether requiring a special use permit for the Featherston home in the circumstances here deprives respondents of the equal protection of the laws. If it does, there will be no occasion to decide whether the special use permit provision is facially invalid where the mentally retarded are involved, or to put it another way, whether the city may never insist on a special use permit for a home for the mentally retarded in an R-3 zone. This is the preferred course of adjudication since it enables courts to avoid making unnecessarily broad constitutional judgments. *Brockett v. Spokane Arcades, Inc.*, 472 U.S. 491, 501-502 (1985); *United States v. Grace*, 461 U.S. 171 (1983); *NAACP v. Button*, 371 U.S. 415 (1963).

The constitutional issue is clearly posed. The city does not require a special use permit in an R-3 zone for apartment houses, multiple dwellings, boarding and lodging houses, fraternity or sorority houses, dormitories, apartment hotels, hospitals, sanitariums, nursing homes for convalescents or the aged (other than for the insane or feebleminded or alcoholics or drug addicts), private clubs or fraternal orders, and other specified uses. It does, however, insist on a special permit for the Featherston home, and it does so, as the District Court found, because it would be a facility for the mentally retarded. May the city require the

15

permit for this facility when other care and multiple-dwelling facilities are freely permitted?

It is true, as already pointed out, that the mentally retarded as a group are indeed different from others not sharing their misfortune, and in this respect they may be different from those who would occupy other facilities that would be permitted in an R-3 zone without a special permit. But this difference is largely irrelevant unless the Featherston home and those who would occupy it would threaten legitimate interests of the city in a way that other permitted uses such as boarding houses and hospitals would not. Because in our view the record does not reveal any rational basis for believing that the Featherston home would pose any special threat to the city's legitimate interests, we affirm the judgment below insofar as it holds the ordinance invalid as applied in this case.

* * *

[The city advanced four justifications for the denial: (1) "The negative attitude of the majority of property owners located within 200 feet of the Featherston facility"; two locational objections — (2) proximity to a high school and (3) being in a flood plain; and (4) "the size of the home and the number of people that would occupy it." The Court found that none of these was rational. Negative attitudes were not a proper basis. Thirty people who would reside in the facility attended the high school. And other buildings with similar characteristics were located in the same area; the only difference was that their occupants were not challenged.]

The short of it is that requiring the permit in this case appears to us to rest on an irrational prejudice against the mentally retarded, including those who would occupy the Featherston facility and who would live under the closely supervised and highly regulated conditions expressly provided for by state and federal law.

The judgment of the Court of Appeals is affirmed insofar as it invalidates the zoning ordinance as applied to the Featherston home. The judgment is otherwise vacated, and the case is remanded.

It is so ordered.

Justice STEVENS, with whom THE CHIEF JUSTICE joins, concurring.

* * *

[Justice STEVENS disagreed that the three tiered standard for equal protection analysis described by Justice WHITE properly described the Court's equal protection jurisprudence, but believed that the Cleburne ordinance failed the test as he understood it.]

Justice MARSHALL, with whom Justice BRENNAN and Justice BLACKMUN join, concurring in the judgment in part and dissenting in part.

The Court holds that all retarded individuals cannot be grouped together as the "feebleminded" and deemed presumptively unfit to live in a community. Underlying this holding is the principle that mental retardation per se cannot be a proxy for depriving retarded people of their rights and interests without regard to variations in individual ability. With this holding and principle I agree. The Equal Protection Clause requires attention to the capacities and needs of retarded people as individuals.

I cannot agree, however, with the way in which the Court reaches its result or with the narrow, as-applied remedy it provides for the city of Cleburne's equal protection violation. The Court holds the ordinance invalid on rational-basis grounds and disclaims that anything special, in the form of heightened scrutiny, is taking place. Yet Cleburne's ordinance surely would be valid under the traditional rational-basis test applicable to economic and commercial regulation. In my view, it is important to articulate, as the Court does not, the facts and principles that justify subjecting this zoning ordinance to the searching review – the heightened scrutiny – that actually leads to its invalidation. Moreover, in invalidating Cleburne's exclusion of the "feebleminded" only as applied to respondents, rather than on its face, the Court radically departs from our equal protection precedents. Because I dissent from this novel and truncated remedy, and because I cannot accept the Court's disclaimer that no "more exacting standard" than ordinary rational-basis review is being applied, ante, at 3256, I write separately.

I

. * * *

[Justice MARSHALL first points out that the ordinance would likely survive if the Court were in fact using a rational-basis test.]

II

I have long believed the level of scrutiny employed in an equal protection case should vary with "the constitutional and societal importance of the interest adversely affected and the recognized invidiousness of the basis upon which the particular classification is drawn." * * * When a zoning ordinance works to exclude the retarded from all residential districts in a community, these two considerations require that the ordinance be convincingly justified as substantially furthering legitimate and important purposes. *Plyler v. Doe*, 457 U.S. 202, 230-231 (1982); * * *.

First, the interest of the retarded in establishing group homes is substantial. The right to "establish a home" has long been cherished as one of the fundamental liberties embraced by the Due Process Clause. See *Meyer v. Nebraska*, 262 U.S. 390, 399 (1923). For retarded adults, this right means living together in group homes, for as deinstitutionalization has progressed, group homes have become the primary means by which retarded adults can enter life in the community. The District Court found as a matter of fact that "[t]he availability of such a home in communities

17

is an essential ingredient of normal living patterns for persons who are mentally retarded, and each factor that makes such group homes harder to establish operates to exclude persons who are mentally retarded from the community." App. to Pet. for Cert. A-8. Excluding group homes deprives the retarded of much of what makes for human freedom and fulfillment – the ability to form bonds and take part in the life of a community.

Second, the mentally retarded have been subject to a "lengthy and tragic history," * * * [Justice MARSHALL reviews the history of discrimination against people with mental retardation.]

In light of the importance of the interest at stake and the history of discrimination the retarded have suffered, the Equal Protection Clause requires us to do more than review the distinctions drawn by Cleburne's zoning ordinance as if they appeared in a taxing statute or in economic or commercial legislation. * * * The searching scrutiny I would give to restrictions on the ability of the retarded to establish community group homes leads me to conclude that Cleburne's vague generalizations for classifying the "feeble-minded" with drug addicts, alcoholics, and the insane, and excluding them where the elderly, the ill, the boarder, and the transient are allowed, are not substantial or important enough to overcome the suspicion that the ordinance rests on impermissible assumptions or outmoded and perhaps invidious stereotypes. See *Plyler v. Doe*, 457 U.S. 202 (1982); *Roberts v. United States Jaycees*, 468 U.S. 609 (1984); *Mississippi University for Women v. Hogan*, 458 U.S. 718 (1982); *Mills v. Habluetzel*, 456 U.S. 91 (1982).

* * *

III

In its effort to show that Cleburne's ordinance can be struck down under no "more exacting standard * * * than is normally accorded economic and social legislation," ante, at 3256, the Court offers several justifications as to why the retarded do not warrant heightened judicial solicitude. These justifications, however, find no support in our heightened-scrutiny precedents and cannot withstand logical analysis.

The Court downplays the lengthy "history of purposeful unequal treatment" of the retarded, see *San Antonio Independent School District v. Rodriguez*, 411 U.S. at 28, by pointing to recent legislative action that is said to "beli[e] a continuing antipathy or prejudice." Ante, at 3257. Building on this point, the Court similarly concludes that the retarded are not "politically powerless" and deserve no greater judicial protection than "[a]ny minority" that wins some political battles and loses others. Ante, at 3257. The import of these conclusions, it seems, is that the only discrimination courts may remedy is the discrimination they alone are perspicacious enough to see. Once society begins to recognize certain practices as discriminatory, in part because previously stigmatized groups

18

have mobilized politically to lift this stigma, the Court would refrain from approaching such practices with the added skepticism of heightened scrutiny.

Courts, however, do not sit or act in a social vacuum. Moral philosophers may debate whether certain inequalities are absolute wrongs, but history makes clear that constitutional principles of equality, like constitutional principles of liberty, property, and due process, evolve over time; what once was a "natural" and "self-evident" ordering later comes to be seen as an artificial and invidious constraint on human potential and freedom. Compare *Plessy v. Ferguson*, 163 U.S. 537 (1896), and *Bradwell v. Illinois*, 16 Wall. 130, 141 (1873) (Bradley, J., concurring in judgment), with *Brown v. Board of Education*, 347 U.S. 483 (1954), and *Reed v. Reed*, 404 U.S. 71 (1971). Shifting cultural, political, and social patterns at times come to make past practices appear inconsistent with fundamental principles upon which American society rests, an inconsistency legally cognizable under the Equal Protection Clause. It is natural that evolving standards of equality come to be embodied in legislation. When that occurs, courts should look to the fact of such change as a source of guidance on evolving principles of equality. In an analysis the Court today ignores, the Court reached this very conclusion when it extended heightened scrutiny to gender classifications and drew on parallel legislative developments to support that extension * * *.

* * *

For the retarded, just as for Negroes and women, much has changed in recent years, but much remains the same; out-dated statutes are still on the books, and irrational fears or ignorance, traceable to the prolonged social and cultural isolation of the retarded, continue to stymie recognition of the dignity and individuality of retarded people. Heightened judicial scrutiny of action appearing to impose unnecessary barriers to the retarded is required in light of increasing recognition that such barriers are inconsistent with evolving principles of equality embedded in the Fourteenth Amendment.

The Court also offers a more general view of heightened scrutiny, a view focused primarily on when heightened scrutiny does not apply as opposed to when it does apply. * * * Two principles appear central to the Court's theory. First, heightened scrutiny is said to be inapplicable where *individuals* in a group have distinguishing characteristics that legislatures properly may take into account in some circumstances. Ante, at 3255, 3258. Heightened scrutiny is also purportedly inappropriate when many legislative classifications affecting the group are likely to be valid. We must, so the Court says, "look to the likelihood that governmental action premised on a particular classification is valid as a general matter, not merely to the specifics of the case before us," in deciding whether to apply heightened scrutiny. Ante, at 3258.

If the Court's first principle were sound, heightened scrutiny would have to await a day when people could be cut from a cookie mold. Women are hardly alike in all their characteristics, but heightened scrutiny applies to them because legislatures can rarely use gender itself as a proxy for these other characteristics. Permissible distinctions between persons must bear a reasonable relationship to their *relevant* characteristics, * * * and gender *per se* is almost never relevant. Similarly, that some retarded people have reduced capacities in some areas does not justify using retardation as a proxy for reduced capacity in areas where relevant individual variations in capacity do exist.

The Court's second assertion – that the standard of review must be fixed with reference to the number of classifications to which a characteristic would validly be relevant – is similarly flawed. Certainly the assertion is not a logical one; that a characteristic may be relevant under some or even many circumstances does not suggest any reason to presume it relevant under other circumstances where there is reason to suspect it is not. A sign that says "men only" looks very different on a bathroom door than a courthouse door. * * *

Our heightened-scrutiny precedents belie the claim that a characteristic must virtually always be irrelevant to warrant heightened scrutiny. *Plyler*, for example, held that the status of being an undocumented alien is not a "constitutional irrelevancy," and therefore declined to review with strict scrutiny classifications affecting undocumented aliens. 457 U.S. at 219, n.19. While *Frontiero* stated that gender "frequently" and "often" bears no relation to legitimate legislative aims, it did not deem gender an impermissible basis of state action in all circumstances. 411 U.S. at 686-687. Indeed, the Court has upheld some gender-based classifications. * * * Heightened but not strict scrutiny is considered appropriate in areas such as gender, illegitimacy, or alienage * * * because the Court views the trait as relevant under some circumstances but not others. * * * That view – indeed the very concept of heightened, as opposed to strict, scrutiny – is flatly inconsistent with the notion that heightened scrutiny should not apply to the retarded because "mental retardation is a characteristic that the government may legitimately take into account in a wide range of decisions." Ante, at 3258. Because the government also may not take this characteristic into account in many circumstances, such as those presented here, careful review is required to separate the permissible from the invalid in classifications relying on retardation.

The fact that retardation may be deemed a constitutional irrelevancy in *some* circumstances is enough, given the history of discrimination the retarded have suffered, to require careful judicial review of classifications singling out the retarded for special burdens. Although the Court acknowledges that many instances of invidious discrimination against the retarded still exist, the Court boldly asserts that "in the vast majority of situations" special treatment of the retarded is "not only legitimate but also desirable." Ante, at 3257. That assertion suggests the Court would somehow have us calculate the percentage of "situations" in which a characteristic is validly and invalidly invoked before determining whether heightened scrutiny is appropriate. But heightened scrutiny has not been "triggered" in our past cases only after some undefined numerical threshold of invalid "situations" has been crossed. An inquiry into constitutional principle, not mathematics, determines whether heightened scrutiny is appropriate. Whenever evolving principles of equality, rooted in the Equal Protection Clause, require that certain classifications be viewed as *potentially* discriminatory, and when history reveals systemic unequal treatment, more searching judicial inquiry than minimum rationality becomes relevant.

Potentially discriminatory classifications exist only where some constitutional basis can be found for presuming that equal rights are required. Discrimination, in the Fourteenth Amendment sense, connotes a substantive constitutional judgment that two individuals or groups are entitled to be treated equally with respect to something. With regard to economic and commercial matters, no basis for such a conclusion exists, for as Justice HOLMES urged the *Lochner* Court, the Fourteenth Amendment was not "intended to embody a particular economic theory. . . ." *Lochner v. New York*, 198 U.S. 45, 75 (1905) (dissenting). As a matter of substantive policy, therefore, government is free to move in any direction, or to change directions, * * * in the economic and commercial sphere. * * * The structure of economic and commercial life is a matter of political compromise, not constitutional principle, and no norm of equality requires that there be as many opticians as optometrists * * *.

But the Fourteenth Amendment does prohibit other results under virtually all circumstances, such as castes created by law along racial or ethnic lines, * * * and significantly constrains the range of permissible government choices where gender or illegitimacy, for example, are concerned. Where such constraints, derived from the Fourteenth Amendment, are present, and where history teaches that they have systemically been ignored, a "more searching judicial inquiry" is required. *United States v. Carolene Products Co.*, 304 U.S. 144, 153, n.4 (1938).

That more searching inquiry, be it called heightened scrutiny or "second order" rational-basis review, is a method of approaching certain classifications skeptically, with judgment suspended until the facts are in and the evidence considered. The government must establish that the classification is substantially related to important and legitimate objectives, see, e.g., *Craig v. Boren*, 429 U.S. 190, 97 S.Ct. 451, 50 L.Ed.2d 397 (1976), so that valid and sufficiently weighty policies actually justify the departure from equality. Heightened scrutiny does not allow courts to second-guess reasoned legislative or professional judgments tailored to the unique needs of a group like the retarded, but it does seek to assure that the hostility or thoughtlessness with which there is reason to be concerned has not carried the day. By invoking heightened scrutiny, the Court recognizes, and compels lower courts to recognize, that a group may well be the target of the sort of prejudiced, thoughtless, or stereotyped action that offends principles of equality found in the Fourteenth Amendment. Where classifications based on a particular characteristic have done so in the past, and the threat that they may do so remains, heightened scrutiny is appropriate.[24]

---

[24]   No single talisman can define those groups likely to be the target of classifications offensive to the Fourteenth Amendment and therefore warranting heightened or strict scrutiny; experience, not abstract logic, must be the primary guide. The "political powerlessness" of a group may be relevant, San Antonio Independent School District v. Rodriguez, 411 U.S. 1, 28 (1973), but that factor is neither necessary, as the gender cases demonstrate, nor sufficient, as the example of minors illustrates. Minors cannot vote and thus might be considered politically powerless to an extreme degree. Nonetheless, we see few statutes reflecting prejudice or indifference to minors, and I am not aware of any suggestion that legislation affecting them be viewed with the suspicion of heightened scrutiny. Similarly, immutability of the trait at issue may be relevant, but many immutable characteristics, such as height or blindness, are valid bases of governmental action and classifications under a variety of circumstances. See ante, at 3256, n.10.

The political powerlessness of a group and the immutability of its defining trait are relevant insofar as they point to a social and cultural isolation that gives the majority little reason to respect or be concerned with that group's interests and needs. Statutes discriminating against the young have not been common nor need be feared because those who do vote and legislate were once themselves young, typically have children of their own, and certainly interact regularly with minors. Their social integration means that minors, unlike discrete and insular minorities, tend to be treated in legislative arenas with full concern and respect, despite their formal and complete exclusion from the electoral process.

The discreteness and insularity warranting a "more searching judicial inquiry," United States v. Carolene Products Co., 304 U.S. 144, 153, n.4 (1938), must therefore be viewed from a social and cultural perspective as well as a political one. To this task judges are well suited, for the lessons of history and experience are surely the best guide as to when, and with respect to what interests, society is likely to stigmatize individuals as members of an inferior caste or view them as not belonging to the community. Because prejudice spawns prejudice, and stereotypes produce limitations that confirm the stereotype on which they are based, a history of unequal treatment requires sensitivity to the prospect that its vestiges endure. In separating those groups that are discrete and insular from those that are not, as in many important legal distinctions, "a page of history is worth a volume of logic." New York Trust Co. v. Eisner, 256 U.S. 345, 349 (1921) (Holmes, J.).

As the history of discrimination against the retarded and its continuing legacy amply attest, the mentally retarded have been, and in some areas may still be, the targets of action the Equal Protection Clause condemns. With respect to a liberty so valued as the right to establish a home in the community, and so likely to be denied on the basis of irrational fears and outright hostility, heightened scrutiny is surely appropriate.

IV

In light of the scrutiny that should be applied here, Cleburne's ordinance sweeps too broadly to dispel the suspicion that it rests on a bare desire to treat the retarded as outsiders, pariahs who do not belong in the community. The Court, while disclaiming that special scrutiny is necessary or warranted, reaches the same conclusion. Rather than striking the ordinance down, however, the Court invalidates it merely as applied to respondents. I must dissent from the novel proposition that "the preferred course of adjudication" is to leave standing a legislative Act resting on "irrational prejudice" ante, at 3260, thereby forcing individuals in the group discriminated against to continue to run the Act's gauntlet.

* * *

[Justice MARSHALL argues that the ordinance is facially invalid.]

V

The Court's opinion approaches the task of principled equal protection adjudication in what I view as precisely the wrong way. The formal label under which an equal protection claim is reviewed is less important than careful identification of the interest at stake and the extent to which society recognizes the classification as an invidious one. Yet in focusing obsessively on the appropriate label to give its standard of review, the Court fails to identify the interests at stake or to articulate the principle that classifications based on mental retardation must be carefully examined to assure they do not rest on impermissible assumptions or false stereotypes regarding individual ability and need. No guidance is thereby given as to when the Court's freewheeling, and potentially dangerous, "rational-basis standard" is to be employed, nor is attention directed to the invidiousness of grouping all retarded individuals together. Moreover, the Court's narrow, as-applied remedy fails to deal adequately with the overbroad presumption that lies at the heart of this case. Rather than leaving future retarded individuals to run the gauntlet of this overbroad presumption, I would affirm the judgment of the Court of Appeals in its entirety and would strike down on its face the provision at issue. I therefore concur in the judgment in part and dissent in part.

Notes & Questions

1. Do you agree with the majority's analysis? Should people with disabilities primarily look to local city councils for protection? On the other hand, are there distinctions to be made? Who should make them?

2. The Court considers this a "mental retardation" case. Would the majority analyze the issue differently it were a diabetes cases? A leg-amputee case? A hearing impairment case? Should there be a different analysis for each kind of disability? As a policy matter should all disabilities be under a common statute?

3. Should there be different levels of scrutiny? You will see in Part 9 that in other countries courts do not distinguish among different groups in the "level of scrutiny." Why do U.S. courts make this distinction? Is it a sensible way to evaluate discrimination cases?

4. What do you think of the Court's use of statutes designed to help people with mental disabilities to argue that there is no need to provide heightened scrutiny?

5. What is the practical difference between the majority's and Justice Marshall's approaches? What *is* "heightened" scrutiny?

6. Disability advocates relied on the dissent to argue that heightened scrutiny, or at least "rational basis with teeth," should apply to disability discrimination. Yeiter v. Sec'y of Health & Human Servs., 818 F.2d 8, 10 (6th Cir. 1987); *see* Heller v. Doe, 509 U.S. 312, 335-36 n.1 (1993) (Souter, J., dissenting); Stephen Mikochik, The Constitution and the Americans with Disabilities Act: Some First Impressions, 64 Temp. L. Rev. 619, 626-27 (1991). However, the application of the rational basis test to disability discrimination was confirmed by the Court in *Board of Trustees of the University of Alabama v. Garrett*, 531 U.S. 356 (2001), discussed *infra* in Parts 3 and 4. For an alternative approach, *see* Michael Waterstone, Disability Constitutional Law, __ Emory L.J. __ (forthcoming 2013).

§ 1.4 ADA Precursors

A. *Vocational Rehabilitation And Benefits*

The ADA was not drawn on a blank canvas. Federal laws addressing the rights of people with disabilities have been in existence since the first half of the twentieth century. In scope and purpose, however, these laws were narrower than the ADA. These early laws generally established vocational or benefits programs that were supervised by professional medical and vocational personnel. They were based on the medical model discussed earlier; that is, the idea that the presence of a disability separated an individual from the rest of society.

The early vocational laws were aimed principally at "rehabilitation." Their premise was that a person with a disability could achieve acceptance into the larger community by "overcoming" the disability and obtaining employment. In the aftermath of the First World War, in 1918, Congress enacted the Smith-Sears Act "[t]o provide for the vocational rehabilitation and return to civil employment of disabled persons discharged from the military or naval forces." Vocational Rehabilitation Acts of 1918, ch. 107, 40 Stat. 617, 617 (1918).

The National Vocational Rehabilitation Act of 1920, the Smith-Fess Act, extended these vocational rehabilitation principles to civilians. National Vocational Rehabilitation Act of 1920, ch. 219, Pub. L. No. 66-236, 41 Stat. 735 (1920) (codified as amended at 29 U.S.C. §§ 731-741 (repealed 1973, and reenacted in the Rehabilitation Act of 1973, Pub. L. No. 93-112, 87 Stat. 355 (codified at 29 U.S.C. §§ 701 et seq. (2006))).

The "voc rehab" law attempted to "provide for the promotion of vocational rehabilitation of persons disabled in industry or in any legitimate occupation and their return to civil employment . . ." and offered services to people "who, by reason of a physical defect or infirmity, whether congenital or acquired by accident, injury, or disease, [are], or may be expected to be, totally or partially incapacitated for remunerative occupation." *Id.* ch. 219, §§ 1-2. The Randolph-Sheppard Act of 1936 subsequently created a federal program to employ qualified blind people as vendors on federal property. Pub. L. No. 74-732, ch. 638, 49 Stat. 1559 (1936) (codified as amended at 20 U.S.C. § 107 (2006)).

A second type of law conferred monetary and other benefits on certain groups of persons with disabilities. The Social Security Act of 1935 established a federal and state system of health services for "crippled" children. Pub. L. No. 74-271, ch. 531, 49 Stat. 620 (codified at 42 U.S.C. §§ 1381-83 (2006)). In 1954, the Act was amended to provide monthly benefits for eligible workers who acquired disabilities. Social Security Amendments of 1954, Pub. L. No. 83-761, § 106, 68 Stat. 1052, 1080 (1954). In 1972, this Act again was amended to provide benefits to limited categories of poor persons with disabilities. Social Security Amendments of 1972, Pub. L. No. 92-603, 86 Stat. 1329-1465 (codified at 42 U.S.C. §§ 1381-83 (2006)).

B.   *Early Disability Civil Rights Statutes (1968-88)*

As part of the Civil Rights era of the 1960s, minority groups began to view equal access to society as a fundamental right. In disability rights, as well, access became central and disability rights statutes began to address the integration of people with disabilities into society as a remedy for discrimination. These statutes increasingly required that society, as opposed to the individual with a disability, make changes to ensure access and integration. This approach draws closer to the ADA model.

1.   Architectural Barriers Act of 1968

The Architectural Barriers Act, Pub. L. No. 90-480, 82 Stat. 718, passed in 1968, requires that new facilities built with federal funds be accessible to people with disabilities. 42 U.S.C. § 4151-4157 (2006). The Act charges the Administrator of General Services, the U.S. Postal Service, and the Secretaries of Housing and Urban Development and of Defense, in consultation with the Secretary of Health and Human Services, with developing accessibility standards for the design, construction, and alteration of their buildings and facilities.

2.   Rehabilitation Act of 1973

The most important ADA precursor was the Rehabilitation Act of 1973. As originally passed, the primary focus of the Rehabilitation Act was vocational training and rehabilitation. Pub. L. No. 93-112; 87 Stat. 355 (1973). The stated purpose of the Act was to "provide a statutory basis for the Rehabilitation Services Administration," an agency charged with carrying out the provisions of the Act, and to authorize various rehabilitation programs. *Id.* § 2. We will return to the Rehabilitation Act in the next subsection.

3.   Individuals With Disabilities Education Act (Education For All Handicapped Children Act of 1975)

In 1975, Congress passed the Education For All Handicapped Children Act. Pub. L. No. 94-142, 89 Stat. 773 (1975). This Act recognized the number and needs of children with disabilities in the public schools. Specifically, Congress found that "there are more than eight million handicapped children in the United States today," the educational needs of which were not being met. *Id.* § 3(b)(1)-(2).

The Act's purpose was to assure that children with disabilities have available to them a "free appropriate" public education which emphasizes special education and related services devoted to meet their unique needs. *Id.* § 3(c). The enforcement provisions and firm commitment to federal spending established in this Act are more aggressive and explicit than some of the later post-Rehabilitation Act statutes.

This Act eventually was amended to become the present-day Individuals with Disabilities Education Act (IDEA). 20 U.S.C. §§ 1400 et seq. (2006). To a greater extent than its predecessor, the IDEA reflects a modern approach to educational opportunities for students with disabilities. This includes a commitment to higher expectations, mainstreaming students where possible, and an increased federal role in ensuring equal educational opportunity for all students. *See* 20 U.S.C. § 1400-(c)(5)(A), (c)(5)(D), (c)(7)(A).

IDEA requires public schools to make available to eligible children with disabilities a free public education in the least restrictive environment appropriate to their individual needs. The law requires public schools to develop appropriate Individualized Education Programs (IEPs) for each child, and ensures certain procedures be followed in developing and implementing these IEPs. Each student's IEP must be developed by a team of knowledgeable persons and reviewed annually. This team includes the child's teacher, parents, and if appropriate the child, and an agency representative who is qualified to provide or supervise the provision of special education. If the parents disagree with the proposed IEP, they can request a due process hearing and a review from the State educational agency, and, subsequently, can appeal this decision to state or federal court. *See id.* §§ 1414-1415. We will return to the IDEA in Part 6, *infra*.

4. Voting Accessibility For The Elderly And Handicapped Act of 1984

In 1984, Congress passed the Voting Accessibility for the Elderly and Handicapped Act ("Voting Accessibility Act"). 42 U.S.C. §§ 1973ee et seq. (2006). With this Act, Congress sought to "promote the fundamental right to vote by improving access for handicapped and elderly individuals to registration facilities and polling places for Federal elections." *Id.* § 1973ee. The Voting Accessibility Act provided that the political subdivisions of the state that are responsible for conducting elections must ensure that polling places for federal elections are accessible to voters with disabilities. *Id.* § 1973ee-1(a).

There are exceptions. This section does not apply if the chief election officer of a State (1) determines there is an emergency; (2) determines that all polling places have been surveyed and no such accessible place is available; or (3) assures that any handicapped or elderly voter assigned to an inaccessible polling place upon request will be assigned to an alternative polling place, or provided with an alternative means for casting a ballot. *Id.* § 1973ee-1(b). The Attorney General, or any person aggrieved by noncompliance with this Act, may bring a civil action to enforce its provisions. *Id.* § 1973ee-4.

The Voting Accessibility Act demonstrates that during this time period, as Congress passed legislation on broad social issues, it was willing to consider and take action to protect the civil rights of people with disabilities. This Act has been criticized as weak, however, for providing no definition of "accessibility," and for leaving the means of compliance entirely to the states. *See* Michael E. Waterstone, Constitutional and Statutory Voting Rights for People with Disabilities, 14 Stan. L. & Pol'y Rev. 353, 358 (2003).

These weaknesses have generated momentum for additional federal legislation on this topic. In October of 2002, with broad bi-partisan support, President Bush signed into law the Help America Vote

Act, 42 U.S.C. § 15301 et seq. (2006). Among other things, this Act provides for accessible voting machines and a secret and independent ballot for voters with disabilities.

5. Air Carrier Access Act of 1986

Congress's next attempt to address the rights of people with disabilities was the Air Carrier Access Act of 1986. Pub. L. No. 99-435, 100 Stat. 1080 (1986). Like the Voting Accessibility Act, this Act focused on a single issue area – airline travel. The Act amended the Federal Aviation Act of 1958 to provide that prohibitions of discrimination by airline carriers applied to individuals with disabilities.

The Air Carrier Access Act's antidiscrimination provision paralleled Section 504 of the Rehabilitation Act, discussed *infra*. As originally passed, the Act provided that "[n]o air carrier may discriminate against any otherwise qualified handicapped individual, by reason of such handicap, in the provision of air transportation." *Id.* § 2(c)(1). The language of the statute was later amended, without any substantive change to its meaning except to include foreign carriers. *See* 49 U.S.C. § 41705(a) (2006) ("In providing air transportation, an air carrier, including any foreign air carrier, may not discriminate against an otherwise qualified individual"). The Act also used the Rehabilitation Act's definition of "handicapped individual." *See* Pub. L. No. 99-435, 100 Stat. 1080 (1986) ("For the purposes of paragraph (1) of this subsection, the term 'handicapped individual' means any individual who has a physical or mental impairment that substantially limits one or more major life activities, has a record of such an impairment, or is regarded as having such an impairment."). As amended, the definition is the same. *See* 49 U.S.C. § 41705.

6. Fair Housing Amendments Act of 1988

In 1988, Congress introduced a series of amendments to the Civil Rights Act of 1968, including a prohibition on housing discrimination against people with disabilities. *See* Pub. L. No. 100-430, 102 Stat. 1619 (1988). These amendments are known as the "Fair Housing Amendments Act of 1988." Like the Voting Accessibility Act and the Air Carrier Access Act, the Fair Housing Amendments Act draws heavily on the approach and language of the Rehabilitation Act. *See* 42 U.S.C. § 3601 et seq. (2006).

The Fair Housing Amendments Act makes it unlawful to discriminate in the sale or rental of housing, and the terms and conditions of such a sale or rental, on the basis of disability. *Id.* § 3604(f). The Act has a broad scope. It protects not only a buyer or renter with a disability, but also a person with a disability who lives with the buyer or renter, or any other person associated with the buyer or renter. *Id.*

The concept of reasonable accommodation is integral to the Fair Housing Act's definition of discrimination. Discrimination includes:

(1) a refusal to permit an occupant with disability, at her own expense, from making "reasonable modifications" of the existing premises;

(2) a refusal to make reasonable accommodations in rules, policies, practices, or services; and

(3) a failure to construct multifamily dwellings, which contain four or more units, 30 months after September 13, 1988 so that specified portions of these facilities are accessible to individuals with disabilities.

Id.

The Department of Housing and Urban Development (HUD), responsible for promulgating regulations pursuant to the new amendments, was cognizant of the difficulties in drawing lines as to what separates a "reasonable" accommodation or modification from one that is unreasonable. HUD offered its own interpretation that major costs or administrative burdens should not be imposed on landlords or sellers.

The Department wishes to stress that a housing provider is not required to provide supportive services, e.g., counseling, medical, or social services that fall outside the scope of the services that the housing provider offers to residents. A housing provider is required to make modifications in order to enable a qualified applicant with handicaps to live in the housing, but is not required to offer housing of a fundamentally different nature. The test is whether, with appropriate modifications, the applicant can live in the housing that the housing provider offers; not whether the applicant could benefit from some other type of housing that the housing provider does not offer.

See Implementation of Fair Housing Amendments of 1988, 54 Fed. Reg. 3231, 3249 (Jan. 23, 1989).

This Act, like the Air Carrier Access Act, began to extend disability discrimination law beyond federal or federally funded entities. The Civil Rights Act of 1968 applied to housing that received federal financial assistance, state and local government housing, *and* private housing. 42 U.S.C. § 3603 (2006). The Fair Housing Amendments Act did not change this. Movement into the private sphere was a significant step that was taken further with the eventual passage of the ADA.

There are statutory exceptions. The "single-family homeowner" exemption applies to any single-family house sold or rented by an owner provided that the owner does not own more than three such houses at any one time, does not try to claim the exemption more than once every twenty-four months, does not own any interest in more than three single-family houses, and does not use a real estate agent in the transaction. *Id.*

§ 3603(b)(1). There is also a "four or less family residence" exception, which applies to rooms or units in dwellings containing living quarters occupied by no more than four families living independently of each other if the owner lives in one of the quarters. *Id.* § 3603(b)(2). We return to the Fair Housing Amendments Act in Part 7, *infra*.

C. *Interpretation Of The Rehabilitation Act*

The Rehabilitation Act set the stage for the ADA in its language and its implementing regulations. The first four Titles of the 1973 Act and the bulk of the Act's text establish incentive programs for states to receive federal grants. These funds are to meet the "current and future needs of handicapped individuals," authorize federal assistance on research relating to rehabilitation of individuals with disabilities, and provide evaluation mechanisms for these various programs. *See* Title I, §§ 100-130 ("Vocational and Rehabilitation Services"); Title II, §§ 200-204 ("Research and Training"); Title III, §§ 300-306 ("Special Federal Responsibilities"); Title IV, §§ 400-407 ("Administration and Program and Project Evaluation").

The final part of the original 1973 Act – Title V ("Miscellaneous") – contains the portions of the Rehabilitation Act that over time have had the greatest impact. Section 501, 29 U.S.C. § 791(b) (2006), requires affirmative action and nondiscrimination in employment by federal agencies of the executive branch. Every department, agency, and instrumentality of the executive branch is required to:

> submit to the [EEOC] and the [Interagency Committee on Employees who are Individuals with Disabilities] an affirmative action program plan for the hiring, placement, and advancement of individuals with disabilities . . . . Such plan shall include a description of the extent to which and methods whereby the special needs of employees who are individuals with disabilities are being met.

Id.

Section 502, 29 U.S.C. § 792, established the Architectural and Transportation Barriers Compliance Board ("Access Board"), which is charged with ensuring compliance with the Architectural Barriers Act. Section 503, 29 U.S.C. § 793, requires that to receive certain government contracts, entities must demonstrate that they are taking affirmative steps to employ people with disabilities. New rules adopted by the Department of Labor include "a hiring goal for federal contractors and subcontractors that 7 percent of each job group in their workforce be qualified individuals with disabilities." Dep't of Labor, Press Release, US Labor Department Announces Final Rules to Improve Employment of Veterans, People with Disabilities (Aug. 27, 2013), http://www.dol.gov/opa/media/press/ofccp/OFCCP20131578.htm. The goal, which is not a quota, will take effect in 2014, 180 days after the rules are published in the Federal Register.

The enduring hallmark of the Rehabilitation Act, however, is Section 504, 29 U.S.C. § 794. This Section provides:

> No otherwise qualified individual with a disability in the United States, as defined in Section 705(20), shall, solely by reason of her or his disability, be excluded from the participation in, be denied the benefits of, or be subjected to discrimination under any program or activity receiving Federal financial assistance.

This sweeping language was the first explicit Congressional statement recognizing "discrimination" against people with disabilities. The scheme of the original statute suggests that Congress may not have expected Section 504 to have a major impact. The conference and committee reports on the Rehabilitation Act paid virtually no attention to this provision. *See* Joseph P. Shapiro, No Pity: People with Disabilities Forging a New Civil Rights Movement 65 (1993) (discussing work of sociologist Richard Scotch, who concluded that Congressional aides could not remember who had suggested adding this civil rights protection).

The statutory definition of disability referenced in Section 504 was taken almost without change from the Vocational Rehabilitation Act of 1920. The original definition in the Rehabilitation Act of 1973 is as follows:

> The term "handicapped individual" means any individual who (A) has a physical or mental disability which for such individual constitutes or result in a substantial hardship to employment and (B) can reasonably be expected to benefit in terms of employability from vocational rehabilitation services provided pursuant to titles I and III of this Act.

§ 7(6), Pub. L. No. 93-112, 87 Stat. 355 (codified as amended 29 U.S.C. § 705(20) (2006)). It is tailored to employment situations, and therefore is ill-suited to support a larger anti-discrimination framework.

This background provided the impetus for two important modifications to Section 504 of the Rehabilitation Act of 1973. The first was a revised definition of "handicapped individual." In the Rehabilitation Act Amendments of 1974, Congress defined a "handicapped" individual as one "who (A) has a physical or mental impairment which substantially limits one or more of such person's major life activities; (B) has a record of such an impairment, or (C) is regarded as having such an impairment." *See* Rehabilitation Act Amendments of 1974, § 111(a), Pub. L. No. 93-651, 89 Stat. 2 (1974) (codified at 29 U.S.C. § 705(20)(B)(i)-(iii)). This phrasing broke free of the earlier vocational and rehabilitation-based roots of the original definition. The definition places less emphasis on an ability to cure or fix a disability, and instead, recognizes that perception of disability is important. *See* Jonathan C. Drimmer, Cripples, Overcomers, and Civil Rights: Tracing the Evolution of Federal Legislation and Social Policy for People with Disabilities, 40 UCLA L. Rev. 1341, 1386 (1993). This is the definition the ADA eventually would use. *See* 42 U.S.C. § 12102(2) (2006).

The second area of development for the Rehabilitation Act was the interpreting regulations. The Department of Health, Education, and Welfare was charged with developing regulations for Section 504. The Section 504 regulations introduced the concept of reasonable accommodation, which is the idea that some affirmative step, as opposed to strictly equal treatment, may be necessary to ensure equal access for people with disabilities to jobs, facilities, and programs. *See infra* ch. 8. For example, the "Employment" section of the Section 504 regulations states:

> A recipient [of federal funds] shall make reasonable accommodation to the known physical or mental limitations of an otherwise qualified handicapped applicant or employee unless the recipient can demonstrate that the accommodation would impose an undue hardship on the operation of its program or activity.

34 C.F.R. § 104.12(a) (2008). "Qualified handicapped person" is elsewhere defined in the regulations with respect to employment as "a handicapped person who, with reasonable accommodation, can perform the essential functions of the job in question." *Id.* § 104.3(l)(1).

The Section 504 regulations provide examples of reasonable accommodations, including altering facilities and modifying work schedules. *Id.* § 104.12(b). The Section 504 regulations provide that "[n]o qualified handicapped person shall, because a recipient's facilities are inaccessible to or unusable by handicapped persons, be denied the benefits of, be excluded from participation in, or otherwise be subjected to discrimination under any program or activity . . . ." *Id.* § 104.21. This is commonly known as the "program access" requirement.

A recipient of federal funds does not have to make its facilities accessible; rather, accessibility is achieved when each program or activity within the facilities, viewed as a whole, is accessible. *Id.* § 104.22. Examples of steps to ensure program accessibility include redesigning equipment, reassigning classes to accessible buildings, and home visits.

Another issue covered by the Section 504 regulations is education. The regulations provide that recipients of federal funds that operate public or secondary schools *shall* provide a free appropriate public education to each qualified handicapped person, regardless of the nature or severity of the individual's handicap. *Id.* § 104.33.

Similarly, the regulations provide that qualified persons with disabilities may not be denied admission or be subjected to discrimination by postsecondary schools on the basis of disability. *Id.* § 104.42. The regulations contain similar language as to "treatment of students":

> No qualified handicapped student shall, on the basis of handicap, be excluded from participation in, be denied the benefits of, or otherwise be subjected to discrimination under any academic, research, occupational training, housing, health insurance, counseling, financial aid, physical education, athletics, recreation, transportation, other extracurricular, or other postsecondary education aid, benefits, or services . . . .

Id. § 104.43(a). A "qualified handicapped person" for the purposes of postsecondary and vocational education services is defined as "a handicapped person who meets the academic and technical standards requisite to admission or participation in the recipient's education program or activity." 34 C.F.R. § 104.3(l)(3).

Many of the terms in the ADA are derived directly from the Rehabilitation Act and its accompanying regulations. The ADA is explicit that Rehabilitation Act regulations and case law are instructive to interpreting the ADA. 42 U.S.C. § 12201(a) (2006). Therefore, much of the dispute about the meaning of the ADA arises out of courts' efforts to interpret the words Congress used in the Rehabilitation Act – did Congress intend those words to reach as broadly as they might?

The Rehabilitation Act and its regulations frame the issues of employment, facility, and educational access for persons with a disability as a balancing test. Accommodation is desirable, so long as the methods of ensuring accessibility are reasonable. Although "reasonable" is not defined, a guiding principle is that a reasonable accommodation or modification does not require a change to the fundamental nature of the job, program, or facility. The early Rehabilitation Act cases reflected that tension.

Southeastern Community College v. Davis was the Supreme Court's first foray into defining the reach of the Rehabilitation Act. When reading this and subsequent cases, observe the tools courts use to divine congressional intent. How clear are the tools? How much play do they give the lower courts? How does a court accurately determine legislative intent?

SOUTHEASTERN COMMUNITY COLLEGE v. DAVIS

Supreme Court of the United States, 1979
442 U.S. 397

Mr. Justice POWELL delivered the opinion of the Court.

This case presents a matter of first impression for this Court: Whether § 504 of the Rehabilitation Act of 1973, which prohibits discrimination against an "otherwise qualified handicapped individual" in federally funded programs "solely by reason of his handicap," forbids professional schools from imposing physical qualifications for admission to their clinical training programs.

I

Respondent, [Davis] who suffers from a serious hearing disability, seeks to be trained as a registered nurse. During the 1973-1974 academic year she was enrolled in the College Parallel program of Southeastern Community College, a state institution that receives federal funds. * * * In the course of her application to the nursing program, she was interviewed by a member of the nursing faculty * * * [and] was advised to consult an audiologist.

* * * [Following a] change in her hearing aid * * * it was expected that she would be able to detect sounds "almost as well as a person would who has normal hearing." [App.] 127a-128a. But this improvement would not mean that she could discriminate among sounds sufficiently to understand normal spoken speech. Her lipreading skills would remain necessary for effective communication: "While wearing the hearing aid, she is well aware of gross sounds occurring in the listening environment. However, she can only be responsible for speech spoken to her, when the talker gets her attention and allows her to look directly at the talker." Id. at 128a.

Southeastern next consulted Mary McRee, Executive Director of the North Carolina Board of Nursing. On the basis of the audiologist's report, McRee recommended that respondent not be admitted to the nursing program. In McRee's view, respondent's hearing disability made it unsafe for her to practice as a nurse. * * * In addition, it would be impossible for respondent to participate safely in the normal clinical training program, and those modifications that would be necessary to enable safe participation would prevent her from realizing the benefits of the program: "To adjust patient learning experiences in keeping with [respondent's] hearing limitations could, in fact, be the same as denying her full learning to meet the objectives of your nursing programs." Id. at 132a-133a. [The College's nursing faculty thereafter denied her admission.]

* * *

[Davis] then filed suit in the United States District Court for the Eastern District of North Carolina, alleging both a violation of § 504 of the Rehabilitation Act of 1973, 87 Stat. 394, as amended, 29 U.S.C. § 794 (1976 ed., Supp. II), * * * and a denial of equal protection and due process. After a bench trial, the District Court entered judgment in favor of Southeastern. 424 F.Supp. 1341 (1976). It confirmed the findings of the audiologist that even with a hearing aid respondent cannot understand speech directed to her except through lipreading, and further found:

> "[I]n many situations such as an operation room intensive care unit, or post-natal care unit, all doctors and nurses wear surgical masks which would make lip reading impossible. Additionally, in many situations a Registered Nurse would be required to instantly follow the physician's instructions concerning procurement of various types of instruments and drugs where the physician would be unable to get the nurse's attention by other than vocal means." Id. at 1343.

Accordingly, the court concluded:

> "[Respondent's] handicap actually prevents her from safely performing in both her training program and her proposed profession. The trial testimony indicated numerous situations where [respondent's] particular disability would render her unable to function properly. Of particular concern to the court in this case is the potential of danger to future patients in such situations." Id. at 1345.

Based on these findings, the District Court concluded that respondent was not an "otherwise qualified handicapped individual" protected against discrimination by § 504. In its view, "[o]therwise qualified, can only be read to mean otherwise able to function sufficiently in the position sought in spite of the handicap, if proper training and facilities are suitable and available." 424 F.Supp. at 1345. Because respondent's disability would prevent her from functioning "sufficiently" in Southeastern's nursing program, the court held that the decision to exclude her was not discriminatory within the meaning of § 504. * * *

On appeal, the Court of Appeals for the Fourth Circuit reversed. 574 F.2d 1158 (1978). It did not dispute the District Court's findings of fact, but held that the court had misconstrued § 504. In light of administrative regulations that had been promulgated while the appeal was pending, see 42 Fed. Reg. 22676 (1977), * * * the appellate court believed that § 504 required Southeastern to "reconsider plaintiff's application for admission to the nursing program without regard to her hearing ability." 574 F.2d at 1160. It concluded that the District Court had erred in taking respondent's handicap into account in determining whether she was "otherwise qualified" for the program, rather than confining its inquiry to her "academic and technical qualifications." Id. at

1161. The Court of Appeals also suggested that § 504 required "affirmative conduct" on the part of Southeastern to modify its program to accommodate the disabilities of applicants, "even when such modifications become expensive." 574 F.2d at 1162.

Because of the importance of this issue to the many institutions covered by § 504, we granted certiorari. 439 U.S. 1065 (1979). We now reverse. * * *

II

As previously noted, this is the first case in which this Court has been called upon to interpret § 504. It is elementary that "[t]he starting point in every case involving construction of a statute is the language itself." *Blue Chip Stamps v. Manor Drug Stores*, 421 U.S. 723, 756 (1975) (POWELL, J., concurring); see *Greyhound Corp. v. Mt. Hood Stages, Inc.*, 437 U.S. 322, 330 (1978); *Santa Fe Industries, Inc. v. Green*, 430 U.S. 462, 472 (1977). Section 504 by its terms does not compel educational institutions to disregard the disabilities of handicapped individuals or to make substantial modifications in their programs to allow disabled persons to participate. Instead, it requires only that an "otherwise qualified handicapped individual" not be excluded from participation in a federally funded program "solely by reason of his handicap," indicating only that mere possession of a handicap is not a permissible ground for assuming an inability to function in a particular context.[6]

The court below, however, believed that the "otherwise qualified" persons protected by § 504 include those who would be able to meet the requirements of a particular program in every respect except as to limitations imposed by their handicap. See 574 F.2d at 1160. Taken literally, this holding would prevent an institution from taking into account any limitation resulting from the handicap, however disabling. It

---

[6] The Act defines "handicapped individual" as follows:

"The term 'handicapped individual' means any individual who (A) has a physical or mental disability which for such individual constitutes or results in a substantial handicap to employment and (B) can reasonably be expected to benefit in terms of employability from vocational rehabilitation services provided pursuant to subchapters I and III of this chapter. For the purposes of subchapters IV and V of this chapter, such term means any person who (A) has a physical or mental impairment which substantially limits one or more of such person's major life activities, (B) has a record of such an impairment, or (C) is regarded as having such an impairment." § 7(6) of the Rehabilitation Act of 1973, 87 Stat. 361, as amended, 88 Stat. 1619, 89 Stat. 2-5, 29 U.S.C. § 706(6). * * *

assumes, in effect, that a person need not meet legitimate physical requirements in order to be "otherwise qualified." We think the understanding of the District Court is closer to the plain meaning of the statutory language. An otherwise qualified person is one who is able to meet all of a program's requirements in spite of his handicap.

The regulations promulgated by the Department of HEW to interpret § 504 reinforce, rather than contradict, this conclusion. According to these regulations, a "[q]ualified handicapped person" is, "[w]ith respect to postsecondary and vocational education services, a handicapped person who meets the academic and technical standards requisite to admission or participation in the [school's] education program or activity . . . ." 45 C.F.R. § 84.3(k)(3) (1978). An explanatory note states:

> "The term 'technical standards' refers to *all* nonacademic admissions criteria that are essential to participation in the program in question." 45 C.F.R. pt. 84, app. A, p. 405 (1978) (emphasis supplied).

A further note emphasizes that legitimate physical qualifications may be essential to participation in particular programs. * * * We think it clear, therefore, that HEW interprets the "other" qualifications which a handicapped person may be required to meet as including necessary physical qualifications.

III

The remaining question is whether the physical qualifications Southeastern demanded of respondent might not be necessary for participation in its nursing program. It is not open to dispute that, as Southeastern's Associate Degree Nursing program currently is constituted, the ability to understand speech without reliance on lipreading is necessary for patient safety during the clinical phase of the program. As the District Court found, this ability also is indispensable for many of the functions that a registered nurse performs.

Respondent contends nevertheless that § 504, properly interpreted, compels Southeastern to undertake affirmative action that would dispense with the need for effective oral communication. First, it is suggested that respondent can be given individual supervision by faculty members whenever she attends patients directly. Moreover, certain required courses might be dispensed with altogether for respondent. It is not necessary, she argues, that Southeastern train her to undertake all the tasks a registered nurse is licensed to perform. Rather, it is sufficient to make § 504 applicable if respondent might be able to perform satisfactorily some of the duties of a registered nurse or to hold some of the positions available to a registered nurse. * * *

Respondent finds support for this argument in portions of the HEW regulations discussed above. In particular, a provision applicable to postsecondary educational programs requires covered institutions to make "modifications" in their programs to accommodate handicapped persons, and to provide "auxiliary aids" such as sign-language interpreters.[9] Respondent argues that this regulation imposes an obligation to ensure full participation in covered programs by handicapped individuals and, in particular, requires Southeastern to make the kind of adjustments that would be necessary to permit her safe participation in the nursing program.

---

[9] This regulation provides:

"(a) Academic *requirements*. A recipient [of federal funds] to which this subpart applies shall make such modifications to its academic requirements as are necessary to ensure that such requirements do not discriminate or have the effect of discriminating, on the basis of handicap, against a qualified handicapped applicant or student. Academic requirements that the recipient can demonstrate are essential to the program of instruction being pursued by such student or to any directly related licensing requirement not be regarded as discriminatory within the meaning of this section. Modifications may include changes in the length of time permitted for the completion of degree requirements, substitution of specific courses required for the completion of degree requirements, and adaptation of the manner in which specific courses are conducted.

* * *

"(d) *Auxiliary aids*. (1) A recipient to which this subpart applies shall take such steps as are necessary to ensure that no handicapped student is denied the benefits of, excluded from participation in, or otherwise subjected to discrimination under the education program or activity operated by the recipient because of the absence of educational auxiliary aids for students with impaired sensory, manual, or speaking skills.

"(2) *Auxiliary* aids may include taped texts, interpreters or other effective methods of making orally delivered materials available to students with hearing impairments, readers in libraries for students with visual impairments, classroom equipment adapted for use by students with manual impairments, and other similar services and actions. Recipients need not provide attendants, individually prescribed devices, readers for personal use or study, or other devices or services of a personal nature." 45 C.F.R. § 84.44 (1978).

38

We note first that on the present record it appears unlikely respondent could benefit from any affirmative action that the regulation reasonably could be interpreted as requiring. Section 84.44(d)(2), for example, explicitly excludes "devices or services of a personal nature" from the kinds of auxiliary aids a school must provide a handicapped individual. Yet the only evidence in the record indicates that nothing less than close, individual attention by a nursing instructor would be sufficient to ensure patient safety if respondent took part in the clinical phase of the nursing program. See 424 F.Supp. at 1346. Furthermore, it also is reasonably clear that § 84.44(a) does not encompass the kind of curricular changes that would be necessary to accommodate respondent in the nursing program. In light of respondent's inability to function in clinical courses without close supervision, Southeastern, with prudence, could allow her to take only academic classes. Whatever benefits respondent might realize from such a course of study, she would not receive even a rough equivalent of the training a nursing program normally gives. Such a fundamental alteration in the nature of a program is far more than the "modification" the regulation requires.

Moreover, an interpretation of the regulations that required the extensive modifications necessary to include respondent in the nursing program would raise grave doubts about their validity. If these regulations were to require substantial adjustments in existing programs beyond those necessary to eliminate discrimination against otherwise qualified individuals, they would do more than clarify the meaning of § 504. Instead, they would constitute an unauthorized extension of the obligations imposed by that statute.

The language and structure of the Rehabilitation Act of 1973 reflect a recognition by Congress of the distinction between the evenhanded treatment of qualified handicapped persons and affirmative efforts to overcome the disabilities caused by handicaps. Section 501(b), governing the employment of handicapped individuals by the Federal Government, requires each federal agency to submit "an affirmative action program plan for the hiring, placement, and advancement of handicapped individuals . . . ." These plans "shall include a description of the extent to which and methods whereby the special needs of handicapped employees are being met." Similarly, § 503(a), governing hiring by federal contractors, requires employers to "take affirmative action to employ and advance in employment qualified handicapped individuals . . . ." The President is required to promulgate regulations to enforce this section.

Under § 501(c) of the Act, by contrast, state agencies such as Southeastern are only "encourage[d] . . . to adopt and implement such policies and procedures." Section 504 does not refer at all to affirmative action, and except as it applies to federal employers it does not provide for implementation by administrative action. A comparison of these provisions demonstrates that Congress understood accommodation of the needs of handicapped individuals may require affirmative action and knew how to provide for it in those instances where it wished to do so. * * *

Although an agency's interpretation of the statute under which it operates is entitled to some deference, "this deference is constrained by our obligation to honor the clear meaning of a statute, as revealed by its language, purpose, and history." *Teamsters v. Daniel*, 439 U.S. 551, 566 n.20 (1979). Here, neither the language, purpose, nor history of § 504 reveals an intent to impose an affirmative-action obligation on all recipients of federal funds. [In a footnote, the Court rejected several statutory interpretation arguments made by the United States as *amicus curiae*.] Accordingly, we hold that even if HEW has attempted to create such an obligation itself, it lacks the authority to do so.

* * *

IV

We do not suggest that the line between a lawful refusal to extend affirmative action and illegal discrimination against handicapped persons always will be clear. It is possible to envision situations where an insistence on continuing past requirements and practices might arbitrarily deprive genuinely qualified handicapped persons of the opportunity to participate in a covered program. * * *

In this case, however, it is clear that Southeastern's unwillingness to make major adjustments in its nursing program does not constitute such discrimination. The uncontroverted testimony of several members of Southeastern's staff and faculty established that the purpose of its program was to train persons who could serve the nursing profession in all customary ways. * * * This type of purpose, far from reflecting any animus against handicapped individuals is shared by many if not most of the institutions that train persons to render professional service. It is undisputed that respondent could not participate in Southeastern's nursing program unless the standards were substantially lowered. Section 504 imposes no requirement upon an educational institution to lower or to effect substantial modifications of standards to accommodate a handicapped person. * * *

* * *

One may admire respondent's desire and determination to overcome her handicap, and there well may be various other types of service for which she can qualify. In this case, however, we hold that there was no violation of § 504 when Southeastern concluded that respondent did not qualify for admission to its program. Nothing in the language or history of § 504 reflects an intention to limit the freedom of an educational institution to require reasonable physical qualifications for admission to a clinical training program. Nor has there been any showing in this case that any action short of a substantial change in Southeastern's program would render unreasonable the qualifications it imposed.

Accordingly, we reverse the judgment of the court below, and remand for proceedings consistent with this opinion.

So ordered.

Notes & Questions

1. Do you agree with Justice Powell's statement of the issue: "Whether § 504 . . . forbids professional schools from imposing physical qualifications for admission to their clinical training programs"? Is there a way to rephrase it that is consistent with what Davis wanted to achieve?

2. Do you think the language of the Rehabilitation Act admits readings other than the Court's? What readings? What evidence is there of Congress's intent?

3. The Department of Health, Education and Welfare (HEW) was later split into the Department of Health and Human Services and the Department of Education. What role do HEW's regulation play in the Court's opinion? An important question in many Rehabilitation Act and ADA cases, and indeed in any case involving the interpretation of administrative regulations, is the level of deference the reviewing court accords the regulations. The leading case in this area is *Chevron U.S.A., Inc. v. Natural Resources Defense Council, Inc.*, 467 U.S. 837 (1984). In *Chevron*, the Court states:

> When a court reviews an agency's construction of the statute which it administers, it is confronted with two questions. First, always, is the question whether Congress has directly spoken to the precise question at issue. If the intent of Congress is clear, that is the end of the matter; for the court, as well as the agency, must give effect to the unambiguously expressed intent of Congress. If, however, the court determines Congress has not directly addressed the precise question at issue, the court does not simply impose its own construction on the statute, as would be necessary in the absence of an administrative interpretation. Rather, if the statute is silent or ambiguous with respect to the specific issue, the question for the court is whether the agency's answer is based on a permissible construction of the statute.

Id. at 842-43 (footnotes omitted).

4. Does the Court properly distinguish between the training function of the College and the ultimate career Davis may wish to pursue? That is, what if Davis only wants to be an administrator? Should the College be required to accommodate her?

5. The Court recognizes that "the line between a lawful refusal to extend affirmative action and illegal discrimination against handicapped persons ... will [not always] be clear." How would you formulate language that permits an easier and less contentious line to be drawn? What societal or economic considerations factor into your language?

6. In *Alexander v. Choate*, 469 U.S. 287, 293 (1985), a class of Medicaid recipients argued that Tennessee's reduction of the number of inpatient hospital days paid for by Medicaid violated the Rehabilitation Act. Although the U.S. Supreme Court declined to find that this was a cognizable claim, it commented on the dangers inherent in interpreting Section 504 too broadly: "Any interpretation of § 504 must ... be responsive to two powerful but countervailing considerations – the need to give effect to the statutory objectives and the desire to keep § 504 within manageable bounds." *Id.* at 299.

Chapter 2 THE ADA'S HISTORY AND PHILOSOPHY

§ 2.1 A Brief Guide To The ADA

The ADA has a preface section and five main parts. In the text of the statute, these five parts are referred to as "Subchapters." But they are commonly referred to as "Titles," and that is how we refer to them herein.

The preface contains two code sections. The first, § 12101, gives Congress's "Findings and Purposes." 42 U.S.C. § 12101 (2006). This section sets the nation's proper goals regarding individuals with disabilities as assuring "equality of opportunity, full participation, independent living, and economic self sufficiency." *Id.* § 12101(a)(8). It also provides that the purpose of the chapter, among other things, is to "provide a clear and comprehensive national mandate for the elimination of discrimination against people with disabilities," *id.* § 12101(b)(1), and to ensure that the federal government plays a central role in enforcing these standards. *Id.* § 12101(b)(3).

The second code section sets forth certain definitions that apply throughout the rest of the Act. 42 U.S.C. § 12102. This includes the definition of "disability," which we discuss in Part 2 of this casebook.

The Act's five Titles come next. Title I deals with employment. *Id.* §§ 12111-12117. The general rule of discrimination it sets forth is that "no covered entity shall discriminate against a qualified individual with a disability because of the disability of such individual in regard to job application procedures, the hiring, advancement, or discharge of employees, employee compensation, job training, and other terms, conditions, and privileges of employment." *Id.* § 12112. Situations of "undue hardship," or where an employee is a significant risk to the health or safety of others in the workplace, provide defenses to employers. *Id.* §§ 12111(3), 12111(10), 12113(a)-(b). These and other employment issues under Title I, ranging from pre-hiring to termination, are explored in Part 3 of this casebook.

The next subchapter, Title II, covers discrimination by public entities. *Id.* §§ 12131-12181. Generally, this means discrimination by state or local governments. 42 U.S.C. § 12131(1)(A). This Title is divided into two parts. Part A sets forth the general rule of non-discrimination by public entities. It provides that "no qualified individual with a disability shall, by reason of such disability, be excluded from participation in or be denied the benefits of the services, programs, or activities of a public entity, or be subjected to discrimination by any such entity." *Id.* § 12132. Part B deals with discrimination by public entities in the context of public transportation. Title II in its entirety is discussed in Part 4 of this casebook.

The next subchapter is Title III. *Id.* §§ 12181-12189. This deals with discrimination in public accommodations and services operated by private entities. The general rule is that "[n]o individual shall be discriminated against on the basis of disability in the full and equal enjoyment of the goods, services, facilities, privileges, advantages, or accommodations of any place of public accommodation by any person who owns, leases (or leases to), or operates a place of public accommodation." *Id.* § 12182(a). A public accommodation must make reasonable modifications in its policies, practices, and procedures, unless that entity can demonstrate that doing so would fundamentally alter the nature of its goods, services, or facilities. *Id.* § 12182(b)(2)(A)(ii). Older facilities must remove architectural barriers if it is "readily achievable" to do so, *id.* § 12182(b)(2)(A)(iv), while facilities (or alterations) that post-date the ADA must be designed to be readily accessible to individuals with disabilities to the "maximum extent possible." 42 U.S.C. § 12183(a)(2). Title III is discussed in Part 5 of this casebook.

As a public law, the ADA contained a Title IV, entitled "Communications." *See* Pub. L. No. 101-336, 104 Stat. 366 (1990). When the ADA became part of the United States Code, the Telecommunications section was codified elsewhere in the U.S. Code. 47 U.S.C. § 255 (2006). This section provides that manufacturers and providers of telecommunications equipment and services must ensure that their equipment and services are accessible to and useable by people with disabilities, if this is readily achievable. *Id. See infra* Part 8, Section 33.7 discussing the Twenty-first Century Communications and Video Accessibility Act of 2010.

The final section, Title V of the public law (but Title IV in the U.S. Code), is entitled "Miscellaneous Provisions." *Id.* §§ 12201-12213. There are various significant provisions in this section that have aided courts in interpreting the ADA. For example, this section solidified the close relationship between the ADA and the Rehabilitation Act of 1973, by noting that nothing in the ADA is to be construed to provide a lesser standard of protection than the Rehabilitation Act. 42 U.S.C. § 12201(a) (2006). This section also provides that states shall not be immune under the Eleventh Amendment for suits brought under the ADA. *Id.* § 12202. Although, as will be discussed *infra* in Parts 3 and 4, the Supreme Court has held that Congress exceeded its authority by authorizing Title I suits for damages against states for discrimination in employment. These and other specific provisions in Title IV will be discussed throughout this casebook.

On September 25, 2008, President Bush signed the ADA Amendments Act of 2008, Pub. L. 110-325, 42 U.S.C.A. § 12101 (et seq.) (2008), into law. This Act, responding to restrictive Supreme Court decisions, primarily amended the definition of disability, originally set forth in 42 U.S.C. § 12102. The ADA Amendments Act, and its impacts on the ADA statutory scheme and case law, will be discussed throughout this casebook.

§ 2.2 ADA Background And Fundamentals

A. *The Story Of The Passage Of The ADA*

The culmination of federal legislative efforts to establish and protect the rights of people with disabilities was the ADA. But the story of the ADA begins earlier than its passage in 1990.

In February 1986, the National Council on the Handicapped (later the National Council on Disability (NCD or "Council")) released its report "Toward Independence: An Assessment of Federal Laws and Programs Affecting Persons with Disabilities – With Legislative Recommendations, a Report to the President and to the Congress of the United States" ("Toward Independence"), http://www.ncd.gov/publications/1986/February 1986. NCD is an independent Federal agency whose fifteen members are appointed by the President and confirmed by the Senate. The Council was originally established under the Rehabilitation Act of 1973 as an advisory board to the Department of Education, but in 1984 it was transformed into an independent agency. 29 U.S.C. § 780 (2006).

The 15-member Council made three general conclusions:

(1) Approximately two-thirds of working-age persons with disabilities do not receive Social Security or other public assistance income;

(2) Federal disability programs reflect an overemphasis on income support and an under-emphasis of initiatives for equal opportunity, independence, prevention, and self-sufficiency;

(3) More emphasis should be given to Federal programs encouraging and assisting private sector efforts to promote opportunities and independence for individuals with disabilities.

Toward Independence, *supra*, at viii.

The Council emphasized the expense of disability governmental benefits programs and concluded that:

The present and future costs of disability to the Nation are directly related to the degree of success we attain in reducing existing barriers, both structural and attitudinal, and in providing appropriate services to individuals with disabilities so that they may reach their full potential and become more independent and self-sufficient.

Id. at 1.

The Council recommended changes to federal disability policy in ten issue areas:

Equal Opportunity Laws: The enactment of a comprehensive law requiring equal opportunity for individuals with disabilities, with broad coverage and setting clear, consistent, and enforceable standards prohibiting discrimination on the basis of handicap.

Employment: To increase employment among people with disabilities – a drastically underemployed segment of the population – several legislative changes, concerning the transition from school to work, supported employment, private sector initiatives, job training, job development, and placement.

Disincentives to Work under Social Security Laws: Ways in which provisions of existing Social Security laws serve to discourage and penalize people with disabilities if they seek to become employed and self supporting. In response to those work disincentives, corrective amendments to the problematic provisions.

Prevention of Disabilities: To promote prevention of disabilities and to assure that individuals with disabilities do not suffer unnecessary secondary disabilities or exacerbation of their impairments, the Federal Government mount a national program for the prevention of disabilities.

Transportation: Amendments to Federal transportation legislation to achieve the Nation's established policy that "disabled people have the same right to use public transportation as nondisabled persons." Proposals relate to urban mass transit, air transportation, intercity and interstate buses, and private vehicles.

Housing: To permit people with disabilities an opportunity to obtain appropriate housing, which is an important prerequisite to obtaining employment, living independently, and avoiding costly institutionalization. Provides recommendations designed to prohibit housing discrimination and to promote increased appropriate and accessible housing for persons with disabilities.

Community-Based Services for Independent Living: To achieve productivity and independence, people with disabilities require a range of support services according to the nature and degree of their disabilities. Measures, including amendments and funding support to promote availability of community-based services for independent living.

Educating Children with Disabilities: Legislative recommendations regarding educational opportunities for children with disabilities. These recommendations respond to: the need for special education and related services during infancy; the need to educate children with special needs in regular education facilities; and the need to assess progress made since the enactment of the Education for All Handicapped Children Act.

Personal Assistance: Attendant Services, Readers, and Interpreters: Because of the critical importance of such services in fostering independence and avoiding expensive institutionalization, a national commitment to developing a quality system of attendant services, readers, and interpreters.

Coordination: To ensure Federal and Federally supported disability-related programs be authorized and required to develop a joint plan for the systematic coordination of services and benefits.

Id. at viii-ix.

The Council's Report was a significant step. It set the stage for many of the same issues that even today are at the forefront of debates on disability civil rights.

Thus, the Council noted that "[v]arious estimates place the number of Americans with disabilities between 20 million and 50 million persons, with a figure of 35 or 36 million being the most commonly quoted estimate. A precise and reliable overall figure is not currently available . . . ." *Id.* at 2. As will be discussed *infra* in Part 2, the number of Americans with disabilities still has never been fully resolved. This continues to affect disability law and policy.

The Council described the two major approaches to the issue of defining disability as the "health conditions approach" and the "work disability approach." It found that neither approach was adequate.

The Council noted the health conditions approach as emphasizing "all conditions or limitations which impair the health or interfere with the normal functional abilities of an individual." *Id.* at 2-3. This approach produces high numbers of people with disabilities, because it includes conditions not typically viewed as disabling. For example, various respiratory, circulatory, digestive, skin, musculoskeletal conditions are included that are not typically categorized as disabilities. "Because of its focus on the medically oriented notions of health, the health conditions approach also does not provide adequate data on such conditions as learning disabilities and mental conditions." *Id.* at 3.

The work disability approach "focus[es] on individuals' reports that they have a condition that prevents them from working or limits their ability to work." Toward Independence, *supra*, at 3. This emphasis over-estimates and under-estimates the number of people with disabilities, because individuals who are not working have a psychological incentive to classify themselves as having a work disability and because individuals with disabilities who are working are not counted.

The Council's Report articulated the idea that disability rights legislation was part of the larger civil rights movement in the United States. It determined that then-existing laws prohibiting disability discrimination were not as broad as those prohibiting discrimination on the basis of race, color, sex, religion, or national origin. Private employers, public accommodations, and housing were covered by other civil rights laws, but not by disability rights laws.

As a result of these findings, the Council proposed the Americans with Disabilities Act of 1986. *Id.* at 11. The proposed legislation would extend to federal government, recipients of federal financial assistance, federal contractors, employers engaged in interstate commerce with fifteen or more employees, housing providers, public accommodations (as defined under Title II of the Civil Rights Act of 1964), interstate transportation, insurance providers, and state, county, and local governments. *Id.*

The Council's proposal identified a broad class of protected individuals. It recommended that there be no eligibility classification for coverage and that the law apply to "all situations in which a person is subjected to unfair or unnecessary exclusion or disadvantage because of some physical or mental impairment, perceived impairment, or history of impairment." *Id.* at 12. The proposal established a realm of prohibited conduct, including intentional and unintentional exclusion, segregation, and unequal treatment.

The proposal required reasonable accommodation and removal of architectural, transportation, and communication barriers. It called for an administrative federal enforcement mechanism and a private right of action if federal enforcement did not occur or at the conclusion of the federal process. Legal remedies included injunctive relief, monetary damages, attorneys' fees, back pay, fines, and termination of federal funding. The ADA of 1986 never became law. But Toward Independence formed the basis for what was to become the Americans with Disabilities Act of 1990.

The Council's second report, "On the Threshold of Independence" was submitted to the President and Congress in January of 1988 and included a proposed bill to implement the Council's recommendations. *See generally*, Nat'l Council on Disability, On the Threshold of Independence (1988), http://www.ncd.gov/publications/1988/Jan1988.

On April 28, 1988, fourteen co-sponsors introduced this bill in the Senate. The next day, thirty-four co-sponsors introduced it in the House of Representatives. Lowell Weicker, Jr., Historical Background of the Americans with Disabilities Act, 64 Temp. L. Rev. 387, 391 (1991). A joint congressional hearing was held on September 27, 1988, but the bills were not acted on by the 100th Congress before it adjourned. *Id.* The bill was modified in response to the information gathered in the congressional hearing and on May 9, 1989, the bill was reintroduced to the 101st Congress. *Id.*

The final bill passed the Senate by a vote of 91 to 6. It passed the House by a vote of 377 to 28. On the morning of July 26, 1990, on the south lawn of the White House, with 3,000 disability rights advocates, members of Congress and the Administration looking on, President George Bush signed the Americans with Disabilities Act into law. It was the largest signing ceremony in history. *See* Nat'l Council on Disability, The Americans with Disabilities Act: Ensuring Equal Access to the American Dream (Jan. 26, 1995), http://www.ncd.gov/publications/1995/ 01262005. President Bush described the ADA as

> [t]he world's first comprehensive declaration of the equality of people with disabilities, and evidence of America's leadership internationally in the cause of human rights. With today's signing of the landmark Americans with Disabilities Act, every man woman and child with a disability can now pass through the closed doors, into a bright new era of equality, independence, and freedom.

Id.

B. *Key Legislative Trade-Offs*

As with any bill, amendments to the ADA were introduced throughout the committee process. The Senate Committee on Labor and Human Resources adopted three amendments. The Committee replaced punitive and compensatory damages with Title VII remedies (i.e., back pay, benefits, and injunctive relief); phased in the employment provisions (e.g., covering employers with 25 or more employees for the first two years, and employers with 15 or more employees later); and eliminated the prohibition against "anticipatory discrimination" (i.e., for individuals who believed they were about to be subjected to discrimination). H.R. Rep. No. 101-485(II), at 164 (1989) (minority views summarizing changes). These amendments were to respond to concerns of the Bush administration. *Id.*

The House Committee on Education and Labor made amendments to the House bill on November 14, 1989, adopting the Senate's changes and making additional changes. The House bill:

excluded current users of illegal drugs from protection;

limited employers' liability for contractors' discrimination to actions regarding the employer's own employees or applicants;

added consideration of site-specific factors to the determination of undue hardship;

clarified when an alteration to a facility would trigger accessibility requirements;

clarified that the Attorney General could not seek punitive damages on behalf of an aggrieved party;

replaced the term "potential places of employment" with "commercial facilities" for purposes of new construction;

required Federal agencies to develop coordination procedures;

required that plaintiffs filing public accommodations suits have reasonable grounds to sue;

authorized certification of state and local building codes by the Attorney General; and

allowed flexibility in applying accessibility requirements to historical buildings. *Id.* at 165-66.

The most controversial issue in committee was the damages provision. As of November 1989, a deal had been struck eliminating punitive and compensatory damages and incorporating by reference the remedies of Title VII. At that time, Title VII required EEOC conciliation as a prerequisite to a suit in federal court and limited remedies to back pay, benefits, and injunctive relief.

However, in early 1990, civil rights reform legislation was proposed that would have changed Title VII to allow direct access to courts, provide for jury trials, and permit compensatory and punitive damages. *See* Henry H. Perritt, Jr., 1 Americans with Disabilities Act Handbook § 2.3 (3d ed. 1997). The minority in the House, who had agreed reluctantly to the original deal, and the Bush administration, objected to the possibility of expanded remedies under the ADA. *Id.* Eventually, over the objections of the Bush administration, the parties relented, and an amendment to de-link the ADA from Title VII was voted down in the House, by a vote of 227 to 192. *Id.*

In the Conference Committee, the changes were minor, and generally followed the House version of the bill. Regarding Title I, the Committee accepted the House definition of "essential functions," which required written job descriptions to be considered as evidence of essential functions and provided for consideration of the employer's judgment as to what job functions are essential. H.R. Conf. Rep. No. 101-596, at 58 (1990).

The Committee adopted the House's definition of "undue hardship." *Id.* It adopted the House's approach to direct threat, which expanded it to all threats to the health or safety of others, rather than just to contagious diseases. *Id.* at 60. The Committee adopted the House's clarification of the exclusion of current users of illegal drugs. *Id.* at 63-65. Regarding Title II, the Committee adopted the House's structure, which split Title II's requirements into two subtitles – one covering general prohibitions and one covering public transportation. *Id.* at 67.

Regarding Title III, the Committee adopted the House's use of "commercial facilities" instead of "potential places of employment." *Id.* at 75. The Committee adopted the House list of factors for determining what barrier removal is "readily achievable," and providing more consideration for the resources of the individual facility. H.R. Conf. Rep. No. 101-596, at 75-76.

The Committee adopted the House's clarification that entities liable for violations of the Act include anyone who owns, leases (or leases to), or operates a place of public accommodation. *Id.* at 76. The Committee adopted the House definition of "direct threat" (the Senate version did not include a definition). *Id.* at 77. The Committee replaced the Senate's alterations provision, which applied to "major structural alterations," with the House's provision, applying to any alteration "that affects . . . a primary function." *Id.*

Finally, the Committee adopted the House's remedies provision, which allowed anticipatory litigation only for an individual with "reasonable grounds" to believe he was about to be subject to discrimination. *Id.* at 80. The Committee adopted the House's clarification that the Attorney General was not authorized to seek punitive damages. *Id.* at 80-81. It adopted the House's grace period for compliance by small businesses, allowing them an additional six or twelve months, depending on size. H.R. Conf. Rep. No. 101-596, at 81.

Regarding Title V, the Committee adopted the House version of the exclusion of current users of illegal drugs. Moreover, it clarified that "[t]he provision is not intended to be limited to persons who use drugs on the day of, or within a matter of days or weeks before, the action in question. Rather, the provision is intended to apply to a person whose illegal use of drugs occurred recently enough to justify a reasonable belief that a person's drug use is current." *Id.* at 87.

The Committee adopted the House provision for use of alternative dispute resolution. It noted, however, that "[i]t is the intent of the conferees that the use of these alternative dispute resolution procedures is completely voluntary. Under no condition would an arbitration clause in a collective bargaining agreement or employment contract prevent an individual from pursuing their rights under the ADA." *Id.* at 89.

C. *Constitutional Basis*

In exercising its authority pursuant to the Equal Protection Clause, Congress signaled a different approach than that taken by the U.S. Supreme Court. Through the ADA, Congress attempted to exercise its full constitutional authority to prohibit and deter discrimination on the basis of disability. 42 U.S.C. § 12101(b)(4) (2006) ("It is the purpose of this chapter . . . to invoke the full sweep of Congressional authority, including the power to enforce the fourteenth amendment and to regulate commerce . . . ."). To do this, Congress relied on the Equal Protection Clause of the Fourteenth Amendment to the Constitution, U.S. Const. amend. XIV, § 5, and on the Interstate Commerce Clause. U.S. Const. art. I, § 8, cl. 3. The limits and reach of these constitutional bases are explored throughout this casebook, particularly *infra* in Part 4.

D. *Role Of Federal Agencies*

The ADA provided two roles for federal agencies: (1) development of regulations, and (2) enforcement.

1. Regulations

The ADA charged several federal agencies with developing regulations. The EEOC was tasked with issuing regulations interpreting and implementing the employment provisions under Title I of the ADA within one year of the ADA's enactment. 42 U.S.C. § 12116. The Department of Justice (DOJ) was charged with issuing regulations interpreting and implementing the state and local government requirements under Title II of the ADA within one year of enactment. *Id.* § 12134.

The DOJ was required to issue regulations implementing the Title III requirements applicable to places of public accommodation. *Id.* § 12186(b). However, the Department of Transportation (DOT) was charged with issuing regulations implementing the transportation requirements under Title II and Title III. *Id.* §§ 12149, 12186(a).

The ADA required significant coordination between federal agencies. The DOJ's construction-related requirements and the DOT's requirements for accessible facilities and vehicles are required to be consistent with guidelines issued by the U.S. Architectural and Transportation Barriers Compliance Board ("Access Board"). *Id.* §§ 12134(c), 12186(c). The agencies responsible for regulation and enforcement were required to develop coordinated regulations and processes for handling complaints with the agencies responsible for enforcing the Rehabilitation Act. *Id.* §§ 12117(b), 12134(b).

2. Enforcement

The ADA did not become effective on enactment in 1990. Instead, different titles of the ADA became effective after different periods. Title I became effective 24 months after enactment, or July 26, 1992, for employers with 25 or more employees. Title I became effective for smaller employers (with 15 or fewer employees) two years later, on July 26, 1994. 42 U.S.C. §§ 12111, 12111(5) (2006).

The EEOC and the DOJ, as well as private individuals, were given enforcement authority, following the powers, remedies, and procedures of the Civil Rights Act of 1964. *Id.* § 12117(a). Thus, individuals who believe they have faced employment discrimination must file a charge with the EEOC within 180 days of the violation. They must await a "right to sue" letter from the EEOC before they can pursue their claim in court. *Id.* § 12117(a), § 2000e-5(e). That time period is extended to up to 300 days if the state has a law prohibiting the same conduct. *See* Bonilla v. Muebles J.J. Alvarez, Inc., 194 F.3d 275, 278 (1st Cir. 1999); *see also* Ebbert v. Daimler Chrysler Corp., 319 F.3d 103 (3d Cir. 2003) (holding that oral notice can be sufficient to start statutory period if it is as comprehensive as written notice).

Title II of the ADA took effect on January 26, 1992. 28 C.F.R. pt. 35, app. B, § 35.140 (2008) ("Employment Discrimination Prohibited"). The ADA provided for enforcing agencies to follow the enforcement procedures and remedies of Section 505 of the Rehabilitation Act of 1973. 42 U.S.C. § 12134(a). Section 505, in turn, incorporates the procedures of Title VI of the Civil Rights Act of 1964.

Under Title VI of the Civil Rights Act, a federal agency that administers federal funding to the entity being challenged has jurisdiction to enforce the law, by seeking voluntary compliance, terminating federal funding through an administrative process, or referral to the DOJ for judicial enforcement. Because the ADA extended the disability discrimination prohibitions to non-federally funded state and local government programs, eight designated federal agencies were given jurisdiction over all programs of the *type* of program they fund (i.e., as opposed to programs they actually fund). Those agencies were:

> Department of Agriculture: activities relating to farming and raising livestock;
>
> Department of Education: activities relating to elementary, secondary, vocational, and higher education (other than health-related schools), and libraries;
>
> Department of Health and Human Services: activities relating to provision of health care and social services, including health-related schools, social services providers, and preschool and daycare programs;
>
> Department of Housing and Urban Development: activities relating to public housing;

Department of Interior: activities relating to lands and natural resources, including water and waste management, energy, historic and cultural preservation, and museums;

Department of Justice: activities relating to law enforcement, public safety, and administration of justice, commerce and industry, government support services (audit, personnel, etc.), and government functions not assigned to another designated agency;

Department of Labor: activities relating to labor and the work force;

Department of Transportation: activities relating to transportation.

28 C.F.R. pt. 35, app. A (1991) ("Section-by-Section Analysis, Subpart F").

The DOJ was given jurisdiction over any entities that did not fall within the jurisdiction of a designated agency. 28 C.F.R. pt. 35, app. B, § 35.190(b)(6) (2003). When the federal agency actually funds the challenged entity, the agency must use the Section 504 process (including the possibility of funding termination), rather than the ADA process (which does not include the option of funding termination). 28 C.F.R. pt. 35, app. A ("Section-by-Section Analysis, Subpart F") (1991).

Complaints under Title II must be filed with a federal agency within 180 days of the alleged violation. 28 C.F.R. pt. 35, app. B, § 35.170(b). The deadline is deemed to have been met if the complaint is filed with any federal agency within 180 days, even if that agency does not, in fact, have jurisdiction. *Id.* However, unlike Title I, filing with a federal agency is not a prerequisite to a private suit.

The appropriate designated federal agency must accept all complete Title II complaints for investigation. Whereas in the past the designated agency must investigate all complaints, the recent revisions removed the word "each," instead providing that the designated agency "shall investigate complaints for which it is responsible under § 35.171." The revised regulations also provide that "the designated agency may conduct compliance reviews of public entities in order to ascertain whether there has been a failure to comply with the nondiscrimination requirements of this part." 28 C.F.R. § 35.172(b). The designated agency will then, "[w]here appropriate . . . attempt informal resolution of any matter being investigated under this section, and, if resolution is not achieved and a violation is found, issue to the public entity and the complainant, if any, a Letter of Findings. . . ." *Id.* § 35.172(c).

After issuance of a Letter of Findings, the designated agency must notify the DOJ of the finding and attempt to negotiate a written, enforceable voluntary compliance agreement with the entity. *Id.* § 35.173. If a voluntary compliance agreement is not reached, the designated agency must refer the matter to the DOJ for appropriate enforcement action. *Id.* § 35.174. The private complainant may pursue independent judicial enforcement at any time during this process, regardless of the federal agency's findings. *Id.* § 35.172(c).

Title III of the ADA became effective January 26, 1992. 42 U.S.C. § 12181(a) (2006). However, businesses employing 25 or fewer employees and having gross receipts less than $1 million were given an additional six months, and businesses employing 10 or fewer employees and having receipts less than $500,000 were given an additional year. *Id.* § 12181(b).

Title III adopted the remedies and procedures of Title II of the Civil Rights Act of 1964. *Id.* § 12188(a)(1). Title III gives the DOJ authority to investigate complaints and to conduct periodic compliance reviews in the absence of complaints. *Id.* § 12188(b)(1)(A)(i). If the DOJ believes an entity has engaged in a pattern or practice of discrimination or believes a violation raises an issue of public importance, the DOJ may file a civil action in federal court. *Id.* § 12188(b)(1)(B).

§ 2.3 The History, Theory And Economics Of The Accommodation Principle

At the heart of ADA and the controversy surrounding it is the requirement that social institutions spend resources to remove barriers confronting people with disabilities. The most prominent example is the command that employers make "reasonable accommodations" for qualified applicants or employees.

The word "discriminate" is defined to include "not making reasonable accommodations to the known physical or mental limitations of an otherwise qualified individual with a disability who is an applicant or employee," in the absence of "undue hardship on the operation of the business," or denying employment opportunities to such a job applicant or employee "if such denial is based on the need for such covered entity to make reasonable accommodations to the physical or mental impairments of the employee or applicant." 42 U.S.C. § 12112(d)(5). The explicit command that employers accept the burden of paying for accommodations – up to the undue hardship ceiling – arguably sets the ADA apart from other civil rights legislation and has created significant theoretical and practical disputes. Title III's requirement that access be given to public accommodations is an example of the same allocation of responsibilities.

৵

Notes & Questions

1. Is it theoretically sound policy to impose on private entities the cost of achieving a societal goal? Would it be better to have the government pay for it? Does it matter that the costs may be minimal in "most" cases?

2. If the goal of economic legislation is "efficiency," is it possible that the ADA will support that goal in some sense? A 2007 cost-benefit study conducted by a consortium of the Illinois Department of Commerce and Economic Opportunity, the City of Chicago, the Chicagoland Chamber of Commerce, and researchers at DePaul University concluded, in part, that:

- Participants with disabilities from the retail and hospitality sectors stayed on the job longer than participants without disabilities.

- Across all sectors, participants with disabilities had fewer scheduled absences than those without disabilities.

- Retail participants with disabilities had fewer days of unscheduled absences than those without disabilities.

- Regardless of sector, participants with and without disabilities had nearly identical job performance ratings.

DePaul Univ. & Ill. Dep't of Commerce & Econ. Opportunity, Exploring the Bottom Line: A Study of the Costs and Benefits of Workers with Disabilities 3 (Oct. 2007), *available at* http://www.disabilityworks.org/downloads/disabilityworksDePaulStudyExecutiveSummary.pdf.

3. Is the method chosen likely to achieve that goal? Is it likely to lead to a public backlash? Is the latter a legitimate objection?

4. How can compliance be enforced? Is the EEOC sufficient? The threat of private suits?

5. In theory it should be possible to measure the effects of the ADA on the employment of people with disabilities. One obvious test of the ADA should be whether it fulfills its goals. Post-ADA, are more people with disabilities employed in productive jobs than pre-ADA? Are workers with disabilities paid at comparable levels as workers without disabilities? Economists have been trying to study these issues, but there remain unresolved questions as to the proper analytic approach and as to interpretation of the results.

A. *The Evolution And Legislative History Of The Reasonable Accommodation Requirement*

As discussed above, the ADA is a product of the civil rights movement. Its roots should be understood in the context of parallel developments in other areas of civil rights. In 1971, in *Griggs v. Duke Power Co.*, 401 U.S. 424 (1971), the Supreme Court interpreted Title VII of the Civil Rights Act of 1964 to preclude facially neutral employment tests that disproportionately excluded African Americans. "The Act proscribes not only overt discrimination but also practices that are fair in form, but discriminatory in operation. The touchstone is business necessity. If an employment practice which operates to exclude Negroes cannot be shown to be related to job performance, the practice is prohibited." *Id.* at 431. Effect, even independent of intent, was deemed sufficient to trigger judicial involvement.

The extrapolation of the underlying argument to people with disabilities is manifest. Offering employment to everyone, without relation to disability, is meaningless if the door to the work place is up a flight of stairs and the applicant uses a wheelchair. That fact, however, does not resolve how the legislature should deal with the dilemma – should governments pay for opening such doors or should private employers?

The phrase "reasonable accommodation" began percolating through another area of civil rights law shortly after Title VII was enacted, in 1964. Title VII provides that it is unlawful for an employer "to discriminate against any individual with respect to his compensation, terms, conditions, or privileges of employment, because of such individual's race, color, religion, sex, or national origin." Civil Rights Act of 1964, § 703(a)(1) (codified as amended at 42 U.S.C. § 2000e-2(a)(1) (2006)).

The prohibition against discrimination based on religion inevitably raises accommodation issues: Is it discriminatory to force a person to work on a day on which her religion forbids working? Is it discriminatory to forbid a person from wearing certain garb that his religion requires?

The EEOC addressed these issues in a regulation in 1966, requiring employers to "accommodate to the reasonable religious needs of employees . . . where such accommodation can be made without serious inconvenience to the conduct of the business." 29 C.F.R. § 1605.1 (1967). A year later, it amended the guidelines to require employers to "make reasonable accommodations to the religious needs of employees and prospective employees where such accommodations can be made without undue hardships on the conduct of the employer's business." 29 C.F.R. § 1605.2 (1968). Those themes – "reasonable accommodations" and "undue hardship" – echo in the ADA.

In 1977, the Supreme Court addressed the meaning of "reasonable accommodations" in *Trans World Airlines, Inc. v. Hardison*, 432 U.S. 63, 64 (1977), a case in which an employee alleged that his employer had discriminated against him by refusing to permit him not to work on Saturdays. The court of appeals had suggested that the employer might have permitted the employee to work a four-day work week, replacing him on Saturday with supervisory or other personnel, or that the employer could have paid premium wages to others to induce them to work on Saturday. *Id.* at 84.

The Supreme Court rejected those alternatives:

> To require [the employer] to bear more than a *de minimis* cost in order to give Hardison Saturdays off is an undue hardship. Like abandonment of the seniority system, to require [the employer] to bear additional costs when no such costs are incurred to give other employees the days off that they want would involve unequal treatment of employees on the basis of their religion. By suggesting that [the employer] should incur certain costs in order to give Hardison Saturdays off, the Court of Appeals would in effect require [the employer] to finance an additional Saturday off and then to choose the employee who will enjoy it on the basis of his religious beliefs.

Id.

The Court's opinion is mixed here. Is it saying solely that incurring more than *de minimis* additional costs would constitute undue hardship? Or, is it that incurring those costs would in effect favor one religion over another (or none)? To the extent the Court's interpretation of "undue hardship" is defined to cover anything more than *de minimis*, it would provide little play for the requirement of accommodations in the disability area. This is because some accommodations will require the expenditure of not insignificant funds. Helen Schartz et al., Workplace Accommodations: Evidence-Based Outcomes, 27 Work 345, 347-78(2006).

The *Hardison* limitation does not necessarily compel a similar result in the disability area, however. Accepting the *Hardison* Court's analysis, accommodating one religious group inevitably means giving it a preferential advantage over another religious group. This may implicate other concerns, such as first amendment freedom of religion issues. However, accommodating people with disabilities, having the practical effect of compensating them at a higher level, does not necessarily come at the expense of other employees, except to the extent that all salaries are reduced. This assumes the employer simply cannot lower the pay of the employee with a disability.

This logic may explain why drafters of disability rights legislation and regulations were willing to adopt the reasonable accommodation formulation that the EEOC had used for religious discrimination. During the 1970s, at the federal and state levels, disability rights legislation deployed this reasonable accommodation/undue hardship model.

The regulations to Sections 503 and 504 of the Rehabilitation Act of 1973, issued by the Department of Health, Education, and Welfare in 1978, adopted the "reasonable accommodation" formulation previously used in the regulations adopted pursuant to the Civil Rights Act of 1964. However, the Rehabilitation Act regulations go further. They require recipients of federal funds to make "reasonable accommodation to the known physical or mental limitations of an otherwise qualified handicapped applicant or employee unless the recipient can demonstrate that the accommodation would impose an undue hardship on the operation of its program." 45 C.F.R. § 84.12(a) (2008).

Although the term reasonable accommodation was not new, the regulations avoid the *de minimis* trap of *Hardison* by defining a series of reasonable accommodations, such as making facilities accessible to people with disabilities, modifying work schedules or requiring assistive devices. By explicitly limiting the requirement of reasonable accommodations only to those situations where they would constitute an undue hardship, the regulations also require more than a *de minimis* effort by the recipient.

In *Southeastern Community College v. Davis*, 442 U.S. 397 (1979), described earlier, the Supreme Court held that the defendant nursing school had not discriminated against the hearing-impaired plaintiff because no program modifications would have permitted her to serve as a nurse. *Id.* at 412-13. Nonetheless, the Court recognized that

> Situations may arise where a refusal to modify an existing program might become unreasonable and discriminatory. Identification of those instances where a refusal to accommodate the needs of a disabled person amounts to discrimination against the handicapped continues to be an important responsibility of HEW.

Id. at 412-13.

Thus, *Davis* sits on the cusp. The case is an exemplar of that body of civil rights law that goes no farther than requiring employers (or others) to treat all people without regard to the stereotyped characteristic, be it race, religion or disability. On the other hand, it explicitly understands that refusing to accommodate the needs of a person with a disability might itself amount to prohibited discrimination.

Perhaps inartfully, *Davis* did focus on the key issue that sets disability rights law apart from other branches of civil rights law. That is, treating qualified applicants or employees equally, without regard to whether they have a disability, will forever leave people with disabilities in a disadvantaged position. This is because there are some factors that may affect their ability to participate equally in jobs, but which do not render them incapable of performing the key or essential functions of those jobs.

Later, in *Alexander v. Choate*, 469 U.S. 287, 300 (1985), the Supreme Court read *Davis* to mean that "it appeared unlikely that [Davis] could benefit from *any* modifications that the relevant HEW regulations required and . . . the further modifications Davis sought . . . would have compromised the essential nature of the college's nursing program." *Id.* That interpretation expands the meaning of reasonable to include the universe of modifications that do not "compromise[ ] the essential nature" of a program. Later courts and commentators, and eventually the Supreme Court itself, limited *Davis*. *See, e.g.*, Camenisch v. Univ. of Tex., 616 F.2d 127, 133 (5th Cir. 1980); Mark Martin, Accommodating the Handicapped: The Meaning of Discrimination Under Section 504 of the Rehabilitation Act, 55 N.Y.U. L. Rev. 881, 884-85 (1980); Donald Olenick, Accommodating the Handicapped: Rehabilitation Section 504 After *Southeastern*, 80 Colum. L. Rev. 171, 185 (1980).

The Rehabilitation Act regulations were not the only venue in which legislators were engrafting "reasonable accommodation" duties on civil rights laws. In 1973, California prohibited employment discrimination on the basis of "physical handicap" – later enlarged to include "medical condition" – in its employment discrimination statute. Cal. Lab. Code § 1420 (recodified as Cal. Gov't Code § 12940 (Deering 1997 & Supp. 2004)). A 1992 amendment rearticulated these categories as physical disability, mental disability, and medical condition. *Id.* ("Former Sections: Amendments").

The California Department of Fair Employment and Housing, which is responsible for enforcing the anti-employment discrimination provisions, adopted a regulation in 1980 that echoes the Rehabilitation Act § 504 regulation. Cal. Code Regs. tit. 2, § 7293.9 (1995). The regulation requires an employer to make "reasonable accommodation to the disability of any individual with a disability" if the employer knows of the disability and unless the employer can "demonstrate that the accommodation would impose an undue hardship." *Id.*; *see* Fisher v. Sup. Ct., 223 Cal.Rptr 203, 205 (Cal. Ct. App. 1986) (reasonable accommodation required for medical condition – cancer).

Like the Section 504 regulations, California Section 7293.9 does not define reasonable accommodation but gives examples. The phrase "reasonable accommodation" or similar ideas have also been interpreted in a variety of other settings, including the Individuals with Disabilities Education Act, 20 U.S.C. § 1400 et seq. (2006); § 503 of the Rehabilitation Act, 29 U.S.C. § 793 (2006); and the Developmental Disabilities Assistance and Bill of Rights Act, 42 U.S.C. § 15001 et seq. (2006). *See generally* U.S. Comm'n on Civil Rights, Accommodating the Spectrum of Individual Abilities 104-06 (1983) ("Accommodating the Spectrum").

As mentioned earlier, in 1988, following a number of years of study, Congress introduced legislation to prohibit discrimination against people with disabilities. *See* S. 2345, 100th Cong. (1988); H.R. 4498, 100th Cong. (1988). In these original bills, each defined reasonable accommodation and declared the failure or refusal to make reasonable accommodations to constitute discrimination. S. 2345, § 5(a)(3). Unlike the Rehabilitation Act and its state variants, these bills defined reasonable accommodation in terms of its goal – to provide "the equal opportunity to participate effectively in a particular program, activity, job or other opportunity." *Id.* § 3(b)(5).

One can argue that the theory of reasonable accommodation as developed in federal and state statutes has been articulated from the wrong perspective. Harlan Hahn, Equality and the Environment: The Interpretation of "Reasonable Accommodations" in the Americans with Disabilities Act, 17 J. Rehab. Admin. 101, 102 (1993). On this model, modifying the environment is simply to balance the scales properly, not to give additional assistance to people with disabilities. Neither proposal had an undue hardship limitation. Neither of the bills became law.

The proponents of the ADA focused on the *de minimis* or zero costs of many accommodations. Accommodating the Spectrum, *supra*, at 106-08. The legislative history of the bills that eventually became the ADA, which were introduced in the first session of the 101st Congress, reflect that concept.

During the Congressional consideration of the ADA, much of the testimony focused on the relative ease with which employers could accommodate people with disabilities. The Senate report cited the minimal costs of specific accommodations and noted that witnesses had explained that there would need to be more expensive accommodations, "[b]ut even costs for these accommodations are frequently exaggerated." Sen. Comm. on Lab. & Human Res., S. Rep. No. 101-116, at 10 (1989); *see also* 135 Cong. Rec. S10,753 (daily ed. Sept. 7, 1989) (statement of Sen. Gore) ("[B]y requiring only modifications that are readily achievable and providing that employers do not have to take actions that are unduly burdensome, the bill establishes flexible, workable and realistic obligations to eliminate discrimination against persons with disabilities.").

A number of supporters of legislation argued that employing people with disabilities would decrease the need for federal funding to support them and increase their tax revenues.

> [W]e must bear the economic costs to our society when the disabled are prevented from fully participating in education, jobs, and community life. If the disabled are locked out of jobs, then society must bear the cost of maintaining these individuals and their families – families that otherwise would be self supporting and paying taxes.

136 Cong. Rec. H2447-448 (daily ed. May 17, 1990) (statement of Rep. Miller); *id.* H2438 (statement of Rep. Mineta) ("Sure, there are costs associated with this bill, but those costs are manageable. But the cost of not allowing disabled Americans to be full participants in our society will be much greater."); *id.* at H2440 (statement of Rep. Fish) ("[T]he bill does not put an undue burden on employers, businesses or the community at large. It strikes a balance.").

ADA Title I, as proposed and eventually adopted, sets forth an inexact concept of reasonable accommodation. Reasonable accommodation is defined not teleologically, but to include "making existing facilities used by employees readily accessible to and useable by individuals with disabilities," 42 U.S.C. § 12111(9)(A) (2006), and by listing a series of examples of accommodations. *Id.* § 12111(9)(B).

The drafters carried over language wholesale from the Section 504 regulations for pragmatic reasons: Congress was familiar with their effect and recipients of federal funds had been complying with the language since the late 1970s. *See* Chai Feldblum, The (R)evolution of Physical Disability Antidiscrimination Law, 20 Mental & Physical Disability L. Rep. 613, 617 (1996). As do the Section 504 regulations, the ADA's definition of undue hardship functions as a limitation on Title I's reasonable accommodation requirement. Title II, which deals with public accommodations, limits facilities modifications to those that are "readily achievable." 42 U.S.C. § 12182(b)(2)(A)(iv) (2006).

As one of the drafters of the ADA has pointed out, the statutory definition of reasonableness creates an ambiguity. In the legislation introduced in 1988, "reasonable" meant effective. If the statute then imposed an undue hardship limitation, the logic of the statute would have been that an employer had to make an effective accommodation *up to* the undue hardship limit. Feldblum, *supra*, at 619.

The predominant way that reasonable is defined, however, is as a limitation on the extent to which one should act. Thus, rather than a description of the nature of the affirmative act, reasonableness and undue hardship appear as limitations on an employer's duty. 136 Cong. Rec. H2,427-428 (daily ed. May 17, 1990) (statement of Rep. Owens) (noting that provisions of ADA "derive largely from § 504 of the Rehabilitation Act of 1973 and its implementing regulations, and the Civil Rights Act of 1964").

In the Congressional debates on the ADA, the business community, and especially small businesses, argued against aspects of reasonable accommodations. *E.g.*, Americans with Disabilities Act: Hearing on H.R. 101-45, Before the House Comm. on Small Bus., 101st Cong. 16-20 (1990) (statement of David Pinkus, Nat'l Small Bus. United), reprinted in Disability Law in the United States: A Legislative History of the Americans with Disabilities Act of 1990 (Pub. L. 101-33) 93 (Bernard D. Reams, Jr. et al., eds. 1992) ("Legislative History"); *see also id.* at 14 (statement of Kenneth Lewis, Nat'l Fed. of Indep. Bus.). One opponent contended that the ADA entails "affirmative action . . . requiring creative efforts to assure access rather than a legal standard against which to determine if an employer was guilty of discrimination." *See* Civil Rights Act of 1990: Hearing on S. 2104, Before the House Comm. on Lab. & Human Res., 101st Cong. 206-14, 287, 290 (1990) (statement of Lawrence Z. Lorber, Am. Soc'y of Personnel Admin.).

Opponents bolstered the "affirmative action" argument by suggesting that unlike other civil rights laws, the ADA would impose its costs on others. *E.g.* Legislative History, *supra*, at 2, 84, 85 (statement of

John J. Mottley III, Nat'l Fed. of Indep. Bus.). They argued that the model for the ADA, Section 504 of the Rehabilitation Act, affects only government contractors, who presumably may build additional costs into their contracts. *Id.* at 4, 87. They did not question the goal, but suggested that it was the government's duty to pay for it, either directly or through tax credits. *Id.* at 98-99 (statement of David Pinkus); *id.* at 78, 83 (statement of Joseph J. Dragonette, U.S. Chamber of Commerce).

To the business community, the open-ended nature of the ADA's central terms, such as "reasonable accommodation," "essential functions" and "undue hardship," amplified the problem of its potential costs. *Id.* at 95 (statement of David Pinkus). This argument took two forms. First, businesses did not accept the *de minimis* projections. *E.g., id.* at 5, 88 (statement of John J. Mottley III) (citing examples of $23/hour for sign language interpreter, $150-$700 to purchase a telecommunications device for the deaf (TDD) and $5000 to purchase a computer with speech synthesizer). They pointed out that for small businesses, an accumulation of "*de minimis*" costs can be painful. *Id.* at 4, 87. These arguments tended to lump the costs of Title III (Public Services) accommodations with Title I (Employment) accommodations. *See, e.g., id.* at 5, 88; *id.* at 19 (statement of David Pinkus) (estimating that over $5 billion will be spent to renovate bathrooms to accommodate wheelchairs).

Second, opponents feared potential liability, based on assertedly unclear statutory language. Legislative History, *supra*, at 86 (statement of Kenneth Lewis, Nat'l Fed. Indep. Bus.). They testified that small businesses could not afford to hire counsel to advise them on their ADA duties. *Id.* at 17 (statement of David Pinkus). Thus, they requested clearer guidelines, including monetary or percentage of income guidelines, on the reasonable accommodation mandate. *E.g., id.* at 92 (statement of Kenneth Lewis). Along with these suggestions, they requested that businesses be given discretion in defining such concepts as essential job functions and that the ADA's effects be phased in over time. *E.g., id.* at 76-84 (statement of Joseph J. Dragonette).

In the end, the ADA and its regulations addressed many such objections, giving substantial weight to an employer's definition of essential job functions. 29 C.F.R. § 1630.2(n)(3)(i)-(ii) (2008) (evidence includes, but is not limited to "the employer's judgment as to which functions are essential" and "[w]ritten job descriptions prepared before advertising or interviewing applicants for the job"). In part to limit the proliferation of litigation, Congress required the EEOC or analogous state agencies first to approve employment discrimination claims by requiring plaintiffs to obtain a "right to sue letter." 42 U.S.C. § 12117(a) (2006). However, the essential structure of the reasonable accommodation regime remained.

Many of the criticisms on the reasonable accommodation mandate were case specific and not empirically based. However, critics generally did not question the underlying assumption of proponents of the ADA that imposing an accommodation requirement on businesses would lead to higher employment levels for people with disabilities, other things being equal.

Today, the wisdom of these assumptions is the subject of debate. Thus, the question is raised whether the cost or benefit of accommodating qualified workers with disabilities affects their employment rates. In 1990, the data did not exist to study that question. In fact, it may not exist yet today. Economists and others have tried to answer the question with available data. Although the answer is far from conclusive, we discuss some of these analyses next, and also in Part 3.

B.   *Theory And Economics Of The Reasonable Accommodation Requirement*

The Rehabilitation Act of 1973 imposed reasonable accommodation duties on the government and government contractors; the ADA extends those duties to private employers. The theory justifying the former does not necessarily work for the latter. Although the government may have aims beyond strictly maximizing its output, such as providing employment to those who might not otherwise find it, a private entity's overriding goal is to maximize its profits. To accomplish that, it presumably aims to operate in the most efficient manner.

Historically, anti-employment discrimination law in the United States has aimed at insuring that a person who fits a particular job is able to obtain that job, despite irrelevant personal features. A person's skin color, gender, sexual orientation or religion generally has little bearing on the match between the person's skills and a particular job. Thus, the Civil Rights Act of 1964 and its later amendments forbid discrimination in employment. Pub L. No. 88-352, 78 Stat. 241, 253-66 (codified as amended principally at 42 U.S.C. §§ 2000e-2000e-17 (2006)). But they do not, except in the minimal sense of *Trans World Airlines v. Hardison*, 432 U.S. 63 (1977), require recognition and amelioration based on protected characteristics.

In effect, such prohibitions insure that those irrelevant characteristics will not limit a person's employment opportunities. One commentator explains this concept by distinguishing among "contingent" equality (equality that depends upon the attitudes of third parties about a worker and not on her work), "intrinsic" equality (equality based upon the intrinsic ability of a person to perform a job), and "constructed" equality (equality created by legal dictates). John J. Donohue, III, Employment Discrimination Law in Perspective: Three Concepts of Equality, 92 Mich. L. Rev. 2583, 2585-86 (1994). To the extent these antidiscrimination laws focus employers' attentions on the actual fit between an employee and a job, they can be explained from an efficiency perspective.

Thus, they require employers properly to evaluate actual and potential employees without regard to irrelevant characteristics. In theory, this should lead to a workforce better able to perform the employers' tasks. Pamela S. Karlen & George Rutherglen, Disabilities, Discrimination, and Reasonable Accommodation, 46 Duke L.J. 1, 23-24 (1996). The antidiscrimination provisions in effect filter out irrelevant signals in the employment process and increase the employers' efficiency.

Least controversially, ADA Title I forbids discrimination against those "regarded as" having a disability. In that respect, it performs the same filtering function that traditional antidiscrimination law performs by removing misleading signals from the employers' information mix.

Title I also performs that function for people who actually have disabilities but who require no accommodations. Much research has shown that many people with disabilities require no, and often *de minimis* cost for, accommodations. In an early study of accommodations for the U.S. Department of Labor, of workers with disabilities, only 22% received some form of accommodations of which half cost nothing and more than 2/3 cost less than $100. U.S. Dep't of Labor, A Study of Accommodations Provided to Handicapped Employees by Federal Contractors: Final Report (1982) (prepared by Berkeley Planning Associates (contract no. J-E 1-0009)); *see* U.S. Comm'n on Civil Rights, *supra*, at 106-07 & nn. 24-29; Frederick C. Collignon, The Role of Reasonable Accommodation in Employing Disabled Persons in Private Industry, in Disability and the Labor Market: Economic Problems, Policies, and Programs 196, 215-16 (Monroe Berkowitz & M. Anne Hill, eds. 1986). However, other studies suggest this is overstated. *See generally* Thomas N. Chirikos, Will the Costs of Accommodating Workers with Disabilities Remain Low?, 17 Behav. Sci. & L. 93 (1999); Thomas N. Chirikos, The Economics of Employment, 69 Milbank Q. 150 (1991).

The issue is more complex when accommodations have a non-zero, above *de minimis*, cost. Arguably, even in this situation, a number of factors could render the statutory requirement efficient.

In the first place, the cost of the accommodation could be less than the increased efficiency or benefit realized by hiring a specific employee. In addition, studies support the proposition that employees with disabilities tend to be more stable workers, have lower turnover, less absenteeism and lower accident risks. Collignon, *supra*, at 208 n.9. This is not an unreasonable assumption in view of the fact that, once they have a job, people with disabilities may be less willing to lose that job to take another.

Certain accommodations also improve the productivity of other employees without disabilities, such as flexible work hours, audible as well as text based documentation, or large print and clearly-labeled storage. Moreover, there may be potential or actual employees with special skills that justify substantial accommodation expenses because others with similar skills are either hard to locate or rare in the labor force. Of course, this expense is no different than the huge costs of "accommodating" film stars or corporate chief executives – it is part of the pay.

Putting aside workers with unique skills and "spillover effects," any efficiency argument for hiring a group of people with disabilities assumes that there is not a parallel group of prospective employees with identical skills, who do not need to be accommodated. In general, that may be counterfactual.

Thus, as a purely theoretical matter, it would appear that one cannot use efficiency arguments to justify accommodation requirements. Karlen & Rutherglen, *supra*, at 24-25. That said, the issue is not purely one of theory: even in view of the minimal or zero costs of most accommodations, arguments based only on a theoretical pool of employees who require an employer to incur no additional costs arguably cannot answer the policy question.

Adopting a program of constructed equality assumes that an end other than efficiency has become the dominant policy goal. Donohue, *supra*, at 2609-10. Arguably, the ADA mandates such a program, at least in part, because people who require accommodations are not always economically equal to others from an employer's perspective.

One implicit assumption of requiring private enterprises to provide accommodation is that the costs of providing accommodations will be offset by the smaller government benefits paid to people with disabilities who will be employed and increased taxes from those workers (i.e., there will be a net gain). A variant on this assumption is that it is more efficient to have individual employers "run" this social welfare program, so that even if there are net costs, they are smaller than if the government ran the program. Yet another possible assumption is that a political decision has been made that costs and economic efficiency are dispensable (presumably within limits), if more people with disabilities are employed.

This accommodation requirement – an "accommodation mandate" as termed by Christine Jolls – departs from prior conceptualizations of discrimination. Robert L. Burgdorf, Jr., 'Substantially Limited' Protection from Disability Discrimination: The Special Treatment Model and Misconstructions of the Definition of Disability, 42 Vill. L. Rev. 409-509 (1997); S. A. Krenek, Beyond Reasonable Accommodation, 72 Tex. L. Rev. 1969, 1996-98 (1994); *see also* Christine Jolls, Accommodation Mandates, 53 Stan. L. Rev. 223 (2000).

Under pre-ADA discrimination theory, in the absence of discrimination, individuals who are equally productive should receive the same compensation (i.e., wages, benefits, and other rewards). This definition of discrimination does not consider employer investments in making some, but not all, workers more productive than they otherwise would be. Under the ADA, an employer must make affirmative changes in response to a qualified individual's needs so they may perform essential job functions. Jolls, *supra*, at 231-32; Mark Kelman, Market Discrimination and Groups, 53 Stan. L. Rev. 833, 834-55 (2001).

In *U.S. Airways, Inc. v. Barnett*, 535 U.S. 391 (2002), the Supreme Court summarized:

> [The ADA] seeks to diminish or to eliminate the stereotypical thought processes, the thoughtless actions, and the hostile reactions that far too often bar those with disabilities from participating fully in the Nation's life, including the workplace. These objectives demand unprejudiced thought and reasonable responsive reaction on the part of employers and fellow workers alike. They will *sometimes require affirmative conduct to promote entry of disabled people into the workforce. They do not, however, demand action beyond the realm of reasonable.*

Id. at 401 (citations omitted, emphasis added) (deciding that a job reassignment in violation of a company's seniority system would not be a "reasonable" accommodation). Moreover, "[t]he simple fact that an accommodation would provide a 'preference' – in the sense that it would permit a worker with a disability to violate a rule that others must obey – cannot, *in and of itself*, automatically show that the accommodation is not 'reasonable'." *Id.* at 398.

But economics cannot be ignored completely. Even if all employers follow the ADA to the letter, the argument may be made that because its requirements may raise employers' costs, they may lead to less overall employment and thus less employment of people with disabilities. Beyond that, any business that fails to provide accommodations to its employees has a price advantage over its competitors who do incur those costs.

Of course, there are documented positive effects of accommodations. First, there are certain tax incentives. *See infra* Part 8 for discussion; *see also* EEOC Facts About Disability-Related Tax Provisions: Disabled Access Tax Credit, http://www.eeoc.gov/facts/fs-disab.html (last visited October 22, 2013) (discussing 26 U.S.C. § 44, and Tax Deduction to Remove Architectural and Transportation Barriers to People with Disabilities and Elderly Individuals, 26 U.S.C. § 190, as applicable to the provision of accommodations by small businesses).

Second, there is evidence that some accommodations boost profits. President's Committee on Employment of People with Disabilities, Job Accommodation Network (JAN) Reports (Oct.-Dec. 1994) (for every dollar invested in an effective accommodation, companies sampled realized an average of $50 in benefits). Finally, one should not overlook that corporate culture and attitudes, in parallel with economic considerations, may motivate using accommodations. *See* Lisa Schur et al., Corporate Culture and the Employment of Persons with Disabilities, 23 Behav. Sci. & L. 3, 13-17 (2005); Lisa Schur et al., Is Disability Disabling in All Workplaces?: Disability, Workplace Disparities, and Corporate Culture, 48 Industrial Relations 381, 384-387 (2009).

Laws like the ADA are largely self-enforcing. Given the difficulties in enforcing any law as broadly applicable and as nuanced as the ADA, employers might not follow it to the letter and face no civil actions or governmental sanctions. Any real-world understanding of the ADA's impact must consider the effects of this differential compliance.

There is an alternative way to view accommodations. If the "average" worker is viewed as unimpaired, the work environment can be expected to build on assumptions that workers have no limitations on their abilities to see, hear, walk, climb stairs, lift, grasp door knobs, write, speak, and so on. This environment becomes the baseline – *the* appropriate, efficient manner to order work given the perceived characteristics of the average individual in the labor market.

Accommodations, thus, represent deviations from the presumptively efficient status quo necessitated by the appearance in the applicant pool, or in the workforce, of individuals with disabilities – individuals whose characteristics differ from those of the "model (able-bodied) worker" around whom the work environment was built. But this is one viewpoint. *See* Burgdorf, *supra*, at 530; cf. Harlan Hahn, Equality and the Environment: The Interpretation of "Reasonable Accommodations" in the Americans with Disabilities Act, 17 J. Rehab. Admin. 101, 103 (1993).

In Part 3, we will come back to the empirical research in this area. As you go through the rights and remedies in the intervening chapters, consider if the ADA's accommodation mandate is the best way to achieve its goals.

Part 2

Definitional Issues
Analysis

Chapter 3   DISABILITY
§ 3.1   Overview
§ 3.2   Actual Disability
    A.   Physical Or Mental Impairment
    B.   Substantially Limits
    C.   Major Life Activity
§ 3.3   Record Of A Disability
§ 3.4   Regarded As Having A Disability
Chapter 4   OTHER PROTECTIONS
§ 4.1   Association
§ 4.2   Retaliation
§ 4.3   Harassment
Chapter 5   QUALIFIED
§ 5.1   Prerequisites
§ 5.2   Essential Requirements
§ 5.3   Estoppel

Chapter 3   DISABILITY

§ 3.1   Overview

The ADA primarily protects individuals with disabilities.   A person is an individual with a disability if he or she falls into one of the following categories:

- An individual with an actual disability;

- An individual with a record of a disability; or

- An individual who is regarded or treated as if he or she has a disability ("regarded as").   42 U.S.C. § 12102(1)(A)-(C).

The definition of disability appears only in the definitional section of the ADA, 42 U.S.C. § 12102(1).   Therefore, the protected class does not vary among the five titles of the ADA.   In addition to having a disability, to be protected under Titles I and II of the ADA, an individual must be a qualified individual with a disability, that is, the individual must be capable of performing the essential functions of the job sought, or meet the essential eligibility requirements for the service or program, with or without a reasonable accommodation.   *Id.* §§ 12111(8), 12131(2).

Moreover, the ADA protects individuals from retaliation if they assert rights on behalf of individuals with disabilities or encourage or assist people with disabilities to assert their rights.   *Id.* § 12203.   Each title of the ADA specifies protection of individuals who associate with individuals with disabilities. *Id.* § 12112(b)(4); 28 C.F.R. §§ 35.130(g), 36.205 (2011).

The ADA definition of disability was taken directly from the definitions in Sections 501, 503, and 504 of the Rehabilitation Act of 1973. 29 U.S.C. § 705(9) (2006); Chai Feldblum, Definition of Disability Under the Federal Anti-Discrimination Law: What Happened? Why? And What Can We Do About It?, 21 Berkeley J. Emp. & Lab. L. 91, 91-92, 128-29 (2000). For nearly twenty years following the passage of the Rehabilitation Act, the regulatory agencies, courts, and even defendants applying the Act had taken a broad approach to the scope of coverage. In fact, courts rarely even reviewed the definitional language. *Id.* at 92.

> Just as courts hearing employment discrimination cases under Title VII [of the Civil Rights Act] never analyzed whether the plaintiff in a case was "really a woman," or "really black," courts hearing Section 504 cases rarely tarried long on the question of whether a plaintiff was "really a handicapped individual." Rather, as with Title VII cases, courts hearing Section 504 cases tended to focus on the essential causation requirement: i.e., had the plaintiff proven the alleged discriminatory action was taken solely *because of* his or her handicap.

Id. at 106 (emphasis added) (citations omitted).

Advocates lobbying for the ADA believed any individual with a serious illness or with a non-trivial impairment would be covered. *Id.* at 156-57. However, courts applying the ADA tended to focus on the limits of the protected class and avoid the question of whether the alleged discrimination was based on the impairment. This resulted in a narrow interpretation of the protection provided by the ADA. In response to the Supreme Court's interpretation of the ADA's definition of disability, disability advocates pursued a statutory amendment to the ADA, originally entitled the ADA Restoration Act and eventually re-named the ADA Amendments Act (ADAAA).

The ADAAA was introduced in the Senate and House of Representatives in 2007 and underwent substantial changes through consultation between national disability advocates and business interests. It was passed and signed into law on September 25, 2008 and became effective January 1, 2009. Pub. L. 110-325, 42 U.S.C.A. §12101 et seq. (2009).

The ADAAA purports to restore the original congressional intent to provide a broad definition of disability "to make it easier for people with disabilities to obtain protection under the ADA." 28 C.F.R. pt. 1630 app. The ADAAA expressly rejects the Supreme Court's decisions in *Sutton v. United Air Lines, Inc.*, 527 U.S. 471 (1999) and *Toyota Motor Mfg.*,

Kentucky, Inc. v. Williams, 534 U.S. 184 (2002), discussed below, and reinstates the reasoning of the Court in *School Board of Nassau County, Fla. v. Arline*, 480 U.S. 273 (1987). The ADAAA also amends the definition of disability in the Rehabilitation Act of 1973 to incorporate the amended ADA definition.

The EEOC promulgated regulations on the definition of disability which were published in the Federal Register on March 25, 2011. These regulations are designed to help implement the ADAAA, focusing on Congress's mandate that the definition of disability be construed broadly. The regulations make explicit that "[t]he primary object of attention in cases brought under the ADA should be whether covered entities have complied with their obligations and whether discrimination has occurred, not whether the individual meets the definition of disability. The question of whether an individual meets the definition of disability under this part should not be deemed part of the analysis." 29 C.F.R. § 16301.4.

§ 3.2 Actual Disability

According to the text of the ADA, "disability" means, with respect to an individual, "a physical or mental impairment that substantially limits one or more of the major life activities of such individual. . . ." 42 U.S.C. § 12102(2)(A) (2009). There are three requirements within this definition:

- A physical or mental impairment;

- A substantial limitation; and

- A major life activity.

The ADAAA does not change these three basic requirements. It does, however, command the courts to construe the key terms broadly, a key development given that much of the case law around the ADA from its passage through the passage of the ADAAA focused on the threshold issue of what qualifies as an actual disability.

A. *Physical Or Mental Impairment*

The statute does not define physical or mental impairment. The regulations define a physical impairment as "[a]ny physiological disorder or condition, cosmetic disfigurement, or anatomical loss affecting one or more body systems, such as meurological, musculoskeletal, special sense organs, respiratory (including speech organs), cardiovascular, reproductive, digestive, genitourinary, immune, circulatory, hemic, lymphatic, skin, and endocrine." 29 C.F.R. § 1630.2(h)(1). A mental impairment is defined by the regulations as "[a]ny mental or psychological disorder, such as an intellectual disability (formerly termed 'mental retardation'), organic brain syndrome, emotional or mental illness, and specific learning disabilities." *Id.* § 1630.2(h)(2).

Conditions, such as pregnancy or advanced age, which are not the result of a physiological disorder, are not covered. However, medical conditions associated with pregnancy or age may be impairments. 29 C.F.R. pt. 1630 app., § 1630.2(h). Predisposition to illness is not an impairment. *Id.*

Homosexuality, bisexuality, sexual behavior disorders, compulsive gambling, kleptomania, and pyromania are specifically excluded from coverage. 42 U.S.C. § 12211(a) (2009). Drug and alcohol addiction are covered. *Id.* § 12210. However, individuals who are currently using illegal drugs are specifically excluded from protection. *Id.* "Current" drug use is use "that occurred recently enough to justify a reasonable belief that a person's drug use is current or that continuing use is a real and ongoing problem." U.S. Dep't of Justice Title III Technical Assistance Manual § 2.3000 (Nov. 1993) ("TAM III"), http://www.usdoj.gov/crt/ada/taman3. html; U.S. Dep't of Justice Title II Technical Assistance Manual § 2.3000 ("TAM II"), http://www.usdoj.gov/crt/ada/taman2.html. Casual drug use is not protected. EEOC, Technical Assistance Manual: Title I of the ADA § 2.2(b) (Jan. 1992) ("TAM I").

B.   *Substantially Limits*

In the post-ADA period, the concept of substantially limits was frequently litigated. Most prominently, in *Sutton v. United Air Lines, Inc.*, the Supreme Court announced that the limiting effect of an impairment must be judged while using any "mitigating measures," such as medications or equipment that reduce the effect of an impairment. As will be discussed below, the ADAAA explicitly rejected the *Sutton* approach. Still, to understand how the law has evolved, it is important to consider the original *Sutton* decision, with the express caveat that it is no longer good law.

SUTTON v. UNITED AIR LINES INC.

Supreme Court of the United States, 1999
527 U.S. 471

* * *

Justice O'CONNOR delivered the opinion of the Court.

The Americans with Disabilities Act of 1990 (ADA or Act), 104 Stat. 328, 42 U.S.C. § 12101 *et seq.*, prohibits certain employers from discriminating against individuals on the basis of their disabilities. See § 12112(a). Petitioners challenge the dismissal of their ADA action for failure to state a claim upon which relief can be granted. We conclude that the complaint was properly dismissed. In reaching that result, we hold that the determination of whether an individual is disabled should be made with reference to measures that mitigate the individual's

impairment, including, in this instance, eyeglasses and contact lenses.
* * *

I

* * *

Petitioners are twin sisters, both of whom have severe myopia. Each petitioner's uncorrected visual acuity is 20/200 or worse in her right eye and 20/400 or worse in her left eye, but "[w]ith the use of corrective lenses, each . . . has vision that is 20/20 or better." Consequently, without corrective lenses, each "effectively cannot see to conduct numerous activities such as driving a vehicle, watching television or shopping in public stores," but with corrective measures, such as glasses or contact lenses, both "function identically to individuals without a similar impairment."

In 1992, petitioners applied to respondent for employment as commercial airline pilots. They met respondent's basic age, education, experience, and Federal Aviation Administration certification qualifications. After submitting their applications for employment, both petitioners were invited by respondent to an interview and to flight simulator tests. Both were told during their interviews, however, that a mistake had been made in inviting them to interview because petitioners did not meet respondent's minimum vision requirement, which was uncorrected visual acuity of 20/100 or better. Due to their failure to meet this requirement, petitioners' interviews were terminated, and neither was offered a pilot position.

In light of respondent's proffered reason for rejecting them, petitioners filed a charge of disability discrimination under the ADA with the Equal Employment Opportunity Commission (EEOC). After receiving a right to sue letter, petitioners filed suit in the United States District Court for the District of Colorado, alleging that respondent had discriminated against them "on the basis of their disability, or because [respondent] regarded [petitioners] as having a disability" in violation of the ADA. Specifically, petitioners alleged that due to their severe myopia they actually have a substantially limiting impairment or are regarded as having such an impairment, and are thus disabled under the Act.

The District Court . . . held that they were not actually substantially limited in any major life activity and thus had not stated a claim that they were disabled within the meaning of the ADA. * * * Employing similar logic, the Court of Appeals for the Tenth Circuit affirmed the District Court's judgment.

* * *

III

[W]e turn first to the question whether petitioners have stated a claim under subsection (A) of the disability definition, that is, whether they have alleged that they possess a physical impairment that substantially limits them in one or more major life activities. See 42 U.S.C. § 12102(2)(A). Because petitioners allege that with corrective measures their vision "is 20/20 or better," they are not actually disabled within the meaning of the Act if the "disability" determination is made with reference to these measures. Consequently, with respect to subsection (A) of the disability definition, our decision turns on whether disability is to be determined with or without reference to corrective measures.

Petitioners maintain that whether an impairment is substantially limiting should be determined without regard to corrective measures. They argue that, because the ADA does not directly address the question at hand, the Court should defer to the agency interpretations of the statute, which are embodied in the agency guidelines issued by the EEOC and the Department of Justice. These guidelines specifically direct that the determination of whether an individual is substantially limited in a major life activity be made without regard to mitigating measures. See 29 C.F.R. pt. 1630 app., § 1630.2(j); 28 C.F.R. pt. 35, App. A, § 35.104 (1998); 28 C.F.R. pt. 36, App. B, § 36.104.

Respondent, in turn, maintains that an impairment does not substantially limit a major life activity if it is corrected. It argues that the Court should not defer to the agency guidelines cited by petitioners because the guidelines conflict with the plain meaning of the ADA. The phrase "substantially limits one or more major life activities," it explains, requires that the substantial limitations actually and presently exist. Moreover, respondent argues, disregarding mitigating measures taken by an individual defies the statutory command to examine the effect of the impairment on the major life activities "of such individual." And even if the statute is ambiguous, respondent claims, the guidelines' directive to ignore mitigating measures is not reasonable, and thus this Court should not defer to it.

We conclude that respondent is correct that the approach adopted by the agency guidelines – that persons are to be evaluated in their hypothetical uncorrected state – is an impermissible interpretation of the ADA. Looking at the Act as a whole, it is apparent that if a person is taking measures to correct for, or mitigate, a physical or mental impairment, the effects of those measures – both positive and negative – must be taken into account when judging whether that person is "substantially limited" in a major life activity and thus "disabled" under the Act. Justice STEVENS relies on the legislative history of the ADA for the contrary proposition that individuals should be examined in their uncorrected state. Because we decide that, by its terms, the ADA cannot be read in this manner, we have no reason to consider the ADA's legislative history.

Three separate provisions of the ADA, read in concert, lead us to this conclusion. The Act defines a "disability" as "a physical or mental impairment that *substantially limits* one or more of the major life activities" of an individual. § 12102(2)(A) (emphasis added). Because the phrase "substantially limits" appears in the Act in the present indicative verb form, we think the language is properly read as requiring that a person be presently – not potentially or hypothetically – substantially limited in order to demonstrate a disability. A "disability" exists only where an impairment "substantially limits" a major life activity, not where it "might," "could," or "would" be substantially limiting if mitigating measures were not taken. A person whose physical or mental impairment is corrected by medication or other measures does not have an impairment that presently "substantially limits" a major life activity. To be sure, a person whose physical or mental impairment is corrected by mitigating measures still has an impairment, but if the impairment is corrected it does not "substantially limi[t]" a major life activity.

The definition of disability also requires that disabilities be evaluated "with respect to an individual" and be determined based on whether an impairment substantially limits the "major life activities of such individual." § 12102(2). Thus, whether a person has a disability under the ADA is an individualized inquiry. See *Bragdon v. Abbott*, 524 U.S. 624, 641-642 (1998) (declining to consider whether HIV infection is a *per se* disability under the ADA); 29 C.F.R. pt. 1630, App. § 1630.2(j) ("The determination of whether an individual has a disability is not necessarily based on the name or diagnosis of the impairment the person has, but rather on the effect of that impairment on the life of the individual").

The agency guidelines' directive that persons be judged in their uncorrected or unmitigated state runs directly counter to the individualized inquiry mandated by the ADA. The agency approach would often require courts and employers to speculate about a person's condition and would, in many cases, force them to make a disability determination based on general information about how an uncorrected impairment usually affects individuals, rather than on the individual's actual condition. For instance, under this view, courts would almost certainly find all diabetics to be disabled, because if they failed to monitor their blood sugar levels and administer insulin, they would almost certainly be substantially limited in one or more major life activities. A diabetic whose illness does not impair his or her daily activities would therefore be considered disabled simply because he or she has diabetes. Thus, the guidelines approach would create a system in which persons often must be treated as members of a group of people with similar impairments, rather than as individuals. This is contrary to both the letter and the spirit of the ADA.

* * *

The dissents suggest that viewing individuals in their corrected state will exclude from the definition of "disab[led]" those who use prosthetic limbs, or take medicine for epilepsy or high blood pressure. This suggestion is incorrect. The use of a corrective device does not, by itself, relieve one's disability. Rather, one has a disability under subsection (A) if, notwithstanding the use of a corrective device, that individual is substantially limited in a major life activity. * * *

Applying this reading of the Act to the case at hand, we conclude that the Court of Appeals correctly resolved the issue of disability in respondent's favor. As noted above, petitioners allege that with corrective measures, their visual acuity is 20/20, and that they "function identically to individuals without a similar impairment." In addition, petitioners concede that they "do not argue that the use of corrective lenses in itself demonstrates a substantially limiting impairment." Accordingly, because we decide that disability under the Act is to be determined with reference to corrective measures, we agree with the courts below that petitioners have not stated a claim that they are substantially limited in any major life activity.

* * *

For these reasons, the judgment of the Court of Appeals for the Tenth Circuit is affirmed.

* * *

Justice STEVENS, with whom Justice BREYER joins, dissenting.

When it enacted the Americans with Disabilities Act of 1990 (ADA or Act), Congress certainly did not intend to require United Air Lines to hire unsafe or unqualified pilots. Nor, in all likelihood, did it view every person who wears glasses as a member of a "discrete and insular minority." Indeed, by reason of legislative myopia it may not have foreseen that its definition of "disability" might theoretically encompass, not just "some 43,000,000 Americans," 42 U.S.C. § 12101(a)(1), but perhaps two or three times that number. Nevertheless, if we apply customary tools of statutory construction, it is quite clear that the threshold question whether an individual is "disabled" within the meaning of the Act – and, therefore, is entitled to the basic assurances that the Act affords – focuses on her past or present physical condition without regard to mitigation that has resulted from rehabilitation, self-improvement, prosthetic devices, or medication. One might reasonably argue that the general rule should not apply to an impairment that merely requires a nearsighted person to wear glasses. But I believe that, in order to be faithful to the remedial purpose of the Act, we should give it a generous, rather than a miserly, construction.

There are really two parts to the question of statutory construction presented by this case. The first question is whether the determination of disability for people that Congress unquestionably intended to cover should focus on their unmitigated or their mitigated condition. If the correct answer to that question is the one provided by eight of the nine Federal Courts of Appeals to address the issue, and by all three of the Executive agencies that have issued regulations or interpretive bulletins construing the statute – namely, that the statute defines "disability" without regard to ameliorative measures – it would still be necessary to decide whether that general rule should be applied to what might be characterized as a "minor, trivial impairment." * * * I shall therefore first consider impairments that Congress surely had in mind before turning to the special facts of this case.

I

"As in all cases of statutory construction, our task is to interpret the words of [the statute] in light of the purposes Congress sought to serve." * * * Congress expressly provided that the "purpose of [the ADA is] to provide a clear and comprehensive national mandate for the elimination of discrimination against individuals with disabilities." 42 U.S.C. § 12101(b)(1). To that end, the ADA prohibits covered employers from "discriminat[ing] against a qualified individual *with a disability* because of the disability" in regard to the terms, conditions, and privileges of employment. 42 U.S.C. § 12112(a) (emphasis added).

The Act's definition of disability is drawn "almost verbatim" from the Rehabilitation Act of 1973, 29 U.S.C. § 706(8)(B). *Bragdon v. Abbott*, 524 U.S. 624, 631 (1998). [The dissent quotes the statute.]

The three parts of this definition do not identify mutually exclusive, discrete categories. On the contrary, they furnish three overlapping formulas aimed at ensuring that individuals who now have, or ever had, a substantially limiting impairment are covered by the Act.

An example of a rather common condition illustrates this point: There are many individuals who have lost one or more limbs in industrial accidents, or perhaps in the service of their country in places like Iwo Jima. With the aid of prostheses, coupled with courageous determination and physical therapy, many of these hardy individuals can perform all of their major life activities just as efficiently as an average couch potato. If the Act were just concerned with their present ability to participate in society, many of these individuals' physical impairments would not be viewed as disabilities. Similarly, if the statute were solely concerned with whether these individuals viewed themselves as disabled – or with whether a majority of employers regarded them as unable to perform most jobs – many of these individuals would lack statutory protection from discrimination based on their prostheses.

The sweep of the statute's three-pronged definition, however, makes it pellucidly clear that Congress intended the Act to cover such persons. The fact that a prosthetic device, such as an artificial leg, has restored one's ability to perform major life activities surely cannot mean that subsection (A) of the definition is inapplicable. Nor should the fact that the individual considers himself (or actually is) "cured," or that a prospective employer considers him generally employable, mean that subsections (B) or (C) are inapplicable. But under the Court's emphasis on "the present indicative verb form" used in subsection (A), that subsection presumably would not apply. And under the Court's focus on the individual's "presen[t] – not potentia[l] or hypothetica[l]" – condition, and on whether a person is "precluded from a broad range of jobs," subsections (B) and (C) presumably would not apply.

In my view, when an employer refuses to hire the individual "because of" his prosthesis, and the prosthesis in no way affects his ability to do the job, that employer has unquestionably discriminated against the individual in violation of the Act. Subsection (B) of the definition, in fact, sheds a revelatory light on the question whether Congress was concerned only about the corrected or mitigated status of a person's impairment. If the Court is correct that "[a] 'disability' exists only where" a person's "present" or "actual" condition is substantially impaired, there would be no reason to include in the protected class those who were once disabled but who are now fully recovered. Subsection (B) of the Act's definition, however, plainly covers a person who previously had a serious hearing impairment that has since been completely cured. See *School Bd. of Nassau Cty. v. Arline*, 480 U.S. 273, 281 (1987). Still, if I correctly understand the Court's opinion, it holds that one who continues to wear a hearing aid that she has worn all her life might not be covered – fully cured impairments are covered, but merely treatable ones are not. The text of the Act surely does not require such a bizarre result.

The three prongs of the statute, rather, are most plausibly read together not to inquire into whether a person is currently "functionally" limited in a major life activity, but only into the existence of an impairment – present or past – that substantially limits, or did so limit, the individual before amelioration. This reading avoids the counterintuitive conclusion that the ADA's safeguards vanish when individuals make themselves more employable by ascertaining ways to overcome their physical or mental limitations.

* * *

II

* * *

I do not mean to suggest, of course, that the ADA should be read to prohibit discrimination on the basis of, say, blue eyes, deformed fingernails, or heights of less than six feet. Those conditions, to the extent that they are even "impairments," do not substantially limit individuals in any condition and thus are different in kind from the impairment in the case before us. While not all eyesight that can be enhanced by glasses is substantially limiting, having 20/200 vision in one's better eye is, without treatment, a significant hindrance. Only two percent of the population suffers from such myopia. Such acuity precludes a person from driving, shopping in a public store, or viewing a computer screen from a reasonable distance. Uncorrected vision, therefore, can be "substantially limiting" in the same way that unmedicated epilepsy or diabetes can be. Because Congress obviously intended to include individuals with the latter impairments in the Act's protected class, we should give petitioners the same protection.

III

[The dissent rejects the majority's position that judging the plaintiffs on the basis of whether they were disabled "is necessary to avoid requiring courts to 'speculate' about a person's 'hypothetical' condition and to preserve the Act's focus on making 'individualized inquiries' into whether a person is disabled."]

Ironically, it is the Court's approach that actually condones treating individuals merely as members of groups. That misdirected approach permits any employer to dismiss out of hand every person who has uncorrected eyesight worse than 20/100 without regard to the specific qualifications of those individuals or the extent of their abilities to overcome their impairment. In much the same way, the Court's approach would seem to allow an employer to refuse to hire every person who has epilepsy or diabetes that is controlled by medication, or every person who functions efficiently with a prosthetic limb.

Under the Court's reasoning, an employer apparently could not refuse to hire persons with these impairments who are substantially limited even with medication, but that group-based "exception" is more perverse still. Since the purpose of the ADA is to dismantle employment barriers based on society's accumulated myths and fears, see Arline, 480 U.S., at 283-284, it is especially ironic to deny protection for persons with substantially limiting impairments that, when corrected, render them fully able and employable. Insofar as the Court assumes that the majority of individuals with impairments such as prosthetic limbs or epilepsy will still be covered under its approach because they are substantially limited "notwithstanding the use of a corrective device," I respectfully disagree as an empirical matter. Although it is of course true that some of these individuals are substantially limited in any condition, Congress enacted the ADA in part because such individuals are *not* ordinarily substantially limited in their mitigated condition, but rather are often the victims of "stereotypic assumptions not truly indicative of the individual ability of such individuals to participate in, and contribute to, society." 42 U.S.C. § 12101(a)(7).

It has also been suggested that if we treat as "disabilities" impairments that may be mitigated by measures as ordinary and expedient as wearing eyeglasses, a flood of litigation will ensue. The suggestion is misguided. Although vision is of critical importance for airline pilots, in most segments of the economy whether an employee wears glasses – or uses any of several other mitigating measures – is a matter of complete indifference to employers. It is difficult to envision many situations in which a qualified employee who needs glasses to perform her job might be fired – as the statute requires – "because of," § 12112, the fact that she cannot see well without them. Such a proposition would be ridiculous in the garden-variety case. On the other hand, if an accounting firm, for example, adopted a guideline refusing to hire any incoming accountant who has uncorrected vision of less than 20/100 – or, by the same token, any person who is unable without medication to avoid having seizures – such a rule would seem to be the essence of invidious discrimination.

In this case the quality of petitioners' uncorrected vision is relevant only because the airline regards the ability to see without glasses as an employment qualification for its pilots. Presumably it would not insist on such a qualification unless it has a sound business justification for doing so (an issue we do not address today). But if United regards petitioners as unqualified because they cannot see well without glasses, it seems eminently fair for a court also to use uncorrected vision as the basis for evaluating petitioners' life activity of seeing.

* * *

IV

* * *

Accordingly, although I express no opinion on the ultimate merits of petitioners' claim, I am persuaded that they have a disability covered by the ADA. I therefore respectfully *dissent*.

୭

The ADAAA explicitly rejected the *Sutton* approach, stating as its purpose, "to reject the requirement enunciated by the Supreme Court in Sutton v. United Airlines, Inc., 527 U.S. 471 (1999) and its companion cases that whether an impairment substantially limits a major life activity is to be determined with reference to the ameliorative effects of mitigating measures." 42 U.S.C. § 12101 note, quoting ADAAA § 2(b)(2).

The ADAAA provides a rule of construction specifying that "the term 'substantially limits' shall be interpreted consistently with the findings and purpose of the ADA Amendments Act of 2008." 42 U.S.C. § 12102(4)(B). The findings and purposes specifically reject the Equal Employment Opportunity Commission's (EEOC) regulations interpreting "substantially limits" under the original ADA to mean "significantly restricted." 42 U.S.C. § 12101(a)(8). Instead, under the ADAAA, "substantially limits" must be construed so that it "is not . . . a demanding standard." 29 C.F.R. 1630.2(j)(1)(ii) (2012). Rather, the phrase must be "construed broadly in favor of expansive coverage." *Id.* Congress's goal was to change the focus from the "threshold inquiry" of whether an individual is disabled to the "primary issue" of whether the individual experienced discrimination because of an actual or perceived disability. 29 C.F.R. pt. 1630 app., 29 C.F.R. § 1630.2(j)(1)(ii) (2012).

Under the EEOC's regulations implementing the ADAAA, "[a]n impairment is a disability . . . if it substantially limits the ability of an individual to perform a major life activity as compared to most people in the general population." 29 C.F.R. § 1630.2(j)(1)(ii) (2012). "An impairment need not prevent, or significantly or severely restrict, the individual from performing a major life activity in order to be considered substantially limiting." *Id.* Moreover, the determination of whether an impairment substantially limits a major life activity "usually will not require scientific, medical, or statistical analysis." *Id.* § 1630.2(j)(1)(v).

Certain impairments "will, as a factual matter, virtually always be found to impose a substantial limitation on a major life activity." *Id.* § 1630.2(j)(3)(ii). Thus, for example, deafness, blindness, intellectual disabilities, mobility limitations requiring the use of a wheelchair will almost certainly satisfy the "substantial limitation" requirement. Moreover, conditions like cancer, diabetes, autism, cerebral palsy, epilepsy, Human Immunodeficiency Virus (HIV) infection, major depressive disorder, bipolar disorder, post-traumatic stress disorder, obsessive compulsive disorder, and schizophrenia also fall into this "virtually always" category. *Id.* § 1630.2(j)(3)(iii).

The factors that may be considered in determining whether an impairment is substantially limiting include, as compared to the general population:

(i) The condition under which the individual performs the major life activity;

(ii) The manner in which the individual performs the major life activity;

(iii) The duration of time it takes the individual to perform the major life activity, or for which the individual can perform the major life activity.

29 C.F.R. § 1630.2(j)(4)(i)-(ii). This may include, among other things, consideration of (1) the difficulty, effort, or time required to perform a major life activity; (2) pain experienced when performing a major life activity; (3) the length of time a major life activity can be performed; (4) the way an impairment affects the operation of a major bodily function, and/or (5) the non-ameliorative effects of mitigating measures, such as negative side effects of medication or burdens associated with following a particular treatment regimen. *Id.*

Short-term temporary impairments without long-term effects are unlikely to be considered substantial. The ADAAA specifies that, for purposes of the "regarded as" prong of the definition of disability, transitory and minor impairments are not covered and specifies that an impairment is transitory if it has an actual or expected duration of six months or less. 42 U.S.C. § 12102(3) (2009); 29 C.F.R. 1630.15(f) (2011). Although this provision applies only to individuals who are "regarded as" having a disability, the six-month limitation may be considered when applying the definition of actual disability. The legislative history of the ADAAA indicates that "A similar exception for the first two prongs of the definition is unnecessary as the functional limitation requirement already excludes claims by individuals with ailments that are minor or short term." Statement of the Managers to Accompany the Americans with Disabilities Act Amendments Act of 2008, Cong. Rec. S8840, S8842 (Sept. 16, 2008). This may be why the implementing regulations specifically provide that the six-month transitory portion of the "transitory and minor" exception does not apply to the actual disability or record of disability prongs. "The effects of an impairment lasting or expected to last fewer than six months can be substantially limiting within the meaning of this section." 29 C.F.R. § 1630.20(j)(1)(ix) (2012).

1.   Individualized inquiry

The determination of whether an impairment substantially limits a person's major life activities is an *individualized* inquiry. Professor Chai Feldblum, however, argues that individualized assessment of a substantial limitation was not foreseen or intended by the drafters of the ADA. Feldblum, Definition of Disability Under the Federal Anti-Discrimination Law: What Happened? Why? And What Can We Do About It?, 21 Berkeley J. Emp. & Lab. L. 91, 151-52 (2000). The individualized inquiry examines the impairment's effect on the individual as of the time of the alleged discrimination, rather than relying on the general medical diagnosis or the average, general, or usual effect. This individualized assessment necessarily leads to different results for individuals with the same impairment.

2.   Mitigation

Impairments often do not exist in a vacuum. Medical science offers a vast array of ways for people to mitigate their impairments. This may be as simple as a pair of eyeglasses, or as complicated as a prosthetic limb. How do these mitigating measures play into the definition of disability analysis?

The ADAAA provides that most mitigating measures must not be considered in determining whether an impairment substantially limits a major life activity. However, Congress took pains not to extend protection to everyone who uses ordinary glasses or contact lenses. The ADAAA provides:

> (E)(i)   The determination of whether an impairment substantially limits a major life activity shall be made

without regard to the ameliorative effects of mitigating measures such as –

      (I)   medication, medical supplies, equipment, or appliances, low-vision devices (which do not include ordinary eyeglasses or contact lenses), prosthetics including limbs and devices, hearing aids and cochlear implants or other implantable hearing devices, mobility devices, or oxygen therapy equipment and supplies;

      (II)   use of assistive technology;

      (III) reasonable accommodations or auxiliary aids or services; or

      (IV) learned behavioral or adaptive neurological modifications.

      (ii)   The ameliorative effects of the mitigating measures of ordinary eyeglasses or contact lenses shall be considered in determining whether an impairment substantially limits a major life activity.

      (iii) As used in this subparagraph –

      (I)   the term "ordinary eyeglasses or contact lenses" means lenses that are intended to fully correct visual acuity or eliminate refractive error; and

      (II)   the term "low-vision devices" means devices that magnify, enhance, or otherwise augment a visual image.

42 U.S.C. § 12102(4) (2009).

Although the ADAAA excludes individuals who use ordinary eyeglasses or contact lenses from protection, it does provide them some ability to challenge qualification standards and exams that exclude them from employment:

(c) Qualification Standards and Tests Related to Uncorrected Vision – Notwithstanding section 3(4)(E)(ii), a covered entity shall not use qualification standards, employment tests, or other selection criteria based on an individual's uncorrected vision unless the standard, test, or other selection criteria, as used by the covered entity, is shown to be job-related for the position in question and consistent with business necessity.

Id. § 12113(c).

Has the ADAAA found the correct balance between providing broad protection for people with disabilities and avoiding over-inclusion of individuals with insubstantial impairments?

Notes & Questions

1. What distinguishes disability civil rights from race or gender civil rights, which cover both men and women and majority as well as minority communities? Is it necessary to limit the size of the group protected by the disability civil rights laws? Is disability discrimination more like age discrimination, which is presumed only to happen to people over age 40? Should coverage be broader when prohibiting exclusion, segregation, and the like and narrower when requiring affirmative activities such as reasonable accommodation?

2. Should the individual effect of a protected trait have any relevance to whether a person is entitled to protection from discrimination? Should race and gender civil rights protections be limited according to the amount of minority ancestry one has or the level of testosterone one carries? Why is disability treated differently?

3. Should a person with no disability have a "reverse discrimination" claim, for example, if she is rejected for a job in favor of a less qualified person with a disability? The ADAAA specifically prohibits such reverse discrimination claims, providing "(g) CLAIMS OF NO DISABILITY. – Nothing in this Act shall provide the basis for a claim by an individual without a disability S. 3406-6 that the individual was subject to discrimination because of the individual's lack of disability." 42 U.S.C. § 12201(g) (2009); 29 C.F.R. § 1630.4(b) (2011).

4. The majority in *Sutton* states that individuals may still be substantially limited in the life activities of walking or running, even while using mitigating equipment. Would a runner who uses a prosthetic limb, but can nonetheless run faster than most nondisabled nonathletes, be considered disabled if a prospective employer refused to hire her for a job that included walking? Consider the case of Oscar Pistorius, a double amputee who sparked a controversy over whether he should be allowed to qualify for the Olympics, because his prosthetics might give him an unfair advantage over nondisabled athletes. Should he be considered a person with a disability? Does it matter whether he claims discrimination by the Olympics if they excluded him or whether he claims discrimination by an employer who refuses to hire him? *See* "Victory for Pistorius Gives Paralympians Hope," Int'l. Herald Trib., 2008 WLNR 9430943 (May 19, 2008).

5. The Court relies heavily on a belief that protecting people who wear eyeglasses would far exceed the statute's finding that there were 43 million people with disabilities in the United States. How much weight should be given to such a Congressional finding? *See* Feldblum, *supra*, at 154 (indicating that the 43 million figure was not extensively researched or considered during the enactment of the ADA). Professor Ruth Colker estimates that the Court's interpretation of the definition of disability has reduced the number of protected individuals from 43 million to approximately 14 million. Ruth Colker, The Mythic 43 Million Americans

The Court of Appeals affirmed. It held respondent's HIV infection was a disability under the ADA, even though her infection had not yet progressed to the symptomatic stage. * * *

II

We first review the ruling that respondent's HIV infection constituted a disability under the ADA. The statute defines disability as:

"(A) a physical or mental impairment that substantially limits one or more of the major life activities of such individual;

"(B) a record of such an impairment; or

"(C) being regarded as having such an impairment." § 12102(2).

We hold respondent's HIV infection was a disability under subsection (A) of the definitional section of the statute. In light of this conclusion, we need not consider the applicability of subsections (B) or (C).

Our consideration of subsection (A) of the definition proceeds in three steps. First, we consider whether respondent's HIV infection was a physical impairment. Second, we identify the life activity upon which respondent relies (reproduction and childbearing) and determine whether it constitutes a major life activity under the ADA. Third, tying the two statutory phrases together, we ask whether the impairment substantially limited the major life activity. In construing the statute, we are informed by interpretations of parallel definitions in previous statutes and the views of various administrative agencies which have faced this interpretive question.

A

The ADA's definition of disability is drawn almost verbatim from the definition of "handicapped individual" included in the Rehabilitation Act of 1973, as amended, 29 U.S.C. § 706(8)(B) (1988 ed.), and the definition of "handicap" contained in the Fair Housing Amendments Act of 1988, 42 U.S.C. § 3602(h)(1) (1988 ed.). Congress' repetition of a well-established term carries the implication that Congress intended the term to be construed in accordance with pre-existing regulatory interpretations. * * *

The directive requires us to construe the ADA to grant at least as much protection as provided by the regulations implementing the Rehabilitation Act.

1

The first step in the inquiry under subsection (A) requires us to determine whether respondent's condition constituted a physical impairment. The Department of Health, Education and Welfare (HEW) issued the first regulations interpreting the Rehabilitation Act in 1977. The regulations are of particular significance because, at the time, HEW was the agency responsible for coordinating the implementation and enforcement of § 504 of that statute. *Consolidated Rail Corporation v. Darrone*, 465 U.S. 624, 634 (1984) (citing Exec. Order No. 11914, 3 C.F.R. § 117 (1976-1980 Comp.)). Section 504 prohibits discrimination against individuals with disabilities by recipients of federal financial assistance. 29 U.S.C. § 794. The HEW regulations, which appear without change in the current regulations issued by the Department of Health and Human Services, define "physical or mental impairment" to mean:

> "(A) any physiological disorder or condition, cosmetic disfigurement, or anatomical loss affecting one or more of the following body systems: neurological; musculoskeletal; special sense organs; respiratory, including speech organs; cardiovascular; reproductive, digestive, genito-urinary; hemic and lymphatic; skin; and endocrine; or

> * * *

In issuing these regulations, HEW decided against including a list of disorders constituting physical or mental impairments, out of concern that any specific enumeration might not be comprehensive. 42 Fed. Reg. 22685 (1977), reprinted in 45 C.F.R. pt. 84, App. A, p. 334 (1997). The commentary accompanying the regulations, however, contains a representative list of disorders and conditions constituting physical impairments, including "such diseases and conditions as orthopedic, visual, speech, and hearing impairments, cerebral palsy, epilepsy, muscular dystrophy, multiple sclerosis, cancer, heart disease, diabetes, mental retardation, emotional illness, and ... drug addiction and alcoholism." *Ibid.*

* * *

HIV infection is not included in the list of specific disorders constituting physical impairments, in part because HIV was not identified as the cause of AIDS until 1983. * * * HIV infection does fall well within the general definition set forth by the regulations, however.

The disease follows a predictable and, as of today, an unalterable course. * * *

The initial stage of HIV infection is known as acute or primary HIV infection. In a typical case, this stage lasts three months. The virus concentrates in the blood. The assault on the immune system is immediate. The victim suffers from a sudden and serious decline in the number of white blood cells. There is no latency period.

* * *

After the symptoms associated with the initial stage subside, the disease enters what is referred to sometimes as its asymptomatic phase.

* * * Although it varies with each individual, in most instances this stage lasts from 7 to 11 years. The virus now tends to concentrate in the lymph nodes, though low levels of the virus continue to appear in the blood. * * *

In light of the immediacy with which the virus begins to damage the infected person's white blood cells and the severity of the disease, we hold it is an impairment from the moment of infection. As noted earlier, infection with HIV causes immediate abnormalities in a person's blood, and the infected person's white cell count continues to drop throughout the course of the disease, even when the attack is concentrated in the lymph nodes. In light of these facts, HIV infection must be regarded as a physiological disorder with a constant and detrimental effect on the infected person's hemic and lymphatic systems from the moment of infection. HIV infection satisfies the statutory and regulatory definition of a physical impairment during every stage of the disease.

2

The statute is not operative, and the definition not satisfied, unless the impairment affects a major life activity. Respondent's claim throughout this case has been that the HIV infection placed a substantial limitation on her ability to reproduce and to bear children. Given the pervasive, and invariably fatal, course of the disease, its effect on major life activities of many sorts might have been relevant to our inquiry. * * *

From the outset, however, the case has been treated as one in which reproduction was the major life activity limited by the impairment. It is our practice to decide cases on the grounds raised and considered in the Court of Appeals and included in the question on which we granted certiorari. * * * We ask, then, whether reproduction is a major life activity.

We have little difficulty concluding that it is. As the Court of Appeals held, "[t]he plain meaning of the word 'major' denotes comparative importance" and "suggest[s] that the touchstone for determining an activity's inclusion under the statutory rubric is its significance." Reproduction falls well within the phrase "major life activity." Reproduction and the sexual dynamics surrounding it are central to the life process itself.

While petitioner concedes the importance of reproduction, he claims that Congress intended the ADA only to cover those aspects of a person's life which have a public, economic, or daily character. The argument founders on the statutory language. Nothing in the definition suggests that activities without a public, economic, or daily dimension may somehow be regarded as so unimportant or insignificant as to fall outside the meaning of the word "major." The breadth of the term confounds the attempt to limit its construction in this manner.

As we have noted, the ADA must be construed to be consistent with regulations issued to implement the Rehabilitation Act. See 42 U.S.C. § 12201(a). Rather than enunciating a general principle for determining what is and is not a major life activity, the Rehabilitation Act regulations instead provide a representative list, defining the term to include "functions such as caring for one's self, performing manual tasks, walking, seeing, hearing, speaking, breathing, learning, and working." 45 C.F.R. § 84.3(j)(2)(ii) (1997); 28 C.F.R. § 41.31(b)(2) (1997). As the use of the term "such as" confirms, the list is illustrative, not exhaustive.

These regulations are contrary to petitioner's attempt to limit the meaning of the term "major" to public activities. The inclusion of activities such as caring for one's self and performing manual tasks belies the suggestion that a task must have a public or economic character in order to be a major life activity for purposes of the ADA. On the contrary, the Rehabilitation Act regulations support the inclusion of reproduction as a major life activity, since reproduction could not be regarded as any less important than working and learning. Petitioner advances no credible basis for confining major life activities to those with a public, economic, or daily aspect. In the absence of any reason to reach a contrary conclusion, we agree with the Court of Appeals' determination that reproduction is a major life activity for the purposes of the ADA.

3

The final element of the disability definition in subsection (A) is whether respondent's physical impairment was a substantial limit on the major life activity she asserts. The Rehabilitation Act regulations provide no additional guidance. 45 C.F.R. pt. 84, App. A, p. 334 (1997).

Our evaluation of the medical evidence leads us to conclude that respondent's infection substantially limited her ability to reproduce in two independent ways. First, a woman infected with HIV who tries to conceive a child imposes on the man a significant risk of becoming infected. The cumulative results of 13 studies collected in a 1994 textbook on AIDS indicates that 20% of male partners of women with HIV became HIV-positive themselves, with a majority of the studies finding a statistically significant risk of infection. * * *

Second, an infected woman risks infecting her child during gestation and childbirth, *i.e.*, perinatal transmission. Petitioner concedes that women infected with HIV face about a 25% risk of transmitting the virus to their children. Published reports available in 1994 confirm the accuracy of this statistic. * * *

Petitioner points to evidence in the record suggesting that antiretroviral therapy can lower the risk of perinatal transmission to about 8%. * * * The United States questions the relevance of the 8% figure, pointing to regulatory language requiring the substantiality of a limitation to be assessed without regard to available mitigating measures. 29 C.F.R. pt. 1630, App., p. 351 (1997)). We need not resolve this dispute in order to decide this case, however. It cannot be said as a matter of law that an 8% risk of transmitting a dread and fatal disease to one's child does not represent a substantial limitation on reproduction.

The Act addresses substantial limitations on major life activities, not utter inabilities. Conception and childbirth are not impossible for an HIV victim but, without doubt, are dangerous to the public health. This meets the definition of a substantial limitation. The decision to reproduce carries economic and legal consequences as well. There are added costs for antiretroviral therapy, supplemental insurance, and long-term health care for the child who must be examined and, tragic to think, treated for the infection. The laws of some States, moreover, forbid persons infected with HIV to have sex with others, regardless of consent. * * *

In the end, the disability definition does not turn on personal choice. When significant limitations result from the impairment, the definition is met even if the difficulties are not insurmountable. For the statistical and other reasons we have cited, of course, the limitations on reproduction may be insurmountable here. Testimony from the respondent that her HIV infection controlled her decision not to have a child is unchallenged. In the context of reviewing summary judgment, we must take it to be true. Fed. R. Civ. P. 56(e). We agree with the District Court and the Court of Appeals that no triable issue of fact impedes a ruling on the question of statutory coverage. Respondent's HIV infection is a physical impairment which substantially limits a major life activity, as the ADA defines it. In view of our holding, we need not address the second question presented, *i.e.*, whether HIV infection is a *per se* disability under the ADA.

B

Our holding is confirmed by a consistent course of agency interpretation before and after enactment of the ADA. Every agency to consider the issue under the Rehabilitation Act found statutory coverage for persons with asymptomatic HIV. * * *

One comprehensive and significant administrative precedent is a 1988 opinion issued by the Office of Legal Counsel of the Department of Justice (OLC) concluding that the Rehabilitation Act "protects symptomatic and asymptomatic HIV-infected individuals against discrimination in any covered program." Application of Section 504 of the Rehabilitation Act to HIV-Infected Individuals, 12 Op. Off. Legal Counsel 264, 264-265 (Sept. 27, 1988) (preliminary print) (footnote omitted). * * *

Every court which addressed the issue before the ADA was enacted in July 1990, moreover, concluded that asymptomatic HIV infection satisfied the Rehabilitation Act's definition of a handicap. * * * We are aware of no instance prior to the enactment of the ADA in which a court or agency ruled that HIV infection was not a handicap under the Rehabilitation Act.

Had Congress done nothing more than copy the Rehabilitation Act definition into the ADA, its action would indicate the new statute should be construed in light of this unwavering line of administrative and judicial interpretation. All indications are that Congress was well aware of the position taken by OLC when enacting the ADA and intended to give that position its active endorsement. * * * As noted earlier, Congress also incorporated the same definition into the Fair Housing Amendments Act of 1988. See 42 U.S.C. § 3602(h)(1). We find it significant that the implementing regulations issued by the Department of Housing and Urban Development (HUD) construed the definition to include infection with HIV. 54 Fed. Reg. 3232, 3245 (1989) (codified at 24 C.F.R. § 100. 201 (1997)) * * *. Again the legislative record indicates that Congress intended to ratify HUD's interpretation when it reiterated the same definition in the ADA * * *.

* * * The uniform body of administrative and judicial precedent confirms the conclusion we reach today as the most faithful way to effect the congressional design.

C

Our conclusion is further reinforced by the administrative guidance issued by the Justice Department to implement the public accommodation provisions of Title III of the ADA. As the agency directed by Congress to issue implementing regulations, see 42 U.S.C. § 12186(b), to render technical assistance explaining the responsibilities of covered individuals and institutions, § 12206(c), and to enforce Title III in court, § 12188(b), the Department's views are entitled to deference. See *Chevron*, 467 U.S. at 844, 104 S.Ct. at 2782-2783.

The Justice Department's interpretation of the definition of disability is consistent with our analysis. The regulations acknowledge that Congress intended the ADA's definition of disability to be given the same construction as the definition of handicap in the Rehabilitation Act. 28 C.F.R. § 36.103(a) (1997); *id.*, pt. 36, App. B, pp. 608, 609. The regulatory definition developed by HEW to implement the Rehabilitation Act is incorporated verbatim in the ADA regulations. § 36.104. The Justice Department went further, however. It added "HIV infection (symptomatic and asymptomatic)" to the list of disorders constituting a physical impairment. § 36.104(1)(iii). The technical assistance the Department has issued pursuant to 42 U.S.C. § 12206 similarly concludes that persons with asymptomatic HIV infection fall within the ADA's definition of disability. * * * Any other conclusion, the Department reasoned, would contradict Congress' affirmative ratification of the administrative interpretations given previous versions of the same definition. 28 C.F.R. pt. 36, App. B, pp. 609, 610 (1997) (citing the OLC opinion and HUD regulations); 56 Fed. Reg. 7455, 7456 (1991) (same) (notice of proposed rulemaking).

We also draw guidance from the views of the agencies authorized to administer other sections of the ADA. * * * These agencies, too, concluded that HIV infection is a physical impairment under the ADA. * * * Most categorical of all is EEOC's conclusion that "an individual who has HIV infection (including asymptomatic HIV infection) is an individual with a disability." EEOC Interpretive Manual § 902.4(c)(1), p. 902-21; accord, id., § 902.2(d), p. 902-14, n.18. In the EEOC's view, "impairments . . . such as HIV infection, are inherently substantially limiting." 29 C.F.R. pt. 1630, App., p. 350 (1997); EEOC Technical Assistance Manual II-4; EEOC Interpretive Manual § 902.4(c)(1), p. 902-21.

The regulatory authorities we cite are consistent with our holding that HIV infection, even in the so-called asymptomatic phase, is an impairment which substantially limits the major life activity of reproduction.

III

* * *

The determination of the Court of Appeals that respondent's HIV infection was a disability under the ADA is affirmed. The judgment is vacated, and the case is remanded for further proceedings consistent with this opinion.

* * *

Chief Justice REHNQUIST, with whom Justice SCALIA and Justice THOMAS join, and with whom Justice O'CONNOR joins as to Part II, concurring in the judgment in part and dissenting in part.

I

Is respondent Abbott (hereinafter respondent) who has tested positive for the human immunodeficiency virus (HIV) but was asymptomatic at the time she suffered discriminatory treatment – a person with a "disability" as that term is defined in the Americans with Disabilities Act of 1990 (ADA)? The term "disability" is defined in the ADA to include:

> "(A) a physical or mental impairment that substantially limits one or more of the major life activities of such individual;

> "(B) a record of such an impairment; or

> "(C) being regarded as having such an impairment." 42 U.S.C. § 12102(2).

It is important to note that whether respondent has a disability covered by the ADA is an individualized inquiry. The Act could not be clearer on this point: Section 12102(2) states explicitly that the disability determination must be made "with respect to an individual." Were this not sufficiently clear, the Act goes on to provide that the "major life activities" allegedly limited by an impairment must be those "of such individual." § 12102(2)(A).

The individualized nature of the inquiry is particularly important in this case because the District Court disposed of it on summary judgment. Thus all disputed issues of material fact must be resolved against respondent. She contends that her asymptomatic HIV status brings her within the first definition of a "disability." She must therefore demonstrate, inter alia, that she was (1) physically or mentally impaired and that such impairment (2) substantially limited (3) one or more of her major life activities.

Petitioner does not dispute that asymptomatic HIV-positive status is a physical impairment. I therefore assume this to be the case, and proceed to the second and third statutory requirements for "disability."

According to the Court, the next question is "whether reproduction is a major life activity." That, however, is only half of the relevant question. As mentioned above, the ADA's definition of a "disability" requires that the major life activity at issue be one "of such individual." § 12102(2)(A). The Court truncates the question, perhaps because there is not a shred of record evidence indicating that, prior to becoming infected with HIV, respondent's major life activities included reproduction (assuming for the moment that reproduction is a major life activity at all). At most, the record indicates that after learning of her HIV status, respondent, whatever her previous inclination, conclusively decided that she would not have children. There is absolutely no evidence that, absent the HIV, respondent would have had or was even considering having children. Indeed, when asked during her deposition whether her HIV infection had in any way impaired her ability to carry out any of *her* life functions, respondent answered "No." It is further telling that in the course of her entire brief to this Court, respondent studiously avoids asserting even once that reproduction is a major life activity *to her*. To the contrary, she argues that the "major life activity" inquiry should not turn on a particularized assessment of the circumstances of this or any other case.

But even aside from the facts of this particular case, the Court is simply wrong in concluding as a general matter that reproduction is a "major life activity." Unfortunately, the ADA does not define the phrase "major life activities." But the Act does incorporate by reference a list of such activities contained in regulations issued under the Rehabilitation Act. 42 U.S.C. § 12201(a); 45 C.F.R. § 84.3(j)(2)(ii) (1997). The Court correctly recognizes that this list of major life activities "is illustrative, not exhaustive," but then makes no attempt to demonstrate that reproduction is a major life activity in the same sense that "caring for one's self, performing manual tasks, walking, seeing, hearing, speaking, breathing, learning, and working" are.

Instead, the Court argues that reproduction is a "major" life activity in that it is "central to the life process itself." In support of this reading, the Court focuses on the fact that " 'major' " indicates " 'comparative importance,' " see also Webster's Collegiate Dictionary 702 (10th ed. 1994) ("greater in dignity, rank, importance, or interest"), ignoring the alternative definition of "major" as "greater in quantity, number, or extent." It is the latter definition that is most consistent with the ADA's illustrative list of major life activities.

No one can deny that reproductive decisions are important in a person's life. But so are decisions as to who to marry, where to live, and how to earn one's living. Fundamental importance of this sort is not the common thread linking the statute's listed activities. The common thread is rather that the activities are repetitively performed and essential in the day-to-day existence of a normally functioning individual. They are thus quite different from the series of activities leading to the birth of a child.

Both respondent, and the Government, argue that reproduction must be a major life activity because regulations issued under the ADA define the term "physical impairment" to include physiological disorders affecting the reproductive system. 28 C.F.R. § 36.104 (1997). If reproduction were not a major life activity, they argue, then it would have made little sense to include the reproductive disorders in the roster of physical impairments. This argument is simply wrong. There are numerous disorders of the reproductive system, such as dysmenorrhea and endometriosis, which are so painful that they limit a woman's ability to engage in major life activities such as walking and working. And, obviously, cancer of the various reproductive organs limits one's ability to engage in numerous activities other than reproduction.

But even if I were to assume that reproduction is a major life activity of respondent, I do not agree that an asymptomatic HIV infection "substantially limits" that activity. The record before us leaves no doubt that those so infected are still entirely able to engage in sexual intercourse, give birth to a child if they become pregnant, and perform the manual tasks necessary to rear a child to maturity. While individuals infected with HIV may choose not to engage in these activities, there is no support in language, logic, or our case law for the proposition that such voluntary choices constitute a "limit" on one's own life activities.

The Court responds that the ADA "addresses substantial limitations on major life activities, not utter inabilities." I agree, but fail to see how this assists the Court's cause. Apart from being unable to demonstrate that she is utterly unable to engage in the various activities that comprise the reproductive process, respondent has not even explained how she is less able to engage in those activities.

Respondent contends that her ability to reproduce is limited because "the fatal nature of HIV infection means that a parent is unlikely to live long enough to raise and nurture the child to adulthood." But the

ADA's definition of a disability is met only if the alleged impairment substantially "limits" (present tense) a major life activity. 42 U.S.C. § 12102(2)(A). Asymptomatic HIV does not presently limit respondent's ability to perform any of the tasks necessary to bear or raise a child. Respondent's argument, taken to its logical extreme, would render every individual with a genetic marker for some debilitating disease "disabled" here and now because of some possible future effects.

In my view, therefore, respondent has failed to demonstrate that any of her major life activities were substantially limited by her HIV infection.[1]

* * *

Notes & Questions

1. On remand, the First Circuit determined that Ms. Abbott's cavity dental procedure would not pose a direct threat to Dr. Bragdon if carried out in his office using universal precautions. Abbott v. Bragdon, 163 F.3d 87 (1st Cir. 1998).

2. Under the ADAAA, HIV infection will "virtually always" be found to substantially limit immune function, a major life activity. 29 C.F.R. § 1630.2(j)(3)(iii). Prior to the ADAAA, one circuit court has held that HIV and AIDS may be treated as different disabilities, such that the EEOC's pleading that a person was "HIV positive" was insufficient to allow evidence and argument that the person had "AIDs." EEOC v. Lee's Log Cabin, 546 F.3d. 438, 443-45 (7th Cir. 2008). *See* dissent at 554 F.3d 1002 (7th Cir. 2009).

3. Some have argued that genetic conditions that have not manifested themselves are protected under the ADA. *See infra* Part 8, ch. 32; *see also* Paul Steven Miller, Is There a Pink Slip in My Genes? Genetic Discrimination in the Workplace, 3 J. Health Care L. & Pol'y 225, 237-38 (2000). Does *Bragdon v. Abbott* support that proposition? Does it depend on the inevitability of manifestation of the genetic disorder? Does it depend on the severity of the physiological effect of a disease, such as HIV, even before symptoms develop? Does the ADAAA strengthen the argument that people with genetic conditions are protected? The Genetic Information Nondiscrimination Act of 2008 (GINA), Pub. L. 110-233 (2008), codified at 42 U.S.C.A. Ch. 21F (2009), prohibits employers from discriminating on the basis of genetic information and generally prohibits employers from gathering genetic information about employees. GINA only protects people with genetic diseases that are not manifested. Is the gap between individuals with non-manifested genetic diseases, protected under GINA, and substantially limiting disabilities, protected under the ADA, significant? Would a person with the early manifestations of rhetinitus pigmentosa (a progressive vision disease that often begins with

---

[1]   Justice O'Conner's concurring and dissenting opinion omitted.

night blindness and progresses over the course of many years to complete blindness) be protected under either law?

4. If reproduction is a major life activity, is infertility a disability? *See* LaPorta v. Wal-Mart Stores, Inc., 163 F.Supp.2d 758 (W.D. Mich. 2001) (infertility is a disability under the ADA). What if the infertility is caused intentionally, such as by tubal ligation or vasectomy, or by age? *See* Krauel v. Iowa Methodist Med. Ctr., 95 F.3d 674, 678 (8th Cir. 1996) (indicating infertility caused by ovarian cancer may be covered, but not infertility caused by age). Should substantial limitation be assessed in comparison to most people or the average person of the plaintiff's age group? Does the ADAAA resolve this issue?

5. Does the context in which the case occurs affect which activities should be considered in determining whether the person is substantially limited? In other words, in an employment case is a person protected only if they are limited in work-related activities?

§ 3.3 Record Of A Disability

Individuals without a current disability, including those whose impairments are found to have been mitigated, can rely on the second prong of the disability definition – i.e., discrimination on the basis of a record of a disability. 42 U.S.C. § 12102(1)(B) (2009). According to the ADA's regulations, having a record of a disability means one "has a history of, or has been misclassified as having, a mental or physical impairment that substantially limits one or more major life activities." 29 C.F.R. § 1630.2(k)(1) (2012). This provision was intended to protect those with a history of disability, "like an individual who was treated for cancer ten years ago but who is now deemed by a doctor to be free of cancer," and to protect "individuals misclassified as disabled," including those misclassified as learning disabled. 29 C.F.R. pt. 1630 app., § 1630.2(k) (2011).

To be protected, the record must be of an impairment that would substantially limit one or more of the individual's major life activities. Thus, the former impairment must, itself, have been a legally-recognized disability. This analysis requires courts to assess the somewhat esoteric question of whether the prior impairment substantially limited a major life activity. In doing so, courts use the same criteria as for an actual disability. Before the ADAAA, individuals who had undergone successful treatment for medical conditions were often found not to have records of disabilities, because the impairments are seen as temporary. *See* Garrett v. University of Alabama, 507 F.3d 1306 (11th Cir. 2007) (cancer); Clevinger v. Intel Corp., 254 F. App'x 615 (9th Cir. 2007) (depression); Winters v. Pasadena Ind. School Dis., 124 F. App'x 822 (5th Cir. 2005) (depression). The new ADAAA regulations suggest that these cases might now come out differently.

The fact that an individual has a record of being classified as disabled for some other purpose (e.g., disabled veteran status, disability retirement, social security, etc.) does not guarantee the individual will be considered to have a record of disability for ADA purposes, because the definitions of disability for other purposes differ from the ADA definition.

§ 3.4 Regarded As Having A Disability

One of the main purposes of the ADA was to combat the long-held assumptions, prejudices, and stereotypes about disabilities that have unnecessarily kept people with disabilities out of the workplace and other aspects of society. The final prong of the ADA's definition of disability is the "regarded as" prong. A person may be protected under the ADA if he is treated as having an impairment that substantially limits a major life activity.   42 U.S.C. § 12102(1)(C) (2009).   According to the ADA's interpretative regulations, the "regarded as" provision applies if an individual has "an actual or perceived physical or mental impairment, whether or not that impairment substantially limits, or is perceived to substantially limit, a major life activity." 29 C.F.R. § 1630.2(l) (2012).

To satisfy the "regarded as" prong, an individual does not need to establish that an employer regarded the plaintiff as meeting the legal definition of disability. "An individual meets the requirement of 'being regarded as having such an impairment' if the individual establishes that he or she has been subjected to an action prohibited under this Act because of an actual or perceived physical or mental impairment whether or not the impairment limits or is perceived to limit a major life activity." 42 U.S.C. § 12102(3) (2009). However, the "regarded as" definition "shall not apply to impairments that are transitory and minor. A transitory impairment is an impairment with an actual or expected duration of six months or less." *Id.* In addition, the ADAAA makes clear that "regarded as" plaintiffs are not entitled to reasonable accommodations or reasonable modifications under Title I or Title II. *Id.* §12201(h). Previously, the Courts of Appeals had split on this issue.

The ADAAA can be viewed as having expanded federal anti-discrimination protections to a whole new category of individuals – those who experience impairment that is not necessarily disabling. This is because the ADAAA specifically eliminates the prior requirement that a "regarded as" plaintiff prove that the employer considered him or her to be substantially limited in a major life activity. "In our post-ADAAA world, the 'regarded as' prong now protects individuals against nearly all forms of impairment-based discrimination, regardless of the real or perceived severity or stigmatizing nature of the impairment." Michelle Travis, Impairment as Protected Status: A New Universality for Disability Rights, 46 Ga. L. Rev. 937, 1001 (2012). Thus, an employer could be found to be discriminating if he or she merely acted on a belief that the plaintiff had a physical or mental impairment.

In the following case, the Supreme Court addressed whether an effect of an impairment that could be harmful to others should disqualify a person from the protection of the ADA. The Court also considered the argument that an employer's action based on the effect of an impairment on third parties should not be considered discrimination on the basis of disability. Rejecting subsequent Supreme Court interpretations, the ADA Amendments Act purports to reestablish the *Arline* Court's approach to the definition of disability. The ADAAA specifically states that its purpose is "(3) to reject the Supreme Court's reasoning in Sutton v. United Airlines, Inc., 527 U.S. 471 (1999) with regard to coverage under the third prong of the definition of disability and to reinstate the reasoning of the Supreme Court in School Board of Nassau County v. Arline, 480 U.S. 273 (1987), which set forth a broad view of the third prong of the definition of handicap under the Rehabilitation Act of 1973."

SCHOOL BOARD OF NASSAU COUNTY, FLORIDA v. ARLINE

Supreme Court of the United States, 1987
480 U.S. 273

* * *

Justice BRENNAN delivered the opinion of the Court.

Section 504 of the Rehabilitation Act of 1973, 87 Stat. 394, as amended, 29 U.S.C. § 794 ([Rehabilitation] Act), prohibits a federally funded state program from discriminating against a handicapped individual solely by reason of his or her handicap. This case presents the questions whether a person afflicted with tuberculosis, a contagious disease, may be considered a "handicapped individual" within the meaning of § 504 of the [Rehabilitation] Act, and, if so, whether such an individual is "otherwise qualified" to teach elementary school.

I

From 1966 until 1979, respondent Gene Arline taught elementary school in Nassau County, Florida. She was discharged in 1979 after suffering a third relapse of tuberculosis within two years. After she was denied relief in state administrative proceedings, she brought suit in federal court, alleging that the school board's decision to dismiss her because of her tuberculosis violated § 504 of the [Rehabilitation] Act.

A trial was held in the District Court, at which the principal medical evidence was provided by Marianne McEuen, M.D., an assistant director of the Community Tuberculosis Control Service of the Florida Department of Health and Rehabilitative Services. According to the medical records reviewed by Dr. McEuen, Arline was hospitalized for tuberculosis in 1957. For the next 20 years, Arline's disease was in remission. Then, in 1977, a culture revealed that tuberculosis was again active in her system; cultures taken in March 1978 and in November 1978 were also positive.

The superintendent of schools for Nassau County, Craig Marsh, then testified as to the school board's response to Arline's medical reports. After both her second relapse, in the spring of 1978, and her third relapse in November 1978, the school board suspended Arline with pay for the remainder of the school year. At the end of the 1978-1979 school year, the school board held a hearing, after which it discharged Arline, "not because she had done anything wrong," but because of the "continued reoccurence [sic] of tuberculosis."

In her trial memorandum, Arline argued that it was "not disputed that the [school board dismissed her] solely on the basis of her illness. Since the illness in this case qualifies the Plaintiff as a 'handicapped person' it is clear that she was dismissed solely as a result of her handicap in violation of Section 504." The District Court held, however, that although there was "[n]o question that she suffers a handicap," Arline was nevertheless not "a handicapped person under the terms of that statute." The court found it "difficult ... to conceive that Congress intended contagious diseases to be included within the definition of a handicapped person." The court then went on to state that, "even assuming" that a person with a contagious disease could be deemed a handicapped person, Arline was not "qualified" to teach elementary school.

The Court of Appeals reversed, holding that "persons with contagious diseases are within the coverage of section 504," and that Arline's condition "falls ... neatly within the statutory and regulatory framework" of the [Rehabilitation] Act. The court remanded the case "for further findings as to whether the risks of infection precluded Ms. Arline from being 'otherwise qualified' for her job and, if so, whether it was possible to make some reasonable accommodation for her in that teaching position" or in some other position. We granted certiorari, and now affirm.

II

In enacting and amending the [Rehabilitation] Act, Congress enlisted all programs receiving federal funds in an effort "to share with handicapped Americans the opportunities for an education, transportation, housing, health care, and jobs that other Americans take for granted." 123 Cong. Rec. 13515 (1977) (statement of Sen. Humphrey). To that end, Congress not only increased federal support for vocational rehabilitation, but also addressed the broader problem of discrimination against the handicapped by including § 504, an antidiscrimination provision patterned after Title VI of the Civil Rights Act of 1964. Section 504 of the Rehabilitation Act reads in pertinent part:

> "No otherwise qualified handicapped individual in the United States, as defined in section 706(7) of this title, shall, solely by reason of his handicap, be excluded from

participation in, be denied the benefits of, or be subjected to discrimination under any program or activity receiving Federal financial assistance . . . ." 29 U.S.C. § 794.

In 1974 Congress expanded the definition of "handicapped individual" for use in § 504 to read as follows:[footnote omitted]

"[A]ny person who (i) has a physical or mental impairment which substantially limits one or more of such person's major life activities, (ii) has a record of such an impairment, or (iii) is regarded as having such an impairment." 29 U.S.C. § 706(7)(B).

The amended definition reflected Congress' concern with protecting the handicapped against discrimination stemming not only from simple prejudice, but also from "archaic attitudes and laws" and from "the fact that the American people are simply unfamiliar with and insensitive to the difficulties confront[ing] individuals with handicaps." S. Rep. No. 93-1297, p. 50 (1974); U.S. Code Cong. & Admin. News 1974, p. 6400. To combat the effects of erroneous but nevertheless prevalent perceptions about the handicapped, Congress expanded the definition of "handicapped individual" so as to preclude discrimination against "[a] person who has a record of, or is regarded as having, an impairment [but who] may at present have no actual incapacity at all." *Southeastern Community College v. Davis*, 442 U.S. 397, 405-406, n.6 (1979).

In determining whether a particular individual is handicapped as defined by the [Rehabilitation] Act, the regulations promulgated by the Department of Health and Human Services are of significant assistance. As we have previously recognized, these regulations were drafted with the oversight and approval of Congress, see *Consolidated Rail Corporation v. Darrone*, 465 U.S. 624, 634-635 * * * (1984); they provide "an important source of guidance on the meaning of § 504." *Alexander v. Choate*, 469 U.S. 287, 304, n.24 (1985). The regulations are particularly significant here because they define two critical terms used in the statutory definition of handicapped individual. "Physical impairment" is defined as follows:

"[A]ny physiological disorder or condition, cosmetic disfigurement, or anatomical loss affecting one or more of the following body systems: neurological; musculoskeletal; special sense organs; respiratory, including speech organs; cardiovascular; reproductive, digestive, genito-urinary; hemic and lymphatic; skin; and endocrine." 45 C.F.R. § 84.3(j)(2)(i) (1985).

In addition, the regulations define "major life activities" as "functions such as caring for one's self, performing manual tasks, walking, seeing, hearing, speaking, breathing, learning, and working." § 84.3(j)(2)(ii).

III

Within this statutory and regulatory framework, then, we must consider whether Arline can be considered a handicapped individual. According to the testimony of Dr. McEuen, Arline suffered tuberculosis "in an acute form in such a degree that it affected her respiratory system," and was hospitalized for this condition. Arline thus had a physical impairment as that term is defined by the regulations, since she had a "physiological disorder or condition . . . affecting [her] . . . respiratory [system]." 45 C.F.R. § 84.3(j)(2)(i) (1985). This impairment was serious enough to require hospitalization, a fact more than sufficient to establish that one or more of her major life activities were substantially limited by her impairment. Thus, Arline's hospitalization for tuberculosis in 1957 suffices to establish that she has a "record of . . . impairment" within the meaning of 29 U.S.C. § 706(7)(B)(ii), and is therefore a handicapped individual.

Petitioners concede that a contagious disease may constitute a handicapping condition to the extent that it leaves a person with "diminished physical or mental capabilities," and concede that Arline's hospitalization for tuberculosis in 1957 demonstrates that she has a record of a physical impairment. Petitioners maintain, however, that Arline's record of impairment is irrelevant in this case, since the school board dismissed Arline not because of her diminished physical capabilities, but because of the threat that her relapses of tuberculosis posed to the health of others.

We do not agree with petitioners that, in defining a handicapped individual under § 504, the contagious effects of a disease can be meaningfully distinguished from the disease's physical effects on a claimant in a case such as this. Arline's contagiousness and her physical impairment each resulted from the same underlying condition, tuberculosis. It would be unfair to allow an employer to seize upon the distinction between the effects of a disease on others and the effects of a disease on a patient and use that distinction to justify discriminatory treatment.

Nothing in the legislative history of § 504 suggests that Congress intended such a result. That history demonstrates that Congress was as concerned about the effect of an impairment on others as it was about its effect on the individual. Congress extended coverage, in 29 U.S.C. § 706(7)(B)(iii), to those individuals who are simply "regarded as having" a physical or mental impairment. The Senate Report provides as an example of a person who would be covered under this subsection "a person with some kind of visible physical impairment which in fact does not substantially limit that person's functioning." S. Rep. No. 93-1297, at 64. Such an impairment might not diminish a person's physical or mental capabilities, but could nevertheless substantially limit that person's ability to work as a result of the negative reactions of others to the impairment.

Allowing discrimination based on the contagious effects of a physical impairment would be inconsistent with the basic purpose of § 504, which is to ensure that handicapped individuals are not denied jobs or other benefits because of the prejudiced attitudes or the ignorance of others. By amending the definition of "handicapped individual" to include not only those who are actually physically impaired, but also those who are regarded as impaired and who, as a result, are substantially limited in a major life activity, Congress acknowledged that society's accumulated myths and fears about disability and disease are as handicapping as are the physical limitations that flow from actual impairment. Few aspects of a handicap give rise to the same level of public fear and misapprehension as contagiousness. Even those who suffer or have recovered from such noninfectious diseases as epilepsy or cancer have faced discrimination based on the irrational fear that they might be contagious. The [Rehabilitation] Act is carefully structured to replace such reflexive reactions to actual or perceived handicaps with actions based on reasoned and medically sound judgments: the definition of "handicapped individual" is broad, but only those individuals who are both handicapped *and* otherwise qualified are eligible for relief. The fact that *some* persons who have contagious diseases may pose a serious health threat to others under certain circumstances does not justify excluding from the coverage of the [Rehabilitation] Act *all* persons with actual or perceived contagious diseases. Such exclusion would mean that those accused of being contagious would never have the opportunity to have their condition evaluated in light of medical evidence and a determination made as to whether they were "otherwise qualified." Rather, they would be vulnerable to discrimination on the basis of mythology – precisely the type of injury Congress sought to prevent. We conclude that the fact that a person with a record of a physical impairment is also contagious does not suffice to remove that person from coverage under § 504.

IV

The remaining question is whether Arline is otherwise qualified for the job of elementary schoolteacher. To answer this question in most cases, the district court will need to conduct an individualized inquiry and make appropriate findings of fact. Such an inquiry is essential if § 504 is to achieve its goal of protecting handicapped individuals from deprivations based on prejudice, stereotypes, or unfounded fear, while giving appropriate weight to such legitimate concerns of grantees as avoiding exposing others to significant health and safety risks.[16] The basic factors

---

[16] A person who poses a significant risk of communicating an infectious disease to others in the workplace will not be otherwise qualified for his or her job if reasonable accommodation will not eliminate that risk. The Act would not require a school board to place a teacher

to be considered in conducting this inquiry are well established. In the context of the employment of a person handicapped with a contagious disease, we agree with *amicus* American Medical Association that this inquiry should include

> "[findings of] facts, based on reasonable medical judgments given the state of medical knowledge, about (a) the nature of the risk (how the disease is transmitted), (b) the duration of the risk (how long is the carrier infectious), (c) the severity of the risk (what is the potential harm to third parties) and (d) the probabilities the disease will be transmitted and will cause varying degrees of harm."

In making these findings, courts normally should defer to the reasonable medical judgments of public health officials. The next step in the "otherwise-qualified" inquiry is for the court to evaluate, in light of these medical findings, whether the employer could reasonably accommodate the employee under the established standards for that inquiry.

Because of the paucity of factual findings by the District Court, we, like the Court of Appeals, are unable at this stage of the proceedings to resolve whether Arline is "otherwise qualified" for her job. The District Court made no findings as to the duration and severity of Arline's condition, nor as to the probability that she would transmit the disease. Nor did the court determine whether Arline was contagious at the time she was discharged, or whether the School Board could have reasonably accommodated her. Accordingly, the resolution of whether Arline was otherwise qualified requires further findings of fact.

V

We hold that a person suffering from the contagious disease of tuberculosis can be a handicapped person within the meaning of § 504 of the Rehabilitation Act of 1973, and that respondent Arline is such a person. We remand the case to the District Court to determine whether Arline is otherwise qualified for her position. The judgment of the Court of Appeals is *Affirmed*.

Chief Justice REHNQUIST, with whom Justice SCALIA joins, dissenting.

* * *

[T]he Rehabilitation Act cannot be read to support the result reached by the Court. The record in this case leaves no doubt that Arline was discharged because of the contagious nature of tuberculosis, and not because of any diminished physical or mental capabilities resulting from

---

with active, contagious tuberculosis in a classroom with elementary schoolchildren. Respondent conceded as much at oral argument.

her condition. Thus, in the language of § 504, the central question here is whether discrimination on the basis of contagiousness constitutes discrimination "by reason of . . . handicap." Because the language of the [Rehabilitation] Act, regulations, and legislative history are silent on this issue, the principles outlined above compel the conclusion that contagiousness is not a handicap within the meaning of § 504. It is therefore clear that the protections of the [Rehabilitation] Act do not extend to individuals such as Arline.

In reaching a contrary conclusion, the Court never questions that Arline was discharged because of the threat her condition posed to others. Instead, it posits that the contagious effects of a disease cannot be "meaningfully" distinguished from the disease's effect on a claimant under the [Rehabilitation] Act. To support this position, the Court observes that Congress intended to extend the [Rehabilitation] Act's protections to individuals who have a condition that does not impair their mental and physical capabilities, but limits their major life activities because of the adverse reactions of others. This congressional recognition of a handicap resulting from the reactions of others, we are told, reveals that Congress intended the Rehabilitation Act to regulate discrimination on the basis of contagiousness.

This analysis misses the mark in several respects. To begin with, Congress' recognition that an individual may be handicapped under the [Rehabilitation] Act solely by reason of the reactions of others in no way demonstrates that, for the purposes of interpreting the [Rehabilitation] Act, the reactions of others to the condition cannot be considered separately from the effect of the condition on the claimant. In addition, the Court provides no basis for extending the [Rehabilitation] Act's generalized coverage of individuals suffering discrimination as a result of the reactions of others to coverage of individuals with contagious diseases. Although citing examples of handicapped individuals described in the regulations and legislative history, the Court points to nothing in these materials suggesting that Congress contemplated that a person with a condition posing a threat to the health of others may be considered handicapped under the [Rehabilitation] Act * * *

* * *

Notes & Questions

1. The Court in *Arline* separates the question of whether a person has a disability from the question whether the person is otherwise qualified for a position. This two-pronged analysis, often requiring expert testimony about the effects of the disability, makes summary judgment more difficult to obtain for employers facing disability discrimination claims.

2. As the Court in *Arline* makes clear, contagiousness, standing alone, does not render a person unprotected by the disability rights laws.

At what point can an employer justify firing an employee with a contagious illness?

3. The dissent in *Arline* argued that actions based on a disability's effect on people other than the person with a disability are not discriminatory. The Court rejected this argument because the Rehabilitation Act explicitly protects people "regarded as" having disabilities. That approach prevents employers from relying on inconvenience to or morale of other employees to argue that a person with a disability is unqualified. Does this approach go too far, as Chief Justice Rehnquist, in dissent, maintains?

4. On remand, the district court assessed whether Ms. Arline was "otherwise qualified for the job of elementary school teacher," *Arline v. Sch. Bd. of Nassau County*, 692 F.Supp. 1286, 1290 (M.D. Fla. 1988), and evaluated the risk she posed to her students. The court found that tuberculosis is not easily transmitted, the risk of transmission is significantly reduced by medication such as Ms. Arline was taking, medical treatment such as that received by Ms. Arline was effective, and Ms. Arline's exposure to students was of a limited duration. In addition, at the time the school fired her, Ms. Arline had ten negative cultures and only one positive. Therefore, the court found that Ms. Arline "posed no threat of communicating tuberculosis to the schoolchildren she was teaching." *Id.* at 1292. The court found that "the decision to terminate Plaintiff . . . was not based on reasonable medical judgments, but rather was based upon 'society's accumulated myths and fears about [tuberculosis].'" *Id.* In light of this conclusion, what do you think about the Supreme Court's approach?

5. The ADAAA makes clear that employers need not provide a reasonable accommodation to policies, practices, or procedures to an individual who proceeds under the "regarded as" prong. Prior to the ADAAA, courts had been divided over this issue. 42 U.S.C.A. § 12201(h). *See* Alex Long, Introducing the New and Improved Americans with Disabilities Act: Assessing the ADA Amendments Act of 2008, 103 Nw. U. L. Rev. Colloquy 217, 225 (2008). In its regulations, the EEOC takes the position that the impact of this provision is that "[w]here an individual is not challenging a covered entity's failure to make reasonable accommodations and does not require a reasonable accommodation, it is generally unnecessary to proceed under the 'actual disability' or 'record of' prongs, which require a showing of an impairment that substantially limits a major life activity or a record of such an impairment." 29 C.F.R § 1630(G)(3).

It is still early to evaluate the impact of the ADAAA and the implementing EEOC regulations. Still, it appears that courts are generally complying with Congress's wishes and moving past the ADA's definition. For examples of cases holding that individuals are covered under the ADA's definition of disability which would likely have come out differently prior to the ADAAA, *see* Berard v. Wal-Mart, 2011 WL 4632062 (M.D. Fla. 2011) (holding an individual with diabetes covered); Johnson v. Farmers Ins., 2012 WL 95387 (W.D. Okla 2012) (sleep apnea), Fleck v. Wilmac, 2012 WL 1033472 (E.D. Pa. 2012) (chronic, non-healing walking injury causing difficulties walking and standing), Dentice v. Farmers Ins., 2012 WL 2504046 (E.D. Wis. 2012) (depression, anxiety, and panic disorder), Durrenberger v. Tex. Dep't of Criminal Justice, 757 F.Supp.2d 640 (S.D. Tex. 2010) (prisoner with hearing difficulty who could not hear well in visitation room). But there are limits. *See* Neely v. PSGE Tex., 2013 WL 5942233 (5th Cir. 2013) (holding that while the ADA Amendments Act made it easier for employees to show that they have a disability, it did not eliminate the requirement).

Chapter 4 OTHER PROTECTIONS

§ 4.1 Association

In addition to protecting people with disabilities from discriminatory actions, the ADA protects individuals, with and without disabilities, who are discriminated against because of their known association with an individual with a disability. 42 U.S.C. §§ 12112(b)(4), 12182(b)(1)(E) (2009); 29 C.F.R. § 1630.8 (2011); 28 C.F.R. §§ 35.130(g), § 36.205 (2010). The protection is not limited to those with a familial relationship with an individual with a disability, but may include business, social, and other relationships as well. 29 C.F.R. § 1630.8. The protection means that, if an entity denies service to an individual with a disability and his or her companions, the entity is liable to the disabled individual and, independently, the companions. U.S. Dep't of Justice Title III Technical Assistance Manual § 3.5000 (Nov. 1993), http://www.usdoj.gov/crt/ada/taman3.html.

To be protected from discrimination on the basis of association, the plaintiff must prove that she was qualified for the job, program, or service that she sought. The plaintiff must also prove that she was associated with a specific person or group with an actual disability or a record of a disability, or who is regarded as having a disability, and that the entity knew of the person's disability. Freilich v. Upper Chesapeake Health, Inc., 313 F.3d 205, 215 (4th Cir. 2002) (discrimination based on generalized advocacy for a type of individual is not sufficient).

Notes & Questions

1. The association provision protects, for instance, an employee who has a dependent with a disability from the denial of benefits available to other employees on the basis of that association. The EEOC provides this example:

> An employer who provides health insurance to the dependents of its employees learns that Jaime, an applicant for a management position, has a spouse with a disability. The employer determines that providing insurance to Jaime's spouse will lead to increased health insurance costs. The employer violates the ADA if it decides not to hire Jaime based on the increased health insurance costs that will be caused by his wife's disability.

U.S. EEOC, Questions and Answers About the Association Provision of the Americans with Disabilities Act, at 3.F, http://www.eeoc.gov/facts/association_ada.html (last modified Feb. 2, 2011). In Part 8 we present the concerns of genetic discrimination, whereby an applicant may not be hired on the basis of genetic testing indicating, for instance, the applicant's heightened likelihood for developing heart disease in the future, and thus imposing perceived burdensome health care expenses on the employer. How would you argue the case of discrimination based on the family member having a predisposition for breast cancer?

2. An employee whose son attends a special program for children with autism requests to start and finish her workday earlier so as to pick up and care for her son at 3 PM. Must an employer provide reasonable accommodations to the employee who is associated with a person who has a disability? *See* Overley v. Covenant Transport, Inc., 178 F. App'x 488 (6th Cir. 2006) (employee with a child with a disability not entitled to reasonable accommodation); Hartog v. Wasatch Academy, 129 F.3d 1076, 1084-85 (10th Cir. 1997) (accommodations not required for disabled relatives of employees).

§ 4.2 Retaliation

The ADA protects individuals with and without disabilities from retaliation or coercion for asserting disability rights. 42 U.S.C. § 12203 (2009). The regulations provide:

> (a) . . . It is unlawful to discriminate against any individual because that individual has opposed any act or practice made unlawful by this part or because that individual made a charge, testified, assisted or participated in any manner in an investigation, proceeding, or hearing to enforce any provision contained in this part.
>
> (b) . . . It is unlawful to coerce, intimidate, threaten, harass or interfere with any individual in the exercise or enjoyment of, or because that individual aided or encouraged any other individual in the exercise of, any right granted or protected by this part.

29 C.F.R. § 1630.12 (2011); *see also* 28 C.F.R. §§ 35.134, 36.206 (2010).

> Illustrations of conduct prohibited by this section include:
>
> (1) Coercing an individual to deny or limit the benefits, services or advantages to which he or she is entitled under the Act . . .;
>
> (2) Threatening, intimidating, or interfering with an individual with a disability who is seeking to obtain or use the goods, services, facilities, privileges, advantages, or accommodations of a public accommodation;
>
> (3) Intimidating or threatening any person because that person is assisting or encouraging an individual or group entitled to claim the rights granted or protected by the Act . . .; or
>
> (4) Retaliating against any person because that person has participated in any investigation or action to enforce the Act . . . .

28 C.F.R. § 36.206(c).

Some courts have held that temporal proximity between the protected activity and adverse employment action is sufficient to establish a causal link. *See* Shellenberger v. Summit Bancorp, 318 F.3d 183, 189 (3d Cir. 2003) (employee had filed Title I employment discrimination claim with EEOC). Other courts have applied a "pretext" theory. For an employee to prevail under the pretext theory, she must show: "(1) protected employee activity [e.g., filing a Title I claim with the EEOC]; (2) adverse action by the employer either after or contemporaneous with the employee's protected activity; and (3) a causal connection between the employee's protected activity and the employer's adverse action." *Id.* at 187. If the plaintiff can establish these three elements, the burden then shifts to the employer to prove a legitimate, non-retaliatory reason for the adverse employment action. If the employer proffers such a reason, the burden then shifts back to the plaintiff to prove that "retaliatory animus played a role in the employer's decision-making process and that it had a determinative effect on the outcome of that process." *Id.* (quoting Krous v. Am. Sterilizer Co., 126 F.3d 494, 501 (3d Cir. 1997).

In Stone v. City of Indianapolis Public Utilities Division, 281 F.3d 640, 644 (7th Cir. 2002), the Seventh Circuit outlined another, slightly different evidentiary procedure for a Title I employment discrimination retaliation claim. The first step is for the plaintiff to present direct evidence that she engaged in protected activity, and as a result suffered an adverse employment action. If the employer does not contradict this evidence, the plaintiff is entitled to summary judgment. If the employer rebuts plaintiff's evidence, the case proceeds to trial unless the employer adduces uncontradicted evidence that the adverse employment action would have been taken against the plaintiff regardless of retaliatory motive. In that case, the employer is entitled to summary judgment because it has established that the plaintiff was not harmed by the retaliation. According to the Seventh Circuit, "mere temporal proximity between the filing of the charge of discrimination and the action alleged to have been taken in retaliation for that filing will rarely be sufficient in and of itself to create a triable issue."

FREILICH v. UPPER CHESAPEAKE HEALTH, INC.

United States Court of Appeals, Fourth Circuit, 2002
313 F.3d 205

WILKINSON, Chief Judge.

* * *

I.

Dr. Linda Freilich is a Board Certified Internist and Nephrologist who maintained unrestricted hospital privileges at defendant Harford

Memorial Hospital (HMH), a private, non-profit hospital, from 1982 until April 12, 2000. During her tenure at HMH, Dr. Freilich states she advocated the rights of her patients in order to improve their quality of care. Specifically, Dr. Freilich complained that the outsourcing of quality assurance and oversight services for dialysis patients led to an improper standard of care.

Maryland state regulations require physicians to apply for reappointment every two years. During the reappointment process, each hospital must collect specific information about the physician applicant. The hospital then must analyze the physician's pattern of performance based upon seven factors, including "adherence to hospital bylaws, policies, and procedures" and "attitudes, cooperation, and ability to work with others." Pursuant to COMAR regulations, HMH Medical Staff Bylaws provide that HMH will consider in the reappointment process "ethics and behavior in the Hospital, cooperation with Hospital personnel as it relates to patient care or the orderly operation of the Hospital, and general demeanor and attitude with respect to the Hospital, its patients and its personnel."

* * * [O]n April 11, 2000, HMH's Board of Directors voted to deny Dr. Freilich's application and terminated her medical privileges. In a letter to Dr. Freilich explaining the basis for its decision, the Board quoted the "ethics and behavior" language in the HMH Bylaws.

On December 11, 2000, Dr. Freilich filed a 14-count, 76-page complaint against HMH and fourteen individuals who were involved in her peer review (collectively the "hospital defendants"), the State of Maryland, and the United States. The complaint alleged that HMH and its Board of Directors denied Dr. Freilich's application for reappointment because she did nothing more than advocate the rights of her patients. * * * Finally, Dr. Freilich alleged violations of both the Americans with Disabilities Act (ADA) and the Rehabilitation Act (RA).

In an extensive opinion, the district court dismissed the federal claims with prejudice and the state law claims without prejudice. Dr. Freilich now appeals. We review a dismissal for failure to state a claim *de novo*, and assume the facts as stated in the complaint are true.

II.

* * *

III.

We next turn to Dr. Freilich's claims against the hospital under Titles II and III of the Americans with Disabilities Act (ADA) and under the Rehabilitation Act (RA). To the extent possible, we construe similar provisions in the two statutes consistently. See *Ennis v. Nat'l Ass'n of Bus. and Educ. Radio, Inc.*, 53 F.3d 55, 57 (4th Cir. 1995). Dr. Freilich makes three claims, which we address in turn.

A.

Dr. Freilich brings her first ADA claim on behalf of her dialysis patients. Dr. Freilich alleges that HMH violated the ADA and the RA by providing in-hospital quality assurance and oversight for all hospital services provided by contractors except for dialysis services. *See* 42 U.S.C. §§ 12132, 12182; 29 U.S.C. § 794. Quality assurance and oversight for dialysis services is provided by an outside contractor. We do not reach the merits of this claim, however, because Dr. Freilich lacks standing to bring such a claim on behalf of her patients.

Our standing inquiry "involves both constitutional limitations on federal-court jurisdiction and prudential limitations on its exercise." *Warth v. Seldin*, 422 U.S. 490, 498, 95 S.Ct. 2197, 45 L.Ed.2d 343 (1975). Even if a plaintiff satisfies Article III standing requirements, "[f]ederal courts must hesitate before resolving a controversy, even one within their constitutional power to resolve, on the basis of the rights of third persons not parties to the litigation." *Singleton v. Wulff*, 428 U.S. 106, 113, 96 S.Ct. 2868, 49 L.Ed.2d 826 (1976). To overcome the prudential limitation on third-party standing, a plaintiff must demonstrate: (1) an injury-in-fact; (2) a close relationship between herself and the person whose right she seeks to assert; and (3) a hindrance to the third party's ability to protect his or her own interests. *Powers v. Ohio*, 499 U.S. 400, 410-11, 111 S.Ct. 1364, 113 L.Ed.2d 411 (1991).

The district court held that even assuming the existence of the first two elements, Dr. Freilich did not sufficiently allege a hindrance to her patients' ability to protect their own interests. Here Dr. Freilich fails to allege sufficient obstacles to the patients bringing suit themselves. The district court correctly pointed out that "the dialysis patients and indigent patients on whose behalf Dr. Freilich advocated are not constrained in bringing suit by any obstacles made known in the Complaint." In her submission to this court, Dr. Freilich argues that dialysis patients are disabled and chronically ill, foreclosing them from presenting their own rights. But we cannot simply assume that every disabled or chronically ill person is incapable of asserting his or her own claims. In fact, such persons are typical and frequent plaintiffs under both the ADA and RA. Faced, then, with no evidence that Dr. Freilich's dialysis patients are hindered from presenting their own claims, we adhere to the longstanding principle that "third parties themselves usually will be the best proponents of their own rights." *Singleton*, 428 U.S. at 114, 96 S.Ct. 2868.

B.

Next, Dr. Freilich asserts a claim of associational discrimination under the ADA. See 42 U.S.C. § 12182(b)(1)(E). Dr. Freilich alleges that HMH denied her reappointment because of her "patient advocacy." Under Title III of the ADA, 42 U.S.C. § 12182(b)(1)(E), it is discriminatory to "exclude or otherwise deny equal goods, services, facilities, privileges, advantages, accommodations, or other opportunities to an individual or entity because of the known disability of an individual with whom the individual or entity is known to have a relationship or association." There is little case law applying this provision. We therefore look for guidance from a similar provision in Title I of the ADA which governs associational discrimination in employment. See 42 U.S.C. § 12112(b)(4).

The associational discrimination provision in Title I "was intended to protect qualified individuals from adverse job actions based on 'unfounded stereotypes and assumptions' arising from the employees' relationships with particular disabled persons." *Oliveras-Sifre v. Puerto Rico Dept. of Health*, 214 F.3d 23, 26 (1st Cir. 2000) (citing *Barker v. Int'l Paper Co.*, 993 F.Supp. 10, 15 (D.Me. 1998)). In *Oliveras-Sifre*, the plaintiffs alleged that they were punished for their advocacy on behalf of AIDS patients. However, the First Circuit rejected the plaintiffs' contention that the defendants' actions violated the associational discrimination provision of the ADA. The plaintiffs did not allege "a specific association with a disabled individual." Instead, they "contend[ed], in essence, that they were punished for their advocacy on behalf of individuals with AIDS." *Id.* In *Barker*, the court granted summary judgment in favor of the defendants along the same lines: the plaintiff alleged that he was terminated because of his advocacy on behalf of the plaintiff's disabled wife, which was held insufficient to support an associational discrimination claim. 993 F.Supp. at 15.

Dr. Freilich's allegations suffer from similar defects as the allegations in *Oliveras-Sifre* and *Barker*. Dr. Freilich alleges that HMH "coerced, intimidated, threatened, or interfered . . . with [her] because she exercised rights protected by the ADA," and that HMH discriminated against her because she refused "to end her advocacy of the dialysis patients' rights that were being violated under [the] ADA." She further alleges that she was "denied equal use of facilities, privileges, advantages or other opportunities because of her association with and her relationship to patients with disabilities." But such generalized references to association with disabled persons or to advocacy for a group of disabled persons are not sufficient to state a claim for associational discrimination under the ADA. Every hospital employee can allege at least a loose association with disabled patients. To allow Dr. Freilich to proceed on such a basis would arm every hospital employee with a potential ADA complaint. A step of that magnitude is for Congress, not this court, to take.

C.

Finally, Dr. Freilich brings a claim for retaliatory discharge under the ADA and the RA. She alleges that HMH terminated her hospital privileges "because she strongly opposed and voiced her concerns about HMH's practices in treating dialysis patients." Specifically, Dr. Freilich contends that her opposition to HMH's decision to outsource quality oversight and quality assurance over dialysis services constitutes protected conduct under the ADA. Under 42 U.S.C. § 12203, "[n]o person shall discriminate against any individual because such individual has opposed any act or practice made unlawful by this chapter or because such individual made a charge, testified, assisted, or participated in any manner in an investigation, proceeding, or hearing under this chapter." In order to establish a prima facie case of retaliation, a plaintiff must allege (1) that she has engaged in conduct protected by the ADA; (2) that she suffered an adverse action subsequent to engaging in the protected conduct; and (3) that there was a causal link between the protected activity and the adverse action. *Rhoads v. FDIC*, 257 F.3d 373, 392 (4th Cir. 2001). In reviewing retaliation claims, courts recognize the need to balance the desire to encourage employees to oppose unlawful discrimination, with "an employer's interest in maintaining a harmonious, productive and loyal workforce." *Fitch v. Solipsys Corp.*, 94 F.Supp.2d 670, 678 (D. Md. 2000).

A plaintiff need not establish that the conduct she opposed actually constituted an ADA violation. *Ross v. Communications Satellite Corp.*, 759 F.2d 355, 357 n.1 (4th Cir. 1985). But a complainant must allege the predicate for a reasonable, good faith belief that the behavior she is opposing violates the ADA. *E.g.*, *Weissman v. Dawn Joy Fashions, Inc.*, 214 F.3d 224, 234 (2d Cir. 2000).

In her complaint, Dr. Freilich alleges what at most are violations of state medical malpractice law, not infractions of the ADA. Dr. Freilich says that she complained orally and/or in writing regarding the failure to transport a patient in a timely manner; the failure to adhere to skin protocols; the failure to address concerns regarding uncertified nurses; the failure to diagnose a cervical fracture on a patient; the unsupervised dialysis of a patient; and the failure to provide correct dialysis services for several patients. While we do not overlook the importance of maintaining adequate levels of patient care, it is not the job of a federal court under the ADA to referee disagreements between a hospital and staff physician over what constitutes the appropriate funding or manner of such care. In essence, Dr. Freilich disagrees with the level of care being provided to some hospital patients, which she attributes to the outsourcing of quality assurance and quality oversight for dialysis patients. She could not, however, reasonably believe that her disagreement with HMH over the expenditure of hospital resources constituted a violation of the ADA.

Every disagreement over the adequacy of hospital expenditures or the provision of patient care is not an ADA issue. If it were, courts would be drawn into medical resource disputes quite beyond their expertise and hospital personnel would be diverted by litigation from their primary task of providing medical attention to those in their charge. Hospitals are in the business of serving persons with many kinds of disabilities, and we have noted that "our federal disability statutes are not designed to ensure that persons with one type of disability are treated the same as persons with another type of disability." *Lewis v. Kmart Corp.*, 180 F.3d 166, 171-

72 (4th Cir. 1999). Recognizing that the medical community is best equipped to conduct the balancing that medical resource allocations inevitably require, Congress declined to give courts a mandate to arbitrate such disputes.

Because Dr. Freilich has failed to allege any set of facts supporting her claim that she opposed practices made unlawful by the ADA, we affirm the district court's dismissal of her retaliation claim.

* * *

AFFIRMED.

Notes & Questions

1. Protection from retaliation does not depend on the ultimate outcome of the enforcement action being pursued. Therefore, the individual claiming retaliation does not have to have been legally correct that the action she opposed was illegal. She simply must have a good faith reasonable belief that she was asserting covered rights. Fogleman v. Mercy Hosp., Inc., 283 F.3d 561, 565 (3d Cir. 2002), cert. denied 537 U.S. 824 (2002); Freilich v. Upper Chesapeake Health, Inc., 313 F.3d 205, 216-17 (4th Cir. 2002); Weissman v. Dawn Joy Fashions, Inc., 214 F.3d 224, 234 (2d Cir. 2000). However, to be protected activity, the individual's actions must have been asserting possible ADA violations. Merely advocating on behalf of individuals with disabilities for non-civil-rights matters will not be protected from retaliation. Oliveras-Sifre v. P.R. Dep't of Health, 214 F.3d 23, 27 (1st Cir. 2000).

2. The retaliation and coercion provisions are not limited in their application to covered public entities, public accommodations, and employers. Rather, private individuals are prohibited from retaliation or coercion as well. 28 C.F.R. pt. 35 app. B, § 35.134 (2011); *id.* pt. 36 app. C, § 36.206 (2011); *see also* Shotz v. City of Plantation, Fla., 344 F.3d 1161 (11th Cir. 2003).

3. How does a plaintiff prove that an employer or business acted with retaliatory animus? As a lawyer, what specific proof would you look for?

§ 4.3 Harassment

Like Title VII, the few courts to consider the issue have held that the ADA includes a cause of action for workplace harassment on the basis of disability. *See, e.g.,* Fox v. Gen. Motors Corp., 247 F.3d 169 (4th Cir. 2001). The relevant statutory provision courts have used is Title I's prohibition of discrimination in the "terms, conditions, and privileges of employment." This is based on an analogy to similar language in Title VII which has been the basis for race and sex harassment claims. Under Title VII, a plaintiff must show that harassment is harsh and invidious.

Applied to disability, courts have held that a parallel requirement is that the workplace is "permeated with discriminatory conduct – intimidation, ridicule, insult – that is sufficiently severe or pervasive as to alter the conditions of employment." Silk v. City of Chicago, 194 F.3d 788, 804 (7th Cir. 1999).

The leading authority on disability harassment law, Professor Mark Weber, has argued that this requirement has precluded many disability-based harassment claims because judges have not appreciated the severity of disability harassment, even in those cases with shocking fact patterns. *See generally* Mark Weber, Disability Harassment (2007); *see also* Michael A. Stein and Michael Waterstone, Disabling Prejudice, 102 Northwestern Univ. L. Rev. 1351 (2008) (reviewing Weber's book). Weber has documented cases where supervisors harassed employees in front of other coworkers by referring to them as "lazy," "crippled," or worthless; managers condoned coworkers ridiculing and jeering the oral communication of an employee with severe speech disorder; and an employee with a mild developmental disability was derided and called "Rick Retardo." Weber suggests that the ADA contains a more specific provision regarding harassment. Specifically, the ADA makes it "unlawful to coerce, intimidate, threaten, or interfere with any individual in the exercise or enjoyment of" any protected right. 42 U.S.C. § 12203(b). Weber views the ADA as containing a "right to be there" which harassment interferes with. Thus, there is no basis for grafting the "severe and pervasive" standard derived from Title VII onto disability harassment claims.

Chapter 5   QUALIFIED

In addition to being a person with a disability, to be protected under Title I or Title II of the ADA, a person must be qualified. 42 U.S.C. § 12112(a) (2009). Qualification is also a requirement for an association claim under Title I, but not under Title II or Title III. *See* 29 C.F.R. § 1630.8 (2011); 28 C.F.R. §§ 35.130(a), 36.205 (2011). Title III does not contain a qualification requirement.

The Title I and II qualification standard requires that the plaintiff be able to meet the essential eligibility requirements of the job, program, or service at issue, with or without reasonable accommodations or reasonable modifications. *Id.* § 35.104; 29 C.F.R. § 1630.2(m) (2012).

§ 5.1 Prerequisites

The first step in the qualification inquiry is determining whether the person meets the nondiscriminatory prerequisites for the position or program, such as educational background, experience, skills, or licenses. 29 C.F.R. pt. 1630 app., § 1630.2(m). To be considered nondiscriminatory in the employment context, these prerequisites must be job-related and consistent with business necessity. 42 U.S.C. § 12113(a) (2009). In the context of government programs, they must be "necessary for the provision of the service, program or activity being offered." 28 C.F.R. § 35.130(b)(8).

∽

ALBERTSON'S, INC. v. KIRKINGBURG

Supreme Court of the United States, 1999
527 U.S. 555

* * *

Justice SOUTER delivered the opinion of the Court.

The question posed is whether, under the Americans with Disabilities Act of 1990 (ADA or Act), as amended, 42 U.S.C. § 12101 *et seq.* (1994 ed. and Supp. III), an employer who requires as a job qualification that an employee meet an otherwise applicable federal safety regulation must justify enforcing the regulation solely because its standard may be waived in an individual case. We answer no.

I

In August 1990, petitioner, Albertson's, Inc., a grocery-store chain with supermarkets in several States, hired respondent, Hallie Kirkingburg, as a truckdriver based at its Portland, Oregon, warehouse. Kirkingburg had more than a decade's driving experience and performed well when petitioner's transportation manager took him on a road test.

119

Before starting work, Kirkingburg was examined to see if he met federal vision standards for commercial truckdrivers. * * * Since 1971, the basic vision regulation has required corrected distant visual acuity of at least 20/40 in each eye and distant binocular acuity of at least 20/40. Kirkingburg, however, suffers from amblyopia, an uncorrectable condition that leaves him with 20/200 vision in his left eye and monocular vision in effect. Despite Kirkingburg's weak left eye, the doctor erroneously certified that he met the DOT's basic vision standards, and Albertson's hired him.

In December 1991, Kirkingburg injured himself on the job and took a leave of absence. Before returning to work in November 1992, Kirkingburg went for a further physical as required by the company. This time, the examining physician correctly assessed Kirkingburg's vision and explained that his eyesight did not meet the basic DOT standards. The physician, or his nurse, told Kirkingburg that in order to be legally qualified to drive, he would have to obtain a waiver of its basic vision standards from the DOT. * * * Kirkingburg applied for a waiver, but because he could not meet the basic DOT vision standard Albertson's fired him from his job as a truckdriver. In early 1993, after he had left Albertson's, Kirkingburg received a DOT waiver, but Albertson's refused to rehire him.

Kirkingburg sued Albertson's, claiming that firing him violated the ADA. Albertson's moved for summary judgment solely on the ground that Kirkingburg was "not 'otherwise qualified' to perform the job of truck driver with or without reasonable accommodation." The District Court granted the motion, ruling that Albertson's had reasonably concluded that Kirkingburg was not qualified without an accommodation because he could not, as admitted, meet the basic DOT vision standards. The court held that giving Kirkingburg time to get a DOT waiver was not a required reasonable accommodation because the waiver program was "a flawed experiment that has not altered the DOT vision requirements."

A divided panel of the Ninth Circuit reversed. * * *

The Court of Appeals then addressed the ground upon which the District Court had granted summary judgment, acknowledging that Albertson's consistently required its truckdrivers to meet the DOT's basic vision standards and that Kirkingburg had not met them (and indeed could not). The court recognized that the ADA allowed Albertson's to establish a reasonable job-related vision standard as a prerequisite for hiring and that Albertson's could rely on Government regulations as a basis for setting its standard. The court held, however, that Albertson's could not use compliance with a Government regulation as the justification for its vision requirement because the waiver program, which Albertson's disregarded, was "a lawful and legitimate part of the DOT regulatory scheme." The Court of Appeals conceded that Albertson's was free to set a vision standard different from that mandated by the DOT, but held that under the ADA, Albertson's would have to justify its independent standard as necessary to prevent " 'a direct threat to the health or safety of other individuals in the workplace.' " Although the court suggested that Albertson's might be able to make such a showing on remand, it ultimately took the position that the company could not, interpreting petitioner's rejection of DOT waivers as flying in the face of the judgment about safety already embodied in the DOT's decision to grant them.

* * *

III

Petitioner's primary contention is that even if Kirkingburg was disabled, he was not a "qualified" individual with a disability, see 42 U.S.C. § 12112(a), because Albertson's merely insisted on the minimum level of visual acuity set forth in the DOT's Motor Carrier Safety Regulations. If Albertson's was entitled to enforce that standard as defining an "essential job functio[n] of the employment position," see 42 U.S.C. § 12111(8), that is the end of the case, for Kirkingburg concededly could not satisfy it.

Under Title I of the ADA, employers may justify their use of "qualification standards . . . that screen out or tend to screen out or otherwise deny a job or benefit to an individual with a disability," so long as such standards are "job-related and consistent with business necessity, and . . . performance cannot be accomplished by reasonable accommodation . . . ." § 12113(a). See also § 12112(b)(6) (defining discrimination to include "using qualification standards . . . that screen out or tend to screen out an individual with a disability . . . unless the standard . . . is shown to be job-related for the position in question and is consistent with business necessity").

Kirkingburg and the Government argue that these provisions do not authorize an employer to follow even a facially applicable regulatory standard subject to waiver without making some enquiry beyond determining whether the applicant or employee meets that standard, yes or no. Before an employer may insist on compliance, they say, the employer must make a showing with reference to the particular job that the waivable regulatory standard is "job-related . . . and . . . consistent with business necessity," see § 12112(b)(6), and that after consideration of the capabilities of the individual a reasonable accommodation could not fairly resolve the competing interests when an applicant or employee cannot wholly satisfy an otherwise justifiable job qualification.

The Government extends this argument by reference to a further section of the statute, which at first blush appears to be a permissive provision for the employer's and the public's benefit. An employer may impose as a qualification standard "a requirement that an individual shall not pose a direct threat to the health or safety of other individuals in the workplace," § 12113(b), with "direct threat" being defined by the Act as "a significant risk to the health or safety of others that cannot be eliminated by reasonable accommodation," § 12111(3); see also 29 C.F.R. § 1630.2(r) (1998). The Government urges us to read subsections (a) and (b) together to mean that when an employer would impose any safety qualification standard, however specific, tending to screen out individuals with disabilities, the application of the requirement must satisfy the ADA's "direct threat" criterion. That criterion ordinarily requires "an individualized assessment of the individual's present ability to safely perform the essential functions of the job," 29 C.F.R. § 1630.2(r) (1998),"based on medical or other objective evidence" * * *.

Albertson's answers essentially that even assuming the Government has proposed a sound reading of the statute for the general run of cases, this case is not in the general run. It is crucial to its position that Albertson's here was not insisting upon a job qualification merely of its own devising, subject to possible questions about genuine appropriateness and justifiable application to an individual for whom some accommodation may be reasonable. The job qualification it was applying was the distant visual acuity standard of the Federal Motor Carrier Safety Regulations * * *. The validity of these regulations is unchallenged, they have the force of law, and they contain no qualifying language about individualized determinations.

If we looked no further, there would be no basis to question petitioner's unconditional obligation to follow the regulations and its consequent right to do so. This, indeed, was the understanding of Congress when it enacted the ADA. But there is more: the waiver program.

The Court of Appeals majority concluded that the waiver program "precludes [employers] from declaring that persons determined by DOT to be capable of performing the job of commercial truck driver are incapable of performing that job by virtue of their disability," and that in the face of a waiver an employer "will not be able to avoid the [ADA's] strictures by showing that its standards are necessary to prevent a direct safety threat." The Court of Appeals thus assumed that the regulatory provisions for the waiver program had to be treated as being on par with the basic visual acuity regulation, as if the general rule had been modified by some different safety standard made applicable by grant of a waiver. * * * On this reading, an individualized determination under a different substantive safety rule was an element of the regulatory regime, which would easily fit with any requirement of 42 U.S.C. §§ 12113(a) and (b) to consider reasonable accommodation. An employer resting solely on the federal standard for its visual acuity qualification would be required to accept a waiver once obtained, and probably to provide an applicant some opportunity to obtain a waiver whenever that was reasonably possible. If this was sound analysis, the District Court's summary judgment for Albertson's was error.

But the reasoning underlying the Court of Appeal's decision was unsound, for we think it was error to read the regulations establishing the waiver program as modifying the content of the basic visual acuity standard in a way that disentitled an employer like Albertson's to insist on it. To be sure, this is not immediately apparent. If one starts with the statutory provisions authorizing regulations by the DOT as they stood at the time the DOT began the waiver program, one would reasonably presume that the general regulatory standard and the regulatory waiver standard ought to be accorded equal substantive significance, so that the content of any general regulation would as a matter of law be deemed modified by the terms of any waiver standard thus applied to it. * * * Safe operation is supposed to be the touchstone of regulation in each instance.

As to the general visual acuity regulations in force under the former provision, affirmative determinations that the selected standards were needed for safe operation were indeed the predicates of the DOT action. Starting in 1937, the federal agencies authorized to regulate commercial motor vehicle safety set increasingly rigorous visual acuity standards, culminating in the current one, which has remained unchanged since it became effective in 1971. When the FHWA proposed it, the agency found that "[a]ccident experience in recent years has demonstrated that reduction of the effects of organic and physical disorders, emotional impairments, and other limitations of the good health of drivers are increasingly important factors in accident prevention," 34 Fed. Reg. 9080, 9081 (1969) (Notice of Proposed Rule Making); the current standard was adopted to reflect the agency's conclusion that "drivers of modern, more complex vehicles" must be able to "withstand the increased physical and mental demands that their occupation now imposes." 35 Fed. Reg. 6458 (1970). Given these findings and "in the light of discussions with the Administration's medical advisers," *id.* at 6459, the FHWA made a considered determination about the level of visual acuity needed for safe operation of commercial motor vehicles in interstate commerce, an "area [in which] the risks involved are so well known and so serious as to dictate the utmost caution." *Id.* at 17419.

For several reasons, one would expect any regulation governing a waiver program to establish a comparable substantive standard (albeit for exceptional cases), grounded on known facts indicating at least that safe operation would not be jeopardized. * * *

And yet, despite this background, the regulations establishing the waiver program did not modify the general visual acuity standards. * * * The FHWA in fact made it clear that it had no evidentiary basis for concluding that the pre-existing standards could be lowered consistently with public safety. When, in 1992, the FHWA published an "[a]dvance notice of proposed rulemaking" requesting comments "on the need, if any, to amend its driver qualification requirements relating to the vision standard," *id.* at 6793, it candidly proposed its waiver scheme as simply a means of obtaining information bearing on the justifiability of revising the binding standards already in place, see *id.* at 10295. The agency explained that the "object of the waiver program is to provide objective data to be considered in relation to a rulemaking exploring the feasibility of relaxing the current absolute vision standards in 49 C.F.R. part 391 in favor of a more individualized standard." *Ibid.* As proposed, therefore, there was not only no change in the unconditional acuity standards, but no indication even that the FHWA then had a basis in fact to believe anything more lenient would be consistent with public safety as a general matter. * * *

In sum, the regulatory record made it plain that the waiver regulation did not rest on any final, factual conclusion that the waiver scheme would be conducive to public safety in the manner of the general acuity standards and did not purport to modify the substantive content of the general acuity regulation in any way. The waiver program was simply an experiment with safety, however well intended, resting on a hypothesis whose confirmation or refutation in practice would provide a factual basis for reconsidering the existing standards.

Nothing in the waiver regulation, of course, required an employer of commercial drivers to accept the hypothesis and participate in the Government's experiment. The only question, then, is whether the ADA should be read to require such an employer to defend a decision to decline the experiment. Is it reasonable, that is, to read the ADA as requiring an employer like Albertson's to shoulder the general statutory burden to justify a job qualification that would tend to exclude the disabled, whenever the employer chooses to abide by the otherwise clearly applicable, unamended substantive regulatory standard despite the Government's willingness to waive it experimentally and without any finding of its being inappropriate? If the answer were yes, an employer would in fact have an obligation of which we can think of no comparable example in our law. The employer would be required in effect to justify *de novo* an existing and otherwise applicable safety regulation issued by the Government itself. The employer would be required on a case-by-case basis to reinvent the Government's own wheel when the Government had merely begun an experiment to provide data to consider changing the underlying specifications. And what is even more, the employer would be required to do so when the Government had made an affirmative record indicating that contemporary empirical evidence was hard to come by. It is simply not credible that Congress enacted the ADA (before there was any waiver program) with the understanding that employers choosing to respect the Government's sole substantive visual acuity regulation in the face of an experimental waiver might be burdened with an obligation to defend the regulation's application according to its own terms.

* * *

1. What reasons did Albertsons offer for not having to comply with the DOT waiver? Why did the Court agree?

2. What statement, if any, does this case make about the DOT's waiver program? Do you think this was an intended consequence of the case? Will it make other public agencies less likely to create similar waiver programs?

3. Since the *Kirkingurg* decision, the Department of Transportation Federal Motor Carrier Safety Administration has granted exemptions to numerous individuals with monocular vision, but has largely maintained the general requirement for binocular vision. The agency described the results of its studies of monocular vision as follows:

> Since 1992, the agency has undertaken studies to determine if this vision standard should be amended. The final report from our medical panel recommends changing the field of vision standard from 70 to 120, while leaving the visual acuity standard unchanged. (*See* Frank C. Berson, M.D., Mark C. Kuperwaser, M.D., Lloyd Paul Aiello, M.D., and James W. Rosenberg, M.D., "Visual Requirements and Commercial Drivers," October 16, 1998, filed in the docket, FHWA-98-4334.) The panel's conclusion supports the agency's view that the present visual acuity standard is reasonable and necessary as a general standard to ensure highway safety. The FMCSA also recognizes that some drivers do not meet the vision standard, but have adapted their driving to accommodate their vision limitation and demonstrated their ability to drive safely.

69 Fed. Reg. 31447 (June 3, 2004). Would the increased number of individuals with monocular vision being found safe to drive commercial vehicles have altered the court's attitude to Mr. Kirkingburg's case?

§ 5.2 Essential Requirements

Under Title I, qualification means the person can perform the essential functions of the job at issue with or without reasonable accommodations. 29 C.F.R. pt. 1630 app., § 1630.2(m). The essential functions of the job are "the fundamental job duties of the employment position . . . . The term 'essential functions' does not include the marginal functions of the position." *Id.* § 1630.2(n)(1).

> A job function may be considered essential for any of several reasons, including but not limited to the following:
>
> (i) The function may be essential because the reason the position exists is to perform that function;

(ii)   The function may be essential because of the limited number of employees available among whom the performance of that job function can be distributed; and/or

(iii)   The function may be highly specialized so that the incumbent in the position is hired for his or her expertise or ability to perform the particular function.

29 C.F.R. § 1630.2(n)(2).

Any one of these factors or combination of factors may make a function an essential one. The number of employees to whom a job function may be distributed can be important either because there is a small workforce at a given company in comparison to the work load, or because the work load fluctuates and it is essential to have all employees do multiple tasks during peak work periods. 29 C.F.R. pt. 1630 app., § 1630.2(n).

The essential functions analysis is a factual one. *Id.* Evidence may include:

(i)   The employer's judgment as to which functions are essential;

(ii)   Written job descriptions prepared before advertising or interviewing applicants for the job;

(iii)   The amount of time spent on the job performing the function;

(iv)   The consequences of not requiring the incumbent to perform the function;

(v)   The terms of a collective bargaining agreement;

(vi)   The work experience of past incumbents in the job; and/or,

(vii)   The current work experience of incumbents in similar jobs.

29 C.F.R. § 1630.2(n)(3).

An employer is not required to modify its production standards. Therefore, production standards, such as the ability to type a certain number of words per minute or accomplish a certain number of tasks in a day, will not be subject to judicial scrutiny regarding whether those standards are actually essential. The EEOC Intepretative Guidance provides:

However, if an employer does require [such a production standard] it will have to show that it actually imposes such

requirements on its employees in fact, and not simply on
paper. . . . [I]f it is alleged that the employer intentionally
selected the particular level of production to exclude
individuals with disabilities, the employer may have to offer
a legitimate, nondiscriminatory reason for its selection.

Id. pt. 1630 app., § 1630.2(n).

As noted, the individual may be qualified because she can perform
the essential functions if she is given reasonable accommodations. Thus,
the qualification standard often incorporates the central question of
whether the employer is required to accommodate the individual.

Under Title II, qualification means the person "meets the essential
eligibility requirements for the receipt of services or the participation in
programs or activities provided by a public entity," with or without
reasonable modification to rules, policies or practices, the removal of
architectural barriers, or the provision of auxiliary aids and services. 28
C.F.R. § 35.104 (2011). The essential eligibility requirements for a
program may fall anywhere on the spectrum, from programs that require
a request for services, to programs that require proof of residency within
the jurisdiction providing the service, to programs requiring proof of low
income status.

For many services, programs, or activities that public entities
offer, the only "essential eligibility requirement" is a desire to participate.
In Concerned Parents to Save Dreher Park Center v. City of W. Palm
Beach, 846 F.Supp. 986, 989 (S.D. Fla. 1994), the City of West Palm Beach
had stopped offering several recreational programs, including programs
that previously had been structured for people with disabilities. In
considering whether the plaintiffs (various individuals with disabilities
and associations of parents and volunteers) were "qualified individuals
with disabilities," the court held that the only "essential eligibility
requirements" of a city's recreational program is a request for benefits of
the program. *Id.* at 990. The Title II Technical Assistance Manual issued
by the DOJ recognizes that oftentimes this will be the case. *See* TAM II
§ 2.8000 ("The 'essential eligibility requirements' for participation in some
activities covered under this part may be minimal. For example, most
public entities provide information about their operations as a public
service to anyone who requests it. In such situations, the only "eligibility
requirement" for receipt of such information would be the request for it.").

In *Southeastern Community College v. Davis*, 442 U.S. 397 (1979),
discussed *supra*, § 1.4.C, the Supreme Court explored the balance between
qualification and modification of eligibility standards under Section 504 of
the Rehabilitation Act.

Notes & Questions

1. Is an employee who is on disability leave "qualified" for purposes of protection under the ADA? Can she be denied insurance benefits offered to other employees while on leave? *See* Johnson v. K-Mart Corp., 273 F.3d 1035 (11th Cir. 2001) (former employee may be a qualified individual with a disability for purposes of ADA claim); Weyer v. Twentieth Century Fox Film Corp., 198 F.3d 1104, 1110 (9th Cir. 2000) (not qualified); EEOC v. CNA Ins. Cos., 96 F.3d 1039, 1045 (7th Cir. 1996) (not qualified). *But see* Ford v. Schering-Plough Corp., 145 F.3d 601, 608 (3d Cir. 1998); Castellano v. City of N.Y., 142 F.3d 58, 68 (2d Cir. 1998). *Cf.* Robinson v. Shell Oil Co., 519 U.S. 337 (1997) (Title VII of the Civil Rights Act covers former employees).

2. In *Southeastern Community College v. Davis*, Ms. Davis argued that she did not intend to practice all the positions available to a registered nurse and, therefore, that the nursing degree program could reasonably be altered to accommodate her. This argument has been made by medical students with disabilities (e.g., a blind medical student intending to practice psychiatry and requesting exemption from surgery requirements). The Court rejected this argument in *Davis*, finding that the school has the right to define the meaning of its degree program broadly. Is it fair to allow a school to exclude students with disabilities from a degree program by pre-judging the possible limits of their careers? With the constant advancement of technology, more careers are available to people with disabilities every day, yet schools may rely on outdated assumptions to prevent them from qualifying for those careers. Should schools be required to focus exclusively on education qualifications, and let future employers focus on employment qualifications?

3. In *Alexander v. Choate*, 469 U.S. 287, 301 (1985), the Court stated:

> The balance struck in *Davis* requires that an otherwise qualified handicapped individual must be provided with meaningful access to the benefit that the grantee offers. The benefit itself, of course, cannot be defined in a way that effectively denies otherwise qualified handicapped individuals the meaningful access to which they are entitled; to assure meaningful access, reasonable accommodations in the grantee's program or benefit may have to be made.

Does this differ from the Court's approach in *Davis* in terms of the level of deference to be accorded to an entity's eligibility criteria? Are the eligibility standards of institutions of higher education entitled to greater deference than other governmental entities? *See* Wynne v. Tufts Univ. Sch. of Med., 976 F.2d 791, 795 (1st Cir. 1992), cert. denied 507 U.S. 1030

(1993) (school demonstrated that it had considered alternatives to multiple-choice testing and "came to a rationally justifiable conclusion" that alternatives would lower academic standards." It was enough that "Tufts decided, rationally if not inevitably, that no further accommodation could be made without imposing an undue (and injurious) hardship on the academic program."); Zukle v. Regents of the Univ. of Cal., 166 F.3d 1041, 1047-48 (9th Cir. 1999) (court defers to school's determination that in-hospital clerkships are essential). Also consider the context of race-based eligibility criteria. *See* Grutter v. Bollinger, 539 U.S. 306 (2003).

4. The ADA regulations provide several reasons for considering a job function essential, such as being the basis for the job or if the function requires highly specialized skills and is distinct to the job. 29 C.F.R. § 1630.2(n)(2). Is a job function essential if it exists for the safety of the employee who performs it? *See* Turner v. Hershey Chocolate USA, 440 F.3d 604 (3d Cir. 2006) (it is a jury question whether participation in job rotation system designed to reduce risk of repetitive motion injuries is an essential function). Is the ability to evacuate the workplace on one's own accord, in the event of an emergency, an essential function? *See* U.S. EEOC v. E.I. DuPont de Nemours & Co., 406 F.Supp.2d 645 (E.D. La. 2005), affirmed in part and reversed in part, 480 F.3d 724 (5th Cir. 2007) (ability to walk in case of an emergency evacuation not an essential function).

§ 5.3 Estoppel

Can an individual with a disability be estopped from claiming she is qualified if she has made contradictory statements about her capabilities? Because applications for some benefits require the applicant to certify that she is unable to work, some defendants have argued that those statements should automatically estop individuals from claiming that they were qualified for positions from which they were excluded.

CLEVELAND v. POLICY MANAGEMENT SYSTEMS CORP.

Supreme Court of the United States, 1999
526 U.S. 795

Mr. Justice BREYER delivered the opinion of the Court.

The Social Security Disability Insurance (SSDI) program provides benefits to a person with a disability so severe that she is "unable to do [her] previous work" and "cannot . . . engage in any other kind of substantial gainful work which exists in the national economy." § 223(a) of the Social Security Act, as set forth in 42 U.S.C. § 423(d)(2)(A). This case asks whether the law erects a special presumption that would significantly inhibit an SSDI recipient from simultaneously pursuing an action for disability discrimination under the Americans with Disabilities Act of 1990 (ADA), claiming that "with . . . reasonable accommodation" she could "perform the essential functions" of her job. § 42 U.S.C. § 12111(8). We believe that, in context, these two seemingly divergent statutory contentions are often consistent, each with the other. Thus pursuit, and receipt, of SSDI benefits does not automatically estop the recipient from pursuing an ADA claim. Nor does the law erect a strong presumption against the recipient's success under the ADA. Nonetheless, an ADA plaintiff cannot simply ignore her SSDI contention that she was too disabled to work. To survive a defendant's motion for summary judgment, she must explain why that SSDI contention is consistent with her ADA claim that she could "perform the essential functions" of her previous job, at least with "reasonable accommodation."

I

After suffering a disabling stroke and losing her job, Carolyn Cleveland sought and obtained SSDI benefits from the Social Security Administration (SSA). She has also brought this ADA suit in which she claims that her former employer, Policy Management Systems Corporation, discriminated against her on account of her disability. The two claims developed in the following way:

> *August 1993*: Cleveland began work at Policy Management Systems. Her job required her to perform background checks on prospective employees of Policy Management System's clients.

> *January 7, 1994*: Cleveland suffered a stroke, which damaged her concentration, memory, and language skills.

> *January 28, 1994*: Cleveland filed an SSDI application in which she stated that she was "disabled" and "unable to work."

> *April 11, 1994*: Cleveland's condition having improved, she returned to work with Policy Management Systems. She reported that fact to the SSA two weeks later.

> *July 11, 1994*: Noting that Cleveland had returned to work, the SSA denied her SSDI application.

> *July 15, 1994*: Policy Management Systems fired Cleveland.

> *September 14, 1994*: Cleveland asked the SSA to reconsider its July 11th SSDI denial. In doing so, she said: "I was terminated [by Policy Management Systems] due to my condition and I have not been able to work since. I continue to be disabled." She later added that she had "attempted to return to work in mid April," that she had "worked for three

130

months," and that Policy Management Systems terminated her because she "could no longer do the job" in light of her "condition."

November 1994: The SSA denied Cleveland's request for reconsideration. Cleveland sought an SSA hearing, reiterating that "I am unable to work due to my disability," and presenting new evidence about the extent of her injuries.

September 29, 1995: The SSA awarded Cleveland SSDI benefits retroactive to the day of her stroke, January 7, 1994.

On September 22, 1995, the week before her SSDI award, Cleveland brought this ADA lawsuit. She contended that Policy Management Systems had "terminat[ed]" her employment without reasonably "accommodat[ing] her disability." She alleged that she requested, but was denied, accommodations such as training and additional time to complete her work. And she submitted a supporting affidavit from her treating physician. The District Court did not evaluate her reasonable accommodation claim on the merits, but granted summary judgment to the defendant because, in that court's view, Cleveland, by applying for and receiving SSDI benefits, had conceded that she was totally disabled. And that fact, the court concluded, now estopped Cleveland from proving an essential element of her ADA claim, namely, that she could "perform the essential functions" of her job, at least with "reasonable accommodation." 42 U.S.C. § 12111(8).

The Fifth Circuit affirmed the District Court's grant of summary judgment. The court wrote:

> "[T]he application for or the receipt of social security disability benefits creates a *rebuttable* presumption that the claimant or recipient of such benefits is judicially estopped from asserting that he is a 'qualified individual with a disability.'"

The Circuit Court noted that it was "at least theoretically conceivable that under some limited and highly unusual set of circumstances the two claims would not necessarily be mutually exclusive." But it concluded that, because

> "Cleveland consistently represented to the SSA that she was totally disabled, she has failed to raise a genuine issue of material fact rebutting the presumption that she is judicially estopped from now asserting that for the time in question she was nevertheless a 'qualified individual with a disability' for purposes of her ADA claim."

We granted certiorari in light of disagreement among the Circuits about the legal effect upon an ADA suit of the application for, or receipt of, disability benefits. * * *

II

The Social Security Act and the ADA both help individuals with disabilities, but in different ways. The Social Security Act provides monetary benefits to every insured individual who "is under a disability." 42 U.S.C. § 423(a)(1). The Act defines "disability" as an "inability to engage in any substantial gainful activity by reason of any . . . physical or mental impairment which can be expected to result in death or which has lasted or can be expected to last for a continuous period of not less than 12 months." § 423(d)(1)(A). The individual's impairment must be

> "of such severity that [she] is not only unable to do [her] previous work but cannot, considering [her] age, education, and work experience, engage in any other kind of substantial gainful work which exists in the national economy . . ." § 423(d)(2)(A).

The ADA seeks to eliminate unwarranted discrimination against disabled individuals in order both to guarantee those individuals equal opportunity and to provide the Nation with the benefit of their consequently increased productivity. See, *e.g.*, 42 U.S.C. §§ 12101(a)(8),(9). The ADA prohibits covered employers from discriminating "against a qualified individual with a disability because of the disability of such individual." § 12112(a). The ADA defines a "qualified individual with a disability" as a disabled person "who . . . can perform the essential functions" of her job, including those who can do so only "with . . . reasonable accommodation." § 12111(8).

* * *

The Court of Appeals thought, in essence, that claims under both Acts would incorporate two directly conflicting propositions, namely, "I am too disabled to work" and "I am not too disabled to work." And in an effort to prevent two claims that would embody that kind of factual conflict, the court used a special judicial presumption, which it believed would ordinarily prevent a plaintiff like Cleveland from successfully asserting an ADA claim. In our view, however, despite the appearance of conflict that arises from the language of the two statutes, the two claims do not inherently conflict to the point where courts should apply a special negative presumption like the one applied by the Court of Appeals here. That is because there are too many situations in which an SSDI claim and an ADA claim can comfortably exist side by side.

For one thing, as we have noted, the ADA defines a "qualified individual" to include a disabled person "who . . . can perform the essential functions" of her job *"with reasonable accommodation."* Reasonable accommodations may include:

"job restructuring, part-time or modified work schedules, reassignment to a vacant position, acquisition or modification of equipment or devices, appropriate adjustment or modifications of examinations, training materials or policies, the provision of qualified readers or interpreters, and other similar accommodations." 42 U.S.C. § 12111(9)(B).

By way of contrast, when the SSA determines whether an individual is disabled for SSDI purposes, it does *not* take the possibility of "reasonable accommodation" into account, nor need an applicant refer to the possibility of reasonable accommodation when she applies for SSDI. The omission reflects the facts that the SSA receives more than 2.5 million claims for disability benefits each year; its administrative resources are limited; the matter of "reasonable accommodation" may turn on highly disputed workplace-specific matters; and an SSA misjudgment about that detailed, and often fact-specific matter would deprive a seriously disabled person of the critical financial support the statute seeks to provide. The result is that an ADA suit claiming that the plaintiff can perform her job *with* reasonable accommodation may well prove consistent with an SSDI claim that the plaintiff could not perform her own job (or other jobs) *without* it.

For another thing, in order to process the large number of SSDI claims, the SSA administers SSDI with the help of a five-step procedure that embodies a set of presumptions about disabilities, job availability, and their interrelation. The SSA asks:

Step One: Are you presently working? (If so, you are ineligible.)

Step Two: Do you have a "severe impairment," *i.e.*, one that "significantly limits" your ability to do basic work activities? (If not, you are ineligible.)

Step Three: Does your impairment "mee[t] or equa[l]" an impairment on a specific (and fairly lengthy) SSA list? (If so, you are eligible *without more*.)

Step Four: If your impairment does not meet or equal a listed impairment, can you perform your "past relevant work?" (If so, you are ineligible.)

Step Five: If your impairment does not meet or equal a listed impairment and you cannot perform your "past relevant work," then can you perform other jobs that exist in significant numbers in the national economy? (If not, you are eligible.)

The presumptions embodied in these questions – particularly those necessary to produce Step Three's list, which, the Government tells us, accounts for approximately 60 percent of all awards, grow out of the need to administer a large benefits system efficiently. But they inevitably simplify, eliminating consideration of many differences potentially relevant to an individual's ability to perform a particular job. Hence, an individual might qualify for SSDI under the SSA's administrative rules and yet, due to special individual circumstances, remain capable of "perform[ing] the essential functions" of her job.

Further, the SSA sometimes grants SSDI benefits to individuals who not only can work, but are working. For example, to facilitate a disabled person's reentry into the workforce, the SSA authorizes a 9-month trial-work period during which SSDI recipients may receive full benefits. * * * Improvement in a totally disabled person's physical condition, while permitting that person to work, will not necessarily or immediately lead the SSA to terminate SSDI benefits. And the nature of an individual's disability may change over time, so that a statement about that disability at the time of an individual's application for SSDI benefits may not reflect an individual's capacities at the time of the relevant employment decision.

Finally, if an individual has merely applied for, but has not been awarded, SSDI benefits, any inconsistency in the theory of the claims is of the sort normally tolerated by our legal system. Our ordinary Rules recognize that a person may not be sure in advance upon which legal theory she will succeed, and so permit parties to "set forth two or more statements of a claim or defense alternately or hypothetically," and to "state as many separate claims or defenses as the party has regardless of consistency." Fed. R. Civ. P. 8(e)(2). We do not see why the law in respect to the assertion of SSDI and ADA claims should differ. (And, as we said, we leave the law in respect to purely factual contradictions where we found it.)

In light of these examples, we would not apply a special legal presumption permitting someone who has applied for, or received, SSDI benefits to bring an ADA suit only in "some limited and highly unusual set of circumstances."

Nonetheless, in some cases an earlier SSDI claim may turn out genuinely to conflict with an ADA claim. Summary judgment for a defendant is appropriate when the plaintiff "fails to make a showing sufficient to establish the existence of an element essential to [her] case, and on which [she] will bear the burden of proof at trial." *Celotex Corp. v. Catrett*, 477 U.S. 317, 322 (1986). An ADA plaintiff bears the burden of proving that she is a "qualified individual with a disability" – that is, a person "who, with or without reasonable accommodation, can perform the essential functions" of her job. 42 U.S.C. §12111(8). And a plaintiff's sworn assertion in an application for disability benefits that she is, for example, "unable to work" will appear to negate an essential element of her ADA case – at least if she does not offer a sufficient explanation. For that reason, we hold that an ADA plaintiff cannot simply ignore the apparent contradiction that arises out of the earlier SSDI total disability claim. Rather, she must proffer a sufficient explanation.

* * * When faced with a plaintiff's previous sworn statement asserting "total disability" or the like, the court should require an explanation of any apparent inconsistency with the necessary elements of an ADA claim. To defeat summary judgment, that explanation must be sufficient to warrant a reasonable juror's concluding that, assuming the truth of, or the plaintiff's good-faith belief in, the earlier statement, the plaintiff could nonetheless "perform the essential functions" of her job, with or without "reasonable accommodation."

III

In her brief in this Court, Cleveland explains the discrepancy between her SSDI statements that she was "totally disabled" and her ADA claim that she could "perform the essential functions" of her job. The first statements, she says, "were made in a forum which does not consider the effect that reasonable workplace accommodations would have on the ability to work." Moreover, she claims the SSDI statements were "accurate statements" if examined "in the time period in which they were made." The parties should have the opportunity in the trial court to present, or to contest, these explanations, in sworn form where appropriate. Accordingly, we vacate the judgment of the Court of Appeals and remand the case for further proceedings consistent with this opinion.

It is so ordered.

Notes & Questions

1. What kinds of explanations would satisfy the Court's requirement that a plaintiff be able to explain the discrepancy between an application for benefits and an ADA lawsuit? *See* Turner v. Hershey Chocolate USA, 440 F.3d 604 (3d Cir. 2006) (explanation was adequate when plaintiff's benefits application stated that she could not perform the essential functions of her job, as defined by her employer, without accommodations, and ADA case challenged the employer's definition of essential functions and refusal to provide reasonable accommodations). *But see* Detz v. Greiner Indus., Inc., 346 F.3d 109 (3d Cir. 2003) (plaintiff's application for benefits stating that he was physically incapable of working conflicted with ADA claim alleging he was fired from job that he was physically capable of performing). Is the explanation more viable in a failure to accommodate case than in a discharge case?

Part 3

Employment Discrimination: ADA Title I
Analysis

Chapter 6   OBJECTS OF TITLE I
§ 6.1   Overview
§ 6.2   Covered Entities
    A. Definition Of Employer
    B. Definition Of Employee
    C. Jurisdictional Versus Merits Analysis Of Covered Entity
    D. States As Employers
    E. Title I Covered Employers: Illustrations
§ 6.3   Hiring, Discipline And Benefits
    A. Hiring
    B. Discipline
    C. Benefits And Privileges Of Employment
Chapter 7   EXAMINATIONS AND INQUIRIES
§ 7.1   Permissible Scope Of Inquiries And Examinations
    A. Pre-Employment
    B. Post-Conditional Offer
    C. Course Of Employment
    D. Return To Work
§ 7.2   Confidentiality Of Information
§ 7.3   Rights Of People Without Disabilities To Bring
    Inquiry/Examination Claims – Standing
Chapter 8   REASONABLE ACCOMMODATION
§ 8.1   Overview And Illustrations
    A. Statutory Definitions
    B. EEOC Regulations
    C. Failure To Accommodate Claim: Summary
    D. Accommodation Illustrations
§ 8.2   The Process
    A. The Request
    B. Interactive Process
    C. Accommodation For "Regarded As" Disability
§ 8.3   Undue Hardship
    A. Statutory Definition
    B. EEOC Regulations
§ 8.4   Burdens Of Production And Proof
    A. Reasonable Accommodation And Undue Hardship
    B. Disparate Treatment – Application Of *McDonnell Douglas Corp.* And *Price Waterhouse*
    C. Disparate Impact – ADA Title I Class Actions

Chapter 9   TITLE I DEFENSES BASED ON QUALIFICATIONS STANDARDS

§ 9.1   Direct Threat Defense To Others And To Self

Chapter 10   TITLE I ENFORCEMENT AND REMEDIES

§ 10.1   Introduction To Remedies

§ 10.2   Title I Remedial Procedure

    A.   Administrative Exhaustion

    B.   Administrative Limitations Periods – Accrual

    C.   Statute Of Limitations

    D.   Role Of The EEOC

§ 10.3   Title I Remedies

    A.   Equitable Remedies

    B.   Compensatory Damages

    C.   Punitive Damages

§ 10.4   Statute Of Limitations

§ 10.5   Attorneys' Fees

    A.   Prevailing Party

    B.   Reasonableness Of Fees

§ 10.6   A Note On The Taxablity Of Attorneys' Fee Awards

Chapter 11   ALTERNATIVE DISPUTE RESOLUTION

§ 11.1   Mediation Of Disability Rights Disputes

§ 11.2   Arbitration Of Disability Rights Disputes

    A.   Arbitrability Of ADA Disputes

    B.   Enforceability Of The Arbitration Agreement: Procedural And Substantive Unconscionability

---

Chapter 6 OBJECTS OF TITLE I

§ 6.1 Overview

Perhaps the most heavily litigated provisions of the ADA have been the employment sections. They impose comprehensive – from application to termination – obligations on covered employers.

Many of the ADA's restrictions may seem counter-intuitive to employers, such as the limitations on pre-employment questioning of applicants, or the need in some circumstances to accommodate an applicant's or employee's disability by restructuring her job or creating another position. Some of the restrictions may run contrary to the prevailing employment at will doctrine that gives substantial discretion to employers.

In this Part we first address the question of which entities are covered under Title I as "employers" and "employees." Next, we turn to the types of inquiries and medical examinations employers may demand. Distinct but related restrictions apply to the pre-employment setting, the post-conditional-offer setting, and the working environment.

A covered entity also has an obligation to reasonably accommodate a qualified person with a disability. We review this obligation in a number of contexts, including those in which an employee requests reassignment and in which an employee must be disciplined. We then briefly delve into wrongful termination law. The Part concludes with a review of the defenses to Title I claims, and the increasing relevance and treatment of expert testimony in Title I cases.

As with much of the Act's interpretation, disputes over the legitimate scope of inquiries and examinations and the degree to which employers must accommodate employees often are fact-specific. Courts may rely on the pragmatics of a situation and this may result in deferring to the employer's judgment of an employee's ability to perform essential functions. Or, it may result in skepticism that a particular examination was a proxy to exclude persons with (or with perceived) disabilities from the workplace.

§ 6.2 Covered Entities

The basic non-discrimination provision of Title I provides:

> No covered entity shall discriminate against a qualified individual "on the basis of disability" in regard to job application procedures, the hiring, advancement, or discharge of employees, employee compensation, job training, and other terms, conditions, and privileges of employment.

42 U.S.C. § 12112(a) (2006).

A.   *Definition Of Employer*

Under Title I, a "covered entity" is defined as "an employer, employment agency, labor organization, or joint labor-management committee." *Id.* § 12111(2). An "employer" is defined as a "person engaged in an industry affecting commerce who has 15 or more employees for each working day in each of 20 or more calendar weeks in the current or preceding calendar year, and any agent of such person . . . ." *Id.* § 12111(5)(A).

An employer does not include the United States, a corporation wholly owned by the United States, an Indian tribe, or a private membership club (other than a labor organization) exempt from taxation under section 501(c) of Title 26 of the Internal Revenue Code of 1986. *Id.* § 12111(5)(B)(i).

The EEOC's Interpretive Guidance on Title I establishes that the term "employer" is to be given the same meaning as under the Civil Rights Act of 1964. *See* 56 Fed. Reg. 35, 740 (1991) (codified at 29 C.F.R. pt 1630 app., § 1630.2 (a)-(f)). The EEOC is the agency designated to administer and enforce ADA Title I. 42 U.S.C. §§ 12116-17. The EEOC's interpretive guidance uses the terms "employer" or "other covered entity" interchangeably to refer to covered entities subject to Title I. The definition of employer in Title I parallels that used in Title VII and in the Age Discrimination in Employment Act of 1967 (ADEA). Williams v. Banning, 72 F.3d 552, 553-54 (7th Cir. 1995). Courts have applied the same standards of individual liability to these statutes. *See, e.g.*, EEOC v. AIC Sec. Investigations, Ltd., 55 F.3d 1276 (7th Cir. 1995) (comparing the ADA, ADEA, and Title VII); Miller v. Maxwell's Int'l, Inc., 991 F.2d 583, 587 (9th Cir. 1993) (comparing ADEA and Title VII).

B. *Definition Of Employee*

Title I defines employers (and therefore covered entities) in terms of having the requisite number of employees. The statutory definition of "employee" is: "an individual employed by an employer." 42 U.S.C. § 12111(4). This definition does not offer much guidance, and the Supreme Court has characterized it as "a mere 'minimal' definition that is 'completely circular and explains nothing.'" Clackamas Gastroenterology Assocs., P.C. v. Wells, 538 U.S. 440, 444 (2003) (quoting Nationwide Mut. Ins. Co. v. Darden, 503 U.S. 318, 323 (1992)).

Confusion often arises regarding the question of how courts should treat an individual who is a shareholder or director of a professional corporation. Are these individuals "employees" for the purposes of the statute? Under the ADA and other federal civil rights statutes, the circuit courts have split on this issue. Some courts have focused on the "economic realties," such as management, control, and ownership, and reasoned that shareholders and directors are more akin to partners and not employees. *See* EEOC v. Dowd & Dowd, Ltd., 736 F.2d 1177, 1178 (1984) (Title VII case).

Other courts have held differently, suggesting that use of corporate form, including a professional corporation, "precludes any examination designed to determine whether the entity is in fact a partnership." Hyland v. New Haven Radiology Ass'n., P.C., 794 F.2d 793, 798 (2d Cir. 1986). In classifying shareholders, directors, and partners as employees, these courts reason that allowing corporations to evade civil rights laws by classifying workers as "partners" or "directors" is unfair. *Id.*

The Supreme Court addressed this conflict in views among the circuits, in *Clackamas Gastroenterology Associates.* The plaintiff worked for the defendant's clinic as a bookkeeper, and brought an action under Title I for disability discrimination. The issue of whether the clinic was a covered entity for purposes of Title I turned on whether its four physician-shareholders (who also constituted the clinic's board of directors) counted as "employees."

℘

CLACKAMAS GASTROENTEROLOGY ASSOCS. v. WELLS

Supreme Court of the United States, 2003
538 U.S. 440

* * *

Justice STEVENS delivered the opinion of the Court.

The Americans with Disabilities Act of 1990 (ADA or Act), * * * like other federal antidiscrimination legislation, is inapplicable to very small businesses. Under the ADA an "employer" is not covered unless its workforce includes "15 or more employees for each working day in each of 20 or more calendar weeks in the current or preceding calendar year." [42 U.S.C.] § 12111(5). The question in this case is whether four physicians actively engaged in medical practice as shareholders and directors of a professional corporation should be counted as "employees."

I

Petitioner, Clackamas Gastroenterology Associates, P. C., is a medical clinic in Oregon. It employed respondent, Deborah Anne Wells, as a bookkeeper from 1986 until 1997. After her termination, she brought this action against the clinic alleging unlawful discrimination on the basis of disability under Title I of the ADA. Petitioner denied that it was covered by the Act and moved for summary judgment, asserting that it did not have 15 or more employees for the 20 weeks required by the statute. It is undisputed that the accuracy of that assertion depends on whether the four physician-shareholders who own the professional corporation and constitute its board of directors are counted as employees.

* * * Relying on an "economic realities" test adopted by the Seventh Circuit in *EEOC v. Dowd & Dowd, Ltd.,* 736 F.2d 1177, 1178 (1984), the District Court concluded that the four doctors were "more analogous to partners in a partnership than to shareholders in a general corporation" and therefore were "not employees for purposes of the federal antidiscrimination laws." App. 89.

A divided panel of the Court of Appeals for the Ninth Circuit reversed. Noting that the Second Circuit had rejected the economic realities approach, the majority held that the use of any corporation, including a professional corporation, "'precludes any examination designed to determine whether the entity is in fact a partnership.'" 271 F.3d 903, 905 (2001) (quoting *Hyland v. New Haven Radiology Associates, P. C.,* 794 F.2d 793, 798 (2d Cir. 1986)). It saw "no reason to permit a professional corporation to secure the 'best of both possible worlds' by allowing it both to assert its corporate status in order to reap the tax and civil liability advantages and to argue that it is like a partnership in order to avoid liability for unlawful employment discrimination." 271 F.3d at 905. * * *

141

We granted certiorari to resolve the conflict in the Circuits, which extends beyond the Seventh and the Second Circuits. * * *

II

"We have often been asked to construe the meaning of 'employee' where the statute containing the term does not helpfully define it." *Nationwide Mut. Ins. Co. v. Darden,* 503 U.S. 318, 322, 112 S.Ct. 1344, 117 L.Ed.2d 581 (1992). The definition of the term in the ADA simply states that an "employee" is "an individual employed by an employer." 42 U.S.C. § 12111(4). That surely qualifies as a mere "nominal definition" that is "completely circular and explains nothing." *Darden,* 503 U.S. at 323, 112 S.Ct. 1344. As we explained in *Darden,* our cases construing similar language give us guidance on how best to fill the gap in the statutory text.

In *Darden* we were faced with the question whether an insurance salesman was an independent contractor or an "employee" covered by the Employee Retirement Income Security Act of 1974 (ERISA). Because ERISA's definition of "employee" was "completely circular," 503 U.S. at 323, 112 S.Ct. 1344, we followed the same general approach that we had previously used in deciding whether a sculptor was an "employee" within the meaning of the Copyright Act of 1976, see *Community for Creative Non-Violence v. Reid,* 490 U.S. 730, 109 S.Ct. 2166, 104 L.Ed.2d 811 (1989), and we adopted a common-law test for determining who qualifies as an "employee" under ERISA. Quoting *Reid,* 490 U.S. at 739-740, 109 S.Ct. 2166, we explained that "'when Congress has used the term "employee" without defining it, we have concluded that Congress intended to describe the conventional master-servant relationship as understood by common-law agency doctrine.'" *Darden,* 503 U.S. at 322-23, 112 S.Ct. 1344.

Rather than looking to the common law, petitioner argues that courts should determine whether a shareholder-director of a professional corporation is an "employee" by asking whether the shareholder-director is, in reality, a "partner." * * * The question whether a shareholder-director is an employee, however, cannot be answered by asking whether the shareholder-director appears to be the functional equivalent of a partner. Today there are partnerships that include hundreds of members, some of whom may well qualify as "employees" because control is concentrated in a small number of managing partners. * * * Thus, asking whether shareholder-directors are partners – rather than asking whether they are employees – simply begs the question.

Nor does the approach adopted by the Court of Appeals in this case fare any better. The majority's approach, which paid particular attention to "the broad purpose of the ADA," 271 F.3d at 905, is consistent with the statutory purpose of ridding the Nation of the evil of discrimination. See 42 U.S.C. § 12101(b). Nevertheless, two countervailing considerations must be weighed in the balance. First, as the dissenting judge noted below, the congressional decision to limit the coverage of the legislation to firms with 15 or more employees has its own justification that must be respected – namely, easing entry into the market and preserving the competitive position of smaller firms. * * * Second, as *Darden* reminds us, congressional silence often reflects an expectation that courts will look to the common law to fill gaps in statutory text, particularly when an undefined term has a settled meaning at common law. Congress has overridden judicial decisions that went beyond the common law in an effort to correct "the mischief" at which a statute was aimed. See *Darden,* 503 U.S. at 324-25, 112 S.Ct. 1344.

Perhaps the Court of Appeals' and the parties' failure to look to the common law for guidance in this case stems from the fact that we are dealing with a new type of business entity that has no exact precedent in the common law. State statutes now permit incorporation for the purpose of practicing a profession, but in the past "the so-called learned professions were not permitted to organize as corporate entities." 1A W. Fletcher, Cyclopedia of the Law of Private Corporations § 112.10 (rev. ed. 1997-2002). Thus, professional corporations are relatively young participants in the market, and their features vary from State to State. * * *

Nonetheless, the common law's definition of the master-servant relationship does provide helpful guidance. At common law the relevant factors defining the master-servant relationship focus on the master's control over the servant. * * * In addition, the Restatement's more specific definition of the term "servant" lists factors to be considered when distinguishing between servants and independent contractors, the first of which is "the extent of control" that one may exercise over the details of the work of the other. [Restatement (Second) of Agency] § 220(2)(a) [(1958)]. We think that the common-law element of control is the principal guidepost that should be followed in this case.

This is the position that is advocated by the Equal Employment Opportunity Commission (EEOC), the agency that has special enforcement responsibilities under the ADA and other federal statutes containing similar threshold issues for determining coverage. It argues that a court should examine "whether shareholder-directors operate independently and manage the business or instead are subject to the firm's control." Brief for United States et al. as Amici Curiae 8. According to the EEOC's view, "[i]f the shareholder-directors operate independently and manage the business, they are proprietors and not employees; if they are subject to the firm's control, they are employees." Ibid.

Specific EEOC guidelines discuss both the broad question of who is an "employee" and the narrower question of when partners, officers, members of boards of directors, and major shareholders qualify as employees. See 2 Equal Employment Opportunity Commission, Compliance Manual §§ 605: 0008-605: 00010 (2000) (hereinafter EEOC

Compliance Manual). With respect to the broad question, the guidelines list 16 factors – taken from *Darden,* 503 U.S. at 323-24, 112 S.Ct. 1344 – that may be relevant to "whether the employer controls the means and manner of the worker's work performance." EEOC Compliance Manual § 605: 0008, and n.71. The guidelines list six factors to be considered in answering the narrower question, which they frame as "whether the individual acts independently and participates in managing the organization, or whether the individual is subject to the organization's control." Id. § 605: 0009.

We are persuaded by the EEOC's focus on the common-law touchstone of control, * * * and specifically by its submission that each of the following six factors is relevant to the inquiry whether a shareholder-director is an employee:

> Whether the organization can hire or fire the individual or set the rules and regulations of the individual's work.

> Whether and, if so, to what extent the organization supervises the individual's work.

> Whether the individual reports to someone higher in the organization.

> Whether and, if so, to what extent the individual is able to influence the organization.

> Whether the parties intended that the individual be an employee, as expressed in written agreements or contracts.

> Whether the individual shares in the profits, losses, and liabilities of the organization.

EEOC Compliance Manual § 605: 0009.

As the EEOC's standard reflects, an employer is the person, or group of persons, who owns and manages the enterprise. The employer can hire and fire employees, can assign tasks to employees and supervise their performance, and can decide how the profits and losses of the business are to be distributed. The mere fact that a person has a particular title – such as partner, director, or vice president – should not necessarily be used to determine whether he or she is an employee or a proprietor. * * * Nor should the mere existence of a document styled "employment agreement" lead inexorably to the conclusion that either party is an employee. * * *

III

Some of the District Court's findings – when considered in light of the EEOC's standard – appear to weigh in favor of a conclusion that the four director-shareholder physicians in this case are not employees of the clinic. For example, they apparently control the operation of their clinic, they share the profits, and they are personally liable for malpractice claims. There may, however, be evidence in the record that would contradict those findings or support a contrary conclusion under the EEOC's standard that we endorse today. Accordingly, as we did in *Darden,* we reverse the judgment of the Court of Appeals and remand the case to that court for further proceedings consistent with this opinion.

It is so ordered.

Justice GINSBURG, with whom Justice BREYER joins, dissenting.

* * * As doctors performing the everyday work of petitioner Clackamas Gastroenterology Associates, P. C., the physician-shareholders function in several respects as common-law employees, a designation they embrace for various purposes under federal and state law. Classifying as employees all doctors daily engaged as caregivers on Clackamas' premises, moreover, serves the animating purpose of the Americans with Disabilities Act of 1990 * * * Seeing no cause to shelter Clackamas from the governance of the ADA, I would affirm the judgment of the Court of Appeals.

An "employee," the ADA provides, is "an individual employed by an employer." 42 U.S.C. § 12111(4). Where, as here, a federal statute uses the word "employee" without explaining the term's intended scope, we ordinarily presume "Congress intended to describe the conventional master-servant relationship as understood by common-law agency doctrine." *Nationwide Mut. Ins. Co. v. Darden,* 503 U.S. 318, 322-23, 112 S.Ct. 1344, 117 L.Ed.2d 581 (1992) (internal quotation marks and citation omitted). The Court today selects one of the common-law indicia of a master-servant relationship – control over the work of others engaged in the business of the enterprise – and accords that factor overriding significance. Ante, at 1679. I would not so shrink the inquiry.

Are the physician-shareholders "servants" of Clackamas for the purpose relevant here? * * * When acting as clinic doctors, the physician-shareholders appear to fit the Restatement definition. The doctors provide services on behalf of the corporation, in whose name the practice is conducted. * * * The doctors have employment contracts with Clackamas, App. 71, under which they receive salaries and yearly bonuses, Tr. of Oral Arg. 8, and they work at facilities owned or leased by the corporation, App. 29, 71. * * *

The physician-shareholders, it bears emphasis, invite the designation "employee" for various purposes under federal and state law. The Employee Retirement Income Security Act of 1974 (ERISA), much like the ADA, defines "employee" as "any individual employed by an employer." 29 U.S.C. § 1002(6). Clackamas readily acknowledges that the physician-shareholders are "employees" for ERISA purposes. Tr. of Oral Arg. 6-7. Indeed, gaining qualification as "employees" under ERISA was the prime reason the physician-shareholders chose the corporate form instead of a partnership. See id. at 7. Further, Clackamas agrees, the physician-shareholders are covered by Oregon's workers' compensation law * * *, a statute applicable to "person [s] * * * who * * * furnish services for a remuneration, subject to the direction and control of an employer," Ore. Rev. Stat. Ann. § 656.005(30) (1996 Supp.). Finally, by electing to organize their practice as a corporation, the physician-shareholders created an entity separate and distinct from themselves, one that would afford them limited liability for the debts of the enterprise. §§ 58.185(4), (5), (10), (11) (1998 Supp.). I see no reason to allow the doctors to escape from their choice of corporate form when the question becomes whether they are employees for purposes of federal antidiscrimination statutes.

Nothing in or about the ADA counsels otherwise. As the Court observes, the reason for exempting businesses with fewer than 15 employees from the Act, was "to spare very small firms from the potentially crushing expense of mastering the intricacies of the antidiscrimination laws, establishing procedures to assure compliance, and defending against suits when efforts at compliance fail." Ante, at 1678-79 (quoting *Papa v. Katy Industries, Inc.,* 166 F.3d 937, 940 (7th Cir. 1999)). The inquiry the Court endorses to determine the physician-shareholders' qualification as employees asks whether they "ac[t] independently and participat[e] in managing the organization, or * * * [are] subject to the organization's control." Ante, at 1680 (quoting 2 Equal Employment Opportunity Commission, Compliance Manual § 605: 0008, and n.71 (2000)). Under the Court's approach, a firm's coverage by the ADA might sometimes turn on variations in ownership structure unrelated to the magnitude of the company's business or its capacity for complying with federal prescriptions.

This case is illustrative. In 1996, Clackamas had 4 physician-shareholders and at least 14 other employees for 28 full weeks; in 1997, it had 4 physician-shareholders and at least 14 other employees for 37 full weeks. * * * Beyond question, the corporation would have been covered by the ADA had one of the physician-shareholders sold his stake in the business and become a "mere" employee. Yet such a change in ownership arrangements would not alter the magnitude of Clackamas' operation: In both circumstances, the corporation would have had at least 18 people on site doing the everyday work of the clinic for the requisite number of weeks.

The Equal Employment Opportunity Commission's approach, which the Court endorses, it is true, "excludes from protection those who are most able to control the firm's practices and who, as a consequence, are least vulnerable to the discriminatory treatment prohibited by the Act." Brief for United States et al. as Amici Curiae 11; see 42 U.S.C. §§ 12111(8), 12112(a) (only "employees" are protected by the ADA). As this dispute demonstrates, however, the determination whether the physician-shareholders are employees of Clackamas affects not only whether they may sue under the ADA, but also — and of far greater practical import — whether employees like bookkeeper Deborah Anne

Wells are covered by the Act. Because the character of the relationship between Clackamas and the doctors supplies no justification for withholding from clerical worker Wells federal protection against discrimination in the workplace, I would affirm the judgment of the Court of Appeals.

Notes & Questions

1. For what purposes do ERISA and the Copyright Act of 1976 define employee? In dissent, Justice Ginsberg expresses concern that "the determination whether . . . physician-shareholders are employees [under the ADA] . . . affects not only whether *they* may [raise a claim]," but also whether other, non-shareholder employees may raise an ADA claim. Clackamas, 538 U.S. at 455 (Ginsburg, J., dissenting) (emphasis added).

2. In *Nationwide Mutual Insurance Co. v. Darden*, 503 U.S. 318 (1992), the plaintiff needed to establish he was an employee under ERISA to have standing to sue his prior employer for denying his retirement plan benefits. In *Community for Creative Non-Violence v. Reid*, 490 U.S. 730 (1989), petitioners sought to establish that respondent (Reid) was an employee under the Copyright Act of 1976 to acquire copyright over the sculpture prepared by respondent under contract with petitioners. Should Well's ADA claim in *Clackamus* turn on whether an individual, who is neither party to the action, nor seeking redress from the court, is an employee under the common law of agency?

3. The dissent criticized the majority's emphasis on the control element, and noted that sheltering shareholder-directors from the ADA ran contrary to the broad purposes of the ADA. *See* Clackamas, 538 U.S. at 451-54 (Ginsburg, J., dissenting). *Clackamas* affects coverage determinations under the Civil Rights Act of 1964 and other employment anti-discrimination laws (e.g., the ADEA), which have language similar to ADA Title I. *See, e.g.*, EEOC v. Dowd & Dowd, Ltd., 736 F.2d 1177, 1178 (7th Cir. 1984) (shareholders of a professional corporation are not employees under Title VII of the Civil Rights Act of 1964); *see also* Nathan Odem & Peter Blanck, Physician-shareholder Practice Groups and ADA Compliance, 28 Spine 3, 309-313 (2003) (discussing other implications of *Clackamas*).

༄

C. *Jurisdictional Versus Merits Analysis Of Covered Entity*

What is the effect of *not* naming a covered entity as a defendant? In other words, is the ADA's requirement that there be discrimination by a "covered entity" who is an "employer" jurisdictional, or is it instead a merits issue? There currently is a split in the Courts of Appeals on this issue. One court has held that a district court lacks subject matter jurisdiction over an ADA claim lodged against a defendant that is neither an employer, employment agency, labor organization, nor a joint labor-management committee as those terms are defined in the ADA. Jones v. Am. Postal Workers Union, 192 F.3d 417, 423 (4th Cir. 1999). Others have held that the question of whether a defendant is a covered entity is not jurisdictional, but merits related. *See* EEOC v. St. Francis Xavier Parochial Sch., 117 F.3d 621, 623-24 (D.C. Cir. 1997).

The Supreme Court has resolved this issue in the Title VII context, where it held that the employee-numerosity requirement for establishing a restaurant's "employer" status was an element of bartender/waitress's claim for relief, whose satisfaction was conceded where not challenged prior to trial on merits, rather than a jurisdictional requirement that could be questioned at any stage of litigation. *See* Arbaugh v. Y&H Corp., 546 U.S. 500 (2006).

D. *States As Employers*

Many individuals are employed by a state or its agencies. However, states are treated differently for ADA Title I purposes than are private employers. One main area of difference has revolved around the question of whether an individual employed by a state may sue the state for money damages in federal court under the ADA's employment discrimination provisions.

୬

**BOARD OF TRUSTEES OF THE
UNIVERSITY OF ALABAMA v. GARRETT**

Supreme Court of the United States, 2001
531 U.S. 356

* * *

Chief Justice REHNQUIST delivered the opinion of the Court.

We decide here whether employees of the State of Alabama may recover money damages by reason of the State's failure to comply with the provisions of Title I of the Americans with Disabilities Act of 1990 (ADA or Act), 104 Stat. 330, 42 U.S.C. §§ 12111-12117. We hold that such suits are barred by the Eleventh Amendment.

The ADA prohibits certain employers, including the States, from "discriminat[ing] against a qualified individual with a disability because of the disability of such individual in regard to job application procedures, the hiring, advancement, or discharge of employees, employee compensation, job training, and other terms, conditions, and privileges of employment." §§ 12112(a), 12111(2), (5), (7). To this end, the Act requires employers to "mak[e] reasonable accommodations to the known physical or mental limitations of an otherwise qualified individual with a disability who is an applicant or employee, unless [the employer] can demonstrate that the accommodation would impose an undue hardship on the operation of the [employer's] business." § 12112(b)(5)(A).

148

[R]easonable accommodation' may include –

(A) making existing facilities used by employees readily accessible to and usable by individuals with disabilities; and (B) job restructuring, part-time or modified work schedules, reassignment to a vacant position, acquisition or modification of equipment or devices, appropriate adjustment or modifications of examinations, training materials or policies, the provision of qualified readers or interpreters, and other similar accommodations for individuals with disabilities.

§ 12111(9).

The Act also prohibits employers from "utilizing standards, criteria, or methods of administration * * * that have the effect of discrimination on the basis of disability." § 12112(b)(3)(A).

* * *

Respondent Patricia Garrett, a registered nurse, was employed as the Director of Nursing, OB/Gyn/Neonatal Services, for the University of Alabama in Birmingham Hospital. See App. 31, 38. In 1994, Garrett was diagnosed with breast cancer and subsequently underwent a lumpectomy, radiation treatment, and chemotherapy. See id. at 38. Garrett's treatments required her to take substantial leave from work. Upon returning to work in July 1995, Garrett's supervisor informed Garrett that she would have to give up her Director position. See id. at 39. Garrett then applied for and received a transfer to another, lower paying position as a nurse manager. See ibid.

Respondent Milton Ash worked as a security officer for the Alabama Department of Youth Services (Department). See id. at 8. Upon commencing this employment, Ash informed the Department that he suffered from chronic asthma and that his doctor recommended he avoid carbon monoxide and cigarette smoke, and Ash requested that the Department modify his duties to minimize his exposure to these substances. See ibid. Ash was later diagnosed with sleep apnea and requested, again pursuant to his doctor's recommendation, that he be reassigned to daytime shifts to accommodate his condition. See id. at 9. Ultimately, the Department granted none of the requested relief. See id. at 8-9. Shortly after Ash filed a discrimination claim with the Equal Employment Opportunity Commission, he noticed that his performance evaluations were lower than those he had received on previous occasions. See id. at 9.

Garrett and Ash filed separate lawsuits in the District Court, both seeking money damages under the ADA. Petitioners moved for summary judgment, claiming that the ADA exceeds Congress' authority to abrogate the State's Eleventh Amendment immunity. See 989 F.Supp. 1409, 1410 (N.D. Ala. 1998). In a single opinion disposing of both cases, the District

Court agreed with petitioners' position and granted their motions for summary judgment. See *id.*, at 1410, 1412. The cases were consolidated on appeal to the Eleventh Circuit. The Court of Appeals reversed, 193 F.3d 1214 (1999), adhering to its intervening decision in *Kimel v. State Bd. of Regents,* 139 F.3d 1426, 1433 (C.A.11 1998), aff'd, 528 U.S. 62, 120 S.Ct. 631, 145 L.Ed.2d 522 (2000), that the ADA validly abrogates the States' Eleventh Amendment immunity.

We granted certiorari, 529 U.S. 1065, 120 S.Ct. 1669, 146 L.Ed.2d 479 (2000), to resolve a split among the Courts of Appeals on the question whether an individual may sue a State for money damages in federal court under the ADA.

I

The Eleventh Amendment provides:

> The Judicial power of the United States shall not be construed to extend to any suit in law or equity, commenced or prosecuted against one of the United States by Citizens of another State, or by Citizens or Subjects of any Foreign State.

Although by its terms the Amendment applies only to suits against a State by citizens of another State, our cases have extended the Amendment's applicability to suits by citizens against their own States. See *Kimel v. Florida Bd. of Regents,* 528 U.S. 62, 72-73, 120 S.Ct. 631, 145 L.Ed.2d 522 (2000); *College Savings Bank v. Florida Prepaid Postsecondary Ed. Expense Bd.,* 527 U.S. 666, 669-670, 119 S.Ct. 2219, 144 L.Ed.2d 605 (1999); *Seminole Tribe of Fla. v. Florida,* 517 U.S. 44, 54, 116 S.Ct. 1114, 134 L.Ed.2d 252 (1996); *Hans v. Louisiana,* 134 U.S. 1, 15, 10 S.Ct. 504, 33 L.Ed. 842 (1890). The ultimate guarantee of the Eleventh Amendment is that nonconsenting States may not be sued by private individuals in federal court. See *Kimel,* supra, at 73, 120 S.Ct. 631.

We have recognized, however, that Congress may abrogate the States' Eleventh Amendment immunity when it both unequivocally intends to do so and "act[s] pursuant to a valid grant of constitutional authority." 528 U.S. at 73, 120 S.Ct. 631. The first of these requirements is not in dispute here. See 42 U.S.C. § 12202 ("A State shall not be immune under the eleventh amendment to the Constitution of the United States from an action in [a] Federal or State court of competent jurisdiction for a violation of this chapter"). The question, then, is whether Congress acted within its constitutional authority by subjecting the States to suits in federal court for money damages under the ADA.

Congress may not, of course, base its abrogation of the States' Eleventh Amendment immunity upon the powers enumerated in Article I. See *Kimel,* supra, at 79, 120 S.Ct. 631 ("Under our firmly established precedent then, if the [Age Discrimination in Employment Act of 1967] rests solely on Congress' Article I commerce power, the private petitioners in today's cases cannot maintain their suits against their state employers"); *Seminole Tribe,* supra, at 72-73, 116 S.Ct. 1114 ("The Eleventh Amendment restricts the judicial power under Article III, and Article I cannot be used to circumvent the constitutional limitations placed upon federal jurisdiction"); * * * In *Fitzpatrick v. Bitzer,* 427 U.S. 445, 96 S.Ct. 2666, 49 L.Ed.2d 614 (1976), however, we held that "the Eleventh Amendment, and the principle of state sovereignty which it embodies, are necessarily limited by the enforcement provisions of § 5 of the Fourteenth Amendment." Id., at 456, 96 S.Ct. 2666 (citation omitted). As a result, we concluded, Congress may subject nonconsenting States to suit in federal court when it does so pursuant to a valid exercise of its § 5 power. See ibid. Our cases have adhered to this proposition. See, e.g., *Kimel,* supra, at 80, 120 S.Ct. 631. Accordingly, the ADA can apply to the States only to the extent that the statute is appropriate § 5 legislation.

Section 1 of the Fourteenth Amendment provides, in relevant part:

No State shall make or enforce any law which shall abridge the privileges or immunities of citizens of the United States; nor shall any State deprive any person of life, liberty, or property, without due process of law; nor deny to any person within its jurisdiction the equal protection of the laws.

Section 5 of the Fourteenth Amendment grants Congress the power to enforce the substantive guarantees contained in § 1 by enacting "appropriate legislation." See *City of Boerne v. Flores,* 521 U.S. 507, 536, 117 S.Ct. 2157, 138 L.Ed.2d 624 (1997). Congress is not limited to mere legislative repetition of this Court's constitutional jurisprudence. "Rather, Congress' power 'to enforce' the Amendment includes the authority both to remedy and to deter violation of rights guaranteed thereunder by prohibiting a somewhat broader swath of conduct, including that which is not itself forbidden by the Amendment's text." *Kimel,* supra, at 81, 120 S.Ct. 631; *City of Boerne,* supra, at 536, 117 S.Ct. 2157.

City of Boerne also confirmed, however, the long-settled principle that it is the responsibility of this Court, not Congress, to define the substance of constitutional guarantees. 521 U.S. at 519-524, 117 S.Ct. 2157. Accordingly, § 5 legislation reaching beyond the scope of § 1's actual guarantees must exhibit "congruence and proportionality between the injury to be prevented or remedied and the means adopted to that end." Id., at 520, 117 S.Ct. 2157.

II

The first step in applying these now familiar principles is to identify with some precision the scope of the constitutional right at issue. Here, that inquiry requires us to examine the limitations § 1 of the Fourteenth Amendment places upon States' treatment of the disabled. As we did last Term in *Kimel,* see 528 U.S. at 83, 120 S.Ct. 631, we look to our prior decisions under the Equal Protection Clause dealing with this issue.

In *Cleburne v. Cleburne Living Center, Inc.,* 473 U.S. 432, 105 S.Ct. 3249, 87 L.Ed.2d 313 (1985), we considered an equal protection challenge to a city ordinance requiring a special use permit for the operation of a group home for the mentally retarded. The specific question before us was whether the Court of Appeals had erred by holding that mental retardation qualified as a "quasi-suspect" classification under our equal protection jurisprudence. Id. at 435, 105 S.Ct. 3249. We answered that question in the affirmative, concluding instead that such legislation incurs only the minimum "rational-basis" review applicable to general social and economic legislation. Id. at 446, 105 S.Ct. 3249. In a statement that today seems quite prescient, we explained that

> if the large and amorphous class of the mentally retarded were deemed quasi-suspect for the reasons given by the Court of Appeals, it would be difficult to find a principled way to distinguish a variety of other groups who have perhaps immutable disabilities setting them off from others, who cannot themselves mandate the desired legislative responses, and who can claim some degree of prejudice from at least part of the public at large. One need mention in this respect only the aging, the disabled, the mentally ill, and the infirm. We are reluctant to set out on that course, and we decline to do so.

Id. at 445-446, 105 S.Ct. 3249.

Under rational-basis review, where a group possesses "distinguishing characteristics relevant to interests the State has the authority to implement," a State's decision to act on the basis of those differences does not give rise to a constitutional violation. Id. at 441, 105 S.Ct. 3249. "Such a classification cannot run afoul of the Equal Protection Clause if there is a rational relationship between the disparity of treatment and some legitimate governmental purpose." *Heller v. Doe,* 509 U.S. 312, 320, 113 S.Ct. 2637, 125 L.Ed.2d 257 (1993) (citing *Nordlinger v. Hahn,* 505 U.S. 1, 112 S.Ct. 2326, 120 L.Ed.2d 1 (1992); *New Orleans v. Dukes,* 427 U.S. 297, 303, 96 S.Ct. 2513, 49 L.Ed.2d 511 (1976) (*per curiam*)). Moreover, the State need not articulate its reasoning at the moment a particular decision is made. Rather, the burden is upon the challenging party to negative " 'any reasonably conceivable state of facts that could provide a rational basis for the classification.' " *Heller,* supra, at 320, 113 S.Ct. 2637 (quoting *FCC v. Beach Communications, Inc.,* 508 U.S. 307, 313, 113 S.Ct. 2096, 124 L.Ed.2d 211 (1993)).

Justice BREYER suggests that *Cleburne* stands for the broad proposition that state decisionmaking reflecting "negative attitudes" or "fear" necessarily runs afoul of the Fourteenth Amendment. See *post,* at 972 (dissenting opinion) (quoting *Cleburne,* 473 U.S. at 448, 105 S.Ct.

3249). Although such biases may often accompany irrational (and therefore unconstitutional) discrimination, their presence alone does not a constitutional violation make. As we noted in *Cleburne:* "[M]ere negative attitudes, or fear, *unsubstantiated by factors which are properly cognizable* in a zoning proceeding, are not permissible bases for treating a home for the mentally retarded differently * * *." Id. at 448, 105 S.Ct. 3249 (emphases added). This language, read in context, simply states the unremarkable and widely acknowledged tenet of this Court's equal protection jurisprudence that state action subject to rational-basis scrutiny does not violate the Fourteenth Amendment when it "rationally furthers the purpose identified by the State." *Massachusetts Bd. of Retirement v. Murgia,* 427 U.S. 307, 314, 96 S.Ct. 2562, 49 L.Ed.2d 520 (1976) (*per curiam*).

Thus, the result of *Cleburne* is that States are not required by the Fourteenth Amendment to make special accommodations for the disabled, so long as their actions toward such individuals are rational. They could quite hardheadedly – and perhaps hardheartedly – hold to job-qualification requirements which do not make allowance for the disabled. If special accommodations for the disabled are to be required, they have to come from positive law and not through the Equal Protection Clause.

III

Once we have determined the metes and bounds of the constitutional right in question, we examine whether Congress identified a history and pattern of unconstitutional employment discrimination by the States against the disabled. Just as § 1 of the Fourteenth Amendment applies only to actions committed "under color of state law," Congress' § 5 authority is appropriately exercised only in response to state transgressions. See *Florida Prepaid,* 527 U.S. at 640, 119 S.Ct. 2199 ("It is this conduct then – unremedied patent infringement by the States – that must give rise to the Fourteenth Amendment violation that Congress sought to redress in the Patent Remedy Act"); *Kimel,* 528 U.S. at 89, 120 S.Ct. 631 ("Congress never identified any pattern of age discrimination by the States, much less any discrimination whatsoever that rose to the level of constitutional violation"). The legislative record of the ADA, however, simply fails to show that Congress did in fact identify a pattern of irrational state discrimination in employment against the disabled.

Respondents contend that the inquiry as to unconstitutional discrimination should extend not only to States themselves, but to units of local governments, such as cities and counties. All of these, they say, are "state actors" for purposes of the Fourteenth Amendment. * * * This is quite true, but the Eleventh Amendment does not extend its immunity to units of local government. See *Lincoln County v. Luning,* 133 U.S. 529, 530, 10 S.Ct. 363, 33 L.Ed. 766 (1890). These entities are subject to private claims for damages under the ADA without Congress' ever having to rely on § 5 of the Fourteenth Amendment to render them so. It would make no sense to consider constitutional violations on their part, as well as by the States themselves, when only the States are the beneficiaries of the Eleventh Amendment.

Congress made a general finding in the ADA that "historically, society has tended to isolate and segregate individuals with disabilities, and, despite some improvements, such forms of discrimination against individuals with disabilities continue to be a serious and pervasive social problem." 42 U.S.C. § 12101(a)(2). The record assembled by Congress includes many instances to support such a finding. But the great majority of these incidents do not deal with the activities of States.

Respondents in their brief cite half a dozen examples from the record that did involve States. A department head at the University of North Carolina refused to hire an applicant for the position of health administrator because he was blind; similarly, a student at a state university in South Dakota was denied an opportunity to practice teach because the dean at that time was convinced that blind people could not teach in public schools. A microfilmer at the Kansas Department of Transportation was fired because he had epilepsy; deaf workers at the University of Oklahoma were paid a lower salary than those who could hear. The Indiana State Personnel Office informed a woman with a concealed disability that she should not disclose it if she wished to obtain employment.

Several of these incidents undoubtedly evidence an unwillingness on the part of state officials to make the sort of accommodations for the disabled required by the ADA. Whether they were irrational under our decision in *Cleburne* is more debatable, particularly when the incident is described out of context. But even if it were to be determined that each incident upon fuller examination showed unconstitutional action on the part of the State, these incidents taken together fall far short of even suggesting the pattern of unconstitutional discrimination on which § 5 legislation must be based. See *Kimel,* supra, at 89-91, 120 S.Ct. 631; *City of Boerne,* 521 U.S. at 530-531, 117 S.Ct. 2157. Congress, in enacting the ADA, found that "some 43,000,000 Americans have one or more physical or mental disabilities." 42 U.S.C. § 12101(a)(1). In 1990, the States alone employed more than 4.5 million people. U.S. Dept. of Commerce, Bureau of Census, Statistical Abstract of the United States 338 (119th ed. 1999) (Table 534). It is telling, we think, that given these large numbers, Congress assembled only such minimal evidence of unconstitutional state discrimination in employment against the disabled.

Justice BREYER maintains that Congress applied Title I of the ADA to the States in response to a host of incidents representing unconstitutional state discrimination in employment against persons with disabilities. A close review of the relevant materials, however, undercuts that conclusion. Justice BREYER's Appendix C consists not of legislative findings, but of unexamined, anecdotal accounts of "adverse, disparate treatment by state officials." * * * Of course, as we have already explained, "adverse, disparate treatment" often does not amount to a constitutional violation where rational-basis scrutiny applies. These accounts, moreover, were submitted not directly to Congress but to the Task Force on the Rights and Empowerment of Americans with Disabilities, which made no findings on the subject of state discrimination in employment.[7] See the Task Force's Report entitled From ADA to Empowerment (Oct. 12, 1990). And, had Congress truly understood this information as reflecting a pattern of unconstitutional behavior by the States, one would expect some mention of that conclusion in the Act's legislative findings. There is none. See 42 U.S.C. § 12101. Although Justice BREYER would infer from Congress' general conclusions regarding societal discrimination against the disabled that the States had likewise participated in such action, *post,* at 970, the House and Senate committee reports on the ADA flatly contradict this assertion. After describing the evidence presented to the Senate Committee on Labor and Human Resources and its subcommittee (including the Task Force Report upon which the dissent relies), the Committee's Report reached, among others, the following conclusion: "Discrimination still persists in such critical areas as *employment in the private sector,* public accommodations, public services, transportation, and telecommunications." S. Rep. No. 101-116, p. 6 (1989) (emphasis added). The House Committee on Education and Labor, addressing the ADA's employment provisions, reached the same conclusion * * * H.R. Rep. No. 101-485, pt. 2, p. 28 (1990), [U.S.C.C.A.N.] 1990 pp. 303, 310. * * * Thus, not only is the inference Justice BREYER draws unwarranted, but there is also strong evidence that Congress' failure to mention States in its legislative findings addressing discrimination in employment reflects that body's judgment that no pattern of unconstitutional state action had been documented.

Even were it possible to squeeze out of these examples a pattern of unconstitutional discrimination by the States, the rights and remedies created by the ADA against the States would raise the same sort of concerns as to congruence and proportionality as were found in *City of Boerne,* supra. For example, whereas it would be entirely rational (and therefore constitutional) for a state employer to conserve scarce financial resources by hiring employees who are able to use existing facilities, the

---

[7]   Only a small fraction of the anecdotes Justice BREYER identifies in his Appendix C relate to state discrimination against the disabled in employment. At most, somewhere around 50 of these allegations describe conduct that could conceivably amount to constitutional violations by the States, and most of them are so general and brief that no firm conclusion can be drawn. The overwhelming majority of these accounts pertain to alleged discrimination by the States in the provision of public services and public accommodations, which areas are addressed in Titles II and III of the ADA.

ADA requires employers to "mak[e] existing facilities used by employees readily accessible to and usable by individuals with disabilities." 42 U.S.C. §§ 12112(5)(B), 12111(9). The ADA does except employers from the "reasonable accommodatio[n]" requirement where the employer "can demonstrate that the accommodation would impose an undue hardship on the operation of the business of such covered entity." § 12112(b)(5)(A). However, even with this exception, the accommodation duty far exceeds what is constitutionally required in that it makes unlawful a range of alternative responses that would be reasonable but would fall short of imposing an "undue burden" upon the employer. The Act also makes it the employer's duty to prove that it would suffer such a burden, instead of requiring (as the Constitution does) that the complaining party negate reasonable bases for the employer's decision. See ibid.

The ADA also forbids "utilizing standards, criteria, or methods of administration" that disparately impact the disabled, without regard to whether such conduct has a rational basis. § 12112(b)(3)(A). Although disparate impact may be relevant evidence of racial discrimination, see *Washington v. Davis,* 426 U.S. 229, 239, 96 S.Ct. 2040, 48 L.Ed.2d 597 (1976), such evidence alone is insufficient even where the Fourteenth Amendment subjects state action to strict scrutiny. See, e.g., ibid. ("[O]ur cases have not embraced the proposition that a law or other official act, without regard to whether it reflects a racially discriminatory purpose, is unconstitutional *solely* because it has a racially disproportionate impact").

The ADA's constitutional shortcomings are apparent when the Act is compared to Congress' efforts in the Voting Rights Act of 1965 to respond to a serious pattern of constitutional violations. In *South Carolina v. Katzenbach,* 383 U.S. 301, 86 S.Ct. 803, 15 L.Ed.2d 769 (1966), we considered whether the Voting Rights Act was "appropriate" legislation to enforce the Fifteenth Amendment's protection against racial discrimination in voting. Concluding that it was a valid exercise of Congress' enforcement power under § 2 of the Fifteenth Amendment, we noted that "[b]efore enacting the measure, Congress explored with great care the problem of racial discrimination in voting." Id. at 308, 86 S.Ct. 803.

In that Act, Congress documented a marked pattern of unconstitutional action by the States. State officials, Congress found, routinely applied voting tests in order to exclude African-American citizens from registering to vote. See id. at 312, 86 S.Ct. 803. Congress also determined that litigation had proved ineffective and that there persisted an otherwise inexplicable 50-percentage-point gap in the registration of white and African-American voters in some States. See id. at 313, 86 S.Ct. 803. Congress' response was to promulgate in the Voting Rights Act a detailed but limited remedial scheme designed to guarantee meaningful enforcement of the Fifteenth Amendment in those areas of the Nation where abundant evidence of States' systematic denial of those rights was identified.

The contrast between this kind of evidence, and the evidence that Congress considered in the present case, is stark. Congressional enactment of the ADA represents its judgment that there should be a "comprehensive national mandate for the elimination of discrimination against individuals with disabilities." 42 U.S.C. § 12101(b)(1). Congress is the final authority as to desirable public policy, but in order to authorize private individuals to recover money damages against the States, there must be a pattern of discrimination by the States which violates the Fourteenth Amendment, and the remedy imposed by Congress must be congruent and proportional to the targeted violation. Those requirements are not met here, and to uphold the Act's application to the States would allow Congress to rewrite the Fourteenth Amendment law laid down by this Court in *Cleburne*. * * * Section 5 does not so broadly enlarge congressional authority. The judgment of the Court of Appeals is therefore

Reversed.

Justice KENNEDY, with whom Justice O'CONNOR joins, concurring.

Prejudice, we are beginning to understand, rises not from malice or hostile animus alone. It may result as well from insensitivity caused by simple want of careful, rational reflection or from some instinctive mechanism to guard against people who appear to be different in some respects from ourselves. Quite apart from any historical documentation, knowledge of our own human instincts teaches that persons who find it difficult to perform routine functions by reason of some mental or physical impairment might at first seem unsettling to us, unless we are guided by the better angels of our nature. There can be little doubt, then, that persons with mental or physical impairments are confronted with prejudice which can stem from indifference or insecurity as well as from malicious ill will.

One of the undoubted achievements of statutes designed to assist those with impairments is that citizens have an incentive, flowing from a legal duty, to develop a better understanding, a more decent perspective, for accepting persons with impairments or disabilities into the larger society. The law works this way because the law can be a teacher. So I do not doubt that the Americans with Disabilities Act of 1990 will be a milestone on the path to a more decent, tolerant, progressive society.

It is a question of quite a different order, however, to say that the States in their official capacities, the States as governmental entities, must be held in violation of the Constitution on the assumption that they embody the misconceived or malicious perceptions of some of their citizens. It is a most serious charge to say a State has engaged in a pattern or practice designed to deny its citizens the equal protection of the laws, particularly where the accusation is based not on hostility but instead on the failure to act or the omission to remedy. States can, and do, stand apart from the citizenry. States act as neutral entities, ready to take instruction and to enact laws when their citizens so demand. The failure of a State to revise policies now seen as incorrect under a new understanding of proper policy does not always constitute the purposeful and intentional action required to make out a violation of the Equal Protection Clause. See *Washington v. Davis,* 426 U.S. 229, 96 S.Ct. 2040, 48 L.Ed.2d 597 (1976).

For the reasons explained by the Court, an equal protection violation has not been shown with respect to the several States in this case. If the States had been transgressing the Fourteenth Amendment by their mistreatment or lack of concern for those with impairments, one would have expected to find in decisions of the courts of the States and also the courts of the United States extensive litigation and discussion of the constitutional violations. This confirming judicial documentation does not exist. That there is a new awareness, a new consciousness, a new commitment to better treatment of those disadvantaged by mental or physical impairments does not establish that an absence of state statutory correctives was a constitutional violation.

It must be noted, moreover, that what is in question is not whether the Congress, acting pursuant to a power granted to it by the Constitution, can compel the States to act. What is involved is only the question whether the States can be subjected to liability in suits brought not by the Federal Government (to which the States have consented, see *Alden v. Maine,* 527 U.S. 706, 755, 119 S.Ct. 2240, 144 L.Ed.2d 636 (1999)), but by private persons seeking to collect moneys from the state treasury without the consent of the State. The predicate for money damages against an unconsenting State in suits brought by private persons must be a federal statute enacted upon the documentation of patterns of constitutional violations committed by the State in its official capacity. That predicate, for reasons discussed here and in the decision of the Court, has not been established. With these observations, I join the Court's opinion.

Justice BREYER, with whom Justice STEVENS, Justice SOUTER, and Justice GINSBURG join, dissenting.

Reviewing the congressional record as if it were an administrative agency record, the Court holds the statutory provision before us, 42 U.S.C. § 12202, unconstitutional. The Court concludes that Congress assembled insufficient evidence of unconstitutional discrimination, * * * that Congress improperly attempted to "rewrite" the law we established in *Cleburne v. Cleburne Living Center, Inc.,* 473 U.S. 432, 105 S.Ct. 3249, 87 L.Ed.2d 313 (1985), * * * and that the law is not sufficiently tailored to address unconstitutional discrimination. * * *

Section 5, however, grants Congress the "power to enforce, by appropriate legislation," the Fourteenth Amendment's equal protection guarantee. U.S. Const., Amdt. 14, § 5. As the Court recognizes, state discrimination in employment against persons with disabilities might

" 'run afoul of the Equal Protection Clause' " where there is no " 'rational relationship between the disparity of treatment and some legitimate governmental purpose.' " Ante * * * (quoting *Heller v. Doe,* 509 U.S. 312, 320, 113 S.Ct. 2637, 125 L.Ed.2d 257 (1993)). See also *Cleburne v. Cleburne Living Center, Inc.,* supra, at 440, 105 S.Ct. 3249 (stating that the Court will sustain a classification if it is "rationally related to a legitimate state interest"). In my view, Congress reasonably could have concluded that the remedy before us constitutes an "appropriate" way to enforce this basic equal protection requirement. And that is all the Constitution requires.

I

The Court says that its primary problem with this statutory provision is one of legislative evidence. It says that "Congress assembled only * * * minimal evidence of unconstitutional state discrimination in employment." * * * In fact, Congress compiled a vast legislative record documenting " 'massive, society-wide discrimination' " against persons with disabilities. S. Rep. No. 101-116, pp. 8-9 (1989) (quoting testimony of Justin Dart, chairperson of the Task Force on the Rights and Empowerment of Americans with Disabilities). In addition to the information presented at 13 congressional hearings * * * and its own prior experience gathered over 40 years during which it contemplated and enacted considerable similar legislation * * * Congress created a special task force to assess the need for comprehensive legislation. That task force held hearings in every State, attended by more than 30,000 people, including thousands who had experienced discrimination first hand. See From ADA to Empowerment, Task Force on the Rights and Empowerment of Americans with Disabilities 16 (Oct. 12, 1990) (hereinafter Task Force Report). The task force hearings, Congress' own hearings, and an analysis of "census data, national polls, and other studies" led Congress to conclude that "people with disabilities, as a group, occupy an inferior status in our society, and are severely disadvantaged socially, vocationally, economically, and educationally." 42 U.S.C. § 12101(a)(6). As to employment, Congress found that "[t]wo-thirds of all disabled Americans between the age of 16 and 64 [were] not working at all," even though a large majority wanted to, and were able to, work productively. S. Rep. No. 101-116, at 9. And Congress found that this discrimination flowed in significant part from "stereotypic assumptions" as well as "purposeful unequal treatment." 42 U.S.C. § 12101(a)(7).

The powerful evidence of discriminatory treatment throughout society in general, including discrimination by private persons and local governments, implicates state governments as well, for state agencies form part of that same larger society. There is no particular reason to believe that they are immune from the "stereotypic assumptions" and pattern of "purposeful unequal treatment" that Congress found prevalent. The Court claims that it "make[s] no sense" to take into consideration constitutional violations committed by local governments. * * * But the substantive obligation that the Equal Protection Clause creates applies to state and local governmental entities alike. E.g., *Richmond v. J.A. Croson Co.,* 488 U.S. 469, 109 S.Ct. 706, 102 L.Ed.2d 854 (1989). Local governments often work closely with, and under the supervision of, state officials, and in general, state and local government employers are similarly situated. Nor is determining whether an apparently "local" entity is entitled to Eleventh Amendment immunity as simple as the majority suggests – it often requires a " 'detailed examination of the relevant provisions of [state] law.' " *Regents of Univ. of Cal. v. Doe,* 519 U.S. 425, 430, n.6, 117 S.Ct. 900, 137 L.Ed.2d 55 (1997) (quoting *Moor v. County of Alameda,* 411 U.S. 693, 719-721, 93 S.Ct. 1785, 36 L.Ed.2d 596 (1973)).

In any event, there is no need to rest solely upon evidence of discrimination by local governments or general societal discrimination. There are roughly 300 examples of discrimination by state governments themselves in the legislative record. * * * I fail to see how this evidence "fall[s] far short of even suggesting the pattern of unconstitutional discrimination on which § 5 legislation must be based." Ante * * *

The congressionally appointed task force collected numerous specific examples, provided by persons with disabilities themselves, of adverse, disparate treatment by state officials. They reveal, not what the Court describes as "half a dozen" instances of discrimination, ibid., but hundreds of instances of adverse treatment at the hands of state officials – instances in which a person with a disability found it impossible to obtain a state job, to retain state employment, to use the public transportation that was readily available to others in order to get to work, or to obtain a public education, which is often a prerequisite to obtaining employment. State-imposed barriers also frequently made it difficult or impossible for people to vote, to enter a public building, to access important government services, such as calling for emergency assistance, and to find a place to live due to a pattern of irrational zoning decisions similar to the discrimination that we held unconstitutional in *Cleburne,* 473 U.S. at 448, 105 S.Ct. 3249. * * *

As the Court notes, those who presented instances of discrimination rarely provided additional, independent evidence sufficient to prove in court that, in each instance, the discrimination they suffered lacked justification from a judicial standpoint. Ante * * * (stating that instances of discrimination are "described out of context"). Perhaps this explains the Court's view that there is "minimal evidence of unconstitutional state discrimination." Ibid. But a legislature is not a court of law. And Congress, unlike courts, must, and does, routinely draw general conclusions – for example, of likely motive or of likely relationship to legitimate need – from anecdotal and opinion-based evidence of this kind, particularly when the evidence lacks strong refutation. See Task Force Report 16, 20 (task force "met many times with significant representatives of groups opposed to [the] ADA," and as to the general public, although the task force received "about 2,000 letters" in support of the ADA, there was only "one letter in opposition"); S. Rep. No. 101-116, at 10 (summarizing testimony that many reasonable accommodations cost "less than $50," and the expense of others, such as hiring employees who can interpret for the deaf, is "frequently exaggerated"). In reviewing § 5 legislation, we have never required the sort of extensive investigation of each piece of evidence that the Court appears to contemplate. [See] *Katzenbach v. Morgan,* 384 U.S. 641, 652-656, 86 S.Ct. 1717, 16 L.Ed.2d 828 (1966) (asking whether Congress' likely conclusions were reasonable, not whether there was adequate evidentiary support in the record). Nor has the Court traditionally required Congress to make findings as to state discrimination, or to break down the record evidence, category by category. Compare ante * * * (noting statements in two congressional Reports that mentioned state discrimination in public services and transportation but not in employment), with *Morgan,* supra, at 654, 86 S.Ct. 1717 (considering what Congress "might" have concluded); 384 U.S. at 652, 86 S.Ct. 1717 (holding that likely discrimination against Puerto Ricans in areas other than voting supported statute abolishing literacy test as qualification for voting).

Regardless, Congress expressly found substantial unjustified discrimination against persons with disabilities. 42 U.S.C. § 12101(9) (finding a pattern of "*unnecessary* discrimination and prejudice" that "costs the United States billions of dollars in *unnecessary* expenses resulting from dependency and nonproductivity" (emphasis added)). See also 2 Legislative History of the Americans with Disabilities Act (Leg. Hist.) (Committee Print compiled for the House Committee on Education and Labor), Ser. No. 102-B, p. 1620 (1990) (testimony of Arlene B. Mayerson) (describing "unjustifiable and discriminatory loss of job opportunities"); *id. at* 1623 (citing study showing " 'strong evidence that employers' fears of low performance among disabled workers are unjustified' "). Moreover, it found that such discrimination typically reflects "stereotypic assumptions" or "purposeful unequal treatment." 42 U.S.C. § 12101(7). See also 2 Leg. Hist. 1622 (testimony of Arlene B. Mayerson) ("Outmoded stereotypes whether manifested in medical or other job 'requirements' that are unrelated to the successful performance of the job, or in decisions based on the generalized perceptions of supervisors and hiring personnel, have excluded many disabled people from jobs for which they are qualified"). In making these findings, Congress followed our decision in *Cleburne,* which established that not only discrimination against persons with disabilities that rests upon " 'a bare * * * desire to harm a politically unpopular group,' " 473 U.S. at 447, 105 S.Ct. 3249 (quoting *Department of Agriculture v. Moreno,* 413 U.S. 528, 534, 93 S.Ct. 2821, 37 L.Ed.2d 782 (1973) (omission in *Cleburne*)), violates the Fourteenth Amendment, but also discrimination that rests solely upon "negative attitude[s]," "fea[r]," 473 U.S. at 448, 105 S.Ct. 3249, or "irrational prejudice," id., at 450, 105 S.Ct. 3249. Adverse treatment that rests upon such motives is unjustified discrimination in *Cleburne's* terms.

The evidence in the legislative record bears out Congress' finding that the adverse treatment of persons with disabilities was often arbitrary or invidious in this sense, and thus unjustified. For example, one study that was before Congress revealed that "most * * * governmental agencies in [one State] discriminated in hiring against job applicants for an average period of five years after treatment for cancer," based in part on coworkers' misguided belief that "cancer is contagious." 2 Leg. Hist. 1619-1620 (testimony of Arlene B. Mayerson). A school inexplicably refused to exempt a deaf teacher, who taught at a school for the deaf, from a "listening skills" requirement. Government's Lodging 1503. A State refused to hire a blind employee as director of an agency for the blind – even though he was the most qualified applicant. Id. at 974. Certain state agencies apparently had general policies against hiring or promoting persons with disabilities. Id. at 1159, 1577. A zoo turned away children with Downs Syndrome "because [the zookeeper] feared they would upset the chimpanzees." S. Rep. No. 101-116, at 7. There were reports of numerous zoning decisions based upon "negative attitudes" or "fear," *Cleburne*, supra, at 448, 105 S.Ct. 3249, such as a zoning board that denied a permit for an obviously pretextual reason after hearing arguments that a facility would house " 'deviants' " who needed " 'room to roam,' " Government's Lodging 1068. A complete listing of the hundreds of examples of discrimination by state and local governments that were submitted to the task force is set forth in Appendix C, *infra*. Congress could have reasonably believed that these examples represented signs of a widespread problem of unconstitutional discrimination.

II

The Court's failure to find sufficient evidentiary support may well rest upon its decision to hold Congress to a strict, judicially created evidentiary standard, particularly in respect to lack of justification. Justice KENNEDY's empirical conclusion – which rejects that of Congress – rests heavily upon his failure to find "extensive litigation and discussion of the constitutional violations," in "*the courts* of the United States." Ante * * * (concurring opinion) (emphasis added). And the Court itself points out that, when economic or social legislation is challenged in court as irrational, hence unconstitutional, the "burden is upon the challenging party to negative any reasonably conceivable state of facts that could provide a rational basis for the classification." Ante * * * (internal quotation marks omitted). Or as Justice BRANDEIS, writing for the Court, put the matter many years ago, " 'if any state of facts reasonably can be conceived that would sustain' " challenged legislation, then " 'there is a presumption of the existence of that state of facts, and one who assails the classification must carry the burden of showing . . . that the action is arbitrary.' " *Pacific States Box & Basket Co. v. White,* 296 U.S. 176, 185, 56 S.Ct. 159, 80 L.Ed. 138 (1935) (quoting *Borden's Farm Products Co. v.*

Baldwin, 293 U.S. 194, 209, 55 S.Ct. 187, 79 L.Ed. 281 (1934)). Imposing this special "burden" upon Congress, the Court fails to find in the legislative record sufficient indication that Congress has "negative[d]" the presumption that state action is rationally related to a legitimate objective. Ante * * *.

The problem with the Court's approach is that neither the "burden of proof" that favors States nor any other rule of restraint applicable to *judges* applies to *Congress* when it exercises its § 5 power. "Limitations stemming from the nature of the judicial process * * * have no application to Congress." *Oregon v. Mitchell,* 400 U.S. 112, 248, 91 S.Ct. 260, 27 L.Ed.2d 272 (1970) (Brennan, White, and Marshall, JJ., concurring in part and dissenting in part). Rational-basis review – with its presumptions favoring constitutionality – is "a paradigm of *judicial* restraint." *FCC v. Beach Communications, Inc.,* 508 U.S. 307, 314, 113 S.Ct. 2096, 124 L.Ed.2d 211 (1993) (emphasis added). And the Congress of the United States is not a lower court.

Indeed, the Court in *Cleburne* drew this very institutional distinction. We emphasized that "courts have been very reluctant, as they should be in our federal system and with our respect for the separation of powers, to closely scrutinize legislative choices." 473 U.S. at 441, 105 S.Ct. 3249. Our invocation of judicial deference and respect for Congress was based on the fact that "[§] 5 of the [Fourteenth] Amendment empowers *Congress* to enforce [the equal protection] mandate." Id. at 439, 105 S.Ct. 3249 (emphasis added). Indeed, we made clear that the absence of a contrary congressional finding was critical to our decision to apply mere rational-basis review to disability discrimination claims – a "congressional direction" to apply a more stringent standard would have been "controlling." Ibid. See also *Washington v. Davis,* 426 U.S. 229, 248, 96 S.Ct. 2040, 48 L.Ed.2d 597 (1976) (refusing to invalidate a law based on the Equal Protection Clause because a disparate impact standard "should await legislative prescription"). Cf. *Mitchell,* supra, at 284, 91 S.Ct. 260 (Stewart, J., concurring in part and dissenting in part) ("Congress may paint with a much broader brush than may this Court, which must confine itself to the judicial function of deciding individual cases and controversies upon individual records"). In short, the Court's claim that "to uphold the Act's application to the States would allow Congress to rewrite the Fourteenth Amendment law laid down by this Court in *Cleburne,*" * * * is repudiated by *Cleburne* itself.

There is simply no reason to require Congress, seeking to determine facts relevant to the exercise of its § 5 authority, to adopt rules or presumptions that reflect a court's institutional limitations. Unlike courts, Congress can readily gather facts from across the Nation, assess the magnitude of a problem, and more easily find an appropriate remedy. Cf. *Cleburne,* supra, at 442-443, 105 S.Ct. 3249 (addressing the problems of the "large and diversified group" of persons with disabilities "is a difficult and often a technical matter, very much a task for legislators guided by qualified professionals and not by the perhaps ill-informed opinions of the judiciary"). Unlike courts, Congress directly reflects public attitudes and beliefs, enabling Congress better to understand where, and to what extent, refusals to accommodate a disability amount to behavior that is callous or unreasonable to the point of lacking constitutional justification. Unlike judges, Members of Congress can directly obtain information from constituents who have firsthand experience with discrimination and related issues.

Moreover, unlike judges, Members of Congress are elected. When the Court has applied the majority's burden of proof rule, it has explained that we, i.e., the courts, do not " 'sit as a superlegislature to judge the wisdom or desirability of legislative policy determinations.' " *Heller,* 509 U.S. at 319, 113 S.Ct. 2637, quoting *New Orleans v. Dukes,* 427 U.S. 297, 303, 96 S.Ct. 2513, 49 L.Ed.2d 511 (1976) (*per curiam*)). To apply a rule designed to restrict courts as if it restricted Congress' legislative power is to stand the underlying principle – a principle of judicial restraint – on its head. But without the use of this burden of proof rule or some other unusually stringent standard of review, it is difficult to see how the Court can find the legislative record here inadequate. Read with a reasonably favorable eye, the record indicates that state governments subjected those with disabilities to seriously adverse, disparate treatment. And Congress could have found, in a significant number of instances, that this treatment violated the substantive principles of justification – shorn of their judicial-restraint-related presumptions – that this Court recognized in *Cleburne.*

III

The Court argues in the alternative that the statute's damages remedy is not "congruent" with and "proportional" to the equal protection problem that Congress found. Ante * * * (citing *City of Boerne v. Flores,* 521 U.S. 507, 520, 117 S.Ct. 2157, 138 L.Ed.2d 624 (1997)). The Court suggests that the Act's "reasonable accommodation" requirement, 42 U.S.C. § 12112(b)(5)(A), and disparate-impact standard, § 12112(b)(3)(A), "far excee[d] what is constitutionally required." Ante * * * But we have upheld disparate-impact standards in contexts where they were not "constitutionally required." Compare *Griggs v. Duke Power Co.,* 401 U.S. 424, 432, 91 S.Ct. 849, 28 L.Ed.2d 158 (1971), with *Washington,* supra, at 239, 96 S.Ct. 2040, and *City of Rome v. United States,* 446 U.S. 156, 172-173, 100 S.Ct. 1548, 64 L.Ed.2d 119 (1980), with *Mobile v. Bolden,* 446 U.S. 55, 62, 100 S.Ct. 1490, 64 L.Ed.2d 47 (1980) (plurality opinion).

And what is wrong with a remedy that, in response to unreasonable employer behavior, requires an employer to make accommodations that are reasonable? Of course, what is "reasonable" in the statutory sense and what is "unreasonable" in the constitutional sense might differ. In other words, the requirement may exceed what is necessary to avoid a constitutional violation. But it is just that power – the power to require more than the minimum that § 5 grants to Congress, as this Court has repeatedly confirmed. As long ago as 1880, the Court wrote that § 5 "brought within the domain of congressional power" whatever "tends to enforce submission" to its "prohibitions" and "to secure to all persons * * * the equal protection of the laws." *Ex parte Virginia,* 100 U.S. 339, 346, 25 L.Ed. 676 (1880). More recently, the Court added that § 5's "draftsmen sought to grant to Congress, by a specific provision applicable to the Fourteenth Amendment, the same broad powers expressed in the Necessary and Proper Clause, Art. I, § 8, cl. 18." *Morgan,* 384 U.S. at 650, 86 S.Ct. 1717 (citing *M'Culloch v. Maryland,* 4 Wheat. 316, 421, 4 L.Ed. 579 (1819)).

In keeping with these principles, the Court has said that "[i]t is not for us to review the congressional resolution of * * * the various conflicting considerations – the risk or pervasiveness of the discrimination in governmental services * * *, the adequacy or availability of alternative remedies, and the nature and significance of the state interests that would be affected." 384 U.S. at 653, 86 S.Ct. 1717. "It is enough that we be able to perceive a basis upon which the Congress might resolve the conflict as it did." Ibid. See also *South Carolina v. Katzenbach,* 383 U.S. 301, 324, 86 S.Ct. 803, 15 L.Ed.2d 769 (1966) (interpreting the similarly worded Enforcement Clause of the Fifteenth Amendment to permit Congress to use "any rational means to effectuate the constitutional prohibition"). Nothing in the words "reasonable accommodation" suggests that the requirement has no "tend[ency] to enforce" the Equal Protection Clause, *Ex parte Virginia,* supra, at 346, that it is an irrational way to achieve the objective, *Katzenbach,* supra, at 324, 86 S.Ct. 803, that it would fall outside the scope of the Necessary and Proper Clause, *Morgan,* supra, at 650, 86 S.Ct. 1717, or that it somehow otherwise exceeds the bounds of the "appropriate," U.S. Const., Amdt. 14, § 5.

The Court's more recent cases have professed to follow the longstanding principle of deference to Congress. See *Kimel v. Florida Bd. of Regents,* 528 U.S. 62, 81, 120 S.Ct. 631, 145 L.Ed.2d 522 (2000) ("Congress' § 5 power is not confined to the enactment of legislation that merely parrots the precise wording of the Fourteenth Amendment." Rather, Congress can prohibit a "somewhat broader swath of conduct, including that which is not itself forbidden by the Amendment's text"); *Florida Prepaid Postsecondary Ed. Expense Bd. v. College Savings Bank,* 527 U.S. 627, 639, 119 S.Ct. 2199, 144 L.Ed.2d 575 (1999) (" 'Congress must have wide latitude' ") (quoting *City of Boerne,* supra, at 519-520, 117 S.Ct. 2157); *City of Boerne,* supra, at 528, 117 S.Ct. 2157 (reaffirming *Morgan*); 521 U.S. at 536, 117 S.Ct. 2157 (Congress' "conclusions are entitled to much deference"). And even today, the Court purports to apply, not to depart from, these standards. * * * But the Court's analysis and ultimate conclusion deprive its declarations of practical significance. The Court "sounds the word of promise to the ear but breaks it to the hope."

The Court's harsh review of Congress' use of its § 5 power is reminiscent of the similar (now-discredited) limitation that it once imposed upon Congress' Commerce Clause power. Compare *Carter v. Carter Coal Co.,* 298 U.S. 238, 56 S.Ct. 855, 80 L.Ed. 1160 (1936), with *United States v. Darby,* 312 U.S. 100, 123, 61 S.Ct. 451, 85 L.Ed. 609 (1941) (rejecting *Carter Coal*'s rationale). I could understand the legal basis for such review were we judging a statute that discriminated against those of a particular race or gender, see *United States v. Virginia,* 518 U.S. 515, 116 S.Ct. 2264, 135 L.Ed.2d 735 (1996), or a statute that threatened a basic constitutionally protected liberty such as free speech, see *Reno v. American Civil Liberties Union,* 521 U.S. 844, 117 S.Ct. 2329, 138 L.Ed.2d 874 (1997); see also Post & Siegel, Equal Protection by Law: Federal Antidiscrimination Legislation After *Morrison* and *Kimel,* 110 Yale L.J. 441, 477 (2000) (stating that the Court's recent review of § 5 legislation appears to approach strict scrutiny); 1 L. Tribe, American Constitutional Law § 5-16, p. 959 (3d ed. 2000) (same). The legislation before us, however, does not discriminate against anyone, nor does it pose any threat to basic liberty. And it is difficult to understand why the Court, which applies "minimum 'rational-basis' review" to statutes that *burden* persons with disabilities, ante * * * subjects to far stricter scrutiny a statute that seeks to *help* those same individuals.

I recognize nonetheless that this statute imposes a burden upon States in that it removes their Eleventh Amendment protection from suit, thereby subjecting them to potential monetary liability. Rules for interpreting § 5 that would provide States with special protection, however, run counter to the very object of the Fourteenth Amendment. By its terms, that Amendment prohibits *States* from denying their citizens equal protection of the laws. U.S. Const., Amdt. 14, § 1. Hence "principles of federalism that might otherwise be an obstacle to congressional authority are necessarily overridden by the power to enforce the Civil War Amendments 'by appropriate legislation.' Those Amendments were specifically designed as an expansion of federal power and an intrusion on state sovereignty." *City of Rome,* 446 U.S. at 179, 100 S.Ct. 1548. See also *Fitzpatrick v. Bitzer,* 427 U.S. 445, 456, 96 S.Ct. 2666, 49 L.Ed.2d 614 (1976); *Ex parte Virginia,* 100 U.S. at 345. And, ironically, the greater the obstacle the Eleventh Amendment poses to the creation by Congress of the kind of remedy at issue here – the decentralized remedy of private damages actions – the more Congress, seeking to cure important national problems, such as the problem of disability discrimination before us, will have to rely on more uniform remedies, such as federal standards and court injunctions, 42 U.S.C. § 12188(a)(2), which are sometimes draconian and typically more intrusive. See *College Savings Bank v. Florida Prepaid Postsecondary Ed. Expense Bd.,* 527 U.S. 666, 704-705, 119 S.Ct. 2219, 144 L.Ed.2d 605 (1999) (BREYER, J., dissenting). * * * For these reasons, I doubt that today's decision serves any constitutionally based federalism interest.

The Court, through its evidentiary demands, its non-deferential review, and its failure to distinguish between judicial and legislative constitutional competencies, improperly invades a power that the Constitution assigns to Congress. *Morgan,* 384 U.S. at 648, n.7, 86 S.Ct. 1717 (The "sponsors and supporters of the [Fourteenth] Amendment were primarily interested in augmenting the power of Congress"). Its decision saps § 5 of independent force, effectively "confin[ing] the legislative power * * * to the insignificant role of abrogating only those state laws that the judicial branch [is] prepared to adjudge unconstitutional." Id. at 648-649, 86 S.Ct. 1717. Whether the Commerce Clause does or does not enable Congress to enact this provision, see, e.g., *Seminole Tribe of Fla. v. Florida,* 517 U.S. 44, 100-185, 116 S.Ct. 1114, 134 L.Ed.2d 252 (1996) (Souter, J., joined by Ginsburg and Breyer, JJ., dissenting); *College Savings Bank*, supra, at 699-700, 119 S.Ct. 2219 (Breyer, J., dissenting), in my view, § 5 gives Congress the necessary authority.

For the reasons stated, I respectfully dissent.

Notes & Questions

1. In *Garrett*, the Court held that Congress had not found a sufficient pattern of unconstitutional discrimination against people with disabilities in the area of state employment. Bd. of Trs. of the Univ. of Ala. v. Garrett, 531 U.S. 356, 374 (2001). The plurality and dissent referenced the evidence in "Appendix C" compiled by the Task Force on Rights and Empowerment of Americans with Disabilities. *Id*. at 394-424. Do you agree with the majority's conclusion?

2. Although they could not sue the state for monetary damages under the ADA, the *Garrett* plaintiffs were not without relief. On remand, the Eleventh Circuit held that they may sue the state of Alabama for monetary damages under the Rehabilitation Act of 1973. Garrett v. Univ. of Ala., 344 F.3d 1288 (11th Cir. 2003). The court held that the state, and by implication its agencies, waived sovereign immunity by accepting federal funds. *Id*. Nevertheless, on remand to the trial court, the court held that plaintiff Garrett was not a qualified individual with a disability for purposes of the ADA, and her case was dismissed. *See* Garrett v. Bd. of Trs. of the Univ. of Ala., 354 F.Supp.2d 1244 (N.D. Ala. 2005).

3. The larger federalism implications of the *Garrett* decision, and its application to ADA Title II in the case of Tennessee v. Lane, 315 F.3d 680 (6th Cir. 2003), cert. granted, 71 U.S.L.W. 3736 (U.S. Jun. 23, 2003) (No. 02-1667), are explored *infra* in Part 4.

E.   *Title I Covered Employers: Illustrations*

   1.   Temporary employment agencies and staffing firms

Increasingly in the workplace, employers are using temporary or "contingent" workers to fill employment functions. Contingent workers lie outside an employer's core work force and include those whose jobs are structured to last only a limited period of time, are sporadic, or differ in any way from the norm of full-time, long-term employment. U.S. Equal Emp. Opportunity Comm'n, Enforcement Guidance: Application of EEOC Laws to Contingent Workers Placed by Temporary Employment Agencies and Other Staffing Firms (Notice No. 915,002), at 8 FEP Man. (BNA) 405: 7551 (Dec. 3, 1997), http://www.eeoc.gov/policy/docs/guidance-contingent. html (hereinafter "Contingent Workers").

There are at least two questions regarding the application of Title I to contingent workers. First, are contingent workers "employees" within the meaning of Title I, or are they independent contractors? Second, if they are employees, who is their employer for the purposes of the ADA – the staffing firm or the company using the staffing firm for its employment needs?

Is the staffing firm worker an employee within the meaning of the ADA, or an independent contractor? If the worker is an independent contractor, the ADA does not apply. Lerohl v. Friends of Minn. Sinfonia, 322 F.3d 486, 489 (8th Cir. 2003). The EEOC Guidance states that the worker qualifies as an "employee" in the great majority of circumstances. Contingent Workers, *supra*.

However, the label alone is not determinative. Rather, the crucial issue arises in regard to whether the staffing firm, its client, or its worker, has the right to control the means and manner of work performance. *Id.* This is an individual inquiry that must be done on a case-by-case basis.

The individual likely will be viewed as an employee if the firm/client has the right to control where, when, and how the worker performs the job; the work does not require a high level of skill or expertise; the firm/client furnishes the tools, materials, and equipment; the work is performed on the premises of the firm/client; there is a continuing relationship between the worker and the firm/client; and the firm/client sets the hours of work and the duration of the job.

Once the determination is made that the worker is an employee, the question must follow: who is the "employer?" Is it the staffing firm, its client, or both? Often, throughout the duration of the employment, both qualify, yet the key object is to find out which entity exercises control over the worker's employment. The same questions discussed above are relevant to this inquiry.

In addressing the relationship between a staffing firm and its workers, the EEOC Guidance states that this relationship generally qualifies as an employer-employee relationship "because the firm typically hires the worker, determines when and where the worker should report to work, pays the wages, is itself in business, withholds taxes and social security, provides workers' compensation coverage, and has the right to discharge the worker." *Id.* In limited circumstances, for example, in which the client firm puts its employees on the staffing firm's payroll solely to transfer the responsibility of administering wages and insurance benefits, the staffing firm still can qualify as an employer despite its lack of adequate control. *See* Astrowsky v. First Portland Mortgage Corp., 887 F.Supp. 332, 337 (D. Me. 1995) (ADEA case).

If the client exercises supervisory control over the worker, the client can be the employer together with the staffing firm (or independently of it). Poff v. Prudential Ins. Co. of Am., 882 F.Supp. 1534, 1536 (E.D. Pa. 1995). For example, while the staffing firm could pay the worker a salary based on the number of hours worked for the client, as well as withhold taxes and provide workers' compensation coverage, the client could set the hours and terms of work, use its equipment on its premises, and report the worker's performance to the staffing agency. In this scenario, the staffing firm and its client likely qualify as joint employers because each have the right to exercise control over the terms of the worker's employment. Of course, either entity would need the requisite number of employees to be a covered entity under Title I. *Id.* (noting that the employer must count each employee from the day that the employment relationship begins until the day that it ends, regardless of whether the employee is present at work or on leave on each working day).

An entity also may be liable for the actions of companies with which it contracts, if those actions have the effect of discriminating against the entity's employees. Therefore, an employer may be liable for the discriminatory acts of its employment agency, labor union, provider of employee benefits, or trainer on its behalf. When it has known or should have known of the discrimination and failed to take prompt corrective measures, the employer may be liable even without having actively participated in the discriminatory policy or practice of the contractor. *See* Contingent Workers, *supra.*

2.   Single and multiple employers

Sometimes, a court must decide whether to treat two entities as a single employer for the purpose of aggregating the number of employees to meet the numerosity requirement of Title I. The courts of appeals have applied at least two different tests to resolve this issue.

The Sixth Circuit has applied an "integrated enterprise" test. In *Swallows v. Barnes & Noble Book Stores, Inc.*, 128 F.3d 990, 994 (6th Cir. 1997), Plaintiffs were allegedly discharged from their jobs at the state university bookstore because of their age and disability. The Defendant, a national bookstore chain, had contracted with the state university to operate and manage the store. Plaintiffs settled their claims with the defendant but appealed the dismissal of their action against the state.

In holding that the state was not a covered entity, the *Swallows* court framed the issue as whether the state and the bookstore were an integrated enterprise. The court considered the interrelation of operations and common management, labor relations, ownership, and financial control. *Id.* Although no single factor was dispositive, the Sixth Circuit placed particular importance on labor relations.

In *Papa v. Kathy Industries, Inc.*, 166 F.3d 937, 940-41 (7th Cir. 1999), the Seventh Circuit took a different approach in determining affiliate liability for age and disability discrimination. The court viewed the factors enunciated in the integrated enterprise test to be vague. Instead, the court adopted a test that requires that a plaintiff show either that the conditions for "piercing the corporate veil" are present, the enterprise split itself into different entities (with fewer than the statutory minimum number of employees) for the purpose of avoiding Title I liability, or the parent corporation directed the discriminatory act against the employee of the subsidiary. *Id.* The Seventh Circuit later applied this new test in *Worth v. Tyer*, 276 F.3d 249, 260 (7th Cir. 2001), and in *Breece v. AmeriCare Living Centers*, No. IP 01-0997-C-K/T, 2002 WL 31132308 (S.D. Ind. Sept. 25, 2002). The *Papa* court reasoned that this restrictive test was consistent with Congress's statutory purpose of sparing small firms the expense of antidiscrimination laws.

3. Extraterritorial application of Title I

As discussed in § 10.1 *infra*, the remedies available under the ADA are based on the remedies established under Title VII of the Civil Rights Act. Until 1991, the Supreme Court had limited the reach of Title VII of the Civil Rights Act (and thereby the remedies of ADA Title I) to U.S. citizens and aliens working in the United States. *See* EEOC v. Arabian Am. Oil Co., 499 U.S. 244, 257-59 (1991) (Title VII does not have an extraterritorial application to the employment of U.S. citizens abroad by U.S. firms). Congress enacted the Civil Rights Act of 1991 (and amended Title VII) to provide increased extraterritorial reach. Pub. L. No. 102-166, 105 Stat. 1071, § 109(a) (1991). The 1991 Act expands Title VII's definition of "employee" to include U.S. citizens employed abroad. 42 U.S.C. § 2000e(f) (2006). In addition, Congress explicitly precluded Title VII's extraterritorial scope from covering aliens. *Id.* § 2000e-1. This coverage is limited to corporations that are controlled by U.S. employers. *Id.* § 2000e-1(c). However, the 1991 amendments to Title VII did not overrule the Supreme Court's determination that Title VII is inapplicable to aliens employed outside the United States. *See* Shekoyan v. Sibley Int'l Corp., 217 F.Supp.2d 59, 64-65 (D.D.C. 2002) (discussing these issues).

In the ADA, Congress qualified Title I's extraterritorial application in two additional ways. First, with respect to an employee in a workplace in a foreign country, actions that would otherwise constitute discrimination would not be unlawful if compliance with Title I would cause the covered entity to violate the law of the foreign country in which the workplace is located. 42 U.S.C. § 12112(c)(1).

Second, Title I does not apply to foreign operations of a foreign corporation unless the foreign corporation is controlled by a U.S. employer. *Id.* § 12112(c)(2). Where a U.S. employer controls a corporation whose place of incorporation is a foreign country, an action in which the corporation has engaged that constitutes discrimination under Title I is imputed to the employer. *Id.* "Control" of a foreign corporation is determined by factors related to the interrelation of operations and common management, labor relations and financial control. *Id.*

At least one court of appeal has determined that the ADEA (and by implication, Title I of the ADA's pre-employment provisions) does not extend coverage to foreign nationals who apply in foreign countries for jobs in the United States. Reyes-Gaona v. N.C. Growers Ass'n, 250 F.3d 861, 866-67 (4th Cir. 2001). However, Title I protects a qualified foreign national with a disability who is legally employed in the United States from discrimination during the course of his employment. *Id.* at 867 (Motz J., concurring).

This last principle is demonstrated in the case of *Torrico v. IBM, Corp.*, 213 F.Supp.2d 390, 393 (S.D.N.Y. 2002), wherein the plaintiff-employee was a non-U.S. citizen who worked in New York as the general manager of a U.S. telecommunications corporation. Torrico traveled frequently to Latin America and agreed to a three-year temporary rotational assignment to Chile. He was subsequently terminated while on medical leave for autoimmune disease.

The district court found that a non-U.S. citizen employee is entitled to Title I protections when asserting a claim with respect to employment in the United States, rather than in a foreign country. *Id.* at 403. However, whether a non-U.S. citizen who is on a temporary assignment in a foreign country is "employed" in the United States depends on factors such as the terms and intent of the employment negotiated, the job duties and reporting relationship, the duration of the employment assignments in various locations, and where the allegedly discriminatory conduct occurred. *Id.* at 400.

4.   Religious entities as employers

Title I does not prohibit a religious corporation, association, educational institution, or society from giving preference in employment to individuals of a particular religion. This employment must include, however, the performance of work connected with the activities of the religious entity. 42 U.S.C. § 12113(c) (2006).

A religious organization may require as a condition of employment that job applicants and employees conform to the religious tenets of the organization. *Id.* Nevertheless, a religious entity may not discriminate against a qualified individual, who satisfies the permitted religious criteria, because of her disability. 29 C.F.R. pt. 1630 app., § 1630.16(a) (2008).

Furthermore, some courts have found that the Religion Clause of the First Amendment provides for a ministerial exception that supersedes employment discrimination laws where the employee alleging discrimination is a ministerial employee. In *Hosanna-Tabor Evangelical Lutheran Church and School v. E.E.O.C.*, 132 S.Ct. 694 (2012), the U.S. Supreme Court took up whether an employee alleging disability employment discrimination under Title I is prevented from raising that claim by the ministerial exception.

ৎ

HOSANNA-TABOR EVANGELICAL LUTHERAN CHURCH AND SCHOOL v. EQUAL EMPLOYMENT OPPORTUNITY COMMISSION

Supreme Court of the United States, 2012
132 S.Ct. 694

* * *

Chief Justice ROBERTS delivered the opinion for a unanimous Court. THOMAS, J., filed a concurring opinion. ALITO, J., filed a concurring opinion, in which KAGAN, J., joined.

* * *

Certain employment discrimination laws authorize employees who have been wrongfully terminated to sue their employers for reinstatement and damages. The question presented is whether the Establishment and Free Exercise Clauses of the First Amendment bar such an action when the employer is a religious group and the employee is one of the group's ministers.

I

A

Petitioner Hosanna-Tabor Evangelical Lutheran Church and School is a member congregation of the Lutheran Church-Missouri Synod, the second largest Lutheran denomination in America. Hosanna-Tabor operated a small school in Redford, Michigan, offering a "Christ-centered education" to students in kindergarten through eighth grade. 582 F.Supp.2d 881, 884 (E.D.Mich.2008) 582 F.Supp. 2d 881 (E.D. Mich. 2008) (internal quotation marks omitted).

The Synod classifies teachers into two categories: "called" and "lay." "Called" teachers are regarded as having been called to their vocation by God through a congregation. * * *

172

"Lay" or "contract" teachers, by contrast, are not required to be trained by the Synod or even to be Lutheran. At Hosanna-Tabor, they were appointed by the school board, without a vote of the congregation, to one-year renewable terms. Although teachers at the school generally performed the same duties regardless of whether they were lay or called, lay teachers were hired only when called teachers were unavailable.

Respondent Cheryl Perich was first employed by Hosanna-Tabor as a lay teacher in 1999. After Perich completed her colloquy later that school year, Hosanna-Tabor asked her to become a called teacher. Perich accepted the call and received a "diploma of vocation" designating her a commissioned minister. * * *

Perich taught kindergarten during her first four years at Hosanna-Tabor and fourth grade during the 2003-2004 school year. She taught math, language arts, social studies, science, gym, art, and music. She also taught a religion class four days a week, led the students in prayer and devotional exercises each day, and attended a weekly school-wide chapel service. Perich led the chapel service herself about twice a year.

Perich became ill in June 2004 with what was eventually diagnosed as narcolepsy. Symptoms included sudden and deep sleeps from which she could not be roused. Because of her illness, Perich began the 2004-2005 school year on disability leave. On January 27, 2005, however, Perich notified the school principal, Stacey Hoeft, that she would be able to report to work the following month. Hoeft responded that the school had already contracted with a lay teacher to fill Perich's position for the remainder of the school year. Hoeft also expressed concern that Perich was not yet ready to return to the classroom.

On January 30, Hosanna-Tabor held a meeting of its congregation at which school administrators stated that Perich was unlikely to be physically capable of returning to work that school year or the next. The congregation voted to offer Perich a "peaceful release" from her call, whereby the congregation would pay a portion of her health insurance premiums in exchange for her resignation as a called teacher. * * * Perich refused to resign and produced a note from her doctor stating that she would be able to return to work on February 22. The school board urged Perich to reconsider, informing her that the school no longer had a position for her, but Perich stood by her decision not to resign.

On the morning of February 22 – the first day she was medically cleared to return to work – Perich presented herself at the school. Hoeft asked her to leave but she would not do so until she obtained written documentation that she had reported to work. Later that afternoon, Hoeft called Perich at home and told her that she would likely be fired. Perich responded that she had spoken with an attorney and intended to assert her legal rights.

Following a school board meeting that evening, board chairman Scott Salo sent Perich a letter stating that Hosanna-Tabor was reviewing the process for rescinding her call in light of her "regrettable" actions. * * * Salo subsequently followed up with a letter advising Perich that the congregation would consider whether to rescind her call at its next meeting. As grounds for termination, the letter cited Perich's "insubordination and disruptive behavior" on February 22, as well as the damage she had done to her "working relationship" with the school by "threatening to take legal action." * * * The congregation voted to rescind Perich's call on April 10, and Hosanna-Tabor sent her a letter of termination the next day.

B

Perich filed a charge with the Equal Employment Opportunity Commission, alleging that her employment had been terminated in violation of the Americans with Disabilities Act * * *

The EEOC brought suit against Hosanna-Tabor, alleging that Perich had been fired in retaliation for threatening to file an ADA lawsuit. Perich intervened in the litigation, claiming unlawful retaliation under both the ADA and the Michigan Persons with Disabilities Civil Rights Act * * * The EEOC and Perich sought Perich's reinstatement to her former position (or frontpay in lieu thereof), along with backpay, compensatory and punitive damages, attorney's fees, and other injunctive relief.

Hosanna-Tabor moved for summary judgment. Invoking what is known as the "ministerial exception," the Church argued that the suit was barred by the First Amendment because the claims at issue concerned the employment relationship between a religious institution and one of its ministers. According to the Church, Perich was a minister, and she had been fired for a religious reason – namely, that her threat to sue the Church violated the Synod's belief that Christians should resolve their disputes internally.

The District Court agreed that the suit was barred by the ministerial exception and granted summary judgment in Hosanna-Tabor's favor. * * *

The Court of Appeals for the Sixth Circuit * * * concluded, however, that Perich did not qualify as a "minister" under the exception, noting in particular that her duties as a called teacher were identical to her duties as a lay teacher. * * *

We granted certiorari. * * *

II

The First Amendment provides, in part, that "Congress shall make no law respecting an establishment of religion, or prohibiting the free exercise thereof." We have said that these two Clauses "often exert conflicting pressures," *Cutter v. Wilkinson*, 544 U.S. 709, 719, 125 S.Ct.

2113, 161 L.Ed.2d 1020 (2005), and that there can be "internal tension . . . between the Establishment Clause and the Free Exercise Clause," *Tilton v. Richardson,* 403 U.S. 672, 677, 91 S.Ct. 2091, 29 L.Ed.2d 790 (1971) (plurality opinion). Not so here. Both Religion Clauses bar the government from interfering with the decision of a religious group to fire one of its ministers.

* * *

B

* * *

This Court reaffirmed these First Amendment principles in *Serbian Eastern Orthodox Diocese for United States and Canada v. Milivojevich,* 426 U.S. 696, 96 S.Ct. 2372, 49 L.Ed.2d 151 (1976), a case involving a dispute over control of the American-Canadian Diocese of the Serbian Orthodox Church, including its property and assets. The Church had removed Dionisije Milivojevich as bishop of the American-Canadian Diocese because of his defiance of the church hierarchy. Following his removal, Dionisije brought a civil action in state court challenging the Church's decision, and the Illinois Supreme Court "purported in effect to reinstate Dionisije as Diocesan Bishop," on the ground that the proceedings resulting in his removal failed to comply with church laws and regulations. *Id.,* at 708, 96 S.Ct. 2372.

Reversing that judgment, this Court explained that the First Amendment "permit[s] hierarchical religious organizations to establish their own rules and regulations for internal discipline and government, and to create tribunals for adjudicating disputes over these matters." *Id.,* at 724, 96 S.Ct. 2372. When ecclesiastical tribunals decide such disputes, we further explained, "the Constitution requires that civil courts accept their decisions as binding upon them." *Id.,* at 725, 96 S.Ct. 2372. We thus held that by inquiring into whether the Church had followed its own procedures, the State Supreme Court had "unconstitutionally undertaken the resolution of quintessentially religious controversies whose resolution the First Amendment commits exclusively to the highest ecclesiastical tribunals" of the Church. *Id.,* at 720, 96 S.Ct. 2372.

C

Until today, we have not had occasion to consider whether this freedom of a religious organization to select its ministers is implicated by a suit alleging discrimination in employment. The Courts of Appeals, in contrast, have had extensive experience with this issue. Since the passage of Title VII of the Civil Rights Act of 1964, 42 U.S.C. § 2000e *et seq.,* and other employment discrimination laws, the Courts of Appeals have uniformly recognized the existence of a "ministerial exception," grounded in the First Amendment, that precludes application of such legislation to claims concerning the employment relationship between a religious institution and its ministers. * * *

We agree that there is such a ministerial exception. The members of a religious group put their faith in the hands of their ministers. Requiring a church to accept or retain an unwanted minister, or punishing a church for failing to do so, intrudes upon more than a mere employment decision. Such action interferes with the internal governance of the church, depriving the church of control over the selection of those who will personify its beliefs. By imposing an unwanted minister, the state infringes the Free Exercise Clause, which protects a religious group's right to shape its own faith and mission through its appointments. According the state the power to determine which individuals will minister to the faithful also violates the Establishment Clause, which prohibits government involvement in such ecclesiastical decisions.

The EEOC and Perich acknowledge that employment discrimination laws would be unconstitutional as applied to religious groups in certain circumstances. They grant, for example, that it would violate the First Amendment for courts to apply such laws to compel the ordination of women by the Catholic Church or by an Orthodox Jewish seminary. * * * According to the EEOC and Perich, religious organizations could successfully defend against employment discrimination claims in those circumstances by invoking the constitutional right to freedom of association – a right "implicit" in the First Amendment. *Roberts v. United States Jaycees,* 468 U.S. 609, 622, 104 S.Ct. 3244, 82 L.Ed.2d 462 (1984). The EEOC and Perich thus see no need – and no basis – for a special rule for ministers grounded in the Religion Clauses themselves.

We find this position untenable. The right to freedom of association is a right enjoyed by religious and secular groups alike. It follows under the EEOC's and Perich's view that the First Amendment analysis should be the same, whether the association in question is the Lutheran Church, a labor union, or a social club. * * * That result is hard to square with the text of the First Amendment itself, which gives special solicitude to the rights of religious organizations. We cannot accept the remarkable view that the Religion Clauses have nothing to say about a religious organization's freedom to select its own ministers.

The EEOC and Perich also contend that our decision in *Employment Div., Dept. of Human Resources of Ore. v. Smith,* 494 U.S. 872, 110 S.Ct. 1595, 108 L.Ed.2d 876 (1990), precludes recognition of a ministerial exception. In *Smith,* two members of the Native American Church were denied state unemployment benefits after it was determined that they had been fired from their jobs for ingesting peyote, a crime under Oregon law. We held that this did not violate the Free Exercise Clause, even though the peyote had been ingested for sacramental purposes, because the "right of free exercise does not relieve an individual of the obligation to comply with a valid and neutral law of general applicability on the ground that the law proscribes (or prescribes) conduct that his religion prescribes (or proscribes)." *Id.,* at 879, 110 S.Ct. 1595 * * *

It is true that the ADA's prohibition on retaliation, like Oregon's prohibition on peyote use, is a valid and neutral law of general applicability. But a church's selection of its ministers is unlike an individual's ingestion of peyote. *Smith* involved government regulation of only outward physical acts. The present case, in contrast, concerns government interference with an internal church decision that affects the faith and mission of the church itself. See *id.,* at 877, 110 S.Ct. 1595 (distinguishing the government's regulation of "physical acts" from its "lend [ing] its power to one or the other side in controversies over religious authority or dogma"). * * *

III

Having concluded that there is a ministerial exception grounded in the Religion Clauses of the First Amendment, we consider whether the exception applies in this case. * * *

Every Court of Appeals to have considered the question has concluded that the ministerial exception is not limited to the head of a religious congregation, and we agree. We are reluctant, however, to adopt a rigid formula for deciding when an employee qualifies as a minister. * * *

To begin with, Hosanna-Tabor held Perich out as a minister, with a role distinct from that of most of its members. When Hosanna-Tabor extended her a call, it issued her a "diploma of vocation" according her the title "Minister of Religion, Commissioned." App. 42. She was tasked with performing that office "according to the Word of God and the confessional standards of the Evangelical Lutheran Church as drawn from the Sacred Scriptures." *Ibid.* * * * [T]he congregation undertook to periodically review Perich's "skills of ministry" and "ministerial responsibilities," and to provide for her "continuing education as a professional person in the ministry of the Gospel." *Id.,* at 49.

Perich's title as a minister reflected a significant degree of religious training followed by a formal process of commissioning. To be eligible to become a commissioned minister, Perich had to complete eight college-level courses in subjects including biblical interpretation, church doctrine, and the ministry of the Lutheran teacher. She also had to obtain the endorsement of her local Synod district by submitting a petition that contained her academic transcripts, letters of recommendation, personal statement, and written answers to various ministry-related questions. Finally, she had to pass an oral examination by a faculty committee at a Lutheran college. It took Perich six years to fulfill these requirements. And when she eventually did, she was commissioned as a minister only upon election by the congregation, which recognized God's call to her to teach. At that point, her call could be rescinded only upon a supermajority vote of the congregation – a protection designed to allow her to "preach the Word of God boldly." * * *

Perich held herself out as a minister of the Church by accepting the formal call to religious service, according to its terms. She did so in other ways as well. For example, she claimed a special housing allowance on her taxes that was available only to employees earning their compensation " 'in the exercise of the ministry.' * * * In a form she submitted to the Synod following her termination, Perich again indicated that she regarded herself as a minister at Hosanna-Tabor, stating: "I feel that God is leading me to serve in the teaching ministry. . . . I am anxious to be in the teaching ministry again soon." App. 53.

* * *

In light of these considerations – the formal title given Perich by the Church, the substance reflected in that title, her own use of that title, and the important religious functions she performed for the Church – we conclude that Perich was a minister covered by the ministerial exception.

In reaching a contrary conclusion, the Court of Appeals committed three errors. First, the Sixth Circuit failed to see any relevance in the fact that Perich was a commissioned minister. Although such a title, by itself, does not automatically ensure coverage, the fact that an employee has been ordained or commissioned as a minister is surely relevant, as is the fact that significant religious training and a recognized religious mission underlie the description of the employee's position. It was wrong for the Court of Appeals – and Perich * * * to say that an employee's title does not matter.

Second, the Sixth Circuit gave too much weight to the fact that lay teachers at the school performed the same religious duties as Perich. We express no view on whether someone with Perich's duties would be covered by the ministerial exception in the absence of the other considerations we have discussed. But though relevant, it cannot be dispositive that others not formally recognized as ministers by the church perform the same functions – particularly when, as here, they did so only because commissioned ministers were unavailable.

Third, the Sixth Circuit placed too much emphasis on Perich's performance of secular duties. It is true that her religious duties consumed only 45 minutes of each workday, and that the rest of her day was devoted to teaching secular subjects. The EEOC regards that as conclusive, contending that any ministerial exception "should be limited to those employees who perform exclusively religious functions." * * * We cannot accept that view. Indeed, we are unsure whether any such employees exist. The heads of congregations themselves often have a mix of duties, including secular ones such as helping to manage the congregation's finances, supervising purely secular personnel, and overseeing the upkeep of facilities.

Although the Sixth Circuit did not adopt the extreme position pressed here by the EEOC, it did regard the relative amount of time

Perich spent performing religious functions as largely determinative. The issue before us, however, is not one that can be resolved by a stopwatch. The amount of time an employee spends on particular activities is relevant in assessing that employee's status, but that factor cannot be considered in isolation, without regard to the nature of the religious functions performed and the other considerations discussed above.

Because Perich was a minister within the meaning of the exception, the First Amendment requires dismissal of this employment discrimination suit against her religious employer. The EEOC and Perich originally sought an order reinstating Perich to her former position as a called teacher. By requiring the Church to accept a minister it did not want, such an order would have plainly violated the Church's freedom under the Religion Clauses to select its own ministers.

Perich no longer seeks reinstatement, having abandoned that relief before this Court. See Perich Brief 58. But that is immaterial. Perich continues to seek frontpay in lieu of reinstatement, backpay, compensatory and punitive damages, and attorney's fees. An award of such relief would operate as a penalty on the Church for terminating an unwanted minister, and would be no less prohibited by the First Amendment than an order overturning the termination. Such relief would depend on a determination that Hosanna-Tabor was wrong to have relieved Perich of her position, and it is precisely such a ruling that is barred by the ministerial exception. * * *

The EEOC and Perich suggest that Hosanna-Tabor's asserted religious reason for firing Perich – that she violated the Synod's commitment to internal dispute resolution – was pretextual. That suggestion misses the point of the ministerial exception. The purpose of the exception is not to safeguard a church's decision to fire a minister only when it is made for a religious reason. The exception instead ensures that the authority to select and control who will minister to the faithful – a matter "strictly ecclesiastical," *Kedroff,* 344 U.S., at 119, 73 S.Ct. 143 – is the church's alone.[4]

---

[4] A conflict has arisen in the Courts of Appeals over whether the ministerial exception is a jurisdictional bar or a defense on the merits. Compare *Hollins,* 474 F.3d, at 225 (treating the exception as jurisdictional); and *Tomic v. Catholic Diocese of Peoria,* 442 F.3d 1036, 1038–1039 (C.A.7 2006) (same), with *Petruska,* 462 F.3d, at 302 (treating the exception as an affirmative defense); *Bryce,* 289 F.3d, at 654 (same); *Bollard v. California Province of Soc. of Jesus,* 196 F.3d 940, 951 (C.A.9 1999) (same); and *Natal,* 878 F.2d, at 1576 (same). We conclude that the exception operates as an affirmative defense to an otherwise cognizable claim, not a jurisdictional bar. That is because the issue presented by the exception is "whether the allegations the plaintiff makes entitle him to relief," not whether the court has "power to hear [the] case." *Morrison v.*

The EEOC and Perich foresee a parade of horribles that will follow our recognition of a ministerial exception to employment discrimination suits. According to the EEOC and Perich, such an exception could protect religious organizations from liability for retaliating against employees for reporting criminal misconduct or for testifying before a grand jury or in a criminal trial. What is more, the EEOC contends, the logic of the exception would confer on religious employers "unfettered discretion" to violate employment laws by, for example, hiring children or aliens not authorized to work in the United States. * * *

Hosanna-Tabor responds that the ministerial exception would not in any way bar criminal prosecutions for interfering with law enforcement investigations or other proceedings. Nor, according to the Church, would the exception bar government enforcement of general laws restricting eligibility for employment, because the exception applies only to suits by or on behalf of ministers themselves. Hosanna-Tabor also notes that the ministerial exception has been around in the lower courts for 40 years, see *McClure v. Salvation Army,* 460 F.2d 553, 558 (C.A.5 1972), and has not given rise to the dire consequences predicted by the EEOC and Perich.

The case before us is an employment discrimination suit brought on behalf of a minister, challenging her church's decision to fire her. Today we hold only that the ministerial exception bars such a suit. We express no view on whether the exception bars other types of suits, including actions by employees alleging breach of contract or tortious conduct by their religious employers. There will be time enough to address the applicability of the exception to other circumstances if and when they arise.

* * *

The judgment of the Court of Appeals for the Sixth Circuit is reversed.

It is so ordered.

Justice THOMAS, concurring.

* * * Our country's religious landscape includes organizations with different leadership structures and doctrines that influence their conceptions of ministerial status. The question whether an employee is a minister is itself religious in nature, and the answer will vary widely. Judicial attempts to fashion a civil definition of "minister" through a

---

National Australia Bank Ltd., 561 U.S. ----, ----, 130 S.Ct. 2869, 2877, 177 L.Ed.2d 535 (2010) (internal quotation marks omitted). District courts have power to consider ADA claims in cases of this sort, and to decide whether the claim can proceed or is instead barred by the ministerial exception.

bright-line test or multi-factor analysis risk disadvantaging those religious groups whose beliefs, practices, and membership are outside of the "mainstream" or unpalatable to some. Moreover, uncertainty about whether its ministerial designation will be rejected, and a corresponding fear of liability, may cause a religious group to conform its beliefs and practices regarding "ministers" to the prevailing secular understanding. See *Corporation of Presiding Bishop of Church of Jesus Christ of Latter-day Saints v. Amos,* 483 U.S. 327, 336, 107 S.Ct. 2862, 97 L.Ed.2d 273 (1987) ("[I]t is a significant burden on a religious organization to require it, on pain of substantial liability, to predict which of its activities a secular court will consider religious. The line is hardly a bright one, and an organization might understandably be concerned that a judge would not understand its religious tenets and sense of mission. Fear of potential liability might affect the way an organization carried out what it understood to be its religious mission" (footnote omitted)). These are certainly dangers that the First Amendment was designed to guard against.

* * *

Justice ALITO, with whom Justice KAGAN joins, concurring.

I join the Court's opinion, but I write separately to clarify my understanding of the significance of formal ordination and designation as a "minister" in determining whether an "employee" * * * of a religious group falls within the so-called "ministerial" exception. The term "minister" is commonly used by many Protestant denominations to refer to members of their clergy, but the term is rarely if ever used in this way by Catholics, Jews, Muslims, Hindus, or Buddhists. * * * In addition, the concept of ordination as understood by most Christian churches and by Judaism has no clear counterpart in some Christian denominations and some other religions. Because virtually every religion in the world is represented in the population of the United States, it would be a mistake if the term "minister" or the concept of ordination were viewed as central to the important issue of religious autonomy that is presented in cases like this one. Instead, courts should focus on the function performed by persons who work for religious bodies.

The First Amendment protects the freedom of religious groups to engage in certain key religious activities, including the conducting of worship services and other religious ceremonies and rituals, as well as the critical process of communicating the faith. Accordingly, religious groups must be free to choose the personnel who are essential to the performance of these functions.

The "ministerial" exception should be tailored to this purpose. It should apply to any "employee" who leads a religious organization, conducts worship services or important religious ceremonies or rituals, or serves as a messenger or teacher of its faith. If a religious group believes that the ability of such an employee to perform these key functions has

181

been compromised, then the constitutional guarantee of religious freedom protects the group's right to remove the employee from his or her position.

* * *

II

A

The Court's opinion today holds that the "ministerial" exception applies to Cheryl Perich (hereinafter respondent), who is regarded by the Lutheran Church-Missouri Synod as a commissioned minister. But while a ministerial title is undoubtedly relevant in applying the First Amendment rule at issue, such a title is neither necessary nor sufficient. As previously noted, most faiths do not employ the term "minister," and some eschew the concept of formal ordination.[3] And at the opposite end of the spectrum, some faiths consider the ministry to consist of all or a very large *714 percentage of their members.[4] Perhaps this explains why, although every circuit to consider the issue has recognized the "ministerial" exception, no circuit has made ordination status or formal title determinative of the exception's applicability.

The Fourth Circuit was the first to use the term "ministerial exception," but in doing so it took pains to clarify that the label was a mere shorthand. See *Rayburn v. General Conference of Seventh-Day Adventists,* 772 F.2d 1164, 1168 (1985) (noting that the exception's applicability "does not depend upon ordination but upon the function of the position"). * * * A decade after *McClure,* the Fifth Circuit made clear that formal ordination was not necessary for the "ministerial" exception to apply. The court held that the members of the faculty at a Baptist seminary were covered by the exception because of their religious function in conveying church doctrine, even though some of them were not ordained ministers. See *EEOC v. Southwestern Baptist Theological Seminary,* 651 F.2d 277 (1981).

The functional consensus has held up over time, with the D.C. Circuit recognizing that "[t]he ministerial exception has not been limited

---

[3]   In Islam, for example, "every Muslim can perform the religious rites, so there is no class or profession of ordained clergy. Yet there are religious leaders who are recognized for their learning and their ability to lead communities of Muslims in prayer, study, and living according to the teaching of the Qur'an and Muslim law." 10 Encyclopedia of Religion 6858 (2d ed. 2005).

[4]   For instance, Jehovah's Witnesses consider all baptized disciples to be ministers. See The Watchtower, Who Are God's Ministers Today? Nov. 15, 2000, p. 16 ("According to the Bible, all Jehovah's worshippers – heavenly and earthly – are ministers").

to members of the clergy." *EEOC v. Catholic Univ.,* 83 F.3d 455, 461 (1996). * * *

The Ninth Circuit too has taken a functional approach, just recently reaffirming that "the ministerial exception encompasses more than a church's ordained ministers." *Alcazar v. Corp. of Catholic Archbishop of Seattle,* 627 F.3d 1288, 1291 (2010) (en banc); see also *Elvig v. Calvin Presbyterian Church,* 375 F.3d 951, 958 (C.A.9 2004). The Court's opinion today should not be read to upset this consensus.

B

The ministerial exception applies to respondent because, as the Court notes, she played a substantial role in "conveying the Church's message and carrying out its mission." *Ante,* at 708. She taught religion to her students four days a week and took them to chapel on the fifth day. She led them in daily devotional exercises, and led them in prayer three times a day. She ***715** also alternated with the other teachers in planning and leading worship services at the school chapel, choosing liturgies, hymns, and readings, and composing and delivering a message based on Scripture.

* * *

Hosanna-Tabor discharged respondent because she threatened to file suit against the church in a civil court. This threat contravened the Lutheran doctrine that disputes among Christians should be resolved internally without resort to the civil court system and all the legal wrangling it entails. * * * In Hosanna-Tabor's view, respondent's disregard for this doctrine compromised her religious function, disqualifying her from serving effectively as a voice for the church's faith. * * *

For civil courts to engage in the pretext inquiry that respondent and the Solicitor General urge us to sanction would dangerously undermine the religious autonomy that lower court case law has now protected for nearly four decades. In order to probe the *real reason* for respondent's firing, a civil court – and perhaps a jury – would be required to make a judgment about church doctrine. The credibility of Hosanna-Tabor's asserted reason for terminating respondent's employment could not be assessed without taking into account both the importance that the Lutheran Church attaches to the doctrine of internal dispute resolution and the degree to which that tenet compromised respondent's religious function. * * *

Notes & Questions

1. The ADA provides two defenses to employment discrimination claims that are applicable to religious entities acting as employers. Such entity is not prohibited "from giving preference in employment to individuals of a particular religion to perform work connected with the

carrying on by such [entity] of its activities." § 12113(d)(1) (2006). Additionally, "a religious organization may require that all applicants and employees conform to the religious tenets of such organization." § 12113(d)(2). Hosanna-Tabor did not assert these defenses. Why?

2. Is this decision likely to lead to "a parade of horribles", that is, "protect[ing] religious organizations from liability for retaliating against employees for reporting criminal misconduct or for testifying before a grand jury or in a criminal trial"? Hosanna-Tabor Evangelical Church & Sch., 132 S.Ct. 694, 710 (2012).

3. How much weight is appropriately given to the title and training associated with being a minister or its equivalent, in comparison to the amount of time spent engaging in ministerial duties, in determining whether the ministerial exception applies?

৵

5. Employers under Section 504 of the Rehabilitation Act

Like Title I of the ADA, Section 504 of the Rehabilitation Act provides a private right of action to qualified individuals with disabilities who have been subjected to employment discrimination. The Rehabilitation Act defines a covered entity as a "program or activity," including the operations of a corporation, partnership, private organization, or a sole proprietorship, as long as federal assistance is provided to the entity engaged in the covered business activities. 29 U.S.C. § 794(b)(3)(A)(ii) (2006).

Until the passage of the ADA, there was no issue of there being a requirement under the Rehabilitation Act that an employer have any requisite number of employees. But in 1992, Congress amended the Rehabilitation Act to provide that in employment discrimination cases, the standards to determine a violation of the Rehabilitation Act are the same as those applied under the ADA. *Id.* § 794(d).

The only federal court of appeal to squarely consider the issue has concluded that, although the Rehabilitation Act incorporates Title I's substantive standards for determining conduct volatile to the Act, it does not incorporate the ADA's definition of covered entity. Schrader v. Ray, 296 F.3d 968, 975 (10th Cir. 2002). Therefore, there is no requirement under the Rehabilitation Act that an employer have 15 employees. *Id.* at 972-75. But other courts have indicated they would decide the other way. *See* Hiler v. Brown, 177 F.3d 542, 547 (6th Cir. 1999) (assuming, without deciding, that Rehabilitation Act's incorporation of ADA standards extends to definition of employer, including requirement of 15 employees).

The Rehabilitation Act permits a plaintiff to prevail on an employment discrimination claim only if she can establish that the adverse employment action was based solely upon the plaintiff's disability.

29 U.S.C. § 794 (2006). In contrast, the ADA demands only that a plaintiff demonstrate that the adverse employment action was based upon disability among other factors. 42 U.S.C. § 12112 (2006). All Circuits that have interpreted this standard have distinguished it from the Rehabilitation Act standard, holding that the failure to include the language of "solely based upon" in the ADA indicate Congress's intent to alter the standard to a more lenient burden of proving only that discrimination was a basis, and not the only basis, for the adverse action. Lewis v. Humboldt Acquisition Corp., Inc., 681 F.3d 312, 315 (6th Cir. 2012); *see also* Lee v. City of Columbus, Ohio, 636 F.3d 245, 250 (6th Cir. 2011) (finding distinction between Rehabilitation Act and ADA standard).

6. Indirect employment relationships

Can a plaintiff sue an employer with whom she only has an indirect employment relationship? What if, for example, the plaintiff's primary employer has contracted with a third-party to regulate and administer some aspect of that plaintiff's employment? Can the plaintiff sue the third party for disability discrimination?

Although there is no hard and fast answer to this question, courts have generally allowed such suits, despite there being no direct employment relationship, if the third party has a significant amount of control over the employment function at issue. In this way, it is a parallel inquiry to the coverage for workers of "temporary employment agencies and staffing firms" discussed *supra*.

In *Carparts Distribution Center, Inc. v. Automotive Wholesaler's Ass'n New England Inc.*, 37 F.3d 13 (1st Cir. 1994), the Plaintiff was an employee (and sole shareholder, president, and chief executive director) of Carparts, an automotive parts wholesaler distributor. Carparts was a participant in a self-funded medical reimbursement plan offered by the Defendants. Plaintiff, who had AIDS, submitted numerous claims for payment for illnesses that were AIDS-related. The Plaintiff alleged that with knowledge of his illness, defendants amended the Plan to limit benefits for AIDS-related illnesses.

To bring a claim for disability discrimination, the Plaintiff had to show that Defendants were his employers for purposes of the ADA. The Defendant argued that it could not be a covered entity for purposes of Title I because the Plaintiff was not one of its employees. In denying the defendant's motion to dismiss, the court held that the defendant could be plaintiff's employer (even though the plaintiff was not Defendant's employee) because the Defendant could have exercised "significant control" over aspects central to Plaintiff's employment. Peter Blanck, et al., AIDS-Related Benefits Equation: Soaring Costs Times Soaring Needs Divided by Federal Law, in 2 Mealey's Litigation Reports: Americans with Disabilities Act 21 (1994). The First Circuit remanded to the District Court to allow the plaintiff to develop the proper factual record.

The *Carparts* court suggested that defendants could have assumed responsibility for providing health care insurance for Carparts' employees. The court also said persuasive factors would include: whether defendants had the authority to determine the level of benefits provided to Carparts employees; whether alternative health plans were available to Carparts employees through their employment; and whether Carparts shared the administrative responsibilities that resulted from its employees. *Id.* at 17. *Carparts* stands for the proposition that an entity may be considered an employer when it acts as an agent of a Title I covered entity by administering important aspects of employment, such as health insurance services and benefits. *Id.* The court also suggested that an entity may be covered under Title I when it significantly affects access of an individual with a disability to employment opportunities. *Id.* at 12, 18. *Carparts* is discussed further as a Title III case, *infra* Part 5.

Although courts have reached different conclusions as to whether a particular "indirect" employer is a covered entity, they have consistently focused on the third-party's control over a key employment function as the most important factor to consider. In *Bloom v. Bexar*, 130 F.3d 722, 725 (5th Cir. 1997), the Plaintiff was hired as a court reporter by a state district court judge. In holding that Bexar County was not a covered entity for Plaintiff's purposes, the court reasoned that the state legislature had exclusively vested the right to control the means and manner of a court reporter's performance in the state district court (controlled by the state, not the county). *Id.* at 724. Although *Bloom* was a Title VII case, the holding applies by implication to the ADA.

Similarly, in *United States v. N.Y. State Dep't of Motor Vehicles*, 82 F.Supp.2d 42, 43 (E.D.N.Y. 2000), a school bus company refused to rehire an individual with a missing limb as a bus driver. Plaintiff named four Defendants as his "employer" for purposes of Title I – the bus company, the school district, the New York Department of Motor Vehicles (DMV) and the New York State Department of Education (SED). The latter two state agencies had regulations barring the operation of a bus by an individual missing a limb and the contract between the bus company and the school district incorporated those regulations.

In a separate decision, the bus company was found liable as plaintiff's employer. EEOC v. Amboy Bus Co., 96-CV-5451, cited in N.Y. State Dep't of Motor Vehicles, 82 F.Supp.2d at 43. The question remained which of the remaining three Defendants (the school district, DMV, and SED) were covered entities and employers for the purposes of Plaintiff's Title I claim.

The district court stated the general rule as being that "a [d]efendant that does not have a direct relationship with a plaintiff may nonetheless be liable under . . . the ADA for its discriminatory acts if it interferes with the plaintiff's employment opportunities with a third party and the defendant controls access to those opportunities." N.Y. State

Dep't of Motor Vehicles, 82 F.Supp.2d at 46. The court held that the school district was a covered entity and plaintiff's employer for the purposes of Title I because the contract between the school district and the bus company provided the district sufficient control over the plaintiff's employment. *Id.* at 49. But the court went on to hold that there was insufficient evidence of causation for the school district to be liable for employment discrimination, because the evidence indicated that the bus company failed to rehire plaintiff because of the DMV regulations, not because of the contract between the school district and the bus company. *Id.* at 56.

The court also held that the state defendants – the DMV and the SED – exercised sufficient control over plaintiff's employment to be considered covered entities and his employers for purposes of Title I. *Id.* at 49. Nevertheless, the court held that these state agencies could not be considered his employers under an indirect employment theory because their actions were regulatory in nature, taken in exercise of the state's police power. *Id.* at 51-53; *see also* George v. N.J. Bd. of Veterinary Med. Exam'rs, 635 F.Supp. 953, 955 (D.N.J. 1985), aff'd, 794 F.2d 113 (3d Cir. 1986). According to the court, when regulating pursuant to its police power, the state is acting as a sovereign and not as employer.

There is a line as to how far the "interference theory" can go – that is, when a non-direct employer can be liable under the ADA if it interferes with plaintiff's employment prospects and controls access to those employment opportunities. In *Satterfield v. Tennessee*, 295 F.3d 611, 619 (6th Cir. 2002), a state employer contracted with a private company to perform pre-employment physical examinations. The doctor employed by the private company found that plaintiff was not physically qualified for the position. The Sixth Circuit held that the private company and the doctor were not covered under Title I as employers because they did not have direct control over plaintiff's employment opportunities. Ultimately, the state employer made the final decision in regard to plaintiff's employment.

7.   Supervisors and other employees

Title I only covers employers. Individuals that are not employers are not covered entities and therefore not subject to liability. *See* Ostrach v. Regents of the Univ. of Cal., 957 F.Supp. 196, 200 (E.D. Cal. 1997); Lund v. J.C. Penny Outlet, 911 F.Supp. 442, 445 (D. Nev. 1996); Hardwick v. Curtis Trailers Inc., 896 F.Supp. 1037, 1038-39 (D. Or. 1995); Gallo v. Bd. of Regents of Univ. of Cal., 916 F.Supp. 1005, 1009-10 (S.D. Cal. 1995). Supervisors and other employees generally are not personally and individually liable under Title VII of the Civil Rights Act (and by extension the ADA). Greenlaw v. Garrett, 59 F.3d 994, 1001 (9th Cir. 1995); Miller v. Maxwell's Int'l, Inc., 991 F.2d 583, 587 (9th Cir. 1993). Although an employee's supervisor is not personally liable for discriminatory actions, that supervisor's actions may give rise to respondeat superior liability. Stern v. Cal. State Archives, 982 F.Supp. 690, 692 (E.D. Cal. 1997).

8. Labor organizations

Congress incorporated Title VII's definition of labor organization into Title I:

> . . . [a]ny organization of any kind, any agency, or employee representation committee, group, association, or plan so engaged in which employees participate and which exists for the purpose, in whole or in part, of dealing with employers concerning grievances, labor disputes, wages, rates of pay, hours, or other terms or conditions of employment, and any conference, general committee, joint or system board, or joint council so engaged which is subordinate to a national or international labor organization.

42 U.S.C. § 2000e(d). Compare *id.* § 12111(2) (2006).

A labor organization is engaged in an industry affecting commerce, when it maintains a hiring office or has 15 or more members and either:

> (1) is the certified representative of employees under the provisions of the National Labor Relation Act . . ., or the Railway Labor Act . . .;

> (2) although not certified, is a national or international labor organization or a local labor organization recognized or acting as the representative of employees of an employer or employers engaged in an industry affecting commerce; or

> (3) has chartered a local labor organization or subsidiary body which is representing or actively seeking to represent employees of employers within the paragraph (1) or (2); or

> (4) has been chartered by a labor organization representing or actively seeking to represent employees within the meaning of paragraph (1) or (2) as the local or subordinate body through which such employees may enjoy membership or become affiliated with such labor organization; or

> (5) is a conference, general committee, joint or system board, or joint council subordinate to a national or international labor organization, which includes a labor organization engaged in an industry affecting commerce within the meaning of any of the preceding paragraphs of this subsection.

Id. § 2000e(e).

Title I adopts the definition of an "industry affecting commerce," *id.* § 12111(7), as an "activity, business, or industry in commerce or in which a labor dispute would hinder or obstruct commerce or the free flow of commerce and includes . . . any governmental industry, business or activity." *Id.* § 20000e(h). A federal district court lacks subject matter jurisdiction over a Title I employment discrimination claim against a defendant that is not a labor organization as defined in the ADA.

In *Jones v. American Postal Workers Union*, 192 F.3d 417, 426 (4th Cir. 1999), the Fourth Circuit confronted the issue of whether a labor organization that represents federal employees is a covered entity under the ADA. Although the court viewed the ADA as ambiguous on this point, it deferred to the EEOC's interpretation of § 2000e(d) of Title VII, holding that where a labor organization representing federal employees exists for the purpose of negotiating with the United States or its agencies concerning grievances and labor disputes, it is engaged in an "industry affecting commerce" and is covered by Title VII and, by implication, the ADA. *Id.* at 427-28.

9. Federal employers and contractors

As used in Title I, the term employer does not include "the United States or a corporation wholly owned by the government of the United States." 42 U.S.C. § 12111(5)(B)(i) (2006). A suit against a federal agency or against an officer of a federal agency in her official capacity constitutes a suit against the United States, and is not permitted under the ADA. *See, e.g.,* Kemer v. Johnson, 900 F.Supp. 677, 681 (S.D.N.Y. 1995), aff'd, 101 F.3d 683 (2d Cir. 1996).

In contrast, federal employers are subject to the employment disability discrimination provisions of Section 501 of the Rehabilitation Act. A federal employee has a private right of action that can be brought against the head of a federal agency for nonaffirmative action employment discrimination, 29 USC § 791(g); 42 USC § 2000e-16b(a)(1), and for "discriminat[ion] against a qualified individual on the basis of disability in regard to job application procedures, the hiring, advancement, or discharge of employees, employee compensation, job training, and other terms, conditions, and privileges of employment." 42 USC § 12112(a); 29 USC § 791(g); Shaw-Campbell v. Runyon, 888 F.Supp. 1111 (M.D. Ala. 1995). On August 25, 2010, the Office of Federal Operations (OFO) issued a decision affirming an ALJ's certification of the class in the EEOC action against the Social Security Administration, *Jantz v. Astrue*, Appeal No. 0720090019, at 8-9 (EEOC Aug. 25, 2010), *available at* http://www. ssadisabilityclassaction.com/OFO_Decision.pdf. The action alleges that the SSA discriminated and continues to discriminate against employees with disabilities with respect to promotion decisions under Section 501. *Id.* at 1-5. The OFO denied the SSA's request for reconsideration in January of 2011. *Jantz v. Astrue*, 2011 WL 121280, at *2 (EEOC Jan. 4,

2011). As of October 2013, the case remains stayed, pending a decision in review of the SSA's motion to decertify the class.

Additionally, under Section 503 of the Rehabilitation Act, federal contractors receiving more than $10,000 to perform a federal contract must

> "not discriminate against any employee or applicant . . . because of physical or mental disability in regard to any position for which the employee or applicant for employment is qualified. . . . [and must] take affirmative action to employ, advance in employment and otherwise treat qualified individuals with disabilities without discrimination based on their physical or mental disability in all employment practices . . . ."

41 CFR §§ 60-741.5(a)(1); 60-741.4(a)(1) (2011).

On September 24, 2013, the U.S. Department of Labor published the final rules for implementing Section 503 of the Rehabilitation Act, including the goal that federal contractor's employ up to 7% qualified people with disabilities for each job group in the contractor's workforce, or for the contractor's entire workforce. Affirmative Action and Nondiscrimination Obligations of Contractors and Subcontractors Regarding Individuals with Disabilities, 78 Fed. Reg. 58,682, 58,745 (Sept. 24, 2013).

§ 6.3 Hiring, Discipline And Benefits

A. *Hiring*

Employers are prohibited from discriminating against people with disabilities in their hiring practices. Thus, an employer may not adopt qualification standards that unnecessarily exclude people with disabilities. "Discrimination" includes:

> using qualification standards, employment tests or other selection criteria that screen out or tend to screen out an individual with a disability or a class of individuals with disabilities unless the standard, test or other selection criteria, as used by the covered entity, is shown to be job-related for the position in question and is consistent with business necessity.

42 U.S.C. § 12112(b)(6) (2006). Qualification standards based on disability, such as vision or hearing, lifting or walking, or reading or learning abilities must be job-related and consistent with business necessity. *Id.* Thus, they must be narrowly tailored to reflect the actual essential functions of the job. In addition, the employer must be prepared to provide reasonable accommodations for people who can do the job but do not meet the restriction. The safer practice, rather than relying on physical or mental attributes, focuses on the ability to do the tasks

required by the job. Thus, instead of a requirement that an emergency medial technician be able to lift 200 pounds, the qualification standard should be the ability to move a 200-pound patient. The latter standard would not disqualify an individual with a prosthetic arm, who, although she could not lift a 200-pound weight, could maneuver a 200-pound person. *See*, *e.g.*, Gillen v. Fallon Ambulance Serv., Inc., 283 F.3d 11, 28 (1st Cir. 2001).

B.   *Discipline*

A disability does not immunize an employee for behavior and performance-based discipline, as long as the discipline also is applied uniformly employees without disabilities. U.S. Equal Emp. Opportunity Comm'n, Enforcement Guidance on the Americans with Disabilities Act and Psychiatric Disabilities, http://www.eeoc.gov/policy/docs/psych.html (June 19, 2012). An employer with no knowledge of an employee's disability may apply its usual behavior, performance, and discipline standards,

> provided that the workplace conduct standard is job-related for the position in question and is consistent with business necessity. . . . An employer must make reasonable accommodation to enable an otherwise qualified individual with a disability to meet such a conduct standard in the future, barring undue hardship. Because reasonable accommodation is always prospective, however, an employer is not required to excuse past misconduct.

Id. at Questions 30 & 31. A request for accommodation made after disciplinary action is taken does not raise a defense to the initial discipline. Yet, if an employer undertakes discipline after refusing to provide reasonable accommodation, an ADA claim may arise. *See also* U.S. Equal Emp. Opportunity Comm'n, The Americans with Disabilities Act: Applying Performance and Conduct Standards to Employees with Disabilities, http://www.eeoc.gov/facts/performance-conduct.html (last modified June 19, 2012).

C.   *Benefits And Privileges Of Employment*

Title I requires employers to provide accommodations to qualified employees with disabilities so that they may enjoy the same terms, benefits and privileges of employment as those comparable employees without disabilities. 29 C.F.R. pt. 1630 app., § 1630.9 (2008). Employment benefits and privileges may include employer-sponsored job training or in-service programs. This may include access to electronic bulletin boards, and Internet and Intranet services, company credit unions, cafeterias, auditoriums, transportation, and social functions. *See* Peter Blanck, eQuality: Web Rights, Human Flourishing and Persons with Cognitive Disabilities (forthcoming 2014).

However, some courts have found that Title I generally does not require an employer to ensure that insurance benefits treat people with disabilities equally. *See* EEOC v. Aramark Corp., Inc., 208 F.3d 266, 268-69 (D.C. Cir. 2000) (Title I "safe harbor" provision, 42 U.S.C. § 12201(c)(3) (2006), exempts insurance plans that pre-exist the ADA); Weyer v. Twentieth Century Fox Film Corp., 196 F.3d 1092, 1109 (9th Cir. 1999) (employee on disability leave is not qualified because she cannot perform essential functions, and therefore cannot challenge long-term disability insurance policy); EEOC v. CNA Ins. Cos., 96 F.3d 1039, 1044-45 (7th Cir. 1996) (same); *see also* Lewis v. KMart Corp., 180 F.3d 166, 170 (4th Cir. 1999) (distinctions within insurance policy are not employment discrimination because all employees are offered access to the same plan); Kimber v. Thiokol Corp., 196 F.3d 1092, 1101-02 (10th Cir. 1999) (same). *But see* Johnson v. KMart Corp., 273 F.3d 1035, 1048-59 (11th Cir. 2001) (long-term disability policy that provides less coverage for mental disability is discriminatory unless covered by safe harbor provision).

The issue whether Title I reaches insurance benefit plans has arisen primarily in the context of long-term disability insurance policies that cap the coverage for mental disabilities, but not physical disabilities. Title I generally does not require employers to alter their insurance benefit plans for employees working part-time as an accommodation to their disability. *See, e.g.*, Tenbrink v. Fed. Home Loan Bank, 920 F.Supp. 1156, 1162 (D. Kan. 1996). Thus, an employer may provide health benefits only to full-time workers, even if this requirement results in a reduction in benefits for workers with disabilities who are accommodated with part-time schedules. For a review, *see* Bonnie P. Tucker, Insurance and the ADA, 46 DePaul L. Rev. 915, 916-17 (1997).

Notes & Questions

1. Employees with disabilities, who are members of labor unions subject to collective bargaining agreements, may have additional benefits in situations involving hiring and discipline. In *Josephs v. Pacific Bell*, 432 F.3d 1006 (9th Cir. 2005) (opinion amended by 443 F.3d 1050 (9th Cir. 2006)), the employee was fired for failing to indicate a misdemeanor conviction on his job application. The service technician's union of which he was a member had a collective bargaining agreement with Pacific Bell requiring a three step grievance process. Josephs took the necessary steps to complete the process including having the misdemeanor conviction expunged, but Pacific Bell refused to reinstate him. The district court concluded that the employer regarded Josephs as having a mental disability substantially limiting his ability to work a broad range of jobs, and the failure to reinstate him was a violation of the ADA. The appellate court affirmed.

2. Under the provisions of the Affordable Care Act (ACA) that take effect January 1, 2014, all employers with more than 50 full-time

employees (30 or more hours per week), will be required to provide health benefits to full-time employees on an equal basis for all employees with and without disability, or face a substantial fine. 42 U.S.C.A. § 4980H(a) (2013). Concerns have arisen that more employees will be classified as part-time by employers to avoid providing health benefits to some or all employees. Karen McVeigh, US Employers Slashing Worker Hours to Avoid Obamacare Insurance Mandate, The Gaurdian (Sept. 30, 2013), http://www.theguardian.com/world/2013/sep/30/us-employers-slash-hours-avoid-obamacare. If a covered employer reduced all employees with disabilities, and no others, to part-time to avoid covering their health insurance, can a Title I claim be made?

3. Commentators also have opined that the ACA will incentivize many employees to cut hours back to part-time, so as to take advantage of low-cost health coverage purchased through ACA health insurance exchanges. Vivian Giang, Millions of Workers May Choose to Go Part-Time Once Obama-Care Kicks In, Business Insider (Oct. 9, 2013), http://www.businessinsider.com/workers-are-opting-for-part-time-positions-2013-10#ixzz2hi7PwaaA. *See also* Part 8, § 32.2 for further coverage of the ACA.

∽

Chapter 7 EXAMINATIONS AND INQUIRIES

Section 12112(d) of the ADA expands the generic prohibition of discrimination in employment on the basis of disability to include certain kinds of inquiries. 42 U.S.C. §§ 12112(d)(2)-(4) (2006).

The restrictions on inquiries and examinations at different phases of employment serve distinct purposes:

- *Pre-employment* (§ 12112(d)(2)): The potential employer may not try to learn if the applicant has a disability. This provision is prophylactic, allowing individuals with a disability "a fair opportunity to be judged on their qualifications, 'to get past that initial barrier' where an employment judgment may be unfairly based on disabilities rather than abilities." Harris v. Harris & Hart, Inc., 206 F.3d 838, 841 (9th Cir. 2000) (quoting 135 Cong. Rec. 10,768 (daily ed. Sept. 7 1989) (statement of Sen. Harkin)).

- *Post-conditional offer* – before start of employment (§ 12112(d)(3)): At this point, an employer already has made an offer and decided the potential employee meets the job's requirements. The employer may require an examination if all employees – or a least all employees performing similar tasks – are required. The examination is subject to rigid confidentiality restrictions and is used to determine if the employee can perform essential job functions.

- *During course of employment* (§ 12112(d)(4)): An employer may not make inquiries or require a medical examination "unless such examination or inquiry is shown to be job-related and consistent with business necessity." Employees may submit to voluntary examinations as part of employee health plans.

Each of these limitations raise difficult questions for employers. What are the position's essential functions? How must the examination be validated? What is a medical examination? How broadly can questions explore applicants' abilities? What is the proper scope of an examination if an applicant reveals she has a disability and requests an accommodation? What precautions must an employer take to protect the privacy of information?

The EEOC has developed guidelines for proper inquiries, to which courts often refer, although they are not obliged to adhere to them. U.S. Equal Emp. Opportunity Comm'n, Enforcement Guidance on Disability-Related Inquiries and Medical Examinations of Employees Under the Americans with Disabilities Act, http://www.eeoc.gov/policy/docs/guidance-inquiries.html (Sept. 27, 2000) (hereinafter "Inquiries and Medical Examinations").

These provisions have the effect of extending the Act's reach beyond people with disabilities. The point of the pre-employment restriction in particular is to forefend certain kinds of questions, so arguably anyone asked such a question may be entitled to relief. This has lead into a thicket of legal standing issues, which we will explore.

§ 7.1 Permissible Scope Of Inquiries And Examinations

A. *Pre-Employment*

The general pre-employment rule is that an employer may not attempt to find out if an applicant has a disability. But an employer can try to ascertain if the applicant can perform tasks that will be important to the job. As set forth in the statute:

> (A) Prohibited examination or inquiry
> Except as provided in paragraph (3), a covered entity shall not conduct a medical examination or make inquiries of a job applicant as to whether such applicant is an individual with a disability or as to the nature or severity of such disability.
>
> (B) Acceptable inquiry
> A covered entity may make preemployment inquiries into the ability of an applicant to perform job-related functions.

42 U.S.C. § 12112(d)(2) (2006).

The standard to ascertain whether an inquiry is "disability-related" is whether it is "a question (or series of questions) that is likely to elicit information about a disability." Inquiries and Medical Examinations, *supra*, at B.1; *see also* Karraker v. Rent-A-Center, Inc., 411 F.3d 831 (7th Cir. 2005) (concluding that the Minnesota Multiphasic Personality Inventory I, required of employees seeking management positions for the sake of "discerning personality traits," was a "medical examination" for purposes of the ADA). This standard is the same pre- and post-offer. The scope of permitted questions increases, however, if the applicant volunteers information about a disability, has an obvious disability, or requests an accommodation.

1. No known disability or requested accommodation

In most cases, the employer will not know if the applicant has a disability. The ADA functions to ensure that the employer cannot consider the applicant's possible hidden disability before evaluating an applicant's non-medical qualifications. *See* Inquiries and Medical Examinations, *supra*. In this way, the ADA channels employers' questioning of job applicants to their abilities, rather than their disabilities.

There are two types of behaviors in which employers are not permitted to engage at the pre-offer stage. First, they cannot ask disability-related questions, whether direct ("do you have a disability?") or indirect ("have you ever taken the medication AZT?"). *Id.* However, an employer may ask questions to which there are many possible answers, only some of which are disability-related (e.g., "do you have an arrest or conviction record?" or "can you meet our attendance policy?"). *Id.*

The prohibition extends to questions, such as the use of prescription drugs, which might imply the existence of a disability. *See* Griffin v. Steeltek, Inc., 160 F.3d 591, 594 (10th Cir. 1998) (application unlawfully asked: "Have you received workers' compensation or disability payments? If yes, describe."); *cf.* Krocka v. Bransfield, 969 F.Supp. 1073, 1079 (N.D. Ill. 1997) (police department implemented a policy of monitoring employees taking psychotropic medication); Roe v. Cheyenne Mountain Conference Resort, Inc., 920 F.Supp. 1153, 1154-55 (D. Colo. 1996), aff'd in pertinent part, 124 F.3d 1221, 1226 (10th Cir. 1997) (employer had a policy of requiring all employees to report every drug, including legal prescription drugs). However, because a person who currently uses illegal drugs is not considered disabled within the Act, questions about current illegal drug use are not forbidden and drug tests are permitted. 42 U.S.C. § 12114(a) (2006); 29 C.F.R. pt. 1630 app, § 1630.3(a) (2008).

An exception to this rule occurs when the questions relate to the essential functions of the job. Under the express language of § 12112(d)(2)(B), employers may ask whether an applicant can perform essential job functions. Courts may defer to an employer's judgment, but an applicant may nonetheless attack the functions as inessential or marginal. In such a circumstance wherein a doubt arises regarding a particular function, it is useful for the employer to validate the inquiry, for instance, by showing that there is a meaningful relation between success in the job and ability to perform the function.

If the essential functions include lifting objects of a certain weight, the employer may ask about lifting objects of a certain weight. The questions may include not merely the intellectual and physical functions, but also the psychological functions. For example, if the job requires working in a small, enclosed space, such as a narrow tunnel, the employer may ask whether an applicant can do so. Grenier v. Cyanimid Plastics, Inc., 70 F.3d 667, 675 (1st Cir. 1995) (citation omitted). Such an inquiry must be limited to seeking information about *current* abilities (not past histories). Any such inquiry must be carefully tailored to allow for reasonable accommodation. Thus, "do you have any condition that limits your ability to perform this job" is impermissible, while "do you have any condition that currently prevents you from performing the essential functions of this job, with or without reasonable accommodation" may be acceptable.

There are, however, other inquiries that, though less traditional, are still acceptable under Title I. For example, an employer may perform general fitness or agility tests, psychological tests, tests that evaluate an employee's ability to read labels or distinguish objects as part of a demonstration of the ability to perform actual job functions, and polygraph examinations (where permitted by law). *See* Inquiries and Medical Examinations, *supra*. Assuming these tests are not interpreted to be medical in nature, their acceptability relies on the employer's ability to prove that they are job-related; an employer may not ask about the applicant's ability to perform functions that are not essential to the job. Gillen v. Falcon Ambulance Serv., 283 F.3d 11, 27 (1st Cir. 2002) (post conditional-offer).

Employers who administer personality tests prior to hiring face the possibility that the test will be construed as a medical examination. *See* Gregory R. Vetter, Comment, Is a Personality Test a Pre-Job-Offer Medical Examination Under the ADA?, 93 Nw. U. L. Rev. 597, 638-639 (1999). The EEOC permits psychological testing as long as it is not a medical examination under the EEOC guidelines. *See* Inquiries and Medical Examinations, *supra*, at 14. For example, an industrial psychologist could evaluate whether an applicant for a sales job could deal with rejection or whether the applicant for a managerial job is detail-oriented. The analysis depends on a number of factors, including whether a health care professional administers or interprets it. *Id.* *Compare* Barnes v. Cochran, 944 F.Supp. 897, 905 (S.D. Fla. 1996) (psychological evaluation administered by licensed psychologist was a medical examination), *with* Thompson v. Borg-Warner Protective Servs. Corp., No. C-94-4015 MHP, 1996 WL 162990, at *6 (N.D. Cal. Mar. 11, 1996) (psychological evaluation not administered or interpreted by health care professional was not a medical examination), and Varnagis v. City of Chi., No. 96 C 6304, 1997 WL 361150 (N.D. Ill. June 20, 1997) (discovery permitted to determine if psychological evaluation is a medical examination).

The other type of prohibited behavior relates to specific medical examinations. Generally, until the employer makes a "conditional offer" – an offer that may be conditioned on the applicant's passing a physical examination administered to all prospective employees – the employer may not require medical examinations. 42 U.S.C. § 12112(d)(3) (2006). The theory behind disallowing medical examinations in the pre-offer context is identical to that behind disability-related questions: such examinations tend to prematurely reveal disabilities that may not be related to an applicant's ability to perform a job with or without reasonable accommodation.

Of course, there is a fine line between what constitutes a "medical examination," and what is a permissible inquiry that tests job-related functions. For example, consider a case where an employer requires an applicant to lift a thirty-pound box and carry it twenty feet. The EEOC Guidance suggests that this is not a medical examination; rather, it is "a test of whether the applicant can perform the task." *See* Contingent Workers, *supra*. For this to be a permissible inquiry, carrying a thirty-pound weight would need to be an essential part of the job. Generally, the distinction between acceptable "inquiries" and prohibited "medical examinations" turns on the nature of the procedure: a medical examination is a "procedure or test that seeks information about an individual's physical or mental impairments or health." *Id*. The EEOC looks to:

> (1) whether the test is administered by a health care professional; (2) whether the test is interpreted by a health care professional; (3) whether the test is designed to reveal an impairment or physical or mental health; (4) whether the test is invasive; (5) whether the test measures an employee's performance of a task or measures his/her physiological responses to performing the task; (6) whether the test normally is given in a medical setting; and, (7) whether medical equipment is used.

Inquiries and Medical Examinations, *supra*.

2. Known disability or requested accommodation

There are two situations in which an applicant might have a "known disability." These are if the applicant has an obvious disability, or if the applicant has voluntarily disclosed a hidden disability. An applicant also may voluntarily disclose to a potential employer that she needs a reasonable accommodation to perform a job. Any one of these three events broadens the range of permissible questions that an employer may ask.

In the first two situations, an employer may ask if the applicant needs a reasonable accommodation to perform the job, and what type of reasonable accommodation that might be. If an applicant with a visual impairment applies for a job involving computer work, the employer may ask whether he will need reasonable accommodation to perform the functions of the job. If the applicant answers "no," this ends the inquiry, although the employer may ask the applicant to describe or demonstrate performance. If the applicant answers "yes," the employer may ask questions about the type of accommodation ("What will you need?" or "Do you need a particular brand of software?"). Similarly, if the applicant requests an accommodation, the employer may inquire about the accommodation but not the underlying disability. This hypothetical is taken from Contingent Workers, *supra*.

The theory behind the courts and the EEOC permitting expanded inquires in the case of a known disability is drawn from the larger purposes of the Act. The primary goal of the ADA's employment provisions is to prevent the unnecessary or stigmatizing discovery of hidden disabilities. No harm is done to this purpose when an applicant has a known disability and the scope of questioning is thus broadened. EEOC guidance indicates:

> [W]here an applicant has an obvious disability, and the employer has a reasonable belief that s/he will need a reasonable accommodation to perform specific job functions, the employer may ask whether the applicant needs a reasonable accommodation and, if so, what type of accommodation. These same two questions may be asked when an individual voluntarily discloses a nonvisible disability or voluntarily tells the employer that s/he will need a reasonable accommodation to perform a job.

Inquiries and Medical Examinations, *supra*, at n.6 (citations omitted).

The underlying notion is that revelation of this information should be useful to both the applicant and the employer. And, when the employer requests more information than the employee can provide, "inquiries" may broaden beyond simply asking the applicant questions. Grenier v. Cyanimid Plastics, Inc., 70 F.3d 667, 673 (1st Cir. 1995); *cf.* Brumley v. Pena, 62 F.3d 277, 280 (8th Cir. 1995) (similar result under Rehabilitation Act of 1973).

B. *Post-Conditional Offer*

After an employer makes an employee a job offer, the range of permissible behavior by an employer again broadens. At this point, the employer may ask disability-related questions and perform medical examinations that need not be job-related. Contingent Workers, *supra*.

A job offer may be conditioned on the results of post-offer disability-related questions or medical examinations. But, if an individual does not get the job because these questions or examinations reveal a disability, the employer must show that the exclusionary criteria are job-related and consistent with business necessity. 42 U.S.C. § 12112(b) (2006); 29 C.F.R. pt. 1630 app., §§ 1630.10, 1630.14(b)(3) (2008).

If an employer elects to ask disability-related questions or require medical examinations after a job offer, it must make sure that all entering employees in the same job category are subjected to the examination or inquiry. The medical information obtained must be kept confidential. 42 U.S.C. § 12112(d)(3); 29 C.F.R. § 1630.14(b)(1)-(2).

1.   What constitutes a "job offer"?

The EEOC defines a job offer as one made after the employer "has evaluated all relevant non-medical information which it reasonably could have obtained and analyzed prior to giving the offer." Equal Emp. Opportunity Comm'n, ADA Enforcement Guidance: Preemployment Disability-Related Questions and Medical Examinations, http://www. eeoc.gov/policy/docs/preemp.html (Oct. 10, 1995). But if the employer can show that it was not reasonable to obtain all non-medical information at the pre-offer stage, an offer still can be enough to move the parties into the post-offer stage.

For example, it may be too costly for a law enforcement employer wishing to administer a polygraph examination to administer both a pre-offer examination asking non-disability related questions, and a post-offer examination asking disability-related questions. *Id.* Or, an applicant might request that a reference not be contacted until after a conditional offer is made. *Id.*

Job offers do not have to be limited to current vacancies. An employer may give offers to fill current vacancies or reasonably anticipated openings. *Id.* An employer even can give offers in increase of this number when it can show that it needs more offers to fill vacancies or reasonably anticipated openings. *Id.* An example is if the employer can demonstrate that a certain percentage of the applicant pool will likely be disqualified or withdraw from the pool.

2.   Post-offer medical examinations and inquiries

After an employer makes a conditional offer, it may require a medical examination if all entering employees are subjected to the examination regardless of disability and the exam is subject to restrictive confidentiality rules. 42 U.S.C. § 12112(d)(3) (2006).

Though Title I does not explicitly state what an employer may properly review in such a medical examination, courts have nonetheless stated that the scope of the examination is unlimited. "The Act 'imposes no restrictions on the scope of entrance examinations; it only guarantees the confidentiality of the information gathered . . . and restricts the use to which an employer may put the information.'" Garrison v. Baker Hughes Oil Field Operations, Inc., 287 F.3d 955, 962 (10th Cir. 2002) (quoting Norman-Bloodsaw v. Lawrence Berkeley Lab., 135 F.3d 1260, 1273 (9th Cir. 1998)). The statute provides some ways that the information may be used.

The employer may use the examination to tailor accommodations and also may alert safety personnel to a disability. 42 U.S.C. § 12112(d)(3)(B)(i)-(ii). Unlike the pre-offer stage, a post-offer medical examination may be used to determine whether the employee can safely perform the essential functions of the job. In *Gillen v. Falcon Ambulance Service, Inc.*, 283 F.3d 11, 33 (1st Cir. 2002), the First Circuit assumed without deciding that a post-conditional-offer medical examination was permissible when designed to determine whether the plaintiff (a genetic amputee with one functioning hand) could lift a specified weight. *See also*

Barnes v. Cochran, 944 F.Supp. 897, 901-02 (S.D. Fla. 1996) (pre-employment psychological examination for sheriff deputy position that reveal psychological problems used to disqualify plaintiff).

Nevertheless, the results of such examinations or inquiries may not be used in a way that is inconsistent with the ADA's purposes. *See* 42 U.S.C. § 12112(d)(3)(C). Once the offer has been given, it is presumed – subject to later refutation – that the applicant is a qualified individual. Employers may not use post-offer responses or examinations to screen people out unless the results demonstrate a direct threat or an inability to perform the job's essential functions that cannot be accommodated.

The scheme of permitting inquiries only at the post-offer stage of the process mitigates the problems of proof that arise when a person is forced to reveal a disability before an offer is made. At that stage, absent an admission by the employer, the applicant will not know whether her exclusion was due to her disability or her qualifications.

C. *Course Of Employment*

The restrictions on an employer's ability to make disability-related inquiries or require medical examinations continue after the person is hired. *Id.* § 12112(d)(4). As in the pre-offer and post-conditional-offer contexts, the prohibitions are tempered by practicalities.

Once again, the basic rule applies that employers may not ask questions seeking information that reveals disabilities. Conroy v. N.Y. State Dep't of Corr. Servs., 333 F.3d 88 (2d Cir. 2003), aff'g in part and remanding Fountain v. N.Y. State Dep't of Corr. Servs., 190 F.Supp.2d 335, 338 (N.D.N.Y. 2002) (question is "whether inquiry would be likely to require employees to disclose their disabilities or perceived disabilities"). For instance, where an employer demanded to know whether "something medical [was] going on" and "continued to insist there was something physical or mental . . . affecting [the employee]," and the employee felt "compelled" to disclose he was HIV positive, the court held there had been an improper medical inquiry. Horgan v. Simmons, 704 F.Supp.2d 814, 820 (N.D. Ill. 2010). Follow-up medical questions after a disclosure based on an improper inquiry, also are improper inquiries. *Id.* at 820-21.

In *Parsons v. First Quality Retail Services*, an employee, who had been injured while working, was given a final warning after a physical altercation with a coworker. He was then terminated after he revealed that he had given some of his prescription Lortab pills to coworkers in violation of the work policy. 2012 WL 174829 (M.D. Ga. Jan. 20, 2012). Plaintiff argued that his termination for failing to report his use of Lortab to his employer was a per se disability. But the court held that because he voluntarily disclosed his use of Lortab, "generally, where an employee voluntarily discloses medical information related to a disability, he cannot assert a claim regarding an improper medical inquiry." *Id.* Because he volunteered the information here, the employer did not violate the ADA.

If the inquiry is "job-related and consistent with business necessity," it is permissible. An objective test, rather than the employer's subjective belief, determines whether an inquiry is consistent with business necessity. Tice v. Cent. Area Transp. Auth., 247 F.3d 506, 518 (3d Cir. 2001) (citation omitted); Kroll v. White Lake Ambulance Auth., 691 F.3d 809 (6th Cir. 2012) (mandatory psychological counseling is a medical examination, and impermissible unless job related and consistent with business necessity). Fitzpatrick v. City of Atlanta, 2 F.3d 1112, 1119 n.6 (11th Cir. 1993). The Second Circuit has articulated the standard:

> [I]n proving a business necessity, an employer must show more than that its inquiry is consistent with "mere expediency." An employer cannot simply demonstrate that an inquiry is convenient or beneficial to its business. Instead, the employer must first show that the asserted "business necessity" is vital to the business. .... The employer must also show that the examination or inquiry genuinely serves the asserted business necessity and that the request is no broader or more intrusive than necessary. The employer need not show that the examination or inquiry is the only way of achieving a business necessity, but the examination or inquiry must be a reasonably effective method of achieving the employer's goal.

Conroy, 333 F.3d at 97-98.

The EEOC's regulations clarify that an employer can seek to determine if the employee can perform essential job functions, if the employer has an objective reasonable belief that the employee has a disability that may interfere with job performance. 29 C.F.R. pt. 1630 app. § 1630.14(c) (2008); *see also* Covelli v. Nat'l Fuel Gas Dist., 49 F. App'x 356, 2002 WL 31422862, at *1 (2d Cir. Oct. 29, 2002) (noting in dicta that employer may require medical examination to determine if employee who had previously claimed to be injured could perform essential functions); Tice, 247 F.3d at 517-18 (based on employer's knowledge of employee's condition and employee's own doctor's failure to justify return to work, request for independent medical examination justified). The legitimate reasons for requiring a medical exam for an employee are

> (1) when an employee is having difficulty performing his or her job effectively; (2) when an employee becomes disabled on the job or wishes to return to work after suffering an illness; (3) if an employee requests an accommodation; and (4) if medical examination, screening, and monitoring is required by other laws.

EEOC v. Prevo's Family Mkt., Inc., 135 F.3d 1089, 1103 (6th Cir. 1998); Chai R. Feldblum, Medical Examinations and Inquiries Under the

Americans with Disabilities Act: A View from the Inside, 64 Temp. L. Rev. 521, 543 (1991).

D. *Return To Work*

A disability-related leave gives rise to an objective basis to question the employee's ability to perform. Therefore, when an employee returns to work after a medical leave, the employer may demand an examination or a medical release stating that the employee can safely perform the job's essential functions. Grenier v. Cyanimid Plastics, Inc., 70 F.3d 667, 669 (1st Cir. 1995); White v. City of Boston, 7 Mass. L. Rptr. 232, 1997 WL 416586, at *2-3 (Mass. Super. Jul. 22 1997). However, an employer may not require a "general diagnosis," which may reveal a disability. Conroy v. N.Y. State Dep't of Corr. Servs., 333 F.3d 88, 95-96 (2d 2003); Roe v. Cheyenne Mountain Conference Resort, 920 F.Supp. 1153, 1154-55 (D. Colo. 1996), aff'd in pertinent part, 124 F.3d 1221 (10th Cir. 1997).

An inquiry also is permitted when a former worker with a known disability is sent to the employer from a union's hiring hall. Harris v. Harris & Hart, Inc., 206 F.3d 838, 843 (9th Cir. 2000) (worker is not considered an employee until employer has agreed to hire the worker after he has been dispatched from the union hall; but, in this case, employer's "request for a medical release as a prerequisite to re-hiring plaintiff, a former employee with a known disability, did not run afoul of the ADA").

The courts have applied these principles in a variety of cases:

- A court granted summary judgment against an employer with a sick leave policy that required an employee returning to work after a leave of any duration to present a doctor's certificate with a diagnosis. The inquiry was prohibited, because it might have revealed a disability and was too broad to be justified by business necessity. Fountain v. N.Y. State Dep't of Corr. Servs., 190 F.Supp.2d 335, 340 (N.D.N.Y. 2002). The court analogized to asking about all an employee's prescription medications, which was found improper in *Roe*, 124 F.3d at 1230-31. In *Conroy*, the Second Circuit found a question of fact about the "business necessity" of the inquiry. 333 F.3d at 97-98.

- An employer properly requested that an employee, returning to work after suffering severe depression, provide a release permitting her doctor to give the employer more information. The employee's refusal caused a breakdown in the interactive accommodation process, such that the employer could not be liable for failing to accommodate the employee. The court affirmed a summary judgment in favor of the defendant. Beck v.

Univ. of Wis. Bd. of Regents, 75 F.3d 1130, 1135-37 (7th Cir. 1995).[1]

- The court denied summary judgment to an employer where the employee challenged the scope of an inquiry. The employer had requested that the employee, who had returned from a lengthy sick leave the previous month, to submit to an independent medical examination to see if she could resume a job she had previously held. The employer's knowledge of the employee's health problems and the fact that she had returned to work earlier than her doctor recommended justified the examination, but did not justify the breadth of the inquiry, which requested all medications. Reichmann v. Cutler-Hammer, Inc., 95 F.Supp.2d 1171, 1175-76, 1186-87 (D. Kan. 2001).

- A court upheld an employer's requirement that all correctional officers fill out biannually a "Disclosure of Disability Form," which asked the employees to check if they had one of six disabilities – "(1) visual; (2) hearing; (3) speech; (4) physical; (5) learning; and (6) other." Martin v. Kansas, 190 F.3d 1120, 1124 (10th Cir. 1999). Although this inquiry seems intended to discover whether the employee has a disability, not whether he can perform the essential functions of the job, the court found that the employee had failed to rebut the employer's statement that the purpose of the inquiries was to "gather information to be used in setting post assignments and establishing reasonable accommodations, which are job-related purposes that are consistent with business necessity." *Id.* at 1134. However, the employee had not refused an

---

[1] In *Conrad v. Board of Johnson County Commissioners*, 237 F.Supp.2d 1204, 1231-36 (D. Kan. 2002), the defendant county properly required a "fitness for duty evaluation and psychiatric testing" of prenatal nurse (plaintiff). Plaintiff worked with high-risk patients and performed excessive duty hours, requiring subordinates to do the same. Additionally, plaintiff sent a "bizarre and inappropriate" e-mail stating: "I am asking the 'force' to release everyone of us from the 'chains that bind' and 'the walls that keep our Spirits apart,' " and spoke in an extremely rapid and "scattered" manner. In *Donofrio v. N.Y. Times*, No. 99CV1576RCCJCF, 2001 WL 1663314, at *8 (S.D.N.Y. Aug. 24, 2001), the employer reasonably requested an independent medical examination after the employee's unexplained three-week absence and a contact from his doctor stating he was suffering from a mental disorder. The employee's refusal to submit to an examination obstructed the interactive process. *See* Swanson v. Allstate Ins. Co., 102 F.Supp.2d 949, 975-78 (N.D. Ill. 2000) (same outcome).

assignment before the inquiry, and had not asked for accommodations.

- An employer may require a fitness for duty examination where an employee suffers an on-the-job injury. Tice v. Cent. Area Transp. Auth., 247 F.3d 506, 517-18 (3d Cir. 2001); Wade v. Knoxville Utils. Bd., 259 F.3d 452, 462 (6th Cir. 2001).

For further EEOC guidance on obtaining and using medical information regarding persons with intellectual disabilities, *see* Equal Emp. Opportunity Comm'n, Questions & Answers About Persons with Intellectual Disabilities in the Workplace and the Americans with Disabilities Act (last modified Mar. 17, 2011), http://www.eeoc.gov/facts/intellectual_disabilities.html. The EEOC provides guidance on a variety of specific disabilities. *See generally* Equal Emp. Opportunity Comm'n, Enforcement Guidances and Related Documents, http://www.eeoc.gov/policy/guidance.html (last modified on June 19, 2012).

§ 7.2 Confidentiality Of Information

If an employer administers any type of medical test or inquiry, the employer must treat the results as confidential medical records. The statute tightly controls how this information can be used, and who has access to the information:

> [I]nformation obtained regarding the medical condition or history of the applicant [must be] collected and maintained on separate forms and in separate medical files and is treated as a confidential medical record, except that – (i) supervisors and managers may be informed regarding necessary restrictions on the work or duties of the employee and necessary accommodations; (ii) first aid and safety personnel may be informed, when appropriate, if the disability might require emergency treatment; and (iii) government officials investigating compliance with this chapter shall be provided relevant information on request . . . .

42 U.S.C. § 12112(d)(3)(B) (2006), also incorporated into § 12112(d)(4).

Not complying with these record-keeping restrictions is a per se violation of the Act. In contrast to § 12112(d)(3)(C), which requires the results of medical examinations to be "used only in accordance with the subchapter," § 12112(d)(3)(B) mandates that information be protected in the same manner as medical records. Employers thus assume a function similar to medical providers and medical information therefore may not be kept in personnel files. 29 C.F.R. pt. 1630 app., § 1630.14 (2008).

The analysis of the consequences of breaches of the mandates should be understood on those terms and on the understanding of privacy violations. Employers, or employees involved in human resources, may view medical records confidentiality as among their less important tasks and may thus be less than completely diligent in insuring the confidentiality of those records. A plaintiff might show emotional distress (with the proof problems entailed therein), as well as more strictly economic consequences. *Cf.* Doe v. U.S. Postal Serv., 317 F.3d 339, 344-45 (D.C. Cir. 2003) (summary judgment in favor of employer reversed where employee show release of medical information in violation of Rehabilitation Act §§ 501(g) and 504(d), 29 U.S.C. §§ 791(g) and 794(d), that incorporate ADA's confidentiality provisions); *but see* Tice, 247 F.3d at 519-20 (plaintiff failed to go beyond "bare allegations" of emotional distress in opposition to summary judgment motion).

This requirement for confidentiality may give rise to tensions in the context of reasonable accommodations, when other employees seek an explanation for the "special" treatment of the employee with a disability. The ADA is clear that such pressures do not justify the employer revealing an employee's disability, for that decision is to be made by the employee with the disability.

Further, if an employer gains knowledge of a medical condition outside of the scope of the inquiry of a medical examination, the employer is not required to keep such learned information confidential. EEOC v. Thrivent Fin. for Lutherans, No. 11-2848, 2012 WL 5846208 (7th Cir. Sept. 7, 2012). In *Thrivent*, after missing a day at work, an employee emailed his employer stating he had a migraine. *See id.* at *1-2. When the employee quit this job and began applying to new positions, his employer told prospective employers that the employee had migraines and would miss work without notifying the employer. *Id.* at *2. The Court held that this information was not gained through the scope of a medical examination, and therefore was not confidential information, for ADA purposes. *Id.* at *7.

§ 7.3 Rights Of People Without Disabilities To Bring Inquiry/Examination Claims – Standing

What happens if a job applicant without a disability is asked an improper question – for example, one designed to find a disability, answers truthfully, and is refused the job for "other" reasons? *E.g.*, Griffin v. Steeltek, Inc., 160 F.3d 591, 593-95 (10th Cir. 1998). Or, in the post-conditional-offer context, if an employee misrepresents her medical history and the employer improperly uses the misrepresentation as a reason for not hiring. *E.g.*, Garrison v. Baker Hughes Oil Field Operations, Inc., 287 F.3d 955, 960-961 (10th Cir. 2002). May such an aggrieved person sue for violation of the ADA? The broader context of the inquiry sometimes is formulated as a standing question. As set forth in *Lujan v. Defenders of Wildlife*, 504 U.S. 555, 560 (1992), the plaintiff must pass a three-part test: (1) "injury in fact – an invasion of a legally protected interest which is (a) concrete and particularized, and (b) actual or imminent, not conjectural or hypothetical;" (2) "a causal connection between the injury and the conduct complained of – the injury has to be fairly . . . trace[able] to the challenged action of the defendant, and not . . . th[e] result [of] the independent action of some third party not before the court;" (3) "[i]t must be likely, as opposed to merely speculative, that the injury will be redressed by a favorable decision." *Id.* at 560-61 (citations and internal quotation marks omitted).

There may be no injury in fact, when the forbidden inquiry has not caused an applicant to lose a job. In *Armstrong v. Turner Industries, Ltd.*, 141 F.3d 554, 561 (5th Cir. 1998), the Fifth Circuit found that an improper inquiry, without more, does not constitute an injury to support damages liability. Thus, the plaintiff, who was not hired based on false answers rather than a discriminatory motive, could not state a claim for damages. *See also* Cossette v. Minn. Power & Light, 188 F.3d 964, 971 (8th Cir. 1999).

Alternatively, the court may frame the issue in terms of whether the plaintiff must prove disability status as part of his claim. *E.g.*, Griffin v. Steeltek, Inc., 160 F.3d 591, 594 (10th Cir. 1998) (plaintiff need not be disabled to bring claim under 42 U.S.C. § 12112(d)(2)(A), distinguishing Armstrong v. Turner Indus., Ltd., 950 F.Supp. 162, 167-168 (M.D. La. 1996), and dealing with question of proving whether one is a person with a disability as an element of the cause of action). Of course, that question may be cast in standing terminology: does the plaintiff have a "legally protected interest?" The confusion stems from the statutory language. While the ADA's general prohibition on discrimination in § 12112 protects "a qualified individual with a disability," 42 U.S.C. § 12112(d)(2)(A), which addresses inquiries, focuses on job applicants.

Some courts conclude that individuals without disabilities may not bring claims for unlawful medical examinations or inquiries. Armstrong, 950 F.Supp. at 166-68. However, the majority of courts have come out the other way. These courts recognize that the statute expressly uses different terms in different sections. Based on this, and to give effect to the policies underlying the ADA, these courts have held that individuals without disabilities may bring claims for unlawful medical examinations or inquiries. Conroy v. N.Y. State Dep't of Corr. Servs., 333 F.3d 88, 94 (2d Cir. 2003); Cossette, 188 F.3d at 969-70; Bates v. Dura Automotive Systems, Inc., 625 F.3d 283 (6th Cir. 2010); Fredenburg v. Contra Costa County Dep't of Health Servs., 172 F.3d 1176, 1182 (9th Cir. 1999) (requiring plaintiffs to prove that they are persons with disabilities to challenge a medical examination would render § 12112(d)(4)(A) of the ADA "nugatory"); Roe v. Cheyenne Mountain Conference Resort, Inc., 124 F.3d 1221, 1234 (10th Cir. 1997); Owusu-Ansah v. Coca-Cola Co., 715 F.3d 1306 (11th Cir. 2013); *see also* Garrison v. Baker Hughes Oil Field Operations, Inc., 287 F.3d 955, 961 (10th Cir. 2002) ("§ 12112(d)(3)(A) and (B) claims arise out of an employer's post-offer hiring practices and are not related to an entering employee's disability status," although

§ 12112(d)(3)(C) claim must be based on "use [of] 'collected medical information to discriminate on the basis of disability' "; "plaintiff need only 'prove injury flowing from' the statutory violation rather than injury from discrimination based on a disability" to recover compensatory damages under § 12112(d)(3)) (citations omitted).

This extension certainly seems well reasoned. In addition to the statutory interpretation argument, applying certain Title I protections to people without disabilities would have a prophylactic effect, and prevent employers from using prohibited inquiries or medical examinations in all circumstances. As the Tenth Circuit has pointed out, it would be incongruous for a statute that prevents inquiries into whether a person has a disability to require a claimant to prove that he had a disability, *Griffin*, 160 F.3d at 594; *Fountain v. N.Y. State Dep't of Corr. Servs.*, 190 F.Supp.2d 335, 335-38 (N.D.N.Y. 2002), or a compensable injury, to avail himself of the protection of the statute. Such a requirement would, as a practical matter, gut the rule – making it clear to every employer that anyone who objects to the question must be a person with a disability. Congress aimed in the ADA to protect people with diseases such as cancer, who "may object merely to being identified, independent of the consequences," because of the stigmatizing effect. H.R. Rep. No. 101-485(2), at 22-23 (1990), reprinted in 1990 U.S.C.C.A. 303, 357-58.

The few courts that have reached the opposite conclusion rely on the fact that § 12112(a) forbids only discrimination against "a qualified individual with a disability," and § 12112(d)(1) refers back to that earlier section. Armstrong, 950 F.Supp. at 166-68; Bates v. Dura Automotive Systems, Inc., 625 F.3d 283 (6th Cir. 2010). However, that argument assumes that the statute protects only against disability discrimination and inquiries that could result in that discrimination. For further review, *see* Natalie R. Azinger, Too Healthy To Sue Under the ADA? The Controversy Over Pre-Offer Medical Inquiries and Tests, 25 Iowa J. Corp. L. 193, 204-07 (1999); William D. Wickard, The New Americans Without a Disability Act: The Surprisingly Successful Plight of the Non-Disabled Plaintiff Under the ADA, 61 U. Pitt. L. Rev. 1023, 1049-50 (2000).

The majority analysis has other implications. If an employer makes an impermissible pre-offer inquiry and the applicant does not answer or misrepresents her health history, may the employer subsequently discipline or dismiss the employee on the basis of the original misrepresentation? The courts have not addressed this issue, but allowing the employer to punish the employee would appear to immunize the employer from its own illegal actions.

Chapter 8 REASONABLE ACCOMMODATION

§ 8.1 Overview And Illustrations

The conceptual foundation of accommodation for purposes of ADA Title I was introduced in Part 1 of this casebook and will be elaborated upon in this chapter. An employee is not a "qualified" person with a disability for purposes of Title I if he cannot perform the essential job functions with or without a reasonable accommodation. *See* 42 U.S.C. 12111(8) (2006); 29 C.F.R. § 1630.1(c)(2) (2012) (noting that the ADA "does not invalidate or limit the remedies, rights, and procedures of any Federal law or law of any State or political subdivision of any State or jurisdiction that provides greater or equal protection for the rights of individuals with disabilities than is afforded by this part").

A. *Statutory Definitions*

Discrimination under Title I includes that of a covered entity:

> (5)(A) not making reasonable accommodations to the known physical or mental limitations of an otherwise qualified individual with a disability who is an applicant or employee, unless such covered entity can demonstrate that the accommodation would impose an undue hardship on the operation of the business of such covered entity; or

> (B) denying employment opportunities to a job applicant or employee who is an otherwise qualified individual with a disability, if such denial is based on the need of such covered entity to make reasonable accommodation to the physical or mental impairments of the employee or applicant;
> . . . .

42 U.S.C. § 12112(b)(5)(A)-(B).

Title I defines reasonable accommodation to include:

> (A) making existing facilities used by employees readily accessible to and usable by individuals with disabilities; and

> (B) job restructuring, part-time or modified work schedules, reassignment to a vacant position, acquisition or modification of equipment or devices, appropriate adjustment or modifications of examinations, training materials or policies, the provision of qualified readers or interpreters, and other similar accommodations for individuals with disabilities.

Id. § 12111(9).

Reasonable accommodations do not include providing personal use items needed to accomplish daily activities off the job, such as a prosthetic limb, a wheelchair, eyeglasses, or hearing aids. ADA Title IV provides that an individual with a disability does not have "to accept an accommodation, aid, service, opportunity, or benefit which such individual chooses not to accept." *Id.* § 12201(d).

B.   *EEOC Regulations*

The EEOC Title I regulations, 29 C.F.R. §§ 1630.2(o)(1), 1630.9, provide guidance on the concept of "reasonable accommodation" and include under their definition:

> (i) Modifications or adjustments to a job application process that enable a qualified applicant with a disability to be considered for the position such qualified applicant desires; or

> (ii) Modifications or adjustments to the work environment, or to the manner or circumstances under which the position held or desired is customarily performed, that enable a qualified individual with a disability to perform the essential functions of that position; or

> (iii) Modifications or adjustments that enable a covered entity's employee with a disability to enjoy equal benefits and privileges of employment as are enjoyed by its other similarly situated employees without disabilities.

Id. § 1630.2(o)(1).

According to EEOC guidance, there are three categories of accommodation: those (1) required to ensure equal opportunity in the job application process; (2) that enable the qualified employee with a disability to perform the essential job functions; and (3) that enable the qualified employee with a disability to enjoy equal benefits and privileges of employment. *Id.*, pt. 1630 app. §§ 1630.2(o)(1), 1630.9. This regulatory guidance clearly states that accommodations may be necessary to ensure equal opportunity in the job application process or to ensure equal enjoyment of the benefits and privileges of employment, as well as in performing essential job functions. However, the Fifth Circuit in *Feist v. Louisiana*, 730 F.3d 450 (5th Cir. 2013), had to overturn a district court decision to hold that the language of ADA and its implementing regulations demonstrate that a reasonable accommodation does not need to relate to the performance of essential job functions. *Id.* at 450.

The concept underlying reasonable accommodation is that an employer must be prepared to change the way an employee with a disability performs a job. The employer need not change the result of the job (e.g., a certain number of items produced), but may need to change the means of accomplishing the result (e.g., the employee sits while producing, instead of standing). Such accommodations are made informally on a regular basis, at least when they impose no costs on the employer. The ADA extends this informal process to those changes that impose some burdens on the employer.

One may describe an accommodation as a case-by-case modification or adjustment to a workplace process or environment that makes it possible for a qualified person with a disability to perform essential job functions. Possible accommodations virtually are unlimited. Accommodations may include physical modifications to a workspace, flexible scheduling of duties, or provision of equipment, assistive technologies, or job training to aid in job performance. *See Vande Zande v. State of Wis. Dept. of Admin.*, 44 F.3d 538, 542 (7th Cir. 1995) (citations omitted) (noting that reasonable accommodations are "not a legal novelty"). A covered employer discriminates against a qualified person with a disability when it refuses to make a reasonable accommodation that does not cause that employer an undue hardship. For general interpretive guidance from the EEOC, *see* the Regulations to Implement the Equal Employment Provisions of the Americans with Disabilities Act, 29 C.F.R. pt. 1630 app.; 67 Fed. Reg. 61,757 (Oct. 1, 2002); Equal Emp. Opportunity Comm'n, Reasonable Accommodation and Undue Hardship Under the ADA, 8 Fair Emp. Prac. Man. (BNA) 405: 7601 (Oct. 17, 2002) (hereinafter "Reasonable Accommodation and Undue Hardship"), http://www.eeoc.gov/policy/docs/accommodation.html.

A discrimination claim premised on a failure to reasonably accommodate does not require that an employer's action be motivated by a discriminatory animus directed at the person with a disability. Higgins v. New Balance Athletic Shoe, Inc., 194 F.3d 252, 263-64 (1st Cir. 1999). The statute provides that the failure to provide a reasonable accommodation for a qualified individual is actionable discrimination. *Id.*; Bultemeyer v. Fort Wayne Cmty. Schs., 100 F.3d 1281, 1283-84 (7th Cir. 1996). An employer who has knowledge of an individual's disability but does not provide reasonable accommodations violates Title I, regardless of intent. *See* Higgins, 194 F.3d at 264 (noting that the *McDonnell Douglas* burden shifting scheme therefore is inapposite in respect to failure to accommodate claims) (citations omitted). Accommodations are required at the application and interview stages, as well as on the job.

C.   *Failure To Accommodate Claim: Summary*

As illustrated below in detail, to survive a motion for summary judgment on a failure to accommodate claim, a plaintiff typically must show evidence that:

- he is a qualified individual with a disability within the meaning of Title I;

- he works (or worked) for an employer covered by Title I;

- the employer, despite knowledge of the employee's disability, did not reasonably accommodate the employee; and,

- the employer's failure to accommodate adversely affected plaintiff's employment.

211

D. *Accommodation Illustrations*

Neither the statute nor the EEOC regulations provide a bright-line definition of reasonable accommodation. *See* 29 C.F.R. pt. 1630 app., § 1630.2(o)(2) (2008). For general examples, *see* Equal Emp. Opportunity Comm'n, The Americans with Disabilities Act: A Primer for Small Business, http://www.eeoc.gov/ada/adahandbook.html#types (last modified June 19, 2012) (hereinafter "EEOC Primer"). The EEOC defines a workplace modification as feasible if it "seems reasonable on its face, i.e., ordinarily or in the run of cases," or if it is feasible and plausible to effectively meet the needs of a qualified person with a disability. Equal Emp. Opportunity Comm'n, ADA Technical Assistance Manual Addendum, http://www.eeoc.gov/policy/docs/adamanual_add.html (Oct. 29, 2002) (citing U.S. Airways, Inc. v. Barnett, 535 U.S. 391, 401-02 (2002)).

Several alternative scenarios introduce what Title I may require of employers facing two hypothetical job applicants, one with a disability under the ADA and one not, in the context of the accommodation process.

Scenario 1: The applicants are identical in terms of education and experience, and each holds necessary licenses and other prerequisites for the position. The individual with a disability can perform (essential and non-essential) job functions without accommodation. The employer under these circumstances is free to choose the applicant without a disability, as long as the choice is not based on the other applicant's disability.

Scenario 2: The applicant without a disability has more education and experience than the individual with a disability, who can perform (essential and non-essential) job functions without accommodation. Here, the employer again is free to choose the applicant without a disability.

Scenario 3: The applicant with a disability has more education and experience than the individual without a disability, and does not require accommodation to perform the essential job functions. Here, an employer hiring the non-disabled individual would be violating Title I.

Scenario 4: The applicant with a disability has more education and experience than the individual without a disability, and requires that accommodations be made to perform essential job functions. Here, an employer violates Title I if it refuses to make reasonable accommodations (unless they impose an "undue hardship"), or if it refuses to hire the applicant with a disability because of the need to make accommodations.

Empirical evidence suggests that on average, employers facing scenario 1 make hiring decisions without considering individuals' disabilities. *See* Peter Blanck, The Economics of the Employment Provisions of the Americans with Disabilities Act, in Employment, Disability, and the Americans with Disabilities Act 201, 212 (Peter Blanck, ed., Nw. Univ. Press 2000). The evidence suggests that employers facing scenario 3 hire those persons with disabilities who can perform essential and non-essential job functions, as well as those whose abilities outweigh the costs associated with the employee being unable to perform non-essential functions. *Id.* at 213-18. Employers facing scenario 4 generally hire only those persons with disabilities whose accommodations pose small costs, or whose wages can be reduced to offset whatever accommodation costs are incurred. *Id.* For related empirical studies, see Helen Schartz et al., Workplace Accommodations: Evidence-Based Outcomes, 27 Work 345 (2006); Helen Schartz et al., Workplace Accommodations: Empirical Study of Current Employees, 75 Miss. L. J. 917 (2006).

Illustrative examples of accommodation principles in the case law follow.

1. Workplace attendance, schedule modifications

Workplace attendance (including work schedule modifications) may be an essential job requirement, thereby not subject to reasonable accommodation. Amadio v. Ford Motor Co., 238 F.3d 919, 927 (7th Cir. 2001); Robert v. Bd. of Cnty. Comm'rs of Brown Cnty., 691 F.3d 1211, **** (10th Cir. 2012). In *Vande Zande v. Wis. Dep't of Administration*, 44 F.3d 538, 544 (7th Cir. 1995), the Seventh Circuit held that regular attendance may be required of clerical worker positions as an essential job function. Cases subsequent to *Vande Zande* have held regular attendance as an essential job function in the positions of teacher, *Nowak v. St. Rita High Sch.*, 142 F.3d 999, 1003-04 (7th Cir. 1998), account representative, *Corder v. Lucent Techs., Inc.*, 162 F.3d 924, 928 (7th Cir. 1998), production employee, *Waggoner v. Olin Corp.*, 169 F.3d 481, 485 (7th Cir. 1999), and plant equipment repairman, *Jovanovic v. In-Sink-Erator Div. of Emerson Elec. Co.*, 201 F.3d 894, 900 (7th Cir. 2000), among others.

Nevertheless, workplace attendance at the work site is not a per se essential function of every employment position. The requirement that an employee be physically in attendance is particularly apparent in factory or manufacturing positions "where the work must be done on the employer's premises; maintenance and production functions cannot be performed if the employee is not at work." Amadio v. Ford Motor Co., 238 F.3d 919, 927 (7th Cir. 2001) (quoting Jovanovic, 201 F.3d at 900); Robert, 691 F.3d at 1218 (requirement that Offender Supervisor Officer physically conduct on-site visits to check on felony offenders is essential function). However, a short medical leave (e.g., one-week), a leave in combination with leave time under the Family Medical Leave Act (FMLA, up to 12 weeks leave), or an insignificant work schedule change that does not affect worker productivity may be a reasonable accommodation in many circumstances. Amadio, 238 F.3d at 928.

Modifications to an employee's work schedule may be appropriate such as in a situation where a specific start and end time is not necessary. Some workers with disabilities may require longer breaks on the job, and either starting work earlier or ending later than co-workers. For example, in *Ward v. Massachusetts Health Research Inst., Inc.*, a plaintiff with pain in the morning caused by his arthritis requested a modified work schedule as an accommodation and his employer refused. 209 F.3d 29, 31 (1st Cir. 2000). The plaintiff was subsequently fired for arriving late to work. The First Circuit held that despite the general presumption that regular and reliable attendance is an essential function of a job, in this case there was little evidence that regular and reliable attendance is an essential function of the part-time lab and data entry assistant, or that his requested modification would pose an undue burden. *Id.* at 33; *see also* Kallail v. Alliant Energy Corporate Services, Inc., No. 11-2202, ___ F.3d ___, 2012 WL 3792609 (8th Cir. Sept. 4, 2012) (ability to work a rotating shift can be an essential function).

Workers with sleep disorders may require a later start time if medications make waking more difficult for them. In *Conneen v. MBNA Am. Bank, N.A.*, the Third Circuit found that a later starting time at work was a reasonable accommodation for plaintiff with a psychiatric disorder who required medication that caused morning sedation. 334 F.3d 318 (3d Cir. 2003). The Third Circuit held that the employer must demonstrate that failing to arrive at 8:00 am would negatively and meaningfully impact the workplace to be essential. *Id.* Additionally, where an employee with a visual impairment needs to avoid driving in the dark, she may need a schedule change during the winter months. *See* Livingston v. Fred Meyer Stores, 388 F. App'x 738, 740 (9th Cir. 2010) (noting prior precedent of "duty to accommodate an employee's [disability-related] limitations in getting to and from work.").

2.   Home work

Courts generally have taken the position that working at home full time is not a reasonable accommodation. Vande Zande, 44 F.3d 538, 545 (7th Cir. 1995); Tyndall v. Nat'l Educ. Ctrs., Inc., 31 F.3d 209, 212 (4th Cir. 1994); Kiburz v. England, 361 F. App'x 326, 2010 WL 165139 (3d Cir. Jan. 19, 2010). In *Vande Zande*, for example, a woman who was a paraplegic prone to pressure ulcers requested that the company provide her with a desktop computer, and allow her to work full-time at home during an eight week recovery period. 44 F.3d at 544-45. The Seventh Circuit held that this request was unreasonable.

The *Vande Zande* court reasoned the employee's job involved teamwork under supervision, and this could not be accomplished at home without substantially diminishing the quality of the employee's performance. Similarly, in *Rauen v. U.S. Tobacco Mfg.*, 319 F.3d 891, 892 (7th Cir. 2003), the Seventh Circuit held that a request for a complete home office was unreasonable. The court based this holding on the fact that the employee's job required immediate resolution of issues raised on the spur of the moment.

The rationale derives from the notion that an employee who requires significant supervision cannot be adequately supervised at home, and that the quality or productivity of such an employee's work thus may decline significantly. Time will tell if, as home office technology improves, and working from home becomes more popular, this general rule will hold firm. The D.C. Circuit already has concluded that a request to work at home full time is a reasonable accommodation in the case of a computer programmer who could do his job at home without loss of productivity. Langdon v. Dep't of Health and Human Servs., 959 F.2d 1053, 1060-61 (D.C. Cir. 1992).

3. Job reassignment – generally

Title I specifically refers to job reassignment as a reasonable accommodation option. However, the task of explaining what this means, as well as sketching out the parameters of what is required, has fallen largely to the courts.

An employee who develops a disability after being employed may be entitled to reassignment if he cannot perform the essential functions of his current job and be accommodated in his current job. Applicants, as opposed to employees, are not entitled to reassignment and an employer may not require reassignment if a reasonable accommodation is available to allow the employee to do his current job.

An employer may attempt to accommodate an employee by placing him in another position, suggested either by the employee or employer. To be considered a reasonable accommodation, the new job duties must be comparable and not entail a substantial cut in pay.

In using job reassignment as an accommodation, the employer is free to first consider lateral moves to other jobs that are equivalent. An employer may consider a job reassignment to "lesser jobs" that constitute a demotion as an accommodation only if there are no equivalent positions available. Dilley v. SuperValu, Inc., 296 F.3d 958, 964 (10th Cir. 2002).

The EEOC takes the position that reassignment does not involve simply allowing the employee with a disability to apply and compete for the open position, but rather transferring said employee to the open position. Equal Emp. Opportunity Comm'n, Title I Technical Assistance Manual (EEOC-M-1A) No. 24 (1992); Reasonable Accommodation and Undue Burden, *supra*, at Question 29 ("Reassignment means that the employee gets the vacant position if s/he is qualified for it. Otherwise, reassignment would be of little value and would not be implemented as Congress intended.").

Accordingly, in E.E.O.C. v. United Airlines, Inc., 693 F.3d 760, 765 (7th Cir. 2012), the Seventh Circuit held that reassignment requires employers to appoint employees, who have become unable to peform the essential functions of their jobs, to vacant positions for which they are qualified, provided that doing so "would not create an undue hardship (or run afoul of a collective bargaining agreement) . . . ." This court overturned prior precedent holding that where an employee with a disability who could no longer perform the essential functions of his position must compete with other applicants for an vacant position. *Id.* The U.S. Supreme Court denied United Airlines its petition for certiorari. United Airlines, Inc. v. E.E.O.C., 133 S.Ct. 2734 (2013).

Lastly, an employer is not required to reassign an employee with a disability to a promotion to satisfy the duty of accommodation.

4.   Job reassignment – collective bargaining or seniority agreement

The job reassignment accommodation option is constrained when it would require an employer to violate its bona fide seniority system or the terms of its collective bargaining agreement. Dilley v. SuperValu, Inc., 296 F.3d 958, 963 (10th Cir. 2002) (citation omitted); Milton v. Scrivner, Inc., 53 F.3d 1118, 1125 (10th Cir. 1995). The following case illustrates the matter of a seniority system.

US AIRWAYS, INC. v. BARNETT

Supreme Court of the United States, 2002
535 U.S. 391

* * *

Justice BREYER delivered the opinion of the Court.

The Americans with Disabilities Act of 1990 (ADA or Act) * * * prohibits an employer from discriminating against an "individual with a disability" who, with "reasonable accommodation," can perform the essential functions of the job. [42 U.S.C.] §§ 12112(a) and (b) (1994 ed.). This case, arising in the context of summary judgment, asks us how the Act resolves a potential conflict between: (1) the interests of a disabled worker who seeks assignment to a particular position as a "reasonable accommodation," and (2) the interests of other workers with superior rights to bid for the job under an employer's seniority system. In such a case, does the accommodation demand trump the seniority system?

In our view, the seniority system will prevail in the run of cases. As we interpret the statute, to show that a requested accommodation conflicts with the rules of a seniority system is ordinarily to show that the accommodation is not "reasonable." Hence such a showing will entitle an employer/defendant to summary judgment on the question – unless there is more. The plaintiff remains free to present evidence of special circumstances that make "reasonable" a seniority rule exception in the particular case. And such a showing will defeat the employer's demand for summary judgment. Fed. R. Civ. P. 56(e).

I

In 1990, Robert Barnett, the plaintiff and respondent here, injured his back while working in a cargo-handling position at petitioner U.S. Airways, Inc. He invoked seniority rights and transferred to a less physically demanding mailroom position. Under U.S. Airways' seniority system, that position, like others, periodically became open to seniority-based employee bidding. In 1992, Barnett learned that at least two employees senior to him intended to bid for the mailroom job. He asked U.S. Airways to accommodate his disability-imposed limitations by making an exception that would allow him to remain in the mailroom. After permitting Barnett to continue his mailroom work for five months while it considered the matter, U.S. Airways eventually decided not to make an exception. And Barnett lost his job.

Barnett then brought this ADA suit claiming, among other things, that he was an "individual with a disability" capable of performing the essential functions of the mailroom job, that the mailroom job amounted to a "reasonable accommodation" of his disability, and that U.S. Airways, in refusing to assign him the job, unlawfully discriminated against him. US Airways moved for summary judgment * * * contending that its "well-established" seniority system granted other employees the right to obtain the mailroom position.

* * *

II

* * *

A

US Airways' claim that a seniority system virtually always trumps a conflicting accommodation demand rests primarily upon its view of how the Act treats workplace "preferences." Insofar as a requested accommodation violates a disability-neutral workplace rule, such as a seniority rule, it grants the employee with a disability treatment that other workers could not receive. Yet the Act, U.S. Airways says, seeks only "equal" treatment for those with disabilities. See, e.g., 42 U.S.C. § 12101(a)(9). It does not, it contends, require an employer to grant preferential treatment. Cf. H.R. Rep. No. 101-485, pt. 2, p. 66 (1990), U.S. Code Cong. & Admin. News 1990, pp. 303, 348-349; S. Rep. No. 101-116, pp. 26-27 (1989) (employer has no "obligation to prefer *applicants* with disabilities over other *applicants*" (emphasis added)). Hence it does not require the employer to grant a request that, in violating a disability-neutral rule, would provide a preference.

While linguistically logical, this argument fails to recognize what the Act specifies, namely, that preferences will sometimes prove necessary to achieve the Act's basic equal opportunity goal. The Act requires preferences in the form of "reasonable accommodations" that are needed for those with disabilities to obtain the *same* workplace opportunities that those without disabilities automatically enjoy. By definition any special "accommodation" requires the employer to treat an employee with a disability differently, i.e., preferentially. And the fact that the difference in treatment violates an employer's disability-neutral rule cannot by itself place the accommodation beyond the Act's potential reach.

Were that not so, the "reasonable accommodation" provision could not accomplish its intended objective. Neutral office assignment rules would automatically prevent the accommodation of an employee whose disability-imposed limitations require him to work on the ground floor. Neutral "break-from-work" rules would automatically prevent the accommodation of an individual who needs additional breaks from work, perhaps to permit medical visits. Neutral furniture budget rules would automatically prevent the accommodation of an individual who needs a different kind of chair or desk. Many employers will have neutral rules governing the kinds of actions most needed to reasonably accommodate a worker with a disability. See 42 U.S.C. § 12111(9)(b) (setting forth examples such as "job restructuring," "part-time or modified work schedules," "acquisition or modification of equipment or devices," "and other similar accommodations"). Yet Congress, while providing such examples, said nothing suggesting that the presence of such neutral rules would create an automatic exemption. Nor have the lower courts made any such suggestion. Cf. *Garcia-Ayala v. Lederle Parenterals, Inc.,* 212 F.3d 638, 648 (C.A.1 2000) (requiring leave beyond that allowed under the company's own leave policy); *Hendricks-Robinson v. Excel Corp.,* 154 F.3d 685, 699 (C.A.7 1998) (requiring exception to employer's neutral "physical fitness" job requirement).

In sum, the nature of the "reasonable accommodation" requirement, the statutory examples, and the Act's silence about the exempting effect of neutral rules together convince us that the Act does not create any such automatic exemption. The simple fact that an accommodation would provide a "preference" – in the sense that it would permit the worker with a disability to violate a rule that others must obey – cannot, *in and of itself,* automatically show that the accommodation is not "reasonable." As a result, we reject the position taken by U.S. Airways and Justice SCALIA to the contrary.

US Airways also points to the ADA provisions stating that a " 'reasonable accommodation' may include * * * reassignment to a *vacant* position." § 12111(9)(B) (emphasis added). And it claims that the fact that an established seniority system would assign that position to another worker automatically and always means that the position is not a "vacant" one. Nothing in the Act, however, suggests that Congress intended the word "vacant" to have a specialized meaning. And in ordinary English, a seniority system can give employees seniority rights allowing them to bid for a "vacant" position. The position in this case was held, at the time of suit, by Barnett, not by some other worker; and that position, under the

U.S. Airways seniority system, became an "open" one. Brief for Petitioner 5. Moreover, U.S. Airways has said that it "reserves the right to change any and all" portions of the seniority system at will. Lodging of Respondent 2 (U.S. Air Personnel Policy Guide for Agents). Consequently, we cannot agree with U.S. Airways about the position's vacancy; nor do we agree that the Act would automatically deny Barnett's accommodation request for that reason.

B

Barnett argues that the statutory words "reasonable accommodation" mean only "effective accommodation," authorizing a court to consider the requested accommodation's ability to meet an individual's disability-related needs, and nothing more. On this view, a seniority rule violation, having nothing to do with the accommodation's effectiveness, has nothing to do with its "reasonableness." It might, at most, help to prove an "undue hardship on the operation of the business." But, he adds, that is a matter that the statute requires the employer to demonstrate, case by case.

In support of this interpretation Barnett points to Equal Employment Opportunity Commission (EEOC) regulations stating that "reasonable accommodation means * * * [m]odifications or adjustments * * * that *enable* a qualified individual with a disability to perform the essential functions of [a] position." 29 C.F.R. § 1630(*o*)(ii) (2001) (emphasis added). See also H.R. Rep. No. 101-485, pt. 2, at 66, [U.S.C.C.A.N.] 1990, pp. 303, 348-349; S. Rep. No. 101-116, at 35 (discussing reasonable accommodations in terms of "effectiveness," while discussing costs in terms of "undue hardship"). Barnett adds that any other view would make the words "reasonable accommodation" and "undue hardship" virtual mirror images – creating redundancy in the statute. And he says that any such other view would create a practical burden of proof dilemma.

The practical burden of proof dilemma arises, Barnett argues, because the statute imposes the burden of demonstrating an "undue hardship" upon the employer, while the burden of proving "reasonable accommodation" remains with the plaintiff, here the employee. This allocation seems sensible in that an employer can more frequently and easily prove the presence of business hardship than an employee can prove its absence. But suppose that an employee must counter a claim of "seniority rule violation" in order to prove that an "accommodation" request is "reasonable." Would that not force the employee to prove what is in effect an absence, i.e., an absence of hardship, despite the statute's insistence that the employer "demonstrate" hardship's presence?

These arguments do not persuade us that Barnett's legal interpretation of "reasonable" is correct. For one thing, in ordinary English the word "reasonable" does not mean "effective." It is the word "accommodation," not the word "reasonable," that conveys the need for effectiveness. An *ineffective* "modification" or "adjustment" will not *accommodate* a disabled individual's limitations. Nor does an ordinary English meaning of the term "reasonable accommodation" make of it a simple, redundant mirror image of the term "undue hardship." The statute refers to an "undue hardship on the operation of the business." 42 U.S.C. § 12112(b)(5)(A). Yet a demand for an effective accommodation could prove unreasonable because of its impact, not on business operations, but on fellow employees – say, because it will lead to dismissals, relocations, or modification of employee benefits to which an employer, looking at the matter from the perspective of the business itself, may be relatively indifferent.

Neither does the statute's primary purpose require Barnett's special reading. The statute seeks to diminish or to eliminate the stereotypical thought processes, the thoughtless actions, and the hostile reactions that far too often bar those with disabilities from participating fully in the Nation's life, including the workplace. See generally §§ 12101(a) and (b). These objectives demand unprejudiced thought and reasonable responsive reaction on the part of employers and fellow workers alike. They will sometimes require affirmative conduct to promote entry of disabled people into the work force. See supra, at 1521. They do not, however, demand action beyond the realm of the reasonable.

Neither has Congress indicated in the statute, or elsewhere, that the word "reasonable" means no more than "effective." The EEOC regulations do say that reasonable accommodations "enable" a person with a disability to perform the essential functions of a task. But that phrasing simply emphasizes the statutory provision's basic objective. The regulations do not say that "enable" and "reasonable" mean the same thing. And as discussed below, no court of appeals has so read them. But see 228 F.3d at 1122-1123 (Gould, J., concurring).

Finally, an ordinary language interpretation of the word "reasonable" does not create the "burden of proof" dilemma to which Barnett points. Many of the lower courts, while rejecting both U.S. Airways' and Barnett's more absolute views, have reconciled the phrases "reasonable accommodation" and "undue hardship" in a practical way.

They have held that a plaintiff/employee (to defeat a defendant/employer's motion for summary judgment) need only show that an "accommodation" seems reasonable on its face, i.e., ordinarily or in the run of cases. See, e.g., *Reed v. LePage Bakeries, Inc.,* 244 F.3d 254, 259 (C.A.1 2001) (plaintiff meets burden on reasonableness by showing that, "at least on the face of things," the accommodation will be feasible for the employer); *Borkowski v. Valley Central School Dist.,* 63 F.3d 131, 138 (C.A.2 1995) (plaintiff satisfies "burden of production" by showing "plausible accommodation"); *Barth v. Gelb,* 2 F.3d 1180, 1187 (C.A.D.C. 1993) (interpreting parallel language in Rehabilitation Act, stating that plaintiff need only show he seeks a *"method of accommodation that is reasonable in the run of cases"* (emphasis in original)).

Once the plaintiff has made this showing, the defendant/employer then must show special (typically case-specific) circumstances that demonstrate undue hardship in the particular circumstances. See *Reed,* supra, at 258-259 ("undue hardship inquiry focuses on the hardships imposed * * * in the context of the particular [employer's] operations'") (quoting *Barth,* supra, at 1187); *Borkowski,* supra, at 138 (after plaintiff makes initial showing, burden falls on employer to show that particular accommodation "would cause it to suffer an undue hardship"); *Barth,* supra, at 1187 ("undue hardship inquiry focuses on the hardships imposed * * * in the context of the particular agency's operations").

Not every court has used the same language, but their results are functionally similar. In our opinion, that practical view of the statute, applied consistently with ordinary summary judgment principles, see Fed. R. Civ. P. 56, avoids Barnett's burden of proof dilemma, while reconciling the two statutory phrases ("reasonable accommodation" and "undue hardship").

III

The question in the present case focuses on the relationship between seniority systems and the plaintiff's need to show that an "accommodation" seems reasonable on its face, i.e., ordinarily or in the run of cases. We must assume that the plaintiff, an employee, is an "individual with a disability." He has requested assignment to a mailroom position as a "reasonable accommodation." We also assume that normally such a request would be reasonable within the meaning of the statute, were it not for one circumstance, namely, that the assignment would violate the rules of a seniority system. See § 12111(9) ("reasonable accommodation" may include "reassignment to a vacant position"). Does that circumstance mean that the proposed accommodation is not a "reasonable" one?

In our view, the answer to this question ordinarily is "yes." The statute does not require proof on a case-by-case basis that a seniority system should prevail. That is because it would not be reasonable in the run of cases that the assignment in question trump the rules of a seniority system. To the contrary, it will ordinarily be unreasonable for the assignment to prevail.

A

Several factors support our conclusion that a proposed accommodation will not be reasonable in the run of cases. Analogous case law supports this conclusion, for it has recognized the importance of seniority to employee-management relations. This Court has held that, in the context of a Title VII religious discrimination case, an employer need not adapt to an employee's special worship schedule as a "reasonable accommodation" where doing so would conflict with the seniority rights of other employees. * * *

* * *

Most important for present purposes, to require the typical employer to show more than the existence of a seniority system might well undermine the employees' expectations of consistent, uniform treatment – expectations upon which the seniority system's benefits depend. That is because such a rule would substitute a complex case-specific "accommodation" decision made by management for the more uniform, impersonal operation of seniority rules. Such management decisionmaking, with its inevitable discretionary elements, would involve a matter of the greatest importance to employees, namely, layoffs; it would take place outside, as well as inside, the confines of a court case; and it might well take place fairly often. Cf. ADA, 42 U.S.C. § 12101(a)(1) (estimating that some 43 million Americans suffer from physical or mental disabilities). We can find nothing in the statute that suggests Congress intended to undermine seniority systems in this way. And we consequently conclude that the employer's showing of violation of the rules of a seniority system is by itself ordinarily sufficient.

B

The plaintiff (here the employee) nonetheless remains free to show that special circumstances warrant a finding that, despite the presence of a seniority system (which the ADA may not trump in the run of cases), the requested "accommodation" is "reasonable" on the particular facts. That is because special circumstances might alter the important expectations described above. * * * The plaintiff might show, for example, that the employer, having retained the right to change the seniority system unilaterally, exercises that right fairly frequently, reducing employee expectations that the system will be followed – to the point where one more departure, needed to accommodate an individual with a disability, will not likely make a difference. The plaintiff might show that the system already contains exceptions such that, in the circumstances, one further exception is unlikely to matter. We do not mean these examples to exhaust the kinds of showings that a plaintiff might make. But we do mean to say that the plaintiff must bear the burden of showing special circumstances that make an exception from the seniority system reasonable in the particular case. And to do so, the plaintiff must explain why, in the particular case, an exception to the employer's seniority policy can constitute a "reasonable accommodation" even though in the ordinary case it cannot.

IV

In its question presented, U.S. Airways asked us whether the ADA requires an employer to assign a disabled employee to a particular position even though another employee is entitled to that position under the employer's "established seniority system." We answer that *ordinarily* the ADA does not require that assignment. Hence, a showing that the assignment would violate the rules of a seniority system warrants summary judgment for the employer – unless there is more. The plaintiff must present evidence of that "more," namely, special circumstances surrounding the particular case that demonstrate the assignment is nonetheless reasonable.

Because the lower courts took a different view of the matter, and because neither party has had an opportunity to seek summary judgment in accordance with the principles we set forth here, we vacate the Court of Appeals' judgment and remand the case for further proceedings consistent with this opinion.

It is so ordered.

* * *

Justice O'CONNOR, concurring.

I agree with portions of the opinion of the Court, but I find problematic the Court's test for determining whether the fact that a job reassignment violates a seniority system makes the reassignment an unreasonable accommodation under the Americans with Disabilities Act of 1990 (ADA or Act) * * * Although a seniority system plays an important role in the workplace, for the reasons I explain below, I would prefer to say that the effect of a seniority system on the reasonableness of a reassignment as an accommodation for purposes of the ADA depends on whether the seniority system is legally enforceable. * * *

The ADA specifically lists "reassignment to a vacant position" as one example of a "reasonable accommodation." 42 U.S.C. § 12111(9)(B) (1994 ed.). In deciding whether an otherwise reasonable accommodation involving a reassignment is unreasonable because it would require an exception to a seniority system, I think the relevant issue is whether the seniority system prevents the position in question from being vacant. The word "vacant" means "not filled or occupied by an incumbent [or] possessor." Webster's Third New International Dictionary 2527 (1976). In the context of a workplace, a vacant position is a position in which no employee currently works and to which no individual has a legal entitlement. For example, in a workplace without a seniority system, when an employee ceases working for the employer, the employee's former position is vacant until a replacement is hired. Even if the replacement does not start work immediately, once the replacement enters into a contractual agreement with the employer, the position is no longer vacant because it has a "possessor." In contrast, when an employee ceases working in a workplace with a legally enforceable seniority system, the employee's former position does not become vacant if the seniority system entitles another employee to it. Instead, the employee entitled to the position under the seniority system immediately becomes the new "possessor" of that position. In a workplace with an unenforceable seniority policy, however, an employee expecting assignment to a position under the seniority policy would not have any type of contractual right to the position and so could not be said to be its "possessor." The position therefore would become vacant.

Given this understanding of when a position can properly be considered vacant, if a seniority system, in the absence of the ADA, would give someone other than the individual seeking the accommodation a legal entitlement or contractual right to the position to which reassignment is sought, the seniority system prevents the position from being vacant. If a position is not vacant, then reassignment to it is not a reasonable accommodation. * * *

* * *

Justice SCALIA, with whom Justice THOMAS joins, dissenting.

The question presented asks whether the "reasonable accommodation" mandate of the Americans with Disabilities Act of 1990 (ADA or Act) requires reassignment of a disabled employee to a position that "another employee is entitled to hold * * * under the employer's bona fide and established seniority system." * * * [T]he Court answers "maybe." It creates a presumption that an exception to a seniority rule is an "unreasonable" accommodation, ante * * * but allows that presumption to be rebutted by showing that the exception "will not likely make a difference," ante * * *

The principal defect of today's opinion, however, goes well beyond the uncertainty it produces regarding the relationship between the ADA and the infinite variety of seniority systems. The conclusion that any seniority system can ever be overridden is merely one consequence of a mistaken interpretation of the ADA that makes all employment rules and practices – even those which (like a seniority system) pose no *distinctive* obstacle to the disabled – subject to suspension when that is (in a court's view) a "reasonable" means of enabling a disabled employee to keep his job. That is a far cry from what I believe the accommodation provision of the ADA requires: the suspension (within reason) of those employment rules and practices *that the employee's disability prevents him from observing.*

* * *

Justice SOUTER, with whom Justice GINSBURG joins, dissenting.

"[R]eassignment to a vacant position," 42 U.S.C. § 12111(9) (1994 ed.), is one way an employer may "reasonabl[y] accommodat[e]" disabled employees under the Americans with Disabilities Act of 1990 (ADA) * * * The Court today holds that a request for reassignment will nonetheless most likely be unreasonable when it would violate the terms of a seniority system imposed by an employer * * *

Nothing in the ADA insulates seniority rules from the "reasonable accommodation" requirement, in marked contrast to Title VII of the Civil Rights Act of 1964 and the Age Discrimination in Employment Act of 1967, each of which has an explicit protection for seniority. * * *

* * *

Because a unilaterally imposed seniority system enjoys no special protection under the ADA, a consideration of facts peculiar to this very case is needed to gauge whether Barnett has carried the burden of showing his proposed accommodation to be a "reasonable" one despite the policy in force at U.S. Airways. The majority describes this as a burden to show the accommodation is "plausible" or "feasible," ante * * * and I believe Barnett has met it.

He held the mailroom job for two years before learning that employees with greater seniority planned to bid for the position, given U.S. Airways's decision to declare the job "vacant." Thus, perhaps unlike ADA claimants who request accommodation through reassignment, Barnett was seeking not a change but a continuation of the status quo. All he asked was that U.S. Airways refrain from declaring the position "vacant"; he did not ask to bump any other employee and no one would have lost a job on his account. There was no evidence in the District Court of any unmanageable ripple effects from Barnett's request, or showing that he would have overstepped an inordinate number of seniority levels by remaining where he was.

In fact, it is hard to see the seniority scheme here as any match for Barnett's ADA requests, since U.S. Airways apparently took pains to ensure that its seniority rules raised no great expectations. In its policy statement, U.S. Airways said that "[t]he Agent Personnel Policy Guide is *not* intended to be a contract" and that "USAir reserves the right to change any and all of the stated policies and procedures in this Guide at any time, without advanced notice." Lodging of Respondent 2 (emphasis in original). While I will skip any state-by-state analysis of the legal treatment of employee handbooks (a source of many lawyers' fees) it is safe to say that the contract law of a number of jurisdictions would treat this disclaimer as fatal to any claim an employee might make to enforce the seniority policy over an employer's contrary decision. * * *

With U.S. Airways itself insisting that its seniority system was noncontractual and modifiable at will, there is no reason to think that Barnett's accommodation would have resulted in anything more than minimal disruption to U.S. Airways's operations, if that. Barnett has shown his requested accommodation to be "reasonable," and the burden ought to shift to U.S. Airways if it wishes to claim that, in spite of surface appearances, violation of the seniority scheme would have worked an undue hardship. I would therefore affirm the Ninth Circuit.

Notes & Questions

1. The *Barnett* decision stands for the proposition that if a "reassignment accommodation" would violate the rules of a bona fide seniority system, then summary judgment typically is warranted for the employer, "unless there is more" shown by plaintiff. 535 U.S. at 406. What more is necessary? If the plaintiff shows that special circumstances surrounding the case demonstrate the reasonableness of the reassignment, then the employer must show evidence of case-specific circumstances that demonstrate undue hardship. What special circumstances might the plaintiff wish to demonstrate?

2. *Barnett* is limited to an actual, as opposed to a potential, violation of a bona fide seniority system. In *Dilley v. SuperValu*, 296 F.3d 958, 963-64 (10th Cir. 2002), the employer SuperValu did not contend that the plaintiff lacked the seniority to be placed in a non-lifting driver position at the company, but that the seniority system would be violated if a more senior employee subsequently requested the plaintiff's new reassigned position, and the employer left the plaintiff in that position. *Id.* (noting that SuperValu's witness testified that Dilley ranked fifth out of forty-two drivers in seniority; and the jury could have concluded that the prospect of Dilley's displacement by a more senior driver was remote). The Tenth Circuit held that the *Barnett* rule does not apply in such situations, wherein only potential violations of the seniority system exist.

3. For further discussion, *see* Carlos A. Ball, Preferential Treatment and Reasonable Accommodation Under the Americans with Disabilities Act, 55 Ala. L. Rev. 951 (2004); Stephen F. Befort, Reasonable Accommodation and Reassignment Under the Americans with Disabilities Act: Answers, Questions and Suggested Solutions After *U.S. Airways, Inc. v. Barnett*, 45 Ariz. L. Rev. 931 (2003); Seth D. Harris, Re-Thinking the Economics of Discrimination: *U.S. Airways v. Barnett*, the ADA, and the Application of Internal Labor Market Theory, 89 Iowa L. Rev. 123 (2003).

5.   Company policies, discipline and termination

The case law under the ADA has not developed a comfortable balance between the ADA's reasonable accommodation standard and an employer's ability to enforce company policies, discipline, and termination decisions. Were it possible to establish a general "rule" or common approach that unifies the ADA's and employers' policies, it would most likely maintain that the ADA's reasonable accommodation standard does not require an employer to abandon "legitimate and non-discriminatory" company policies. *See, e.g.*, EEOC v. Sara Lee Corp., 237 F.3d 349, 354 (4th Cir. 2001); Burns v. Coca-Cola Enters., 222 F.3d 247, 257 (6th Cir. 2000); Cravens v. Blue Cross & Blue Shield of Kan. City, 214 F.3d 1011, 1020 (8th Cir. 2000); Aka v. Wash. Hosp. Ctr., 156 F.3d 1284, 1305 (D.C. Cir. 1998) (en banc); Daugherty v. City of El Paso, 56 F.3d 695, 700 (5th

Cir. 1995). But, of course, this "rule" only can go so far in deciding the hard cases.

The Supreme Court dealt with this tension in *Barnett*. There, it held that, in the run of cases, a company's seniority system trumps a conflicting accommodation demand. Sometimes, therefore, a requested accommodation may violate a "disability-neutral" workplace rule, such as a seniority rule, and provide the job applicant or employee with a disability accommodation with "treatment that other workers could not receive." U.S. Airways, Inc. v. Barnett, 535 U.S. 391, 397 (2002).

But the Court was clear that asking for a difference in treatment in the face of a "neutral" rule would not always make an accommodation unreasonable. If that were not the rule, the Court concluded:

> Neutral office assignment rules would automatically prevent the accommodation of an employee whose disability-imposed limitations require him to work on the ground floor. Neutral "break-from-work" rules would automatically prevent the accommodation of an individual who needs additional breaks from work, perhaps to permit medical visits. Neutral furniture budget rules would automatically prevent the accommodation of an individual who needs a different kind of chair or desk.

Id. at 397-98. Most employers have neutral rules governing the kinds of actions most needed to reasonably accommodate a worker with a disability. *See* 42 U.S.C. § 12111(9)(b) (2006) (setting forth examples such as "job restructuring," "part-time or modified work schedules," "acquisition or modification of equipment or devices," "and other similar accommodations").

To be sure, the ADA is not a license for "insubordination in the workplace." Reed v. Le Page Bakeries, 244 F.3d 254, 262 (1st Cir. 2001). Despite a covered disability and a request for a reasonable accommodation, an employee may be disciplined or terminated for behavior that is not consistent with a normal workplace, such as, for example, threatening behavior toward co-workers or supervisors. *Id.* (upholding termination of employee with bipolar disorder). Similarly, an employee with alcoholism may be terminated for related behavior that is unacceptable in the workplace, even when that behavior is a result of alcoholism. Employers are allowed to have drug and alcohol free workplaces. Inquiries and Medical Examinations, *supra*.

However, it would be incorrect to suggest that employment policies and rules – even non-discriminatory ones – are not completely subject to the reasonable accommodation requirement. The EEOC guidance indicates that modifying workplace rules for a qualified employee with a disability often is considered a reasonable accommodation. The Guidance suggests that allowing an employee with a psychiatric impairment more frequent breaks during the work day, but not more break time in the aggregate, may be a reasonable and cost-effective accommodation. *Cf.* Equal Emp. Opportunity Comm'n, Enforcement Guidance on the Americans with Disabilities Act and Psychiatric Disabilities No. 25, http://www.eeoc.gov/policy/docs/psych.html (Mar. 25, 1997) (accommodating dry mouth caused by prescription medication). The Guidance also suggests that although the reasonable accommodation requirement does not require an employer to provide an employee with a new supervisor, it may require an alteration of supervisory methods. *Id.* at No. 26.

Moreover, certain facially valid company employment policies may be invalid as applied under the ADA. In *Hernandez v. Hughes Missile Systems Co.*, 298 F.3d 1030, 1032 (9th Cir. 2002), the plaintiff worked as a technician for Hughes. During his employment, he was addicted to drugs and alcohol, and eventually tested positive for cocaine. *Id.* The plaintiff was given the option to resign in lieu of termination, which he chose to do. *Id.* Hernandez did not challenge the legality of this action on the basis of his then-current drug use.

Two years later, Hernandez applied to be rehired with Hughes, attaching a letter from his counselor to his application. His counselor indicated Hernandez had been attending AA and staying sober. Hughes declined to rehire the plaintiff based on an unwritten policy of not rehiring former employees whose employment had ended due to termination or resignation in lieu of termination. *Id.*

The Ninth Circuit found this facially neutral policy could be discriminatory if Hughes regarded Hernandez as having a disability – by virtue of being a previous drug and alcohol user – at the time it failed to rehire him. *Id.* at 1036. The Ninth Circuit found that Hughes had an obligation to determine the underlying reason for the plaintiff's resignation and to accommodate him by modifying its no-rehire policy if the original reason was disability-related. The Supreme Court granted certiorari.

RAYTHEON CO. v. HERNANDEZ

Supreme Court of the United States, 2003
540 U.S. 44

Justice THOMAS delivered the opinion of the Court.

The Americans with Disabilities Act of 1990 (ADA), 104 Stat. 327, as amended, 42 U.S.C. § 12101 et seq., makes it unlawful for an employer, with respect to hiring, to "discriminate against a qualified individual with a disability because of the disability of such individual." § 12112(a). We are asked to decide in this case whether the ADA confers preferential rehire rights on disabled employees lawfully terminated for violating workplace conduct rules. The United States Court of Appeals for the Ninth Circuit held that an employer's unwritten policy not to rehire employees who left the company for violating personal conduct rules contravenes the ADA, at least as applied to employees who were lawfully forced to resign for illegal drug use but have since been rehabilitated. Because the Ninth Circuit improperly applied a disparate-impact analysis in a disparate-treatment case in order to reach this holding, we vacate its judgment and remand the case for further proceedings consistent with this opinion. We do not, however, reach the question on which we granted certiorari. * * *

I

Respondent, Joel Hernandez, worked for Hughes Missile Systems for 25 years. On July 11, 1991, respondent's appearance and behavior at work suggested that he might be under the influence of drugs or alcohol. Pursuant to company policy, respondent took a drug test, which came back positive for cocaine. Respondent subsequently admitted that he had been up late drinking beer and using cocaine the night before the test. Because respondent's behavior violated petitioner's workplace conduct rules, respondent was forced to resign. Respondent's "Employee Separation Summary" indicated as the reason for separation: "discharge for personal conduct (quit in lieu of discharge)." App. 12a.

More than two years later, on January 24, 1994, respondent applied to be rehired by petitioner. Respondent stated on his application that he had previously been employed by petitioner. He also attached two reference letters to the application, one from his pastor, stating that respondent was a "faithful and active member" of the church, and the other from an Alcoholics Anonymous counselor, stating that respondent attends Alcoholics Anonymous meetings regularly and is in recovery. Id. at 13a-15a.

Joanne Bockmiller, an employee in the company's Labor Relations Department, reviewed respondent's application. Bockmiller testified in her deposition that since respondent's application disclosed his prior employment with the company, she pulled his personnel file and reviewed his employee separation summary. She then rejected respondent's application. Bockmiller insisted that the company had a policy against rehiring employees who were terminated for workplace misconduct. Id. at 62a. Thus, when she reviewed the employment separation summary and found that respondent had been discharged for violating workplace conduct rules, she rejected respondent's application. She testified, in particular, that she did not know that respondent was a former drug addict when she made the employment decision and did not see anything that would constitute a "record of" addiction. Id. at 63a-64a.

Respondent subsequently filed a charge with the Equal Employment Opportunity Commission (EEOC). Respondent's charge of discrimination indicated that petitioner did not give him a reason for his nonselection, but that respondent believed he had been discriminated against in violation of the ADA.

Petitioner responded to the charge by submitting a letter to the EEOC, in which George M. Medina, Sr., Manager of Diversity Development, wrote:

> The ADA specifically exempts from protection individuals currently engaging in the illegal use of drugs when the covered entity acts on the basis of that use. Contrary to Complainant's unfounded allegation, his non-selection for rehire is not based on any legitimate disability. Rather, Complainant's application was rejected based on his demonstrated drug use while previously employed and the complete lack of evidence indicating successful drug rehabilitation.
>
> The Company maintains [the] right to deny re-employment to employees terminated for violation of Company rules and regulations * * *. Complainant has provided no evidence to alter the Company's position that Complainant's conduct while employed by [petitioner] makes him ineligible for rehire. Id. at 19a-20a.

This response, together with evidence that the letters submitted with respondent's employment application may have alerted Bockmiller to the reason for respondent's prior termination, led the EEOC to conclude that petitioner may have "rejected [respondent's] application based on his record of past alcohol and drug use." Id. at 94a EEOC Determination Letter, Nov. 20, 1997. The EEOC thus found that there was "reasonable cause to believe that [respondent] was denied hire to the position of Product Test Specialist because of his disability." Id. at 95a. The EEOC issued a right-to-sue letter, and respondent subsequently filed this action alleging a violation of the ADA.

Respondent proceeded through discovery on the theory that the company rejected his application because of his record of drug addiction and/or because he was regarded as being a drug addict. See 42 U.S.C. §§ 12102(2)(B)-(C). In response to petitioner's motion for summary judgment, respondent for the first time argued in the alternative that if the company really did apply a neutral no-rehire policy in his case, petitioner still violated the ADA because such a policy has a disparate impact. The District Court granted petitioner's motion for summary judgment with respect to respondent's disparate-treatment claim. However, the District Court refused to consider respondent's disparate-impact claim because respondent had failed to plead or raise the theory in a timely manner.

The Court of Appeals agreed with the District Court that respondent had failed timely to raise his disparate-impact claim.

Hernandez v. Hughes Missile Systems Co., 298 F.3d 1030, 1037, n.20 (9th Cir. 2002). In addressing respondent's disparate-treatment claim, the Court of Appeals proceeded under the familiar burden-shifting approach first adopted by this Court in *McDonnell Douglas Corp. v. Green*, 411 U.S. 792, 93 S.Ct. 1817, 36 L.Ed.2d 668 (1973). First, the Ninth Circuit found that with respect to respondent's prima facie case of discrimination, there were genuine issues of material fact regarding whether respondent was qualified for the position for which he sought to be rehired, and whether the reason for petitioner's refusal to rehire him was his past record of drug addiction.[4] 298 F.3d at 1034-35. The Court of Appeals thus held that with respect to respondent's prima facie case of discrimination, respondent had proffered sufficient evidence to preclude a grant of summary judgment. Id. at 1035. Because petitioner does not challenge this aspect of the Ninth Circuit's decision, we do not address it here.

* * *

II

This Court has consistently recognized a distinction between claims of discrimination based on disparate treatment and claims of discrimination based on disparate impact. The Court has said that " '[d]isparate treatment' * * * is the most easily understood type of discrimination. The employer simply treats some people less favorably than others because of their race, color, religion, sex, or [other protected characteristic]." * * * Liability in a disparate-treatment case "depends on whether the protected trait * * * actually motivated the employer's decision." Id. at 610, 113 S.Ct. 1701. By contrast, disparate-impact claims "involve employment practices that are facially neutral in their treatment of different groups but that in fact fall more harshly on one group than another and cannot be justified by business necessity." *Teamsters v. United States*, 431 U.S. 324, 335-36, 97 S.Ct. 1843, 52 L.Ed.2d 396 (1977). * * *

Both disparate-treatment and disparate-impact claims are cognizable under the ADA. See 42 U.S.C. § 12112(b) (defining "discriminate" to include "utilizing standards, criteria, or methods of

---

[4]   The Court of Appeals noted that "it is possible that a drug *user* may not be 'disabled' under the ADA if his drug use does not rise to the level of an addiction which substantially limits one or more of his major life activities." 298 F.3d, at 1033-34, n.9. The parties do not dispute that respondent was "disabled" at the time he quit in lieu of discharge and thus a record of the disability exists. We therefore need not decide in this case whether respondent's employment record constitutes a "record of addiction," which triggers the protections of the ADA.

The parties are also not disputing in this Court whether respondent was qualified for the position for which he applied.

administration * * * that have the effect of discrimination on the basis of disability" and "using qualification standards, employment tests or other selection criteria that screen out or tend to screen out an individual with a disability"). Because "the factual issues, and therefore the character of the evidence presented, differ when the plaintiff claims that a facially neutral employment policy has a discriminatory impact on protected classes," *Texas Dept. of Community Affairs v. Burdine*, 450 U.S. 248, 252, n.5, 101 S.Ct. 1089, 67 L.Ed.2d 207 (1981), courts must be careful to distinguish between these theories. Here, respondent did not timely pursue a disparate-impact claim. Rather, the District Court concluded, and the Court of Appeals agreed, that respondent's case was limited to a disparate-treatment theory, that the company refused to rehire respondent because it regarded respondent as being disabled and/or because of respondent's record of a disability. 298 F.3d, at 1037, n.20.

Petitioner's proffer of its neutral no-rehire policy plainly satisfied its obligation under *McDonnell Douglas* to provide a legitimate, nondiscriminatory reason for refusing to rehire respondent. Thus, the only relevant question before the Court of Appeals, after petitioner presented a neutral explanation for its decision not to rehire respondent, was whether there was sufficient evidence from which a jury could conclude that petitioner did make its employment decision based on respondent's status as disabled despite petitioner's proffered explanation. Instead, the Court of Appeals concluded that, as a matter of law, a neutral no-rehire policy was not a legitimate, nondiscriminatory reason sufficient to defeat a prima facie case of discrimination.[6] The Court of Appeals did not even attempt, in the remainder of its opinion, to treat this claim as one involving only disparate treatment. Instead, the Court of Appeals observed that petitioner's policy "screens out persons with a record of addiction," and further noted that the company had not raised a business necessity defense, 298 F.3d at 1036-37 & n.19, factors that pertain to disparate-impact claims but not disparate-treatment claims. * * * By improperly focusing on these factors, the Court of Appeals ignored the fact that petitioner's no-rehire policy is a quintessential legitimate, nondiscriminatory reason for refusing to rehire an employee who was terminated for violating workplace conduct rules. If petitioner did indeed apply a neutral, generally applicable no-rehire policy in rejecting

---

[6] The Court of Appeals characterized respondent's workplace misconduct as merely "testing positive because of [his] addiction." 298 F.3d at 1036. To the extent that the court suggested that, because respondent's workplace misconduct is related to his disability, petitioner's refusal to rehire respondent on account of that workplace misconduct violated the ADA, we point out that we have rejected a similar argument in the context of the Age Discrimination in Employment Act. See Hazen Paper Co. v. Biggins, 507 U.S. 604, 611, 113 S.Ct. 1701, 123 L.Ed.2d 338 (1993).

respondent's application, petitioner's decision not to rehire respondent can, in no way, be said to have been motivated by respondent's disability.

The Court of Appeals rejected petitioner's legitimate, nondiscriminatory reason for refusing to rehire respondent because it "serves to bar the re-employment of a drug addict despite his successful rehabilitation." 298 F.3d at 1036-37. We hold that such an analysis is inapplicable to a disparate-treatment claim. Once respondent had made a prima facie showing of discrimination, the next question for the Court of Appeals was whether petitioner offered a legitimate, nondiscriminatory reason for its actions so as to demonstrate that its actions were not motivated by respondent's disability. To the extent that the Court of Appeals strayed from this task by considering not only discriminatory intent but also discriminatory impact, we vacate its judgment and remand the case for further proceedings consistent with this opinion.

It is so ordered.

Notes & Questions

1. What are the implications of the *Hernandez* decision for employers' hiring, accommodation and retention policies and practices? And, what about for recovering alcoholics and drug addicts seeking work?

2. How is a court to separate behavior or conduct that is not acceptable in the workplace from behavior that is the result of a protected ADA disability?

৵

6. Job rotation

Most courts have held that it is not a reasonable accommodation to require an employer to create new jobs tailored to an employee with a disability. *See*, *e.g.*, Watson v. Lithonia Lighting, 304 F.3d 749, 751 (7th Cir. 2002) (citations omitted). Where an employer shows a business purpose in rotating its manual workers through positions on its assembly line, an employee with a disability will be considered not "otherwise qualified" if she is unable to perform one or more of the individual positions. *Id.* (citing 42 U.S.C. § 12112(b)(5)(A)).

The unreasonableness of a proposed accommodation that compromises an employer's job rotation scheme is magnified where that system is the employer's norm and serves a legitimate business purpose. It is ordinarily not discriminatory (nor a pretext to avoid ADA obligations) when an employer's mandatory job rotation system is used to reduce the risk of injury caused by long-term repetition of particular motions.

Similarly, it would not necessarily violate Title I for an employer to require that every worker be qualified to perform each essential task on a production line. This is particularly true where job rotation is shown to facilitate production tasks by making it easier for the employer to substitute among workers when injury occurs, when some take leave or are absent, or during peak production periods when employees must perform all tasks. *Id.*; *see also* Barnard v. ADM Milling Co., 987 F.Supp. 1337, 1343 (D. Kan. 1997) (accommodation which results in other employees having to work longer hours or to work harder in the same time is not reasonable and therefore not required).

7. "Light duty" positions

An employer may need to establish a pool of light duty positions as an accommodation. Hendricks-Robinson v. Excel Corp., 154 F.3d 685, 696 (7th Cir. 1998)); Dalton v. Subaru-Isuzu Auto., Inc., 141 F.3d 667, 680 (7th Cir. 1998). Historically, the primary function of light duty work is to enable an injured employee to continue to work after injury.

The ADA does not require an employer who establishes light duty positions for employees with disabilities (for instance, recovering from a workplace injury) to maintain these positions indefinitely. This may be particularly true when an employee's "recovery" period has ended without restoration to original health and work capabilities. Dalton, 141 F.3d at 680.

8. Equipment modifications/computer technology/ accessible materials

Purchasing equipment or modifying existing equipment is a form of accommodation when it enables the job applicant or employee with a disability to perform essential job functions. Whether involving acquisition or modification of equipment or provision of other workplace changes, an equipment modification is not required where it would prevent the employee from conducting an essential job function. Gilbert v. Frank, 949 F.2d 637, 643 (2d Cir. 1991).

As an example, the ability to contact the public by telephone would be an essential job function for many occupations. An accommodation for an employee with a hearing impairment would be to provide access to a TTY system to call a relay service operator (who then places the telephone call and relays the conversation between the parties).

New technology has revolutionized the range of available accommodations. *See generally* David Klein et al., Electronic Doors to Education: Study of High School Website Accessibility in Iowa, 21 Behav. Sci. & L. 27 (2003); Heather Ritchie & Peter Blanck, The Promise of the Internet for Disability: A Study of Online Services and Web Site Accessibility of Centers for Independent Living Web Sites, 20 Behav. Sci. & L. 5 (2003); Kevin Schartz et al., Employment of Persons with Disabilities in Information Technology Jobs: for Individuals with Disabilities: Literature Review for "IT Works," 20 Behav. Sci. & L. 637 (2002). This has become especially significant with the growing prevalence of computers in the everyday workplace. Computer technologies accommodate for the physical and cognitive limitations inherent in some disabilities – for example, while people without finger dexterity can use voice-recognition software to run a computer, people with vision and learning impairments may use software to make their computers read documents aloud, and those with severe speech impairments may use software that allows them to "speak" through the computer by using a keyboard. *See, e.g.*, Abledata, Welcome to ABLEDATA, the Premier Source for Information on Assistive Technology!, http://www.abledata.com (last visited Jun. 19, 2012); Peter Blanck, eQuality: Web Rights, Human Flourishing and Persons with Cognitive Disabilities (forthcoming 2014).

Apart from accommodations provided by technologies, computers play a role in increasing the productivity levels of people with disabilities. *See, e.g.*, Peter Blanck et al., Calibrating the Impact of the ADA's Employment Provisions, 14 Stan. L. & Pol'y Rev. 267, 284 (2003). Among people with spinal cord injuries (SCIs), for instance, those using computers prior to the SCI had more rapid returns to work. Doug Kruse & Alan Krueger, Nat'l Bureau of Econ. Research, Labor Market Effects of Spinal Cord Injuries in the Dawn of the Computer Age (Working Paper No. 5302 Oct. 1995), *available at* http://www.nber.org/papers/w5302.pdf. Despite the positive effects of computer use on the employment and earnings of people with SCI, they are less likely than other workers to be computer users and receive computer training following the injury. *See* Doug Kruse et al., Computer Use, Computer Training, and Employment Outcomes Among People with Spinal Cord Injuries, 21 Spine 891, 891-96 (1996).

Another potential accommodation would be the distribution of work-related materials (written or otherwise) in an alternative format such as an electronic file, Braille – one could even have a co-worker read or explain written materials. For other examples, *see* EEOC Primer, *supra*.

9.   Provision of services such as interpreters and job coaches

The EEOC's Interpretative Guidance endorses the reasonable accommodations of sign interpreters, video describers, or other such aids for qualified applicants or employees with sensory impairments. The EEOC also endorses "supported employment" accommodation strategies that include providing a temporary job coach to assist a qualified individual with a cognitive disability, absent undue hardship. 29 C.F.R. pt. 1630 app., § 1630.9 (2008); *see* Peter Blanck, The Americans with Disabilities Act and the Emerging Workforce: Employment of People with Mental Retardation 46-47 (1998) (discussing job coaching as a reasonable accommodation).

The EEOC provides an example of an employee with an intellectual disability, who is qualified for the position and may obtain a job coach as an accommodation. This strategy often helps the worker learn and maintain essential job tasks. In *EEOC v. Hertz*, the court considered whether an employer has a duty under the ADA to employ job coaches as an accommodation for two employees with intellectual disabilities to continue their training and employment.

ॐ

EEOC v. HERTZ CORP.

United States District Court, Eastern District Michigan, 1998
No. 96-72421, 1998 WL 5694

OPINION AND ORDER

FEIKENS, District J.

I. Background

Chief Justice Earl Warren would often ask when judging a case: "Is it fair, is it just?" That question must be asked in this case. The Equal Employment Opportunity Commission (EEOC) and Arkay, Inc. (Arkay), a federally-funded entity which supplies job coaches to assist handicapped persons, have combined in this suit to seek sanctions against the Hertz Corporation (Hertz). They now have been joined by several groups, Disability Rights Advocates and Michigan Protection and Advisory Services, as amici, who support that effort.

With this array, one must ask what it is in this case that brings the EEOC and these rights advocate agencies together to pursue this matter.

One need not look far.

Arkay, Inc. is the motivator.

Arkay has an appealing approach. It seeks out employers, like Hertz, and makes a proposal: that if the employer will hire a handicapped person, it (Arkay) will provide a job coach, free of charge, to the employer, who will assist the handicapped person in doing some work for the employer. Arkay is paid for these efforts by federal government funding.

This is what happened in this case. In early 1994, Arkay went to Hertz and pointed out to it that at its rental car operations at Detroit Metropolitan Airport, it could hire two handicapped persons (mentally retarded) who could work a limited number of hours each day (approximately four hours – the record is not clear), and they would be trained and assisted by two job coaches provided by Arkay. It is clear in the record that these handicapped persons (Donald Klem and Kenneth Miller) would not be able to do the intended work, picking up trash in the Hertz parking lot, without training by and the actual supervision of the job coaches.

Hertz agreed, and the venture started. But it soon went awry. It appears that the job coaches furnished by Arkay had other distracting interests. One day (the record is not clear if this was the first time, or the only time), the job coaches had Mr. Klem and Mr. Miller seated in the back seat of a car while they, a man and a woman, according to current jargon, were "making out" in the front seat. It is not clear from the record just what was going on. Hertz claims that four or five of its supervisors saw rather passionate lovemaking, while EEOC and Arkay claim the two were exchanging gifts and thanking each other with kisses.

When the event in the car was observed by the Hertz supervisors, the job coaches were ordered off the premises and the jobs of Messrs. Klem and Miller were terminated. What happened next is that Arkay went to the EEOC and claimed that a violation of the Americans With Disabilities Act (ADA) had occurred and EEOC had better do something about it.

This suit followed.

Plaintiff's major contention is that Hertz, having hired Messrs. Klem and Miller, now have a continuing duty to employ them, and that Hertz must provide reasonable accommodation to continue their training and employment. That reasonable accommodation, EEOC argues, would require Hertz to find other job coaches to train and supervise Mr. Klem and Mr. Miller.

When Arkay first approached Hertz, and asked it to hire Mr. Klem and Mr. Miller, Hertz had no legal obligation to do so. See *Reigel v. Kaiser Foundation Health Plan of N.C.,* 859 F.Supp. 963 (E.D.N.C. 1994).

When it did hire these men, it was essential that they be accompanied, while being trained and working on Hertz's premises, to be supervised by competent job coaches. Arkay committed itself to provide this important accommodation; it was the essential element, the consideration for the contract. That employment contract was breached by Arkay because of the conduct of its incompetent job coaches.

In this bizarre situation, EEOC, Arkay and the amici now seek to impose a legal obligation on Hertz that they say is compelled by 42 U.S.C. § 12112 (ADA). Their complaint "relates solely to Hertz's failure to reasonably accommodate Klem and Miller . . . ." This alleged failure to so accommodate, they claim, is discrimination.

Now to the facts that are not in dispute.

This case has its origins in defendant Hertz's April 1994 decision to contract with Arkay, Inc., for an employment service for individuals with developmental disabilities. * * * Arkay representative Susan Skibo contacted Hertz as to the possibility of employing Arkay personnel. Ms. Skibo eventually contacted Keith Lamb, one of Hertz's senior station managers at its Detroit Metropolitan Airport location, and outlined to him the arrangement that Arkay wanted to structure with Hertz: in exchange for Hertz's provision of menial tasks for Arkay's developmentally handicapped individuals, Arkay promised to provide job coaches to train them, to closely supervise them and, if necessary, tend to any of their medical needs. If Hertz would agree to employ and pay the handicapped individuals, Arkay would provide and pay the job coaches.

Mr. Lamb expressed some misgivings, but promised to speak to his supervisor, Gary Wellman, about Arkay's proposal. Mr. Lamb spoke with Mr. Wellman and told him that, in light of litter problems Hertz had on its premises, Arkay's proposal "might be something that would be good to try." * * * Mr. Wellman, in turn, took the matter to his supervisor, Michael Kieleszewski, who sought and then obtained permission from Hertz Headquarters to accept Arkay's offer.[3]

Arkay is funded by Medicald in an arrangement that it has with Wayne Community Living Services (WCLS), and that entity works with and through Arkay to provide supported employment for mentally retarded persons. The record indicates that on behalf of WCLS, Arkay entered into this employment agreement with Hertz, which Arkay states in its Answer to Hertz's Third-Party Complaint against it, Para. 9, would be on a trial basis.

The term " 'supported employment,' which has been applied to a wide variety of programs to assist individuals with severe disabilities in both competitive and non-competitive employment, is not synonymous with reasonable accommodation." The *Interpretative Guidance* to Reg. 29 C.F.R. 1630.9 states that an example of supported employment might include providing "a temporary job coach to assist in the training of a qualified individual with a disability . . . ."

Before Messrs. Klem and Miller could be hired, however, Hertz had to make additional accommodations. First, Hertz agreed to waive its usual application and interview process. Hertz also allowed Messrs. Klem and Miller to take a paid half-hour break, even though their shift lasted only four hours. Most important, Hertz allowed Messrs. Klem and Miller to have supportive "job coaches."

The record also indicates that Hertz did not hold Messrs. Klem and Miller to the higher standards of its other employees. On one occasion, Mr. Lamb saw Mr. Klem spit on the floor inside Hertz's car return building, an area used by Hertz customers. Mr. Lamb did not discipline Mr. Klem; he wanted to give Mr. Klem an opportunity to adjust to his new environment. Mr. Miller and Mr. Klem also were not held to the attendance standards of other employees. Mr. Lamb testified that the pair missed work without penalty. Deposition testimony also raises serious questions whether, even with a job coach, Mr. Klem could perform

---

[3]   Prior to accepting Arkay's offer, Hertz had no employees assigned specifically to cleaning the parking lot. Hertz created positions for Messrs. Klem and Miller to do this. The positions have not been filled since Mr. Klem's and Mr. Miller's employment was terminated.

the essential functions of his job. Both Mr. Lamb and one of Mr. Klem's job coaches testified as to incidents in which Mr. Klem spent part of a workday staring at airplanes overhead and refused orders from his job coach to do his job.

Hertz did accommodate to this. Hertz claims, however, that it could not tolerate problems created by the job coaches assigned to Messrs. Klem and Miller. The first job coach that Arkay sent was "mean" to Messrs. Klem and Miller. Hertz requested that this coach be replaced. Arkay granted this request and, for a time, provided a job coach that met Hertz's expectations. This second job coach was subsequently replaced by another coach who, on June 7, 1994, was involved in the incident which precipitated the termination of Hertz's relationship with Arkay.

To this incident, Hertz's response was swift. One of its managers confronted the job coaches and promptly told them to leave Hertz property. Hertz then contacted Arkay and severed its relationship with that company. Even though, at that point, it could have easily have done so, Arkay refused to turn Messrs. Klem and Miller over to another job agency performing the same function that Arkay performed. * * * Instead, Arkay threatened to, and eventually did, contact EEOC and induced it to institute this action. The record is not clear that Arkay ever informed Wayne Community Living Services, of this situation, or that Arkay received WCLS's consent to secure other job coaches, i.e., organizations that, like Arkay, could have provided this type of employment support to Messrs. Klem and Miller.

II. Analysis

The comment of Judge Richard Posner in *Vande Zande v. State of Wisc. Dept. of Admin.*, 44 F.3d 538, 545 (7th Cir. 1995), is instructive:

> [I]f the employer * * * bends over backwards to accommodate a disabled worker – goes farther than the law requires – * * * it must not be punished for its generosity by being deemed to have conceded the reasonableness of so far reaching an accommodation. That would hurt rather than help disabled workers.

While, as is pointed out hereinafter, EEOC cannot even come close to establishing a prima facie case of disability discrimination against Hertz, this is a case in which there is no discrimination whatever. * * * The teaching of the ancient fable is instructive: It took a child to point out to the crowd admiring what they thought was an ornately dressed emperor riding a horse, that the emperor had no clothes on at all. EEOC's position fits that fable. One wonders why that agency is unable to see clearly what it is attempting to claim. Hertz should be complimented for what it tried to do here – not sued. How does EEOC expect to further the goal of assisting handicapped persons that employers will hire if it seeks to punish them for their generosity?

Putting that aside for the moment, and taking on EEOC's argument that it has here a prima facie case, EEOC cannot and does not establish a prima facie case of discrimination required by ADA.

Monette v. Electronic Data Systems Corp., 90 F.3d 1173 (6th Cir. 1996), teaches that, to establish a prima facie case, a plaintiff must show that

> *1) he or she is disabled, 2) is otherwise qualified for the job, with or without "reasonable" accommodation, 3) suffered an adverse employment decision, 4) the employer knew or had reason to know of his or her disability, and 5) after rejection or termination the position remained open, or the disabled individual was replaced.* (Citations omitted)

It is clear that plaintiff does not and cannot establish factor 2). Messrs. Klem and Miller are not qualified for the job because accommodation to permit them to function was not provided by Arkay (or anyone else). It is not the duty, obligation or responsibility of Hertz to provide job coaches, either on a temporary basis or on a permanent basis, to train and supervise these handicapped individuals.

It is also clear that after Messrs. Klem and Miller were terminated due to Arkay's breach of the trial arrangement, that these positions [Klem's and Miller's] did not remain open. These positions ceased when the arrangement failed. It is also clear that they [Klem and Miller] were not replaced.

The result in this case was not brought about by Hertz. Arkay and, perhaps, Wayne Community Living Services had a responsibility for "picking up the pieces," and should have initiated a reopening of the arrangement with Hertz. The record indicates that had Arkay "made such an offer, Hertz would have seriously considered extending the employment" of Mr. Klem and Mr. Miller.

But, even more important, the position of the EEOC is troublesome. This case should not have been brought against Hertz; EEOC's focus was misplaced. EEOC should have advised Arkay that this was not a case of discrimination against handicapped persons but rather a breakdown in Arkay's procedures in affording assistance to handicapped people.

Even EEOC's *Interpretative Guidance* stands in its way. The guidelines provide at [29 C.F.R. part 1630 app. §]1630.9 that:

> *The term "supported employment," which has been applied to a wide variety of programs to assist individuals with severe disabilities in both competitive and non-competitive employment is not synonymous with reasonable accommodation. Examples of supported employment include modified training materials, restructuring essential*

functions to enable an individual to perform a job, or hiring an outside professional ("job coach") to assist in job training. Whether a particular form of assistance would be required as a reasonable accommodation must be determined on an individualized, case by case basis without regard to whether that assistance is referred to as "supported employment." For example, an employer, under certain circumstances, may be required to provide modified training materials or a temporary "job coach" to assist in the training of a qualified individual with a disability as a reasonable accommodation.[6] (Emphasis added)

If a temporary job coach providing job training to a qualified individual *may* be a reasonable accommodation, the clear implication is that a full-time job coach providing more than training to unqualified Individuals is not. Case law supports this view. *Ricks v. Xerox Corp.*, 877 F.Supp. 1468 (D. Kan. 1995), is on point. In that case, the district court ruled that an employee's request for a full-time "helper" to assist in the performance of the essential functions of his job was unreasonable as a matter of law. A similar result was reached in *Gilbert v. Frank*, 949 F.2d 637 (C.A.2 1991), in which the U.S. Court of Appeals for the Second Circuit held that it was unreasonable to have two people performing the same tasks normally performed by one. Insisting that Messrs. Miller and Klem have a full-time job coach to assist in the performance of job duties on a permanent basis is, likewise, unreasonable.

Neither party disputes that Hertz had no initial obligation to hire Messrs. Klem and Miller. *See Reigel*, supra, at 963, 973: *"[The ADA] cannot be construed to require an employer to make fundamental or substantial modifications in its operations to assure every disabled individual the benefit of employment."*

EEOC, in the face of this precedent and in spite of its inability to point to any case mandating that a full-time job coach is a reasonable accommodation, advances the incredible argument that, because Hertz could have obtained a job coach for Messrs. Klem and Miller at no cost to

---

[6]   * * * [T]here is no dispute here that the role of the job coaches in this case went far beyond that of "job training." The record reflects that the coaches supervised, disciplined, and assisted in the performance of work. In addition, Arkay representative Susan Skibo testified that neither Mr. Klem nor Mr. Miller had ever worked without the full-time assistance of a job coach. Ms. Skibo further testified that they would always need this full-time assistance. Finally, while there is an issue of fact with regard to whether Messrs. Klem and Miller were qualified individuals, the fact that they required full-time assistance for more than job training moots, for purposes of summary judgment, the factual dispute.

itself, the provision of a job coach is a *per se* reasonable accommodation, and must be provided.

Plaintiff seeks to establish an expanded liability for putative employers who consider hiring handicapped persons, i.e., that once an employer evidences an intent to and does provide employment for a handicapped person with support for that person of a job coach, it is obligated to continue that relationship in perpetuity and without regard to any event(s) that make that employment relationship untenable. The ADA does not require this.

III. Conclusion

The motion brought by Hertz for summary judgment is GRANTED.

IT IS SO ORDERED.

Notes & Questions

1. In *Hertz*, the job coach was provided by a third-party non-profit provider without expense to the employer. In the absence of outside funding, when may the provision of a job coach present an undue burden?

2. In *EEOC v. Dollar General Corp.*, 252 F.Supp.2d 277, 293 (M.D.N.C. 2003), the court found a genuine issue of material fact remaining as to whether a job coach for an employee with moderate intellectual disability was temporary, "such that she might, at some point, have been able to perform her job functions without a job coach . . . ." In light of varying disabilities, how long might "temporary" be? *See* Miami Univ. v. Ohio Civil Rights Comm'n, 726 N.E.2d 1032, 1043 (Ohio Ct. App., 1999) (accommodation of job coach was reasonable for plaintiff with intellectual disability who did not require job coaching beyond the first week or so in any of her previous jobs).

3. Is it conceivable under the ADA that a job coach as a reasonable accommodation could be permanent? Consider the potential needs of employees who are deaf, vision, reading, or intellectually impaired. *See* Dollar Gen. Corp., 252 F.Supp.2d at 290 (citation omitted).

4. In *EEOC v. Home Depot, USA Inc.*, No. 03 Civ. 4860, the EEOC argued that Home Depot hastily fired a worker with an intellectual disability and a job coach over an issue that was easily resolvable if the job coach had been contacted. The employee missed two days of work, reasonably believing he was not needed to work those days. What is the extent of the job coach's role in relation to the employee and employer? Should the job coach have a role in discussing job performance and discipline issues? Arising from a settlement agreement, Home Depot established new guidelines permitting performance issues to be discussed directly with the employee who has a job coach, however, encouraging the job coach's presence in the event of a disciplinary action or performance evaluation. Molly McDonough, Job Coach a 'Reasonable Accommodation': Home Depot Agrees to Consultations on Developmentally Disabled

Workers, ABA J. Rep., Nov. 4, 2005. Does such a policy diminish an employer's control over workers?

5. For further information on the appropriateness and use of job coaches, *see* Louis Orslene et al. Job Accommodation Network (JAN), Personal Assistance Services (PAS) in the Workplace (Aug. 23, 2006), *available at* http://www.jan.wvu.edu/media/pas.pdf.

10. Leave of absence

A leave of absence from work poses a different scenario, and depending on the circumstances, may or may not be a reasonable accommodation. The Eleventh Circuit has held that an indefinite leave of absence is not a reasonable accommodation. In *Wood v. Green*, 323 F.3d 1309 (11th Cir. 2003), the court concluded that a reasonable accommodation was an accommodation that enables the employee to perform the essential functions of his job presently or in the immediate future. *Id.* at 1313. Wood did not seek an accommodation that would allow him to continue his work presently; rather, he sought an indeterminate leave of absence that would allow him to work at a future, indefinite time. *Id.* at 1314. Because the ADA covers those individuals who "can perform the essential functions of their jobs presently or in the immediate future," the court concluded that Wood was not a qualified individual under the ADA. *Id.* The length of a requested leave also will affect whether the leave constitutes an undue burden for the employer regarding the expense of replacement workers, the difficulty of shifting tasks, or the difficulty of planning.

§ 8.2 The Process

A. *The Request*

To be eligible for an accommodation, an employee must make his disability known to the employer and request an accommodation. Reed v. LePage Bakeries, Inc., 244 F.3d 254, 258-61 (1st Cir. 2001). The request need not be phrased in terms of "reasonable modification" or any other particular language. The employee need not identify the particular change needed. However, the employee must identify her disability and its effect on her job performance. The accommodation request must be "sufficiently direct and specific," giving notice that she needs a "special accommodation." Wynne v. Tufts Univ., 976 F.2d 791, 795 (1st Cir. 1992) (quoting Nathanson v. Med. Coll. of Pa., 926 F.2d 1368, 1381 (3d Cir. 1991)).

At a minimum, the request must explain how the proposed accommodation is linked to some disability. "The employer has no duty to divine the need for a special accommodation where the employee merely makes a mundane request for a change at the workplace." *See* Equal Emp. Opportunity Comm'n, Reasonable Accommodation and Undue

Hardship Under the ADA, 8 Fair Emp. Prac. Man. (BNA) 405: 7601 (Oct. 17, 2002) ("Reasonable Accommodation and Undue Hardship") (request for new office chair because current one is "uncomfortable" does not provide sufficient notice that accommodation is needed due to a disability), http://www.eeoc.gov/policy/docs/accommodation.html.

Reasonable accommodations must be provided to qualified job applicants and employees whether they work part-time or full-time, or are probationary employees. Contingent Workers, *supra*. The accommodation requirement places a particular burden on an individual with a hidden and non-obvious impairment to disclose the claimed disability and request the employer to provide an accommodation. But it is still a process that places obligations on both parties. "[P]roperly participating in the interactive process means that an employer cannot expect an employee to read its mind and know that he or she must specifically say 'I want a reasonable accommodation,' particularly when the employee has a mental illness." Bultemeyer v. Fort Wayne Cmty. Schs., 100 F.3d 1281, 1285 (7th Cir. 1996). However, "[t]he employer has to meet the employee half-way, and if it appears that the employee may need an accommodation but doesn't know how to ask for it, the employer should do what it can to help." *Id.*

An employee need not make the accommodation request before accepting the job or when she first begins the job. She may attempt to work without accommodation and only request accommodation if she finds she cannot perform the job without it. However, she may face normal discipline for any performance failures prior to the request. *See* Reasonable Accommodation and Undue Hardship, *supra*, at Question 4. Generally, an applicant or employee can request an accommodation at any time. An employer, generally, may not instigate the reasonable accommodation process itself or impose accommodations on an employee.

An employee is not required to use particular language when requesting an accommodation. There are no magic words; an employee need only "inform the employer of the need for an adjustment due to a medical condition," for example. Barnett v. U.S. Airways, Inc., 228 F.3d 1105, 1114 n.5, 1115 (9th Cir. 2000) (en banc).

Once an accommodation request is made, an employer generally may not disclose to co-workers or others that an employee is receiving a reasonable accommodation. 42 U.S.C. § 12112(d)(3)(B), (d)(4)(C) (2006); 29 C.F.R. § 1630.14(b)(1) (2008). The exceptions to the ADA confidentiality requirements include the following: supervisors and managers may be told about restrictions on the work duties of the employee and about necessary accommodations; safety personnel may be informed; and government officials investigating ADA compliance may be provided appropriate information. In addition, the EEOC has interpreted Title I to allow employers to disclose medical information in accordance with state workers' compensation laws and for insurance purposes. *See* 29

C.F.R. § 1630.14(b); *see also* Enforcement Guidance on Pre-employment Inquiries Under the Americans with Disabilities Act, 8 Fair Emp. Prac. Man. (BNA) 405: 7191, 7193-94 (1995).

In addition, a plaintiff likely will lose on a failure to accommodate claim if he does not request accommodation until after termination. Amadio v. Ford Motor Co., 238 F.3d 919, 929 (7th Cir. 2001). Similarly, an employee cannot dictate exactly which reasonable accommodation he wants. An employer is not necessarily obligated to provide the specific accommodation requested or preferred by the applicant or employee, but only a reasonable accommodation. *See* Zivkovic v. S. Cal. Edison Co., 302 F.3d 1080, 1089 (9th Cir. 2002); EEOC v. Yellow Freight Sys. Inc., 253 F.3d 943, 951 (7th Cir. 2001) (en banc); Barnett v. U.S. Airways, Inc., 228 F.3d 1105, 1115 (9th Cir. 2000) (en banc) (requiring the selected accommodation to be reasonable and effective).

B. *Interactive Process*

Once the accommodation request is made, the ADA strongly encourages a flexible consultative "interactive process." 29 C.F.R. § 1630.2(o)(3) (2003). The EEOC regulations note that the interactive process should "identify the precise limitations resulting from the disability and potential reasonable accommodations that could overcome those limitations." *Id.*

The interactive process further requires direct and good faith communication between the employer and the qualified individual, consideration of the request, and an offer of an accommodation that is reasonable and effective. *Id.* §§ 1630.2(o)(3), 1630.9.

At this point, an employer may request supporting documentation of the disability from an appropriate professional, such as a doctor or rehabilitation counselor, in furtherance of the consultative process. Vinson v. Thomas, 288 F.3d 1145, 1153 (9th Cir. 2002); Grenier v. Cyanamid Plastics, Inc., 70 F.3d 667, 674 (1st Cir. 1995) (citing Inquiries and Medical Examinations, *supra.*

Most federal courts of appeal have endorsed the interactive process. *See* U.S. Airways, Inc. v. Barnett, 535 U.S. 391, 407 (2002) (Stevens, J., concurring) (noting that the Ninth Circuit's holding with respect to interactive process was "correct" and "is untouched by the Court's opinion"); Lovejoy-Wilson v. NOCO Motor Fuel, Inc., 263 F.3d 208, 218-19 (2d Cir. 2001). In *Mengine v. Runyon*, 114 F.3d 415, 420 (3d Cir. 1997), for instance, the Third Circuit explained that the process furthers the purposes of the ADA because employers typically do not know the job abilities of qualified individuals with disabilities, and an applicant or worker may not be aware of the available employment opportunities or job requirements.

An employer who does not engage in the interactive process proceeds at its peril, and the evidentiary deck will be stacked against it.

The Ninth Circuit has held that a failure to participate in the interactive process may preclude an employer from obtaining summary judgment on an ADA failure to accommodate claim. *See* Barnett v. U.S. Airways, Inc., 228 F.3d 1105, 1112 (9th Cir. 2000) (en banc), vacated on other grounds, 535 U.S. 391, 407 (2002). Similarly, California law provides that an employer's failure to engage in the interactive process, alone, constitutes a violation. Cal. Gov't Code § 12940(n) (West 2003). However, the Tenth Circuit has held that a reasonable accommodation claim cannot be based solely on the allegation that the employer failed to engage in an interactive process. "[T]he interactive process is a means and not an end in itself." Lowe v. Indep. Sch. Dist. No. 1, 363 F. App'x 548, 558 (10th Cir. 2010) (quoting Rehling v. City of Chicago, 207 F.3d 1009, 1016 (7th Cir. 2000)). "Clearly an employer could, with impunity, ignore the interactive process so long as it reasonably accommodated employee needs." Lowe, 363 F. App'x at 558.

The EEOC recognizes that, as part of this process, an employer may be forced to disclose confidential medical information about its job applicants or employees with disabilities to supervisors and managers when necessary for the development of an effective accommodation. EEOC Primer, *supra*.

The interactive process is just that, a *process*. The Ninth Circuit has held that the duty to accommodate is an ongoing duty that is "not exhausted by one effort." Humphrey v. Mem'l Hosps. Ass'n, 239 F.3d 1128, 1138 (9th Cir. 2001) (citation omitted). In *Humphrey*, the court stated that:

> the employer's obligation to engage in the interactive process extends beyond the first attempt at accommodation and continues when the employee asks for a different accommodation or where the employer is aware that the initial accommodation is failing and further accommodation is needed. This rule fosters the framework of cooperative problem-solving contemplated by the ADA, by encouraging employers to seek to find accommodations that really work, and by avoiding the creation of a perverse incentive for employees to request the most drastic and burdensome accommodation possible out of fear that a lesser accommodation might be ineffective.

Id.

C.   *Accommodation For "Regarded As" Disability*

On its face, Title I's reasonable accommodation requirement does not distinguish between the rights of those individuals with actual disabilities and those individuals who are "regarded as" having a disability or have a "record" of disability. But do employers have a duty to accommodate employees who do not actually have a covered disability but fall into one of the latter two categories?

The First Circuit, however, endorsed the possibility of accommodation for a regarded as plaintiff in certain circumstances. Katz v. City Metal Co., Inc., 87 F.3d 26, 33-34 (1st Cir. 1996) (employer's knowledge of employee's heart attack). Nevertheless, *see* Barker v. Int'l Paper Co., 993 F.Supp. 10, 14 (D. Me. 1998) (individuals with a relationship or association with a person with a disability typically are not entitled to receive reasonable accommodation (citing Den Hartog v. Wasatch Acad., 129 F.3d 1076, 1084 (10th Cir. 1997))).

Prior to the ADA Amendments Act of 2008, the circuit courts split on this question. *See* Weber v. Strippit, 186 F.3d 907, 915 (8th Cir. 1999) (no duty to reasonably accommodate employee who was regarded as having a disability); *see also* Mack v. Great Dane Trailers, 308 F.3d 776, 783 n.2 (7th Cir. 2002); Workman v. Frito-Lay, Inc., 165 F.3d 460, 467 (6th Cir. 1999); Newberry v. E. Tex. State Univ., 161 F.3d 276, 280 (5th Cir 1998); *but see* Katz v. City Metal Co., Inc., 87 F.3d 26, 33-34 (1st Cir. 1996) (allowing for possibility of accommodation for regarded as plaintiff in certain circumstances); D'Angelo v. ConAgra Foods, Inc., 422 F.3d 1220 (11th Cir. 2005) (same).

The ADA Amendments Act of 2008, Public Law 110-325, resolved this debate. The Act specifically provides that "[a] covered entity under title I . . . need not provide a reasonable accommodation or a reasonable modification to policies, practices, or procedures to an individual who meets the [regarded as] definition of disability. . . ." Sec. 6(a)(1).

§ 8.3 Undue Hardship

A common critique of Title I is that accommodations for qualified individuals create economic hardships that are costly and burdensome for employers. The statutory mechanism for dealing with this criticism is the "undue hardship" defense.

Employers only are required to make accommodations that do not impose undue hardships on them. Morton v. United Parcel Serv., Inc., 272 F.3d 1249, 1257 (9th Cir. 2001) (citing 42 U.S.C. § 12112(b)(5)(A)). An undue hardship is a significant difficulty or expense when considered in light of various factors (discussed below). The undue hardship analysis is "a fact-intensive inquiry, rarely suitable for resolution on summary judgment." *Id.*; Bates v. United Parcel Service, Inc., 511 F.3d 974 (9th Cir. 2007) (overruling *Morton*, in part, however, upholding the undue hardship analysis).

Undue hardship is an affirmative defense that must be raised and proved by the employer. The degree of the difficulty of accommodation, central to the undue hardship analysis, will turn on evidence regarding the accommodation expense, compared to the firm's size and resources. Lovejoy-Wilson v. NOCO Motor Fuel, Inc., 263 F.3d 208, 221 (2d Cir.

2001). When determining undue hardship in the application and interview stage of employment, only the cost of providing the accommodation in the application or interview, not the cost for the full course of employment, may be considered. For example, providing a sign language interpreter every day of work may be an undue hardship, whereas providing an interpreter for an interview may not. At that interview, the applicant then may explain that she will not need an interpreter every day on the job.

An employer may not claim undue hardship based on other employees' or customers' fears or prejudices. Also, undue hardship may not be based on the view that an accommodation might have a negative impact on the morale of co-workers. 29 C.F.R. pt. 1630 app., § 1630.15(d) (2008).

A. *Statutory Definition*

Title I defines undue hardship in detailed but inexact terms:

(A) In general

The term "undue hardship" means an action requiring significant difficulty or expense, when considered in light of the factors set forth in subparagraph (B).

(B) Factors to be considered

In determining whether an accommodation would impose an undue hardship on a covered entity, factors to be considered include:

(i) the nature and cost of the accommodation needed under this chapter;

(ii) the overall financial resources of the facility or facilities involved in the provision of the reasonable accommodation; the number of persons employed at such facility; the effect on expenses and resources, or the impact otherwise of such accommodation upon the operation of the facility;

(iii) the overall financial resources of the covered entity; the overall size of the business of a covered entity with respect to the number of its employees; the number, type, and location of its facilities; and

(iv) the type of operation or operations of the covered entity, including the composition, structure, and functions of the workforce of such entity; the geographic separateness, administrative, or fiscal relationship of the facility or facilities in question to the covered entity.

42 U.S.C. § 12111(10) (2000).

B.   *EEOC Regulations*

The EEOC regulations expand on the statutory definition. They define undue hardship in regard to accommodation as:

> (1) . . . significant difficulty or expense incurred by a covered entity, when considered in light of the factors set forth in paragraph (p)(2) of this section.

> (2) Factors to be considered.   In determining whether an accommodation would impose an undue hardship on a covered entity, factors to be considered include:

> (i) The nature and net cost of the accommodation needed under this part, taking into consideration the availability of tax credits and deductions, and/or outside funding;

> (ii) The overall financial resources of the facility or facilities involved in the provision of the reasonable accommodation, the number of persons employed at such facility, and the effect on expenses and resources;

> (iii) The overall financial resources of the covered entity, the overall size of the business of the covered entity with respect to the number of its employees, and the number, type and location of its facilities;

> (iv) The type of operation or operations of the covered entity, including the composition, structure and functions of the workforce of such entity, and the geographic separateness and administrative or fiscal relationship of the facility or facilities in question to the covered entity; and

> (v) The impact of the accommodation upon the operation of the facility, including the impact on the ability of other employees to perform their duties and the impact on the facility's ability to conduct business.

29 C.F.R. § 1630.2(p).

Employers frequently are concerned that the costs of workplace accommodations are an undue hardship. Peter Blanck et al., Calibrating the Impact of the ADA's Employment Provisions, 14 Stan. L. & Pol'y Rev. 267, 272-73 (2003).   Data from an in-depth study of workplace accommodation costs and effectiveness indicate that 50.5% of accommodations implemented following guidance provided by JAN were at no cost.   D.J. Hendricks, et al., Cost and Effectiveness of Accommodations in the Workplace: Preliminary Results of a Nationwide Study, 25 Disability Stud. Q. (Fall 2005), http://dsq-sds.org/article/view/623/800. The median cost of the remaining accommodations was

$600. *Id.* JAN customers (778 employers, 882 persons with disabilities) reported making effective and highly effective accommodations with JAN guidance. *Id.* See also Helen Schartz et al., Workplace Accommodations: Evidence-Based Outcomes, 27 Work 345 (2006); Helen Schartz et al., Workplace Accommodations: Empirical Study of Current Employees, 75 Miss. L. J. 917 (2006).

§ 8.4 Burdens Of Production And Proof

A. *Reasonable Accommodation And Undue Hardship*

In many instances an accommodation will be reasonable as long as it does not cause an undue hardship on the employer (and no other affirmative defense applies). Courts have created a judicial model that gives structure to this by allocating the burdens of proof differently as to reasonable accommodation and undue hardship. For a full discussion of this issue, *see* Reed v. LePage Bakeries, Inc., 244 F.3d 254, 258-61 (1st Cir. 2001).

Federal courts of appeal generally have concluded that the qualified applicant or employee bears the burden of production to show that an accommodation is possible. *See, e.g.,* Shapiro v. Twp. of Lakewood, 292 F.3d 356, 358-60 (3d Cir. 2002) (citing Jackan v. N.Y. State Dep't of Lab., 205 F.3d 562, 567 (2d Cir. 2000)); Smith v. Midland Brake, Inc., 180 F.3d 1154, 1174 (10th Cir. 1999) (en banc); Willis v. Conopco, Inc., 108 F.3d 282, 285 (11th Cir. 1997) ("[W]here a plaintiff cannot demonstrate 'reasonable accommodation,' the employer's lack of investigation into reasonable accommodation is unimportant."). When a plaintiff produces evidence "sufficient to make a facial showing that accommodation is possible, the burden of production shifts to the employer to present evidence of its inability to accommodate." White v. York Int'l Corp., 45 F.3d 357, 361 (10th Cir. 1995) (citation omitted). Where an employer does not engage in the interactive process, the burden of proof shifts from the employee to the employer concerning the availability of an accommodation. Mays v. Principi, 301 F.3d 866, 870 (7th Cir. 2002).

Ordinarily, a plaintiff cannot pursue a claim for failure to accommodate without showing that an accommodation within reason existed. This is where the interactive process, discussed above, becomes important from an evidentiary perspective. A plaintiff likely will lose a claim where he causes a breakdown of the interactive process, for example, by refusing to release necessary medical records. Beck v. Univ. of Wis. Bd. of Regents, 75 F.3d 1130, 1136-37 (7th Cir. 1996). Where an employee cannot document the existence of an accommodation because the employer did not engage in the interactive process, "the fault in the failure to make the accommodation available would be the employer's. . . ." Mays, 301 F.3d at 870 (citing Emerson v. N. States Power Co., 256 F.3d 506, 515 (7th Cir. 2001); Ozlowski v. Henderson, 237 F.3d 837, 840 (7th Cir. 2001)).

A qualified job applicant or employee is not required to initiate the interactive process where the employer has said it will not engage in the process. *See, e.g.*, Davoll v. Webb, 194 F.3d 1116, 1132-33 (10th Cir. 1999). The majority view is that failure of an employer to engage in the interactive process does not itself give rise to per se liability under Title I, although for summary judgment purposes such failure often is considered evidence that the employer acted in bad faith. *See, e.g.*, Ballard v. Rubin, 284 F.3d 957, 960 (8th Cir. 2002) (citing Taylor v. Phoenixville Sch. Dist., 174 F.3d 142, 165 (3d Cir. 1999)).

In *Mays v. Principi*, Judge Posner summarizes one view of the evidentiary utility of the interactive process:

> The purpose of the consultative process is to find a reasonable accommodation for the particular disabled employee, and if she proves that ... there was no consultative process, suspicion arises that the reason her disability was not accommodated was not that she turned down a reasonable accommodation but that the employer failed to explain her options to her and thus did not make it "available" to her in a practical sense. The burden shifts to the employer to produce some evidence that even if he failed to consult or "interact" with her, soliciting her suggestions for a reasonable accommodation, etc., he offered her such an accommodation with sufficient clarity to make the accommodation available to her in a practical sense, so that her rejecting it was her own fault.
>
> The principal significance of the consultative process is not that the employee is likely to come up with a reasonable accommodation if only she is consulted, but that she is quite likely to turn it down and either quit or sue unless the employer explains why he can't do more to enable her to work despite her disability. That can be presumed from the employer's failure to consult but he can meet the presumption with evidence that he said enough to avoid being blamed for her failure to accept his offer.

Mays, 301 F.3d at 870-71.

In accord with this view, the Seventh and other circuits have followed a burden-shifting consequence of the employer's failure to engage in the interactive process. *Id.* at 871 (citing Shapiro v. Twp. of Lakewood, 292 F.3d 356, 359-60 (3d Cir. 2002); Frazier v. Simmons, 254 F.3d 1247, 1261 (10th Cir. 2001); *cf.* Lucas v. W.W. Grainger, Inc., 257 F.3d 1249, 1256 n.2 (11th Cir. 2001)). Yet, when no reasonable accommodation is possible, the failure to engage in the interactive process is harmless. *Id.* (citing, e.g., Kvorjak v. Maine, 259 F.3d 48, 53 (1st Cir. 2001)).

In contrast, the Ninth Circuit has come closer to adopting a view that an employer's failure to engage in the interactive process in and of itself constitutes a violation of the ADA. In *Barnett v. U.S. Airways, Inc.*, the court held that when a job applicant or employee requests an accommodation (or an employer recognizes the employee's need for an accommodation but the employee cannot or does not request it because of a disability) the employer *must* engage in an interactive process to determine any possible reasonable accommodation. 228 F.3d 1105, 1112 (9th Cir. 2000) (en banc), vacated on other grounds, 535 U.S. 391, 407 (2002).

The First Circuit, alternatively, resolves the consequences of a failure by an employer to engage in the interactive process on a case-by-case basis. It maintains that although there may be situations in which failure to engage in the process constitutes a violation, the omission is not considered if the trial record "forecloses a finding that the plaintiff could perform the duties of the job, with or without reasonable accommodation," that is, is not a qualified individual with a disability. Kvorjak, 259 F.3d at 53.

The defendant then bears the burden to show that the accommodation would impose an undue hardship. 42 U.S.C. § 12112(b)(5)(A) (2006). However, courts of appeal have varied in their interpretation of whether Title I imposes the same evidentiary burdens on the plaintiff with a disability requesting accommodation as on the defendant employer.

The approach of the First, Second, Third, Eighth and Tenth Circuits shifts the burden of persuasion from plaintiff to defendant, such that the burden of identifying an accommodation is one of production. Reed v. LePage Bakeries, Inc., 244 F.3d 254, 258-59 (1st Cir. 2001) (citing Borkowski v. Valley Cent. Sch. Dist., 63 F.3d 131, 138 (2d Cir. 1995); Walton v. Mental Health Ass'n, 168 F.3d 661, 670 (3d Cir. 1999); Fjellestad v. Pizza Hut of Am., Inc., 188 F.3d 944, 950 (8th Cir. 1999); Benson v. Nw. Airlines, Inc., 62 F.3d 1108, 1112 (8th Cir. 1995); White v. York Int'l Corp., 45 F.3d 357, 361 (10th Cir. 1995)). In this approach, the "plaintiff's burden is not a heavy one." Reed, 244 F.3d at 258. The plaintiff must show a plausible and reasonable accommodation (e.g., where the costs on its face do not clearly exceed its benefits). If the plaintiff then meets its burden of showing that an accommodation is available, plausible and reasonable, the burden then shifts to the defendant.

An alternative approach has been adopted by the D.C. Circuit, and the Fifth, Sixth, and Seventh Circuits. *See, e.g.*, Barth v. Gelb, 2 F.3d 1180, 1186 (D.C. Cir. 1993) (Rehabilitation Act case finding that the burden remains with the plaintiff to prove his case "by a preponderance of the evidence"). These circuits place the burden on the plaintiff to prove by a preponderance of the evidence that the accommodation is reasonable. Hoskins v. Oakland County Sheriff's Dep't, 227 F.3d 719, 728 (6th Cir.

2000); Willis v. Conopco, Inc., 108 F.3d 282, 285-86 (11th Cir. 1997); Riel v. Elec. Data Sys. Corp., 99 F.3d 678, 682-83 (5th Cir. 1996); Monette v. Elec. Data Sys. Corp., 90 F.3d 1173, 1183, n.10, 1186 n.12 (6th Cir. 1996); Vande Zande v. Wis. Dep't of Admin., 44 F.3d 538, 542-43 (7th Cir. 1995). The plaintiff must make a facial showing of reasonableness (e.g., proportionality to costs). The defendant then must show undue burden with careful consideration that the costs involved are excessive. Vande Zande, 44 F.3d at 542.

But the burden-shifting paradigm does not go all the way in defining the relationship between reasonable accommodation and undue burden. As the First Circuit has stated in *Reed v. LePage Bakeries, Inc.*, some courts "are reluctant to examine the relationship between 'reasonable accommodation' and 'undue hardship' as one of shifting burdens." 244 F.3d 254, 258-59 (1st Cir. 2001). "The real issue is the quantum of proof needed to show reasonable accommodation vis-à-vis the quantum of proof needed to show undue hardship." *Id.* at 259.

In *Reed,* the First Circuit rejected the position of the EEOC that a plaintiff need only show that the accommodation would effectively enable her to perform essential job functions and that a defendant then must show that the accommodation would be too costly or difficult. *Id.* Stated differently, the "reasonable" element is not proven by the lack of undue hardship, but by effectiveness. The First Circuit required that a plaintiff demonstrate more to show that her requested accommodation is "reasonable," because Title I limits the plaintiff's accommodation request only to those within reason of difficulty or expense.

The majority view is that to prove "reasonable accommodation," a plaintiff needs to show that the accommodation would enable her to perform essential job functions, and that, facially, it is feasible for the employer to implement the accommodation in the circumstances. *See, e.g.,* Reed, 244 F.3d at 259. If a plaintiff succeeds in this showing, the defendant must show that the accommodation is not "as feasible as it appears but rather that there are further costs to be considered, certain devils in the details." *Id.* at 259-60 (noting that where the costs of an accommodation are obvious, plaintiff's burden and defendant's burden may be similar).

The burdens will differ when the costs of an accommodation are not evident on the face of things, but rather are better known to the employer. *Cf.* Barnett v. U.S. Airways, Inc., 228 F.3d 1105, 1113 (9th Cir. 2000) (finding employer's "superior knowledge" as to certain matters relevant to determining extent of parties' burdens). For example, an employee's proposal that her work area be modified might be facially reasonable, but the employer may still show that, given the particular limitations on its financial resources, or other hidden costs, such accommodation imposes an undue hardship. *Id.* (citing 42 U.S.C. § 12111(10)(B)). Given the inexactness of the burdens of proof for accommodation and hardship, counsel typically "errs on the side of offering proof beyond what their burdens require." Reed, 244 F.3d at 260.

B. *Disparate Treatment – Application Of McDonnell Douglas Corp. And Price Waterhouse*

Above, we have discussed the evidentiary burden-shifting scheme when a Title I plaintiff attempts to prove her case. Here, we discuss an additional evidentiary twist that must be considered in a limited number of ADA cases. For a related discussion, *see* the *Raytheon v. Hernandez* decision discussed *supra* § 8.1.D.5, in which the Supreme Court recognized the distinction between claims of discrimination based on disparate treatment and claims based on disparate impact.

Broadly speaking, under Title VII of the Civil Rights Act (prohibiting employment discrimination on the basis of race, color, religion, sex, or national origin), and ADA Title I, a plaintiff may proceed under one of two discrimination theories. First, a plaintiff may show that she was intentionally treated differently on the basis of a prohibited characteristic (for purposes of the ADA, disability, or for Title VII, race, color, religion, sex, or national origin). This is referred to as a "disparate treatment" claim. Or second, a plaintiff may argue that the effect of a facially non-discriminatory, or "neutral" rule, had a greater statistical impact on the member of the plaintiff's protected group. This is referred to as a "disparate impact" claim, and as will be discussed below, often is used in connection with class action lawsuits. Harold S. Lewis, Jr. & Elizabeth J. Norman, Employment Discrimination Law and Practice 115 (West Group 2001).

Proving intentional discrimination in a disparate treatment theory often is difficult; typically, there is no "smoking gun" document to show intent. To give structure to the plaintiff's burden of proof in this situation, courts have used a burden-shifting scheme set out in *McDonnell Douglas Corp. v. Green*, 411 U.S. 792 (1973).

Under the *McDonnell Douglas* analysis, the plaintiff must establish a prima facie case of discrimination. The burden then shifts to the defendant to present a legitimate, nondiscriminatory reason for the challenged employment action. The burden then shifts back to the plaintiff to demonstrate that the defendant's proffered reason is a pretext for discrimination. This *McDonnell Douglas* framework has been applied to disparate treatment ADA Title I cases. Hardy v. S. F. Phosphates Ltd. Co., 185 F.3d 1076, 1079 (10th Cir. 1999); Kiel v. Select Artificials, Inc., 169 F.3d 1131, 1135-36 (8th Cir. 1999); Skomsky v. Speedway Superamerica, LLC, 267 F.Supp.2d 995, 998 (D. Minn. 2003).

However, if the employer admits that disability played a prominent part in the decision, or the plaintiff has other direct evidence of discrimination based on disability, the *McDonnell Douglas* framework typically is not used. Morgan v. Hilti, Inc., 108 F.3d 1319, 1323 n.3 (10th

Cir. 1995) (citation omitted). Where an employer's reason for a non-hire or other adverse action is that the action was not based on disability per se, but rather, for example, on hiring a more qualified individual, the usual evidentiary approach for resolving the issue is through the ADA's "qualified individual" analysis, not the *McDonnell Douglas* framework.

This distinction is demonstrated in *Davidson v. America Online, Inc.*, 337 F.3d 1179 (10th Cir. 2003). In this case, America Online's (AOL) Call Center in the Philippines only was set up to handle non-voicemail communications. *Id.* at 1182. The admitted effect of this was that people with deafness were not considered for employment at AOL. *Id.* Davidson, who had unsuccessfully applied for a job with AOL, brought an ADA Title I claim.

AOL argued that the reason it did not hire Davidson was not because he was deaf, but rather because he was unable to perform the jobs available for hire, that is, voicemail positions. *Id.* at 1189. AOL therefore suggested that the *McDonnell Douglas* framework was appropriate, and that Davidson should have to counter AOL's proffered non-discriminatory reason. *Id.*

The court disagreed with AOL. In the court's view, defendant's "non-discriminatory" reason was linked to plaintiff's disability. *Id.* ("In other words, AOL's explanation for its action established that it relied on Davidson's disability when it refused to hire him."). The court viewed the defendant essentially as arguing that Davidson was not a "qualified individual" with a disability, and therefore the *McDonnell Douglas* framework was inappropriate and unnecessary. Davidson v. Am. Online, 337 F.3d at 1189.

Sometimes, in ADA Title I and Civil Rights Act Title VII cases, legitimate and illegitimate reasons may have motivated the employment action. These are referred to as "mixed motive" cases. The Supreme Court discussed the evidentiary burden used in these cases in the Title VII case of *Price Waterhouse v. Hopkins*, 490 U.S. 228, 269-70 (1989).

The *Price Waterhouse* Court found that the employer had an affirmative defense that it would have taken the same action regardless of race or gender. However, the Court was divided on the question whether the burden should shift to the defense. Desert Palace, Inc. v. Costa, 539 U.S. 90, 93-94 (2003) (citing the concurring opinions of Justices White and O'Connor in *Price Waterhouse*, 490 U.S. at 244, 261). The *Price Waterhouse* plurality would have shifted the burden to the defense if the plaintiff showed gender was a motivating factor, while Justice White would have shifted the burden only if gender were a substantial factor. *Id.* at 258 (plurality); *id.* at 259 (White, J., concurring). Justice O'Connor's concurring opinion provided a standard that was widely followed, finding that the burden should shift to the defense only if the plaintiff showed, by *direct evidence*, that the illegitimate consideration was a substantial factor in the employment action. *Id.* at 276 (O'Connor, J., concurring).

Congress, in the Civil Rights Act of 1991, Pub. L. No. 102-166, 105 Stat. 1071 (codified in scattered sections of 2 U.S.C.), disagreed with the Court's *Price Waterhouse* analysis and provided that Title VII would be violated if an illegitimate consideration was "a motivating factor for any employment practice, even though other factors also motivated the practice." 42 U.S.C. § 2000e-2(m) (2006). Congress went on to provide that, if the employer proves it would have taken the same action in the absence of the impermissible factor, that affirmative defense would limit the remedies available to declaratory and injunctive relief. However, under this approach, the employer would not avoid liability. *Id.* § 2000e-5(g)(2)(B). Relief would also include costs and attorneys' fees. *Id.*

The Civil Rights Act of 1991 only expressly applies to employment actions on the basis of race, color, religion, sex, or national origin. It is unclear that, as a strictly textual matter, the amendments embodied in the 1991 Act apply to employment claims for disability discrimination under the ADA. Courts have applied *Price Waterhouse*, and not the changes embodied in the 1991 Act, to ADEA cases. Lewis v. Young Men's Christian Ass'n, 208 F.3d 1303 (11th Cir. 2000); Miller v. Cigna Corp., 47 F.3d 586 (3d Cir. 1995). Nevertheless, in the ADA context, the vast majority of courts have applied the framework set forth in the 1991 Civil Rights Act – motivating, as opposed to substantial factor, and no liability affirmative defense for same action – and not *Price Waterhouse*. *See, e.g.,* Foster v. Arthur Anderson, LLP, 168 F.3d 1029, 1033-34 (7th Cir. 1999); Doane v. City of Omaha, 115 F.3d 624, 629 (9th Cir. 1997); Katz v. City Metal Co., 87 F.3d 26, 33 (1st Cir. 1996); Buchanan v. City of San Antonio, 85 F.3d 196, 200 (5th Cir. 1996); Pedigo v. P.A.M. Transp., Inc., 60 F.3d 1300, 1301-02 (8th Cir. 1995).

After 1991, the courts were divided as to whether a plaintiff's proof of an impermissible factor must be by *direct*, as opposed to circumstantial, evidence to shift the burden under the *Price Waterhouse* analysis. Desert Palace, Inc. v. Costa, 539 U.S. 90, 93-94 (2003); Mohr v. Dustrol, Inc., 306 F.3d 636, 640-41 (8th Cir. 2002); Fernandes v. Costa Bros. Masonry, Inc., 199 F.3d 572, 580 (1st Cir. 1999); Trotter v. Bd. of Tr. Univ. of Ala., 91 F.3d 1449, 1453-54 (11th Cir. 1996); Fuller v. Phipps, 67 F.3d 1137, 1142 (4th Cir. 1995).

In *Desert Palace, Inc. v. Costa*, the Supreme Court found that Congress did not intend to impose a heightened standard on plaintiffs and that circumstantial evidence is appropriate for civil rights cases. Therefore, it held that direct evidence of discrimination is not required to shift the burden of proof to the defendant in a mixed-motive discrimination case. 539 U.S. at 101-02. Rather, "a plaintiff need only present sufficient evidence for a reasonable jury to conclude, by a preponderance of the evidence, that 'race, color, religion, sex, or national origin was a motivating factor for any employment practice.'" *Id.* at 101 (quoting 42 U.S.C. §2000e-2(m)).

After *Desert Palace*, the *Price Waterhouse* and *McDonnell Douglas* burden-shifting analyses will be applicable in far fewer ADA and other Title VII cases. This is because circumstantial evidence that an employment action was based on disability will be sufficient to shift the burden of proof to the defense, and increasing the likelihood of surviving a summary judgment motion. *See* Dare v. Wal-Mart Stores, Inc., 267 F.Supp.2d 987, 990-993 (D. Minn. 2003) (challenging the false dichotomy established in *McDonnell Douglas* and applying the "same decision test" in a single-motive, rather than mixed-motive, case).

In a recent mixed motives case, *Serwatka v. Rockwell*, 591 F.3d 957, 962 (7th Cir. 2010), the court required the plaintiff to show that "the employer would not have fired him but for his . . . disability; [and that] proof of mixed motives will not suffice." Other circuits have disagreed about whether to adopt a mixed motive analysis. The Sixth Circuit has held that the mixed motive or "motivating factor" language from Title VII should not be used in ADA cases. Lewis v. Humboldt Acquisition Corp., Inc., 681 F.3d 312, 319 (6th Cir. 2012). The Fourth Circuit has ruled that if "disability played a motivating role in the employment decision, the plaintiff is entitled to relief." Baird ex rel. Baird v. Rose, 192 F.3d 462, 470 (4th Cir. 1999). *See also* Brown v. J. Kaz, Inc., 581 F.3d 175, 182 (3d Cir. 2009).

C.   *Disparate Impact – ADA Title I Class Actions*

At times, ADA Title I plaintiffs have attempted to proceed on a disparate impact class action theory. These plaintiffs have argued that a given employer's policy or practice (for example, a hiring or firing policy) is an adverse employment action on the employees or applicants with disabilities. By and large, the class action strategy has not been successful in ADA Title I cases. This is in contrast to access cases under Title II or Title III, where the class action procedure has been more of a viable tool. *See* Barden v. City of Sacramento, 292 F.3d 1073 (9th Cir. 2002) (Title II); Colo. Cross-Disability Coalition v. Taco Bell Corp., 184 F.R.D. 354 (D. Colo. 1999) (Title III).

To certify a class in federal court, the class representatives must show that the requirements of Federal Rule of Civil Procedure 23(a) are met. This includes a showing that (1) the class is so numerous that joinder of all members is impracticable; (2) there are questions of law or fact common to the class; (3) the claims or defenses of the representative parties are typical of the claims or defenses of the class, and (4) the representative parties will fairly and adequately protect the interest of the class. Fed. R. Civ. P. 23(a). The class representative also must show that the class should be certified pursuant to one of the three categories set forth in Fed. R. Civ. P. 23(b).

Because the ADA and its interpreting regulations require an individualized analysis of a plaintiff's disability, potential reasonable accommodations, and employer's defenses, courts have been hesitant to find that a class representatives' claims are typical of and common to the class. Lintemuth v. Saturn Corp., No. 1: 93-0211, 1994 WL 760811 (M.D. Tenn. Aug. 29, 1994); Chandler v. City of Dallas, 2 F.3d 1385, 1396 (5th Cir. 1993) (Rehabilitation Act); Davoll v. Webb, 160 F.R.D. 142, 143 (D. Colo 1995); David T. Wiley, If You Can't Fight 'Em, Join 'Em: Class Actions Under Title I of the Americans With Disabilities Act, 13 Lab. Law. 197 (1997).

An example of this is found in the case of *Lintemuth v. Saturn Corp.* Six employees with different disabilities sued an auto manufacturer, claiming that the manufacturer discriminated against them in violation of Title I by using placement procedures that did not reasonably accommodate their known medical conditions. 1994 WL 760811 at *3. In holding that the proposed class representatives could not establish the typicality needed for a class to be certified, the court reasoned:

> The variance in the named plaintiffs' personal characteristics, coupled with the individualized, case-by-case analysis required by the ADA, renders the proposed representatives in this action unable to establish the necessary elements of the claims of the class in the course of establishing their own. Furthermore, the highly personal nature of each representative's disability also subjects their claims to unique defenses under the ADA which are significant enough to destroy typicality.

Id. at *4.

However, some courts have held that ADA Title I class actions are appropriate vehicles to challenge employment policies. In *Hendricks-Robinson v. Excel Corp.*, 164 F.R.D. 667 (C.D. Ill. 1996), a group of employees challenged their employer's medical leave policy. The employees proposed a class of all employees "whom Excel perceives to have permanent medical restrictions and who were placed on medical layoff pursuant to Excel's medical layoff policy. . . ." *Id.* at 669. The court held that "we see no reason why a case which challenges a *policy* cannot proceed as a class action under the ADA." *Id.* at 670. Because plaintiffs were not seeking to support their claims by reference to their respective injuries and defenses, but merely sought to attack the policy, the court held that there was typicality. *Id.*; *see also* Wilson v. Pa. St. Police Dep't, No. CIV. A. 94-CV-6547, 1995 WL 422750 (E.D. Pa. July 17, 1995) (certifying a class of plaintiffs who challenged the Pennsylvania State Police Department's employment policy against applicants with poor eyesight as violative of the ADA).

Notes & Questions

1. In *Wal-Mart Stores, Inc. v. Dukes*, 131 S.Ct. 2541 (2011), the U.S. Supreme Court in a Title VII sex discrimination class action brought by Wal-Mart employees, held that

> Commonality requires the plaintiff to demonstrate that the class members 'have suffered the same injury,' . . . . This does not mean merely that they have all suffered a violation of the same provision of law. . . . Their claims must depend upon a common contention . . . . That common contention, moreover, must be of such a nature that it is capable of class-wide resolution – which means that determination of its truth or falsity will resolve an issue that is central to the validity of each one of the claims in one stroke." *Id.* at 2551.

How may *Dukes* impact the ability of attorneys to bring Title I class actions?

2. For an argument that the goals of Title I, including reducing structural barriers to employment, would be furthered by a robust interpretation of disparate impact and class action law in the disability context, *see* Michael A. Stein & Michael Waterstone, 56 Duke L.R. 861 (2006).

&

Chapter 9 TITLE I DEFENSES BASED ON QUALIFICATIONS STANDARDS

Congress acknowledged in the ADA that discrimination takes many forms, including paternalism and stereotyping. H.R. Rep. No. 101-485, pt. 2, at 74 (1990), reprinted in 1990 U.S.C.C.A.N. 303, 356. An insidious aspect of this type of discrimination is the assumption that people with disabilities are not competent to make informed and safe life choices in the employment context. The myth is apparent in employment given employers' assumption that many persons with disabilities are likely to be injured and thereby enhance exposure to tort liability. Peter Blanck & Glen Pransky, Workers with Disabilities, 14 Occupational Med. 581, 587 (1999). In the ADA, Congress addressed discrimination resulting from over-protective qualification rules and policies, as well as intentional discrimination, that relegated individuals with disabilities to lesser and inferior jobs and foreclosed their employment opportunities. H.R. Rep. No. 101-485, pt. 2, at 28-29 (1990), reprinted in 1990 U.S.C.C.A.N. 303, 310-11.

However, Title I permits certain employer defenses to a charge of discrimination based on qualification standards that are job-related and consistent with business necessity. 42 U.S.C. § 12113(a) (2006). One of those defenses is the requirement that an employee not pose a "direct threat" to others in the workplace. *Id.* § 12113(b). Direct threat is "a significant risk to the health or safety of others that cannot be eliminated by reasonable accommodation." *Id.* § 12111(3). As will be discussed below, although Title I does not define direct threat as a risk to self, the EEOC subsequently issued regulations that expanded the direct threat defense to include a "significant risk of substantial harm to the . . . individual" that cannot be addressed by accommodation. 29 C.F.R. § 1630.2(r) (2008).

Employer assessment of the direct threat to the employee historically served as a reason for the unwarranted exclusion – well-meaning or otherwise – of qualified individuals from work. The ADA tightens the reins on what an employer may consider on this point. Employers only may consider health or safety to the extent an individual's condition or behavior imperils health or safety in the workplace, or the individual fails to meet specific health or safety standards imposed by government authorities, such as Occupational Safety & Health Administration (OSHA) workplace requirements. Albertson's Inc. v. Kirkingburg, 527 U.S. 555, 557 (1999).

Under Title I, the direct threat defense does not arise as part of the plaintiff's showing that he is a "qualified individual." *See, e.g.,* 42 U.S.C. § 12111(8). In others words, health and safety factors are not a required aspect of the plaintiff's Title I showing that he is a qualified individual. Rather, the issue arises as part of a defense by the employer that the job applicant does not meet necessary qualification standards. *Id.* §§ 12112(b)(6), 12113(a).

Qualification standards are "personal and professional attributes including skill, experience, education, physical, medical, safety and other requirements" necessary for an individual to be eligible for the position. 29 C.F.R. § 1630.2(q); 42 U.S.C. § 12113(a). In general, health and safety considerations are a critical component of the Act's tiered analysis, but are not to be confused with essential job functions or qualifications, except in limited circumstances. There are instances where essential functions implicate issues of safety; for instance, a firefighter who could not "carry an unconscious adult out of a burning building," would not be qualified to perform the essential functions of the position and would be unsafe. 29 C.F.R. pt. 1630, app. § 1630.2(n) ("Essential Functions"). In such instances, the essential functions are not analyzed in terms of safety but, rather, the inability to perform job tasks.

Congress placed the evidentiary burden on the employer to demonstrate that such qualification standards are job-related and necessary to business functioning. 42 U.S.C. §§ 12112(b)(6), 12113(a); H.R. Rep. No. 101-485, pt. 3, at 42 (1990), reprinted in 1990 U.S.C.C.A.N. 445, 465 ("[A] facially neutral qualification standard, employment test or other selection criterion that has a discriminatory effect on persons with disabilities . . . would be discriminatory unless the employer can demonstrate that it is job related and required by business necessity."). With respect to business necessity and direct threat, the employer often will have superior information and knowledge about workplace requirements and operations.

§ 9.1 Direct Threat Defense To Others And To Self

The direct threat to others defense is a subset of the qualifications defense, specifically carved out by Congress to meet the health and safety aspects of the more general defense. 42 U.S.C. § 12113(a-b) (2006). The statute provides that " 'qualification standards' may include a requirement that an individual shall not pose a direct threat to the health or safety of other individuals in the workplace." *Id.* § 12113(b). The EEOC subsequently issued regulations that expanded the direct threat defense beyond the language of the statute to include a significant risk of harm to *the individual* or others that cannot be addressed by reasonable accommodation. 29 C.F.R. §§ 1630.2(r), 1630.15(b)(2) (2008). In *Chevron U.S.A. v. Echazabal*, 536 U.S. 73 (2002) , the Supreme Court considered the validity of these regulations.

CHEVRON U.S.A. INC. v. ECHAZABAL

Supreme Court of the United States, 2002
536 U.S. 73

* * *

Justice SOUTER delivered the opinion of the Court.

A regulation of the Equal Employment Opportunity Commission authorizes refusal to hire an individual because his performance on the job would endanger his own health, owing to a disability. The question in this case is whether the Americans with Disabilities Act of 1990 * * * permits the regulation.[1] We hold that it does.

I

Beginning in 1972, respondent Mario Echazabal worked for independent contractors at an oil refinery owned by petitioner Chevron U.S.A. Inc. Twice he applied for a job directly with Chevron, which offered to hire him if he could pass the company's physical examination. See 42 U.S.C. § 12112(d)(3) (1994 ed.). Each time, the exam showed liver abnormality or damage, the cause eventually being identified as Hepatitis C, which Chevron's doctors said would be aggravated by continued exposure to toxins at Chevron's refinery. In each instance, the company withdrew the offer, and the second time it asked the contractor employing Echazabal either to reassign him to a job without exposure to harmful chemicals or to remove him from the refinery altogether. The contractor laid him off in early 1996.

Echazabal filed suit, ultimately removed to federal court, claiming, among other things, that Chevron violated the Americans with Disabilities Act (ADA or ACT) in refusing to hire him, or even to let him continue working in the plant, because of a disability, his liver condition.[2]

---

[1] We do not consider the further issue passed upon by the Ninth Circuit, which held that the respondent is a " 'qualified individual' " who "can perform the essential functions of the employment position," 42 U.S.C. § 12111(8) (1994 ed.). 226 F.3d 1063, 1072 (9th Cir. 2000). That issue will only resurface if the Circuit concludes that the decision of respondent's employer to exclude him was not based on the sort of individualized medical enquiry required by the regulation, an issue on which the District Court granted summary judgment for petitioner and which we leave to the Ninth Circuit for initial appellate consideration if warranted.

[2] Chevron did not dispute for purposes of its summary-judgment motion that Echazabal is "disabled" under the ADA, and Echazabal did not argue that Chevron could have made a " 'reasonable accommodation.' " App. 184, n.6.

Chevron defended under a regulation of the Equal Employment Opportunity Commission (EEOC) permitting the defense that a worker's disability on the job would pose a "direct threat" to his health, see 29 C.F.R. § 1630.15(b)(2) (2001). Although two medical witnesses disputed Chevron's judgment that Echazabal's liver function was impaired and subject to further damage under the job conditions in the refinery, the District Court granted summary judgment for Chevron. It held that Echazabal raised no genuine issue of material fact as to whether the company acted reasonably in relying on its own doctors' medical advice, regardless of its accuracy.

On appeal, the Ninth Circuit asked for briefs on a threshold question not raised before, whether the EEOC's regulation recognizing a threat-to-self-defense, ibid., exceeded the scope of permissible rulemaking under the ADA. 226 F.3d 1063, 1066, n.3 (9th Cir. 2000). The Circuit held that it did and reversed the summary judgment. * * *

* * *

II

* * *

The first strike against the expression-exclusion rule here is right in the text that Echazabal quotes. Congress included the harm-to-others provision as an example of legitimate qualifications that are "job-related and consistent with business necessity." These are spacious defensive categories, which seem to give an agency (or in the absence of agency action, a court) a good deal of discretion in setting the limits of permissible qualification standards. That discretion is confirmed, if not magnified, by the provision that "qualification standards" falling within the limits of job relation and business necessity "may include" a veto on those who would directly threaten others in the workplace. Far from supporting Echazabal's position, the expansive phrasing of "may include" points directly away from the sort of exclusive specification he claims. * * *

* * *

Strike two in this case is the failure to identify any such established series, including both threats to others and threats to self, from which Congress appears to have made a deliberate choice to omit the latter item as a signal of the affirmative defense's scope. The closest Echazabal comes is the EEOC's rule interpreting the Rehabilitation Act of 1973, 87 Stat. 357, as amended, 29 U.S.C. § 701 et seq., a precursor of the ADA. That statute excepts from the definition of a protected "qualified individual with a handicap" anyone who would pose a "direct threat to the health or safety of other individuals," but, like the later ADA, the Rehabilitation Act says nothing about threats to self that particular employment might pose. 42 U.S.C. § 12113(b). The EEOC nonetheless extended the exception to cover threat-to-self employment, 29 C.F.R. § 1613.702(f) (1990), and Echazabal argues that Congress's adoption only of the threat-to-others exception in the ADA must have been a deliberate omission of the Rehabilitation Act regulation's tandem term of threat-to-self, with intent to exclude it.

But two reasons stand in the way of treating the omission as an unequivocal implication of congressional intent. The first is that the EEOC was not the only agency interpreting the Rehabilitation Act, with the consequence that its regulation did not establish a clear, standard pairing of threats to self and others. While the EEOC did amplify upon the text of the Rehabilitation Act exclusion by recognizing threats to self along with threats to others, three other agencies adopting regulations under the Rehabilitation Act did not. * * *

Even if we put aside this variety of administrative experience, however, and look no further than the EEOC's Rehabilitation Act regulation pairing self and others, the congressional choice to speak only of threats to others would still be equivocal. Consider what the ADA reference to threats to others might have meant on somewhat different facts. If the Rehabilitation Act had spoken only of "threats to health" and the EEOC regulation had read that to mean threats to self or others, a congressional choice to be more specific in the ADA by listing threats to others but not threats to self would have carried a message. The most probable reading would have been that Congress understood what a failure to specify could lead to and had made a choice to limit the possibilities. The statutory basis for any agency rulemaking under the ADA would have been different from its basis under the Rehabilitation Act and would have indicated a difference in the agency's rulemaking discretion. But these are not the circumstances here. Instead of making the ADA different from the Rehabilitation Act on the point at issue, Congress used identical language, knowing full well what the EEOC had made of that language under the earlier statute. Did Congress mean to imply that the agency had been wrong in reading the earlier language to allow it to recognize threats to self, or did Congress just assume that the agency was free to do under the ADA what it had already done under the earlier Act's identical language? There is no way to tell. Omitting the EEOC's reference to self-harm while using the very language that the EEOC had read as consistent with recognizing self-harm is equivocal at best. No negative inference is possible.

There is even a third strike against applying the expression-exclusion rule here. It is simply that there is no apparent stopping point to the argument that by specifying a threat-to-others defense Congress intended a negative implication about those whose safety could be considered. When Congress specified threats to others in the workplace, for example, could it possibly have meant that an employer could not defend a refusal to hire when a worker's disability would threaten others outside the workplace? If Typhoid Mary had come under the ADA, would a meat packer have been defenseless if Mary had sued after being turned away? See 42 U.S.C. § 12113(d). * * *

B

Since Congress has not spoken exhaustively on threats to a worker's own health, the agency regulation can claim adherence under the rule in *Chevron,* 467 U.S. at 843, 104 S.Ct. 2778, so long as it makes sense of the statutory defense for qualification standards that are "job-related and consistent with business necessity." 42 U.S.C. § 12113(a). Chevron's reasons for calling the regulation reasonable are unsurprising: moral concerns aside, it wishes to avoid time lost to sickness, excessive turnover from medical retirement or death, litigation under state tort law, and the risk of violating the national Occupational Safety and Health Act of 1970, 84 Stat. 1590, as amended, 29 U.S.C. § 651 et seq. Although Echazabal claims that none of these reasons is legitimate, focusing on the concern with OSHA will be enough to show that the regulation is entitled to survive.

Echazabal points out that there is no known instance of OSHA enforcement, or even threatened enforcement, against an employer who relied on the ADA to hire a worker willing to accept a risk to himself from his disability on the job. In Echazabal's mind, this shows that invoking OSHA policy and possible OSHA liability is just a red herring to excuse covert discrimination. But there is another side to this. The text of OSHA itself says its point is "to assure so far as possible every working man and woman in the Nation safe and healthful working conditions," § 651(b), and Congress specifically obligated an employer to "furnish to each of his employees employment and a place of employment which are free from recognized hazards that are causing or are likely to cause death or serious physical harm to his employees," § 654(a)(1). Although there may be an open question whether an employer would actually be liable under OSHA for hiring an individual who knowingly consented to the particular dangers the job would pose to him, see Brief for United States et al. as Amici Curiae 19, n.7, there is no denying that the employer would be asking for trouble: his decision to hire would put Congress's policy in the ADA, a disabled individual's right to operate on equal terms within the workplace, at loggerheads with the competing policy of OSHA, to ensure the safety of "each" and "every" worker. Courts would, of course, resolve the tension if there were no agency action, but the EEOC's resolution exemplifies the substantive choices that agencies are expected to make when Congress leaves the intersection of competing objectives both imprecisely marked but subject to the administrative leeway found in 42 U.S.C. § 12113(a).

Nor can the EEOC's resolution be fairly called unreasonable as allowing the kind of workplace paternalism the ADA was meant to outlaw. It is true that Congress had paternalism in its sights when it passed the ADA, see § 12101(a)(5) (recognizing "overprotective rules and policies" as a form of discrimination). But the EEOC has taken this to mean that Congress was not aiming at an employer's refusal to place disabled workers at a specifically demonstrated risk, but was trying to get at refusals to give an even break to classes of disabled people, while claiming to act for their own good in reliance on untested and pretextual stereotypes. Its regulation disallows just this sort of sham protection, through demands for a particularized enquiry into the harms the employee would probably face. The direct threat defense must be "based on a reasonable medical judgment that relies on the most current medical knowledge and/or the best available objective evidence," and upon an expressly "individualized assessment of the individual's present ability to safely perform the essential functions of the job," reached after considering, among other things, the imminence of the risk and the severity of the harm portended. 29 C.F.R. § 1630.2(r) (2001). The EEOC was certainly acting within the reasonable zone when it saw a difference between rejecting workplace paternalism and ignoring specific and documented risks to the employee himself, even if the employee would take his chances for the sake of getting a job. * * *

Finally, our conclusions that some regulation is permissible and this one is reasonable are not open to Echazabal's objection that they reduce the direct threat provision to "surplusage." * * * The mere fact that a threat-to-self defense reasonably falls within the general "job related" and "business necessity" standard does not mean that Congress accomplished nothing with its explicit provision for a defense based on threats to others. The provision made a conclusion clear that might otherwise have been fought over in litigation or administrative rulemaking. It did not lack a job to do merely because the EEOC might have adopted the same rule later in applying the general defense provisions, nor was its job any less responsible simply because the agency was left with the option to go a step further. A provision can be useful even without congressional attention being indispensable.

Accordingly, we reverse the judgment of the Court of Appeals and remand the case for proceedings consistent with this opinion.

It is so ordered.

Notes & Questions

1. What limits, if any, do Title I's defense provisions place on EEOC rulemaking? Consider 42 U.S.C. §§ 12113(b) and 12111(3).

2. Although the *Echazabal* Court acknowledged that it is not clear whether an employer would be liable under OSHA for hiring an individual with a disability who consented to the particular dangers of a job, it reasoned that:

> there is no denying that the employer would be asking for trouble: his decision to hire would put Congress's policy in the ADA, a disabled individual's right to operate on equal terms within the workplace, at loggerheads with the competing policy of OSHA, to ensure the safety of "each" and "every" worker.

Echazabal, 536 U.S. at 85; *see* 29 U.S.C. §§ 651(b), 654(a)(1) (2006).

3. In *Chao v. Conocophillips Co.* a federal district court considered whether the non-disclosure of medical records requirements in the ADA foreclose access to employee medical records by OSHA. No. Civ. A. 03-MC-0136, 2003 WL 22794705 (E.D. Pa. Nov. 5, 2003). The court reasoned that maintaining records that assure compliance with the OSH Act is job-related and consistent with business necessity, *id.* at *3, and that although "the ADA does not expressly authorize other federal agencies to view [medical] records," the court held that the ADA "does not foreclose such access either, particularly where . . . the OSH Act authorizes it." *Id.*

4. Is the EEOC's direct threat-to-self guidance a reasonable balance between OSHA's objectives of workplace safety and the ADA's rejection of employer paternalism? Consider Orr v. Wal-Mart Stores, Inc., 297 F.3d 720 (8th Cir. 2002). *Orr* held that a Wal-Mart pharmacist who was a diabetic did not have an actual disability that presently and substantially limited a major life activity, and therefore, was not an individual with a disability under the ADA. *Id.* at 725. The Eighth Circuit went on to note in dicta that, had the plaintiff established a prima facie case of actual disability under Title I, Wal-Mart could have raised the threat-to-self defense that working in a single-pharmacist pharmacy, which did not provide for uninterrupted meal breaks, posed a direct threat to plaintiff's health and that Wal-Mart was justified in not continuing his employment. *Id.* at 725 n.5 (citing Echazabal, 536 U.S. 73).

5. How may an employer's threat-to-self defense be overcome by a plaintiff's showing of relevant technological or medical advances? *See* Kapche v. City of San Antonio, 304 F.3d 493, 495 (5th Cir. 2002) (remanding for a "determination whether today there exists new or improved technology . . . that could now permit insulin-dependent diabetic drivers in general, and Kapche in particular, to operate a vehicle safely").

6. In *Taylor v. Rice*, a federal district court held that under § 501 of the Rehabilitation Act, using the ADA's Title I employment discrimination standards, the federal government could not succeed with its direct threat defense without performing an individualized assessment of the individual's ability to perform the job's essential functions. No. 05-5257, 2006 WL 1736199 (D.C. Cir. June 27, 2006) (citing *Chevron U.S.A. Inc. v. Echazabal*, 536 U.S. 73, 86 (2002)). The plaintiff, who was HIV-positive, was offered a job as a Foreign Service Agent, conditioned on successfully passing a medical exam. After the plaintiff's positive status was revealed, the job offer was revoked on the basis that he was not qualified for the position, as he would not be able to potentially serve at a broad enough scope of overseas posts because of the lack of available medical services. The court found that the defendant had not provided evidence sufficient to conclude that the threat to self could not be

overcome with a reasonable accommodation, one not causing an undue burden to the government.

7. In *Wurzel v. Whirlpool Corp.*, No. 10-3629, 2012 WL 1449683 (6th Cir. Apr. 27, 2012), the Sixth Circuit held that an employer did not need to wait for a serious injury to occur to determine that an employee posed a direct threat, where the employer based its determination on an individualized assessment of objective medical evidence.

8. For additional post-*Echazabal* cases addressing the threat-to-self defense, *see* Collins v. Raytheon Aircraft Co., No. 01-1415-JTM, 2003 WL 192553 (D. Kan. Jan. 16, 2003); *Parks v. Potter*, No. 01A12128, EEOC DOC 1A12128, 2002 WL 31232213, at *1 (EEOC Sept. 27, 2002).

൧

ECHAZABAL v. CHEVRON U.S.A., INC.

United States Court of Appeals, Ninth Circuit, 2003
336 F.3d 1023

* * *

Opinion by Judge TASHIMA; Dissent by Judge TROTT.

OPINION

TASHIMA, Circuit Judge:

* * *

In light of *Echazabal*, [536 U.S. 73 (2002),] the only * * * issue on remand is whether Chevron has met the requirements for assertion of the direct threat defense. * * *

* * *

ANALYSIS

* * *

Before excluding an individual from employment as a direct threat, an employer must demonstrate that it has made an "individualized assessment" of the employee's ability to perform the essential functions of the job, "based on a reasonable medical judgment that relies on the most current medical knowledge and/or on the best available objective evidence." 29 C.F.R. § 1630.2(r). The factors to be considered include: "(1) The duration of the risk; (2) The nature and severity of the potential harm; (3) The likelihood that the potential harm will occur; and (4) The imminence of the potential harm."[2] Id. The Supreme Court emphasized

---

[2] These factors were first articulated by the Supreme Court in School Board of Nassau County v. Arline, 480 U.S. 273, 288, 107 S.Ct. 1123, 94 L.Ed.2d 307 (1987), and are commonly referred to as the "Arline factors."

the requirement of a "particularized enquiry into the harms the employee would probably face." *Echazabal*, 122 S.Ct. at 2053.

A. The "individualized assessment" requirement

Chevron defends its assessment disqualifying Echazabal from employment with three arguments: (1) It satisfied the individualized assessment requirement by relying on the "facially proper" opinions of "competent physicians." (2) There were no genuine issues of material fact with regard to the four *Arline* factors. (3) The opinions of Echazabal's medical experts cannot be considered in evaluating its employment decision because they were made "long after the fact."

1. The standard for evaluating medical judgments

Chevron argues that its reliance on the advice of its own doctors, and allegedly upon that of Echazabal's doctors, constitutes a "facially reasonable" and thus a legally sufficient "individualized assessment" of Echazabal. This is an erroneous interpretation of the governing standard.[3] The regulation presents a much more specific matrix against which to measure the reasonableness of the employer's action * * *

In *Bragdon v. Abbott,* 524 U.S. 624, 118 S.Ct. 2196, 141 L.Ed.2d 540 (1998), the Supreme Court considered a direct threat defense presented by a dentist concerned about treating an HIV-infected patient. The Court stated that the health care provider had a duty to assess the risk based on "the objective, scientific information available to him and others in his profession." Id. at 649, 118 S.Ct. 2196. A subjective belief in the existence of a risk, even one made in good faith, will not shield the decisionmaker from liability. Id. This Circuit has held that an employer must gather "substantial information" about an employee's work history and medical status. *Nunes,* 164 F.3d at 1248. The decision must be based upon "particularized facts using the best available objective evidence as required by the regulations." *Lowe v. Ala. Power Co.,* 244 F.3d 1305, 1309 (11th Cir. 2001); cf. *McGregor v. Nat'l R.R. Passenger Corp.,* 187 F.3d 1113, 1116 (9th Cir. 1999) (holding that policies requiring employees to be "100% healed" before returning to work violate the ADA because they preclude individualized assessment of whether employee can perform the essential functions of the job with or without accommodation).

Echazabal has raised a material issue of fact as to whether Chevron's decision was "based on a reasonable medical judgment that

---

[3]   Chevron's argument that it did not rely upon stereotypes in assessing Echazabal's condition is besides the point. While the ADA was passed, in part, to counter stereotypical assumptions about the disabled that result in discrimination, 42 U.S.C. § 12101(a)(7), the mere fact that an employer avoids stereotypes does not satisfy its affirmative obligation to make an assessment based on "the most current medical knowledge and/or on the best available objective evidence."

relies on the most current medical knowledge and/or the best available objective evidence." 29 C.F.R. § 1630.2(r). As part of the physical examinations ordered by Chevron, Dr. Baily, and later Dr. McGill, administered and relied upon tests that measure the levels of three enzymes in the bloodstream. Based on results demonstrating abnormally high levels of certain enzymes, Drs. Baily and McGill concluded that Echazabal's liver was not functioning properly, and recommended that Echazabal not be exposed to chemicals that could be toxic to his liver. * * * Neither Dr. Baily nor Dr. McGill has any special training in liver disease. Baily's area of medical expertise is in preventive medicine, while McGill is a generalist, with no board certification in any specialty. In contrast, Echazabal's experts, Dr. Fedoruk and Dr. Gitnick, are specialists in toxicology and liver disease. * * * Their opinions demonstrate that enzyme tests do not produce information regarding liver function. Rather, enzyme tests reflect only that an infection is ongoing. According to Fedoruk and Gitnick, the only tests that do measure liver function – blood albumin levels and prothrombin time – revealed that Echazabal's liver was functioning properly. Far from showing "cutting edge research," as Chevron argues, these opinions offered the unequivocal assessment that Echazabal could work at the refinery without facing a substantial risk of harm, beyond that faced by other workers. The required assessment could not be based upon "common sense," as Chevron argues, but rather only after – at a minimum – a consultation with a medical professional who had made an "objective, scientific" judgment. *Bragdon*, 524 U.S. at 629, 118 S.Ct. 2196.

* * * Both Dr. Gitnick and Dr. Fedoruk stated that "there is no medical or scientific evidence" supporting a finding that Echazabal's chemical exposures from working as a plant helper or in the coker unit would present an appreciable or clinically significant risk. Dr. Fedoruk indicated that for some of the chemicals identified as potentially risky for Echazabal, an individual would receive a higher dosage from a daily multivitamin tablet than Echazabal would receive from working in the refinery. Based on the opinions of Drs. Fedoruk and Gitnick, a reasonable jury could conclude that Chevron failed to rely upon a "reasonable medical judgment that relies on the most current medical knowledge and/or on the best available objective evidence."

In addition, the record does not support the district court's conclusion that the medical opinion letters from Echazabal's doctors evaluating his specific position all concurred that the job posed a "serious, immediate risk to him." On April 5, 1993, Dr. Ha wrote: "In my opinion the patient is now capable of carrying on with the work that he has applied for and there is no restriction on his activity at work as outlined by the working condition sheet GO 308 that was sent to me."[6] Dr. Ha

---

[6] The GO-308 is Chevron's job summary for the coke handler and coke plant helper positions. It identifies airborne contaminants and

stated that Echazabal's prognosis "should be very good." Dr. Ha's opinion, based on her knowledge of Echazabal's potential work environment, does not support the view that she concurred in Chevron's assessment.[7] On November 10, 1993, and July 20, 1994, Dr. Suchov wrote two letters indicating that there was "no limitation" on Echazabal's ability to work and that he could return to his "usual duties." Although the district court dismissed these letters because they did not address Echazabal's specific job duties, Echazabal's declaration states that he informed all of his doctors of the type of work that he performed. These letters, together with Echazabal's own declaration, raise a material issue of fact as to the objective reasonableness of Chevron's opinion.

The dissent describes as "clincher" the communications between Dr. McGill and Dr. Weingarten, one of Echazabal's treating physicians, in which Dr. Weingarten recommended against exposure to hepatotoxic hydrocarbons. The sum total of the recommendation was as follows:

> In your letter, it is mentioned that Mr. Echazabal has applied for return of his job and it mentioned that "this may entail exposure to hepatotoxic hydrocarbons." This, of course, is recommended not to be the case.

This general statement, which followed a statement that Echazabal was in good health and showed no sign of liver failure, is insufficient to carry Chevron's burden of establishing that it relied on the "most current medical knowledge and/or the best available objective evidence" and that it considered the likelihood of harm, its possible severity, and imminence. Notably missing from this statement is any indication that Dr. Weingarten was asked to consider the specific chemical exposures, to indicate the levels at which they would become dangerous or the likelihood that they would injure Echazabal, or even whether the risk to Echazabal was any greater than that for a healthy individual. (Indeed, it is difficult to imagine that any responsible doctor would recommend exposure of even his healthiest patient to an unspecified amount of hepatotoxic chemicals.) The district court notably found that "Dr. Weingarten was not informed by Dr. McGill about the specific chemicals

---

chemicals in the work environment, including "hydrocarbon liquids and vapors, acid, caustic, refinery waste water and sludge, petroleum solvents, oils, greases [and] chlorine bleach."

[7] The district court incorrectly states that this letter did not relate to the 1995 job offer and that there was no record evidence that the letter was seen by Chevron's doctors or Irwin's expert, Dr. Tang. The job that Echazabal applied for in 1995 was a "plant helper" position at the coker unit described in GO 308, which was reviewed by Dr. Ha. In addition, Dr. Tang specifically references Dr. Ha's letter in his deposition when describing the contents of Echazabal's medical file. Dr. Ha's letter was directed to Chevron and was part of Echazabal's record.

to which plaintiff would be exposed, or the levels of concentration of those chemicals."

Chevron was required to do more than consider generalized statements of potential harm. Before refusing to hire Echazabal, Chevron was required, under the terms of 29 C.F.R. § 1630.2(r), to consider the severity, imminence, and potential likelihood of harm. Based on consideration of these factors, Chevron had the burden of demonstrating at least a "significant risk of substantial harm" to Echazabal. Id. The EEOC's Interpretive Guidance for this section explains that where the employer invoking the direct threat defense relies on threats to the employee, the employer must determine that there is a "high probability of substantial harm" to the individual. 29 C.F.R. pt. 1630 App. (EEOC Interpretive Guidance on Title I of the ADA) ("*Interpretive Guidance*"). Echazabal has raised a material question of fact as to whether Chevron made an adequate analysis. Dr. Weingarten's general statement, unrelated to the demands and conditions of the particular position or the likelihood, imminence, or potential severity of harm (or even whether Echazabal was at greater risk than a healthy individual), would not preclude a reasonable juror from concluding that Chevron failed to make the required assessment.

2. Evaluation of the *Arline* factors

Had Chevron conducted the individualized assessment required by law, it would have considered in detail the four *Arline* factors as they applied to Echazabal's condition. Chevron argues that there are no genuine issues of material fact with regard to the four *Arline* factors to be considered in assessing whether Echazabal's condition posed a "direct threat." While Echazabal concedes that the first *Arline* factor − the duration of his condition − is not disputed, he has raised material issues of fact about the three remaining factors.

First, Echazabal has raised a material issue of fact as to whether Chevron properly assessed the nature of the potential harm. The record indicates that the Chevron doctors were unfamiliar with the specific risks of Echazabal's position. Dr. Baily stated in his deposition that he did not know the types or concentrations of toxin, liquid, or vapor exposures Echazabal would face in the coker unit, that he made no attempt to ascertain this information and did not contact either the Industrial Hygiene Department or an outside specialist to determine whether Echazabal could perform the plant helper job. He indicated that solvents are only liver toxic "in sufficient quantities," but he made a blanket recommendation that all exposure be avoided. He made only a general recommendation that Echazabal not be exposed to hepatotoxins, unrelated to any specific position, assuming that it was management's responsibility to determine Echazabal's fitness for a particular job, and that he was not charged with considering specific exposure levels or chemicals. In fact, Dr. Baily anticipated that management would contact a specialist. He stated that the limitations "were not specifically based on any . . . individual work place exposure. The limitations were placed in general fashion to give guidance to management so that they would then be able to work with the specialist in determining which jobs might be appropriate for that applicant or employee."

Similarly, Dr. McGill testified in his deposition that, at the time he assessed Echazabal, he did not know the levels of hydrocarbons to which a plant helper would be exposed, was not aware if any regulatory levels would be exceeded, and that he did not attempt to contact the Industrial Hygiene Department to determine whether the industrial setting in the coker unit would be harmful to Echazabal. * * * Although he contacted Industrial Hygiene with regard to other employees, Dr. McGill did not do so in Echazabal's case because he assumed that it "had been thoroughly worked over in the 1992 phase [a]nd [he] was assuming that it had been investigated."[9]

Moreover, neither of the Chevron doctors had expertise in this area. Dr. Baily stated that he was not a liver specialist, that his experience with patients with chronic liver diseases was "very limited," that he was "not familiar with the specific biochemistry of liver abnormalities," that he had not spoken with a liver specialist about Echazabal's case, and that he was not aware of specific evidence that hepatotoxins pose a risk to individuals with hepatitis. Dr. Baily had no knowledge of whether Chevron ever contacted a specialist about the position. Similarly, Dr. McGill had not treated any patients in the prior 15 years for chronic liver disease, did not consult any treatises on the issue, did not research the likelihood of liver failure due to exposure to liver toxins, and did not consult a specialist.

According to Dr. Fedoruk, who did review Chevron's records, the level of toxins present at the coker unit placed Echazabal at no greater risk of injury than other workers. He also stated that there was no reliable scientific or medical evidence to suggest that the other exposures would lead to hepatoxicity and most of the potential exposures identified by Chevron were insignificant. Dr. Gitnick opined that Echazabal was "at

---

[9]   Thus, the dissent is incorrect in suggesting that the Chevron doctors based their determination on considerations of the specific risks of the position for which Echazabal applied. It states that Drs. Baily and McGill were "personally familiar with the conditions and demands of the work at issue," and that Dr. McGill "determined that the chemicals and solvents to which Mr. Echazabal would be exposed at the refinery would further damage his reduced liver capacity and seriously endanger his health and his life." In fact, neither doctor considered the risks of the specific position. As we have shown in the text above, Dr. Baily assumed that this would be done by management in conjunction with a specialist and Dr. McGill assumed that it had already been done.

no greater risk of injuring himself and specifically his liver than any other employee." He stated that the contrary opinions of Chevron's doctors were simply wrong and unsupported by medical evidence.

Second, the declarations of Fedoruk and Gitnick suggest that, at the time of Chevron's evaluation, there was little indication that Echazabal faced potential harm that was (a) likely, or (b) imminent. For example, Dr. Gitnick stated that "I can say to a reasonable degree of medical certainty that Mr. Echazabal is in no greater risk of injuring himself and specifically his liver by working in the refinery than other employee [sic]. His liver is functioning properly and there is no evidence of liver failure." Dr. Fedoruk also indicated that his tests had remained stable over years of work at the refinery. These statements were not, as Chevron implies, merely differences of medical opinion. In several instances, Fedoruk and Gitnick declared that Chevron doctors were simply wrong in their assessment of Echazabal's condition and that their analysis is inconsistent with the literature on liver function. The Chevron doctors, unlike Fedoruk and Gitnick, were not experts in this field.

Finally, this Circuit has cautioned that individualized risk assessment also requires consideration of relevant information about an employee's past work history. See *Nunes,* 164 F.3d at 1248; *Mantolete v. Bolger,* 767 F.2d 1416, 1423 (9th Cir. 1985) (holding that, in assessing elevated risk to an employee under the Rehabilitation Act, the employer must "gather [and assess] all relevant information regarding the applicant's work history and medical history"); see also *Anderson v. Little League Baseball, Inc.,* 794 F.Supp. 342, 345 (D. Ariz. 1992) (giving "great weight" to fact of disabled plaintiff's three years of service without incident in rejecting employer's direct threat defense). Chevron gave no weight to the fact that Echazabal had worked at the El Segundo refinery, without incident or injury, for over 20 years. A reasonable jury could find that this injury-free work history provided evidence that Echazabal would not pose a direct threat to himself as a coker unit employee.[10]

3. Consideration of Echazabal's medical experts' opinions

Chevron argues that the opinions offered by Echazabal's experts, Drs. Fedoruk and Gitnick, should not be considered because they were offered after the employment decision to exclude Echazabal from the refinery. Expert evidence of this nature, however, elucidates the very issue the court must assess – whether the opinion that a direct threat existed was *objectively* reasonable. See *Bragdon,* 524 U.S. at 649, 118

---

[10]   Chevron and the dissent emphasize the risk to Echazabal during an explosion or other emergency. * * * [T]he *Interpretive Guidance* indicates that "generalized fears about risks to individuals with disabilities in the event of an evacuation or other emergency [cannot] be used by an employer to disqualify an individual with a disability." 29 C.F.R. pt. 1630 App.

S.Ct. 2196; *Nunes,* 164 F.3d at 1248 (analysis of direct threat "requires the employer to gather 'substantial information' about the employee's work history and medical status, and disallows reliance on subjective evaluations by the employer"). The two expert opinions were directed in significant part to the state of medical knowledge – the best available objective evidence – at the time of Chevron's employment action. At the very least, they were highly relevant to that question. The subjective belief of Chevron's doctors is not relevant. Id.

Chevron also argues that to consult the Fedoruk and Gitnick opinions would be contrary to *Cook v. United States Dep't of Labor,* 688 F.2d 669 (9th Cir. 1982). *Cook* addressed a claim under the Comprehensive Employment and Training Act of 1973, and preceded *Bragdon,* as well as the 1990 enactment of the ADA and the 1991 issuance of the EEOC regulation. See Equal Employment Opportunity for Individuals With Disabilities, 56 Fed. Reg. 35734 (1991) (codified at 29 C.F.R. pt. 1630) * * * Moreover, *Cook* did not involve the application of a regulatory requirement that the employer's assessment be "based on a reasonable medical judgment that relies on the most current medical knowledge." Thus, because of these differing circumstances, *Cook* is unhelpful, much less controlling, in determining whether an employer has complied with the EEOC's ADA regulations requiring an individualized assessment based on the *Arline* factors and "the most current medical knowledge and/or the best available objective evidence." As the Supreme Court emphasized, the requirement of an individualized assessment in 29 C.F.R. § 1630.2(r) serves an important role in protecting against the risk of paternalism the ADA was enacted to discourage. *See Echazabal,* 122 S.Ct. at 2052-53.

Finally, we note that there is no medical evidence in the record to support Chevron's assertion that the opinions of Drs. Fedoruk and Gitnick were not "available" to Chevron when it made its assessment. Neither is there a showing that the body of medical knowledge on which those opinions were based was not available at the time, i.e., was beyond the then "most current medical knowledge." Given this medical knowledge, there is an issue of material fact whether the medical judgments which formed the basis of Chevron's assessment were based on "the most current medical knowledge and/or the best available objective evidence," as required by the EEOC's regulation. 29 C.F.R. § 1630.2(r). * * *

At the heart of Chevron's arguments lies an unfounded fear that a proper application of the "individualized assessment" standard requires employer awareness of cutting-edge medical research not generally known to or accepted within the medical community. This is not the case. Chevron asserts that by relying primarily upon the advice of a generalist and an expert in preventive medicine in order to come to a conclusion about Echazabal's *liver* problem, it met the statute's requirements. Before terminating an individual's livelihood, the ADA requires more.

The dissent contends that Chevron did enough. The dissent's quibble, however, is less with our opinion and more with the requirements of the ADA. The dissent makes little mention of the rigorous requirements of § 1630.2(r) and the employer's burden of proving that it complied with those requirements before it can rely on the direct threat defense. Rather, it states vaguely that Chevron's decision was made "after appropriately and thoroughly considering all relevant factors," that "the process [was not] defective or unreasonable," that Chevron did not have to seek an outside expert in liver disease so long as its decision was "objectively reasonable under the circumstances," and it dismisses the Fedoruk and Gitnick opinions as irrelevant "to the bona fides and quality of Chevron's decision." None of these statements, however, expresses the governing standard for reviewing Chevron's decision.

Were we reviewing an administrative agency's decision under the substantial evidence standard of review and limited to the administrative record made before the agency, we might agree that the decision was not an abuse of discretion. That, however, is not our task on this appeal. Rather, without weighing the evidence at this summary judgment stage, we must decide only whether Echazabal has raised a material question of fact as to whether Chevron has met its burden under § 1630.2(r). * * * See *Suzuki Motor Corp. v. Consumers Union of United States, Inc.,* 330 F.3d 1110, 2003 WL 21137731, at *18 (9th Cir. 2003) ("it is not our role, at this stage, to take sides in this way"). He has succeeded in doing so.

B. Accommodation and the Interactive Process

Finally, Echazabal contends that Chevron failed adequately to address its duty to accommodate Echazabal and to initiate an interactive process prior to terminating his position. Echazabal, however, did not raise this issue in the district court in opposition to Chevron's motion for summary judgment, and we decline to consider it here. See *Bolker v. Comm'r,* 760 F.2d 1039, 1042 (9th Cir. 1985) (stating that, subject to limited exceptions, "we will not consider an issue raised for the first time on appeal"). Moreover, it is unnecessary to address this issue in the absence of an opportunity for the district court to address it, given that the grant of summary judgment must be reversed.

CONCLUSION

For the foregoing reasons, we conclude that disputed issues of material fact remain with respect to Chevron's obligations under the EEOC's direct threat regulation. We therefore reverse the district court's summary judgment in favor of Chevron and remand for further proceedings consistent with this opinion and the Supreme Court's opinion in *Echazabal.* * * *

REVERSED and REMANDED.

TROTT, Circuit Judge, dissenting:

In making its decision not to hire Mr. Echazabal, Chevron relied on the recommendation of his own treating physician who agreed with Chevron's examining doctors that the job in question would jeopardize the applicant's health. Mr. Echazabal now attacks not only the opinion of Chevron's doctors, but also the medical opinion of the doctor he chose to treat him. His "ammunition?" Two competing academic opinions never communicated to Chevron in connection with its hiring decision and not produced until the filing of his lawsuit. On this record, I conclude that this past-posted evidence cannot create a genuine issue of material fact as to the equity of Chevron's good faith decision. At best, this lawsuit is a misguided attempt by plaintiff's lawyers belatedly to put Chevron's *and his own* doctors' opinions on trial, an adventure which is not germane on this set of facts to whether Chevron's decision when it was made comported with what the law required. As such, this case stands for the proposition that securing the opinion of a health-compromised job applicant's own treating doctor is not enough to protect an employer from costly litigation, litigation that comes complete with a prayer for punitive damages.

This case is important in the scheme of things, however, not so much because of its mistaken outcome, but for the bodeful implications it has for those to whom this law applies. My colleagues' opinion dismissing the opinions of the doctors upon whom Chevron relied will have a significant pernicious impact on all employers in this Circuit who are doing their best in good faith to comply with the law. Moreover, it will encourage lawyers to choose lawsuits for their clients rather than employment. * * *

* * *

Notes & Questions

1. How accurate do you suppose Judge Tashima was in characterizing Chevron's central argument as "an unfounded fear" that the individualized assessment standard will require employers to be fully-informed on "cutting-edge medical research not generally known to or accepted within the medical community?"

2. Mr. Echazabal passed away early in 2004. His case was settled soon thereafter.

3. In *EEOC v. E. I. DuPont de Nemours & Co.*, No. 03-1605, 2004 WL 2347570, at *1 (E.D. La. Oct. 15, 2004), DuPont argued that it was justified in requiring a lab employee (Laura Barrios) with physical disabilities to undergo a highly physical functional capacity examination, in part, to determine if she posed a direct threat to herself and others by virtue of an alleged inability to evacuate the chemical plant independently. DuPont further argued that Barrios, an eighteen-year veteran of the company, was not qualified, claiming that evacuation was

an essential function of all jobs at the plant. *Id.* The jury returned a $1.29 million verdict in favor of Barrios, one million of which was in punitive damages. Press Release, Equal Emp. Opportunity Comm'n, EEOC Obtains $1.29 Million Jury Verdict Against DuPont for Disability Discrimination (Oct. 25, 2004), http://www.eeoc.gov/press/10-25-04.html.

4. For a case analyzing the threat-to-self defense under state law involving a plaintiff with Gender Identity Disorder (GID), and the question whether an otherwise reasonable accommodation in a particular setting endangers the plaintiff and co-residents and thus, becomes unreasonable, *see* Plumo ex rel. Doe v. Bell, 754 N.Y.S.2d 846 (N.Y. Sup. Ct. 2003).

5. Other courts have not taken as stringent an approach as to what quality of expert testimony will be sufficient for an employer to meet his burden by showing that an employee is a direct threat to himself or others in the workplace (or, correspondingly, for an employee to show that he can perform the essential functions of a job with or without reasonable accommodation). As pointed out in dissent in *Echazabal*, the Ninth Circuit's majority opinion on remand could penalize an employer who has made a good faith attempt (by utilizing the opinion of its own trained professionals) to comply with the law. 336 F.3d at 1035-38 (Trott J., dissenting). The dissent argues that the Ninth Circuit's rule effectively requires an employer to second-guess its own doctors, and be responsible for making the "correct" decision in light of conflicting medical opinions. To safeguard against these concerns, other courts have required less of an employer to prove their direct threat defense as a matter of law. Under this view, a court's role is to make sure that an employer has considered sufficient medical evidence specific to the individual, but *not* to itself weigh the medical evidence.

For example, in *Knapp v. Northwestern University*, 101 F.3d 473, 477 (7th Cir. 1996), a student was barred from participation in intercollegiate basketball because of a heart defect. The student brought suit under the Rehabilitation Act, seeking an injunction that would allow him to play. In discussing whether the student was an "otherwise qualified individual" within the meaning of the Rehabilitation Act, the court considered evidence as to the player's risk of injury or death if he played (if the risk was severe enough, he could not be a "qualified individual."). The university considered the medical opinion of its team doctor in making the determination that the risk was significant. In spite of a conflicting opinion by Knapp's testifying doctor, the court held that the university had satisfied its evidentiary burden. The Seventh Circuit held that it was the province of the employer decision-maker, not the courts, to weigh conflicting evidence and decide which medical professional's opinion on which to base its decision. The court's role was limited to making sure the university considered individualized, medically acceptable evidence. *Id.* at 485.

Time will tell if the Ninth Circuit's *Echazabal* decision on remand is followed widely, and whether courts will rigorously inquire into the propriety of the employer's medical decisions (as well as the expertise of the testifying physician) before granting an employer summary judgment. At a minimum, though, some courts will inquire deeper into what type of medical information an employer considers before making a summary judgment determination.

6.   See EEOC v. Hussey Copper Ltd., 696 F.Supp.2d 505 (W.D. Pa. March 12, 2010) (involving applicant who received methadone treatment); Mayes v. Whitlock Packaging Corp., 2010 WL 1754200 (E.D. Okla. Apr. 29, 2010) (Plaintiff with epilepsy that could not be controlled with medication posed a direct threat); Wurzel v. Whirlpool Corp., 2010 WL 1495197 (N.D. Ohio Apr. 14, 2010).

Chapter 10 TITLE I ENFORCEMENT AND REMEDIES

§ 10.1   Introduction To Remedies

As any wronged person knows, having a right is only a start: one must have a way to enforce that right. The ADA provides a wide array of enforcement tools, from administrative remedies before state or federal agencies to judicial remedies, such as specific performance or damages. For Title I purposes, the administrative remedies are at least nominally favored, as a litigant must – formally at least – step through them before getting to the harsher judicial remedies. Thus, one must understand both structures.

Not wanting to depart markedly from existing legislation, the drafters of the ADA looked to familiar statutes for the ADA's enforcement and remediation provisions. The business community, which was used to dealing with the EEOC and coordinate state agencies, concurred.   In response, Congress constructed enforcement mechanisms that explicitly rest on those in the Rehabilitation Act of 1973 and the Civil Rights Act of 1964, as amended.   Chai R. Feldblum, Medical Examinations and Inquiries Under the Americans with Disabilities Act: A View from the Inside, 64 Temp. L. Rev. 521, 521-23 (1991). However, the ADA covers a broader swath of territory than those acts, from employment to telecommunications to public accommodations, which results in some complexity.

- The remedies for employment discrimination in violation of Title I are those provided in Title VII of the Civil Rights Act. 42 U.S.C. § 12117 (2006) (citing sections 705, 706, 707, 709 and 710 of the Civil Rights Act of 1964, 42 U.S.C. §§ 2000e-4, 2000e-5, 2000e-6, 2000e-8 and 2000e-9 (2000)). Cases interpreting other statutes that rest on Title VII, such as the Age Discrimination in Employment Act (ADEA), 29 U.S.C. § 621, et seq. (2006), thus inform the interpretation of the ADA. The remedies include the traditional equitable remedies for employment discrimination: back pay, front pay, reinstatement and attorneys' fees. They also include both compensatory damages, such as for emotional distress, and, upon a showing of "malice or . . . reckless indifference to the federally protected rights of an aggrieved individual," punitive damages.

The ADA likewise parcels out enforcement responsibilities broadly. Both the EEOC and the Attorney General are granted power to investigate and enforce various titles of the ADA. The EEOC may investigate Titles I and II and may enforce Title I. *See* 42 U.S.C. §§ 12117, 12133. Individuals, of course, may bring their own actions. *Id*. The Title I procedures contain some complications. States that have equivalent civil rights protections have the first opportunity to respond to employment discrimination complaints. Only after a "deferral period" may the EEOC act and only after the EEOC determines not to pursue a case itself, or not to refer it to the Department of Justice, can an individual sue.

In an effort to streamline the process, the EEOC has developed a process for nonbinding mediation. Equal Emp. Opportunity Comm'n, Mediation, http://www.eeoc.gov/eeoc/mediation/index.cfm (last modified Jun. 19, 2012). We will address this in § 11.1 *infra*. In parallel, many employers insert mandatory arbitration provisions in their employment contracts, to preclude resort to judicial fora. The applicability, scope and enforceability of those provisions, which affect important statutory rights, have been the subject of litigation and are discussed in § 11.2 *infra*.

Notes & Questions

Assuming no background, i.e., no preexisting statutes, what kind of remedies should be available? Should the remedy depend on the number of employees or revenue of the defendant? On whether the defendant is a private or governmental body?

§ 10.2   Title I Remedial Procedure

An individual who perceives that he has been the subject of disability-based employment discrimination by a private entity may seek relief under Title I of the ADA. The Act makes available – and forces the individual to use – the procedures and remedies of Title VII of the Civil Rights Act of 1964, as amended. ADA section 107(a) reads:

> The powers, remedies, and procedures set forth in sections 705, 706, 707, 709, and 710 of the Civil Rights Act of 1964 (42 U.S.C. 2000e-4, 2000e-5, 2000e-6, 2000e-8, and 2000e-9) shall be the powers, remedies, and procedures this title provides to the Commission, to the Attorney General, or to any person alleging discrimination on the basis of disability in violation of any provision of this Act, or regulations promulgated under section 106, concerning employment.

42 U.S.C. § 12117(a) (2006); *see* Jacob A. Stein et al., Stein on Personal Injury Damages, § 5:9 (3d ed. West 2012). That Act lays out a detailed set of procedures, as well as available remedies.

A.   *Administrative Exhaustion*

Prior to seeking relief in court, a person with a grievance against an employer or potential employer must apply for relief to the EEOC or, in many states, to the state or local agency with jurisdiction over discrimination claims. These sequential procedures can add complexity sufficient to trip up an unwary litigant. They also set time limits, because the person has only 180 days from the discriminatory act (300 days in "deferral states," those with their own agencies that can review a complaint before or in lieu of EEOC review).

The Supreme Court has also held that the EEOC can file a complaint, which had previously been filed with it, with the state agency on the aggrieved party's behalf, wait for that agency to decline to act, and then reactivate the federal complaint. *Love v. Pullman Co.*, 404 U.S. 522, 525-27 (1972):

> We hold that the filing procedure followed here fully complied with the intent of the Act, and we thus reverse the judgment of the Court of Appeals. Nothing in the Act suggests that the state proceedings may not be initiated by the EEOC acting on behalf of the complainant rather than by the complainant himself, nor is there any requirement that the complaint to the state agency be made in writing rather than by oral referral. Further, we cannot agree with the respondent's claim that the EEOC may not properly hold a complaint in "suspended animation," automatically filing it upon termination of the state proceedings.

> We see no reason why further action by the aggrieved party should be required. The procedure complies with the purpose both of [§] 706(b), to give state agencies a prior opportunity to consider discrimination complaints, and of [§] 706 (d), to ensure expedition in the filing and handling of those complaints. The respondent makes no showing of prejudice to its interests. To require a second "filing" by the aggrieved party after termination of state proceedings would serve no purpose other than the creation of an additional procedural technicality. Such technicalities are particularly inappropriate in a statutory scheme in which laymen, unassisted by trained lawyers, initiate the process.

Notes & Questions

1. What is the point of requiring people who think they have suffered some variant of employment discrimination to go to an administrative agency?

2. Note the expansive view of the court on the way a claim must be filed. What accounts for that?

The pre-suit administrative process contains rigid timelines. The first time limit is the time to file a claim with the appropriate administrative agency. The basic rule is that a claim must be filed with the EEOC within 180 days of the "alleged unlawful employment practice." 42 U.S.C. § 2000e-5(e). *See also* 29 C.F.R. § 1601.13. However, where the complainant has instituted proceedings "with a State or local agency with authority to grant or seek relief from such practice or to institute criminal proceedings with respect thereto" the complainant has 300 days after the alleged unlawful employment practice or 30 days after receiving notice that the state or local agency has terminated proceedings, whichever is earlier, to file with the EEOC. 42 U.S.C. § 2000e-5(e)(1). The complainant must serve the claim on the opposing party within ten days of filing. *Id.*

B.   *Administrative Limitations Periods - Accrual*

The principal issue with a statute of limitation is often when an action "accrues," here, when the violation occurred. In general, the violation occurs when the employee receives notice of it, for example, a discharge, demotion or failure to hire. "The 300-day limit . . . begins to run when the defendant has taken the action that injures the plaintiff and when the plaintiff knows [he] has been injured . . . 'not when [plaintiff] determines that the injury was unlawful.'" Sharp v. United Airlines, Inc., 236 F.3d 368, 372 (7th Cir. 2001) (quoting Thelen v. Marc's Big Boy Corp., 64 F.3d 264, 267 (7th Cir. 1995)) (citation omitted).

There can be ambiguity in the act that causes the violation to accrue. In *Flannery v. Recording Industry Ass'n Of America*, 354 F.3d 632 (7th Cir. 2004), the plaintiff and defendant viewed different acts as constituting the accrual event:

> We therefore return to the question of the proper date of the "unlawful employment practice" with our focus solely on the amended complaint. Two principles guide our determination on this question. First, it bears repeating that, because this case comes to us on a motion to dismiss, we must consider all the alleged facts in the amended complaint as true, draw all reasonable inferences in favor of Mr. Flannery, and ask "whether there is any possible interpretation of the complaint under which it can state a claim." [Citation omitted.] Second, our cases hold that the date on which an unlawful employment practice occurs – in this case, when a termination decision is final and when unequivocal notice is given – is a question of fact. [Citation omitted.]

> Taking these two principles together, the amended complaint alleges that, at the March 2000 meeting, RIAA officials initially told Mr. Flannery he would "have to leave," but that, by the end of the meeting, they had agreed, at Mr. Flannery's request, to keep him on and see how things went. Under these facts, a plausible interpretation of the March 2000 decision is that any decision was

"tentative," *Ricks*, 449 U.S. at 261, 101 S.Ct. 498, not a "concrete act [which] smack[ed] of finality," *Lever*, 979 F.2d at 554. It also is at least as plausible that the other date presented to us by Mr. Flannery, June 14, 2001, was the date of the final termination decision. According to his allegations, on or about June 14, 2001, Mr. Flannery was told that he would be terminated effective October 1, 2001. The letter from Mr. Walters describing the benefits he would receive upon his termination was also dated June 14, 2001. Finally, that letter was subsequently identified by Mr. Creighton as Mr. Flannery's "official notice" of his "current and future status with RIAA." Am. Compl., Ex.B. We do not mean to imply that *Ricks* and *Lever* necessarily require that a definitive termination date must be given, or that the termination decision must be memorialized in an "official" communication, in order for the employer's decision to be "final." *See Ricks*, 449 U.S. at 257, 101 S.Ct. 498 ("Mere continuity of employment, without more, is insufficient to prolong the life of a cause of action for employment discrimination.") * * * Our only holding is that these facts, taken together, and assumed to be true, permit the conclusion that the final termination decision was not made until June 14, 2001.

Furthermore, even assuming that a final decision was made at the March 2000 meeting, the tentativeness of RIAA officials at that meeting permit an interpretation that, at that time, RIAA failed to give Mr. Flannery the requisite unequivocal notice. As we have previously noted, notice to the employee is only sufficient if it provides a *"clear intention to dispense with the employee's services." Dvorak*, 289 F.3d at 486 (emphasis added). Requiring employees like Mr. Flannery to file EEOC charges on the basis of ambiguous conversations regarding termination would cause a flood of false charges; litigants would be forced to file a charge at every hint of termination in order to preserve their claims. * * * The concomitant burden upon the EEOC would impact significantly the enforcement function of the agency.

Flannery, 354 F.3d at 640-41.

Notes & Questions

1. When the act that violates the ADA is an improper transfer of an employee to a different position, the claim accrues upon the transfer. Ramirez v. City of San Antonio, 312 F.3d 178, 181-82 (5th Cir. 2002).

2. The *Flannery* case involves termination. What causes a claim to accrue when an employer will not accommodate an employee with a disability? When the employer first refuses? Throughout the entire period of the refusal? *See* Jones v. United Parcel Serv., No. Civ. A-00-1049-SLR, 2002 WL 1268050, at *2 (D. Del. May 23, 2002) (last day of wrongful denial of accommodations). *See also* Herr v. City of Chi., 447 F.Supp.2d 915, 919 (N.D. Ill. 2006) (claim based on failure to accommodate did not accrue while defendant continuing to ask plaintiff to provide information to substantiate requested accommodation).

3. If the plaintiff is discriminatorily discharged, but subsequently reapplies for other jobs, when does the claim accrue? *See* Chedwick v. UPMC, 2007 WL 4390327 at *5-*7 20 A.D. Cases 677 (W.D. Pa. 2007) (termination and hiring are separate events under ADA, so refusal to hire claim was timely, although claim based on termination would not have been).

୨

1.   Violations outside the limitations period

Often discriminatory acts are ongoing, so that the violation may include acts before the 180/300 day period. But the failure to remedy a preexisting violation is not itself a violation. Stepney v. Naperville School Dist. 203, 392 F.3d 236, 240 (7th 2004) ("continuing violation doctrine does not provide an avenue for circumventing this rule. The doctrine applies to claims like sexual harassment, where an individual act cannot be made the subject of a lawsuit when it occurs because 'its character as a violation did not become clear until it was repeated during the limitations period.' *Dasgupta v. Univ. of Wis. Bd. of Regents*, 121 F.3d 1138, 1139 (7th Cir.1997). In those cases, duration and repetition are necessary to convert merely offensive behavior into an actionable change in the plaintiff's working conditions. *Id*. The courts developed the "continuing violation doctrine" to permit employees to bring claims encompassing acts of discrimination that occurred outside the limitations period. The elements of the doctrine varied by jurisdiction. *Compare* Williams v. Owens-Ill., Inc., 665 F.2d 918, 924 (9th Cir. 1982) (systematic policy of discrimination that continues into statutory period), *with* Moskowitz v. Trs. of Purdue Univ., 5 F.3d 279, 281-82 (7th Cir. 1993) (equitable tolling basis for doctrine). In *National Railroad Passenger Corp. v. Morgan*, 536 U.S. 101 (2002), the Supreme Court rejected this device, except in cases of hostile work environment claims.

୨

Notes & Questions

1. Some states follow the continuing violation doctrine, even for claims of discrete discrimination or retaliation. Interpreting the California Fair Employment and Housing Act, Cal. Gov't Code § 12900 et

seq., the California Supreme Court held in *Richards v. CH2M Hill*, 111 Cal.Rptr.2d 87, 106-107 (Cal. 2001):

> [A]n employer's persistent failure to reasonably accommodate a disability, or to eliminate a hostile work environment targeting a disabled employee, is a continuing violation if the employer's unlawful actions are (1) sufficiently similar in kind – recognizing, as this case illustrates, that similar kinds of unlawful employer conduct, such as acts of harassment or failures to reasonably accommodate disability, may take a number of different forms . . .; (2) have occurred with reasonable frequency; (3) and have not acquired a degree of permanence. (*Berry [v. Board of Sup's of L.S.U.*, 715 F.2d 971 (5th Cir. 1983)], *supra*, 715 F.2d at p. 981.) But consistent with our case law and with the statutory objectives of the FEHA, we further hold that "permanence" in the context of an ongoing process of accommodation of disability, or ongoing disability harassment, should properly be understood to mean the following: that an employer's statements and actions make clear to a reasonable employee that any further efforts at informal conciliation to obtain reasonable accommodation or end harassment will be futile.

> Thus, when an employer engages in a continuing course of unlawful conduct under the FEHA by refusing reasonable accommodation of a disabled employee or engaging in disability harassment, and this course of conduct does not constitute a constructive discharge, the statute of limitations begins to run not necessarily when the employee first believes that his or her rights may have been violated, but rather, *either* when the course of conduct is brought to an end, as by the employer's cessation of such conduct or by the employee's resignation, *or* when the employee is on notice that further efforts to end the unlawful conduct will be in vain. Accordingly, an employer who is confronted with an employee seeking accommodation of disability or relief from disability harassment may assert control over its legal relationship with the employee either by accommodating the employee's requests, or by making clear to the employee in a definitive manner that it will not be granting any such requests, thereby commencing the running of the statute of limitations.

* * *

Who got it right, the United States Supreme Court or the California Supreme Court? Other courts have adopted a continuing violation theory.

2. The first bill signed by President Barak Obama was the Lilly Ledbetter Fair Pay Restoration Act, Pub. L. 111-2 (2009). That statute reversed the Supreme Court's decision, *Ledbetter v. Goodyear Tire & Rubber Co.*, 550 U.S. 618 (2007), a Title VII case. In *Ledbetter*, the Supreme Court dealt with salary payments that were the result of decisions made outside the statutory period. The Court held: "[t]he EEOC charging period is triggered when a discrete unlawful practice takes place. A new violation does not occur, and a new charging period does not commence, upon the occurrence of subsequent nondiscriminatory acts that entail adverse effects resulting from the past discrimination. But if an employer engages in a series of separately actionable intentionally discriminatory acts, then a fresh violation takes place when each act is committed." *Id.* at 619. Receiving a paycheck was a discrete act from a discriminatory pay setting decision, and therefore did not restart the limitations period. Thus, if the employee received lower pay as a result of discriminatory decisions outside the 180-day period, the claim was lost.

The Lilly Ledbetter Fair Pay Restoration Act contains the following:

Section 706(e) of the Civil Rights Act of 1964 (42 U.S.C. 2000e-5(e)) is amended by adding at the end the following:

(3)(A)   For purposes of this section, an unlawful employment practice occurs, with respect to discrimination in compensation in violation of this title, when a discriminatory compensation decision or other practice is adopted, when an individual becomes subject to a discriminatory compensation decision or other practice, or when an individual is affected by application of a discriminatory compensation decision or other practice, including each time wages, benefits, or other compensation is paid, resulting in whole or in part from such a decision or other practice.

(B)   In addition to any relief authorized by section 1977A of the Revised Statutes (42 U.S.C. 1981a), liability may accrue and an aggrieved person may obtain relief as provided in subsection (g)(1), including recovery of back pay for up to two years preceding the filing of the charge, where the unlawful employment practices that have occurred during the charge filing period are similar or related to unlawful employment practices with regard to discrimination in compensation that occurred outside the time for filing a charge.

. . .

SEC. 5. APPLICATION TO OTHER LAWS.

(a) AMERICANS WITH DISABILITIES ACT OF 1990. – The amendments made by section 3 shall apply to claims of discrimination in compensation brought under title I and section 503 of the Americans with Disabilities Act of 1990 (42 U.S.C. 12111 et seq., 12203), pursuant to section 107(a) of such Act (42 U.S.C. 12117(a)), which adopts the powers, remedies, and procedures set forth in section 706 of the Civil Rights Act of 1964 (42 U.S.C. 2000e-5).

৵

2. Equitable grounds for relief from a delayed filing

The filing requirements of Title VII are not jurisdictional, and thus may be extended upon a proper showing. Zipes v. Trans World Airlines, Inc., 455 U.S. 385, 393 (1982); Wilson v. MVM, Inc., 475 F.3d 166, 173-75 (3d Cir. 2007) (Rehabilitation Act claims). *See generally* U.S. Equal Emp. Opportunity Comm'n, EEOC Compliance Manual, http://www.eeoc.gov/policy/compliance.html (last visited Jun. 19, 2012). *But see* Sizova v. Nat'l Inst. of Standards & Tech., 282 F.3d 1320, 1325 (10th Cir. 2002) (distinguishing between failure to timely exhaust and complete failure to exhaust, finding the latter to be a jurisdictional bar); Davis v. N.C. Dep't of Corr., 48 F.3d 134, 137 (4th Cir. 1995) (same); Bullard v. Sercon Corp., 846 F.2d 463, 468 (7th Cir. 1988) (same).

First, they may be equitably tolled. The EEOC's Guidance lists four reasons for equitable tolling: (1) No reason to suspect discrimination at the time of the disputed event; (2) mental incapacity; (3) misleading information or mishandling of charge by the EEOC or FEPA; and (4) timely filing in the wrong forum, as long as the charging party diligently pursued the action.

Second, the employer may be estopped from raising the limitation period. It is not uncommon for these equitable doctrines to be raised in the same case.

Third, the employer may waive the bar of the period. Waiver is the intentional relinquishment of a known right. The most obvious example occurs when the employer informs the employee that it will not use the passage of time against the employee. *See* Coll. Sav. Bank v. Fla. Prepaid Postsecondary Educ. Expense Bd., 527 U.S. 666, 680-82 (1999) ("The classic description of an effective waiver of a constitutional right is the 'intentional relinquishment or abandonment of a known right or privilege.'") (citations omitted).

C. *Statute Of Limitations*

Title I requires exhaustion of administrative remedies. Those remedies are exhausted when the claimant receives notice that the EEOC has issued a right to sue letter. Title VII's 90-day limitation period to file suit then takes over. At that point, the cause of action has accrued and the complainant has 90 days to file a lawsuit. 42 U.S.C. § 12117(a) (2006), incorporating 42 U.S.C. § 2000e-5(f)(1) (2006).

◈

Notes & Questions

1. What kind of notice must a person have of the EEOC's decision? In *Ebbert v. DaimlerChrysler Corp.*, 319 F.3d 103, 114 (3d Cir. 2003), the Third Circuit held that oral notice may suffice, if it is as complete as written notice, i.e., states that the claimant has 90 days to file a suit.

2. Does the notice of the EEOC's decision have to be to the claimant? Title VII cases indicate "no." In *Irwin v. Dep't Of Veterans Affairs*, 498 U.S. 89, 92-93 (1990), the Supreme Court held that notice to the claimant's lawyer, although not received by the claimant sufficed under 42 U.S.C. § 2000e-16(c) sufficed. In *Ball v. Abbott Advertising, Inc.*, 864 F.2d 419, 421 (6th Cir. 1988), the court held that oral notice to the claimant's attorney sufficed, without saying anything about the completeness of the notice.

◈

D.   *Role Of The EEOC*

The U.S. Equal Employment Opportunity Commission (EEOC) is charged with enforcing federal employment discrimination laws including the ADA. The EEOC has the authority to investigate charges of discrimination against employers covered by the ADA. The EEOC's role is to assess charge allegations and make findings based on that assessment. If the EEOC finds that discrimination has occurred, they will attempt to settle the charge, or if settlement is not an option the EEOC has the authority to file a lawsuit to protect the rights of individuals and the interests of the public. In 2012, more people filed charges with the EEOC against their employers alleging disability discrimination under Title I (26,379) than in any previous year in the ADA's history. U.S. Equal Emp. Opportunity Comm'n, Americans with Disabilities Act of 1990 (ADA) Charges FY 1997-FY 2012, http://www.eeoc.gov/eeoc/statistics/enforcement/ada-charges.cfm (last visited October 1, 2013).

1.   EEOC's authority

EQUAL EMPLOYMENT OPPORTUNITY COMMISSION v. WAFFLE HOUSE, INC.

Supreme Court of the United States, 2002
534 U.S. 279

Justice STEVENS delivered the opinion of the Court.

The question presented is whether an agreement between an employer and an employee to arbitrate employment-related disputes bars the Equal Employment Opportunity Commission (EEOC) from pursuing victim-specific judicial relief, such as backpay, reinstatement, and damages, in an enforcement action alleging that the employer has violated Title I of the Americans with Disabilities Act of 1990(ADA), 104 Stat. 328, 42 U.S.C. § 12101 *et seq.* (1994 ed. and Supp. V).

I

In his application for employment with respondent, Eric Baker agreed that "any dispute or claim" concerning his employment would be "settled by binding arbitration." As a condition of employment, all prospective Waffle House employees are required to sign an application containing a similar mandatory arbitration agreement. See App. 56. Baker began working as a grill operator at one of respondent's restaurants on August 10, 1994. Sixteen days later he suffered a seizure at work and soon thereafter was discharged. *Id.* at 43-44. Baker did not initiate arbitration proceedings, nor has he in the seven years since his termination, but he did file a timely charge of discrimination with the EEOC alleging that his discharge violated the ADA.

After an investigation and an unsuccessful attempt to conciliate, the EEOC filed an enforcement action against respondent in the Federal District Court for the District of South Carolina, pursuant to § 107(a) of the ADA, 42 U.S.C. § 12117(a) (1994 ed.), and § 102 of the Civil Rights Act of 1991, as added, 105 Stat. 1072, 42 U.S.C. § 1981a (1994 ed.). Baker is not a party to the case. The EEOC's complaint alleged that respondent engaged in employment practices that violated the ADA, including its discharge of Baker "because of his disability," and that its violation was intentional, and "done with malice or with reckless indifference to [his] federally protected rights." The complaint requested the court to grant injunctive relief to "eradicate the effects of [respondent's] past and present unlawful employment practices," to order specific relief designed to make Baker whole, including backpay, reinstatement, and compensatory damages, and to award punitive damages for malicious and reckless conduct. App. 38-40.

Respondent filed a petition under the Federal Arbitration Act (FAA), 9 U.S.C. § 1 *et seq.*, to stay the EEOC's suit and compel arbitration, or to dismiss the action. [Both the district court and the court of appeals held the EEOC could pursue an action, despite the arbitration agreement.] Nevertheless, the court [of appeals] held that the EEOC was precluded from seeking victim-specific relief in court because the policy goals expressed in the FAA required giving some effect to Baker's arbitration agreement. * * *

Therefore, according to the Court of Appeals, when an employee has signed a mandatory arbitration agreement, the EEOC's remedies in an enforcement action are limited to injunctive relief.

* * *

II

Congress has directed the EEOC to exercise the same enforcement powers, remedies, and procedures that are set forth in Title VII of the Civil Rights Act of 1964 when it is enforcing the ADA's prohibitions against employment discrimination on the basis of disability. 42 U.S.C. § 12117(a) (1994 ed.). Accordingly, the provisions of Title VII defining the EEOC's authority provide the starting point for our analysis.

When Title VII was enacted in 1964, it authorized private actions by individual employees and public actions by the Attorney General in cases involving a "pattern or practice" of discrimination. 42 U.S.C. § 2000e-6(a) (1994 ed.). The EEOC, however, merely had the authority to investigate and, if possible, to conciliate charges of discrimination. See *General Telephone Co. of Northwest v. EEOC*, 446 U.S. 318, 325, 100 S.Ct. 1698, 64 L.Ed.2d 319 (1980). In 1972, Congress amended Title VII to authorize the EEOC to bring its own enforcement actions; indeed, we have observed that the 1972 amendments created a system in which the EEOC was intended "to bear the primary burden of litigation," id. at 326, 100 S.Ct. 1698. Those amendments authorize the courts to enjoin employers from engaging in unlawful employment practices, and to order appropriate affirmative action, which may include reinstatement, with or without backpay. Moreover, the amendments specify the judicial districts in which such actions may be brought. They do not mention arbitration proceedings.

In 1991, Congress again amended Title VII to allow the recovery of compensatory and punitive damages by a "complaining party." 42 U.S.C. § 1981a(a)(1) (1994 ed.). The term includes both private plaintiffs and the EEOC, § 1981a(d)(1)(A), and the amendments apply to ADA claims as well, §§ 1981a(a)(2), (d)(1)(B). As a complaining party, the EEOC may bring suit to enjoin an employer from engaging in unlawful employment practices, and to pursue reinstatement, backpay, and compensatory or punitive damages. Thus, these statutes unambiguously authorize the EEOC to obtain the relief that it seeks in its complaint if it can prove its case against respondent.

* * *

Against the backdrop of our decisions in *Occidental* [*Life Ins. Co. of Cal. v. EEOC*, 432 U.S. 355, 97 S.Ct. 2447, 53 L.Ed.2d 402 (1977)] and *General Telephone* [*Co. of Northwest v. EEOC*, 446 U.S. 318, 100 S.Ct. 1698, 64 L.Ed.2d 319 (1980)], Congress expanded the remedies available in EEOC enforcement actions in 1991 to include compensatory and punitive damages. There is no language in the statutes or in either of these cases suggesting that the existence of an arbitration agreement between private parties materially changes the EEOC's statutory function or the remedies that are otherwise available.

III

[The Court discusses the Federal Arbitration Act.]

IV

The Court of Appeals based its decision on its evaluation of the "competing policies" implemented by the ADA and the FAA, rather than on any language in the text of either the statutes or the arbitration agreement between Baker and respondent. 193 F.3d, at 812. It recognized that the EEOC never agreed to arbitrate its statutory claim, * * *, and that the EEOC has "independent statutory authority" to vindicate the public interest, but opined that permitting the EEOC to prosecute Baker's claim in court "would significantly trample" the strong federal policy favoring arbitration because Baker had agreed to submit his claim to arbitration. *Id.* at 812. To effectuate this policy, the court distinguished between injunctive and victim-specific relief, and held that the EEOC is barred from obtaining the latter because any public interest served when the EEOC pursues "make whole" relief is outweighed by the policy goals favoring arbitration. Only when the EEOC seeks broad injunctive relief, in the Court of Appeals' view, does the public interest overcome the goals underpinning the FAA.[7]

If it were true that the EEOC could prosecute its claim only with Baker's consent, or if its prayer for relief could be dictated by Baker, the court's analysis might be persuasive. But once a charge is filed, the exact opposite is true under the statute – the EEOC is in command of the process. The EEOC has exclusive jurisdiction over the claim for 180 days.

---

[7]   This framework assumes the federal policy favoring arbitration will be undermined unless the EEOC's remedies are limited. The court failed to consider, however, that some of the benefits of arbitration are already built into the EEOC's statutory duties. Unlike individual employees, the EEOC cannot pursue a claim in court without first engaging in a conciliation process. 42 U.S.C. § 2000e-5(b) (1994 ed.). Thus, before the EEOC ever filed suit in this case, it attempted to reach a settlement with respondent. The court also neglected to take into account that the EEOC files suit in a small fraction of the charges employees file. * * *

During that time, the employee must obtain a right-to-sue letter from the agency before prosecuting the claim. If, however, the EEOC files suit on its own, the employee has no independent cause of action, although the employee may intervene in the EEOC's suit. 42 U.S.C. § 2000e-5(f)(1) (1994 ed.). In fact, the EEOC takes the position that it may pursue a claim on the employee's behalf even after the employee has disavowed any desire to seek relief. Brief for Petitioner 20. The statute clearly makes the EEOC the master of its own case and confers on the agency the authority to evaluate the strength of the public interest at stake. Absent textual support for a contrary view, it is the public agency's province – not that of the court – to determine whether public resources should be committed to the recovery of victim-specific relief. And if the agency makes that determination, the statutory text unambiguously authorizes it to proceed in a judicial forum.

Respondent and the dissent contend that Title VII supports the Court of Appeals' bar against victim-specific relief, because the statute limits the EEOC's recovery to "appropriate" relief as determined by a court. * * * They rely on § 706(g)(1), which provides that, after a finding of liability, "the court may enjoin the respondent from engaging in such unlawful employment practice, and order *such affirmative action as may be appropriate*, which may include, but is not limited to, reinstatement or hiring of employees, with or without back pay . . . *or any other equitable relief as the court deems appropriate*." 42 U.S.C. § 2000e-5(g)(1) (1994 ed.) (emphasis added). They claim this provision limits the remedies available and directs courts, not the EEOC, to determine what relief is appropriate.

The proposed reading is flawed for two reasons. First, under the plain language of the statute the term "appropriate" refers to only a subcategory of claims for equitable relief, not damages. The provision authorizing compensatory and punitive damages is in a separate section of the statute, § 1981a(a)(1), and is not limited by this language. The dissent responds by pointing to the phrase "may recover" in § 1981a(a)(1), and arguing that this too provides authority for prohibiting victim-specific relief. * * * But this contention only highlights the second error in the proposed reading. If "appropriate" and "may recover" can be read to support respondent's position, then any discretionary language would constitute authorization for judge-made, *per se* rules. This is not the natural reading of the text. These terms obviously refer to the trial judge's discretion in a particular case to order reinstatement and award damages in an amount warranted by the facts of that case. They do not permit a court to announce a categorical rule precluding an expressly authorized form of relief as inappropriate in all cases in which the employee has signed an arbitration agreement.

The Court of Appeals wisely did not adopt respondent's reading of § 706(g). Instead, it simply sought to balance the policy goals of the FAA against the clear language of Title VII and the agreement. While this may be a more coherent approach, it is inconsistent with our recent arbitration cases. The FAA directs courts to place arbitration agreements on equal footing with other contracts, but it "does not require parties to arbitrate when they have not agreed to do so." *Volt Information Sciences, Inc. v. Board of Trustees of Leland Stanford Junior Univ.*, 489 U.S. 468, 478, 109 S.Ct. 1248, 103 L.Ed.2d 488 (1989). * * * Because the FAA is "at bottom a policy guaranteeing the enforcement of private contractual arrangements," *Mitsubishi Motors Corp. v. Soler Chrysler-Plymouth, Inc.*, 473 U.S. 614, 625, 105 S.Ct. 3346, 87 L.Ed.2d 444 (1985), we look first to whether the parties agreed to arbitrate a dispute, not to general policy goals, to determine the scope of the agreement. *Id.*, at 626, 105 S.Ct. 3346. While ambiguities in the language of the agreement should be resolved in favor of arbitration, *Volt*, 489 U.S. at 476, 109 S.Ct. 1248, we do not override the clear intent of the parties, or reach a result inconsistent with the plain text of the contract, simply because the policy favoring arbitration is implicated. "Arbitration under the [FAA] is a matter of consent, not coercion." *Id.*, at 479, 109 S.Ct. 1248. Here there is no ambiguity. No one asserts that the EEOC is a party to the contract, or that it agreed to arbitrate its claims. It goes without saying that a contract cannot bind a nonparty. Accordingly, the proarbitration policy goals of the FAA do not require the agency to relinquish its statutory authority if it has not agreed to do so.

* * *

Even if the policy goals underlying the FAA did necessitate some limit on the EEOC's statutory authority, the line drawn by the Court of Appeals between injunctive and victim-specific relief creates an uncomfortable fit with its avowed purpose of preserving the EEOC's public function while favoring arbitration. For that purpose, the category of victim-specific relief is both overinclusive and underinclusive. For example, it is overinclusive because while punitive damages benefit the individual employee, they also serve an obvious public function in deterring future violations. * * * Punitive damages may often have a greater impact on the behavior of other employers than the threat of an injunction, yet the EEOC is precluded from seeking this form of relief under the Court of Appeals' compromise scheme. And, it is underinclusive because injunctive relief, although seemingly not "victim-specific," can be seen as more closely tied to the employees' injury than to any public interest. * * *

The compromise solution reached by the Court of Appeals turns what is effectively a forum selection clause into a waiver of a nonparty's statutory remedies. But if the federal policy favoring arbitration trumps the plain language of Title VII and the contract, the EEOC should be barred from pursuing any claim outside the arbitral forum. If not, then the statutory language is clear; the EEOC has the authority to pursue victim-specific relief regardless of the forum that the employer and employee have chosen to resolve their disputes. Rather than attempt to split the difference, we are persuaded that, pursuant to Title VII and the

ADA, whenever the EEOC chooses from among the many charges filed each year to bring an enforcement action in a particular case, the agency may be seeking to vindicate a public interest, not simply provide make-whole relief for the employee, even when it pursues entirely victim-specific relief. To hold otherwise would undermine the detailed enforcement scheme created by Congress simply to give greater effect to an agreement between private parties that does not even contemplate the EEOC's statutory function.

V

It is true, as respondent and its *amici* have argued, that Baker's conduct may have the effect of limiting the relief that the EEOC may obtain in court. If, for example, he had failed to mitigate his damages, or had accepted a monetary settlement, any recovery by the EEOC would be limited accordingly. * * * As we have noted, it "goes without saying that the courts can and should preclude double recovery by an individual." *General Telephone*, 446 U.S. at 333, 100 S.Ct. 1698.

But no question concerning the validity of his claim or the character of the relief that could be appropriately awarded in either a judicial or an arbitral forum is presented by this record. Baker has not sought arbitration of his claim, nor is there any indication that he has entered into settlement negotiations with respondent. It is an open question whether a settlement or arbitration judgment would affect the validity of the EEOC's claim or the character of relief the EEOC may seek. The only issue before this Court is whether the fact that Baker has signed a mandatory arbitration agreement limits the remedies available to the EEOC. The text of the relevant statutes provides a clear answer to that question. They do not authorize the courts to balance the competing policies of the ADA and the FAA or to second-guess the agency's judgment concerning which of the remedies authorized by law that it shall seek in any given case.

Moreover, it simply does not follow from the cases holding that the employee's conduct may affect the EEOC's recovery that the EEOC's claim is merely derivative. We have recognized several situations in which the EEOC does not stand in the employee's shoes. * * * And, in this context, the statute specifically grants the EEOC exclusive authority over the choice of forum and the prayer for relief once a charge has been filed. The fact that ordinary principles of res judicata, mootness, or mitigation may apply to EEOC claims does not contradict these decisions, nor does it render the EEOC a proxy for the employee.

The judgment of the Court of Appeals is reversed, and the case is remanded for further proceedings consistent with this opinion.

It is so ordered.

[Dissenting opinion by Justice THOMAS, joined by Chief Justice REHNQUIST and Justice SCALIA, omitted.]

Notes & Questions

1. Why does it make sense to have a two-track system – EEOC and private litigation? And why does it make sense to let both the EEOC and a private plaintiff seek victim-specific relief?

2. What do you think about the Court's discussion of section 706? May courts impose limits on broad classes of relief?

2.　　　　EEOC procedures – administrative exhaustion

The EEOC has been given the authority to issue regulations regarding Title I. 42 U.S.C. § 12116 (2006).[9] The EEOC's administrative process for pursuing ADA claims follows that of other discrimination claims. The EEOC assigns an investigator to the case and the investigator may seek information from the employer. The EEOC may obtain documents from the entity against which a charge is made. *Id.* § 2000e-8(b). It will determine whether "there is reasonable cause to believe that an unlawful employment practice has occurred or is occurring." 29 C.F.R. § 1601.24 (2008). If it finds reasonable cause, it must attempt to conciliate the matter with the employer. *Id.*; 42 U.S.C. § 2000e-5(b). It may not file a suit without first going through the conciliation process. In *EEOC v. Argo Distribution, LLC*, 55 F.3d 462 (5th Cir. 2009), the court held that the EEOC's failure to conciliate did not deprive the court of subject matter jurisdiction of the claim, but could be a basis on which a prevailing defendant could recover attorneys' fees from the EEOC.

If the EEOC successfully conciliates the matter, it may dismiss the claim. 29 C.F.R. § 1601.20. During this process, it may ask the parties if they will mediate the dispute. Eventually, if the EEOC does not resolve the matter, it either will issue a "determination that reasonable cause exists to believe that an unlawful employment practice has occurred or is occurring under title VII or the ADA," *id.* § 1601.21, or find there is "not reasonable cause to believe that an unlawful employment practice has occurred or is occurring as to all issues addressed in the determination" and issue a "right to sue letter." *Id.* § 1601.19.

The EEOC has 30 days after a charge is filed or after the end of a period of reference to a deferral agency to obtain an acceptable conciliation

---

[9]　　　　The EEOC's Procedural Regulations are in 29 C.F.R. pt. 1601 (2008). The regulations in 29 C.F.R. pt. 37 (2003) set forth procedures for resolving conflicts of jurisdiction that might arise when complaints are filed under both Title I of the ADA and section 504 of the Rehabilitation Act. *Id.* § 37.2(a). Part 37 also covers complaints that fall within the overlapping jurisdiction of Titles I and II and complaints that fall within Title II. *Id.* § 37.2(2).

agreement. 42 U.S.C. § 2000e-5(f)(1). Failing that, the EEOC may bring a civil action against the respondent, unless the respondent is a government, governmental agency, or political subdivision. 29 C.F.R. § 1601.27. In that case, the EEOC "shall" refer that matter to the Attorney General who may bring a civil action against the respondent. *Id.* Only a relatively minor number of claims result in civil actions by the EEOC or the Attorney General.

If the EEOC dismisses the charge or, if within 180 days from the filing of the charge or the expiration of the reference period, whichever is later, neither the EEOC nor the Attorney General has filed a civil action against the employer, the EEOC or the Attorney General must notify the complainant. After 180 days, at the request of the charging party, the EEOC must issue a right to sue letter. 29 C.F.R. § 1601.28 (2008).

In by far the majority of cases with potentially meritorious claims, the EEOC does not itself pursue the investigation, but issues a "right to sue" letter to the complainant. In Fiscal Year 2012, the EEOC reported receiving 26,379 charges (up from 19,453 in 2008 when the Amendments Act was passed), of which it settled 10.1%, found 64.4% had no reasonable cause and issued a right to sue letter, found 4.5% had reasonable cause, which can lead to conciliation, administratively closed 15.1%, and noted a withdrawal of the charge with benefits in 6.0% of cases. There were merits resolutions in 20.5% of the cases, and $103.4 million (up from $57.2 million in 2008) in monetary benefits were paid. U.S. Equal Emp. Opportunity Comm'n, Americans with Disabilities Act of 1990 (ADA) Charges FY 1997-FY 2012.

An individual may not bring her own case in court before exhausting her administrative remedies. Taylor v. Books A Million, Inc., 296 F.3d 376, 379 (5th Cir. 2002) (citing Dao v. Auchan Hypermarket, 96 F.3d 787, 788-89 (5th Cir. 1996)). The Fifth Circuit in *Dao* concluded:

> We join those courts in holding that an employee must comply with the ADA's administrative prerequisites prior to commencing an action in federal court against her employer for violation of the ADA. . . . .
>
> Section 2000e-5(e)(1) provides that, before a plaintiff can commence a civil action under Title VII in federal court, she must file a timely charge with the EEOC, or with a state or local agency with authority to grant or seek relief from the alleged unlawful employment practice. 42 U.S.C. § 2000e-5(e)(1) . . . .

Dao, 96 F.3d at 789. The right to sue letter, in that circumstance, constitutes exhaustion of the complainant's administrative remedies.

Within 90 days of receipt of the right to sue letter, the complainant may herself bring a civil action against the respondent. 42 U.S.C. § 2000e-5(f)(1) (2006).

Notes & Questions

1.   What, exactly, is exhausted by issuance of a right to sue letter? All discrimination claims by the plaintiff against the defendants? Only those set out in the EEOC claim? Williams v. Little Rock Mun. Water Works, 21 F.3d 218, 222 (8th Cir. 1994) ("A plaintiff will be deemed to have exhausted administrative remedies as to allegations contained in a judicial complaint that are like or reasonably related to the substance of charges timely brought before the EEOC."); *see* Faibisch v. Univ. of Minn., 304 F.3d 797, 803 (8th Cir. 2002) (same; Title VII claim).

2.   Is the EEOC entitled to the deference accorded an agency interpreting its own ordinances when determining what tolls the limitations period? *See* Ebbert v. DaimlerChrysler Corp., 319 F.3d 103, 114 (3d Cir. 2003).

3.   May the EEOC begin or re-open an investigation after the employee complaining of disability discrimination has initiated a private lawsuit against the employer? *See* EEOC v. Federal Exp. Corp., 558 F.3d 842, 854 (9th Cir. 2009) ("EEOC retains the authority to issue an administrative subpoena against an employer even after the charging party has been issued a right-to-sue notice and instituted a private action based upon that charge.").

4.   For the scope of the EEOC's authority, *see* EEOC v. Dillon Co., Inc., 310 F.3d 1271, 1274-75 (10th Cir. 2002).

§ 10.3   Title I Remedies

The default remedy under the ADA for intentional discrimination is equitable – enjoining the respondent from continuing to engage in the unlawful employment action and ordering reinstatement or hiring, as the case may be.   42 U.S.C. § 2000e-5(g)(1) (2006).   As an adjunct to reinstatement or hiring, the court may order back pay or other appropriate equitable relief. *Id.* The time period for back pay is limited to two years. *Id.* In the event reinstatement is not appropriate, the court may order front pay. *Id.* § 2000e-5(f)(1); Taylor v. Books A Million, Inc., 296 F.3d 376, 379 (5th Cir. 2002).

In addition, an injured party may receive other compensatory damage pursuant to 42 U.S.C. § 1981a, including damages for "future pecuniary losses, emotional pain, suffering, inconvenience, mental anguish, loss of enjoyment of life, and other nonpecuniary losses." 42 U.S.C. § 1981a-(b)(3). Section 1981a also authorizes punitive damages when the respondent acts with "malice or with reckless indifference to the federally protected rights of an aggrieved individual." *Id.* § 1981a(b)(1). As Justice Stevens has written:

In enacting the Civil Rights Act of 1991 (1991 Act), Congress established a three-tiered system of remedies for a broad range of discriminatory conduct, including violations of Title VII of the Civil Rights Act of 1964 . . . 4 as well as some violations of the Americans with Disabilities Act of 1990 (ADA), 42 U.S.C. § 12101 *et seq.* (1994 ed. and Supp. III). Equitable remedies are available for disparate impact violations; compensatory damages for intentional disparate treatment; and punitive damages for intentional discrimination "with malice or with reckless indifference to the federally protected rights of an aggrieved individual." § 1981a(b)(1).

Kolstad v. Am. Dental Ass'n, 527 U.S. 526, 547-48 (1999) (Stevens, J., concurring and dissenting). The Civil Rights Act imposes monetary limitations on damage awards, depending on the size of the employer. 42 U.S.C. § 1981a(b)(3).

A. *Equitable Remedies*

1. Injunctive relief – reinstatement

The ADA's remedies for employment discrimination are those of Title VII. The favored remedy is equitable relief – ordering the reinstatement or hiring of the aggrieved individual. Salitros v. Chrysler Corp., 306 F.3d 562, 572 (8th Cir. 2002). In the ADA context, reinstatement or hiring often will mean making a reasonable accommodation to the complaining individual's disability. Dilley v. SuperValu, Inc., 296 F.3d 958, 963-64 (10th Cir. 2002).

ৎ

Notes & Questions

1. If the job no longer exists, what is an employer to do? Shea v. Tisch, 870 F.2d 786, 788-90 (1st Cir. 1989) (reinstatement not required if job does not exist).

2. Reinstatement must, of course, be actual reinstatement.

Chrysler argues that the district court erred in awarding front pay when Chrysler had already reinstated Salitros. . . . Extreme animosity between the employer and employee may make an amicable and productive work relationship impossible and thus justify an award of front pay. . . . In this case, the district court found that the reinstatement Chrysler offered Salitros was illusory, because Salitros was never able to work after he was reinstated, and his inability to work resulted from Chrysler's ill-treatment: "He remained on medical leave because of physically and psychologically damaging harassment experienced at the worksite." Salitros's income while on medical leave showed

299

a "sharp disparity" with his normal income. The court further held that Salitros could not be expected to return to Chrysler in the future. "Given the animosity between the parties, an order reinstating plaintiff to defendant's workplace would be antithetical to his health and is entirely impracticable . . . ." Accordingly, the court held an award of front pay was necessary. We cannot say that this reasoning reveals an abuse of discretion.

Salitros v. Chrysler Corp., 306 F.3d 562, 572 (8th Cir. 2002).

3.   Because the remedy is equitable, it is within the discretion of the trial court. Newhouse v. McCormick & Co., Inc., 110 F.3d 635, 641 (8th Cir. 1997).   On appeal, it is thus unlikely that the trial court's determination not to order reinstatement of an employee will be reversed.

2.   Back pay; front pay

Back pay and front pay are equitable remedies in this context, and are within the discretion of the trial court, but each serves a distinct purpose. Back pay provides a remedy for the time when the aggrieved party was not employed, but should have been. Front pay, on the other hand, is a surrogate for hiring or reinstatement. The entitlement to and computation of each entails somewhat different factors.

a.   *Back pay*

Back "pay" is somewhat of a misnomer, because back pay can include a range of benefits in addition to pay that the complainant would have received. Those include: (1) pay at the rate the complainant would have been paid; (2) overtime if the complainant can show that he would have worked overtime; (3) prejudgment interest on the back pay award, *McKnight v. Gen. Motors Corp.*, 973 F.2d 1366, 1372 (7th Cir. 1992); and (4) the amount of contributions to pension plans and the accumulated growth thereon. Best v. Shell Oil Co., 4 F.Supp.2d 770, 772-74 (N.D. Ill. 1998).

Because back pay replaces time when an employee would have been working, if the employee would not have been working for part of that period, for example, if the employee were on an extended sick leave, back pay would not be awarded for the period. Flowers v. Komatsu Mining Sys., Inc., 165 F.3d 554, 557-58 (7th Cir. 1999).

b.   *Front pay*

In *Pollard v. E.I. du Pont de Nemours & Co.*, 532 U.S. 843 (2001), the Supreme Court held (in a Title VII case) that a front pay award was not an element of compensatory damages. It was therefore excluded from the statutory $300,000 statutory cap set forth in damages in 42 U.S.C. § 1981a(b)(3).

Notes & Questions

1. What difference does it make if the remedy is termed equitable? Why should courts have broad discretion in awarding front pay?

2. The calculation of front pay has an inherent uncertainty. Courts look to a number of factors:

> Courts are able to alleviate the uncertainty of future damages by taking into account a discharged employee's duty to mitigate, "the availability of employment opportunities, the period within which one by reasonable efforts may be re-employed, the employee's work and life expectancy, the discount tables to determine the present value of future damages and other factors that are pertinent on prospective damages awards."

Carr v. Fort Morgan Sch. Dist., 4 F.Supp.2d 989, 995 (D. Colo. 1998). However, the court ordered instatement because "there was little evidence to suggest that the relations between the parties were actually so strained that insurmountable hostility would prevent plaintiff from performing teaching duties in the district." *Id.* at 996.

3. In addition to front pay (or, in some cases, as part of it), courts may order other benefits that an employee would be entitled to. Davoll v. Webb, 194 F.3d 1116, 1144 (10th Cir. 1999). They may include the monetary equivalent of essentially anything that an employee might earn during her future tenure.

∾

c.   *Limitations on back and front pay –*
mitigation and collateral sources

The mitigation inquiry, like other factors discussed here, depends on the particular facts. What if the plaintiff rejects an unconditional offer of reinstatement? *See* Ford Motor Co. v. EEOC, 458 U.S. 219, 230-31 (1982) (ADEA claim; such refusal terminates the backpay obligation); Saladin v. Turner, 936 F.Supp. 1571, 1582 (N.D. Okla. 1996). Why should the refusal to mitigate going forward have anything to do with the backpay obligation?

But what if an employee refuses to take a test designed to determine whether she might be able to perform a job or if she declines a conditional offer of reinstatement. Hogan v. Bangor & Aroostook R.R. Co., 61 F.3d 1034, 1038 (1st Cir. 1995) (does not constitute failure to mitigate).

If an employee can return to the job, why award front pay? Che v. Mass. Bay Transp. Auth., 342 F.3d 31, 43 (1st Cir. 2003) ("overarching preference" in employment discrimination cases is "for reinstatement"). Following *Che*, the court in *Harding v. Cianbro Corp.*, 473 F.Supp.2d 89 (D. Me. 2007) refused to order frontpay, where reinstatement was possible, despite concerns about potential co-worker hostility; the employer offered to put the plaintiff in a job where the potentially hostile co-workers would not be present.

Mitigation, including looking for other jobs, also figures into the front pay assessment. *See* Gotthardt v. Nat'l R.R. Passenger Corp., 191 F.3d 1148, 1157 (9th Cir. 1999) (ADEA case; front pay contemplates reasonable mitigation; "An award of front pay does not contemplate that a plaintiff will sit idly by and be compensated for doing nothing."); Castle v. Sangamo Weston, Inc., 837 F.2d 1550, 1562 (11th Cir. 1988) (ADEA plaintiff has a duty to mitigate). However, courts have not demanded that employees accept any job. The job must be "comparable." "[A] position constitutes comparable employment if it would afford the plaintiff virtually identical promotional opportunities, compensation, job responsibilities, working conditions and status as the position from which she was discharged." Hutchison v. Amateur Elec. Supply, 42 F.3d 1037, 1044 (7th Cir. 1994); Ward v. Tipton County Sheriff Dep't, 937 F.Supp. 791, 797 (S.D. Ind. 1996) ("Title VII claimants are not obliged to go into another line of work, accept a demotion, or take a demeaning position, in order to mitigate their damages.") (citations and internal quotations omitted).

d.   *Limitations on back and front pay –*
        collateral payments

Often a plaintiff will have been terminated, but also will have received benefits as a consequence of the termination, such as unemployment or increased pension benefits. Any front pay award must compensate the ex-employee plaintiff for losing his job, while avoiding a windfall for either the ex-employee or the employer.

Courts have analyzed these situations using a variant of the collateral source rule. If the additional funds received by the ex-employee come from a source independent of the employer, such as unemployment benefits, courts will not deduct them from the back or front pay award, because to do so would give the employer, assumedly a wrongdoer, an unfair windfall. *See* Moysis v. DTG Datanet, 278 F.3d 819, 828 (8th Cir. 2002) (workers compensation will not reduce back pay award) (citing Gaworski v. ITT Commercial Fin. Corp., 17 F.3d 1104, 1112 (8th Cir. 1994). *But see* Flowers v. Komatsu Mining Sys., Inc., 165 F.3d 554, 559 (7th Cir. 1999) (district court had discretion to deduct social security disability payments for periods plaintiff received back pay, despite collateral nature of payments).

On the other hand, a terminated employee may receive additional pension benefits because of her early (and wrongful) termination. While she may be entitled to front pay, permitting her to retain additional benefits as a result of the early termination would put her in a better position than if she had remained on the job. Accordingly, courts tend to deduct them from the front pay award. *See* Giles v. Gen. Elec. Co., 245 F.3d 474, 493-95 (5th Cir. 2001) (long term disability payments and disability pension used to reduce front pay award, because benefits designed to "compensate for [plaintiff's] inability to work in the future," just as front pay award is).

In the area of pension benefits, some courts have used the following test:

> (1) whether the employee makes any contribution to funding of the disability payment; (2) whether the benefit plan arises as the result of a collective bargaining agreement; (3) whether the plan and payments thereunder cover both work-related and nonwork-related injuries; (4) whether payments from the plan are contingent upon length of service of the employee; and (5) whether the plan contains any specific language contemplating a set-off of benefits received under the plan against a judgment received in a tort action.

Phillips v. W. Co. of N. Am., 953 F.2d 923, 932 (5th Cir. 1992); *see also* Hamlin v. Charter Twp. of Flint, 165 F.3d 426, 435 (6th Cir. 1999) (following *Phillips*). If the first four factors listed are affirmative and the fifth negative, it suggests that the employer should not benefit from the pension payout.

࿐

Notes & Questions

1. What if the employee receives sick pay benefits that may compensate for time she would have worked, but the employer caused the illness? *See* Salitros v. Chrysler Corp., 306 F.3d 562, 573-74 (8th Cir. 2002) (employer may not use sick pay, resulting from illness employer caused, to reduce front pay award).

2. What is the proper standard of review for these decisions? Some courts use an abuse of discretion standard, *Lussier v. Runyon*, 50 F.3d 1103, 1109-10 (1st Cir. 1995) (whether to deduct collateral source payments within district court's discretion), while others consider it as part of a broader policy issue and thus treat it as a question for de novo review. *See* Salitros, 306 F.3d at 573. Since the issue is one of the court's equitable powers, why should de novo review be used?

࿐

B.   *Compensatory Damages*

Compensatory damages include standard tort remedies, future monetary loss, pain and suffering, and the like. In 1991, Congress amended the Civil Rights Act to erase a number of decisions that had cut back on civil rights remedies and at the same time made equivalent compensatory and punitive damages available to those who suffered sex, religious, or ethnic discrimination. H.R. Rep. No. 40(II), 102d Cong., 1st Sess. 1991, reprinted in 1991 U.S.C.C.A.N. 549. The statute provides compensatory damages if the defendant engages in "unlawful intentional discrimination (not an employment practice that is unlawful because of its disparate impact)." 42 U.S.C. § 1981a(a)(1) (2006). It extended the same remedies to violations of the ADA and the Rehabilitation Act. 42 U.S.C. § 1981a(a)(2). However, it provides a safe harbor for employees who engage in good faith efforts to find a reasonable accommodation for the employee that will not impose undue hardship on the employer. *Id.* § 1981a(a)(3).

కొ

Notes & Questions

1. Most circuit courts had previously concluded that compensatory damages are in addition to front pay. *See* Giles v. Gen. Elec. Co., 245 F.3d 474, 490 n.28 (*comparing* Pals v. Schepel Buick & GMC Truck, Inc., 220 F.3d 495, 499-500 (7th Cir. 2000) (holding front pay exempt from cap); EEOC v. W & O, Inc., 213 F.3d 600, 618, n.10 (11th Cir. 2000) (same); Gotthardt v. Nat'l R.R. Passenger Corp., 191 F.3d 1148, 1153-54 (9th Cir. 1999) (same); Martini v. Fed. Nat'l Mortgage Ass'n, 178 F.3d 1336, 1348-49 (D.C. Cir. 1999) (same); Medlock v. Ortho Biotech, Inc., 164 F.3d 545, 556 (10th Cir. 1999) (same); Kramer v. Logan County Sch. Dist., 157 F.3d 620, 626 (8th Cir. 1998) (same), *with* Pollard v. E.I. DuPont de Nemours & Co., 213 F.3d 933, 945 (6th Cir. 2000) (reasoning that front pay is compensatory in nature and therefore subject to the cap), rev'd, 532 U.S. 843 (2001); Hudson v. Reno, 130 F.3d 1193, 1202-03 (6th Cir. 1997) (same)).

2. As seen in *Pollard*, the consequence of excluding front pay from compensatory damages is that the monetary limits of section 1981a(a) do not apply. While authorizing compensatory and punitive damages, Congress placed limits on those damages. The sum of compensatory and punitive damages is limited as follows:

> (A) for an employer with 15 to 100 employees in each of 20 or more calendar weeks in the current or preceding calendar year, $50,000;

> (B) for an employer with 101 to 200 employees in each of 20 or more calendar weeks in the current or preceding calendar year, $100,000;

> (C) for an employer with 201 to 500 employees in each of 20 or more calendar weeks in the current or preceding calendar year, $200,000; and

(D) for an employer with more than 500 employees in each of 20 or more calendar weeks in the current or preceding calendar year, $300,000.

42 U.S.C. § 1981a(b)(3)(A)-(D) (2006). The cap might be construed to cover compensatory and punitive damages separately, but courts have found that the correct reading is that the cap is an overall cap. Hogan v. Bangor & Aroostook R.R. Co., 61 F.3d 1034, 1037 (1st Cir. 1995) (citing Gately v. Commonwealth of Massachusetts, 2 F.3d 1221, 1228 (1st Cir. 1993)).

3. An individual may also seek state law remedies for the same behavior. If the state remedies are more generous, a court may award them. Gagliardo v. Connaught Lab., Inc., 311 F.3d 565, 570 (3d Cir. 2002). The Third Circuit relied on the statutory language: "Nothing in this chapter shall be construed to invalidate or limit the remedies, rights, and procedures of any Federal law or law of any State . . . that provides greater or equal protection for the rights of individuals with disabilities than are afforded by this chapter." Gagliardo, 311 F.3d at 570 (quoting 42 U.S.C. § 12201(b) (2000)).

4. Can a plaintiff receive compensatory (or punitive) damages for every type of discrimination claim? In *Kramer v. Banc of America Sec., LLC,* 355 F.3d 961 (7th Cir. 2004), the Seventh Circuit held that they were not available in a retaliation case.

5. The prohibition on retaliation is found in Title V – Miscellaneous Provisions. 42 U.S.C. § 12203. That section does not lay out specific remedies, but states, "The remedies and procedures available under sections 12117, 12133, and 12188 of this Act shall be available to aggrieved persons for violations of subsection[ ](a) . . . with respect to title I, title II and title III, respectively." Why would Congress have excluded compensatory and punitive damages for retaliation claims?

> The Fourth Circuit, however, in *Baird v. Rose*, 192 F.3d 462, 471-72 (4th Cir. 1999), noted that the remedies available for a violation of 42 U.S.C. § 12203 in the employment context are set forth in 42 U.S.C. § 12117, which "specifically makes the remedies available under Title VII applicable to actions under the ADA." *See also Fox v. Gen. Motors Corp.*, 247 F.3d 169, 175-76 (4th Cir. 2001) (stating that Congress evinced its knowledge of the parallel nature of Title VII and the ADA when it provided that " 'the powers, remedies, and procedures set forth in [Title VII] shall be the powers, remedies, and procedures [the ADA] provides' ") (quoting 42 U.S.C. § 12117(a)). It is undisputed that the Civil Rights Act of 1991, codified at 42 U.S.C. § 1981a, provides that compensatory damages are available for Title VII violations. *See* Lissau v. S. Food Serv., Inc., 159 F.3d 177, 180-81 (4th Cir. 1998).

The legislative history of the ADA supports the proposition that compensatory damages available under Title VII are also available in actions brought under the ADA. * * * [A] committee report stated that "if the powers, remedies, and procedures change in Title VII of the 1964 Act, they will change identically under the ADA for persons with disabilities . . . the Committee's intent is that the remedies of Title VII, currently and as amended in the future, will be applicable to persons with disabilities." *Id.* (quoting H.R. Rep. No. 101-485, pt. 3, at 48 (1990)).

Rhoads v. FDIC, No. CCB-94-1548, 2002 WL 31755427, *1-*2 (D. Md. Nov. 7, 2002).

6. In *Edwards v. Brookhaven Science Associates, LLC*, 390 F.Supp.2d 225, 236 (E.D.N.Y. 2005), the court rejected *Kramer* and found that a retaliation claim could result in compensatory damages and required a jury trial. *But see* Cantrell v. Nissan N. Am., Inc., No. 3:03-0082, 2006 WL 724549 (M.D. Tn. Mar. 21, 2006) (following *Kramer*); Santana v. Lehigh Valley Hosp. & Health Network, No. Civ.A.05-CV-01496, 2005 WL 1941654 (E.D. Pa. Aug. 11, 2005) (same).

7. ADA compensatory damages are subject to the same standards of proof as standard tort damages for emotional distress, pain and suffering, and loss of the enjoyment of life. The size of compensatory damages is, in the first instance, a question for the jury. "There is a strong presumption in favor of affirming a jury award of damages. The damage award may be overturned only upon a clear showing of excessiveness." Giles v. Gen. Elec. Co., 245 F.3d 474, 488 (5th Cir. 2001) (quoting Eiland v. Westinghouse Elec. Corp., 58 F.3d 176, 183 (5th Cir. 1995) (believing a $300,000 verdict was excessive, the Fifth Circuit cut it in half)). On the other hand, where an employer refused to permit an employee to return to work, viewing him as having a disability, and thereby cut his $28,000 income in less than half, causing his wife to go to work, instead of caring for their small children, the First Circuit approved a $200,000 compensatory award. Hogan v. Bangor & Aroostook R. Co., 61 F.3d 1034, 1037 (1st Cir. 1995).

8. In 2009, a federal court approved the largest settlement award in ADA history for a single ADA claim. The settlement was obtained in *EEOC v. Sears, Roebuck, and Co.* for $6.2 million after the EEOC alleged that Sears maintained an inflexible workers compensation policy for the exhaustion of leaves of absence and terminated employees with disabilities rather than provide them with accommodations. EEOC, Press Release, Sears, Roebuck to Pay $6.2 Million for Disability Bias (Sept. 9, 2009), http://www.eeoc.gov/eeoc/newsroom/release/9-29-09.cfm.

C. *Punitive Damages*

Congress added punitive damages to plaintiffs' arsenal of ADA Title I remedies in 1991. Section 1981a adopts its own standard for imposing those damages, which is not necessarily congruent with common-law tests. The statute provides that a defendant must have engaged in intentional discrimination and has done so "with malice or with reckless indifference to the federally protected rights of an aggrieved individual." Rev. Stat. § 1977, as amended, 42 U.S.C. § 1981a(b)(1). In *Kolstad v. American Dental Ass'n,* 527 U.S. 526 (1999), a sex discrimination case, the Court held that punitive damages are only available when the plaintiff has shown that the employer has discriminated with the knowledge that so doing violates federal law. The Court also held that an employer may not be vicariously liable for the discriminatory employment decisions of managerial agents where these decisions are contrary to the employer's good-faith efforts to comply with Title VII.

In Title I ADA cases, following *Kolstad,* courts have affirmed juries' imposition of punitive damages on employers based on their knowledge in a range of situations. For instance, in *Gagliardo,* 311 F.3d at 573, the court found: (1) the employer showed reckless indifference to plaintiff's rights, where the supervisor and human resources (HR) representative knew the plaintiff had multiple sclerosis and the HR representative, who also had MS, knew that the requested accommodation was reasonable, but the employer failed after various requests to provide accommodation; and (2) the employer was aware of plaintiff's rights because the HR representative, who was familiar with the ADA and responsible for ensuring the employer followed the ADA, was a sufficiently high manager that her knowledge was imputed to the defendant corporation.

In *Salitros,* the jury had awarded punitive damages. The court of appeals wrote:

> [The] manager . . . was quoted as saying he was going to teach Salitros a lesson, in circumstances that support the inference that the lesson to be learned was either not to file EEOC charges or not to protest work assignments that he thought exceeded his medical restrictions. [The manager] testified that he had received training on the Americans With Disabilities Act. A jury could conclude that [he] acted in reckless indifference to whether he was violating Salitros's federally protected rights.

Salitros v. Chrysler Corp., 306 F.3d 562, 570 (8th Cir. 2002). "[The manager's] malice may be imputed to [the corporate defendant] because he was serving in a managerial capacity and acting in the scope of his employment." *Id. But see* Dilley v. SuperValu, Inc., 296 F.3d 958, 966-67

(10th Cir. 2002) (court properly did not submit punitive damage issue to jury: evidence insufficient to show disregard of right).

§ 10.4 Statute Of Limitations

Once an ADA claim has accrued – given rise to a claim for relief – the statute of limitations begins to run: if the complainant does not file within the statutory period, the claim is barred, unless it was tolled or the defendant is estopped from relying on it. Title I requires exhaustion of administrative remedies. Those remedies are exhausted when the claimant receives notice that the EEOC has issued a right to sue letter. Title VII's 90-day limitation period to file suit then takes over. At that point, the cause of action has accrued and the complainant has 90 days to file a lawsuit. 42 U.S.C. § 2000e-5(f)(1) (2006).

Notes & Questions

1. What kind of notice must a person have of the EEOC's decision? In *Ebbert v. DaimlerChrysler Corp.*, 319 F.3d 103, 114 (3d Cir. 2003), the Third Circuit held that oral notice may suffice, if it is as complete as written notice, i.e., states that the claimant has 90 days to file a suit.

2. Does the notice of the EEOC's decision have to be to the claimant? In *Ball v. Abbott Advertising, Inc.*, 864 F.2d 419, 421 (6th Cir. 1988), the court held that oral notice to the claimant's attorney sufficed, without saying anything about the completeness of the notice. The *Ebbert* court speculated that the *Ball* court might have assumed the attorney was or should have been aware of the limitations period. Ebbert, 319 F.3d at 116 n.16.

3. Actual receipt of a letter from the EEOC is not always required; constructive receipt will suffice in many jurisdictions. Zillyette v. Capital One Fin. Corp., 179 F.3d 1337, 1340-41 (11th Cir. 1999) (giving a survey of cases in different jurisdictions accepting various forms of constructive receipt as causing the start of the 90-day period). *But see* Hornsby v. U.S. Postal Serv., 787 F.2d 87, 91, nn.4-7 (3d Cir. 1986) (postal form notifying the plaintiff that a letter addressed to him could be picked up at the Post Office but not identifying the sender, did not, by itself, constitute notice of an EEOC final action even if other circumstances short of actual receipt of the written notice would have sufficed).

§ 10.5 Attorneys' Fees

In any action or administrative proceeding commenced pursuant to [the Americans with Disabilities Act], the court or agency, in its discretion, may allow the prevailing party, other than the United States, a reasonable attorney's fee, including litigation expenses, and costs, and the United States shall be liable for the foregoing the same as a private individual.[10]

42 U.S.C. § 12205 (2006).

The last battle in an ADA case is often waged over the parties' attorneys' fees requests.[11] Fees go to the prevailing party – other than the government. The disputes over attorneys' fees typically take two forms: (1) is the person seeking fees the prevailing party; (2) are the fees requested reasonable?

A. *Prevailing Party*

On the first issue, the law presently seems to confer prevailing party status on someone who obtains a judgment and on someone who obtains a judicially enforceable agreement – a consent decree or a court-supervised settlement agreement, but not someone who, by filing an action, simply caused the defendant to change its practices. This issue is discussed thoroughly in Part 5 in the context of the Supreme Court's decision in *Buckhannon Board & Care Home, Inc. v. W. Va. Department of Health and Human Resources.*

There are some Title I quirks, however. In a "mixed-motive" case, the plaintiff may show, for example, that the defendant violated the ADA in firing her; but the defendant shows it would have taken the same action in the absence of the discrimination, so the plaintiff takes only a declaratory judgment. In those cases, the plaintiff is not entitled to attorneys' fees, because she is not a prevailing party under Section 12205. Pedigo v. P.A.M. Transp., Inc., 98 F.3d 396, 398 (8th Cir. 1996) ("*Pedigo II*"); *see also* Dehne v. Med. Shoppe Int'l, Inc., 261 F.Supp.2d 1142, 1147-48 (E.D. Mo. 2003). Section 107 of the Civil Rights Act of 1991, 42 U.S.C. § 2000e-5(g)(2)(B)(i) (2006), which should apply to ADA Title I cases, allows attorneys' fees even when only declaratory relief is awarded. Pedigo v. P.A.M. Transp., Inc., 60 F.3d 1300, 1301 (8th Cir. 1995). However, in *Pedigo II*, a later case involving the same parties, the Eighth Circuit looked to ADA section 505 and found the plaintiff had not prevailed for attorneys' fees purposes. The ADA-specific statute trumped the more general Title VII provision.

---

[10]   Note that section 107 of the ADA, 42 U.S.C. § 12117, which sets Title I's remedies, incorporates the remedies of Title VII of the Civil Rights Act of 1964. The latter permits attorneys' fees in cases section 505 might not. However, courts have applied the ADA-specific statute, rather than Title VII.

[11]   The prevailing party is also entitle to costs under Federal Rule of Civil Procedure 54(d)(1). *See* Miles v. State, 320 F.3d 986, 988-89 (9th Cir. 2003).

Similarly, a "prevailing party" may mean different things for a plaintiff or a defendant. Consider the following case.

❧

ADKINS v. BRIGGS & STRATTON CORP.

United States Court of Appeals, Seventh Circuit, 1998
159 F.3d 306

TERENCE T. EVANS, Circuit Judge.

The Briggs & Stratton Corporation fired Thomas Adkins after finding him sleeping at the wheel of his forklift. As it turned out, Adkins may have had a legitimate excuse for dozing off: narcolepsy, a condition characterized by an uncontrollable need for short periods of sleep. But Adkins admitted that the company had no knowledge of the disease when it fired him; in fact, Adkins' narcolepsy wasn't diagnosed until 4 months later. Nevertheless, Adkins sued under the ADA, alleging that the company fired him "because of" his disability.

Citing *Hedberg v. Indiana Bell Telephone Co.,* 47 F.3d 928 (7th Cir.1995), the district court found that "[a]s a matter of both logic and law, it is impossible for an employer to take action 'because of' a disability the employer knew nothing about." The court therefore dismissed Adkins' complaint for failure to state a claim. Emboldened by the court's ruling, Briggs & Stratton then moved for attorney's fees. But the district court denied the motion and Briggs & Stratton appeals. We review the denial of a motion for fees for abuse of discretion. See *Eichman v. Linden & Sons, Inc.,* 752 F.2d 1246, 1248 (7th Cir.1985).

The ADA gives the district court discretion to award attorney's fees to a "prevailing party." 42 U.S.C. § 12205. Although both employers and employees may "prevail" and therefore recover fees under the Act, the standard for awarding fees to employers is higher: an award of fees to an employer is appropriate only when the suit is brought in bad faith or when it is frivolous, unreasonable, or without foundation. *Christiansburg Garment Co. v. EEOC,* 434 U.S. 412, 421-22, 98 S.Ct. 694, 54 L.Ed.2d 648 (1978).

Despite its earlier ruling on the motion to dismiss – and the strong language that the claim defied both logic and law – the district court concluded that Briggs & Stratton was not entitled to fees because Adkins' claim was sufficiently distinguishable from *Hedberg* to save it from being frivolous. We disagree. No matter how you slice it, Adkins' claim was frivolous. *Hedberg*'s lesson is simple and straightforward: "an employer cannot be liable under the ADA for firing an employee when it indisputably had no knowledge of the disability." 47 F.3d at 932. Adkins admitted in his complaint that Briggs & Stratton had no knowledge of his narcolepsy – he himself did not know he had the disease until several months after he was fired. Thus, Adkins had no ADA claim. Period.

Briggs & Stratton argues that the district court's ruling on the fees motion was inconsistent with the ruling on the motion to dismiss and we agree. The court cannot adopt one standard of frivolousness for purposes of deciding a motion to dismiss and another standard for purposes of deciding a motion for attorney's fees. Because the court appeared to do just that, we reverse. In ruling on the motion to dismiss, the district court correctly found Adkins' claim to be frivolous (though the court didn't use that exact word); it should have made the same finding in ruling on the attorney's fees motion.

But does a frivolous finding necessarily mean that Briggs & Stratton is entitled to fees? In a word: no. Nothing in § 12205 suggests that the court *must* award fees to a party defending against a frivolous claim; indeed, the statute expressly states that the court "*in its discretion may* allow the prevailing party . . . a reasonable attorney's fee . . ." (emphasis added). Similarly, *Christiansburg* counsels that fees are *appropriate* – not mandatory – when a claim is frivolous. In exercising its discretion, the court is free to weigh equitable considerations (including the employee's ability to pay) and to award a nominal fee – or even no fee – if the court, for acceptable reasons, deems it appropriate. Certainly the court need not award the full amount requested, even if the fee request is reasonable. A district court cannot, however, backpedal from a frivolous finding on a motion to dismiss to avoid imposing fees. Accordingly, we reverse the order denying costs and remand the case to the distinguished and experienced district judge for further proceedings consistent with this opinion.

Notes & Questions

1. The courts uniformly have held that the standard for awarding attorneys' fees to defendants is higher than that for awarding them to plaintiffs. Why? As the Seventh Circuit put it in *Adkins*, "an award of fees to an employer is appropriate only when the suit is brought in bad faith or when it is frivolous, unreasonable, or without foundation." *See also* Bercovitch v. Baldwin Sch., Inc., 191 F.3d 8, 10 (1st Cir. 1999) (citing Hughes v. Rowe, 449 U.S. 5, 14 (1980) (per curiam) (noting that the Supreme Court has applied the same rule under 42 U.S.C. § 1983)). This asymmetry is a result of Congress's recognition that attorneys' fees under the ADA should be "interpreted in a manner consistent with the Civil Rights Attorneys' Fees Act [42 U.S.C. § 1988], including that statute's definition of prevailing party, as construed by the Supreme Court." H.R. Doc. No. 101-485 (III), at 73 (1990), 1990 U.S.C.C.A.N. 445, 496 (citing Christiansburg Garment Co. v. EEOC, 434 U.S. 412, 422 (1978), and Hughes, 449 U.S. at 5). The court is not required to award attorneys' fees to a prevailing defendant even if the action is frivolous. *See* Greenier v. Pace, Local No. 1188, 245 F.Supp.2d 247, 249, 250 (D. Me. 2003) ("[T]he frivolity showing required of a prevailing party applies with 'special force' in pro se actions. *Hughes v. Rowe*, 449 U.S. 5, 14-16 * * * (applying the *Christiansburg* standard to pro se plaintiffs under the fee-shifting

provision 42 U.S.C. § 1988)," and refusing to award fees to defendant, "[i]n light of Plaintiff's limited ability to grasp the legal significance of his actions as well as the sanctions already imposed in this matter").

2. Generally, subjective bad faith is not required to show frivolousness, rather it is sufficient that the action objectively arguably lacks a basis in law or fact. Neitzke v. Williams, 490 U.S. 319, 325 (1989). In *Schutts v. Bently Nev. Corp.*, 966 F.Supp. 1549 (D. Nev. 1997), the plaintiff was fired by the defendant after the plaintiff was arrested for and eventually convicted of hitting a person with a gun and holding the gun to the person's head, threatening to "blow his brains out." The Court held that the law in the Ninth Circuit and elsewhere clearly gave an employer the right to fire an employee for improper acts even if those acts arose out of an alleged disability – here depression. The Court found that the facts and "controlling federal judicial authority extant prior to the initiation of this action, should have made plain to Plaintiff and his lawyer the futility – and impropriety – of filing the complaint and of opposing Defendant's meritorious summary judgment motion." *Id*. at 1557. On those facts, the court awarded the defendant attorneys' fees under 42 U.S.C. § 12205 (2006) and, showing its displeasure, under Federal Rule of Civil Procedure 11.

B.   *Reasonableness Of Fees*

The calculation of reasonable attorneys' fees in ADA cases is the same as that in other civil rights cases. Because those fees can be a substantial percentage or even exceed the damages, their overhanging shadow can influence settlement discussions in even apparently defensible cases. The following case addresses a range of issues that arise when a court awards fees.

LANNI v. NEW JERSEY

United States Court of Appeals, Third Circuit, 2001
259 F.3d 146

STAPLETON, Circuit Judge.

This appeal involves a dispute over attorney's fees awarded in a suit brought under the Americans with Disabilities Act ("ADA") and the New Jersey Law Against Discrimination ("LAD"). Phillip Lanni prevailed below, but argues on appeal that the District Court erred in its calculation of his attorney's fees. * * *.

I.

[Lanni had a learning disability and alleged his employer, the State of New Jersey, and various of its employees discriminated against him. He signed a "partial contingency fee" agreement with Linda Wong of the law firm Wong Fleming, P.C., procuring her representation in an action against the state. Wong Fleming filed a 10 count complaint against nine defendants and "the District Court dismissed the majority of these claims on summary judgment, leaving only one count against three individual defendants and the [State]".] * * *

After nineteen days of testimony, the jury returned a verdict finding violations of the ADA and LAD by two defendants and the [State] and finding no liability on the part of the third individual defendant. Lanni was awarded $70,930.00 in economic damages and $156,100.00 in non-economic damages. No punitive damages were assessed.

Pursuant to the ADA and the LAD, Lanni was permitted to recover reasonable attorney's fees as a result of prevailing in his law suit. Six months after the verdict, Lanni filed an application that claimed his lawyers were entitled to $1,165,444.88 in attorney's fees and $49,412.75 in costs, for a total fee of $1,214,857.63. Six months later, following hearings and the submission of briefs on the issue of fees, the District Court awarded Lanni $277,723.50 in fees and $24,706.00 in costs. The correctness of the process by which the District Court calculated this award is the primary matter disputed.

II.

We review the District Court's decision to award attorney's fees under an abuse of discretion standard. * * * Whether the correct standards were applied by the District Court in determining the allowable fee is a question of law subject to plenary review. *See Rode v. Dellarciprete,* 892 F.2d 1177, 1182 (3d Cir.1990). The District Court's factual findings will be disturbed only if they are clearly erroneous. *Id.* at 1182-83.

As the prevailing party on an ADA claim, Lanni is permitted to recover an award of attorney's fees. 42 U.S.C. § 12205 ("the court or agency, in its discretion, may allow the prevailing party [in a discrimination case] . . . a reasonable attorney's fee, including litigation expenses, and costs . . ."). The LAD has a similar provision. N.J.S.A. 10: 5-27.1 ("the prevailing party may be awarded a reasonable attorney's fee . . .").

The jury's damage award in this case was made under both the ADA and LAD. Accordingly, to the extent the applicable standards for an award of attorney's fees and costs differ under the two statutes and an appropriate award under one exceeds an appropriate award under the other, Lanni is entitled to elect to receive the higher award. As we discuss hereafter, an award under the LAD may reflect any risk of nonpayment of a fee assumed by counsel. An award under the ADA may not reflect that risk. In other respects, the ADA and LAD law applicable here does not materially differ.

Under both ADA and LAD law, a "lodestar" amount provides the starting point for determining reasonable attorney's fees. *See Rode,* 892 F.2d at 1183. The lodestar is obtained by multiplying the number of hours reasonably expended on the litigation by a reasonable hourly rate. *See id.* A District Court has substantial discretion in determining what constitutes a reasonable rate and reasonable hours, but once the lodestar is determined, it is presumed to be the reasonable fee. *See id.* Following a determination of the lodestar, either party may seek adjustment. If that party meets the burden of proving that an adjustment is appropriate, the lodestar amount may be increased or reduced at the discretion of the District Court. *See id.*

Wong Fleming utilized an electronic billing system that tracked time spent by each employee of the firm to the tenth of an hour. Both Ms. Wong and Mr. Fleming alleged that they currently charge $325 an hour for their services. Wong Fleming asserted that its associates were due fees in the $180 an hour range (depending upon experience), while its paralegals and other firm staff were due payment at a lesser rate, but not below $70 an hour. Multiplying these rates by the hours recorded in their billing system, Wong Fleming calculated its lodestar. Wong Fleming then argued that a multiplier of 75% was warranted in this case due to the substantially contingent nature of the compensation structure and the legal risk associated with taking the case.[12] In this way, Wong Fleming arrived at its total requested attorney's fees of $1,165,444 .88. Costs and expenses were claimed at $49,412.75.

While accepting that Lanni, as a prevailing party, was entitled to his reasonable attorney's fees, the District Court did not accept Wong Fleming's calculations. Lanni raises five challenges to the District Court's decision regarding costs and fees.

A.

First, Lanni contends that the District Court erred in its determination of reasonable hourly market rates for Wong Fleming's services. The District Court rejected Wong Fleming's asserted rate of $325 an hour for Linda Wong and Daniel Fleming. The District Court instead concluded that the reasonable hourly rates of Wong and Fleming should be calculated on a graduated scale, varying according to the time period during which the services were performed.

The party seeking fees bears the burden of producing sufficient evidence of what constitutes a reasonable market rate for the essential character and complexity of the legal services rendered in order to make out a prima facie case. * * * If the prima facie case has been made, the opposing party bears the burden of producing record evidence that will

---

12   Perhaps it would be more accurate to say the multiplier is 175%.

contest this rate. *Id.* If reasonable market rates are in dispute, a hearing must be conducted. *Id.*

When attorney's fees are awarded, the current market rate must be used. *See Rode,* 892 F.2d at 1183; *Rendine v. Pantzer,* 141 N.J. 292, 661 A.2d 1202 (1995). The current market rate is the rate at the time of the fee petition, not the rate at the time the services were performed. *See Rode,* 892 F.2d at 1188-89 (describing petition based on current rates as premised on a theory of "delay compensation"); *Rendine,* 661 A.2d at 1227 ("To take into account delay in payment, the hourly rate at which compensation is to be awarded should be based on current rates rather than those in effect when the services were performed.").

The District Court was apparently well aware of these rules, and stated that it was using a "current market rate" to determine the proper attorney's fees due to appellant. It then inexplicably calculated the fees on a graduated scale roughly tracking the actual historic rates of Linda Wong. The District Court observed that the "method of applying current rates is flexible within the discretion of the Court" and then concluded that calculating rates on a graduated scale would be "consistent with the rationale behind calculating a reasonable hourly rate" because it would "offset the costs of the delay in payment to plaintiff's counsel, while still avoiding a 'windfall' to counsel beyond their reasonable rate." We are uncertain how the District Court believed its professed use of the current market rate could be harmonized with a graduated scale that awarded historic rates. A current market rate is exactly that – a reasonable rate based on the currently prevailing rates in the community for comparable legal services. It is not a graduated schedule of past rates. We conclude that the District Court's use of an historical graduated scale to calculate a current market rate for partners at Wong Fleming was a misapplication of the appropriate legal standard.

[The court reaches a similar conclusion regarding the district court's calculation of associate and paralegal rates.]

While we agree with the appellant that the testimony of appellee's expert contains very little in the way of probative "contradictory evidence" of currently prevailing market rates and agree that in some instances, a district court may be justified in awarding rates similar to those requested by Wong Fleming, * * * we conclude defendants met their burden of coming forward with sufficient other evidence to support a finding that the market rate in this situation was well below the rates claimed by Wong Fleming. On remand, the District Court should determine the currently prevailing rates in the community for comparable legal services at the time the fee petition was filed.

B.

Second, Lanni claims the District Court erred when it found that the presence of both named partners of Wong Fleming at trial was excessive and determined that allowance of the claimed hours for the presence of a second partner would be unreasonable. The District Court accordingly disallowed the 138.7 hours spent by Mr. Fleming at trial. Wong Fleming asserts that this case was unusually challenging and novel and required the time of two attorneys.

Rendine admonishes that "[t]rial courts should not accept passively the submission of counsel to support the lodestar amount. . . . For example, where three attorneys are present at a hearing when one would suffice, compensation should be denied for the excess time." *Rendine*, 661 A.2d at 1226. * * * It is therefore clearly permissible as a general matter under the LAD for a court to find the presence of two named partners during a trial to constitute an excessive and unreasonable expenditure of hours.

The District Court did not abuse its discretion. Given Wong's professed expertise in this area, it would have not been unreasonable to expect her to conduct the trial alone or with the help of an associate. While we believe awarding fees for Fleming's time multiplied by an associate's rate may been justifiable here, it is not our role under an abuse of discretion standard to substitute our inclinations for those of the District Court. * * * Accordingly, the District Court's disallowance of Fleming's trial time will stand.

C.

Third, Lanni claims the District Court erred by deducting 25% from the lodestar because Lanni did not prevail on all of his claims. The District Court's downward adjustment was made under the rubric of *Hensley v. Eckerhart,* 461 U.S. 424, 433-35, 103 S.Ct. 1933, 76 L.Ed.2d 40 (1983), which teaches that where a plaintiff prevails on one or more claims but not on others, fees shall not be awarded for time that would not have been spent had the unsuccessful claims not been pursued. The *Hensley* Court termed this a downward adjustment for "limited success." *Id.* at 436-37, 103 S.Ct. 1933.

The District Court noted that only two of the original ten claims had succeeded and that only the DEP and two of the original nine individual defendants had been found liable. Wong Fleming has failed to persuade us that the time spent pursuing the unsuccessful claims contributed in any way to Lanni's success on his remaining claims. Accordingly, we find no abuse of discretion in connection with the *Hensley* reduction of the lodestar for limited success.

D.

Fourth, Lanni claims the District Court erred by denying its request for a multiplier enhancing the lodestar by 75% based on the risk of counsel's being inadequately compensated. The law of the ADA and LAD diverge on the question of the availability of multiplier enhancements for contingency of compensation. While there is no basis for such enhancements under the ADA, they are permissible under the LAD. *Compare City of Burlington v. Dague,* 505 U.S. 557, 563, 112 S.Ct. 2638, 120 L.Ed.2d 449 (1992) (finding, under a comparable federal fees provision that contingency fees would "amount[ ] to double counting") *with Rendine v. Pantzer,* 661 A.2d at 1202 (N.J.1995) (rejecting *Dague* and approving of contingency enhancements under the LAD).

* * *

LAD cases have not required "pure" contingency in order to warrant an enhancement, but instead have awarded multipliers in cases where fees were "substantially" or "predominantly" contingent. *Rendine,* 661 A.2d at 1216-17. The agreement in this case was hardly a straightforward contingency arrangement. Lanni paid $32,000 to Wong Fleming during the course of the litigation and was required by contract to pay Wong Fleming a minimum of $125 per hour, whether he won or lost at trial. Lanni points out, however, that the $125 an hour rate was a reduced "partial contingency" rate below Wong Fleming's normal rate (which was $175 for Linda Wong, at least initially). Wong Fleming also represents that it took Lanni's case knowing that he was considering filing for bankruptcy in order to prevent a foreclosure on his home.

The District Court stated: "The Court has considered plaintiff's entitlement to an enhancement under the LAD. While plaintiff's attorneys in this case were competent and the case was well argued, the Court concludes that counsel's performance does not warrant an enhancement in this case." Wong Fleming argues that the District Court misperceived the claim it was making. Wong Fleming makes no argument that Lanni is entitled to an enhancement based on the quality of its performance. Rather, it argues for a contingency enhancement under *Rendine,* 661 A.2d at 1228 ("We hold that the trial court, after having carefully established the amount of the lodestar fee, should consider whether to increase that fee to reflect the risk of nonpayment in all cases in which the attorney's compensation entirely or substantially is contingent on a successful outcome.").

The District Court failed to address the *Rendine* argument. On remand, the District Court must consider whether this is a "substantially contingent" case under the *Rendine* analysis, and if so, whether a contingency enhancement is warranted.

E.

Fifth, Lanni contends that the District Court erred by reducing all of its costs by 50% based solely on the finding that Wong Fleming had charged what the Court thought to be unreasonable rates for photocopies and faxes. Wong Fleming charged twenty-five cents per page for photocopies and a dollar per page for faxes. The defendants offered evidence tending to show that copies could be purchased for two to six cents per page and faxes should have cost closer to fifty cents per page.

The District Court concluded that the costs and expenses requested by Wong Fleming were "excessive and extreme" and awarded only half the requested amount.

Like Lanni, we read the District Court's opinion as offering the disparity between faxing and photocopying costs and the actual costs of those services as the sole justification for the Court's fifty percent reduction. We can understand the District Court's indignation at what it understandably perceived to be overreaching with respect to faxing and photocopying, and we acknowledge that district courts have broad discretion in the imposition of costs. * * * Nevertheless, without more explanation than we have been given, we can only characterize the Court's fifty percent reduction as arbitrary. This is not a case in which the District Court has found a pattern of overreaching and has made a reasoned estimate of the overcharges. Here, we find ourselves simply unable to tell from whence the District Court's fifty percent figure came. On remand, the District Court will re-assess the costs and expenses.

* * *

CONCLUSION

We will vacate the District Court's award of attorney's fees and remand for further proceedings consistent with this opinion.

Notes & Questions

1. Does it make the least bit of sense to allow the plaintiff's lawyer to recover substantially more than the plaintiff? Why not, defense counsel will be paid their hourly fees even if their client loses? There are typically differences in the economics of plaintiff-side firms and defense-side firms. The former usually experience sporadic (but sometimes quite large) payments; the latter experience steady payments, but only rarely a premium. How, if at all, does the possibility of recovering essentially hourly fees change the incentives for plaintiff's counsel?

2. What is the purpose of a fee award? Are fees awarded in most cases? *See* Alyeska Pipeline Serv. Co. v. Wilderness Soc'y, 421 U.S. 240, 247 (1975) (discussing "American Rule" – a "general practice" of not awarding fees to a prevailing party absent explicit statutory authority).

3. As *Lanni* demonstrates, the first element in calculating a fee is to compute a "lodestar": the number of hours reasonably expended on the litigation multiplied by the reasonable hourly rate of the individuals working on the matter. *E.g.*, Staton v. Boeing Co., 327 F.3d 938, 964 (9th Cir. 2003); Giles v. Gen. Elec. Co., 245 F.3d 474, 490-91 (5th Cir. 2001). "A 'strong presumption' exists that the lodestar figure represents a 'reasonable fee,' and therefore, it should only be enhanced or reduced in 'rare and exceptional cases.'" Fischer v. SJB-P.D. Inc., 214 F.3d 1115, 1119 n.4 (9th Cir. 2000) (quoting Pennsylvania v. Del. Valley Citizens' Council for Clean Air, 478 U.S. 546, 565 (1986) (internal quotations

omitted)). *But see* No Barriers, Inc., v. Brinker Chili's Tex., Inc., 262 F.3d 496, 500-01 (5th Cir. 2001) (court not required to use lodestar in simple case when court familiar with work done). But a court has discretion to determine both the reasonable hours and the reasonable rates; *see, e.g.,* Giles, 245 F.3d at 490-91 (rates too high); Greenway v. Buffalo Hilton Hotel, 951 F.Supp. 1039, 1069 (W.D.N.Y. 1997) (attorneys seeking fees had not properly established the reasons for having two attorneys at depositions).

4.   May courts take into account the complexity of a case? *See* Roland v. Cellucci, 106 F.Supp.2d 128, 135-36 (D. Mass. 2000) (case involving a large class of individuals with disabilities and a number of novel time-consuming claims entitled to greater staffing). Should courts reduce fees if a case is particularly straightforward?

5.   Counsel who anticipate seeking fees, should carefully prepare their bills from the outset. Interestingly, often these cases involve litigation on behalf of clients to whom no bills are sent, but that should not lead to laxity in preparing statements. It is not uncommon for courts to refuse to award fees where statements are not sufficiently detailed. *E.g.,* No Barriers, Inc., 262 F.3d at 500.

6.   What factors ought a court to consider in awarding fees? A number of courts have approved a list of 12 factors that may be used to assess attorneys' fees:

(1)   The time and labor required;
(2)   The novelty and difficulty of the questions;
(3)   The skill requisite to perform a legal service properly;
(4)   The preclusion of employment by the attorney due to acceptance of the case;
(5)   The customary fees;
(6)   Whether the fee is fixed or contingent;
(7)   The time limitations imposed by the client or the circumstances;
(8)   The amount involved and the results obtained;
(9)   The experience, reputation, and ability of the attorney;
(10) The "undesirability" of the case;
(11) The nature and length of the professional relationship with the client; and
(12) Awards in similar cases.

Hamlin v. Charter Twp. of Flint, 165 F.3d 426, 437 (6th Cir. 1999) (citing Hensley v. Eckerhart, 461 U.S. 424, 430 n.3 (1983)); Johnson v. Ga. Highway Express, Inc., 488 F.2d 714, 717-19 (5th Cir. 1974). What determines the "undesirability" of a case? Suing the mill in a town where it is the largest employer? Seeking services for incarcerated juveniles?

7. How important is the measure of success in assessing fees? Where a party prevails only on a fraction of its claims, the court may reduce the award to reflect services on the losing claims. Lanni v. New Jersey, 259 F.3d 146, 151 (3d Cir. 2001) (approving reduction to account for lack of success on several claims). On the other hand, where counsel achieves a particularly good result, for example, prevailing in a complex case, the court has discretion to award more than the lodestar. Daggitt v. United Food & Commercial Workers Int'l Union, Local 304A, 245 F.3d 981, 989-90 (8th Cir. 2001). But what if the plaintiff obtains only nominal damages? The Supreme Court has written, "When a plaintiff recovers only nominal damages because of his failure to prove an essential element of his claim for monetary relief, the only reasonable fee is usually no fee at all." Farrar v. Hobby, 506 U.S. 103, 115 (1992) (citation omitted). That is, the size of the award determines, not whether a party prevails, but the size of the appropriate fee. For example, in *Red Cloud-Owen v. Albany Steel, Inc.*, 958 F.Supp. 94 (N.D.N.Y. 1997), the jury awarded the plaintiff $1. The court cited *Carroll v. Blinken*, 105 F.3d 79, 81 (2d Cir. 1997) for the proposition:

> *Pino* [*v. Locasio*, 101 F.3d 235, 237 (2d Cir. 1996)] stands for the proposition that in determining the reasonableness of a fee award . . ., the quantity and quality of relief obtained is a critical factor. Where the damage award is nominal or modest, the injunctive relief has no systemic effect of importance, and no substantial public interest is served, a substantial fee award cannot be justified.

Red Cloud-Owen, 958 F.Supp. at 96. The court declined to award the plaintiff attorneys' fees.

8. What is the measure of fees if the only relief awarded is an injunction?

9. And if the defendant wins, does it obtain fees? Courts are reluctant to do so. What should the test be? A prevailing defendant only recovers if plaintiff's claim is "frivolous, unreasonable, or groundless, or . . . the plaintiff continued to litigate after it clearly became so." Christiansburg Garment Co. v. EEOC, 434 U.S. 412, 422 (1978). Is it sufficient that the defendant prevails? One court has written: "[W]here evidence is introduced that, if credited, would suffice to support a judgment, fees [for the defendant] are unjustified." Am. Fed'n of State, County & Mun. Employees v. County of Nassau, 96 F.3d 644, 652 (2d Cir. 1996). In *Red Cloud-Owen*, there was such evidence, so it was inappropriate to award fees to the defendant. 958 F.Supp. at 98.

৯

§ 10.6   A Note On The Taxability Of Attorneys' Fee Awards

Tax law is beyond the general scope of this casebook. However, taxes permeate everything, so it is important to bear them in mind when settling litigation.

Compensatory damages in ADA litigation generally will be taxable. *See generally*, Internal Revenue Service, IRS Publication 4345, Settlements-Taxability (2004). To the extent a settlement is for back pay or front pay, it would not be excludable from income under section 104 of the Internal Revenue Code. Comm'r of Internal Revenue v. Schleier, 515 U.S. 323, 328-32 (1995) (finding damages under ADEA to be taxable, since ADEA allows only lost pay and liquidated damages). To the extent the settlement or award is for emotional distress and other forms of compensatory damages, unless it flows directly from personal injury or illness, it is not excludable, because it does not constitute personal injury under section 104(a)(2). Banaitis v. Comm'r of Internal Revenue, 340 F.3d 1074, 1077-80 (9th Cir. 2003). Finally, all punitive damages are taxable. O'Gilvie v. United States, 519 U.S. 79, 84-89 (1996).

The treatment of attorneys' fees has been problematic. The nature of a settlement for tax purposes depends upon the "nature and basis of the action settled; and amounts received in compromise of a claim must be considered as having the same nature as the right compromised." Alexander v. Internal Revenue Serv., 72 F.3d 938, 942 (1st Cir. 1995). Thus, in employment discrimination cases, where virtually all of the settlement will be taxable, courts that view the attorneys' fees portion of the settlement as income to the plaintiff, view the attorneys' fees as income as well. It may, of course, be possible to allocate attorneys' fees to parts of a settlement that are not taxable, if such exist. In that event, the proponent of the fee allocation must prove that allocation. Although such evidence as attorneys' timesheets will be permitted, courts need not allocate pro rata based on the amounts of the settlement. Alexander, 72 F.3d at 940.

Some courts had held that the taxability may depend on the way state law treats such fees. Where state law treated them as property of the plaintiff, they were taxable. Coady v. Comm'r, 213 F.3d 1187, 1190-91 (9th Cir. 2000) (Alaska law; wrongful termination). Where state law gave the attorney a lien or other right to a portion of the settlement, the fees were not income to the plaintiff, and thus not taxable. Banaitis v. Comm'r of Internal Revenue, 340 F.3d 1074, 1082-83 (9th Cir. 2003) (California law), rev'd sub nom. Comm'r v. Banks, 543 U.S. 426 (2005). However, courts have refused to defer to state-law characterizations of the property interest in the part of the settlement or judgment that represents the fee. Young v. Comm'r, 240 F.3d 369, 377-79 (4th Cir. 2001) (property dispute between former spouses; rejecting theory that state law controls and finding North Carolina law differs from Alabama law).

The Supreme Court in *Comm'r v. Banks*, 543 U.S. 426 (2005) rejected the plaintiff's argument that because he had a contingent fee agreement with his attorney, entered into prior to the suit, his fee award was not income to him, but to his counsel. The Court wrote:

> The Internal Revenue Code defines "gross income" for federal tax purposes as "all income from whatever source derived." 26 U.S.C. § 61(a). The definition extends broadly to all economic gains not otherwise exempted. *Commissioner v. Glenshaw Glass Co.*, 348 U.S. 426, 429-30, 75 S.Ct. 473, 99 L.Ed. 483 (1955); *Commissioner v. Jacobson*, 336 U.S. 28, 49, 69 S.Ct. 358, 93 L.Ed. 477 (1949). A taxpayer cannot exclude an economic gain from gross income by assigning the gain in advance to another party. *Lucas v. Earl,* 281 U.S. 111, 50 S.Ct. 241, 74 L.Ed. 731 (1930) * * *. The rationale for the so-called anticipatory assignment of income doctrine is the principle that gains should be taxed "to those who earn them," *Lucas, supra*, at 114, 50 S.Ct. 241, a maxim we have called "the first principle of income taxation," *Commissioner v. Culbertson*, 337 U.S. 733, 739-740, 69 S.Ct. 1210, 93 L.Ed. 1659 (1949). The anticipatory assignment doctrine is meant to prevent taxpayers from avoiding taxation through "arrangements and contracts however skillfully devised to prevent [income] when paid from vesting even for a second in the man who earned it." *Lucas*, 281 U.S., at 115, 50 S.Ct. 241. The rule is preventative and motivated by administrative as well as substantive concerns, so we do not inquire whether any particular assignment has a discernible tax avoidance purpose. . . .

> Respondents argue that the anticipatory assignment doctrine is a judge-made antifraud rule with no relevance to contingent-fee contracts of the sort at issue here. The Commissioner maintains that a contingent-fee agreement should be viewed as an anticipatory assignment to the attorney of a portion of the client's income from any litigation recovery. We agree with the Commissioner.

> . . . Though the value of the plaintiff's claim may be speculative at the moment the fee agreement is signed, the anticipatory assignment doctrine is not limited to instances when the precise dollar value of the assigned income is known in advance. *Lucas, supra*; *United States v. Basye*, 410 U.S. 441, 445, 450-452, 93 S.Ct. 1080, 35 L.Ed.2d 412 (1973).

Id. at 433-35.

If taxpayers have to take the attorneys' fees part of the award into their gross income, some might argue that they should be able to treat the inevitable "payment" to the attorney as a trade or business expense. *See* 26 U.S.C. § 162(a) (2006). However, courts have rejected this approach. The attorneys' fees must be treated as a "miscellaneous itemized deduction" under Section 63 of the Internal Revenue Code. *See* Alexander v. Internal Revenue Serv., 72 F.3d 938, 944-46 (1st Cir. 1995).

However, the question of the taxability of fees is largely historic. In 2004, the American Jobs Creation Act of 2004, Pub. L. No. 108-357, 118 Stat. 1418 (codified in scattered sections of 26 U.S.C.), added Section 62(a)(19) to the Internal Revenue Code, which permits a taxpayer to deduct "attorney fees and court costs paid by, or on behalf of, the taxpayer in connection with any action involving a claim of unlawful discrimination." Unlawful discrimination is defined in Section 62(e) and specifically includes "Section 102, 202, 302, or 503 of the Americans with Disabilities Act of 1990 (42 U.S.C. 12112, 12132, 12182, or 12203)" as well as

> Any provision of Federal, State, or local law, or common law claims permitted under Federal, State, or local law –
> (i) providing for the enforcement of civil rights, or
> (ii) regulating any aspect of the employment relationship, including claims for wages, compensation, or benefits, or prohibiting the discharge of an employee, the discrimination against an employee, or any other form of retaliation or reprisal against an employee for asserting rights or taking other actions permitted by law.

Id. § 62(e)(18). Thus, a person settling an ADA case and receiving substantial attorney's fees in the future should not wind up paying taxes on those fees. *Banks* controls for prior settlements. This validates commentators who argued that, as a policy matter, taxing attorney fees undermines the statutes that provide attorneys' fees and promote the concept of a "private attorney general," by taking away a substantial part of the benefit. *See* Lara Sager & Stephen Cohen, How the Income Tax Undermines Civil Rights Law, 73 S. Cal. L. Rev. 1075, 1101 (2000).

Chapter 11 ALTERNATIVE DISPUTE RESOLUTION

§ 11.1   Mediation Of Disability Rights Disputes

The ADA encourages alternative dispute resolution as a way to resolve ADA claims. Section 513 of the Act, 42 U.S.C. § 12212 (2006), reads as follows:

> Where appropriate and to the extent authorized by law, the use of alternative means of dispute resolution, including settlement negotiations, conciliation, facilitation, mediation, factfinding, minitrials, and arbitration, is encouraged to resolve disputes under this [Act].

Mediation is a voluntary procedure in which the parties to a dispute meet with a third party, typically an individual trained in assisting people to resolve their disputes. The third party has no power to impose a resolution on the individuals. However, at the conclusion of the mediation, the parties may enter into a settlement agreement that is binding. In carrying out their obligations under the Act, the EEOC and the Department of Justice (DOJ) have established mediation programs. The EEOC's program deals with employment disputes under Title I, *see generally* Equal Emp. Opportunity Comm'n, Mediation, http://www.eeoc.gov/eeoc/mediation/index.cfm (last modified Jun. 19, 2012), while the Justice Department's program addresses disputes under Titles II and III. *See generally* U.S. Dep't of Justice, ADA Mediation Program, http://www.usdoj.gov/crt/ada/mediate.htm (last modified June 25, 2002).

The EEOC's mediation program applies, not just to the ADA, but also to Title VII of the Civil Rights Act of 1964, the Age Discrimination In Employment Act, and the Equal Pay Act.[13] The EEOC offers mediation to parties when a charge is filed. During the time the dispute is in mediation, the charge is not processed by the EEOC. If the EEOC has decided that the charge is without merit, it is not eligible for mediation. The EEOC maintains a staff of personnel, attorneys and non-attorneys, who have received training in mediation. Alternatively, the parties to the dispute may request a mediator outside the EEOC's structure. The process is confidential and is without charge to the parties. In 2000, the EEOC spent approximately $13 million on its mediation program. Equal Emp. Opportunity Comm'n, History of EEOC Mediation Program, http://www.eeoc.gov/eeoc/mediation/history.cfm (last modified Jun. 19, 2012).

---

[13]   In addition to the language in specific statutes, the EEOC's program rests on the Administrative Dispute Resolution Act, 5 U.S.C. §§ 571-84 (2006).

§ 11.2 Arbitration Of Disability Rights Disputes

Unlike mediation, arbitration results in a holding that binds the parties. Agreeing to arbitrate means giving up the right to a trial, and in particular a jury trial. In theory, the benefit of the agreement for potential (or actual) claimants is the speed of the process compared to a judicial resolution. The advantages for potential (or actual) defendants lie in the relative inexpensiveness and the avoidance of a jury. Arbitration awards may or may not be appealable, depending on the arbitration agreement, but where they are, the appellate review is generally quite limited. Gilmer v. Interstate/Johnson Lane Corp., 500 U.S. 20, 32 n.4 (1991) (noting that judicial review of arbitration awards " 'is sufficient to ensure that arbitrators comply with the requirements of the statute' at issue") (citation omitted). Parties must agree to arbitrate their disputes, although they can do so in advance, before the dispute has arisen, or after it has arisen. Often the "agreement" is a clause in a more comprehensive document, such as an employment contract.

The core issue in any dispute over the applicability of an arbitration provision is whether a party to it effectively has waived her right to a jury trial, which would otherwise be available in any action for damages. The arbitration of ADA disputes and, more generally, of disputes under civil rights statutes, has been, unlike the mediation of such disputes, a matter of some contention. Many parties, of course, elect to submit to binding arbitration, but problems arise where one party – an employer or a service provider – attempts to impose arbitration on the other party via the employment or service contract. Plaintiffs often object to mandatory arbitration clauses because of the perceived bias of arbitrators in favor of defendants, who are the repeat-users of their services.

Situations in which arbitration is part of a broader agreement have posed a number of questions:

- Is arbitration even permissible for civil rights disputes?

- If it is permissible, does the particular arbitration clause cover the dispute?

- If the clause covers the dispute, is the arbitration procedure "effective"; i.e., is it fair?

Many states have their own analogues to the ADA and other civil rights statutes. Those states may, of course, authorize or reject arbitration of disputes under their civil rights statutes independently of what the federal government does under its statutes. See Armendariz v. Found. Psychcare Servs., Inc., 24 Cal. 4th 83 (2000).

A. *Arbitrability Of ADA Disputes*

The backdrop of questions of arbitrability is the Federal Arbitration Act (FAA), 9 U.S.C. §§ 1-14 (2006). Relying upon the federal policy favoring arbitration embodied in the Act, the Supreme Court said that "statutory claims may be the subject of an arbitration agreement, enforceable pursuant to the FAA." Gilmer, 500 U.S. at 26. Thus, arbitration agreements have been enforceable for claims under the Sherman Act, the Racketeer Influenced and Corrupt Organizations Act (RICO), the Securities Exchange Act of 1934, and the Securities Act of 1933. *Id.* (citing e.g. Shearson/Am. Express, Inc. v. McMahon, 482 U.S. 220 (1987) (holding Securities Exchange Act and RICO claims arbitrable); Mitsubishi Motors Corp. v. Soler Chrysler-Plymouth, Inc., 473 U.S. 614 (1985) (arbitration in an antitrust action in part under the Sherman Act)).

The Supreme Court, however, has created a measure of confusion in the civil rights area. In *Alexander v. Gardner-Denver Co.*, 415 U.S. 36 (1974) ("Gardner-Denver"), the Court held that an employee "does not forfeit his right to a judicial forum for claimed discriminatory discharge in violation of Title VII of the Civil Rights Act of 1964 . . . if 'he first pursues his grievance through final arbitration under the non-discrimination clause of the collective bargaining agreement.' " Wright v. Universal Mar. Serv. Corp., 525 U.S. 70, 75-76 (1998) (quoting Gardner-Denver, 415 U.S. at 49). That is, rights under the employee's collective bargaining agreement are separate from the employee's statutory rights under Title VII and "there can be no prospective waiver of an employee's rights under Title VII." Gardner-Denver, 415 U.S. at 51.

On the other hand, in *Gilmer*, 500 U.S. at 22-36, the Supreme Court held that a claim under the Age Discrimination in Employment Act, 29 U.S.C. § 621, et seq. (2006) (ADEA), could be the subject of a compulsory arbitration agreement in the standard U-4 Form used by the securities industry. In *Mitsubishi Motors Corp. v. Soler Chrysler-Plymouth, Inc.*, 473 U.S. 614, 628 (1985), the Court had held that if the "parties' agreement to arbitrate reached the statutory issues," the court had to decide "whether legal constraints external to the parties' agreement foreclosed the arbitration of those claims." *Id.* at 628. The court could look to the text, the legislative history and the policy of the statute. The plaintiff in *Gilmer* argued that the FAA did not permit arbitration of a civil rights claim. The Court rejected that argument. It held that the party opposing arbitration has the burden of showing the words of the agreement are foreclosed. Gilmer, 500 U.S. at 26. It found that neither the language of the ADEA, which does not mention arbitration, nor its history precluded arbitration. *Id.* at 27-30. Nor was there any "inherent conflict" between arbitration and the statutory goals, since an arbitral panel was competent to provide all legal remedies. *Id.* at 32.

With some understatement, the Court has recognized that, "there is obviously some tension between these two lines of cases." Wright v. Universal Mar. Serv. Corp., 525 U.S. 70, 76 (1998). In *Wright*, various parties and amici suggested ways of resolving the two lines of cases. Certain parties advocated permitting individually executed (the U-4 is not individually negotiated) agreements prospectively to waive the right to a judicial proceeding, but not permitting collective bargaining agreements or, presumably, other collectively negotiated agreements to do so. On the other side, certain amici argued that the attitude toward arbitration had evolved to such an extent that all agreements could validly require compulsory arbitration. The Court found it did not need to resolve the conflict in view of the contractual language in the case before it. Nonetheless, circuit courts must plow on.

What is the impact of the ADA's arbitration section? That section reads identically to section 118 of the Civil Rights Act: "Where appropriate and to the extent authorized by law, the use of alternative means of dispute resolution, including . . . arbitration, is encouraged to resolve disputes arising under this chapter." ADA § 513, 42 U.S.C. § 12212 (2006). One court discussed section 513 as follows:

> If this language were not interpreted to permit prospective waiver of a judicial forum, it would be superfluous. Litigants are always permitted to resolve their disputes extrajudicially, with or without statutory language authorizing such action. This language adds nothing if it does not mean that litigants can anticipatorily waive a judicial forum for ADA claims.

Bercovitch v. Baldwin Sch., Inc., 133 F.3d 141, 150 (1st Cir. 1998).

Two things distinguish ADA section 513 from section 118 of the Civil Rights Act. First, it was enacted before *Gilmer* came down. Unlike section 118, not even a plausible argument can be made that Congress had *Gilmer* in mind. Second, it has specific legislative history. The House Judiciary Committee Report, incorporated into the House Conference Report stated:

> The Committee wishes to emphasize, however, that the use of alternative dispute resolution mechanisms is intended to supplement, not supplant, the remedies provided by this Act. Thus, for example, the Committee believes that any agreement to submit disputed issues to arbitration, whether in the context of a collective bargaining agreement or in an employment contract, does not preclude the affected person from seeking relief under the enforcement provisions of this Act. This view is consistent with the Supreme Court's interpretation of title VII of the Civil Rights Act of 1964, whose remedial provisions are incorporated by reference in title I. The Committee believes that the approach articulated by the Supreme Court in *Alexander v. Gardner-Denver Co.* applies equally to the ADA and does not intend that the inclusion of Section 513 [the ADA arbitration section] be used to preclude rights and remedies that would otherwise be available to persons with disabilities.

H.R. Rep. No. 101-485 (III) (1990), reprinted in 1990 U.S.C.C.A.N. 445, 499 (footnote omitted); *see also* H.R. Rep. No. 101-596 (1990), reprinted in 1990 U.S.C.C.A.N. 445, 598. (This language reads uncannily like that quoted by the *Luce, Forward* court.) Do those differences matter?

The courts of appeals that have considered whether ADA claims may be subject to a compulsory arbitration regime have found that they can, at least where there is an individualized agreement. *See* Bercovitch, 133 F.3d at 148-51 (ADA does not preclude waiver of the judicial forum in parents' agreement with private school); Miller v. Pub. Storage Mgmt., Inc., 121 F.3d 215, 218 (5th Cir. 1997) ("Congress did not intend to exclude the ADA from the scope of the FAA"); *cf.* Gibson v. Neighborhood Health Clinics, Inc., 121 F.3d 1126, 1130 (7th Cir. 1997) ("[t]he parties agree that an employee and employer may contractually agree to submit federal claims, including Title VII and ADA claims, to arbitration" (citing Gilmer, 500 U.S. at 35).

B. *Enforceability Of The Arbitration Agreement: Procedural And Substantive Unconscionability*

Although most courts have found that there is no statutory impediment to employers requiring employees to arbitrate ADA disputes, rather than take those disputes to court, courts still may police the fairness of the arbitration proceedings themselves.[14] Arbitration agreements are interpreted pursuant to the FAA, but are to be treated on an "equal footing with other contracts," *Waffle House, Inc.*, 534 U.S. at 293, so generally applicable state law governs the formation of the agreement. First Options of Chi., Inc. v. Kaplan, 514 U.S. 938, 943-44 (1995); Morrison v. Circuit City Stores, Inc., 317 F.3d 646, 666 (6th Cir. 2003). "Thus, generally applicable contract defenses, such as fraud, duress, or unconscionability, may be applied to invalidate arbitration agreements without contravening the FAA." Doctor's Assocs., Inc. v. Casarotto, 517 U.S. 681, 687 (1996), quoted in Posadas v. Pool Depot, Inc., 858 So.2d 611, 614 (La. App. 2003) (arbitration agreement unenforceable because print too small and relative positions of buyer and seller made enforcement unreasonable).

State courts have, in a number of cases, established criteria for the propriety of arbitration agreements. For example, the California Supreme Court adopted a five part test for the

> minimum requirements for the lawful arbitration of [civil] rights [disputes] pursuant to a mandatory employment arbitration agreement. Such an arbitration agreement is lawful if it "(1) provides for neutral arbitrators, (2) provides for more than minimal discovery, (3) requires a written

---

[14] Most, but not all, ADA-based arbitration disputes arise in the employment context.

award, (4) provides for all of the types of relief that would otherwise be available in court, and (5) does not require employees to pay either unreasonable costs or any arbitrators' fees or expenses as a condition of access to to the arbitration forum."

Armendariz v. Found. Health Psychcare Servs., Inc., 24 Cal.4th 83, 102 (Cal. 2000). While states differ, many follow these themes.

Part 4

Access To Public Services: ADA Title II
Analysis

Chapter 12 STATUTORY BACKGROUND
§ 12.1 Statutory And Regulatory Scheme
§ 12.2 Constitutionality
    A. Did Congress Validly Abrogate The States' Sovereign Immunity?
    B. Other Constitutional Issues
Chapter 13   COVERAGE
§ 13.1 Introduction
    A. "Public Entity"
    B. Service, Program, Or Activity
§ 13.2 Elements Of Title II Claim
§ 13.3 "Qualified Person With A Disability"
§ 13.4 Not Excluding, Denying, Or Discriminating – Affirmative Responsibilities Of Public Entities
    A. Reasonable Modifications To Policies, Practices, And Procedures
    B. Opportunity For Equal Benefit
    C. Integration
    D. Facilities Modification
    E. Effective Communication
    F. Transportation
§ 13.5 By Reason Of Disability – Intentional Discrimination Versus Disparate Impact
Chapter 14   Remedies And Enforcement
§ 14.1 Introduction
§ 14.2 Procedure
§ 14.3 Remedies
    A. Private Rights Of Action
    B. Available Types Of Relief
    C. Attorneys' Fees And Statute Of Limitations

Chapter 12 STATUTORY BACKGROUND

Think of the ways that you interact with your state and local governments. The government acts as an educational provider, the furnisher of important social services, a licensing body, and law enforcement, amongst other things. Before passing the ADA, Congress heard testimony from individuals with disabilities who documented accounts of state-sponsored discrimination in all of these areas. The ADA's Findings and Purposes state the Congressional finding that discrimination against individuals with disabilities persists in such critical areas as education, transportation, communication, recreation, institutionalization, health services, voting, and access to public services.

Title II of the ADA prohibits discrimination by state and local governmental entities. It requires that the services, programs, and activities of public entities be accessible to people with disabilities. Before the ADA was enacted, the Rehabilitation Act of 1973 prohibited some public entities from discriminating on the basis of disability. Section 504 provided that "[n]o otherwise qualified individual with a disability in the United States . . . shall, solely by reason of his or her disability, be excluded from the participation in, or be denied the benefits of, or be subjected to discrimination under any program or activity receiving Federal financial assistance . . . ." 29 U.S.C. § 794 (2006). This protection, however, was limited to public entities that received federal financial assistance.

A primary purpose of Title II was to extend the existing prohibition on discrimination to state and local government entities, regardless of whether they received federal financial assistance.

The implementation of Title II has not been without controversy. Like the other titles of the law, courts have grappled with questions concerning what entities should be covered, what proactive steps covered entities must take, and what exactly constitutes discrimination. These issues, and others, will be explored in this Part.

§ 12.1   Statutory And Regulatory Scheme

ADA Title II is divided into two main sections. Part A, entitled "Prohibition Against Discrimination And Other Generally Applicable Provisions," sets forth the general definitions and prohibitions against discrimination by public entities. The two major terms for the purposes of Title II, "public entity" and "qualified individual with a disability," are defined as follows:

(1)   Public entity

The term "public entity" means –

(A)   any State or local government;

(B)   any department, agency, special purpose district, or other instrumentality of a State or States or local government; and

(C)   the National Railroad Passenger Corporation, and any commuter authority (as defined in Section 24102(4) of Title 49).

(2)   Qualified individual with a disability

The term "qualified individual with a disability" means an individual with a disability who, with or without reasonable modifications to rules, policies, or practices, the removal of architectural, communication, or transportation barriers, or the provision of auxiliary aids and services, meets the essential eligibility requirements for the receipt of services or the participation in programs or activities provided by a public entity.

42 U.S.C. § 12131 (2006).

Title II's discrimination provision reads:

Subject to the provisions of this subchapter, no qualified individual with a disability shall, by reason of such disability, be excluded from participation in or be denied the benefits of the services, programs, or activities of a public entity, or be subjected to discrimination by any such entity.

Id. § 12132.

Part A of Title II contains an extensive regulatory scheme. The law requires the Attorney General to promulgate regulations implementing Part A. *See id.* § 12134 ("Regulations"). The regulations can be found in Section 35 of Title 28 of the Code of Federal Regulations. *See* 28 C.F.R. §§ 35.101-35.190 (2008). The regulations are intentionally patterned after, and to be interpreted consistently with, the regulations written pursuant to the Rehabilitation Act of 1973. 42 U.S.C. § 12134(b); see also 28 C.F.R. § 35.103 ("Relationship to other laws").

On July 23, 2010, Attorney General Eric Holder signed final regulations revising the Department's ADA Title II regulations. The revisions cover a wide range of areas, including effective communication, examinations and courses, lodging, service animals, ticketing, wheelchairs, correctional facilities, and accessible parking.

Part B, entitled "Actions Applicable To Public Transportation Provided By Public Entities Considered Discriminatory," addresses the specialized issue of discrimination in public transportation. One purpose of Title II is to clarify and extend the Rehabilitation Act's requirements for public transportation entities, regardless of whether they receive federal aid. Part B is divided into two Subparts: "Subpart I – Public Transportation Other Than by Aircraft or Certain Rail Provisions," and "Subpart II – Public Transportation by Intercity and Commuter Rail."

The Subparts describe in detail the compliance requirements for public entities in the context of public transportation. Section 12132 provides a general prohibition on discrimination. Part B also has an extensive regulatory scheme, which the statute directs will be promulgated by the U.S. Department of Transportation. *See* 42 U.S.C. §§ 12149, 12164 (2006).

§ 12.2 Constitutionality

A. *Did Congress Validly Abrogate The States' Sovereign Immunity?*

The U.S. Supreme Court has addressed the question of whether Congress exceeded its constitutional authority in abrogating or limiting states' sovereign immunity in civil rights statutes like the ADA. The Eleventh Amendment to the Constitution, as interpreted by the Court, provides that states generally are immune from suits by citizens for monetary damages.

In certain circumstances, however, Congress may abrogate states' sovereign immunity pursuant to Section 5 of the 14th Amendment. *See* U.S. Const. amend. XIV, § 1 ("No State shall make or enforce any law which shall abridge the privileges or immunities of citizens of the United States; nor shall any State deprive any person of life, liberty, or property, without due process of law; *nor deny to any person within its jurisdiction the equal protection of the laws.*") (emphasis added); *id.* § 5 ("The Congress shall have power to enforce, by appropriate legislation, the provisions of this article."). The Rehnquist Court took a narrow view of when such action is appropriate.

In *City of Boerne v. Flores*, 521 U.S. 507 (1997), the Court struck down the Religious Freedom Restoration Act, holding that Congress may only use its Section 5 powers to provide *remedies* for constitutional rights recognized by the Courts. The Court held that Congress may not create new constitutional rights or expand the scope of existing rights. Moreover, legislation passed pursuant to Congress's Section 5 powers must have "congruence" and "proportionality" to the constitutional wrong to be prevented. *Id.* at 530-33.

In *Kimel v. Florida Board of Regents*, 528 U.S. 62 (2000), the Court held that the Age Discrimination in Employment Act (ADEA) was not a valid exercise of Congress's Section 5 power to enforce the 14th Amendment. Thus, Congress exceeded its constitutional authority and could not abrogate states' immunity from suit. The Court held that there was not a documented constitutional wrong that Congress was attempting to remedy, because there was insufficient evidence of a pattern of unconstitutional discrimination by the states on the basis of age. *Id.* at 88-89.

Similarly, in *Florida Prepaid Postsecondary Education Expense Board v. College Savings Bank*, 527 U.S. 627 (1999), the Court struck down the Patent and Plant Variety Protection Remedy Clarification Act, a federal statute authorizing private persons to sue a state for patent infringement. The Court again held that Congress had exceeded its constitutional authority in abrogating the states' immunity because it had not identified a pattern of patent infringement by the states. *Id.* at 640.

Thereafter, in *Nevada Department of Human Resources v. Hibbs*, 538 U.S. 721 (2003), the Court ruled that state employees may recover money damages in federal court in the event of a state's failure to comply with the Family and Medical Leave Act (FMLA). Here, the Court was satisfied that Congress, in passing the FMLA, had acted to correct and deter documented constitutional wrongs. *Id.* at 735.

The ADA has played a prominent role in the development of this Eleventh Amendment jurisprudence. It is clear that Congress' intent in ADA Title II is to abrogate the states' sovereign immunity; it says as much. The question for purposes of constitutional analysis is whether Congress has the power to do so.

Four years after *City of Boerne*, in *Board of Trustees of the University of Alabama v. Garrett*, 531 U.S. 356 (2001), the Court held that, pursuant to the Eleventh Amendment, a state is immune to suits for money damages under ADA Title I. *Id.* at 374; *see supra*, Part 3, § 6.2.D.

The Court's reasoning in *Garrett* may be summarized as follows: To abrogate the states' Eleventh Amendment sovereign immunity pursuant to Section 5 of the Fourteenth Amendment, Congress must find sufficient proof of a pattern of unconstitutional discrimination against people with disabilities in the specific area of state employment.

As discussed in Part 3, § 6.2.D, *supra*, the Supreme Court had previously held in *City of Cleburne v. Cleburne Living Center, Inc.*, 473 U.S. 432 (1985), that people with disabilities do not invoke a heightened scrutiny analysis under the Equal Protection Clause. Instead, states are free to discriminate on the basis of disability whenever it is *rational* to do so (a rational basis standard). To find that there was a pattern of unconstitutional wrongs, the Court in *Garrett* held that Congress would have needed to find a pattern of states irrationally discriminating against people with disabilities in employment.

The *Garrett* Court held that Congress failed to demonstrate such a pattern when it passed the ADA. Moreover, Congress' actions in Title I as applied to states, prohibiting discrimination and requiring reasonable accommodation, were not a congruent and proportional remedy to the harms it did find. In *Garrett*, the Court declined to decide whether Congress validly abrogated sovereign immunity in enacting ADA Title II. This issue carries somewhat greater importance than it does in the Title I context because of the large number of covered Title II entities with potential sovereign immunity protection. The next case starts to address this issue.

TENNESSEE v. LANE

Supreme Court of the United States, 2004
541 U.S. 509

Justice STEVENS delivered the opinion of the Court.

Title II of the Americans with Disabilities Act of 1990 provides that "no qualified individual with a disability shall, by reason of such disability, be excluded from participation in or be denied the benefits of the services, programs or activities of a public entity, or be subjected to discrimination by any such entity." § 12132. The question presented in this case is whether Title II exceeds Congress' power under § 5 of the Fourteenth Amendment.

I

In August 1998, respondents George Lane and Beverly Jones filed this action against the State of Tennessee and a number of Tennessee counties, alleging past and ongoing violations of Title II. Respondents, both of whom are paraplegics who use wheelchairs for mobility, claimed that they were denied access to, and the services of, the state court system by reason of their disabilities. Lane alleged that he was compelled to appear to answer a set of criminal charges on the second floor of a county courthouse that had no elevator. At his first appearance, Lane crawled up two flights of stairs to get to the courtroom. When Lane returned to the courthouse for a hearing, he refused to crawl again or to be carried by officers to the courtroom; he consequently was arrested and jailed for failure to appear. Jones, a certified court reporter, alleged that she has not been able to gain access to a number of county courthouses, and, as a result, has lost both work and an opportunity to participate in the judicial process. Respondents sought damages and equitable relief.

* * *

II

The ADA was passed by large majorities in both Houses of Congress after decades of deliberation and investigation into the need for comprehensive legislation to address discrimination against persons with disabilities. In the years immediately preceding the ADA's enactment, Congress held 13 hearings and created a special task force that gathered evidence from every State in the Union. The conclusions Congress drew from this evidence are set forth in the task force and Committee Reports, described in lengthy legislative hearings, and summarized in the preamble to the statute. Central among these conclusions was Congress' finding that

> "individuals with disabilities are a discrete and insular
> minority who have been faced with restrictions and

336

limitations, subjected to a history of purposeful unequal treatment, and relegated to a position of political powerlessness in our society, based on characteristics that are beyond the control of such individuals and resulting from stereotypic assumptions not truly indicative of the individual ability of such individuals to participate in, and contribute to, society." 42 U.S.C. § 12101(a)(7).

Invoking "the sweep of congressional authority, including the power to enforce the fourteenth amendment and to regulate commerce," the ADA is designed "to provide a clear and comprehensive national mandate for the elimination of discrimination against individuals with disabilities." §§ 12101(b)(1), (b)(4). It forbids discrimination against persons with disabilities in three major areas of public life: employment, which is covered by Title I of the statute; public services, programs, and activities, which are the subject of Title II; and public accommodations, which are covered by Title II. . . .

* * *

IV

The first step of the Boerne inquiry requires us to identify the constitutional right or rights that Congress sought to enforce when it enacted Title II. *Garrett*, 531 U.S. at 365. In Garrett we identified Title I's purpose as enforcement of the Fourteenth Amendment's command that "all persons similarly situated should be treated alike." *Cleburne v. Cleburne Living Center, Inc.*, 473 U.S. 432, 439 (1985). As we observed, classifications based on disability violate that constitutional command if they lack a rational relationship to a legitimate governmental purpose. *Garrett*, 531 U.S. at 366 (citing *Cleburne*, 473 U.S. at 446).

Title II, like Title I, seeks to enforce this prohibition on irrational disability discrimination. But it also seeks to enforce a variety of other basic constitutional guarantees, infringements of which are subject to more searching judicial review. . . . These rights include some, like the right of access to the courts at issue in this case, that are protected by the Due Process Clause of the Fourteenth Amendment. The Due Process Clause and the Confrontation Clause of the Sixth Amendment, as applied to the States via the Fourteenth Amendment, both guarantee to a criminal defendant such as respondent Lane the "right to be present at all stages of the trial where his absence might frustrate the fairness of the proceedings." *Faretta v. California*, 422 U.S. 806, 819, n.15 (1975). The Due Process Clause also requires the States to afford certain civil litigants a "meaningful opportunity to be heard" by removing obstacles to their full participation in judicial proceedings. *Boddie v. Connecticut*, 401 U.S. 371, 379 (1971); *M.L.B. v. S.L.J.*, 519 U.S. 102 (1996). We have held that the Sixth Amendment guarantees to criminal defendants the right to trial by a jury composed of a fair cross section of the community, noting that the exclusion of "identifiable segments playing major roles in the community cannot be squared with the constitutional concept of jury trial." *Taylor v. Louisiana*, 419 U.S. 522, 530 (1975). And, finally, we have recognized that members of the public have a right of access to criminal proceedings secured by the First Amendment. *Press-Enterprise Co. v. Superior Court of Cal., County of Riverside*, 478 U.S. 1, 8-15 (1986).

Whether Title II validly enforces these constitutional rights is a question that "must be judged with reference to the historical experience which it reflects." *South Carolina v. Katzenbach*, 383 U.S. 301, 308 (1966). See also *Florida Prepaid*, 527 U.S. at 639-640. While § 5 authorizes Congress to enact reasonably prophylactic remedial legislation, the appropriateness of the remedy depends on the gravity of the harm it seeks to prevent. "Difficult and intractable problems often require powerful remedies," *Kimel*, 528 U.S. at 88, but it is also true that "[s]trong measures appropriate to address one harm may be an unwarranted response to another, lesser one," *Boerne*, 521 U.S. at 530.

It is not difficult to perceive the harm that Title II is designed to address. Congress enacted Title II against a backdrop of pervasive unequal treatment in the administration of state services and programs, including systematic deprivations of fundamental rights. For example, "[a]s of 1979, most States . . . categorically disqualified 'idiots' from voting, without regard to individual capacity." The majority of these laws remain on the books, and have been the subject of legal challenge as recently as 2001. Similarly, a number of States have prohibited and continue to prohibit persons with disabilities from engaging in activities such as marrying and serving as jurors. The historical experience that Title II reflects is also documented in this Court's cases, which have identified unconstitutional treatment of disabled persons by state agencies in a variety of settings, including unjustified commitment, e.g., *Jackson v. Indiana*, 406 U.S. 715 (1972); the abuse and neglect of persons committed to state mental health hospitals, *Youngberg v. Romeo*, 457 U.S. 307 (1982); and irrational discrimination in zoning decisions, *Cleburne v. Cleburne Living Center, Inc.*, 473 U.S. 432 (1985). The decisions of other courts, too, document a pattern of unequal treatment in the administration of a wide range of public services, programs, and activities, including the penal system, public education, and voting. Notably, these decisions also demonstrate a pattern of unconstitutional treatment in the administration of justice.

This pattern of disability discrimination persisted despite several federal and state legislative efforts to address it. In the deliberations that led up to the enactment of the ADA, Congress identified important shortcomings in existing laws that rendered them "inadequate to address the pervasive problems of discrimination that people with disabilities are facing." S. Rep. No. 101-116, at 18. See also H.R. Rep. No. 101-485, pt. 2, at 47, U.S. Code Cong. & Admin. News 1990, pp. 303, 329. It also uncovered further evidence of those shortcomings, in the form of hundreds of examples of unequal treatment of persons with disabilities by States and their political subdivisions. See *Garrett*, 531 U.S. at 379 (Breyer, J., dissenting). See also id. at 391 (App. C to opinion of Breyer, J., dissenting). As the Court's opinion in Garrett observed, the "overwhelming majority" of these examples concerned discrimination in the administration of public programs and services. Id. at 371, n.7; Government's Lodging in Garrett, O.T. 2000, No. 99-1240 (available in Clerk of Court's case file).

With respect to the particular services at issue in this case, Congress learned that many individuals, in many States across the country, were being excluded from courthouses and court proceedings by reason of their disabilities. A report before Congress showed that some 76% of public services and programs housed in state-owned buildings were inaccessible to and unusable by persons with disabilities, even taking into account the possibility that the services and programs might be restructured or relocated to other parts of the buildings. U.S. Civil Rights Commission, Accommodating the Spectrum of Individual Abilities 39 (1983). Congress itself heard testimony from persons with disabilities who described the physical inaccessibility of local courthouses. Oversight Hearing on H.R. 4468 before the House Subcommittee on Select Education of the Committee on Education and Labor, 100th Cong., 2d Sess., 40-41, 48 (1988). And its appointed task force heard numerous examples of the exclusion of persons with disabilities from state judicial services and programs, including exclusion of persons with visual impairments and hearing impairments from jury service, failure of state and local governments to provide interpretive services for the hearing impaired, failure to permit the testimony of adults with developmental disabilities in abuse cases, and failure to make courtrooms accessible to witnesses with physical disabilities. Government's Lodging in Garrett, O.T. 2000, No. 99-1240. See also Task Force on the Rights and Empowerment of Americans with Disabilities, From ADA to Empowerment (Oct. 12, 1990).

Given the sheer volume of evidence demonstrating the nature and extent of unconstitutional discrimination against persons with disabilities in the provision of public services, the dissent's contention that the record is insufficient to justify Congress' exercise of its prophylactic power is puzzling, to say the least. Just last Term in Hibbs, we approved the family-care leave provision of the FMLA as valid § 5 legislation based primarily on evidence of disparate provision of parenting leave, little of which concerned unconstitutional state conduct. 538 U.S. at 728-733. We explained that because the FMLA was targeted at sex-based classifications, which are subject to a heightened standard of judicial scrutiny, "it was easier for Congress to show a pattern of state constitutional violations" than in Garrett or Kimel, both of which concerned legislation that targeted classifications subject to rational-basis review. 538 U.S. at 735-737. Title II is aimed at the enforcement of a variety of basic rights, including the right of access to the courts at issue in this case, that call for a standard of judicial review at least as searching, and in some cases more searching, than the standard that applies to sex-based classifications. And in any event, the record of constitutional violations in this case – including judicial findings of unconstitutional state action, and statistical, legislative, and anecdotal evidence of the widespread exclusion of persons with disabilities from the enjoyment of public services – far exceeds the record in Hibbs.

The conclusion that Congress drew from this body of evidence is set forth in the text of the ADA itself: "[D]iscrimination against individuals with disabilities persists in such critical areas as . . . education, transportation, communication, recreation, institutionalization, health services, voting, and access to *public services*." 42 U.S.C. § 12101(a)(3) (emphasis added). This finding, together with the extensive record of disability discrimination that underlies it, makes clear beyond peradventure that inadequate provision of public services and access to public facilities was an appropriate subject for prophylactic legislation.

V

The only question that remains is whether Title II is an appropriate response to this history and pattern of unequal treatment. At the outset, we must determine the scope of that inquiry. Title II – unlike RFRA, the Patent Remedy Act, and the other statutes we have reviewed for validity under § 5 – reaches a wide array of official conduct in an effort to enforce an equally wide array of constitutional guarantees. Petitioner urges us both to examine the broad range of Title II's applications all at once, and to treat that breadth as a mark of the law's invalidity. According to petitioner, the fact that Title II applies not only to public education and voting-booth access but also to seating at state-owned hockey rinks indicates that Title II is not appropriately tailored to serve its objectives. But nothing in our case law requires us to consider Title II, with its wide variety of applications, as an undifferentiated whole. Whatever might be said about Title II's other applications, the question presented in this case is not whether Congress can validly subject the States to private suits for money damages for failing to provide reasonable access to hockey rinks, or even to voting booths, but whether Congress had the power under § 5 to enforce the constitutional right of access to the courts. Because we find that Title II unquestionably is valid § 5 legislation as it applies to the class of cases implicating the accessibility of judicial services, we need go no further. See *United States v. Raines*, 362 U.S. 17, 26 (1960).

Congress' chosen remedy for the pattern of exclusion and discrimination described above, Title II's requirement of program accessibility, is congruent and proportional to its object of enforcing the right of access to the courts. The unequal treatment of disabled persons in the administration of judicial services has a long history, and has persisted despite several legislative efforts to remedy the problem of disability discrimination. Faced with considerable evidence of the shortcomings of previous legislative responses, Congress was justified in concluding that this "difficult and intractable proble[m]" warranted "added prophylactic measures in response." *Hibbs*, 538 U.S. at 737 (internal quotation marks omitted).

The remedy Congress chose is nevertheless a limited one. Recognizing that failure to accommodate persons with disabilities will often have the same practical effect as outright exclusion, Congress required the States to take reasonable measures to remove architectural and other barriers to accessibility. 42 U.S.C. § 12131(2). But Title II does not require States to employ any and all means to make judicial services accessible to persons with disabilities, and it does not require States to compromise their essential eligibility criteria for public programs. It requires only "reasonable modifications" that would not fundamentally alter the nature of the service provided, and only when the individual seeking modification is otherwise eligible for the service. Ibid. As Title II's implementing regulations make clear, the reasonable modification requirement can be satisfied in a number of ways. In the case of facilities built or altered after 1992, the regulations require compliance with specific architectural accessibility standards. 28 C.F.R. § 35.151 (2003). But in the case of older facilities, for which structural change is likely to be more difficult, a public entity may comply with Title II by adopting a variety of less costly measures, including relocating services to alternative, accessible sites and assigning aides to assist persons with disabilities in accessing services. § 35.150(b)(1). Only if these measures are ineffective in achieving accessibility is the public entity required to make reasonable structural changes. Ibid. And in no event is the entity required to undertake measures that would impose an undue financial or administrative burden, threaten historic preservation interests, or effect a fundamental alteration in the nature of the service. §§ 35.150(a)(2), (a)(3).

This duty to accommodate is perfectly consistent with the well-established due process principle that, "within the limits of practicability, a State must afford to all individuals a meaningful opportunity to be heard" in its courts. *Boddie*, 401 U.S. at 379 (internal quotation marks and citation omitted). Our cases have recognized a number of affirmative obligations that flow from this principle: the duty to waive filing fees in certain family-law and criminal cases, the duty to provide transcripts to criminal defendants seeking review of their convictions, and the duty to provide counsel to certain criminal defendants. Each of these cases makes clear that ordinary considerations of cost and convenience alone cannot justify a State's failure to provide individuals with a meaningful right of access to the courts. Judged against this backdrop, Title II's affirmative obligation to accommodate persons with disabilities in the administration of justice cannot be said to be "so out of proportion to a supposed remedial or preventive object that it cannot be understood as responsive to, or designed to prevent, unconstitutional behavior." *Boerne*, 521 U.S. at 532;

Kimel, 528 U.S. at 86. It is, rather, a reasonable prophylactic measure, reasonably targeted to a legitimate end.

For these reasons, we conclude that Title II, as it applies to the class of cases implicating the fundamental right of access to the courts, constitutes a valid exercise of Congress' § 5 authority to enforce the guarantees of the Fourteenth Amendment. The judgment of the Court of Appeals is therefore affirmed.

Chief Justice REHNQUIST, with whom Justice KENNEDY and Justice THOMAS join, dissenting.

In *Board of Trustees of Univ. of Ala. v. Garrett*, 531 U.S. 356 (2001), we held that Congress did not validly abrogate States' Eleventh Amendment immunity when it enacted Title I of the Americans with Disabilities Act of 1990(ADA), 42 U.S.C. §§ 12111-12117. Today, the Court concludes that Title II of that Act, §§ 12131-12165, does validly abrogate that immunity, at least insofar "as it applies to the class of cases implicating the fundamental right of access to the courts." Ante, at 1993. Because today's decision is irreconcilable with Garrett and the well-established principles it embodies, I dissent.

The Eleventh Amendment bars private lawsuits in federal court against an unconsenting State. E.g., *Nevada Dept. of Human Resources v. Hibbs,* 538 U.S. 721, 726 (2003); *Garrett,* supra, at 363; *Kimel v. Florida Bd. of Regents,* 528 U.S. 62, 73 (2000). Congress may overcome States' sovereign immunity and authorize such suits only if it unmistakably expresses its intent to do so, and only if it "acts pursuant to a valid exercise of its power under § 5 of the Fourteenth Amendment." *Hibbs,* supra, at 726. While the Court correctly holds that Congress satisfied the first prerequisite, ante, at 1985, I disagree with its conclusion that Title II is valid § 5 enforcement legislation.

Section 5 of the Fourteenth Amendment grants Congress the authority "to enforce, by appropriate legislation," the familiar substantive guarantees contained in § 1 of that Amendment. U.S. Const., Amdt. 14, § 1 ("No State shall . . . deprive any person of life, liberty, or property, without due process of law; nor deny to any person within its jurisdiction the equal protection of the laws"). Congress' power to enact "appropriate" enforcement legislation is not limited to "mere legislative repetition" of this Court's Fourteenth Amendment jurisprudence. *Garrett,* supra, at 365. Congress may "remedy" and "deter" state violations of constitutional rights by "prohibiting a somewhat broader swath of conduct, including that which is not itself forbidden by the Amendment's text." *Hibbs,* 538 U.S. at 727 (internal quotation marks omitted). Such "prophylactic" legislation, however, "must be an appropriate remedy for identified constitutional violations, not 'an attempt to substantively redefine the States' legal obligations.'" Id. at 727-728 (quoting *Kimel,* supra, at 88); *City of Boerne v. Flores,* 521 U.S. 507, 525 (1997) (enforcement power is "corrective or preventive, not definitional"). To ensure that Congress does not usurp this Court's responsibility to define the meaning of the Fourteenth Amendment, valid § 5 legislation must exhibit " 'congruence and proportionality between the injury to be prevented or remedied and the means adopted to that end.' " *Hibbs*, supra, at 728 (quoting *City of Boerne*, supra, at 520). While the Court today pays lipservice to the "congruence and proportionality" test, see ante, at 1986, it applies it in a manner inconsistent with our recent precedents.

In *Garrett*, we conducted the three-step inquiry first enunciated in *City of Boerne* to determine whether Title I of the ADA satisfied the congruence-and-proportionality test. A faithful application of that test to Title II reveals that it too " 'substantively redefine[s],' " rather than permissibly enforces, the rights protected by the Fourteenth Amendment. *Hibbs*, supra, at 728.

The first step is to "identify with some precision the scope of the constitutional right at issue." *Garrett*, supra, at 365. This task was easy in *Garrett, Hibbs, Kimel,* and *City of Boerne* because the statutes in those cases sought to enforce only one constitutional right.

* * *

In this case, the task of identifying the scope of the relevant constitutional protection is more difficult because Title II purports to enforce a panoply of constitutional rights of disabled persons: not only the equal protection right against irrational discrimination, but also certain rights protected by the Due Process Clause. Ante, at 1988. However, because the Court ultimately upholds Title II "as it applies to the class of cases implicating the fundamental right of access to the courts," ante, at 1993, the proper inquiry focuses on the scope of those due process rights. The Court cites four access-to-the-courts rights that Title II purportedly enforces: (1) the right of the criminal defendant to be present at all critical stages of the trial, *Faretta v. California*, 422 U.S. 806, 819 (1975); (2) the right of litigants to have a "meaningful opportunity to be heard" in judicial proceedings, *Boddie v. Connecticut*, 401 U.S. 371, 379 (1971); (3) the right of the criminal defendant to trial by a jury composed of a fair cross section of the community, *Taylor v. Louisiana*, 419 U.S. 522, 530 (1975); and (4) the public right of access to criminal proceedings, *Press-Enterprise Co. v. Superior Court of Cal., County of Riverside*, 478 U.S. 1, 8-15 (1986). Ante, at 1988.

Having traced the "metes and bounds" of the constitutional rights at issue, the next step in the congruence-and-proportionality inquiry requires us to examine whether Congress "identified a history and pattern" of violations of these constitutional rights by the States with respect to the disabled. *Garrett*, 531 U.S. at 368. This step is crucial to determining whether Title II is a legitimate attempt to remedy or prevent actual constitutional violations by the States or an illegitimate attempt to rewrite the constitutional provisions it purports to enforce. Indeed, "Congress' § 5 power is appropriately exercised *only* in response to state transgressions." Ibid. (emphasis added). But the majority identifies nothing in the legislative record that shows Congress was responding to widespread violations of the due process rights of disabled persons.

Rather than limiting its discussion of constitutional violations to the due process rights on which it ultimately relies, the majority sets out on a wide-ranging account of societal discrimination against the disabled. Ante, at 1988-1990. This digression recounts historical discrimination against the disabled through institutionalization laws, restrictions on marriage, voting, and public education, conditions in mental hospitals, and various other forms of unequal treatment in the administration of public programs and services. Some of this evidence would be relevant if the Court were considering the constitutionality of the statute as a whole; but the Court rejects that approach in favor of a narrower "as-applied" inquiry. We discounted much the same type of outdated, generalized evidence in *Garrett* as unsupportive of Title I's ban on employment discrimination. 531 U.S. at 368-372; see also *City of Boerne*, 521 U.S. at 530 (noting that the "legislative record lacks . . . modern instances of . . . religious bigotry"). The evidence here is likewise irrelevant to Title II's purported enforcement of Due Process access-to-the-courts rights.

Even if it were proper to consider this broader category of evidence, much of it does not concern unconstitutional action by the States. The bulk of the Court's evidence concerns discrimination by nonstate governments, rather than the States themselves. We have repeatedly held that such evidence is irrelevant to the inquiry whether Congress has validly abrogated Eleventh Amendment immunity, a privilege enjoyed only by the sovereign States. *Garrett*, supra, at 368-369,; *Florida Prepaid Postsecondary Ed. Expense Bd. v. College Savings Bank*, 527 U.S. 627, 640 (1999); *Kimel*, 528 U.S. at 89. Moreover, the majority today cites the same congressional task force evidence we rejected in *Garrett*. Ante, at 1990 (citing *Garrett*, supra, at 379 (BREYER, J., dissenting), and 531 U.S. at 391-424 (App. C to opinion of BREYER, J., dissenting) (chronicling instances of "unequal treatment" in the "administration of public programs")). As in *Garrett*, this "unexamined, anecdotal" evidence does not suffice. 531 U.S. at 370. Most of the brief anecdotes do not involve States at all, and those that do are not sufficiently detailed to determine whether the instances of "unequal treatment" were irrational, and thus unconstitutional under our decision in Cleburne. *Garrett*, supra, at 370-371. Therefore, even outside the "access to the courts" context, the Court identifies few, if any, constitutional violations perpetrated by the States against disabled persons.

With respect to the due process "access to the courts" rights on which the Court ultimately relies, Congress' failure to identify a pattern of actual constitutional violations by the States is even more striking. Indeed, there is nothing in the legislative record or statutory findings to indicate that disabled persons were systematically denied the right to be present at criminal trials, denied the meaningful opportunity to be heard in civil cases, unconstitutionally excluded from jury service, or denied the right to attend criminal trials.

* * *

The near-total lack of actual constitutional violations in the congressional record is reminiscent of Garrett, wherein we found that the same type of minimal anecdotal evidence "f[e]ll far short of even suggesting the pattern of unconstitutional [state action] on which § 5 legislation must be based." Id. at 370. See also *Kimel*, 528 U.S. at 91 ("Congress' failure to uncover any significant pattern of unconstitutional discrimination here confirms that Congress had no reason to believe that broad prophylactic legislation was necessary"); *Florida Prepaid*, supra, at 645 ("The legislative record thus suggests that the Patent Remedy Act did not respond to a history of 'widespread and persisting deprivation of constitutional rights' of the sort Congress has faced in enacting proper prophylactic § 5 legislation" (quoting *City of Boerne*, 521 U.S. at 526)).

The barren record here should likewise be fatal to the majority's holding that Title II is valid legislation enforcing due process rights that involve access to the courts. This conclusion gains even more support when Title II's nonexistent record of constitutional violations is compared with legislation that we have sustained as valid § 5 enforcement legislation. See, e.g., *Hibbs*, 538 U.S. at 729-732 (tracing the extensive legislative record documenting States' gender discrimination in employment leave policies); *South Carolina v. Katzenbach*, 383 U.S. 301, 312-313 (1966) (same with respect to racial discrimination in voting rights). Accordingly, Title II can only be understood as a congressional attempt to "rewrite the Fourteenth Amendment law laid down by this Court," rather than a legitimate effort to remedy or prevent state violations of that Amendment. *Garrett*, supra, at 374.

The third step of our congruence-and-proportionality inquiry removes any doubt as to whether Title II is valid § 5 legislation. At this stage, we ask whether the rights and remedies created by Title II are congruent and proportional to the constitutional rights it purports to enforce and the record of constitutional violations adduced by Congress. *Hibbs*, supra, at 737-739; *Garrett*, supra, at 372-373.

Title II provides that "no qualified individual with a disability shall, by reason of such disability, be excluded from participation in or be denied the benefits of the services, programs, or activities of a public entity, or be subjected to discrimination by any such entity." 42 U.S.C. § 12132. A disabled person is considered "qualified" if he "meets the essential eligibility requirements" for the receipt of the entity's services or participation in the entity's programs, "*with or without reasonable modifications to rules, policies, or practices, the removal of architectural, communication, or transportation barriers, or the provision of auxiliary aids and services.*" § 12131(2) (emphasis added). The ADA's findings make clear that Congress believed it was attacking "discrimination" in all areas of public services, as well as the "discriminatory effect" of "architectural, transportation, and communication barriers." §§ 12101(a)(3), (a)(5). In sum, Title II requires, on pain of money damages, special accommodations for disabled persons in virtually every interaction they have with the State.

"Despite subjecting States to this expansive liability," the broad terms of Title II "d[o] nothing to limit the coverage of the Act to cases involving arguable constitutional violations." *Florida Prepaid*, 527 U.S. at 646. By requiring special accommodation and the elimination of programs that have a disparate impact on the disabled, Title II prohibits far more state conduct than does the equal protection ban on irrational discrimination. We invalidated Title I's similar requirements in *Garrett*, observing that "[i]f special accommodations for the disabled are to be required, they have to come from positive law and not through the Equal Protection Clause." 531 U.S. at 368; id. at 372-373 (contrasting Title I's reasonable accommodation and disparate impact provisions with the Fourteenth Amendment's requirements). Title II fails for the same reason. Like Title I, Title II may be laudable public policy, but it cannot be seriously disputed that it is also an attempt to legislatively "redefine the States' legal obligations" under the Fourteenth Amendment. *Kimel*, 528 U.S. at 88.

The majority, however, claims that Title II also vindicates fundamental rights protected by the Due Process Clause – in addition to access to the courts – that are subject to heightened Fourteenth Amendment scrutiny. Ante, at 1988 (citing *Dunn v. Blumstein*, 405 U.S. 330, 336-337 (1972) (voting); *Shapiro v. Thompson*, 394 U.S. 618, 634 (1969) (right to move to a new jurisdiction); *Skinner v. Oklahoma ex rel. Williamson*, 316 U.S. 535, 541 (1942) (marriage and procreation)). But Title II is not tailored to provide prophylactic protection of these rights; instead, it applies to any service, program, or activity provided by any entity. Its provisions affect transportation, health, education, and recreation programs, among many others, all of which are accorded only rational-basis scrutiny under the Equal Protection Clause. A requirement of accommodation for the disabled at a state-owned amusement park or sports stadium, for example, bears no permissible prophylactic relationship to enabling disabled persons to exercise their fundamental constitutional rights. Thus, as with Title I in *Garrett*, the Patent Remedy Act in Florida Prepaid, the Age Discrimination in Employment Act of 1967 in *Kimel*, and the RFRA in *City of Boerne*, all of which we invalidated as attempts to substantively redefine the Fourteenth Amendment, it is unlikely "that many of the [state actions] affected by [Title II] ha[ve] any likelihood of being unconstitutional." *City of Boerne*, supra, at 532. Viewed as a whole, then, there is little doubt that Title II of the ADA does not validly abrogate state sovereign immunity.

The majority concludes that Title II's massive overbreadth can be cured by considering the statute only "as it applies to the class of cases implicating the accessibility of judicial services." Ante, at 1993 (citing *United States v. Raines*, 362 U.S. 17, 26, 80 (1960)). I have grave doubts about importing an "as applied" approach into the § 5 context. While the majority is of course correct that this Court normally only considers the application of a statute to a particular case, the proper inquiry under *City of Boerne* and its progeny is somewhat different. In applying the congruence-and-proportionality test, we ask whether Congress has attempted to statutorily redefine the constitutional rights protected by the Fourteenth Amendment. This question can only be answered by measuring the breadth of a statute's coverage against the scope of the constitutional rights it purports to enforce and the record of violations it purports to remedy.

In conducting its as-applied analysis, however, the majority posits a hypothetical statute, never enacted by Congress, that applies only to courthouses. The effect is to rig the congruence-and-proportionality test by artificially constricting the scope of the statute to closely mirror a recognized constitutional right. But Title II is not susceptible of being carved up in this manner; it applies indiscriminately to all "services," "programs," or "activities" of any "public entity." Thus, the majority's approach is not really an assessment of whether Title II is "appropriate *legislation*" at all, U.S. Const., Amdt. 14, § 5 (emphasis added), but a test of whether the Court can conceive of a hypothetical statute narrowly tailored enough to constitute valid prophylactic legislation.

Our § 5 precedents do not support this as-applied approach. In each case, we measured the full breadth of the statute or relevant provision that Congress enacted against the scope of the constitutional right it purported to enforce. If we had arbitrarily constricted the scope of the statutes to match the scope of a core constitutional right, those cases might have come out differently. In *Garrett*, for example, Title I might have been upheld "as applied" to irrational employment discrimination; or in *Florida Prepaid*, the Patent Remedy Act might have been upheld "as applied" to intentional, uncompensated patent infringements. It is thus not surprising that the only authority cited by the majority is Raines, supra, a case decided long before we enunciated the congruence-and-proportionality test.

I fear that the Court's adoption of an as-applied approach eliminates any incentive for Congress to craft § 5 legislation for the purpose of remedying or deterring actual constitutional violations. Congress can now simply rely on the courts to sort out which hypothetical applications of an undifferentiated statute, such as Title II, may be enforced against the States. All the while, States will be subjected to substantial litigation in a piecemeal attempt to vindicate their Eleventh Amendment rights. The majority's as-applied approach simply cannot be squared with either our recent precedent or the proper role of the Judiciary.

Even in the limited courthouse-access context, Title II does not properly abrogate state sovereign immunity. As demonstrated in depth above, Congress utterly failed to identify any evidence that disabled persons were denied constitutionally protected access to judicial proceedings. Without this predicate showing, Title II, even if we were to hypothesize that it applies only to courthouses, cannot be viewed as a congruent and proportional response to state constitutional violations. *Garrett*, 531 U.S. at 368 ("Congress' § 5 authority is appropriately exercised only in response to state transgressions").

Moreover, even in the courthouse-access context, Title II requires substantially more than the Due Process Clause. Title II subjects States to private lawsuits if, *inter alia*, they fail to make "reasonable modifications" to facilities, such as removing "architectural . . . barriers." 42 U.S.C. §§ 12131(2), 12132. Yet the statute is not limited to occasions when the failure to modify results, or will likely result, in an actual due process violation – i.e., the inability of a disabled person to participate in a judicial proceeding. Indeed, liability is triggered if an inaccessible building results in a disabled person being "subjected to discrimination" – a term that presumably encompasses any sort of inconvenience in accessing the facility, for whatever purpose. § 12132.

* * *

For the foregoing reasons, I respectfully dissent.

Notes & Questions

1. What is the key difference between *Garrett* and *Lane*? How are the constitutional theories inapposite? How was the Court persuaded by the difference? How does Chief Justice Rehnquist, in his dissent, respond to this difference?

2. In *Lane*, the Court had to decide whether to evaluate the constitutionality of Title II in its entirety, or just as to claims involving access to the courts. What were the considerations on either side? If you were the lawyers for the Plaintiff, which way would you have argued the case (not having the benefit of knowing the outcome beforehand)? The *Lane* briefing actually reflected both approaches: George Lane's brief primarily argued the "as applied" approach, and the Solicitor General's office mainly argued the Title II as a whole approach. *See* Brief for Respondents, Tennessee v. Lane, 541 U.S. 509 (2004) (No. 02-1667), available at 2003 WL 22733904; *see also* Brief for the United States, Tennessee v. Lane, 541 U.S. 509 (2004) (No. 02-1667), available at 2003 WL 22733902.

3. The decision in *Lane* discusses voting at length, and we will return to voting challenges under the ADA later in this Part. Consider

the following scenario: a group of plaintiffs who are mobility-impaired and vision-impaired retain you as their lawyer. They are upset because voting in their state does not provide them the opportunity to vote secretly and independently, or in their polling place (they are typically directed to vote absentee). After *Lane*, how would you argue the case under Title II of the ADA? *See* Michael Waterstone, *Lane*, Fundamental Rights, & Voting, 56 Ala. L. Rev. 793 (2005).

4. *Lane* chose not to address Title II in its entirety. The lower courts have not been in universal agreement on its reach. In *Bill M. ex rel. William M. v. Nebraska Dep't of Health & Human Services, Finance, & Support*, 408 F.3d 1096 (8th Cir. 2005), the Eighth Circuit took a restrictive view of *Lane*, holding that *Lane* was limited to access-to-court cases. This case was subsequently vacated by the Supreme Court and remanded back to the Eighth Circuit. *See* United States v. Neb. Dept. of Health & Human Servs. Finance & Support, 547 U.S. 1067 (2006). The case then settled. 2008 WL 2550648 (D. Neb. 2008). The Tenth Circuit also took a restrictive view of *Lane* in *Guttman v. Khalsa*, 669 F.3d 1101, 1119 (10th Cir. 2012) ("Congress did not identify a history of irrational discrimination in professional licensing when enacting Title II"). The Tenth Circuit also explicitly distinguished its approach from both cases in Note 5 below. *See id.* at 1117.

5. Other courts, however, have interpreted Lane more expansively. In *Association for American for Disabled Americans, Inc. v. Florida International University*, No. 02-10360, 2005 WL 768129 (11th Cir. 2005), plaintiffs argued that Florida International University (FIU) violated Title II of the ADA by failing to provide qualified sign language interpreters, failing to provide adequate auxiliary aids and services such as effective note takers, and failing to furnish appropriate aids to its students with disabilities such as physical access to certain programs and facilities. FIU argued that plaintiff's claim was barred by the Eleventh Amendment, and the district court agreed. The Eleventh Circuit reversed, holding that Title II of the ADA, as applied to access to public education, constitutes a valid exercise of Congress's enforcement power under the Fourteenth Amendment. Although the court conceded that classifications relating to education only involve rational basis review under the Equal Protection Clause, it distinguished public education from other rights subject to rational basis review, holding that the right to public education "is vital to the future success of our society." In evaluating a history of unconstitutional discrimination, the court considered the record supporting Title II as a whole, instead of just looking at examples of discrimination in education. *See also* Constantine v. Rectors & Visitors of George Mason Univ., 411 F.3d 474, 490 (4th Cir. 2005) (holding that Title II of the ADA is valid § 5 legislation insofar as it applies to public higher education).

ॐ

In the following case, the Supreme Court addressed – somewhat – the scope of *Lane*.

९

UNITED STATES v. GEORGIA

Supreme Court of the United States, 2006
546 U.S. 151

SCALIA, J., delivered the opinion for a unanimous Court. STEVENS, J., filed a concurring opinion, in which GINSBURG, J., joined.

I

* * *

B

Petitioner Tony Goodman is a paraplegic inmate in the Georgia prison system who, at all relevant times, was housed at the Georgia State Prison in Reidsville. After filing numerous administrative grievances in the state prison system, Goodman filed a *pro se* complaint in the United States District Court for the Southern District of Georgia challenging the conditions of his confinement. He named as defendants the State of Georgia and the Georgia Department of Corrections (state defendants) and several individual prison officials. He brought claims under Rev. Stat. § 1979, 42 U.S.C. § 1983, Title II of the ADA, and other provisions not relevant here, seeking both injunctive relief and money damages against all defendants.

Goodman's *pro se* complaint and subsequent filings in the District Court included many allegations, both grave and trivial, regarding the conditions of his confinement in the Reidsville prison. Among his more serious allegations, he claimed that he was confined for 23-to-24 hours per day in a 12-by-3-foot cell in which he could not turn his wheelchair around. He alleged that the lack of accessible facilities rendered him unable to use the toilet and shower without assistance, which was often denied. On multiple occasions, he asserted, he had injured himself in attempting to transfer from his wheelchair to the shower or toilet on his own, and, on several other occasions, he had been forced to sit in his own feces and urine while prison officials refused to assist him in cleaning up the waste. He also claimed that he had been denied physical therapy and medical treatment, and denied access to virtually all prison programs and services on account of his disability.

The District Court adopted the Magistrate Judge's recommendation that the allegations in the complaint were vague and constituted insufficient notice pleading as to Goodman's § 1983 claims. It therefore dismissed the § 1983 claims against all defendants without providing Goodman an opportunity to amend his complaint. The District

Court also dismissed his Title II claims against all individual defendants. * * *

Goodman appealed to the United States Court of Appeals for the Eleventh Circuit. The United States, petitioner, intervened to defend the constitutionality of Title II's abrogation of state sovereign immunity. The Eleventh Circuit determined that the District Court had erred in dismissing all of Goodman's § 1983 claims, because Goodman's multiple *pro se* filings in the District Court alleged facts sufficient to support "a limited number of Eighth-Amendment claims under § 1983" against certain individual defendants. * * * The Court of Appeals held that the District Court should have given Goodman leave to amend his complaint to develop three Eighth Amendment claims relating to his conditions of confinement:

"First, Goodman alleges that he is not able to move his wheelchair in his cell. If Goodman is to be believed, this effectively amounts to some form of total restraint twenty-three to twenty-four hours-a-day without penal justification. Second, Goodman has alleged several instances in which he was forced to sit in his own bodily waste because prison officials refused to provide assistance. Third, Goodman has alleged sufficient conduct to proceed with a § 1983 claim based on the prison staff's supposed 'deliberate indifference' to his serious medical condition of being partially paraplegic. . . ." * * *

The Court remanded the suit to the District Court to permit Goodman to amend his complaint, while cautioning Goodman not to reassert all the § 1983 claims included in his initial complaint, "some of which [we]re obviously frivolous." *Id.,* at 18a.

The Eleventh Circuit did not address the sufficiency of Goodman's allegations under Title II. Instead, relying on its prior decision in *Miller v. King,* 384 F.3d 1248 (2004) the Court of Appeals affirmed the District Court's holding that Goodman's Title II claims for money damages against the State were barred by sovereign immunity. We granted certiorari to consider whether Title II of the ADA validly abrogates state sovereign immunity with respect to the claims at issue here. * * *.

II

In reversing the dismissal of Goodman's § 1983 claims, the Eleventh Circuit held that Goodman had alleged actual violations of the Eighth Amendment by state agents on the grounds set forth above. The State does not contest this holding, and we did not grant certiorari to consider the merits of Goodman's Eighth Amendment claims; we assume without deciding, therefore, that the Eleventh Circuit's treatment of these claims was correct. Moreover, Goodman urges, and the State does not dispute, that this same conduct that violated the Eighth Amendment also violated Title II of the ADA. In fact, it is quite plausible that the alleged deliberate refusal of prison officials to accommodate Goodman's disability-related needs in such fundamentals as mobility, hygiene, medical care, and virtually all other prison programs constituted "exclu[sion] from participation in or . . . den[ial of] the benefits of" the prison's "services, programs, or activities." 42 U.S.C. § 12132; see also *Yeskey*, 524 U.S., at 210, 118 S.Ct. 1952 (noting that the phrase "services, programs, or activities" in § 12132 includes recreational, medical, educational, and vocational prison programs). Therefore, Goodman's claims for money damages against the State under Title II were evidently based, at least in large part, on conduct that independently violated the provisions of § 1 of the Fourteenth Amendment. See *Louisiana ex rel. Francis v. Resweber*, 329 U.S. 459, 463, 67 S.Ct. 374, 91 L.Ed. 422 (1947) (the Due Process Clause of the Fourteenth Amendment incorporates the Eighth Amendment's guarantee against cruel and unusual punishment). In this respect, Goodman differs from the claimants in our other cases addressing Congress's ability to abrogate sovereign immunity pursuant to its § 5 powers. * * *

While the Members of this Court have disagreed regarding the scope of Congress's "prophylactic" enforcement powers under § 5 of the Fourteenth Amendment, see, *e.g., Lane*, 541 U.S., at 513, 124 S.Ct. 1978 (majority opinion of STEVENS, J.); *id.*, at 538, 124 S.Ct. 1978 (Rehnquist, C.J., dissenting); *id.*, at 554, 124 S.Ct. 1978 (SCALIA, J., dissenting), no one doubts that § 5 grants Congress the power to "enforce . . . the provisions" of the Amendment by creating private remedies against the States for *actual* violations of those provisions. "Section 5 authorizes Congress to create a cause of action through which the citizen may vindicate his Fourteenth Amendment rights." *Id.*, at 559-560, 124 S.Ct. 1978 (SCALIA, J., dissenting) (citing the Ku Klux Klan Act of April 20, 1871, 17 Stat. 13); see also *Fitzpatrick v. Bitzer*, 427 U.S. 445, 456, 96 S.Ct. 2666, 49 L.Ed.2d 614 (1976) ("In [§ 5] Congress is expressly granted authority to enforce . . . the *substantive provisions* of the Fourteenth Amendment" by providing actions for money damages against the States (emphasis added)); *Ex parte Virginia*, 100 U.S. 339, 346, 25 L.Ed. 676 (1880) ("The prohibitions of the Fourteenth Amendment are directed to the States . . . . It is these which Congress is empowered to enforce . . ."). This enforcement power includes the power to abrogate state sovereign immunity by authorizing private suits for damages against the States. See *Fitzpatrick, supra*, at 456, 96 S.Ct. 2666. Thus, insofar as Title II creates a private cause of action for damages against the States for conduct that *actually* violates the Fourteenth Amendment, Title II validly abrogates state sovereign immunity. The Eleventh Circuit erred in dismissing those of Goodman's Title II claims that were based on such unconstitutional conduct.

From the many allegations in Goodman's *pro se* complaint and his subsequent filings in the District Court, it is not clear precisely what conduct he intended to allege in support of his Title II claims. Because the Eleventh Circuit did not address the issue, it is likewise unclear to what extent the conduct underlying Goodman's constitutional claims also violated Title II. Moreover, the Eleventh Circuit ordered that the suit be remanded to the District Court to permit Goodman to amend his complaint, but instructed him to revise his factual allegations to exclude his "frivolous" claims – some of which are quite far afield from actual constitutional violations (under either the Eighth Amendment or some other constitutional provision), or even from Title II violations. See, *e.g.,* App. 50 (demanding a "steam table" for Goodman's housing unit). It is therefore unclear whether Goodman's amended complaint will assert Title II claims premised on conduct that does *not* independently violate the Fourteenth Amendment. Once Goodman's complaint is amended, the lower courts will be best situated to determine in the first instance, on a claim-by-claim basis, (1) which aspects of the State's alleged conduct violated Title II; (2) to what extent such misconduct also violated the Fourteenth Amendment; and (3) insofar as such misconduct violated Title II but did not violate the Fourteenth Amendment, whether Congress's purported abrogation of sovereign immunity as to that class of conduct is nevertheless valid.

* * *

The judgment of the Eleventh Circuit is reversed, and the suit is remanded for further proceedings consistent with this opinion.

It is so ordered.

Justice STEVENS, with whom Justice GINSBURG joins, concurring.

The Court holds that Title II of the Americans with Disabilities Act of 1990 validly abrogates state sovereign immunity at least insofar as it creates a private cause of action for damages against States for conduct that violates the Constitution. And the state defendants have correctly chosen not to challenge the Eleventh Circuit's holding that Title II is constitutional insofar as it authorizes prospective injunctive relief against the State. See *Miller v. King,* 384 F.3d 1248, 1264 (C.A.11 2004). Rather than attempting to define the outer limits of Title II's valid abrogation of state sovereign immunity on the basis of the present record, the Court's opinion wisely permits the parties, guided by *Tennessee v. Lane,* 541 U.S. 509, 124 S.Ct. 1978, 158 L.Ed.2d 820 (2004), to create a factual record that will inform that decision.[v] I therefore join the opinion.

It is important to emphasize that although petitioner Goodman's Eighth Amendment claims provide a sufficient basis for reversal, our opinion does not suggest that this is the only constitutional right applicable in the prison context and therefore relevant to the abrogation

---

[v]   Such definition is necessary because Title II prohibits " 'a somewhat broader swath of conduct' " than the Constitution itself forbids. *Lane,* 541 U.S., at 533, n. 24, 124 S.Ct. 1978 (quoting *Kimel v. Florida Bd. of Regents,* 528 U.S. 62, 81, 120 S.Ct. 631, 145 L.Ed.2d 522 (2000)). * * *

issue. As we explain, when the District Court and the Court of Appeals revisit that issue, they should analyze Goodman's claims to see whether they state "actual constitutional violations (under either the Eighth Amendment *or some other constitutional provision*)," (emphasis added), and to evaluate whether "Congress's purported abrogation of sovereign immunity in such contexts is nevertheless valid." This approach mirrors that taken in *Lane,* which identified a constellation of "basic constitutional guarantees" that Title II seeks to enforce and ultimately evaluated whether Title II was an appropriate response to the "class of cases" at hand. 541 U.S., at 522–523, 531, 124 S.Ct. 1978. The Court's focus on Goodman's Eighth Amendment claims arises simply from the fact that those are the only constitutional violations the Eleventh Circuit found him to have alleged properly.

Moreover, our approach today is fully consistent with our recognition that the history of mistreatment leading to Congress' decision to extend Title II's protections to prison inmates was not limited to violations of the Eighth Amendment. * * * In fact, as the Solicitor General points out in his brief arguing that Title II's damage remedy constitutes appropriate prophylactic legislation in the prison context, the record of mistreatment of prison inmates that Congress reviewed in its deliberations preceding the enactment of Title II was comparable in all relevant respects to the record that we recently held sufficient to uphold the application of that title to the entire class of cases implicating the fundamental right of access to the courts. See *Lane,* 541 U.S., at 533-534, 124 S.Ct. 1978. And while it is true that cases involving inadequate medical care and inhumane conditions of confinement have perhaps been most numerous, courts have also reviewed myriad other types of claims by disabled prisoners, such as allegations of the abridgment of religious liberties, undue censorship, interference with access to the judicial process, and procedural due process violations. See, *e.g., Vitek v. Jones,* 445 U.S. 480, 100 S.Ct. 1254, 63 L.Ed.2d 552 (1980) (procedural due process); *May v. Sheahan,* 226 F.3d 876 (C.A.7 2000) (access to judicial process, lawyers, legal materials, and reading materials); *Littlefield v. Deland,* 641 F.2d 729 (C.A.10 1981) (access to reading and writing materials); *Nolley v. County of Erie,* 776 F.Supp. 715 (W.D.N.Y. 1991) (access to law library and religious services).

Indeed, given the constellation of rights applicable in the prison context, it is clear that the Eleventh Circuit has erred in identifying only the Eighth Amendment right to be free from cruel and unusual punishment in performing the first step of the "congruence and proportionality" inquiry set forth in *City of Boerne v. Flores,* 521 U.S. 507, 117 S.Ct. 2157, 138 L.Ed.2d 624 (1997). * * * By reversing the Eleventh Circuit's decision in this case and remanding for further proceedings, we not only provide the parties an opportunity to create a more substantial factual record, but also provide the District Court and the Court of Appeals the opportunity to apply the *Boerne* framework properly. Given these benefits, I agree with the Court's decision to await further proceedings before trying to define the extent to which Title II validly abrogates state sovereign immunity in the prison context.

Notes & Questions

1.   *Goodman* is opaque on the key Title II question post-*Lane*; that is, for what other rights besides access to courts is Title II's abrogation of state sovereign immunity constitutional? After *Goodman,* the two courts of appeal to consider the issue have held that that Title II's abrogation of sovereign immunity is valid insofar as it applies to public education. *See* Bowers v. National Collegiate Athletic Association, 475 F.3d 524, 550-56 (3d Cir. 2007); *see also* Toledo v. Sanchez, 454 F.3d 24, 40 (1st Cir. 2006). *But see* Klinger v. Director, Dept. of Revenue, 455 F.3d 888 (holding that Title II did not validly abrogate state sovereign immunity insofar as it related to claims that people with disabilities had been charged for handicap parking placards).

2.   The holding in *Goodman* – that Congress can abrogate state sovereign immunity to protect actual constitutional violations – brings Title II theoretically closer to Section 1983. As Justice Scalia notes in the majority opinion, there is a difference in opinion on the Court regarding the scope of Congress's prophylactic authority (i.e., how much room does Congress have to provide a damage remedy for a "somewhat broader swath of conduct" than what the Constitution itself forbids).

3.   The type of claim matters to the sovereign immunity analysis. In *Bolmer v. Oliveira,* 594 F.3d 134 (2d Cir. 2010), the plaintiff alleged that the Connecticut Department of Mental Health and Addiction Services violated Title II of the ADA by involuntarily committing him. The Second Circuit rejected defendant's sovereign immunity defense, holding that plaintiff's claims were based in substantive due process, which are considered not under a rational basis framework but whether or not the alleged conduct was substantially below the standard generally accepted in the medical community.

ॐ

B.   *Other Constitutional Issues.*

Thus far, we have discussed scenarios where an individual sues a state for a violation of Title II seeking money damages. In these cases, the individual typically names a state official in his official capacity, which is interpreted as a suit against the state. *See* Hafer v. Melo, 502 U.S. 21 (1991). A state therefore may raise its Eleventh Amendment sovereign immunity as a defense, as Tennessee did in *Lane.*

However, when a claim is made against a state officer in his official capacity and only requests the remedy of prospective injunctive relief, there is an exception to the sovereign immunity rule. Under the doctrine of *Ex Parte Young*, 209 U.S. 123 (1908), the Eleventh Amendment is no bar to "federal jurisdiction over a suit against a state official when that suit seeks only prospective injunctive relief in order to 'end a continuing violation of federal law.' " *See* Seminole Tribe of Fla. v. Florida, 517 U.S. 44, 73 (1996) (quoting Green v. Mansour, 474 U.S. 64, 68 (1985)). The *Ex Parte Young* doctrine rests on the premise that "a suit against a state official to enjoin an ongoing violation of federal law is not a suit against the State." Idaho v. Coeur d'Alene Tribe, 521 U.S. 261, 295 (1997).

In *Armstrong v. Wilson*, 124 F.3d 1019 (9th Cir. 1997), a class of inmates with various disabilities claimed that the state prison system violated Title II by not providing adequate evacuation plans for prisoners with disabilities. They also claimed that the range of vocational programs for disabled inmates was more limited than those for non-disabled prisoners. The plaintiffs named the state prison officials in their official capacities, and sought only prospective injunctive relief. The Ninth Circuit held that even though the plaintiffs in essence were asking for wide-ranging, wholesale institutional reforms, their claims fell squarely within the *Ex Parte Young* exception to Eleventh Amendment sovereign immunity. *See also* Miller v. King, 384 F.3d 1248 (11th Cir. 2004); McCarthy v. Hawkins, 381 F.3d 407 (5th Cir. 2003); Chaffin v. Kan. State Fair Bd., 348 F.3d 850, 866-67 (10th Cir. 2003); Henrietta D. v. Bloomberg, 331 F.3d 261, 288 (2d Cir. 2003); Bruggeman ex rel. Bruggeman v. Blagojevich, 324 F.3d 906, 913 (7th Cir. 2003).

Other courts have held that the ADA and Rehabilitation Act of 1973 allow plaintiffs to sue state officials in their individual capacities for money damages in certain circumstances. *See* Shotz v. City of Plantation, 344 F.3d 1161 (11th Cir. 2003). In these cases, however, the state officers typically raise the defense of *qualified immunity* (also referred to as *good faith immunity).* This defense provides immunity from liability to government officials engaged in discretionary government activities unless their conduct violates "clearly established statutory or constitutional rights." Harlow v. Fitzgerald, 457 U.S. 800, 818 (1982). The right must be established such that a reasonable official would have understood that his behavior violated that right.

In enacting the ADA, Congress expressly invoked its commerce clause power, stating: "It is the purpose of this chapter . . . (4) to invoke the sweep of congressional authority, including the power . . . to regulate commerce, in order to address the major areas of discrimination faced day-to-day by people with disabilities." 42 U.S.C. § 12101(b). While Congress cannot abrogate sovereign immunity pursuant to the Commerce Clause, it does allow Congress to create statutes, like the ADA, that provide for prospective injunctive relief against state actors. But "new federalism" has also limited Congressional power under the Commerce Clause. *See* United States v. Lopez, 514 U.S. 549 (1995) (holding that the Gun Free School Zones Act of 1990 exceeded Congress's Commerce Clause authority); *see also* United States v. Morrison, 529 U.S. 598 (2000) (holding that a provision in the Violence Against Women Act, providing victims of gender-motivated violence with a federal civil action against perpetrators, could not be justified as an exercise of Congress's power to regulate interstate commerce).

In *Klingler v. Director, Department of Revenue*, 366 F.3d 614 (8th Cir. 2004), the court applied *Lopez* and *Morrison* to ADA Title II, holding that Congress lacked power under the Commerce Clause to prohibit Missouri's assessment of a $2.00 fee for handicapped parking placards. In a spirited dissent, Judge Richard Arnold criticized the majority opinion for not giving Congress the benefit of the doubt as to whether Title II regulated a substantial amount of commercial activity. *Id.* at 621. The Supreme Court granted *certiorari*, vacated the case, and remanded for reconsideration in light of *Tennessee v. Lane*, 541 U.S. 509 (2004).

On remand, the State of Missouri dropped its commerce clause challenge to the Klingler appeal, and the Eighth Circuit determined the "annual fee for the parking placards is a discriminatory surcharge." Klingler v. Dir., Dep't of Revenue, 433 F.3d 1078, 1079 (2006). By this point, plaintiffs only had claims for injunctive relief (the Court had earlier dismissed, on sovereign immunity grounds, their claims for monetary damages, and declined to reinstate them after *Goodman*, *see Klinger v. Director*, 455 F.3d 888 (8th Cir. 2006)), and on remand the Eighth Circuit declined plaintiff's request to reinstate their monetary claims. Klingler v. Dir., Dep't of Revenue, 433 F.3d 1078, 1082 (8th Cir. 2006).

Section 504 of the Rehabilitation Act has also been challenged on federalism grounds. Generally, the applicable Eleventh Amendment jurisprudence has tracked the ADA cases. There is a split among the courts of appeals as to whether a plaintiff may bring suit against a state for money damages under the Rehabilitation Act. In *Reickenbacker v. Foster*, 274 F.3d 974, 983 (5th Cir. 2001), the Fifth Circuit held that the Rehabilitation Act did not represent a valid exercise of Congress's power under Section 5 of the Fourteenth Amendment, despite a clear Congressional intent to abrogate the states' sovereign immunity. But in *Miranda B. v. Kitzhaber*, 328 F.3d 1181, 1186 (9th Cir. 2003), the Ninth Circuit held that with the Rehabilitation Act, Congress validly abrogated the states' sovereign immunity.

The Rehabilitation Act contains a unique wrinkle on this issue. It is settled that, even if Congress does not validly abrogate state sovereign immunity using its Section 5 powers, a state may voluntarily waive its sovereign immunity by consenting to a suit. *See* Coll. Sav. Bank v. Fla. Prepaid Postsecondary Educ. Expense Bd., 527 U.S. 666, 670 (1999). For example, a state can choose to waive its immunity in exchange for some "gratuity" (i.e., funds) from Congress, or because it for other reasons wishes to submit itself to federal jurisdiction. In the wake of *Board of Trustees of the University of Alabama v. Garrett*, 531 U.S. 356, 374 (2001), several states have waived their sovereign immunity to suits under Title I of the ADA. *See supra* § 12.2.

Some courts have held that by accepting federal funds under the Rehabilitation Act, states consent to suit in federal court and waive their Eleventh Amendment sovereign immunity. *See* Clark v. Cal. Dep't of Corr., 123 F.3d 1267, 1271 (9th Cir. 1997); *see also* A.W. v. Jersey City Pub. Schs., 341 F.3d 234 (3d Cir. 2003); Miranda B. v. Kitzhaber, 328 F.3d 1181, 1186 (9th Cir. 2003); Miller v. Tx. Tech Univ. Health Scis. Ctr., 421 F.3d 342, 349 (5th Cir. 2005).

There is an additional layer of complexity relating to whether Rehabilitation Act suits can proceed against a state in *state* court. In *Robinson v. Kansas*, 295 F.3d 1183 (10th Cir. 2002), the Tenth Circuit held that Kansas waived its sovereign immunity and consented to suit under the Rehabilitation Act in federal court. However, in *Purvis v. Williams*, 73 P.3d 740 (Kan. 2003), the Supreme Court of Kansas reached the opposite conclusion as to Rehabilitation Act suits for money damages in state courts. The high state court held that Kansas' sovereign immunity – which it had not waived by accepting federal funds – precluded suit in Kansas' state courts under the Rehabilitation Act for money damages.

A separate sub-issue is whether the acceptance of federal money requires an institution or even a state as a whole to refrain from discrimination, or whether only the specific program or agency funded has that obligation. Federal regulations have been issued to clarify that there is broad coverage for institutions that receive federal funds. *See generally* Nondiscrimination on the Basis of Race, Color, National Origin, Handicap, or Age in Programs or Activities Receiving Federal Financial Assistance; Final Rule, 68 Fed. Reg. 51,334 (Aug. 26, 2003).

Chapter 13 COVERAGE

§ 13.1 Introduction

Title II applies to the services, programs, and activities that are offered by public entities.

A. *"Public Entity"*

As a threshold matter, the text of the statute unambiguously defines "public entities" as state and local governments. The question has arisen, however, as to how expansively this phrase should be interpreted. The Supreme Court considered this issue in the following case.

ം

PENNSYLVANIA DEPARTMENT OF CORRECTIONS v. YESKEY

Supreme Court of the United States, 1998
524 U.S. 206

Justice SCALIA delivered the opinion of the Court.

The question before us is whether Title II of the Americans with Disabilities Act of 1990 (ADA), 104 Stat. 337, 42 U.S.C. § 12131 et seq., which prohibits a "public entity" from discriminating against a "qualified individual with a disability" on account of that individual's disability, see § 12132, covers inmates in state prisons.

* * *

Petitioners argue that state prisoners are not covered by the ADA for the same reason we held in *Gregory v. Ashcroft*, 501 U.S. 452 (1991), that state judges were not covered by the Age Discrimination in Employment Act of 1967 (ADEA), 29 U.S.C. § 621 et seq. *Gregory* relied on the canon of construction that absent an "unmistakably clear" expression of intent to "alter the usual constitutional balance between the States and the Federal Government," we will interpret a statute to preserve rather than destroy the States' "substantial sovereign powers." 501 U.S. at 460-461 (citations and internal quotation marks omitted). It may well be that exercising ultimate control over the management of state prisons, like establishing the qualifications of state government officials, is a traditional and essential state function subject to the plain-statement rule of *Gregory*. "One of the primary functions of government," we have said, "is the preservation of societal order through enforcement of the criminal law, and the maintenance of penal institutions is an essential part of that task." *Procunier v. Martinez*, 416 U.S. 396, 412 (1974), overruled on other grounds, *Thornburgh v. Abbott*, 490 U.S. 401, 414 (1989). "It is difficult to imagine an activity in which a State has a stronger interest," *Preiser v. Rodriguez*, 411 U.S. 475, 491 (1973).

* * *

Assuming, without deciding, that the plain-statement rule does govern application of the ADA to the administration of state prisons, we think the requirement of the rule is amply met: the statute's language unmistakably includes State prisons and prisoners within its coverage. The situation here is not comparable to that in *Gregory*. There, although the ADEA plainly covered state employees, it contained an exception for " 'appointee[s] on the policymaking level' " which made it impossible for us to "conclude that the statute plainly cover[ed] appointed state judges." 501 U.S. at 467. Here, the ADA plainly covers state institutions *without* any exception that could cast the coverage of prisons into doubt. Title II of the ADA provides:

> "Subject to the provisions of this subchapter, no qualified individual with a disability shall, by reason of such disability, be excluded from participation in or be denied the benefits of the services, programs, or activities of a public entity, or be subjected to discrimination by any such entity." 42 U.S.C. § 12132.

State prisons fall squarely within the statutory definition of "public entity," which includes "any department, agency, special purpose district, or other instrumentality of a State or States or local government." § 12131(1)(B).

* * *

[P]etitioners point out that the statute's statement of findings and purpose, 42 U.S.C. § 12101, does not mention prisons and prisoners. That is perhaps questionable, since the provision's reference to discrimination "in such critical areas as . . . institutionalization," § 12101(a)(3), can be thought to include penal institutions. But assuming it to be true, and assuming further that it proves, as petitioners contend, that Congress did not "envisio[n] that the ADA would be applied to state prisoners," Brief for Petitioners 13-14, in the context of an unambiguous statutory text that is irrelevant. As we have said before, the fact that a statute can be " 'applied in situations not expressly anticipated by Congress does not demonstrate ambiguity. It demonstrates breadth.' " *Sedima, S.P.R.L. v. Imrex Co.*, 473 U.S. 479, 499 (1985) (citation omitted).

* * *

Because the plain text of Title II of the ADA unambiguously extends to state prison inmates, the judgment of the Court of Appeals is affirmed.

Notes & Questions

1. Prison cases make up a large percentage of ADA Title II claims. Most are unsuccessful. Some courts have held that to prevail on a claim that statutory rights have been violated, inmates must show that the challenged prison policy or regulation is unreasonable. *See* Gates v.

Rowland, 39 F.3d 1439, 1447 (9th Cir. 1994). In *Pierce v. County of Orange*, 526 F.3d 1190 (9th Cir. 2008), the court held that the defendant County was in violation of both Title II's physical barriers and program access requirements. Whereas the district court had excused the County on the grounds that it was making compliance progress, the Court of Appeals held that this conclusion was unwarranted given the County's track record. *Id.* at 1217-20. In *Armstrong v. Schwarzenegger*, 622 F.3d 1058 (9th Cir. 2010), the court held that contractual arrangements between state and county for incarceration of state prison inmates and parolees in county jails were subject to Title II of the ADA. But in *Edison v. Douberly*, 604 F.3d 1307 (11th Cir. 2010), the court held that a private prison management corporation operating a Florida state prison was not a public entity subject to liability under Title II.

2. Other courts have held that public entities include:

- State universities. *See* Coleman v. Zatechka, 824 F.Supp. 1360 (D. Neb. 1993); *see also* Bowers v. Nat'l Collegiate Athletic Ass'n, 9 F.Supp.2d 460 (D.N.J. 1998); Darian v. Univ. of Mass. Boston, 980 F.Supp. 77 (D. Mass. 1997).

- State and municipal courts. *See* Galloway v. Sup. Ct. of D.C., 816 F.Supp. 12 (D.D.C. 1993); *see also* Soto v. City of Newark, 72 F.Supp.2d 489 (D.N.J. 1999); People v. Caldwell, 603 N.Y.S.2d 713 (N.Y. City Crim. Ct. 1993).

- State bars and board of law examiners. *See* Petition of Rubenstein, 637 A.2d 1131 (Del. 1994); *see also* Ware v. Wyo. Bd. of Law Exam's, 973 F.Supp. 1339 (D. Wyo. 1997), affirmed, 161 F.3d 19 (10th Cir. 1998); State ex rel. Okla. Bar Ass'n v. Busch, 919 P.2d 1114 (Okla. 1996).

- Local police departments. *See* Gorman v. Bartch, 152 F.3d 907 (8th Cir. 1998).

- City planning and zoning boards. *See* Innovative Health Sys., Inc. v. City of White Plains, 117 F.3d 37 (2d Cir. 1997); Bay Area Addiction Research v. City of Antioch, 179 F.3d 725, 730-32 (9th Cir. 1999); Wisconsin Community Services, Inc. v. City of Milwaukee, 465 F.3d 737, 750 (7th Cir. 2006).

- High school athletic associations. *See* Cruz ex rel. Cruz v. Pa. Interscholastic Athletic Ass'n, Inc., 157 F.Supp.2d 485 (E.D. Pa. 2001).

- State judicial nominating commissions. *See* Doe v. Judicial Nominating Comm'n, 906 F.Supp. 1534 (S.D. Fla. 1995).

- State pension funds. *See* Piquard v. City of E. Peoria, 887 F.Supp. 1106 (C.D. Ill. 1995).

This generally broad construction has one important limit. Courts have declined to classify federal agencies as public entities for the purposes of Title II. For example, in *Isle Royale Boaters Ass'n v. Norton*, 154 F.Supp.2d 1098 (W.D. Mich. 2001), the National Park Service, a unit of federal government, was held not to be a "public entity" for purposes of Title II. Similarly, in *Zingher v. Yacavone*, 30 F.Supp.2d 446 (D. Vt. 1997), the court held that the U.S. Department of Education and Secretary of Education were not "public entities" for purposes of Title II.

3. What about a hospital that is established by the state, but run as a public corporation? Is this a public entity? The general test for this situation is set out in *Fresnius Medical Care Cardiovascular Resources, Inc. v. Puerto Rico*, 322 F.3d 56, 68 (1st Cir. 2003). The First Circuit started by examining whether the state had "clearly structured the entity to share its sovereignty." If the answer to that question is clear, it ends the analysis. If the answer to that question is unclear, the court examines whether the state treasury is liable for damages caused by the entity. In *Fresnius*, the court found the first question did not resolve the issue. The court then concluded, under the second part of the test, that the hospital was not an arm of the state because the state was not obligated on the debt of the hospital. *Id.* at 68-72.

4. Consider the following scenario: A nurse with a disability requests a workplace accommodation, which the hospital declines to make. The nurse sues under Title II of the ADA, claiming that the hospital is a public entity because it was established by the State. Using the test set forth in *Fresnius*, the court holds that the hospital is not an arm of the state, and therefore not a public entity. Does the nurse have any other options under the ADA?

ৎ

B. *Service, Program, Or Activity*

1. The general rule – broad construction

Title II applies to "services, programs, and activities" of public entities. At various times, litigants have attempted to use this language to limit the functions of a public entity that falls within Title II's ambit. Consider how this argument played out in *Pennsylvania Department of Corrections v. Yeskey*, discussed above.

> Petitioners contend that the phrase "benefits of the services, programs, or activities of a public entity," § 12132, creates an ambiguity, because state prisons do not provide prisoners with "benefits" of "programs, services, or activities" as those terms are ordinarily understood. We disagree. Modern prisons provide inmates with many recreational "activities," medical "services," and educational and vocational "programs," all of which at least theoretically "benefit" the prisoners (and any of which

disabled prisoners could be "excluded from participation in"). . . . The text of the ADA provides no basis for distinguishing these programs, services, and activities from those provided by public entities that are not prisons. We also disagree with petitioners' contention that the term "qualified individual with a disability" is ambiguous insofar as concerns its application to state prisoners. The statute defines the term to include anyone with a disability "who, with or without reasonable modifications to rules, policies, or practices, the removal of architectural, communication, or transportation barriers, or the provision of auxiliary aids and services, meets the essential eligibility requirements for the receipt of services or the participation in programs or activities provided by a public entity." 42 U.S.C. § 12131(2). Petitioners argue that the words "eligibility" and "participation" imply voluntariness on the part of an applicant who seeks a benefit from the State, and thus do not connote prisoners who are being held against their will. This is wrong on two counts: First, because the words do not connote voluntariness. *See, e.g.,* Webster's New International Dictionary 831 (2d ed. 1949) ("eligible": "Fitted or qualified to be chosen or elected; legally or morally suitable; as, an eligible candidate"); *id.* at 1782 ("participate": "To have a share in common with others; to partake; share, as in a debate"). While "eligible" individuals "participate" voluntarily in many programs, services, and activities, there are others for which they are "eligible" in which "participation" is mandatory. A drug addict convicted of drug possession, for example, might, as part of his sentence, be required to "participate" in a drug treatment program for which only addicts are "eligible." And secondly, even if the words did connote voluntariness, it would still not be true that all prison "services," "programs," and "activities" are excluded from the ADA because participation in them is not voluntary. The prison law library, for example, is a service (and the use of it an activity), which prisoners are free to take or leave. . . . In the very case at hand, the governing law makes it clear that participation in the Boot Camp program is voluntary. See Pa. Stat. Ann., Tit. 61, § 1126(a) (Purdon Supp. 1998) ("An eligible inmate may make an application to the motivational boot camp selection committee for permission to participate in the motivational boot camp program"); § 1126(c) ("[c]onditio[n]" of "participa[tion]" is that applicant "agree to be bound by" certain "terms and conditions").

Pa. Dep't of Corr. v. Yeskey, 524 U.S. 206, 210-11 (1998).

This broad construction is not absolute. One area of disagreement involves proceedings that adjudicate parental termination of rights. This is an important issue to the disability community, who argues that stereotypes about parenting abilities of people with disabilities (especially mental disabilities) are rampant in these types of proceedings. Despite *Yeskey's* expansive holding, courts have split on whether or not these proceedings are covered under Title II. *Compare* M.C. v. Dept. of Children and Families, 750 So.2d 705, 706 (Fla.Dist.Ct.App. 2000) ("such proceedings are held for the benefit of the child, not the parent. Therefore, the ADA is inapplicable when used as a defense by the parent(s) in proceedings as here under review."), *with* In re C.M., 2004 WL 1900100 at *2 (Iowa App. 2004) (the "ADA requires a public entity to make 'reasonable accommodation' to allow a disabled person to participate in services," but finding that the reunification services provided to the mother were reasonable."). In 2006, the Supreme Court declined *certiorari* on this issue in the case of *In re Kayla*, 900 A.2d 1202, 1208 (S.C. Rhode Island 2006).

Nevertheless, the generally expansive view of "service, program, or activity" has greatly concerned city and state officials. In *Barden v. City of Sacramento*, 292 F.3d 1073 (9th Cir. 2002), at issue was whether sidewalks were a service, program, or activity within the meaning of Title II. Consider the arguments raised by the amicus brief of the National League of Cities, supporting the City of Sacramento, which is followed by the Ninth Circuit's opinion.

ও

BARDEN v. CITY OF SACRAMENTO

Brief of the National League of Cities and 76 California Cities as Amici Curiae in Support of Appellees, City of Sacramento

* * *

The imposition of the program access standard on sidewalks and other structures in the public rights-of-way where no public programs, services or activities are offered would jeopardize public entities' ability to achieve the levels of accessibility mandated by Title II of the ADA and Section 504 of the Rehabilitation Act. Public entities have only limited funds and other resources available to spend on public facilities and infrastructure, and need to preserve their ability to concentrate the expenditure of these resources where it will actually improve the accessibility of their programs, services and activities to persons with disabilities. Appellants' efforts to broaden the program access standard to encompass all physical structures, regardless of whether public programs are offered at those structures, would divert public expenditures to facilities where no programs are offered, and would thereby reduce the overall benefit to disabled persons while greatly increasing the cost of accessibility compliance.

In California, the enormous scale of the public rights-of-way ensures that an adverse decision would have profound impacts on public entities' ability to comply with the program access standard. California's cities obtain public funds from finite Federal, State and local sources, and their ability to generate additional tax revenues is subject to numerous legal, political and economic constraints. In order to meet the cities' legal responsibility to provide for the public safety, utilities, health and other needs, most of their tax revenues must be spent on governmental functions other than transportation. Of the estimated 8% of total revenues available for city streets and roads, all but a small fraction must be spent on new construction, reconstruction, signals and safety devices In the most recent fiscal year reported, only approximately $57 million in public funds were available to California's cities to spend on pedestrian ways and bicycle paths.

California has an estimated 166,971 miles of public roadway, of which 69,422 miles (approximately three times the Earth's circumference) are city streets. At an estimated per-mile sidewalk construction cost of $36,000 (for both sides of the street, at the four-foot width that Appellants contend is required), the costs to California cities of rebuilding their existing sidewalks to conform with the design standards sought by Appellants would total approximately $2.5 billion, exclusive of the costs of demolition and acquisition of enlarged rights-of-way. Given the fundamental sidewalk design changes that Appellants contend is required to make the public rights-of-way accessible, the costs of altering existing sidewalks to implement such changes would likely exceed the costs of demolition and rebuilding, such that a total cost of $2.5 billion would be likely regardless of whether the changes were achieved through rebuilding, alteration, or both.

The extraordinary magnitude of such an undertaking would overwhelm the cities' resources and be impossible to achieve. Yet despite the enormous costs that would be required to rebuild the existing sidewalk infrastructure, there would be no commensurate benefit in the accessibility of public programs, services and activities, since Appellants seek to require the cities to rebuild sidewalks and other structures in rights-of-way where no programs, services or activities are offered.

&

BARDEN v. CITY OF SACRAMENTO

United States Court of Appeals, Ninth Circuit, 2002
292 F.3d 1073

TASHIMA, Circuit Judge.

We must decide whether public sidewalks in the City of Sacramento are a service, program, or activity of the City within the meaning of Title II of the Americans with Disabilities Act ("ADA"), 42 U.S.C. § 12132, or § 504 of the Rehabilitation Act, 29 U.S.C. § 794. We hold that they are and, accordingly, that the sidewalks are subject to program accessibility regulations promulgated in furtherance of these statutes. We therefore reverse the order of the district court and remand for further proceedings. We have jurisdiction pursuant to 28 U.S.C. § 1292(b).

BACKGROUND

Appellants, various individuals with mobility and/or vision disabilities, commenced this class action against the City of Sacramento. Appellants alleged that the City violated the ADA and the Rehabilitation Act by failing to install curb ramps in newly-constructed or altered sidewalks and by failing to maintain existing sidewalks so as to ensure accessibility by persons with disabilities. The parties stipulated to the entry of an injunction regarding the curb ramps; however, they did not reach agreement on the City's obligation to remove other barriers to sidewalk accessibility, such as benches, sign posts, or wires.

* * *

DISCUSSION

Title II of the ADA provides that "no qualified individual with a disability shall, by reason of such disability, be excluded from participation in or be denied the benefits of the services, programs, or activities of a public entity, or be subjected to discrimination by any such entity." 42 U.S.C. § 12132. Similarly, § 504 of the Rehabilitation Act provides that "[n]o otherwise qualified individual with a disability . . . shall, solely by reason of her or his disability, be excluded from the participation in, be denied the benefits of, or be subjected to discrimination under any program or activity receiving Federal financial assistance." 29 U.S.C. § 794(a). One form of prohibited discrimination is the exclusion from a public entity's services, programs, or activities because of the inaccessibility of the entity's facility – thus, the program accessibility regulations at issue here.

The access requirements are set forth in 28 C.F.R. §§ 35.149-35.151. Section 35.150 requires a public entity to "operate each service, program, or activity so that the service, program, or activity, when viewed in its entirety, is readily accessible to and usable by individuals with disabilities." 28 C.F.R. § 35.150(a). The public entity is required to develop a transition plan for making structural changes to facilities in order to make its programs accessible. Id. at § 35.150(d)(1). The regulation also requires the transition plan to include a schedule for providing curb ramps to make pedestrian walkways accessible. Id. at § 35.150(d)(2). Section 35.151 similarly requires newly-constructed or altered roads and walkways to contain curb ramps at intersections. 28 C.F.R. § 35.151(e).

The district court's order was based on its conclusion that sidewalks are not a service, program, or activity of the City. Rather than determining whether each function of a city can be characterized as a service, program, or activity for purposes of Title II, however, we have construed "the ADA's broad language [as] bring[ing] within its scope 'anything a public entity does.'" *Lee v. City of Los Angeles*, 250 F.3d 668, 691 (9th Cir. 2001) (quoting *Yeskey v. Pa. Dep't of Corr.*, 118 F.3d 168, 171 (3d Cir. 1997), *aff'd*, 524 U.S. 206 (1998)); see also *Johnson v. City of Saline*, 151 F.3d 564, 569 (6th Cir. 1998) (finding that "the phrase 'services, programs, or activities' encompasses virtually everything that a public entity does"); *Innovative Health Sys., Inc. v. City of White Plains*, 117 F.3d 37, 45 (2d Cir. 1997) (reasoning that the phrase "programs, services, or activities" is "a catch-all phrase that prohibits all discrimination by a public entity, regardless of the context"), superseded on other grounds, *Zervos v. Verizon New York, Inc.*, 252 F.3d 163, 171 n.7 (2d Cir. 2001). Attempting to distinguish which public functions are services, programs, or activities, and which are not, would disintegrate into needless "hair-splitting arguments." *Innovative Health Sys.*, 117 F.3d at 45. The focus of the inquiry, therefore, is not so much on whether a particular public function can technically be characterized as a service, program, or activity, but whether it is "'a normal function of a governmental entity.'" *BAART*, 179 F.3d at 731 (quoting *Innovative Health Sys.*, 117 F.3d at 44). Thus, we have held that medical licensing is a service, program, or activity for purposes of Title II, *Hason v. Med. Bd.*, 279 F.3d 1167, 1173 (9th Cir. 2002), as is zoning, *BAART*, 179 F.3d at 731, and parole hearings, *Thompson v. Davis*, 282 F.3d 780, 786-87 (9th Cir. 2002). See also *Johnson*, 151 F.3d at 569-70 (reasoning that the word "'activities,' on its face, suggests great breadth and offers little basis to exclude any actions of a public entity," and thus holding that a contract to operate the city's public access cable station was an activity within the meaning of Title II); *Innovative Health Sys.*, 117 F.3d at 44 (holding that the ADA and the Rehabilitation Act encompass zoning decisions because zoning is "a normal function of a governmental entity").

In keeping with our precedent, maintaining public sidewalks is a normal function of a city and "without a doubt something that the [City] 'does.'" *Hason*, 279 F.3d at 1173. Maintaining their accessibility for individuals with disabilities therefore falls within the scope of Title II.

This broad construction of the phrase, "services, programs, or activities," is supported by the plain language of the Rehabilitation Act because, although the ADA does not define "services, programs, or activities," the Rehabilitation Act defines "program or activity" as "all of the operations of" a qualifying local government. 29 U.S.C. § 794(b)(1)(A). The legislative history of the ADA similarly supports construing the language generously, providing that Title II "essentially 8515 simply extends the anti-discrimination prohibition embodied in section 504 [of the Rehabilitation Act] to *all actions of state and local governments*." H.R. Rep. No. 101-485(II), at 84 (1990), reprinted in 1990 U.S.C.C.A.N. 303, 367 (emphasis added); see also id. at 151, reprinted in 1990 U.S.C.C.A.N.

303, 434 ("Title II . . . makes *all activities* of State and local governments subject to the types of prohibitions against discrimination . . . included in section 504 . . . .") (emphasis added). In fact, the ADA must be construed "broadly in order to effectively implement the ADA's fundamental purpose of 'provid[ing] a clear and comprehensive national mandate for the elimination of discrimination against individuals with disabilities.'" *Hason*, 279 F.3d at 1172 (quoting *Arnold v. United Parcel Serv., Inc.*, 136 F.3d 854, 861 (1st Cir. 1998)) (alteration in the original).

Requiring the City to maintain its sidewalks so that they are accessible to individuals with disabilities is consistent with the tenor of § 35.150, which requires the provision of curb ramps, "giving priority to walkways serving" government offices, "transportation, places of public accommodation, and employers," but then "followed by walkways serving other areas." 28 C.F.R. § 35.150(d)(2). Section 35.150's requirement of curb ramps in all pedestrian walkways reveals a general concern for the accessibility of public sidewalks, as well as a recognition that sidewalks fall within the ADA's coverage, and would be meaningless if the sidewalks between the curb ramps were inaccessible.

* * *

CONCLUSION

Title II's prohibition of discrimination in the provision of public services applies to the maintenance of public sidewalks, which is a normal function of a municipal entity. The legislative history of Title II indicates that all activities of local governments are subject to this prohibition of discrimination. This conclusion is also supported by the language of § 35.150, which requires the provision of curb ramps in order for sidewalks to be accessible to individuals with disabilities. The order of the district court accordingly is reversed and the case remanded for further proceedings.

Notes & Questions

1. Did the Ninth Circuit in *Barden* give enough attention to the types of concerns raised by the League of Cities in its brief? Will this decision, and others like it, overwhelm a city's resources and make the fair administration of city resources impossible to achieve? If so, does it also fail to establish a commensurate benefit in the accessibility of public programs, services and activities? *See* Frame v. City of Arlington, 657 F.3d 215, 231 (5th Cir. 2012) (in sidewalk case, noting city's financial burden and acknowledged that a city's obligation to make newly built and altered sidewalks readily accessible is not "boundless.").

2. Other circuit courts considering the issue of sidewalk access under Title II have similarly reasoned that plaintiffs have a private right of action to enforce the DOJ's regulations with respect to newly built and altered sidewalks. *See, e.g.,* Ability Ctr. of Greater Toledo v. City of Sandusky, 385 F.3d 901 (6th Cir. 2004); Kinney v. Yerusalim, 9 F.3d 1067

(3d Cir. 1993); Frame v. City of Arlington, 657 F.3d 215, 231 (5th Cir. 2011), *cert denied* 132 S.Ct. 1561 (2012).

3. Courts have followed substantially similar logic in holding that various state and local government functions are services, programs, or activities within the meaning of Title II. *See, e.g.,* Bay Area Addiction Research Treatment, Inc. v. City of Antioch, 179 F.3d 725 (9th Cir. 1999) (zoning); Layton v. Elder, 143 F.3d 469, 471 (8th Cir. 1998) (meetings at state courthouses); Lightbourn v. County of El Paso, Tex., 118 F.3d 421 (5th Cir. 1997) (voting); Save Our Summers v. Wash. State Dep't of Ecology, 132 F.Supp.2d 896 (E.D. Wash. 1999) (farmers' practices of burning wheat stubble); Soto v. City of Newark, 72 F.Supp.2d 489, 493-94 (D. N.J. 1999) (municipal wedding ceremonies); Niece v. Fitzner, 922 F.Supp. 1208, 1217 (E.D. Mich. 1996) (use of telephones in prisons).

4. There are limits, however. Courts have held that incarceration or sleeping in one's prison cell, *Bryant v. Madigan*, 84 F.3d 246, 249 (7th Cir. 1996), and cable television reception for inmates, *Aswegan v. Bruhl*, 113 F.3d 109, 110 (8th Cir. 1997), are not services, programs, or activities for Title II purposes. In *Noel v. New York City Taxi & Limousine Comm'n*, 687 F.3d 63, 72 (2d Cir. 2012), the Second Circuit held that the Taxi and Limousine Commission's (TLC) control over the regulation of the taxi industry does not make the private taxi industry a program, service, or activity of a public entity. Accordingly, the TLC did not violate Title II of the ADA by licensing and regulating a private taxi industry that fails to afford meaningful access to passengers with disabilities.

୭

2. Employment under Title II

As discussed in Part 3, § 6.2.D, claims that involve discrimination in employment typically proceed under Title I of the ADA. However, legislative history suggests that Congress intended Title II, as well as Title I, to reach employment. *See* H.R. Rep. No. 101-485(III), at 84 (1990). Similarly, the regulations promulgated by the Attorney General provide that Title II applies to employment: "No qualified individual with a disability shall, on the basis of disability, be subjected to discrimination in employment under any service, program, or activity conducted by a public entity." 28 C.F.R. § 35.140(a) (2008).

The Courts of Appeals have split on whether employment cases (for employees of state and local governments) can be brought under Title II of the ADA. *Compare* Bledsoe v. Palm Beach County Soil and Water Conservation District, 133 F.3d 816 (11th Cir. 1998) (holding that Title II of the ADA encompasses employment discrimination claims) *with* Zimmerman v. Oregon Department of Justice, 170 F.3d 1169 (9th Cir. 1999) (holding that Title II does not cover employment claims). *See also* Elwell v. Oklahoma ex rel. Bd. of Regents of Univ. of Oklahoma, 693 F.3d

1303 (10th Cir. 2012) (holding that employment is not a service, program or activity). It is unclear if this latter position has been made impermissible by the analysis in *Lane* and *Goodman*.

§ 13.2   Elements Of Title II Claim

We turn next to what a plaintiff must show to make out a claim under ADA Title II. Because of the close relationship between Title II and the Rehabilitation Act, generally this showing is the same for both statutes.

Under both statutes, courts have required a plaintiff to show that:

(1) he or she is a qualified individual with a disability;

(2) he or she was either excluded from participation in or denied the benefits of some public entity's services, programs, or activities or was otherwise discriminated against; and

(3) such exclusion, denial of benefits, or discrimination was by reason of the plaintiff's disability.

The various issues involved in interpreting and testing the limits of these requirements are discussed below.

§ 13.3   "Qualified Person With A Disability"

To bring a claim for discrimination under Title II, a plaintiff must demonstrate that she is a "qualified person with a disability." This means that the plaintiff is an individual with a disability who can meet the essential eligibility requirements with or without reasonable modification.

This definition was derived from the Rehabilitation Act and its implementing regulations. The key parts of this definition are: individual with a disability, essential eligibility requirements, and reasonable modification. The definition of disability is constant throughout the ADA, and therefore, the discussion of disability in Part 2, *supra*, applies here. The concept of reasonable modification is discussed below.

A full discussion of "essential eligibility requirements" also is presented in Part 2, *supra*. But, there are some unique wrinkles on this issue, in the Title II context, that merit discussion.

Often, the determination of an "essential eligibility requirement" triggers the question of what rules or policies are proper subjects of a request for reasonable accommodation. What about the case where a public entity has a threshold rule for participation, and when the rule is waived so that a person with a disability can participate; are the purposes behind the rule are altered?

One well-litigated example of this issue involves age eligibility rules in high school athletics. Many high school athletic associations have requirements that high school athletes be below a certain age, or that

370

athletes only may participate in high school athletics for a certain number of semesters. The purposes behind these rules are to maintain fair levels of competition (so that significantly older and more physically mature children do not skew the balance), to reduce the risk of injury, and to discourage parents from holding back their children in school so that the children have a competitive advantage over their younger peers.

This issue has come up where a child with a learning disability has been held back in school, and therefore, is too old to participate in high school athletics. Are the age requirements "essential eligibility" criteria, such that these students cannot participate?

✑

POTTGEN v. MISSOURI STATE HIGH SCHOOL ACTIVITIES ASS'N

United States Court of Appeals, Eighth Circuit, 1994
40 F.3d 926

BEAM, Circuit Judge.

The Missouri State High School Activities Association (hereinafter "MSHSAA") appeals the issuance of a preliminary injunction which restrains it from enforcing its age limit for interscholastic sports against Edward Leo Pottgen. Pottgen repeated two grades in elementary school due to an undiagnosed learning disability. By his senior year, this delay in completing his education made him too old to play interscholastic baseball under MSHSAA eligibility standards. In district court, Pottgen challenged the age limit as violating section 504 of the Rehabilitation Act of 1973, Title II of the Americans with Disabilities Act, and section 1983. Because we find that Pottgen is not a qualified individual under these statutes, we reverse.

I. BACKGROUND

After Pottgen repeated two grades in elementary school, the school tested him to see whether he needed special classroom assistance. When the school discovered that Pottgen had several learning disabilities, it placed him on an individualized program and provided him with access to special services. With these additional resources, Pottgen progressed through school at a normal rate. It is not clear from the evidence whether he attempted to make up the lost time through summer school or other remedial activities.

Pottgen was active in sports throughout junior high and high school. He played interscholastic baseball for three years in high school and planned to play baseball his senior year as well. However, because he had repeated two grades, Pottgen turned nineteen shortly before July 1 of his senior year. Consequently, MSHSAA By-Laws rendered Pottgen ineligible to play. The MSHSAA By-Law states, in relevant part, "A student shall not have reached the age of nineteen prior to July 1

371

preceding the opening of school. If a student reaches the age of nineteen on or following July 1, the student may be considered eligible for [interscholastic sports during] the ensuing school year."

Pottgen petitioned MSHSAA for a hardship exception to the age limit since he was held back due to his learning disabilities. Pottgen struck out. MSHSAA determined that waiving the requirement violated the intent of the age eligibility rule.

Pottgen then brought this suit, alleging MSHSAA's age limit violated the Rehabilitation Act of 1973 (the "Rehabilitation Act"), the Americans with Disabilities Act (the "ADA"), and section 1983. The district court granted a preliminary injunction enjoining MSHSAA from "(i) preventing [Pottgen] from competing in any Hancock High School baseball games or district or state tournament games; and (ii) imposing any penalty, discipline or sanction on any school for which or against which [Pottgen] competes in these games." *Pottgen v. Missouri State High Sch. Activities Ass'n*, 857 F.Supp. 654, 666 (E.D. Mo. 1994).

II. DISCUSSION

[The court concludes that Pottgen is not "otherwise qualified" under the Rehabilitation Act because he cannot meet the essential requirement of the age limit.]

* * *

2. Title II of the ADA

MSHSAA also appeals the district court's ruling that Pottgen would likely prevail on his ADA claim. MSHSAA contends Pottgen is not a "qualified individual with a disability" under Title II of the ADA.

* * *

To determine whether Pottgen was a "qualified individual" for ADA purposes, the district court conducted an individualized inquiry into the necessity of the age limit in Pottgen's case. Such an individualized inquiry is inappropriate at this stage. Instead, to determine whether Pottgen is a "qualified individual" under the ADA, we must first determine whether the age limit is an essential eligibility requirement by reviewing the importance of the requirement to the interscholastic baseball program. If this requirement is essential, we then determine whether Pottgen meets this requirement with or without modification. It is at this later stage that the ADA requires an individualized inquiry.

The dissent disagrees with this holding and would impose an individualized "essential eligibility requirement" inquiry at the first stage. We think this is not required, and for good reason. A public entity could never know the outer boundaries of its "services, programs or activities." A requirement could be deemed essential for one person with a disability but immaterial for another similarly, but not identically, situated individual.

MSHSAA's interscholastic baseball program demonstrates this proposition. The dissent admits that the age requirement is "admittedly salutary" but believes it must fall away for Pottgen because an individualized fact-finding inquiry found him "not appreciably larger than the average eighteen-year-old" and not "a threat to the safety of others." If this is the query, MSHSAA would need to establish a fact-finding mechanism for each individual seeking to attack a program requirement. At that time, MSHSAA would have to show the essential nature of each allegedly offending program requirement as it applies to the complaining individual. The dissent's approach requires thorough evidentiary hearings at each stage of the process. Clearly the ADA imposes no such duty. Indeed, such an approach flies in the face of the *Arline* Court's statement that "[a]ccommodation is not reasonable if it either imposes 'undue financial and administrative burdens' [on the public entity] or requires 'a fundamental alteration in the nature of [the] program.'" 480 U.S. at 287 n.17 (citations omitted).

Consistent with our Rehabilitation Act analysis, we find MSHSAA has demonstrated that the age limit is an essential eligibility requirement of the interscholastic baseball program. Again, Pottgen alleges he can meet the eligibility requirement if MSHSAA waives it for him. In conformity with our previous finding, we conclude that this is not a reasonable modification.

Thus, we find that Pottgen is not a "qualified individual" under the ADA. The district court erred in granting a preliminary injunction based on recovery under this Act.

* * *

RICHARD S. ARNOLD, Chief Judge, dissenting.

In my view, the courts are obligated by statute to look at plaintiffs as individuals before they decide whether someone can meet the essential requirements of an eligibility rule like the one before us in the present case. Such an individualized inquiry, I believe, shows that the age requirement, as applied to Ed Pottgen, is not essential to the goals of the Missouri State High School Activities Association. I therefore respectfully dissent.

I have little to add to Judge Shaw's excellent opinion for the District Court. For me, this case is largely controlled by the words of the Americans with Disabilities Act of 1990, 42 U.S.C. § 12132, and by regulations issued under the Act. The statute provides, in relevant part, that

> no qualified individual with a disability shall, by reason of
> such disability, be excluded from participation in or be

denied the benefits of the services, programs, or activities of a public entity, or be subjected to discrimination by any such entity.

There is no doubt that Ed Pottgen has a learning disability (for which he is now adequately compensating), and that, by reason of this disability, he has become unable to meet the Activities Association's age requirements. The Court today holds, however, that Ed is not a "qualified individual."

The statute itself defines this term. "Qualified individual with a disability" means

an individual with a disability, who, with or without reasonable modifications to rules, policies, or practices . . . meets the essential eligibility requirements for . . . participation in programs or activities provided by a public entity.

42 U.S.C. § 12131(2).

So, by the express words of Congress, it is not necessary for a person to meet all eligibility requirements. Instead, if a proposed modification of those requirements is "reasonable," a person can be a "qualified individual." The question therefore is whether it is "reasonable" to require the Activities Association to modify or waive the age requirement in the case of Ed Pottgen. The age criterion would not have to be abandoned completely: Ed would have been eligible if the requirement had been modified by only thirty-five days. He was that close to complete and literal compliance with all of the Activities Association's rules.

I agree with the Court that if a requirement is "essential" to a program or activity, a waiver or modification of that requirement would not be "reasonable" within the meaning of the statute. But how do we determine what is "essential"? The regulations interpreting the statute are of some help in answering that question. Under 28 C.F.R. § 35.130(b)(7) (1994),

A public entity shall make reasonable modifications in policies, practices, or procedures when the modifications are necessary to avoid discrimination on the basis of disability, unless the public entity can demonstrate that making the modifications would fundamentally alter the nature of the service, program, or activity.

Was high-school baseball competition in Missouri fundamentally altered when Ed Pottgen was allowed to play one more year? I think not, and here the District Court's findings of fact become important. According to the Activities Association itself, there are three reasons for the age requirement. First, there is a desire to protect the safety of younger athletes against whom an older athlete might compete. Second, the Association wishes to reduce the competitive advantage that results when older students play, because of their presumed greater maturity. And third, the Association wishes to discourage students from delaying their education to gain athletic maturity. There is no contention whatever in the present case that Ed Pottgen deliberately repeated the first and third grades in order to make himself eligible to play baseball another year at age nineteen. The District Court found, moreover, "that any competitive advantage resulting from plaintiff's age is de minimis." 857 F.Supp. at 662 n.3. The Court further found that the Activities Association made no individualized review of plaintiff's circumstances and gave no consideration to the issue of safety when it denied plaintiff's request for a waiver of the age rule. Finally, the Court found that "plaintiff does not appear to constitute a threat to the safety of others." Id. at 662. Plaintiff is not appreciably larger than the average eighteen-year-old.

In other words, the age requirement could be modified for this individual player without doing violence to the admittedly salutary purposes underlying the age rule. But instead of looking at the rule's operation in the individual case of Ed Pottgen, both the Activities Association and this Court simply recite the rule's general justifications (which are not in dispute) and mechanically apply it across the board. But if a rule can be modified without doing violence to its essential purposes, as the District Court has found in the present case, I do not believe that it can be "essential" to the nature of the program or activity to refuse to modify the rule.

The Court avoids this issue by holding that "an individualized inquiry into the necessity of the age limit in Pottgen's case . . . is inappropriate. . . ." With respect, I find no such principle in the words of the statute. If an eligibility requirement can be reasonably modified to make someone eligible, that person is a qualified individual. In determining this issue, it seems to me entirely appropriate to focus on the effect that modification of the requirement for the individual in question would have on the nature of the program. When the case is looked at from this point of view, it becomes clear that the Association could easily bend to accommodate Ed Pottgen without breaking anything essential. For these reasons, I would affirm the preliminary injunction entered by the District Court.

Notes & Questions

1. Do you agree with the approach taken by the majority or Judge Arnold's dissent? If a rule can be modified without doing offense to the reasons the rule exists, can the rule really be "essential?" Are courts the proper party to make this determination?

2. Courts have split on this issue. In *Sandison v. Michigan High School Athletic Ass'n*, 64 F.3d 1026 (6th Cir. 1995), the Sixth Circuit held that the age rule was "essential," and no reasonable modification would

allow the plaintiff to meet the rule. The plaintiff could not be made younger, and it would be unreasonable to force the association to decide on a case-by-case basis whether the rule should or could be waived. Likewise, in *McPherson v. Michigan High School Athletic Ass'n*, 119 F.3d 453 (6th Cir. 1997), the Sixth Circuit found that making a determination on a case-by-case basis whether to waive an eight semester high school athletic eligibility rule would require too much of an administrative and financial burden. Therefore, the court would not entertain the plaintiff's argument that as applied to him, one individual waiver was not unreasonable. But in *Washington v. Indiana High School Athletic Ass'n*, 181 F.3d 840, 852 (7th Cir. 1999), the Seventh Circuit adopted the approach of the *Pottgen* dissent, and held that the rule was not "essential" if modifying the rule for this particular athlete caused no competitive advantage or safety threat.

3. Unlike these difficult cases, and unlike most employment situations, for many services, programs, or activities that public entities offer, the only "essential eligibility requirement" is a desire to participate. In *Concerned Parents to Save Dreher Park Center v. City of West Palm Beach*, 846 F.Supp. 986, 989 (S.D. Fla. 1994), the City stopped offering recreational programs that had been structured for people with disabilities. In considering whether the plaintiffs were "qualified individuals with disabilities," the court held that the only "essential eligibility requirement" of a city's recreational program is a request for benefits of the program. As discussed *supra* in Part 2, the DOJ regulations recognize that often this will be the case. *See* 28 C.F.R. pt. 35 app. A, § 35.104 (2008).

4. In *Mary Jo C. v. New York State & Local Ret. Sys.*, 707 F.3d 144 (2d Cir. 2013), a librarian fired for behavior symptomatic of her mental illness sought a waiver of a missed deadline to collect disability retirement benefits. The Second Circuit held that the district court erred in determining that essential eligibility requirements means "all formal legal requirements," finding that because the deadline had been waived before it was not essential.

∾

§ 13.4 Not Excluding, Denying, Or Discriminating – Affirmative Responsibilities Of Public Entities

To have a viable Title II claim, a plaintiff must demonstrate that she was either excluded from participation in or denied the benefits of some public entity's services, programs, or activities, or was otherwise discriminated against.

Perhaps more than in any other title, the regulations offer extensive guidance on what this means, and in some cases require that public entities make proactive changes. The regulations provide that by one year after their effective date, every public entity must complete a self-evaluation of their "services, policies, and practices," and develop a transition plan to make any necessary modifications. 28 C.F.R. § 35.105 (2008). Notably, there is a circuit split on whether failure to comply with the self-evaluation and transition regulations creates a private right of action. *Compare* Chaffin v. Kan. State Fair Bd., 348 F.3d 850, 857-60 (10th Cir. 2003) (holding there is a private right of action) *with* Ability Ctr. of Greater Toledo, 385 F.3d at 913-15 (no private right of action); Iverson v. City of Boston, 452 F.3d 94, 96 (1st Cir. 2006) (same).

In the "General prohibitions against discrimination" section, the regulations set out a list of activities that a public entity may *not* do on the basis of disability in providing benefits or services:

> (i) Deny a qualified individual with a disability the opportunity to participate in or benefit from the aid, benefit, or service;

> (ii) Afford a qualified individual with a disability an opportunity to participate in or benefit from the aid, benefit, or service that is not equal to that afforded others;

> (iii) Provide a qualified individual with a disability with an aid, benefit, or service that is not as effective in affording equal opportunity to obtain the same result, to gain the same benefit, or to reach the same level of achievement as that provided to others;

> (iv) Provide different or separate aids, benefits, or services to individuals with disabilities or to any class of individuals with disabilities than is provided to others unless such action is necessary to provide qualified individuals with disabilities with aids, benefits, or services that are as effective as those provided to others;

> (v) Aid or perpetuate discrimination against a qualified individual with a disability by providing significant assistance to an agency, organization, or person that discriminates on the basis of disability in providing any aid, benefit, or service to beneficiaries of the public entity's program;

> (vi) Deny a qualified individual with a disability the opportunity to participate as a member of planning or advisory boards;

> (vii) Otherwise limit a qualified individual with a disability in the enjoyment of any right, privilege, advantage, or opportunity enjoyed by others receiving the aid, benefit, or service.

Id. § 35.130(b)(1).

Conceptually, it is useful to think about the affirmative responsibilities of public entities in six areas:

(a) making reasonable modifications to policies, practices, and procedures;

(b) providing people with disabilities the opportunity to the same benefits of public services;

(c) administering services, programs, or activities in the most integrated setting appropriate to the needs of qualified individuals with disabilities;

(d) modifications to facilities;

(e) communications modifications, and

(f) accommodations in transportation.

The six categories are not completely isolated from one another; rather, as the cases below demonstrate, any given case can be conceived of as falling into one or more.

A. *Reasonable Modifications To Policies, Practices, And Procedures*

The concept of reasonable modifications for Title II purposes has its roots in the Rehabilitation Act. In *School Board of Nassau County v. Arline*, 480 U.S. 273 (1987), a Rehabilitation Act case discussed *supra* in Part 2, the Supreme Court stated an "accommodation is not reasonable if it either imposes 'undue financial and administrative burdens' on a grantee, or requires 'a fundamental alteration in the nature of [the] program.'" *Id.* at 287, n.17.

The Title II regulations offer extensive guidance on the reasonable modification requirement. Consistent with *Southeastern Community College v. Davis*, 480 U.S. 273 (1987), and other Rehabilitation Act precedent, the regulations provide that reasonable modifications must be made *unless* the public entity can demonstrate that making the modifications would fundamentally alter the nature of the program, service, or activity. *See* 28 C.F.R. § 35.130(b)(7). Consider the request for reasonable accommodation discussed in the following case.

HENRIETTA D. v. BLOOMBERG

United States Court of Appeals, Second Circuit, 2003
331 F.3d 261

KATZMANN, Circuit Judge.

The plaintiffs in this civil rights litigation, indigent New York City residents who suffer from AIDS and other HIV-related illnesses, are clients of New York City's Division of AIDS Services and Income Support

("DASIS"), an agency whose sole function is to assist persons with HIV-related diseases in obtaining public assistance benefits and services. The plaintiffs allege that in spite of DASIS's existence (and in part due to DASIS's ineffectiveness), New York City and New York State are failing to provide them with adequate access to public benefits, and are thereby violating various federal and state statutes, regulations, and constitutional provisions.

* * *

Background

* * * The members of the class assert that they face unique physical hurdles in attempting to access certain public assistance benefits and services. They claim that DASIS, the New York City agency charged with helping them access such benefits and services, is ineffective and systemically fails to achieve its goals. The plaintiffs seek injunctive relief ordering the defendants, various city and state officials charged with implementing New York's social services system, to provide the benefits to which the plaintiff class is entitled. * * *

As an initial matter, the District Court, after hearing the testimony of several individuals afflicted with HIV-related illness, agreed with the plaintiffs that the physical challenges and medical risks faced by the plaintiff class create unique barriers with respect to obtaining access to public benefits and services:

> People living with HIV and AIDS develop numerous illnesses and physical conditions not found in the general population, and experience manifestations of common illnesses that are much more aggressive, recurrent, and difficult to treat. Infections and cancers spread rapidly in a person whose immune system has been compromised, and the effectiveness of medicine is diminished by nutritional problems that limit the body's ability to absorb what is ingested. Illnesses that are not lethal to the general population can kill an HIV-infected person. For all these reasons, persons with AIDS and HIV-related disease experience serious functional limitations that make it extremely difficult, if not impossible in some cases, to negotiate the complicated City social service system on their own.
>
> * * *
>
> The opportunistic infections and chronic conditions that result from a weakened immune system limit the HIV-infected person's ability to engage in regular activities of daily life such as traveling, standing in line, attending scheduled appointments, completing paper work, and

otherwise negotiating medical and social service bureaucracies . . . .

Functional limitations also develop from the primary drugs used to combat AIDS and HIV-related disease. . . . An individual receiving this common regime of prescription drugs likely will be restricted in his or her ability to walk, stand, or travel. Other side effects include enhanced neuropathy, diarrhea, nausea, and vomiting.

* * *

The requirement that persons with AIDS and advanced HIV disease travel to and wait in infection-ridden public waiting rooms can be dangerous, and even life-threatening, for this population, all of whom suffer from severely weakened immune systems.

Id. at 185-86 (internal citations and paragraph numbering omitted).

The District Court concluded that DASIS was designed to address these obstacles, and most of the testimony at trial dealt with the plaintiffs' allegations that DASIS generally failed to provide the services that it was mandated by law to provide. After hearing testimony from DASIS clients, DASIS employees, advocates for DASIS clients, and experts, the District Court concluded that the allegations were well-founded, finding that DASIS was "chronically and systematically failing to provide plaintiffs with meaningful access to critical subsistence benefits and services, with devastating consequences." * * *

The District Court held that the plaintiffs had demonstrated that they required special accommodations in order to access public benefits and services, and concluded that the DASIS law, if properly complied with, would provide the necessary accommodations to the HIV-positive population, id. at 208, but that DASIS was not functioning as the DASIS law had intended:

At this time, the Court finds that plaintiffs demonstrated at trial that . . . DASIS . . . is broken, i.e., that defendants are failing to make the reasonable accommodations necessary to ensure plaintiffs meaningful access to, and an equal opportunity to benefit from, the social welfare benefits and services that defendants provide to eligible New York City residents. The extensive evidence proffered at trial – from representative plaintiffs, from some of the City's largest providers of services to the plaintiff class, from expert testimony, and from the City's own performance-tracking reports – establishes unequivocally that defendants are chronically and systematically failing to provide plaintiffs with meaningful access to critical subsistence benefits and services, with devastating consequences.

Id. at 209.

Based on these findings and conclusions, the District Court ruled in the plaintiffs' favor, holding that New York City had failed to provide the plaintiffs with meaningful access to public assistance benefits and services in violation of Title II of the ADA and section 504 of the Rehabilitation Act. Specifically, the District Court found that the DASIS law provided the reasonable accommodations requested by the plaintiffs, and that the City's failure to comply with the DASIS law violated the ADA and the Rehabilitation Act. Id. at 208-09, 214. * * *

* * *

Discussion

* * *

I. The ADA and the Rehabilitation Act

* * *

B. Whether the Relief Granted Constitutes
a Reasonable Accommodation * * *

We agree with the District Court that the DASIS law represents an attempt at reasonable accommodation and can properly form a basis for the injunctive relief granted in this case. See *Henrietta D. v. Giuliani*, No. 95 Civ. 0641, 1996 WL 633382, at *9 (E.D.N.Y. Oct. 25, 1996) ("[I]n its most basic, facilitory efforts, DAS is a necessary modification to, and not a fundamental alteration of, the public assistance services that the City provides to all eligible New Yorkers."). The avowed purpose of the DASIS law is to "provide access to [publicly subsidized benefits and services] . . . to every person with clinical/symptomatic HIV illness . . . or with AIDS," N.Y. City Admin. Code § 21-126, and the DASIS law makes clear that "[a]ny eligible person shall receive only those benefits and services for which such person qualifies in accordance with the applicable eligibility standards established pursuant to local, state or federal statute, law, regulation or rule," id. at § 21-128(b). We do not intimate that either the mere fact that the DASIS law was enacted or the fact that it was viewed as "access" legislation per se makes it a reasonable accommodation under the relevant federal statutes. We find it to be a prima facie reasonable accommodation because we agree with the District Court that its provisions are consistent with its goal of serving as a reasonable accommodation, and it does not appear to impose costs that obviously outweigh its benefits. As the District Court noted, the vast majority of services created by the DASIS law are fundamentally procedural in nature. The law provides for intensive case management, for low client-caseworker ratios, and for imposition of clear deadlines. We thus share the District Court's view that the plaintiffs have established that requiring DASIS to comply with the DASIS law represents appropriate reasonable accommodation relief.

381

The regulations implementing both the Rehabilitation Act and the ADA give a public entity defendant the opportunity to show that a requested accommodation is unreasonable. The regulations provide that such a defendant need not make the requested accommodation if it "would fundamentally alter the nature of the service, program, or activity," 28 C.F.R. § 35.130(b)(7), or "impose an undue hardship on the operation of [the] program," 28 C.F.R. § 41.53. Similarly, in outlining the burdens of proof in a reasonable accommodation claim under Title I of the ADA, we have held that a defendant will not be required to adopt an accommodation if it successfully demonstrates that the proposed accommodation is unreasonable, i.e., that it "would cause it to suffer an undue hardship." *Borkowski*, 63 F.3d at 138. The Supreme Court in Olmstead noted that:

> the undue hardship inquiry requires not simply an assessment of the cost of the accommodation in relation to the recipient's overall budget, but a case-by-case analysis weighing factors that include: (1)[t]he overall size of the recipient's program with respect to number of employees, number and type of facilities, and size of budget; (2)[t]he type of the recipient's operation, including the composition and structure of the recipient's workforce; and (3) [t]he nature and cost of the accommodation needed.

527 U.S. at 606 n.16, (internal citation and quotation marks omitted).

The defendants in this case have not, however, alleged that the proposed accommodation would cause them or their programs undue hardship. Perhaps that is because, at least at the time this litigation was before the District Court, in the defendants' estimation, the accommodation provided by the DASIS law was not causing such a hardship. We note that if at any time such hardship arises the defendants would undoubtedly have the ability to return to the District Court to seek a modification of its order to reflect that condition.

Instead of challenging the requested accommodations based on the burden of their implementation, the defendants argue that no accommodations are required because the plaintiffs have not demonstrated that they are suffering a negative disparate impact relative to similarly situated persons without disabilities. See *Henrietta D.*, 119 F.Supp.2d at 208 n.17 ("Defendants provided no evidence that DASIS and its special functions represent[ ] a fundamental alteration of defendants' service, program, or activity. The reasonableness of the modifications that plaintiffs seek, moreover, is evidenced by the fact that virtually all are modifications that defendants have long purported – but failed – to provide, and that they are now required by local law to provide."). As we have observed, no such demonstration is necessary. Accordingly, we affirm the injunction as a reasonable accommodative measure.

We pause, however, to address two additional issues raised by the defendants in other contexts that might provide bases for challenging the scope of the accommodation ordered by the District Court. First, while the defendants frame their disparate treatment argument as an attack on the need for a reasonable accommodation itself, their point also might support an argument that the plaintiffs already are being reasonably accommodated. There would be no need for injunctive relief if the plaintiffs were already being reasonably accommodated. See *Wernick v. Fed. Reserve Bank of N.Y.*, 91 F.3d 379, 385 (2d Cir.1996) (affirming dismissal of ADA claim because "the accommodations offered by the [defendant] were plainly reasonable."). The defendants' disparate impact argument suggests that had the defendants been able to prove that the plaintiffs are faring no worse in accessing benefits than the non-disabled, they would have proven that the plaintiffs were already being reasonably accommodated.

We reject this argument. A "reasonable accommodation" is one that gives the otherwise qualified plaintiff with disabilities "meaningful access" to the program or services sought. *Alexander v. Choate*, 469 U.S. 287, 301 (1985). That others cannot avail themselves of the services does not make the minimal access provided to the plaintiff "meaningful." As we have held, meaningful access must be defined with reference to the plaintiff's facial entitlement to benefits. In this case, the District Court made specific findings to the effect that qualified plaintiffs cannot obtain benefits without aid, and that the current accommodative regime is dysfunctional. That is sufficient to justify relief. The mere fact that the plaintiffs, in the current apparently broken overall social services system, might not be doing worse than persons without disabilities, does not render the dysfunctional DASIS "reasonable."

Second, the defendants assert that the DASIS law fundamentally represents a grant to the plaintiff class of substantive benefits unavailable to persons without disabilities rather than an attempt to accommodate the plaintiff class's disabilities with respect to public benefits available to all qualifying individuals. While the defendants frame this issue as an attack on the plaintiffs' right to any accommodation, it could merit consideration as a basis for questioning whether the injunctive relief granted is overbroad. Even though the plaintiffs have demonstrated that they are entitled to a reasonable accommodation, an accommodation that served as a grant of special substantive rights would not constitute appropriate relief. See *Doe v. Pfrommer*, 148 F.3d 73, 84 (2d Cir.1998). The DASIS law nominally provides the plaintiffs with certain additional substantive benefits, such as nutritional supplements and transportation allowances. There is language in the District Court's opinion arguably to suggest that the plaintiffs might be able to state a claim to some of these substantive benefits. See *Henrietta D.*, 119 F.Supp.2d at 212 n.22 (commenting that even the "nutritional supplements and transportation allowances act as reasonable modifications allowing persons with AIDS and HIV access to their benefits, not as benefits additional to those received by the non-disabled public").

In spite of this footnote, we do not construe the injunction of the District Court in fact to order access to any of the additional benefits provided only to the plaintiff class. The overall discussion of the opinion and the language of the injunction make clear that the District Court's holding does not ultimately embrace so broad a theory of accommodation. The District Court recognized that the

> [p]laintiffs have made no claim under the ADA or the [Rehabilitation] Act for additional or better benefits and services than provided to the non-disabled. To the contrary, plaintiffs' ADA and [Rehabilitation] Act claims seek meaningful access to the very same benefits and services provided to the non-disabled. Plaintiffs seek, and this Court requires, only the modifications – such as intensive case management and low case manager-to-client ratios – required to ensure meaningful access to the same benefits and services.

Id. at 212; see also *Henrietta D. v. Giuliani*, 81 F.Supp.2d 425, 432 (E.D.N.Y.2000) ("Plaintiffs do not challenge the amount or adequacy of the benefits available to them; they seek equal and meaningful access to benefits already available to them."). The injunction itself specifically limits the "benefits and services" to which it orders access to "public assistance, Medicaid, Food Stamps, housing, and other benefits and services available to qualifying members of the general public comparable to public assistance and welfare benefits." This language restricts the injunctive relief to benefits available to both the plaintiffs and the eligible non-disabled.

Thus, while we affirm the injunctive relief ordered, we note that we do not read the injunction to require provision of extra substantive benefits unavailable to the non-disabled – including, without limitation, enhanced rental assistance, nutritional supplements, and transportation allowances – nor do we construe it to permit an action based on procedural ineffectiveness if the ineffectiveness relates solely to provision of such "additional" substantive benefits.

* * *

These observations aside, we agree, as set forth above, with the District Court that the overwhelming purpose of DASIS is to provide access to public benefits available to all, and that the plaintiffs have demonstrated, and the defendants have not rebutted, evidence that DASIS offers a reasonable accommodation to the challenges faced by the plaintiff class. Indeed, counsel for the city defendants commented in colloquy in the District Court that "DASIS itself is a reasonable modification of the public assistance programs administered by HRA to all non-DASIS clients." We are thus comfortable affirming the injunction.

Notes & Questions

1. What was the reasonable accommodation the plaintiffs in *Henrietta D.* asked for? Was it the creation of DASIS in the first place? Or that DASIS do their job better? Should the latter have to be a request for reasonable accommodation?

2. Although the reasonable modification requirement of Title II does not include an undue hardship defense, the courts have read undue hardship into the fundamental alteration defense. Thus, courts determining whether a modification will constitute a fundamental alteration consider whether the change will cause an undue financial or administrative burden on the entity. *See, e.g.*, Olmstead v. Zimring, 527 U.S. 581, 597, 603-04 (1999).

3. Under the statute, even if a given program, service, or activity has an essential eligibility requirement, the plaintiff still can be a "qualified individual with a disability" if she can meet that requirement with or without "reasonable modifications to rules, policies, or practices, the removal of architectural, communication, or transportation barriers, or the provisions of auxiliary aids and services." 42 U.S.C. § 12131(2) (2006). These two terms – "essential eligibility requirements" and "reasonable modification" – are related. As discussed above, courts have split on the issue of whether the waiver of an essential eligibility requirement in a given case can in and of itself be a reasonable modification. Courts also vary in how much deference to pay to defendant's characterization of what is "essential." For example, in *Fialka-Feldman v. Oakland Univ. Bd. of Trustees*, 678 F.Supp.2d 576 (E.D. Mich. 2009), plaintiff was a continuing education student with a disability who sought on-campus housing. Defendant refused, arguing that plaintiff was not a degree seeking student, and that this was an essential requirement to live in an on campus dormitory. The court disagreed, finding that none of the rationales for this justification were sufficient. *Id.* at 586-587.

4. There have been several cases brought where plaintiffs challenge a defendant police department's training procedures as they relate to people with disabilities. Most cases have held that police responses are a covered program, service, or activity of a public entity. *See, e.g.*, Schorr v. Borough of Lemoyne, 243 F.Supp.2d 232 (M.D. Pa. 2003). But courts have also been reticent to hold police departments in violation of the ADA for inadequate training, often reasoning that officers do not have time to make proper accommodations. For example, in Bircoll v. Miami-Dade County, 480 F.3d 1072 (11th Cir. 2007), the court held that waiting for an oral interpreter before taking a field sobriety test was not a reasonable modification of police procedures. *See also* Sanders v. City of Minneapolis, 474 F.3d 523, 527 (8th Cir. 2007) ("It was not the City's

failure to train its police officers, but [the deceased's] apparent attempt to run over the officers that precipitated the shooting."); Hainze v. Richards, 207 F.3d 795, 801 (5th Cir. 2000) ("Title II does not apply to an officer's on-the-street responses to reported disturbances or other similar incidents, whether or not those calls involve subjects with mental disabilities, prior to the officer's securing the scene and ensuring that there is no threat to human life."); Thao v. City of St. Paul, 481 F.3d 565 (8th Cir. 2007) (["W]e conclude that the Plaintiffs have failed to demonstrate that more 'adequate' training to accommodate the mentally ill would have required a different response."); Buchanan v. Maine, 469 F.3d 158, 177 (1st Cir. 2006) ("An argument that police training, which was provided, was insufficient does not present a viable claim . . . .").

5. Voting is a frequent area of ADA Title II litigation. Some commentators and litigants have suggested that Title II's nondiscrimination provision requires that individuals with disabilities should have a protected right to a secret and independent voting commensurate with other votes. *See* Michael Waterstone, Constitutional and Statutory Voting Rights for People with Disabilities, 14 Stan. L. & Pol'y Rev. 353, 358-61 (2003). *See generally* Kay Schriner & Andrew Batavia, The Americans with Disabilities Act: Does It Secure the Fundamental Right to Vote?, 29 Pol'y Stud. J. 663 (2001). There are several potential regulatory sources of such an argument. Public entities are required to "make reasonable modifications in policies, practices, or procedures when the modifications are necessary to avoid discrimination on the basis of disability, unless the entity can demonstrate that making the modifications would fundamentally later the nature of the service program, or activity. 28 C.F.R. § 35130(b)(7). Public entities are prohibited from "providing any aid, benefit, or service" that "affords a qualified individual with a disability an opportunity to participate in or benefit from the aid, benefit, or service that is not equal to that afforded others." *Id.,* § 130(b)(1)(ii). Public entities are prohibited from using "methods of administration . . . that have the purpose or effect of defeating or substantially impairing accomplishments of the objectives of the public entity's program with respect to individuals with disabilities." *Id.,* § 35.130(b)(3)(ii). And, public entities must take "appropriate steps to ensure that communications with applicants, participants, members o the public, and companions with disabilities are as effective as communications with others." *Id.* § 35.160(a)(1). Nevertheless, courts have generally not accepted this argument, and instead have held that the ADA does not require a secret and independent vote for people with disabilities. *See, e.g.*, Am. Ass'n of People with Disabilities v. Harris, 647 F.3d 1093 (11th Cir. 2011); Am. Ass'n of People with Disabilities v. Shelley, 324 F.Supp.2d 1120 (C.D. Cal. 2004).

6. The ADA is not the only statute impacting the voting rights of people with disabilities. The Voting Rights Act, as amended in 1982, provides that "[a]ny voter who requires assistance to vote by reason of

blindness, disability, or inability to read or write may be given assistance by a person of the voter's choice . . . ." 42 U.S.C. § 1973aa-6 (2006). The Voting Accessibility for the Elderly and Handicapped Act provides that "[w]ithin each state . . . each political subdivision responsible for conducting elections shall assure that all polling places for Federal elections are accessible to handicapped and elderly voters." Id. § 1973ee-1(a).

In 2002, Congress passed the Help America Vote Act, Pub. L. No. 107-252, 116 Stat. 1666 (2002) (signed into law on Oct. 29, 2002). Regarding polling place access, the Act provides funds to states and units of local governments to "mak[e] polling places, including the path of travel, entrances, exits, and voting areas of each polling facility, accessible to individuals with disabilities, including the blind and visually impaired, in a manner that provides the same opportunities for access and participation (including privacy and independence) as for other voters." 42 U.S.C. § 15421(b)(1) (2006). The Act's provisions regarding secret and independent voting are more absolute. It states that voting systems shall "be accessible for individuals with disabilities, including nonvisual accessibility for the blind and visually impaired, in a manner that provides the same opportunity for access and participation (including privacy and independence) as for other voters." Id. § 15481(a)(3)(A).

For the first time, federal legislation offers a federal guarantee of a secret and independent right to vote for people with disabilities. But HAVA implementation has not been smooth. A report commissioned by the Electoral Assistance Commission in 2004 found that less than a quarter of polling places allowed voters with visual impairments to cast a secret ballot. See U.S. Election Assistance Comm'n, *A Summary of the 2004 Election Day Survey: Access to Voting for the Disabled* 14-4 (2005) (noting that more than half the states failed to even respond to the survey questions on accessibility). These numbers had improved by 2006. See *2006 Election Administration and Voting Survey* 26 (2006). HAVA's enforcement mechanisms also are weak: it provides for no private right of action for individuals who are denied their right to a secret and independent ballot, and the Department of Justice (DOJ) has opposed a judicial recognition of one. See Federal Defendants' Opposition to Plaintiff's Motion for Preliminary Injunction, 2006 WL 1505602, *2 (arguing HAVA confers no private right of action) in Taylor v. Onorato, 428 F.Supp.2d 384 (W.D. Pa. 2006) (holding that private plaintiffs have no private right of action HAVA access provisions). The DOJ does have the power to bring "civil actions against any State or jurisdiction in an appropriate United States District Court for such declaratory and injunctive relief as may be necessary." 42 U.S.C. § 15511.

7. Title II of the ADA applies to the disaster relief plans and efforts of state and local governments. In *Communities Actively Living Indep. & Free v. City of Los Angeles*, CV 09-0287 CBM RZX, 2011 WL 4595993 (C.D. Cal. Feb. 10, 2011), citing the reasonable modification

regulations, the court found that Los Angeles denied individuals with disabilities meaningful access to the emergency preparedness program in violation of Title II (as well as § 504, and California state disability discrimination laws). In November of 2013, a federal court held that New York City had discriminated against people with disabilities in its failure to plan for their needs in large scale disasters. At the trial, witnesses with disabilities had testified about the harm they had experienced during Hurricanes Sandy and Irene. Expert witnesses had testified about major deficiencies in the City's planning for a wide range of emergencies, and city officials had admitted that there were no emergency plans specific to evacuating people with disabilities during disasters.

8. The 2010 DOJ regulations make clear that service animals, which must be permitted in public facilities, are limited to dogs that are trained to do work or perform task for the benefit of an individual with a disability. Other species of animals cannot be considered service animals. 28 C.F.R. §35.104, although public entities may have to make reasonable modifications to permit the use of miniature horses in some contexts. *Id.* at § 35.136.

9. The 2010 revision regulations offered clarifications on wheelchairs and other power-driven mobility devices. A wheelchair is defined as "a manually operated or power-driven device designed primarily for use by an individual with a mobility disability. . . ." 28 C.F.R. §104. Individuals with disabilities must be permitted to use wheelchairs in any areas open to pedestrian traffic. Other power-driven mobility devices are "any mobility device powered by batteries, fuel, or other engines that is used by individuals with mobility disabilities for the purpose of locomotion, whether or not it was designed primarily for use for individuals with mobility disabilities." *Id.* Covered entities must make reasonable modifications in their policies, practices, and procedures to permit individuals with mobility devices to use these unless the entity can demonstrate that they cannot be operated in accordance with legitimate safety requirements.

10. Finally, the 2010 revisions offer important guidance on ticketing, an area which had not been addressed in previous regulations. 28 C.F.R. §35.138. Although the regulations are detailed, to summarize, public entities which sell tickets have to modify their policies, practices, and procedures to ensure that individuals with disabilities have an equal opportunity to purchase tickets during the same hours as others, during the same stages of tickets sales, through the same methods of distribution, in the same types and numbers of ticketing sales outlets, and under the same terms and conditions. The prices of tickets for accessible seating must not be higher than the price of other tickets in the same seating section. For each ticket for accessible seating purchased by or for an individual with a disability, an entity must make available for purchase three additional tickets for seats in the same row that are contiguous with the wheelchair space, provided that the seats are available at the time of

purchase. Tickets for accessible seating may be released to sale for individuals without disabilities only in certain limited circumstances.

B.   *Opportunity For Equal Benefit*

In the *Henrietta D.* case discussed above, the defendants argued that plaintiffs were asking for an "additional benefit" not conferred on the general population. Said differently, defendants argued that plaintiffs could not show discrimination because they could not demonstrate a negative disparate impact relative to similarly situated persons without disabilities. While rejecting this argument, the court did hold that ADA Title II does not require "additional benefits" for people with disabilities. Rather, the standard is meaningful and equal access.

But this line is not always easy to discern. Consider the following case.

RODDE v. BONTA

United States Court of Appeals, Ninth Circuit, 2004
357 F.3d 988

Pregerson, Circuit Judge.

Los Angeles County and Thomas Garthwaite, Director and Chief Medical Officer of Los Angeles County's Department of Health Services, (the County) plan to reduce the County's health care spending by closing Rancho Los Amigos National Rehabilitation Center (Rancho). Rancho is a County hospital dedicated primarily to providing inpatient and outpatient rehabilitative care to disabled individuals. Plaintiffs are current and future Medi-Cal patients with special needs that require medical services offered at Rancho. They challenged the impending closure of Rancho through this action. The district court granted plaintiffs' request for a preliminary injunction that barred the County from going forward with its planned closure without providing plaintiffs with necessary medical and rehabilitative services elsewhere. The County appealed. We have jurisdiction under 28 U.S.C. § 1292(a), and we affirm.

I.

Rancho – one of six County hospitals – is a 207-bed facility that specializes in rehabilitation and the acute care needs of patients with chronic diseases. Rancho provides care to about 2,600 inpatients and 8,600 outpatients annually. While most County hospitals predominantly treat the indigent and uninsured, Rancho has a high percentage of patients with public and private insurance. About 67 percent of Rancho's inpatients and 58 percent of Rancho's outpatients are Medi-Cal recipients.

Rancho has served Los Angeles's homeless, mentally ill, disabled and elderly populations since it opened in 1888. Important health care innovations, including the "halo" device used to support the head and neck of spinal cord injury patients, were invented at Rancho. Rancho was also the first facility to replace wood with plastic for prosthetic limbs. By the early 1930s, Rancho was becoming legendary for its occupational therapy. Later, during World War II, Rancho began providing long-term care and rehabilitation for polio patients; in 1954, the majority of the 1,865 Los Angeles area polio victims were treated at Rancho.

In 2002, in an effort to increase efficiency and reduce costs, the County consolidated its clinical services for certain severe disabilities. It did so by moving all acute inpatient rehabilitation, chronic ventilator/pulmonary services, and pediatric orthopedic surgery for selected neuromuscular disorders to Rancho. Before that time, these services were also offered at other County facilities. Because of the consolidation, currently about 60 percent of Rancho's inpatients are transferred to Rancho from the other five County hospitals.

Rancho is a unique facility; no other facility in the area currently provides many of the services it offers. Because many disabled patients will be unable to find necessary medical treatment elsewhere if Rancho closes, doctors anticipate that closing Rancho will have a devastating effect on the facility's disabled patients, including plaintiffs. Doctors are also concerned that closing Rancho will negatively impact the treatment of patients at other County facilities as well as important medical training and research.

Nevertheless, on January 28, 2003, the County decided to close Rancho because of anticipated future budget deficits. The County planned to reduce services at Rancho beginning May 1, 2003, and to fully close the hospital by June 30, 2003. The County expects to save $58.6 million annually by closing Rancho. However, the County's calculation does not take into account the cost of providing Rancho patients with care at other County facilities.

Although the County was expecting a budget deficit when it began studying cost-cutting proposals, a new infusion of Medicaid funding has helped the County's health care system end the 2002-2003 fiscal year with over $300 million in its fund balance. The County now projects that it will have almost the same amount in its fund balance for fiscal year 2003-2004 and nearly $200 million at the end of fiscal year 2004-2005. No shortfall is expected until 2006-2007.

II.

* * *

In support of its ruling, the district court found that the County consolidated services for the severely disabled at Rancho, which annually serves more than 9,500 patients, about 50 percent of which are covered by

Medi-Cal. The court found that plaintiffs' needs "could not and would not be met in the Los Angeles community" without Rancho, and that closing the facility would harm many of its Medi-Cal patients because they would be unable to obtain substitute care elsewhere. The district court also concluded that closing Rancho as planned would violate federal law because there was no evidence the County could transition Rancho patients before the closure, and further that the County's contract with the state required it to comply with Medicaid regulations. Further, the district court held that plaintiffs' ADA claim was likely to succeed on the merits.

* * *

IV.

A. Likelihood of Success: Title II of the ADA

The district court did not abuse its discretion in concluding that plaintiffs established a likelihood of success on the merits of their ADA claim.

Title II of the ADA prohibits discrimination in public services and programs. To establish a violation of the ADA, a plaintiff must demonstrate: "(1) he is a 'qualified individual with a disability'; (2) he was either excluded from participation in or denied the benefits of a public entity's services, programs or activities, or was otherwise discriminated against by the public entity; and (3) such exclusion, denial of benefits, or discrimination was by reason of his disability." *Weinreich v. Los Angeles County MTA*, 114 F.3d 976, 978 (9th Cir.1997) (emphasis omitted).

Applying this standard, the district court concluded that plaintiffs demonstrated a likelihood of success on their ADA claim. The County does not dispute that plaintiffs are qualified individuals with disabilities, or that as a public entity its health care program is covered by the ADA. Instead, the County's arguments focus on whether the services plaintiffs would lose with Rancho's closure fall within the scope of care the County must provide to plaintiffs consistent with the ADA. For the reasons set forth below, we conclude that they do.

The County attacks "the very premise of the district court's definition of the benefit" at issue – the notion that plaintiffs are entitled to "the specialized medical expertise" they need for adequate medical care – as contrary to Supreme Court precedent. The district court considered this argument, but found the County's precedent distinguishable and its contention unpersuasive. We agree.

At the core of the County's argument is *Alexander v. Choate*, 469 U.S. 287 (1985). In *Alexander*, to save money, Tennessee proposed reducing the number of annual days of inpatient care covered by the state Medicaid program from 20 to 14 for all program participants. The evidence suggested that about 27 percent of disabled participants required more than 14 days of care, while only about 8 percent of non-disabled participants required more than 14 days. Id. at 289-90. Plaintiffs challenged the proposed reduction as discriminatory (under Section 504 of the Rehabilitation Act) because it would have a disproportionate effect on the disabled. The Supreme Court concluded that the planned reduction was not discriminatory because it did not deny the disabled the benefits of the 14 days of care the state chose to provide; rather, the plan left all patients

> with identical and effective hospital services fully available for their use, with both classes of users subject to the same durational limitation.
>
> . . .
>
> Medicaid programs do not guarantee that each recipient will receive that level of health care precisely tailored to his or her particular needs. Instead, the benefit provided through Medicaid is a particular package of health care services, such as 14 days of inpatient coverage. That package of services has the general aim of assuring that individuals will receive necessary medical care, but the benefit provided remains the individual services offered – not "adequate health care." . . .
>
> Section 504 seeks to assure evenhanded treatment and the opportunity for handicapped individuals to participate in and benefit from programs receiving federal assistance. . . . The Act does not, however, guarantee the handicapped equal results from the provision of state Medicaid.

Id. at 302-04 (internal citation omitted).

The *Alexander* Court specifically noted that there was no "suggestion" in the record "that the illnesses uniquely associated with the handicapped or occurring with greater frequency among them cannot be effectively treated, at least in part, with fewer than 14 days' coverage." Id. at 302 n.22.

We applied *Alexander* in *Crowder v. Kitagawa*, 81 F.3d 1480 (9th Cir.1996), where we held that a Hawaii law requiring carnivorous animals entering the state to be quarantined violated the ADA:

> Although Hawaii's quarantine requirement applies equally to all persons entering the state with a dog, its enforcement burdens visually-impaired persons in a manner different and greater than it burdens others. Because of the unique dependence upon guide dogs among many of the visually-impaired, Hawaii's quarantine effectively denies these persons . . . meaningful access to state services, programs, and activities while such services, programs, and activities

remain open and easily accessible by others. The quarantine, therefore, discriminates against the plaintiffs by reason of their disability.

Id. at 1484.

Concerned Parents to Save Dreher Park Center v. City of West Palm Beach, 846 F.Supp. 986 (S.D.Fla.1994), cited by plaintiffs and the district court, also relied on *Alexander*. In Dreher Park, a Florida city had made available recreational and social programs and activities for disabled individuals at Dreher Park. Id. at 988. Budget constraints caused the city to make various cuts, including effectively eliminating the existing recreational programs for disabled individuals. Id. at 989. Plaintiffs challenged the cuts under the ADA, and the court granted their request for a preliminary injunction. The court concluded that the complete elimination of the programs at Dreher Park likely violated the ADA because there were no equivalent programs available to fill the void left by the closure. Although disabled individuals could theoretically participate in the general recreational programs the city offered at other locations,

> it is clear that many of the general programs are unable to offer the benefits of recreation to individuals with disabilities because of the nature of the recreational activities and the physical and other limitations of persons with disabilities. . . . It appears from the evidence that City had offered the Dreher Park Center programs precisely because they were needed to give equal benefits of recreation to persons with disabilities. When these programs were eliminated, Plaintiffs were denied the benefits of the City's leisure services in contravention of Title II.
>
> . . .
>
> Title II . . . require[s] that any benefits provided to non-disabled persons must be equally made available for disabled persons.

Id. at 991-92.

Alexander is distinguishable from the instant case. The reduction at issue in *Alexander* was facially neutral – the maximum hospital stay for all patients was reduced to 14 days. The County's argument that its proposed cuts are similarly "across-the-board" because it also plans to reduce the beds at County-USC Hospital (and already has eliminated some clinics) is unpersuasive. Reductions analogous to the cut in Alexander might include eliminating X dollars or Y percent of funding from the budget of each of the County's six hospitals or from each medical department or type of service offered therein. Eliminating entirely the only hospital of six that focuses on the needs of disabled individuals (because the County earlier decided to consolidate such services at that hospital) and that provides services disproportionately required by the disabled and available nowhere else in the County is simply not the sort of facially neutral reduction considered in *Alexander*. *Alexander* may allow the County to step down services equally for all who rely on it for their healthcare needs, but it does not sanction the wholesale elimination of services relied upon disproportionately by the disabled because of their disabilities.

Moreover, the Court in *Alexander* specifically noted that nothing in the record suggested "that the illnesses uniquely associated with the handicapped or occurring with greater frequency among them cannot be effectively treated, at least in part, with fewer than 14 days' coverage." 469 U.S. at 302 n.22. Here, in contrast, plaintiffs presented ample evidence that rehabilitative services and treatment for complex and disabling medical conditions, such as paralysis and conditions associated with severe diabetes, cannot currently be provided effectively anywhere in the County system but Rancho. While the proposed cutback in Alexander did not uniquely affect disabled individuals, the County's planned cutback specifically targets services for the disabled. Even after Alexander, the ADA prohibits the County from eliminating healthcare services for the disabled in this manner.

Further, in *Crowder*, we confirmed that, even in the wake of Alexander, state action that disproportionately burdens the disabled because of their unique needs remains actionable under the ADA. 81 F.3d 1480. As in *Crowder*, the closure of Rancho would deny certain disabled individuals meaningful access to government-provided services because of their unique needs, while others would retain access to the same class of services.

Like the district court, we find the *Dreher Park* decision persuasive; it presents an analogous fact pattern, applies *Alexander*, and reaches a fair and well-reasoned result. In both *Dreher Park* and this case, the government first consolidated services for the disabled at a single facility. Then, due to budget shortages, the government decided to close the single facility providing specialized programs for the disabled, while continuing to operate the facilities providing the same category of services to non-disabled individuals. While the disabled could theoretically seek service from the remaining facilities, the evidence suggested in *Dreher Park*, as it does here, that the services designed for the general population would not adequately serve the unique needs of the disabled, who therefore would be effectively denied services that the non-disabled continued to receive. In light of all these parallels, the district court did not abuse its discretion in adopting *Dreher Park's* conclusion that such action violates the ADA and warrants an injunction.

In sum, plaintiffs demonstrated that if the County closes Rancho, it will reduce, and in some instances eliminate, necessary medical services for disabled Medi-Cal patients while continuing to provide the medical care required and sought by Medi-Cal recipients without disabilities. The district court relied on the correct legal standards and its factual findings are supported by the record. Therefore, the district court did not abuse its discretion in concluding that closing Rancho without continuing to provide medically necessary services to disabled individuals elsewhere would constitute discrimination on the basis of disability.

Notes & Questions

1. Do you agree with *Rodde's* characterization of the County's action as fundamentally different from the hospital reduction plan in *Alexander,* or does this case signal that the Ninth Circuit is moving away from a strict view of *Alexander?* Will this limit city officials as they make difficult decisions about resource allocation?

2. Consider the following scenario: Prior to 1994, Hawaii provided medical benefits to some of its most financially needy residents through a fee-for-service Medicaid program that served three populations: the aged, blind, and disabled; those receiving Aid to Families with Dependent Children (AFDC); and those receiving general assistance benefits. In addition to fitting into one of these three categories, program participants also had to have an income no greater than 100% of the federal poverty level and assets not in excess of $2000. Recognizing that these income and asset tests left the working poor uninsured, the State extended medical and dental benefits to members of the same three populations whose income was no greater than 300% of the federal poverty level through the State Health Insurance Program (SHIP), which did not contain an asset test. Faced with serious budget deficits, Hawaii ended its SHIP program and began a new HMO-based plan called QUEST. Hawaii allowed SHIP participants who received AFDC or General Assistance to transition into QUEST, but it eliminated coverage of the aged, blind, and disabled with incomes over a certain percentage of the federal poverty level. How would you construct an argument that this violates Title II of the ADA? Should such an argument be successful? *See* Lovell v. Chandler, 303 F.3d 1039 (9th Cir. 2002) (holding Title II violation on these facts).

&

C.   *Integration*

The regulations provide that public entities must administer services, programs, or activities in the most integrated setting appropriate to the needs of qualified individuals with disabilities. 28 C.F.R. § 35.130(d) (2008). In *Olmstead v. Zimring,* the Supreme Court considered the interplay between this integration mandate and the "fundamental alteration" limit on reasonable accommodation.

၁၈

OLMSTEAD v. ZIMRING

Supreme Court of the United States, 1999
527 U.S. 581

Justice GINSBURG announced the judgment of the Court and delivered the opinion of the Court with respect to Parts I, II, and III-A, and an opinion with respect to Part III-B, in which Justice O'CONNOR, Justice SOUTER, and Justice BREYER join.

This case concerns the proper construction of the anti-discrimination provision contained in the public services portion (Title II) of the Americans with Disabilities Act of 1990 (ADA), 104 Stat. 337, 42 U.S.C. § 12132. Specifically, we confront the question whether the proscription of discrimination may require placement of persons with mental disabilities in community settings rather than in institutions. The answer, we hold, is a qualified yes.

* * *

II

. . . [W]e summarize the facts underlying this dispute. Respondents L.C. and E.W. are mentally retarded women; L.C. has also been diagnosed with schizophrenia, and E.W. with a personality disorder. Both women have a history of treatment in institutional settings. In May 1992, L.C. was voluntarily admitted to Georgia Regional Hospital at Atlanta (GRH), where she was confined for treatment in a psychiatric unit. By May 1993, her psychiatric condition had stabilized, and L.C.'s treatment team at GRH agreed that her needs could be met appropriately in one of the community-based programs the State supported. Despite this evaluation, L.C. remained institutionalized until February 1996, when the State placed her in a community-based treatment program.

E.W. was voluntarily admitted to GRH in February 1995; like L.C., E.W. was confined for treatment in a psychiatric unit. In March 1995, GRH sought to discharge E.W. to a homeless shelter, but abandoned that plan after her attorney filed an administrative complaint. By 1996, E.W.'s treating psychiatrist concluded that she could be treated appropriately in a community-based setting. She nonetheless remained institutionalized until a few months after the District Court issued its judgment in this case in 1997.

In May 1995, when she was still institutionalized at GRH, L.C. filed suit in the United States District Court for the Northern District of Georgia, challenging her continued confinement in a segregated environment. Her complaint invoked 42 U.S.C. § 1983 and provisions of the ADA, §§ 12131-12134, and named as defendants, now petitioners, the Commissioner of the Georgia Department of Human Resources, the Superintendent of GRH, and the Executive Director of the Fulton County

Regional Board (collectively, the State). L.C. alleged that the State's failure to place her in a community-based program, once her treating professionals determined that such placement was appropriate, violated, *inter alia*, Title II of the ADA. L.C.'s pleading requested, among other things, that the State place her in a community care residential program, and that she receive treatment with the ultimate goal of integrating her into the mainstream of society. E.W. intervened in the action, stating an identical claim.

* * *

The Court of Appeals for the Eleventh Circuit affirmed the judgment of the District Court, but remanded for reassessment of the State's cost-based defense. See 138 F.3d at 905. As the appeals court read the statute and regulations: When "a disabled individual's treating professionals find that a community-based placement is appropriate for that individual, the ADA imposes a duty to provide treatment in a community setting – the most integrated setting appropriate to that patient's needs"; "[w]here there is no such finding [by the treating professionals], nothing in the ADA requires the deinstitutionalization of th[e] patient." Id. at 902.

* * *

We granted certiorari in view of the importance of the question presented to the States and affected individuals.

* * *

III

Endeavoring to carry out Congress' instruction to issue regulations implementing Title II, the Attorney General, in the integration and reasonable-modifications regulations . . . made two key determinations. The first concerned the scope of the ADA's discrimination proscription, 42 U.S.C. § 12132; the second concerned the obligation of the States to counter discrimination. As to the first, the Attorney General concluded that unjustified placement or retention of persons in institutions, severely limiting their exposure to the outside community, constitutes a form of discrimination based on disability prohibited by Title II. See 28 C.F.R. § 35.130(d) (1998) ("A public entity shall administer services . . . in the most integrated setting appropriate to the needs of qualified individuals with disabilities."); Brief for United States as Amicus Curiae in *Helen L. v. DiDario*, No. 94-1243 (C.A.3 1994), pp. 8, 15-16 (unnecessary segregation of persons with disabilities constitutes a form of discrimination prohibited by the ADA and the integration regulation). Regarding the States' obligation to avoid unjustified isolation of individuals with disabilities, the Attorney General provided that States could resist modifications that "would fundamentally alter the nature of the service, program, or activity." 28 C.F.R. § 35.130(b)(7) (1998).

The Court of Appeals essentially upheld the Attorney General's construction of the ADA. . . . [T]he appeals court ruled that the unjustified institutionalization of persons with mental disabilities violated Title II; the court then remanded with instructions to measure the cost of caring for L.C. and E.W. in a community-based facility against the State's mental health budget.

We affirm the Court of Appeals' decision in substantial part. Unjustified isolation, we hold, is properly regarded as discrimination based on disability. But we recognize, as well, the States' need to maintain a range of facilities for the care and treatment of persons with diverse mental disabilities, and the States' obligation to administer services with an even hand. Accordingly, we further hold that the Court of Appeals' remand instruction was unduly restrictive. In evaluating a State's fundamental-alteration defense, the District Court must consider, in view of the resources available to the State, not only the cost of providing community-based care to the litigants, but also the range of services the State provides others with mental disabilities, and the State's obligation to mete out those services equitably.

A

We examine first whether, as the Eleventh Circuit held, undue institutionalization qualifies as discrimination "by reason of . . . disability." The Department of Justice has consistently advocated that it does. Because the Department is the agency directed by Congress to issue regulations implementing Title II, its views warrant respect. We need not inquire whether the degree of deference described in *Chevron U.S.A. Inc. v. Natural Resources Defense Council, Inc.*, 467 U.S. 837, 844 (1984), is in order; "[i]t is enough to observe that the well-reasoned views of the agencies implementing a statute 'constitute a body of experience and informed judgment to which courts and litigants may properly resort for guidance.'" *Bragdon v. Abbott*, 524 U.S. 624, 642 (1998) (quoting *Skidmore v. Swift & Co.*, 323 U.S. 134, 139-140 (1944)).

* * *

The ADA stepped up earlier measures to secure opportunities for people with developmental disabilities to enjoy the benefits of community living. The Developmentally Disabled Assistance and Bill of Rights Act, a 1975 measure, stated in aspirational terms that "[t]he treatment, services, and habilitation for a person with developmental disabilities . . . *should* be provided in the setting that is least restrictive of the person's personal liberty." 89 Stat. 502, 42 U.S.C. § 6010(2) (1976 ed.) (emphasis added); see also *Pennhurst State School and Hospital v. Halderman*, 451 U.S. 1, 24 (1981) (concluding that the § 6010 provisions "were intended to be hortatory, not mandatory"). In a related legislative endeavor, the Rehabilitation Act of 1973, Congress used mandatory language to proscribe discrimination against persons with disabilities. See 87 Stat. 394, as amended, 29 U.S.C. § 794 (1976 ed.) ("No otherwise qualified individual with a disability in the United States . . . *shall*, solely by reason of her or his disability, be excluded from the participation in, be denied the benefits of, or be subjected to discrimination under any program or activity receiving Federal financial assistance." (Emphasis added.)) Ultimately, in the ADA, enacted in 1990, Congress not only required all public entities to refrain from discrimination, see 42 U.S.C. § 12132; additionally, in findings applicable to the entire statute, Congress explicitly identified unjustified "segregation" of persons with disabilities as a "for[m] of discrimination." See § 12101(a)(2) ("historically, society has tended to isolate and segregate individuals with disabilities, and, despite some improvements, such forms of discrimination against individuals with disabilities continue to be a serious and pervasive social problem"); § 12101(a)(5) ("individuals with disabilities continually encounter various forms of discrimination, including . . . segregation").

Recognition that unjustified institutional isolation of persons with disabilities is a form of discrimination reflects two evident judgments. First, institutional placement of persons who can handle and benefit from community settings perpetuates unwarranted assumptions that persons so isolated are incapable or unworthy of participating in community life. Cf. *Allen v. Wright*, 468 U.S. 737, 755 (1984) ("There can be no doubt that [stigmatizing injury often caused by racial discrimination] is one of the most serious consequences of discriminatory government action."); *Los Angeles Dept. of Water and Power v. Manhart*, 435 U.S. 702, 707, n.13, (1978) (" 'In forbidding employers to discriminate against individuals because of their sex, Congress intended to strike at the entire spectrum of disparate treatment of men and women resulting from sex stereotypes.' ") (quoting *Sprogis v. United Air Lines, Inc.*, 444 F.2d 1194, 1198 (C.A.7 1971)). Second, confinement in an institution severely diminishes the everyday life activities of individuals, including family relations, social contacts, work options, economic independence, educational advancement, and cultural enrichment. See Brief for American Psychiatric Association et al. as Amici Curiae 20-22. Dissimilar treatment correspondingly exists in this key respect: In order to receive needed medical services, persons with mental disabilities must, because of those disabilities, relinquish participation in community life they could enjoy given reasonable accommodations, while persons without mental disabilities can receive the medical services they need without similar sacrifice. See Brief for United States as Amicus Curiae 6-7, 17.

The State urges that, whatever Congress may have stated as its findings in the ADA, the Medicaid statute "reflected a congressional policy preference for treatment in the institution over treatment in the community." Brief for Petitioners 31. The State correctly used the past tense. Since 1981, Medicaid has provided funding for state-run home and community-based care through a waiver program. See 95 Stat. 812-813, as amended, 42 U.S.C. § 1396n(c); Brief for United States as Amicus Curiae 20-21. Indeed, the United States points out that the Department of Health and Human Services (HHS) "has a policy of encouraging States to take advantage of the waiver program, and often approves more waiver slots than a State ultimately uses." Id. at 25-26 (further observing that, by 1996, "HHS approved up to 2109 waiver slots for Georgia, but Georgia used only 700").

We emphasize that nothing in the ADA or its implementing regulations condones termination of institutional settings for persons unable to handle or benefit from community settings. Title II provides only that "qualified individual[s] with a disability" may not "be subjected to discrimination." 42 U.S.C. § 12132. "Qualified individuals," the ADA further explains, are persons with disabilities who, "with or without reasonable modifications to rules, policies, or practices, . . . mee[t] the essential eligibility requirements for the receipt of services or the participation in programs or activities provided by a public entity." § 12131(2).

Consistent with these provisions, the State generally may rely on the reasonable assessments of its own professionals in determining whether an individual "meets the essential eligibility requirements" for habilitation in a community-based program. Absent such qualification, it would be inappropriate to remove a patient from the more restrictive setting. See 28 C.F.R. § 35.130(d) (1998) (public entity shall administer services and programs in "the most integrated setting *appropriate* to the needs of qualified individuals with disabilities" (emphasis added)); cf. *School Bd. of Nassau Cty. v. Arline*, 480 U.S. 273, 288 (1987) ("[C]ourts normally should defer to the reasonable medical judgments of public health officials."). Nor is there any federal requirement that community-based treatment be imposed on patients who do not desire it. See 28 C.F.R. § 35.130(e)(1) (1998) ("Nothing in this part shall be construed to require an individual with a disability to accept an accommodation . . . which such individual chooses not to accept."); 28 C.F.R. pt. 35 app. A p. 450 (1998) ("[P]ersons with disabilities must be provided the option of declining to accept a particular accommodation."). In this case, however, there is no genuine dispute concerning the status of L.C. and E.W. as individuals "qualified" for noninstitutional care: The State's own professionals determined that community-based treatment would be appropriate for L.C. and E.W., and neither woman opposed such treatment.

B

The State's responsibility, once it provides community-based treatment to qualified persons with disabilities, is not boundless. The reasonable-modifications regulation speaks of "reasonable modifications" to avoid discrimination, and allows States to resist modifications that entail a "fundamenta[l] alter[ation]" of the States' services and programs. 28 C.F.R. § 35.130(b)(7) (1998). The Court of Appeals construed this regulation to permit a cost-based defense "only in the most limited of circumstances," 138 F.3d at 902, and remanded to the District Court to consider, among other things, "whether the additional expenditures necessary to treat L.C. and E.W. in community-based care would be unreasonable given the demands of the State's mental health budget." Id. at 905.

The Court of Appeals' construction of the reasonable-modifications regulation is unacceptable for it would leave the State virtually defenseless once it is shown that the plaintiff is qualified for the service or program she seeks. If the expense entailed in placing one or two people in a community-based treatment program is properly measured for reasonableness against the State's entire mental health budget, it is unlikely that a State, relying on the fundamental-alteration defense, could ever prevail. See Tr. of Oral Arg. 27 (State's attorney argues that Court of Appeals' understanding of the fundamental-alteration defense, as expressed in its order to the District Court, "will always preclude the State from a meaningful defense"); cf. Brief for Petitioners 37-38 (Court of Appeals' remand order "mistakenly asks the district court to examine [the fundamental-alteration] defense based on the cost of providing community care to just two individuals, not all Georgia citizens who desire community care"); 1: 95-cv-1210-MHS (ND Ga., Oct. 20, 1998), p. 3, App. 177 (District Court, on remand, declares the impact of its decision beyond L.C. and E.W. "irrelevant"). Sensibly construed, the fundamental-alteration component of the reasonable-modifications regulation would allow the State to show that, in the allocation of available resources, immediate relief for the plaintiffs would be inequitable, given the responsibility the State has undertaken for the care and treatment of a large and diverse population of persons with mental disabilities.

* * *

[T]he ADA is not reasonably read to impel States to phase out institutions, placing patients in need of close care at risk. Nor is it the ADA's mission to drive States to move institutionalized patients into an inappropriate setting, such as a homeless shelter, a placement the State proposed, then retracted, for E.W. Some individuals, like L.C. and E.W. in prior years, may need institutional care from time to time "to stabilize acute psychiatric symptoms." App. 98 (affidavit of Dr. Richard L. Elliott); see 138 F.3d at 903 ("[T]here may be times [when] a patient can be treated in the community, and others whe[n] an institutional placement is necessary."); Reply Brief 19 (placement in a community-based treatment program does not mean the State will no longer need to retain hospital accommodations for the person so placed). For other individuals, no placement outside the institution may ever be appropriate. See Brief for American Psychiatric Association et al. as Amici Curiae 22-23 ("Some individuals, whether mentally retarded or mentally ill, are not prepared at particular times – perhaps in the short run, perhaps in the long run – for the risks and exposure of the less protective environment of community settings"; for these persons, "institutional settings are needed and must remain available."); Brief for Voice of the Retarded et al. as Amici Curiae 11 ("Each disabled person is entitled to treatment in the most integrated setting possible for that person – recognizing that, on a case-by-case basis, that setting may be in an institution."); *Youngberg v. Romeo*, 457 U.S. 307, 327 (1982) (Blackmun, J., concurring) ("For many mentally retarded people, the difference between the capacity to do things for themselves within an institution and total dependence on the institution for all of their needs is as much liberty as they ever will know.").

To maintain a range of facilities and to administer services with an even hand, the State must have more leeway than the courts below understood the fundamental-alteration defense to allow. If, for example, the State were to demonstrate that it had a comprehensive, effectively working plan for placing qualified persons with mental disabilities in less restrictive settings, and a waiting list that moved at a reasonable pace not controlled by the State's endeavors to keep its institutions fully populated, the reasonable-modifications standard would be met. See Tr. of Oral Arg. 5 (State's attorney urges that, "by asking [a] person to wait a short time until a community bed is available, Georgia does not exclude [that] person by reason of disability, neither does Georgia discriminate against her by reason of disability"); see also id. at 25 ("[I]t is reasonable for the State to ask someone to wait until a community placement is available."). In such circumstances, a court would have no warrant effectively to order displacement of persons at the top of the community-based treatment waiting list by individuals lower down who commenced civil actions.

* * *

For the reasons stated, we conclude that, under Title II of the ADA, States are required to provide community-based treatment for persons with mental disabilities when the State's treatment professionals determine that such placement is appropriate, the affected persons do not oppose such treatment, and the placement can be reasonably accommodated, taking into account the resources available to the State and the needs of others with mental disabilities. The judgment of the Eleventh Circuit is therefore affirmed in part and vacated in part, and the case is remanded for further proceedings.

It is so ordered.

Notes & Questions

1. Consider the Court's statement that

[s]ensibly construed, the fundamental-alteration component of the reasonable modifications regulation would allow the State to show that, in the allocation of available resources, immediate relief for the plaintiffs would be inequitable, given the responsibility the State has undertaken for the care and treatment of a large and diverse population of persons with mental disabilities.

Olmstead, 527 U.S. at 584. Does this give lower courts sufficient guidance? Or will this create litigation over what states' "integration plans" need to look like? In *Frederick L. v. Department of Public Welfare*, No. Civ. A 00-4510, 2004 WL 1945565, at *6 (E.D. Pa. Sept. 1, 2004), the court indicated that

> while Defendants' plan need not be a formal document, it must consist of (1) an "assurance" or "commitment" to "take all reasonable steps" so that there will be "ongoing progress" toward community placement in the future; (2) the commitment must be "communicated in some manner"; and (3) [the defendant] must be "held accountable."

The district court went on to enter judgment for the Department of Public Welfare. On appeal, the Third Circuit reversed, holding that under *Olmstead*, a state may avoid liability only by providing a comprehensive, effective working plan for placing qualified persons with mental disabilities in community based programs with a waiting list that moved at a reasonable pace. The plan had to demonstrate a specific and measurable commitment to deinstitutionalization for which they could be held accountable. *See* Frederick L. v. Department of Public Welfare, 422 F.3d 151 (3d Cir. 2005). But in *Sanchez v. Johnson*, 416 F.3d 1051 (9th Cir. 2005), plaintiffs were a class of people with developmental disabilities and their providers who argued that inadequate staff salaries for employees that worked in community based programs violated Title II's integration mandate. California offered a fundamental alteration defense, arguing that its plan was sufficient. The court agreed, holding that California had a comprehensive, effectively working plan, so that the relief requested would result in a fundamental alteration of the state's programs. *Id.* at 1067-68.

2. Integration cases may be intensely fact-specific, and they can ignite issues of whether people with disabilities are getting "special" or "extra" benefits that people without disabilities do not, or whether there is some baseline standard of adequate medical care a state must provide. In *Radaszewski ex rel. Radaszewski v. Maram*, 383 F.3d 599 (7th Cir. 2004), Eric Radaszewski required around-the-clock medical care in order to survive. Until he reached the age of 21, the Illinois Department of Public Aid (IDPA) provided funding through a Medicaid program for children that enabled Eric to receive 16 hours of private-duty nursing at home each day. After he turned 21, Eric was no longer eligible to participate in that program, and he would have been sent to a long-term facility to receive the required care (there were factual questions in the record as to whether Eric could even get the constant care he required in an institution, and whether being there would put his life in danger). Eric's mother filed suit on Eric's behalf, arguing that the IDPA's failure to fully fund at-home, private-duty nursing for Eric amounted to discrimination in violation of Title II of the ADA, in that Illinois was failing to provide the medical services that Eric required in order to remain in the most community-

integrated setting appropriate for his needs (his home). The state argued that this was not discriminatory, because in-home nursing care is not a service that Illinois provided to any adult individual. The District Court agreed with Illinois, holding that "[t]he IDPA is not required to provide the handicapped more coverage than the non-handicapped individual to ensure 'adequate health care.'" *Id.* at 606 (citation omitted). The Seventh Circuit disagreed, holding that

> [a]lthough a State is not obligated to create entirely new services or to otherwise alter the substance of the care that it provides to Medicaid recipients in order to accommodate an individual's desire to be cared for at home, the integration mandate may well require the State to make reasonable modifications to the form of existing services in order to adapt them to community-integrated settings.

Id. at 611. The court remanded for a factual determination of these issues.

3. At least one U.S. Court of Appeal has held that to have standing to bring an *Olmstead* claim, a plaintiff does not have to currently be in an institutionalized setting. In *Fisher v. Oklahoma Health Care Authority*, 335 F.3d 1175 (10th Cir. 2003), a group of participants in a community-based Medicaid program challenged a decision by the State of Oklahoma to cease providing unlimited, medically-necessary prescription benefits for program participants. The plaintiffs claimed that placing them at risk of premature institutionalization in nursing homes was violative of the *Olmstead* integration mandate. The state of Oklahoma argued that because the plaintiffs were not currently institutionalized, they could not bring an *Olmstead* claim. The Tenth Circuit, noting that there was nothing in the text of the statute nor in the *Olmstead* decision supporting such an interpretation, disagreed. *See also* Pashby v. Delia, 709 F.3d 307 (4th Cir. 2013) (holding that plaintiffs only need to face the risk of institutionalization to bring an *Olmstead* claim). But in *Cohon v. New Mexico Dept. of Health*, 646 F.3d 717, 730 (10th Cir. 2011), the court declined to recognize a claim that in-home health was insufficiently funded for people with severe disabilities as an *Olmstead* claim.

4. While the integration mandate is important, it is not absolute. The regulations and case law are sensitive to integration concerns working *against* the creation of programs tailored to particular types of individuals with disabilities. This was the issue in *Easley by Easley v. Snider*, 36 F.3d 297 (3d Cir. 1994). The state of Pennsylvania had a program whereby individuals with physical disabilities could receive home assistance to enable them to live at home, instead of institutions. A prerequisite for this program was that the individual be "mentally alert." The *Easley* plaintiffs, who had intellectual disabilities, requested a modification of the mental alertness requirement to allow a surrogate to supervise the assistant. The Third Circuit court found that "mental

alertness" was an essential eligibility requirement, and that any modification (i.e., use of surrogates) would "change the entire focus of the program." *Id.* at 305. The court concluded that the Rehabilitation Act case law protected the ability of a public entity to offer a service to a certain class of people with disabilities and not extend it to everyone, and that the ADA regulations supported this view.

5. *Olmstead* implementation has been hard. In July of 2001, President George W. Bush issued an Executive Order reinforcing the *Olmstead* decision, and providing guidance to the Attorney General, the Secretaries of Health and Human Services, Education, Labor, and Housing and Urban Development, and the Commissioner of the Social Security Administration in its implementation. Exec. Order No. 13,217, 66 F.R. 33155 (June 18, 2001) ("Community-Based Alternatives for Individuals with Disabilities"). As part of the Bush administration's "New Freedom" initiative, the Centers for Medicare and Medicaid Services distributed over $120 million in grants in 2001 and 2002 to help states increase community based integration for people with disabilities.

However, years after the *Olmstead* decision, states still face a lack of coordinated community-based services and a shortfall of funds in carrying out the integration mandate. One reason is what is referred to as an "institutional bias," which results in institutions receiving a disproportionate share of Medicaid funding and which is the primary source of funding for long-term care. An increased emphasis on community alternatives also causes concern on the part of some state employees, as state-funded institutions serve as a key economic force in certain areas. *See* Johanna M. Donlin, Moving Ahead with *Olmstead*: To Comply with the Americans with Disabilities Act, States Are Working Hard to Find Community Placements for People with Disabilities, 29 State Legislatures 28 (Mar. 1, 2003), available at 2003 WL 8909235. There has been litigation in this area. In *M.R. v. Dreyfus,* 697 F.3d 706 (9th Cir. 2012), the Ninth Circuit ordered a preliminary injunction where a regulation promulgated by Washington's Department of Social and Health Services (DSHS) reduced the amount of in-home "personal care services" available under the state's Medicaid plan.

For an example of one state's road to implementation, on July 1, 2008, the Governor of Georgia (the state at issue in *Olmstead*) announced that state officials signed a voluntary compliance agreement with the U.S. Department of Health and Human Services Office of Civil Rights that would formalize an effort to transition mentally ill and developmentally disabled Georgians out of state hospitals. The features of this agreement included: an Olmstead coordinator who reports to the governor and is charged with developing and implementing Georgia's Olmstead Plan objectives; annual estimates of the need for community services for mentally and developmentally disabled Georgians who are institutionalized or at risk of institutionalization; the maintenance of "Olmstead lists" and "transition lists" that document all institutionalized individuals who do not actively oppose receiving services in the community, as well as specific individuals Georgia is planning to discharge into the community in a given fiscal year; and proper notification and explanation of denial of discharge based on determination of state treatment professionals, as well as methods of recourse available to individuals who wish to contest these decisions. *See* The Chatanooga.com, Governor Perdue Announces Olmstead Agreement, signed July 2, 2008. The Department of Justice and Georgia have since entered into another agreement, focusing on Georgia's failure to serve individuals with developmental disabilities and mental illness in the most integrated setting appropriate to those individuals' needs, that supersedes the former agreement. *See* Settlement Agreement between United States of America and the State of Georgia, Civil No. 1:10-CV-249-CAP (N.D. Ga. Oct. 19, 2010) (settlement agreement), *available at* http://www.hhs.gov/ocr/civilrights/activities/examples/Olmstead/gaolmstreadagree.pdf; United States v. Georgia Settlement Agreement Fact Sheet (Oct. 19, 2010), *available at* http://www.hhs.gov/ocr/civilrights/activities/examples/Olmstead/gaolmsteadagreefs.pdf.

6. The Georgia settlement has been part of a recent Department of Justice commitment to *Olmstead* implementation. The DOJ has been a party to *Olmstead* litigation in Texas, New York, Florida, Rhode Island, Florida, as well as other states. For a summary, *see* U.S. Department of Justice, DOJ Olmstead Litigation, http://www.ada.gov/olmstead/olmstead_enforcement.htm (last visited Oct. 22, 2013). As one example, the DOJ notified the State of Mississippi that it believed it was in violation of the ADA's integration mandate in its provision of services to people with developmental disabilities and mental illness. *See* Letter from Thomas E. Perez, Assistant Attorney General, U.S. Department of Justice, to Hon. Haley R. Barbour, Governor of the State of Mississippi (Dec. 22, 2011), *available at* http://www.ada.gov/olmstead/documents/miss_findings_letter.pdf. The DOJ is currently in negotiations with the State to reach a settlement to resolve the violations of law identified in the findings letter.

D. *Facilities Modification*

Title II applies to a public entity's physical structures. Courts have interpreted this reach to include, among other things, city buildings, Johnson v. City of Saline, 151 F.3d 564 (6th Cir. 1998), botanical gardens on the premises of a state university, *Parker v. Universidad de P.R.*, 225 F.3d 1 (1st Cir. 2000), publicly owned sporting arenas and theatres, *Ass'n for Disabled Americans, Inc. v. City of Orlando*, 153 F.Supp.2d 1310 (M.D. Fla. 2001), and, as discussed above, city sidewalks. *See* Barden v. City of Sacramento, 292 F.3d 1073 (9th Cir. 2002).

The regulations speak in terms of physical structures as "facilities," which are defined as:

all or any portion of buildings, structures, sites, complexes, equipment, rolling stock or other conveyances, roads, walks, passageways, parking lots, or other real or personal property, including the site where the building, property, structure, or equipment is located.

28 C.F.R. § 35.104 (2008).

The regulations' prohibition of discrimination in facility access is patterned after the Title II general discrimination provision:

[N]o qualified individual with a disability shall, because a public entity's facilities are inaccessible to or unusable by individuals with disabilities, be excluded from participation in, or be denied the benefits of the services, programs, or activities of a public entity, or be subjected to discrimination by any public entity.

Id. § 35.149.

Therefore, textually, facilities serve two functions. They may themselves be "programs, services, or activities" within the meaning of the statutory text, or conduits (e.g., websites) to other "programs, services, or activities" public entities may offer.

The regulations set forth the "program access" standards for facilities. What a public entity must do to ensure "program access" to its facilities varies according to whether the facility is an "existing" facility, a new facility, or a facility that has been altered.

1. Existing facilities

The regulations provide that each service, program, or activity conducted by a public entity, when viewed in its entirety, must be readily accessible to and useable by individuals with disabilities. 28 C.F.R. § 35.150(a). This does not mean, however, that each existing facility must be physically accessible to and usable by individuals with disabilities. *Id.* § 35.150(a)(1).

In ensuring program access in existing facilities, a public entity does not have to take action that will result in a fundamental alteration in the nature of a service, program, or activity, or cause an undue financial or administrative burden. *Id.* § 35.150(a)(3). The public entity has the burden of showing that compliance with the program access standard would result in such alteration or burden. The decision that compliance would result in such an alteration or burden must be made by the head of the public entity, in writing. *Id.* These principles play out in the following case.

GREER v. RICHARDSON INDEPENDENT SCHOOL DISTRICT

United States Court of Appeals, Fifth Circuit, 2012
472 F. App'x 287

EDITH BROWN CLEMENT, Circuit Judge:

* * * Greer, who uses a wheelchair for mobility as a result of a spinal cord injury, attended her son's junior varsity football game at RISD's Berkner B stadium, located at Berkner High School in Richardson, Texas, on October 4, 2007. After entering the stadium, Greer realized that the only way to access the stadium's bleacher seating was by climbing a flight of stairs. Unable to access the stadium's bleachers, Greer maneuvered her wheelchair to an accessible paved area adjacent to the bleachers where she watched the football game through a chain link fence that surrounds the field while her husband watched the game from the bleachers. From her viewpoint, Greer claims she was only able to observe roughly 15% of the game due to her view being blocked by football players standing on the sideline. She also claims the area, while accessible by a wheelchair, was slightly sloped, which required her to hold on to the fence to avoid slowly rolling backwards. It is not disputed that Greer was able to access other aspects of the stadium, including being able to park at the stadium, navigate from the parking lot to the stadium, buy a ticket to the game, and buy a hot dog and beverage at the concession stand.

On February 1, 2008, Greer sued RISD, claiming that it discriminated against her by excluding her from participation in the benefits, programs and activities of a governmental entity receiving federal assistance, in violation of Title II of the ADA, 42 U.S.C. § 12101, et seq. and the Rehabilitation Act of 1973, 29 U.S.C. §§ 794 and 794a. * * *

Greer appeals the district court's rulings on summary judgment.

* * *

Title II of the ADA states that "no qualified individual with a disability shall, by reason of such disability, be excluded from participation in or be denied the benefits of the services, programs, or activities of a public entity, or be subjected to discrimination by any such entity." * * *

When considering ADA compliance for * * * existing structures, the touchstone is thus not the facility's technical compliance with the ADAAG, but is instead "program accessibility." "A public entity shall operate each service, program, or activity so that the service, program, or activity, when viewed in its entirety, is readily accessible to and usable by individuals with disabilities." 28 C.F.R. § 35.150(a). Making a program or activity accessible under this standard does not require a public entity to make all of its existing facilities accessible to disabled individuals nor does it require a public entity to take an action that would place an undue burden on the entity. Id. at (a)(1), (3). Furthermore, the regulations do not provide any objective criteria for evaluating program accessibility. While an existing facility's compliance with the ADAAG regulations may be informative, program accessibility is ultimately a subjective determination by viewing the program or activity at issue in its entirety and not solely by evaluating individual elements of the facility where the program is held. * * *

[The] primary question before this court is whether the district court properly found that Greer failed to * * * [show] that there was insufficient program access when she attended the football game at Berkner B. * * *

The following exchange between the district court and Greer's counsel at the hearing on the parties' cross-motions for summary judgment is instructive.

The district court:

That the key issue with respect to this subject, as the plaintiff would characterize it, is that [providing alternative accessible viewing areas] doesn't do because it's not just watching the game that matters, which Ms. Greer, or others, seated in one of those areas could do, but it is the experience of watching the game with the other fans.

Greer's counsel in response:

But to the extent that the basic argument is that are you entitled to keep the disabled out of the general seating area versus not, then I would agree that that is a fair assessment of one of the central issues before the Court.

In light of the prior proceedings and the parties' briefs, we understand Greer's general contention to be this: "program access" is more than just the ability to watch the football game at the Berkner B stadium. Instead program access requires that a disabled individual such as Greer not only be able to watch the game but also experience the game from the general admission public bleachers so as to not be separated from other attendees.

There is an aspect of Greer's segregation argument that rings true as noted by the district * * *. It would likely not be permissible for a public entity such as RISD to claim it provides program access if it required disabled individuals to sit alone in an area far removed from her companions and other attendees, such as behind the goal posts at the end of the field, when all other attendees were seated along the sidelines. Yet we need not determine where that line exists here – how far away is too far away – because, as the photos in the record show, all of the accessible seating offered by RISD is either immediately adjacent to or in front of the bleacher seating for the general public.

However, we disagree with Greer's suggestion that any separation from the general public seating area is ipso facto discrimination and we do not agree with Greer's argument that she was denied program access at the Berkner B stadium. * * * In making these arguments, Greer attempts to completely nullify the "program access" standard of review by asserting that, based on RISD's admission that the bleachers are not accessible and therefore wheel-chair-bound visitors to Berkner B are provided alternate seating areas, RISD must prove that modifying the stadium seating would constitute an undue financial burden in order for RISD to avoid summary judgment. This however is not an accurate interpretation of the law. As an operator of an existing facility, RISD need only show that the program offered at Berkner B, when viewed in its entirety, is readily accessible to and usable by individuals with disabilities. 28 C.F.R. § 35.150(a). Thus, despite Greer's protests that RISD's repeated statements that it "is not legally obligated to provide bleacher access for a mobility-impaired individual who has designated accessible seating available in an alternate area" are incorrect, RISD's statement is a valid interpretation of the law. As an existing facility, RISD's duty is to provide program access to events at Berkner B, which may be achieved without providing access to the bleachers.

Furthermore, Greer's argument that "Keeping the disabled out of the public seating – without any justification – is a denial of program access on its face," would render the "program access" standard meaningless. Under such a reading, a public entity would be required in all cases to modify existing facilities whenever the general public seating area was not wheelchair accessible or ADAAG compliant. Yet this is precisely what the program access standard for existing facilities was meant to avoid by allowing public entities to ensure that disabled individuals can readily access the program at the facility but not necessarily all aspects of the facility itself.

* * * RISD provided sworn statements from two individuals that use wheelchairs when they attend events at Berkner B, both of whom stated that they had no issues attending events. Greer herself admitted she was able to access the parking lot, navigate into the stadium, buy a ticket, make a purchase from the concession stand, and view a portion of the game.

Nonetheless, as Greer points out, "seeing the program is the entire reason for going." Most attendees at a high school football game, particularly parents of students playing in the game, are not going to the stadium for the quality of the hot dogs at the concession stand. Thus, being able to do things such as buying a ticket and visiting the concession stand would not be sufficient to provide program access if she was unable to view the actual football game.

Even taking as true Greer's claim that she was only able to see 15% of the game from her vantage point next to the bleachers, the problem with Greer's single experience is that it appears to be, at least in part, a product of her own choices and was strongly contradicted by RISD's evidence. She acknowledges that she never asked if she could be accommodated by sitting somewhere else in the stadium, such as the track that surrounds the football field that would have provided an unobstructed view. She did not ask anyone at the stadium if her husband or friends could be accommodated by being provided chairs to sit next to her. * * *

Notes & Questions

1. Was the court correct that Greer had meaningful access to the football game "when viewed in its entirety?" For a case coming out the other way, *see* Disabled in Action of Pennsylvania v. Se. Pennsylvania Transp. Auth., 635 F.3d 87 (3d Cir. 2011) (holding that an inaccessible train station was not accessible because another connected station was accessible).

2. A Recent report by the National Disability Rights Network details rampant inaccessibility in Amtrak service. Nat'l Disability Rights Network, All Aboard (Except People with Disabilities): Amtrak's 23 Years of ADA Compliance Failure (Oct. 2013), *available at* http://dadsupport. ndrn.org/pub/NDRN_Amtrak_Report.pdf.

3. The regulations allow public entities latitude in determining how to make existing facilities meet the program access standard for existing facilities. Structural changes are not required necessarily. The regulations suggest alternatives, such as redesign of equipment, reassignment of services to accessible buildings (either permanently or on request), assignment of aids to beneficiaries, and home visits. Preference should be given to methods that offer the most integrated setting appropriate.

4. If a public entity chooses structural modifications, there are additional regulations with which the public entity must comply. These include transition plans for public entities with 50 or more employees, setting forth the steps necessary to achieve program access. 28 C.F.R. § 35.150(d)(1).

5. In facilities cases, like others, funding is always an issue. In *Bacon v. City of Richmond, Virginia*, 475 F.3d 633 (4th Cir. 2007), a group of school children with disabilities entered into a settlement agreement with their school board to make their schools more physically accessible. The agreement was contingent on the board receiving funding from the City. *Id.* at 637. When that did not happen, the plaintiffs sued the City. The court held that the city could not be ordered to provide funding for a system-wide retrofitting of city schools without a finding of fault on the part of the city.

6. The 2010 revisions to the DOJ regulations added a safe harbor provision for some existing facilities. The regulations provide that

"[E]lements that have not been altered in existing facilities on or after March 15, 2012, and that comply with the corresponding technical and scoping specifications for those elements in either the 1991 Standards or in the Uniform Federal Accessibility Standards (UFAS), Appendix A to 41 CFR part 101-19.6 (July 1, 2002 ed.), 49 FR 31528, app. A (Aug. 7, 1984) are not required to be modified in order to comply with the requirements set forth in the 2010 Standards ... [this safe harbor] does not apply to those elements in existing facilities that are subject to supplemental requirements (i.e., elements for which there are neither technical nor scoping specifications in the 1991 Standards)." 28 C.F.R. § 35.150(b)(2). These include residential facilities dwelling units, amusement rides, and golf facilities, amongst others.

༄

2. New or modified facilities

The regulations create a different set of responsibilities for public entities for construction of new facilities and alterations of existing facilities. For new construction, the regulations provide:

> Each facility or part of a facility constructed by, on behalf of, or for the use of a public entity shall be designed and constructed in such manner that the facility or part of the facility is readily accessible to and usable by individuals with disabilities, if the construction was commenced after January 26, 1992.

28 C.F.R. § 35.151(a).

> For alterations of existing facilities, the regulations provide:

> Each facility or part of a facility altered by, on behalf of, or for the use of a public entity in a manner that affects or could affect the usability of the facility or part of the facility shall, to the maximum extent feasible, be altered in such manner that the altered portion of the facility is readily accessible to and useable by individuals with disabilities, if the alteration was commended after January 26, 1992.

Id. § 35.151(b).

Construction or alteration commenced after March 15, 2012, must be according to the 2010 ADA Standards for Accessible Design (which consist of the 2004 Americans with Disabilities Act Accessibility Guidelines for Buildings and Facilities AAG and the requirements contained in revised § 35.151, which offer additional clarity on path of travel, in addition to other areas. Previously, public entities could choose between ADAAG and the Uniform Federal Accessibility Standards (UFAS).

In contrast to the regulations governing existing facilities (where entities are exempted from making fundamental alterations and bearing undue financial burdens), the regulations for new construction and alteration are more stringent. There is no "undue burden" provision, with the regulations stating facilities "shall" be accessible. The 2010 revisions clarify that there is a narrow exception for structural impracticability: "[f]ull compliance will be considered structurally impracticable only in those rare circumstances when the unique characteristics of terrain prevent the incorporation of accessibility features." 28 C.F.R. § 35.151(a)(2).

There has been litigation over what constitutes an alteration of an existing facility, thus triggering the need to comply with the accessibility standards. Consider the following case.

ൟ

KINNEY v. YERUSALIM

United States Court of Appeals, Third Circuit, 1993
9 F.3d 1067

ROTH, Circuit Judge:

This appeal requires us to determine whether 28 C.F.R. § 35.151(e)(1) (1992), issued by the Attorney General pursuant to Section 204 of the Americans with Disabilities Act (the "ADA"), 42 U.S.C. § 12134 (Supp. 1991), requires the City of Philadelphia (the "City") to install curb ramps at intersections when it resurfaces city streets. At issue is whether resurfacing constitutes an "alteration" within the scope of the regulation. The district court held that it does and ordered the City to install curb ramps on those portions of city streets for which resurfacing bids had been taken since January 26, 1992, the effective date of the ADA. On appeal, the City challenges the district court's reading of the term "alteration."

* * *

We agree with the district court's interpretation of the regulation and, consequently, we will affirm. Moreover, we agree that the applicability of the "undue burden" defense has been carefully limited to existing facilities and programs. Thus, that defense is not available in the context of alterations.

I.

Plaintiffs are Disabled in Action, a non-profit organization, and twelve individuals with ambulatory disabilities who live and work in Philadelphia. In their complaint, plaintiffs sought injunctive relief under 42 U.S.C. § 1983 (1988) for alleged violations of the ADA. These allegations were based on the City's practice of installing curb cuts only when work on the city streets otherwise affected the curb or sidewalk or when a complete reconstruction of the street was required.

413

The lack of curb cuts is a primary obstacle to the smooth integration of those with disabilities into the commerce of daily life. Without curb cuts, people with ambulatory disabilities simply cannot navigate the city; activities that are commonplace to those who are fully ambulatory become frustrating and dangerous endeavors. At present, people using wheelchairs must often make the Hobson's choice between traveling in the streets – with cars and buses and trucks and bicycles – and traveling over uncut curbs which, even when possible, may result in the wheelchair becoming stuck or overturning, with injury to both passenger and chair.

The City of Philadelphia has some 2,400 miles of streets, roads and highways. These streets typically consist of three components: a sub-base of stone, covered by a concrete base, finished with a layer of asphalt. For routine maintenance – patching, pothole repairs, and limited resurfacing – the City maintains a crew of roughly 300 people. For more extensive work, including most resurfacing, bids are solicited from outside contractors.

Resurfacing of the streets is done in a variety of ways, affecting different parts of the street structure. Resurfacing at its simplest is "paving," which consists of placing a new layer of asphalt over the old. In other instances, a more complicated process of "milling" is used to ensure proper drainage or contouring of the road. Milling requires the use of heavy machinery to remove the upper 2 to 3 1/2 inches of asphalt. During an ordinary milling and resurfacing job, cracks in the concrete base may be discovered, and, if so, repaired. The most extensive form of resurfacing is "reconstruction," which involves removal and replacement of both the asphalt and the concrete or stone layers.

Whatever the extent of work performed under a contract, the City has certain minimum requirements for resurfacing. Thus, by the City's own specifications, resurfacing requires laying at least 1 1/2 inches of new asphalt, sealing open joints and cracks, and patching depressions of more than one inch. At issue in this appeal are those resurfacings which cover, at a minimum, an entire street from intersection to intersection. Thus, we are not called upon to decide whether minor repairs or maintenance trigger the obligations of accessibility for alterations under the ADA.

At present the City does not include the installation of curb cuts in its milling and resurfacing contracts unless the curb is independently intended to be altered by the scope of the contract. Thus, only those contracts calling for alterations to curbs include curb cuts; contracts for alterations limited to the street surface itself do not.

Plaintiffs brought this class action against Alexander Hoskins, the Commissioner of the Philadelphia Streets Department, and Howard Yerusalim, the Secretary of the Pennsylvania Department of Transportation (PennDOT), to compel the installation of curb cuts on all streets resurfaced since the effective date of the ADA. After the parties filed cross-motions for summary judgment, the district court granted plaintiffs' motion, ordering the City to "install curb ramps or slopes on every City street, at any intersection having curbs or other barriers to access, where bids for resurfacing were let after January 26, 1992." *Kinney v. Yerusalim*, 812 F.Supp. 547, 553 (E.D. Pa. 1993). The City brought a timely appeal.

* * *

III.

* * *

[T]he Department of Justice issued regulations maintaining the previously established distinction between existing facilities, which are covered by 28 C.F.R. § 35.150 (1992), and new construction and alterations, which are covered by 28 C.F.R. § 35.151 (1992). With limited exceptions, the regulations do not require public entities to retrofit existing facilities immediately and completely. Rather, a flexible concept of accessibility is employed, and entities are generally excused from making fundamental alterations to existing programs and bearing undue financial burdens. 28 C.F.R. § 35.150(a) & (b) (1992). In contrast, the regulations concerning new construction and alterations are substantially more stringent. When a public entity independently decides to alter a facility, it "shall, to the maximum extent feasible, be altered in such a manner that the altered portion of the facility is readily accessible to and usable by individuals with disabilities." 28 C.F.R. § 35.151(b) (1992). This obligation of accessibility for alterations does not allow for non-compliance based upon undue burden.

Consistent with the emphasis on architectural barriers, the installation of curb cuts is specifically given priority in both the "existing facilities" and the "new constructions and alterations" sections of the regulations. Streets are considered existing facilities under the regulations, and, as such, they are subject to the more lenient provisions of § 35.150. However, because of the importance attributed to curb cuts, the regulations direct public entities to fashion a transition plan for existing facilities, containing a "schedule for providing curb ramps or other sloped areas where pedestrian walks cross curbs, giving priority to walkways serving entities covered by the Act." 28 C.F.R. § 35.150(d)(2) (1992). These changes must be completed by January 26, 1995. 28 C.F.R. § 35.150(c) (1992).

The existence of a transition plan for the installation of curb cuts on existing streets does not, however, negate the City's obligations under § 35.151, governing alterations. In addition to the general provision in subpart (b), § 35.151 has a second subpart addressed solely to the installation of curb ramps. This subpart provides that when a public entity undertakes to construct new streets or to alter existing ones, it shall take that opportunity to install curb ramps.

Newly constructed or altered streets, roads, and highways must contain curb ramps or other sloped areas at any intersection having curbs or other barriers to entry from a street level pedestrian walkway. 28 C.F.R. § 35.151(e) (1992). The City does not dispute the literal requirement that the regulation mandates the installation of curb cuts when the City "alters" a street. The City does, however, protest the notion that the resurfacing of a street constitutes an "alteration."

Subpart (e) does not explicitly define "alteration," either in general or as applied in particular instances. Our focus here is the specific application of the general provision in subpart (b) (alterations to existing facilities) to one subject in subpart (e) (streets). We will look first to subpart (b) for guidance:

> Alteration. Each facility or part of a facility altered by, on behalf of, or for the use of a public entity in a manner that affects or could affect the usability of the facility or part of the facility shall, to the maximum extent feasible, be altered in such a manner that the altered portion of the facility is readily accessible to and usable by individuals with disabilities, if the alteration was commenced after January 26, 1992.

28 C.F.R. § 35.151(b) (1992). In addition, subpart (c) provides that alterations made in conformity with the Americans with Disabilities Act Accessibility Guidelines for Buildings and Facilities (the "ADAAG") or with the Uniform Federal Accessibility Standards (the "UFAS") shall be deemed to comply with the requirements of this section. Both guidelines provide technical and engineering specifications. The ADAAG definition of "alteration" is substantially the same as that in the regulation: "a change to a building or facility . . . that affects or could affect the usability of the building or facility or part thereof." 28 C.F.R. pt. 36 app. A. It continues: "[n]ormal maintenance . . . [is] not [an] alteration[ ] unless [it] affect[s] the usability of the building or facility." Id.

These provisions lead one to the conclusion that an "alteration" within the meaning of the regulations is a change that affects the usability of the facility involved. If we then read the "affects usability" definition into subpart (e), the regulation serves the substantive purpose of requiring equal treatment: if an alteration renders a street more "usable" to those presently using it, such increased utility must also be made fully accessible to the disabled through the installation of curb ramps.

Subpart (e) effectively unifies a street and its curbs for treatment as interdependent facilities. If a street is to be altered to make it more usable for the general public, it must also be made more usable for those with ambulatory disabilities. At the time that the City determines that funds will be expended to alter the street, the City is also required to modify the curbs so that they are no longer a barrier to the usability of the streets by the disabled. This interpretation helps to implement the legislative vision, for Congress felt that it was discriminatory to the disabled to enhance or improve an existing facility without making it fully accessible to those previously excluded.

* * *

Thus, while Congress chose not to mandate full accessibility to existing facilities, it required that subsequent changes to a facility be undertaken in a non-discriminatory manner. The use of such changes must be made available to all. The emphasis on equal treatment is furthered, as well, by an expansive, remedial construction of the term "usability." "Usability should be broadly defined to include renovations which affect the use of a facility, and not simply changes which relate directly to access." H. Rep. No. 485, 101st Cong., 2d Sess., pt. 3, at 64 (1990), reprinted in 1990 U.S.C.C.A.N. 445, 487.

With this directive, we must now determine whether resurfacing a street affects its usability. Both physically and functionally, a street consists of its surface; from a utilitarian perspective, a street is a two-dimensional, one-plane facility. As intended, a street facilitates smooth, safe, and efficient travel of vehicles and pedestrians – in the language above, this is its "primary function."

As such, we can only agree with the district court that resurfacing a street affects it in ways integral to its purpose. As discussed above, "resurfacing" involves more than minor repairs or maintenance. At a minimum, it requires the laying of a new asphalt bed spanning the length and width of a city block. The work is substantial, with substantial effect. As the district court described in its opinion granting plaintiffs' motion for summary judgment:

> Resurfacing makes driving on and crossing streets easier and safer. It also helps to prevent damage to vehicles and injury to people, and generally promotes commerce and travel. The surface of a street is the part of the street that is "used" by both pedestrians and vehicular traffic. When that surface is improved, the street becomes more usable in a fundamental way.

Kinney, 812 F.Supp. at 551.

* * *

V.

For the foregoing reasons, we find that resurfacing of the city streets is an alteration within the meaning of 28 C.F.R. § 35.151(b) which must be accompanied by the installation of curb cuts under 28 C.F.R. § 35.151(e). We will affirm the decision of the district court.

Notes & Questions

1. What test do the regulations set forth for whether modifications affect the usability of a facility? How does the *Kinney* court treat these regulations?

2. In *Disabled in Action of Pennsylvania v. Se. Pennsylvania Transp. Auth.*, 635 F.3d 87 (3d Cir. 2011), the court elaborated on its decision in *Kinney*. The case involved claims against the Southeastern Pennsylvania Transportation Authority (SEPTA) for not making three subway stations accessible to wheelchair users when they undertook extensive repairs to a staircase at one station and an escalator at another. Rejecting SEPTA's argument that these were not major structural renovations, the court held that the construction at subway stations constituted "alterations" within meaning of ADA, and, as a matter of first impression, the phrase "maximum extent feasible," referred to technical, rather than economic, feasibility

3. *Civic Association of the Deaf of New York City, Inc. v. Giuliani*, 970 F.Supp. 352, 359 (S.D.N.Y. 1997), had a similar result to *Kinney*. The court held that changing over from one emergency call box system to another constituted an alteration of public facilities. But in *Molloy v. Metropolitan Transportation Authority*, 94 F.3d 808, 811-12 (2d Cir. 1996), the Second Circuit held that a staff reduction plan, whereby human ticket clerks were replaced with ticket vending machines, was not an "alteration" within the meaning of Title II's transportation regulations.

4. As discussed above, voting has been an important area of litigation under Title II. The facilities aspect of this was addressed in *Am. Ass'n of People with Disabilities v. Harris*, 647 F.3d 1093 (11th Cir. 2011). Following the 2000 election, Florida implemented new optical scanning voter machines. Plaintiffs alleged that new machines were inaccessible in that some individuals with manual and visual impairments could not vote without third party assistance and that change in machine was an alteration to a Title II facility. The Eleventh Circuit held that the voting machines were not facilities because only permanent, physical structures and the fixed items attached to those structures are facilities that may be altered under Title II.

℘

E. *Effective Communication*

Like the program access standard, Title II's communications provisions have a statutory and regulatory component. Title II's definition of qualified person with a disability links the "provision of auxiliary aids and services" to the concept of reasonable accommodations. The Title II regulations have a separate section devoted to "Communication," which makes clear that communication is an integral part of a public entity's responsibilities under Title II.

Title II's communication regulations and the case law interpreting them stand for the proposition that a public entity must offer *effective* communication alternatives. The "General" provision in the regulations dealing with communications states: "A public entity shall take appropriate steps to ensure that communications with applicants, participants, and members of the public with disabilities are as effective as communications with others." 28 C.F.R. § 35.160(a) (2008). Most cases involve the question of exactly how effective a communication alternative has to be.

৯

DUFFY v. RIVELAND

United States Court of Appeals, Ninth Circuit, 1996
98 F.3d 447

POOLE, Circuit Judge:

* * *

II. BACKGROUND

The facts of this case are relatively straightforward and undisputed. Sean Duffy is a hearing-impaired inmate at the Washington State Reformatory (WSR) in Monroe, Washington. He has been incarcerated since 1983. Although Duffy is hearing-impaired, he can read and write, and frequently communicates with others through an exchange of written notes. However, he communicates most effectively with the assistance of an interpreter.

A. The Disciplinary Hearing

On July 23, 1992, Duffy was charged by a corrections officer with indecent exposure under Washington Administrative Code § 137-28-030(507) and Revised Criminal Code of Washington Chapter 9A.88.010(1). WSR officials placed Duffy in the segregation unit following the incident. The next day, Officer Jerry Sorenson attempted to serve Duffy with a notice of the infraction and the upcoming disciplinary hearing, but he refused to accept it.

The disciplinary hearing was originally scheduled for July 24, 1992. However, because of the serious nature of the infraction, WSR officials continued the matter so that an interpreter could be secured for Duffy.

On July 28, 1992, Duffy again refused service of the infraction papers and notice of the hearing. That same day, WSR's Disciplinary Court Clerk Peggy Williams arranged for a meeting between Duffy and Frances Linder, a mental health counselor at a different state correctional facility, who apparently knows some sign language. Linder learned how to sign through experiences with her hearing-impaired parents. At all times relevant to these proceedings, Linder had no formal training in sign language, nor was she certified by the Registry of Interpreters for the Deaf (RID). However, Williams hoped that Linder would be able to assist them by serving Duffy with the notice of the hearing and the infraction.

Duffy was escorted from the segregation unit to meet with Williams and Linder. However, as soon as Duffy saw Linder, he refused to enter the office where she sat, went directly to Sorenson's office, and wrote, "I request an (sic) qualified interpreter for this hearing." Duffy testified in his deposition that he did not know the nature of the meeting on the 28th with Linder, and he apparently assumed that it was the actual hearing.

Linder had provided services as an interpreter in several previous hearings at WSR. She had even attended an earlier disciplinary hearing involving Duffy to serve as his interpreter. However, this hearing was related to a minor infraction and, according to Duffy, the charges were dismissed largely because of the documentary evidence that he was able to provide. Duffy also testified that based on his prior experience with Linder, however, his ability to communicate with her was "not one hundred percent."

After Duffy refused to meet with Linder on the 28th, Williams sought counsel from the State Attorney General's Office regarding Duffy's refusal to accept service. She was advised that under Washington law the hearing could be held in his absence if he refused to attend.

Williams then wrote Duffy a memorandum advising him that his hearing was scheduled for July 30, 1992, if he wished to attend. The memorandum also explicitly stated that the hearing would be conducted without an interpreter. Despite Duffy's earlier recalcitrance, Officer Christopher Gerstbrein finally completed service of all papers-including the disciplinary infraction report and Williams' memo-on the morning of July 29th. At that point, the following written exchange occurred between Gerstbrein and Duffy:

Gerstbrein: Do you want to attend your hearing?

Duffy: No. Without an (sic) qualified interpreter present, I refused (sic) to attend a hearing.

Gerstbrein: Is Francis (sic) Linder qualified?

Duffy: No. She's a correctional officer and she hasn't registered with the RID (Registry of Interpreter [sic] for the Deaf) so she's not an interpreter under the law.

* * *

Gerstbrein: I'll talk to the hearing officer about this. Do you know anyone who is qualified?

Duffy shook his head no to Gerstbrein's final inquiry.

On the morning of July 30th, Duffy attracted the attention of another corrections officer. He gestured for a pen and paper, then wrote, "What happened to the hearing at 9: 00 a.m.?" Duffy also showed the officer the Hearing Notice/Appearance Waiver Form that Gerstbrein had served the previous day. After reading Duffy's note and the hearing notice, the officer responded in writing "Sometimes they run late. But I'll check on it." Sometime later, the officer returned and passed Duffy a note indicating that the WSR officials were still "looking for a signer."

The disciplinary hearing took place, however, in Duffy's absence on July 30, 1992, and he was found guilty of the infraction. Duffy was sentenced to 15 days in disciplinary segregation, with credit for the eight days already served.

Based on these events, Duffy filed a pro se civil action seeking declaratory and monetary relief under the ADA, RA, § 1983 and Washington State law. By order dated January 28, 1994, the district court granted summary judgment to the defendants on all Duffy's claims. Duffy filed a timely notice of appeal on February 15, 1994.

B. The Classification Hearings

Classification hearings are held approximately every six months in Washington prisons by the Department of Corrections in order to discuss issues of programming with the inmates. Since his original incarceration, Duffy had attended these meetings and participated through written communications.

On September 25, 1992, Duffy was notified about an upcoming classification meeting, and again he requested a "qualified interpreter." Duffy's classification counselor offered the services of Frances Linder but, again, Duffy refused. The classification counselor did, however, offer to provide a certified interpreter at Duffy's eventual parole hearing.

Duffy subsequently refused to attend his classification hearing scheduled for October 28, 1992, as well as his next hearing, scheduled for March 3, 1993. Duffy was reviewed in absentia, and was denied "camp and pre-release placement."

On May 4, 1994, Duffy filed his second pro se civil suit, again seeking declaratory and monetary relief, based on the denial of his request for an interpreter at his classification hearings. Again, the district court granted summary judgment to the defendants on all Duffy's claims by order dated April 19, 1994. Duffy filed his timely notice of appeal on April 28, 1994.

* * *

IV. ANALYSIS

* * *

D. Duffy's ADA Claims

* * *

Duffy's principal argument is that the Appellees were implicitly required under the ADA to honor his requests for a RID-certified interpreter at his hearings. Without such an interpreter, Duffy argues, he was discriminated against due to his disability because he would be unable to communicate effectively.

Duffy's argument regarding the certification requirement of a "qualified interpreter" is based largely on 28 C.F.R. Part 35 App. A, Subpart E, § 35.160, which focuses on the complexity and importance of the proceedings, and 28 C.F.R. § 35.160(b)(2), which requires public entities to "give primary consideration to the requests of the individual with disabilities" in determining "what type of auxiliary aid and service is necessary."

Duffy alleges that the requirement that an interpreter be certified is implicit in the ADA's definition of a "qualified interpreter." See 28 C.F.R. § 35.104 ("Qualified interpreter means an interpreter who is able to interpret effectively, accurately, and impartially, both receptively and expressively, using any necessary specialized vocabulary."). He cites several district court decisions from other circuits as support for this proposition. See, e.g., *Clarkson v. Coughlin*, 145 F.R.D. 339, 341 (S.D.N.Y.1993)("A qualified sign language interpreter is one who has obtained certification from the National Registry of Interpreters for the Deaf. . . ."); *DeLong v. Brumbaugh*, 703 F.Supp. 399, 403 (W.D.Pa.1989)("[q]ualified interpreters are available from the Registry of Interpreters for the Deaf, Inc., ..."); *Pyles v. Kamka*, 491 F.Supp. 204, 205 (D.Md.1980)(approving consent decree in which prison officials agreed that "an interpreter shall be deemed qualified if he/she is certified by the National Registry of Interpreters for the Deaf").

However, we cannot agree that, as a matter of law, the ADA regulations require an interpreter to be certified by the RID. The appendix of the DOJ's implementing regulations contains the extensive discussion of the definition of "qualified interpreter" that Duffy cites. The DOJ recognized the concerns of many commentators that, absent a clear definition of the phrase, "qualified interpreter" would be interpreted to mean any "available interpreter."

The definition promulgated by the DOJ "focuses on the actual ability of the interpreter in a particular interpreting context to facilitate effective communication between the public entity and the individual with disabilities." 28 C.F.R. Part 35, App. A. However, the DOJ did not go so far as to suggest that the definition of "qualified interpreter" requires formal certification. That restraint is evident in the statement that the definition "does not invalidate or limit standards . . . of any State or local law that are equal to or more stringent . . . [nor] supersede any requirement of State law for use of a certified interpreter in court proceedings." Id.

However, based on the definition of qualified interpreter under the ADA, we conclude that Duffy has raised a significant factual issue as to whether Linder is a qualified interpreter. In addition to his earlier complaint to Appellee Riveland, Duffy maintained in his deposition that Linder "signed in a different way and not related to my signs and some of her signs I did not understand." Duffy also stated that Linder also "interrupted" and "would removed (sic) herself from the role of interpreter."

It is undisputed that Linder had no formal training in sign language and is not a professional interpreter. Instead, she is a correctional mental health counselor, employed by the Washington State Department of Corrections, who learned how to sign through her relationship with her parents. These facts give rise to issues regarding the accuracy of her signing and her ability to be impartial-both of which are material to the definition of "qualified interpreter" as provided in the ADA regulations.

Appellees argue that the ADA regulations are "flexible" and permit the use of written communications between deaf inmates and prison officials in proceedings of this nature instead of a qualified interpreter. Appellees rely on the same discussion of the requirements for qualified interpreters contained in Appendix Part 35, specifically the comments that:

> Although in some circumstances a notepad and written materials may be sufficient to permit effective communication, in other circumstances they may not be sufficient. For example, a qualified interpreter may be necessary when the information being communicated is complex, or is exchanged for a lengthy period of time. Generally, factors to be considered in determining whether an interpreter is required include the context in which the communication is taking place, the number of people involved, and the importance of the communication.

Appellees argue further that the disciplinary proceeding, in particular, was not a complicated matter. However, at the very least, this presents another factual issue that is more properly resolved in the district court.

We therefore reverse both district courts' grants of summary judgment for the Appellees on Duffy's ADA claims, so that these issues may be properly addressed by a fact-finder.

* * *

V. CONCLUSIONS

We reverse the district court's dismissal of Duffy's ADA and RA claims against the WSR and Department of Corrections on the ground of Eleventh Amendment immunity. Because Duffy has raised genuine issues of material fact as to Linder's qualifications, and his ability to communicate effectively with her, we reverse both district courts' grants of summary judgment to Appellees on Duffy's ADA and RA claims, and remand for further proceedings.

Notes & Questions

1. Consider the following hypothetical: Two individuals with hearing-impairments want to get married in a municipal court. They request that the city provide a sign language interpreter at their wedding so that they might understand the marriage proceedings. The city refuses. What result? What other information would you want to know? *See* Soto v. City of Newark, 72 F.Supp.2d 489 (D.N.J. 1999) (holding city failed to provide an effective means of communication).

2. The regulations provide that auxiliary aids and services be furnished when necessary to afford an individual with a disability (including applicants, participants, companions, and members of the public) an equal opportunity to participate in and enjoy the programs, services, or activities of the public entity. 28 C.F.R. § 35.160(b)(1). The effective communication obligation is owed to people with hearing, speech, vision and print disabilities. In terms of types of auxiliary aids and services, a public entity is to "give primary consideration to the requests of the individual with disabilities." *Id.* at § 35.160(b)(2). Auxiliary aids and services for people with hearing impairments include qualified interpreters, notetakers, written materials, amplifiers, captioning, TTYs and others. *Id.* at § 35.104(a). For people with vision and print impairments they include qualified readers, taped text, Braille, large print, assistance locating items, and others. *Id.* at § 35.104(b). For people with speech disabilities they include TTDs, computer terminals, speech synthesizers, communication boards, and others. The regulations provide that a public entity does not need to take any action that it can demonstrate would result in a fundamental alteration or an undue financial and administrative burden. *Id.* at § 35.164. As mentioned, the public entity has the burden of proving undue burden or fundamental alteration, and the decision must be made by the head of the public agency in writing.

3. Does "effective" mean equal? Imagine that a prisoner with hearing and speech impairments brings a Title II claim, arguing that other prisoners get unlimited use of public telephones, while he is forced to use a TDD telephone in a special office in limited intervals. What result? *See* Spurlock v. Simmons, 88 F.Supp.2d 1189, 1192 (D. Kan. 2000) (holding that prisoner's access was "meaningful," and therefore there was no ADA violation). *See also* Loye v. County of Dakota, 625 F.3d 494 (8th

Cir. 2010) (holding that interpreters being present at most, but not all, community meetings dealing with decontamination proceedings, constituted effective communication).

4. What is "meaningful" often turns on circumstances and practical realities. This often comes up in encounters individuals with disabilities have with law enforcement. In *Bircoll v. Miami-Dade County*, 480 F.3d 1072, 1087 (11th Cir. 2007), in holding that a police department had effectively accommodated a deaf inmate, the court had occasion to discuss "what steps are reasonably necessary to establish effective communication with a hearing-impaired person after a DUI arrest. . . ." These included the abilities of and the usual and preferred method of communication used by the arrestee, the nature of the criminal activity involved and the importance and complexity of the police communication at issue, the location of the communication, and whether the arrestee's requested method of communication would impose an undue burden or fundamental change. *Folkerts v. City of Waverly, Iowa*, 707 F.3d 975 (8th Cir. 2013), involved a police interrogation of a criminal suspect with an intellectual disability. The suspect later sued under Title II, claiming that interrogator had not evaluated his level of function, did not have his guardians present during questioning, and that the aggressive questioning did not allow him to effectively communicate. The Eight Circuit affirmed the district court's granting of defendants' summary judgment motion, holding that the interrogator's modifications, including an alteration of questioning style and moving the interview to a less intimidating room, created circumstances for effective communication. *See also* Seremeth v. Bd. of County Com'rs Frederick County, 673 F.3d 333, 337 (4th Cir. 2012) (handcuffing of Deaf father during suspected domestic child abuse investigation, which limited his ability to communicate via ASL, did not violate ADA because "[w]hile police investigations are subject to the ADA's framework, the exigent circumstances involved in a suspected domestic violence situation render the accommodations provided reasonable under the ADA.").

5. Another issue involves the scope of a public entity's responsibility to make the particular requested communication accommodation. Generally, provided the accommodation that is offered is effective, courts have not been swayed by a request for a specific type of accommodation. For example, in *Petersen v. Hastings Public Schools*, 31 F.3d 705 (8th Cir. 1994), plaintiffs with hearing impairments brought a Title II claim challenging the school district's decision to educate students by use of a sign language system that was different than that used in their homes. The Eighth Circuit, while noting that the regulations provide that primary consideration be given to the expressed accommodation choice made by the person with a disability, nevertheless held that the sign language system that was employed was an "effective" means of communication, and that there was no ADA violation. *Id.* at 709. *See also* Dobard v. S.F. Bay Area Rapid Transit Dist., No. C-92-3563-DLJ, 1993

WL 372256, at *1 (N.D. Cal. Sept. 7, 1993) (refusing plaintiff's request of a computer aided transcription auxiliary aid so that he could participate fully in a BART board meeting).

6. The 2010 revised regulations offer additional guidance on auxiliary aids and services, providing that the term includes "[q]ualified interpreters on-site or through video remote interpreting (VRI) services; notetakers; real-time computer-aided transcription services; written materials; exchange of written notes; telephone handset amplifiers; assistive listening devices; assistive listening systems; telephones compatible with hearing aids; closed caption decoders; open and closed captioning, including real-time captioning; voice, text, and video-based telecommunications products and systems, including text telephones (TTYs), videophones, and captioned telephones, or equally effective telecommunications devices; videotext displays; accessible electronic and information technology; or other effective methods of making aurally delivered information available to individuals who are deaf or hard of hearing; Qualified readers; taped texts; audio recordings; Brailled materials and displays; screen reader software; magnification software; optical readers; secondary auditory programs (SAP); large print materials; accessible electronic and information technology; or other effective methods of making visually delivered materials available to individuals who are blind or have low vision." 28 C.F.R. § 104. The revised regulations also clarified that public entities cannot require an individual with a disability to bring another individual to interpret for him or her.

F.   *Transportation*

Title II has a separate part dedicated to nondiscrimination in transportation provided by public entities. Transportation was an area where the ADA's framers recognized an existing pattern of discrimination and inequity.

The ADA explicitly states that "[d]iscrimination against individuals with disabilities persists in such critical areas as . . . transportation" and "[i]ndividuals with disabilities continually encounter various forms of discrimination, including . . . transportation . . . barriers." 42 U.S.C. §§ 12101(a)(3), (a)(5) (2006). The debates on ADA passage suggest that the framers viewed transportation as crucial in unlocking other opportunities that the ADA would help create. *See* S. Rep. No. 101-116, at 11 (1989); 135 Cong. Rec. S10792 (daily ed. Sept. 7, 1989) (statement of Sen. Biden) ("Too many persons with impaired mobility have been blocked from taking part in a variety of opportunities, because simple physical access has not been provided."); *see also* 136 Cong. Rec. H2438 (daily ed. May 17, 1990) (statement of Rep. Mineta) ("[D]isabled Americans are ready, willing and able, to use their talents, skills, and energy in communities across the country; but today many wait for full access to our transportation systems.").

Public transportation is especially important to people with disabilities because the evidence suggests that they are more reliant on public transportation than the general population. The legal and policy tensions specific to transportation issues are a microcosm of the entire Act. These issues include mainstreaming of existing transportation to accommodate people with disabilities versus paratransit (i.e., transportation services usually performed by vans that are provided separate from mass transit's normal operations), and whether there should be a "threshold" or "necessary" level of spending on mass transportation options for people with disabilities.

1.   Pre-ADA statutes and regulations

As with the rest of the ADA, the law's transportation provisions were not drawn on a blank slate. There is a history of federal legislation aimed at improving public transportation options and accessibility for people with disabilities. One court dubbed the pre-ADA federal statutory and regulatory scheme a "welter of statutory provisions." *See* Ams. Disabled for Accessible Pub. Transp. v. Skinner, 881 F.2d 1184, 1186 (3d Cir. 1989). For an extensive discussion of the pre-ADA statutes and regulations, *see* Blanck, et al., Disability Civil Rights Law & Policy, at ch. 11 (2004).

2.   ADA transportation provisions

Title II has an entire part dedicated to discrimination in public transportation. *See* Title II, Part B, "Actions Applicable to Public Transportation Provided by Public Entities Considered Discriminatory." 42 U.S.C. §§ 12141-12165 (2006). This evidences recognition by Congress of the importance of transportation to achieve the ADA's other goals, and of the history of overbroad and under-enforced transportation statutes discussed above.

The Act's transportation provisions generally should be thought of as an explanation of how public entities must comply with Title II's general discrimination prohibition in their capacity as providers of public transportation. There are jurisdictional divisions, however, in terms of regulations. For example, in *Boose v. Tri-County Metro. Transp. Dist. of Oregon,* 587 F.3d 997 (9th Cir. 2009), citing Title II's general reasonable modification regulation, 28.C.F.R. § 35.130(b)(7) (promulgated by the DOJ), plaintiff argued that defendant public entity should be required to make a reasonable modification to its paratransit system. The Ninth Circuit held that only the Department of Transportation has authority to promulgate regulations pursuant to Part B of Title II, and therefore 28 C.F.R. § 35.130(b)(7) did not apply.

a.   *Subpart I – trains, cabs, buses, and other paratransit*

The first "subpart" of Title II's transportation provisions covers "public transportation other than by aircraft or certain rail operations."

This excludes air travel, which is covered by the Air Carrier Access Act, 49 U.S.C. § 41705 (2006), and "intercity and commuter rail" operations, which are covered in the second transportation subpart. This subpart covers fixed route systems (e.g., buses and rails that run on fixed schedules), paratransit, and demand response systems (e.g., any system, such as taxicab service, that is not a fixed route).

i. Fixed route systems

This Part of the ADA has two main sections. Section 12142 deals with accessibility of "fixed route systems," which are defined elsewhere as "a system of providing designated public transportation on which a vehicle is operated along a prescribed route according to a fixed schedule." 42 U.S.C. § 12141(3). This may be buses or rails that run on regular schedules. Section 12143 deals with accessibility for paratransit as a complement to fixed route systems.

How accessible does service have to be? In one case, *Midgett v. Tri County Metropolitan Transportation District*, 254 F.3d 846 (9th Cir. 2001), plaintiff met with three bus lifts with varying degrees of malfunction, all on one particularly cold day. The court declined to grant plaintiff an injunction that would require the transportation provider to modify its policies, reasoning that "[p]laintiff's evidence establishes several frustrating, but isolated, instances of malfunctioning lift service on Tri-Met. The evidence also shows that, unfortunately, a few individual Tri-Met operators have not treated passengers as they are required and are trained to so. Under the regulations, these occasional problems do not, without more, establish violations of the ADA." *Id.* at 850.

Notes & Questions

1. Who can bring a lawsuit under the ADA's transportation provisions? Specifically, can testers, who may not ride a city's fixed-route bus system on a regular basis, have standing to challenge ADA non-compliance? *See* Tandy v. City of Wichita, 380 F.3d 1277 (10th Cir. 2004) (holding that tester standing exists under Title II of the ADA).

2. Under 42 U.S.C. § 12142 (2006), transit systems must purchase and lease vehicles (buses, rapid rail vehicles, and other vehicles) that are "readily accessible to and usable by individuals with disabilities, including individuals who use wheelchairs." Otherwise, they have discriminated. Transit systems may not purchase and lease used vehicles that are inaccessible unless they have demonstrated "good faith efforts" to purchase or lease a used accessible vehicle. Again, failure to do so constitutes discrimination. It also is discriminatory for transit systems to "remanufacture" (i.e., extend a vehicle's usable life for 5 years or more) without, to the maximum extent possible, making the vehicle readily accessible to and usable by people with disabilities. The same applies to

the purchase or lease of remanufactured vehicles. There is an exception for historic vehicles. *Id.* at § 12142(c)(2).

3. Section 12143 deals with accessibility for paratransit as a complement to fixed route systems. The general rule is that it is considered discrimination for a public entity that operates a fixed route system (i.e., other than a system which provides solely commuter bus service) to fail to provide paratransit and other special transportation services to individuals with disabilities, including individuals who use wheelchairs. The level of service must be one which:

(1)   is comparable to the level of designated public transportation services provided to individuals without disabilities using such system; or

(2)   in the case of response time, is comparable, to the extent practicable, to the level of designated public transportation services provided to individuals without disabilities using such system.

Id. § 12143(a).

This section provides the Secretary of Transportation specific directives on issuing regulations. In accordance with these directives, the regulations require public entities to provide paratransit to individuals with disabilities whether or not they need the assistance of other people to use paratransit, and to one other individual to ride with the person with a disability (and for additional people if this will not take space away from other people with disabilities).

4. The regulations provide an undue financial burden defense for public entities. *Id.* § 12143(c)(4). Also, under the regulations each public entity that operates a fixed route system, after holding a public hearing, must submit a plan to the Secretary of Transportation, which is to be updated annually to ensure compliance with services. *Id.* § 12143(c)(7). Failure to abide by these regulations constitutes discrimination. 42 U.S.C. § 12143(e).

৯৹

ii.   Demand responsive systems

Section 12144 takes a similar approach for "demand response systems," which are defined in § 12141 as "any system of providing designated public transportation which is not a fixed route system." An example would be a city-owned taxi-cab service.

This section provides that a public entity operating a demand responsive system must buy or lease only accessible vehicles. Otherwise, they have discriminated. The exception is when the demand responsive system, when viewed in its entirety, "provides a level of service to such individuals [with disabilities] equivalent to the level of service such system provides to individuals without disabilities." *Id.* § 12144. There is no paratransit requirement for demand responsive systems.

In *Noel v. New York City Taxi & Limousine Comm'n*, 837 F.Supp.2d 268 (S.D.N.Y. 2011), the district court found that the New York City Taxi and Limousine Commission was a demand responsive system, but held it was not subject to Part B of Title II because it did not operate the system. It did hold, however, that it did have to comply with the general prohibition on discrimination in Part A of Title II. The Second Circuit vacated and remanded, holding that the Commission's control over the private taxi industry does not make it "a 'program or activity' of a public entity." *Noel*, 687 F.3d at 72.

iii. Transportation facilities

The facilities modification issue, discussed above, has a statutory basis as far as transportation facilities. Similar to the regulations promulgated under the first part of Title II, the statute provides different standards for new and existing transportation facilities.

It is discriminatory to construct a new facility "unless such facility is readily accessible to and usable by individuals with disabilities, including individuals who use wheelchairs." *Id.* § 12146. Altered areas also must be accessible and entities must spend additional money on making the path of travel to the altered area accessible if it is a primary function area. 49 C.F.R. § 37.43 (2008). Moreover, public entities discriminate if they make alterations to public transit facilities in a manner that does not, to the maximum extent feasible, make the altered portions of the facilities useable and readily accessible to people with disabilities. 42 U.S.C. § 12147.

Section 12148 provides that transportation programs and activities operated in existing facilities must be conducted so that, when viewed in their entirety, the program or activity is readily accessible to and usable by individuals with disabilities. *Id.* § 12148. The exception is that public entities are not required to make structural changes in order to make existing facilities accessible to individuals who use wheelchairs, unless they would be required to do so under § 12147(a) or (b). *Id.*; *see also* 49 C.F.R. § 37.61. Section 12148 sets forth a "one car per train rule": if a light or rapid rail system has two or more vehicles, at least one vehicle per train must be accessible. 42 U.S.C. § 12148. There is an exception for historic trains. *Id.* § 12148(b)(1).

b. *Subpart II – intercity and commuter rail*

The second "subpart" of the ADA's transportation provisions covers rail service that is dedicated to commuters and that runs between cities. *Id.* § 12161. Like subpart I, the statute details specific acts that are "discriminatory," and many of these prohibited acts echo the first subpart.

Commuter service and intercity rail are required to provide one accessible car per train, and public entities operating such systems must purchase accessible new cars to meet that standard. *Id.* §§ 12162 (a)(1), a(2)(A), (b)(1), b(2)(A). For commuter service and intercity rail, the statute goes into detail as to what is required (i.e., so as not to be discriminatory) in each car. This includes entrance, exit, and restroom accessibility for single level passenger coaches for individuals who use wheelchairs, *id.* §§ 12162 (a)(2)(B), b(2)(B); rules for single level and bi-level dining cars, *id.* §§ 12162(a)(2)(C)-(D), (a)(4); required wheelchair spaces and storage facilities for single level cars, *id.* § 12162(a)(3) (2000); "remanufactured" cars, *id.* § 12162(d); and station accessibility, *id.* § 12162(e).

෧

Notes & Questions

1. In *Wray v. National Railroad Passenger Corp.*, 10 F.Supp.2d 1036 (E.D. Wis. 1998), two disabled passengers brought suit against Amtrak. These passengers had attempted to sit in a wheelchair accessible Amtrak train, but were removed from their seats to make room for other disabled passengers who had reserved their disabled-accessible seats beforehand. The court held for Amtrak, reasoning that the ADA did not grant plaintiffs a right to sit in the disabled section when there were other disabled passengers who had made advance reservations. Although the court pointed out that the one-car-per-train rule "might be worthy of review" because it does not address the number of seats which must be accessible, the court held that Amtrak's reservation system was a reasonable response to the problem of excess demand. *Id.* at 1040.

2. As a final reflection on the ADA's transportation provision, consider how it represents a different approach than the rest of the ADA. The ADA's transportation provisions are some of the most, if not the most, detailed in the statute. At no other point in the statute do we see explicit provisions of comparable specificity: bathroom accessibility in station cars, provisions for types of eating facilities in rail cars, and so on. Also, nowhere else does the statute spell out so precisely what constitutes discrimination. This is, at least in part, an explicit recognition on the part of the framers of the crucial nature of transportation. This specificity should be judged against the backdrop of the pre-ADA transportation related statutes, whose failure had been attributed to a lack of clear guidance. *See* ADAPT v. Skinner, 881 F.2d 1184, 1186 (3d Cir. 1989). Has this specificity helped? To be sure, there are fewer reported cases dealing with public transportation than the rest of Title II, and most of the ADA. However, some suggest that the ADA's transportation provisions fail to adequately protect the transportation needs of the disabled. *See* Nat'l Disability Rights Network, All Aboard (Except People with Disabilities): Amtrak's 23 Years of ADA Compliance Failure (Oct. 2013), *available at* http://dadsupport.ndrn.org/pub/NDRN_Amtrak_Report.pdf; Michael Lewyn, "Thou Shalt Not Put a Stumbling Block Before the Blind":

The Americans with Disabilities Act and Public Transportation for the Disabled, 52 Hastings L. J. 1037, 1064 (2001). Nevertheless, it is inescapable that the ADA's transportation provisions provide public entities more guidance than operators of other public functions like voting and public education. It is worth keeping in mind this principle as future modifications and amendments to the ADA are debated and adopted.

3. There is evidence that inadequate and inaccessible transportation services and facilities continue to pose one of the greatest barriers to increasing employment rates for persons with disabilities. *See* Ruben Castaneda, Md., Disabled Commuters Settle Suit, Wash. Post, Dec. 28, 2005, at B4 (spokesperson for the Maryland Department of Disabilities "said 60 to 70 percent of the state's disabled people are unemployed, and transportation problems prevent many of them from finding or keeping jobs"). Accessible buses have increased from 36% to 91% since 1989. Report: Transport Fails to Serve Disabled, USA Today, June 13, 2005. Nonetheless, bus drivers forget to announce stops (essential information for passengers who are blind or visually impaired); bus drivers can be reluctant to stop for a passenger using a wheelchair for fear the bus will fall behind schedule; and "[w]heelchairs can get stuck in the wide spaces between platforms and trains." *Id.* Finally, there are major shortcomings in transportation services for persons with disabilities living in rural areas or in need of paratransit. *Id.*

&

§ 13.5 By Reason Of Disability – Intentional Discrimination Versus Disparate Impact

Title II's discrimination provision provides that "no qualified individual with a disability shall, *by reason of such disability*, be excluded from participation in or be denied the benefits of services, programs, or activities of the public entity, or be subjected to discrimination by any such entity." 42 U.S.C. § 12132 (2006) (emphasis added). Does this impute an "intentional discrimination" standard on Title II claims, analogous to claims under the Equal Protection Clause of the Fourteenth Amendment?

Generally not. In one case, the Third Circuit addressed the issue as follows:

> Because the ADA evolved from an attempt to remedy the effects of "benign neglect" resulting from the "invisibility" of the disabled, Congress could not have intended to limit the Act's protections and prohibitions to circumstances involving deliberate discrimination. Such discrimination arises from "affirmative animus" which was not the focus of the ADA or section 504. The Supreme Court elaborates upon this distinction noting that, although discrimination against the disabled normally results from "thoughtless-

ness" and "indifference," not "invidious animus", such "animus" did exist. 469 U.S. at 295 n.12. ("To be sure, well-cataloged instances of invidious discrimination against the handicapped do exist"). However, that was not the focus of section 504, or the ADA. Rather, the ADA attempts to eliminate the effects of that "benign neglect," "apathy," and "indifference." The 504 coordination regulations, and the ADA "make clear that the unnecessary segregation of individuals with disabilities in the provision of public services is itself a form of discrimination within the meaning of those statutes, independent of the discrimination that arises when individuals with disabilities receive different services than those provided to individuals without disabilities."

Helen L. v. DiDario, 46 F.3d 325, 335 (3d Cir. 1995).

Similarly, in the *Olmstead* case, discussed above, the Supreme Court observed:

The State argues that L.C. and E.W. encountered no discrimination "by reason of" their disabilities because they were not denied community placement on account of those disabilities. . . . Nor were they subjected to "discrimination," the State contends, because " 'discrimination' necessarily requires uneven treatment of similarly situated individuals," and L.C. and E.W. had identified no comparison class, i.e., no similarly situated individuals given preferential treatment. We are satisfied that Congress had a more comprehensive view of the concept of discrimination advanced in the ADA.

Olmstead, 527 U.S. at 598.

Justice Thomas's dissenting opinion in *Olmstead*, however, disagreed:

[I]t is also clear petitioners did not "discriminate" against respondents "by reason of [their] disabili[ties]," as § 12132 requires. We have previously interpreted the phrase "by reason of" as requiring proximate causation. *See, e.g., Holmes v. Securities Investor Protection Corporation*, 503 U.S. 258, 265-266 (1992); *see also id.* at 266, n.11 (citation of cases). Such an interpretation is in keeping with the vernacular understanding of the phrase. *See* American Heritage Dictionary 1506 (3d ed. 1992) (defining "by reason of" as "because of"). This statute should be read as requiring proximate causation as well. Respondents do not contend that their disabilities constituted the proximate cause for their exclusion. Nor could they – community

433

placement simply is not available to those without disabilities. Continued institutional treatment of persons who, though now deemed treatable in a community placement, must wait their turn for placement does not establish that the denial of community placement occurred "by reason of" their disability. Rather, it establishes no more than the fact that petitioners have limited resources.

Olmstead, 527 U.S. at 626 (Thomas, J., dissenting).

Notes & Questions

1. *Helen L.*'s holding – that Congress did not intend Title II's coverage to be limited to cases of deliberate discrimination – has its roots in *Alexander v. Choate*, 469 U.S. 287 (1985). In *Alexander*, the Supreme Court rejected the contention that Section 504 of the Rehabilitation Act only reached purposeful discrimination against persons with disabilities. The Court indicated that there is strong support in the legislative history for the proposition that the Rehabilitation Act was not intended to prohibit solely intentional discrimination: "[d]iscrimination against the handicapped was perceived by Congress to be most often the product, not of invidious animus, but rather of thoughtlessness and indifference – of benign neglect." *Id.* at 295. The Court noted that "much of the conduct that Congress sought to alter in passing the Rehabilitation Act would be difficult if not impossible to reach were the Act construed to proscribe only conduct fueled by a discriminatory intent." *Id.* at 296-97.

2. For the most part, as reflected in *Helen L.* courts have imparted this principle whole-cloth to the ADA, and held that a plaintiff need not prove impermissible intent under either Section 504 of the Rehabilitation Act or Title II of the ADA. Courts have offered guidance on what a plaintiff must show to demonstrate that he was discriminated against "by reason of such disability" for purposes of the Rehabilitation Act and Title II. In *Washington v. Indiana High School Athletic Ass'n*, 181 F.3d 840 (7th Cir. 1999), the Seventh Circuit stated:

> Discrimination under both acts may be established by evidence that (1) the defendant intentionally acted on the basis of disability, (2) the defendant refused to provide a reasonable accommodation, or (3) the defendant's rule disproportionably impacts disabled people.

Id. at 847.

3. An example of discriminatory intent proved through discriminatory effect can be found in *Henrietta D. v. Giuliani*, 119 F.Supp.2d 181 (E.D.N.Y. 2000). The plaintiffs challenged the City of New York's provision of social welfare benefits to persons with HIV and related illnesses. Plaintiffs offered proof that under existing New York law, they

were not receiving adequate services, and there was no proof that the New York legislature required discriminatory intent. The court held the disparate impact was sufficient to prove a Title II violation.

4. On appeal to the Second Circuit, the city of New York argued that plaintiffs, who were city residents with HIV who claimed inadequate city services, could not make out a case of discrimination under Title II because *nobody* was receiving adequate services. New York argued that plaintiff would need to demonstrate a disparate impact – i.e., that there was another category of people without disabilities who were receiving the requested services. The court rejected this argument, holding that the concept of discrimination embraced by the ADA does not demand that plaintiffs identify a comparison class of similarly situated individuals given preferential treatment. *See* Henrietta D. v. Bloomberg, 331 F.3d 261, 273 (2d Cir. 2003), discussed *supra* § 13.4.

5. Although intentional discrimination generally is not required to make out a Title II claim, a plaintiff may have to demonstrate deliberate discrimination to receive a compensatory damage award. This was the result in *Ferguson v. City of Phoenix*, 157 F.3d 668 (9th Cir. 1998). The Ninth Circuit held that a Title II plaintiff could not receive compensatory damages without showing discriminatory intent. In its ruling, the Ninth Circuit relied on Fifth and Eleventh Circuit decisions that concluded compensatory damages were unavailable for unintentional violations of the Rehabilitation Act.

6. Not requiring deliberate discrimination seems the preferred result, and more in line with Rehabilitation Act case law and the legislative history of Title II. But in close cases, some courts have moved toward requiring a higher standard of discriminatory intent. Ironically, this approach also has its genesis in *Alexander v. Choate*, the same case establishing that the Rehabilitation Act applies to more than just intentional discrimination. A limited number of courts have interpreted *Alexander* to mean that if a rule is "neutral," it does not discriminate on the basis of disability, but instead on some other non-prohibited criteria. For example, in *Sandison v. Michigan High School Athletic Ass'n,* 64 F.3d 1026, 1036 (6th Cir. 1995), a student with a learning disability who had been held back in school challenged a high school association's "age-rule" that declared 19-year old students ineligible to compete. The Sixth Circuit found that this was a "neutral" rule and therefore did not discriminate against the student because of his disability, but rather because of his age.

7. While repeating the general mantra that the ADA does not require intentional discrimination, there are other similar cases taking a restrictive view of the basis of alleged discrimination. For example, in *Wisconsin Community Services, Inc. v. City of Milwaukee*, 465 F.3d 737 (7th Cir. 2006), the operator of a mental health clinic challenged a city zoning board's denial of its request for a permit to operate their clinic. Specifically, the operator argued that as an accommodation, the city had

to modify its zoning practices in order to accommodate the needs of its disabled clients. The court held that plaintiff's "inability to meet the City's special use criteria appears due not to its client's disabilities but to its plan to open a non-profit health clinic in a location where the City desired a commercial, taxpaying tenant instead. As far as this record indicates, the City would have rejected similar proposals from non-profit health clinics serving the non-disabled." *Id.* at 754. And in *Brown v. City of Los Angeles*, 521 F.3d 1238 (9th Cir. 2008), two retired police officers alleged that the city violated Title II by reducing their disability retirement pension payments by the amount of workers' compensation awards that they received. Assuming without deciding that their claim could proceed under Title II (as opposed to Title I), the court held that this was not discrimination "by reason of" disability; rather, they were classified according to whether their injuries were sufficiently work related to receive worker's compensation awards.

Chapter 14 Remedies And Enforcement

§ 14.1 Introduction

Title II's remedial provision reads simply, but in fact points in a set of confusing directions, because it proceeds from a base that is incongruent with its goals. The remedial provisions were tailored to federal executive branch agencies and entities that receive federal funds, rather than state and local entities that do not receive federal funding. Confusion results, which the drafters might have avoided if they had been less wedded to following existing legislation and judicial decisions.[1]

The remedial language takes just one sentence:

> The remedies, procedures, and rights set forth in [section 505 of the Rehabilitation Act of 1973 (29 U.S.C. § 794a)] shall be the remedies, procedures, and rights this [title] provides to any person alleging discrimination on the basis of disability in violation of [section 202]. . . .

42 U.S.C. § 12133 (2006).

That would be fine if section 505 articulated remedies, but *that* section refers to

> [t]he remedies, procedures, and rights set forth in section 717 of the Civil Rights Act of 1964 (42 U.S.C. 2000e-16), including the application of sections 706(f) through 706 (k) (42 U.S.C. 2000e-5(f) through (k)), shall be available, with respect to any complaint under Section 791 of this title, to any employee or applicant for employment aggrieved by the final disposition of such complaint . . . .

29 U.S.C. § 794a(a)(1) (2006). With respect to non-employment disputes, it goes on,

> [t]he remedies, procedures, and rights set forth in Title VI of the Civil Rights Act of 1964 (42 U.S.C. 2000d et seq.)

---

[1]   On Title II's remedies, *see* Cheryl L. Anderson, Damages for Intentional Discrimination by Public Entities Under Title II of the Americans with Disabilities Act: A Rose by Any Other Name, but Are the Remedies the Same?, 9 BYU J. Pub. L. 235, 244 (1995); Sande Buhai & Nina Golden, Adding Insult to Injury: Discriminatory Intent As a Prerequisite to Damages Under the ADA, 52 Rutgers L. Rev. 1121, 1128-32 (2000); John J. Coleman, III & Marcel L. Debruge, A Practitioner's Introduction to ADA Title II, 45 Ala. L. Rev. 55, 92-96 (1993); Mark C. Weber, Disability Discrimination by State and Local Government: The Relationship Between Section 504 of the Rehabilitation Act and Title II of the Americans with Disabilities Act, 36 Wm. & Mary L. Rev. 1089, 1104 (1995).

> shall be available to any person aggrieved by any act or
> failure to act by any recipient of Federal assistance or
> Federal provider of such assistance under section 794 of
> this title.

Id. § 794a(a)(2). It also authorizes the recovery of attorneys' fees. 29 U.S.C. § 794a(b). However, Title VI of the Civil Rights Act of 1964 does not spell out any remedies, so courts must imply them by divining congressional intent. Cannon v. Univ. of Chi., 441 U.S. 677, 711-12 (1979). To quote one judge: "By incorporating one section after another by reference – sections that mesh only imperfectly – Congress could not have made its meaning less clear." Tyler v. City of Manhattan, 118 F.3d 1400, 1409 (10th Cir. 1997) (Jenkins, J., dissenting).

Although the ADA was enacted pursuant to the Commerce Clause and section 5 of the Fourteenth Amendment, Title VI of the Civil Rights Act was enacted pursuant to the Constitution's Spending Clause, article I, § 8, clause 1. The Supreme Court has, therefore, interpreted the remedies available under Title II to be those available pursuant to the Spending Clause. Barnes v. Gorman, 536 U.S. 181, 184-89 (2002). Those remedies are such as would flow from a contract, expressed or implied, between the United States and the defendant. As we will see, this imposes limitations on the available relief; tort remedies, for example, are unavailable.

§ 14.2 Procedure

Title II adopts the remedial scheme of section 504 of the Rehabilitation Act, including the procedures of section 505.[2] As noted, those, in turn, rest on Title VI of the Civil Rights Act. Individuals have two courses of action to attack alleged violations of Title II.[3]

First, they may pursue administrative remedies. As with Title I, the claimant must file within 180 days of the violation, 28 C.F.R. § 35.170(b) (2008), unless the time is extended for good cause.

> An individual may file a complaint with any agency that he
> or she believes to be the appropriate agency designated
> under subpart G of this part, or with any agency that
> provides funding to the public entity that is the subject of
> the complaint, or with the Department of Justice for
> referral as provided in [28 C.F.R.] § 35.171(a)(2).

Id. § 35.170. Certain agencies have jurisdiction under section 504; agencies that do not have section 504 jurisdiction may be "designated agencies" – "for components of State and local governments that exercise responsibilities, regulate, or administer services, programs, or activities in

---

[2]   Those procedures apply to the entire subchapter, parts A and B.

[3]   The Department of Justice regulations regarding Title II are found in 28 C.F.R. pt. 35.

[specified] functional areas." *Id.* § 35.190(b).[4] The regulations specify how complaints are to be processed if filed with agencies other than the Department of Justice.

The designated agency, which may be the Department of Justice, must investigate a complaint and attempt informal resolution. 28 C.F.R. § 35.172. If informal resolution fails, it issues findings of fact and conclusions of law, a description of the appropriate remedy and a notice to the complainant and the public entity. *Id.* § 35.172(a). If it finds non-compliance, it issues a letter of non-compliance, notifies the Assistant Attorney General in charge of the Civil Rights Division of the Department of Justice and attempts to negotiate to secure compliance. *Id.* § 35.173(a). If that fails it refers the matter to the Assistant Attorney General for litigation.

When the covered entity receives federal funding, the designated agency also may seek to revoke the federal funding under Section 504. *Id.* § 42.108(a). The regulations cabin that authority with a series of barriers that make attacks on funded programs quite difficult. The relevant regulation reads:

> No order suspending, terminating, or refusing to grant or continue Federal financial assistance shall become effective until: (1) The responsible Department official has advised the applicant or recipient of his failure to comply and has determined that compliance cannot be secured by voluntary means, (2) there has been an express finding on the record, after opportunity for hearing, of a failure by the applicant or recipient to comply with a requirement imposed by or pursuant to this subpart, (3) the action has been approved by the Attorney General pursuant to § 42.110, and (4) the expiration of 30 days after the Attorney General has filed with the committee of the House and the committee of the Senate having legislative jurisdiction over the program involved, a full written report of the circumstances and the grounds for such action.

Id. § 42.108(c).

Individuals' second option is a private suit. While individuals may elect to pursue administrative remedies, the courts have found uniformly that there is no need to exhaust administrative remedies in actions that

---

[4] The designated agencies are the Departments of Agriculture, Education, Health and Human Services, Housing and Urban Development, Interior, Justice, Labor and Transportation. *Id.* Other departments' ADA responsibilities are spelled out in their own regulation. For example, the Department of Transportation's regulations are found at 49 C.F.R. pt. 27.

are not against the federal government under the Rehabilitation Act. Tuck v. HCA Health Servs., 7 F.3d 465, 470-71 (6th Cir. 1993); *cf.* Smith v. Barton, 914 F.2d 1330, 1338 (9th Cir. 1990) (exhaustion not required under Rehabilitation Act). *See* 28 C.F.R. § 35.17(b) (2008).

In *Cannon v. University of Chicago*, 441 U.S. 677, 677 (1979), the Supreme Court found that those seeking relief under Title IX of the Civil Rights Act need not exhaust administrative remedies. Because the same enforcement procedures apply to Title IX of the Civil Rights Act, section 504 of the Rehabilitation Act, and Title II of the ADA, which all rest on Title VI of the Civil Rights Act, there is no exhaustion requirement under those statutes. Zimmerman v. Or. Dep't of Justice, 170 F.3d 1169, 1178 (9th Cir. 1999) (citing Barton, 914 F.2d at 1338 ("[P]rivate plaintiffs suing under section 504 [of the Rehabilitation Act] need not first exhaust administrative remedies")); Davoll v. Webb, 194 F.3d 1116, 1124 (10th Cir. 1999) (dictum); Petersen v. Univ. of Wis. Bd. of Regents, 818 F.Supp. 1276, 1280 (W.D. Wis. 1993); *see also* Camenisch v. Univ. of Tex., 616 F.2d 127 (5th Cir. 1980), vacated on other grounds, 451 U.S. 390 (1981) (same, but pre-ADA).

The absence of an exhaustion requirement follows from the fact that the "administrative remedies, which result in suspension or termination of the federal assistance to the institutional recipient, do not afford individual complainants adequate relief." Barton, 914 F.2d at 1338; *see also* Greater L.A. Council on Deafness, Inc. v. Cmty. Television of S. Cal., 719 F.2d 1017, 1021 (9th Cir. 1983) (exhaustion not required under Rehabilitation Act); Pushkin v. Regents of Univ. of Colo., 658 F.2d 1372, 1380-82 (10th Cir. 1981) (same). If there were any doubt that exhaustion is not required under Title II of the ADA, Congress made it clear in the legislative history that it intended no such requirement. H.R. Rep. No. 101-485, at 98 (1990), reprinted in 1990 U.S.C.C.A.N. 267, 381 ("As with § 504, there is also a private right of action . . . which includes the full panoply of remedies. Again, consistent with section 504, it is not the Committee's intent that persons with disabilities need to exhaust Federal administrative remedies before exercising their private right of action.").

⤸

Notes & Questions

1. What if the claimant must exhaust his administrative remedies under another statute? Can he avoid that by pleading a Title II claim? The cases have held that other exhaustion requirements trump Title II's silence. *See, e.g.,* Babicz v. Sch. Bd. of Broward County, 135 F.3d 1420, 1422 (11th Cir. 1998) (must exhaust Individuals with Disabilities Education Act remedies); Zulauf v. Ky. Educ. Television, 28 F.Supp.2d 1022, 1024 (E.D. Ky. 1998) (must exhaust remedies under Video Programming Accessibility Act); *cf.* Nieves-Marquez v. Puerto Rico, 353 F.3d 108 (1st Cir. 2003) (plaintiffs properly exhausted administrative

remedies under Individuals with Disabilities Education Act, before seeking relief under Title II).

2. One must, of course, be careful: Employment claims against the federal government, rather than recipients of federal funds, arise under section 501 of the Rehabilitation Act, 29 U.S.C. § 794 (2006), which does require exhaustion. Spence v. Straw, 54 F.3d 196, 200-02 (3d Cir. 1995); Boyd v. U.S. Postal Serv., 752 F.2d 410, 412-13 (9th Cir. 1985).

3. Title II, like Title III, is perhaps uniquely dependent on public enforcement: in a broad category of cases, individuals will not be able to sue states for damages, *see Board of Trustees of the University of Alabama v. Garrett* and *Tennessee v. Lane* (discussed *supra* § 12.2), and a defendant may be able to moot out a claim for attorneys fees by changing a challenged practice, *see Buckhannon Bd. & Care Home, Inc. v. W. Va. Dep't of Health & Human Res.*, 532 U.S. 598 (2001). For an argument that federal enforcement efforts have not been up to the task, *see* Michael Waterstone, *A New Vision of Public Enforcement*, 92 Minn. L. Rev. 434 (2007).

ॐ

§ 14.3   Remedies

Both the federal government and private individuals may seek relief under Title II. They may not sue people in their individual capacity, since those targets are not defined "entities" under Title II. But there are – or were – a number of questions about the range of relief available.

A.   *Private Rights Of Action*

In *Cannon v. University of Chicago*, 441 U.S. 677, 677 (1979), the Court held that individuals have a private right of action under Title VI. Because this is the statute on which Title II's remedies are based, individuals also have a private right of action under Title II.

Cannon left unanswered whether individuals may seek relief for government actions that have a "disparate impact" on the subject group, as opposed to intentional discrimination; i.e., they have no private right of action for disparate impact discrimination. The answer to that did not come until *Alexander v. Sandoval*, 532 U.S. 275, 285-93 (2001), where the Court held that Title VI of the Civil Rights Act of 1964 does not imply a right of action for private litigants to sue recipients of federal funds for "disparate impact" violations. Applying *Sandoval* in the ADA Title II context, in *Chaffin v. Kansas State Fair Bd.*, 348 F.3d 850 (10th Cir. 2003), the Tenth Circuit held that with § 504 and Title II Congress sought to remedy a broad, comprehensive concept of discrimination against individuals with disabilities, including disparate impact discrimination. The regulations provided context to these Congressional goals. Thus, an individual had a private right of action to enforce an inaccessible state fairgrounds.

B. *Available Types Of Relief*

Because the remedies for Title VI are those for breaches of contract – the recipient's contract with the federal government – those remedies, even in the absence of a contract, are the remedies for Title II of the ADA.

BARNES v. GORMAN

Supreme Court of the United States, 2002
536 U.S. 181

JUSTICE SCALIA delivered the opinion of the Court.

We must decide whether punitive damages may be awarded in a private cause of action brought under § 202 of the Americans with Disabilities Act of 1990(ADA), 104 Stat. 337, 42 U.S.C. § 12132 (1994 ed.), and § 504 of the Rehabilitation Act of 1973, 87 Stat. 394, 29 U.S.C. § 794(a).

I

Respondent Jeffrey Gorman, a paraplegic, is confined to a wheelchair and lacks voluntary control over his lower torso, including his bladder, forcing him to wear a catheter attached to a urine bag around his waist. In May 1992, he was arrested for trespass after fighting with a bouncer at a Kansas City, Missouri, nightclub. While waiting for a police van to transport him to the station, he was denied permission to use a restroom to empty his urine bag. When the van arrived, it was not equipped to receive respondent's wheelchair. Over respondent's objection, the officers removed him from his wheelchair and used a seatbelt and his own belt to strap him to a narrow bench in the rear of the van. During the ride to the police station, respondent released his seatbelt, fearing it placed excessive pressure on his urine bag. Eventually, the other belt came loose and respondent fell to the floor, rupturing his urine bag and injuring his shoulder and back. The driver, the only officer in the van, finding it impossible to lift respondent, fastened him to a support for the remainder of the trip. Upon arriving at the station, respondent was booked, processed, and released; later he was convicted of misdemeanor trespass. After these events, respondent suffered serious medical problems – including a bladder infection, serious lower back pain, and uncontrollable spasms in his paralyzed areas – that left him unable to work full time.

[Gorman sued under the ADA and the Rehabilitation Act. He recovered actual damages and punitive damages of $1 million. The Sixth Circuit affirmed.]

Section 202 of the ADA prohibits discrimination against the disabled by public entities; § 504 of the Rehabilitation Act prohibits discrimination against the disabled by recipients of federal funding, including private organizations, 29 U.S.C. § 794(b)(3). Both provisions are enforceable through private causes of action. Section 203 of the ADA declares that the "remedies, procedures, and rights set forth in [§ 505(a)(2) of the Rehabilitation Act] shall be the remedies, procedures, and rights this subchapter provides" for violations of § 202. 42 U.S.C. § 12133. Section 505(a)(2) of the Rehabilitation Act, in turn, declares that the "remedies, procedures, and rights set forth in title VI of the Civil Rights Act of 1964 ... shall be available" for violations of § 504, as added, 92 Stat. 2983, 29 U.S.C. § 794a(a)(2). Thus, the remedies for violations of § 202 of the ADA and § 504 of the Rehabilitation Act are coextensive with the remedies available in a private cause of action brought under Title VI of the Civil Rights Act of 1964, 42 U.S.C. § 2000d *et seq.*, which prohibits racial discrimination in federally funded programs and activities.

Although Title VI does not mention a private right of action, our prior decisions have found an *implied* right of action, *e.g.*, *Cannon v. University of Chicago*, 441 U.S. 677, 703, 99 S.Ct. 1946, 60 L.Ed.2d 560 (1979), and Congress has acknowledged this right in amendments to the statute, leaving it "beyond dispute that private individuals may sue to enforce" Title VI, *Alexander v. Sandoval*, 532 U.S. 275, 280, 121 S.Ct. 1511, 149 L.Ed.2d 517 (2001). It is less clear what remedies are available in such a suit. In *Franklin* [*v. Gwinnett County Public Schools,* 503 U.S. 60, 112 S.Ct. 1028, 117 L.Ed.2d 208 (1992)], supra, at 73, 112 S.Ct. 1028, we recognized "the traditional presumption in favor of any appropriate relief for violation of a federal right," and held that since this presumption applies to suits under Title IX of the Education Amendments of 1972, 20 U.S.C. §§ 1681-1688, monetary damages were available. (Emphasis added.) And the Court has interpreted Title IX consistently with Title VI, see Cannon, supra, at 694-698, 99 S.Ct. 1946. *Franklin*, however, did not describe the scope of "appropriate relief." We take up this question today.

Title VI invokes Congress's power under the Spending Clause, U.S. Const., Art. I, § 8, cl. 1, to place conditions on the grant of federal funds. * * * We have repeatedly characterized this statute and other Spending Clause legislation as "much in the nature of a contract: in return for federal funds, the [recipients] agree to comply with federally imposed conditions." *Pennhurst State School and Hospital v. Halderman*, 451 U.S. 1, 17, 101 S.Ct. 1531, 67 L.Ed.2d 694 (1981) (emphasis added); see also *Davis* [*v. Monroe County Bd. of Ed.,* 526 U.S. 629, 640, 119 S.Ct. 1661, 143 L.Ed.2d 839 (1999)], supra, at 640, 119 S.Ct. 1661; *Gebser v. Lago Vista Independent School Dist.*, 524 U.S. 274, 286, 118 S.Ct. 1989, 141 L.Ed.2d 277 (1998); *Guardians Assn. v. Civil Serv. Comm'n of New York City*, 463 U.S. 582, 599, 103 S.Ct. 3221, 77 L.Ed.2d 866 (1983) * * *. Just as a valid contract requires offer and acceptance of its terms, "[t]he legitimacy of Congress' power to legislate under the spending power . . . rests on whether the [recipient] voluntarily and knowingly accepts the terms of the 'contract.' . . . Accordingly, if Congress intends to impose a condition on the grant of federal moneys, it must do so unambiguously." *Pennhurst*, supra, at 17, 101 S.Ct. 1531 * * *. Although we have been careful not to imply that *all* contract-law rules apply to Spending Clause legislation, see, *e.g.*, *Bennett v. Kentucky Dept. of Ed.*, 470 U.S. 656, 669, 105 S.Ct. 1544, 84 L.Ed.2d 590 (1985) (Title I), we have regularly applied the contract-law analogy in cases defining the scope of conduct for which funding recipients may be held liable for money damages. Thus, a recipient may be held liable to third-party beneficiaries for intentional conduct that violates the clear terms of the relevant statute, *Davis*, supra, at 642, 119 S.Ct. 1661, but not for its failure to comply with vague language describing the objectives of the statute, *Pennhurst*, supra, at 24-25, 101 S.Ct. 1531; and, if the statute implies that only violations brought to the attention of an official with power to correct them are actionable, not for conduct unknown to any such official, see *Gebser*, supra, at 290, 118 S.Ct. 1989. We have also applied the contract-law analogy in finding a damages remedy available in private suits under Spending Clause legislation. *Franklin*, supra, at 74-75, 112 S.Ct. 1028.

The same analogy applies, we think, in determining the scope of damages remedies. We said as much in *Gebser*: "Title IX's contractual nature has implications for our construction of the scope of available remedies." 524 U.S. at 287, 118 S.Ct. 1989. One of these implications, we believe, is that a remedy is "appropriate relief," * * * only if the funding recipient is *on notice* that, by accepting federal funding, it exposes itself to liability of that nature. A funding recipient is generally on notice that it is subject not only to those remedies explicitly provided in the relevant legislation, but also to those remedies traditionally available in suits for breach of contract. Thus we have held that under Title IX, which contains no express remedies, a recipient of federal funds is nevertheless subject to suit for compensatory damages, *id.* at 76, 112 S.Ct. 1028, and injunction, *Cannon*, supra, at 711-712, 99 S.Ct. 1946, forms of relief traditionally available in suits for breach of contract. * * * Like Title IX, Title VI mentions no remedies – indeed, it fails to mention even a private right of action (hence this Court's decision finding an *implied* right of action in *Cannon*). But punitive damages, unlike compensatory damages and injunction, are generally not available for breach of contract, see 3 E. Farnsworth, Contracts § 12.8, pp. 192-201 (2d ed. 1998); Restatement (Second) of Contracts § 355; 1 T. Sedgwick, Measure of Damages § 370 (8th ed. 1891).

Nor (if such an interpretive technique were available) could an *implied* punitive damages provision reasonably be found in Title VI. Some authorities say that reasonably implied contractual terms are those that the parties would have agreed to if they had adverted to the matters in question. * * * More recent commentary suggests that reasonably implied contractual terms are simply those that "comport with community standards of fairness," Restatement (Second) of Contracts § 204, Comment d; see also 2 Farnsworth, *supra*, § 7.16, at 334-336. Neither approach would support the implication here of a remedy that is not normally available for contract actions and that is of indeterminate magnitude. We have acknowledged that compensatory damages alone "might well exceed a recipient's level of federal funding," *Gebser, supra*, at 290, 118 S.Ct. 1989; punitive damages on top of that could well be disastrous. Not only is it doubtful that funding recipients would have agreed to exposure to such unorthodox and indeterminate liability; it is doubtful whether they would even have *accepted the funding* if punitive damages liability was a required condition. "Without doubt, the scope of potential damages liability is one of the most significant factors a school would consider in deciding whether to receive federal funds." *Davis, supra*, at 656, 119 S.Ct. 1661 (KENNEDY, J., dissenting). And for the same reason of unusual and disproportionate exposure, it can hardly be said that community standards of fairness support such an implication. In sum, it must be concluded that Title VI funding recipients have not, merely by accepting funds, implicitly consented to liability for punitive damages.

Our conclusion is consistent with the "well settled" rule that "where legal rights have been invaded, and a federal statute provides for a general right to sue for such invasion, federal courts may use any available remedy to make good the wrong done." *Bell v. Hood*, 327 U.S. 678, 684, 66 S.Ct. 773, 90 L.Ed. 939 (1946) * * *. When a federal-funds recipient violates conditions of Spending Clause legislation, the wrong done is the failure to provide what the contractual obligation requires; and that wrong is "made good" when the recipient *compensates* the Federal Government or a third-party beneficiary (as in this case) for the loss caused by that failure. * * * Punitive damages are not compensatory, and are therefore not embraced within the rule described in *Bell*.

* * *

Because punitive damages may not be awarded in private suits brought under Title VI of the 1964 Civil Rights Act, it follows that they may not be awarded in suits brought under § 202 of the ADA and § 504 of the Rehabilitation Act. * * *

It is so ordered.

Notes & Questions

1. The forms of relief that might be available are equitable relief (principally injunctions) and damages. The United States may seek injunctive relief for violations of Title II. United States v. City & County of Denver, 927 F.Supp. 1396 (D. Colo. 1996) (United States seeking injunctive relief). Individuals may obtain injunctive relief, in general, following *Cannon*. *See* First Step, Inc. v. City of New London, 247 F.Supp.2d 135, 156-57 (D. Conn. 2003); Bertrand v. City of Mackinac

Island, 662 N.W.2d 77, 78, 81-88 (Mich. Ct. App. 2003) (city required to permit resident to use electric-assist tricycle, despite ordinance forbidding "motor vehicles").

2. Individuals may obtain prospective relief from state officials for continuing violations of federal law under the *Ex Parte Young* doctrine, 209 U.S. 123 (1908). *See* Carten v. Kent State Univ., 282 F.3d 391, 395-97 (6th Cir. 2002). Under *Carten*, a request for reinstatement falls under the "continuing act" umbrella of *Carten*, because the termination is a continuing violation. *Id. Young* is an exception to Eleventh Amendment immunity, because the official is "stripped" of his mantle as a part of the state by virtue of his violation.

3. Courts generally have found that plaintiffs may recover compensatory damages in Title VI cases. *E.g.*, Guardians Ass'n v. Civil Serv. Comm'n., 463 U.S. 582, 602-03 (1983); *see also* Franklin v. Gwinnett County Pub. Schs., 503 U.S. 60, 70 (1992) (noting that "a clear majority" in *Guardians* would allow damages in actions for intentional violations of Title VI). In Rehabilitation Act § 504 cases, prevailing plaintiffs are entitled to the "full spectrum of legal and equitable remedies needed to redress their injuries." Matthews v. Jefferson, 29 F.Supp.2d 525, 535 (W.D. Ark. 1998) (quoting Gorman v. Bartch, 152 F.3d 907, 908 (8th Cir. 1998)). Accordingly, ADA Title II plaintiffs may recover compensatory damages, including damages for emotional distress, pain and suffering, and economic losses. "Where legal rights have been invaded, and a federal statute provides for a general right to sue for such invasion, federal courts may use any available remedy to make good the wrong done." Niece v. Fitzner, 922 F.Supp. 1208, 1219 (E.D. Mich. 1996) (quoting Franklin, 503 U.S. at 66 (quoting Bell v. Hood, 327 U.S. 678, 684 (1946) (Title IX case))).

4. What a plaintiff must show regarding the defendant's state of mind to recover compensatory damages has been disputed, but a consensus has developed. The backdrop is *Alexander v. Sandoval,* 532 U.S. 275 (2001), which held that Title VI of the Civil Rights Act of 1964 does not imply a right of action for private litigants to sue recipients of federal funds for "disparate impact" violations. In terms of allowing compensatory damages, courts distinguish between discrimination caused by the disparate impact of facially neutral actions and discrimination caused by discriminatory intent. In *Meagley v. City of Little Rock*, 639 F.3d 384 (8th Cir. 2011), the court refused to award compensatory damages for Title II violations resulting in the injury of the disabled plaintiff at the defendant's zoo without a showing of intentional discrimination. Similarly, in *Ferguson v. City of Phoenix*, 157 F.3d 668 (9th Cir. 1998), the Ninth Circuit held that a Title II plaintiff could not receive compensatory damages without showing discriminatory intent

5. Some courts characterize the necessary level of intent for damages as "deliberate indifference." Duvall v. County of Kitsap, 260 F.3d 1124, 1139 (9th Cir. 2001). The obvious case is when there is "facial

discrimination." Lovell v. Chandler, 303 F.3d 1039, 1057 (9th Cir. 2002) (court affirmed summary judgment giving right to compensatory damages against Hawaii, because it (a) was chargeable with knowledge of the discrimination in violation of federally protected rights when it categorically excluded classes of people with disabilities from state healthcare programs, and (b) deliberately failed to protect their rights by denying them benefits). But less may suffice. "Deliberate indifference requires both knowledge that a harm to a federally protected right is substantially likely, and a failure to act upon that likelihood." Duvall, 260 F.3d at 1139 (citing City of Canton v. Harris, 489 U.S. 378, 389 (1989)). The entity must know, for example, that an accommodation is required and must fail to make the accommodation in a way that bespeaks more than negligence, but has "an element of deliberateness," *id.*, by, for example, failing to consider an individual's needs. *Id*; *see also* Lovell, 303 F.3d at 1056-58. *See* Ms. K v. City of South Portland, 407 F.Supp.2d 290, 295 (D. Me. 2006) (no facts showing intentional discrimination; moreover, icy sidewalk "that led to S.B.'s unfortunate injury constituted a hazard for the disabled and non-disabled alike, and did not rise to the level of a permanent barrier to the disabled").

6.   The government, as opposed to private parties, has a range of remedies available:

- It may seek injunctive relief. Barnes v. Gorman, 536 U.S. 181, 187 (2002).

- It may seek compensatory damages in court. *See, e.g.,* Martin v. Metro. Atlanta Rapid Transit Auth., 225 F.Supp.2d 1362, 1372 (N.D. Ga. 2002); People ex rel. Spitzer v. County of Del., 82 F.Supp.2d 12, 15-18 (N.D.N.Y. 2000).

- It may take administrative actions, such as cutting off funds for programs. 42 U.S.C. §§ 2000e-5(f), 2000e-16 (2006); see 28 C.F.R. § 42.108 (2008) ("the responsible Department official may suspend or terminate, or refuse to grant or continue, Federal financial assistance, or use any other means authorized by law, to induce compliance with this subpart").

C.   *Attorneys' Fees And Statute Of Limitations*

The somewhat limited set of issues involved in attorneys' fees and statutes of limitations are similar under Title II as Title III. *See* review under Title III. Part 5, ch. 17.

Part 5

Access To Public Accommodations: ADA Title III
Analysis

Chapter 15 COVERED ENTITIES
§ 15.1 Places Of Public Accommodation And Commercial Facilities
    A. General
    B. Responsible Parties
    C. Covered Areas
    D. Physical Structures
§ 15.2 Examinations And Courses
§ 15.3 Exempt Entities
§ 15.4 Relationship To Title II
§ 15.5 Geographic Limits
Chapter 16 PROHIBITED CONDUCT
§ 16.1 General
§ 16.2 Reasonable Modifications
    A. Burdens Of Proof
    B. Reasonableness/Fundamental Alteration
§ 16.3 Effective Communication
    A. General
    B. Distance Education
§ 16.4 Architectural Barriers
    A. Existing Facilities
    B. Alterations
    C. New Construction
§ 16.5 The Complexity Of Compliance
Chapter 17 ENFORCEMENT AND REMEDIES
§ 17.1 Procedure
    A. Notice
    B. Statute Of Limitations
    C. Alternative Dispute Resolution
§ 17.2 Remedies
    A. Injunctive Relief
    B. Enforcement By The Attorney General – Compensatory
        Damages And Civil Penalties
    C. Attorneys' Fees

Chapter 15 COVERED ENTITIES

Title III extends the ADA's antidiscrimination mandate to places of public accommodation and commercial facilities. The overarching requirement of Title III is as follows:

No individual shall be discriminated against on the basis of disability in the **full and equal enjoyment** of the goods, services, facilities, privileges, advantages, or accommodations of any place of public accommodation by any person who owns, leases (or leases to) or operates a place of public accommodation.

42 U.S.C. § 12182 (2006) (emphasis added). For a discussion of this concept of "full and equal enjoyment" *see* Peter Blanck, eQuality: Web Rights, Human Flourishing and Persons with Cognitive Disabilities (forthcoming 2014).

Discrimination under Title III is defined broadly to include failure to make reasonable modifications of policies, practices and procedures, failure to ensure effective communication, and failure to take steps to make facilities physically accessible. The defenses to a charge of discrimination rely on the concepts of undue burden, fundamental alteration, and what is "readily achievable."

§ 15.1 Places Of Public Accommodation And Commercial Facilities

A. General

Title III covers "places of public accommodation" and "commercial facilities." Public accommodations consist of twelve specified categories of businesses that affect commerce:

(1) Place of lodging, except for an establishment located within a building that contains not more than five rooms for rent or hire and that is actually occupied by the proprietor of such establishment as the residence of such proprietor . . . or (ii) A facility that – (A) Provides guest rooms for sleeping for stays that primarily are short-term in nature . . . and (B) Provides guest rooms under conditions and with amenities similar to a hotel, motel, or inn;

(2) a restaurant, bar, or other *establishment serving food or drink*;

(3) a motion picture house, theater, concert hall, stadium, or other *place of exhibition or entertainment*;

(4) an auditorium, convention center, lecture hall, or other *place of public gathering*;

(5) a bakery, grocery store, clothing store, hardware store, shopping center, or other *sales or rental establishment*;

(6) a laundromat, dry-cleaner, bank, barber shop, beauty shop, travel service, shoe repair service, funeral parlor, gas station, office of an accountant or

lawyer, pharmacy, insurance office, professional office of a health care provider, hospital, or other *service establishment*;

(7)   a terminal, depot, or other station used for *specified public transportation* [air travel is not included in the definition of specified public transportation];

(8)   a museum, library, gallery, or other *place of public display or collection*;

(9)   a park, zoo, amusement park, or other *place of recreation*;

(10)   a nursery, elementary, secondary, under-graduate, or postgraduate private school, or other *place of education*;

(11)   a day care center, senior citizen center, homeless shelter, food bank, adoption agency, or other *social service center establishment*; and

(12)   a gymnasium, health spa, bowling alley, golf course, or other *place of exercise or recreation.*

28 C.F.R § 36.104 (2013) (emphases added).

The twelve categories are exhaustive, but the examples therein are not. 28 C.F.R. § 36.104 (2008). If a business does not fit into one of the twelve categories, it is not a place of public accommodation. U.S. Dep't of Justice, Title III Technical Assistance Manual § 1.2000 (Nov. 1993) ("TAM III"), http://www.usdoj.gov/crt/ada/taman3.html. Similarly, wholesale establishments that sell to the public are included as sales or rental establishments, but wholesale establishments that sell exclusively to other businesses are not. 28 C.F.R. pt. 36, app. B, § 36.104 (2008); *see* Torres v. AT&T Broadband, LLC, 158 F.Supp.2d 1035, 1038 (N.D. Cal. 2001) (digital cable television system is not a place of public accommodation). Private airports, which do not fall in one of the twelve categories, are not places of public accommodation. TAM III, *supra*, at § 1.3100; *see also* 28 C.F.R. § 36.104.

Instead, places that do not fall within the twelve categories are considered "commercial facilities." Commercial facilities do not include rail vehicles, or facilities covered or specifically exempted by the Fair Housing Act (e.g., residential dwelling units, or owner-occupied rooming houses occupied by four or fewer families). TAM III, *supra*, at § 1.3100. Public accommodations are subject to the nondiscrimination obligations of Title III, while commercial facilities are subject only to the requirements for new construction and alterations. Lonberg v. Sanborn Theaters Inc., 259 F.3d 1029, 1035 n.7 (9th Cir. 2001) (citations omitted).

A single facility may contain both public accommodations and commercial facilities. TAM III, *supra*, at § 1.3000 (e.g., stores within a private airport are public accommodations, even though the airport itself is a commercial facility). *See also* Johnson v. Gambrinus Co./Spoetzl Brewery, 116 F.3d 1052, 1057 (5th Cir. 1997) (public areas of brewery are public accommodations, while non-public areas are commercial facilities). In addition, a single entity may operate a public accommodation and a commercial facility. However, policies or decisions made in the commercial facility that affect the public accommodation must comply with Title III. TAM III, *supra*, at § 1.2000.

Title III does not cover residential facilities. *Id.* § 1.200; *see also* Lancaster v. Phillips Investments, LLC, 482 F.Supp.2d 1362, 1366 (M.D. Ala. 2007). However, common areas within residential facilities that are open to the public (e.g., not restricted to residents and their guests) may be considered Title III public accommodations. TAM III, *supra*, at § 1.200, at illus. 1. Similarly, sales or rental offices within a residential facility or within a model home may be places of public accommodation covered by Title III. *Id.* § 1.200, at illus. 3. A vacation timeshare may be a place of public accommodation if its operation resembles that of a hotel or other place of transient lodging. *Id.* at 4–5.

Areas of a private home that are used as a place of public accommodation will be covered under Title III. 28 C.F.R. pt. 36, app. B., § 36.207 (2008). Therefore, a home that houses a daycare facility or a physician's office will be covered under Title III, at least in those areas used for the public accommodation or used for residential and public activities. *Id.* § 36.104. Similarly, a homeless shelter that allows stays ranging from overnight to long-term may be a place of lodging covered by Title III and a residential facility covered by the Fair Housing Act. TAM III, *supra*, at § 1.2000.

B.   Responsible Parties

Title III regulates the conduct of a private entity that owns, leases (or leases to) or operates a place of public accommodation or commercial facility. 42 U.S.C. § 12182(a) (2006). Therefore, landlords, tenants, and operators of public accommodations are responsible for ensuring compliance with Title III. These entities may contractually allocate responsibility among themselves for complying with particular responsibilities. However, such an allocation is effective only between the parties and each party remains fully liable to an individual with a disability who encounters discrimination at the public accommodation. TAM III, *supra*, § 1.2000.

Nevertheless, to be responsible under Title III, an individual or entity must have some ability to control the place of public accommodation.

NEFF v. AMERICAN DAIRY QUEEN CORP.

United States Court of Appeals, Fifth Circuit, 1995
58 F.3d 1063

GARZA, Circuit Judge:

Margo Neff appeals from the district court's entry of summary judgment on her claims against American Dairy Queen Corporation ("ADQ") under the Americans with Disabilities Act, 42 U.S.C. §§ 12101-12213 (West Supp.1995) ("ADA"). We affirm.

I

ADQ owns the federally registered "Dairy Queen" trade name and various trademarks and service marks used in connection with the operation of licensed Dairy Queen stores. ADQ, through franchise agreements with franchisees throughout the United States, licenses franchisees to establish and operate Dairy Queen retail stores. Among those franchisees is R & S Dairy Queens, Inc., a Texas corporation that owns two Dairy Queen stores in San Antonio * * *.

Margo Neff is disabled and requires a wheelchair to gain mobility. Neff filed suit under section 308 of the ADA, * * * alleging that ADQ had violated section 302 of the ADA, * * * by failing to make the San Antonio Stores accessible to her. In her complaint, Neff pointed to numerous barriers that she alleged made the San Antonio Stores inaccessible to the disabled. Neff sought an injunction requiring ADQ to modify "its" San Antonio Stores to eliminate the alleged barriers, a declaratory judgment concerning ADQ's violation of the ADA, and attorneys' fees.

ADQ moved for summary judgment on the grounds that it did not own, lease, or operate the San Antonio Stores and therefore was not responsible for removing the alleged barriers. Its summary judgment pleadings included an affidavit by ADQ's Vice President for Franchise Operations stating that ADQ neither owned nor operated the San Antonio Stores. ADQ also offered copies of the franchise agreements between ADQ and R & S Dairy Queens relating to the San Antonio Stores. According to ADQ, the agreements established as a matter of law that it did not "operate" the stores within the meaning of section 302.

In response, Neff contended that the terms of the franchise agreement between ADQ and R & S Dairy Queens regarding the Nacogdoches Store supported her claim that ADQ retained sufficient control over the operation of the San Antonio Stores to make it an "operator" of the stores for the purposes of section 302.

The district court granted summary judgment, * * * concluding that the Nacogdoches Store franchise agreement established no more than that ADQ held the power to veto modifications to the store's facilities, and

453

that this amount of control was insufficient to bring ADQ within the scope of section 302. Neff appeals from the district court's entry of summary judgment, contending that the existence of genuine issues of material fact regarding whether ADQ "operates" the San Antonio Stores should have precluded summary judgment on her ADA claims.

II

* * *

B

Neff's appeal thus presents a narrowly defined issue of first impression: whether a franchisor with limited control over a franchisee's store "operates a place of public accommodation" within the meaning of section 302(a). Section 302(a) provides in pertinent part that "[n]o individual shall be discriminated against on the basis of disability in the full and equal enjoyment of . . . [the] facilities . . . or accommodations of any place of public accommodation *by any person who owns, leases (or leases to), or operates a place of public accommodation.*" (emphasis added). Because the ADA does not define the term "operates," we "construe it in accord with its ordinary and natural meaning." * * * To "operate," in the context of a business operation, means "to put or keep in operation," *The Random House College Dictionary* 931 (Rev. ed. 1980), "[t]o control or direct the functioning of," *Webster's II: New Riverside University Dictionary* 823 (1988), "[t]o conduct the affairs of; manage," *The American Heritage Dictionary* 1268 (3d ed. 1992).

Neff argues that the terms of the Nacogdoches Store Franchise Agreement demonstrate that ADQ exercises sufficient control over the San Antonio Stores to bring ADQ within the scope of section 302. We hold that the relevant inquiry in a case such as this one is whether ADQ specifically controls the modification of the franchises to improve their accessibility to the disabled. Cf. *Carparts Distribution Center, Inc. v. Automotive Wholesalers' Ass'n,* 37 F.3d 12, 16-18 (1st Cir. 1994) (interpreting "employer" as used in Title I of ADA by looking to defendant's control over allegedly discriminatory denial of employee benefits). Although we have found no circuit court of appeals case law interpreting the scope of "operates" as used in § 302 of the ADA, the existing district court authority is consistent with our approach. All three district courts that have addressed the question of ADQ's liability for allegedly discriminatory conditions at franchisee stores have concluded that ADQ does not "operate" the stores for the purposes of § 302, and all three looked to ADQ's authority over structural modifications to the franchisee stores in reaching their conclusions. * * *

Neff and the United States point to numerous non-structural aspects of the San Antonio Stores' operations that they contend ADQ controls, such as accounting, personnel uniforms, use of trademarks, etc. While ADQ's control over these aspects may be relevant in other contexts, we hold that because it does not relate to the allegedly discriminatory conditions at the San Antonio Stores, it does not bear on the question of whether ADQ "operates" the franchises for the purposes of the ADA's prohibition on discrimination in public accommodations. Instead, the relevant question in this case is whether ADQ, according to the terms of its franchise agreements with R & S Dairy Queens, controls modification of the San Antonio Stores to cause them to comply with the ADA.

Neff points to the following language in the Nacogdoches Store franchise agreement to support her position that ADQ controls the San Antonio stores:

> B.   Company makes available to its licensees a system to establish, equip and operate a retail store facility as part of the "Dairy Queen" system using distinctive, uniform and approved designs, equipment, supplies . . . which Licensee desires to adopt and use to operate a "Dairy Queen" retail store . . . in accordance with this Agreement and the system standards and requirements established and periodically revised by the Company . . . .

> 5.1   The retail Store shall be constructed and equipped in accordance with Company's approved specifications and standards in effect at the time pertaining to design and layout of the building, and as to equipment, inventory, signage, fixtures, location and design and accessory features. Licensee shall not commence construction of the Store until he has received the written consent of Company to his building plans.

> 5.2   Any replacement, reconstruction, addition or modification in building, interior or exterior decor or image, equipment or signage, to be made after Company's consent is granted for initial plans, whether at the request of Licensee or of Company, shall be made in accordance with written specifications which have received the prior written consent of Company, which shall not be unreasonably withheld.

> 5.3   The building, equipment and signage employed in the conduct of Licensee's business shall be maintained in accordance with requirements established periodically by Company, or reasonable, specific lists prepared by Company based upon periodic inspections of the premises by Company's representatives. Within a period of ninety (90) days after the receipt of any particular maintenance list, Licensee shall effect the items of maintenance designated therein including the repair of defective items and/or the replacement of unrepairable or obsolete items of equipment

and signage. Routine maintenance shall be conducted in accordance with general schedules published by Company.

* * *

6.7   Licensee shall adopt and use as his continuing operational routine the standard "Dairy Queen" management system, as prescribed in the Store Management Operations Manual, including Company's standards with respect to product preparation, merchandising, employee training, equipment and facility maintenance and sanitation. Company will revise the Manual and these programs periodically to meet changing conditions of retail operation in the best interest of "Dairy Queen" retail stores . . . .

* * * However, we agree with the district court that this language does not establish sufficient control on ADQ's part such that ADQ can be said to "operate" the San Antonio stores. Paragraph B is simply a general statement regarding the purpose of the agreement, and even it makes clear that R & S Dairy Queens, not ADQ, will "operate" the store. Paragraph 5.1 provides for the greatest level of control over the accessibility of the Nacogdoches Store to the disabled, but it relates to the construction of the store, and it is undisputed that the Nacogdoches store was constructed and equipped before the ADA was enacted. Consequently, even if ADQ "operated" the store with respect to its construction, such operation is irrelevant because the issue in Neff's case is whether ADQ "operates" the San Antonio Stores with respect to the removal of existing architectural barriers. In addition, ADQ's pre-ADA control over the San Antonio Stores cannot form the basis of Neff's discrimination claim because the ADA is not to be given retroactive effect. See *Burfield v. Brown, Moore & Flint, Inc.,* 51 F.3d 583, 588 (5th Cir. 1995) (holding that employment discrimination claim was barred because "[t]he ADA is not retroactive and it does not apply to actions allegedly taken prior to the effective date of the Act").

Paragraph 5.2, the only paragraph that relates to modifications to the structure of the Nacogdoches Store, simply provides that ADQ may disapprove any proposed modifications to the Nacogdoches Store building and equipment. While this does amount to a limited form of control over structural modifications, we agree with the district court that this right, which is essentially negative in character, cannot support a holding that ADQ "operates" the Nacogdoches Store with respect to its removal of architectural barriers to the disabled. We note that Neff has not alleged or offered any summary judgment evidence to show that ADQ has withheld its consent to proposed modifications to the Nacogdoches Store designed to bring it into compliance with the ADA.

In its brief, Neff specifically emphasizes paragraphs 5.3 and 6.7. Paragraph 5.3 refers to building and equipment maintenance and not the modification of the store structure or removal of architectural barriers. ADQ's control in this regard, while more relevant than its control over employee uniforms, accounting standards, etc., is not directly relevant to the Neff's suit. Neff's complaint is not based on R & S's failure to perform maintenance on the Nacogdoches Store building or equipment; rather, she complains of the equipment itself. Further, while Paragraph 5.3 does provide that such maintenance must be conducted in accordance with ADQ-established maintenance lists, Neff has not alleged, or offered any summary judgment evidence to show, that these lists prevent R & S from modifying the Nacogdoches Store to bring it into compliance with the ADA.

Paragraph 6.7 states that R & S must adhere to the routine prescribed by ADQ's "Store Management Operations Manual," through which ADQ sets standards for "product preparation, merchandising, employee training, equipment and facility maintenance and sanitation." The effect of this provision is similar in kind to the effect of Paragraph 5.3. It does not relate to the modification of the physical structure or accessibility of the Nacogdoches Store, and Neff has not alleged or offered summary judgment to show that the Store Management Operations Manual prevents R & S Dairy Queens from making such modifications.

In sum, while the terms of the Nacogdoches Store franchise agreement demonstrate that ADQ retains the right to set standards for building and equipment maintenance and to "veto" proposed structural changes, we hold that this supervisory authority, without more, is insufficient to support a holding that ADQ "operates," in the ordinary and natural meaning of that term, the Nacogdoches Store.

Because Neff rested her claim that ADQ "operates" the San Antonio stores exclusively on the terms of the Nacogdoches Store franchise agreement, and did not allege that ADQ has prevented R & S Dairy Queens from complying with the ADA, either as a practical matter or by exercising its rights under its franchise agreements, we hold that ADQ met its burden under Rule 56(c) in its motion for summary judgment. ADQ established the absence of a genuine issue of material fact and further that it was entitled to judgment as a matter of law based on the terms of its franchise agreements with R & S Dairy Queens. Because Neff offered no summary judgment evidence other than the Nacogdoches Store franchise agreement in response to ADQ's motion, we further hold that Neff's summary judgment evidence was insufficient to raise a genuine issue for trial.

Neff and the United States argue that to exclude ADQ from the scope of section 302(a) would be inconsistent with the canon of construction requiring courts to interpret civil rights statutes liberally to effectuate their remedial purposes. * * * Even assuming the canon applies in this context, we hold that Neff's interpretation of the term "operates" would require more than just a liberal construction of that term. Neff's argument in this case would require us to bend "operates" too far beyond its natural meaning for us to rely on the canon of statutory interpretation requiring that we interpret civil rights legislation liberally.

Furthermore, we fail to see how our interpretation of "operates" to exclude ADQ under the circumstances involved in this case will interfere with the remedial purposes of the ADA. Assuming conditions at the San Antonio stores do not comply with the ADA, it is Neff's decision not to sue the owner and operator of those stores, R & S Dairy Queens, that will prevent her from obtaining the injunction she seeks.

Neff also argues that because "a franchisor is held responsible under the Civil Rights Act, a franchisor is held responsible under the ADA." This argument fails on several levels. First, it depends on Neff's premise that "the Title III [of the ADA] rights and remedies are the same as those rights and remedies available under the Civil Rights Act of 1964." However, the statutory provision Neff cites for this proposition states only that the *remedies* available under the ADA shall be the same as the *remedies* available under the Civil Rights Act. See 42 U.S.C. § 12188(a)(1). Second, because the Civil Rights Act does not define the scope of defendants who may potentially be liable with reference to who "operates" a public accommodation, Civil Rights Act cases are unlikely to be informative on the meaning of that term. Third, the two cases on which Neff relies to argue that franchisors "are liable" under the Civil Rights Act, *Wheeler v. Hurdman,* 825 F.2d 257 (10th Cir. 1987), and *Bradley v. Pizzaco,* 7 F.3d 795 (8th Cir. 1993), are factually distinguishable.

III

For the foregoing reasons, we AFFIRM the district court's order granting ADQ's motion for summary judgment.

Notes & Questions

1. Title II of the Civil Rights Act of 1964 also covers "public accommodations." However, the Civil Rights Act definition is different. Title II of the Civil Rights Act only covers places of transient lodging, restaurants and places of exhibition or entertainment. 42 U.S.C. § 2000a (2006). What do you think is the reason for the different definitions of the same term?

2. Both landlords and tenants are responsible for ADA compliance. Botosan v. Paul McNally Realty, 216 F.3d 827, 832 (9th Cir. 1999). In light of *Neff*, when will a tenant, rather than the landlord, be held responsible for barriers in a common area, or vice versa? *See* Emerick v. Kahala L & L, Inc., No. Civ. 97-01174 FIY, 2000 WL 687662 (D. Haw. May 16, 2000). How will a plaintiff restaurant patron know whether the franchisor or franchisee is responsible for a particular discriminatory barrier or policy at the complaint-filing stage of litigation? Must the plaintiff always sue both parties? *See* Pona v. Cecil Shitaker's,

Inc., 155 F.3d 1034, 1036 (8th Cir. 1998) (restaurant franchisor could not be held liable to customer who was asked to leave restaurant because she had service dog because franchisor did not reserve right under franchise agreement to control entry to restaurant).

3.   Independent contractors may also appear to exercise control in some public accommodations.   To be responsible under Title III, an individual or entity must have some ability to control the place of public accommodation.   Thus, in *Aikins v. St. Helena Hospital*, 843 F.Supp. 1329 (N.D. Cal. 1994), a doctor who worked as an independent contractor, and who did not control the relevant operations or policies of the hospital, was not liable under Title III for the hospital's actions.   *Id.* at 1335.   *But see* Howe v. Hull, 874 F.Supp. 779, 787-788 (N.D. Ohio 1994) (doctor was "operator" of hospital because he had role in admitting patients).

ॐ

C.   Covered Areas

There have been questions raised as to what areas are considered "public" for purposes of determining a public accommodation.   For instance, the argument is made that certain individuals, such as college students, theatre performers, independent contractors, or competitors in sports contests, are not protected by Title III because they are not clients nor customers.   Nor are they employees subject to the requirements of Title I.   Therefore, areas reserved for those groups may not be covered by the ADA.

This argument would exempt from coverage areas that are restricted for the use of certain designated individuals (e.g., locker rooms, playing fields, and class rooms).   Under this theory, only the general public (e.g., spectators of a football game, but not athletes) would be able to assert rights or have legal standing under Title III.

In *PGA Tour Inc. v. Martin*, 532 U.S. 661, 679-680 (2001), the U.S. Supreme Court found that, for the purposes of Title III, sports competitors are clients or customers of a place of public accommodation.   The Court found that players in competitive sports, such as those on the PGA Tour, are members of the general public.   Indeed, they constitute a sub-group of the general public who have paid a fee and/or met a qualification standard.   Therefore, the playing areas, rules of play, and so on are subject to the Title III requirements for places of public accommodation.

In some cases, simultaneous questions have arisen as to whether an individual was an employee covered under Title I, a member of the public covered under Title III, or some other category without protection of the ADA.   As a general matter, the courts have been careful to ensure that individuals are not denied coverage under both Title I and Title III.   Thus, a physician may be covered under Title III for the purposes of accommodations in hospital privileges, because his independent contractor status does not bring him within Title I's employment protections.

Menkowitz v. Pottstown Mem'l Med. Ctr., 154 F.3d 113, 122-23 (3d Cir. 1998); Hetz v. Aurora Med. Ctr. of Minitowoc Cty., 2007 WL 1753428 (E.D. Wis. 2007). *But see* Wojewski v. Rapid City Reg'l Hosp., Inc., 394 F.Supp.2d 1134 (D.S.D. 2005) (holding physician with staff privileges is not protected by Title III), affirmed in part, vacated in part, remanded by Wojewski v. Rapid City Regional Hosp., Inc., 450 F.3d 338 (8th Cir. 2006).

༆

Notes & Questions

1. Should an employee of a business not covered under Title I of the ADA (e.g., with fewer than 15 employees) have a right to assert disability discrimination under Title III? Should an employee of a business that is covered by Title I also be able to assert rights under Title III? Should the employee be restricted to non-employment-related rights (e.g., access to public areas as opposed to access to employee areas or reasonable modification of employment-related policies)? *Compare* DeWyer v. Temple Univ., No. CIV.A.00-CV-1665, 2001 WL 115461, at *3 (E.D. Pa. Feb. 5, 2001) (employee can assert employment-related rights under Title I, not Title III; also possible for an employee to assert Title III for non-employment related rights), *with* Motzkin v. Boston Univ., 938 F.Supp. 983, 995-96 (D. Mass 1996) (employment practices are covered exclusively by Title I, not Title III). *See also* Weyer v. Twentieth Century Fox Film Corp., 198 F.3d 1104 (9th Cir. 2000) (questioning, but not deciding, whether employee can pursue rights against employer under Title III). Notably, some courts have found that Title II covers employment, thus potentially allowing employees of government agencies to assert both Title I and Title II claims. *See* Bledsoe v. Palm Beach County Soil & Water Conservation Dist., 133 F.3d 816, 820-22 (11th Cir. 1998). Other courts have disagreed and restricted employment rights to Title I. *See* Zimmerman v. Or. Dep't of Justice, 170 F.3d 1169, 1173-74 (9th Cir. 1999).

2. Are volunteers working for a Title III entity protected? *See* Bauer v. Muscular Dystrophy Ass'n., Inc., 268 F.Supp.2d 1281 (D. Kan. 2003).

3. May the customer's motive in patronizing a business affect her protection? Jarek Molski, a man with paraplegia and a reputation for suing hundreds of establishments for alleged inaccessible public accommodations, has been labeled a "vexatious litigant," *Molski v. Evergreen Dynasty Corp.*, 500 F.3d 1047, 1050 (9th Cir. 2007), and "purportedly in the business of tracking down public accommodations with ADA violations and extorting settlements out of them." Molski v. M.J. Cable, Inc., 481 F.3d 724, 728 (9th Cir. 2007). In *M.J. Cable, Inc.*, the Ninth Circuit reversed a jury finding that Molski was not a member of the protected class, concluding the jury verdict had no basis to this end. But in *Evergreen Dynasty*, the Ninth Circuit "upheld the ruling that Mr. Molski was an abusive litigant" even though "many of the establishments

he sued probably were violating federal law, and the U.S. Supreme Court denied certiorari." Evergreen Dynasty Corp., 500 F.3d 1047 (9th Cir. 2007), cert. denied, 77 U.S.L.W. 3295 (U.S. Nov. 17, 2008) (No. 08-38).

✌

D. Physical Structures

There is a split among the federal circuit courts regarding whether an entity may be a place of public accommodation when it does not occupy a physical "place" that is open to the public. Consider the different approaches set forth in the following cases.

✌

CARPARTS DISTRIBUTION CENTER, INC. v. AUTOMOTIVE WHOLESALER'S ASS'N OF NEW ENGLAND, INC.

United States Court of Appeals, First Circuit, 1994
37 F.3d 12

TORRUELLA, Chief Judge.

Plaintiffs-appellants Carparts Distribution Center, Inc., Daniel W. Dirsh, and Shirley M. Senter, appeal from the district court's order dismissing their complaint for illegal discrimination based on disability under state and federal laws. The court granted judgment under Fed.R.Civ.P. 12(b)(6) in favor of defendants.

* * *

II.

BACKGROUND

In May 1986, Plaintiff Ronald J. Senter ("Senter") was diagnosed as infected with Human Immunodeficiency Virus ("HIV positive"). In March 1991, he was diagnosed as suffering from Acquired Immune Deficiency Syndrome ("AIDS"). He died on January 17, 1993.

Senter was the sole shareholder, president, chief executive director, and an employee of Carparts Distribution Center, Inc. ("Carparts"), an automotive parts wholesale distributor incorporated in New Hampshire.

Since 1977, Carparts has been a participant in a self-funded medical reimbursement plan known as Automotive Wholesalers Association of New England Health Benefit Plan ("the Plan") offered by the defendants in this case, Automotive Wholesalers Association of New England, Inc. ("AWANE") and its administering trust, Automotive Wholesalers Association of New England, Inc. Insurance Plan ("AWANE Plan"). Senter was enrolled in the Plan since 1977. In October 1990, AWANE Plan informed members of AWANE, including Carparts, of its intention to amend the Plan in order to limit benefits for AIDS-related illnesses to $25,000, effective January 1, 1991. Otherwise, lifetime benefits under the Plan were, and are, afforded in the amount of $1 million per eligible plan member.

On a number of occasions during and after 1989, Senter had several serious illnesses, many of which were HIV or AIDS related. Senter directly submitted claims for payment of his medical treatment and medications to AWANE and the AWANE Plan until spring or summer of 1991, when Carparts submitted the claims on Senter's behalf because he became too sick or matters were too complicated for him to do so.

Senter and Carparts ("plaintiffs" or "appellants") alleged, that the Trustees of the Plan were aware of Senter's condition at the time the amendments to the plan were adopted. Plaintiffs claim that the cap on AIDS-related illnesses was instituted by defendants with knowledge that Senter was diagnosed HIV positive, suffering from AIDS, and subject to AIDS-related medical expenses and that the lifetime cap on AIDS related expenses was instituted in response to Senter's illness and related claims that he had filed during the previous several months. According to plaintiffs, after Senter reached the lifetime cap on AIDS related illnesses, defendants breached their contractual obligation to provide, at a minimum, medical coverage to Senter for non-AIDS related treatments, by failing, neglecting or refusing to make payments for non-AIDS related matters in a complete or consistent manner.

Plaintiffs brought this action alleging that the lifetime cap on health benefits for individuals with AIDS, instituted by defendants, represented illegal discrimination on the basis of a disability. Such a discriminatory provision allegedly rendered Carparts responsible for payments to healthcare providers on Senter's behalf and effectively put Carparts out of compliance with anti-discrimination laws, subjecting Carparts to potential liability under * * * a state anti-discrimination law, and the Americans with Disabilities Act ("the ADA"), 42 U.S.C. § 12101, et seq.

The district court dismissed all of plaintiffs' claims on July 19, 1993. This appeal followed.

* * *

C. Title III of the ADA

Title III of the ADA provides:

(a). General Rule. No individual shall be discriminated against on the basis of disability in the full and equal enjoyment of the goods, services, facilities, privileges, advantages, or accommodations of any place of public accommodation by any person who owns, leases (or leases to), or operates a place of public accommodation. 42 U.S.C. § 12182(a).

Prohibited discrimination under Title III includes the denial, on the basis of disability, of the opportunity to benefit from the goods, services, privileges, advantages or accommodations of an entity. 42 U.S.C. § 12182(b) 28 C.F.R. § 36.202.

The district court interpreted the term "public accommodation" as "being limited to actual physical structures with definite physical boundaries which a person physically enters for the purpose of utilizing the facilities or obtaining services therein." Because the court found that neither of the defendants possessed those characteristics, it dismissed Senter's Title III claim. Plaintiffs contend that the district court erred in finding that Title III of the ADA did not apply to defendants because they were not places of "public accommodation" within the meaning of the Act.

Whether establishments of "public accommodation" are limited to actual physical structures is a question of first impression in this Circuit. For the following reasons we find that they are not so limited and remand to the district court to allow plaintiffs the opportunity to adduce further evidence supporting their view that the defendants are places of "public accommodation" within the meaning of Title III of the ADA.

We begin our analysis by looking at the language of the statute. * * * The definition of "public accommodation" states that "[t]he following private entities are considered public accommodations for purposes of this subchapter, if the operations of such entities affect commerce –" and then provides an illustrative list which includes a "travel service," a "shoe repair service," an "office of an accountant, or lawyer," an "insurance office," a "professional office of a healthcare provider," and "other service establishment[s]." 42 U.S.C. § 12181(7)(F). The plain meaning of the terms do not require "public accommodations" to have physical structures for persons to enter. Even if the meaning of "public accommodation" is not plain, it is, at worst, ambiguous. This ambiguity, considered together with agency regulations and public policy concerns, persuades us that the phrase is not limited to actual physical structures.

By including "travel service" among the list of services considered "public accommodations," Congress clearly contemplated that "service establishments" include providers of services which do not require a person to physically enter an actual physical structure. Many travel services conduct business by telephone or correspondence without requiring their customers to enter an office in order to obtain their services. Likewise, one can easily imagine the existence of other service establishments conducting business by mail and phone without providing facilities for their customers to enter in order to utilize their services. It would be irrational to conclude that persons who enter an office to purchase services are protected by the ADA, but persons who purchase the same services over the telephone or by mail are not. Congress could not have intended such an absurd result.

Our interpretation is also consistent with the legislative history of the ADA. The purpose of the ADA is to "invoke the sweep of Congressional authority . . . in order to address the major areas of discrimination faced day-to-day by people with disabilities," 42 U.S.C. § 12101(b). The ADA was enacted to "provide a clear and comprehensive national mandate for the elimination of discrimination against individuals with disabilities." 42 U.S.C. § 12101(b)(1). The purpose of Title III of the ADA, is "to bring individuals with disabilities into the economic and social mainstream of American life ... in a clear, balanced, and reasonable manner." H.R. Rep. No. 485, 101st Cong., 2d Sess., pt. 2, at 99 (1990), reprinted in 1990 U.S.C.C.A.N. 303, 382. In drafting Title III, Congress intended that people with disabilities have equal access to the array of goods and services offered by private establishments and made available to those who do not have disabilities. S. Rep. No. 116, 101st Cong., 1st Sess. at 58 (1989).

Beyond our threshold determination, we must tread with care. Some of the critical language of Title III is both general and ambiguous – for example, a key provision concerns the denial based on a disability "of the opportunity of the individual or class to participate in or benefit from the goods, services, facilities, privileges, advantages, or accommodations of an entity." 42 U.S.C. § 12182(b)(1)(A)(i). As a matter of bare language, one could spend some time arguing about whether this is intended merely to provide access to whatever product or service the subject entity may offer, or is intended in addition to shape and control which products and services may be offered. Indeed, there may be areas in which a sharp distinction between these two concepts is illusory.

One who simply reads the Committee Report describing the operations of Title III could easily come away with the impression that it is primarily concerned with access in the sense of either physical access to a place of public accommodation or something analogous, such as access provided through telephone lines, messengers or some other medium. At the same time, there is nothing in that history that explicitly precludes an extension of the statute to the substance of what is being offered. Suppose, for example, a company that makes and distributes tools provides easy access to its retail outlets for persons with every kind of disability, but declines to make even minor adjustments in the design of the tools to make them usable by persons with only quite limited disabilities.

The statute's treatment of insurance is a good example of these ambiguities. On the one hand, the ADA carves out a safe harbor of sorts for anyone who is "an insurer, hospital, or medical service company, health maintenance organization, or any agent, or entity that administers benefit plans, or similar organizations . . . ." 42 U.S.C. § 12201(c)(1). *See also id.* at (C)(2), (3). One might initially suppose that this is because Title III would otherwise cover the substance of the insurance plans. However, there is some indication in the legislative history that the industry received this exemption not because its policies would otherwise be substantively regulated under Title III, but because "there is some uncertainty over the possible interpretations of the language contained in titles I, II and III as it applies to insurance . . . ." See S. Rep. No. 116, 101 Cong., 1st Sess. at 84 (1989).

We think that at this stage it is unwise to go beyond the *possibility* that the plaintiff may be able to develop some kind of claim under Title III even though this may be a less promising vehicle in the present case than Title I. Not only the facts but, as we have already noted, even the factual allegations are quite sparse. In addition, because of our resolution of the Title I claims, this case must be remanded and is subject to further proceedings regardless of whether Title III remains in the case. While it is tempting to seek to provide further guidance, the nature of the record and the way the issues are addressed in the appellate briefs make it imprudent to do so.

Neither Title III nor its implementing regulations make any mention of physical boundaries or physical entry. Many goods and services are sold over the telephone or by mail with customers never physically entering the premises of a commercial entity to purchase the goods or services. To exclude this broad category of businesses from the reach of Title III and limit the application of Title III to physical structures which persons must enter to obtain goods and services would run afoul of the purposes of the ADA and would severely frustrate Congress's intent that individuals with disabilities fully enjoy the goods, services, privileges and advantages, available indiscriminately to other members of the general public.

* * *

V.

CONCLUSION

Because the district court dismissed plaintiffs' complaint without providing notice of its intended dismissal and erred in interpreting the term "employer" under Title I of the ADA and in concluding that defendants were not "public accommodations" under Title III, we hold that the district court erred in dismissing plaintiffs' complaint.

&

PARKER v. METROPOLITAN LIFE INSURANCE CO.

United States Court of Appeals, Sixth Circuit, 1997
121 F.3d 1006

KENNEDY, Circuit Judge.

Title III of the Americans with Disabilities Act, 42 U.S.C. §§ 12182-12189 ("ADA"), prohibits discrimination on the basis of disability in the full and equal enjoyment of the goods, services, facilities, privileges, advantages or accommodations of any place of public accommodation. In the instant case, we are asked to determine whether Title III of the ADA prohibits an employer from providing to its employees a long-term disability plan issued by an insurance company which contains longer benefits for employees who become disabled due to a physical illness than for those who become disabled due to a mental illness. For the reasons set forth below, we conclude that such a distinction is not prohibited.

I.

Plaintiff, Ouida Sue Parker, was employed by Schering-Plough Health Care Products, Inc. ("Schering-Plough") from April 20, 1981 through October 29, 1990. During her employment, Parker participated in a long-term disability plan offered by Schering-Plough to its employees; the plan was issued by Metropolitan Life Insurance Co. ("MetLife"). Under the plan, an individual who is deemed to be totally disabled due to a mental or nervous disorder may receive benefits for up to twenty-four months, unless at the termination of the twenty-four month period, the individual was hospitalized or receiving inpatient care for the disorder. For physical disorders, however, the plan provides for benefits until the individual reaches sixty-five years of age.

On October 29, 1990, Parker became disabled due to severe depression. On April 29, 1991, Parker began to receive benefit payments under the plan. Because Parker suffered from a mental disorder, Schering-Plough terminated her payments twenty-four months later, on April 28, 1993, pursuant to the terms of the plan. Following Schering-Plough's denial of two administrative appeals filed by Parker, plaintiff filed this action alleging violations of the Americans with Disabilities Act, 42 U.S.C. §§ 12101-12213, and the Employee Retirement Income Security Act, 29 U.S.C. §§ 1001-1461 ("ERISA"). The District Court granted the defendants' motion for summary judgment. The District Court first found that Parker did not have standing to sue under Title I of the ADA, 42 U.S.C. §§ 12111-12117, because only a "qualified individual with a disability" may obtain relief under Title I and Parker was not a "qualified individual with a disability" when her benefits were terminated because her disorder prevented her from performing the essential functions of her employment position. The District Court also dismissed Parker's claim against the defendants under Title III of the ADA, 42 U.S.C. §§ 12165-12189. MetLife was not a proper defendant under Title III, the court concluded, because Title III only covers discrimination in the physical access to goods and services, not discrimination in the terms of insurance policies. The Title III claim against Schering-Plough, Parker's employer, was dismissed because Title I, not Title III, governs discrimination in employment practices. Because Parker was not a qualified individual under Title I, a suit against her employer could not be maintained under the ADA. Lastly, the District Court granted summary judgment in favor of the defendants on Parker's ERISA claim because the classification of her disorder as "nervous/mental" was not arbitrary or capricious.

On appeal from the District Court's order, a panel of this Court affirmed the District Court's judgment as to Parker's ERISA * * * claim and Title I claim under the ADA. The panel, however, reversed the District Court's judgment as to plaintiff's claim under Title III of the ADA. Disagreeing with the District Court, the panel concluded that Title III "prohibits discrimination in the contents of the goods and services offered at places of public accommodation, rather than just discrimination in terms of physical access to places of public accommodation." * * * Accordingly, the panel found that Title III covers insurance products because "insurance products are 'goods' or 'services' provided by a 'person' who owns a 'public accommodation.'" * * *

Because the panel concluded that the contents of insurance products are governed by Title III, it then turned to whether Title IV of the ADA, 42 U.S.C. § 12201(c), commonly referred to as the "safe harbor provision," precluded application of Title III to insurance products. The panel concluded that the safe harbor provision was ambiguous on its face as to whether it intended to exempt insurance products from ADA coverage. It, therefore, looked to legislative history for guidance. The panel concluded that the legislative history indicated that "insurance practices are protected by the 'safe harbor' provision, but only to the extent that they are consistent with 'sound actuarial principles,' 'actual reasonably anticipated experience,' and 'bona fide risk classification.'" * * * Responding to the defendants' argument that an insurance plan violates the ADA only if it is a "subterfuge" under § 12201(c), the panel declined to adopt the Supreme Court's definition of subterfuge pronounced in *Ohio Public Employees Retirement System v. Betts,* 492 U.S. 158 (1989). In *Betts,* the Court defined the term subterfuge in the Age Discrimination in Employment Act ("ADEA") as an intent to discriminate. * * * Declining to follow the ADEA definition of subterfuge, the panel held that an insurance plan is a subterfuge under the ADA if it is "based on speculation, and not on sound actuarial principles, actual or reasonably anticipated experience, or bona fide risk classification." * * *

Finally, in response to Schering-Plough's contention that Title I, not Title III, governs employment practices, the panel held that "based on our affirmance of Plaintiff's Title I claim, it is not clear whether Schering remains a proper defendant to the remaining claim [Title III] of this suit." * * * The panel did not resolve this question of law; rather, it instructed the lower court that the issue was ripe for its determination on remand. * * *

Following the panel's decision, the defendants sought rehearing *en banc* on the panel's disposition of Parker's Title III claim. We granted their petition and vacated our prior judgment. * * * Accordingly, the case is again before us for our determination. Upon review, we conclude that the judgment of the District Court will be AFFIRMED.

    * * *

III.

A. Title III: Places of Public Accommodation

To determine whether a benefit plan provided by an employer falls within the prohibitions of Title III, we must begin by examining the statutory text. * * * The ADA generally prohibits discrimination against the disabled by employers, public entities, and by operators of public accommodations. See 42 U.S.C. §§ 12101-12213. Title III of the ADA specifically addresses discrimination by owners, lessors, and operators of public accommodations. It provides as follows:

> No individual shall be discriminated against on the basis of disability in the full and equal enjoyment of the goods, services, facilities, privileges, advantages, or accommodations of any place of public accommodation by any person who owns, leases (or leases to), or operates a place of public accommodation.

42 U.S.C. § 12182(a).

Section 12181 sets forth the following list of private entities that are considered public accommodations for purposes of Title III:

* * *

> (F) a laundromat, dry-cleaner, bank, barber shop, beauty shop, travel service, shoe repair service, funeral parlor, gas station, office of an accountant or lawyer, pharmacy, *insurance office,* professional office of a health care provider, hospital, or other service establishment;

* * *

42 U.S.C. § 12181(7) (emphasis added).

Title III specifically prohibits, *inter alia,* the provision of unequal or separate benefits by a place of public accommodation. See 42 U.S.C. §§ 12182(b)(1)(A)(i)-(iii). For example, 42 U.S.C. § 12182(b)(1)(A)(ii) provides that it is "discriminatory to afford an individual or class of individuals, on the basis of a disability ... with the opportunity to participate in or benefit from a good, service, facility, privilege, advantage, or accommodation that is not equal to that afforded to other individuals ...," 42 U.S.C. § 12182(b)(1)(a)(ii). To the extent that subsections (i), (ii), and (iii) do not explicitly state that they apply only to public accommodations, subsection (iv) expressly provides that "... the term 'individual or class of individuals' refers to the clients or customers of the covered public accommodation ..." 42 U.S.C. § 12182(b)(1)(a)(iv).

While we agree that an insurance office is a public accommodation as expressly set forth in § 12181(7), plaintiff did not seek the goods and services of an insurance office. Rather, Parker accessed a benefit plan provided by her private employer and issued by MetLife. A benefit plan offered by an employer is not a good offered by a place of public accommodation. As is evident by § 12187(7), a public accommodation is a physical place and this Court has previously so held. In *Stoutenborough v. National Football League, Inc.*, 59 F.3d 580 (6th Cir. 1995), Thomas Stoutenborough and an association of hearing impaired persons filed suit against the National Football League ("NFL") and several television stations under Title III of the ADA alleging that the NFL's "blackout rule" discriminates against them because hearing impaired individuals have no other means of accessing football games when live telecasts are prohibited. They cannot, for example, listen to the broadcast on the radio. * * * To place the blackout rule within the purview of Title III, the plaintiffs argued that they were denied substantially equal access to live television transmissions of football games which is a service of a public accommodation. * * * This Court rejected the plaintiffs' contention holding that the defendants did not fall within any of the twelve categories enumerated in § 12181(7). * * * Furthermore, we held that "the prohibitions of Title III are restricted to 'places' of public accommodation ..." A "place," as defined by the applicable regulations, is " 'a facility, operated by a private entity, whose operations affect commerce and fall within at least one of the' twelve 'public accommodation' categories." * * * " 'Facility,' in turn, is defined as 'all or any portion of buildings, structures, sites, complexes, equipment, rolling stock or other conveyances, roads, walks, passageways, parking lots, or other real or personal property, including the site where the building, property, structure, or equipment is located.' " * * * Although the court acknowledged that the football games were played in a place of accommodation and that the television broadcasts were a service provided by the defendants, the court concluded that the broadcasts "do[ ] not involve a 'place of public accommodation.' " * * * Accordingly, we held that the service offered by the defendants did not involve a place of public accommodation. * * * Quoting the district court's opinion, we explained that " '[i]t is all of the services which the public accommodation offers, not all services which the lessor of the public accommodation offers which fall within the scope of Title III.' " * * * Finally, the court noted that "plaintiffs' argument that the prohibitions of Title III are not solely limited to 'places' of public accommodation contravenes the plain language of the statute." * * *

Similarly, the good that plaintiff seeks is not offered by a place of public accommodation. The public cannot enter the office of MetLife or Schering-Plough and obtain the long-term disability policy that plaintiff obtained. Parker did not access her policy from MetLife's insurance office. Rather, she obtained her benefits through her employer. There is, thus, no nexus between the disparity in benefits and the services which MetLife offers to the public from its insurance office.[3] * * *

---

[3] Judge Merritt's dissent suggests that our opinion concludes that Parker's disability plan obtained through her employer is not covered by

The Department of Justice's explanation of whether wholesale establishments are places of public accommodation supports our conclusion that MetLife's offering of a disability plan to Schering-Plough is not a service offered by a place of public accommodation. As the Department explains:

> ... The Department intends for wholesale establishments to be covered ... as places of public accommodation except in cases where they sell exclusively to other businesses and not to individuals.... [However], [i]f th[e wholesale company] operates a road side stand where its crops are sold to the public, the road side stand would be a sales establishment covered by the ADA.... Of course, a company that operates a place of public accommodation is subject to this part only in the operation of that place of public accommodation. In the example given above, the wholesale produce company that operates a road side stand would be a public accommodation only for the purposes of the operation of that stand. The company would be prohibited from discriminating on the basis of disability in the operation of the road side stand, and it would be required to remove barriers to physical access . . . .

28 C.F.R. pt. 36, app. B, at 604 (1996). Thus, the offering of disability policies on a discounted rate solely to a business is not a service or good offered by a place of public accommodation.

Furthermore, Title III does not govern the content of a long-term disability policy offered by an employer. The applicable regulations clearly set forth that Title III regulates the availability of the goods and services the place of public accommodation offers as opposed to the contents of goods and services offered by the public accommodation. According to the Department of Justice:

> The purpose of the ADA's public accommodations requirements is to ensure accessibility to the goods offered by a public accommodation, not to alter the nature or mix of goods that the public accommodation has typically provided. In other words, a bookstore, for example, must make its facilities and sales operations accessible to individuals with disabilities, but is not required to stock Brailled or large

---

Title III because she physically did not access her policy from MetLife's insurance office. We have not so held. The policy Parker obtained is not covered by Title III because Title III covers only physical places. We have expressed no opinion as to whether a plaintiff must physically enter a public accommodation to bring suit under Title III as opposed to merely accessing, by some other means, a service or good provided by a public accommodation.

470

print books. Similarly, a video store must make its facilities and rental operations accessible, but is not required to stock closed-captioned video tapes.[5]

* * * While Title IV of the ADA, 42 U.S.C. § 12201(c), may address the contents of insurance policies provided by a public accommodation,[7]

---

[5]   The Department of Justice has in other writings interpreted Title III to include regulation of the substantive terms of insurance contracts. See DOJ Technical Assistance Manual, § III-3.11000, reprinted in Americans with Disabilities Act Manual (BNA) at 90:0917. That provision of the technical assistance manual provides:

> Insurance offices are places of public accommodation and, as such, may not discriminate on the basis of disability in the sale of insurance contracts or in the terms or conditions of the insurance contracts they offer. Because of the nature of the insurance business, however, consideration of disability in the sale of insurance contracts does not always constitute "discrimination." An insurer or other public accommodation may underwrite, classify, or administer risks that are based on or not inconsistent with State law, provided that such practices are not used to evade the purposes of the ADA.

> Thus, a public accommodation may offer a plan that limits certain kinds of coverage based on classification of risk, but may not refuse to insure, or refuse to continue to insure, or limit the amount, extent, or kind of coverage available to an individual, or charge a different rate for the same coverage solely because of a physical or mental impairment, except where the refusal, limitation, or rate differential is based on sound actuarial principles or is related to actual or reasonably anticipated experience. The ADA, therefore, does not prohibit use of legitimate actuarial considerations to justify differential treatment of individuals with disabilities in insurance.

As this interpretation is inconsistent with its regulations and the statutory text of Title IV, we decline to adopt it. * * *

[7]   Title IV and its accompanying regulations only require that an insurance policy offered by a place of public accommodation be consistent with state law and not a subterfuge to evade the purposes of the ADA to fall within the safe harbor provision. However, it is the opinion of both the Department of Justice and the Equal Employment Opportunity Commission that disparities in insurance policies must be supported by sound actuarial principles. * * *

Title IV does not address the contents of a long-term disability plan offered by an employer because it is not a place of public accommodation. We, therefore, disagree with the First Circuit's decision in *Carparts Distribution Center, Inc. v. Automotive Wholesaler's Association of New England, Inc.,* 37 F.3d 12 (1st Cir. 1994). * * *

In arriving at this conclusion, the First Circuit disregarded the statutory canon of construction, *noscitur a sociis.* * * * The doctrine of *noscitur a sociis* instructs that "a . . . term is interpreted within the context of the accompanying words 'to avoid the giving of unintended breadth to the Acts of Congress.'" * * * Black's Law Dictionary defines the term as:

> It is known from its associates. The meaning of a word is or may be known for the accompanying words. Under the doctrine of "noscitur a sociis", the meaning of questionable or doubtful words or phrases in a statute may be ascertained by reference to the meaning of other words or phrases associated with it.

BLACK'S LAW DICTIONARY 1060 (6th ed. 1990).

The clear connotation of the words in § 12181(7) is that a public accommodation is a physical place. Every term listed in § 12181(7) and subsection (F) is a physical place open to public access. The terms travel service, shoe repair service, office of an accountant or lawyer, insurance office, and professional office of a healthcare provider do not suggest otherwise. Rather than suggesting that Title III includes within its purview entities other than physical places, it is likely that Congress simply had no better term than "service" to describe an office where travel agents provide travel services and a place where shoes are repaired. Office of an accountant or lawyer, insurance office, and professional office of a healthcare provider, in the context of the other terms listed, suggest a physical place where services may be obtained and nothing more. To interpret these terms as permitting a place of accommodation to constitute

---

The discrepancy between the statute, the regulations, and the agency interpretations is due to Congress' failure to define the term "subterfuge" in Title IV of the ADA. The EEOC and the Justice Department, in certain writings, have expressed the view that, in order for a policy to not be a subterfuge, it must be based on sound actuarial principles. This definition is inconsistent with the Supreme Court's definition of the term subterfuge contained in the Age Discrimination in Employment Act. See *Ohio Public Employees Retirement Sys. v. Betts*, 492 U.S. 158, (1989). In *Betts*, the Court defined subterfuge as a specific intent to discriminate. * * * We leave the resolution of the proper definition of subterfuge in Title IV for another day because we conclude that a long-term disability plan provided by an employer is not covered by Title III; the safe harbor provision is, therefore, not implicated.

something other than a physical place is to ignore the text of the statute and the principle of *noscitur a sociis*.

Accordingly, we conclude that the provision of a long-term disability plan by an employer and administered by an insurance company does not fall within the purview of Title III.

* * *

For the foregoing reasons, the judgment of the District Court is AFFIRMED.

BOYCE F. MARTIN, JR., Chief Judge, dissenting.

I join Judge Merritt and others in dissenting from the opinion of the Court in this case. I write separately to highlight my agreement with Judge Merritt regarding congressional intent and to emphasize my disagreement with the majority's interpretation of *Stoutenborough v. National Football League, Inc.,* 59 F.3d 580 (6th Cir. 1995).

In *Stoutenborough,* a hearing impaired individual and an association of hearing impaired individuals sought to prohibit the National Football League, its member clubs, and several broadcast companies from using the so-called "blackout rule" to avoid broadcasting live local football games when tickets to the live game had not been completely sold seventy-two hours before the game. With regard to Stoutenborough's Title III claim, we stated that "plaintiff's argument that the prohibitions of Title III are not solely limited to 'places' of public accommodation contravenes the plain language of the statute." * * *

The majority takes this language to mean that Title III's mandates are limited to physical structures. However, *Stoutenborough* recognized that, in the context of a Title III claim, the term "place" is a defined term; we recognized that "a 'place' is '[1] a facility, [2] operated by a private entity, [3] whose operations affect commerce and [4] fall within at least one of the twelve "public accommodation" categories.'" * * * Because the defendants in *Stoutenborough,* did not fall within one of the twelve public accommodation categories, they were not "places" of public accommodation as required for Title III protection. Thus, although *Stoutenborough* limited Title III's applicability to "places," it did so in the context of the defined meaning of the term "place." Unlike the defendants in *Stoutenborough,* Title III specifically identifies an "insurance office" as a public accommodation. 42 U.S.C. § 12181(7)(F).

Not only does the majority view incorrectly apply *Stoutenborough,* it also directly conflicts with the conclusion reached by the First Circuit. In *Carparts Distribution Ctr. v. Automotive Wholesalers Ass'n of New England,* 37 F.3d 12 (1st Cir. 1994), the First Circuit held that, by including travel services in the list of public accommodations, Congress chose not to limit Title III protections to physical structures. The *Carparts* court wrote: "It would be irrational to conclude that persons who enter an office to purchase services are protected by the ADA, but persons who purchase the same services over the telephone or by mail are not. Congress could not have intended such an absurd result." * * * Similarly, Judge Merritt notes that, under the majority view, individuals who purchase insurance through an insurance office are entitled to Title III protections while those who purchase insurance through their employers receive no Title III protections.

In my view, Judge Merritt and the First Circuit present a more compelling argument. As the First Circuit noted, "[t]he purpose of Title III is 'to bring individuals with disabilities into the economic and social mainstream of American life ... in a clear, balanced, and reasonable manner.' " * * *

By limiting Title III's applicability to physical structures, the majority interprets Title III in a manner completely at odds with clear congressional intent. In recent years, the economic and social mainstream of American life has experienced significant change due to technological advances. An increasing array of products and services are becoming available for purchase by telephone order, through the mail, via the Internet, and other communications media. Unfortunately, under the majority view, the same technological advances that have offered disabled individuals unprecedented freedom may now operate to deprive them of rights that Title III would otherwise guarantee. As the modern economy increases the percentage of goods and services available through a marketplace that does not consist of physical structures, the protections of Title III will become increasingly diluted.

In my view, the majority view incorrectly applies a prior opinion of this Court and reaches a conclusion clearly at odds with congressional intent. Accordingly, I join Judge Merritt and respectfully dissent.

MERRITT, Circuit Judge, dissenting.

I would adhere to the panel's interpretation with respect to the application to group health and disability insurance policies of Titles III and IV of the Americans with Disabilities Act, 42 U.S.C. §§ 12182, 12201. The panel's reasoning is fully set out in its published decision, *Parker v. Metropolitan Life Ins. Co.,* 99 F.3d 181 (6th Cir.1996). It reaches the conclusion that the statute covers group health and disability insurance provided by insurance companies through an insured's employer, as well as insurance provided by walk-in insurance agencies.

Our Court has now held that the provisions of the Disabilities Act simply do not cover employee health and disability insurance plans because "a benefit plan offered by an employer is not a good offered by a place of public accommodation." * * * Footnotes 4 and 9 of the Court's opinion notwithstanding, according to the express language of the Court's opinion, Parker is not covered because she got her coverage from MetLife

474

through the employer instead of walking into a MetLife office and buying it.

* * *

Footnotes 3 and 8 are *post hoc* efforts by the Court to do an about face and march off in a different direction, or at least bury its head in the sand.

Our Court's decision that the Disabilities Act does not cover employer-sponsored plans flies in the face of § 501(c) of the Act, 42 U.S.C. § 12201(e), entitled "Insurance" (attached as an addendum to this opinion), which immediately follows the Title III coverage provision prohibiting discrimination. It provides a "safe harbor" for insurance companies in certain respects. If Title III does not cover the millions of employees covered by health and disability insurance policies, as our Court has now held, it is difficult to see why Congress would provide a qualified exemption for insurance companies. It is also difficult to see why the House and Senate Committee Reports would treat such insurance as covered by the Act, as the following quotes clearly demonstrate:

> Under the [Disabilities Act], a person with a disability cannot be denied insurance or be subject to different terms or conditions of insurance based on disability alone, if the disability does not impose increased risks.
>
> . . . .
>
> Moreover, while a plan which limits certain kinds of coverage based on classification of risk would be allowed under this section * * *, the plan may not refuse to insure, or refuse to continue to insure, or limit the amount, extent, or kind of coverage available to an individual, or charge a different rate for the same coverage solely because of a physical or mental impairment, except where the refusal, limitation, or rate differential is based on sound actuarial principles or is related to actual or reasonably anticipated experience.
>
> For example, a blind person may not be denied coverage based on blindness independent of actuarial risk classification.
>
> * * * The explanation continues:
>
> In sum, section 501(c) [the safe-harbor provision] is intended to afford to insurers and employers the same opportunities they would enjoy in the absence of the legislation to design and administer insurance products and benefit plans in a manner that is consistent with basic principles of insurance risk classification. This legislation assures that decisions concerning the insurance of persons

with disabilities which are not based on bona fide risk classification be made in conformity with non-discrimination requirements. Without such clarification, this legislation could arguably find violative of its provisions any action taken by an insurer or employer which treats disabled persons differently under an insurance or benefit plan because they represent an increased hazard of death or illness.

. . . .

* * * Another House report states:

[Section 12201] specifies that titles I, II, and III shall not be construed to restrict various insurance practices on the part of insurance companies and employers, as long as such practices are not used to evade the purposes of this Act.

. . . .

Specifically, [Section 12201(c)(1)] makes it clear that insurers may continue to sell to and underwrite individuals applying for life, health, or other insurance on an individually underwritten basis, or to service such products, so long as the standards used are based on sound actuarial data and not on speculation.

. . . .

In sum, [the Disabilities Act] requires that underwriting and classification of risks be based on sound actuarial principles or be related to actual or reasonably anticipated experience. * * * The Senate report contains an explanation nearly identical to those quoted above. * * * In addition, the Senate Report states:

> The Committee does not intend that any provisions of this legislation should affect the way the insurance industry does business in accordance with the State laws and regulations under which it is regulated. Virtually all States prohibit unfair discrimination among persons of the same class and equal expectation of life. The [Disabilities Act] adopts this prohibition of discrimination. Under the [Disabilities Act], a person with a disability cannot be denied insurance or be subject to different terms or conditions of insurance based on disability alone, if the disability does not pose increased risks.

* * *

476

It is strange, indeed, that Congress would put § 501(c) in the Act and write these committee reports if Congress did not include employer-sponsored health and disability insurance in the prohibition against discrimination based on disability. It boggles the mind to think that Congress would include only the few people who walk into an insurance office to buy health insurance but not the millions who get such insurance at work. This distinction drawn by the Court produces an absurd result.

The Court limits § 12182(a) "to physical access to an office," rejecting the contrary view of the other circuit and district courts that have decided the issue, as well rejecting the Department of Justice and the EEOC view that employer group health insurance is covered. In the end, the unnecessary conflict between these two views will now have to be resolved by the Supreme Court.

The fact that Congress intended that health and disability insurance for employees is covered by Titles III and IV does not necessarily mean that insurance companies lose. It means merely, as noted in the panel decision, that insurance practices, including the insurance industry's justification for its distinction between mental and physical disabilities, are fully protected to the extent they are in accord with sound actuarial principles, reasonably anticipated experience and bona fide risk classification. The case, as the panel held, should be remanded to the district court for further consideration of the factual and legal issues arising under Title IV from the insurance industry's asserted distinction between mental and physical disabilities.

ADDENDUM

(c) Insurance

Subchapters I through III of this chapter and title IV of this Act shall not be construed to prohibit or restrict –

(1) an insurer, hospital or medical service company, health maintenance organization, or any agent, or entity that administers benefit plans, or similar organizations from underwriting risks, classifying risks, or administering such risks that are based on or not inconsistent with State law; or

(2) a person or organization covered by the chapter from establishing, sponsoring, observing or administering the terms of a bona fide benefit plan that are based on understanding risks, classifying risks, or administering such risks that are based on or not inconsistent with State law; or

(3) a person or organization covered by this chapter from establishing, sponsoring, observing or administering the terms of a bona fide benefit plan that is not subject to State laws that regulate insurance.

Paragraphs (1), (2), and (3) shall not be used as a subterfuge to evade the purposes of subchapter I and III of this chapter.

Notes & Questions

1. In *Parker*, the court concludes, in part, that a health insurance plan offered by an employer to its employees is not the goods or services of a Title III entity. Additionally, the court distinguishes "the content of a long-term disability policy offered by an employer" from "the availability of the goods and services the place of public accommodation offers." *Id.* at 1012. How clear is this distinction of content and availability? *See* Fletcher v. Tufts Univ., 367 F.Supp.2d 99, 114-15 (D. Mass. 2005) (applying Title III to the substance of insurance policies). *But see* Weyer v. Twentieth Century Fox Film Corp., 198 F.3d 1104, 1115 (9th Cir. 2000); Ford v. Schering-Plough Corp., 145 F.3d 601, 612-13 (3d Cir. 1998). For a detailed discussion of this distinction, see Blanck: eQuality, *supra*.

2. Professor Elizabeth A. Pendo, The Politics of Infertility: Recognizing Coverage Exclusions as Discrimination, 11 Conn. Ins. L. J. 293, 325-35 (2005) (discussing generally the merits of claims for Title III violations arising from an insurance company's refusal to cover infertility treatments). Professor Pendo presents a significant distinction between self-funded benefits plans and employer-purchased health care policies. She notes that the majority of health plans available to employees are "completely or partially self-funded," self-funded plans are exempt from state regulation via ERISA's preemption, and thus "[they] enjoy significantly less protection under the ADA." *Id.* at 332-33.

The Internet's World Wide Web raises similar "place" issues. *See* discussion, *infra*, Part 8, ch. 33.

ACCESS NOW, INC. v. SOUTHWEST AIRLINES, CO.

United States District Court, Southern District of Florida, 2002
227 F. Supp. 2d 1312

SEITZ, District Judge.

THIS MATTER is before the Court on Defendant Southwest Airlines, Co.'s ("Southwest") Motion to Dismiss Plaintiffs' Complaint. * * * Plaintiffs, Access Now, Inc. ("Access Now"), a non-profit, access advocacy organization for disabled individuals, and Robert Gumson ("Gumson"), a blind individual, filed this four-count Complaint for injunctive and declaratory relief under the Americans with Disabilities Act ("ADA"), 42 U.S.C. §§ 12101, *et seq.* Plaintiffs contend that Southwest's Internet website, southwest.com, excludes Plaintiffs in violation of the ADA, as the goods and services Southwest offers at its "virtual ticket counters" are inaccessible to blind persons. Southwest has moved to dismiss Plaintiffs' Complaint on the grounds that southwest.com is not a "place of public accommodation" and, therefore, does not fall within the scope of Title III of

478

the ADA. The Court has considered the parties' thorough papers, the extremely informative argument of counsel, and the exhibits presented during oral argument. For the reasons stated below, the Court will grant Southwest's motion to dismiss.

Background

Having found that nearly forty-three million Americans have one or more mental or physical disabilities, that such individuals continually encounter various forms of discrimination, and that "the continuing existence of unfair and unnecessary discrimination and prejudice denies people with disabilities the opportunity to compete on an equal basis and to pursue those opportunities for which our free society is justifiably famous," Congress enacted the ADA in 1990. * * * Congress' stated purposes in enacting the ADA were, among other things, to provide "a clear and comprehensive national mandate for the elimination of discrimination against individuals with disabilities," and "clear, strong, consistent, enforceable standards addressing discrimination against individuals with disabilities." * * * Among the statutorily created rights embodied within the ADA, is Title III's prohibition against discrimination in places of public accommodation. 42 U.S.C. § 12182(a).

Since President George Bush signed the ADA into law on July 26, 1990, this Nation, as well as the rest of the world, has experienced an era of rapidly changing technology and explosive growth in the use of the Internet. Today, millions of people across the globe utilize the Internet on a regular basis for communication, news gathering, and commerce. Although this increasingly widespread and swiftly developing technology provides great benefits for the vast majority of Internet users, individuals who suffer from various physical disabilities may be unable to access the goods and services offered on many Internet websites. According to Plaintiffs, of the nearly ten million visually impaired persons in the United States, approximately 1.5 million of these individuals use the Internet.

In an effort to accommodate the needs of the visually impaired, a number of companies within the computer software industry have developed assistive technologies, such as voice-dictation software, voice-navigation software, and magnification software to assist visually impaired persons in navigating through varying degrees of text and graphics found on different websites. However, not only do each of the different assistive software programs vary in their abilities to successfully interpret text and graphics, but various websites also differ in their abilities to allow different assistive technologies to effectively convert text and graphics into meaningful audio signals for visually impaired users. This lack of coordination between website programmers and assistive technology manufacturers has created a situation where the ability of a visually impaired individual to access a website depends upon the particular assistive software program being used and the particular website being visited.

In light of this rapidly developing technology, and the accessibility problems faced by numerous visually impaired Internet users, the question remains whether Title III of the ADA mandates that Internet website operators modify their sites so as to provide complete access to visually impaired individuals. Because no court within this Circuit has squarely addressed this issue, the Court is faced with a question of first impression, namely, whether Southwest's Internet website, southwest.com, is a place of public accommodation as defined by the ADA, and if so, whether Title III of the ADA requires Southwest to make the goods and services available at its "virtual ticket counters" accessible to visually impaired persons.

Southwest, the fourth largest U.S. airline (in terms of domestic customers carried), was the first airline to establish a home page on the Internet. See Southwest Airlines Fact Sheet, http://www.southwest.com/about_swa/press/factsheet.html * * *. Southwest's Internet website, southwest.com, provides consumers with the means to, among other things, check airline fares and schedules, book airline, hotel, and car reservations, and stay informed of Southwest's sales and promotions. Employing more than 35,000 employees, and conducting approximately 2,800 flights per day, Southwest reports that "approximately 46 percent, or over $500 million, of its passenger revenue for first quarter 2002 was generated by online bookings via southwest.com." * * * According to Southwest, "[m]ore than 3.5 million people subscribe to Southwest's weekly Click 'N Save e-mails." * * * Southwest prides itself on operating an Internet website that provides "the highest level of business value, design effectiveness, and innovative technology use achievable on the Web today." * * *

Despite the apparent success of Southwest's website, Plaintiffs contend that Southwest's technology violates the ADA, as the goods and services offered on southwest.com are inaccessible to blind persons using a screen reader. * * * Plaintiffs allege that although "southwest.com offers the sighted customer the promise of independence of on-line airline/hotel booking in the comfort and safety of their home . . . even if a blind person like [Plaintiff] Gumson has a screen reader with a voice synthesizer on their computer, they are prevented from using the southwest.com website because of its failure to allow access." * * * Specifically, Plaintiffs maintain that "the southwest.com website fails to provide 'alternative text' which would provide a 'screen reader' program the ability to communicate via synthesized speech what is visually displayed on the website." * * * Additionally, Plaintiffs assert that the southwest.com website "fails to provide online forms which can be readily filled out by [Plaintiffs] and fails to provide a 'skip navigation link' which facilitates access for these blind consumers by permitting them to bypass the navigation bars on a website and proceed to the main content." * * *

Plaintiffs' four-count Complaint seeks a declaratory judgment that Southwest's website violates the communication barriers removal provision of the ADA (Count I), violates the auxiliary aids and services provision of the ADA (Count II), violates the reasonable modifications provisions of the ADA (Count III), and violates the full and equal enjoyment and participation provisions of the ADA (Count IV). Plaintiffs ask this Court to enjoin Southwest from continuing to violate the ADA, to order Southwest to make its website accessible to persons who are blind, and to award Plaintiffs attorneys' fees and costs. Southwest has moved to dismiss Plaintiffs' Complaint pursuant to Fed. R. Civ. P. 12(b)(6). * * *

Discussion

* * *

B. Plaintiffs Have Failed to State a Claim Upon Which Relief Can be Granted

The threshold issue of whether an Internet website, such as southwest.com, is a "place of public accommodation" as defined by the ADA, presents a question of statutory construction. As in all such disputes, the Court must begin its analysis with the plain language of the statute in question. *Rendon v. Valleycrest Prods., Ltd.,* 294 F.3d 1279, 1283 n.6 (11th Cir. 2002). * * * The "first step in interpreting a statute is to determine whether the language at issue has a plain and unambiguous meaning with regard to the particular dispute in the case." *Rendon,* 294 F.3d at 1283 n.6. A court need look no further where the statute in question provides a plain and unambiguous meaning. *Rendon,* 294 F.3d at 1283 n.6.

1. Southwest.com is Not a "Place of Public Accommodation" as Defined by the Plain and Unambiguous Language of the ADA

Title III of the ADA sets forth the following general rule against discrimination in places of public accommodation:

> No individual shall be discriminated against on the basis of disability in the full and equal enjoyment of the goods, services, facilities, privileges, advantages, or accommodations of any *place of public accommodation* by any person who owns, leases (or leases to), or operates a *place of public accommodation.*

42 U.S.C. § 12182(a) (emphasis added). The statute specifically identifies twelve (12) particularlized categories of "places of public accommodation." 42 U.S.C. § 12181(7).* * *

Furthermore, pursuant to Congress' grant of authority to the Attorney General to issue regulations to carry out the ADA, the applicable federal regulations also define a "place of public accommodation" as "a facility, operated by a private entity, whose operations affect commerce and fall within at least one of the [twelve (12) enumerated categories set

481

forth in 42 U.S.C. § 12181(7).]" 28 C.F.R. § 36.104. Section 36.104 defines "facility" as "all or any portion of buildings, structures, sites, complexes, equipment, rolling stock or other conveyances, roads, walks, passageways, parking lots, or other real or personal property, including the site where the building, property, structure, or equipment is located." 28 C.F.R. § 36.104. In interpreting the plain and unambiguous language of the ADA, and its applicable federal regulations, the Eleventh Circuit has recognized Congress' clear intent that Title III of the ADA governs solely access to physical, concrete places of public accommodation. *Rendon,* 294 F.3d at 1283-84; *Stevens v. Premier Cruises, Inc.,* 215 F.3d 1237, 1241 (11th Cir. 2000) (noting that "[b]ecause Congress has provided such a comprehensive definition of 'public accommodation,' we think that the intent of Congress is clear enough"). Where Congress has created specifically enumerated rights and expressed the intent of setting forth "clear, strong, consistent, enforceable standards," courts must follow the law as written and wait for Congress to adopt or revise legislatively-defined standards that apply to those rights. Here, to fall within the scope of the ADA as presently drafted, a public accommodation must be a physical, concrete structure. To expand the ADA to cover "virtual" spaces would be to create new rights without well-defined standards.

Notwithstanding the fact that the plain and unambiguous language of the statute and relevant regulations does not include Internet websites among the definitions of "places of public accommodation," Plaintiffs allege that the southwest.com website falls within the scope of Title III, in that it is a place of "exhibition, display and a sales establishment." * * * Plaintiffs' argument rests on a definition they have created by selecting language from three separate statutory subsections of 42 U.S.C. § 12181(7). * * *[6] While Plaintiffs can, as advocates, combine general terms from three separate statutory subsections, and apply them to an unenumerated specific term, namely Internet websites, the Court must view these general terms in the specific context in which Congress placed each of them.

---

[6]   Plaintiffs created their definition from the following italicized language in three subsections of 42 U.S.C. § 12181(7):

> "a motion picture house, theater, concert hall, stadium, or other *place of exhibition* or entertainment," 42 U.S.C. § 12181(7)(C);

> "a museum, library, gallery, or other place of public *display* or collection," 42 U.S.C. § 12181(7)(H); and

> "a bakery, grocery store, clothing store, hardware store, shopping center, or other *sales* or rental *establishment*," 42 U.S.C. § 12181(7)(E).

Under the rule of *ejusdem generis,* "where general words follow a specific enumeration of persons or things, the general words should be limited to persons or things similar to those specifically enumerated." *Allen v. A.G. Thomas,* 161 F.3d 667, 671 (11th Cir. 1998) * * *. Here, the general terms, "exhibition," "display," and "sales establishment," are limited to their corresponding specifically enumerated terms, all of which are physical, concrete structures, namely: "motion picture house, theater, concert hall, stadium"; "museum, library, gallery"; and "bakery, grocery store, clothing store, hardware store, shopping center," respectively. 42 U.S.C. §§ 12181(7)(C), (H) & (E). Thus, this Court cannot properly construe "a place of public accommodation" to include Southwest's Internet website, southwest.com.

2. Plaintiffs Have Not Established a Nexus Between Southwest.com and a Physical, Concrete Place of Public Accommodation

Although Internet websites do not fall within the scope of the ADA's plain and unambiguous language, Plaintiffs contend that the Court is not bound by the statute's plain language, and should expand the ADA's application into cyberspace. As part of their argument, Plaintiffs encourage the Court to follow *Carparts Distribution Ctr., Inc. v. Automotive Wholesaler's Assoc. of New England,* in which the First Circuit broadly held that the ADA's definition of "public accommodation" is not limited to actual physical structures, but includes, *inter alia,* health-benefit plans. *Carparts,* 37 F.3d 12, 19 (1st Cir. 1994). While application of the broad holding and dicta in *Carparts* to the facts in this case might arguably require this Court to include Internet websites within the ADA's definition of "public accommodations," the Eleventh Circuit has not read Title III of the ADA nearly as broadly as the First Circuit.[9] See *Rendon,* 294 F.3d 1279.

---

[9]   In addition to Carparts, Plaintiffs encourage this Court to follow Doe v. Mutual of Omaha Ins. Co., 179 F.3d 557, 559 (7th Cir. 1999), in which Chief Judge Posner approvingly cited to Carparts and stated in dicta that:

> The core meaning of [42 U.S.C. § 12182(a)], plainly enough, is that the owner or operator of a store, hotel, restaurant, dentist's office, travel agency, theater, Web site, or other facility (whether in physical space or in electronic space, [Carparts]), that is open to the public cannot exclude disabled persons from entering the facility and, once in, from using the facility in the same way that the nondisabled do. * * *

Plaintiffs also cite to a September 9, 1996 letter from Deval L. Patrick, Assistant Attorney General, Civil Rights Division, United States Department of Justice, to U.S. Senator Tom Harkin, advising the Senator

In *Rendon,* a recent Eleventh Circuit case addressing the scope of Title III, a group of individuals with hearing and upper-body mobility impairments sued the producers of the television game show, "Who Wants To Be A Millionaire," alleging that the use of an automated fast finger telephone selection process violated the ADA because it excluded disabled individuals from participating. The district court dismissed the complaint on grounds that the automated telephone selection process was not conducted at a physical location, and therefore, was not a "place of public accommodation" as defined by the ADA. The Eleventh Circuit reversed, holding that the telephone selection process was "a discriminatory screening mechanism . . . which deprives [the plaintiffs] of the opportunity to compete for the privilege of being a contestant on the [game show]." *Rendon,* 294 F.3d at 1286. The Eleventh Circuit observed that "[t]here is nothing in the text of the statute to suggest that discrimination via an imposition of screening or eligibility requirements must occur on site to offend the ADA." Id. at 1283-84. Most significantly, the Eleventh Circuit noted that the plaintiffs stated a claim under Title III because they demonstrated "a nexus between the challenged service and the premises of the public accommodation," namely the concrete television studio. Id. at 1284 n.8.

---

that "[c]overed entities that use the Internet for communications regarding their programs, goods, or services must be prepared to offer those communications through accessible means as well." * * * Finally, Plaintiffs cite the recent unpublished opinion in *Vincent Martin et al. v. Metro. Atlanta Rapid Transit Authority,* 225 F.Supp.2d 1362 (N.D. Ga. 2002), in which U.S. District Judge Thomas W. Thrash, Jr. held that until the Metropolitan Atlanta Rapid Transit Authority (MARTA) reformats its Internet website in such a way that it can be read by visually impaired persons using screen readers, MARTA is "violating the ADA mandate of 'making adequate communications capacity available, through accessible formats and technology, to enable users to obtain information and schedule service.'" * * * *Vincent Martin.,* 225 F.Supp.2d 1362, 1374 * * * (quoting 49 C.F.R. § 37.167(f). That case, however, is distinguishable in one critical respect: Plaintiffs in *Vincent Martin* filed suit under both the Rehabilitation Act of 1973, as amended, 29 U.S.C. § 794 *et seq.,* and Title II of the ADA, 42 U.S.C. § 12132, not Title III as in the present case. Title II prohibits qualified individuals from being "excluded from participation in or [being] denied the benefits of the services, programs, or activities of a public entity, or [being] subjected to discrimination by any such entity." 42 U.S.C. § 12132. Title II of the ADA defines "public entity" as "(A) any State or local government; (B) any department, agency, special purpose district, or other instrumentality of a State or States or local government; and (C) the National Railroad Passenger Corporation, and any commuter authority. . . ." 42 U.S.C. § 12131. * * *

Plaintiffs contend that the Eleventh Circuit in *Rendon* aligned itself with the First Circuit in *Carparts,* and that *Rendon* requires a broad reading of the ADA to include Internet websites within the "public accommodations" definition. However, these arguments, while emotionally attractive, are not legally viable for at least two reasons. First, contrary to Plaintiffs' assertion that the Eleventh Circuit aligned itself with *Carparts,* the Eleventh Circuit in *Rendon* not only did not approve of *Carparts,* it failed even to cite it.

Second, whereas the defendants in *Rendon* conceded, and the Eleventh Circuit agreed, that the game show at issue took place at a physical, public accommodation (a concrete television studio), and that the fast finger telephone selection process used to select contestants tended to screen out disabled individuals, the Internet website at issue here is neither a physical, public accommodation itself as defined by the ADA, nor a means to accessing a concrete space such as the specific television studio in *Rendon.*[11] 294 F.3d at 1284. Although Plaintiffs contend that this "is a case seeking equal access to Southwest's virtual 'ticket counters' as they exist on-line," * * * the Supreme Court and the Eleventh Circuit have both recognized that the Internet is "a unique medium – known to its users as 'cyberspace' – *located in no particular geographical location* but available to anyone, anywhere in the world, with access to the Internet." *Voyeur Dorm, L.C. v. City of Tampa,* 265 F.3d 1232, 1237 n.3 (11th Cir. 2001). * * * Thus, because the Internet website, southwest.com, does not exist in any particular geographical location, Plaintiffs are unable to demonstrate that Southwest's website impedes their access to a specific, physical,

---

[11]   In recognizing the requirement that a plaintiff establish "a nexus between the challenged service and the premises of the public accommodation," the Eleventh Circuit noted that the plaintiffs in *Rendon* stated a claim under Title III of the ADA because they sought "the privilege of competing in a contest held in a *concrete space.* . . ." *Rendon,* 294 F.3d at 1284 (emphasis added); compare Stoutenborough v. Nat'l Football League, Inc., 59 F.3d 580 (6th Cir. 1995) (holding that hearing impaired plaintiffs, who alleged that National Football League "blackout rule" violated Title III of ADA, failed to state a cause of action, as there was no nexus between televised broadcast of football game and physical place of public accommodation). See also Torres v. AT & T Broadband, LLC, 158 F.Supp.2d 1035 (N.D. Cal. 2001) (dismissing Title III claim that cable service provider must make a list of available programs accessible to the visually impaired, and holding that "neither the digital cable system nor its on-screen channel menu can be considered a place of public accommodation within the meaning of the ADA"); *Access Now, Inc. v. Claire's Stores, Inc.,* 2002 WL 1162422, at *5 (S.D. Fla. May 7, 2002) (noting in approving a Title III class settlement that "[n]o court has held that internet websites made available to the public by retail entities must be accessible").

concrete space such as a particular airline ticket counter or travel agency. Having failed to establish a nexus between southwest.com and a physical, concrete place of public accommodation, Plaintiffs have failed to state a claim upon which relief can be granted under Title III of the ADA.

Conclusion

Accordingly, based upon the foregoing reasons, it is hereby

ORDERED that Defendant Southwest's Motion to Dismiss Plaintiffs' Complaint is GRANTED, and this action is DISMISSED WITH PREJUDICE. * * *

Notes & Questions

1. Access Now appealed this case to the Eleventh Circuit. The court dismissed the appeal, holding that Access Now had only on appeal raised the argument that Southwest's travel service was a place of public accommodation to which the website was connected. *See* Access Now, Inc. v. Southwest Airlines Co., 385 F.3d 1324 (11th Cir. 2004).

2. As more and more businesses offer goods and services only through the Internet or by telephone, will the requirement that there be a nexus to a "place" severely limit ADA coverage? *National Federation of the Blind v. Target Corp.* was the first major case to address inaccessibility of the website services of business with a physical place of public accommodation. In *Target Corp.*, the District Court for the Northern District of California found that a subclass of all legally blind individuals in California attempted and were denied full access to the goods and services of Target.com, in violation of California state law. *See* Part 8, § 33.4.A for further discussion.

3. Professor Blanck suggests there are at least two next generation questions regarding the accessible cyberworld as affecting persons with disabilities: (1) Do the ADA's antidiscrimination provisions cover U.S. businesses as public accommodations operating only in cyberplaces (on the Web) and not with a physical store presence either in the United States or abroad? And, (2) Are foreign businesses – otherwise public accommodations – doing business in the U.S. "cyberwaters" and without a physical presence in the United States covered by the ADA? *See* Peter Blanck, Closing: Special Issue on Disability Policy and Law, Flattening the (In-Accessible) Cyber World for People with Disabilities, *Assistive Technology Journal*, 20, 175-80 (2008) (noting also disability laws in other countries that cover the Internet as a place of public accommodation). For ideas on the second question, compare the U.S. Supreme Court decision in *Spector v. Norwegian Cruise Line Ltd.*, 545 U.S. 119 (2005), discussed *infra*, in which the Court held ADA title III applies to foreign-flag cruise ships operating in U.S. waters.

4. The Sixth Circuit in *Parker v. Metropolitan Life Insurance Co.*, 121 F.3d 1006 (6th Cir. 1997), likened insurance policies to books in a

bookstore and found that, like books, the policies do not have to be accessible. Is there a basis for distinguishing insurance policies from books? Electronic books? Is that distinction enough to exempt insurance policies from coverage? According to the Department of Justice, even though a bookstore is not required to stock Braille books, it may be required to special order accessible books on request? How would this policy work as applied to insurance?

5. Insurance has posed particular problems for the courts. Although the analyses vary, most circuits, except the First and Second, have not applied the provisions of Title III to the substance of insurance policies, under one or more of several theories:

> Only policies bought at a physical office will be covered;

> Only policies bought directly, as opposed to through an employer, will be covered (i.e., insurance companies as wholesalers);

> Title III is limited to "access" to places, and it does not cover "content" of the goods or services offered (i.e., insurance companies, like bookstores, are not required to sell accessible goods (e.g., Braille books));

> Title V's "safe harbor" provision would exempt insurance policies, even if they were otherwise covered under Title III.

Like the First Circuit in *Carparts,* the Second Circuit has held that the substance of insurance policies is covered under Title III. *See* Pallozzi v. Allstate Life Ins. Co., 198 F.3d 28, 33 (2d Cir. 2000). In this case, Allstate refused to issue a life insurance policy to a couple because of their mental disabilities. The Second Circuit found that "an entity covered by Title III is not only obligated by the statute to provide disabled persons with physical access, but is also prohibited from refusing to sell them its merchandise by reason of discrimination against their disability." *Id.*

§ 15.2 Examinations And Courses

Title III covers private entities that offer certain examinations or courses:

> Any person that offers examinations or courses related to applications, licensing, certification, or credentialing for secondary or postsecondary education, professional, or trade purposes shall offer such examinations or courses in a place and manner accessible to persons with disabilities or offer alternative accessible arrangements for such individuals.

42 U.S.C. § 12189 (2006).

The requirements for providers of examinations and courses are similar, but not identical, to the public accommodations requirements of Title III. These requirements apply to providers of examinations and courses, regardless of whether or not they qualify for treatment as places of public accommodation.

At the district court level, courts have grappled with the effects of this section on various types of tests and exams, such as bar exams, medical licensing exams, and law school admissions exams. *See, e.g.,* Biank v. Nat'l Bd. of Med. Exam'rs, 130 F.Supp.2d 986, 989 (N.D. Ill. 2000) (national medical examination board was subject to ADA requirements); Agranoff v. Law Sch. Admission Council, 97 F.Supp.2d 86, 87 (D. Mass. 1999) (applying Title III to law school admission exam); Argen v. N.Y. State Bd. of Law Exam'rs, 860 F.Supp. 84, 90-91 (W.D.N.Y. 1994) (denying special accommodation on bar exam because of failure to prove learning disability); Ellen S. v. Fla. Bd. of Bar Exam'rs, 859 F.Supp. 1489, 1490-91 (S.D. Fla. 1994) (challenging questions on bar application); Pazer v. N.Y. State Bd. of Law Exam'rs, 849 F.Supp. 284, 285 (S.D.N.Y. 1994) (detailing visually disabled person's claim for accommodation).

In *Doe v. National Board of Medical Examiners*, 199 F.3d 146, 148 (3d Cir. 1999), the Third Circuit addressed the National Board of Medical Examiners' practice of "flagging" examinations on which it granted accommodations to indicate that it deemed such scores non-comparable with other test-takers (for example, providing extra time to students with learning disabilities or alternative formats to blind and deaf students). The court first held that these types of challenges were properly considered under 42 U.S.C. § 12189 (Title III's section on examinations and courses), as opposed to the more general antidiscrimination provisions in § 12182.

The plaintiff argued that because he would be discriminated against (stigmatized) when his examination was "flagged," the Board did not offer the exam in a manner that was "accessible" to people with disabilities. The court rejected this argument, concluding that he had not proven that he would face discrimination when his exam was flagged, and that he had not shown that the Board was incorrect in terming his scores incomparable.

In *Enyart v. National Conference of Bar Examiners*, 630 F.3d 1153 (9th Cir. 2011), a law school graduate who was blind sought to take the California bar exam using assistive techonology software, but the developer did not make the exam in electronic format and the graduate was offered other accommodations. Here, the Ninth Circuit applied the "best ensure" standard, holding that the required administration of the exams was to best ensure that the test results reflected the graduate's ability, rather than her disability. The court noted that the plaintiff's disability was progressive and that testing accommodations should advance as technology progresses. *See also* Argenyi v. Creighton Univ.,

703 F.3d 441 (8th Cir. 2013) (material issue of fact as to whether medical student was denied opportunity to gain the same benefit from medical school as his non-disabled peers).

§ 15.3   Exempt Entities

Religious entities and private clubs are exempt from the requirements of Title III, including the nondiscrimination and construction requirements. 42 U.S.C. § 12187 (2006). A religious entity is one controlled by a religious organization; the term refers not only to places of worship, but also to facilities that, but for religious ownership, would be places of public accommodation, such as hospitals, schools, and day care facilities. TAM III, *supra*, § 1.5200. The existence of a lay board of directors does not mean the entity is not a religious entity. "The test is a factual one – whether the church or other religious organization controls the operations [of the entity]." 28 C.F.R. pt. 36 app. B, § 36.104 (2008).

The religious entity exemption applies to all activities of the religious entity. However, it does not extend to activities of non-religious entities because they are associated with a religious entity or located on a religious entity's facility. Thus, a private day care provider who leases space in a religious facility is not exempt from Title III, as long as the space is not a place of worship, a lease exists, and consideration is paid. *Id.*

Private clubs are exempt from Title III and are defined as those clubs exempted from coverage under Title II of the Civil Rights Act of 1964. 42 U.S.C. § 12187. Factors to determine whether a private entity constitutes an exempt private club include:

> Whether members exercise a high degree of control over club operations;
>
> Whether the membership process is highly selective;
>
> "[W]hether substantial membership fees are charged"; and
>
> "[W]hether the entity is operated on a non-profit basis."

28 C.F.R. pt. 36 app. B. The club must not have been founded to avoid compliance with federal civil rights laws. TAM III, *supra*, § 1.6000. A private club loses its exemption to the extent it allows nonmembers to use the facility as a place of public accommodation. *Id.*

§ 15.4   Relationship To Title II

Title III is limited to private entities, defined as those that are not public entities within the meaning of Title II of the ADA. 42 U.S.C. § 12181(6) (2006). Therefore, no entity may be covered both by Titles II and III. However, there are situations in which private and public entities are closely related.

Because public entities are prohibited from discriminating through contract, a state or local government that contracts with a private entity for the provision of a service to the public must ensure that the service complies with Title II. The private entity, itself, may be covered by Title III or may not be covered by the ADA, for instance, if it is a religious organization.

Regardless of the private entity's separate obligations, the public entity must ensure (e.g., by contract) that the service complies with Title II. TAM III, *supra*, § 1.7000. In determining whether an undue burden is present in such an instance, the private entity will be judged according to its own resources. However, the public entity will be judged by its own, likely more substantial resources. Therefore, a public entity must be prepared to make its resources available to the private entity to ensure compliance with Title II.

§ 15.5 Geographic Limits

There has been some question regarding the application of Title III to foreign-flagged cruise ships who enter United States waters. To date, most disability advocates generally agree that the ADA is not applicable extraterritorially, at least in regard to physical as opposed to virtual (e.g., web-based services) presences abroad. Nevertheless, they argue that Title III's provisions should be enforced on foreign-flagged ships who choose to avail themselves of U.S. waters, at least to the extent Title III is consistent with international law. They argue this would not result in extraterritorial application because enforcement would be limited to U.S. boundaries. *Cf.* discussion regarding the Internet, *supra* § 15.1.

Cruise ship operators argue a presumption against extraterritorial application of domestic statutes. They claim that the architectural requirements of Title III would necessarily have extraterritorial effects because they are permanent and would have to be carried into international waters when the cruise ships leave the United States. The circuits have split on the issue.

In 2004, the Supreme Court Granted certiorari to address the issue in Spector, 356 F.3d 641 (5th Cir. 2004), *cert. granted*, 72 U.S.L.W. 3644 (U.S. Sept. 28, 2004) (No. 03-1388), cert. granted, 125 S.Ct. 26, 72 U.S.L.W. 3644 (U.S. Sep 28, 2004) (No. 03-1388).

SPECTOR v. NORWEGIAN CRUISE LINE LTD.

Supreme Court of the United States, 2005
545 U.S. 119

* * *

Justice KENNEDY announced the judgment of the Court and delivered the opinion of the Court with respect to Parts I, II-A-1, and II-B-

2, an opinion with respect to Parts II-A-2, II-B-1, II-B-3, and III-B, in which Justice STEVENS and Justice SOUTER join, and an opinion with respect to Part III-A, in which Justice STEVENS, Justice SOUTER, and Justice THOMAS join.

This case presents the question whether Title III of the Americans with Disabilities Act of 1990 (ADA), 104 Stat. 353, 42 U.S.C. § 12181 *et seq.*, applies to foreign-flag cruise ships in United States waters. The Court of Appeals for the Fifth Circuit held Title III did not apply because of a presumption, which it sought to derive from this Court's case law, that, absent a clear indication of congressional intent, general statutes do not apply to foreign-flag ships. 356 F.3d 641, 644-646 (2004). The Court of Appeals for the Eleventh Circuit, on the other hand, has held that the ADA does apply to foreign-flag cruise ships in United States waters. See *Stevens v. Premier Cruises, Inc.,* 215 F.3d 1237 (2000). We granted certiorari to resolve the conflict. * * *

Our cases hold that a clear statement of congressional intent is necessary before a general statutory requirement can interfere with matters that concern a foreign-flag vessel's internal affairs and operations, as contrasted with statutory requirements that concern the security and well-being of United States citizens or territory. While the clear statement rule could limit Title III's application to foreign-flag cruise ships in some instances, when it requires removal of physical barriers, it would appear the rule is inapplicable to many other duties Title III might impose. We therefore reverse the decision of the Court of Appeals for the Fifth Circuit that the ADA is altogether inapplicable to foreign vessels; and we remand for further proceedings.

I

The respondent Norwegian Cruise Line Ltd. (NCL), a Bermuda Corporation with a principal place of business in Miami, Florida, operates cruise ships that depart from, and return to, ports in the United States. The ships are essentially floating resorts. They provide passengers with staterooms or cabins, food, and entertainment. The cruise ships stop at different ports of call where passengers may disembark. Most of the passengers on these cruises are United States residents; under the terms and conditions of the tickets, disputes between passengers and NCL are to be governed by United States law; and NCL relies upon extensive advertising in the United States to promote its cruises and increase its revenues.

Despite the fact that the cruises are operated by a company based in the United States, serve predominately United States residents, and are in most other respects United States-centered ventures, almost all of NCL's cruise ships are registered in other countries, flying so-called flags of convenience. The two NCL cruise ships that are the subject of the present litigation, the Norwegian Sea and the Norwegian Star, are both registered in the Bahamas.

The petitioners are disabled individuals and their companions who purchased tickets in 1998 or 1999 for round-trip cruises on the Norwegian Sea or the Norwegian Star, with departures from Houston, Texas. Naming NCL as the defendant, the petitioners filed a class action in the United States District Court for the Southern District of Texas on behalf of all persons similarly situated. They sought declaratory and injunctive relief under Title III of the ADA, which prohibits discrimination on the basis of disability. The petitioners asserted that cruise ships are covered both by Title III's prohibition on discrimination in places of "public accommodation," § 12182(a), and by its prohibition on discrimination in "specified public transportation services," § 12184(a). Both provisions require covered entities to make "reasonable modifications in policies, practices, or procedures" to accommodate disabled individuals, §§ 12182(b)(2)(A)(ii), 12184(b)(2)(A), and require removal of "architectural barriers, and communication barriers that are structural in nature" where such removal is "readily achievable," §§ 12182(b)(2)(A)(iv), 12184(b)(2)(C).

The District Court held that, as a general matter, Title III applies to foreign-flag cruise ships in United States territorial waters. Civ. Action No. H-00-2649 (SD Tex., Sept. 10, 2002), App. to Pet. for Cert. 35a. The District Court found, however, that the petitioners' claims regarding physical barriers to access could not go forward because the agencies charged with promulgating architectural and structural guidelines for ADA compliance (the Architectural and Transportation Barriers Compliance Board, the Department of Transportation, and the Department of Justice) had not done so for cruise ships. In these circumstances, the court held, it is unclear what structural modifications NCL would need to make. *Id.,* at 36a-42a. The District Court granted NCL's motion to dismiss the barrier-removal claims, but denied NCL's motion with respect to all the other claims. *Id.,* at 47a.

The Court of Appeals for the Fifth Circuit affirmed in part and reversed in part. It reasoned that our cases, particularly *Benz v. Compania Naviera Hidalgo, S. A.,* 353 U.S. 138, 77 S.Ct. 699, 1 L.Ed.2d 709 (1957), and *McCulloch v. Sociedad Nacional de Marineros de Honduras,* 372 U.S. 10, 83 S.Ct. 671, 9 L.Ed.2d 547 (1963), stand for the proposition that general statutes do not apply to foreign-flag vessels in United States territory absent a clear indication of congressional intent. 356 F.3d, at 644 * * * As Title III does not contain a specific provision mandating its application to foreign-flag vessels, the Court of Appeals sustained the District Court's dismissal of the petitioners' barrier-removal claims on this alternative ground and reversed the District Court on the remaining Title III claims. 356 F.3d, at 650-651.

* * *

II

A

1

Title III of the ADA prohibits discrimination against the disabled in the full and equal enjoyment of public accommodations, 42 U.S.C. § 12182(a), and public transportation services, § 12184(a). * * * Entities that provide public accommodations or public transportation: (1) may not impose "eligibility criteria" that tend to screen out disabled individuals, §§ 12182(b)(2)(A)(i), 12184(b)(1); (2) must make "reasonable modifications in polices, practices, or procedures, when such modifications are necessary" to provide disabled individuals full and equal enjoyment, §§ 12182(b)(2)(A)(ii), 12184(b)(2)(A); (3) must provide auxiliary aids and services to disabled individuals, §§ 12182(b)(2)(A)(iii), 12184(b)(2)(B); and (4) must remove architectural and structural barriers, or if barrier removal is not readily achievable, must ensure equal access for the disabled through alternative methods, §§ 12182(b)(2)(A)(iv)-(v), 12184(b)(2)(C).

These specific requirements, in turn, are subject to important exceptions and limitations. Eligibility criteria that screen out disabled individuals are permitted when "necessary for the provision" of the services or facilities being offered, §§ 12182(b)(2)(A)(i), 12184(b)(1). Policies, practices, and procedures need not be modified, and auxiliary aids need not be provided, if doing so would "fundamentally alter" the services or accommodations being offered. §§ 12182(b)(2)(A)(ii)-(iii). Auxiliary aids are also unnecessary when they would "result in an undue burden," § 12182(b)(2)(A)(iii). As we have noted, moreover, the barrier removal and alternative access requirements do not apply when these requirements are not "readily achievable," §§ 12182(b)(2)(A)(iv)-(v). Additionally, Title III does not impose nondiscrimination or accommodation requirements if, as a result, disabled individuals would pose "a significant risk to the health or safety of others that cannot be eliminated by a modification of policies, practices, or procedures or by the provision of auxiliary aids or services," § 12182(b)(3).

Although the statutory definitions of "public accommodation" and "specified public transportation" do not expressly mention cruise ships, there can be no serious doubt that the NCL cruise ships in question fall within both definitions under conventional principles of interpretation. §§ 12181(7)(A)-(B),(I),(L), 12181(10). The Court of Appeals for the Fifth Circuit, nevertheless, held that Title III does not apply to foreign-flag cruise ships in United States waters because the statute has no clear statement or explicit text mandating coverage for these ships. This Court's cases, particularly *Benz* and *McCulloch,* do hold, in some circumstances, that a general statute will not apply to certain aspects of the internal operations of foreign vessels temporarily in United States waters, absent a clear statement. The broad clear statement rule adopted by the Court of Appeals, however, would apply to every facet of the business and operations of foreign-flag ships. That formulation is inconsistent with the Court's case law and with sound principles of statutory interpretation.

2

This Court has long held that general statutes are presumed to apply to conduct that takes place aboard a foreign-flag vessel in United States territory if the interests of the United States or its citizens, rather than interests internal to the ship, are at stake. See *Cunard S.S. Co. v. Mellon,* 262 U.S. 100, 43 S.Ct. 504, 67 L.Ed. 894 (1923) * * * *Uravic v. F. Jarka Co.,* 282 U.S. 234, 240, 51 S.Ct. 111, 75 L.Ed. 312 (1931) * * * The general rule that United States statutes apply to foreign-flag ships in United States territory is subject only to a narrow exception. Absent a clear statement of congressional intent, general statutes may not apply to foreign-flag vessels insofar as they regulate matters that involve only the internal order and discipline of the vessel, rather than the peace of the port. This qualification derives from the understanding that, as a matter of international comity, "all matters of discipline and all things done on board which affec[t] only the vessel or those belonging to her, and [do] not involve the peace or dignity of the country, or the tranquility of the port, should be left by the local government to be dealt with by the authorities of the nation to which the vessel belonged." *Wildenhus's Case,* 120 U.S. 1, 12, 7 S.Ct. 385, 30 L.Ed. 565 (1887). This exception to the usual presumption, however, does not extend beyond matters of internal order and discipline. "[I]f crimes are committed on board [a foreign-flag vessel] of a character to disturb the peace and tranquility of the country to which the vessel has been brought, the offenders have never by comity or usage been entitled to any exemption from the operation of the local laws." * * *

The two cases in recent times in which the presumption against applying general statutes to foreign vessels' internal affairs has been invoked, *Benz* and *McCulloch,* concern labor relations. The Court held that the general terms of the National Labor Relations Act (NLRA), 49 Stat. 449, 29 U.S.C. § 151 *et seq.,* did not govern the respective rights and duties of a foreign ship and its crew because the NLRA standards would interfere with the foreign vessel's internal affairs in those circumstances. These cases recognized a narrow rule, applicable only to statutory duties that implicate the internal order of the foreign vessel rather than the welfare of American citizens. * * * The Court held the NLRA inapplicable to labor relations between a foreign vessel and its foreign crew not because foreign ships are generally exempt from the NLRA, but because the particular application of the NLRA would interfere with matters that concern only the internal operations of the ship. In contrast, the Court held that the NLRA is fully applicable to labor relations between a foreign vessel and American longshoremen because this relationship, unlike the one between a vessel and its own crew, does not implicate a foreign ship's internal order and discipline. *Longshoremen v. Ariadne Shipping Co.,* 397 U.S. 195, 198-201, 90 S.Ct. 872, 25 L.Ed.2d 218 (1970).

This narrow clear statement rule is supported by sound principles of statutory construction. It is reasonable to presume Congress intends no interference with matters that are primarily of concern only to the ship and the foreign state in which it is registered. It is also reasonable, however, to presume Congress does intend its statutes to apply to entities in United States territory that serve, employ, or otherwise affect American citizens, or that affect the peace and tranquility of the United States, even if those entities happen to be foreign-flag ships.

Cruise ships flying foreign flags of convenience offer public accommodations and transportation services to over 7 million United States residents annually, departing from and returning to ports located in the United States. Large numbers of disabled individuals, many of whom have mobility impairments that make other kinds of vacation travel difficult, take advantage of these cruises or would like to do so. To hold there is no Title III protection for disabled persons who seek to use the amenities of foreign cruise ships would be a harsh and unexpected interpretation of a statute designed to provide broad protection for the disabled. § 12101. The clear statement rule adopted by the Court of Appeals for the Fifth Circuit, moreover, would imply that other general federal statutes – including, for example, Title II of the Civil Rights Act of 1964, 78 Stat. 243, 42 U.S.C. § 2000a *et seq.* – would not apply aboard foreign cruise ships in United States waters. A clear statement rule with this sweeping application is unlikely to reflect congressional intent.

The relevant category for which the Court demands a clear congressional statement, then, consists not of all applications of a statute to foreign-flag vessels but only those applications that would interfere with the foreign vessel's internal affairs. This proposition does not mean the clear statement rule is irrelevant to the ADA, however. If Title III by its terms does impose duties that interfere with a foreign-flag cruise ship's internal affairs, the lack of a clear congressional statement can mean that those specific applications of Title III are precluded. On remand, the Court of Appeals may need to consider which, if any, Title III requirements interfere with the internal affairs of foreign-flag vessels. As we will discuss further, however, Title III's own limitations and qualifications may make this inquiry unnecessary.

B

1

The precise content of the category "internal affairs" (or, as it is variously denoted in the case law, "internal order" or "internal operations") is difficult to define with precision. There is, moreover, some ambiguity in our cases as to whether the relevant category of activities is restricted to matters that affect only the internal order of the ship when there is no effect on United States interests, or whether the clear statement rule further comes into play if the predominant effect of a statutory requirement is on a foreign ship's internal affairs but the requirement also promotes the welfare of United States residents or territory. We need not attempt to define the relevant protected category with precision. It suffices to observe that the guiding principles in determining whether the clear statement rule is triggered are the desire for international comity and the presumed lack of interest by the territorial sovereign in matters that bear no substantial relation to the peace and tranquility of the port.

It is plain that Title III might impose any number of duties on cruise ships that have nothing to do with a ship's internal affairs. The pleadings and briefs in this case illustrate, but do not exhaust, the ways a cruise ship might offend such a duty. The petitioners allege the respondent charged disabled passengers higher fares and required disabled passengers to pay special surcharges * * *; maintained evacuation programs and equipment in locations not accessible to disabled individuals * * *; required disabled individuals, but not other passengers, to waive any potential medical liability and to travel with a companion * * *; and reserved the right to remove from the ship any disabled individual whose presence endangers the "comfort" of other passengers * * *. The petitioners also allege more generally that respondent "failed to make reasonable modifications in policies, practices, and procedures" necessary to ensure the petitioners' full enjoyment of the services respondent offered * * *. These are bare allegations, and their truth is not conceded. We express no opinion on the factual support for those claims. We can say, however, that none of these alleged Title III violations implicate any requirement that would interfere with the internal affairs and management of a vessel as our cases have employed that term.

At least one subset of the petitioners' allegations, however, would appear to involve requirements that might be construed as relating to the internal affairs of foreign-flag cruise ships. These allegations concern physical barriers to access on board. For example, according to the petitioners, most of the cabins on the respondent's cruise ships, including the most attractive cabins in the most desirable locations, are not accessible to disabled passengers * * *. The petitioners also allege that the ships' coamings – the raised edges around their doors – make many areas of the ships inaccessible to mobility-impaired passengers who use wheelchairs or scooters * * *. Removal of these and other access barriers, the petitioners suggest, may be required by Title III's structural barrier removal requirement, §§ 12182(b)(2)(A)(iv), 12184(b)(2)(C).

Although these physical barriers affect the passengers as well as the ship and its crew, the statutory requirement could mandate a permanent and significant alteration of a physical feature of the ship – that is, an element of basic ship design and construction. If so, these applications of the barrier removal requirement likely would interfere

496

with the internal affairs of foreign ships. A permanent and significant modification to a ship's physical structure goes to fundamental issues of ship design and construction, and it might be impossible for a ship to comply with all the requirements different jurisdictions might impose. The clear statement rule would most likely come into play if Title III were read to require permanent and significant structural modifications to foreign vessels. It is quite a different question, however, whether Title III would require this. The Title III requirements that might impose permanent and substantial changes to a ship's architecture and design, are, like all of Title III's requirements, subject to the statute's own specific limitations and qualifications. These limitations may make resort to the clear statement rule unnecessary.

2

Title III requires barrier removal if it is "readily achievable," § 12182(b)(2)(A)(iv). The statute defines that term as "easily accomplishable and able to be carried out without much difficulty or expense," § 12181(9). Title III does not define "difficulty" in § 12181(9), but use of the disjunctive – "easily accomplishable and able to be carried out without much difficulty or expense" – indicates that it extends to considerations in addition to cost. Furthermore, Title III directs that the "readily achievable" determination take into account "the impact . . . upon the operation of the facility," § 12181(9)(B).

Surely a barrier removal requirement under Title III that would bring a vessel into noncompliance with the International Convention for the Safety of Life at Sea (SOLAS), Nov. 1, 1974, [1979-1980], 32 U.S.T. 47, T.I.A.S. No. 9700, or any other international legal obligation, would create serious difficulties for the vessel and would have a substantial impact on its operation, and thus would not be "readily achievable." This understanding of the statute, urged by the United States, is eminently reasonable * * * If, moreover, Title III's "readily achievable" exemption were not to take conflicts with international law into account, it would lead to the anomalous result that American cruise ships are obligated to comply with Title III even if doing so brings them into noncompliance with SOLAS, whereas foreign ships – which unlike American ships have the benefit of the internal affairs clear statement rule – would not be so obligated. Congress could not have intended this result.

It is logical and proper to conclude, moreover, that whether a barrier modification is "readily achievable" under Title III must take into consideration the modification's effect on shipboard safety. A separate provision of Title III mandates that the statute's nondiscrimination and accommodation requirements do not apply if disabled individuals would pose "a significant risk to the health or safety of others that cannot be eliminated by a modification of policies, practices, or procedures or by the provision of auxiliary aids or services," § 12182(b)(3). This reference is to a safety threat posed by a disabled individual, whereas here the question would be whether the structural modification itself may pose the safety threat. It would be incongruous, nevertheless, to attribute to Congress an intent to require modifications that threaten safety to others simply because the threat comes not from the disabled person but from the accommodation itself. The anomaly is avoided by concluding that a structural modification is not readily achievable within the meaning of § 12181(9) if it would pose a direct threat to the health or safety of others.

3

Because Title III does not require structural modifications that would conflict with international legal obligations or pose any real threat to the safety of the crew or other passengers, it may well follow – though we do not decide the question here – that Title III does not require any permanent and significant structural modifications that interfere with the internal affairs of any cruise ship, foreign flag or domestic. If that is indeed the case, recourse to the clear statement rule would not be necessary.

Cases may arise, however, where it is prudent for a court to turn first to the internal affairs clear statement rule rather than deciding the precise scope and operation of the statute. Suppose, for example, it is a difficult question whether a particular Title III barrier removal requirement is readily achievable, but the requirement does entail a permanent and significant structural modification, interfering with a foreign ship's internal affairs. In that case a court sensibly could invoke the clear statement rule without determining whether Title III actually imposes the requirement. On the other hand, there may be many cases where it is not obvious that a particular physical modification relates to a vessel's basic architecture and construction, but it is clear the modification would conflict with SOLAS or some other international legal obligation. In those cases, a court may deem it appropriate to hold that the physical barrier modification in question is not readily achievable, without resort to the clear statement rule.

III

A

In light of the preceding analysis, it is likely that under a proper interpretation of "readily achievable" Title III would impose no requirements that interfere with the internal affairs of foreign-flag cruise ships. If Title III did impose a duty that required cruise ships to make permanent and significant structural modifications that did not conflict with international law or threaten safety, or if the statute otherwise interfered with a foreign ship's internal affairs, the clear statement rule recognized in *Benz* and *McCulloch* would come into play at that point. The Title III requirement in question, however, would still apply to domestic cruise ships, and Title III requirements having nothing to do with internal affairs would continue to apply to domestic and foreign ships alike.

This application-by-application use of the internal affairs clear statement rule is consistent with how the rule has traditionally operated. In *Benz* and *McCulloch,* the Court concluded that the NLRA did not apply to labor relations between a foreign-flag ship and its foreign crew because of interference with the foreign ships' internal affairs. In *Ariadne Shipping,* however, the Court held that the NLRA does apply to labor relations between a foreign-flag ship and American longshoremen. *Ariadne Shipping* acknowledged the clear statement rule invoked in *Benz* and *McCulloch* but held that the "considerations that informed the Court's construction of the statute in [those cases] are clearly inapplicable" to the question whether the statute applies to foreign ships' labor relations with American longshoremen. 397 U.S., at 199, 90 S.Ct. 872. *Ariadne Shipping* held that the longshoremen's "short-term, irregular and casual connection with the [foreign] vessels plainly belied any involvement on their part with the ships' 'internal discipline and order.'" *Id.,* at 200, 90 S.Ct. 872. Therefore, application of the NLRA to foreign ships' relations with American longshoremen "would have threatened no interference in the internal affairs of foreign-flag ships." *Ibid.* If the clear statement rule restricts some applications of the NLRA to foreign ships (*e.g.,* labor relations with the foreign crew), but not others (*e.g.,* labor relations with American longshoremen), it follows that the case-by-case application is also required under Title III of the ADA. The rule, where it is even necessary to invoke it, would restrict some applications of Title III to foreign ships (*e.g.,* certain structural barrier modification requirements), but not others (*e.g.,* the prohibition on discriminatory ticket pricing).

The internal affairs clear statement rule is an implied limitation on otherwise unambiguous general terms of the statute. It operates much like the principle that general statutes are construed not to apply extraterritorially, *EEOC v. Arabian American Oil Co.,* 499 U.S. 244, 260, 111 S.Ct. 1227, 113 L.Ed.2d 274 (1991), or the rule that general statutes are presumed not to impose monetary liability on nonconsenting States, *Atascadero State Hospital v. Scanlon,* 473 U.S. 234, 105 S.Ct. 3142, 87 L.Ed.2d 171 (1985). Implied limitation rules avoid applications of otherwise unambiguous statutes that would intrude on sensitive domains in a way that Congress is unlikely to have intended had it considered the matter. In these instances, the absence of a clear congressional statement is, in effect, equivalent to a statutory qualification saying, for example, "Notwithstanding any general language of this statute, this statute shall not apply extraterritorially"; or ". . . this statute shall not abrogate the sovereign immunity of nonconsenting States"; or ". . . this statute does not regulate the internal affairs of foreign-flag vessels." These clear statement rules ensure Congress does not, by broad or general language, legislate on a sensitive topic inadvertently or without due deliberation. An all-or-nothing approach, under which a statute is altogether inapplicable if but one of its specific applications trenches on the domain protected by a clear statement rule, would convert the clear statement rule from a principle of interpretive caution into a trap for an unwary Congress. If Congress passes broad legislation that has some applications that implicate a clear statement rule – say, some extraterritorial applications, or some applications that would regulate foreign ships' internal affairs – an all-or-nothing approach would require that the entire statute, or some arbitrary set of applications larger than the domain protected by the clear statement rule, would be nullified. We decline to adopt that posture.

B

Our holding that the clear statement rule operates only when a ship's internal affairs are affected does not implicate our holding in *Clark v. Martinez,* 543 U.S. ----, 125 S.Ct. 716, 160 L.Ed.2d 734 (2005). *Martinez* held that statutory language given a limiting construction in one context must be interpreted consistently in other contexts, "even though other of the statute's applications, standing alone, would not support the same limitation." *Id.,* * * * at 724. This was simply a rule of consistent interpretation of the statutory words, with no bearing on the implementation of a clear statement rule addressed to particular statutory applications.

The statute in *Martinez,* 8 U.S.C. § 1231(a)(6), authorized detention of aliens pending their removal. In *Zadvydas v. Davis,* 533 U.S. 678, 696-699, 121 S.Ct. 2491, 150 L.Ed.2d 653 (2001), the Court had interpreted this statute to impose time limits on detention of aliens held for certain reasons stated in the statute. The Court held that an alternative interpretation, one allowing indefinite detention of lawfully admitted aliens, would raise grave constitutional doubts. Having determined the meaning of § 1231(a)(6)'s text in *Zadvydas,* we were obliged in *Martinez* to follow the same interpretation even in a context where the constitutional concerns were not present. *Martinez,* * * * 125 S.Ct., at 721-724. As already made clear, the question was one of textual interpretation, not the scope of some implied exception. The constitutional avoidance canon simply informed the choice among plausible readings of § 1231(a)(6)'s text: "The canon of constitutional avoidance," *Martinez* explained, "comes into play only when, after the application of ordinary textual analysis, the statute is found to be susceptible of more than one construction; and the canon functions as a means of choosing between them." *Id.,* * * * at 726 (emphasis deleted).

Martinez gives full respect to the distinction between rules for resolving textual ambiguity and implied limitations on otherwise unambiguous text. Indeed, *Martinez* relies on the distinction to reconcile its holding with two cases which did involve a clear statement rule, *Raygor v. Regents of Univ. of Minn.,* 534 U.S. 533, 122 S.Ct. 999, 152 L.Ed.2d 27 (2002), and *Jinks v. Richland County,* 538 U.S. 456, 123 S.Ct.

1667, 155 L.Ed.2d 631 (2003). *Raygor* had held that the tolling provision in the supplemental jurisdiction statute, 28 U.S.C. § 1367(d), does not apply to nonconsenting States because the statute lacks the required clear statement that States are within its coverage. Later, in *Jinks,* we held that the § 1367(d) tolling provision does apply to suits against counties. The counties were not protected by a clear statement rule analogous to the one applicable to States. See *Martinez,* * * * 125 S.Ct., at 726 and n.6; * * * "This progression of decisions," we held in *Martinez,* "does not remotely establish that § 1367(d) has two different meanings, equivalent to the unlimited-detention/limited-detention meanings of § 1231(a)(6) urged upon us here. They hold that the single and unchanging disposition of § 1367(d) ... does not apply to claims against States that have not consented to be sued in federal court." * * * 125 S.Ct., at 726. The distinction between *Zadvydas* and *Martinez,* on the one hand, and *Raygor* and *Jinks,* on the other, is the distinction between a canon for choosing among plausible meanings of an ambiguous statute and a clear statement rule that implies a special substantive limit on the application of an otherwise unambiguous mandate.

The internal affairs clear statement rule is an implied limitation rule, not a principle for resolving textual ambiguity. Our cases, then, do not compel or permit the conclusion that if any one application of Title III might interfere with a foreign-flag ship's internal affairs, Title III is inapplicable to foreign ships in every other instance.

* * *

The Court of Appeals for the Fifth Circuit held that general statutes do not apply to foreign-flag ships in United States waters. This Court's cases, however, stand only for the proposition that general statutes are presumed not to impose requirements that would interfere with the internal affairs of foreign-flag vessels. Except insofar as Title III regulates a vessel's internal affairs – a category that is not always well defined and that may require further judicial elaboration – the statute is applicable to foreign ships in United States waters to the same extent that it is applicable to American ships in those waters.

Title III's own limitations and qualifications prevent the statute from imposing requirements that would conflict with international obligations or threaten shipboard safety. These limitations and qualifications, though framed in general terms, employ a conventional vocabulary for instructing courts in the interpretation and application of the statute. If, on remand, it becomes clear that even after these limitations are taken into account Title III nonetheless imposes certain requirements that would interfere with the internal affairs of foreign ships – perhaps, for example, by requiring permanent and substantial structural modifications – the clear statement rule would come into play. It is also open to the court on remand to consider application of the clear statement rule at the outset if, as a prudential matter, that appears to be the more appropriate course.

We reverse the judgment of the Court of Appeals and remand the case for further proceedings.

It is so ordered.

Justice GINSBURG, with whom Justice BREYER joins, concurring in part and concurring in the judgment.

I agree with the Court's holding that Title III of the Americans with Disabilities Act of 1990 covers cruise ships, *ante,* at 2177, and allows them to resist modifications "that would conflict with international legal obligations," *ante,* at 2180-2181. I therefore join Parts I, II-A-1, and II-B-2 of the Court's opinion. I would give no wider berth, however, to the "internal affairs" clear statement rule in determining Title III's application to respondent's cruise ships, the Norwegian Sea and Norwegian Star. * * * That rule, as I understand it, derives from, and is moored to, the broader guide that statutes "should not be interpreted to regulate foreign persons or conduct if that regulation would conflict with principles of international law." *Hartford Fire Ins. Co. v. California,* 509 U.S. 764, 815, 113 S.Ct. 2891, 125 L.Ed.2d 612 (1993) (Scalia, J., dissenting) * * * Title III is properly read to avoid such conflict, but should not be hemmed in where there is no potential for international discord.[1]

* * *

Justice THOMAS, concurring in part, dissenting in part, and concurring in the judgment in part.

[omitted]

Justice THOMAS concurs in part IIIA of the plurality opinion holding that Title III of the ADA applies to foreign vessels when it does not impact their internal affairs. Justice THOMAS disagrees with the plurality approach that structural changes do not impact internal affairs.

Justice SCALIA, with whom THE CHIEF JUSTICE and Justice O'CONNOR join, and with whom Justice THOMAS joins as to Part I-A, dissenting.

I respectfully dissent. * * * Title III plainly affects the internal order of foreign-flag cruise ships, subjecting them to the possibility of conflicting international obligations. I would hold that, since there is no clear statement of coverage, Title III does not apply to foreign-flag cruise ships.

---

[1]   Were a clear statement rule in order, I would agree with the plurality's application-by-application approach.

I

A

As the plurality explains, where a law would interfere with the regulation of a ship's internal order, we require a clear statement that Congress intended such a result. * * *

* * *

As the plurality concedes, *ante,* at 2179, the structural modifications that Title III of the ADA requires under its barrier-removal provisions, see 42 U.S.C. §§ 12182(b)(2)(A)(iv), 12184(b)(2)(C), would plainly affect the ship's "internal order." Rendering exterior cabins handicapped-accessible, changing the levels of coamings, and adding public restrooms – the types of modifications petitioners request – would require alteration of core physical aspects of the ship, some of which relate to safety. (Safety has, under international law, traditionally been the province of a ship's flag state.) This is quite different from prohibiting alcohol in United States waters or imposing tort liability for injuries sustained on foreign ships in port – the laws at issue in *Cunard* and the Jones Act cases. Those restrictions affected the ship only in limited circumstances, and in ways ancillary to its operation at sea. A ship's design and construction, by contrast, are at least as integral to the ship's operation and functioning as the bargaining relationship between shipowner and crew at issue in *Benz* and *McCulloch.*

Moreover, the structural changes petitioners request would be permanent. Whereas a ship precluded from serving or carrying alcohol in United States waters may certainly carry and serve alcohol on its next trip from Italy to Greece, structural modifications made to comply with American laws cannot readily be removed once the ship leaves our waters and ceases to carry American passengers. This is again much like the situation presented in *Benz* and *McCulloch,* where the application of American labor laws would have continued to govern contracts between foreign shipowners and their foreign crews well beyond their time in our waters.

The purpose of the "internal order" clear-statement requirement is to avoid casually subjecting oceangoing vessels to laws that pose obvious risks of conflict with the laws of the ship's flag state, the laws of other nations, and international obligations to which the vessels are subject. That structural modifications required under Title III qualify as matters of "internal order" is confirmed by the fact that they may already conflict with the International Convention for the Safety of Life at Sea (SOLAS), Nov. 1, 1974, [1979-1980] 32 U.S.T. 47, T.I.A.S. No. 9700. That treaty, which establishes the safety standards governing the design and maintenance of oceangoing ships, has been ratified by 155 countries. * * * The ADA Accessibility Guidelines (ADAAG) Review Advisory Committee – the Government body Congress has charged with formulating the Title III barrier-removal guidelines – has promulgated rules requiring at least one accessible means of egress to be an elevator, whereas SOLAS, which requires at least two means of escape, does not allow elevators to be one of them. See Passenger Vessel Access Advisory Committee, Final Report: Recommendations for Accessibility Guidelines for Passenger Vehicles, ch. 13, pt. I (Dec. 2000), https://access-board.gov/pvaac/commrept/index.htm (hereinafter PVAAC Report) (explaining potential conflicts between ADAAG regulations and SOLAS). The ADAAG rules set coaming heights for doors required to be accessible at one-half inch; SOLAS sets coaming heights for some exterior doors at three to six inches to ensure that those doors will be watertight. *Ibid.*

Similar inconsistencies may exist between Title III's structural requirements and the disability laws of other countries. The United Kingdom, for example, is considering the promulgation of rules to govern handicapped accessibility to passenger vehicles, including cruise ships. The rules being considered currently include exact specifications, down to the centimeter, for the height of handrails, beds and electrical switches, and the width of door openings. See Disabled Persons Transport Advisory Committee, The design of large passenger ships and passenger infrastructure: Guidance on meeting the needs of disabled people (Nov. 2000), http://www.dptac.gov.uk/pubs/guideship/pdf/dptacbroch.pdf. Though many of these regulations may be compatible with Title III, it is easy to imagine conflicts arising, given the detailed nature of ADAAG's regulations. See PVAAC Report, chs. 1-11. As we have previously noted, even this "*possibility* of international discord" with regard to a seagoing vessel's internal order, *McCulloch*, 372 U.S. at 21, 83 S.Ct. 671 (emphasis added), gives rise to the presumption of noncoverage absent clear statement to the contrary.

* * * It has never been a condition for application of the foreign-flag clear-statement rule that an actual conflict with foreign or international law be established – any more than that has been a condition for application of the clear-statement rule regarding extraterritorial effect of congressional enactments. The reason to apply the rule here is that the structure of a ship pertains to the ship's internal order, which is a matter presumably left to the flag state unless Congress indicates otherwise. The basis for that presumption of congressional intent is principally (though perhaps not exclusively) that subjecting such matters to the commands of various jurisdictions raises the *possibility* (not necessarily the certainty) of conflict among jurisdictions and with international treaties. Even if the Court could, by an imaginative interpretation of Title III, demonstrate that in this particular instance there would be no conflict with the laws of other nations or with international treaties, * * * it would remain true that a ship's structure is preeminently part of its internal order; and it would remain true that subjecting ship structure to multiple national requirements invites conflict. *That* is what triggers application of the clear-statement rule.

Safety concerns – and specifically safety as related to ship structure – are traditionally the responsibility of the flag state. Which is to say they are regarded as part of the ship's internal order. And even if Title III makes ample provision for a safety exception to the barrier-removal requirements, what *it* considers necessary for safety is not necessarily what other nations or international treaties consider necessary.

* * * In any event, the application of Title III to oceangoing vessels under American flag is not at issue here. I would therefore hold that, because Title III's barrier-removal provisions clearly have the possibility of subjecting foreign-flag ships to conflicting international obligations, no reading of Title III – no matter how creative – can alter the presumption that Title III does not apply to foreign-flag ships without a clear statement from Congress.[2]

B

The plurality holds that, even "[i]f Title III did impose a duty that required [foreign-flag] cruise ships to make permanent and significant structural modifications[,] or . . . otherwise interfered with a foreign ship's internal affairs . . . Title III requirements having nothing to do with internal affairs would continue to apply to domestic and foreign ships alike." *Ante,* at 2181. I disagree. Whether or not Title III's prescriptions regarding such matters implicate the "internal order" of the ship, they still relate to the ships' maritime operations and are part of the same Title III.[3] The requirements of that enactment either apply to foreign-flag ships or they do not. It is not within our power to design a statute some of whose provisions apply to foreign-flag ships and other of whose provisions do not – any more than it is within our power to prescribe that the statute applies to foreign-flag cruise ships 60% of whose passengers are United States citizens and does not apply to other foreign-flag cruise ships.

* * * The plurality seems to forget that it is a matter of determining whether Congress *in fact intended* that its enactment cover foreign-flag ships. To believe that there was any such intent section-by-section and paragraph-by-paragraph is delusional. Either Congress enacted Title III only with domestic entities (and not foreign-flag ships) in

---

[2]   Of course this clear-statement rule would not apply to the onshore operations of foreign cruise companies, which would be treated no differently from the operations of other foreign companies on American soil.

[3]   This includes the pricing and ticketing policies, which are intimately related to the ships' maritime operations (and perhaps to internal order) because they are designed to defray the added cost and provide the added protection that the cruise-ship companies deem necessary for safe transport of disabled passengers. * * *

mind, or it intended Title III to apply across-the-board. It could not possibly be the real congressional intent that foreign-flag cruise ships be considered "place[s] of public accommodation" or "specified public transportation" for purposes of certain provisions but not for others. That Congress had separate foreign-flag intent with respect to each requirement – and would presumably adopt a clear statement provision-by-provision – is utterly implausible. And far from its being the case that this creates "a trap for an unwary Congress," *ante,* at 2182, it is the plurality's disposition that, in piecemeal fashion, applies to foreign-flag ships provisions never enacted with foreign-flag vessels in mind. * * * We recently addressed a similar question in *Clark v. Martinez,* 543 U.S. ----, 125 S.Ct. 716, 160 L.Ed.2d 734 (2005), where we explained that a statutory provision must be interpreted consistently from case to case. "It is not at all unusual to give a statut[e] . . . a limiting construction called for by one of the statute's applications, even though other of the statute's applications, standing alone, would not support the same limitation." *Id.,* * * * at 724. That principle should apply here. Since some applications of Title III plainly affect the internal order of foreign-flag ships, the absence of a clear statement renders the statute inapplicable – even though some applications of the statute, if severed from the rest, would not require clear statement.

* * *

The fine-tuning of legislation that the plurality requires would be better left to Congress. To attempt it through the process of case-by-case adjudication is a recipe for endless litigation and confusion. The plurality's resolution of today's case proves the point. It requires this Title III claimant (and every other one who brings a claim against a foreign shipowner) to show that each particular remedy he seeks does not implicate the internal order of the ship. That showing, where structural modification is involved, would not only require the district court to determine what is "readily achievable," * * * and what would "pose 'a significant risk to the health or safety of others,'" * * * but would also require it to determine the obligations imposed by foreign law and international treaties. * * * All this to establish the preliminary point that Title III applies and the claim can proceed to adjudication. * * *

II

* * * Though Congress gave a seemingly exhaustive list of entities constituting "public accommodation[s]" – including inns, hotels, restaurants, theaters, banks, zoos, and laundromats – it failed to mention ships, much less foreign-flag ships. See § 12181(7). * * * Petitioners also claim that, because cruise ships are essentially floating hotels that contain restaurants and other facilities explicitly named in § 12181(7), they should be covered. While this may support the argument that *cruise ships* are "public accommodations," it does not support the position that Congress intended to reach *foreign-flag* cruise ships.

The "specified public transportation" provision prohibits discrimination on the basis of disability "in the full and equal enjoyment of specified public transportation services provided by a private entity that is primarily engaged in the business of transporting people and whose operations affect commerce." § 12184(a). The definition of "specified public transportation" includes "transportation by bus, rail, or any other conveyance (other than by aircraft) that provides the general public with general or special service (including charter service) on a regular and continuing basis." § 12181(10). "[A]ny other conveyance" clearly covers ships. But even if the statute specifically *mentioned* ships, that would not be a clear statement that *foreign-flag* ships are included – any more than the reference to "employer" in the NLRA constituted a clear statement that foreign-flag ship employers were covered, see *McCulloch*, 372 U.S., at 19-21 * * *

Title III of the ADA stands in contrast to other statutes in which Congress *has* made clear its intent to extend its laws to foreign ships. For example, the Maritime Drug Law Enforcement Act, 94 Stat. 1159, 46 U.S.C.App. § 1901 *et seq.*, which permits the inspection and apprehension of vessels suspected of possessing controlled substances, applies to "vessel[s] subject to the jurisdiction of the United States," § 1903(a) * * *

That the Department of Justice and the Department of Transportation – the Executive agencies charged with enforcing the ADA – appear to have concluded that Congress intended Title III to apply to foreign-flag cruise ships does not change my view. We "accept only those agency interpretations that are reasonable in light of the principles of construction courts normally employ." *ARAMCO*, 499 U.S. 244, 260, 111 S.Ct. 1227, 113 L.Ed.2d 274 (1991) (Scalia, J., concurring in part and concurring in judgment) (declining to adopt the Equal Employment Opportunity Commission's determination that Title VII applied to employers abroad); see also *id.*, at 257-258 * * * (opinion of the Court) (same). In light of our longstanding clear-statement rule, it is not reasonable to apply Title III here.

I would therefore affirm the Fifth Circuit's judgment that Title III of the ADA does not apply to foreign-flag cruise ships in United States territorial waters.

Notes & Questions

1. The Court remanded the case to determine whether necessary modifications under Title III would require "permanent and significant structural modifications to foreign vessels," possibly implicating the clear statement rule. Spector v. Norwegian Cruise Line Ltd., 545 U.S. 119, 135, 142 (2005). The Fifth Circuit remanded to the district court noting "that the district court's original basis for denying relief – the Government's failure to promulgate uniform physical accessibility guidelines for cruise ships – has not been eliminated by the Supreme Court's decision as at

least a factor in the liability determination." Spector v. Norwegian Cruise Line Ltd., 427 F.3d 285, 285 (5th Cir. 2005) (per curium).

Chapter 16 PROHIBITED CONDUCT

§ 16.1 General

Title III provides general and specific prohibitions on discriminatory conduct. Discrimination generally prohibited by a public accommodation under Title III includes:

- Denial of participation

- Participation in unequal benefit

- Providing a separate benefit when separation is not necessary

- Failure to ensure that people with disabilities receive goods or services in the most integrated setting appropriate to their needs

- Denying an individual with a disability the opportunity to participate in an integrated benefit because of the availability of a separate benefit

- Using contractual or administrative methods that have the effect of discriminating or that perpetuate the discrimination of others who are subject to common control

- Discrimination on the basis of association with a person with a known disability

As discussed *supra* Section 15.1, a place of public accommodation is a facility and service operated by a private entity that affects commerce and falls within one of twelve categories (e.g., hotel, restaurant, hardware store, doctor's office, museum, zoo, private school, senior center). 42 U.S.C. § 12182(b)(1) (2006).

Specific types of discrimination under Title III include:

- Discriminatory eligibility criteria

- Failure to make reasonable modifications of policy, practice, or procedure when necessary to permit a person with a disability to benefit from a place of public accommodation

- Failure to ensure effective communication through the provision of auxiliary aids

- Failure to remove architectural barriers to access when it is readily achievable to do so

Id. § 12182(b)(2).

A place of public accommodation may not assess any charge to a person with a disability for any action, aid, or service required by the ADA, even to cover the actual costs of the action, aid, or service. 28 C.F.R.

§ 36.301(c) (2008). Rather, the cost of compliance must be considered an overhead expense.

The DOJ's 2010 ADA Standards for Accessible Design recognize that public accommodations may not prohibit access or otherwise deny an equal benefit to an individual with a mobility impairment because the individual uses a "power-driven mobility device" other than a traditional wheelchair. This includes various powered devices "for the purpose of locomotion, including golf cars, electronic personal assistance mobility devices (EPAMDs), such as the Segway® PT, or any mobility device designed to operate in areas without defined pedestrian routes," but not including federal wildreness areas. 28 C.F.R. § 36.104 (2013).

Furthermore, these new regulations provide higher standards for the provision of accessible seating in places of public accommodation that require ticketing, including equal opportunity to purchase individual and multiple tickets, the pricing of tickets, right to transfer tickets, and providing accessible "seating maps, plans, brochures, pricing charts, or other information, that identify accessible seating . . .", (f).

Notes & Questions

1. The ADA also prohibits retaliation against people with disabilities for exercising their opposition (e.g., filing charges, testifying) to acts or practices made unlawful under the Act, and prohibits interference (e.g., intimidation, coercion, threat) with the right of people with disabilities to exercise their civil rights under the Act. 42 U.S.C. § 12203(a)-(b) (2006). In making out a prima facie case of retaliation, does the plaintiff as a customer of a Title III entity have to demonstrate that the retaliatory action had a "detrimental and substantial effect"? What standard do you suggest? *See* Wilson v. Murillo, 163 Cal. Rptr. 3d 214 (Cal. Ct. App. 2008).

§ 16.2 Reasonable Modifications

In addition to prohibiting direct discrimination, Title III provides that discrimination includes:

> a failure to make reasonable modifications in policies, practices, or procedures, when such modifications are necessary to afford such goods, services, facilities, privileges, advantages, or accommodations to individuals with disabilities, unless the entity can demonstrate that making such modifications would fundamentally alter the nature of such goods, services, facilities, privileges, advantages, or accommodations.

42 U.S.C. § 12182(b)(2)(a)(ii); 28 C.F.R. § 36.302(a).

A reasonable modification, like a reasonable accommodation in the employment context, can be any change to the way a good or service is provided. *See, e.g.,* Dudley v. Hannaford Bros. Co., 190 F.Supp.2d 69, 77 (D. Me. 2002), aff'd, 333 F.3d 299 (1st Cir. 2003) (reconsidering a cashier's determination that a customer is drunk when the customer has a disability that can mimic drunkenness); Baughman v. Walt Disney World Co., 685 F.3d 1131, 1137 (9th Cir. 2012) (allowing the use of Segways within park unless demonstrated that Segways pose a safety issue); Matthews v. Nat'l Collegiate Athletic Ass'n, 179 F.Supp.2d 1209, 1227 (E.D. Wash. 2001) (reducing academic eligibility requirements for participation in sports for a student with learning disability that prevents him from meeting the requirements); Burriola v. Greater Toledo YMCA, 133 F.Supp.2d 1034, 1040 (N.D. Ohio 2001) (allowing parents to provide a one-on-one aide in order to enable a child with autism to participate in a daycare program); Anderson v. Ross Stores, No. C 99-4056 CRB, 2000 WL 1585269, at *2 (N.D. Cal. Oct. 10, 2000) (allowing a woman to use the men's dressing room when her personal assistant is male); United States v. Venture Stores, Inc., No. 92 C 6677, 1994 WL 86068, at *1 (N.D. Ill. Mar. 15, 1994) (accepting a state-issued ID card in lieu of a driver's license for paying by check for a person who's disability prevents driving).

Additionally, in *Savage v. City Place Ltd. Partnership*, No. 240306, 2004 WL 3045404 (Md. Cir. Ct. Dec. 20, 2004), a Maryland state court in 2004 held that the ADA applied to the evacuation procedures of a place of public accommodation under Title III.

Allowing service dogs is generally a reasonable modification for places of public accommodations. Following a complaint of a Title III violation where a woman, her husband, and attorney were barred from entering a law office for a deposition because the woman had a service dog, the Department of Justice approved a consent decree requiring places of public accommodation to "adopt an ADA-compliant service animal policy and post the policy in a conspicuous location," among other requirements. *See* Press Release, Department of Justice, *Justice Department Reaches Consent Decree with Colorado Attorney Resolving Lawsuit Alleging Disability Discrimination* (Mar. 30, 2010), http://www.justice.gov/opa/pr/2010/March/10-crt-344.html; *see also* 28 C.F.R. §36.104 (2012).

A.   Burdens Of Proof

JOHNSON v. GAMBRINUS CO./SPOETZL BREWERY

United States Court of Appeals, Fifth Circuit, 1997
116 F.3d 1052

KING, Circuit Judge:

* * *

Gambrinus Company/Spoetzl Brewery appeals the district court's judgment and injunctive order entered after the district court found a violation of the Americans with Disabilities Act and Texas law when it refused to permit Franklin Johnson, who is blind, to tour the Spoetzl Brewery with his guide dog. Finding no error, we affirm.

I. Background

The Gambrinus Company ("Gambrinus") owns the Spoetzl Brewery (the "brewery") in Shiner, Texas. The brewery offers free daily public tours. A brief description of the tour is necessary to understand the issues in this case. The tour begins at the gift shop where tourists watch a video about the brewery. After seeing the video, the tour group is guided through a long hallway and up a flight of metal stairs that leads to the brewhouse. The tour then roughly traces the production process for Shiner Beer.

* * *

On July 8, 1993, Franklin Johnson and his guide dog visited the brewery, along with Johnson's friend Scott Bowman and Bowman's son, to take the tour. * * * [The brewery] informed Johnson that he would not be allowed to take the tour with his dog, but that he could take the tour with a personal human guide such as herself. Johnson informed Fikac that he had a legal right to take the tour with his guide dog, but the brewery would not budge on its blanket no animals policy. Johnson declined to take the tour without his dog, and he waited outside while Bowman and his son took the tour. Although Hybner instructed Fikac to inform Johnson that he could visit the hospitality room, Fikac forgot to do so. However, the brewery's blanket no animals policy at that time applied to the hospitality room also.

On July 1, 1994, Johnson filed suit against Gambrinus, seeking relief under Title III of the Americans with Disabilities Act ("ADA"), 42 U.S.C. §§ 12181-12189, and Texas law. A bench trial was held on July 18 and 19, 1995. In its findings of fact and conclusions of law, the district court determined that Gambrinus's blanket no animals policy, which included service animals, was not compelled by any law and violated the ADA. The court ordered Gambrinus "to modify or establish policies, practices, or procedures to ensure that disabled persons with guide dogs or other service animals have the broadest feasible access to the public tour of the Spoetzl Brewery consistent with the brewery's safe operation," to seek guidance from the Justice Department, and to submit to the court a written policy carrying out its order. Gambrinus timely appealed.

* * *

IV. Standards Of Proof Under The Americans With Disabilities Act

Title III of the ADA, which applies to public accommodations, establishes the general rule that "[n]o individual shall be discriminated against on the basis of disability in the full and equal enjoyment of the goods, services, facilities, privileges, advantages, or accommodations of any place of public accommodation by any person who owns, leases (or leases to), or operates a place of public accommodation." 42 U.S.C. § 12182(a). The ADA then defines discrimination to include

> a failure to make reasonable modifications in policies, practices, or procedures, when such modifications are necessary to afford such goods, services, facilities, privileges, advantages, or accommodations to individuals with disabilities, unless the entity can demonstrate that making such modifications would fundamentally alter the nature of such goods, services, facilities, privileges, advantages, or accommodations.

Id. § 12182(b)(2)(A)(ii).

The central issue for us to address in this case is the allocation of the burdens of proof in a "reasonable modifications" case under Title III. Because no Fifth Circuit case sets forth these burdens in the context of Title III, we will look to the more fully developed case law under Title I of the ADA, which prohibits disability discrimination in employment. See id. § 12112.

In *Riel v. Electronic Data Sys. Corp.,* 99 F.3d 678 (5th Cir. 1996), the plaintiff brought suit under the ADA after he was fired for repeatedly failing to meet milestone deadlines on projects. Id. at 681. He claimed that his failure to meet those deadlines was caused by his disability, which was fatigue attributed to renal failure and diabetes, and he requested accommodations. Id. at 680-81. The district court granted summary judgment for the employer, in part by concluding that the plaintiff's requested accommodations were not reasonable. Id. at 680. We reversed and remanded. Id.

Title I of the ADA provides that discrimination includes "not making reasonable accommodations to the known physical or mental limitations of an otherwise qualified individual with a disability . . . unless [the employer] can demonstrate that the accommodation would impose an undue hardship on the operation of the business." 42 U.S.C. § 12112(b)(5)(A). The *Riel* court noted that the statutory language, by requiring a reasonable accommodation unless the employer "can demonstrate" undue hardship, clearly placed the burden of proof with respect to undue hardship on the employer. 99 F.3d at 682. As to the burden of proving the reasonableness of the accommodation, the court noted that "[i]n contrast, discrimination is defined to be a 'failure to implement reasonable accommodations,' suggesting that the plaintiff bears the burden of proof on that issue." Id. The court went on to describe the substance of these burdens: "[A] reasonable accommodation is 'a method of accommodation that is reasonable in the run of cases, whereas the undue hardship inquiry focuses on the hardships imposed by the plaintiff's preferred accommodation in the context of the particular [employer's] operations.'" Id. at 683 * * * Thus, a plaintiff meets the burden of proof on reasonableness by proposing and putting forth evidence of an accommodation that is generally reasonable, or reasonable "in the run of cases." The employer can challenge the reasonableness of the accommodation only by evidence showing that the accommodation generally would not be reasonable. Moving on to the affirmative defense, if the employer introduces evidence that disputes the appropriateness of the accommodation in the specific circumstances, that constitutes evidence of undue hardship (on which the employer bears the burden of proof). The *Riel* court held that an employer's only mechanism for challenging a requested accommodation (that is reasonable in the run of cases) on grounds that are specific to the circumstances is through the undue hardship defense. Id. at 683-84.

The plaintiff in *Riel* requested that his employer accommodate him either by transferring him to a position without milestone deadlines or by adjusting the deadlines for him. Id. at 683. The employer argued that relaxing the milestone deadlines would disrupt its work structure. Id. The court concluded that there was a fact issue on that question and accordingly determined that summary judgment was inappropriate. Id. The employer also argued that its internal polices would not allow it to transfer the plaintiff because the plaintiff had received ratings of "below average" as a result of missing milestone deadlines. Id. The court concluded that this evidence focused upon the plaintiff's specific circumstances and thus could not be used to rebut the plaintiff's showing of an accommodation reasonable in the run of cases, but instead was relevant only to meeting the employer's burden of showing undue hardship. Id. at 683-84. The employer, however, did not plead undue hardship, which is an affirmative defense. Id. at 684. The employer's evidence therefore was not sufficient to show that it was entitled to judgment as a matter of law and that there were no genuine issues of material fact. Id.

While *Riel* was a Title I reasonable accommodations case, its analysis is easily transferrable to the Title III reasonable modifications context. The language of both provisions is very similar: Title I defines discrimination to include "not making reasonable accommodations ... unless [the defendant] can demonstrate that the accommodation would impose an undue hardship." 42 U.S.C. § 12112(b)(5)(A). Title III defines discrimination to include "a failure to make reasonable modifications ... unless the entity can demonstrate that making such modifications would fundamentally alter the nature of [the public accommodation]." Id. § 12182(b)(2)(A)(ii). In light of the statutes' parallel language, we find no basis for distinguishing their respective burdens of proof. While Title I provides an undue hardship defense and Title III provides a fundamental alteration defense, fundamental alteration is merely a particular type of undue hardship. See 29 C.F.R. pt. 1630, app., § 1630.2(p). Consequently, while the scope of the affirmative defense under Title III is more narrow than that provided by Title I, the type of proof – that is, proof focusing on the specific circumstances rather than on reasonableness in general – is the same.

Applying the *Riel* framework to the Title III reasonable modifications context yields the following allocation of burdens of proof. The plaintiff has the burden of proving that a modification was requested and that the requested modification is reasonable. The plaintiff meets this burden by introducing evidence that the requested modification is reasonable in the general sense, that is, reasonable in the run of cases. While the defendant may introduce evidence indicating that the plaintiff's requested modification is not reasonable in the run of cases, the plaintiff bears the ultimate burden of proof on the issue. * * * If the plaintiff meets this burden, the defendant must make the requested modification unless the defendant pleads and meets its burden of proving that the requested modification would fundamentally alter the nature of the public accommodation. The type of evidence that satisfies this burden focuses on the specifics of the plaintiff's or defendant's circumstances and not on the general nature of the accommodation. Under the statutory framework, such evidence is relevant only to a fundamental alteration defense and not relevant to the plaintiff's burden to show that the requested modification is reasonable in the run of cases.

Service animals present potential concerns not encountered with other types of personal assistance mechanisms for individuals with disabilities. The Justice Department, which Congress directed to issue regulations to carry out the provisions of Title III, 42 U.S.C. § 12186(b), has promulgated a regulation and commentary discussing the use of service animals in places of public accommodation. The regulation states: "Generally, a public accommodation shall modify policies, practices, or procedures to permit the use of a service animal by an individual with a disability." 28 C.F.R. § 36.302(c)(1). In its interpretive commentary, the Justice Department has stated as follows:

> Section 36.302(c)(1) of the final rule now provides that "[g]enerally, a public accommodation shall modify policies, practices, and procedures to permit the use of a service animal by an individual with a disability." This formulation reflects the general intent of Congress that

public accommodations take the necessary steps to accommodate service animals and to ensure that individuals with disabilities are not separated from their service animals. It is intended that the broadest feasible access be provided to service animals in all places of public accommodation, including movie theaters, restaurants, hotels, retail stores, hospitals, and nursing homes. The section also acknowledges, however, that, in rare circumstances, accommodation of service animals may not be required because a fundamental alteration would result in the nature of the goods, services, facilities, privileges, advantages, or accommodations offered or provided, or the safe operation of the public accommodation would be jeopardized.

28 C.F.R. pt. 36, app. B, at 623. * * * This Justice Department interpretation fits well within the *Riel* framework. Under the *Riel* framework, the plaintiff must show a modification that is reasonable generally or in the run of cases. The regulation and commentary reflect an administrative determination that modifying a no animals policy to allow a service animal full access with its owner in a place of public accommodation is generally reasonable, or, in *Riel* language, reasonable in the run of cases. The commentary also mirrors the *Riel* framework by stating that a public accommodation must modify its animal restriction policy to allow a service animal to accompany its owner unless it can demonstrate that such modifications would cause a fundamental alteration or jeopardize the safety of the public accommodation.

* * *

We agree with the district court that the Justice Department's interpretation is not arbitrary, capricious, or manifestly contrary to the statute. As previously discussed, the regulation corresponds with the ADA's statutory framework as discussed in *Riel*. Furthermore, the legislative history of Title III makes clear that Congress concluded that it is a reasonable modification for places of public accommodation with animal restriction policies to allow individuals with disabilities full use of service animals. We also defer to the Justice Department's commentary concerning service animals because it is not inconsistent with the plain language of the regulation. * * *

* * *

[Court agreed with the district court's finding that contamination of the beer by the service animal was very unlikely.]

VI. Application Of ADA Standards In Light Of The FDA Findings

After analyzing the district court's interpretations and findings regarding the FDA regulation, we now turn to a discussion of whether each party has met its burdens under the ADA.

As previously stated, Johnson has the burden to show that he requested a modification that is reasonable in the run of cases. Johnson has met that burden: he requested a modification of Gambrinus's blanket no animals policy to allow full access for his guide dog in Gambrinus's place of public accommodation. As indicated in the Justice Department's regulation and commentary, this modification is generally reasonable.[11]

Thus, as established by *Riel* and the Justice Department regulation and commentary, Gambrinus must make modifications to allow guide dogs on the tour unless it can demonstrate either 1) that such modifications would fundamentally alter the nature of the public accommodation or 2) that such modifications would jeopardize the safety of the public accommodation.[12] Gambrinus has failed to make such a showing.

Gambrinus argues that it is not required to allow guide dogs on the tour because it would either require Gambrinus to violate the FDA regulation or to shut down beer production while a dog was present to avoid exposure. According to Gambrinus, shutting down the production process would fundamentally alter the nature of the tour, which is to see beer actually being made. However, as we have previously discussed, Gambrinus's interpretation and application of the FDA regulation are flawed because the district court did not err in finding that there are parts of the tour where a guide dog could go without a likelihood of contamination and thus without violating the FDA regulation.

Gambrinus further complains that the district court erred by "not considering" its fundamental alteration argument. However, a reading of the district court's findings of fact and conclusions of law reveals that the district court found that "[a] modification to provide Plaintiff and his support dog the broadest feasible access to the public tour of the Spoetzl

---

[11]   Gambrinus agrees that the burden to prove reasonableness is on Johnson but argues that this burden also requires Johnson to prove that there are no obstacles to full access, such as the FDA regulation. However, the fact that FDA regulations apply to a particular public accommodation shows only that in Gambrinus's unique circumstances there may be a barrier to full access for service animals. That type of evidence is irrelevant to Johnson's burden to show that his requested accommodation is reasonable in the run of cases, but instead is relevant only to Gambrinus's affirmative defenses, on which it bears the burden of proof.

[12]   Because we have concluded that the FDA regulation did not mandate Gambrinus's blanket no animals policy, the asserted justification for its proposed modification – a human escort – disappears. Thus, our discussion assumes only one proposed modification (the plaintiff's), and we make no comment on the situation in which there are two competing proposed reasonable modifications.

Brewery consistent with the safe operation of its manufacturing facilities will not work a fundamental alteration of the nature of the goods, services, facilities, privileges, or accommodations offered or provided." Gambrinus complains that this finding is clearly erroneous because the district court could not assess whether any modifications would cause a fundamental alteration when the exact nature of the changes to be made is still uncertain. Basically, Gambrinus is arguing that the district court had a duty to delineate the exact nature of the changes Gambrinus must make before it could conclude that Gambrinus had violated the ADA. The district court had no such duty because Johnson met his burden of showing that modification of a blanket no animals policy is reasonable in the run of cases and therefore Gambrinus must make the modification unless it can demonstrate an affirmative defense. As previously discussed, the district court found many areas of the tour where a guide dog could be present without a likelihood of contamination. It was not clearly erroneous to determine that a modification to allow service animals on those parts of the tour would not result in a fundamental alteration. Findings concerning fundamental alterations relating to other modifications will come later. * * *

* * *

For the foregoing reasons, we AFFIRM.

Notes & Questions

1. Is the allocation of the burdens of proof in *Johnson* appropriate? Why or why not? Was the court correct to adopt the burdens of proof established in Title I cases? Are there differences between Title I cases and Title III cases that may call for a different allocation of burdens?

2. It is notable that, while Title I provides an "undue hardship" defense, the Title III reasonable modification provision does not. It only provides a "fundamental alteration" defense. The court in *Johnson* treats the two defenses as if they are identical. Do you agree with the court? Why might Congress have intended them to be different?

3. What range of accommodations could the defendants have offered in this case? In the actual case, Brewery offered to provide a staff member to accompany Mr. Johnson through the tour. Is this accommodation acceptable?

4. Under the 2008 ADA Amendments Act, a service animal has been more narrowly defined as:

> any *dog* that is individually trained to do work or perform tasks for the benefit of an individual with a disability, including a physical, sensory, psychiatric, intellectual, or other mental disability. Other species of animals, whether wild or domestic, trained or untrained, are not service

animals for the purposes of this definition. 28 C.F.R. § 36.104 (2013) (emphasis added).

Additionally, "work or tasks performed by a service animal must be directly related to the individual's disability." *Id.*

The care and supervision of a service animal is the responsibility of the individual with a disability. 28 C.F.R. § 36.302(c)(4)-(5) (2013). Similarly, the behavior of the service animal is the responsibility of its owner. *Id.* § 36.302(c)(2), (4) A service animal may be excluded if "[t]he animal is out of control and the animal's handler does not take effective action to control it; or . . . [it] is not housebroken." *Id.* § 36.302(c)(2)(i)-(ii). A business may impose limitations on the admittance of service animals if those limitations respond to legitimate safety or health risks. Thus, a hospital may ban a service animal from an emergency treatment room. Pool v. Riverside Health Serv., Inc., No. 94-1430-PFK, 1995 WL 519129, at *4 (D. Kan. Aug. 25, 1995).

Further, a public accommodation may make two types of inquiries to determine whether a dog is a qualified service animal, when this fact is unclear. The public accommodation may only "ask if the animal is required because of a disability and what work or task the animal has been trained to perform." 28 C.F.R. § 36.302(c)(6) (2013). The Title II entity may not require a surcharge for admittance of the service animal. *Id.* § 36.302(c)(8). Alternately, miniature horses may be used by an individual with a disability if it has been "trained to do work or perform tasks for the benefit of the individual with a disability." § 36.302(c)(9)(i).

B.   Reasonableness/Fundamental Alteration

PGA TOUR, INC. v. MARTIN

Supreme Court of the United States, 2001
532 U.S. 661

Justice STEVENS delivered the opinion of the Court.

This case raises two questions concerning the application of the Americans with Disabilities Act of 1990, 104 Stat. 328, 42 U.S.C. § 12101 *et seq.*, to a gifted athlete: first, whether the Act protects access to professional golf tournaments by a qualified entrant with a disability; and second, whether a disabled contestant may be denied the use of a golf cart because it would "fundamentally alter the nature" of the tournaments, § 12182(b)(2)(A)(ii), to allow him to ride when all other contestants must walk.

I

Petitioner PGA TOUR, Inc., a nonprofit entity formed in 1968, sponsors and cosponsors professional golf tournaments conducted on three annual tours. About 200 golfers participate in the PGA TOUR; about 170 in the NIKE TOUR; and about 100 in the SENIOR PGA TOUR. PGA TOUR and NIKE TOUR tournaments typically are 4-day events, played on courses leased and operated by petitioner. The entire field usually competes in two 18-hole rounds played on Thursday and Friday; those who survive the "cut" play on Saturday and Sunday and receive prize money in amounts determined by their aggregate scores for all four rounds. The revenues generated by television, admissions, concessions, and contributions from cosponsors amount to about $300 million a year, much of which is distributed in prize money.

There are various ways of gaining entry into particular tours. For example, a player who wins three NIKE TOUR events in the same year, or is among the top-15 money winners on that tour, earns the right to play in the PGA TOUR. Additionally, a golfer may obtain a spot in an official tournament through successfully competing in "open" qualifying rounds, which are conducted the week before each tournament. Most participants, however, earn playing privileges in the PGA TOUR or NIKE TOUR by way of a three-stage qualifying tournament known as the "Q-School."

Any member of the public may enter the Q-School by paying a $3,000 entry fee and submitting two letters of reference from, among others, PGA TOUR or NIKE TOUR members. The $3,000 entry fee covers the players' greens fees and the cost of golf carts, which are permitted during the first two stages, but which have been prohibited during the third stage since 1997. Each year, over a thousand contestants compete in the first stage, which consists of four 18-hole rounds at different locations. Approximately half of them make it to the second stage, which also includes 72 holes. Around 168 players survive the second stage and advance to the final one, where they compete over 108 holes. Of those finalists, about a fourth qualify for membership in the PGA TOUR, and the rest gain membership in the NIKE TOUR. The significance of making it into either tour is illuminated by the fact that there are about 25 million golfers in the country.

Three sets of rules govern competition in tour events. First, the "Rules of Golf," jointly written by the United States Golf Association (USGA) and the Royal and Ancient Golf Club of Scotland, apply to the game as it is played, not only by millions of amateurs on public courses and in private country clubs throughout the United States and worldwide, but also by the professionals in the tournaments conducted by petitioner, the USGA, the Ladies' Professional Golf Association, and the Senior Women's Golf Association. Those rules do not prohibit the use of golf carts at any time.

Second, the "Conditions of Competition and Local Rules," often described as the "hard card," apply specifically to petitioner's professional tours. The hard cards for the PGA TOUR and NIKE TOUR require players to walk the golf course during tournaments, but not during open qualifying rounds. On the SENIOR PGA TOUR, which is limited to golfers age 50 and older, the contestants may use golf carts. Most seniors, however, prefer to walk.

Third, "Notices to Competitors" are issued for particular tournaments and cover conditions for that specific event. Such a notice may, for example, explain how the Rules of Golf should be applied to a particular water hazard or manmade obstruction. It might also authorize the use of carts to speed up play when there is an unusual distance between one green and the next tee.

The basic Rules of Golf, the hard cards, and the weekly notices apply equally to all players in tour competitions. As one of petitioner's witnesses explained with reference to "the Masters Tournament, which is golf at its very highest level, . . . the key is to have everyone tee off on the first hole under exactly the same conditions and all of them be tested over that 72-hole event under the conditions that exist during those four days of the event." * * *

II

Casey Martin is a talented golfer. As an amateur, he won 17 Oregon Golf Association junior events before he was 15, and won the state championship as a high school senior. He played on the Stanford University golf team that won the 1994 National Collegiate Athletic Association (NCAA) championship. As a professional, Martin qualified for the NIKE TOUR in 1998 and 1999, and based on his 1999 performance, qualified for the PGA TOUR in 2000. In the 1999 season, he entered 24 events, made the cut 13 times, and had 6 top-10 finishes, coming in second twice and third once.

Martin is also an individual with a disability as defined in the Americans with Disabilities Act of 1990 (ADA or Act). Since birth he has been afflicted with Klippel-Trenaunay-Weber Syndrome, a degenerative circulatory disorder that obstructs the flow of blood from his right leg back to his heart. The disease is progressive; it causes severe pain and has atrophied his right leg. During the latter part of his college career, because of the progress of the disease, Martin could no longer walk an 18-hole golf course. Walking not only caused him pain, fatigue, and anxiety, but also created a significant risk of hemorrhaging, developing blood clots, and fracturing his tibia so badly that an amputation might be required. For these reasons, Stanford made written requests to the Pacific 10 Conference and the NCAA to waive for Martin their rules requiring players to walk and carry their own clubs. The requests were granted.

When Martin turned pro and entered petitioner's Q-School, the hard card permitted him to use a cart during his successful progress through the first two stages. He made a request, supported by detailed medical records, for permission to use a golf cart during the third stage. Petitioner refused to review those records or to waive its walking rule for the third stage. Martin therefore filed this action. A preliminary injunction entered by the District Court made it possible for him to use a cart in the final stage of the Q-School and as a competitor in the NIKE TOUR and PGA TOUR. Although not bound by the injunction, and despite its support for petitioner's position in this litigation, the USGA voluntarily granted Martin a similar waiver in events that it sponsors, including the U.S. Open.

III

* * *

On the merits, because there was no serious dispute about the fact that permitting Martin to use a golf cart was both a reasonable and a necessary solution to the problem of providing him access to the tournaments, the Court of Appeals regarded the central dispute as whether such permission would "fundamentally alter" the nature of the PGA TOUR or NIKE TOUR. Like the District Court, the Court of Appeals viewed the issue not as "whether use of carts generally would fundamentally alter the competition, but whether the use of a cart by Martin would do so." * * * That issue turned on "an intensively fact-based inquiry," and, the court concluded, had been correctly resolved by the trial judge. In its words, "[a]ll that the cart does is permit Martin access to a type of competition in which he otherwise could not engage because of his disability." * * *

The day after the Ninth Circuit ruled in Martin's favor, the Seventh Circuit came to a contrary conclusion in a case brought against the USGA by a disabled golfer who failed to qualify for "America's greatest – and most democratic – golf tournament, the United States Open." *Olinger v. United States Golf Assn.*, 205 F.3d 1001 (C.A. 7 2000). The Seventh Circuit endorsed the conclusion of the District Court in that case that "the nature of the competition would be fundamentally altered if the walking rule were eliminated because it would remove stamina (at least a particular type of stamina) from the set of qualities designed to be tested in this competition." Id. at 1006 (internal quotation marks omitted). In the Seventh Circuit's opinion, the physical ordeals endured by Ken Venturi and Ben Hogan when they walked to their Open victories in 1964 and 1950 amply demonstrated the importance of stamina in such a tournament. As an alternative basis for its holding, the court also concluded that the ADA does not require the USGA to bear "the administrative burdens of evaluating requests to waive the walking rule and permit the use of a golf cart." Id. at 1007.

* * *

V

As we have noted, 42 U.S.C. § 12182(a) sets forth Title III's general rule prohibiting public accommodations from discriminating against individuals because of their disabilities. The question whether petitioner has violated that rule depends on a proper construction of the term "discrimination," which is defined by Title III to include

> "a failure to make reasonable modifications in policies, practices, or procedures, when such modifications are necessary to afford such goods, services, facilities, privileges, advantages, or accommodations to individuals with disabilities, *unless the entity can demonstrate that making such modifications would fundamentally alter the nature* of such goods, services, facilities, privileges, advantages, or accommodations." § 12182(b)(2)(A)(ii) (emphasis added).

Petitioner does not contest that a golf cart is a reasonable modification that is necessary if Martin is to play in its tournaments. Martin's claim thus differs from one that might be asserted by players with less serious afflictions that make walking the course uncomfortable or difficult, but not beyond their capacity. In such cases, an accommodation might be reasonable but not necessary. In this case, however, the narrow dispute is whether allowing Martin to use a golf cart, despite the walking requirement that applies to the PGA TOUR, the NIKE TOUR, and the third stage of the Q-School, is a modification that would "fundamentally alter the nature" of those events.

In theory, a modification of petitioner's golf tournaments might constitute a fundamental alteration in two different ways. It might alter such an essential aspect of the game of golf that it would be unacceptable even if it affected all competitors equally; changing the diameter of the hole from three to six inches might be such a modification. Alternatively, a less significant change that has only a peripheral impact on the game itself might nevertheless give a disabled player, in addition to access to the competition as required by Title III, an advantage over others and, for that reason, fundamentally alter the character of the competition. We are not persuaded that a waiver of the walking rule for Martin would work a fundamental alteration in either sense.

As an initial matter, we observe that the use of carts is not itself inconsistent with the fundamental character of the game of golf. From early on, the essence of the game has been shotmaking – using clubs to cause a ball to progress from the teeing ground to a hole some distance away with as few strokes as possible. That essential aspect of the game is still reflected in the very first of the Rules of Golf, which declares: "The Game of Golf consists in playing a ball from the *teeing ground* into the hole by a *stroke* or successive strokes in accordance with the rules." Rule 1-1, Rules of Golf, App. 104. * * * Over the years, there have been many changes in the players' equipment, in golf course design, in the Rules of Golf, and in the method of transporting clubs from hole to hole. Originally, so few clubs were used that each player could carry them without a bag. Then came golf bags, caddies, carts that were pulled by hand, and eventually motorized carts that carried players as well as clubs. "Golf carts started appearing with increasing regularity on American golf courses in the 1950's. Today they are everywhere. And they are encouraged. For one thing, they often speed up play, and for another, they are great revenue producers." There is nothing in the Rules of Golf that either forbids the use of carts or penalizes a player for using a cart. That set of rules, as we have observed, is widely accepted in both the amateur and professional golf world as the rules of the game. The walking rule that is contained in petitioner's hard cards, based on an optional condition buried in an appendix to the Rules of Golf, is not an essential attribute of the game itself.

Indeed, the walking rule is not an indispensable feature of tournament golf either. As already mentioned, petitioner permits golf carts to be used in the SENIOR PGA TOUR, the open qualifying events for petitioner's tournaments, the first two stages of the Q-School, and, until 1997, the third stage of the Q-School as well. * * * Moreover, petitioner allows the use of carts during certain tournament rounds in both the PGA TOUR and the NIKE TOUR. In addition, although the USGA enforces a walking rule in most of the tournaments that it sponsors, it permits carts in the Senior Amateur and the Senior Women's Amateur championships.

Petitioner, however, distinguishes the game of golf as it is generally played from the game that it sponsors in the PGA TOUR, NIKE TOUR, and (at least recently) the last stage of the Q-School – golf at the "highest level." According to petitioner, "[t]he goal of the highest-level competitive athletics is to assess and compare the performance of different competitors, a task that is meaningful only if the competitors are subject to identical substantive rules." The waiver of any possibly "outcome-affecting" rule for a contestant would violate this principle and therefore, in petitioner's view, fundamentally alter the nature of the highest level athletic event. The walking rule is one such rule, petitioner submits, because its purpose is "to inject the element of fatigue into the skill of shot-making," and thus its effect may be the critical loss of a stroke. As a consequence, the reasonable modification Martin seeks would fundamentally alter the nature of petitioner's highest level tournaments even if he were the only person in the world who has both the talent to compete in those elite events and a disability sufficiently serious that he cannot do so without using a cart.

The force of petitioner's argument is, first of all, mitigated by the fact that golf is a game in which it is impossible to guarantee that all competitors will play under exactly the same conditions or that an individual's ability will be the sole determinant of the outcome. For example, changes in the weather may produce harder greens and more head winds for the tournament leader than for his closest pursuers. A lucky bounce may save a shot or two. Whether such happenstance events are more or less probable than the likelihood that a golfer afflicted with Klippel-Trenaunay-Weber Syndrome would one day qualify for the NIKE TOUR and PGA TOUR, they at least demonstrate that pure chance may have a greater impact on the outcome of elite golf tournaments than the fatigue resulting from the enforcement of the walking rule.

Further, the factual basis of petitioner's argument is undermined by the District Court's finding that the fatigue from walking during one of petitioner's 4-day tournaments cannot be deemed significant. The District Court credited the testimony of a professor in physiology and expert on fatigue, who calculated the calories expended in walking a golf course (about five miles) to be approximately 500 calories – " 'nutritionally ... less than a Big Mac.' " * * * What is more, that energy is expended over a 5-hour period, during which golfers have numerous intervals for rest and refreshment. In fact, the expert concluded, because golf is a low intensity activity, fatigue from the game is primarily a psychological phenomenon in which stress and motivation are the key ingredients. And even under conditions of severe heat and humidity, the critical factor in fatigue is fluid loss rather than exercise from walking.

Moreover, when given the option of using a cart, the majority of golfers in petitioner's tournaments have chosen to walk, often to relieve stress or for other strategic reasons. As NIKE TOUR member Eric Johnson testified, walking allows him to keep in rhythm, stay warmer when it is chilly, and develop a better sense of the elements and the course than riding a cart.

Even if we accept the factual predicate for petitioner's argument – that the walking rule is "outcome affecting" because fatigue may adversely affect performance – its legal position is fatally flawed. Petitioner's refusal to consider Martin's personal circumstances in deciding whether to accommodate his disability runs counter to the clear language and purpose of the ADA. As previously stated, the ADA was enacted to eliminate discrimination against "individuals" with disabilities, 42 U.S.C. § 12101(b)(1), and to that end Title III of the Act requires without exception that any "policies, practices, or procedures" of a public accommodation be reasonably modified for disabled "individuals" as necessary to afford access unless doing so would fundamentally alter what is offered, § 12182(b)(2)(A)(ii). To comply with this command, an individualized inquiry must be made to determine whether a specific modification for a particular person's disability would be reasonable under the circumstances as well as necessary for that person, and yet at the same time not work a fundamental alteration. See S. Rep. No. 101-116, at 61; H.R. Rep. No. 101-485, pt. 2, at 102 * * * (public accommodations "are required to make decisions based on facts applicable to individuals"). * * *

To be sure, the waiver of an essential rule of competition for anyone would fundamentally alter the nature of petitioner's tournaments. As we have demonstrated, however, the walking rule is at best peripheral to the nature of petitioner's athletic events, and thus it might be waived in individual cases without working a fundamental alteration. Therefore, petitioner's claim that all the substantive rules for its "highest-level" competitions are sacrosanct and cannot be modified under any circumstances is effectively a contention that it is exempt from Title III's reasonable modification requirement. But that provision carves out no exemption for elite athletics, and given Title III's coverage not only of places of "exhibition or entertainment" but also of "golf course[s]," 42 U.S.C. §§ 12181(7)(C), (L), its application to petitioner's tournaments cannot be said to be unintended or unexpected, see §§ 12101(a)(1), (5). Even if it were, "the fact that a statute can be applied in situations not expressly anticipated by Congress does not demonstrate ambiguity. It demonstrates breadth." *Pennsylvania Dept. of Corrections v. Yeskey,* 524 U.S. at 212. * * *

Under the ADA's basic requirement that the need of a disabled person be evaluated on an individual basis, we have no doubt that allowing Martin to use a golf cart would not fundamentally alter the nature of petitioner's tournaments. As we have discussed, the purpose of the walking rule is to subject players to fatigue, which in turn may influence the outcome of tournaments. Even if the rule does serve that purpose, it is an uncontested finding of the District Court that Martin "easily endures greater fatigue even with a cart than his able-bodied competitors do by walking." 994 F.Supp. at 1252. The purpose of the walking rule is therefore not compromised in the slightest by allowing Martin to use a cart. A modification that provides an exception to a peripheral tournament rule without impairing its purpose cannot be said to "fundamentally alter" the tournament. What it can be said to do, on the other hand, is to allow Martin the chance to qualify for, and compete in, the athletic events petitioner offers to those members of the public who have the skill and desire to enter. That is exactly what the ADA requires. As a result, Martin's request for a waiver of the walking rule should have been granted.

The ADA admittedly imposes some administrative burdens on the operators of places of public accommodation that could be avoided by strictly adhering to general rules and policies that are entirely fair with respect to the able-bodied but that may indiscriminately preclude access by qualified persons with disabilities.[53] But surely, in a case of this kind,

---

[53] However, we think petitioner's contention that the task of assessing requests for modifications will amount to a substantial burden is overstated. As Martin indicates, in the three years since he requested the use of a cart, no one else has sued the PGA, and only two other golfers (one of whom is Olinger) have sued the USGA for a waiver of the walking

Congress intended that an entity like the PGA not only give individualized attention to the handful of requests that it might receive from talented but disabled athletes for a modification or waiver of a rule to allow them access to the competition, but also carefully weigh the purpose, as well as the letter, of the rule before determining that no accommodation would be tolerable.

The judgment of the Court of Appeals is AFFIRMED.

It is so ordered.

Justice SCALIA, with whom Justice THOMAS joins, dissenting.

In my view today's opinion exercises a benevolent compassion that the law does not place it within our power to impose. The judgment distorts the text of Title III, the structure of the ADA, and common sense. I respectfully dissent.

* * *

II

Having erroneously held that Title III applies to the "customers" of professional golf who consist of its practitioners, the Court then erroneously answers – or to be accurate simply ignores – a second question. The ADA requires covered businesses to make such reasonable modifications of "policies, practices, or procedures" as are necessary to "afford" goods, services, and privileges to individuals with disabilities; but it explicitly does not require "modifications [that] would fundamentally alter the nature" of the goods, services, and privileges. § 12182(b)(2)(A)(ii). In other words, disabled individuals must be given *access* to the same goods, services, and privileges that others enjoy. The regulations state that Title III "does not require a public accommodation to alter its inventory to include accessible or special goods with accessibility features that are designed for, or facilitate use by, individuals with disabilities." 28 CFR § 36.307 (2000). As one Court of Appeals has explained:

> The common sense of the statute is that the content of the goods or services offered by a place of public accommodation is not regulated. A camera store may not refuse to sell cameras to a disabled person, but it is not required to stock cameras specially designed for such persons. Had Congress purposed to impose so enormous a burden on the retail sector of the economy and so vast a supervisory responsibility on the federal courts, we think it would have made its intention clearer and would at least have imposed

rule. In addition, we believe petitioner's point is misplaced, as nowhere in § 12182(b)(2)(A)(ii) does Congress limit the reasonable modification requirement only to requests that are easy to evaluate.

some standards. It is hardly a feasible judicial function to decide whether shoestores should sell single shoes to one-legged persons and if so at what price, or how many Braille books the Borders or Barnes and Noble bookstore chains should stock in each of their stores.

Doe v. Mutual of Omaha Ins. Co., 179 F.3d 557, 560 (C.A.7 1999).

Since this is so, even if respondent here is a consumer of the "privilege" of the PGA TOUR competition, * * * I see no basis for considering whether the rules of that competition must be altered. It is as irrelevant to the PGA TOUR's compliance with the statute whether walking is essential to the game of golf as it is to the shoe store's compliance whether "pairness" is essential to the nature of shoes. If a shoe store wishes to sell shoes only in pairs it may; and if a golf tour (or a golf course) wishes to provide only walk-around golf, it may. The PGA TOUR cannot deny respondent *access* to that game because of his disability, but it need not provide him a game different (whether in its essentials or in its details) from that offered to everyone else.

Since it has held (or assumed) professional golfers to be customers "enjoying" the "privilege" that consists of PGA TOUR golf; and since it inexplicably regards the rules of PGA TOUR golf as merely "policies, practices, or procedures" by which access to PGA TOUR golf is provided, the Court must then confront the question whether respondent's requested modification of the supposed policy, practice, or procedure of walking would "fundamentally alter the nature" of the PGA TOUR game, § 12182(b)(2)(A)(ii). The Court attacks this "fundamental alteration" analysis by asking two questions: first, whether the "essence" or an "essential aspect" of the sport of golf has been altered; and second, whether the change, even if not essential to the game, would give the disabled player an advantage over others and thereby "fundamentally alter the character of the competition." * * * It answers no to both.

Before considering the Court's answer to the first question, it is worth pointing out that the assumption which underlies that question is false. Nowhere is it writ that PGA TOUR golf must be classic "essential" golf. Why cannot the PGA TOUR, if it wishes, promote a new game, with distinctive rules (much as the American League promotes a game of baseball in which the pitcher's turn at the plate can be taken by a "designated hitter")? If members of the public do not like the new rules – if they feel that these rules do not truly test the individual's skill at "real golf" (or the team's skill at "real baseball") they can withdraw their patronage. But the rules are the rules. They are (as in all games) entirely arbitrary, and there is no basis on which anyone – not even the Supreme Court of the United States – can pronounce one or another of them to be "nonessential" if the rulemaker (here the PGA TOUR) deems it to be essential.

If one assumes, however, that the PGA TOUR has some legal obligation to play classic, Platonic golf – and if one assumes the correctness of all the other wrong turns the Court has made to get to this point – then we Justices must confront what is indeed an awesome responsibility. It has been rendered the solemn duty of the Supreme Court of the United States, laid upon it by Congress in pursuance of the Federal Government's power "[t]o regulate Commerce with foreign Nations, and among the several States," U.S. Const., Art. I, § 8, cl. 3, to decide What Is Golf. I am sure that the Framers of the Constitution, aware of the 1457 edict of King James II of Scotland prohibiting golf because it interfered with the practice of archery, fully expected that sooner or later the paths of golf and government, the law and the links, would once again cross, and that the judges of this august Court would some day have to wrestle with that age-old jurisprudential question, for which their years of study in the law have so well prepared them: Is someone riding around a golf course from shot to shot *really* a golfer? The answer, we learn, is yes. The Court ultimately concludes, and it will henceforth be the Law of the Land, that walking is not a "fundamental" aspect of golf.

Either out of humility or out of self-respect (one or the other) the Court should decline to answer this incredibly difficult and incredibly silly question. To say that something is "essential" is ordinarily to say that it is necessary to the achievement of a certain object. But since it is the very nature of a game to have no object except amusement (that is what distinguishes games from productive activity), it is quite impossible to say that any of a game's arbitrary rules is "essential." Eighteen-hole golf courses, 10-foot-high basketball hoops, 90-foot baselines, 100-yard football fields – all are arbitrary and none is essential. The only support for any of them is tradition and (in more modern times) insistence by what has come to be regarded as the ruling body of the sport – both of which factors support the PGA TOUR's position in the present case. (Many, indeed, consider walking to be *the central feature* of the game of golf – hence Mark Twain's classic criticism of the sport: "a good walk spoiled.") I suppose there is some point at which the rules of a well-known game are changed to such a degree that no reasonable person would call it the same game. If the PGA TOUR competitors were required to dribble a large, inflated ball and put it through a round hoop, the game could no longer reasonably be called golf. But this criterion – destroying recognizability as the same generic game – is surely not the test of "essentialness" or "fundamentalness" that the Court applies, since it apparently thinks that merely changing the diameter of the *cup* might "fundamentally alter" the game of golf. * * *

Having concluded that dispensing with the walking rule would not violate federal-Platonic "golf" (and, implicitly, that it is federal-Platonic golf, and no other, that the PGA TOUR can insist upon), the Court moves on to the second part of its test: the competitive effects of waiving this nonessential rule. In this part of its analysis, the Court first finds that the effects of the change are "mitigated" by the fact that in the game of golf weather, a "lucky bounce," and "pure chance" provide different conditions for each competitor and individual ability may not "be the sole determinant of the outcome." * * * I guess that is why those who follow professional golfing consider Jack Nicklaus the *luckiest* golfer of all time, only to be challenged of late by the phenomenal *luck* of Tiger Woods. The Court's empiricism is unpersuasive. "Pure chance" is randomly distributed among the players, but allowing respondent to use a cart gives him a "lucky" break every time he plays. Pure chance also only matters at the margin – a stroke here or there; the cart substantially improves this respondent's competitive prospects beyond a couple of strokes. But even granting that there are significant nonhuman variables affecting competition, that fact does not justify adding another variable that always favors one player.

In an apparent effort to make its opinion as narrow as possible, the Court relies upon the District Court's finding that even with a cart, respondent will be at least as fatigued as everyone else. * * * This, the Court says, *proves* that competition will not be affected. Far from thinking that reliance on this finding cabins the effect of today's opinion, I think it will prove to be its most expansive and destructive feature. Because step one of the Court's two-part inquiry into whether a requested change in a sport will "fundamentally alter [its] nature," § 12182(b)(2)(A)(ii), consists of an utterly unprincipled ontology of sports (pursuant to which the Court is not even sure whether golf's "essence" requires a 3-inch hole), there is every reason to think that in future cases involving requests for special treatment by would-be athletes the second step of the analysis will be determinative. In resolving that second step – determining whether waiver of the "nonessential" rule will have an impermissible "competitive effect" – by measuring the athletic capacity of the requesting individual, and asking whether the special dispensation would do no more than place him on a par (so to speak) with other competitors, the Court guarantees that future cases of this sort will have to be decided on the basis of individualized factual findings. Which means that future cases of this sort will be numerous, and a rich source of lucrative litigation. One can envision the parents of a Little League player with attention deficit disorder trying to convince a judge that their son's disability makes it at least 25% more difficult to hit a pitched ball. (If they are successful, the only thing that could prevent a court order giving the kid four strikes would be a judicial determination that, in baseball, three strikes are metaphysically necessary, which is quite absurd.)

The statute, of course, provides no basis for this individualized analysis that is the Court's last step on a long and misguided journey. The statute seeks to assure that a disabled person's disability will not deny him *equal access* to (among other things) competitive sporting events – not that his disability will not deny him an *equal chance to win* competitive sporting events. The latter is quite impossible, since the very *nature* of competitive sport is the measurement, by uniform rules, of unevenly distributed excellence. This unequal distribution is precisely what determines the winners and losers – and artificially to "even out" that distribution, by giving one or another player exemption from a rule that emphasizes his particular weakness, is to destroy the game. That is why the "handicaps" that are customary in social games of golf – which, by adding strokes to the scores of the good players and subtracting them from scores of the bad ones, "even out" the varying abilities – are *not* used in professional golf. In the Court's world, there is one set of rules that is "fair with respect to the able-bodied" but "individualized" rules, mandated by the ADA, for "talented but disabled athletes." * * * The ADA mandates no such ridiculous thing. Agility, strength, speed, balance, quickness of mind, steadiness of nerves, intensity of concentration – these talents are not evenly distributed. No wild-eyed dreamer has ever suggested that the managing bodies of the competitive sports that test precisely these qualities should try to take account of the uneven distribution of God-given gifts when writing and enforcing the rules of competition. And I have no doubt Congress did not authorize misty-eyed judicial supervision of such a revolution.

* * *

My belief that today's judgment is clearly in error should not be mistaken for a belief that the PGA TOUR clearly *ought not* allow respondent to use a golf cart. *That* is a close question, on which even those who compete in the PGA TOUR are apparently divided; but it is a *different* question from the one before the Court. Just as it is a different question whether the Little League *ought* to give disabled youngsters a fourth strike, or some other waiver from the rules that makes up for their disabilities. In both cases, whether they *ought* to do so depends upon (1) how central to the game that they have organized (and over whose rules they are the master) they deem the waived provision to be, and (2) how competitive – how strict a test of raw athletic ability in all aspects of the competition – they want their game to be. But whether Congress has said they *must* do so depends upon the answers to the legal questions I have discussed above – not upon what this Court sententiously decrees to be " 'decent, tolerant, [and] progressive'." * * *

And it should not be assumed that today's decent, tolerant, and progressive judgment will, in the long run, accrue to the benefit of sports competitors with disabilities. Now that it is clear courts will review the rules of sports for "fundamentalness," organizations that value their autonomy have every incentive to defend vigorously the necessity of every regulation. They may still be second-guessed in the end as to the Platonic requirements of the sport, but they will *assuredly* lose if they have at all wavered in their enforcement. The lesson the PGA TOUR and other sports organizations should take from this case is to make sure that the same written rules are set forth for all levels of play, and never voluntarily to grant any modifications. The second lesson is to end open tryouts. I doubt that, in the long run, even disabled athletes will be well served by these incentives that the Court has created.

Complaints about this case are not "properly directed to Congress." * * * They are properly directed to this Court's Kafkaesque determination that professional sports organizations, and the fields they rent for their exhibitions, are "places of public accommodation" to the competing athletes, and the athletes themselves "customers" of the organization that pays them; its Alice in Wonderland determination that there are such things as judicially determinable "essential" and "nonessential" rules of a made-up game; and its Animal Farm determination that fairness and the ADA mean that everyone gets to play by individualized rules which will assure that no one's lack of ability (or at least no one's lack of ability so pronounced that it amounts to a disability) will be a handicap. The year was 2001, and "everybody was finally equal." K. Vonnegut, Harrison Bergeron, in Animal Farm and Related Readings 129 (1997).

Notes & Questions

1. In the build up and aftermath to the *Martin* case, there was significant commentary – both academic and in the media – as to how this case would impact other amateur and professional sports. How would you articulate an application of the "*Martin*" rule in the following scenario? A talented racquetball player who uses a wheelchair wishes to compete against players who compete on foot. In wheelchair competitions, the rules provide that the ball can bounce twice before the player needs to return the ball ("two bounce rule"). This player requests that in his competition with a player competing on foot, the two bounce rule apply to him, but his opponent (competing on foot) should be only allowed one bounce before he needs to return the ball (the "one-bounce" rule, which typically governs racquetball competitions). What result? *See* Kuketz v. Petronelli, 821 N.E.2d 473 (Mass. 2005) (holding that this rule modification would fundamentally alter the competition). For other examples, *see* Michael E. Waterstone, Let's Be Reasonable Here: Why the ADA Will Not Ruin Professional Sports, 00 BYU L. Rev. 1489 (2000).

2. The Department of Justice has provided several illustrations of reasonable modifications:

> ILLUSTRATION 1: A private health clinic, in collaboration with its local public safety officials, has developed an evacuation plan to be used in the event of fire or other emergency. The clinic occupies several floors of a multistory building. During an emergency, elevators, which are the normal means of exiting from the clinic, will be shut off. The health clinic is obligated to modify its evacuation procedures, if necessary, to provide alternative means for

clients with mobility impairments to be safely evacuated from the clinic without using the elevator. The clinic should also modify its plan to take into account the needs of its clients with visual, hearing, and other disabilities.

ILLUSTRATION 2: Under its obligation to remove architectural barriers where it is readily achievable to do so, a local motel has greatly improved physical access in several of its rooms. However, under its present reservation system, the motel is unable to guarantee that, when a person requests an accessible room, one of the new rooms will actually be available when he or she arrives. The ADA requires the motel to make reasonable modifications in its reservation system to ensure the availability of the accessible room. Also, if the motel's only available accessible rooms were offered at higher rates than the room initially requested, it may be a reasonable modification of policy for the hotel to make the more expensive rooms available at the lower rate.

ILLUSTRATION 3: A retail store has a policy of not taking special orders for out-of-stock merchandise unless the customer appears personally to sign the order. The store would be required to reasonably modify its procedures to allow the taking of special orders by phone from persons with disabilities who cannot visit the store. If the store's concern is obtaining a guarantee of payment that a signed order would provide, the store could, for example, take orders by mail or take credit card orders by telephone from persons with disabilities.

ILLUSTRATION 4: An individual requires assistance in order to use toilet facilities and his only companion is a person of the opposite sex. Permitting a person of the opposite sex to assist an individual with a disability in a toilet room designated for one sex may be a required reasonable modification of policy.

ILLUSTRATION 5: A car rental company has a policy that customers who wish to secure car rentals with cash must have been employed at their present jobs for a year or more. A responsible, cash-paying customer with other sources of income, who is unemployed due to a disability, applies to rent a car and is rejected. The ADA requires the car rental company to reasonably modify its procedures to permit rentals by individuals with other adequate sources of income, including disability-related sources of income such as SSI, SSDI, Veteran's Administration disability benefits, or employer's disability benefits.

ILLUSTRATION 6: An individual is unable to wait in a long line for an amusement park ride because of a disability that carries with it a heightened sensitivity to heat. Another individual cannot wait in line because the line moves along an inaccessible path. In both cases the park may be required to modify its policy requiring all patrons to wait in line for attractions. For example, the amusement park could make available a marker to hold an individual's place in line.

ILLUSTRATION 7: A movie theater has a policy prohibiting patrons from consuming food and beverages purchased outside the theater. The theater may be required to make an exception to permit a parent to bring in appropriate food for a child with diabetes.

Title III, *supra*, § 4.2100.

3. The 2010 ADA Standards for Accessible Design set higher standards for places of lodging in making reservations for individual with disabilities, such as ensuring the customer has the necessary information to assess whether a given room will meet their needs, will be held for the customer, reservations can be made by the individual with a disability "during the same hours and in the same manner as individuals who do not need accessible rooms . . . ." 28 C.F.R. Pt. 36, App. A § 36.302(e).

4. What is "reasonable?"

- Is it reasonable for a business to adopt a policy forbidding its employees from wearing perfume to accommodate a customer with chemical sensitivity? *See* Stuart Oneglia, Core Letter #116, U.S. Dep't of Justice, Civil Rights Div., http://www.usdoj.gov/crt/foia/cltr116.txt (Sept. 8, 1993); John Wodatch, Core Letter #159, U.S. Dep't of Justice, Civil Rights Div., http://www.usdoj.gov/crt/foia/cltr159.txt (Feb. 16, 1995).

- Is a private child care facility required to provide diapering for a child whose disability prevents toilet training if the facility's rules require children to be toilet trained? *See* Christopher Kuczynski, Core Letter #127, U.S. Dep't of Justice, Civil Rights Div., http://www.usdoj.gov/crt/foia/cltr127.txt (Mar. 31, 1994).

- Is a teacher required to allow tape recording of lectures for a person whose disability prevents note taking? *See* James Turner, Core Letter #132, U.S. Dep't of Justice, Civil Rights Div., http://www.usdoj.gov/crt/foia/cltr132.txt (Nov. 16, 1993).

- Is a bank required to modify its policy of requiring people to sign their names if a person's disability prevents them from signing? *See* Deval Patrick, Core Letter #149, U.S. Dep't of

Justice, Civil Rights Div., http://www.usdoj.gov/crt/foia/cltr149. txt (Dec. 29, 1994).

- Is an inaccessible gas station required to provide full service for the self service price for a person whose disability prevents them from accessing the machines? *See* Deval Patrick, Core Letter #172, U.S. Dep't of Justice, Civil Rights Div., http://www.usdoj.gov/crt/foia/cltr172.txt (July 26, 1995).

- Is a shopping mall with accessible bathrooms and toilet stalls required to provide personal assistance to persons who cannot transfer independently from their wheelchair to the toilet seat? What if the mall already caters to a large elderly consumer community with personal assistance provided upon request to carry shopping bags, takes and serves food orders at the customer's table in the food court, or provides a valet parking service?

- For new approaches to such accommodation issues, the Global Universal Design Commission, Inc., (GUDC) a not-for-profit corporation, was established to develop Universal Design (UD) standards for buildings, products and services. GUDC is currently developing UD voluntary consensus standards for commercial buildings, which will expand access to buildings for all people, regardless of physical stature and varying abilities. *See* Global Universal Design Comm'n, Inc., Welcome (2008), http://www.globaluniversaldesign.org/.

5. A place of public accommodation need not change its specialty to accommodate a person with a disability. Thus, if a person with a disability is seeking a service outside the business' area of specialization, the business appropriately may refer the individual elsewhere, if it would do the same for a customer without a disability. 28 C.F.R. § 36.302(b)(1) (2008). A public accommodation generally is not required to alter its inventory to carry accessible goods. *Id.* § 36.307(a). Thus, a video store need not carry captioned videos, and a grocery store need not sell diabetic foods. *Id.* § 36.307(c). However, a public accommodation may be required to special order accessible goods if it regularly makes such orders on request for other goods not in its inventory and if it can obtain the accessible goods from its usual suppliers without significant hardship. *Id.* § 36.307(b).

6. The *Martin* Court, in part, determined that allowing a professional golfer with a disability, causing severe pain and fatigue with prolonged walking, to use a golf cart in tournaments was not a fundamental alteration of the competition rules as applied. Note that the PGA did not dispute that the provision of the golf cart may be a reasonable modification of PGA policies. What obligations might a golf course have to an amateur golfer who uses a wheelchair due to a spinal cord injury? Half Moon Bay Golf Links has entered into a settlement

agreeing to provide two adaptive golf carts that permit a person seated in the cart to play golf. Dave Murphy, Half Moon Bay: Golf Course to Offer Carts for Disabled, S.F. Chron., Mar. 10, 2006, at B5.

7. Title III provides that a public accommodation does not discriminate on the basis of disability if goods, services, facilities, privileges, advantages or accommodations are denied because a customer or patron "poses a direct threat to the health or safety of others." 42 U.S.C. § 12182(b)(3). Compare Title I "direct threat," *supra* Part 3, § 9.1. In *Bragdon v. Abbott*, 524 U.S. 624 (1998), in which a dentist refused to see a patient with HIV in his practice, the Supreme Court found in order for a Title III direct threat defense to stand, the ADA requires a "significant risk to the health or safety of others that cannot be eliminated by a modification of policies, practices, or procedures or by the provision of auxiliary aids or services." *Id.* at 648-49 (quoting 42 U.S.C. § 12182(b)(3)). Likewise, in *Doe v. Deer Mountain Day Camp*, 682 F.Supp.2d 324 (S.D.N.Y. 2010), a ten year-old boy living with HIV was denied admission to a basketball camp based on the boy's HIV status. The camp claimed they were unable to make reasonable accommodations for him. However, the camp failed to show his participation posed a significant risk of substantial harm.

§ 16.3 Effective Communication

A. *General*

Title III requires covered entities to communicate effectively with individuals with hearing, vision, and speech disabilities.

Discrimination under Title III includes:

a failure to take such steps as may be necessary to ensure that no individual with a disability is excluded, denied services, segregated or otherwise treated differently than other individuals because of the absence of auxiliary aids and services, unless the entity can demonstrate that taking such steps would fundamentally alter the nature of the good, service, facility, privilege, advantage, or accommodation being offered or would result in an undue burden.

42 U.S.C. § 12182(b)(2)(A)(iii) (2006); 28 C.F.R. pt. 36 app. B, § 36.303(a) (2008).

According to the regulations implementing Title III, a public accommodation must provide auxiliary aids and services in order to meet the standard of "effective communication." 28 C.F.R. § 36.303(c). Auxiliary aids and services include:

(1)   Qualified interpreters, note-takers, computer-aided transcription services, written materials, telephone handset amplifiers, assistive listening devices, assistive listening systems, telephones compatible with hearing aids, closed caption decoders, open and closed captioning, telecommunications devices for deaf persons (TDDs), videotext displays, or other effective methods of making aurally delivered materials available to individuals with hearing impairments;

(2)   Qualified readers, taped texts, audio recordings, Brailled materials, large print materials, or other effective methods of making visually delivered materials available to individuals with visual impairments;

(3)   Acquisition or modification of equipment or devices; and

(4)   Other similar services and actions.

Id. § 36.303(b).

The effective communication requirement is balanced by a defense that the requested auxiliary aid would impose an undue burden on the covered entity or create a fundamental alteration.

AIKINS v. ST. HELENA HOSPITAL

United States District Court, Northern District of California, 1994
843 F.Supp. 1329

SMITH, District Judge.

INTRODUCTION

Plaintiffs Elaine Aikins ("Mrs. Aikins") and California Association of the Deaf ("CAD") have brought suit against defendants St. Helena Hospital ("St. Helena," "the hospital") and Dr. James Lies ("Dr. Lies") under the Americans with Disabilities Act ("the ADA"), the Rehabilitation Act of 1973, and various California civil rights statutes. Both defendants have filed motions to dismiss or, in the alternative, for summary judgment. Defendants have also sought to have CAD dismissed from the lawsuit on the basis that CAD lacks standing.

BACKGROUND

The events giving rise to this lawsuit occurred between October 30 and November 4, 1992. Mrs. Aikins is a deaf woman whose husband, Harvey Aikins, suffered a massive cardiac arrest at approximately 8: 00 p.m. on October 30, 1992. Following Mr. Aikins's attack, Mrs. Aikins went to the home of some neighbors and had them call 911. According to Mrs. Aikins, the paramedics arrived at her home approximately four minutes after the call to 911, which defendants assert was approximately fifteen minutes after Mr. Aikins suffered the attack.[1]   The paramedics then transported Mr. Aikins to St. Helena Hospital.

Dr. Lies was working in St. Helena's emergency room when Mr. Aikins was brought in. Dr. Lies is an independent contractor on staff at the hospital. He exercises no authority over hospital policy. When the paramedics informed Dr. Lies that they had arrived within four minutes of Mr. Aikins's attack, Dr. Lies decided to perform an emergency angioplasty. He attempted to consult Mrs. Aikins and to obtain her consent, but Mrs. Aikins could not understand him and requested that interpreters be provided. A hospital operator with some knowledge of fingerspelling was summoned and attempted to fingerspell Dr. Lies's comments for Mrs. Aikins. The woman became frustrated, however, and gave up her efforts within a minute. Shortly thereafter, Mrs. Aikins's neighbors arrived and attempted to mediate between Dr. Lies and Mrs. Aikins.   Dr. Lies asserts that the neighbors "were quite able to communicate with [Mrs. Aikins]" and relayed to her his opinion that, with immediate medical intervention, Dr. Lies might be able to save Mr. Aikins's life. Mrs. Aikins submits that the neighbors only passed her a terse note stating that Mr. Aikins may have had a massive cardiac arrest and that he was "brain dead."

Subsequently, Mrs. Aikins went to the hospital's administrative office and made further attempts to secure interpreter services.   At approximately 9: 00 p.m., she was approached by a member of the hospital staff who sought to obtain her signature on forms consenting to the emergency procedure. Although the forms say that "[y]our signature on this form indicates . . . (2) that the operation procedure set forth above has been adequately explained to you by your physician, (3) that you have had a chance to ask questions, [and] (4) that you have received all of the information you desire concerning the operation or procedure . . .," Mrs. Aikins claims that she was told only that "Dr. Lies needed [her] signature to permit him to perform surgery to save [her] husband's life." Dr. Lies claims that, although he believed that it was unnecessary under the

---

[1]   There is some conflict among the parties as to the timing of these events. Mrs. Aikins maintains that the paramedics arrived four minutes after the call and worked on Mr. Aikins for another fifteen minutes. Defendants initially thought that the paramedics arrived four minutes after the attack but assert that they later learned that they had not arrived until fifteen minutes after the attack. As Mrs. Aikins's claims relate not to the propriety of her husband's treatment but rather to the hospital's and Dr. Lies's ineffective communication with her, the difference in these time estimates is relevant only to the issue of the effectiveness of the communication between Mrs. Aikins and hospital officials.

circumstances to obtain Mrs. Aikins's consent to the surgery, "given [her] disability, [he] wanted her to be involved."

Later that evening, Dr. Lies contacted Mrs. Aikins's daughter, Francine Stern, to request that she fly up to Calistoga from Los Angeles to help her mother. Ms. Stern, who was Mr. Aikins's stepdaughter, is a fluent signer. Ms. Stern told Dr. Lies that she would be unable to come up until November 2nd.

Mrs. Aikins went to her husband's room at approximately 12:30 on the night of the operation. She claims that the nurse on duty told her that Mr. Aikins would not survive without life support and that Mrs. Aikins then requested that life support be discontinued. She then went to the administrative office, accompanied by a deaf friend, to request interpreter services again. Both the office and another nurse whom Mrs. Aikins and her friend later encountered in Mr. Aikins's room allegedly told Mrs. Aikins that the hospital had no means of procuring interpreter services.

The following day, October 31, 1992, Mr. Aikins showed no neurologic improvement, prompting Dr. Lies to question Mrs. Aikins about the length of time between the heart attack and the arrival of the paramedics. Dr. Lies submits that it was during this questioning, seemingly conducted through Mrs. Aikins's in-laws, that he first learned that fifteen minutes, not four, had elapsed between Mr. Aikins's heart attack and the commencement of CPR. Based on this new information, Dr. Lies ordered an EEG. The EEG was performed on November 1, 1992, at 9:00 a.m. and revealed that Mr. Aikins had no brain activity.

On November 2nd, Mrs. Aikins's daughter arrived and participated in a meeting with Dr. Lies and Mrs. Aikins. Mrs. Aikins claims that this meeting was the first opportunity that she had to communicate directly with Dr. Lies and to receive complete answers to her questions. As a result of the meeting, Mrs. Aikins requested that her husband's life support be discontinued. Mr. Aikins died two days later.

Defendants have each filed motions to dismiss or, in the alternative, for summary judgment. Dr. Lies argues that he is not covered by the ADA; that the Rehabilitation Act is inapplicable; and that plaintiffs cannot recover against him on their state law causes of action. St. Helena argues that it complied with both the ADA and the Rehabilitation Act as a matter of law. Both defendants also submit that CAD is not a proper party to the action and that monetary relief is unavailable under the federal statutes.

DISCUSSION

* * *

539

II. Plaintiffs' Claims under the Americans with Disabilities Act

Plaintiffs claim that defendants violated the Americans with Disabilities Act ("ADA") by denying Mrs. Aikins access to information in connection with the treatment of her husband. The ADA provides, in pertinent part: "No individual shall be discriminated against on the basis of disability in the full and equal enjoyment of the goods, services, facilities, privileges, advantages, or accommodations of any place of public accommodation by any person who owns, leases (or leases to), or operates a place of public accommodation." 42 U.S.C. § 12182(a) (West Supp.1993).

A. The ADA Does Not Apply to Dr. Lies

Dr. Lies contends that plaintiffs' claims against him under the ADA must fail because the Act does not apply to him in his capacity as an independent contractor with St. Helena. The regulations implementing the ADA alter the language of the statute slightly to read as follows: "No individual shall be discriminated against on the basis of disability . . . by any private entity who owns, leases (or leases to), or operates a place of public accommodation." 28 C.F.R. § 36.201(a) (1993). The preamble to the regulation notes that the change was designed to make clear that the regulation "places the ADA's nondiscrimination obligations on 'public accommodations' rather than on 'persons' or 'places of public accommodation.'" 36 C.F.R. app. B, § 36.104 (1993).

The statute and the regulation both indicate that individuals may be liable under the ADA if they "own, lease[ ] (or lease[ ] to), or operate[ ]" a place of public accommodation. 42 U.S.C. § 12182(a); 28 C.F.R. § 35.201(a) (1993). The use of language relating to ownership or operation implies a requirement of control over the place providing services. Dr. Lies, however, is an independent contractor with St. Helena. * * * He is not on the hospital's board of directors, and he has no authority to enact or amend hospital policy. * * * Because he lacks the power to control hospital policy on the use of interpreters, this Court holds that Dr. Lies is not a proper defendant under the ADA.

Plaintiffs contend that this construction of the ADA undercuts the Act's purpose. Noting that the Act defines "public accommodation" to include the "professional office of a health care provider," 42 U.S.C. § 12181(7)(F) * * *, plaintiffs maintain that the Act would clearly cover Dr. Lies had he provided services to Mr. and Mrs. Aikins at his own office. They argue that he should not be able to escape liability under the ADA merely because in this case he provided services outside his office. "To hold otherwise," plaintiffs suggest, "would allow individuals to discriminate whenever they provide part of their services outside of their place of public accommodation while disallowing the very same type of discrimination for those services provided at the place of public accommodation."

Plaintiffs' policy argument does not warrant a departure from the statute's implicit requirement of ownership or control. The Court's construction of the Act is not at odds with the ADA's fundamental purpose of eliminating discrimination against individuals with disabilities, see 42 U.S.C. § 12101(b)(1) * * *, because it retains accountability for those in a position to ensure nondiscrimination.

B. St. Helena Has Not Shown That It Complied with the Act as a Matter of Law

St. Helena does not dispute that the ADA applies to it, see 42 U.S.C. § 12181(7)(F), but claims that it complied with the Act as a matter of law. Alternatively, St. Helena argues that compliance is excused, as it would impose an undue burden on the hospital. The regulations implementing the ADA provide that a "public accommodation shall furnish appropriate auxiliary aids and services where necessary to ensure effective communication with individuals with disabilities." 28 C.F.R. § 36.303(c) (1993). This requirement is tempered by the general qualification that a public accommodation may treat disabled individuals in need of auxiliary aids and services differently from other individuals if "the public accommodation can demonstrate that [ensuring equality of treatment] would . . . result in an undue burden, i.e. significant difficulty or expense." § 36.303(a) (1993).

St. Helena bases its contention that it complied with the ADA as a matter of law on the following evidence and allegations: that its human resources department had in place a policy of providing interpreters to those in need of them; that the hospital posted signs notifying the public that information about T.D.D. services could be obtained by going to the switchboard; that the switchboard operator and the office of human resources maintained lists of interpreters; that Mr. Aikins's medical records contain a statement that "there were interpreters present at all times during the discussion with the patient and the family"; and that "the complaint is replete with descriptions of instances where information was exchanged between plaintiff Aikins and members of the St. Helena hospital staff." Defendant argues alternatively that provision of an interpreters on a twenty-four hour a day basis would impose an undue burden on the hospital.

The record does not reveal that St. Helena complied with the ADA as a matter of law. St. Helena has not demonstrated that it communicated effectively with plaintiff Aikins during her husband's stay in the hospital. Indeed, the hospital's allegations that communication was effective are undercut not only by plaintiff's own account of the episode but also by the fact that, for between twenty-four to thirty-six hours, Dr. Lies was under the concededly mistaken impression that Mr. Aikins had been without CPR for only four minutes following his heart attack, a critical fact. * * * Furthermore, although the regulations provide that the hospital "shall furnish" appropriate auxiliary aids and services for non-hearing individuals, § 36.303(c), it appears that St. Helena relied almost exclusively on Mrs. Aikins to provide her own interpreters. There exists a genuine dispute as to the issue of St. Helena's compliance with the ADA.

Finally, the Court cannot say as a matter of law that provision of interpreters would have imposed an undue burden on the hospital. The regulations set out criteria for determining whether a proposed accommodation imposes an undue burden within the meaning of section 36.303(a). Section 36.104 provides, in pertinent part:

> In determining whether an action would result in an undue burden, factors to be considered include – (1) The nature and cost of the action needed under this part; (2) The overall financial resources of the site or sites involved in the action; the number of persons employed at the site; the effect on expenses and resources; legitimate safety requirements that are necessary for safe operation . . .; or the impact otherwise of the action upon the operation of the site; (3) The geographic separateness, and the administrative or fiscal relationship of the site or sites in question to any parent corporation or entity; (4) If applicable, the overall financial resources of any parent corporation or entity; the overall size of the parent corporation or entity with respect to the number of its employees; the number, type, and location of its facilities; and (5) If applicable, the type of operation or operations of any parent corporation or entity, including the composition, structure, and functions of the workforce of the parent corporation or entity. * * *

The question whether provision of interpreter services on some basis would pose an undue burden on St. Helena raises material issues of fact.

Dobard v. San Francisco Bay Area Rapid Transit District, 1993 WL 372256 (N.D. Cal. Sept. 7, 1993), cited by defendant, does not warrant a different conclusion. In that case defendant transit authority provided plaintiff with both a sign language interpreter and a sound amplification device in connection with his attendance at a public board meeting. Plaintiff argued that defendant nonetheless violated the ADA by refusing to provide plaintiff with a computer aided transcription device, the auxiliary aid of his choice. The court in *Dobard* found that plaintiff had failed to state a claim for violation of the ADA, as defendant was not required to employ the most advanced technology but only to ensure that communication was effective. Plaintiffs herein are not arguing for an absolute right to a particular auxiliary aid. Rather, they claim a right to effective communication with the hospital. St. Helena, unlike the defendant in *Dobard*, allegedly made no effort to provide Mrs. Aikins with auxiliary aids, relying upon Mrs. Aikins to marshal her own communication resources.

III. Plaintiffs' Claims under the Rehabilitation Act

A. Mrs. Aikins Is an "Otherwise Qualified" Individual Within the Meaning of the Act

Plaintiffs have raised claims under section 504 of the Rehabilitation Act of 1973. Section 504 provides, in pertinent part: "No otherwise qualified individual with a disability in the United States . . . shall, solely by reason of her or his disability, be excluded from participation in, be denied the benefits of, or be subjected to discrimination under any program or activity receiving Federal financial assistance. . . ." 29 U.S.C. § 794(a) (West Supp. 1993). Section 794a provides a private right of action for violations of section 794. * * * Defendant Lies argues that plaintiffs' claims under section 504 should be dismissed because plaintiff Aikins is not an "otherwise qualified" individual within the meaning of the Act.

In *Rothschild v. Grottenthaler*, 907 F.2d 286 (2d Cir. 1990), the Second Circuit addressed a similar issue. The plaintiffs in *Rothschild* were deaf parents of hearing students who claimed that their school district was violating the Rehabilitation Act by refusing to provide interpreters for plaintiffs at meetings to which the school invited parents. Defendants argued that plaintiffs were not "otherwise qualified" to take advantage of the school district's primary service, education.

The *Rothschild* court found that defendants had "seriously misapprehend[ed] the import of section 504." Observing that the regulations interpreting section 504 define "qualified handicapped person" broadly to include "a handicapped person who meets the essential eligibility requirements for the receipt of such services," see 34 C.F.R. § 104.3(k) (1993), the Second Circuit concluded that the Act applies to all services offered by a covered entity, not just those relating to the entity's central function. "The fact that a particular recipient institution is primarily engaged in the provision of one category of service does not exempt it from Regulation 104.3(k) in its provision of other services." 907 F.2d at 291.

Although *Rothschild* is not binding upon this Court, its reasoning is sound. That Mrs. Aikins was not a patient at St. Helena should not preclude her from raising claims under the Rehabilitation Act based on the hospital's failure to communicate effectively with her in connection with its treatment of her husband. Mrs. Aikins was "otherwise qualified" to discuss her husband's condition with hospital officials, including Dr. Lies.

Defendant Lies next argues that California law precludes Mrs. Aikins from being "otherwise qualified" in the circumstances presented by this case. He submits that Mrs. Aikins's consent to the procedures performed on her husband was not necessary; as a consequence she was not required to be consulted or kept informed of her husband's condition. Defendant attempts to analogize from *Bowen v. American Hospital Association*, 476 U.S. 610, 630 * * * (1986), wherein a plurality of the Court stated that a "hospital's withholding of treatment when no parental consent has been given cannot violate § 504." The plurality reasoned that, in the absence of the required parental consent, the infant is neither "otherwise qualified" within the meaning of the Act, nor denied treatment "solely because of his handicap." Defendant maintains that Mrs. Aikins is not "otherwise qualified" because her consent to her husband's treatment was not required.

Defendant's argument is unavailing. Dr. Lies's argument that emergency circumstances vitiated the requirement of informed consent is undercut by his own statement that, "[t]hough it was clear to me that Mr. Aikins presented an immediate medical emergency, thus making informed consent unnecessary, I had time to, and so did seek to, advise Mrs. Aikins and obtain her consent." Having undertaken to obtain Mrs. Aikins's consent, defendant was obligated to do so in a nondiscriminatory manner. See Rothschild, 907 F.2d 286; 34 C.F.R. § 104.4(b)(1) (1993) ("A recipient, in providing any . . . service, may not . . . on the basis of handicap . . . [a]fford a qualified handicapped person an opportunity to participate in or benefit from the . . . service that is not equal to that provided others. . . ."). More important, Mrs. Aikins's claims relating to inadequate communication span a period of almost seventy-two hours, from the time of her husband's admission to the hospital until the time that his life support was disconnected. Whatever emergency existed at the time of Mr. Aikins's admission to the hospital had subsided by the time the decision was made to discontinue his life support. * * * Finally, *Bowen* is distinguishable. That case essentially involved a failure of causation. It was the parents' refusal of consent, not the infant's disability, that would have resulted in the denial of treatment. By contrast, it was precisely Mrs. Aikins's disability that caused defendants to communicate with her in an allegedly inadequate manner.

B. Defendants Have Not Shown That They Complied with the Act as a Matter of Law

Defendants finally argue that they complied with the Rehabilitation Act as a matter of law. Defendant Lies argues that Mr. Aikins received precisely the same treatment that he would have received had Mrs. Aikins not been deaf. Defendant St. Helena maintains that it provided all that it was required to provide under the Act.

Both arguments are without merit. Even if Mr. Aikins received exactly the care that he would have received had Mrs. Aikins not been deaf, Dr. Lies misses the point. Mrs. Aikins's claims relate to her exclusion from meaningful participation in the decisions affecting her husband's treatment, not to the appropriateness of the treatment itself.

See § 794(a); *Rothschild*, 907 F.2d 286. As to the hospital's argument, the Court cannot infer from defendant's reference to its policies on interpreters and its own self-serving statements that it communicated effectively with plaintiff at all times that it complied with the Rehabilitation Act as a matter of law.

IV. Availability of Damages under the Federal Statutes

Defendants argue that Mrs. Aikins is not entitled to compensatory relief under either the ADA or the Rehabilitation Act. They are correct about the ADA. In cases involving claims under subchapter three of the ADA, the Act provides only for injunctive relief. Section 12188(a)(1) states that the remedies available to persons subjected to discrimination in violation of that subchapter are those set forth in 42 U.S.C. section 2000a-3(a). * * * Section 2000a-3(a) provides: "Whenever any person has engaged or there are reasonable grounds to believe that any person is about to engage in any act or practice prohibited by section 2000a-2 of this title, a civil action for preventive relief . . . may be instituted by the person aggrieved . . . ." 42 U.S.C. § 2000a-3(a) (West 1981). In *Newman v. Piggie Park Enterprises, Inc.*, 390 U.S. 400, 401-02 (1968), the Supreme Court held that a plaintiff suing under section 2000a-3(a) cannot recover damages. Plaintiffs appear to concede the unavailability of compensatory relief under the ADA in their opposition papers. * * *

Because plaintiffs lack standing on the present record to assert claims for injunctive relief, the unavailability of damages under the ADA requires dismissal of all claims under the ADA. Such dismissal is without prejudice to plaintiffs' reinstating the ADA claims for injunctive relief upon a proper showing of standing.

As to Mrs. Aikins's claims under the Rehabilitation Act, the Ninth Circuit has held that damages are available for violations of the Act. Section 794a provides, in pertinent part: "The remedies, procedures, and rights set forth in title VI of the Civil Rights Act of 1964 [codified at 42 U.S.C. section 2000d et seq.] shall be available to any person aggrieved by any act or failure to act by any recipient of Federal assistance . . . under section 794 of this title." 29 U.S.C. § 794a(a)(2). * * * Exhaustion of administrative remedies is not a prerequisite to suit in the Ninth Circuit. * * * The settled interpretation of section 794a in the Ninth Circuit is that money damages are available for violations of section 504 of the Rehabilitation Act. * * *

* * *

CONCLUSION

For the foregoing reasons, the Court hereby DISMISSES the following claims WITHOUT LEAVE TO AMEND: CAD's claims for damages; Mrs. Aikins's claims for damages under the ADA; plaintiffs' claims against Dr. Lies under the ADA; and plaintiffs' claims under California Government Code section 11135 and Health and Safety Code section 1259.

Plaintiffs' remaining claims for injunctive relief are DISMISSED WITH LEAVE TO AMEND. * * *

Summary judgment is DENIED to both defendants on Mrs. Aikins's claims for damages under the Rehabilitation Act. * * *

Notes & Questions

1. In *Aikins,* the plaintiff's mere allegation that she was a deaf woman who lived part of the year close to a particular hospital that failed to provide a sign language interpreter was not sufficient to demonstrate that she was likely to use the hospital again or that the hospital was likely to discriminate against her again. 843 F.Supp. 1329, 1333-34 (N.D. Cal. 1994). On the other hand, a plaintiff who desires to visit the same health care provider in the future likely would have standing to bring a claim of discrimination under Title III. Majocha v. Turner, 166 F.Supp.2d 316, 324-25 (W.D. Penn. 2001); Gillespie v. Dimensions Health Corp., 369 F.Supp.2d 636, 641-46 (D.Md. 2005).

2. The type of aid that will be effective depends on the cognitive, reading, and linguistic ability of the individual with a disability and on the length and complexity of the communication at issue. While a simple conversation, such as a question about a book in a bookstore, may be conducted using handwritten notes, a complex conversation, such as a medical visit concerning the possibility of surgery, may require a sign language interpreter. Majocha v. Turner, 166 F.Supp.2d 316, 324-25 (W.D. Pa. 2001). The type of auxiliary aid needed will also depend on the person receiving the communication. An individual who was born deaf and has spoken only American Sign Language (ASL) his entire life is likely to have difficulty understanding complex notes in English. *Id.* at 317. The Department of Justice has provided several illustrations:

> ILLUSTRATION 1: H, an individual who is deaf, uses sign language as his primary means of communication and also communicates by writing. He is shopping for film at a camera store. Exchanging notes with the sales clerk would be adequate to ensure effective communication.

> ILLUSTRATION 2: H then stops by a new car showroom to look at the latest models. The car dealer would be able to communicate effectively general information about the models available by providing brochures and exchanging notes by pen and notepad, or perhaps by means of taking turns at a computer terminal keyboard. If H becomes serious about making a purchase, the services of a qualified interpreter may be necessary because of the complicated nature of the communication involved in buying a car.

> ILLUSTRATION 2a: H goes to his doctor for a bi-weekly check-up, during which the nurse records H's blood pressure and weight. Exchanging notes and using gestures

are likely to provide an effective means of communication at this type of check-up. BUT: Upon experiencing symptoms of a mild stroke, H returns to his doctor for a thorough examination and battery of tests and requests that an interpreter be provided. H's doctor should arrange for the services of a qualified interpreter, as an interpreter is likely to be necessary for effective communication with H, given the length and complexity of the communication involved.

ILLUSTRATION 3: S, an individual who is blind, visits an electronics store to purchase a clock radio and wishes to inspect the merchandise information cards next to the floor models in order to decide which one to buy. Reading the model information to S should be adequate to ensure effective communication. Of course, if S is unreasonably demanding or is shopping when the store is extremely busy, it may be an undue burden to spend extended periods of time reading price and product information.

ILLUSTRATION 4: S also has tickets to a play. When S arrives at the theater, the usher notices that S is an individual who is blind and guides S to her seat. An usher is also available to guide S to her seat following intermission. With the provision of these services, a Brailled ticket is not necessary for effective communication in seating S.

ILLUSTRATION 5: The same theater provides S with a tape-recorded version of its printed program for the evening's performance. A Brailled program is not necessary to effectively communicate the contents of the program to S, if an audio cassette and tape player are provided.

TAM III, *supra*, § 4.3200.

3. The ADA refers to "qualified interpreters." An interpreter need not meet any particular licensing or certification standard to be qualified. Alvarez v. N.Y. City Health & Hosps. Corp., No. 99 Civ. 3215(RCC), 2002 WL 1585637, at *4 (S.D.N.Y. July 17, 2002). A qualified interpreter "is able to interpret effectively, accurately and impartially both receptively and expressively, using any necessary specialized vocabulary." 28 C.F.R. pt. 36 app. B, § 36.104 (2008). To ensure impartiality, public accommodations generally should avoid using relatives or other interested parties as interpreters.

In certain circumstances, notwithstanding that the family member or friend is able to interpret or is a certified interpreter, the family member or friend may not be qualified to render the necessary interpretation because of factors such as emotional or personal involvement or considerations of confidentiality that may adversely affect the ability to interpret "effectively, accurately, and impartially."

Id. § 36.104.

The presence of a professional interpreter does not interfere with the confidentiality of a communication between a health care provider or attorney and a patient or client. Certified interpreters must comply with a code of ethics that ensures that assignment-related information is kept confidential. *See* Registry of Interpreters for the Deaf, NAD-RID Code of Professional Conduct (2005), *available at* http://www.rid.org/UserFiles/File/pdfs/codeofethics.pdf.

4. Courts have reached different conclusions about whether Title III requires movie theatres to provide films that are accessible to people with hearing impairments through captioning. Following the Ninth Circuit's holdings in *Arizona v. Harkins Amusement Enterprises, Inc.*, 603 F.3d 666 (9th Cir. 2010), closed captioning and audio descriptions are "auxiliary aids and services" that may be required by movie theater operators and owners, absent undue burden or fundamental alteration. However, the Court noted that open captioning is not mandated by the ADA as a matter of law.

The Department of Justice commentary on the issue provides that movie theaters are not required to present open-captioned films. 28 C.F.R. pt. 36 app. B, § 36.303. Relying on that language, an Oregon district court found that movie theatres are not required to provide either open captioning or rear-window captioning of films, which hearing patrons cannot view. Cornilles v. Regal Cinemas, Inc., No. Civ. 00-173-AS, 2002 WL 31440885, at *7 (D. Or. Jan. 3, 2002). The court treated movie films like a store's inventory and relied on the DOJ's statement that public accommodations are not required to change their inventory to provide accessible goods, such as Braille books or captioned videotapes. *Id.* at *6; *see also* Todd v. Am. Multi-Cinema, Inc., No. Civ. A. H-02-1944, 2004 WL 1764686 (S.D. Tex. Aug. 5, 2004).

However, a Washington, D.C. district court reached the opposite conclusion. Ball v. AMC Entm't, Inc., 246 F.Supp.2d 17, 19 (D.D.C. 2003). That court relied on the statutory language, which does not address captioning, and minimized the importance of the Department of Justice comment about open captioning, finding that when the Department issued its regulation only open captioning was available. Therefore, the Department's opinion about open captioning did not address whether theaters were required to offer closed captioning. That court went on to conclude that movie theatres are not like bookstores, in that they are providing the service of showing movies, rather than goods. Therefore, requiring them to show captioned movies would not constitute requiring them to change their inventory. *Id.* at 24-25. In addition, the screening of closed-captioned films would not fundamentally alter the service, because deaf moviegoers can see the captions without changing how other patrons see the films. *Id.* at 20. Nor did the fact that most films are not yet compatible with rear-window captioning (RWC) serve as a defense, as "requiring installation of RWC does not require exhibition of all RWC-compatible films." *Id.* at 25.

On March 13, 2013, the Captioning and Image Narration to Enhance Movie Accesibility (CINEMA) Act, S. 555, 113th Cong. (2013), and the Air Carrier Access Amendments (ACAA) Act, S. 556, 113th Cong. (2013), were introduced to the Senate. The CINEMA Act seeks to amend the ADA to ensure that all movie theaters are accessible to individuals who are blind, visually impaired, deaf, or hard of hearing. The ACAA Act seeks to ensure that all in-flight entertainment is accessible to individuals who are blind, visually impaired, deaf, or hard of hearing.

5. In *Feldman v. Pro Football Inc.*, 419 F. App'x 381 (4th Cir. 2011), the 4th Circuit upheld Maryland's federal district court decision that ordered Pro Football "to provide deaf and hard of hearing fans equal access to the aural information broadcast over the stadium bowl public address system at FedExField, which includes music with lyrics, play information, advertisements, referee calls, safety/emergency information, and other announcements . . . ." What options does Pro Football have to implement this order without fundamentally altering its services?

6. Unlike the reasonable modification provision of Title III, the effective communication requirement provides a defense of undue burden. 28 C.F.R. § 36.303(a) (2008). Undue burden means significant difficulty or expense. *Id.* In determining whether an action would result in an undue burden, several factors to be considered include the nature and cost of the action, the overall financial resources of the covered entity, the staff resources, safety concerns, other impacts of the action on the covered entity, and the overall resources, size, and proximity of any parent entities. *Id.* § 36.104.

ॐ

B.   *Distance Education*

Distance education services, provided extensively via the Internet, frequently are offered by Title III entities. William Myhill and colleagues, in a comprehensive study of distance education initiatives and their implications for learners with disabilities, documented extensive training, education, and employment opportunities for individuals with disabilities, the "growing popularity in strictly distance learning degree and certification programs," and the use of distance education as a popular K-12 approach for improving learning among children in under-resourced schools, rural regions, and for students who are academically at-risk. William N. Myhill, et al., Distance Education Initiatives and their Early 21st Century Role in the Lives of People with Disabilities, in Focus on Distance Education Developments 2 (Edward P. Bailey ed., 2007). To date, there is no known litigation alleging violation of Title III by a distance education provider. The issue, however, is ripe.

Distance education may pose significant concern for students with disabilities, in part, due to the "the absence of teacher preparation and professional development standards for the unique environments of distance education." *Id.* at 9. Additionally, the tendency of faculty to attempt "one-for-one transfer of course materials into online content" may create unintended communication barriers and difficulty locating required online materials. *Id.* at 10.

Myhill conducted a Title III analysis involving an administrative assistant, Eleanor, who is blind and who seeks to take online courses in client interviewing, business writing, and auditing to advance in her insurance firm. *Id.* at 27. The authors conclude, in part, the private educational company 1) "cannot deny Eleanor the full and equal enjoyment of their services on the basis her disability," 2) "is obligated to make reasonable modifications to their procedures, practices, and policies necessary to accommodate Eleanor's unique needs as a person with a significant visual impairment," and 3) "must ensure that its distance learning materials are compatible with screen readers so that Eleanor effectively can navigate the course content." *Id.* at 27-28 (citations omitted). Moreover, none of the necessary modifications "are likely to 'fundamentally alter' the nature of [the company's] services." Myhill, et al., *supra*, at 28. *See also* Blanck, eQuality, *supra* (related discussion of Title III coverage of massive open online course (MOOCs)).

§ 16.4 Architectural Barriers

Unlike previous civil rights laws, the drafters of the ADA had to contend with the fact that overcoming traditional discriminatory attitudes alone would not be sufficient to bring people with disabilities into mainstream society. Rather, societal prejudice had been "built" into our physical environment. Because of the expense of retrofitting existing buildings to make them accessible, the drafters of the ADA reached a compromise that provides for a gradual approach to facility accessibility.

The National Council on Disability issued a comprehensive assessment of progress toward achieving the goals of the ADA in July 2007. Nat'l Council on Disability, The Impact of the Americans with Disabilities Act: Assessing the Progress Toward Achieving the Goals of the ADA 52 (July 26, 2007). The report notes that relevant systematic data "measuring the accessibility of public accommodations and commercial facilities pre-ADA does not exist and the law makes no specific provisions for tracking such information." *Id.* at 45. Survey data and interviews with individuals with disabilities, however, are encouraging. For instance, "the percentage of people with disabilities going out to restaurants regularly has increased from 34 percent in 1986 to 57 percent in 2004." *Id.* (citing Nat'l Org. on Disability, 2004 National Organization on Disability/Harris Survey of Americans with Disabilities, at exhibit 3 (2004)).

Nonetheless, major trade associations including the National Restaurant Association, the Building Owners and Managers Association International, the American Hotel and Lodging Association, and the U.S. Chamber of Commerce were unable to provide information "on the number of their members that have made their facilities more accessible to people with mobility impairments in the last 15 years." *Id.* at 46. Businesses counter, arguing that unlike other federal and state safety and building code regulations, government entities, such as zoning boards, offer little assistance to businesses for complying with the ADA. *Id.* at 48.

Assistance to businesses in the form of tax credits to renovate or provide accommodations for greater accessibility are underutilized. A 2003 survey concluded "77 percent of surveyed businesses were not accessing any of the tax incentives for accessibility." *Id.* at 47 (citing Ctr. for an Accessible Soc'y, Employers Know Little about Tax Credits, Says Study (Apr. 29, 2003). NCD, in part, recommends the National Institute on Disability and Rehabilitation Research survey businesses "to determine the degree to which businesses have instituted readily achievable barrier removal efforts, and provide guidance to Congress on adequately funding the Department of Justice to enforce this part of the statute." *Id.* at 53.

A. *Existing Facilities*

1. Barrier removal

In facilities existing on or after March 15, 2012, the 2010 ADA Standards for Accessible Design require elements in existing facilities that do not comply with the corresponding technical and scoping specifications for those elements in the 1991 Standards must be modified to the extent readily achievable to comply with the requirements set forth in the 2010 Standards. 28 C.F.R. § 36.304(d)(2)(ii)(B) (2013).

"Readily achievable" is defined as "easily accomplishable and able to be carried out without much difficulty or expense." 28 C.F.R. § 36.104(a). The "readily achievable" standard considers (i) the nature and cost of barrier removal; (ii) the overall financial resources, number of persons employed, effect on expenses and resources, and legitimate safety requirements; (iii) the geographic separateness from, and administrative or fiscal relationship to a parent entity; and (iv) the overall financial resources and types of operation of a parent entity. *Id.* § 36.104.

There are additional limits on the readily achievable standard. Even if it is readily achievable to do so, entities are not required to remove barriers, if doing so would exceed the requirements of 28 C.F.R. §§ 36.401-.406 (Subpart D) for alterations or new construction. 28 C.F.R. § 36.304(g)(1) (2013). A covered entity does not have to rearrange removable features if doing so would result in "a significant loss of selling or serving space." *Id.* § 36.304(f). However, these limits do not apply to guest rooms in existing places of lodging that "are not owned by the entity that owns, leases, or operates the overall facility and the physical features of the guest room interiors are controlled by their individual owners." *Id.* § 36.304(g)(4).

If removal of a barrier or barriers is not readily achievable, a place of public accommodation " shall not fail to make its goods, services, facilities, privileges, advantages, or accommodations available through alternative methods, if those methods are readily achievable." 28 C.F.R.§ 36.305(a) (2013). Alternative methods to barrier removal may include:

    (1)   Providing curb service or home delivery;

    (2)   Retrieving merchandise from inaccessible shelves or racks;

    (3)   Relocating activities to accessible locations.

Id. § 36.305(b).

COLORADO CROSS DISABILITY COALITION v. HERMANSON FAMILY LTD. PARTNERSHIP I

United States Court of Appeals, Tenth Circuit, 2001
264 F.3d 999

BALDOCK, Circuit Judge.

Defendant Hermanson Family Limited Partnership I owns certain commercial buildings in Larimer Square, an historic block of shops and restaurants located in downtown Denver, Colorado. Plaintiff Kevin W. Williams is a Denver attorney who, as a result of a spinal cord injury, is paralyzed from the chest down and uses a power wheel chair for mobility. Since he moved to Denver around 1990, Plaintiff Williams has visited Larimer Square frequently. On his trips to Larimer Square, Plaintiff Williams noticed that architectural barriers prevented him from accessing many of the stores. Specifically, a 5.5 inch iron stoop at the entrance to the Crawford Building, owned by Defendant, prevents wheelchair access. In addition, the door to the store is recessed from the storefront and adds another barrier to wheelchair access of one to three inches.

In 1996, Plaintiff Williams and his employer, the Colorado Cross Disability Coalition, filed four separate lawsuits in the federal district court against Defendants under Title III of the Americans with Disabilities Act (ADA), 42 U.S.C. §§ 12181 thru 12189, and the Colorado Anti Discrimination Act * * * In their suits, Plaintiffs asked the district court to compel Defendants to install ramps at four locations in Larimer Square. The district court consolidated the cases for both discovery and trial.

The consolidated cases proceeded to a bench trial. At the close of Plaintiff's case, the district court granted Defendants' motions for judgment as a matter of law, * * * concluding that Plaintiff failed to establish that removal of architectural barriers at the four locations was readily achievable. Plaintiff appeals the district court's ruling as to only one of the four locations, the Crawford Building. * * * Applying this standard, we affirm.

I.

Title III of the ADA prohibits discrimination against persons with disabilities in places of public accommodation. 42 U.S.C. § 12182(a). The ADA provides a private right of action for preventative relief, including an application for a permanent or temporary injunction or restraining order for "any person who is being subjected to discrimination on the basis of disability in violation of" Title III. Id. §§ 12182(a)(1), 2000a-3(a). A successful plaintiff may also be entitled to attorney fees and costs. Id. § 2000a-3(b). Section 12182(a) provides: "No individual shall be discriminated against on the basis of disability in the full and equal enjoyment of the goods, services, facilities, privileges, advantages, or accommodations of any place of public accommodation by any person who owns, leases (or leases to), or operates a place of public accommodation." Id. § 12182(a). Under Title III of the ADA, "discrimination" specifically includes "failure to remove architectural barriers . . . in existing facilities . . . where such removal is readily achievable." Id. § 12182(b)(2)(A)(iv).

The ADA defines "readily achievable" as "easily accomplishable and able to be carried out without much difficulty or expense." Id. § 12181(9). The ADA further sets out several factors to be considered in determining whether removal of architectural barriers is readily achievable: (1) nature and cost of the action; (2) overall financial resources of the facility or facilities involved; (3) number of persons employed at such facility; (4) effect on expenses and resources; (5) impact of such action upon the operation of the facility; (6) overall financial resources of the covered entity; (7) overall size of the business of a covered entity with respect to the number of its employees; (8) the number, type, and location of its facilities; (9) type of operation or operations of the covered entity, including composition, structure, and functions of the workforce of such entity; and (10) geographic separateness, administrative or fiscal relationship of the facility or facilities in question to the covered entity. Id. § 12181(9)(A)-(D). * * *

Title III of the ADA, however, remains silent as to who bears the burden of proving that removal of an architectural barrier is, or is not, readily achievable. See *Pascuiti v. New York Yankees,* No. 98 CIV. 8186(SAS), 1999 WL 1102748, at *1 (S.D.N.Y. Dec. 6, 1999) (unpublished). Plaintiff argues that subsection (iv), when read in conjunction with subsection (v), places the burden on Defendant to prove the proposed architectural barrier removal is not readily achievable. Subsection (v) states that discrimination includes, *"where an entity can demonstrate that the removal of a barrier under clause (iv) is not readily achievable,* a failure to make such goods, services, facilities, privileges, advantages, or accommodations available through alternative methods if such methods are readily achievable." 42 U.S.C. § 12182(b)(2)(A)(v) (emphasis added). Subsection (v) clearly contemplates that the entity, rather than the plaintiff, bears the burden to demonstrate that barrier removal under subsection (iv) is not readily achievable. Read together, subsections (iv) and (v) provide an affirmative defense for an entity. Accordingly, we conclude Plaintiff must initially present evidence tending to show that the suggested method of barrier removal is readily achievable under the particular circumstances. If Plaintiff does so, Defendant then bears the ultimate burden of persuasion that barrier removal is not readily achievable under subsection (iv).

Placing the burden of persuasion on Defendant to prove the affirmative defense that barrier removal is not readily achievable is consistent with the remaining subsections of Title III. Section 12182(b)(2)(A)(i) provides that discrimination includes the imposition of eligibility criteria that "screen out" or "tend to screen out" individuals with disabilities unless the eligibility criteria can be shown to be necessary. Several district courts have placed the burden of showing that the eligibility criteria are necessary on the proponent of such criteria. * * *

Similarly, sections 12182(b)(2)(A)(ii) and (iii) provide an affirmative defense for an entity to demonstrate that compliance would fundamentally alter the nature of the goods and services provided. Consequently, the entity bears the burden of persuasion regarding fundamental alteration and undue burden. See *Johnson v. Gambrinus Co./Spoetzl Brewery,* 116 F.3d 1052, 1059 (5th Cir. 1997) * * *; *Mayberry v. Von Valtier,* 843 F.Supp. 1160, 1166 (E.D. Mich. 1994) * * *

In *Johnson,* 116 F.3d at 1059, the Fifth Circuit addressed the burden of proof in a § 12182(b)(2)(A)(ii) reasonable modification claim. The court held that the plaintiff bears the burden of proving that a modification was requested and that the requested modification was reasonable. Id. Once the plaintiff meets the burden of showing that an accommodation is reasonable in the general sense, the court held the defendant must make the requested accommodation unless defendant pleads and meets its burden of proving that the requested accommodation would fundamentally alter the nature of the public accommodation. Id. The plaintiff bears the ultimate burden of proof on the issue of reasonableness, while the defendant bears the burden of proving the requested accommodation would fundamentally alter the nature of the public accommodation. Id.

Several district courts have adopted *Johnson's* allocation of the burden of proof in subsection (ii) cases. See *Dahlberg v. Avis Rent A Car Sys., Inc.,* 92 F.Supp.2d 1091, 1105-06 (D. Colo. 2000) * * *; *Bingham v.*

Oregon Sch. Activities Ass'n, 24 F.Supp.2d 1110, 1116-17 (D. Or. 1998) * * * Our conclusion that Congress also intended to create an affirmative defense for an entity to establish a proposed barrier removal is not readily achievable under subsection (iv) once Plaintiff meets the initial burden of tending to show barrier removal is readily achievable comports with the remaining subsections of Title III setting forth affirmative defenses.

The Department of Justice (DOJ) Regulations regarding Title III similarly support our conclusion that "readily achievable" is an affirmative defense. The regulations specifically refer to the "readily achievable defense." 28 C.F.R. pt. 36, app. B, at 647 (2000). Furthermore, the regulations compare the "readily achievable defense" to the "undue burden defense" of § 12182(b)(2)(A)(iii), which limits a public accommodation's obligation to provide auxiliary aids, and the "undue hardship defense" of § 12112(b)(5)(A), which limits an employer's obligation to make reasonable accommodations in the employment context. Id. While the regulations state the readily achievable defense is less demanding than the undue burden or undue hardship defenses, they nevertheless explicitly place the burden of persuasion on the entity. Id.

While no circuit court has addressed the issue of who bears the burden of proving readily achievable under subsection (iv), several district courts have done so. In *Pascuiti,* 1999 WL 1102748, at *1, after considering the text of Title III, its legislative history, and implementing regulations, the district court allocated the burden of proof on the issue of whether the removal is readily available in the following manner: "The plaintiffs bear the initial burden of suggesting a method of barrier removal and proffering evidence that their suggested method meets the statutory definition of 'readily achievable.'" The court further stated that plaintiffs must consider the factors identified in § 12181(9) and proffer evidence, including expert testimony, as to the ease and inexpensiveness of their proposed method of barrier removal. Id. at *4. "If plaintiffs satisfy their burden of proffering evidence that a suggested method of barrier removal can be accomplished easily and without much difficulty or expense, the burden then shifts to the [defendants] to rebut that showing and prove that the suggested method is not readily achievable." Id. at *5. Finally, the court noted that "[p]lacing this burden on the defendant gives meaning to subsection (v), which contains the phrase 'where an entity can demonstrate that the removal of a barrier under clause (iv) is not readily achievable.' 42 U.S.C. § 12182(b)(2)(A)(v)." Id.

The district court employed a similar approach in *Parr v. L & L Drive-Inn Rest.,* 96 F.Supp.2d 1065, 1085 (D. Haw. 2000). * * * [T]he district court concluded that "[t]o succeed on an ADA claim of discrimination on account of one's disability due to an *architectural barrier,* the plaintiff must also prove that: (1) the existing facility at the defendant's place of business presents an architectural barrier prohibited under the ADA, and (2) the removal of the barrier is readily achievable." Id. (emphasis in original). The court discussed the shifting burden, stating, "[i]f Plaintiff satisfies his burdens, he has made out a prima facie case of discrimination, upon which the burden shifts to Defendant to present sufficient evidence to rebut such a showing." Id. While the court in *Pascuiti* shifted the burden of persuasion to Defendant, the court in *Parr* appears to have shifted only the burden of production to Defendant.

We find the burden allocation of *Pascuiti* to be well-reasoned and consistent with the language of Title III of the ADA. We therefore adopt the same approach wherein Plaintiff bears the initial burden of production to present evidence that a suggested method of barrier removal is readily achievable, i.e., can be accomplished easily and without much difficulty or expense. If Plaintiff satisfies this burden, Defendant then has the opportunity to rebut that showing. Defendant bears the ultimate burden of persuasion regarding its affirmative defense that a suggested method of barrier removal is not readily achievable. * * *

Further, our conclusion that subsections (iv) and (v), read together, place the burden of persuasion on Defendant to prove the affirmative defense that barrier removal is not readily achievable comports with the overall operation of the ADA. The ADA has three separate titles: Title I covers employment discrimination * * *; Title II covers discrimination by government entities * * *; and Title III covers discrimination by places of public accommodation * * * Title I provides that impermissible employment disability discrimination includes "not making reasonable accommodations to the known physical or mental limitations of an otherwise qualified individual with a disability . . . unless such covered entity can demonstrate that the accommodation would impose an undue hardship on the operation of the business of such covered entity." * * * " 'The employer . . . bears the burden of persuasion on whether a proposed accommodation would impose an undue hardship.' " * * *

Similarly, Title II states that "no qualified individual with a disability shall, by reason of such disability, be excluded from participation in or be denied the benefits of the services, programs, or activities of a public entity, or be subjected to discrimination by any such entity." * * * The DOJ regulations provide: "A public entity shall operate each service, program, or activity so that the service, program, or activity, when viewed in its entirety, is readily accessible to and useable by individuals with disabilities." 28 C.F.R. § 35.150(a). Under the regulations, however, a public entity is not required to "take any action that it can demonstrate would result in a fundamental alteration in the nature of a service, program, or activity or in undue financial and administrative burdens." 28 C.F.R. § 35.150(a)(3). Further, the regulations specifically state that "a public entity has the burden of proving that compliance with § 35.150(a) of this part would result in such alterations or burdens." * * *

According to the plain language of Title III and the allocation of burdens we have adopted, Plaintiff must initially introduce evidence tending to establish that the proposed method of architectural barrier removal is "readily achievable," i.e., "easily accomplishable and able to be carried out without much difficulty or expense" under the particular circumstances. 42 U.S.C. § 12181(9). Only if Plaintiff satisfies this initial burden does the burden of persuasion shift to Defendant to prove that the requested barrier removal method is not readily achievable.

II.

We now turn to the question of whether Plaintiff in this case produced sufficient evidence to satisfy his burden that his suggested method of barrier removal is readily achievable. At trial, Plaintiff introduced evidence regarding the installation of a ramp at the entrance to the Crawford Building. Plaintiff called Nore Winter, an expert in historical preservation in architecture and urban design. Winter owns a company called Winter & Company, which provides consultation to property owners, architects, and municipalities in developing preservation policies and design concepts. Winter testified that the front entrance to the Crawford Building could be made accessible without threatening or destroying the historic significance of the building or the district.

Winter prepared a sketch for a concept of a warped-plane sidewalk to provide access to the Crawford Building. He testified that did not intend for the sketch to be a construction drawing, but rather to illustrate an approach for achieving accessibility that would be compatible with the historic character of the building. Winter acknowledged that his sketch was "conceptual." Further, he stated that "[w]hen you start talking about real building design, et cetera, it's going to take a team of collaboration of all the parties involved with all the different viewpoints and interests to come up with the solutions that are going to best meet everyone's needs." Winter did not provide precise cost estimates. Instead, he estimated probable costs associated with the ramps of $10,750 based on his experience with similar projects. Winter testified that he reviewed a report by John Salmen, Defendant's consultant. According to Winter, Salmen's report suggested that Winter's approach would be valid, but Salmen would recommend extending the ramp out the full width of the sidewalk.

On cross-examination, Winter appeared to be unaware that the rise of the threshold of the building was three inches, bringing the total rise from the sidewalk elevation into the building to nine inches. To address the nine-inch rise, Winter suggested extending the elevation out for the full width of the sidewalk. When cross examined about designing the ramp to accommodate both wheelchair access and people with vision impairments who could fail to discern the change in grade and trip on such a ramp, Winter responded that —

you're getting beyond what my focus has been, which is on the historic impacts on these properties. As I stated earlier, I would work in collaboration with the design team to help solve these kinds of problems and these kinds of questions. I can't give you the design for that altering of the ramp right here.

Winter also suggested slanting the stoop to address the nine-inch rise. He acknowledged, however, that "I haven't really inspected this, but only to say I believe it could be possible."

Plaintiff next presented the testimony of expert accountant Robert Aucone regarding Defendant's financial resources. Aucone concluded that the financial impacts of installing ramps would be relatively immaterial and easily accomplishable. Aucone testified that in his opinion, even if the actual cost of a ramp was twice as much as estimated, his opinion would not change.

Plaintiff further introduced testimony and documentary evidence that Defendant and its predecessor had received estimates to ramp the Crawford Building. Plaintiff called Susan Spencer, the general manager of Larimer Square from 1986 until 1995. Spencer acted as general manager when Defendant purchased the Crawford Building in 1993. As general manager of Larimer Square, Spencer's duties included property management and leasing responsibilities. In addition, Spencer's responsibilities included discerning costs and making recommendations concerning whether ramps would be installed at buildings in Larimer Square. In July 1992, Rich Langston, a contractor, sent Spencer an estimate for a ramp at the Crawford building in the amount of $2,195.00. In the memo, Langston recommended against the ramp because it would require cutting the iron stoop. In November 1992, Langston sent Spencer an estimate in the amount of $2,272.00 to ramp the Crawford Building.

Spencer testified that she considered ramping the Crawford Building, but decided against it. According to Spencer, a ramp extending to the side of the building would have extended into the doorway or into the neighboring property. Further, Spencer expressed concern that a ramp extending straight out from the building would have created a trip hazard for persons with visual impairments.

Finally, Plaintiff introduced Title III DOJ regulations and commentary concerning whether a method of architectural barrier removal is readily achievable under subsection (iv). The regulations specifically list "[i]nstalling ramps" as an example of barrier removal under § 12182(b)(2)(A)(iv). 28 C.F.R. § 36.304(b)(1). The commentary points out, however, that

> the inclusion of a measure on this list does not mean that it is readily achievable in all cases. Whether or not any of these measures is readily achievable is to be determined on

a case-by-case basis in light of the particular circumstances presented and the factors listed in the definition of readily achievable (§ 36.104).

28 C.F.R. pt. 36, app. B, at 647 (2000). The commentary further explains when ramping steps may be required:

> A public accommodation generally would not be required to remove a barrier to physical access posed by a flight of steps, if removal would require extensive ramping or an elevator. Ramping a single step, however, will likely be readily achievable, and ramping several steps will in many circumstance also be readily achievable.

Id. The DOJ regulations also urge public accommodations –

> to comply with the barrier removal requirements of this section in accordance with the following order of priorities.

> (1) First, a public accommodation should take measures to provide access to a place of public accommodation from public sidewalks, parking, or public transportation. These measures include, for example, installing an entrance ramp. . . .

28 C.F.R. § 36.304(c)(1).

While the regulations specifically mention ramping a single step as a top priority and likely to be readily achievable, the regulations also state that whether removal of a barrier is readily achievable is subject to a case by case inquiry. 28 C.F.R. pt. 36, app. B, at 647. Accordingly, Plaintiff must show that installation of a ramp at the Crawford Building is readily achievable in light of the particular circumstances.

While this is a close case, we conclude Plaintiff introduced evidence regarding only speculative concepts of ramp installation, rather than evidence that a specific design was readily achievable. For instance, Plaintiff failed to present any evidence to establish the likelihood that the City of Denver would approve a proposed modification to the historical building. Plaintiff also failed to provide any precise cost estimates regarding the proposed modification. Perhaps most importantly, Plaintiff's expert testimony failed to demonstrate that under the particular circumstances installing a ramp would be readily achievable. Instead, expert Winter provided speculative conceptual ideas, rather than a specific design which would be easily accomplishable and able to be carried out without much difficulty or expense. Winter acknowledged that his sketch was conceptual and that he did not intend the sketch to be a construction drawing. Notably, Winters appeared unaware of the exact height of the architectural barrier.

While the regulations state that ramping a single step will likely be readily achievable, such an inquiry must be based on a case by case basis under the particular circumstances and factors listed in the definition of readily achievable. Because Plaintiff failed to present sufficient evidence that removal of the architectural barrier is readily achievable, the district court properly granted Defendant's motion for judgment as a matter of law.

The judgment of the district court is AFFIRMED.

LUCERO, Circuit Judge, concurring and dissenting.

I concur in the majority's Section I analysis concerning the burden of proof in cases brought to remove architectural barriers under 42 U.S.C. § 12182(b)(2)(A)(iv). In particular, I agree that the approach outlined in *Pascuiti v. New York Yankees,* 1999 WL 1102748 (S.D.N.Y. Dec. 6, 1999), and adopted by the majority is well-reasoned. However, I dissent from the resolution of this case in Section II of the majority opinion. In my judgment, the majority demands too much of ADA Title III plaintiffs. Moreover, in simply premising its holding on a negative – that Williams presented too little evidence showing his proposal was readily achievable – the majority provides inadequate guidance to trial courts in this undeveloped area of ADA law.

I

The majority opinion does not clarify the type and quantum of evidence a plaintiff must present to show that removal of an architectural barrier is "readily achievable" pursuant to 42 U.S.C. § 12182(b)(2)(A)(iv). As to the type of evidence, an obvious starting place is the language of the ADA itself, which defines "readily achievable" as "easily accomplishable and able to be carried out without much difficulty or expense." 42 U.S.C. § 12181(9). A clear reading of that definition is that it requires a plaintiff to show two things related to the removal of an architectural barrier: (1) that it can be done with ease and (2) that it can be done inexpensively. See *Pascuiti,* 1999 WL 1102748, at *4 (holding that plaintiffs must "proffer evidence . . . as to the ease and inexpensiveness of their proposed method of barrier removal" to make out a prima facie case).

The first requirement addresses non-monetary qualitative issues such as feasibility, engineering/structural concerns, historic preservation, and so forth. These concerns will vary with the design of the building, the character of the neighborhood, local laws and regulations, and other variables. In most cases, plaintiffs should provide expert testimony presenting a plan and assuring its feasibility, keeping in mind any applicable engineering, structural, and historic preservation concerns.

The second requirement addresses quantitative, monetary issues and includes such considerations as "cost," 42 U.S.C. § 12181(9)(A), "overall financial resources," § 12181(9)(B), (C), and "the effect on expenses and resources," § 12181(9)(B). Plaintiffs can satisfy their burden through the testimony of a financial expert who can relate the estimated costs of the proposal to the defendant's financial position and ability to pay those costs.

It is the quantum of evidence – the amount of detail and precision – as to which the majority requires too much. In the vast majority of cases, there will be an information imbalance between plaintiffs and defendants. Defendants, who possess the practical experience and knowledge gained by owning and operating the building containing the architectural barrier, will have a much better sense of the true impact and feasibility of a barrier removal proposal. As a result, while plaintiffs bear the burden of advancing a reasonable plan, defendants ultimately are in a better position to produce – as part of their affirmative defense – the detailed evidence the majority apparently wishes to see in these types of cases. I find it unreasonable to require ADA Title III plaintiffs to anticipate and counter any and all potential objections as part of their prima facie case. Placing too high a burden on ADA plaintiffs risks ignoring Congressional intent and gutting the ADA's private right of action. If plaintiffs must all but present the court with a pre-approved construction contract for a sum certain which includes detailed plans, impact statements, engineering studies, and permits to meet their threshold burden, virtually no plaintiff could afford to bring an architectural barrier removal claim under 42 U.S.C. § 12182(b)(2)(A)(iv). Plaintiffs should present some evidence as to cost and feasibility that recognizes and addresses these considerations but should not be required to have final, detailed answers as to any of them.

II

Turning to the facts of this case, I believe that Williams satisfied his burden of proffering a plan for barrier removal that is readily achievable. It is quite evident from the record that the only concern that separates this case from the "garden variety" ramping of a nine-inch entrance elevation is the subject property's inclusion on the National Register of Historic Places. As the majority discusses, Williams called expert witnesses Noré Winter, an architect and authority on historical preservation, who discussed the ramping plan, a possible design, and estimated costs, and Robert Aucone, an accountant, who testified regarding Hermanson's financial resources. The majority faults this evidence for three reasons: (1) it included only "speculative conceptual ideas, rather than a specific design"; (2) it "failed to provide any precise cost estimates"; and (3) it "failed to present any evidence that the City of Denver would approve" the ramp. * * *

The majority's criticisms of the "speculative" nature of the proposed barrier removal plan, which appear to critique Williams's evidence addressing the qualitative prong of the "readily achievable" standard, are undermined by the fact that both Winter and Hermanson's expert, John Salmen, approved the same approach to removing the challenged architectural barrier: warping and raising the sidewalk gradually from the curb to the entrance of the Crawford Building. At the very least, this demonstrates that the basic approach advocated by Winter was sound. That is enough, in my view, to satisfy Williams's burden. Hermanson would have ample opportunity to demonstrate whatever flaws exist in Winter's plan during Hermanson's presentation of his affirmative defense.

There is no need for "precise" cost estimates in this case because there was no uncertainty surrounding Hermanson's ability to pay for the proposed barrier removal plan. Aucone testified that "even if the actual cost of a ramp was twice as much as estimated, his opinion" that Hermanson could easily afford to install the ramp "would not change." * * * In fact, Aucone testified that Hermanson could well afford, by a factor of six, the estimated cost of Salmen's Crawford Building proposal. Perhaps precise estimates would be necessary if the cost of the barrier removal plan were at the margin of Hermanson's ability to pay for it, but that was not the situation. The issue is "could Hermanson easily afford to remove the barrier?" The clear answer, even assuming a six-fold error by Winter in estimating the cost of the proposal, is "yes."

I do not believe Williams should be required to present evidence demonstrating the likelihood of approval by the City of Denver as part of his prima facie case. No reason is advanced to suspect that the City of Denver would not approve the proposed plan – the only evidence on this subject indicated that the City of Denver had approved other barrier removal projects in the Larimer Square area. We are not presented with a complicated and expensive project such as incorporating an elevator into an antiquated building, and absent such evidence or a similar reason – such as unusually large scope or novelty – we should not presume significant hurdles to planning approval. Moreover, given the character of Larimer Square, the most likely obstacle to the City of Denver's approval of the barrier removal plan would be historic preservation concerns. However, that was exactly the area of Winter's expertise and the area he most thoroughly addressed in his testimony.

I would hold that Williams met his burden and reverse the district court.

Notes & Questions

1. Does the burden of production as to whether barrier removal is readily achievable and which party has the burden differ when Title III entities are historical landmarks? *Compare* Colo. Cross Disability Coalition v, Hermanson Family Ltd. P'Ship I, 264 F.3d 999 (10th Cir. 2001) *with* Molski v. Foley Estates Vineyard & Winery, LLC, 531 F.3d 1043 (9th Cir. 2008).

LIEBER v. MACY'S WEST, INC.

United States District Court, Northern District of California, 1999
80 F.Supp.2d 1065

PATEL, Chief Judge

* * *

FINDINGS OF FACT

1. Macy's Union Square is a landmark retail facility in San Francisco. Macy's Union Square consists of a Main Store occupying almost an entire city block and a Men's Store located across the street.

2. The Main Store contains eight levels and a basement which have display areas open to customers. The Men's Store has five floors each of which has display areas open to the public. Altogether Macy's Union Square contains 567,000 square feet of space, approximately 450,000 sq. ft. of which is currently used to display merchandise for sale to the public. The court notes that Macy's Union Square has recently undergone a major renovation project, affecting both the Main Store and the Men's Store. Macy's witnesses testified that this renovation was slated to cost over $130 million.

* * *

Plaintiffs established that numerous barriers to access still exist at Macy's Union Square. Such barriers include restrooms with various features mounted at heights that exceed ADAAG's reach requirements (including toilet paper dispensers, towel dispensers, soap dispensers, and seat cover dispensers); lack of proper signage at entry doors; locking devices that require grasping, pinching, or twisting of the wrist; and other features that affect the usability of the restroom for people with mobility disabilities. Plaintiffs also established that numerous fitting rooms which purport to be accessible contain features that fail to conform to ADAAG requirements, such as benches that are not 24" by 48", and door handles that require tight grasping.

7. The court finds that Macy's conceded that removal of many of these barriers was readily achievable. Martin Gusky, the Vice President of Properties for Macy's West, testified that he recently reviewed the barriers described by Mr. Margen, in consultation with an access expert hired by Macy's for the purposes of this litigation. Mr. Gusky testified that, based on such review, he initiated plans to remove most of the barriers described by Mr. Margen (other than cash wraps and crowded pathways) within two months of the date of the trial.

8. Overall, the court finds that, despite limited efforts to remove barriers at Macy's Union Square, multiple and pervasive access barriers still existed at the time of trial. With regard to many of the barriers that

are structural in nature, such as inaccessible fitting rooms, restrooms, bridal registries and elevation changes, the court notes that, at trial, Macy's announced new plans to remedy such barriers.

9. Plaintiffs also presented credible evidence that Macy's has repeatedly blocked even the main and secondary aisles (those leading between pads) by placing merchandise displays in the aisles so as to constrict the paths of travel to less than 36" wide. Various plaintiffs and class members testified that they have difficulty getting from the main store entrance to the elevators because of such obstacles. Defendant presented no explanation or justification for the presence of such barriers, and did not claim it was not readily achievable to remedy them. Accordingly, the court finds that Macy's failed to make adequate efforts under the readily achievable standard to maintain even the main and secondary aisles in an accessible condition at all times.

10. In areas of alteration, Macy's is also required to maintain at least one 36" accessible route to all fitting rooms and cash wraps, regardless of whether such routes pass through merchandise areas. Plaintiffs established that Macy's has failed to maintain 36" accessible routes to fitting rooms and cashwraps in areas of alteration. Peter Margen identified numerous pathways in altered areas of the Men's Store in which routes to fitting rooms and cashwraps were blocked by moveable merchandise display units.

11. While Macy's witnesses [claim] that they seek to maintain accessible routes to fitting rooms and cashwraps, this testimony is not credible, since Macy's did not present or name any person at the Union Square Store who directly accepts responsibility to maintain such pathways. Macy's Director of Stores, Rebecca Canfield, who previously served as the store manager of Macy's Union Square indicated that this issue has never been addressed by any Macy's or Federated policy, or even by a memo.

12. Throughout the display areas, most of the merchandise is placed on racks, shelves and other structures designed to hold and display the merchandise. Some of these structures such as shelving are clearly attached to walls as are heavy display counters called "caselines." Mr. Heitzmann testified that case lines are fixed, despite the fact that they are not physically attached to the floor. He indicated that they are considered fixed because they are "wired," or electronically attached to their locations on the floor. Macy's presented no evidence to contradict Mr. Heitzmann. The court thus finds that caselines are fixed so as to be subject to ADAAG § 4.1.3(12)(b) in all areas of alteration. Other various types of tables and display structures are moveable, according to Macy's personnel. These include a variety of metal racks variously called 2-ways (or T-stands), 4-ways, and rounders. Within the retail industry all of these display features, whether fixed or moveable, are termed "fixtures." To avoid confusion with the legal definition of a fixture in real estate law, however,

the court will refer to all of the merchandise display features at issue here as "display units," a term utilized in the Americans with Disabilities Act Access Guidelines.

13. The merchandise display units throughout Macy's Union Square are generally "self service" such that customers are expected to obtain merchandise by independently browsing and/or searching through the display areas for an item that they wish to purchase, removing that item from the display unit on their own, and bringing the item to a cash register to process their purchase.

14. Although Macy's sales clerks (called "associates" by Macy's) are to some extent available to assist customers in locating and/or obtaining merchandise to the extent permitted by the clerk's other duties (such as processing purchases at the sales counter), Macy's admits that the Store is generally operated according to a self-service model.

15. Macy's merchandise display areas are generally organized according to departments, each of which focuses on a particular type of merchandise. Each department consists of one or more "pads" in which the merchandise is placed on display units.

16. "Main" and "secondary" aisles lead patrons into the facility from various entrances and from one pad to another. Macy's admits that the display units are generally positioned within the pads with a certain clearance between each unit for the purpose of enabling customers to get to the merchandise.

17. Ms. Canfield, who previously served as the store manager of Macy's Union Square, testified that Macy's practice generally is to try to provide 24" to 30" clear space between its merchandise display units.

18. Macy's stipulated at trial that a 30" pathway was, in fact, unusable for various class members.

19. Ms. Canfield estimated that, at the time of trial, 15%-25% of the display units would have to be removed just to provide a 30" clear space between all display units. In the Men's Store, Ms. Canfield testified that 5%-15% of the units likely would need to be removed to provide 30" of clearance.

20. Defendant's professional floor planner, Kevin Ellis, the head of Macy's West Planning, Design and Construction Departments, testified that his departments use 36" between display units as the standard. Once the facility is designed and constructed, however, he turns responsibility for maintaining clearance over to the store's operational personnel, such as Ms. Canfield.

21. Similar testimony was presented by Andrew Brezina, the head of Federated's planning and design department. Mr. Brezina's department is responsible for designing the layout of the display areas in newly constructed and renovated Federated Stores, including most of the

Macy's Union Square Store which has been undergoing a comprehensive renovation. (The Men's Store renovation was completed in early 1997; the Main Store renovation was ongoing at the time of trial.) Mr. Brezina testified that he plans such layouts to provide 30" to 36" of clear space between the merchandise placed on units. He testified that this is a "comfort zone" required for customers to be comfortable shopping.

22. Mr. Brezina admitted that he had no control over the merchandise layouts once the operations people (such as Ms. Canfield) take control of the facility, and that he routinely observed unit layouts at Macy's Union Square that did not comport with the plans prepared by his planning and design departments.

23. Plaintiffs' expert, Peter Margen, documented numerous instances at the Union Square Store facility where pathways between merchandise racks in pads provided substantially less than 36" of clear width. Pathways often start out with sufficient clearance and then narrow at one or more points due to a lack of organized layout within the pads.

24. Ms. Canfield initially claimed that this limited spacing was designed to provide a "comfort zone" for all shoppers, including wheelchair users. On cross-examination, Ms. Canfield admitted that the 24"-30" spacing practice is based solely on her personal perception of the needs of able-bodied customers. In fact, she admitted that she has no idea how wheelchair users actually get to the merchandise display at Macy's Union Square and admitted in her deposition that wheelchair users would have difficulty accessing at least 25% of all the merchandise on display units even at the slowest time of the year when inventories are lowest. She further admitted that conditions get even more congested at the holiday season (Thanksgiving to New Years) when inventories are significantly higher.

25. Ms. Canfield testified that she had never consulted with Mr. Brezina, Federated's in-house expert on department store planning, and that she was unaware that he considered 30-36" spacing to be necessary for able-bodied patrons to be comfortable.

26. Ms. Canfield testified that she is unaware of any formal policy or memo directing staff to maintain any minimum clearance between display units, and does not know if anyone within Macy's or Federated has gone through the Union Square store at any time to try to maximize the extent to which wheelchair users can get up to the merchandise on displays inside of pads, even without losing any selling space.

27. Ms. Canfield admitted that she doesn't know the extent to which her 24"-30" standard is generally followed at the stores under her supervision.

28. Ms. Canfield testified that her unwritten policy of providing 24" to 30" between merchandise display racks has been in effect since the

1980's. She testified that this policy has not been adjusted at any time, and specifically has not been modified in response to the Americans With Disabilities Act.

29. Macy's witnesses testified that the merchandising strategy at Macy's Union Square consists of placing all inventory on the selling floor when it arrives at the store, and requiring each department to "clear" all of its own inventory. Macy's personnel stated that the store generally does not use stock rooms to hold duplicates of items, nor does it generally use clearance outlets to dispose of items that are not selling at its mainline stores. Further, Macy's witnesses testified that Macy's Union Square does not transfer merchandise from one store to another within the Macy's West chain, nor does it attempt to renegotiate inventory purchases with vendors, except on very rare occasion. Thus, according to Macy's personnel, when stock does not sell as well as expected, the merchandise generally remains on the floor even as more merchandise is delivered and placed out on displays.

30. The primary mechanism specifically described by Macy's for promoting inventory control is the use of price mark-downs on inventory.

31. Various witnesses testified that certain of the display units utilized at the store are substantially more efficient in terms of holding more merchandise in a given area. Rounders generally hold the most merchandise in a given space, while tables and two-ways generally hold the least. Macy's personnel testified that many of the display units used at Macy's Union Square are chosen for the "look" they present to customers (i.e., the visual appeal) even though they are not the most efficient use of space.

32. Macy's vice president of floor planning, Kevin Ellis, admitted that Macy's occasionally uses high efficiency units, but generally relies upon less-efficient units. Macy's also utilizes display units provided by vendors apparently without evaluating the efficiency of the units.

33. The evidence thus indicates that Macy's could improve access at Macy's Union Square by changing the type of units used without necessarily reducing the amount of merchandise on display. The court does not find that Macy's must disregard all visual "look" in selecting display units. Rather, the court finds that Macy's must at least consider and evaluate the feasibility of alternative display practices given that the current practices systematically prevent many people with disabilities from even getting to the merchandise on display.

34. To the extent that Macy's witnesses claimed that they were obligated to place merchandise display units closer together than 30" in order to maximize sales, the usefulness of this strategy is contradicted by their own in-house expert, Mr. Brezina. The evidence indicates that 30" – 36" clearance is the minimum spacing needed before the facility begins passing the point of diminishing returns.

35. Macy's presented no evidence at trial that it would lose sales if it increased its current merchandise display practices to provide 36" between its merchandise display units. In fact, the evidence indicates that Macy's may already be past the point of diminishing returns, such that widening pathways might encourage shoppers who would otherwise be deterred from shopping at Macy's Union Square as much as they would if the store environment were less crowded.

36. The court notes that Federated in recent Annual Reports claims that its newest stores are designed to be more "open" and provide wider aisles in order to provide a more comfortable shopping environment. * * * Federated's 1995 Annual Report notes that "wider aisles . . . enhance store vistas and the shopping experience." * * * Ms. Canfield admitted that she is not knowledgeable concerning Federated's overall store planning guidelines and was not even aware of these efforts by Federated to increase the openness of its newer stores.

37. Prior to trial, Macy's had designated several experts, including an economist and a retail consultant, to testify about the effects of widening the pathways inside the pads. At trial, however, Macy's chose not to call these experts and instead sought to rely on the testimony of two lay witnesses employed by Macy's – Rebecca Canfield, Macy's Director of Stores, and Liz Hauer, Macy's Head of Merchandise Planning – to discuss the potential impact of providing improved access at Macy's Union Square. The testimony of these witnesses on this issue, however, was purely speculative.

38. Neither Ms. Canfield nor Ms. Hauer had looked at the effect of widening the pathways inside merchandise pads until the middle of the trial. Ms. Canfield admitted that, prior to trial, she had never made any effort to assess the potential impact of widening the pathways inside the pads to improve access. The only effort she made to address this issue was a one-time, 1-3 hour visit during the trial when she went to Macy's Union Square in the company of Macy's attorneys, and made some mental "guesstimates" of the potential effects of widening the pathways inside the store to 30 inches between the units. These mental guesstimates, however, were too speculative to be probative.

39. Ms. Canfield also claimed that any reduction in the amount of merchandise displayed on the sales floor would necessarily have an equivalent effect on sales volume at the store. This testimony, however, was also too speculative to be probative. Ms. Canfield admitted that she had no knowledge of any empirical study designed to assess how widening pathways at Union Square (or any other store) would affect sales, and she had never even looked at the operations and/or financial performance of other department stores that do provide access for people with mobility disabilities.

40. Ms. Canfield's sole professional experience is in the hands-on management of several Macy's stores. She holds no professional degrees

in economics or retailing and has never done any studies or written any articles concerning retailing. It is undisputed that Macy's has never tried reducing the density of merchandise displays at an existing store to improve shopper access or comfort. Ms. Canfield thus has no direct experience upon which to base any opinions concerning this issue. Moreover, prior to trial, Ms. Canfield had never even considered this issue, much less analyzed or investigated it in any formal manner.

41. Any proper study or investigation of this issue would have to consider the extent to which shoppers, both able-bodied and disabled, would be more likely to shop more often at Macy's if the environment were more comfortable and accessible.

42. From all the evidence, the court finds that Macy's generally does not make any significant effort to adjust the layout of the display units so as to maximize access even without changing or losing any units, and ignores this basic access requirement under the ADA barrier removal requirements

43. Ms. Canfield also assumed that any reduction in merchandise on the floor would lead to reduced sales, without considering the ability of Macy's to increase utilization of stock rooms to store duplicates. Ms. Canfield made no analysis of the potential positive effects of having fewer duplicates out on display in terms of shopper satisfaction and resulting increased sales. Ms. Canfield claimed that utilizing stock rooms would lead to some increased labor costs, but made no effort to try to quantify this. She also ignored certain factors that might off-set such labor costs, such as increased sales to customers who would shop more often in an uncluttered, comfortable environment. Different stock planning and display practices might also reduce the extent to which Macy's has to mark down inventory in order to clear it from the floor and make room for new deliveries. Defendant's witnesses admitted that Macy's has to mark down substantial portions of its merchandise in order to clear it from the floor, thus losing substantial opportunities for improved revenue.

44. Ms. Canfield admitted that Macy's also uses stockrooms to some extent and admitted that Macy's could increase the extent to which such stockrooms are used to hold duplicate merchandise rather than putting all of the merchandise in a shipment out on the floor. She also admitted that Macy's has in the past utilized stockrooms to a greater extent than currently used at Macy's Union Square. However, she made no analysis of the effect on Macy's operations of increasing the use of stockrooms to hold duplicate merchandise in order to reduce the crowding of the sales floor. As noted above, this court does not suggest that Macy's is required to adopt the specific methods that have been implemented at Nordstrom's. However, the Nordstrom's example remains instructive, particularly in light of the testimony by Macy's witnesses that the use of stockrooms at Macy's is currently in flux and Federated's admission that it is constantly experimenting with new merchandising strategies.

45. Ms. Hauer, Head of Merchandise Planning, also claimed that any reduction in the amount of merchandise out on display would have a proportional negative effect on Macy's overall sales. Ms. Hauer, however, also admitted that she has never done any study or investigation of this issue Ms. Hauer testified that she had no experience with any Macy's store, or even any department in a Macy's store, where the actual density of the merchandise display area had been reduced in terms of the amount of merchandise displayed in a given space. She, too, admitted that there is a point of diminishing returns beyond which adding more merchandise to a display area would lead to overcrowding such that total sales will actually be reduced. In her deposition, Ms. Hauer admitted repeatedly that she did not know whether or not Macy's Union Square was already beyond that point of diminishing returns. She also claimed in her deposition that she could estimate whether or not the Union Square store was over-crowded based on her experience in developing stock plans, but no evidence was presented by defendant to support this claim. In fact, Ms. Hauer admitted that she had no actual knowledge of display area conditions at Macy's Union Square and that she would have to guess on the issue of whether widening pathways within the store to 36 inches would even require removing units.

46. Ms. Hauer further admitted that she had no knowledge concerning the extent to which Macy's Union Square is actually using its display area to maximum efficiency. She admitted that she never investigated to see what the effect would be of widening the pathways in Union Square so that wheelchair users could get to the merchandise. She was also unaware of anyone within Macy's who had made any such investigation.

47. Ms. Hauer also claimed that crowding of the floor in Macy's stores was necessary due to defendant's six-month planning cycle in which defendant purchases inventory to be delivered at future dates. Ms. Hauer claimed that, to the extent merchandise does not sell as well as expected, the floor inevitably gets more crowded.

48. The court notes that defendant engaged and disclosed an economist and retail consultant to testify on these issues at trial. The court finds defendant's decision at trial not to call these expert witnesses and instead to rely solely on lay witnesses is revealing. Under these facts, the court may infer that defendant's decision not to call its expert witnesses means that their evidence would not have supported defendant's case.

49. Overall, the court finds that Macy's has failed to make any effort to modify or even review its stock planning and display practices to assess the feasibility of alternative methods that would improve access. Ms. Canfield failed to do a reliable analysis of the potential economic effects of widening the pathways inside the pads, and her testimony on the issue was thus speculative.

50. Macy's asserted as a defense at trial that it provides customer service to the extent it fails to provide actual physical access to merchandise for patrons with disabilities. However, the court finds that Macy's presented no credible evidence to sustain this defense.

51. The plaintiffs and class members all testified credibly that they generally have difficulty just getting the attention of sales clerks at Macy's Union Square and rarely, if ever, are able to get adequate customer assistance.

52. The court also notes that Macy's failed to produce any witness to testify the extent to which Macy's actually provides customer service as an alternative to direct access to merchandise. In the middle of trial, Macy's determined that it would not call Patricia Stromberg, the person in charge of training sales associates, despite the fact that she had previously been identified as a potential witness on the role of service in providing access to patrons with disabilities. The court finds, based on the facts, that Ms. Stromberg's testimony would have not have benefited Macy's. Ms. Stromberg was within Macy's power to produce at trial, and would have been expected to testify if her testimony would have been favorable.

53. Instead of producing a witness directly knowledgeable on the issue of customer service, Macy's chose to rely again on the testimony of Rebecca Canfield, who admitted that she did not have any direct knowledge of the substance of the training program for sales associates. Ms. Canfield further testified that she was not aware of any training given to sales associates specifically with regard to providing assistance for customers with disabilities. Ms. Canfield admitted that sales clerks frequently have to serve many customers all at the same time.

54. Through Ms. Canfield, Macy's presented a plan being developed to institute necessary procedures to insure a minimal level of access for disabled customers. Under the plan, Macy's was to consider designating a store manager to be responsible for providing access to customers with disabilities. Macy's was also reviewing the possibility of installing customer service phones and signage instructing disabled customers to call for assistance.

55. Macy's witnesses have further testified that their use of "vendor shops" prevents them from controlling merchandise density. However, Macy's presented no evidence that it attempts to provide for access in its contractual arrangements with vendors. Macy's further presented no credible evidence that vendors would actually refuse to provide merchandise for sale at Macy's if access standards were included in the vendor shop agreements. Macy's Director of Store Planning, Mr. Brezina, admitted that Macy's retains ultimate control over spacing of displays, even in vendor shops. The court finds that Macy's cannot, and has not, ceded control over its floor areas to the point of denying access simply in order to maintain contractual advantages from vendors.

Conclusions of Law

A. Jurisdiction

* * *

2. Macy's is a "place of public accommodation" under the operation of the Americans with Disabilities Act ("ADA"). 28 C.F.R. § 36.104. Macy's Union Square is owned and operated by Macy's West, Inc., a wholly-owned subsidary of Federated Department Stores. Macy's Union Square is subject to all requirements of a public accommodation under Title III of the Americans with Disabilities Act ("ADA") of 1990, 42 U.S.C. § 12101, et seq. * * *

3. The Americans with Disabilities Act ("ADA") is a comprehensive civil rights law for people with disabilities. In enacting the ADA, Congress sought to remedy discrimination in public accommodations whether such discrimination is intentional or not. 42 U.S.C. § 12101(a); *Helen L. v. DiDario,* 46 F.3d 325, 335 (3d Cir. 1995).

4. Title III of the ADA provides that "[n]o individual shall be discriminated against on the basis of disability" in places of public accommodation. 42 U.S.C. § 12182(a) (1994). The ADA further defines "discrimination" as a failure to remove "barriers . . . where such removal is readily achievable." 42 U.S.C. § 12182(b)(2)(A)(iv) (1994).

* * *

II. Areas of Current Construction

A. Burden of Proof

26. The Americans with Disabilities Act, enacted in 1990, requires places of public accommodation such as Macy's Union Square to remove barriers to the extent readily achievable 42 U.S.C. § 12182(b)(2). Continued efforts are required of places of public accommodation over time to remove any remaining barriers to the extent readily achievable. 42 U.S.C. § 12181(9); 28 C.F.R. § 36.304. The U.S. Department of Justice issued regulations pursuant to Title III of the ADA detailing such barrier removal obligations. 28 C.F.R. Part 36.

27. Plaintiffs bear the burden of establishing the existence of access barriers throughout Macy's Union Square. Plaintiffs also bear the burden of putting forward reasonable modifications. The burden then shifts to Macy's to show that the requested modifications would fundamentally alter the nature of its public accommodation. * * *

B. Access to Merchandise in Areas of
Current Construction – Moveable Displays

28. The thrust of plaintiffs' argument as it relates to areas of current construction is that Macy's violates the ADA in regards to the placement of merchandise racks within the display pads. Plaintiffs

testified at trial about their difficulties in obtaining access to merchandise at Macy's Union Square. The court was not persuaded by plaintiffs' video exhibit. Nor was the court convinced that access problems were as widespread and pernicious as plaintiffs complained. The court concluded from plaintiffs' anecdotal testimony as well as the testimony of plaintiffs' access expert that access problems vary in degree and also vary from department to department and over time. However, the court was persuaded that taken as a whole, plaintiffs' testimony demonstrated a pattern overall of lack of access which worsens at certain times of the year when Macy's increases its merchandise inventory.

29. The question remains then: what are Macy's obligations under the ADA in terms of providing access to moveable displays? The explicit language of the ADA, Department of Justice ("DOJ") ADA regulations, and the legislative history of the ADA uniformly indicate that the statute does not contemplate that customers in wheelchairs will have 100% physical access to merchandise at Macy's or at any other retail store. Section 302(b)(2)(A)(iv) of the ADA, 42 U.S.C. § 12182(b)(2)(A)(iv) (1994).

30. The ADA contemplates the likelihood that the removal of *all* barriers will not be "readily achievable." The ADA specifically states that where barrier removal is not "readily achievable," retailers should provide access to their merchandise "through alternative methods if such methods are readily achievable." 42 U.S.C. § 12182(b)(2)(A)(v) (1994).

31. Neither the ADA nor its implementing regulations contain any specific spacing requirement for moveable merchandise display racks. The regulatory spacing requirement for self-service merchandise units, the 36-inch requirement in 4.1.3(12)(b) of the ADA Guidelines for Accessible Design ("ADAAG"), applies to *fixed* display units. No provision of the ADA or DOJ regulations applies this 36-inch standard to *moveable* display racks. The ADA's "physical access" requirement does not mandate 36 inches of clearance on all sides of a moveable display rack, nor even on one side. ADAAG § 4.1.3. (12)(b). Therefore the spacing of moveable display racks is governed by the more general "readily achievable" standard of the ADA.

32. Nor are DOJ publications to the contrary. The DOJ publication *ADA Guide to Small Business* states that retailer must "provide a 36" minimum width route between displays and shelves if readily achievable." * * *

33. The ADA defines "readily achievable" as "easily accomplishable and able to be carried out without much difficulty or expense." 42 U.S.C. § 12181(9). The ADA sets forth the following factors, among others, in deciding whether an action is to be considered readily achievable: (i) the nature and cost of the action; (ii) the overall financial resources of the facility involved and the effect on expenses and resources, or the impact otherwise of such action upon the operation of the facility; (iii) the overall financial resources of the covered entity, including the

number of its employees; and (iv) the type of operation of the covered entity. 42 U.S.C. § 12181(9). The Title III regulations specify that if applicable the overall financial resources of any parent corporation or entity should also be considered. 28 C.F.R. § 36.104 (definition of "readily achievable"). The DOJ ADA regulations include rearranging tables and display racks among the examples of efforts that it considers to be readily achievable. 28 C.F.R. § 36.304(b).

34. DOJ regulations explain that "the rearrangement of temporary or movable structures, such as furniture, equipment or display racks is not readily achievable to the extent that it results in a significant loss of selling or serving space." Section 301(9) of the ADA, 42 U.S.C. § 12182(b)(2)(A)(iv) (1994); 28 C.F.R. § 36.304(f).

35. While Macy's has argued that the effect on its revenues of loss of selling space is relevant, the court does not concur. The "significant loss of selling space" standard is only meaningful to the extent that it affects operations. The ADA statute makes clear that the readily achievable barrier removal obligation must consider the "overall financial resources," "effect on expenses and resources," and the "effect on operations" of the facilities involved in the action. 42 U.S.C. § 12181(9), ("Definitions"). Moreover, the Department of Justice ("DOJ"), which promulgated the Title III regulations, has interpreted the provisions dealing with reconfiguration of display racks as requiring the retailer to consider the effect on operations in determining the extent to which barrier removal is readily achievable. DOJ ADA Title III Technical Manual * * *; DOJ Guide to Small Businesses * * *.

36. The testimony offered by Macy's witnesses regarding the supposed loss of selling space was speculative. Defendant failed to present the testimony of their expert witnesses, relying solely upon the opinions of lay witnesses. The opinion testimony of Macy's lay witnesses was not probative. It was not based on more than "guesstimates" of the impact of providing more space between racks and the concomitant impact on selling space. There was an absence of any empirical or other studies or investigation into the feasibility of providing access.

37. However, the court finds that placing 36" between each display rack is not mandated by the ADA or by Title 24. * * *

* * *

40. Congress did conclude that certain areas of a store will not be fully accessible to a customer in a wheelchair. However, the DOJ regulations state that in such instances "selected widening should be undertaken to maximize the amount of merchandise * * * accessible to individuals who use wheelchairs." 56 Fed. Reg. 35538 (July 26, 1991). The evidence indicates that Macy's has failed to make any efforts to even selectively widen its pathways inside the pads. For example, none of

defendant's lay witnesses even looked at whether Macy's could improve access inside the merchandise pads until the middle of trial.

41. The court concludes that the conditions within the merchandise pads at Macy's Union Square obligated Macy's to take steps to maximize access within those areas to the extent readily achievable, as specifically contemplated by the ADA. 28 C.F.R. § 36.304(b)(3)-(4).

42. Macy's Director of Stores testified at trial that Macy's practice and goal in operating the facility is to provide only 24"-30" clear space between merchandise display units. The evidence presented at trial showed that in fact clearances are at times substantially less than 24", with barely enough room for even able-bodied customers to squeeze through. The evidence shows that Macy's has never even tried to provide more accessible routes in merchandise pads. The court finds that Macy's admitted practice of providing only 24"-30" pathways between merchandise display units violates the requirement that accessible routes be provided in merchandise areas to the extent readily achievable.

43. In fact, the evidence presented supports the claim that it is readily achievable for Macy's to take steps to increase access within merchandise pads. First of all, Macy's own witness testified that access could be improved in many pads simply by adjusting the placement of merchandise display units.

44. The testimony of Macy's own Director of Design and Planning, Andrew Brezina, contradicts Macy's assertion that it cannot provide greater accessibility without adversely affecting its business operations. Mr. Brezina testified that he regularly sets out fixture plans providing 30-36" clearance between display units. He testified that this clearance is a comfort zone required even for able-bodied shoppers. To the extent Macy's is crowding the display areas by narrowing pathways below this comfort zone for able-bodied shoppers, Macy's may actually improve its operations by widening the pathways even if this required using different display units and/or reducing the total amount of merchandise on the display floor.

45. The barrier removal requirements of the ADA mandate that Macy's make efforts to improve access in merchandise display areas. Macy's has failed to even consider various alternative means of providing access such as those utilized by other department stores. Defendant has thus violated the ADA's requirement that places of public accommodation "take such steps as may be necessary" to provide access. 42 U.S.C. § 12182(b)(2)(A)(iii). Defendant's witnesses admitted that they never even examined their merchandising practices to see if they could be modified to address the pervasive access barriers at issue.

46. While the court does not find that Macy's is obligated to follow the methodology of any other department store in providing access, the methods used by other stores are relevant as examples of alternative

approaches. The evidence presented at trial concerning Nordstrom's, (a direct competitor of Macy's) showing its practice of providing 36" pathways between merchandise display units by use of stockrooms, clearance centers, and more careful planning demonstrates that there are in fact alternate methods through which retail department stores can generally provide access without a significant burden or fundamental alteration.

47. The court further concludes that Macy's has violated its ADA obligations by failing to even consider alternative methods necessary to provide full and equal access. The ADA specifically requires public accommodations to modify their policies and practices where necessary for access, subject to the fundamental alteration defense. 42 U.S.C. § 12182(b)(2)(A)(ii). Federated's Annual Reports claim that Federated is constantly experimenting, trying new strategies, and adjusting to changing conditions. Yet defendant has done *nothing* to try to improve access to the merchandise inside the pads. It has not experimented with different methods, it has not tried adjusting its planning and display practices, it has not even tried to maximize access by simply repositioning existing display units in the pads to maximize access. Defendant has simply ignored the problem.

48. The court thus concludes that Macy's failure to make any effort to improve access within the pads violates the requirement that readily achievable efforts be made to provide access. 42 U.S.C. § 12182(b)(2)(A)(iii).

C. Customer Service Defense

49. The ADA requires the merchant to provide sales assistance to retrieve merchandise that is physically inaccessible. House Committee on Education and Labor, H.R. Rep. No. 485(II), at 110 (1990). Also, DOJ regulations state that "[e]xamples of alternatives to barrier removal include ... [r]etrieving merchandise from inaccessible shelves or racks." 28 C.F.R. § 36.305(b)(2). The DOJ commentary published contemporaneously with its ADA regulations state "[I]f it is not readily achievable for a retail store ... to rearrange display racks to provide accessible aisles, the store must, if readily achievable, provide a clerk ... to retrieve inaccessible merchandise." 56 Fed. Reg. 35544, 35570, Vol. 56, No. 144 (July 26, 1991).

50. Contrary to the defense presented by Macy's, on all the evidence the court concludes that, at the time of trial, Macy's had not adequately provided access to merchandise pads through readily achievable "alternative methods" such as customer service. 42 U.S.C. § 12182(b)(2)(v). Under the readily achievable standard, Macy's is specifically obligated to provide service to people with disabilities as an alternative to access in any areas where it does not provide actual physical access to the merchandise offered for sale to the public. 28 C.F.R. § 36.305(b)(2).

51. Plaintiffs and class members testified that they were impeded in their ability to view merchandise they were interested in buying at Macy's Union Square because sales clerks were unable or unwilling to provide adequate service. The trial evidence indicated that while Macy's stated an intention to improve customer assistance to people with disabilities, at the time of trial it had taken insufficient steps to ensure that shoppers with disabilities actually get adequate assistance from sales clerks. Macy's witness on this issue, Rebecca Canfield, was aware of no special training given to sales clerks to assist disabled customers, and no procedures were in place to ensure that shoppers with disabilities actually receive adequate, or any, assistance obtaining items when the clerks are busy processing the purchases of other customers at the sales counter.

D. Contractual Arrangements Defense

52. The ADA specifically prohibits public accommodations from discriminating against person with disabilities "through contractual . . . or other arrangements." 42 U.S.C. § 12182(b). Macy's claimed that the vendors would not "like" seeing merchandise adjusted between pads. Even if this were the case, the ADA clearly prohibits Macy's from maintaining access barriers that discriminate against patrons with disabilities through contractual arrangements with vendors. 42 U.S.C. § 12182(b). Moreover, Macy's failed to present any evidence of actual vendor contracts or testimony from any vendor showing that Macy's could not retain the flexibility to move merchandise display units as needed to provide access for people with disabilities. Plaintiffs submitted evidence that competing department stores with vendor presences maintain accessible layouts. Thus, the court finds that Macy's contracts with vendors are no excuse for failing to provide greater access within vendor shops.

E. Fundamental Alteration Defense

53. The ADA does not require Macy's to alter the fundamental nature of its business. 302(b)(2)(A)(ii) of the ADA * * *

54. The fundamental nature of Macy's business, and the essence of its role as a place of public accommodation, is to provide goods available for sale to the general public, including sale merchandise.

55. To the extent that defendant is claiming that providing improved access is not required because it would involve changing Macy's policies and practices, then defendant is required to meet the ADA's fundamental alteration standard, a higher standard than the readily achievable standard. 42 U.S.C. § 12182. Under this standard, Macy's must show that the nature of the goods and services it provides would in fact be fundamentally altered by providing changes needed to improve access. 42 U.S.C. § 12182(b)(2)(A).

56. While Macy's argues that the adoption of Nordstrom's strategy of removing clearance merchandise from the store would be a fundamental

change to Macy's business, the court is not suggesting or requiring that Macy's adopt any particular strategy for providing additional access, thus this defense is not relevant to the case at bar.

THE COURT ENTERS AN ORDER AS FOLLOWS:

1. Macy's is liable for violating the Americans with Disabilities Act, 42 U.S.C. 12101 *et seq.*, California Civil Code § 54 *et seq.*, and California Health and Safety Code § 19955 *et seq.*

2. Macy's West is ordered to take the following actions to improve access at Macy's Union Square:

(A) Prepare written materials and provide training to all responsible managers and sales associates regarding placement of merchandise in the display pads to ensure that access is maximized. Designate a party responsible for overseeing this process and for reviewing display pads on an ongoing basis. This person or persons shall also have responsibility for ensuring that main and secondary aisles remain passable. Department Managers shall be informed as to the existence and identity of this person or persons and customers with disabilities shall be provided with that information upon request. Provide within sixty (60) days of the date of this order a plan for effective customer service for customers with mobility disabilities, including signage informing such patrons of the availability of such service.

(B) In those areas of the store not subject to new construction/alterations standards, make at least one fitting room in each distinct functional sales area, and any unique features such as bridal registries, fully ADAAG/Title 24 accessible to patrons with mobility disabilities, and provide at least one clearly accessible route to each such feature from the main aisles.

(C) In those areas of the store not subject to new construction/alterations standards, provide auxiliary (fold-out) shelves at all inaccessible counters or ensure that clipboards are available at every counter that fails to provide an area 36" wide that is no more than 36" above the floor, and that such clipboards are actually offered to patrons with disabilities.

* * *

IT IS SO ORDERED.

Notes & Questions

1. In deciding which barriers to remove, a public accommodation must prioritize according to the significance of the barrier to the disabled

person's attempt to access the goods and services of the public accommodation. Thus, the first priority includes access to, and into, the facility. Elements to be addressed under this first priority include parking, entrances, and curbs, among others.

The second priority level includes access to the goods and services of the public accommodation. Elements to be addressed include aisles, shelves, signage, doorways, and so on.

The third priority includes restroom access and involves elements such as toilet stalls, dispensers, grab bars, and mirrors. The final priority includes any other barriers to access to the goods and services of the public accommodation. 28 C.F.R. § 36.304(c) (2008).

Are these priorities logical? Does a person requiring a fully accessible restroom shop at a grocery without an accessible restroom? What about a department store? A shopping mall? The DOJ has entered into hundreds of settlement agreements and consent decrees with Title III entities since 1994. *See* U.S. Dep't of Justice, ADA Enforcement Cases 2006 - Present: Title III, http://www.ada.gov/enforce_current. htm#TitleIII (last visited Oct. 30, 2013). Do these agreements place less emphasis on accessible restrooms than entryways or curb cuts?

2. Moving portable furniture, such as trash cans or chairs, out of space needed for accessibility is specifically identified in the regulations as an example of readily achievable barrier removal. Parr v. L & L Drive-Inn Restaurant, 96 F.Supp.2d 1065 (D. Haw. 2000). However, some courts have refused to require it when such items are moved by customers not under the control of the facility, finding that an injunction requiring keeping the accessible spaces clear of portable furniture would not be enforceable. Ass'n for Disabled Ams., Inc. v. Key Largo Bay Beach, LLC, 407 F.Supp.2d 1321, 1343-44, 1346 (S.D. Fla. 2005).

3. The courts apply the readily achievable standard on a case-by-case basis and often reach varying results. In *Alford v. City of Cannon Beach*, No. CV-00-303-HU, 2002 WL 31439173, at *1 (D. Or. Jan. 15, 2002), the court found that the cost of the needed alterations must be compared with the gross profits of the business, rather than the net profits. It was determined to be a question of fact whether an $8,344 expense was readily achievable when compared with $308,000 in gross profits. In *Parr v. L & L Drive-Inn Restaurant*, 96 F.Supp.2d 1065 (D. Haw. 2000), the court found that installation of an accessible parking space was not readily achievable because, although it was inexpensive, it would require the business not only to lose a parking space in a small parking lot that it shared with other businesses, but also to violate a local parking ordinance. In *Guzman v. Denny's, Inc.*, 40 F.Supp.2d 930, 936 n.4 (S.D. Ohio 1999), the court did not find that the reduction of a restaurant's storage space by one quarter to one third constituted a significant loss as a matter of law. In *Alford*, the court found that, as a matter of law, a loss of

over 41 percent of a shop's inventory and retail space made a proposed alteration not readily achievable. Alford, 2002 WL 31439173, at *10.

4. The parties in *Lieber* use expert witnesses abundantly. What standards apply to expert witness testimony? For instance, in recommending building modifications, must testimony include a "detailed cost analysis"? *Compare* Lieber v. Macy's West, Inc. 80 F. Supp. 2d 1065, 1065-73 (N.D. Cal. 1999) *with* Gathright-Dietrich v. Atlanta Landmarks, Inc., No. 05-14229, 2006 WL 1716751, at *4 (11th Cir. June 23, 2006) ("these proposals were non-specific, conceptual proposals that did not provide any detailed cost analysis").

5. Federal buildings, including buildings leased by federal agencies, and those designed, built, or altered with federal funds, are subject to the Architectural Barriers Act (ABA), 42 U.S.C. §§ 4151-57 (2006), rather than the ADA. In December 2005, the U.S. Access Board released the ABA guidelines that will supercede the Uniform Federal Accessibility Standards. U.S. Access Bd., Update of ADA and ABA Standards (2005), http://www.access-board.gov/ada-aba/standards-update. htm.

6. The Department of Justice treats hand controls on vehicles as a matter of readily achievable barrier removal. Therefore, rental car companies must install hand controls on a vehicle when necessary to allow a person with a disability to drive. Whether the request is readily achievable may depend on the amount of notice needed to acquire and install the controls. *See* TAM III, *supra*, § 4.4200. Why are hand controls an issue of barrier removal rather than reasonable modification of policy?

7. Because Title III provides only for prospective injunctive relief, to have standing, a plaintiff must demonstrate that he or she will return to the business in the future. How can a person with a disability demonstrate standing? Should a person with one type of disability be allowed to challenge barriers to people with other types of disabilities (e.g., should a wheelchair user be allowed to challenge a restaurant's failure to provide Braille signage)? Should a person with a disability be allowed to challenge access barriers at an entire chain of restaurants that are built according to the same design but that she has not visited? *See* Parr, 96 F.Supp.2d at 1079; *see also* Eve L. Hill & Peter Blanck, *Future of Disability Rights: Parte Three Statutes of Limitations in the Americans with Disabilites Act "Design and Construction Cases,"* 60 Syracuse L. Rev. 125 (2009).

৵

B. *Alterations*

Title III entities, including both public accommodations and commercial facilities, making alterations or renovations to existing facilities for other than barrier removal purposes must "make such alterations . . . in such a manner that, to the maximum extent feasible, the altered portions of the facility are readily accessible to and usable by individuals with disabilities, including individuals who use wheelchairs. . . ." 42 U.S.C. § 12147(a) (2006). This requirement applies to alterations that began after January 26, 1992. 28 C.F.R. § 36.402(a)(1) (2008). Any construction that starts on or after March 15, 2012, must adhere to the updated 2010 ADA Standards for accessible design. These new standards include both the 2004 ADAAG Standards at 36 C.F.R. part 1191, appendices B and D and the Title II regulations at 28 C.F.R. part 35.151. *See* Department of Justice, *2010 ADA Standards for Accessible Design*, (Sept. 15, 2010), *available at* http://www.ada.gov/regs2010/2010ADA Standards/2010ADAStandards.pdf.

Both public accommodations and commercial facilities must comply with the requirements for alterations. *Id.* § 36.402(a). *See generally* TAM III, *supra*. Alterations that make a facility less accessible than before the alteration are not permitted. *Id.* pt. 36 app. A, ADAAG, § 4.1.6(a). Alterations generally must comply with the ADAAG standards for new construction unless compliance is technically infeasible. 28 C.F.R. § 36.406(a).

An alteration covered by Title III is "a change to a place of public accommodation or a commercial facility that affects or could affect the usability of the building or facility or any part thereof." *Id.* § 36.402(b). Additions are treated as alterations. *Id.* pt. 36 app. A, § 4.1.5.

A "facility" is defined broadly as "all or any portion of buildings, structures, sites, complexes, equipment, rolling stock or other conveyances, roads, walks, passageways, parking lots, or other real or personal property, including the site where the building, property, structure, or equipment is located." *Id.* § 36.104. Therefore, changes to equipment, such as rail ticket vending machines and emergency alarm boxes have been treated as alterations required to be made accessible. Molloy v. Metro. Transp. Auth., 94 F.3d 808, 812 (2d Cir. 1996) (ticket vending machines). However, the term facility only includes objects that are in a fixed location and "connected to a broader infrastructure." American Ass'n of People with Disabilities v. Harris, 647 F.3d 1093, 1106 (11th Cir. 2011) (holding that voting machines were not part of the facility). The same principles apply to alterations under Title II and Title III. Civic Ass'n of the Deaf of N.Y. City v. Giuliani, 970 F.Supp. 352, 359 (S.D.N.Y. 1997) (emergency alarm boxes).

Historic buildings are not exempted from compliance. Instead, alterations to historic buildings generally are required to comply with the ADAAG, to the maximum extent possible, including the path of travel requirement, unless providing access will threaten or destroy the historic significance of the building. 28 C.F.R. § 36.405(b) (2008); *id.* pt. 36 app. A, § 4.1.7 (providing procedures for determination of threat to historic significance). Historic buildings are those listed or eligible for listing on the National Register of Historic Places under the National Historic

Preservation Act or designated as historic under state or local law. 28 C.F.R. § 36.405(a).

1.   Path of travel

In addition to making any altered element accessible, a public accommodation or commercial facility has additional obligations whenever it undertakes an alteration that affects or could affect the usability of an area that contains a primary function. *Id.* § 36.403(a). A primary function is "a major activity for which the facility is intended." *Id.* § 36.403(b). Examples include:

> the customer service lobby of a bank, the dining area of a cafeteria, the meeting rooms in a conference center, as well as offices and other work areas in which the activities of the [entity] are carried out. Mechanical rooms, boiler rooms, supply storage rooms, employee lounges or locker rooms, janitorial closets, entrances, corridors, and restrooms are not areas containing a primary function.

Id. Alterations to primary function areas include:

> (i) Remodeling merchandise display areas or employee work areas in a department store; (ii) Replacing an inaccessible floor surface in the customer service or employee work areas of a bank; (iii) Redesigning the assembly line area of a factory; or (iv) Installing a computer center in an accounting firm.

Id. § 36.403(c)(1).

When a primary function area is altered, the covered entity must dedicate an additional 20 percent of the overall cost of the alteration to ensure that the path of travel to the altered area and the restrooms, telephones, and drinking fountains that serve the altered area, are accessible. *Id.* § 36.403(a), (f). A path of travel is a pedestrian "passage by means of which the altered area may be approached, entered, and exited, and which connects the altered area with an exterior approach, . . . an entrance to the facility, and other parts of the facility." 28 C.F.R. § 36.403(e).

2.   Technically infeasible

Alterations and path of travel alterations only have to be made accessible "to the maximum extent feasible." *Id.* § 36.402(c). Put another way, accessibility modifications that are technically infeasible do not have to be made. This is a fairly narrow exception "where the nature of the existing facility makes it virtually impossible to comply fully with applicable accessibility standards." *Id.* If it is technically infeasible to comply with the ADAAG new construction standards, ADAAG provides fall-back standards for alterations. 28 C.F.R. pt. 36 app. A, § 4.1.6.

Notes & Questions

1.   When should the statute of limitations begin running on an alteration that does not comply with the ADA standards? When the alteration is completed? When the individual with a disability visits the altered site? Plaintiffs argue typically that failure to comply with the ADA requirements is an ongoing violation and the statute of limitations should begin to run whenever an individual with a disability actually encounters the inaccessible feature. This argument has merit, as a plaintiff probably does not have standing to challenge a barrier until he has actually encountered it. Moreno v. G&M Oil Co., 88 F.Supp.2d 1116, 1117 (C.D. Cal. 2000). However, one court has held that the statute of limitations should run from the date of the alteration's completion. Speciner v. Nationsbank, N.A., 215 F.Supp.2d 622, 634-35 (D. Md. 2002). *See also* Hill & Blanck, *supra.*

2.   Do alterations to automated check-in kiosks at airports trigger the ADAAG?

C.   *New Construction*

Buildings constructed for first occupancy after January 26, 1993 must be fully accessible in accordance with the ADAAG standards. 28 C.F.R. § 36.401 (2008). The exception to full compliance with ADAAG occurs when the entity can demonstrate that full compliance is structurally impracticable. *Id.* § 36.401(c). Structural impracticability will be found "only in those rare circumstances when the unique characteristics of terrain prevent the incorporation of accessibility features." *Id.*

1.   ADAAG

The ADA Accessibility Guidelines provide general, scoping (i.e., how many of each element must be accessible), and technical (i.e., what an accessible element looks like) standards and are codified at 28 C.F.R. pt. 36 app. A (2008). The general provisions, including definitions, are in ADAAG sections 1-3.

The scoping provisions are in sections 4.1.1-4.1.7, while the technical standards are in sections 4.2-4.35. Additional scoping and technical standards for particular types of facilities are provided in:

Section 5 for restaurants and cafeterias,

Section 6 for medical facilities,

Section 7 for business and mercantile facilities,

Section 8 for libraries,

Section 9 for transient lodging,

Section 10 for transportation facilities,

Section 11 (proposed) for judicial, legislative and regulatory facilities, and

Section 12 (proposed) for detention facilities.

Section 15 for recreation facilities

Sections 11, 12, and 15 have been proposed by the Architectural and Transportation Barriers Compliance Board but have not been adopted by the Department of Justice and, therefore, are not enforceable. Proposed standards for residential facilities and for public rights of way have been reserved. 28 C.F.R. pt. 36 app. A, §§ 11-12. The proposed sections have been adopted by the U.S. Architectural and Transportation Barriers Compliance Board ("Access Board"), but have not been approved by the U.S. Department of Justice and, therefore, are not in effect at the time of printing. The Access Board published the final regulations for outdoor recreational facilities in September 2013. Architectural Barriers Act Accessibility Guidelines; Outdoor Developed Areas, 78 Fed. Reg. 59476-01 (Sept. 26, 2013).

The ADAAG allows departures from particular technical and scoping requirements if other designs and technologies will provide substantially equivalent or greater access to and usability of the facility. 28 C.F.R. pt. 36 app. A, § 2.2. Means of equivalent facilitation are acceptable only if they are at least as accessible as the ADAAG standards.

CARUSO v. BLOCKBUSTER-SONY MUSIC ENTERTAINMENT CENTRE

United States Court of Appeals, Third Circuit, 1999
193 F.3d 730

ALITO, Circuit J.

The Blockbuster-Sony Music Entertainment Centre ("E-Centre") is a music and entertainment facility located in Camden, New Jersey. An interior pavilion at the E-Centre provides fixed seating for 6,200 patrons, and an uncovered lawn area located behind the pavilion can accommodate approximately 18,000 spectators who either stand or sit on portable chairs or blankets.

Appellant William Caruso, a Vietnam veteran who uses a wheelchair as a result of his disability, attended a concert at the E-Centre on July 13, 1995. The following day, Caruso and the Advocates for Disabled Americans filed a complaint in federal district court alleging, *inter alia,* that the E-Center does not comply with Title III of the Americans with Disabilities Act (ADA) * * * 42 U.S.C. § 12181 et seq.,

* * * because: 1) the wheelchair areas in the pavilion do not provide wheelchair users with lines of sight over standing spectators and 2) the lawn area is not wheelchair accessible. The District Court granted summary judgment in favor of the defendants on both claims. We now affirm in part and reverse in part.

I.

Title III of the ADA protects individuals against discrimination "on the basis of disability in the full and equal enjoyment of the goods, services, facilities, privileges, advantages, or accommodations of any place of public accommodation." 42 U.S.C. § 12182(a). Title III requires that newly constructed facilities be "readily accessible to and usable by individuals with disabilities, except where an entity can demonstrate that it is structurally impracticable." 42 U.S.C. § 12183. In order to carry out these provisions, Congress has directed the Department of Justice (DOJ) to "issue regulations . . . that include standards applicable to facilities" covered by Title III. 42 U.S.C. § 12186(b). Congress has further required that any standards included by the DOJ in its regulations "be consistent with the minimum guidelines and requirements issued by the Architectural and Transportation Barriers Compliance Board" ("Access Board"). 42 U.S.C. § 12186(c).

Pursuant to its statutory authority under Title III, the DOJ has issued numerous regulations, see 28 C.F.R. §§ 36.101-36.608 (1998), one of which adopts the Access Board's guidelines as the DOJ's own Standards for New Construction and Alterations ("Standards"). * * * Both of the issues in this case require us to interpret portions of the DOJ Standards.

A. Lines of Sight

Appellants contend that DOJ Standard 4.33.3, which was adopted after notice and comment, requires wheelchair seats in the E-Center pavilion to afford sightlines over standing spectators. Standard 4.33.3 provides:

> Placement of Wheelchair Locations. Wheelchair areas shall be an integral part of any fixed seating plan and shall be provided so as to provide people with physical disabilities a choice of admission prices and lines of sight comparable to those for members of the general public. They shall adjoin an accessible route that also serves as a means of egress in case of emergency. At least one companion fixed seat shall be provided next to each wheelchair seating area. When the seating capacity exceeds 300, wheelchair spaces shall be provided in more than one location. . . .

28 C.F.R. pt. 36, app. A, 4.33.3.

Appellants first argue that the plain meaning of the phrase "lines of sight comparable to those for members of the general public" requires that "if standing spectators can see the stage even when other patrons stand, wheelchair users, too, must be able to see the stage when other patrons stand." * * * While this argument has considerable force, it does not account for the rest of the language in Standard 4.33.3, which helps the reader to place the phrase "lines of sight comparable" in context. Standard 4.33.3 is entitled "Placement of Wheelchair Locations" and includes at least two provisions concerning the dispersal of wheelchair locations in facilities with fixed seating plans. In addition, one of these dispersal provisions appears in the same sentence that contains the "lines of sight" requirement. Given this focus on the dispersal of wheelchair locations, it seems plausible to read the "lines of sight comparable" requirement as follows: if a facility's seating plan provides members of the general public with different lines of sight to the field or stage (e.g., lines of sight at a baseball game from behind the plate, on either side of the diamond, and from the outfield bleachers), it must also provide wheelchair users with a comparable opportunity to view the field or stage from a variety of angles.

Appellants reject this suggestion that the "lines of sight" provision might require dispersal rather than vertical enhancement, contending that such a reading would impermissibly render other portions of Standard 4.33.3 superfluous. They argue:

> Standard 4.33.3 . . . contains an explicit dispersal provision, wholly independent of the "comparable" line of sight provision. It requires, in pertinent part, that "[w]heelchair areas . . . shall be provided so as to provide persons with disabilities a choice of admission prices." For facilities, such as modern sports and entertainment venues, that offer tickets at a range of prices depending on seating location, dispersal of wheelchair locations is required by this provision. Moreover, a requirement for dispersal is also derived from the language in Standard 4.33.3 that "[w]hen the seating capacity exceeds 300, wheelchair spaces shall be provided in more than one location." Construing the phrase "lines of sight comparable to those provided to members of the general public" as simply requiring dispersal of wheelchair locations, as the E-Centre urges, is contrary to the plain language of that regulation and would deprive important parts of the regulation of any meaning. * * *

This attempt to divorce the "lines of sight" requirement from the two provisions in 4.33.3 that are indisputably about dispersion overlooks the possibility that the three provisions are designed to work together so that: 1) at a minimum, facilities with over 300 seats provide at least two wheelchair locations and 2) larger facilities provide wheelchair users with the option of choosing from among seats that afford a variety of views for a variety of *corresponding* prices. Contrary to appellants' assertion, this second result is not accomplished by the "choice of admission prices" language alone. For, if Standard 4.33.3 is read in piecemeal fashion as appellants suggest, a facility, regardless of its size and the number of views that it offers to the general public, would be able to place all wheelchair users in just two locations so long at it offers some choice of prices in those locations. See Independent Living Resources v. Oregon Arena Corp., 982 F.Supp. 698, 743 n.61 (D. Or. 1997).

In the end, it seems that both interpretations of the "lines of sight" language are plausible and would provide some benefit to wheelchair users. Appellants' reading would benefit wheelchair users by allowing them to see when other patrons stand. The E-Centre's reading would benefit wheelchair users by providing them with a greater opportunity to view a performance or event from a variety of viewpoints. Since both readings of the rule are plausible and are consistent with the ADA's purpose of enabling people with disabilities to share equally in the benefits provided by a public accommodation, we conclude that the "lines of sight" language is ambiguous.

Appellants' second contention is that, even if Standard 4.33.3 is ambiguous, the court should follow the interpretation that has been given to the rule by the DOJ. * * *

> In addition to requiring companion seating and dispersion of wheelchair locations, [Standard 4.33.3] requires that wheelchair locations provide people with disabilities lines of sight comparable to those for members of the general public. *Thus, in assembly areas where spectators can be expected to stand during the event or show being viewed, the wheelchair locations must provide lines of sight over spectators who stand.* This can be accomplished in many ways, including placing wheelchair locations at the front of a seating section, or by providing sufficient additional elevation for wheelchair locations placed at the rear of seating sections to allow those spectators to see over the spectators who stand in front of them.

1994 DOJ TAM Supp. ¶ III-7.5180, Conditional App. at 49 (emphasis added).

In response, appellees maintain that the 1994 TAM Supplement is not an interpretive rule entitled to deference, but rather, an invalid attempt to adopt a new substantive requirement without notice and comment. The E-Centre bases this argument on the history of Standard 4.33.3, which, according to the E-Centre, reveals that the rule was not intended to address the issue of lines of sight over standing patrons.

Standard 4.33.3 was originally proposed by the Access Board on January 22, 1991. At that time, the provision provided:

> Placement of Wheelchair Locations. Wheelchair areas shall be an integral part of any fixed seating plan and shall be

dispersed throughout the seating area. They shall ... be located to provide lines of sight comparable to those for all viewing areas.

56 Fed. Reg. 2380. In its public notice regarding the proposed rule, the Access Board explicitly invited comments on the issue of sightlines over standing spectators:

> Section 4.33.3 provides that seating locations for people who use wheelchairs shall be dispersed throughout the seating area and shall be located to provide lines of sight comparable to those for all viewing areas. *This requirement appears to be adequate for theaters and concert halls, but may not suffice in sports arenas or race tracks where the audience frequently stands throughout a large portion of the game or event.* In alterations of existing sports arenas, accessible spaces are frequently provided at the lower part of a seating tier projecting out above a lower seating tier or are built out over existing seats at the top of a tier providing a great differential in height. These solutions can work in newly constructed sports arenas as well, if sight lines relative to standing patrons are considered at the time of the initial design. *The Board seeks comments on whether full lines of sight over standing spectators in sports arenas and other similar assembly areas should be required.*

56 Fed. Reg. 2314 (emphasis added).

On February 22, 1991, the DOJ published a notice in which it proposed to adopt the Access Board's Proposed Guidelines "with any amendments made by the [Access Board] during the rulemaking process." 56 Fed. Reg. 7478-79. The DOJ notice stated that "any comments" on the Access Board's Proposed Guidelines should be sent directly to the Board. Id. at 7479.

On July 26, 1991, the Access Board announced its proposed final guidelines. Along with the guidelines, the Board published commentary, including two passages relevant to the meaning of the "lines of sight comparable" language in 4.33.3. First, the Board gave the following response to comments on dispersal:

> Response. The requirements in 4.33.3 for dispersal of wheelchair seating spaces have been modified. Wheelchair seating spaces must be an integral part of any fixed seating plan and be situated so as to provide wheelchair users a choice of admission prices and lines of sight comparable to those available to the rest of the public. . . .

56 Fed. Reg. 35440. By discussing the "lines of sight" requirement in the section of the commentary concerning dispersal, the Board appeared to be indicating that it was treating this requirement, like the choice of price

requirement, as a dispersal requirement. The Board then went on to consider the issue of sightlines over standing patrons in a separate section of the commentary:

> Comment. The [Board] asked questions regarding . . . lines of sight over standing spectators in sports arenas and other similar assembly areas. . . . Many commenters . . . recommended that lines of sight should be provided over standing spectators.

> Response. . . . *The issue of lines of sight over standing spectators will be addressed in guidelines*[5] *for recreational facilities.*

Id. (emphasis added).

On the same day that the Access Board issued its proposed guidelines, including the above comment and response seemingly deferring the issue of standing lines of sight, the DOJ promulgated Standard 4.33.3, which is worded identically to the Access Board's final proposed text, which addressed the sight-line issue. Unlike the Board, the Department did not initially express a view in its commentary on the issue of sightlines over standing spectators. Rather, in explaining its adoption of the Access Board's guidelines, the DOJ made the following general statement:

> The Department put the public on notice, through the proposed rule, of its intention to adopt the proposed [guidelines], with any changes made by the Board, as the accessibility standards. As a member of the Board and of its ADA Task Force, the Department participated actively in the public hearings held on the proposed guidelines and in preparation of both the proposed and final versions of [the guidelines] . . . [All] comments on the Department's proposed rule . . . have been addressed adequately in the final [guidelines]. Largely in response to comments, the Board made numerous changes from its proposal.

28 C.F.R. pt. 36, app. B, at 632-33.

The next discussion of the sightlines issue came in a 1992 Notice of Proposed Rulemaking published by the Access Board. There the Board

---

[5]   It is important to note the difference between Access Board guidelines and DOJ guidelines. For the Access Board, guidelines are the substantive rules they develop and promulgate. Thus, in speaking of a future guideline, the Board was not referring to a future interpretation of 4.33.3, but rather, a separate substantive rule it would develop. By contrast, a DOJ guideline is an interpretation of a substantive rule, not the substantive rule itself.

summarized what had occurred during the 1991 notice and comment period with regard to 4.33.3 and expressed its future intentions:

> During the initial rulemaking, the Board requested information on lines of sight at seating locations for persons who use wheelchairs. . . . An overwhelming majority of responses favored including a provision requiring lines of sight over standing spectators in sports arenas and other similar assembly areas. A few commenters opposed such a provision because it would be either unenforceable, add significant cost or reduce seating capacity. . . . *The Board intends to address the issue of lines of sight over standing spectators in the guidelines for recreational facilities which will be proposed at a future date.*
>
> Question 17: *The Board is seeking comments on the design issues associated with providing integrated and dispersed accessible seating locations with a clear line of sight over standing spectators in arenas, stadiums or other sports facilities.* Clearly, not all seats in sports facilities afford clear lines of sight over standing spectators. Tall persons, guard railings or other fixed elements in the facility may block one's view of the playing field. However, since persons with disabilities have fewer choices of seating locations, *should all the accessible seating locations be required to have lines of sight over standing spectators?* Would such a requirement compromise the requirement for dispersed wheelchair seating by providing seating in fewer locations? If maximum dispersal of accessible seating locations is provided, what percentage of such locations can be provided with a clear line of sight over standing spectators? The Board encourages commenters to provide cost information and examples (including drawings, pictures or slides) of sports facilities where the accessible seating locations are dispersed, integrated and provide clear lines of sight over standing spectators.

57 Fed. Reg. 060618 (emphasis added).

Based on this regulatory history, the E-Centre contends that Standard 4.33.3 was intended to leave unresolved the issue of lines of sight over standing spectators, and, as a result, the DOJ was not entitled to "interpret" Standard 4.33.3 in 1994 in a fashion that did resolve the issue of sightlines over standing spectators. * * * The E-Centre maintains that, if the DOJ wanted to impose a new requirement that wheelchair users be able to see over standing patrons, it had to engage in notice and comment, since such a requirement would constitute a new substantive rule. See 5 U.S.C. § 553(b) & (c) (notice and comment procedure required for substantive rules but not interpretive rules); *Dia Navigation Co. v.*

Pomeroy, 34 F.3d 1255, 1264 (3d Cir. 1994) (explaining that a rule is substantive if "the agency intends to create new law, rights or duties").

Appellants dispute the E-Centre's characterization of the 1994 DOJ statement as a "substantive" rule. They argue that, because the DOJ did not explicitly adopt the Access Board's commentary, the meaning of Standard 4.33.3 was not limited by that commentary when it was adopted, and thus the 1994 statement does not constitute a "change" in the requirements under 4.33.3. They also maintain that even if the Access Board's commentary can be attributed to the DOJ, the DOJ was entitled to change its interpretation of Standard 4.33.3 in 1994 without notice and comment.

With regard to the threshold question of whether the Access Board's commentary can be attributed to the DOJ, the appellants rely on the District of Columbia Circuit's analysis in *Paralyzed Veterans of America v. D.C. Arena L.P.,* 117 F.3d 579 (D.C. Cir. 1997):

> If the Department, when it promulgated the regulation, had said what the Board said, or even clearly adopted what the Board said, it would be hard to conclude that the Department did not subsequently "amend" the regulation in violation of the APA. But Justice did not do so in its statement of basis and purpose. It never referred to the Board's concern, nor did it imply that its regulation did not address the problem of lines of sight over standing spectators. It may well be that it is a plausible inference that Justice, at the time, deliberately intended the regulation to mean the same thing as did the Board – but it is not a necessary inference. . . . We admit the issue is not easy: appellants almost but do not quite establish that the Department significantly changed its interpretation of the regulation when it issued the 1994 technical manual.

Id. at 587.

We agree that "the issue is not easy," 117 F.3d at 587, but we respectfully disagree with the District of Columbia Circuit's conclusion that the DOJ did not adopt what the Access Board had said. Instead, we conclude that the DOJ implicitly adopted the Access Board's analysis of 4.33.3. This conclusion is strongly supported by the following factors: 1) the DOJ referred all comments to the Board; 2) the DOJ relied on the Board to make adequate changes based on those comments; 3) the Board specifically changed the language of 4.33.3 in response to comments and explained that change in its commentary; 4) the DOJ was a "member of the Board" and "participated actively . . . in preparation of both the proposed and final versions of the [guidelines]," 28 C.F.R. pt. 36, app. B, at 632; and 5) the DOJ's commentary stated that the final guidelines promulgated by the Board adequately addressed all comments. *Accord*

Independent Living Resources v. Oregon Arena Corporation, 982 F.Supp. 698, 741 (D. Or. 1997).

[2] We thus agree with the appellants that 4.33.3, when viewed in light of the regulatory history recounted above, does not reach the issue of sightlines over standing spectators. A court should not defer to an agency's interpretation of its own regulation if "an alternative reading is compelled by . . . indications of the [agency's] intent at the time of the regulation's promulgation." *Thomas Jefferson University v. Shalala,* 512 U.S. 504, 512 (1994). Thus, we do not accept the interpretation set out in the DOJ Technical Assistance manual. "An agency is not allowed to change a legislative rule retroactively through the process of disingenuous interpretation of the rule to mean something other than its original meaning." 1 Kenneth Culp Davis And Richard J. Pierce, Jr., Administrative Law Treatise § 6.10 at 283 (1994).

The DOJ could, of course, adopt a new substantive regulation to require that wheelchair users be given lines of sight equivalent to standing patrons – and such a rule certainly has much to recommend it – but to do this it must proceed with notice-and-comment rulemaking.

B. Access to the Lawn Area

Appellants' second contention is that the E-Centre does not comply with the ADA because there is no wheelchair access to the lawn area. In relevant part, Title III requires that the facilities of a public accommodation be "readily accessible to and usable by individuals with disabilities, except where an entity can demonstrate that it is structurally impracticable." 42 U.S.C. § 12183(a)(1). To implement this mandate, the DOJ has adopted a regulation requiring that "[a]t least one accessible route . . . connect accessible buildings, accessible facilities, accessible elements, and accessible *spaces* that are on the same site." Standard 4.1.2(3) (emphasis added). Consistent with this provision, the appellants seek "at least one wheelchair lift to . . . provide access to the lawn area from the two outdoor plazas." * * * The E-Centre would appear obligated to provide such access unless it can demonstrate structural impracticability.

The DOJ has explained in its regulations that the structural impracticability exception is reserved for "those rare circumstances when the unique characteristics of terrain prevent the incorporation of accessibility features." 28 C.F.R. § 36.401(c). Additional guidance, some of which is directly on point, can be found in the DOJ commentary that was published with the regulations:

> Consistent with the legislative history of the ADA, this narrow exception will apply only in rare and unusual circumstances where unique characteristics of terrain make accessibility unusually difficult. . . . Almost all commenters supported this interpretation. *Two commenters argued that*

the DOJ requirement is too limiting. . . . These commenters suggested consistency with HUD's Fair Housing Accessibility Guidelines, which generally would allow exceptions from accessibility requirements, or allow compliance with less stringent requirements, on sites with slopes exceeding 10%.

The Department is aware of the provisions in HUD's guidelines. . . . The approach taken in these guidelines, *738 which apply to different types of construction and implement different statutory requirements for new construction, does not bind this Department in regulating under the ADA . . . .

The limited structural impracticability exception means that it is acceptable to deviate from accessibility requirements only where unique characteristics of terrain prevent the incorporation of accessibility features and where providing accessibility would destroy the physical integrity of a facility. A situation in which a building must be built on stilts because of its location in marshlands or over water is an example of one of the few situations in which the exception for structural impracticability would apply.

This exception to accessibility requirements should not be applied to situations in which a facility is located in "hilly" terrain or on a plot of land upon which there are steep grades. In such circumstances, accessibility can be achieved without destroying the physical integrity of a structure, and is required in the construction of new facilities.

28 C.F.R. pt. 36, app. B, at 649 (emphasis added).

This passage indicates that public accommodations cannot demonstrate structural impracticability merely by providing evidence of a slope of over 10%. Yet, this is precisely how the E-Centre tries to show that "it is impossible to make the lawn area wheelchair accessible." * * * The E-Centre has presented no argument as to why it cannot provide a ramp or a lift that would enable wheelchair users to reach the lawn area. Moreover, Caruso has introduced affidavits from people who have visited other concert venues with sloping grass areas that are wheelchair accessible. * * *

Not surprisingly, the E-Centre does not focus on the "structural impracticability" issue, and instead presses two other arguments. First, it contends that it need not provide wheelchair access to the lawn area because the DOJ Standards only require wheelchair seating to be provided when there is fixed seating for the general public. * * * This argument, however, misconstrues the issue being appealed. Caruso is not asking that the E-Centre be required to construct wheelchair seating areas on the lawn that comply with the various requirements governing fixed seating plans. Rather, he is merely seeking an accessible route to the lawn area. Caruso is entitled to such a route under the regulations regardless of whether or not the facility is also required to meet the more specific DOJ Standards concerning fixed seating plans. See 28 C.F.R. § 36.401(c)(2) ("[A]ny portion of the facility that can be made accessible shall be made accessible to the extent that is not structurally impracticable."); id., pt. 36, app. A, Standard 4.1.1(5)(a) (same); id. Standard 4.1.2(2) ("At least one accessible route . . . shall connect . . . accessible spaces that are on the same site."). Accordingly, we reject the argument that assembly areas without fixed seating need not provide access to people in wheelchairs.

The E-Centre's other justification for failing to provide access is based on the "Equivalent Facilitation" provision in the DOJ Standards. It states:

> Departures from particular technical and scoping requirements of this guideline by the use of other designs and technologies are permitted where the alternative designs and technologies used will provide substantially equivalent or greater access to and usability of the facility.

DOJ Standard 2.2. The E-Centre contends that it has provided "equivalent facilitation" for wheelchair users by placing additional wheelchair locations in the interior pavilion. * * * The District Court agreed and granted summary judgment for the E-Centre on this basis.

The principal problem with the E-Centre's "equivalent facilitation" argument is that it treats the ADA's requirement of equal access for people with disabilities as a "particular technical and scoping requirement." This is simply not the case. Rather, equal access is an explicit requirement of both the statute itself and the general provisions of the DOJ's regulations. See 42 U.S.C. § 12183; 28 C.F.R. § 36.401. Properly read, the "Equivalent Facilitation" provision does not allow facilities to deny access under certain circumstances, but instead allows facilities to bypass the technical requirements laid out in the Standards when alternative designs will provide "equivalent or greater access to and usability of the facility." Therefore, we conclude that the E-Centre cannot rely on the "Equivalent Facilitation" provision to excuse its failure to provide any wheelchair access to an assembly area that accommodates 18,000 people.

Furthermore, as noted by Caruso in his appellate brief, the language of Title III itself precludes a reading of the "Equivalent Facilitation" provision that would allow venues to restrict wheelchair access to certain areas based on a belief that wheelchair users will be better off elsewhere. See 42 U.S.C. § 12182(b)(1)(A)(iii) (discriminatory to provide a separate benefit unless necessary to provide equal benefit); id. at (b)(1)(B) (benefits of a public accommodation must be provided in the most integrated setting appropriate to the needs of the individual). As the DOJ explains in its commentary:

> Taken together, [the statutory and regulatory provisions concerning separate benefits and integrated settings] are intended to prohibit exclusion and segregation of individuals with disabilities and the denial of equal opportunities enjoyed by others, based on, among other things, presumptions, patronizing attitudes, fears, and stereotypes about individuals with disabilities. Consistent with these standards, public accommodations are required to make decisions based on facts applicable to individuals and not on the basis of presumptions as to what a class of individuals with disabilities can or cannot do. . . . Separate, special, or different programs that are designed to provide a benefit to persons with disabilities cannot be used to restrict the participation of persons with disabilities in general, integrated activities.

28 C.F.R. pt. 36, app. B., at 622.

The District Court, in concluding that the E-Centre had not violated Title III by failing to provide access to the lawn area, appeared to give precisely the type of justification that the DOJ commentary finds repugnant to the ADA:

> The E-Centre provides the disabled with higher quality (i.e. closer) seats in the pavilion for the same price as lawn seats. Plaintiffs do not offer any reasons why the interior seats are not equivalent or superior to lawn seating. In our view, the E-Centre provides equal, if not greater, access to its facility for wheelchair users in the interior than it does for non-wheelchair users on the lawn.

968 F.Supp. at 218. On appeal, the E-Centre reiterates this argument that it is acceptable to restrict wheelchair users from the lawn area because they provide "higher quality (i.e. closer) seats in the pavilion." * * * We reject this contention as inconsistent with the plain language of Title III. See 42 U.S.C. § 12182(b)(1)(c) ("Notwithstanding the existence of separate or different programs or activities . . . an individual with a disability shall not be denied the opportunity to participate in such programs or activities that are not separate or different."). We further conclude that the only way the E-Centre can justify its failure to provide access to the lawn area is by showing structural impracticability. Since the E-Centre has not yet made such a showing, we reverse the grant of summary judgment on Caruso's lawn-access claim and remand for further proceedings related to this claim.

II.

For the reasons explained above, we affirm the decision of the District Court in part, and we reverse in part, and we remand for further proceedings consistent with this opinion.

Notes & Questions

1. The Department of Justice has taken the position that stadiums and other venues where spectators may be expected to stand up during events must ensure that wheelchair seats provide lines of sight above the shoulders and between the head of spectators standing in front of the wheelchair seating. *See* Disability Rights Section, U.S. Dep't of Justice, Accessible Stadiums 2, *available at* http://www.ada.gov/stadium. pdf (last visited Apr. 7, 2009). However, courts have split on the issue. *Compare* Caruso, *supra, with* Paralyzed Veterans of America v. D.C. Arena L.P., 117 F.3d 579, 589 (D.C. Cir. 1997) (applying the Department of Justice's interpretation requiring substantially all wheelchair seats to provide lines of sight over standing spectators) and *Miller v. California Speedway*, 536 F.3d 1020, 1027-28 (9th Cir. 2008) ("[T]he parties all concede that the Attorney General's lines-of-sight regulations would clearly pass muster if challenged under the ADA.").

2. The legal question regarding lines of sight revolves around whether the Department's informal interpretation, published without notice and comment, is entitled to judicial deference. As a practical matter, however, do you believe Congress intended to require wheelchair seating to provide lines of sight over standing spectators when inaccessible seating does not guarantee that a spectator will be able to see over the spectator standing in front? Is such seating "comparable"?

3. Is it more important to require specificity in accessibility guidelines for building-related access (such as the ADA Accessibility Guidelines), than it is for program-related access (which often simply require "effective" or "reasonable" access)? Why or why not? Should the government be held to a higher standard of clarity or specificity in building design guidelines?

Another contested issue regarding ADAAG § 4.33.3 is whether wheelchair seating in stadium-style movie theatres has to offer choices of position within the theater and whether it has to be integrated into the stadium seating section of the theatre. The dispute has centered on 4.33.3's requirements that patrons with disabilities be offered "comparable" "lines of sight" to nondisabled viewers, and that wheelchair seating be "an integral part of any fixed seating plan." In *Lara v. Cinemark USA, Inc.*, 207 F.3d 783 (5th Cir. 2000), the Fifth Circuit held that § 4.33.3 required only lines of sight that are unobstructed, and held that it did not require viewing angles that are as comfortable as those required by the general public. Therefore, Cinemark theatres were permitted to put wheelchair seats at the bottom of the theatres, forcing patrons in wheelchairs to crane their necks uncomfortably to see the screen.

In *United States v. Hoyts Cinemas Corp.*, 380 F.3d 558, 568-69 (1st Cir. 2004), the First Circuit disagreed, finding that wheelchair accessible seating must be placed in the stadium section of a theater if the view from the non-stadium section is worse. The Central District of California also has found that stadium-style movie seating must include wheelchair accessible seats in the stadium section of the theatre. United States v. Am. Multi-Cinema, Inc., 232 F.Supp.2d 1092, 1112 (C.D. Cal. 2002); *see* United States v. AMC Entm't, Inc., 549 F.3d 760 (9th Cir. 2008) (reversing on other grounds).

In *Oregon Paralyzed Veterans of America v. Regal Cinemas, Inc.*, 339 F.3d 1126 (9th Cir. 2003), *cert. denied Regal Cinemas, Inc. v. Stewmon,* 124 S.Ct. 2903 (2004), the Ninth Circuit reversed a district court's award of summary judgment to the defendant theater owners. The district court had followed the reasoning of the Fifth Circuit in *Lara.* The Ninth Circuit found that the Department of Justice's interpretation of ADAAG § 4.33.3 as requiring comparable viewing angles for wheelchair users, was reasonable and, therefore, entitled to deference.

In *United States v. Hoyts Cinemas Corp.*, 380 F.3d 558 (1st Cir. 2004), the First Circuit disagreed with *Lara,* finding that the "comparable lines of sight" requirement of § 4.33.3 includes angles of sight, not just obstructions. However, the court found that the requirement that wheelchair seating be "integral" did not necessarily require them to be placed within the stadium section of every theater. The U.S. Central District Court of California has also found that stadium style movie seating must include wheelchair accessible seats in the stadium section of the theatre. United States v. Am. Multi-Cinema, Inc. 232 F.Supp.2d 1092 (C.D. Cal. 2002).

§ 16.5   The Complexity Of Compliance

Voluntary compliance with Title III by public accommodations has been disappointing. Some degree of threat or risk associated with a lawsuit generally is more successful. Several studies discussed by the NCD in their 2007 report "Implementation of the Americans with Disabilities Act" found that encouraging voluntary compliance with free mediation services, business-specific technical assistance, monetary incentives (e.g., tax credits, government funds), free compliance surveys, and information and referral services, among others, produced minimal voluntary compliance. Nat'l Council on Disability, Implementation of the Americans with Disabilities Act: Challenges, Best Practices, and New Opportunities for Success 169-79 (July 26, 2007).

Offering free mediation, the Disability Law Center in Massachusetts explained:

We first ask the individual calling with the complaint if he or she is willing to mediate the complaint. In most cases, the individual says yes. They just want access. We then contact the respondent (the owner or manager of the public accommodation), and in most cases the business owner declines to participate. They prefer to hedge their bet and wait to see if someone files the lawsuit.

Id. at 170 (quoting ADA Notification Act, Hearing on H.R. 3590 Before Subcomm. on the Constitution of the House Comm. on the Judiciary, 106th Cong. (2000), at 2000 WL 19303719 (statement of Christine Griffin)).

Similarly, a consortium of small business trade organizations and an Independent Living Center in San Francisco provided extensive outreach over an eighteen month period. This included direct informational mailings containing random $500-$1,000 coupons for technical assistance (TA) to neighborhood merchants, a $25,000 TA fund for accessibility needs surveys and architectural plans (displayed prominently in the Department of Building Inspection), free "easy-to-understand print materials about what accessibility means," media outreach, voluntary dispute resolution, and training by architects on accessibility and other practical solutions. *Id.* at 173. At the end of the TA period, "less than 3% of those offered information responded. Less than .2% requested funds for accessibility surveys or modification planning." *Id.* at 174 (quoting San Francisco Collaborative, Access to San Francisco Small Businesses a Problem for Customers with Disabilities or Risk Management Approach to Small Businesses Failing 2 (2004)).

In contrast, Work Incentives Act (WIA) youth service providers in Chicago, unmotivated by free compliance information and assistance, became highly motivated when the city administrator of WIA funds stepped in. Surveys conducted by Access Living and presented to the 41 WIA youth service providers found that 75% of their entries and bathrooms were inaccessible, and none voluntarily chose to improve accessibility. *Id.* at 171 (citing Telephone interview with Sarah Triano, currently program director at Access Living in Chicago, and then youth and education team leader and project director for the 2001-2003 WIA-funded accessibility project (July 10, 2006)). Then, the Chicago Mayor's Office of Workforce Development, administering local WIA funds, "incorporate[d] an access survey requirement and prefunding policy and procedure for enforcing physical and programmatic accessibility into its WIA funding request for proposals (RFP). . . . "[and] agreed to provide funds for grants to the WIA youth contractors to improve accessibility." *Id.* The threat of not being eligible for future funds prompted WIA service providers, in part, to request replacement copies of the surveys they previously received. Nat'l Council on Disability, *supra*, at 171.

Further investigation into the underlying causes for lacking voluntary Title III compliance indicated significant complexity.

> [I]ronically, some of its complexity arises from an attempt to ensure that small businesses in particular are not subject to an inflexible burden of compliance. Whether barrier removal is readily achievable in any particular business is a case-by-case judgment that depends on factors that include the nature and cost of barrier removal and the size and financial resources of the public accommodation. While this flexibility allows the small mom-and-pop grocery store to avoid being held to the level of barrier removal that could be expected of a supermarket chain store, it also means that businesses in existing facilities cannot follow a simple, industry-wide formula for achieving compliance.

Id. at 179-80 (citations omitted).

Small business owners note that ADA Title III is one of many sets of regulations to which they are subject, including building, fire, health, and other codes. These codes typically are more standardized and easy to follow, and can shut a business down for noncompliance. As such, they take a higher priority for many small business owners. *Id.* at 181. Also, unlike others codes, Title III compliance is not subject to a local or state inspection to approve business operation. *Id.* at 182. Standard inspection procedures provide notice to businesses and typically include a period for correcting identified problems.

Moreover, small business may have economic rationales for avoiding the issue. Especially in states without provisions for recovering compensatory damages, because "enforcement is unlikely to be as expensive as compliance from the date of enactment of the ADA," a business may conclude non-compliance over time is less expensive than paying a modest statutory fine or compensatory award. *Id.* at 185 (quoting Ruth Colker, ADA Title III: A Fragile Compromise, 21 *Berkeley J. Emp. & Lab. L.* 377, 411-412 (2000)).

Chapter 17 ENFORCEMENT AND REMEDIES

Title III aims to provide "full and equal enjoyment" of "goods, services, facilities, privileges, advantages, or accommodations of any place of public accommodation" to people with disabilities. *See supra* Part 5.

Title III does not look retrospectively. The remedies it gives to private parties are prospective and are based on section 204(a) of the Civil Rights Act of 1964. 42 U.S.C. § 2000a-3(a) (2006). Injunctive relief is available, including restraining orders. Obviously, those remedies do not include damages, which are retrospective. *See* Goodwin v. C.N.J., Inc., 436 F.3d 44, 50-51 (1st Cir. 2006), and cases cited therein (restitution not available, because retrospective, like damages; also, no grounds for restitution on facts).

As Professor Colker has chronicled, the breadth of Title III's coverage was purchased at the cost of the strength of its remedies. Ruth Colker, ADA Title III: A Fragile Compromise, 21 Berkeley J. Emp. & Lab. L. 377, 382-85 (2000); *see also* Molly Hughes, Title III of the ADA: More Than an Employment Statute, S.C. Law. (Jan./Feb. 2001), at 18. However, in addition to equitable remedies available to private parties, the Attorney General may seek monetary remedies and civil penalties in appropriate cases.

The ADA's remedial language for private parties asking for relief under Title III, section 308, reads:

(a) In General.

(1) Availability of remedies and procedures. The remedies and procedures set forth in section 204(a) of the Civil Rights Act of 1964 (42 U.S.C. 2000a-3(a)) are the remedies and procedures this title provides to any person who is being subjected to discrimination on the basis of disability in violation of this title or who has reasonable grounds for believing that such person is about to be subjected to discrimination in violation of section 303. Nothing in this section shall require a person with a disability to engage in a futile gesture if such person has actual notice that a person or organization covered by this title does not intend to comply with its provisions.

(2) Injunctive relief. In the case of violations of sections 302(b)(2)(A)(iv) and section 303(a), injunctive relief shall include an order to alter facilities to make such facilities readily accessible to and usable by individuals with disabilities to the extent required by this title. Where appropriate, injunctive relief shall also include requiring the provision of an auxiliary aid or service, modification of a policy, or provision of alternative methods, to the extent required by this title.

42 U.S.C. § 12188(a).

The principal remedial issues under these sections is whether a claimant must hurdle a procedural barrier – notice – before bringing suit, and what constitutes appropriate standing and remediation.

§ 17.1 Procedures

A.   *Notice*

Title III does not by its terms require exhaustion of any administrative process. Nonetheless, early on, some courts found a *notice* requirement implied in the Act. *E.g.*, Burkhart v. Asean Shopping Ctr., Inc., 55 F.Supp.2d 1013 (D. Ariz. 1999), superseded by Botosan v. Paul McNally Realty, 216 F.3d 827, 832 (9th Cir. 2000); Snyder v. San Diego Flowers, 21 F.Supp.2d 1207, 1210-1211 (S.D. Cal. 1998); Mayes v. Allison, 983 F.Supp. 923, 925 (D. Nev. 1997); Daigle v. Friendly Ice Cream Corp., 957 F.Supp. 8, 10 (D.N.H. 1997); Howard v. Cherry Hills Cutters, Inc., 935 F.Supp. 1148, 1150 (D. Colo. 1996). In order to resort to extrinsic interpretive aids, courts must find a statute ambiguous and the *Burkhart*, *Mayes*, *Daigle*, and *Howard* courts did so. Although it refers only to section 204(a) of the Civil Rights Act of 1964, those courts held that it could be read to indicate that Congress intended to import a notice requirement from section 204(c). *See* Adam A. Milani, Go Ahead. Make My 90 Days: Should Plaintiffs Be Required to Provide Notice to Defendants Before Filing Suit Under Title III of the Americans with Disabilities Act?, 2001 Wis. L. Rev. 107, 118-125 (2001).

Notes & Questions

1.   Even where courts found a notice "requirement" in the statute, two factors limit the effect of the requirement on people with disabilities and on property owners. First, even some courts that apply section 204(c) hold it is only a notice, not an exhaustion, requirement. Burkhart v. Asean Shopping Ctr., Inc., 55 F.Supp.2d 1013, 1017 (D. Ariz. 1999). A plaintiff must simply wait 30 days. Second, those courts required only minimal notice and, at that, only substantial compliance. Daigle v. Friendly Ice Cream Corp., 957 F.Supp. 8, 10-11 (D.N.H. 1997) (unregistered letter to state attorney general asking for assistance, plus response from attorney general, obviated need for registered letter).

2.   Championed by a well-known film actor/local politician,[1] legislation has been introduced several times that would require

---

[1]   John M. Williams, Clint Eastwood Explains His Beef with the ADA, Business Week online (May 17, 2000), http://www.businessweek. com:/print/bwdaily/dnflash/may2000/nf00517c.htm?tc;   LawGuru.com Legal News, Congress Weighs 90-Day Delay for All Litigation Under ADA

claimants to notify non-accommodating businesses of an alleged violation, followed by a 90-day wait before taking legal action. *See* ADA Notification Act of 2007, H.R. 3479, 2007 Cong. U.S. 3479. One federal district judge noted the apparent inefficiency in the statute:

> Requiring potential plaintiffs to notify offenders and provide an opportunity to remediate before filing suit is likely to solve access problems more efficiently than allowing all violators to be dragged into litigation regardless of their willingness to comply voluntarily with the ADA once informed if its infractions. The goals of the ADA do not include creating an incentive for attorneys to seek statutory fees by laying traps for those who are ignorant of the law. The Court believes that the purposes of the ADA are best served by reserving private enforcement actions for knowing violators who refuse to comply without an injunction.

Snyder v. San Diego Flowers, 21 F.Supp.2d 1207, 1210-1211 (S.D. Cal. 1998) (notice required), superceded by Botosan v. Paul McNally Realty, 216 F.3d 827, 832 (9th Cir. 2000).

On the one hand, the ADA's requirements are complex in some areas. The ADA's building accessibility standards are contained in the ADA Accessibility Guidelines (ADAAG). Access Board, ADA Accessibility Guidelines for Buildings and Facilities (ADAAG), http://www.access-board.gov/adaag/html/adaag.htm (Sept. 2002). It would not be hard to envision owners of facilities not being familiar with all of ADAAG's details. Moreover, the burden on a potential plaintiff in giving notice of an architectural barrier is far less than that of litigation imposed on a defendant who is prepared to modify its facility. Because no action for damages lies under Title III, there is little redress for someone turned away from an establishment because of a disability. Congress' goal was not redress, but to change accessibility, for which notice before a suit might be most expeditious.

On the other hand, the ADA has been in effect for over 20 years (plus a nearly three-year grace period) and the standards are available, so it is difficult for owners of buildings and facilities to plead ignorance at this stage. Indeed, at least one court has held that a failure to follow ADAAG for new construction constitutes intentional discrimination. Access Now, Inc. v. S. Fla. Stadium Corp., 161 F.Supp.2d 1357, 1357, 1362 (S.D. Fla. 2001) (citing Ass'n for Disabled Americans, Inc. v. Concorde Gaming Corp., 158 F.Supp. 2d 1353, 1362 n.5 (S.D. Fla. 2001)). Moreover, the ADA is not limited to physical access requirements and there is little

---

(June 16, 2000), http://www.lawguru.com/newsletters/2000/06/35368. html (2000).

purpose to notifying a business that its obviously exclusionary practices are illegal.

The drafters of the ADA may have believed that a business that had not made itself accessible years after the Act's passage and with the ADAAG readily available was not likely voluntarily to change. Most important, they may have believed that people with disabilities should have access without recourse to notifying businesses, just as, for example, African-Americans have access without having to notifying businesses that the law requires it.

To date, no federal legislation has been passed to add a notice requirement to Title III. Nevertheless, a notice statute was passed under California law providing, in part, standards for the statement of facts to be articulated in a demand letter alleging a construction-related accessibility violation, Cal. Civ. Code Ann. § 55.31 (West 2012), and duties of the attorney submitting the demand letter, which are subject to disciplinary procedures if not followed. § 55.32.

～

B. *Statute Of Limitations*

Like Title II, there is no express statutory limitations scheme under Title III of the ADA. Therefore, one must look to state law to determine the limitations period. As with Title II, federal courts will generally look to state personal injury law to identify the statute of limitations in Title III cases. *See* discussion and cases, *supra* Part 3, ch. 10; Hill & Blanck, *supra*.

C. *Alternative Dispute Resolution*

The U.S. Department of Justice offers a free mediation service for ADA Title II and Title III claims. They have over 400 mediators nationwide and claim that 75% of completed mediations result in successful resolutions. U.S. Dep't of Justice, Enforcing the ADA: A Status Report from the Department of Justice (April-June 2008), http://www.ada.gov/aprjun08.htm. In the first ten years following enactment of the ADA, the Department referred over 1,000 complaints to mediation. Enforcing the ADA: Looking Back on a Decade of Progress, July 2000, http://www.ada.gov/pubs/10thrpt.htm (last visited Apr. 14, 2009).

Arbitration is also available for Title III cases. Pre-dispute arbitration agreements, similar to those discussed in the employment context, *supra*, Part 3, are being used to require submission of Title III cases to arbitration, rather than litigation. This is particularly occurring in the health care context, where medical service providers frequently require patients to sign arbitration agreements before providing medical services.

§ 17.2 Remedies

A. *Injunctive Relief*

1. Consequences of lack of damages

As noted above, an essential feature of this remedy is the exclusion of damages for private plaintiffs.[2] This is not a matter that has been seriously disputed. Section 308 of the ADA refers to section 204(a) of the Civil Rights Act of 1964. Early on, the Supreme Court found – based on the unambiguous language quoted above – that private parties could not recover damages. Newman v. Piggie Park Enters., Inc., 390 U.S. 400, 402 (1968) (per curiam); *see also* Pickern v. Holiday Quality Foods Inc., 293 F.3d 1133, 1136 (9th Cir. 2002). Courts deciding the issue under the ADA have followed suit. *E.g.*, A.R. v. Kogan, 964 F.Supp. 269, 271 (N.D. Ill. 1997). Indeed, the District of Columbia Circuit rejected Department of Transportation regulations that would have imposed money damages, to be paid to passengers of bus companies whose trips were disrupted because the companies did not use accessible buses, because the ADA's remedies, which do not include damages, are exclusive. Am. Bus Ass'n v. Slater, 231 F.3d 1, 4-6 (D.C. Cir. 2000).

The unavailability of a damage remedy may diminish the overall effectiveness of Title III. Professor Colker has surveyed the appellate decisions and verdicts in Title III cases. Colker, ADA Title III: A Fragile Compromise, 21 Berkeley J. Emp. & Lab. L. 377, 399-406 (2000). As of 2000, she found far fewer Title III appellate decisions (25) than Title I decisions (475). *Id*. at 399-400. Only 16% of ADA verdicts were in Title III cases. *Id*. at 401.[3] Professor Waterstone extended the analysis through 2004 and found 82 appellate cases under Title III, still substantially below both Title I and Title II cases. Waterstone, The Untold Story of the Rest of the Americans with Disabilities Act, 58 Vand. L. Rev. 1807, 1853-54 (2005). Colker suggests that the relatively small number of Title III cases is due to the absence of a damage remedy incentive. In addition, cases must go to judges, who may be less plaintiff-oriented than juries. *Id*. at 402-03.[4] The evidence, however, is not

---

[2] Plaintiffs may seek damages for the same acts under applicable state statutes. *E.g.*, Dudley v. Hannaford Bros. Co., 190 F.Supp.2d 69, 76-77 (D. Me. 2002) (plaintiff could recover penalty under Maine Human Rights Act).

[3] Of course, Title III cases will not go to a jury unless there is an associated state law claim for damages, because Title III's remedies are equitable.

[4] She notes that, ironically, equitable relief to be decided by judges was the favored remedy for racial discrimination under the Civil Rights Act, because civil rights advocates feared judges less than prejudiced

completely convincing, because there are far more employees than business establishments, so one might anticipate more Title I suits, in general. Moreover, loss of or failure to obtain a job may be more significant, and thus more likely to lead to litigation, than the inability to use a business. *See* Bonnie Poitras Tucker, The ADA's Revolving Door: Inherent Flaws in the Civil Rights Paradigm, 62 Ohio St. L.J. 335, 382-83 (2001) (citing examples of changes in public accommodations since enactment of the ADA).

In *Jenkins v. National Board of Medical Examiners* [NBME], No. 08-5371, 2009 WL 331638 (6th Cir. Feb. 11, 2009), the Sixth Circuit applied the ADAAA retroactively to a case where the only remedy sought was prospective injuctive relief, *i.e.*, a request for future accommodations, rather than monetary damages for past acts. Here, the NBME denied the student's request for additional time on the exam, stating that he was not disabled under the ADA. Following the ruling, the case settled, and as a term of the settlement, the NBME granted the student double the standard time and a separate testing area for his exam. U.S. DOJ, Press Release, *Justice Department Settles with National Board of Medical Examiners Over Refusal to Provide Testing Accommodations to Yale Medical School Student* (Feb. 22, 2011), http://www.justice.gov/opa/pr/2011/February/11-crt-220.html; Settlement Agreement Between United States of America and Nat'l Bd. of Med. Exam's, DJ#202-16-181 (Feb. 23, 2011), http://www.ada.gov/nbme.htm.

2.   Standing

Unlike Titles I and II, Title III presents issues of standing to sue. A private plaintiff seeking relief under Title III must plead and prove not only the traditional level of standing – injury-in-fact – but must also show that the harm is likely to occur to him again.

> "[T]he plaintiff must have suffered an 'injury in fact' – an invasion of a legally protected interest which is (a) concrete and particularized; and (b) 'actual or imminent', not 'conjectural' or 'hypothetical.' " * * * Second, there must be a causal connection between the injury and the conduct complained of. * * * Finally, a plaintiff must show that it is likely that the injury will be redressed by a favorable decision.

Deck v. Am. Hawaiian Cruises, Inc., 121 F.Supp.2d 1292, 1296-97 (D. Haw. 2000) (quoting and citing Lujan v. Defenders of Wildlife, 504 U.S. 555, 560 (1992)); *see also* Betancourt v. Federated Dept. Stores, 732 F.Supp.2d 693 (W.D.T.X. 2010) (holding that plaintiff had standing to assert her architectural barrier claims under Title III because she had

---

juries in southern states. In ADA cases, in contrast, juries appear to be more sympathetic to plaintiffs than judges.

visited the store where she encountered ADA violations that discriminated against her and endangered her safety; the alleged barriers existed at the time plaintiff filed her complaint; and, plaintiff alleges she plans to return to the store once it is compliant); Castaneda v. Burger King, 597 F.Supp.2d 1035, 1042 (N.D. Cal. 2009) (holding that although the complaint was not site specific and the plaintiff had not visited all locations, it was sufficiently detailed to allow defendants to understand the claims against them); Kreisler v. Second Ave. Diner Corp., No. 12-4093, slip op. at 9 (2d Cir. 2013) (holding that once plaintiff established standing for one barrier they may bring challenges to all other barriers on premise that affect their disability despite not personally encountering them). *But see* Scherr v. Mariott Int'l Inc., 703 F.3d 1069, 1075 (7th Cir. 2013) (standing to sue a individual Mariott hotel for ADA violations does not extend to other Mariott hotels with the same violation absent an intent to visit those hotels).

Even if he has used the Title III service or good, may he assert the rights of others with different disabilities?

PICKERN v. HOLIDAY QUALITY FOODS INC.

United States Court of Appeals, Ninth Circuit, 2002
293 F.3d 1133

WILLIAM A. FLETCHER, Circuit Judge.

Plaintiff Jerry Doran appeals the district court's dismissal of his suit seeking injunctive relief for an alleged violation of Title III of the Americans with Disabilities Act, 42 U.S.C. § 12181 et seq. ("ADA" or "Title III"). Doran, a paraplegic who uses a wheelchair, alleges that because defendant Holiday Quality Foods' ("Holiday") grocery stores are "public accommodations" within the meaning of the ADA, 42 U.S.C. § 12181(7)(E), Holiday is required to remove architectural barriers that make it difficult for Doran to gain access to one of Holiday's stores. On motion for summary judgment, the district court held that because Doran had not attempted to enter the store during the limitations period, and thus had not actually encountered any barriers during that period, his claim was time-barred and he did not have standing.

We hold that when a plaintiff who is disabled within the meaning of the ADA has actual knowledge of illegal barriers at a public accommodation to which he or she desires access, that plaintiff need not engage in the "futile gesture" of attempting to gain access in order to show actual injury during the limitations period. When such a plaintiff seeks injunctive relief against an ongoing violation, he or she is not barred from seeking relief either by the statute of limitations or by lack of standing.

We therefore reverse and remand.

I. Background

* * * Doran's grandmother lives in Paradise, and Doran visits Paradise frequently to see her. He states in his deposition that "I try to go every Sunday to see my grandmother. She lives there [in Paradise], so I go up all the time." At some time prior to 1998, Doran visited the Paradise store and encountered the architectural barriers of which he now complains. He states that he would like to patronize the Paradise store when he visits his grandmother, but is deterred from doing so by the store's allegedly unlawful barriers.

* * *

Doran alleges that the Paradise store has inadequate access to and from the parking lot; inadequate checkstand access; inadequate signs; and inadequate access to the restroom and to vending machines. After visiting the store prior to 1998, he visited it again only once before filing his complaint on March 1, 1999. On that second visit, in late 1998, he was obliged, because of the barriers, to wait in the parking lot while his companion went into the store on his behalf. Because Doran delayed for more than a year in filing his complaint after he first became aware of the barriers at the Paradise store, the district court dismissed his complaint. Doran timely appealed from the dismissal.

* * *

II. Statute of Limitations

The enforcement provisions of Title III provide only for injunctive relief. * * * Injunctive relief is available to "any person who *is being subjected to* discrimination on the basis of disability" or who has "reasonable grounds for believing that such person *is about to be subjected to* discrimination." 42 U.S.C. § 12188(a)(1) (emphases added). By employing the phrases "is being subjected to" and "is about to be subjected to," the statute makes clear that either a continuing or a threatened violation of the ADA is an injury within the meaning of the Act. A plaintiff is therefore entitled to injunctive relief to stop or to prevent such injury.

Seeking to avoid unreasonable burdens on ADA plaintiffs, Title III explicitly provides that it does not require "a person with a disability to engage in a *futile gesture* if such person has actual notice that a person or organization . . . does not intend to comply" with the ADA. *Id.* (emphasis added). The "futile gesture" language of Title III is taken from *Teamsters v. United States,* 431 U.S. 324, 366, 97 S.Ct. 1843, 52 L.Ed.2d 396 (1977). In *Teamsters,* the Court held that plaintiffs who did not actually apply for promotions could nevertheless challenge the employer's racially discriminatory seniority system under Title VII of the Civil Rights Act of 1964, Pub. L. No. 88-352, *codified as amended at* 42 U.S.C. § 2000e et seq., if they could show that they would have applied for the job if not for the employer's discriminatory practices. *See Teamsters,* 431 U.S. at 367-68,

97 S.Ct. 1843. The Court reasoned that "[w]hen a person's desire for a job is not translated into a formal application *solely because of his unwillingness to engage in a futile gesture he is as much a victim of discrimination* as is he who goes through the motions of submitting an application." *Id.* at 365-66, 97 S.Ct. 1843 (emphasis added).

Congress specifically intended that *Teamsters'* "futile gesture" reasoning be applied to ADA claims. *See* H. Rep. No. 101-485(II) at 82-83 (1990) *reprinted in* 1990 U.S.C.C.A.N. 303, 365 ("The Committee intends for this doctrine to apply to this title"); S. Rep. No. 101-116 at 43 (1989). Thus, under the ADA, once a plaintiff has actually become aware of discriminatory conditions existing at a public accommodation, and is thereby deterred from visiting or patronizing that accommodation, the plaintiff has suffered an injury. * * * So long as the discriminatory conditions continue, and so long as a plaintiff is aware of them and remains deterred, the injury under the ADA continues.

A plaintiff has no cause of action under the ADA for an injury that occurred outside the limitations period.[2] But he or she has a cause of action, and is entitled to injunctive relief, for an injury that is occurring within the limitations period, as well as for threatened future injury. Doran states that he is currently aware of barriers to access that now exist at the Paradise store, and that these barriers currently deter him. Indeed, he states that the barriers deterred him from entering the store just before filing suit, when he needed something from the store and was obliged to remain in the parking lot. Doran's suit for injunctive relief is therefore not time-barred.

III. Standing

If Doran's statements are true, he has suffered and is suffering an injury within the meaning of Title III of the ADA. However, his injury must also satisfy the "case" or "controversy" requirement of Article III of the Constitution. [The court cites and quotes *Lujan*.] The second and third elements are not at issue; Holiday's noncompliance with Title III has caused Doran's injury, and an injunction requiring Holiday to comply with the ADA would redress it. The only question is whether Doran is suffering a sufficiently "concrete and particularized" and "actual or imminent" injury to satisfy the Court's "injury in fact" requirement.

---

[2] The parties agree that a one-year limitations period applies. Because the ADA does not contain a statute of limitations, the court must apply the statute of limitations of the most analogous state law. * * * Most district courts have applied California's one-year limit for personal injury actions to federal disability discrimination claims brought in California. * * * Because the parties agree that the applicable limitations period is one year and do not argue the point to us, we assume without deciding that they are correct.

"By particularized, we mean that the injury must affect the plaintiff in a personal and individual way." *Lujan,* 504 U.S. at 560 n.1, 112 S.Ct. 2130. In the context of the ADA, we understand that to mean that Doran must himself suffer an injury as a result of the Paradise store's noncompliance with the ADA. We hold that in stating that he is currently deterred from attempting to gain access to the Paradise store, Doran has stated sufficient facts to show concrete, particularized injury.

In so holding, we agree with *Steger v. Franco, Inc.,* 228 F.3d 889 (8th Cir. 2000), in which the Eighth Circuit held that a blind plaintiff who had only once attempted to enter the defendant's building had standing to bring an ADA challenge. The plaintiff was thwarted in his attempt to gain access to the men's restroom in the building because the signage did not comply with the ADA. *Id.* at 893-94. Like that plaintiff, Doran has personally encountered certain barriers that bar his access to Holiday's Paradise store. Further, the *Steger* court rejected the defendant's argument that the blind plaintiff could challenge the ADA violation only as to the restroom he had attempted to access, stating that such a "narrow construction" of the ADA would be "not only . . . inefficient, but impractical." *Id.* * * * We agree with the Eighth Circuit that Doran need not necessarily have personally encountered all the barriers that 8765 bar his access to the Paradise store in order to seek an injunction to remove those barriers.

In addition to suffering a concrete injury particular to himself, Doran must also have suffered actual or imminent injury. We hold that a disabled individual who is currently deterred from patronizing a public accommodation due to a defendant's failure to comply with the ADA has suffered "actual injury." Similarly, a plaintiff who is threatened with harm in the future because of existing or imminently threatened non-compliance with the ADA suffers "imminent injury."

Doran has visited Holiday's Paradise store in the past and states that he has actual knowledge of the barriers to access at that store. Doran also states that he prefers to shop at Holiday markets and that he would shop at the Paradise market if it were accessible. This is sufficient to establish actual or imminent injury for purposes of standing. *Compare Dudley v. Hannaford Bros. Co.,* 146 F.Supp.2d 82, 86 (D.Me. 2001) (disabled plaintiff alleged actual injury where he evinced a desire to patronize a store that had discriminated against him in the past and had not changed its discriminatory policies or practices; the plaintiff "[did] not simply allege that he suffered one act of discrimination in the past. Rather, he also alleges that Defendant's discriminatory practice continues to exist.") *with Moreno v. G & M Oil Co.,* 88 F.Supp.2d 1116, 1116 (C.D.Cal. 2000) (disabled plaintiff could not show actual injury with respect to defendant's other gas stations, because plaintiff "[did] not claim he wants to visit the other stations, or will ever do so."). * * *

IV. Conclusion

Viewing the evidence in the light most favorable to Doran, we hold that his suit for injunctive relief is not time-barred and that he has standing under the ADA and under Article III.

REVERSED AND REMANDED.

Notes & Questions

1. Note the relationship between standing and statutes of limitations. What if the only actual injury the plaintiff suffered fell outside the limitations period?

2. Where a plaintiff seeks prospective relief, the causality and redressability prongs of the *Lujan* test have been interpreted to demand the possibility of repeated harm.

> Thus, although a plaintiff need not repeatedly suffer discrimination in order to assert her rights under Title III, ADA plaintiffs who seek injunctive relief must demonstrate that they themselves face a real and immediate threat of future harm; there must be sufficient immediacy, reality and causality between defendant's conduct and plaintiffs' allegations of future injury to warrant injunctive relief.

Deck v. Am. Hawaiian Cruises, 121 F.Supp.2d 1292, 1297 (D. Haw. 2000) (citing O'Shea v. Littleton, 414 U.S. 488, 495-96 (1974)). The Eleventh Circuit has held that a plaintiff must allege "a real and immediate – as opposed to a merely conjectural or hypothetical – threat of *future* injury." Wooden v. Bd. of Regents of Univ. Sys. of Ga., 247 F.3d 1262, 1284 (11th Cir. 2001); *see also* Shotz v. Cates, 256 F.3d 1077, 1081 (11th Cir. 2001); Malowney v. Fed. Collection Deposit Group, 193 F.3d 1342, 1348 (11th Cir. 1999).

3. Of course, if a plaintiff has never visited the facility, she lacks standing. Steger v. Franco, Inc., 228 F.3d 889, 894 (8th Cir. 2000) (denying standing to three plaintiffs who never visited facility before initiation of suit); Resnick v. Magical Cruise Co., Ltd., 148 F.Supp.2d 1298, 1301-02 (M.D. Fla. 2001) (no standing for person who never attempted to take cruise and only learned from defendant's website that its ships might not be accessible). But what if a person has used an accommodation once, but has no intention of using it again? In a case in which a plaintiff sued a cruise line after using it for one voyage, but could not show that she planned a trip on one of its ships in the future, she lacked standing. Deck v. Am. Hawaiian Cruises, 121 F.Supp.2d 1292, 1298-99 (D. Haw. 2000). The court cited a number of like cases. *See also* Moreno v. G & M Oil Co., 88 F.Supp.2d 1116 (C.D. Cal. 2000) (disabled plaintiff could not show actual injury with respect to defendant's other gas stations, because plaintiff "[did] not claim he wants to visit the other stations, or will ever do so").

4. But how much can one extrapolate from cruise-ship cases? Perhaps more *financially* accessible accommodations furnish a better model. For example, a court found that a plaintiff had standing where he had previously gone to a stadium, continued to reside in the area, and stated that he would visit the stadium in the future. Access Now, Inc. v. S. Fla. Stadium Corp., 161 F.Supp.2d 1357 (S.D. Fla. 2001); accord Pickern v. Holiday Quality Foods Inc., 293 F.3d 1133, 1138 (9th Cir. 2002); Dudley v. Hannaford Bros. Co., 146 F.Supp.2d 82, 86 (D. Me. 2001) (plaintiff's attempt to purchase liquor had occurred outside the limitations period, but "a single past incident of discrimination can provide . . . grounds for a plaintiff's standing, as long as the lack of accommodation continues to exist" (citing Parr v. L & L Drive-Inn Restaurant, 96 F.Supp.2d 1065, 1077-83 (D. Haw. 2000))). The issue whether a plaintiff will return to an accommodation often is a question of fact, so that summary judgment for the defendant is inappropriate where the plaintiff can assert an intention to return.

5. If a person has standing to seek relief for one kind of barrier, should she have standing to seek relief for others at the same location? After all, she has never encountered them. One court found that a person who used a wheelchair had standing to attack all barriers that affected the use of a wheelchair, whether or not previously encountered. Parr, 96 F.Supp.2d at 1080-81 ("This Court is reluctant to embrace a rule of standing that would allow an alleged wrongdoer to evade the court's jurisdiction so long as he does not injure the same person twice. . . . Plaintiff should not be required to encounter every barrier seriatim . . . to obtain effective relief." (internal quotations and citation omitted)).

> Plaintiff has standing to allege ADA violations in which he did not encounter, as long as Plaintiff is "among the injured." The legal interest at stake is Plaintiff's right to patronize L & L free from discrimination. The discrimination occurred as soon as Plaintiff encountered an architectural barrier. Plaintiff should not be required to encounter every barrier seriatim within L & L to obtain effective relief.

Id. at 1081 (citation omitted).

A second court held that a plaintiff using a wheelchair who was suing a stadium only could obtain an injunction with respect to those aspects of the stadium with which he "encountered difficulty." Access Now, Inc., 161 F.Supp.2d at 1363-66. The court distinguished *Parr*, 96 F.Supp.2d at 1081, on the ground that the plaintiff in *Parr* "had experienced certain barriers personally, and had 'actual notice' of their recurrence throughout the facility; as such, would not be required to confront each of those incidents of discrimination in order to demonstrate his entitlement to standing." Access Now, Inc., 161 F.Supp.2d at 1365. *Parr* did not say that, however. It stated,

[t]o satisfy standing requirements to file suit, '[a]ctual notice' of an intent not to comply with the ADA is sufficient." * * * Once Plaintiff either encountered discrimination or learned of the alleged violations through expert findings or personal observation, he had 'actual notice' that Defendant did not intend to comply with the ADA. Because Plaintiff is not required to engage in a 'futile gesture,' Plaintiff should be allowed to sue for the violations he did not encounter. *See* 42 U.S.C. § 12188(a)(1).

Parr, 96 F.Supp.2d at 1081.

The distinction seems to be that the plaintiff in *Parr* learned about the ADAAG violations he had not personally encountered through an expert's evaluation of them, but the plaintiff in *Access Now* learned of those he had not seen personally via a non-expert. Convincing? Note that the statute does not by its terms require knowledge of specific violations.

6. Should a sighted person using a wheelchair be able to sue for the lack of Braille signs? Why not? Parr, 96 F.Supp.2d at 1082 ("Plaintiff seeks relief for barriers that are not related to his personal disability of non-mobility. For example, Plaintiff seeks ADA compliance for braille sign violations which relate to sight impaired individuals. Such barriers do not specifically constitute discrimination against Plaintiff, yet are prohibited by the ADA nonetheless."). In theory, this restriction may not be limiting, because the Attorney General can enforce the statute. *Id.* at 1083. However, private parties still must convince the Attorney General to act.

Why are there standing requirements? Does this case differ from the situation where a wheelchair user who couldn't enter a store because it lacked ramps can also seek wider aisles, although he never tried to use them? The courts have denied standing to sue for others' disabilities. A person with various kinds of psychological impairments did not have standing to seek relief for people who use wheelchairs or have vision or hearing impairments. Vandermolen v. City of Roosevelt Park, No. 1:97CV 200, 1997 WL 853505, at *1-*2 (W.D. Mich. Oct. 28, 1997) (plaintiff who suffered from "depression, post-traumatic stress disorder, agoraphobia, claustrophobia, panic attacks, extreme sensitivity to sunlight, obesity, hypertension, hyperventilation, dizziness and a problem of the vocal cords" could not sue to make City "hall accessible to wheelchair-disabled, deaf and blind persons, [because] he himself is neither wheelchair-disabled, deaf or blind").

7. What if a group sues for the rights of its members? Do all have to have been injured? In the same way?

Access Now claims that it has associational standing to bring this lawsuit on behalf of its members. * * * An association has standing to sue on behalf of its members when: (1) at least one of its members has standing to sue in his own right; (2) the interests at stake are germane to the organization's purpose; and (3) neither the claim asserted nor the relief requested requires the participation of the individual members in the lawsuit. *See United Food & Commercial Workers Union Local 751 v. Brown Group, Inc.*, 517 U.S. 544, 552-53, 116 S.Ct. 1529, 134 L.Ed.2d 758 (1996) (citing *Hunt v. Wash. State Apple Advertising Comm'n*, 432 U.S. 333, 343, 97 S.Ct. 2434, 53 L.Ed.2d 383 (1977)).

Defendant cites an unpublished case from the District of New Hampshire to support its argument that even if Access Now satisfies the three prong test set forth in *Hunt*, this Court should find, based on prudential limits on the exercise of jurisdiction, that Access Now lacks standing. * * * First, this decision is not binding upon this Court. Second, the facts of [that case] are easily distinguishable from the facts currently before this Court. [There], the court found that no other member of Access 123, besides the co-plaintiff Muehe, had visited the defendant's restaurant. * * * Therefore, Access 123's associational standing was based upon Muehe's injury alone. * * * Here, Access Now has alleged that other members of its organization have visited American Huts' Restaurant. * * * The Court finds, based on the facts alleged in the Complaint, that Access Now's claims are not solely based upon Wein's injury.

Wein v. Am. Huts, Inc., 313 F.Supp.2d 1356, 1359-60 (S.D. Fla. 2004). If a person may not sue for others' injuries, why should an organization be able to do so?

୬

3.   Examples of injunctive relief

Given the range of behavior prohibited by Title III, the range of injunctive relief is broad, limited principally by: (1) reasonableness; (2) the avoidance of "fundamental alterations" in a program; (3) the avoidance of "direct threats" to safety; and (4) if the remedy entails modifying an existing structure, the modification must be "readily achievable." 42 U.S.C. § 12182(b) (2006). We address these substantive defenses in Chapter 13, §§ 13.2-13.4.

In deciding whether a requested modification is reasonable, poses a direct threat, or fundamentally alters the "goods, services, facilities, privileges, advantages, or accommodations," the "need of a disabled person [must] be evaluated on an individual basis." PGA Tour, Inc. v. Martin, 532 U.S. 661, 690 (2001). Presumably, therefore, an accommodation proper for one person might not be necessary for another, although as a practical matter, if it is determined that a particular modification does not constitute a fundamental alteration, it would seem difficult to deny the benefit of that finding to others with a range of similar impairments. In *PGA Tour, Inc. v. Martin*, for example, the PGA Tour had to modify its rules to permit Casey Martin to use a golf cart in tournaments. Others with similar impairments will certainly be able to take advantage of the change, absent a showing that the alteration is not "necessary" for them.

The range of injunctions requested has been broad:

- A sports arena was required to modify its seating to accommodate wheelchair users and was ordered not to "infill" seats for wheelchair patrons, until all seats for ambulatory patrons were sold. "If an ambulatory patron could still purchase a ticket for a conventional seat, then wheelchair users must be able to purchase tickets for comparable wheelchair spaces." Indep. Living Res. v. Or. Arena Corp., 1 F.Supp.2d 1159, 1165, 1170-71 (D. Or. 1998). The court also ordered changes in the arena's sales of season tickets. *Id.*; *see* Or. Paralyzed Veterans of Am. v. Regal Cinemas, Inc., 339 F.3d 1126 (9th Cir. 2003) (appeals court reversed district court and ordered that summary judgment be entered ordering movie theatre chain to offer patron in wheelchairs "lines of sight comparable to those for members of the general public," in accordance with Justice Department regulation, 28 C.F.R. pt. 36 app. A, § 4.33.3); Ball v. AMC Entm't, Inc., 246 F.Supp.2d 17, 25-26 (D.D.C. 2003) (requiring installation of rear-window captioning system in 101 theatres would not fundamentally alter the nature of the service the theatres provide; factual question as to burden). *But see* Lara v. Cinemark USA, Inc., 207 F.3d 783 (5th Cir. 2000) (declining to interpret Justice Department regulations to require comparable lines of sight); Cornilles v. Regal Cinemas, Inc., No. Civ. 00-173-AS, 2002 WL 31469787, at *1 (D. Or. Mar. 19, 2002) (approving a magistrate's recommendation that a theatre chain is not required to install a rear-window captioning system in all theatres due to the unduly burdensome cost of $9,000 to $14,000 per theatre).

- A court issued a preliminary injunction requiring a preschool to have its personnel undergo inhalation therapy training to assist an asthmatic child. Alvarez v. Fountainhead, Inc., 55 F.Supp.2d 1048, 1055-56 (N.D. Cal. 1999).

- An airport making extensive alterations to its terminal was permanently enjoined to conform those alterations to ADAAG, by using an elevator, rather than a platform lift, to carry people with disabilities to the airport's restaurant. Coalition of Montanans Concerned with Disabilities, Inc. v. Gallatin Airport Auth., 957 F.Supp. 1166, 1171 (D. Mont. 1997).

- A restaurant had to modify its entrance and parking spaces to conform to ADAAG. Parr v. L & L Drive-Inn Restaurant, 96 F.Supp.2d 1065, 1087-88 (D. Haw. 2000).

- The National Board of Medical Examiners was required to give a medical student with a reading disability additional time to take Step I of the Medical Licensing Examination. Rush v. Nat'l Bd. of Med. Exam'rs, 268 F.Supp.2d 673, 679 (N.D. Tex. 2003).

B.   *Enforcement By The Attorney General –*
       Compensatory Damages And Civil Penalties

The statute gives the Attorney General broad powers to enforce Title III. The Attorney General has substantial investigative powers. 42 U.S.C. § 12188(b)(1) (2006).   Moreover, unlike private parties, the Attorney General has authority to obtain compensatory damages in addition to the equitable relief available when individuals sue on their own behalf. *Id.* § 12188(b)(2). However, "[f]or purposes of subsection (b)(2)(B), the term monetary damages and such other relief does not include punitive damages." *Id.* § 12188(b)(4). The Attorney General may – "to vindicate the public interest" – also seek civil penalties, which may not exceed $50,000 for a first violation or $100,000 for any subsequent violation. *Id.* § 12188(b)(2)(C).

Much of the Justice Department's work is done through settlement agreements and consent decrees, rather than reported cases. Since 2000, The Department of Justice has entered into 260 Title III consent decrees and settlement agreements.   Enforcment Activities, United States Department of Justice Civil Rights Division (Nov. 2013) *at* hhtp://www.ada.gov/enforce_activities.htm#settlements.   At trial, both monetary damages and civil penalties are within the court's discretion. United States v. York Obstetrics & Gynecology, No. 00-8-P-DMC, 2001 WL 80082, at *1 n.3 (D. Me. Jan. 30, 2001). However, the statute instructs the court to take the defendant's good faith into account in assessing penalties.

> In a civil action under paragraph (1)(B), the court, when considering what amount of civil penalty, if any, is appropriate, shall give consideration to any good faith effort or attempt to comply with this chapter by the entity. In evaluating good faith, the court shall consider, among other factors it deems relevant, whether the entity could have reasonably anticipated the need for an appropriate type of auxiliary aid needed to accommodate the unique needs of a particular individual with a disability.

42 U.S.C. § 12188(b)(5) (2006).

Damages can be substantial when awarded by a jury. Enforcing the ADA, *supra*, at I.A.2 (jury awarded $30,000 to a blind person denied the right to sit on a jury). On the other hand, in most cases the settlement amounts negotiated by the Justice Department are relatively modest.[5] The penalties the Justice Department obtains serve two functions – to punish past behavior and to ensure that a defendant adheres to a settlement agreement. However, the principal function of the Justice Department is to obtain broad relief, so the damages often appear calibrated to compensate the individual plaintiffs for their trouble in the litigation.

---

[5] For example:

- $28,000 against a national bar review course operator which had "failed to provide appropriate auxiliary aids to students with vision and hearing impairments." Enforcing the ADA, *supra*, at I.B.2.

- $7,500 against Duke University for failing to provide a campus accessible to a wheelchair-using student. *Id.*

- an agreement by a CPA course to "pay $20,000 in damages to be distributed to deaf and hearing impaired students, and establish a $25,000 scholarship fund for accounting students at California State University who have hearing impairments." *Id.*

- "The American Association of State Social Work Boards and Assessment Systems, Inc., agreed to . . . pay $3,000 to a [blind] complainant who was not allowed to use his own reader for the social work license examination. Instead, he was allegedly required to use a college student who had been hired to work at the registration table and had never read for a person with a vision impairment. During the exam, the reader allegedly stumbled over technical terms and made mistakes in marking and recording the answers." *Id.*

- A 30-store discount department store chain agreed to pay $15,000 for not having ADA-compliant stores; a brokerage firm paid $1,500 for not having monthly statements legible to clients with vision impairments. *Id.* at I.C.1.

- However, in one case, the Department of Justice got a $550,000 damage award against a major real estate company that had refused to lease space to an advocacy group for people with disabilities. *Id.*

UNITED STATES v. YORK OBSTETRICS & GYNECOLOGY, P.A.

United States District Court, District of Maine, 2001
No. 00-8-P-DMC, 2001 WL 80082

COHEN, Magistrate J.

Trial was held in this case over five days between November 7 and November 14, 2000. The jury returned a verdict in favor of plaintiff-intervenor Raymond McLaren on the count of the complaint that alleged violation of the Americans with Disabilities Act ("ADA"), 42 U.S.C. § 12101 *et seq.*, and in favor of the defendant on all other counts. The jury awarded Mr. McLaren $60,000 in damages pursuant to 42 U.S.C. § 12188(b)(2)(B). The government indicated at that time, consistent with the request for relief contained in its complaint, that it also seeks injunctive relief and imposition of a civil penalty pursuant to 42 U.S.C. § 12188(b)(2). * * *

[Court quotes the statute.] The government seeks imposition of an unspecified but "substantial" civil penalty both "to reimburse the U.S. Department of Justice" and to serve as a deterrent to the defendant and others, Government Memorandum at 7, 8, and entry of a specific order of injunctive relief, *id.* Exh. 2.[3] The defendant opposes any monetary penalty and has submitted its own proposed order of injunctive relief. * * *.

There is apparently no reported case law applying the penalty provisions of the ADA that are at issue here. The government cites extensively to case law construing civil penalty provisions of other federal statutes, but such statutes are often written in language that is significantly different from that of section 12188(b)(2).

In this case, the violations of the ADA found by the jury consist of the failure to provide Raymond McLaren with a sign language interpreter upon his request on four to six occasions when he accompanied his wife to the defendant obstetrical practice for pre-natal visits. The scope of the injunctive relief sought by the government under these circumstances is excessive. I will enter an order granting injunctive relief that is appropriate under all the circumstances.

With respect to the government's request for imposition of a civil penalty, I find that the amount of compensatory damages awarded by the jury under the circumstances can and will serve a public deterrent function. I would ordinarily conclude that these damages would also serve

---

[3]   It is also important to note, notwithstanding the government's suggestion that the court "must" impose such a penalty, * * * that the statute clearly provides that imposition of a civil penalty is a matter entirely within the court's discretion.

to deter the defendant from future violation of the ADA in similar circumstances, but I am troubled by the statements of the defendant's managing partner to the press after the trial emphasizing that Raymond McLaren "was not [its] patient" and was "not even our patient," Exhs. 6-8 to Government's Memorandum, suggesting that the defendant still does not accept the fact that its duties under the ADA extend to all individuals who can reasonably be expected to use its services in any way, 42 U.S.C. § 12182(a). The defendant made no objection to the jury instruction setting forth its duty to Raymond McLaren under the ADA. While it may disagree with the jury's verdict and its decision to credit Mr. McLaren's testimony that he repeatedly requested an interpreter over the testimony offered by the defendant that he did not do so, the defendant should not continue to believe that it had no duty to Mr. McLaren under the ADA.

The government has submitted in connection with its advocacy of a substantial civil penalty to "reimburse" the government the affidavits of Martha A. Barron and James M. Moore. * * * Mr. Moore represented the government at trial. Ms. Barron states that the Office of the United States Attorney "has incurred $38,819.71 in expenses" associated with this case and that "[m]ost of the expenses incurred in this case were for payment of expert witness fees, sign language interpretation, deposition transcripts, private investigation and travel." * * * Mr. Moore states that "the U.S. Department of Justice devoted in excess of 1,000 attorney hours to the investigation, discovery and motions states as well as the trial" of this case. * * * Assuming without deciding that reimbursement of investigation costs is a purpose of the ADA's civil penalty provision which provides for the imposition of such a penalty "to vindicate the public interest," the government's submissions in this case do not support the imposition of any penalty for this purpose.

The Department of Justice itself has issued regulations implementing the ADA. One of those regulations significantly provides as follows:

> In any action or administrative proceeding commenced pursuant to the Act or this part, the court or agency, in its discretion, may allow the prevailing party, other than the United States, a reasonable attorney's fee, including litigation expenses, and costs, and the United States shall be liable to the foregoing the same as a private individual.

28 C.F.R. § 36.505. Surely the government may not recoup indirectly, via the imposition of a civil penalty, that which it may not recover directly by virtue of its own regulation. Attorney fees (or the equivalent value of attorney time), litigation expenses and costs may not be recovered in this manner. So far as appears from the Barron affidavit, all of the asserted expenses incurred are those traditionally incurred in connection with litigation; many of the individual items listed are treated as litigation costs under Fed. R. Civ. P. 54. * * *

While I see no evidence of any good faith effort by the defendant to comply with the ADA with respect to Raymond McLaren in this case, I do not reach consideration of section 12188(b)(5) because I conclude, albeit with some reluctance given the post-trial statements of the defendant's managing partner, that the imposition of a civil penalty is not appropriate under the circumstances.

In addition to the damages awarded to Raymond McLaren by the jury, the judgment in this case shall include the following injunctive relief:

1. York Obstetrics & Gynecology, P.A., and its officers, physicians, employees and agents (hereafter "York Obstetrics"), are hereby enjoined from violating the Americans with Disabilities Act (hereafter "ADA") or otherwise discriminating on the basis of hearing impairment or any other disability against any individual with a disability who seeks any service from them.

2. York Obstetrics shall furnish all appropriate auxiliary aids and services, at no cost, to persons who are deaf or hearing-impaired, including, but not limited to, qualified sign language and oral interpreters, when necessary for effective communication.

3. York Obstetrics shall produce a written policy for effective communication that will ensure compliance with Title III of the ADA. * * *

4. York Obstetrics shall distribute copies of its written policy to all personnel at any of its offices who have contact with members of the public, including York Hospital birthing nurses.

5. York Obstetrics shall develop and implement an appropriate training program to ensure that all personnel (including, but not limited to, York Hospital birthing nurses) who have contact with patients who are deaf or hearing-impaired as well as other deaf or hearing-impaired persons associated with its patients, are sensitive to the communication needs of such persons and knowledgeable about York Obstetrics' written policy described in paragraph 3 hereof.

6. York Obstetrics shall post signage of conspicuous size and print at a prominent place in each of its waiting rooms and scheduling areas stating: "York Women's Care Associates recognizes its legal obligations to ensure effective communication with persons who are deaf or hearing impaired. Sign language interpreters and other auxiliary aids and services are available to provide equal access to our staff and services for deaf and hearing-impaired persons. Please contact any member of our staff for further information or to request this service." * * *

* * *

Notes & Questions

1. Why no penalties in *York Obstetrics*? In *DeVinney v. Maine Medical Center*, No. Civ. 97-276-P-C, 1998 WL 271495, at *16 (D. Me. May

18, 1998), which also involved the failure "to provide auxiliary aids and services, including qualified sign language interpreters, where such aids and services were necessary for effective communication with persons who are deaf or hard of hearing or who have other communication-related disabilities," *id.* at *1, the court approved a consent decree that imposed an initial $10,000 penalty on the defendant – less than the statutory $50,000 for an initial penalty, because of the defendant's good faith in complying. It also approved potential future penalties to be set by the court, in view of the defendant's good faith, for non-compliance, but levied a $3,000 penalty on the defendant each time it failed to provide a sign-language interpreter to a deaf person in accordance with the decree. All penalties were taken to be subsequent penalties under 42 U.S.C. § 12188(b)(2)(C)(ii) (2006). How does one deal with the fact that different results appear to depend on the whim of the judge?

C. *Attorneys' Fees*

The ADA provides for prevailing parties to recover reasonable attorney's fees from the losing party. This is similar to the approach taken in other civil rights laws.

> In any action or administrative proceeding commenced pursuant to the Americans with Disabilities Act, the court or agency, in its discretion, may allow the prevailing party, other than the United States, a reasonable attorneys fee, including litigation expenses, and costs, and the United States shall be liable for the foregoing the same as a private individual.[6]

42 U.S.C. § 12205 (2006).

Because damages are unavailable under Title III, and, therefore, attorneys' fees cannot be paid on a traditional contingency fee basis (where the attorney takes a portion of the damages recovery), the recoverability of attorneys' fees by the prevailing party is important. Recovery of attorneys' fees is also important in all ADA cases, because many people with disabilities cannot afford the often-substantial costs of litigation.

Disputes over attorneys' fees typically take two forms: (1) is the person seeking fees the prevailing party; (2) are the fees requested reasonable? On the first issue, the law presently seems to confer

---

[6] Note that section 107 of the ADA, 42 U.S.C. § 12117, which sets Title I's remedies, incorporates the remedies of Title VII of the Civil Rights Act of 1964. The latter permits attorneys' fees in cases section 505 might not. However, courts have applied the ADA-specific statute, rather than Title VII.

prevailing party status on someone who obtains a judgment and on someone who obtains a judicially enforceable agreement – a consent decree or a court-supervised settlement agreement, but not someone who, by filing an action, simply caused the defendant to change its practices. On the second issue, the courts have devised a multipart test to assess reasonableness.

1.   Prevailing Party

The Supreme Court has held:

> The touchstone of the prevailing party inquiry must be the material alteration of the legal relationship of the parties in a manner which Congress sought to promote in the fee statute. Where such a change has occurred, the degree of the plaintiff's overall success goes to the reasonableness of the award under *Hensley* [*v. Eckerhart*, 461 U.S. 424 (1983)] not to the availability of a fee award *vel non*.

Tex. State Teachers Ass'n v. Garland Indep. Sch. Dist., 489 U.S. 782, 792 (1989).

Obviously, one who obtains a judgment is a prevailing party. A difficult question has arisen when the plaintiff does not actually obtain a judgment, but the defendant changes its practices in response to the litigation – the "catalyst" theory. The following opinions – majority, concurrence and dissent – address the arguments in some detail.

BUCKHANNON BOARD & CARE HOME, INC. v. WEST VIRGINIA DEPARTMENT OF HEALTH & HUMAN RESOURCES

Supreme Court of the United States, 2001
532 U.S. 598

CHIEF JUSTICE REHNQUIST delivered the opinion of the Court.

Numerous federal statutes allow courts to award attorney's fees and costs to the "prevailing party." The question presented here is whether this term includes a party that has failed to secure a judgment on the merits or a court-ordered consent decree, but has nonetheless achieved the desired result because the lawsuit brought about a voluntary change in the defendant's conduct. We hold that it does not.

Buckhannon Board and Care Home, Inc., which operates care homes that provide assisted living to their residents, failed an inspection by the West Virginia Office of the State Fire Marshal because some of the residents were incapable of "self-preservation" as defined under state law. See W. Va.Code §§ 16-5H-1, 16-5H-2 (1998) (requiring that all residents of residential board and care homes be capable of "self-preservation," or capable of moving themselves "from situations involving imminent danger, such as fire"); W. Va.Code of State Rules, tit. 87, ser. 1, § 14.07(1)

(1995) (same). On October 28, 1997, after receiving cease and desist orders requiring the closure of its residential care facilities within 30 days, Buckhannon Board and Care Home, Inc., on behalf of itself and other similarly situated homes and residents (hereinafter petitioners), brought suit in the United States District Court for the Northern District of West Virginia against the State of West Virginia, two of its agencies, and 18 individuals (hereinafter respondents), seeking declaratory and injunctive relief that the "self-preservation" requirement violated the Fair Housing Amendments Act of 1988 (FHAA), 102 Stat. 1619, 42 U.S.C. § 3601 et seq., and the Americans with Disabilities Act of 1990 (ADA), 104 Stat. 327, 42 U.S.C. § 12101 et seq.

Respondents agreed to stay enforcement of the cease-and-desist orders pending resolution of the case and the parties began discovery. In 1998, the West Virginia Legislature enacted two bills eliminating the "self-preservation" requirement, see S. 627, I 1998 W. Va. Acts 983-986 (amending regulations); H.R. 4200, II 1998 W. Va. Acts 1198-1199 (amending statute), and respondents moved to dismiss the case as moot. The District Court granted the motion, finding that the 1998 legislation had eliminated the allegedly offensive provisions and that there was no indication that the West Virginia Legislature would repeal the amendments.

Petitioners requested attorney's fees as the "prevailing party" under the FHAA, 42 U.S.C. § 3613(c)(2) ("[T]he court, in its discretion, may allow the prevailing party . . . a reasonable attorney's fee and costs"), and ADA, 42 U.S.C. § 12205 ("[T]he court . . ., in its discretion, may allow the prevailing party . . . a reasonable attorney's fee, including litigation expenses, and costs"). Petitioners argued that they were entitled to attorney's fees under the "catalyst theory," which posits that a plaintiff is a "prevailing party" if it achieves the desired result because the lawsuit brought about a voluntary change in the defendant's conduct. Although most Courts of Appeals recognize the "catalyst theory," the Court of Appeals for the Fourth Circuit rejected it in *S-1 and S-2 v. State Bd. of Ed. of N.C.*, 21 F.3d 49, 51 (C.A.4 1994) (en banc) ("A person may not be a 'prevailing party' . . . except by virtue of having obtained an enforceable judgment, consent decree, or settlement giving some of the legal relief sought"). The District Court accordingly denied the motion and, for the same reason, the Court of Appeals affirmed in an unpublished, *per curiam* opinion. * * *

To resolve the disagreement amongst the Courts of Appeals, we granted certiorari, 530 U.S. 1304, 121 S.Ct. 28, 147 L.Ed.2d 1050 (2000), and now affirm.

In the United States, parties are ordinarily required to bear their own attorney's fees–the prevailing party is not entitled to collect from the loser. See *Alyeska Pipeline Service Co. v. Wilderness Society*, 421 U.S. 240, 247, 95 S.Ct. 1612, 44 L.Ed.2d 141 (1975). Under this "American Rule," we follow "a general practice of not awarding fees to a prevailing party absent explicit statutory authority." *Key Tronic Corp. v. United States,* 511 U.S. 809, 819, 114 S.Ct. 1960, 128 L.Ed.2d 797 (1994). Congress, however, has authorized the award of attorney's fees to the "prevailing party" in numerous statutes in addition to those at issue here, such as the Civil Rights Act of 1964, 78 Stat. 259, 42 U.S.C. § 2000e-5(k), the Voting Rights Act Amendments of 1975, 89 Stat. 402, 42 U.S.C. § 1973l (e), and the Civil Rights Attorney's Fees Awards Act of 1976, 90 Stat. 2641, 42 U.S.C. § 1988. See generally *Marek v. Chesny,* 473 U.S. 1, 43-51, 105 S.Ct. 3012, 87 L.Ed.2d 1 (1985) (Appendix to opinion of Brennan, J., dissenting).[4]

In designating those parties eligible for an award of litigation costs, Congress employed the term "prevailing party," a legal term of art. Black's Law Dictionary 1145 (7th ed.1999) defines "prevailing party" as "[a] party in whose favor a judgment is rendered, regardless of the amount of damages awarded <in certain cases, the court will award attorney's fees to the prevailing party>. – Also termed *successful party*." This view that a "prevailing party" is one who has been awarded some relief by the court can be distilled from our prior cases.[5]

In *Hanrahan v. Hampton,* 446 U.S. 754, 758, 100 S.Ct. 1987, 64 L.Ed.2d 670 (1980) (*per curiam*), we reviewed the legislative history of § 1988 and found that "Congress intended to permit the interim award of counsel fees only when a party has prevailed on the merits of at least some of his claims." Our "[r]espect for ordinary language requires that a plaintiff receive at least some relief on the merits of his claim before he can be said to prevail." *Hewitt v. Helms,* 482 U.S. 755, 760, 107 S.Ct.

---

[4]   We have interpreted these fee-shifting provisions consistently, see *Hensley v. Eckerhart,* 461 U.S. 424, 433, n.7, 103 S.Ct. 1933, 76 L.Ed.2d 40 (1983), and so approach the nearly identical provisions at issue here.

[5]   We have never had occasion to decide whether the term "prevailing party" allows an award of fees under the "catalyst theory" described above. Dictum in *Hewitt v. Helms,* 482 U.S. 755, 760, 107 S.Ct. 2672, 96 L.Ed.2d 654 (1987), alluded to the possibility of attorney's fees where "voluntary action by the defendant . . . affords the plaintiff all or some of the relief . . . sought," but we expressly reserved the question, see *id.* at 763, 107 S.Ct. 2672 ("We need not decide the circumstances, if any, under which this 'catalyst' theory could justify a fee award"). And though the Court of Appeals for the Fourth Circuit relied upon our decision in *Farrar v. Hobby,* 506 U.S. 103, 113 S.Ct. 566, 121 L.Ed.2d 494 (1992), in rejecting the "catalyst theory," *Farrar* "involved no catalytic effect." *Friends of Earth, Inc. v. Laidlaw Environmental Services (TOC), Inc.,* 528 U.S. 167, 194, 120 S.Ct. 693, 145 L.Ed.2d 610 (2000). Thus, there is language in our cases supporting both petitioners and respondents, and last Term we observed that it was an open question here. See *ibid.*

2672, 96 L.Ed.2d 654 (1987). We have held that even an award of nominal damages suffices under this test. See *Farrar v. Hobby*, 506 U.S. 103, 113 S.Ct. 566, 121 L.Ed.2d 494 (1992).

In addition to judgments on the merits, we have held that settlement agreements enforced through a consent decree may serve as the basis for an award of attorney's fees. See *Maher v. Gagne*, 448 U.S. 122, 100 S.Ct. 2570, 65 L.Ed.2d 653 (1980). Although a consent decree does not always include an admission of liability by the defendant, see, *e.g.*, *id.* at 126, n.8, 100 S.Ct. 2570, it nonetheless is a court-ordered "chang[e][in] the legal relationship between [the plaintiff] and the defendant." *Texas State Teachers Assn. v. Garland Independent School Dist.*, 489 U.S. 782, 792, 109 S.Ct. 1486, 103 L.Ed.2d 866 (1989) (citing Hewitt, supra, at 760-761, 107 S.Ct. 2672, and *Rhodes v. Stewart*, 488 U.S. 1, 3-4, 109 S.Ct. 202, 102 L.Ed.2d 1 (1988) (*per curiam*)). These decisions, taken together, establish that enforceable judgments on the merits and court-ordered consent decrees create the "material alteration of the legal relationship of the parties" necessary to permit an award of attorney's fees. * * *.

We think, however, the "catalyst theory" falls on the other side of the line from these examples. It allows an award where there is no judicially sanctioned change in the legal relationship of the parties. Even under a limited form of the "catalyst theory," a plaintiff could recover attorney's fees if it established that the "complaint had sufficient merit to withstand a motion to dismiss for lack of jurisdiction or failure to state a claim on which relief may be granted." * * * This is not the type of legal merit that our prior decisions, based upon plain language and congressional intent, have found necessary. * * * A defendant's voluntary change in conduct, although perhaps accomplishing what the plaintiff sought to achieve by the lawsuit, lacks the necessary judicial *imprimatur* on the change. Our precedents thus counsel against holding that the term "prevailing party" authorizes an award of attorney's fees *without* a corresponding alteration in the legal relationship of the parties.

The dissenters chide us for upsetting "long-prevailing *Circuit* precedent." *Post*, at 1850 (opinion of GINSBURG, J.) (emphasis added). But, as Justice SCALIA points out in his concurrence, several Courts of Appeals have relied upon dicta in our prior cases in approving the "catalyst theory." See *post*, at 1849; see also *supra*, at 1839, n.5. Now that the issue is squarely presented, it behooves us to reconcile the plain language of the statutes with our prior *holdings*. We have only awarded attorney's fees where the plaintiff has received a judgment on the merits, see, *e.g.*, *Farrar*, *supra*, at 112, 113 S.Ct. 566, or obtained a court-ordered consent decree, *Maher*, *supra*, at 129-130, 100 S.Ct. 2570 — we have not awarded attorney's fees where the plaintiff has secured the reversal of a directed verdict, see *Hanrahan*, 446 U.S. at 759, 100 S.Ct. 1987, or acquired a judicial pronouncement that the defendant has violated the Constitution unaccompanied by "*judicial* relief," *Hewitt*, *supra*, at 760, 107

S.Ct. 2672 (emphasis added). Never have we awarded attorney's fees for a nonjudicial "alteration of actual circumstances." *Post*, at 1856 (dissenting opinion). While urging an expansion of our precedents on this front, the dissenters would simultaneously abrogate the "merit" requirement of our prior cases and award attorney's fees where the plaintiff's claim "was at least colorable" and "not . . . groundless." *Post*, at 1852 (internal quotation marks and citation omitted). We cannot agree that the term "prevailing party" authorizes federal courts to award attorney's fees to a plaintiff who, by simply filing a nonfrivolous but nonetheless potentially meritless lawsuit (it will never be determined), has reached the "sought-after destination" without obtaining any judicial relief. *Post*, at 1856 (internal quotation marks and citation omitted).

Petitioners nonetheless argue that the legislative history of the Civil Rights Attorney's Fees Awards Act supports a broad reading of "prevailing party" which includes the "catalyst theory." We doubt that legislative history could overcome what we think is the rather clear meaning of "prevailing party" – the term actually used in the statute. Since we resorted to such history in *Garland*, 489 U.S. at 790, 109 S.Ct. 1486, *Maher*, 448 U.S. at 129, 100 S.Ct. 2570, and *Hanrahan*, *supra*, at 756-757, 100 S.Ct. 1987, however, we do likewise here.

The House Report to § 1988 states that "[t]he phrase 'prevailing party' is not intended to be limited to the victor only after entry of a final judgment following a full trial on the merits," H.R. Rep. No. 94-1558, p. 7 (1976), while the Senate Report explains that "parties may be considered to have prevailed when they vindicate rights through a consent judgment or without formally obtaining relief," S. Rep. No. 94-1011, p. 5 (1976), U.S. Code Cong. & Admin. News 1976, pp. 5908, 5912. Petitioners argue that these Reports and their reference to a 1970 decision from the Court of Appeals for the Eighth Circuit, *Parham v. Southwestern Bell Telephone Co.*, 433 F.2d 421 (C.A.8 1970), indicate Congress' intent to adopt the "catalyst theory." We think the legislative history cited by petitioners is at best ambiguous as to the availability of the "catalyst theory" for awarding attorney's fees. Particularly in view of the "American Rule" that attorney's fees will not be awarded absent "explicit statutory authority," such legislative history is clearly insufficient to alter the accepted meaning of the statutory term. * * *

Petitioners finally assert that the "catalyst theory" is necessary to prevent defendants from unilaterally mooting an action before judgment in an effort to avoid an award of attorney's fees. They also claim that the rejection of the "catalyst theory" will deter plaintiffs with meritorious but expensive cases from bringing suit. We are skeptical of these assertions, which are entirely speculative and unsupported by any empirical evidence (*e.g.*, whether the number of suits brought in the Fourth Circuit has declined, in relation to other Circuits, since the decision in S-1 and S-2).

Petitioners discount the disincentive that the "catalyst theory" may have upon a defendant's decision to voluntarily change its conduct, conduct that may not be illegal. "The defendants' potential liability for fees in this kind of litigation can be as significant as, and sometimes even more significant than, their potential liability on the merits," *Evans v. Jeff D.*, 475 U.S. 717, 734, 106 S.Ct. 1531, 89 L.Ed.2d 747 (1986), and the possibility of being assessed attorney's fees may well deter a defendant from altering its conduct.

And petitioners' fear of mischievous defendants only materializes in claims for equitable relief, for so long as the plaintiff has a cause of action for damages, a defendant's change in conduct will not moot the case. Even then, it is not clear how often courts will find a case mooted: "It is well settled that a defendant's voluntary cessation of a challenged practice does not deprive a federal court of its power to determine the legality of the practice" unless it is "absolutely clear that the allegedly wrongful behavior could not reasonably be expected to recur." *Friends of Earth, Inc. v. Laidlaw Environmental Services (TOC), Inc.*, 528 U.S. 167, 189, 120 S.Ct. 693, 145 L.Ed.2d 610 (2000) (internal quotation marks and citations omitted). If a case is not found to be moot, and the plaintiff later procures an enforceable judgment, the court may of course award attorney's fees. Given this possibility, a defendant has a strong incentive to enter a settlement agreement, where it can negotiate attorney's fees and costs. *Cf. Marek v. Chesny*, 473 U.S. at 7, 105 S.Ct. 3012 ("[M]any a defendant would be unwilling to make a binding settlement offer on terms that left it exposed to liability for attorney's fees in whatever amount the court might fix on motion of the plaintiff" (internal quotation marks and citation omitted)).

We have also stated that "[a] request for attorney's fees should not result in a second major litigation," *Hensley v. Eckerhart*, 461 U.S. 424, 437, 103 S.Ct. 1933, 76 L.Ed.2d 40 (1983), and have accordingly avoided an interpretation of the fee-shifting statutes that would have "spawn[ed] a second litigation of significant dimension," *Garland, supra*, at 791, 109 S.Ct. 1486. Among other things, a "catalyst theory" hearing would require analysis of the defendant's subjective motivations in changing its conduct, an analysis that "will likely depend on a highly factbound inquiry and may turn on reasonable inferences from the nature and timing of the defendant's change in conduct." * * * Although we do not doubt the ability of district courts to perform the nuanced "three thresholds" test required by the "catalyst theory" – whether the claim was colorable rather than groundless; whether the lawsuit was a substantial rather than an insubstantial cause of the defendant's change in conduct; whether the defendant's change in conduct was motivated by the plaintiff's threat of victory rather than threat of expense, see *post*, at 1852 (dissenting opinion) – it is clearly not a formula for "ready administrability." *Burlington v. Dague*, 505 U.S. 557, 566, 112 S.Ct. 2638, 120 L.Ed.2d 449 (1992).

Given the clear meaning of "prevailing party" in the fee-shifting statutes, we need not determine which way these various policy arguments cut. In *Alyeska*, 421 U.S. at 260, 95 S.Ct. 1612, we said that Congress had not "extended any roving authority to the Judiciary to allow counsel fees as costs or otherwise whenever the courts might deem them warranted." To disregard the clear legislative language and the holdings of our prior cases on the basis of such policy arguments would be a similar assumption of a "roving authority." For the reasons stated above, we hold that the "catalyst theory" is not a permissible basis for the award of attorney's fees under the FHAA, 42 U.S.C. § 3613(c)(2), and ADA, 42 U.S.C. § 12205.

The judgment of the Court of Appeals is

Affirmed.

JUSTICE SCALIA, with whom JUSTICE THOMAS joins, concurring.

* * *

I

"Prevailing party" is not some newfangled legal term invented for use in late-20th-century fee-shifting statutes. "[B]y the long established practice and universally recognized rule of the common law, in actions at law, the prevailing party is entitled to recover a judgment for costs . . . ." *Mansfield, C. & L.M.R. Co. v. Swan*, 111 U.S. 379, 387, 4 S.Ct. 510, 28 L.Ed. 462 (1884).

> "Costs have usually been allowed to the prevailing party, as incident to the judgment, since the statute 6 Edw. I, c. 1, § 2, and the same rule was acknowledged in the courts of the States, at the time the judicial system of the United States was organized. * * *

"Weighed in the light of these several provisions in the Judiciary Act [of 1789], the conclusion appears to be clear that Congress intended to allow costs to the prevailing party, as incident to the judgment. . . ." *The Baltimore*, 8 Wall. 377, 388, 390 [19 L.Ed. 463] (1869).

The term has been found within the United States Statutes at Large since at least the Bankruptcy Act of 1867, which provided that "[t]he party prevailing in the suit shall be entitled to costs against the adverse party." Act of Mar. 2, 1867, ch. 176, § 24, 14 Stat. 528. See also Act of Mar. 3, 1887, ch. 359, § 15, 24 Stat. 508 ("If the Government of the United States shall put in issue the right of the plaintiff to recover the court may, in its discretion, allow costs to the prevailing party from the time of joining such issue"). A computer search shows that the term "prevailing party" appears at least 70 times in the current United States Code; it is no stranger to the law.

At the time 42 U.S.C. § 1988 was enacted, I know of no case, state or federal, in which – either under a statutory invocation of "prevailing party" or under the common-law rule – the "catalyst theory" was enunciated as the basis for awarding costs. * * * The other state or state-law cases the dissent cites as awarding costs despite the absence of a judgment all involve a judicial finding – or its equivalent, an acknowledgment by the defendant – of the merits of plaintiff's case. Moreover, the dissent cites *not a single case* in which this Court – or even any other federal court applying federal law prior to enactment of the fee-shifting statutes at issue here – has regarded as the "prevailing party" a litigant who left the courthouse emptyhanded. If the term means what the dissent contends, that is a remarkable absence of authority.

That a judicial finding of liability was an understood requirement of "prevailing" is confirmed by many statutes that use the phrase in a context that *presumes* the existence of a judicial ruling. * * *

The dissent points out, *post*, at 1853, that the Prison Litigation Reform Act of 1995 limits attorney's fees to an amount "proportionately related to the court ordered relief for the violation." This shows that *sometimes* Congress *does* explicitly "tightly bind fees to judgments," *ibid.*, inviting (the dissent believes) the conclusion that "prevailing party" does *not* fasten fees to judgments. That conclusion does not follow from the premise. What this statutory provision demonstrates, *at most*, is that use of the phrase "prevailing party" is not the *only* way to impose a requirement of court-ordered relief. That is assuredly true. But it would be no more rational to reject the normal meaning of "prevailing party" because some statutes produce the same result with different language, than it would be to conclude that, since there are many synonyms for the word "jump," the word "jump" must mean something else.

It is undoubtedly true, as the dissent points out by quoting a nonlegal dictionary, see *post*, at 1855-1856, that the word "prevailing" can have other meanings in other contexts: "prevailing winds" are the winds that predominate, and the "prevailing party" in an election is the party that wins the election. But when "prevailing party" is used by courts or legislatures in the context of a lawsuit, it is a term of art. It has traditionally – and to my knowledge, prior to enactment of the first of the statutes at issue here, *invariably* – meant the party that wins the suit or obtains a finding (or an admission) of liability. * * * Words that have acquired a specialized meaning in the legal context must be accorded their *legal* meaning.

> "[W]here Congress borrows terms of art in which are accumulated the legal tradition and meaning of centuries of practice, it presumably knows and adopts the cluster of ideas that were attached to each borrowed word in the body of learning from which it was taken and the meaning its use will convey to the judicial mind unless otherwise instructed.

In such case, absence of contrary direction may be taken as satisfaction with widely accepted definitions, not as a departure from them." *Morissette v. United States*, 342 U.S. 246, 263 (1952).

The cases cited by the dissent in which we have "not treated Black's Law Dictionary as preclusively definitive," *post*, at 1853, are inapposite. In both *Pioneer Investment Services Co. v. Brunswick Associates Ltd. Partnership*, 507 U.S. 380, 113 S.Ct. 1489, 123 L.Ed.2d 74 (1993), and *United States v. Rodgers*, 466 U.S. 475, 104 S.Ct. 1942, 80 L.Ed.2d 492 (1984), we rejected Black's definition because it conflicted with our precedent. See *Pioneer*, *supra*, at 395-396, n.14, 113 S.Ct. 1489; *Rodgers*, *supra*, at 480, 104 S.Ct. 1942. We did not, as the dissent would do here, simply reject a relevant definition of a word tailored to judicial settings in favor of a more general definition from another dictionary.

II

The dissent distorts the term "prevailing party" beyond its normal meaning for policy reasons, but even those seem to me misguided. They rest upon the presumption that the catalyst theory applies when "*the suit's merit* led the defendant to abandon the fray, to switch rather than fight on, to accord plaintiff sooner rather than later the principal redress sought in the complaint," *post*, at 1850 (emphasis added). As the dissent would have it, by giving the term its normal meaning the Court today approves the practice of denying attorney's fees to a plaintiff with a proven claim of discrimination, simply because the very *merit* of his claim led the defendant to capitulate before judgment. That is not the case. To the contrary, the Court *approves* the result in *Parham v. Southwestern Bell Tel. Co.*, 433 F.2d 421 (C.A.8 1970), where attorney's fees were awarded "after [a] finding that the defendant had acted unlawfully," *ante*, at 1842, and n.9. What the dissent's stretching of the term produces is something more, and something far less reasonable: an award of attorney's fees when the merits of the plaintiff's case remain unresolved – when, for all one knows, the defendant only "abandon[ed] the fray" because the cost of litigation – either financial or in terms of public relations – would be too great. In such a case, the plaintiff may have "prevailed" as Webster's defines that term – "gain[ed] victory by virtue of strength or superiority," see *post*, at 1855. But I doubt it was greater strength in financial resources, or superiority in media manipulation, rather than *superiority in legal merit*, that Congress intended to reward.

It could be argued, perhaps, that insofar as abstract justice is concerned, there is little to choose between the dissent's outcome and the Court's: If the former sometimes rewards the plaintiff with a phony claim (there is no way of knowing), the latter sometimes denies fees to the plaintiff with a solid case whose adversary slinks away on the eve of judgment. But it seems to me the evil of the former far outweighs the evil of the latter. There is all the difference in the world between a rule that denies the extraordinary boon of attorney's fees to some plaintiffs who are no less "deserving" of them than others who receive them, and a rule that causes the law to be the very instrument of wrong – exacting the payment of attorney's fees to the extortionist.

It is true that monetary settlements and consent decrees can be extorted as well, and we have approved the award of attorney's fees in cases resolved through such mechanisms. See *ante*, at 1840 (citing cases). Our decision that the statute makes plaintiff a "prevailing party" under such circumstances was based entirely on language in a House Report, see *Maher v. Gagne*, 448 U.S. 122, 129, 100 S.Ct. 2570, 65 L.Ed.2d 653 (1980), and if this issue were to arise for the first time today, I doubt whether I would agree with that result. See *Hewitt v. Helms*, 482 U.S. 755, 760, 107 S.Ct. 2672, 96 L.Ed.2d 654 (1987) (SCALIA, J.) (opining that "[r]espect for ordinary language requires that a plaintiff receive at least some relief *on the merits* of his claim before he can be said to prevail" (emphasis added)). But in the case of court-approved settlements and consent decrees, even if there has been no judicial determination of the merits, the outcome is at least the product of, and bears the sanction of, judicial action *in the lawsuit*. There is at least *some* basis for saying that the party favored by the settlement or decree prevailed *in the suit*. Extending the holding of Maher to a case in which no judicial action whatever has been taken stretches the term "prevailing party" (and the potential injustice that *Maher* produces) beyond what the normal meaning of that term in the litigation context can conceivably support. * * *

The dissent's ultimate worry is that today's opinion will "impede access to court for the less well-heeled," *post*, at 1850. But, of course, the catalyst theory also harms the "less well-heeled," putting pressure on them to avoid the risk of massive fees by abandoning a solidly defensible case early in litigation. Since the fee-shifting statutes at issue here allow defendants as well as plaintiffs to receive a fee award, we know that Congress did not intend to *maximize* the quantity of "the enforcement of federal law by private attorneys general," *ibid*. Rather, Congress desired an *appropriate* level of enforcement – which is more likely to be produced by limiting fee awards to plaintiffs who prevail "on the merits," or at least to those who achieve an enforceable "alteration of the legal relationship of the parties," than by permitting the open-ended inquiry approved by the dissent.

III

The dissent points out that the catalyst theory has been accepted by "the clear majority of Federal Circuits," *ibid*. But our disagreeing with a "clear majority" of the Circuits is not at all a rare phenomenon. Indeed, our opinions sometimes contradict the *unanimous* and longstanding interpretation of lower federal courts. * * *

The dissent's insistence that we defer to the "clear majority" of Circuit opinion is particularly peculiar in the present case, since that majority has been nurtured and preserved *by our own misleading dicta* (to which I, unfortunately, contributed). Most of the Court of Appeals cases cited by the dissent, *post*, at 1852, and n.5, as reaffirming the catalyst theory after our decision in *Farrar v. Hobby*, 506 U.S. 103, 113 S.Ct. 566, 121 L.Ed.2d 494 (1992), relied on our earlier opinion in *Hewitt*. * * * Deferring to our colleagues' own error is bad enough; but enshrining the error that we ourselves have improvidently suggested and blaming it on the near-unanimous judgment of our colleagues would surely be unworthy. Informing the Courts of Appeals that our ill-considered dicta have misled them displays, it seems to me, not "disrespect," but a most becoming (and well-deserved) humility.

* * *

The Court today concludes that a party cannot be deemed to have prevailed, for purposes of fee-shifting statutes such as 42 U.S.C. §§ 1988, 3613(c)(2) (1994 ed. and Supp. V), unless there has been an enforceable "alteration of the legal relationship of the parties." That is the normal meaning of "prevailing party" in litigation, and there is no proper basis for departing from that normal meaning. Congress is free, of course, to revise these provisions – but it is my guess that if it does so it will not create the sort of inequity that the catalyst theory invites, but will require the court to determine that there was at least a substantial likelihood that the party requesting fees would have prevailed.

JUSTICE GINSBURG, with whom JUSTICE STEVENS, JUSTICE SOUTER, and JUSTICE BREYER join, dissenting.

The Court today holds that a plaintiff whose suit prompts the precise relief she seeks does not "prevail," and hence cannot obtain an award of attorney's fees, unless she also secures a court entry memorializing her victory. The entry need not be a judgment on the merits. Nor need there be any finding of wrongdoing. A court-approved settlement will do.

The Court's insistence that there be a document filed in court – a litigated judgment or court-endorsed settlement – upsets long-prevailing Circuit precedent applicable to scores of federal fee-shifting statutes. The decision allows a defendant to escape a statutory obligation to pay a plaintiff's counsel fees, even though the suit's merit led the defendant to abandon the fray, to switch rather than fight on, to accord plaintiff sooner rather than later the principal redress sought in the complaint. Concomitantly, the Court's constricted definition of "prevailing party," and consequent rejection of the "catalyst theory," impede access to court for the less well heeled, and shrink the incentive Congress created for the enforcement of federal law by private attorneys general.

In my view, the "catalyst rule," as applied by the clear majority of Federal Circuits, is a key component of the fee-shifting statutes Congress adopted to advance enforcement of civil rights. Nothing in history, precedent, or plain English warrants the anemic construction of the term "prevailing party" the Court today imposes.

I

[Justice GINSBURG recites the facts.]

II

A

The Court today detects a "clear meaning" of the term prevailing party, *ante*, at 1843, that has heretofore eluded the large majority of courts construing those words. "Prevailing party," today's opinion announces, means "one who has been awarded some relief by the court," *ante*, at 1839. The Court derives this "clear meaning" principally from Black's Law Dictionary, which defines a "prevailing party," in critical part, as one "in whose favor a judgment is rendered," *ibid.* (quoting Black's Law Dictionary 1145 (7th ed.1999)).

One can entirely agree with Black's Law Dictionary that a party "in whose favor a judgment is rendered" prevails, and at the same time resist, as most Courts of Appeals have, any implication that only such a party may prevail. In prior cases, we have not treated Black's Law Dictionary as preclusively definitive; instead, we have accorded statutory terms, including legal "term [s] of art," *ante*, at 1839 (opinion of the Court); *ante*, at 1846 (SCALIA, J., concurring), a contextual reading. See, *e.g.*, *Pioneer Investment Services Co. v. Brunswick Associates Ltd. Partnership*, 507 U.S. 380, 395-396, n.14, 113 S.Ct. 1489, 123 L.Ed.2d 74 (1993) (defining "excusable neglect," as used in Federal Rule of Bankruptcy Procedure 9006(b)(1), more broadly than Black's defines that term); *United States v. Rodgers*, 466 U.S. 475, 479-480, 104 S.Ct. 1942, 80 L.Ed.2d 492 (1984) (adopting "natural, nontechnical" definition of word "jurisdiction," as that term is used in 18 U.S.C. § 1001, and declining to confine definition to "narrower, more technical meanings," citing Black's). Notably, this Court did not refer to Black's Law Dictionary in *Maher v. Gagne*, 448 U.S. 122, 100 S.Ct. 2570, 65 L.Ed.2d 653 (1980), which held that a consent decree could qualify a plaintiff as "prevailing." The Court explained:

> "The fact that [plaintiff] prevailed through a settlement rather than through litigation does not weaken her claim to fees. Nothing in the language of [42 U.S.C.] § 1988 conditions the District Court's power to award fees on full litigation of the issues or on a judicial determination that the plaintiff's rights have been violated." *Id.* at 129, 100 S.Ct. 2570.

The spare "prevailing party" language of the fee-shifting provision applicable in *Maher*, and the similar wording of the fee-shifting provisions now before the Court, contrast with prescriptions that so tightly bind fees to judgments as to exclude the application of a catalyst concept. The Prison Litigation Reform Act of 1995, for example, directs that fee awards to prisoners under § 1988 be "proportionately related to the *court ordered relief* for the violation." 110 Stat. 1321-72, as amended, 42 U.S.C. § 1997e(d)(1)(B)(i) (1994 ed., Supp. V) (emphasis added). That statute, by its express terms, forecloses an award to a prisoner on a catalyst theory. But the FHAA and ADA fee-shifting prescriptions, modeled on 42 U.S.C. § 1988 unmodified, see *supra*, at 1851, n.1, do not similarly staple fee awards to "court ordered relief." Their very terms do not foreclose a catalyst theory.

B

It is altogether true, as the concurring opinion points out, *ante*, at 1843-1844, that litigation costs other than attorney's fees traditionally have been allowed to the "prevailing party," and that a judgment winner ordinarily fits that description. It is not true, however, that precedent on costs calls for the judgment requirement the Court ironly adopts today for attorney's fees. Indeed, the first decision cited in the concurring opinion, *Mansfield, C. & L.M.R. Co. v. Swan*, 111 U.S. 379, 4 S.Ct. 510, 28 L.Ed. 462 (1884), see *ante*, at 1843, tugs against the restrictive rule today's decision installs.

In *Mansfield*, plaintiffs commenced a contract action in state court. Over plaintiffs' objections, defendants successfully removed the suit to federal court. Plaintiffs prevailed on the merits there, and defendants obtained review here. See 111 U.S. at 380-381, 4 S.Ct. 510. This Court determined, on its own motion, that federal subject-matter jurisdiction was absent from the start. Based on that determination, the Court reversed the lower court's judgment for plaintiffs. Worse than entering and leaving this Courthouse equally "emptyhanded," *ante*, at 1845 (concurring opinion), the plaintiffs in *Mansfield* were stripped of the judgment they had won, including the "judicial finding . . . of the merits" in their favor, *ante*, at 1844 (concurring opinion). The *Mansfield* plaintiffs did, however, achieve this small consolation: The Court awarded them costs here as well as below. Recognizing that defendants had "prevail[ed]" in a "formal and nominal sense," the *Mansfield* Court nonetheless concluded that "[i]n a true and proper sense" defendants were "the losing and not the prevailing party." 111 U.S. at 388, 4 S.Ct. 510.

While *Mansfield* casts doubt on the present majority's "formal and nominal" approach, that decision does not consider whether costs would be in order for the plaintiff who obtains substantial relief, but no final judgment. Nor does "*a single case* " on which the concurring opinion today relies, *ante*, at 1845 (emphasis in original). There are, however, enlightening analogies. In multiple instances, state high courts have regarded plaintiffs as prevailing, for costs taxation purposes, when defendants' voluntary conduct, mooting the suit, provided the relief that plaintiffs sought. The concurring opinion labors unconvincingly to distinguish these state-law cases. A similar federal practice has been observed in cases governed by Federal Rule of Civil Procedure 54(d), the default rule allowing costs "to the prevailing party unless the court otherwise directs." * * *

In short, there is substantial support, both old and new, federal and state, for a costs award, "in [the court's] discretion," *supra*, at 1851, n.1, to the plaintiff whose suit prompts the defendant to provide the relief plaintiff seeks.

C

Recognizing that no practice set in stone, statute, rule, or precedent, see *infra*, at 1861, dictates the proper construction of modern civil rights fee-shifting prescriptions, I would "assume . . . that Congress intends the words in its enactments to carry 'their ordinary, contemporary, common meaning.'" *Pioneer*, 507 U.S. at 388, 113 S.Ct. 1489 (defining "excusable neglect") (quoting *Perrin v. United States*, 444 U.S. 37, 42, 100 S.Ct. 311, 62 L.Ed.2d 199 (1979) (defining "bribery")); see also, *e.g.*, *Sutton v. United Air Lines, Inc.*, 527 U.S. 471, 491, 119 S.Ct. 2139, 144 L.Ed.2d 450 (1999) (defining "substantially" in light of ordinary usage); *Rutledge v. United States*, 517 U.S. 292, 299-300, n.10, 116 S.Ct. 1241, 134 L.Ed.2d 419 (1996) (similarly defining "in concert"). In everyday use, "prevail" means "gain victory by virtue of strength or superiority: win mastery: triumph." Webster's Third New International Dictionary 1797 (1976). There are undoubtedly situations in which an individual's goal is to obtain approval of a judge, and in those situations, one cannot "prevail" short of a judge's formal declaration. In a piano competition or a figure skating contest, for example, the person who prevails is the person declared winner by the judges. However, where the ultimate goal is not an arbiter's approval, but a favorable alteration of actual circumstances, a formal declaration is not essential. Western democracies, for instance, "prevailed" in the Cold War even though the Soviet Union never formally surrendered. Among television viewers, John F. Kennedy "prevailed" in the first debate with Richard M. Nixon during the 1960 Presidential contest, even though moderator Howard K. Smith never declared a winner. See T. White, The Making of the President 1960, pp. 293-294 (1961).

A lawsuit's ultimate purpose is to achieve actual relief from an opponent. Favorable judgment may be instrumental in gaining that relief. Generally, however, "the judicial decree is not the end but the means. At the end of the rainbow lies not a judgment, but some action (or cessation of action) by the defendant * * *." *Hewitt v. Helms*, 482 U.S. 755, 761, 107 S.Ct. 2672, 96 L.Ed.2d 654 (1987). On this common understanding, if a party reaches the "sought-after destination," then the party "prevails" regardless of the "route taken." *Hennigan v. Ouachita Parish School Bd.*, 749 F.2d 1148, 1153 (C.A.5 1985).

Under a fair reading of the FHAA and ADA provisions in point, I would hold that a party "prevails" in "a true and proper sense," *Mansfield*, 111 U.S. at 388, 4 S.Ct. 510, when she achieves, by instituting litigation, the practical relief sought in her complaint. The Court misreads Congress, as I see it, by insisting that, invariably, relief must be displayed in a judgment, and correspondingly that a defendant's voluntary action never suffices. In this case, Buckhannon's purpose in suing West Virginia officials was not narrowly to obtain a judge's approbation. The plaintiffs' objective was to stop enforcement of a rule requiring Buckhannon to evict residents like centenarian Dorsey Pierce as the price of remaining in business. If Buckhannon achieved that objective on account of the strength of its case, see *supra*, at 1852-1853 – if it succeeded in keeping its doors open while housing and caring for Ms. Pierce and others similarly situated – then Buckhannon is properly judged a party who prevailed.

III

As the Courts of Appeals have long recognized, the catalyst rule suitably advances Congress' endeavor to place private actions, in civil rights and other legislatively defined areas, securely within the federal law enforcement arsenal.

The catalyst rule stemmed from modern legislation extending civil rights protections and enforcement measures. The Civil Rights Act of 1964 included provisions for fee awards to "prevailing parties" in Title II (public accommodations), 42 U.S.C. § 2000a-3(b), and Title VII (employment), 42 U.S.C. § 2000e-5(k), but not in Title VI (federal programs). The provisions' central purpose was "to promote vigorous enforcement" of the laws by private plaintiffs; although using the two-way term "prevailing party," Congress did not make fees available to plaintiffs and defendants on equal terms. * * *

Once the 1964 Act came into force, courts commenced to award fees regularly under the statutory authorizations, and sometimes without such authorization. See *Alyeska Pipeline Service Co. v. Wilderness Society,* 421 U.S. 240, 262, 270-271, n.46, 95 S.Ct. 1612, 44 L.Ed.2d 141 (1975). In *Alyeska,* this Court reaffirmed the "American rule" that a court generally may not award attorney's fees without a legislative instruction to do so. See *id*. at 269, 95 S.Ct. 1612. To provide the authorization *Alyeska* required for fee awards under Title VI of the 1964 Civil Rights Act, as well as under Reconstruction Era civil rights legislation, 42 U.S.C. §§ 1981-1983, 1985, 1986 (1994 ed. and Supp. IV), and certain other enactments, Congress passed the Civil Rights Attorney's Fees Awards Act of 1976, 42 U.S.C. § 1988 (1994 ed. and Supp. IV).

As explained in the Reports supporting § 1988, civil rights statutes vindicate public policies "of the highest priority," S. Rep. No. 94-1011, p. 3 (1976), U.S. Code Cong. & Admin. News 1976, pp. 5908, 5910 (quoting *Newman v. Piggie Park Enterprises, Inc.,* 390 U.S. 400, 402, 88 S.Ct. 964, 19 L.Ed.2d 1263 (1968) *(per curiam)*), yet "depend heavily on private enforcement," S. Rep. No. 94-1011, at 2, U.S. Code Cong. & Admin. News 1976, pp. 5908, 5910. Persons who bring meritorious civil rights claims, in this light, serve as "private attorneys general." *Id.* at 5, U.S. Code Cong. & Admin. News 1976, pp. 5908, 5912; H.R. Rep. No. 94-1558, p. 2 (1976). Such suitors, Congress recognized, often "cannot afford legal counsel." *Id.* at 1. They therefore experience "severe hardshi[p]" under the "American Rule." *Id.* at 2. Congress enacted § 1988 to ensure that nonaffluent plaintiffs would have "effective access" to the Nation's courts to enforce civil rights laws. *Id.* at 1.[9] That objective accounts for the fee-shifting provisions before the Court in this case, prescriptions of the FHAA and the ADA modeled on § 1988. See *supra*, at 1851, n.1.

Under the catalyst rule that held sway until today, plaintiffs who obtained the relief they sought through suit on genuine claims ordinarily qualified as "prevailing parties," so that courts had discretion to award them their costs and fees. Persons with limited resources were not impelled to "wage total law" in order to assure that their counsel fees would be paid. They could accept relief, in money or of another kind, voluntarily proffered by a defendant who sought to avoid a recorded decree. And they could rely on a judge then to determine, in her equitable discretion, whether counsel fees were warranted and, if so, in what amount.

Congress appears to have envisioned that very prospect. The Senate Report on the 1976 Civil Rights Attorney's Fees Awards Act states: "[F]or purposes of the award of counsel fees, parties may be considered to have prevailed when they vindicate rights through a consent judgment *or without formally obtaining relief.*" S. Rep. No. 94-1011, at 5, U.S. Code Cong. & Admin. News 1976, pp. 5908, 5912 (emphasis added). In support, the Report cites cases in which parties recovered fees in the absence of any court-conferred relief.[11] The House Report corroborates: "[A]fter a

---

[9]   See H.R. Rep. No. 94-1558, at 1, U.S. Code Cong. & Admin. News 1976, pp. 5908, 5910 ("Because a vast majority of the victims of civil rights violations cannot afford legal counsel, they are unable to present their cases to the courts . . . . [This statute] is designed to give such persons effective access to the judicial process . . . ."); S. Rep. No. 94-1011, at 2 ("If private citizens are to be able to assert their civil rights, and if those who violate the Nation's fundamental laws are not to proceed with impunity, then citizens must have the opportunity to recover what it costs them to vindicate these rights in court.") * * *.

[11]   See S. Rep. No. 94-1011, at 5, U.S. Code Cong. & Admin. News 1976, pp. 5908, 5912-5913 (citing *Kopet v. Esquire Realty Co.*, 523 F.2d 1005, 1008-1009 (C.A.2 1975) (partner sued his firm for release of documents, firm released the documents, court awarded fees because of the release, even though the partner's claims were "dismissed for lack of subject matter jurisdiction"), and *Thomas v. Honeybrook Mines, Inc.*, 428 F.2d 981, 984, 985 (C.A.3 1970) (union committee twice commenced suit

complaint is filed, a defendant might voluntarily cease the unlawful practice. *A court should still award fees* even though it might conclude, as a matter of equity, that *no formal relief,* such as an injunction, is needed." H.R. Rep. No. 94-1558, at 7 (emphases added). These Reports, Courts of Appeals have observed, are hardly ambiguous. * * * Congress, I am convinced, understood that " '[v]ictory' in a civil rights suit is typically a practical, rather than a strictly legal matter." *Exeter-West Greenwich Regional School Dist. v. Pontarelli,* 788 F.2d 47, 51 (C.A.1 1986) (citation omitted).

IV

The Court identifies several "policy arguments" that might warrant rejection of the catalyst rule. See *ante,* at 1842-1843. A defendant might refrain from altering its conduct, fearing liability for fees as the price of voluntary action. See *ante,* at 1842. Moreover, rejection of the catalyst rule has limited impact: Desisting from the challenged conduct will not render a case moot where damages are sought, and even when the plaintiff seeks only equitable relief, a defendant's voluntary cessation of a challenged practice does not render the case moot "unless it is 'absolutely clear that the allegedly wrongful behavior could not reasonably be expected to recur.' " *Ante,* at 1843 (quoting *Friends of Earth, Inc.,* 528 U.S. at 189, 120 S.Ct. 693). Because a mootness dismissal is not easily achieved, the defendant may be impelled to settle, negotiating fees less generous than a court might award. See *ante,* at 1843. Finally, a catalyst rule would "require analysis of the defendant's subjective motivations," and thus protract the litigation. *Ibid.*

The Court declines to look beneath the surface of these arguments, placing its reliance, instead, on a meaning of "prevailing party" that other jurists would scarcely recognize as plain. See *ibid.* Had the Court

---

for pension fund payments, suits prompted recovery, and court awarded fees even though the first suit had been dismissed and the second had not yet been adjudicated)).

The Court features a case cited by the House as well as the Senate in the Reports on § 1988, *Parham v. Southwestern Bell Tel. Co.,* 433 F.2d 421 (C.A.8 1970). The Court deems Parham consistent with its rejection of the catalyst rule, alternately because the Eighth Circuit made a "finding that the defendant had acted unlawfully," and because that court ordered the District Court to " 'retain jurisdiction over the matter . . . to insure the continued implementation of the [defendant's] policy of equal employment opportunities.' " *Ante,* at 1842, n.9 (quoting 433 F.2d at 429). Congress did not fix on those factors, however: Nothing in either Report suggests that judicial findings or retention of jurisdiction is essential to an award of fees. The courts in Kopet and Thomas awarded fees based on claims as to which they neither made "a finding" nor "retain[ed] jurisdiction." * * *

inspected the "policy arguments" listed in its opinion, I doubt it would have found them impressive.

In opposition to the argument that defendants will resist change in order to stave off an award of fees, one could urge that the catalyst rule may lead defendants promptly to comply with the law's requirements: the longer the litigation, the larger the fees. Indeed, one who knows noncompliance will be expensive might be encouraged to conform his conduct to the legal requirements before litigation is threatened. * * * No doubt, a mootness dismissal is unlikely when recurrence of the controversy is under the defendant's control. But, as earlier observed, see *supra*, at 1857, why should this Court's fee-shifting rulings drive a plaintiff prepared to accept adequate relief, though out-of-court and unrecorded, to litigate on and on? And if the catalyst rule leads defendants to negotiate not only settlement terms but also allied counsel fees, is that not a consummation to applaud, not deplore?

As to the burden on the court, is it not the norm for the judge to whom the case has been assigned to resolve fee disputes (deciding whether an award is in order, and if it is, the amount due), thereby clearing the case from the calendar? If factfinding becomes necessary under the catalyst rule, is it not the sort that "the district courts, in their factfinding expertise, deal with on a regular basis"? * * * Might not one conclude overall, as Courts of Appeals have suggested, that the catalyst rule "saves judicial resources," * * *, by encouraging "plaintiffs to discontinue litigation after receiving through the defendant's acquiescence the remedy initially sought"? * * *

The concurring opinion adds another argument against the catalyst rule: That opinion sees the rule as accommodating the "extortionist" who obtains relief because of "greater strength in financial resources, or superiority in media manipulation, rather than *superiority in legal merit.*" *Ante*, at 1847 (emphasis in original). This concern overlooks both the character of the rule and the judicial superintendence Congress ordered for all fee allowances. The catalyst rule was auxiliary to fee-shifting statutes whose primary purpose is "to promote the vigorous enforcement" of the civil rights laws. *Christiansburg Garment Co.*, 434 U.S. at 422, 98 S.Ct. 694. To that end, courts deemed the conduct-altering catalyst that counted to be the substance of the case, not merely the plaintiff's atypically superior financial resources, media ties, or political clout. See *supra*, at 1852-1853. And Congress assigned responsibility for awarding fees not to automatons unable to recognize extortionists, but to judges expected and instructed to exercise "discretion." See *supra*, at 1851, n.1. So viewed, the catalyst rule provided no berth for nuisance suits, see *Hooper*, 37 F.3d, at 292, or "thinly disguised forms of extortion," *Tyler v. Corner Constr. Corp.*, 167 F.3d 1202, 1206 (C.A.8 1999) (citation omitted).

V

As to our attorney's fee precedents, the Court correctly observes, "[w]e have never had occasion to decide whether the term 'prevailing party' allows an award of fees under the 'catalyst theory,'" and "there is language in our cases supporting both petitioners and respondents." *Ante*, at 1839, n.5. It bears emphasis, however, that in determining whether fee shifting is in order, the Court in the past has placed greatest weight not on any "judicial *imprimatur*," *ante*, at 1840, but on the practical impact of the lawsuit. In *Maher v. Gagne*, 448 U.S. 122, 100 S.Ct. 2570, 65 L.Ed.2d 653 (1980), in which the Court held fees could be awarded on the basis of a consent decree, the opinion nowhere relied on the presence of a formal judgment. See *supra*, at 1853; *infra*, n.14. Some years later, in *Hewitt v. Helms*, 482 U.S. 755, 107 S.Ct. 2672, 96 L.Ed.2d 654 (1987), the Court suggested that fees might be awarded the plaintiff who "obtain[ed] relief without [the] benefit of a formal judgment." *Id.* at 760, 107 S.Ct. 2672. The Court explained: "If the defendant, under the pressure of the lawsuit, pays over a money claim before the judicial judgment is pronounced," or "if the defendant, under pressure of [a suit for declaratory judgment], alters his conduct (or threatened conduct) towards the plaintiff," *i.e.*, conduct "that was the basis for the suit, the plaintiff will have prevailed." *Id.* at 761, 107 S.Ct. 2672. I agree, and would apply that analysis to this case.

The Court posits a "'merit' requirement of our prior cases." *Ante*, at 1841. *Maher*, however, affirmed an award of attorney's fees based on a consent decree that "did not purport to adjudicate [plaintiff's] statutory or constitutional claims." 448 U.S. at 126, n.8, 100 S.Ct. 2570. The decree in *Maher* "explicitly stated that 'nothing [therein was] intended to constitute an admission of fault by either party.'" *Ibid.* The catalyst rule, in short, conflicts with none of "our prior *holdings*," *ante*, at 1841.

* * *

Notes & Questions

1. *Buckhannon* raises a number of questions about statutory interpretation. How clear are the words "prevailing party"? The concurrence looks to the historical context in which the words were used, but the dissent looks to the present context of the statute. Which would Congress have looked to? Does it matter?

2. Should the Court's majority have considered legislative history in more depth? Which side – concurrence or dissent – has the better of that argument?

3. Which side in *Buckhannon* has the better of the policy argument regarding the need for the catalyst theory? Are defendants coerced more from the possibility of attorneys' fees' being awarded in questionable suits than plaintiffs are deterred by the possibility of not recovering because the defendant will voluntarily change? Again, does that matter?

4. The Supreme Court's rejection of the catalyst theory did not go unnoticed in Congress. In November 2002, Senators Feingold, Kennedy and Jeffords introduced S. 3161, which would have expressly provided that the definition of "prevailing party" includes:

> in addition to a party who substantially prevails through a judicial or administrative judgment or order, or an enforceable written agreement, a party whose pursuit of a non-frivolous claim or defense was a catalyst for a voluntary or unilateral change in position by the opposing party that provides any significant part of the relief sought.

S. 3161, 107th Cong. § 8(a) (2002). However, the bill has not been passed.

5. How far does *Buckhannon* go in limiting the availability of fees? A series of cases in the Ninth Circuit have explored the limits of *Buckhannon* when the parties enter into a settlement agreement. In *Barrios v. California Interscholastic Federation*, 277 F.3d 1128 (9th Cir. 2002), the plaintiff had entered into a settlement agreement with the defendant providing for the payment of $10,000 to the plaintiff and providing that the plaintiff, a baseball coach using a wheelchair, would be allowed to coach on the field, contrary to the prior decisions of the defendant. *Id.* at 1133. Although the Court initially had entered the settlement agreement as an order of the court, it later granted the defendant's motion to set aside its order. Accordingly, only an agreement existed between the plaintiff and the defendant. Nonetheless, the Ninth Circuit concluded that the plaintiff was a prevailing party for purposes of recovering attorneys' fees. Under prior Ninth Circuit law,

> [A] plaintiff 'prevails' when he or she enters into a legally enforceable settlement agreement against the defendant: "[A] plaintiff 'prevails' when actual relief on the merits of his claim materially alters the legal relationship between the parties by modifying the defendant's behavior in a way that directly benefits the plaintiff." The Court explained that "a material alteration of the legal relationship occurs [when] the plaintiff becomes entitled to enforce a judgment, consent decree, or settlement against the defendant."

Id. at 1134 (citing Fischer v. SJB-P.D. Inc., 214 F.3d 1115, 1118 (9th Cir. 2000) (quoting Farrar v. Hobby, 506 U.S. 103, 111-12 (1992)).

Thus, the issue was whether there was a material change in the relationship between the parties that is enforceable by a court. The Ninth Circuit concluded that *Buckhannon* did not alter that standard, because the plaintiff in *Barrios* did not claim merely to be a catalyst, but had obtained a legally enforceable settlement. *Id.* at 1134 n.5. The Ninth Circuit distinguished as dictum a footnote in *Buckhannon*, which stated that attorneys' fees are recoverable only with a judgment or a consent decree. *Id.*

6. Subsequently, the Ninth Circuit may have implicitly limited *Barrios*. In *Richard S. v. Department of Developmental Services*, 317 F.3d 1080 (9th Cir. 2003), the court had awarded preliminary injunctive relief in favor of the individual plaintiffs and permanent injunctive relief on a motion brought by an advocacy group as an intervener. The parties entered into a settlement agreement in open court, agreeing that its terms would be binding and enforceable as if reduced to writing. *Id.* at 1088.

On the plaintiffs' motion for attorneys' fees, the court originally awarded fees based in part on a catalyst theory, but held that the plaintiffs were not entitled to a fee due to their preliminary injunction, which only preserved the status quo. *Id.* The Supreme Court then decided *Buckhannon* and the district court reversed its prior award of attorneys' fees. In so doing, the court relied upon a footnote in *Buckhannon*, which states, "Private settlements do not entail the *judicial approval and oversight* involved in consent decrees." Richard S., 317 F.3d at 1088 (emphasis added) (quoting Buckhannon, 532 U.S. at 604 n.7). The Ninth Circuit again distinguished this footnote, which is itself arguably *dicta*, but now on the grounds that the magistrate judge presiding over the settlement negotiations had issued a minute order stating that the parties had entered into a binding and enforceable settlement agreement and retained jurisdiction to enforce the agreement. *Id.* at 1088. Similarly, in *American Disability Association v. Chmielarz*, 289 F.3d 1315, 1319-20 (11th Cir. 2002), the Eleventh Circuit stated:

> Thus, it is clear that, even absent the entry of a formal consent decree, if the district court either incorporates the terms of a settlement into its final order of dismissal *or* expressly retains jurisdiction to enforce a settlement, it may thereafter enforce the terms of the parties' agreement. Its authority to do so clearly establishes a "judicially sanctioned change in the legal relationship of the parties," as required by *Buckhannon*, because the plaintiff thereafter may return to court to have the settlement enforced.

Id. at 1320.

One might ask whether this holding cuts back on prior holdings, which did not require that the settlement agreement be entered on the record. There are several arguments why that might not be the case, assuming that the settlement agreement does result in a change in the relationship between or among the parties. First, to the extent that a settlement agreement provides that parties will change their behavior, it would be enforceable by a judicial proceeding. Second, it would appear to put form over substance to require that the settlement be entered on the record. Nonetheless, the Supreme Court may indeed follow what appears to be *dictum* in *Buckhannon*'s footnote 7, so plaintiffs who intend to seek attorneys' fees should embody any settlement agreement in a consent decree or at least a judicially enforceable order.

7. The *Richard S.* court also found that a preliminary injunction could constitute a basis for finding that a plaintiff was a prevailing party. Richard S., 317 F.3d at 1088-89 (citing Watson v. County of Riverside, 300 F.3d 1092, 1093 (9th Cir. 2002) and Williams v. Alioto, 625 F.2d 845, 847-48 (1980)). However, other circuits have rejected that conclusion, finding that prevailing party status may not be based upon a decision that is not on the merits of a claim. Christopher P. v. Marcus, 915 F.2d 794, 805 (2d Cir. 1990). Of course, neither of these cases involves the ADA. In short, the limits of the Supreme Court's rejection of the catalyst theory have yet to be fully explored.

8. How much does a plaintiff have to prevail in order to be a "prevailing party"? In *Buckhannon*, the Court decided that a prevailing party is "[a] party in whose favor a judgment is rendered, regardless of the amount of damages awarded." Buckhannon, 532 U.S. at 603 (quoting Black's Law Dictionary 1145 (7th ed. 1999)). Prevailing party status is not determined by the degree of success achieved, assuming there is some degree of success. Richard S., 317 F.3d at 1087. Rather, the degree of success may determine the amount of attorneys' fees. *Id.* at 1087 n.3. However, that formula may change when the plaintiff obtains only nominal damages. If parties recover injunctive relief, that alone suffices for attorneys' fees. Fischer v. SJB-P.D. Inc., 214 F.3d 1115, 1118 (9th Cir. 2000).

9. In a "mixed-motive" case, the plaintiff may show, for example, that the defendant violated the ADA in firing her; but the defendant may show that it would have taken the same action in the absence of the discrimination, so the plaintiff would take only a declaratory judgment. In those cases, the plaintiff is not entitled to attorneys' fees, because she is not a prevailing party under Section 12205. Pedigo v. P.A.M. Transp., Inc., 98 F.3d 396, 398 (8th Cir. 1996) ("*Pedigo II*"); *see also* Dehne v. Med. Shoppe Int'l, Inc., 261 F.Supp.2d 1142, 1147-48 (E.D. Mo. 2003). Section 107 of the Civil Rights Act of 1991, 42 U.S.C. § 2000e-5(g)(2)(B)(i) (2006), which should apply to ADA Title I cases, allows attorneys' fees even when only declaratory relief is awarded. Pedigo v. P.A.M. Transp., Inc., 60 F.3d 1300, 1301 (8th Cir. 1995). However, in *Pedigo II*, a later case involving the same parties, the Eighth Circuit looked to ADA section 505 and found the plaintiff had not prevailed for attorneys' fees purposes. The ADA-specific statute trumped the more general Title VII provision.

10. Plaintiffs often may be entitled to attorneys' fees under the appropriate state law if their award rests on state law claims. The Ninth Circuit certified the question whether the catalyst theory applies under California law to the California Supreme Court. On the reference from the Ninth Circuit, in *Tipton-Whittingham v. City of Los Angeles*, 34 Cal.4th 604 (Cal. 2004), the California Supreme Court held that the catalyst theory does justify attorney's fees in California.

☙

Importantly, although the ADA appears to allow awards of attorneys' fees to any prevailing party, whether she is the plaintiff or the defendant, the courts have generally found that fees are to be awarded only to the victims of discrimination (generally the plaintiffs). Defendants who prevail in ADA and other civil rights cases are generally held to be entitled to fees only if the plaintiff's case was brought in bad faith or when it is frivolous, unreasonable, or without foundation. Christiansburg Garment Co. v. EEOC, 434 U.S. 412, 421-22, 98 S.Ct. 694, 54 L.Ed.2d 648 (1978).

As the Seventh Circuit put it in *Adkins v. Briggs Stratton Corp.,* 159 F.3d 306 (7th Cir. 1998), "an award of fees to an employer is appropriate only when the suit is brought in bad faith or when it is frivolous, unreasonable, or without foundation." *See also* Bercovitch v. Baldwin Sch., Inc., 191 F.3d 8, 10 (1st Cir. 1999) (citing Hughes v. Rowe, 449 U.S. 5, 14 (1980) (per curiam) (noting that the Supreme Court has applied the same rule under 42 U.S.C. § 1983)). This asymmetry is a result of Congress's recognition that attorneys' fees under the ADA should be "interpreted in a manner consistent with the Civil Rights Attorneys' Fees Act [42 U.S.C. § 1988], including that statute's definition of prevailing party, as construed by the Supreme Court." H.R. Doc. No. 101-485 (III), at 73 (1990), 1990 U.S.C.C.A.N. 445, 496 (citing Christiansburg Garment Co. v. EEOC, 434 U.S. 412, 422 (1978), and Hughes, 449 U.S. at 5). The court is not required to award attorneys' fees to a prevailing defendant even if the action is frivolous. *See* Greenier v. Pace, Local No. 1188, 245 F.Supp.2d 247, 249, 250 (D. Me. 2003) ("[T]he frivolity showing required of a prevailing party applies with 'special force' in pro se actions. *Hughes v. Rowe*, 449 U.S. 5, 14-16 * * * (applying the *Christiansburg* standard to pro se plaintiffs under the fee-shifting provision 42 U.S.C. § 1988)," and refusing to award fees to defendant, "[i]n light of Plaintiff's limited ability to grasp the legal significance of his actions as well as the sanctions already imposed in this matter").

Generally, subjective bad faith is not required to show frivolousness, rather it is sufficient that the action objectively arguably lacks a basis in law or fact. Neitzke v. Williams, 490 U.S. 319, 325 (1989). In *Schutts v. Bently Nevada Corp.*, 966 F.Supp. 1549 (D. Nev. 1997), the plaintiff was fired by the defendant after the plaintiff was arrested for and eventually convicted of hitting a person with a gun and holding the gun to the person's head, threatening to "blow his brains out." Holding that the law in the Ninth Circuit and elsewhere clearly gave an employer the right to fire an employee for improper acts even if those acts arose out of an alleged disability – here depression – the Court found that the facts and "controlling federal judicial authority extant prior to the initiation of this action, should have made plain to Plaintiff and his lawyer the futility – and impropriety – of filing the complaint and of opposing Defendant's meritorious summary judgment motion." *Id.* at 1557. On those facts, the court awarded the defendant attorneys' fees under 42 U.S.C. § 12205

(2006) – and, showing its displeasure, under Federal Rule of Civil Procedure 11.

2.   Reasonableness Of Fees

The calculation of reasonable attorneys' fees in ADA cases is the same as that in other civil rights cases. In Title I and Title II cases, those fees can be a substantial percentage or even exceed the damages, and in Title III cases, fees are the only form of monetary relief. Therefore, their overhanging shadow can influence settlement discussions in even apparently defensible cases. The following case addresses a range of issues that arise when a court awards fees.

HANSEN v. DEERCREEK PLAZA, LLC.

United States District Court, S.D. Florida, 2006
420 F.Supp.2d 1346

SELTZER, United States Magistrate Judge.

THIS CAUSE is before the Court on Plaintiff's Verified Motion for Attorneys' Fees and Litigation Expenses and Costs (DE 28) and was referred to the undersigned United States Magistrate Judge pursuant to the consent of the parties.

PROCEDURAL BACKGROUND

Donald Hansen ("Plaintiff") filed this action for injunctive relief against Deercreek Plaza, LLC ("Defendant") pursuant to Title III of the Americans with Disabilities Act, 42 U.S.C. § 12181 *et seq.* Subsequently, the parties entered into a Consent Decree, whereby Defendant agreed to pay Plaintiff's reasonable attorneys' fees, litigation expenses, expert's fees, and costs.[1] The Court approved and adopted the Consent Decree and retained jurisdiction to enforce the Consent Decree (DE 27). Plaintiff thereafter filed the instant Verified Motion for Attorneys' Fees and Litigation Expenses and Costs (DE 28). Plaintiff seeks a total award – fees, expenses, and costs – of $13,483.56. Defendant filed a response to the Motion (DE 32), and Plaintiff filed a reply (DE 33); Defendant then filed a surreply (DE 36), to which Plaintiff again filed a response (DE 37).

The matter is now ripe for decision.

---

[1]   Under the Consent Decree, the parties were to negotiate the amount of fees, expenses, and costs that Defendant was to pay and, if they could not agree, they would submit the matter to the Court for determination of the amount. The parties were unable to agree on the amount, and the instant motion ensued.

The Americans with Disabilities Act ("ADA") has been appropriately described as "one of the landmark civil rights laws in this country." *Access Now, Inc. v. Southwest Airlines Co.,* 385 F.3d 1324, 1335 (11th Cir.2004). To promote the interests of this legislation, Congress turned to the private bar, as it had to promote the interests of our nation's other civil rights laws. *Hensley v. Eckerhart,* 461 U.S. 424, 445, 103 S.Ct. 1933, 76 L.Ed.2d 40 (1983) (action brought under § 1988; "Congress could, of course, have provided public funds or government attorneys for litigating private civil rights claims, but it chose to limit the growth of the enforcement bureaucracy . . . by continuing to rely on the private bar and by making defendants bear the full burden of paying for enforcement of their civil rights obligations."). For that reason, Congress expressly authorized awards of reasonable attorneys' fees, including litigation expenses and costs, to prevailing parties in ADA actions[2]:

> In any action or administrative proceeding commenced pursuant to this Act, the court or agency, in its discretion, may allow the prevailing party, other than the United States, a reasonable attorney's fee, including litigation expenses, and costs . . . . 42 U.S.C. § 12205. Indeed, were it not for the efforts of those attorneys willing to undertake the representation of ADA plaintiffs, there would be little, if any, enforcement of this landmark statute. *See Newman v. Piggie Park Enters., Inc.,* 390 U.S. 400, 402, 88 S.Ct. 964, 19 L.Ed.2d 1263 (1968) (action brought under the Civil Rights Act of 1964; "If successful plaintiffs were routinely forced to bear their own attorney's fees, few aggrieved persons would be in a position to advance the public interest by invoking the injunctive powers of the federal court."). Furthermore, Defendant here expressly agreed to "pay [Plaintiff's] counsel . . . for [Plaintiff's] attorneys' fees, litigation expenses, and costs incurred in this matter, and [Plaintiff's] expert, . . . for [Plaintiff's] expert fees and costs incurred in this matter." Consent Decree ¶ 4 (Ex. A to Motion (DE 28)).

---

[2]   It is undisputed that Plaintiff is the prevailing party herein. In *Buckhannon Board & Care Home, Inc. v. West Virginia Department of Health and Human Resources,* 532 U.S. 598, 121 S.Ct. 1835, 149 L.Ed.2d 855 (2001), the Supreme Court noted that a "material alteration of the legal relationship of the parties" is necessary to permit an attorney's fee award under a "prevailing party" fee-shifting statute. *Id.* at 604, 121 S.Ct. 1835 (quoting *Tex. State Teachers Ass'n v. Garland Indep. Sch. Dist.,* 489 U.S. 782, 792-93, 109 S.Ct. 1486, 103 L.Ed.2d 866 (1989)). The Court ruled that a settlement agreement "enforced through a consent decree" is a "court-ordered change in the legal relationship" between the parties sufficient to support a fee award. Id.

In the Motion, Plaintiff seeks attorneys' fees in the amount of $11,511.[3] This Circuit has adopted the lodestar method to determine a reasonable attorneys' fee. *Norman v. Hous. Auth. of City of Montgomery,* 836 F.2d 1292 (11th Cir.1988). To establish a lodestar amount, a court must ascertain the number of hours an attorney reasonably expended on the litigation and then multiply that figure by a reasonable hourly rate. Id. at 1299-1302. Under appropriate circumstances, the lodestar amount may be adjusted to reach a more appropriate attorneys' fee. Id. at 1302. The fee applicant bears the burden of documenting the reasonable hours expended and reasonable hourly rates. *ACLU of Georgia v. Barnes,* 168 F.3d 423, 427 (11th Cir.1999).

A. Reasonable Hourly Rates

In calculating a lodestar amount, the Court must first determine whether the hourly rates sought are reasonable. "A reasonable hourly rate is the prevailing market rate in the relevant legal community for similar services by lawyers of reasonably comparable skills, experience, and reputation." *Norman,* 836 F.2d at 1299. *Norman* discussed the evidence needed to satisfy a fee applicant's burden of demonstrating reasonable rates:

Satisfactory evidence at a minimum is more than the affidavit of the attorney *performing* the work. *Blum [v. Stenson],* 465 U.S. [886] at 896 n. 11, 104 S.Ct. at 1547 n. 11, 79 L.Ed.2d 891. It should also be noted that in line with the goal of obtaining objectivity, satisfactory evidence necessarily must speak to rates actually billed and paid in similar lawsuits. Testimony that a given fee is reasonable is therefore unsatisfactory evidence of market rate. *See Hensley,* 461 U.S. [424] at 439 n. 15, 103 S.Ct. [1933] at 1943 n. 15, 76 L.Ed.2d 40. Evidence of rates may

---

[3]   Neither Plaintiff nor Defendant has requested a hearing, and the Court concludes that a hearing is not necessary. In *Norman v. Housing Authority of City of Montgomery,* 836 F.2d 1292, 1303-04 (11th Cir.1988), the Eleventh Circuit ruled that a hearing on a fee petition is required only "where an evidentiary hearing [is] requested, where there [are] disputes of fact, and where the written record [is] not sufficiently clear to allow the trial court to resolve the disputes of fact. . . ." More recently, the Eleventh Circuit has explained that "[a]n evidentiary hearing is unnecessary for issues about which the district court possesses sufficient expertise: 'Such matters might include the reasonableness of the fee, the reasonableness of the hours and the significance of [the] outcome.'" *Thompson v. Pharmacy Corp. of Am.,* 334 F.3d 1242, 1245 (11th Cir.2003) (quoting *Norman,* 836 F.2d at 1304). The primary issues presented herein are the reasonableness of counsel's hourly rate and the reasonableness of the number of hours expended, matters over which the Court possesses sufficient expertise. Moreover, the written record here is of sufficient clarity to permit the Court to resolve any issues of fact that may exist.

be adduced through direct evidence of charges by lawyers under similar circumstances or by opinion evidence. The weight to be given to opinion evidence of course will be affected by the detail contained in the testimony on matters such as similarity of skill, reputation, experience, similarity of case and client, and breadth of the sample of which the expert has knowledge.

Norman, 836 F.2d at 1299. Satisfactory evidence may also include "citations to prior precedents showing reasonable rate adjudications for the fee applicant, for comparable attorneys, or for comparable cases." *Haugh v. Sec'y of Dep't of HHS*, No. 90-3128V, 1999 WL 525539, at *2 (Fed.Cl. June 30, 1999); *Design & Prod., Inc. v. United States*, 20 Cl.Ct. 207, 220 (1990) (same).

Throughout this litigation, Plaintiff was represented by the firm of Aurilio & Associates; attorneys Samuel Aurilio and Cynthia Mitchell provided the representation for the firm, assisted by paralegal Iris Thorn. Plaintiff seeks to be awarded a fee at an hourly rate for attorney Aurilio of $295, for attorney Mitchell of $225, and for paralegal Thorn of $90.

Plaintiff proffers that attorney Aurilio normally charges an hourly rate of $295 to represent plaintiffs in ADA Title III cases. He further proffers that attorney Aurilio has practiced law in Florida for more than 15 years and has been involved in more than 120 ADA cases. In addition, he has been named Advocate of the Year for Palm Beach County and granted a citation by the Governor of Florida for his advocacy. Plaintiff also attaches to his motion the affidavits of two other ADA attorneys, who opine that $295 is within the range of the prevailing market rate in the South Florida legal community for similar services by lawyers of reasonably comparable skills, experience, and reputation. Finally, Plaintiff submits that attorney Aurilio has previously been awarded fees in ADA cases at an hourly rate of $295 by other judges in this District. *See* Motion at 6-7 (citing decisions awarding attorney Aurilio $295 per hour). Significantly, Defendant does not object to awarding attorney Aurilio the requested rate. Furthermore, as *Norman* made clear, "The court . . . is itself an expert on the question and may consider its own knowledge and experience concerning reasonable and proper fees and may form an independent judgment either with or without the aid of witnesses as to value." 836 F.2d at 1303 (citing *Hensley,* 461 U.S. at 433, 103 S.Ct. 1933). Based on Plaintiff's submissions, Defendant's failure to object, and the Court's own experience and knowledge of prevailing market rates for similar services in the South Florida legal community, the Court agrees that an hourly rate of $295 for attorney Aurilio is reasonable and appropriate.

Plaintiff proffers that attorney Mitchell, for whom a $225 hourly rate is requested, was admitted to the practice of law in September 2002; accordingly, she had approximately two to three years experience during the time she worked on the instant litigation. Plaintiff further proffers that attorney Mitchell has been lead counsel in more than 80 ADA Title III cases, and he attaches the affidavits of two other attorneys attesting to the reasonableness of her requested rate. Finally, Plaintiff references two other cases from judges in this District, wherein attorney Mitchell was awarded her $225 requested rate. *See* Motion at 7 (DE 28). But the cases cited by Plaintiff do not reflect any defense objection to the requested rate; here, the defense does object. Moreover, this Court had previously awarded an hourly rate of $150 to attorney Mitchell after she had been admitted to practice for one year. *See Access 4 All, Inc. v. Ramos-Mejia, Inc.,* No. 02-60733-Civ-Dimitrouleas (S.D.Fla. Sept. 22, 2003) (Seltzer, M.J.) (DE 34). Based on the Court's own experience and familiarity with ADA litigation and prevailing hourly rates in this District, and considering that attorney Mitchell had been litigating ADA cases for two to three years when she rendered the legal services, the Court concludes that a rate of $185 per hour for attorney Mitchell is reasonable and appropriate.

Finally, Plaintiff requests that the paralegal – Iris Thorn – be compensated at a rate of $90 per hour. Plaintiff proffered that paralegal Thorn has two and a half years experience handling ADA cases. Defendant does not contest the reasonableness of this rate, and the Court believes that it is within the range of prevailing paralegal rates for this District. Accordingly, the Court will issue an award for the work of paralegal Thorn at a rate of $90 per hour.

B. Hours Reasonably Expended

The Court must next determine the reasonableness of the hours expended by Plaintiff's counsel. A fee applicant must set out the general subject matter of the time expended by the attorney "with sufficient particularity so that the court can assess the time claimed for each activity." *Norman,* 836 F.2d at 1303. "[A] lawyer may not be compensated for hours spent on activities for which he would not bill a client of means who was seriously intent on vindicating similar rights." *Id.* at 1301. Thus, fee applicants are required to use "billing judgment." *Id.* In ascertaining the number of reasonable hours, a court must deduct "excessive, redundant or otherwise unnecessary hours" from those claimed. Id.

In support of his Motion, Plaintiff has submitted his attorneys' itemized time records. Those records reflect that attorney Aurilio expended 6.9 hours, that attorney Mitchell expended 40.3 hours, and that paralegal Thorn expended 4.7 hours in litigating this action and in negotiating the settlement.

Defendant objects to any award of fees because Plaintiff proceeded with this litigation knowing that Defendant was making improvements to the property pursuant to a previous ADA settlement agreement. Alternatively, Defendant requests that Plaintiff's fees be substantially reduced because he (Plaintiff) resisted settling the matter earlier in the litigation. The Court, however, does not agree.

Plaintiff's entitlement to fees was memorialized in the Consent Decree to which Defendant agreed: "[Defendant] shall pay [Plaintiff's] counsel . . . for [Plaintiff's] attorneys' fees, . . . incurred in this matter." Consent Decree ¶ 4 (Ex. A to Motion (DE 28)). Furthermore, the ADA authorizes an award of fees to a prevailing party, and, by virtue of the Consent Decree, Plaintiff here was clearly the prevailing party. *See supra* note 2. Nor does the Court find persuasive Defendant's argument that Plaintiff extended the litigation to inflate its fees. Although the parties did attend a mediation conference and exchange settlement documents months before entering into the Consent Decree, not all issues were able to be resolved at (or immediately following) the mediation.[4] For other reasons, however, the Court does find that some reduction in the hours claimed is warranted.

Attorney Aurilio seeks compensation for a total of 6.9 hours. The Court, however, finds that certain billing entries are excessive or otherwise non-compensable. His billing record for September 23, 2005, shows that he billed .3 hours to read and review an order continuing trial. Because this task could reasonably have been accomplished in .1 hours, the Court will disallow .2 hours. On September 21, 2004, attorney Aurilio billed .2 hours to review the summons and original complaint. Yet, attorney Mitchell had already billed 1.2 hours on August 16, 2004, to prepare the complaint. Attorney Aurilio's review was therefore duplicative; and the Court will disallow the .2 hours claimed. Accordingly, the Court will permit Plaintiff to be awarded a total of 6.5 hours of attorney Aurilio's time.

Attorney Mitchell seeks compensation for 40.3 hours. Certain of her billing entries as well warrant reduction or disallowance. Attorney Mitchell's billing statements contain numerous entries bearing the sole description "Activity: Status review file"; this description is unaccompanied by any further information. These billing entries lack the requisite particularity to enable this Court to assess the necessity and reasonableness of the time claimed. These entries, totaling 1.5 hours, appear for the following dates and times: Feb. 7, 2005–.2 hours; Feb. 22, 2005–.2 hours; March 1, 2005–.2 hours; March 8, 2005–.2 hours; March 15, 2005–.2 hours; April 8, 2005–.1 hours; May 2, 2005–.1 hours; October 8, 2005–.1 hours; October 31, 2005–.1 hours; December 1, 2005–.1 hours. Accordingly, the Court will disallow 1.5 hours billed by attorney Mitchell but denoted merely as "status review." Furthermore, in his Reply,

---

[4]   By way of example, there existed an issue involving overlapping parking with a neighboring Albertsons store, and Plaintiff was awaiting a court ruling on certain parking issues in that matter before he could finalize the instant litigation.

Plaintiff acknowledges, and the Court agrees, that attorney Mitchell's billings contain some duplication. Attorney Mitchell billed .5 hours for drafting a joint scheduling conference report on January 21, 2005. Because she had previously billed for revising and emailing this document on January 18, 2005, this duplicative billing will be disallowed. In addition, on May 25, 2005, attorney Mitchell billed .7 hours for reviewing a notice of mediation and discussing the results of the mediation with attorney Aurilio. Although Plaintiff acknowledges that some reduction is warranted because she billed .1 hours on May 9 for reviewing the same notice, the Court will disallow the full .7 hours. Finally, the billing statements contain an excessive entry that warrants reduction. On March 28, 2005, attorney Mitchell billed .3 hours to review a one page letter from defense counsel; the Court will reduce this number by .2 hours and award Plaintiff .1 hours for reviewing the letter. The Court, therefore, will deduct 2.9 hours from the 40.3 hours claimed; it will award Plaintiff fees for 37.4 hours expended by attorney Mitchell.

Paralegal Thorn seeks compensation for 4.7 hours expended on this litigation. Defendant contends that administrative work by the paralegal should be disallowed. A court may award fees for the work of paralegals, but "only to the extent that [they] perform work traditionally done by an attorney." *Scelta v. Delicatessen Support Servs., Inc.,* 203 F.Supp.2d 1328, 1334 (M.D.Fla.2002) (quoting *Jean v. Nelson,* 863 F.2d 759, 778 (11th Cir.1988)). By contrast, "work that is clerical or secretarial in nature is not separately recoverable." *Id.* (denying attorney's fees for such clerical and secretarial work as gathering materials and copying, mailing, and refiling them). The Court has reviewed paralegal Thorn's billing statements and finds that the work for which Plaintiff seeks compensation – telephoning opposing counsel, conferencing with Plaintiff's expert, attending the onsite inspection, drafting cover letters and emails – was the type of work traditionally performed by an attorney. Accordingly, the Court will award Plaintiff the full 4.7 hours claimed for paralegal Thorne.

In sum, the undersigned will award Plaintiff attorneys' fees based on a total of 48.6 hours – 6.5 hours by attorney Aurilio, 37.4 hours by attorney Mitchell, and 4.7 hours by paralegal Thorn – reasonably expended in this litigation.

C. Lodestar Amount

Multiplying the reasonable number of hours expended by Plaintiff's counsel by the reasonable hourly rates – 6.5 hours at a $295 hourly rate (Aurilio), 37.4 hours at a $185 hourly rate (Mitchell), and 4.7 hours at a $90 hourly rate (Thorn) – results in a lodestar amount of $9,259.50. The Court will enter an attorneys' fee award in this amount.

EXPERT FEES, COSTS, AND LITIGATION EXPENSES

A prevailing ADA plaintiff may recover expert fees as a litigation expense. *Lovell v. Chandler,* 303 F.3d 1039, 1058 (9th Cir.2002) ("[B]ecause the term 'litigation expenses' normally encompasses expert witness fees, we hold that [the ADA, § 12205] provides direct authority for the award of expert fees"; noting that the preamble to ADA regulations also identifies expert fees as part of litigation expenses); *see also Shepard v. Honda of Am. Mfg., Inc.,* 160 F.Supp.2d 860, 875-76 (S.D. Ohio 2001) (awarding expert fees to prevailing ADA plaintiff).

Plaintiff has submitted the invoices of his expert, who billed at an hourly rate of $150. Plaintiff seeks an expert fee award of $1,350; this sum is composed of $600[5] for a pre-suit investigatory inspection of the property and $750 for a second inspection. These charges reflect the expert's time traveling to and from the subject property, inspecting the property, producing the reports, researching, and otherwise preparing the matter. Defendant challenges the $600 sought for the initial inspection because no report was produced nor were the results utilized in this litigation. The Court, however, disagrees. Conducting a pre-suit investigatory inspection to confirm the existence of the barriers complained of is sound legal practice. Furthermore, Plaintiff's counsel represents that a report was generated, which would have been provided to Defendant had it made such a request. Because the invoices describe necessary expert services rendered at a reasonable rate, the Court finds that the requested expert's fee of $1,350 is appropriate and in line with ADA expert fees awarded in this District. *See, e.g., Ass'n for Disabled Americans v. North Beach Hotel, Inc.,* 97-133-Civ-Highsmith (S.D. Fla. June 21, 1998) (DE 35) (awarding expert fees of $3,755.50 based on $185 hourly rate).

In his Motion, Plaintiff also seeks reimbursement for other costs and expenses in the total amount of $622.56: filing fee–$150; photocopies–$72.50; mediation services–$325; service of process–$35; travel–$30.73; and postage–$9.33. Of these costs, Defendant does not dispute the propriety of awarding costs for the filing fee, service of process fee, postage charges, and travel charges, which total $225.06. The balance, to which Defendant does object, is composed of the photocopies ($72.50) and the mediation services ($325).

Photocopying charges are taxable as costs to a prevailing party under 28 U.S.C. § 1920(4). Beyond the costs authorized in § 1920, the ADA authorizes an award of litigation expenses under 42 U.S.C. § 12205. "Section 12205's allowance of 'litigation expenses' is much broader than

---

[5] The expert's invoice shows a $1,200 charge, but this amount includes the charge for inspecting the adjacent Albertsons grocery store, which Plaintiff sued separately. Accordingly, Plaintiff here is seeking compensation for only one-half of the amount charged–$600.

the provisions of § 1920," and it includes expenditures for items that are related to the advancement of the litigation. *Corbett v. Nat'l Prods.*, No. 94-2652, 1995 WL 284248, at *4 (E.D.Pa. May 9, 1995); *accord Chaffin v. Kansas*, No. 01-1110-JTM, 2005 WL 387654, at *2 (D.Kan. Feb. 17, 2005); *Robins v. Scholastic Book Fairs*, 928 F.Supp. 1027, 1036-37 (D.Or.1996). Finally, in the Consent Decree, Defendant expressly agreed to compensate Plaintiff for all litigation expenses and costs incurred in this matter. Although Defendant asserts that Plaintiff made the disputed photocopies solely for the convenience of counsel, it fails to specify the number of copies that it alleges were so made. Moreover, these copy charges are expenses all of a type routinely billed to a client and are therefore compensable. *See United States v. Adkinson*, 256 F.Supp.2d 1297, 1320 (N.D.Fla.2003). Accordingly, the Court will award Plaintiff the $72.50 sought for photocopies.

Defendant also objects to the Court awarding Plaintiff the $325 he incurred for mediation services on the ground that such costs are not compensable under § 1920. The Court disagrees. Although mediation fees are not compensable under § 1920, they are compensable litigation expenses under the ADA. *See Clark v. Peco, Inc.*, No. 97-737-HU, 1999 WL 398012, *12 (D.Or. April 16, 1999) (awarding mediation fee as an ADA litigation expense); *see also Robins*, 928 F.Supp. at 1036-37 (interpreting 42 U.S.C. § 12205 to allow recovery for "all necessary litigation expenses, so long as they are not overhead expenses absorbed by counsel"). Accordingly, the Court will allow Plaintiff to recover his $325 mediation fee.

The Court, therefore, finds that all the costs – $622.56 – sought by Plaintiff are compensable and will include this sum in its award.

CONCLUSION

Based on the foregoing, the Plaintiff's Verified Motion for Attorneys' and Litigation Expenses and Costs (DE 28) is GRANTED and Defendant shall pay to Plaintiff attorneys' fees in the amount of $9,259.50, an expert fee in the amount of $1,350, and costs and expenses in the amount of $622.56, for a total award of $11,232.06. Pursuant to the terms of the Consent Decree, Defendant shall make this payment on or before ten days from the date hereof.

The Court will enter a separate Judgment for fees, expenses, and costs simultaneously herewith.

Notes & Questions

1. As *Hansen* demonstrates, the first element in calculating a fee is to compute a "lodestar": the number of hours reasonably expended on the litigation multiplied by the reasonable hourly rate of the individuals working on the matter. *See, e.g.*, Staton v. Boeing Co., 327 F.3d 938, 964 (9th Cir. 2003); Giles v. Gen. Elec. Co., 245 F.3d 474, 490-91 (5th Cir. 2001). "A 'strong presumption' exists that the lodestar figure represents a

'reasonable fee,' and therefore, it should only be enhanced or reduced in 'rare and exceptional cases.'" Fischer v. SJB-P.D. Inc., 214 F.3d 1115, 1119 n.4 (9th Cir. 2000) (quoting Pennsylvania v. Del. Valley Citizens' Council for Clean Air, 478 U.S. 546, 565 (1986) (internal quotations omitted)). *But see* No Barriers, Inc., v. Brinker Chili's Tex., Inc., 262 F.3d 496, 500-01 (5th Cir. 2001) (court not required to use lodestar in simple case when court familiar with work done). But a court has discretion to determine both the reasonable hours and the reasonable rates; *see, e.g.*, Giles, 245 F.3d at 490-91 (rates too high); Greenway v. Buffalo Hilton Hotel, 951 F.Supp. 1039, 1069 (W.D.N.Y. 1997) (attorneys seeking fees had not properly established the reasons for having two attorneys at depositions).

2. May courts take into account the complexity of a case? *See* Roland v. Cellucci, 106 F.Supp.2d 128, 135-36 (D. Mass. 2000) (case involving a large class of individuals with disabilities and a number of novel time-consuming claims entitled to greater staffing). Should courts also reduce fees if a case is particularly straightforward?

3. Counsel who anticipate seeking fees should carefully prepare their bills from the outset. Interestingly, often these cases involve litigation on behalf of clients to whom no bills are sent, but that should not lead to laxity in preparing statements. It is not uncommon for courts to refuse to award fees where statements are not sufficiently detailed. *See, e.g.*, No Barriers, Inc., 262 F.3d at 500.

4. What factors ought a court to consider in awarding fees? A number of courts have approved a list of 12 factors that may be used to assess attorneys' fees:

(1) The time and labor required;
(2) The novelty and difficulty of the questions;
(3) The skill requisite to perform a legal service properly;
(4) The preclusion of employment by the attorney due to acceptance of the case;
(5) The customary fees;
(6) Whether the fee is fixed or contingent;
(7) The time limitations imposed by the client or the circumstances;
(8) The amount involved and the results obtained;
(9) The experience, reputation, and ability of the attorney;
(10) The "undesirability" of the case;
(11) The nature and length of the professional relationship with the client; and
(12) Awards in similar cases.

Hamlin v. Charter Township of Flint, 165 F.3d 426, 437 (6th Cir. 1999) (citing Hensley v. Eckerhart, 461 U.S. 424, 430 n.3 (1983)); Johnson v. Ga.

Highway Express, Inc., 488 F.2d 714, 717-19 (5th Cir. 1974). What determines the "undesirability" of a case? Suing the mill in a town where it is the largest employer? Seeking services for incarcerated juveniles?

5. How important is the measure of success in assessing fees? Where a party prevails only on a fraction of its claims, the court may reduce the award to reflect services on the losing claims. Lanni v. New Jersey, 259 F.3d 146, 151 (3d Cir. 2001) (approving reduction to account for lack of success on several claims). On the other hand, where counsel achieves a particularly good result, for example, prevailing in a complex case, the court has discretion to award more than the lodestar. Daggitt v. United Food & Commercial Workers Int'l Union, Local 304A, 245 F.3d 981, 989-90 (8th Cir. 2001). But what if the plaintiff obtains only nominal damages? The Supreme Court has written, "When a plaintiff recovers only nominal damages because of his failure to prove an essential element of his claim for monetary relief, the only reasonable fee is usually no fee at all." Farrar v. Hobby, 506 U.S. 103, 115 (1992) (citation omitted). That is, the size of the award determines, not whether a party prevails, but the size of the appropriate fee. For example, in *Red Cloud-Owen v. Albany Steel, Inc.*, 958 F.Supp. 94 (N.D.N.Y. 1997), the jury awarded the plaintiff $1. The court cited *Carroll v. Blinken*, 105 F.3d 79, 81 (2d Cir. 1997) for the proposition:

> *Pino* [*v. Locasio*, 101 F.3d 235, 237 (2d Cir. 1996)] stands for the proposition that in determining the reasonableness of a fee award . . ., the quantity and quality of relief obtained is a critical factor. Where the damage award is nominal or modest, the injunctive relief has no systemic effect of importance, and no substantial public interest is served, a substantial fee award cannot be justified.

Red Cloud-Owen, 958 F.Supp. at 96. The court declined to award the plaintiff attorneys' fees.

In Title III cases, of course, no damages are available. How should a court assess the significance of purely injunctive relief in determining the measure of success?

ॐ

Part 6

Special Education:
Individuals with Disabilities Education Act
Analysis

Chapter 18 BACKGROUND
§ 18.1 Precursors To IDEA
§ 18.2 General Statutory Requirements Of IDEA
Chapter 19 PERSONS PROTECTED
§ 19.1 General
§ 19.2 Infants And Toddlers With Disability
§ 19.3 Specific Learning Disability
§ 19.4 Other Health Impairment
§ 19.5 Eligibility, Child Find, And Re-Evaluation
Chapter 20 FREE APPROPRIATE PUBLIC EDUCATION
§ 20.1 FAPE Standard
§ 20.2 FAPE Applications
Chapter 21 LEAST RESTRICTIVE ENVIRONMENT
Chapter 22 RELATED SERVICES
§ 22.1 Health Services
§ 22.2 Speech / Language Services
§ 22.3 Extended School Year (ESY) Services
Chapter 23 SPECIAL SITUATIONS
§ 23.1 Discipline, Behavior And Restraint
§ 23.2 Residential Placement, Private School Placement, And Juvenile Justice Issues
§ 23.3 Distance Learning
Chapter 24 PROCEDURAL SAFEGUARDS, EXHAUSTION AND REMEDIES
§ 24.1 Special Education Process
§ 24.2 Exhaustion Of Administrative Remedies
§ 24.3 Civil Action
§ 24.4 *Pro Se* Representation In Federal Court
§ 24.5 Remedies

Chapter 18 BACKGROUND

§ 18.1 Precursors To IDEA

"The history of educating children with disabilities in the United States is a tale of neglect and exclusion." Daniel H. Melvin II, The Desegregation of Children with Disabilities, 44 DePaul L. Rev. 599, 603 (1995). Prior to the advent of special education law, children with disabilities were generally educated, if at all, in separate specialized institutions.

In 1975, in enacting the first comprehensive special education law, Congress found that of the eight million children with disabilities in the country, one million were excluded entirely from the public school system and over four million were not receiving appropriate educational services. Education for All Handicapped Children Act, Pub. L. 94-142, Sec. 3(b)(1)-(5), 89 Stat. 773 (codified as amended at 20 U.S.C. § 1400 et seq. (2006)).

The special education law of the United States has its origins in race discrimination law and, specifically, in the landmark Supreme Court decision of *Brown v. Board of Education of Topeka*, 347 U.S. 483 (1954). In that case, the Supreme Court found that, although there is no constitutional right to public education, "where the state has undertaken to provide it, [public education] is a right which must be made available to all on equal terms." *Id.* at 493. The Court went on to conclude: "in the field of public education the doctrine of 'separate but equal' has no place. Separate educational facilities are inherently unequal. Therefore, we hold that [black students] . . . are, by reason of the segregation complained of, deprived of equal protection of the laws guaranteed by the Fourteenth Amendment." *Id.* at 495.

While this decision did not involve children with disabilities, its finding that segregation in education based solely on race was inherently unequal formed the basis for disability advocates to argue that unnecessary segregation or exclusion of children with disabilities was similarly violative of the Fourteenth Amendment's Equal Protection and Due Process Clauses. Thus, in the 1970s, coincident with the independent living movement, courts in Pennsylvania and the District of Columbia issued landmark decisions requiring education and integration of students with disabilities in public education.

In *Pennsylvania Ass'n for Retarded Children v. Pennsylvania*, 334 F.Supp. 1257 (E.D. Pa. 1971) (*"PARC"*), the court approved a consent decree finding that, under the Equal Protection Clause, having undertaken to provide free public education, Pennsylvania must educate all children, including those with disabilities. Moreover, "[i]t is the Commonwealth's obligation to place each mentally retarded child in a free, public program of education and training *appropriate to the child's capacity.*" *Id.* at 1260 (emphasis added). The court also applied the principle from *Brown* that separate education is inherently unequal and, therefore, applied a presumption that "placement in a regular public school class is preferable to placement in a special public school class and placement in a special public school class is preferable to placement in any other type of program of education and training." *Id.*

In *Mills v. Board of Education of District of Columbia*, 348 F.Supp. 866, 875 (D.D.C. 1972), the court granted summary judgment to a class of children with disabilities, finding that the Equal Protection Clause required inclusion of children with disabilities in public education and that the additional cost of such education was not a defense. The court stated:

> [T]he District of Columbia's interest in educating the excluded children clearly must outweigh its interest in preserving its financial resources. If sufficient funds are not available to finance all of the services and programs that are needed and desirable in the system then the available funds must be expended equitably in such a manner that no child is entirely excluded from a publicly supported education consistent with his needs and ability to benefit there from. The inadequacies of the District of Columbia Public School System whether occasioned by insufficient funding or administrative inefficiency, certainly cannot be permitted to bear more heavily on the "exceptional" or handicapped child than on the normal child.

Id. at 876. In addition, recognizing the common practice of suspending and expelling students with disabilities as a method of discrimination, the court found that "due process of law requires a hearing prior to exclusion, termination of [sic] classification into a special program." *Id.* at 875. Therefore, the court mandated rights to hearing, appeal, access to records and written notice. *Id.* at 878-83.

In 1973, Congress enacted § 504 of the Rehabilitation Act, prohibiting discrimination "solely by reason of . . . handicap" in any program or activity receiving Federal financial assistance. 29 U.S.C. § 794 (2006). Because most states received such financial assistance, most public school programs were, and are, covered by § 504. However, the Rehabilitation Act only purported to require modifications of the general education program, thus leaving it unclear to what extent states had to provide different education services for children with disabilities. In addition, the regulations implementing § 504 were not issued until 1978, thus leaving schools without a clear understanding of how to satisfy their obligations.

§ 18.2 General Statutory Requirements Of IDEA

Against this background, Congress enacted the Education of All Handicapped Children Act, Pub. L. 94-142, 89 Stat. 773 in 1975 (codified as amended, Individuals with Disabilities Education Act, 20 U.S.C. § 1400-1487 (2006)) (IDEA). The IDEA was reauthorized in 1997, and on December 3, 2004 was reauthorized again by the Individuals with Disabilities Education Improvement Act of 2004, Pub. L. No. 108-446, 118 Stat. 2647 (2004) (hereinafter IDEA 2004). IDEA 2004 went into effect on July 1, 2005.

The primary stated purposes of the IDEA 2004, as amended, are:

(1)(A) to ensure that all children with disabilities have available to them a free appropriate public education that emphasizes special education and related services designed to meet their unique needs and prepare them for further education, employment and independent living;

(B) to ensure that the rights of children with disabilities and parents of such children are protected; and

(C) to assist States, localities, educational service agencies, and Federal agencies to provide for the education of all children with disabilities;

20 U.S.C.A § 1400(d) (West 2006). The U.S. Department of Education's final regulations implementing IDEA 2004 became effective on October 13, 2006. 34 C.F.R. § 300.1 et seq. (2008).

IDEA 2004 provides federal funding to states to support special education services in public elementary and secondary schools. This funding is based on the number of children in the state receiving special education services multiplied by the average per-pupil cost of public education in the United States. However, the IDEA 2004 is not intended to fund the entire cost of special education. The IDEA 2004 authorizes federal funding grants of 40% of that average cost.

Congress has not allocated sufficient funds to cover its entire 40% portion of special education costs, leaving states to fund much of their own compliance with their constitutional and statutory obligations. It is important to recognize that, while federal IDEA 2004 funding is important, the IDEA itself is not the sole source of the states' special education obligations. Rather, as the courts in *PARC* and *Mills* determined, the basic special education obligations arise from the Fourteenth Amendment to the Constitution and are independent from any promise of federal funding. The IDEA can be viewed as imposing some additional requirements or simply formalizing and standardizing the mechanisms for complying with the constitutional obligations.

The primary requirements of the IDEA 2004 are Free Appropriate Public Education (FAPE), Least Restrictive Environment (LRE), Procedural Due Process, and "Child Find." Regarding FAPE, the IDEA 2004 requires each state to provide "[a] free appropriate public education . . . to all children with disabilities residing in the State between the ages of 3 and 21, inclusive, including children with disabilities who have been suspended or expelled from school." *Id.* § 1412(a)(1)(A). To ensure that FAPE is provided to every eligible child, the IDEA 2004 includes a "child find" provision. *Id.* § 1412(a)(3)(A). Child find requires states to identify, locate, and evaluate "[a]ll children with disabilities residing in the State, including children with disabilities who are homeless . . . or wards of the State and children with disabilities attending private schools, regardless of the severity of their disabilities, and who are in need of special education and related services." *Id.*

The IDEA 2004 requires that public education for children with disabilities be provided in the least restrictive environment (LRE) appropriate to them, meaning,

> children with disabilities ... are educated with children who are not disabled, and special classes, separate schooling, or other removal of children with disabilities from the regular educational environment occurs only when the nature or severity of the disability of a child is such that education in regular classes with the use of supplementary aids and services cannot be achieved satisfactorily.

Id. § 1412(a)(5)(A).

IDEA 2004 newly requires that the state's funding scheme does not create placements in conflict with the LRE requirement or the provision of a student's individualized FAPE. *Id.* § 1412(a)(5)(B)(i). Additionally, the 2004 Amendments require states that receive IDEA funds to implement the National Instructional Materials Accessibility Standard (NIMAS) for accessible electronic text. 20 U.S.C. § 1412(a)(23)(A) (2006). [NIMAS] see 34 C.F.R. Part 300, App. C. (2006).

> The NIMAS require the production of electronic files by publishers (e.g., of school textbooks) that possess print rights and which are conducting business with state and local governments must be available in Extensible Markup Language (XML) upon request. XML is intended to facilitate simple conversion to a variety of specialized formats (e.g., Braille, audio books, text-to-speech, html, large print).

William N. Myhill, Law and Policy Challenges for Achieving an Accessible eSociety, in 2 Euro. Yrbk. Disability L. 103, 111 (2010). The NIMAS requirement became effective on July 19, 2006. *Id.*

The procedural due process provisions of the IDEA include: the requirement to evaluate children to determine their eligibility for special education services; provide individualized education programs (IEPs) developed by IEP teams; ensure parental notice, consent, and access to records; and offer mediation and access to impartial hearings to resolve disputes. *Id.* § 1415. In addition, the IDEA 2004 imposes a "stay-put" requirement preventing schools from expelling or suspending students with disabilities or otherwise changing their educational placements without meeting due process requirements. *Id.* § 1415(j).

Notes & Questions

1. The IDEA provides for federal funding of 40% of the average per-pupil cost of public education in the United States. President's Comm'n on Excellence in Special Educ., *A New Era: Revitalizing Special Education for Children and their Families*, 31 (July 2002), *available at* http://www.ed.gov/inits/commissionsboards/whspecialeducation/reports/images/Pres_Rep.pdf. This funding formula has led to problems of overfunding in states where the actual cost of public education is lower than the national average and underfunding in states where the actual cost of education is higher than average. *Id.* This formula also takes a one-size-fits-all approach based on the average general cost of public education, rather than on the costs of special education or the cost of special education for the particular children receiving services. *Id.* at 32. This approach neglects the fact that it costs more to educate students with severe disabilities than it does to educate students with mild disabilities. *Id.* Finally, the lack of clear definition of children with disabilities for funding purposes leads to differences from state to state in how children are identified and counted for special education purposes. *Id.* at 21-22.

2. IDEA § 1412(a)(1)(B)(i) provides:

> The obligation to make a free appropriate public education available to all children with disabilities does not apply with respect to children aged 3 through 5 and 18 through 21 in a State to the extent that its application to those children would be inconsistent with State law or practice. . . .

This conflict of law arose in *E.R.K. v. State of Hawaii Department of Education,* 728 F.3d 982 (9th Cir. 2013), where a state statute barred students "from attending public school after the last day of the school year in which they turned 20." Haw. Rev. Stat. § 302A-1134(c) (West 2013). Interpreting the IDEA's exception provision, § 1412(a)(1)(B)(i), by citing its legislative history, S.Rep. No. 94-168, 1975 U.S.C.C.A.N. 1425, 1442-43 (1975), the Court ruled that as long as the state provides a free public education to students without disabilities over age 20, it must provide a FAPE to those students with disabilities over age 20 who are eligible for IDEA. *E.R.K.*, 728 F.3d at 986-88. In the present case, the state provided a free public education to adults attending Community Schools, which specialized in instruction to earn the General Education Development (GED) and Competency Based (i.e., life skills) credentials, and thus was required to provide a FAPE to the plaintiffs. *Id.* at 986-92.

3. For a more complete history of the IDEA and its integration requirement, *see generally* Daniel H. Melvin II, The Desegregation of Children with Disabilities, 44 DePaul L. Rev. 599 (1995).

Chapter 19 PERSONS PROTECTED

§ 19.1 General

The Rehabilitation Act, like the ADA, protects all participants in a program. In the school setting, this would include students, parents, visitors, spectators, visiting athletes, and teachers. Unlike the ADA and Rehabilitation Act, which cover any qualified individual with a mental or physical impairment that substantially limits a major life activity, the IDEA 2004 protects "children with disabilities" ages three through twenty-one, *id.* § 1412(a)(1)(B), defined as those

> (i) with intellectual disabilities, hearing impairments (including deafness), speech or language impairments, visual impairments (including blindness), serious emotional disturbance (hereinafter referred to as "emotional disturbance"), orthopedic impairments, autism, traumatic brain injury, other health impairments, or specific learning disabilities; and

> (ii) who, by reason thereof, needs special education and related services.

Id. § 1401(3)(A). For children ages 3 through 9, states have discretion to cover children with other impairments, such as developmental delay, who need special education and related services as a result of those impairments. *Id.* § 1401(3)(B).

Notably, to be eligible for special education, a child must meet the requirements of one of the 10 categories of disabilities *and*, "by reason thereof", need special education and related services. However, there is no requirement that the child be "otherwise qualified' for education or be able to benefit from the education. As the First Circuit found in *Timothy W. v. Rochester School District*,

> The language of the Act could not be more unequivocal. The statute is permeated with the words "*all* handicapped children" whenever it refers to the target population. It never speaks of any exceptions for severely handicapped children. Indeed, . . . the Act gives priority to the most severely handicapped. Nor is there any language whatsoever which requires as a prerequisite to being covered by the Act, that a handicapped child must demonstrate that he or she will "benefit" from the educational program. Rather, the Act speaks of the state's responsibility to design a special education and related services program that will meet the unique "needs" of all handicapped children . . . . In summary, the Act mandates an appropriate public education for all handicapped children, regardless of the level of achievement that such children might attain.

875 F.2d 954, 960-61 (1st Cir. 1989).

§ 19.2   Infants And Toddlers With Disability

Infants and toddlers (from infancy to age two) with identified disabilities or experiencing developmental delays are entitled to services from their local school district under IDEA 2004 Part C to ensure children are ready for school. Currently, Part C is a $436 million program that provides Federal funds to states to provide these early intervention services. U.S. Dep't of Educ., IDEA 2004 Part C Regulations, Notice of Proposed Rule Making (NPRM), http://www.ed.gov/policy/speced/guid/idea/part-c/nprm/index.html (last visited June 7, 2012). New regulations took effect October 28, 2011, explaining that "[e]arly intervention services . . . [a]re designed to meet the developmental needs of an infant or toddler with a disability and the needs of the family to assist appropriately in the infant's or toddler's development, as identified by the IFSP [individualized family service plan] Team . . . ." 34 C.F.R. § 303.13(a)(4) (2013).

Early intervention services include: assistive technology devices and services, audiology and vision services, family training, counseling, and home visits, health, medical and nursing services, nutrition services, occupational and physical therapy, psychological and social work services, sign language and cued language services, special instruction, speech-language pathology services, transportation and related costs, and service coordination services.   34 C.F.R § 303.13(b)(1)-(13).   In part, early intervention regulations ensure that an infants and toddlers with surgically implanted device, such as a cochlear implant, is entitled to receive early intervention services identified in the child's IFSP as being necessary to meet the child's developmental needs.   34 C.F.R. § 303.16(c)(1)(iii)(A). The new regulations also clarify that each state must implement a comprehensive child find system. 34 C.F.R. § 303.115; *see infra* § 19.5 (regarding child find requirements).

§ 19.3   Specific Learning Disability

"Specific learning disability" is defined as "a disorder in one or more of the basic psychological processes involved in understanding or in using language, spoken or written, which disorder may manifest itself in the imperfect ability to listen, think, speak, read, write, spell, or do mathematical calculations." 20 U.S.C. § 1401(30)(A) (2006). "Such term includes such conditions as perceptual disabilities, brain injury, minimal brain dysfunction, dyslexia, and developmental aphasia."   *Id.* § 1401(30)(B). "Such term does not include a learning problem that is primarily the result of visual, hearing, or motor disabilities, of intellectual disabilities, of emotional disturbance, or of environmental, cultural, or economic disadvantage." *Id.* § 1401(30)(C).

§ 19.4 Other Health Impairment

According to the Department of Education regulations implementing the IDEA:

> Other health impairment means having limited strength, vitality or alertness, including a heightened alertness to environmental stimuli, that results in limited alertness with respect to the educational environment, that –
>
> (i) Is due to chronic or acute health problems such as asthma, attention deficit disorder or attention deficit hyperactivity disorder, diabetes, epilepsy, a heart condition, hemophilia, lead poisoning, leukemia, nephritis, rheumatic fever, sickle cell anemia, and Tourette syndrome; and
>
> (ii) Adversely affects a child's educational performance.

34 C.F.R. § 300.8(c)(9) (2008).

§ 19.5 Eligibility, Child Find, And Re-Evaluations

Individual assessment of possible disability to determine eligibility for special education services requires written notice and informed parental consent. *Id.* § 1414(a)(1)(D). Evaluators must use a variety of assessment tools, *id.* § 1414(b)(2), and avoid exclusive use of IQ and other standardized tests, because they are inherently biased toward non-white and minority populations. Larry P. v. Riles, 793 F.2d 969, 981 (9th Cir. 1984); Robert D. Hernandez, Reducing Bias in the Assessment of Culturally and Linguistically Diverse Populations, 14 J. Educ'l Issues Language Minority Students 269, 269-70 (1994). Assessment methodologies specifically must be "selected and administered so as not to be discriminatory on a racial or cultural basis." 20 U.S.C. § 1414(b)(3)(A)(i) (2006). For instance, assessments must be "provided and administered" in the "language and form most likely to yield accurate information on what the child knows and can do academically, developmentally, and functionally, unless it is not feasible." *Id.* § 1414(b)(3)(A)(ii).

When the parents or guardian of a child with a disability disagrees with the evaluation conducted by the educational agency, some courts have upheld the IDEA regulation, 34 C.F.R. § 300.502(b) (2012), that requires the educational agency to pay for an independent educational evaluation (IEE). Phillip C. ex. Rel. A.C. v. Jefferson Bd. of Educ., 701 F.3d 691, 695-98 (11th Cir. 2012); *see* S.F. v. McKinney Indep. Sch. Dist., No. 4:10-CV-323-RAS-DDB, 2012 WL 718589, *6-9 (E.D. Tex. Mar. 6, 2012) (finding plaintiff prevailed in school district's challenge to their request for an IEE arising from the failure of the school district to comply with the IDEA's procedural evaluation requirements); *accord* Lyons v. Lower Merrion Sch. Dist., No. 09-5576, 2010 WL 8913276 (E.D. Pa. Dec. 14, 2010) (rejecting school district's argument that hearing officer could not conduct a due process hearing as requested by parents so as to order the school to provide an IEE at public expense). The regulation specifically provides that the parents must request an IEE; then the educational agency must file a due process complaint requesting a hearing to demonstrate its evaluation is appropriate, or ensure that an IEE is provided at public expense, 34 C.F.R. § 300.502(b)(2), and provide the parents with "information about where an [IEE] may be obtained, and the agency criteria applicable for [IEEs] . . . ." 34 C.F.R. § 300.502(a)(2).

The "child find" requirement imposes duties on states to seek out and evaluate children to determine whether they are eligible for special education services. 20 U.S.C. § 1412(a)(3)(A) (2006). States may use simple, routine group assessments or "sweep-screening" without parental consent to identify hearing and vision problems. They may also use group assessments, such as achievement and ability tests. However, these standardized achievement tests are generally inadequate to identify disabilities without the use of other assessment methods.

In *Jamie S. v. Milwaukee Public Schools*, 519 F.Supp.2d 870 (D. Wis. 2007), *vacated in part as to class certification*, 668 F.3d 481 (7th Cir. 2012), a class of students eligible for special education services from Milwaukee Public Schools (MPS) claimed that MPS did not meet its obligations under the child find provision. The district court concluded that MPS violated the child find provision by failing to identify, locate, and evaluate children with disabilities who were in need of special education and related services. *Id.* at 903. Specifically, the court concluded that MPS (1) failed to timely, within the 90 day requirement, refer children with a suspected disability for an initial evaluation; (2) improperly extended that 90 day requirement; (3) improperly used suspensions so as to delay the initial evaluation; and (4) "failed to insure that the child's parents or guardians attend the initial evaluation." *Id.*

Additionally, the court held that the state Department of Public Instruction (DPI) was aware of its responsibility under the IDEA to assert supervisory obligations over MPS, and because they failed to effectively do so, DPI was liable for MPS's failure to comply with the IDEA and related state statutes. *Id.* at 903-04. DPI did not establish deadlines for imposing sanctions and did not withhold funds when IDEA violations occurred. *Id.* at 888-89. In 2012, however, the Seventh Circuit Court of Appeals, vacated the judgment of class certification and remanded the case for further consistent proceedings, holding that IDEA claims such as the one brought in this case are highly individualized and diverse, making class certification inappropriate. Jamie S., 668 F.3d 481, 485-86 (7th Cir. 2012).

Students receiving special education services must be reevaluated at least every three years unless the parent and education agency agree that a reevaluation is unnecessary. *Id.* § 1414(a)(2). A parent's revocation of consent for reevaluation alone is insufficient. In *G.J. ex rel. E.J. v. Muscogee County Sch. Dist.*, the parents of a child with autism and a brain injury refused consent for a triennial review of his IEP. 704 F.Supp.2d 1299 (M.D. Ga. 2010), aff'd sub nom. G.J. v. Muscogee County Sch. Dist., 668 F.3d 1258 (11th Cir. 2012). The court found that where the parents would not consent to the evaluation until the school district agreed to an extensive set of conditions, they had effectively refused to consent to the evaluation. *Id.* at 1309. However, the court declined to hold that the refusal to consent to reevaluation amounted to a waiver of the child's rights to a FAPE under the IDEA. *Id.* at 1310. Since the parents expressed a willingness to have their child reevaluated but withheld the consent until the school district agreed to their terms, and since the court found that failure to consent was a grounds for summary determination in the school district's favor, the court ordered the child's parents to consent to a reevaluation. *Id.* The court stressed that if the parents refused to reply, their son would become ineligible for services under IDEA. *Id.* at 1313.

In IDEA 2004, Congress found that inappropriate referral and assessment procedures can mislabel limited English proficient, African-American, and other minority children as having a disability. 20 U.S.C. § 1400(c)(11)-(12) (2006); Mitylene Arnold & Marie E. Lassmann, Overrepresentation of Minority Students in Special Education, 124 Educ. 230, 232 (2003) (discussing "the misdiagnosis of intellectual disabilities among African American students").

In 2005, eighteen of Maryland's twenty-four school systems served a "significantly disproportional" number of African-American students in programs for children with intellectual disabilities. Daniel de Vise, Special-Ed Racial Imbalance Spurs Sanctions: Number of Black Students in Montgomery, Arundel Programs Seen as Too High, Washington Post, Aug. 2, 2005, at B4 (African Americans comprising 22% of the student population in Montgomery County schools, though 42% were considered to have intellectual disabilities). Studies document a history of the overrepresentation of English language learners (ELLs) in special education programs, arising in part from incorrectly administered or biased assessment methodologies. Jim Cummins, Bilingualism and Special Education: Issues in Assessment and Pedagogy 1-2 (1984); Chandra Keller-Allen, English Language Learners with Disabilities: Identification and Other State Policies and Issues (Aug. 2006), *available at* http://www.projectforum.org/docs/EnglishLanguageLearners withDisabilities-IdentificationandOtherStatePoliciesandIssues.pdf; *see also* Eve Müller & Joy Markowitz, Project Forum, Synthesis Brief: English Language Learners with Disabilities 2 (Mar. 2004) (discussing "the disproportionately high number of ELLs receiving special education services and the problem of distinguishing . . . those who have true disabilities . . . [from those] who are failing for other reasons"), *available at* http://www.nasdse.org/Portals/0/Documents/Download%20Publications/ DFR-0401.pdf.

As to the ELL population, one commentator explains:

> ELLs experiencing difficulties in school are inappropriately referred for a special education evaluation on the basis of behaviors that simply do not fit the expectations of educators, yet which are appropriate in the child's native culture, or for lack of academic success in part due to linguistic, cultural, economic, and other background characteristics perceived as deviant. . . . Errors in determining the needs of ELLs often occur when school personnel lack an understanding of second language acquisition and educationally relevant cultural differences.

William N. Myhill, The State of Public Education and the Needs of English Language Learners in the Era of 'No Child Left Behind,' 8 J. Gender Race & Just. 393, 447 (2004) (citations omitted).

Notes & Questions

1. The ADA and IDEA define disabilities differently. The ADA defines it as a physical or mental impairment that substantially limits a major life activity. The IDEA specifies a list of types of disabilities and provides protection if a specified disability requires special education and related services. Why would Congress provide such different definitions?

2. The IDEA's list of covered disabilities may leave some gaps in coverage. Children with developmental delays and "slow learners?" *See* Ward ex rel. Carter v. Prince George's County Pub. Schs., 23 F.Supp.2d 585, 591-93 (D. Md. 1998) (stating that the child's performance was below average but not so discrepant from ability to be eligible for special education services). Children who are "medically fragile" or who have serious medical conditions, such as HIV/AIDS or diabetes? *See* Doe v. Belleville Pub. Sch. Dist., 672 F.Supp. 342, 345 (S.D. Ill. 1987) (Child with AIDS who was excluded from school was not covered by IDEA, but by Rehabilitation Act). Children with social maladjustments? *See* A.E. v. Indep. Sch. Dist. No. 25, 936 F.2d 472, 476 (10th Cir. 1991) (socially maladjusted child whose behavior did not arise to the level of serious emotional disturbance is not covered by IDEA). Children with Attention Deficit Disorders (ADD/ADHD)? *See* W. Chester Area Sch. Dist. v. Bruce C., 194 F.Supp.2d 417, 421 (E.D. Pa. 2002) (ADD covered under IDEA if it impairs educational performance). *But see* Lyons v. Smith, 829 F.Supp. 414, 419 (D.D.C. 1993) (ADHD not covered under IDEA as an "other health impairment" if it does not affect alertness and does not impair educational performance).

3. The language of the IDEA only covers children with the listed disabilities if they need "special education and related services." How will children with physical disabilities who are intellectually normal be treated

if they only need related services, such as accessible transportation, assistance eating, or catheterization?

4. In 2010, President Barack Obama signed into law Rosa's Law, Pub. L. 111-256, 124 Stat 2643 (Oct. 5, 2010), which changed references in federal law from "mental retardation" to "intellectual disability," and references to a "mentally retarded individual" to an "individual with an intellectual disability." § 2. The impact of Rosa's law goes beyond the IDEA and other civil rights statutes discussed in this text, to reach many acts utilizing a medical model of disability, such as the Health Professions Education Partnerships Act of 1998, the Public Health Service Act, and the National Sickle Cell Anemia, Cooley's Anemia, Tay-Sachs, and Genetic Diseases Act. § 2(a)-(j).

Chapter 20   FREE APPROPRIATE PUBLIC EDUCATION

The IDEA guarantees students with disabilities a free appropriate public education (FAPE). Pursuant to the IDEA, the vehicle for determining what constitutes FAPE is the Individualized Education Program (IEP). The IEP must be memorialized in a written document containing:

(I)   . . . the child's present levels of academic achievement and functional performance, including –

> (aa) how the child's disability affects the child's involvement and progress in the general education curriculum; . . .

> (cc)   for children with disabilities who take alternate assessments aligned to alternate achievement standards, a description of benchmarks or short-term objectives;

(II)   . . . measurable annual goals, including academic and functional goals, designed to, –

> (aa) meet the child's needs that result from the child's disability to enable the child to be involved in and progress in the general education curriculum; and

> (bb) meet each of the child's other educational needs that result from the child's disability;

(III) a description of how the child's progress toward meeting the annual goals . . . will be measured and when periodic reports on the progress the child is making toward meeting the annual goals . . . will be provided;

(IV) . . . the special education and related services and supplementary aids and services, based on peer-reviewed research to the extent practicable, to be provided to the child, or on behalf of the child, and a statement of the program modifications or supports for school personnel that will be provided for the child –

> (aa) to advance appropriately toward attaining the annual goals;

> (bb) to be involved and progress in the general curriculum . . . and to participate in extracurricular and other nonacademic activities; and

> (cc)   to be educated and participate with other children with disabilities and nondisabled children . . .

(V)   an explanation of the extent, if any, to which the child will not participate with nondisabled children in the regular class and in the activities . . .

(VI) (aa) . . . individual appropriate accommodations that are necessary to measure the academic achievement and functional performance of the child on State and districtwide assessments . . . and

> (bb) if the IEP Team determines that the child shall take an alternate assessment on a particular State or districtwide assessment of student achievement), a statement of why –

>> (AA)   the child cannot participate in the regular assessment; and

>> (BB)   the particular alternate assessment selected is appropriate for the child;

(VII) the projected date for the beginning of the services and modifications . . . and the anticipated frequency, location, and duration of those services and modifications . . .

20 U.S.C. § 1414(d)(1)(A)(i) (2006).

The IEP is created by the IEP Team, which must include the parent(s), at least one regular education teacher, at least one special education teacher, a representative of the local educational agency, an individual who can interpret the assessment results, other individuals with special expertise, and, when appropriate, the student. *Id.* § 1414(d)(1)(B).

The IEP must be reviewed by the IEP Team at least annually. *Id.* § 1414(d)(4)(A)(i). The IDEA provides for special consideration to be given to the need for behavioral interventions, limited English proficiency, Braille instruction for blind children, direct communication methods for children with hearing impairments, and provision of assistive technology. *Id.* § 1414(d)(3)(B).

§ 20.1   FAPE Standard

While the procedural methods of achieving Free Appropriate Public Education are laid out in the IDEA, the substantive meaning of the requirement has fallen to the courts.

BOARD OF EDUCATION v. ROWLEY

Supreme Court of the United States, 1982
458 U.S. 176

Justice REHNQUIST delivered the opinion of the Court.

This case presents a question of statutory interpretation. Petitioners contend that the Court of Appeals and the District Court misconstrued the requirements imposed by Congress upon States which receive federal funds under the Education of the Handicapped Act. We agree and reverse the judgment of the Court of Appeals.

I

The Education of the Handicapped Act (Act), 84 Stat. 175, as amended, 20 U.S.C. § 1401 *et seq.* (1976 ed. and Supp.IV), provides federal money to assist state and local agencies in educating handicapped children, and conditions such funding upon a State's compliance with extensive goals and procedures. The Act represents an ambitious federal effort to promote the education of handicapped children, and was passed in response to Congress' perception that a majority of handicapped children in the United States "were either totally excluded from schools or [were] sitting idly in regular classrooms awaiting the time when they were old enough to 'drop out.'" H.R.Rep.No. 94-332, p. 2 (1975) (H.R.Rep.). The Act's evolution and major provisions shed light on the question of statutory interpretation which is at the heart of this case.

Congress first addressed the problem of educating the handicapped in 1966 when it amended the Elementary and Secondary Education Act of 1965 to establish a grant program "for the purpose of assisting the States in the initiation, expansion, and improvement of programs and projects . . . for the education of handicapped children." Pub.L. 89-750, § 161, 80 Stat. 1204. That program was repealed in 1970 by the Education of the Handicapped Act, Pub.L. 91-230, 84 Stat. 175, Part B of which established a grant program similar in purpose to the repealed legislation. Neither the 1966 nor the 1970 legislation contained specific guidelines for state use of the grant money; both were aimed primarily at stimulating the States to develop educational resources and to train personnel for educating the handicapped.

Dissatisfied with the progress being made under these earlier enactments, and spurred by two District Court decisions holding that handicapped children should be given access to a public education, Congress in 1974 greatly increased federal funding for education of the handicapped and for the first time required recipient States to adopt "a goal of providing full educational opportunities to all handicapped children." Pub.L. 93-380, 88 Stat. 579, 583 (1974 statute). The 1974 statute was recognized as an interim measure only, adopted "in order to give the Congress an additional year in which to study what if any additional Federal assistance [was] required to enable the States to meet the needs of handicapped children." H.R.Rep., at 4. The ensuing year of study produced the Education for All Handicapped Children Act of 1975.

* * *

The "free appropriate public education" required by the Act is tailored to the unique needs of the handicapped child by means of an "individualized educational program" (IEP). § 1401(18). * * *

In addition to the state plan and the IEP already described, the Act imposes extensive procedural requirements upon States receiving federal funds under its provisions. * * *

Thus, although the Act leaves to the States the primary responsibility for developing and executing educational programs for handicapped children, it imposes significant requirements to be followed in the discharge of that responsibility. Compliance is assured by provisions permitting the withholding of federal funds upon determination that a participating state or local agency has failed to satisfy the requirements of the Act, §§ 1414(b)(2)(A), 1416, and by the provision for judicial review. At present, all States except New Mexico receive federal funds under the portions of the Act at issue today.

II

This case arose in connection with the education of Amy Rowley, a deaf student at the Furnace Woods School in the Hendrick Hudson Central School District, Peekskill, N.Y. Amy has minimal residual hearing and is an excellent lipreader. During the year before she began attending Furnace Woods, a meeting between her parents and school administrators resulted in a decision to place her in a regular kindergarten class in order to determine what supplemental services would be necessary to her education. Several members of the school administration prepared for Amy's arrival by attending a course in sign-language interpretation, and a teletype machine was installed in the principal's office to facilitate communication with her parents who are also deaf. At the end of the trial period it was determined that Amy should remain in the kindergarten class, but that she should be provided with an FM hearing aid which would amplify words spoken into a wireless receiver by the teacher or fellow students during certain classroom activities. Amy successfully completed her kindergarten year.

As required by the Act, an IEP was prepared for Amy during the fall of her first-grade year. The IEP provided that Amy should be educated in a regular classroom at Furnace Woods, should continue to use the FM hearing aid, and should receive instruction from a tutor for the deaf for one hour each day and from a speech therapist for three hours each week. The Rowleys agreed with parts of the IEP, but insisted that Amy also be provided a qualified sign-language interpreter in all her academic classes in lieu of the assistance proposed in other parts of the IEP. Such an interpreter had been placed in Amy's kindergarten class for a 2-week experimental period, but the interpreter had reported that Amy did not need his services at that time. The school administrators likewise concluded that Amy did not need such an interpreter in her first-grade classroom. They reached this conclusion after consulting the school district's Committee on the Handicapped, which had received expert evidence from Amy's parents on the importance of a sign-language interpreter, received testimony from Amy's teacher and other persons familiar with her academic and social progress, and visited a class for the deaf.

When their request for an interpreter was denied, the Rowleys demanded and received a hearing before an independent examiner. After receiving evidence from both sides, the examiner agreed with the administrators' determination that an interpreter was not necessary because "Amy was achieving educationally, academically, and socially" without such assistance. The examiner's decision was affirmed on appeal by the New York Commissioner of Education on the basis of substantial evidence in the record. Pursuant to the Act's provision for judicial review, the Rowleys then brought an action in the United States District Court for the Southern District of New York, claiming that the administrators' denial of the sign-language interpreter constituted a denial of the "free appropriate public education" guaranteed by the Act.

The District Court found that Amy "is a remarkably well-adjusted child" who interacts and communicates well with her classmates and has "developed an extraordinary rapport" with her teachers. It also found that "she performs better than the average child in her class and is advancing easily from grade to grade," but "that she understands considerably less of what goes on in class than she could if she were not deaf" and thus "is not learning as much, or performing as well academically, as she would without her handicap." This disparity between Amy's achievement and her potential led the court to decide that she was not receiving a "free appropriate public education," which the court defined as "an opportunity to achieve [her] full potential commensurate with the opportunity provided to other children." According to the District Court, such a standard "requires that the potential of the handicapped child be measured and compared to his or her performance, and that the resulting differential or 'shortfall' be compared to the shortfall experienced by nonhandicapped children." The District Court's definition arose from its assumption that the responsibility for "giv[ing] content to the requirement of an 'appropriate education'" had "been left entirely to the [federal] courts and the hearing officers."

A divided panel of the United States Court of Appeals for the Second Circuit affirmed. The Court of Appeals "agree[d] with the [D]istrict [C]ourt's conclusions of law," and held that its "findings of fact [were] not clearly erroneous."

We granted certiorari to review the lower courts' interpretation of the Act. Such review requires us to consider two questions: What is meant by the Act's requirement of a "free appropriate public education"? And what is the role of state and federal courts in exercising the review granted by 20 U.S.C. § 1415? We consider these questions separately.

III

A

This is the first case in which this Court has been called upon to interpret any provision of the Act. As noted previously, the District Court and the Court of Appeals concluded that "[t]he Act itself does not define 'appropriate education,'" but leaves "to the courts and the hearing officers" the responsibility of "giv[ing] content to the requirement of an 'appropriate education.'" See also 632 F.2d, at 947. * * *

We are loath to conclude that Congress failed to offer any assistance in defining the meaning of the principal substantive phrase used in the Act. It is beyond dispute that, contrary to the conclusions of the courts below, the Act does expressly define "free appropriate public education":

> The term 'free appropriate public education' means *special education* and *related services* which (A) have been provided at public expense, under public supervision and direction, and without charge, (B) meet the standards of the State educational agency, (C) include an appropriate preschool, elementary, or secondary school education in the State involved, and (D) are provided in conformity with the individualized education program required under section 1414(a)(5) of this title.

§ 1401(18) (emphasis added).

"Special education," as referred to in this definition, means "specially designed instruction, at no cost to parents or guardians, to meet the unique needs of a handicapped child, including classroom instruction, instruction in physical education, home instruction, and instruction in hospitals and institutions." § 1401(16). "Related services" are defined as "transportation, and such developmental, corrective, and other supportive services . . . as may be required to assist a handicapped child to benefit from special education." § 1401(17).

Like many statutory definitions, this one tends toward the cryptic rather than the comprehensive, but that is scarcely a reason for abandoning the quest for legislative intent. Whether or not the definition is a "functional" one, as respondents contend it is not, it is the principal tool which Congress has given us for parsing the critical phrase of the Act. We think more must be made of it than either respondents or the United States seems willing to admit.

According to the definitions contained in the Act, a "free appropriate public education" consists of educational instruction specially designed to meet the unique needs of the handicapped child, supported by such services as are necessary to permit the child "to benefit" from the instruction. Almost as a checklist for adequacy under the Act, the definition also requires that such instruction and services be provided at public expense and under public supervision, meet the State's educational standards, approximate the grade levels used in the State's regular education, and comport with the child's IEP. Thus, if personalized instruction is being provided with sufficient supportive services to permit the child to benefit from the instruction, and the other items on the definitional checklist are satisfied, the child is receiving a "free appropriate public education" as defined by the Act.

Other portions of the statute also shed light upon congressional intent. Congress found that of the roughly eight million handicapped children in the United States at the time of enactment, one million were "excluded entirely from the public school system" and more than half were receiving an inappropriate education. 89 Stat. 774, note following § 1401. In addition, as mentioned in Part I, the Act requires States to extend educational services first to those children who are receiving no education and second to those children who are receiving an "inadequate education." § 1412(3). When these express statutory findings and priorities are read together with the Act's extensive procedural requirements and its definition of "free appropriate public education," the face of the statute evinces a congressional intent to bring previously excluded handicapped children into the public education systems of the States and to require the States to adopt *procedures* which would result in individualized consideration of and instruction for each child.

Noticeably absent from the language of the statute is any substantive standard prescribing the level of education to be accorded handicapped children. Certainly the language of the statute contains no requirement like the one imposed by the lower courts – that States maximize the potential of handicapped children "commensurate with the opportunity provided to other children." That standard was expounded by the District Court without reference to the statutory definitions or even to the legislative history of the Act. Although we find the statutory definition of "free appropriate public education" to be helpful in our interpretation of the Act, there remains the question of whether the legislative history indicates a congressional intent that such education meet some additional substantive standard. For an answer, we turn to that history.

B

(i)

As suggested in Part I, federal support for education of the handicapped is a fairly recent development. Before passage of the Act

674

some States had passed laws to improve the educational services afforded handicapped children, but many of these children were excluded completely from any form of public education or were left to fend for themselves in classrooms designed for education of their nonhandicapped peers. * * *

This concern, stressed repeatedly throughout the legislative history, confirms the impression conveyed by the language of the statute: By passing the Act, Congress sought primarily to make public education available to handicapped children. But in seeking to provide such access to public education, Congress did not impose upon the States any greater substantive educational standard than would be necessary to make such access meaningful. Indeed, Congress expressly "recognize[d] that in many instances the process of providing special education and related services to handicapped children is not guaranteed to produce any particular outcome." S. Rep., at 11, U.S. Code Cong. & Admin. News 1975, p. 1435. Thus, the intent of the Act was more to open the door of public education to handicapped children on appropriate terms than to guarantee any particular level of education once inside.

Both the House and the Senate Reports attribute the impetus for the Act and its predecessors to two federal-court judgments rendered in 1971 and 1972. * * * The first case, *Pennsylvania Assn. for Retarded Children v. Commonwealth*, 334 F.Supp. 1257 (E.D. Pa. 1971) and 343 F.Supp. 279 (1972) (*PARC*), was a suit on behalf of retarded children challenging the constitutionality of a Pennsylvania statute which acted to exclude them from public education and training. The case ended in a consent decree which enjoined the State from "deny[ing] to any [child with an intellectual disability] *access* to a free public program of education and training." 334 F.Supp., at 1258 (emphasis added).

PARC was followed by *Mills v. Board of Education of District of Columbia*, 348 F.Supp. 866 (D.C. 1972), a case in which the plaintiff handicapped children had been excluded from the District of Columbia public schools. The court's judgment, quoted in S. Rep., at 6, provided that

> no [handicapped] child eligible for a publicly supported education in the District of Columbia public schools shall be *excluded* from a regular school assignment by a Rule, policy, or practice of the Board of Education of the District of Columbia or its agents unless such child is provided (a) *adequate* alternative educational services suited to the child's needs, which may include special education or tuition grants, and (b) a constitutionally adequate prior hearing and periodic review of the child's status, progress, and the *adequacy* of any educational alternative.

348 F.Supp., at 878 (emphasis added).

Mills and *PARC* both held that handicapped children must be given *access* to an adequate, publicly supported education. Neither case purports to require any particular substantive level of education. Rather, like the language of the Act, the cases set forth extensive procedures to be followed in formulating personalized educational programs for handicapped children. See 348 F.Supp., at 878-883; 334 F.Supp., at 1258-1267. The fact that both *PARC* and *Mills* are discussed at length in the legislative Reports suggests that the principles which they established are the principles which, to a significant extent, guided the drafters of the Act. Indeed, immediately after discussing these cases the Senate Report describes the 1974 statute as having "incorporated the major principles of the right to education cases." S. Rep., at 8, U.S. Code Cong. & Admin. News 1975, p. 1432. Those principles in turn became the basis of the Act, which itself was designed to effectuate the purposes of the 1974 statute. H.R. Rep., at 5.

That the Act imposes no clear obligation upon recipient States beyond the requirement that handicapped children receive some form of specialized education is perhaps best demonstrated by the fact that Congress, in explaining the need for the Act, equated an "appropriate education" to the receipt of some specialized educational services. The Senate Report states: "[T]he most recent statistics provided by the Bureau of Education for the Handicapped estimate that of the more than 8 million children ... with handicapping conditions requiring special education and related services, only 3.9 million such children are receiving an appropriate education." S. Rep., at 8, U.S. Code Cong. & Admin. News 1975, p. 1432. This statement, which reveals Congress' view that 3.9 million handicapped children were "receiving an appropriate education" in 1975, is followed immediately in the Senate Report by a table showing that 3.9 million handicapped children were "served" in 1975 and a slightly larger number were "unserved." A similar statement and table appear in the House Report. H.R. Rep., at 11-12.

It is evident from the legislative history that the characterization of handicapped children as "served" referred to children who were receiving some form of specialized educational services from the States, and that the characterization of children as "unserved" referred to those who were receiving no specialized educational services. * * * By characterizing the 3.9 million handicapped children who were "served" as children who were "receiving an appropriate education," the Senate and House Reports unmistakably disclose Congress' perception of the type of education required by the Act: an "appropriate education" is provided when personalized educational services are provided.

(ii)

Respondents contend that "the goal of the Act is to provide each handicapped child with an equal educational opportunity." We think, however, that the requirement that a State provide specialized

676

educational services to handicapped children generates no additional requirement that the services so provided be sufficient to maximize each child's potential "commensurate with the opportunity provided other children." Respondents and the United States correctly note that Congress sought "to provide assistance to the States in carrying out their responsibilities under . . . the Constitution of the United States to provide equal protection of the laws." S. Rep., at 13, U.S. Code Cong. & Admin. News 1975, p. 1437. But we do not think that such statements imply a congressional intent to achieve strict equality of opportunity or services.

The educational opportunities provided by our public school systems undoubtedly differ from student to student, depending upon a myriad of factors that might affect a particular student's ability to assimilate information presented in the classroom. The requirement that States provide "equal" educational opportunities would thus seem to present an entirely unworkable standard requiring impossible measurements and comparisons. Similarly, furnishing handicapped children with only such services as are available to nonhandicapped children would in all probability fall short of the statutory requirement of "free appropriate public education"; to require, on the other hand, the furnishing of every special service necessary to maximize each handicapped child's potential is, we think, further than Congress intended to go. Thus to speak in terms of "equal" services in one instance gives less than what is required by the Act and in another instance more. The theme of the Act is "free appropriate public education," a phrase which is too complex to be captured by the word "equal" whether one is speaking of opportunities or services.

The legislative conception of the requirements of equal protection was undoubtedly informed by the two District Court decisions referred to above. But cases such as *Mills* and *PARC* held simply that handicapped children may not be excluded entirely from public education. In *Mills*, the District Court said:

> If sufficient funds are not available to finance all of the services and programs that are needed and desirable in the system then the available funds must be expended equitably in such a manner that no child is entirely excluded from a publicly supported education consistent with his needs and ability to benefit therefrom.

348 F.Supp., at 876.

The *PARC* court used similar language, saying "[i]t is the commonwealth's obligation to place each mentally retarded child in a free, public program of education and training appropriate to the child's capacity. . . ." 334 F.Supp., at 1260. The right of access to free public education enunciated by these cases is significantly different from any notion of absolute equality of opportunity regardless of capacity. * * *

677

In explaining the need for federal legislation, the House Report noted that "no congressional legislation has required a precise guarantee for handicapped children, i.e. a basic floor of opportunity that would bring into compliance all school districts with the constitutional right of equal protection with respect to handicapped children." H.R. Rep., at 14. Assuming that the Act was designed to fill the need identified in the House Report – that is, to provide a "basic floor of opportunity" consistent with equal protection – neither the Act nor its history persuasively demonstrates that Congress thought that equal protection required anything more than equal access. Therefore, Congress' desire to provide specialized educational services, even in furtherance of "equality," cannot be read as imposing any particular substantive educational standard upon the States.

The District Court and the Court of Appeals thus erred when they held that the Act requires New York to maximize the potential of each handicapped child commensurate with the opportunity provided nonhandicapped children. Desirable though that goal might be, it is not the standard that Congress imposed upon States which receive funding under the Act. Rather, Congress sought primarily to identify and evaluate handicapped children, and to provide them with access to a free public education.

(iii)

Implicit in the congressional purpose of providing access to a "free appropriate public education" is the requirement that the education to which access is provided be sufficient to confer some educational benefit upon the handicapped child. It would do little good for Congress to spend millions of dollars in providing access to a public education only to have the handicapped child receive no benefit from that education. The statutory definition of "free appropriate public education," in addition to requiring that States provide each child with "specially designed instruction," expressly requires the provision of "such ... supportive services ... as may be required to assist a handicapped child *to benefit* from special education." § 1401(17) (emphasis added). We therefore conclude that the "basic floor of opportunity" provided by the Act consists of access to specialized instruction and related services which are individually designed to provide educational benefit to the handicapped child.

The determination of when handicapped children are receiving sufficient educational benefits to satisfy the requirements of the Act presents a more difficult problem. The Act requires participating States to educate a wide spectrum of handicapped children, from the marginally hearing-impaired to the profoundly retarded and palsied. It is clear that the benefits obtainable by children at one end of the spectrum will differ dramatically from those obtainable by children at the other end, with infinite variations in between. One child may have little difficulty competing successfully in an academic setting with nonhandicapped children while another child may encounter great difficulty in acquiring even the most basic of self-maintenance skills. We do not attempt today to establish any one test for determining the adequacy of educational benefits conferred upon all children covered by the Act. Because in this case we are presented with a handicapped child who is receiving substantial specialized instruction and related services, and who is performing above average in the regular classrooms of a public school system, we confine our analysis to that situation.

The Act requires participating States to educate handicapped children with nonhandicapped children whenever possible. When that "mainstreaming" preference of the Act has been met and a child is being educated in the regular classrooms of a public school system, the system itself monitors the educational progress of the child. Regular examinations are administered, grades are awarded, and yearly advancement to higher grade levels is permitted for those children who attain an adequate knowledge of the course material. The grading and advancement system thus constitutes an important factor in determining educational benefit. Children who graduate from our public school systems are considered by our society to have been "educated" at least to the grade level they have completed, and access to an "education" for handicapped children is precisely what Congress sought to provide in the Act.

C

When the language of the Act and its legislative history are considered together, the requirements imposed by Congress become tolerably clear. Insofar as a State is required to provide a handicapped child with a "free appropriate public education," we hold that it satisfies this requirement by providing personalized instruction with sufficient support services to permit the child to benefit educationally from that instruction. Such instruction and services must be provided at public expense, must meet the State's educational standards, must approximate the grade levels used in the State's regular education, and must comport with the child's IEP. In addition, the IEP, and therefore the personalized instruction, should be formulated in accordance with the requirements of the Act and, if the child is being educated in the regular classrooms of the public education system, should be reasonably calculated to enable the child to achieve passing marks and advance from grade to grade.

IV

A

As mentioned in Part I, the Act permits "[a]ny party aggrieved by the findings and decision" of the state administrative hearings "to bring a civil action" in "any State court of competent jurisdiction or in a district court of the United States without regard to the amount in controversy."

§ 1415(e)(2). The complaint, and therefore the civil action, may concern "any matter relating to the identification, evaluation, or educational placement of the child, or the provision of a free appropriate public education to such child." § 1415(b)(1)(E). In reviewing the complaint, the Act provides that a court "shall receive the record of the [state] administrative proceedings, shall hear additional evidence at the request of a party, and, basing its decision on the preponderance of the evidence, shall grant such relief as the court determines is appropriate." § 1415(e)(2).

* * *

Thus the provision that a reviewing court base its decision on the "preponderance of the evidence" is by no means an invitation to the courts to substitute their own notions of sound educational policy for those of the school authorities which they review. The very importance which Congress has attached to compliance with certain procedures in the preparation of an IEP would be frustrated if a court were permitted simply to set state decisions at nought. The fact that § 1415(e) requires that the reviewing court "receive the records of the [state] administrative proceedings" carries with it the implied requirement that due weight shall be given to these proceedings. And we find nothing in the Act to suggest that merely because Congress was rather sketchy in establishing substantive requirements, as opposed to procedural requirements for the preparation of an IEP, it intended that reviewing courts should have a free hand to impose substantive standards of review which cannot be derived from the Act itself. In short, the statutory authorization to grant "such relief as the court determines is appropriate" cannot be read without reference to the obligations, largely procedural in nature, which are imposed upon recipient States by Congress.

Therefore, a court's inquiry in suits brought under § 1415(e)(2) is twofold. First, has the State complied with the procedures set forth in the Act? And second, is the individualized educational program developed through the Act's procedures reasonably calculated to enable the child to receive educational benefits? If these requirements are met, the State has complied with the obligations imposed by Congress and the courts can require no more.

B

In assuring that the requirements of the Act have been met, courts must be careful to avoid imposing their view of preferable educational methods upon the States. The primary responsibility for formulating the education to be accorded a handicapped child, and for choosing the educational method most suitable to the child's needs, was left by the Act to state and local educational agencies in cooperation with the parents or guardian of the child. * * *

Therefore, once a court determines that the requirements of the Act have been met, questions of methodology are for resolution by the States.

V

* * *

VI

Applying these principles to the facts of this case, we conclude that the Court of Appeals erred in affirming the decision of the District Court. Neither the District Court nor the Court of Appeals found that petitioners had failed to comply with the procedures of the Act, and the findings of neither court would support a conclusion that Amy's educational program failed to comply with the substantive requirements of the Act. On the contrary, the District Court found that the "evidence firmly establishes that Amy is receiving an 'adequate' education, since she performs better than the average child in her class and is advancing easily from grade to grade." In light of this finding, and of the fact that Amy was receiving personalized instruction and related services calculated by the Furnace Woods school administrators to meet her educational needs, the lower courts should not have concluded that the Act requires the provision of a sign-language interpreter. Accordingly, the decision of the Court of Appeals is reversed, and the case is remanded for further proceedings consistent with this opinion.

So ordered.

Justice BLACKMUN, concurring in the judgment.

Although I reach the same result as the Court does today, I read the legislative history and goals of the Education of the Handicapped Act differently. * * *

* * * The clarity of the legislative intent convinces me that the relevant question here is not, as the Court says, whether Amy Rowley's individualized education program was "reasonably calculated to enable [her] to receive educational benefits," measured in part by whether or not she "achieve[s] passing marks and advance[s] from grade to grade." Rather, the question is whether Amy's program, *viewed as a whole*, offered her an opportunity to understand and participate in the classroom that was substantially equal to that given her nonhandicapped classmates. This is a standard predicated on equal educational opportunity and equal access to the educational process, rather than upon Amy's achievement of any particular educational outcome.

* * *

As the Court demonstrates, petitioner Board has provided Amy Rowley considerably more than "a teacher with a loud voice." By concentrating on whether Amy was "learning as much, or performing as well academically, as she would without her handicap," the District Court and the Court of Appeals paid too little attention to whether, on the entire record, respondent's individualized education program offered her an educational opportunity substantially equal to that provided her nonhandicapped classmates. Because I believe that standard has been satisfied here, I agree that the judgment of the Court of Appeals should be reversed.

Justice WHITE, with whom Justice BRENNAN and Justice MARSHALL join, dissenting.

In order to reach its result in this case, the majority opinion contradicts itself, the language of the statute, and the legislative history. Both the majority's standard for a "free appropriate education" and its standard for judicial review disregard congressional intent.

I

The majority first turns its attention to the meaning of a "free appropriate public education." The Act provides:

> The term 'free appropriate public education' means special education and related services which (A) have been provided at public expense, under public supervision and direction, and without charge, (B) meet the standards of the State educational agency, (C) include an appropriate preschool, elementary, or secondary school education in the State involved, and (D) are provided in conformity with the individualized education program required under section 1414(a)(5) of this title.

20 U.S.C. § 1401(18).

The majority reads this statutory language as establishing a congressional intent limited to bringing "previously excluded handicapped children into the public education systems of the States and [requiring] the States to adopt *procedures* which would result in individualized consideration of and instruction for each child." In its attempt to constrict the definition of "appropriate" and the thrust of the Act, the majority opinion states: "Noticeably absent from the language of the statute is any substantive standard prescribing the level of education to be accorded handicapped children. Certainly the language of the statute contains no requirement like the one imposed by the lower courts – that States maximize the potential of handicapped children 'commensurate with the opportunity provided to other children.'"

I agree that the language of the Act does not contain a substantive standard beyond requiring that the education offered must be "appropriate." However, if there are limits not evident from the face of the statute on what may be considered an "appropriate education," they must be found in the purpose of the statute or its legislative history. The Act itself announces it will provide a *full* educational opportunity to all handicapped children." 20 U.S.C. § 1412(2)(A) (emphasis added). This goal is repeated throughout the legislative history, in statements too frequent to be "'passing references and isolated phrases.'" These statements elucidate the meaning of "appropriate." According to the Senate Report, for example, the Act does "guarantee that handicapped children are provided *equal* educational opportunity." S. Rep.No.94-168, p. 9 (1975), U.S. Code Cong. & Admin. News 1975, p. 1433 (emphasis added). This promise appears throughout the legislative history. * * * Indeed, at times the purpose of the Act was described as tailoring each handicapped child's educational plan to enable the child "to achieve his or her maximum potential." H.R. Rep.No.94-332, pp. 13, 19 (1975); see 121 Cong. Rec. 23709 (1975). Senator Stafford, one of the sponsors of the Act, declared: "We can all agree that education [given a handicapped child] should be equivalent, at least, to the one those children who are not handicapped receive." *Id.*, at 19483. The legislative history thus directly supports the conclusion that the Act intends to give handicapped children an educational opportunity commensurate with that given other children.

The majority opinion announces a different substantive standard, that "Congress did not impose upon the States any greater substantive educational standard than would be necessary to make such access meaningful." While "meaningful" is no more enlightening than "appropriate," the Court purports to clarify itself. Because Amy was provided with *some* specialized instruction from which she obtained *some* benefit and because she passed from grade to grade, she was receiving a meaningful and therefore appropriate education.

This falls far short of what the Act intended. The Act details as specifically as possible the kind of specialized education each handicapped child must receive. It would apparently satisfy the Court's standard of "access to specialized instruction and related services which are individually designed to provide educational benefit to the handicapped child," for a deaf child such as Amy to be given a teacher with a loud voice, for she would benefit from that service. The Act requires more. It defines "special education" to mean "specifically designed instruction, at no cost to parents or guardians, to *meet the unique needs* of a handicapped child . . . ." § 1401(16) (emphasis added). Providing a teacher with a loud voice would not meet Amy's needs and would not satisfy the Act. The basic floor of opportunity is instead, as the courts below recognized, intended to eliminate the effects of the handicap, at least to the extent that the child will be given an equal opportunity to learn if that is reasonably possible. Amy Rowley, without a sign-language interpreter, comprehends less than half of what is said in the classroom – less than half of what normal children comprehend. This is hardly an equal opportunity to learn, even if Amy makes passing grades.

* * *

II

The Court's discussion of the standard for judicial review is as flawed as its discussion of a "free appropriate public education." According to the Court, a court can ask only whether the State has "complied with the procedures set forth in the Act" and whether the individualized education program is "reasonably calculated to enable the child to receive educational benefits." Both the language of the Act and the legislative history, however, demonstrate that Congress intended the courts to conduct a far more searching inquiry.

The majority assigns major significance to the review provision's being found in a section entitled "Procedural safeguards." But where else would a provision for judicial review belong? The majority does acknowledge that the current language, specifying that a court "shall receive the records of the administrative proceedings, shall hear additional evidence at the request of a party, and, basing its decision on the preponderance of the evidence, shall grant such relief as the court determines is appropriate," § 1415(e)(2), was substituted at Conference for language that would have restricted the role of the reviewing court much more sharply. It is clear enough to me that Congress decided to reduce substantially judicial deference to state administrative decisions.

The legislative history shows that judicial review is not limited to procedural matters and that the state educational agencies are given first, but not final, responsibility for the content of a handicapped child's education. The Conference Committee directs courts to make an "independent decision." S. Conf. Rep. No.94-455, p. 50 (1975). The deliberate change in the review provision is an unusually clear indication that Congress intended courts to undertake substantive review instead of relying on the conclusions of the state agency.

* * *

Thus, the Court's limitations on judicial review have no support in either the language of the Act or the legislative history. Congress did not envision that inquiry would end if a showing is made that the child is receiving passing marks and is advancing from grade to grade. Instead, it intended to permit a full and searching inquiry into any aspect of a handicapped child's education. The Court's standard, for example, would not permit a challenge to part of the IEP; the legislative history demonstrates beyond doubt that Congress intended such challenges to be possible, even if the plan as developed is reasonably calculated to give the child some benefits.

* * *

Notes & Questions

1. Consider the four possible standards for compliance with Free Appropriate Public Education: (1) mere access to public school education

without significant modifications to the curriculum; (2) procedural compliance and programming reasonably calculated to provide some educational benefit (the standard chosen by the *Rowley* majority); (3) substantially equal opportunity to participate (Justice Blackmun's standard); and (4) educational services designed to maximize the child's educational potential. Which of these comports with the stated goal of the IDEA to "[i]mprov[e] educational results for children with disabilities [as] an essential element of our national policy of ensuring equality of opportunity, full participation, independent living, and economic self-sufficiency for individuals with disabilities"? Which of these standards is most equivalent to the standard for education of children without disabilities in public school?

2. How can parents or schools prove that an IEP is (or is not) "reasonably calculated" to provide a meaningful educational benefit? Is the child's progress (or lack thereof) toward IEP goals dispositive? For further discussion of the grounds for a FAPE violation, *see* William N. Myhill, Note, No FAPE for Children with Disabilities in the Milwaukee Parental Choice Program: Time to Redefine a Free Appropriate Public Education, 89 Iowa. L. Rev. 1051, 1070-71 (2004).

3. Schools often require minimum competency testing to graduate or move from grade to grade. Courts have upheld these requirements, even though they may prevent students with disabilities from receiving a diploma, if adequate notice is given to the students of the testing requirements. Debra P. v. Turlington, 730 F.2d 1405, 1407 (11th Cir. 1984); Brookhart v. Ill. State Bd. of Educ., 697 F.2d 179 (7th Cir. 1983). IEPs commonly are geared, not toward minimum competencies, but toward addressing the individual disabilities of a student. These students often receive certificates that recognize achievement but do not carry the same weight as a diploma. Is awarding a diploma to a student whose disability prevents her from passing a minimum competency test unfair to students without disabilities who must pass the test? Does it mislead prospective employers or providers of higher education? For a discussion of diploma options, *see generally* David R. Johnson et al., Diploma Options for Students with Disabilities, Information Brief (Nat'l Ctr. on Secondary Educ. & Transition Feb. 2005), *available at* http://www.ncset.org/publications/info/NCSETInfoBrief_4.1.pdf.

4. What constitutes FAPE may vary, even among children with similar disabilities, depending on their environment. Thus, for example one deaf child may be most appropriately educated in an environment with hearing children, while another deaf child may be better educated in a classroom with deaf children. *Compare* Visco v. Sch. Dist. of Pittsburgh, 684 F.Supp. 1310, 1316 (W.D. Penn. 1988), *with* Briggs v. Bd. of Educ. Conn., 882 F.2d 688, 693 (2d Cir. 1989).

5. How does the FAPE requirement of the IDEA compare with the requirements of the ADA and Rehabilitation Act (e.g., reasonable

accommodation, reasonable modification of policy, effective communication, and removal of physical barriers)? Are the requirements of the ADA and Rehabilitation Act inappropriate for the public education context?

6. For further discussion of the issue of the correct standard of FAPE, *see* Lester Aron, Too Much or Not Enough: How Have the Circuit Courts Defined a Free and Appropriate Public Education After *Rowley*, 39 Suffolk U. L. Rev. 1 (2005).

❧

§ 20.2 FAPE Applications

The obligation to provide a FAPE may extend to services after a student has reached the age of 21, if a court orders compensatory services for failure to provide adequate FAPE while the student was in school. In *Ferren C. v. Sch. Dist. of Philadelphia*, 612 F.3d 712 (3d Cir. 2010), a twenty-four year old woman with autism, speech and language deficits, and pervasive developmental disorder was awarded $200,000 and three years of compensatory education beyond the age of 21 because the school district failed to provide her with adequate special education for which she was eligible. *Id.* at 715. In formulating equitable relief, the court stated that it must consider all relevant factors, and must weigh "the interests of finality, efficiency, and use of the School District's resources with the compelling needs of [the student] and her family." *Id.* at 718.

The FAPE requirement generally will not extend to participation in extracurricular activities. *See* Rettig v. Kent City Sch. Dist., 788 F.2d 328 (6th Cir. 1986) (concluding the student "would receive no significant educational benefit" from extra-curricular programs due to "sporadic and recurring behavior, including, regurgitation, lack of interest, self-stimulating activities and bladder accidents," thus, the school was not obligated to provide them); Jane Parent ex rel. John Student v. Osceola County Sch. Bd., 59 F.Supp.2d 1243, 1249 (M.D. Fla. 1999) ("Alternative School provided Student with a basic floor of opportunity . . ., although the Alternative School offered limited extra-curricular activities.").

Courts may order school districts to reimburse families for providing home-based educational programs when the school has failed to provide a FAPE. In *T.B. ex rel. W.B. v. St. Joseph Sch. District*, 677 F.3d 844 (8th Cir. 2012), the Eighth Circuit Court of Appeals affirmed a lower court's decision that a school district did not violate the IDEA when it failed to provide a FAPE to a child with autism, and that the parents were therefore not entitled to reimbursement for the expense of the child's home-based program. *Id.* at 845. The court ultimately held that the parents could not show that the home-based care was proper under the IDEA in this case because, although such care need not include certified special education standards, an IEP, or satisfy the IDEA's least restrictive environment requirement, it must still be "reasonably calculated to enable the child to receive educational benefits" as required by the Supreme Court in *Rowley*. T.B. ex rel. W.B., 677 F.3d at 847-48.

Beginning at age 16, a student's IEP must contain needed transition services and be updated annually. 20 U.S.C. § 1414(d)(1)(A)(i)(VIII) (2006).

> The term "transition services" means a coordinated set of activities for a child with a disability that –
>
> (A) is designed within a results-oriented process, ... focused on improving the academic and functional achievement of the child ... to facilitate the child's movement from school to post-school activities, including post-secondary education, vocational training, integrated employment (including supported employment), continuing and adult education, adult services, independent living, or community participation;
>
> (B) is based upon the individual child's needs, taking into account the child's strengths, preferences and interests; and
>
> (C) includes instruction, related services, community experiences, the development of employment and other post-school adult living objectives, and, when appropriate, acquisition of daily living skills and functional vocational evaluation.

Id. § 1401(34).

In *J.L.*, the Ninth Circuit Court of Appeals rejected a district court's ruling that a student who was not provided with adequate transition services violated the IDEA. J.L. v. Mercer Island Sch. Dist., 592 F.3d 938 (9th Cir. 2010). The court below held that the amendments to the IDEA, which discussed transition services and emphasized self-sufficiency, set a new standard that superseded the *Rowley* standard to measure whether a school district was in compliance with the IDEA's requirements. J.L. v. Mercer Island Sch. Dist., No. C06-494P, 2006 WL 3628033, at *6 (W.D.Wash. Dec. 8, 2006); 592 F.3d at 949. The Ninth Circuit indicated that Congress expressed no specific intent to alter the meaning of a FAPE in its amendments to the Act. *Id.* at 947-48. Therefore, although the statutes added transition services to its language, as long as a student was receiving an "educational benefit" as set forth in *Rowley*, IDEA requirements are satisfied. *Id.* at 951.

The school's obligation to provide assistive technologies (ATs) and AT services must be addressed in a child's IEP to become part of the FAPE to which the child is entitled. *See* 34 C.F.R. § 300.105; *see also* 20 U.S.C. § 1414(d)(3)(B)(v). Personal ATs such as eyeglasses and hearing aids generally are not included in the IEP as they are used by the student in all life activities and are not limited to implementing the IEP. The family is responsible for the costs and maintaining such items. Cochlear implants, likewise, are personal ATs. *Petit v. U.S. Dept. of Educ.*, 675 F.3d 769, 774 (D.C. Cir. 2012). As such, school districts are not required to provide or replace cochlear implant devices as either an AT or a related service. *Id.* at 775.

However, the DOE has clarified that school districts are still required to provide *some* services to students with cochlear implants, including "related services that are determined by the IEP Team to be necessary for the child to receive FAPE," 34 C.F.R. § 300.113(b)(1) (2011), and "ensur[ing] that the external components of surgically implanted medical devices are functioning properly." *Petit*, 675 F.3d at 776 (citing 34 C.F.R. § 300.113(b)(2)). However, the school "is not responsible for the post-surgical maintenance, programming, or replacement of the medical device that has been surgically implanted (or of an external component of the surgically implanted medical device)." *Id.*

Notes & Questions

1. Melanie, a high school student with grade level cognitive abilities, has limited use of hands and slurred speech due to cerebral palsy. She receives special education and related services under the IDEA including speech-language services, occupational therapy, adaptive physical education, and use of assistive technologies to facilitate written and spoken communication. She intends to enroll in an advanced civics elective available through the state's virtual high school for credit toward high school graduation. The IEP team agrees the course is appropriate to meet her personal academic goals of applying for admission into a competitive liberal arts college. The course is designed to be self-paced and reached from any computer with Internet access. It entails extensive reading and writing assignments using specified online and/or library resources. The course includes mini multimedia lectures, online progress quizzes, and major assignments submitted via email.

Melanie will be one of 30 students taking the course from around her state. The instructor provides general information to the students via a Listserv, and is reachable during set office hours via phone or email. What legal obligations to the student may arise for her local school and for the state virtual school to ensure a FAPE? *See* William N. Myhill et al., Distance Education Initiatives and Their Early 21st Century Role in the Lives of People with Disabilities, in Focus on Distance Education Developments 24-25 (2007) (discussing this and related scenarios).

Chapter 21 LEAST RESTRICTIVE ENVIRONMENT

Parents of children with disabilities who seek integrated classrooms for their children cite studies indicating:

> [E]ven children with the most severe disabilities learn better in integrated settings. Disabled students set higher goals for themselves when they have nondisabled peers to model. And the teachers in integrated classrooms are more likely to push them as well .... Studies of disabled children show that they master social skills far more easily when they go to school with nondisabled children. In addition, the other classmates learn empathy and many take on a sense of responsibility for helping a disabled classmate.

Joseph P. Shapiro, No Pity: People with Disabilities Forging a New Civil Rights Movement (Times Books 1994). In response to these findings and the disability community's calls for integration, the IDEA requires that:

> To the maximum extent appropriate, children with disabilities ... are educated with children who are not disabled, and special classes, separate schooling, or other removal of children with disabilities from the regular educational environment occurs only when the nature or severity of the disability of a child is such that education in regular classes with the use of supplementary aids and services cannot be achieved satisfactorily.

20 U.S.C. § 1412(a)(5)(A) (2006). This requirement is often referred to as "mainstreaming."

Professor Martha Minow has written that IDEA "embodies an express tension between its two substantive commitments to the 'appropriate education' and to the 'least restrictive alternative.' This tension invokes the choice between specialized services and some degree of separate treatment on the one side and minimized labeling and minimized segregation on the other." Martha Minow, Learning to Live with the Dilemma of Difference: Bilingual and Special Education, Law & Contemp. Probs., Winter 1985, at 181.

The requirement to provide a Free Appropriate Public Education to children with disabilities while ensuring inclusion in the Least Restrictive Environment is accomplished by the provision of a continuum of alternative placements. 34 C.F.R. § 300.115 (2008). The continuum can range from (1) instruction in regular classes, to (2) special classes, to (3) special schools, to (4) home instruction, to (5) instruction in hospitals and institutions. 34 C.F.R. § 300.115(b) (2008).

The Sixth Circuit in *Roncker v. Walker*, 700 F.2d 1058 (6th Cir. 1983), addressed the interaction between the FAPE requirement and the mainstreaming requirement, stating:

> The Act does not require mainstreaming in every case but its requirement that mainstreaming be provided to the *maximum* extent appropriate indicates a very strong congressional preference. The proper inquiry is whether a proposed placement is appropriate under the Act. In some cases, a placement which may be considered better for academic reasons may not be appropriate because of the failure to provide for mainstreaming. . . . In a case where the segregated facility is considered superior, the court should determine whether the services which make that placement superior could be feasibly provided in a non-segregated setting. If they can, the placement in the segregated school would be inappropriate under the Act. Framing the issue in this manner accords the proper respect for the strong preference in favor of mainstreaming while still realizing the possibility that some handicapped children simply must be educated in segregated facilities either because the handicapped child would not benefit from mainstreaming, because any marginal benefits received from mainstreaming are far outweighed by the benefits gained from services which could not feasibly be provided in the non-segregated setting, or because the handicapped child is a disruptive force in the non-segregated setting. Cost is a proper factor to consider since excessive spending on one handicapped child deprives other handicapped children. . . . Cost is no defense, however, if the school district has failed to use its funds to provide a proper continuum of alternative placements for handicapped children. The provision of such alternative placements benefits all handicapped children.

Id. at 1063 (citations omitted). Thus, mainstreaming is not intended to be provided at the expense of FAPE. Rather, the necessary services to provide FAPE should be determined and then applied in an integrated setting if possible. The Ninth Circuit further addressed the interaction between FAPE and integration in *Sacramento City Unified School District v. Rachel H.*, 14 F.3d 1398 (9th Cir. 1994).

SACRAMENTO CITY UNIFIED SCHOOL DISTRICT v. RACHEL H.

United States Court of Appeals, Ninth Circuit, 1994
14 F.3d 1398

SNEED, Circuit Judge:

The Sacramento Unified School District ("the District") timely appeals the district court's judgment in favor of Rachel Holland ("Rachel") and the California State Department of Education. The court found that the appropriate placement for Rachel under the Individuals with Disabilities Act ("IDEA") was full-time in a regular second grade classroom with some supplemental services. The District contends that the appropriate placement for Rachel is half-time in special education classes and half-time in a regular class. We affirm the judgment of the district court.

I.

FACTS AND PRIOR PROCEEDINGS

Rachel Holland is now 11 years old and is mentally retarded. She was tested with an I.Q. of 44. She attended a variety of special education programs in the District from 1985-89. Her parents sought to increase the time Rachel spent in a regular classroom, and in the fall of 1989, they requested that Rachel be placed full-time in a regular classroom for the 1989-90 school year. The District rejected their request and proposed a placement that would have divided Rachel's time between a special education class for academic subjects and a regular class for non-academic activities such as art, music, lunch, and recess. The district court found that this plan would have required moving Rachel at least six times each day between the two classrooms. The Hollands instead enrolled Rachel in a regular kindergarten class at the Shalom School, a private school. Rachel remained at the Shalom School in regular classes and at the time the district court rendered its opinion was in the second grade.

The Hollands and the District were able to agree on an Individualized Education Program ("IEP") for Rachel. Although the IEP is required to be reviewed annually, *see* 20 U.S.C. § 1401a(20)(B), because of the dispute between the parties, Rachel's IEP has not been reviewed since January 1990.

The Hollands appealed the District's placement decision to a state hearing officer pursuant to 20 U.S.C. § 1415(b)(2). They maintained that Rachel best learned social and academic skills in a regular classroom and would not benefit from being in a special education class. The District contended Rachel was too severely disabled to benefit from full-time placement in a regular class. The hearing officer concluded that the District had failed to make an adequate effort to educate Rachel in a regular class pursuant to the IDEA. The officer found that (1) Rachel had benefitted from her regular kindergarten class – that she was motivated to learn and learned by imitation and modeling; (2) Rachel was not disruptive in a regular classroom; and (3) the District had overstated the cost of putting Rachel in regular education – that the cost would not be so great that it weighed against placing her in a regular classroom. The hearing officer ordered the District to place Rachel in a regular classroom with support services, including a special education consultant and a part-time aide.

The District appealed this determination to the district court. * * * The court affirmed the decision of the hearing officer that Rachel should be placed full-time in a regular classroom.

In considering whether the District proposed an appropriate placement for Rachel, the district court examined the following factors: (1) the educational benefits available to Rachel in a regular classroom, supplemented with appropriate aids and services, as compared with the educational benefits of a special education classroom; (2) the non-academic benefits of interaction with children who were not disabled; (3) the effect of Rachel's presence on the teacher and other children in the classroom; and (4) the cost of mainstreaming Rachel in a regular classroom.

1. Educational Benefits

The district court found the first factor, educational benefits to Rachel, weighed in favor of placing her in a regular classroom. Each side presented expert testimony * * *. The court noted that the District's evidence focused on Rachel's limitations but did not establish that the educational opportunities available through special education were better or equal to those available in a regular classroom. Moreover, the court found that the testimony of the Hollands' experts was more credible because they had more background in evaluating children with disabilities placed in regular classrooms and that they had a greater opportunity to observe Rachel over an extended period of time in normal circumstances. The district court also gave great weight to the testimony of Rachel's current teacher, Nina Crone, whom the court found to be an experienced, skillful teacher. Ms. Crone stated that Rachel was a full member of the class and participated in all activities. Ms. Crone testified that Rachel was making progress on her IEP goals: She was learning one-to-one correspondence in counting, was able to recite the English and Hebrew alphabets, and was improving her communication abilities and sentence lengths.

The district court found that Rachel received substantial benefits in regular education and that all of her IEP goals could be implemented in a regular classroom with some modification to the curriculum and with the assistance of a part-time aide.

2. Non-academic Benefits

The district court next found that the second factor, non-academic benefits to Rachel, also weighed in favor of placing her in a regular classroom. The court noted that the Hollands' evidence indicated that Rachel had developed her social and communications skills as well as her self-confidence from placement in a regular class, while the District's evidence tended to show that Rachel was not learning from exposure to other children and that she was isolated from her classmates. The court concluded that the differing evaluations in large part reflected the predisposition of the evaluators. The court found the testimony of Rachel's mother and her current teacher to be the most credible. These witnesses testified regarding Rachel's excitement about school, learning, and her new friendships and Rachel's improved self-confidence.

3. Effect on the Teacher and Children in the Regular Class

The district court next addressed the issue of whether Rachel had a detrimental effect on others in her regular classroom. The court looked at two aspects: (1) whether there was detriment because the child was disruptive, distracting or unruly, and (2) whether the child would take up so much of the teacher's time that the other students would suffer from lack of attention. The witnesses of both parties agreed that Rachel followed directions and was well-behaved and not a distraction in class. The court found the most germane evidence on the second aspect came from Rachel's second grade teacher, Nina Crone, who testified that Rachel did not interfere with her ability to teach the other children and in the future would require only a part-time aide. Accordingly, the district court determined that the third factor, the effect of Rachel's presence on the teacher and other children in the classroom weighed in favor of placing her in a regular classroom.

4. Cost

Finally, the district court found that the District had not offered any persuasive or credible evidence to support its claim that educating Rachel in a regular classroom with appropriate services would be significantly more expensive than educating her in the District's proposed setting.

The District contended that it would cost $109,000 to educate Rachel full-time in a regular classroom. This figure was based on the cost of providing a full-time aide for Rachel plus an estimated $80,000 for school-wide sensitivity training. The court found that the District did not establish that such training was necessary. Further, the court noted that even if such training were necessary, there was evidence from the California Department of Education that the training could be had at no cost. Moreover, the court found it would be inappropriate to assign the total cost of the training to Rachel when other children with disabilities would benefit. In addition, the court concluded that the evidence did not suggest that Rachel required a full-time aide.

In addition, the court found that the District should have compared the cost of placing Rachel in a special class of approximately 12 students with a full-time special education teacher and two full-time aides and the cost of placing her in a regular class with a part-time aide. The District provided no evidence of this cost comparison.

The court also was not persuaded by the District's argument that it would lose significant funding if Rachel did not spend at least 51% of her time in a special education class. The court noted that a witness from the California Department of Education testified that waivers were available if a school district sought to adopt a program that did not fit neatly within the funding guidelines. The District had not applied for a waiver.

By inflating the cost estimates and failing to address the true comparison, the District did not meet its burden of proving that regular placement would burden the District's funds or adversely affect services available to other children. Therefore, the court found that the cost factor did not weigh against mainstreaming Rachel.

The district court concluded that the appropriate placement for Rachel was full-time in a regular second grade classroom with some supplemental services and affirmed the decision of the hearing officer.

* * *

IV.

DISCUSSION

* * *

B. Mainstreaming Requirements of the IDEA

1. The Statute

The IDEA provides that each state must establish:

> [P]rocedures to assure that, to the maximum extent appropriate, children with disabilities . . . are educated with children who are not disabled, and that special classes, separate schooling, or other removal of children with disabilities from the regular educational environment occurs only when the nature or severity of the disability is such that education in regular classes with the use of supplementary aids and services cannot be achieved satisfactorily. . . .

20 U.S.C. § 1412(5)(B).

This provision sets forth Congress's preference for educating children with disabilities in regular classrooms with their peers. *Department of Educ. v. Katherine D.*, 727 F.2d 809, 817 (9th Cir. 1983), *cert. denied,* 471 U.S. 1117, 105 S.Ct. 2360, 86 L.Ed.2d 260 (1985); *see also Oberti v. Board of Educ.*, 995 F.2d 1204, 1213 (3d Cir. 1993) (as corrected, June 23, 1993); *Greer v. Rome City Sch. Dist.*, 950 F.2d 688, 695 (11th Cir. 1991), *withdrawn,* 956 F.2d 1025 (1992), and *reinstated,* 967 F.2d 470 (1992); *Daniel R.R.,* 874 F.2d at 1044.

2. Burden of Proof

There is a conflict regarding which party bears the burden of proof. The Third Circuit has held that a school district has the initial burden of justifying its educational placement at the administrative level *and* the burden in the district court if the student is challenging the agency decision. *See Oberti,* 995 F.2d at 1219. Other circuits have held that the burden of proof in the district court rests with the party challenging the agency decision. *See Roland M. v. Concord Sch. Comm.,* 910 F.2d 983, 991 (1st Cir. 1990), *cert. denied,* 499 U.S. 912, 111 S.Ct. 1122, 113 L.Ed.2d 230 (1991); *Kerkam v. McKenzie,* 862 F.2d 884, 887 (D.C. Cir. 1988). Under either approach, in this case the District, which was challenging the agency decision, had the burden of demonstrating in the district court that its proposed placement provided mainstreaming to "the maximum extent appropriate."

3. Test for Determining Compliance with the IDEA's Mainstreaming Requirement

We have not adopted or devised a standard for determining the presence of compliance with 20 U.S.C. § 1412(5)(B). The Third, Fifth and Eleventh Circuits use what is known as the *Daniel R.R.* test. *Oberti,* 995 F.2d at 1215; *Greer,* 950 F.2d at 696; *Daniel R.R.,* 874 F.2d at 1048. The Fourth, Sixth and Eighth Circuits apply the *Roncker* test. *Devries v. Fairfax County Sch. Bd.,* 882 F.2d 876, 879 (4th Cir.1989); *A.W. v. Northwest R-1 Sch. Dist.,* 813 F.2d 158, 163 (8th Cir.), *cert. denied,* 484 U.S. 847, 108 S.Ct. 144, 98 L.Ed.2d 100 (1987); *Roncker v. Walter,* 700 F.2d 1058, 1063 (6th Cir.), *cert. denied,* 464 U.S. 864, 104 S.Ct. 196, 78 L.Ed.2d 171 (1983).

Although the district court relied principally on *Daniel R.R.* and *Greer,* it did not specifically adopt the *Daniel R.R.* test over the *Roncker* test. Rather, it employed factors found in both lines of cases in its analysis. The result was a four-factor balancing test in which the court considered (1) the educational benefits of placement full-time in a regular class; (2) the non-academic benefits of such placement; (3) the effect Rachel had on the teacher and children in the regular class; and (4) the costs of mainstreaming Rachel. This analysis directly addresses the issue of the appropriate placement for a child with disabilities under the requirements of 20 U.S.C. § 1412(5)(B). Accordingly, we approve and adopt the test employed by the district court.

4. The District's Contentions on Appeal

The District strenuously disagrees with the district court's findings that Rachel was receiving academic and non-academic benefits in a regular class and did not have a detrimental effect on the teacher or other students. It argues that the court's findings were contrary to the evidence of the state Diagnostic Center and that the court should not have been persuaded by the testimony of Rachel's teacher, particularly her testimony that Rachel would need only a part-time aide in the future. The district court, however, conducted a full evidentiary hearing and made a thorough analysis. The court found the Hollands' evidence to be more persuasive. Moreover, the court asked Rachel's teacher extensive questions regarding Rachel's need for a part-time aide. We will not disturb the findings of the district court.

The District is also not persuasive on the issue of cost. The District now claims that it will lose up to $190,764 in state special education funding if Rachel is not enrolled in a special education class at least 51% of the day. However, the District has not sought a waiver pursuant to California Education Code § 56101. This section provides that (1) any school district may request a waiver of any provision of the Education Code if the waiver is necessary or beneficial to the student's IEP, and (2) the Board may grant the waiver when failure to do so would hinder compliance with federal mandates for a free appropriate education for children with disabilities. Cal.Educ.Code § 56101(a) & (b) (Deering 1992).

Finally, the District, citing *Wilson v. Marana Unified Sch. Dist.,* 735 F.2d 1178 (9th Cir.1984), argues that Rachel must receive her academic and functional curriculum in special education from a specially credentialed teacher. *Wilson* does not stand for this proposition. Rather, the court in *Wilson* stated:

> The school district argues that under state law a child who qualifies for special education *must* be taught by a teacher who is certificated in that child's particular area of disability. We do not agree and do not reach a decision on that broad assertion. We hold only, under our standard of review, that the school district's decision was a reasonable one under the circumstances of this case.

735 F.2d at 1180 (emphasis in original). More importantly, the District's proposition that Rachel must be taught by a special education teacher runs directly counter to the congressional preference that children with disabilities be educated in regular classes with children who are not disabled. *See* 20 U.S.C. § 1412(5)(B).

We affirm the judgment of the district court. While we cannot determine what the appropriate placement is for Rachel at the present time, we hold that the determination of the present and future appropriate placement for Rachel should be based on the principles set forth in this opinion and the opinion of the district court.

AFFIRMED.

Notes & Questions

1. The IDEA provides a presumption in favor of integration of children with and without disabilities. This presumption responds to the negative effects of traditional segregation of children with disabilities, which often resulted in low expectations, inadequate education, and even abuse. In addition, segregation is believed by many disability advocates to leave children with disabilities unprepared to participate in their communities and interact with people without disabilities. *See* Shapiro, *supra*, at 168-69.

2. The least restrictive environment mandate requires supplementary aids and services in the regular classroom curriculum when necessary to integrate a child with a disability. 20 U.S.C. § 1412(a)(5)(A) (2006). Does it also require modifications to the regular curriculum? *Compare* Daniel R.R. v. State Bd. of Educ., 874 F.2d 1036, 1048 (5th Cir. 1989) (changes to the regular curriculum not required), *with* Oberti v. Bd. of Educ., 995 F.2d 1204, 1217 (3d Cir. 1993) (modifications to regular curriculum may be required). Does it require substantial modifications to classrooms? *See* Espino v. Besteiro, 520 F.Supp. 905, 911-14 (S.D. Tex. 1981) (requiring air conditioning of classroom for a child whose disability prevents him from regulating body temperature; enclosure of child in plexiglass cubicle violated least restrictive environment requirement, even though the child got good grades).

3. Children with disabilities often face bullying and exclusion at the hands of their peers without disabilities in integrated settings. Paul M. Secunda, At the Crossroads of Title IX and a New "IDEA": Why Bullying Need Not Be "A Normal Part of Growing Up" for Special Education Children, 12 Duke J. Gender L. & Pol'y 1, 13-17 (2005). This often leads parents and teachers to propose segregated settings as better able to protect children with disabilities and provide them FAPE. *See* Shore Reg'l High Sch. Bd. of Educ. v. P.S., 381 F.3d 194 (3d Cir. 2004) (finding that the original school where the child was bullied relentlessly could not provide a FAPE). If, however, bullying is accepted as a reason to exclude children with disabilities from integrated settings or from their neighborhood schools, it becomes possible that schools wishing to exclude children with disabilities will unnecessarily allow bullying to continue. Thus, it is important to consider the school's obligations to protect its students from bullying and ensure that the school is making such efforts before permitting removal of a child with a disability.

4. Courts have agreed that mainstreaming is to be considered only when FAPE can be provided in the integrated environment. Thus,

the primary obligation is to provide FAPE. Lachman v. Ill. State Bd. of Educ., 852 F.2d 290, 295 (7th Cir. 1988).

5. The facts of *Rachel H.*, as the court applied them to the four factor balancing test, produced a 4-0 win in Rachel's favor. Rachel H., 14 F.3d at 1404-05 (accepting the test and conclusions of the district court's four factor analysis, *id.* at 1400-02). How would a court handle an even 2-2 split? Which factors might weigh more heavily? *See* M.L. v. Fed. Way Sch. Dist., 341 F.3d 1052, 1070 (9th Cir. 2003) (applying only the first three factors as relevant); Beth B. v. Van Clay, 211 F.Supp.2d 1020, 1030-35 (N.D. Ill. 2001) (discussing the four *Rachel H.* factors under the Fifth Circuit's, two part *Daniel R.R. v. State Board of Education,* 874 F.2d 1036, 1046 (5th Cir. 1989) test and the Sixth Circuit's test in *Roncker v. Walter,* 700 F.2d 1058, 1063 (6th Cir. 1983)).

પ્ર

Chapter 22 RELATED SERVICES

In addition to educational services, the IDEA also requires schools to provide related services that a child with a disability needs to benefit from his or her education.

> The term "related services" means transportation and such developmental, corrective, and other supportive services (including speech-language pathology and audiology services, interpreting services, psychological services, physical and occupational therapy, recreation, including therapeutic recreation, social work services, school nurse services designed to enable a child with a disability to receive a free appropriate public education as described in the individualized education program of the child, counseling services, including rehabilitation counseling, orientation and mobility services, and medical services, except that such medical services shall be for diagnostic and evaluation purposes only) . . . and includes the early identification and assessment of disabling conditions in children.

20 U.S.C. § 1401(26)(A) (2006).

§ 22.1   Health Services

Medical services are defined as "services provided by a licensed physician to determine a child's medically related disability that results in the child's need for special education and related services." 34 C.F.R § 300.34(c)(5) (2008). By comparison, "[s]chool nurse services are services provided by a qualified school nurse. School health services are services that may be provided by either a qualified school nurse or other qualified person." *Id.* at § 300.34(c)(13). Consider the line between medical services and health/nurse services in the following case.

IRVING INDEPENDENT SCHOOL DISTRICT v. TATRO

Supreme Court of the United States, 1984
468 U.S. 883

Chief Justice BURGER delivered the opinion of the Court.

We granted certiorari to determine whether the Education of the Handicapped Act or the Rehabilitation Act of 1973 requires a school district to provide a handicapped child with clean intermittent catheterization during school hours.

I

Amber Tatro is an 8-year-old girl born with a defect known as spina bifida. As a result, she suffers from orthopedic and speech impairments and a neurogenic bladder, which prevents her from emptying her bladder voluntarily. Consequently, she must be catheterized every three or four hours to avoid injury to her kidneys. In accordance with accepted medical practice, clean intermittent catheterization (CIC), a procedure involving the insertion of a catheter into the urethra to drain the bladder, has been prescribed. The procedure is a simple one that may be performed in a few minutes by a layperson with less than an hour's training. * * *

In 1979 petitioner Irving Independent School District agreed to provide special education for Amber, who was then three and one-half years old. * * * The individualized education program provided that Amber would attend early childhood development classes and receive special services such as physical and occupational therapy. That program, however, made no provision for school personnel to administer CIC.

Respondents unsuccessfully pursued administrative remedies to secure CIC services for Amber during school hours. * * *

II

This case poses two separate issues. The first is whether the Education of the Handicapped Act requires petitioner to provide CIC services to Amber. The second is whether § 504 of the Rehabilitation Act creates such an obligation. We first turn to the claim presented under the Education of the Handicapped Act.

States receiving funds under the Act are obliged to satisfy certain conditions. A primary condition is that the state implement a policy "that assures all handicapped children the right to a free appropriate public education." 20 U.S.C. § 1412(1). * * *

A "free appropriate public education" is explicitly defined as "special education and related services." § 1401(18). The term "special education" means "specially designed instruction, at no cost to parents or guardians, to meet the unique needs of a handicapped child, including classroom instruction, instruction in physical education, home instruction, and instruction in hospitals and institutions." § 1401(16).

"Related services" are defined as

> "transportation, and such developmental, corrective, and other *supportive services* (*including* speech pathology and audiology, psychological services, physical and occupational therapy, recreation, and *medical* and counseling *services, except that such medical services shall be for diagnostic and evaluation purposes only) as may be required to assist a handicapped child to benefit from special education*, and includes the early identification and assessment of handicapping conditions in children."

§ 1401(17) (emphasis added).

The issue in this case is whether CIC is a "related service" that petitioner is obliged to provide to Amber. We must answer two questions: first, whether CIC is a "supportive servic[e] . . . required to assist a handicapped child to benefit from special education"; and second, whether CIC is excluded from this definition as a "medical servic[e]" serving purposes other than diagnosis or evaluation.

A

The Court of Appeals was clearly correct in holding that CIC is a "supportive servic[e] . . . required to assist a handicapped child to benefit from special education." It is clear on this record that, without having CIC services available during the school day, Amber cannot attend school and thereby "benefit from special education." CIC services therefore fall squarely within the definition of a "supportive service."

As we have stated before, "Congress sought primarily to make public education available to handicapped children" and "to make such access meaningful." A service that enables a handicapped child to remain at school during the day is an important means of providing the child with the meaningful access to education that Congress envisioned. The Act makes specific provision for services, like transportation, for example, that do no more than enable a child to be physically present in class, see 20 U.S.C. § 1401(17); and the Act specifically authorizes grants for schools to alter buildings and equipment to make them accessible to the handicapped, § 1406; see S. Rep. No. 94-168, p. 38 (1975), U.S. Code Cong. & Admin. News 1975, p. 1425; 121 Cong. Rec. 19483-19484 (1975) (remarks of Sen. Stafford). Services like CIC that permit a child to remain at school during the day are no less related to the effort to educate than are services that enable the child to reach, enter, or exit the school.

We hold that CIC services in this case qualify as a "supportive servic[e] . . . required to assist a handicapped child to benefit from special education."

B

We also agree with the Court of Appeals that provision of CIC is not a "medical servic[e]," which a school is required to provide only for purposes of diagnosis or evaluation. See 20 U.S.C. § 1401(17). We begin with the regulations of the Department of Education, which are entitled to deference. See, e.g., *Blum v. Bacon*, 457 U.S. 132, 141 (1982). The regulations define "related services" for handicapped children to include "school health services," 34 C.F.R. § 300.13(a) (1983), which are defined in turn as "services provided by a qualified school nurse or other qualified person," § 300.13(b)(10). "Medical services" are defined as "services provided by a licensed physician." § 300.13(b)(4). Thus, the Secretary has determined that the services of a school nurse otherwise qualifying as a "related service" are not subject to exclusion as a "medical service," but that the services of a physician are excludable as such.

This definition of "medical services" is a reasonable interpretation of congressional intent. Although Congress devoted little discussion to the "medical services" exclusion, the Secretary could reasonably have concluded that it was designed to spare schools from an obligation to provide a service that might well prove unduly expensive and beyond the range of their competence. From this understanding of congressional purpose, the Secretary could reasonably have concluded that Congress intended to impose the obligation to provide school nursing services.

Congress plainly required schools to hire various specially trained personnel to help handicapped children, such as "trained occupational therapists, speech therapists, psychologists, social workers and other appropriately trained personnel." S. Rep. No. 94-168, supra, at 33, U.S. Code Cong. & Admin. News 1975, p. 1457. School nurses have long been a part of the educational system, and the Secretary could therefore reasonably conclude that school nursing services are not the sort of burden that Congress intended to exclude as a "medical service." By limiting the "medical services" exclusion to the services of a physician or hospital, both far more expensive, the Secretary has given a permissible construction to the provision.

Petitioner's contrary interpretation of the "medical services" exclusion is unconvincing. In petitioner's view, CIC is a "medical service," even though it may be provided by a nurse or trained layperson; that conclusion rests on its reading of Texas law that confines CIC to uses in accordance with a physician's prescription and under a physician's ultimate supervision. Aside from conflicting with the Secretary's reasonable interpretation of congressional intent, however, such a rule would be anomalous. Nurses in petitioner School District are authorized to dispense oral medications and administer emergency injections in accordance with a physician's prescription. This kind of service for nonhandicapped children is difficult to distinguish from the provision of CIC to the handicapped. It would be strange indeed if Congress, in attempting to extend special services to handicapped children, were unwilling to guarantee them services of a kind that are routinely provided to the nonhandicapped.

To keep in perspective the obligation to provide services that relate to both the health and educational needs of handicapped students, we note several limitations that should minimize the burden petitioner fears. First, to be entitled to related services, a child must be handicapped so as to require special education. See 20 U.S.C. § 1401(1); 34 C.F.R. § 300.5 (1983). In the absence of a handicap that requires special education, the need for what otherwise might qualify as a related service does not create an obligation under the Act. See 34 C.F.R. § 300.14, Comment (1) (1983).

Second, only those services necessary to aid a handicapped child to benefit from special education must be provided, regardless how easily a school nurse or layperson could furnish them. For example, if a particular medication or treatment may appropriately be administered to a handicapped child other than during the school day, a school is not required to provide nursing services to administer it.

Third, the regulations state that school nursing services must be provided only if they can be performed by a nurse or other qualified person, not if they must be performed by a physician. See 34 C.F.R. §§ 300.13(a), (b)(4), (b)(10) (1983). It bears mentioning that here not even the services of a nurse are required; as is conceded, a layperson with minimal training is qualified to provide CIC. See also, e.g., Department of Education of Hawaii v. Katherine D., 727 F.2d 809 (CA9 1983).

Finally, we note that respondents are not asking petitioner to provide equipment that Amber needs for CIC. They seek only the services of a qualified person at the school.

We conclude that provision of CIC to Amber is not subject to exclusion as a "medical service," and we affirm the Court of Appeals' holding that CIC is a "related service" under the Education of the Handicapped Act.

* * *

Notes & Questions

1. The Supreme Court upheld its *Tatro* decision in *Cedar Rapids Community School District v. Garret F.*, 526 U.S. 66 (1999). The Court in that case found that "school health services" included frequent services, such as daily urinary bladder catheterization, tracheotomy tube suctioning, hourly re-positioning, and occasional ambu bagging for a student who uses a ventilator. Justices Thomas and Kennedy dissented, arguing that *Tatro* was wrongly decided and that schools should not be required to provide such extensive and frequent services, requiring hiring of additional staff. *Id.* at 79-83. The dissent argued that, because the IDEA was enacted pursuant to the Spending Clause of the Constitution, it must be interpreted narrowly so as not to impose obligations the states did not anticipate when they accepted federal funding. *Id.* at 83-85 (Thomas, J., dissenting). Advocates have argued that health services required under *Garret F.* include continuous mental health services. Ellen A. Callegary, The IDEA's Promise Unfulfilled: A Second Look at Special Education & Related Services for Children with Mental Health Needs After *Garret F.*, 5 J. Health Care L. & Pol'y 164, 167 (2002).

2. Is requiring that a school provide services that are "medically necessary" to ensure a child receives a FAPE, at odds with *Tatro*? *See* 42 U.S.C. § 1396b(c) (2006) (discussing "treatment of educationally-related services" with Medicaid funds); *cf.* Hornstine v. Township of Moorestown, 263 F.Supp.2d 887, 894 (D.N.J. 2003) (noting agreement among the "IEP team and treating physician that . . . a reduction in course load was medically necessary").

3. In *Dekalb County School District v. M.T.V. ex rel. C.E.V.*, 413 F.Supp.2d 1322 (N.D. Ga. 2005), behavioral optometrists diagnosed plaintiff with a vision disorder that produced symptoms including double-vision and words appearing fuzzy or three-dimensional. *Id.* at 1326. The optometrists found it was "medically necessary" to provide regular vision therapy "in order to reduce . . . visual loss and increase the visual and motor efficiencies." *Id.* An IEP Team disagreed and denied the services. *Id.* On appeal, the administrative law judge (ALJ) concluded that without vision therapy, plaintiff would experience increasing visual difficulty greatly impairing reading. *Id.* 1326-27. The district court and Eleventh Circuit affirmed the ALJ's ruling.

4. Relying on *Tatro*, in *John A. v. Board of Education for Howard County*, 400 Md. 363, 387 (Md. App., 2007), the Maryland Court of Appeals held that although "administration of medication" was not stated in the child's IEP, the IDEA did require that the child receive those services. This dispute arose when the Howard County Public Schools (HCPS) refused to allow their school nurse to administer three medications used to treat a child's ADHD and bipolar disorder. *Id.* at 378. HCPS refused because the child's parents forbade her psychiatrist from releasing any portion of her confidential medical file to the school nurse without written consent, and the parents did not permit HCPS staff to communicate with the child's physician directly. *Id.*

HCPS's health services manager consulted with the Maryland Board of Nursing and was advised that administration of medications without the ability to communicate with the prescribing doctor is inappropriate. *Id.* The parents claimed that refusing to administer the three medications in accordance with the psychiatrist's instructions denied their child a FAPE. *Id.* at 379. HCPS admitted that administration of medication typically would be a "related service" under the IDEA, however, it was not included in the IEP, and argued it thus could not be enforced under the IDEA. *Id.*

The Maryland Court of Appeals held that the administration of medicine is a "related service" required by the IDEA regardless of whether it is enumerated in the IEP. *Id.* at 385. Additionally, because the administration of medication does not have to be performed by a physician, and can be administered by the school nurse or other qualified person, the administering of medication is not an excluded medical service, and must be paid for and provided by the school. *Id.* at 387 (citing *Tatro*, 468 U.S. at 884). Do you agree?

5. Among related service providers, who is qualified to make decisions about the medical necessity of IEP services? Speech-language pathologists? Audiologists? Psychiatrists, psychologists, or counselors? Physical or occupational therapists? Only medical doctors?

6. IDEA 2004 states that related services do not include surgically-implanted medical devices. 20 U.S.C. § 1401(26)(B) (2006). Why would this be?

§ 22.2   Speech / Language Services

The IDEA defines a speech or language disorder as a communication disorder, for example stuttering, impaired articulation, a language impairment, or a voice impairment, that adversely affects a child's educational performance. 34 C.F.R. § 300.8(c)(11)(2012). Children who qualify for services under IDEA due to a speech or language disorder may receive speech-pathology services. These include initial identification and diagnosis of the specific speech or language impairment, referral for medical or professional treatment, provision of habilitation or prevention services, and counseling and guidance for parents, children, and teachers regarding speech and language impairments. *Id.* at § 300.34(c)(15).

However, the student may be reassessed and if a determination is made that he or she no longer has a speech or language disorder, the services may be halted. In *M.L. v. El Paso Indep. Sch. Dist.*, the school district halted speech services after reporting to the child's mother that the school had a shortage of speech therapists. The school later conducted several assessments of the child's progress and determined that he no longer had a speech or language disorder. The Fifth Circuit decided that a school district was not required to provide services for speech and language impairments to a child who had previously received such services after the district determined that he no longer needed them. M.L. v. El Paso Indep. Sch. Dist., 369 F. App'x 573 (5th Cir. 2010).

§ 22.3   Extended School Year (ESY) Services

Extended year services, otherwise known as the extended school year (ESY), are educational programs and services provided beyond the conventional school year, generally to prevent students with significant disabilities from seriously regressing during the summer break. Hoeft v. Tuscon Unified Sch. Dist., 967 F.2d 1298, 1301 (9th Cir, 1992). The IDEA statute does not provide specifically for ESY services; ESY services are mandated by the IDEA regulations only when the IEP determines they are necessary to provide FAPE. 34 C.F.R. § 300.106 (2008). The regulations articulate the services as, "special education and related services that – (1) Are provided to a child with a disability – (i) Beyond the normal school year of the public agency; (ii) In accordance with the child's IEP; and (iii) At no cost to the parents of the child; and (2) Meet the standards of the [State Education Agency]." *Id.* § 300.106(b).

There is no requirement on the part of the school district to provide ESY services to all children with disabilities, even if doing so would confer educational benefit. There is, however, a legal obligation to evaluate a student's need for ESY when developing an IEP. Reusch v. Fountain, 872 F.Supp. 1421, 1424 (D. Md. 1994). While IDEA guarantees the right to FAPE in states receiving IDEA funds, individual states must enact compatible legislation to implement IDEA's guarantees. *Id.* at 1425. Thus, ESY legislation may vary between states, so long as it remains within IDEA's boundaries. For example, the Maryland Code requires schools to notify parents of the availability of ESY, and requires ESY to be reviewed at annual IEP meetings. *Id.* at 1427 (citing Md. Code Ann. Educ. § 8-402 (2008)). State statutes may impose additional procedural requirements to obtain ESY services, provided they do not frustrate the purpose of providing students with disabilities FAPE. Reusch, 872 F.Supp. at 1431.

In *Reusch v. Fountain*, the Maryland District Court held that a school district's process for determining ESY eligibility violated IDEA by obstructing access to the system. Reusch, 872 F.Supp. at 1431. The district's process requires that a request for ESY services be evaluated first by a School Admission, Review and Dismissal committee, which could deny the request or refer it for final review by the Central Admissions, Review and Dismissal committee. This two-step process was unique to ESY services, and not required in other areas of special education. *Id.* at 1430. Children with autism, for instance, were not subject to the two-step process; rather, the two committees met in joint session. *Id.* at 1431.

The court found that the school district failed to provide adequate notice to parents of their child's rights to ESY services, in violation of Maryland law. *Id.* at 1429. Additionally, the school district's two-step program for ESY determinations was an intentional obstacle for parents seeking ESY services for their child, and frustrated timely and effective decision making. *Id.* at 1430-1432. Finally, the court found that the school district violated IDEA by delaying ESY decisions, and failed to address ESY at annual reviews as required by Maryland statute. *Id.* at 1433.

When determining whether a student requires ESY services to receive FAPE, IEP teams consider several factors. A primary test is a regression-recoupment analysis. The *Reusch* court explained that such a standard is satisfied and a student thus entitled to ESY services, "when it is shown that the student will suffer some significant regression of skills or knowledge without a summer program, followed by an insufficient recoupment of the same during the next school year." Reusch, 872 F.Supp. at 1434; *see also* Johnson v. Independent Sch. Dist. No. 4 of Bixby, Tulsa County, Oklahoma, 921 F.2d 1022 (10th Cir. 1990).

However, the regression-recoupment analysis is not the only measure used to determine the necessity of ESY services. Johnson, 921 F.2d at 1027. The *Reusch* court warned, "[a]ny student evaluation that uses a single-criterion test to determine an appropriate educational program would violate the Act." Reusch, 872 F.Supp. at 1434. Other factors to consider may include: the nature and severity of the disability, the student's IEP objectives, and the severity of past or projected regression. *Id.* at 1435. The Tenth Circuit in *Johnson* considered

> the degree of impairment and the ability of the child's parents to provide the educational structure at home, . . . the child's rate of progress, his or her behavioral and physical problems, the availability of alternative resources, the ability of the child to interact with non-handicapped children, the areas of the child's curriculum which need continuous attention, and the child's vocational needs . . .; and whether the requested service is "extraordinary" to the child's condition, as opposed to an integral part of a program for those with the child's condition."

Johnson, 921 F.2d at 1027 (citing Battle v. Pennsylvania, 629 F.2d 269, 280 (3d Cir. 1980); Yaris v. Special School Dist., 558 F.Supp. 545, 551 (E.D. Mo. 1983), *aff'd* 728 F.2d 1055 (8th Cir. 1984).

Notes & Questions

1. School districts are obligated to evaluate students' needs for ESY services when developing their IEPs. They are not, however, obligated to provide ESY services to all children with disabilities, even if doing so would benefit the child. What policy arguments could be made in favor of requiring schools to provide ESY services to all children who request them?

2. Courts have articulated a number of factors in considering whether a student is entitled to ESY services. These may include past skill regression, the likelihood of future skill regression, program requirements to implement specific IEP objectives, and the nature or severity of the child's disability. What other factors might be relevant?

3. What other related services – developmental, corrective, or supportive – may be necessary to ensure a child's FAPE? Nutrition? Augmentative communication devices and services? For students who are blind or have visual impairments, IEP teams are statutorily required to provide the use of, and instruction in, Braille, unless an evaluation of the child's skills and needs lead to a determination that Braille is not appropriate. 20 U.S.C. § 1414(d)(3)(B)(iii)(2006).

Chapter 23 SPECIAL SITUATIONS

§ 23.1   Discipline, Behavior And Restraint

As originally enacted, the IDEA did not address discipline. However, disciplinary actions were frequently brought to the courts in the context of special education rights.

HONIG v. DOE

Supreme Court of the United States, 1988
484 U.S. 305

Justice BRENNAN delivered the opinion of the Court.

As a condition of federal financial assistance, the Education of the Handicapped Act requires States to ensure a "free appropriate public education" for all disabled children within their jurisdictions. In aid of this goal, the Act establishes a comprehensive system of procedural safeguards designed to ensure parental participation in decisions concerning the education of their disabled children and to provide administrative and judicial review of any decisions with which those parents disagree. Among these safeguards is the so-called "stay-put" provision, which directs that a disabled child "shall remain in [his or her] then current educational placement" pending completion of any review proceedings, unless the parents and state or local educational agencies otherwise agree. 20 U.S.C. § 1415(e)(3). Today we must decide whether, in the face of this statutory proscription, state or local school authorities may nevertheless unilaterally exclude disabled children from the classroom for dangerous or disruptive conduct growing out of their disabilities. * * *

In the Education of the Handicapped Act (EHA or the Act), 84 Stat. 175, as amended, 20 U.S.C. § 1400 *et seq.*, Congress sought "to assure that all handicapped children have available to them . . . a free appropriate public education which emphasizes special education and related services designed to meet their unique needs, [and] to assure that the rights of handicapped children and their parents or guardians are protected." § 1400(c). * * *

* * *

Accordingly, the Act establishes various procedural safeguards that guarantee parents both an opportunity for meaningful input into all decisions affecting their child's education and the right to seek review of any decisions they think inappropriate. These safeguards include the right to examine all relevant records pertaining to the identification, evaluation, and educational placement of their child; prior written notice whenever the responsible educational agency proposes (or refuses) to change the child's placement or program; an opportunity to present complaints concerning any aspect of the local agency's provision of a free appropriate public education; and an opportunity for "an impartial due process hearing" with respect to any such complaints. §§ 1415(b)(1), (2).

At the conclusion of any such hearing, both the parents and the local educational agency may seek further administrative review and, where that proves unsatisfactory, may file a civil action in any state or federal court.   §§ 1415(c), (e)(2).   In addition to reviewing the administrative record, courts are empowered to take additional evidence at the request of either party and to "grant such relief as [they] determine[ ] is appropriate." § 1415(e)(2). The "stay-put" provision at issue in this case governs the placement of a child while these often lengthy review procedures run their course. It directs that: "During the pendency of any proceedings conducted pursuant to [§ 1415], unless the State or local educational agency and the parents or guardian otherwise agree, the child shall remain in the then current educational placement of such child. . . ." § 1415(e)(3).

The present dispute grows out of the efforts of certain officials of the San Francisco Unified School District (SFUSD) to expel two emotionally disturbed children from school indefinitely for violent and disruptive conduct related to their disabilities.   In November 1980, respondent John Doe assaulted another student at the Louise Lombard School, a developmental center for disabled children. Doe's April 1980 IEP identified him as a socially and physically awkward 17-year-old who experienced considerable difficulty controlling his impulses and anger. Among the goals set out in his IEP was "[i]mprovement in [his] ability to relate to [his] peers [and to] cope with frustrating situations without resorting to aggressive acts." Frustrating situations, however, were an unfortunately prominent feature of Doe's school career: physical abnormalities, speech difficulties, and poor grooming habits had made him the target of teasing and ridicule as early as the first grade; his 1980 IEP reflected his continuing difficulties with peers, noting that his social skills had deteriorated and that he could tolerate only minor frustration before exploding. On November 6, 1980, Doe responded to the taunts of a fellow student in precisely the explosive manner anticipated by his IEP: he choked the student with sufficient force to leave abrasions on the child's neck, and kicked out a school window while being escorted to the principal's office afterwards. Doe admitted his misconduct and the school subsequently suspended him for five days.   Thereafter, his principal referred the matter to the SFUSD Student Placement Committee (SPC or Committee) with the recommendation that Doe be expelled. On the day the suspension was to end, the SPC notified Doe's mother that it was proposing to exclude her child permanently from SFUSD and was therefore extending his suspension until such time as the expulsion proceedings were completed. The Committee further advised her that she was entitled to attend the November 25 hearing at which it planned to discuss the proposed expulsion.

After unsuccessfully protesting these actions by letter, Doe brought this suit against a host of local school officials and the State Superintendent of Public Instructions. Alleging that the suspension and proposed expulsion violated the EHA, he sought a temporary restraining order canceling the SPC hearing and requiring school officials to convene an IEP meeting. The District Judge granted the requested injunctive relief and further ordered defendants to provide home tutoring for Doe on an interim basis; shortly thereafter, she issued a preliminary injunction directing defendants to return Doe to his then current educational placement at Louise Lombard School pending completion of the IEP review process. Doe reentered school on December 15, 5 1/2 weeks, and 24 school-days, after his initial suspension.

Respondent Jack Smith was identified as an emotionally disturbed child by the time he entered the second grade in 1976. School records prepared that year indicated that he was unable "to control verbal or physical outburst[s]" and exhibited a "[s]evere disturbance in relationships with peers and adults." Further evaluations subsequently revealed that he had been physically and emotionally abused as an infant and young child and that, despite above average intelligence, he experienced academic and social difficulties as a result of extreme hyperactivity and low self-esteem. Of particular concern was Smith's propensity for verbal hostility; one evaluator noted that the child reacted to stress by "attempt [ing] to cover his feelings of low self worth through aggressive behavior [,] . . . primarily verbal provocations."

Based on these evaluations, SFUSD placed Smith in a learning center for emotionally disturbed children. His grandparents, however, believed that his needs would be better served in the public school setting and, in September 1979, the school district acceded to their requests and enrolled him at A.P. Giannini Middle School. His February 1980 IEP recommended placement in a Learning Disability Group, stressing the need for close supervision and a highly structured environment. Like earlier evaluations, the February 1980 IEP noted that Smith was easily distracted, impulsive, and anxious; it therefore proposed a half-day schedule and suggested that the placement be undertaken on a trial basis.

At the beginning of the next school year, Smith was assigned to a full-day program; almost immediately thereafter he began misbehaving. School officials met twice with his grandparents in October 1980 to discuss returning him to a half-day program; although the grandparents agreed to the reduction, they apparently were never apprised of their right to challenge the decision through EHA procedures. The school officials also warned them that if the child continued his disruptive behavior – which included stealing, extorting money from fellow students, and making sexual comments to female classmates – they would seek to expel him. On November 14, they made good on this threat, suspending Smith for five days after he made further lewd comments. His principal referred the matter to the SPC, which recommended exclusion from SFUSD. As it did in John Doe's case, the Committee scheduled a hearing and extended the suspension indefinitely pending a final disposition in the matter. On November 28, Smith's counsel protested these actions on grounds essentially identical to those raised by Doe, and the SPC agreed to cancel the hearing and to return Smith to a half-day program at A.P. Giannini or to provide home tutoring. Smith's grandparents chose the latter option and the school began home instruction on December 10; on January 6, 1981, an IEP team convened to discuss alternative placements.

After learning of Doe's action, Smith sought and obtained leave to intervene in the suit. The District Court subsequently entered summary judgment in favor of respondents on their EHA claims and issued a permanent injunction. In a series of decisions, the District Judge found that the proposed expulsions and indefinite suspensions of respondents for conduct attributable to their disabilities deprived them of their congressionally mandated right to a free appropriate public education, as well as their right to have that education provided in accordance with the procedures set out in the EHA. The District Judge therefore permanently enjoined the school district from taking any disciplinary action other than a 2- or 5-day suspension against any disabled child for disability-related misconduct, or from effecting any other change in the educational placement of any such child without parental consent pending completion of any EHA proceedings. * * *

On appeal, the Court of Appeals for the Ninth Circuit affirmed the orders with slight modifications. *Doe v. Maher*, 793 F.2d 1470 (1986). Agreeing with the District Court that an indefinite suspension in aid of expulsion constitutes a prohibited "change in placement" under § 1415(e)(3), the Court of Appeals held that the stay-put provision admitted of no "dangerousness" exception and that the statute therefore rendered invalid those provisions of the California Education Code permitting the indefinite suspension or expulsion of disabled children for misconduct arising out of their disabilities. The court concluded, however, that fixed suspensions of up to 30 schooldays did not fall within the reach of § 1415(e)(3), and therefore upheld recent amendments to the state Education Code authorizing such suspensions. Lastly, the court affirmed that portion of the injunction requiring the State to provide services directly to a disabled child when the local educational agency fails to do so.

Petitioner Bill Honig, California Superintendent of Public Instruction, sought review in this Court, claiming that the Court of Appeals' construction of the stay-put provision conflicted with that of several other Courts of Appeals which had recognized a dangerousness exception, * * * and that the direct services ruling placed an intolerable burden on the State. We granted certiorari to resolve these questions * * * and now affirm.

* * *

III

The language of § 1415(e)(3) is unequivocal. It states plainly that during the pendency of any proceedings initiated under the Act, unless the state or local educational agency and the parents or guardian of a disabled child otherwise agree, "the child *shall* remain in the then current educational placement." § 1415(e)(3) (emphasis added). Faced with this clear directive, petitioner asks us to read a "dangerousness" exception into the stay-put provision on the basis of either of two essentially inconsistent assumptions: first, that Congress thought the residual authority of school officials to exclude dangerous students from the classroom too obvious for comment; or second, that Congress inadvertently failed to provide such authority and this Court must therefore remedy the oversight. Because we cannot accept either premise, we decline petitioner's invitation to rewrite the statute.

Petitioner's arguments proceed, he suggests, from a simple, commonsense proposition: Congress could not have intended the stay-put provision to be read literally, for such a construction leads to the clearly unintended, and untenable, result that school districts must return violent or dangerous students to school while the often lengthy EHA proceedings run their course. We think it clear, however, that Congress very much meant to strip schools of the *unilateral* authority they had traditionally employed to exclude disabled students, particularly emotionally disturbed students, from school. In so doing, Congress did not leave school administrators powerless to deal with dangerous students; it did, however, deny school officials their former right to "self-help," and directed that in the future the removal of disabled students could be accomplished only with the permission of the parents or, as a last resort, the courts.

As noted above, Congress passed the EHA after finding that school systems across the country had excluded one out of every eight disabled children from classes. * * *

Congress attacked such exclusionary practices in a variety of ways. It required participating States to educate all disabled children, regardless of the severity of their disabilities, 20 U.S.C. § 1412(2)(C), and included within the definition of "handicapped" those children with serious emotional disturbances. § 1401(1). It further provided for meaningful parental participation in all aspects of a child's educational placement, and barred schools, through the stay-put provision, from changing that placement over the parent's objection until all review proceedings were completed. Recognizing that those proceedings might prove long and tedious, the Act's drafters did not intend § 1415(e)(3) to operate inflexibly, see 121 Cong. Rec. 37412 (1975) (remarks of Sen. Stafford), and they therefore allowed for interim placements where parents and school officials are able to agree on one. Conspicuously absent from § 1415(e)(3), however, is any emergency exception for dangerous students. This absence is all the more telling in light of the injunctive decree issued in *PARC*, which permitted school officials unilaterally to remove students in " 'extraordinary circumstances.' " 343 F.Supp., at 301. Given the lack of any similar exception in *Mills*, and the close attention Congress devoted to these "landmark" decisions, see S. Rep., at 6, U.S. Code Cong. & Admin. News p. 1430, we can only conclude that the omission was intentional; we are therefore not at liberty to engraft onto the statute an exception Congress chose not to create.

Our conclusion that § 1415(e)(3) means what it says does not leave educators hamstrung. The Department of Education has observed that, "[w]hile the [child's] placement may not be changed [during any complaint proceeding], this does not preclude the agency from using its normal procedures for dealing with children who are endangering themselves or others." Comment following 34 C.F.R. § 300.513 (1987). Such procedures may include the use of study carrels, timeouts, detention, or the restriction of privileges. More drastically, where a student poses an immediate threat to the safety of others, officials may temporarily suspend him or her for up to 10 schooldays. This authority, which respondent in no way disputes, not only ensures that school administrators can protect the safety of others by promptly removing the most dangerous of students, it also provides a "cooling down" period during which officials can initiate IEP review and seek to persuade the child's parents to agree to an interim placement. And in those cases in which the parents of a truly dangerous child adamantly refuse to permit any change in placement, the 10-day respite gives school officials an opportunity to invoke the aid of the courts under § 1415(e)(2), which empowers courts to grant any appropriate relief.

Petitioner contends, however, that the availability of judicial relief is more illusory than real, because a party seeking review under § 1415(e)(2) must exhaust time-consuming administrative remedies, and because under the Court of Appeals' construction of § 1415(e)(3), courts are as bound by the stay-put provision's "automatic injunction," as are schools. It is true that judicial review is normally not available under § 1415(e)(2) until all administrative proceedings are completed, but as we have previously noted, parents may bypass the administrative process where exhaustion would be futile or inadequate. See *Smith v. Robinson*, 468 U.S. 992, 1014, n. 17 (1984) (citing cases); see also 121 Cong. Rec. 37416 (1975) (remarks of Sen. Williams) ("[E]xhaustion . . . should not be required . . . in cases where such exhaustion would be futile either as a legal or practical matter"). While many of the EHA's procedural safeguards protect the rights of parents and children, schools can and do seek redress through the administrative review process, and we have no reason to believe that Congress meant to require schools alone to exhaust in all cases, no matter how exigent the circumstances. The burden in such cases, of course, rests with the school to demonstrate the futility or inadequacy of administrative review, but nothing in § 1415(e)(2) suggests that schools are completely barred from attempting to make such a showing. Nor do we think that § 1415(e)(3) operates to limit the equitable powers of district courts such that they cannot, in appropriate cases, temporarily enjoin a dangerous disabled child from attending school. As the EHA's legislative history makes clear, one of the evils Congress sought to remedy was the unilateral exclusion of disabled children by *schools*, not courts, and one of the purposes of § 1415(e)(3), therefore, was "to prevent school officials from removing a child from the regular public school classroom over the parents' objection pending completion of the review proceedings." *Burlington School Committee v. Massachusetts Dept. of Education*, 471 U.S., at 373 (emphasis added). The stay-put provision in no way purports to limit or pre-empt the authority conferred on courts by § 1415(e)(2), see *Doe v. Brookline School Committee*, 722 F.2d 910, 917 (CA1 1983); indeed, it says nothing whatever about judicial power.

In short, then, we believe that school officials are entitled to seek injunctive relief under § 1415(e)(2) in appropriate cases. In any such action, § 1415(e)(3) effectively creates a presumption in favor of the child's current educational placement which school officials can overcome only by showing that maintaining the child in his or her current placement is substantially likely to result in injury either to himself or herself, or to others. In the present case, we are satisfied that the District Court, in enjoining the state and local defendants from indefinitely suspending respondent or otherwise unilaterally altering his then current placement, properly balanced respondent's interest in receiving a free appropriate public education in accordance with the procedures and requirements of the EHA against the interests of the state and local school officials in maintaining a safe learning environment for all their students.

IV

We believe the courts below properly construed and applied § 1415(e)(3), except insofar as the Court of Appeals held that a suspension in excess of 10 schooldays does not constitute a "change in placement." We therefore affirm the Court of Appeals' judgment on this issue as modified herein.

Affirmed.

୬

In 1997, after the *Honig* decision, the IDEA was amended to codify a balance between protecting children with disabilities from being excluded from education and schools' interests in providing safe environments. Most common forms of school discipline are available to children with disabilities to the same extent they now are available to children without disabilities. Terry Jean Seligmann, Not as Simple as ABC: Disciplining Children with Disabilities Under the 1997 IDEA Amendments, 42 Ariz. L. Rev. 77, 92 (2000). In some instances, disciplinary actions, such as time-outs or loss of privileges, may be specified in the child's IEP. However, in response to the traditional exclusion of students with disabilities, the IDEA limited schools' ability to expel, suspend or otherwise unilaterally change the placements of students with disabilities. The IDEA provides:

> [D]uring the pendency of any proceedings conducted pursuant to [the procedural safeguards], unless the State or local educational agency and the parents otherwise agree, the child shall remain in the then-current educational placement of the child, or, if applying for initial admission to a public school, shall, with the consent of the parents, be placed in the public school program until all such proceedings have been completed.

20 U.S.C. § 1415(j) (2006).

A suspension of more than ten days generally is considered a prohibited change of placement. *Id.* § 1415(k)(1)(B). However, a school may unilaterally suspend a child with a disability for up to 45 days if the child, while on school grounds or attending a school function (1) brings a weapon to school, (2) knowingly possesses, uses, sells, or buys illegal drugs at school, or (3) "has inflicted serious bodily injury upon another person . . . ." *Id.* § 1415(k)(1)(G). The school district must provide educational services to the child during the suspension or expulsion period, including those services necessary to "enable the child to continue to participate in the general education curriculum," make progress toward achieving their IEP goals, and prevent the behavior violation from recurring. *Id.* § 1415(k)(1)(D).

A hearing officer may suspend a child with a disability up to 45 days "if the hearing officer determines that maintaining the current placement . . . is substantially likely to result in injury to the child or to others." 20 U.S.C. § 1415(k)(3)(B)(ii) (2006). When a suspension is implemented, the school must determine whether the offensive behavior of the student is a manifestation of the student's disability or a result of the school's failure to implement the child's IEP. *Id.* § 1415(k)(1)(E).

Prior to IDEA 2004, the language of the statute favored a presumption that the offending conduct was a manifestation of the disability. Previously, the IEP Team could conclude "the behavior . . . was not a manifestation of such child's disability *only if*" three standards were met. 20 U.S.C. § 1415(k)(4)(C)(ii)(I)-(III) (2000) (emphasis added). The new language removes this presumption in favor of the school and simply provides:

> [T]he local educational agency, the parent, and relevant members of the IEP Team . . . shall review all relevant information in the student's file, including the child's IEP, any teacher observations, and any relevant information provided by the parents to determine –

(I) if the conduct in question was caused by, or had a direct and substantial relationship to, the child's disability; or

(II) if the conduct in question was the direct result of the local educational agency's failure to implement the IEP.

§ 1415(k)(1)(E)(i). If either clause (I) or (II) is applicable, then the conduct is considered a manifestation of the disability. *Id.* § 1415(k)(1)(E)(ii). To rule out a manifestation of disability, the team no longer needs to specifically determine that:

(I) the child's IEP and placement were appropriate and the special education services, supplementary aids and services, and behavior intervention strategies were provided consistent with the child's IEP and placement;

(II) the child's disability did not impair the ability of the child to understand the impact and consequences of the behavior subject to disciplinary action; and

(III) the child's disability did not impair the ability of the child to control the behavior subject to disciplinary action.

20 U.S.C. § 1415(k)(4)(C)(ii) (2000).

If the IEP Team determines that the action was not a manifestation of disability, the regular disciplinary systems applicable to nondisabled students may be applied to the student with a disability. 20 U.S.C. § 1415(k)(1)(C) (2006). If the behavior is determined to be a manifestation, the child is protected by the IDEA's disciplinary provisions. Id. § 1415(k)(1)(F). For instance, this means that "it is unlawful to punish the child for [the manifested] behavior." John Dayton, Special Education Disability Law, 163 West's Educ. L. Rep. 17, 28 (2002). Also, the school must either (1) "conduct a functional behavioral assessment, and implement a behavioral intervention plan" (BIP) to address the manifested behavior if a relevant BIP was not in place prior to the behavior; or (2) "review the [existing plan] . . . and modify it, as necessary, to address the behavior." 20 U.S.C. § 1415(k)(1)(F)(i)-(ii). Additionally, the team must return the student to his/her placement before the removal, unless the local educational agency and parent(s) agree otherwise. *Id.* § 1415(k)(1)(F)(iii).

Notes & Questions

1. Why should children with disabilities be subject to different discipline standards than children without disabilities? Why not?

2. The 1997 IDEA amendments included the ten-day limit on suspensions. Why do you think the *Honig* Court found ten days to be the limit, as opposed to the 30-day limit proposed by the Ninth Circuit? Is this line-setting activity appropriate for a court or should it be reserved to

Congress? Is ten days enough time? Too much? What about the 45 days allowed when a Hearing Officer makes the decision? *See* Allan G. Osborne, Jr., Discipline of Special-Education Students Under the Individuals with Disabilities Act, 29 Fordham Urb. L.J. 513, 523 (2001) (*Honig* Court envisioned a "cooling off" period to allow parents and school to come to agreement).

3. What is a risk of "injury" sufficient to meet the standard for expulsion of a child with a disability? Must it be a risk of major injury or will minor injuries suffice? Prior to the Supreme Court's decision in *Honig*, the Eighth Circuit held:

> [W]e emphatically reject the contention that an 'injury' is inflicted only when blood is drawn or the emergency room visited. Bruises, bite marks, and poked eyes all constitute "injuries" in the context of this analysis. More broadly, we reject the proposition that a child must first inflict serious harm before that child can be deemed substantially likely to cause injury.

Light v. Parkway C-2 Sch. Dist., 41 F.3d 1223, 1230 (8th Cir. 1994).

4. What constitutes "substantial evidence" of risk? The "substantial evidence" standard in other settings is generally a lesser standard than "presumption of the evidence." However, in the special education context, it is a higher standard. Courts have struggled with how to apply this new standard. Seligmann, *supra*, at 98-99.

5. The IDEA allows 45-day suspensions for possession, use, or sale of illegal drugs. Should alcohol also be covered?

6. Some school districts have "no tolerance" policies toward drugs, including over-the-counter and prescription drugs, at school. *See, e.g.,* Prescription Medication Gets Girl Suspended for the School Year, Zero Intelligence, Jan. 12, 2005, http://zerointelligence.net/archives/000255.php. How should such policies be implemented in light of the schools' obligations under the IDEA?

7. The Center for Civil Rights Remedies found that in the 2009-10 school year, twice as many students with disabilities (13%) were suspended compared to students without disabilities (7%), despite the fact that the IDEA procedural safeguards are intended "to safeguard against unjust exclusion of children with disabilities." Daniel J. Losen & Jonathan Gillespie, Opportunities Suspended: The Disparate Impact of Disciplinary Exclusion from School 16 (Aug. 2012), *available at* http://civilrightsproject.ucla.edu/resources/projects/center-for-civil-rights-remedies/school-to-prison-folder/federal-reports/upcoming-ccrr-research/losen-gillespie-opportunity-suspended-ccrr-2012.pdf (last visited Aug. 9, 2012). Moreover, one in four (25%) of Black students with disabilities were suspended from school at least once. *Id.*

§ 23.2 Residential Placement, Private School Placement, And Juvenile Justice Issues

Some disabilities may require residential settings for appropriate treatment. If a child is unable to benefit from his or her education without such residential placement and treatment, the school must provide and pay for the residential placement. *See* 34 C.F.R. § 300.104 (2008) ("If placement in a public or private residential program is necessary to provide special education and related services to a child with a disability, the program, including non-medical care and room and board, must be at no cost to the parents of the child."); Indep. Sch. Dist. No. 284 v. A.C., 258 F.3d 769 (8th Cir. 2001) (school must provide residential placement for student with emotional disability that otherwise prevented education).

Even residential facilities that provide some medical care may be required under the IDEA, although the school will not be required to pay for the strictly medical expenses. *See* Seattle Sch. Dist. No. 1 v. B.S., 82 F.3d 1493, 1502 (9th Cir. 1996) ("That A.S.'s disability, like most disabilities under the IDEA, stems from medical or psychiatric disorders, and that Intermountain's program addresses these disorders in an attempt to ensure that A.S. is able to benefit from her education, does not render the program invalid or remove the District's financial responsibility.") (citations omitted). Moreover, such residential placement may be required, even if some part of the child's need for treatment is due to social or emotional rather than educational problems.

> Analysis must focus, then, on whether full-time placement may be considered necessary for educational purposes, or whether the residential placement is a response to medical, social or emotional problems that are segregable from the learning process. . . . [T]he unseverability of such needs is the very basis for holding that the services are an essential prerequisite for learning.

Kruelle v. New Castle County Sch. Dist., 642 F.2d 687, 693 (3d Cir. 1981).

If FAPE is not available in public school, the school district may be required to pay for a child's attendance at a private (secular or religious) school. 20 U.S.C. § 1412(a)(10)(B)(i) (2006); *see* Zelman v. Simmons-Harris, 536 U.S. 639, 651-63 (2002) (state funded school voucher for use at private school not in violation of Establishment Clause); Zobrest v. Catalina Foothills Sch. Dist., 509 U.S. 1, 13 (1993) (public school provision of sign-language interpreter at a Catholic school not in violation of Establishment Clause). If the public school is refusing to provide FAPE, or refusing to provide services the family deems necessary to ensure FAPE, the parents may unilaterally place their child in private school and seek tuition reimbursement from the public school district. 20 U.S.C. § 1412(a)(10)(C)(ii); Florence County Sch. Dist. Four v. Carter, 510 U.S. 7, 12-13 (1993).

Congress did not intend, however, to require that public schools provide benefits to all students with disabilities who are "voluntarily placed in private schools," comparable with those of their public school counterparts. The extent of the public obligation to fund all or part of these costs depends upon the reason for placement. Public schools are responsible for the full cost of a child's education when the IEP team has determined that a private school placement offers necessary services that the public school cannot. In contrast, a student with a disability placed by her parents in a private school is loosely entitled to special education services limited to the proportional amount the public school would have spent under the IDEA.

Myhill, No FAPE in MPCP, *supra*, at 1060 (citations omitted).

Recent and ongoing litigation has addressed the circumstances under which states are required to reimburse parents for their child's private school education. Amendments made in 1997 to the IDEA and retained in IDEA 2004 have proven to be a source of statutory confusion. In pertinent part, the amendments provide:

If the parents of a child with a disability, *who previously received special education and related services under the authority of a public* agency, enroll the child in a private preschool, elementary school or secondary school, without the consent of or referral by the public agency, a court or hearing officer may require the agency to reimburse the parents for the cost of that enrollment if the court or hearing officer finds that the agency had not made FAPE available to the child in a timely manner prior to that enrollment and that placement is appropriate.

34 C.F.R. § 300.148 (2008) (emphasis added).

A district court held that the 1997 amendments to IDEA amounted to a threshold requirement for reimbursement. In *Board of Education of the City School District of the City of New York v. Tom F.*, defendant's son, a student receiving special education services, had attended a private school since kindergarten. Bd. of Educ. of the City Sch. Dist. of the City of New York v. Tom F., No. 01 Civ. 6845 (GBD), 2005 WL 22866 (S.D.N.Y. Jan. 4, 2005). Despite a Committee on Special Education (CSE) Notice of Recommendation placing the student in a public school, defendant continued to enroll his son in the private school. *Id.* at 1. Defendant then requested an impartial hearing to seek reimbursement for tuition, which an Independent Hearing Officer (IHO) awarded. *Id.* The School District appealed, and the State Education Department State Review Officer (SRO) affirmed the award. *Id.* The School District then brought suit to reverse the decision of the SRO.

In overturning the decision of the SRO, the district court interpreted the 1997 amendments to IDEA to require students to have "previously received special education . . . under the authority of a public agency." *Id.* at 3. Because the child had not previously received special education under the authority of a public agency, the district court denied the parents reimbursement for their son's enrollment in private school.

On appeal, the Second Circuit Court of Appeals vacated and remanded the judgment of the district court to reflect its decision in *Frank G. v. Board of Education of Hyde Park*. Bd. of Educ. of the City Sch. Dist. of the City of New York v. Tom F., 193 Fed. App'x 26 (2d Cir. 2006). In February of 2007, the Supreme Court granted certiorari to hear *Tom F.* Bd. of Educ. of the City Sch. Dist. of New York v. Tom F., 127 S.Ct. 1393 (2007). Oral arguments took place on October 1, 2007. Transcript of Oral Argument at 1, Bd. of Educ. of the City Sch. Dist. of the City of New York v. Tom F., No. 06-637 (Nov. 3, 2006), *available at* http://www.supreme court.gov/oral_arguments/argument_transcripts/06-637.pdf. The Court split 4-4 on the issue (with Justice Kennedy having recused himself), and on October 10, 2007, the Supreme Court, in a *per curium* decision, affirmed the Court of Appeals. Bd. of Educ. of the City Sch. Dist. of New York v. Tom F., 128 S. Ct. 1 (2007).

In *Frank G.*, a school district appealed from a district court ruling awarding tuition reimbursement to parents whose son with Attention Deficit Hyperactivity Disorder (ADHD) previously had not received special education services from a public agency, on the grounds that the 1997 amendments to IDEA required students to have previously received such services. Frank G. v. Bd. of Educ. of Hyde Park, 459 F.3d 356 (2d Cir. 2006). The Court of Appeals affirmed, demonstrating a marked departure from previous interpretation of the IDEA amendments. The court's statutory analysis suggested that construing the IDEA amendment so as to require a "first bite at failure" was incorrect, and plaintiffs were therefore entitled to reimbursement. *Id.* at 372.

In *Gagliardo*, the Second Circuit identified the following criteria to determine if a school is providing an appropriate placement for a student:

> '[C]ourts assessing the propriety of a unilateral placement consider the totality of the circumstances in determining whether that placement reasonably serves a child's individual needs. To qualify for reimbursement under the IDEA, parents need not show that a private placement furnishes every special service necessary to maximize their child's potential. They need only demonstrate that the placement provides educational *instruction specially designed to meet the unique needs of a handicapped child,* supported by such services as are necessary to permit the child to benefit from instruction.'

Gagliardo v. Arlington Cent. Sch. Dist., 489 F.3d 105, 112 (2d Cir. 2007) (quoting Frank G., 459 F.3d at 364-65) (emphasis added). *See also* Ka.D.

ex rel. Ky.D. v. Nest, 10-56320, 2012 WL 1144291 (9th Cir. Apr. 6, 2012) (finding the school district's general education classroom did not meet the student's unique needs and their subsequent offer substantively failed to provide a FAPE, therefore, a parents unilateral placement of the child in a private school was appropriate and qualified for reimbursement).

Students with disabilities who are placed by their parents in private schools for reasons other than the lack of FAPE in their public school have only a generalized entitlement to special education and related services. 34 C.F.R. §§ 300.130-.144 (2008). The Local Education Agency must consult with private school representatives, conduct child find activities in private schools located in the district, and spend a proportionate amount of IDEA funds to provide "equitable participation" in special education services for parentally-placed private school students with disabilities. *Id.*

However, the students themselves do not have an individualized right to any portion of those services. 34 C.F.R. § 300.137(a). Thus, a private school student with a disability is not entitled to FAPE. Parentally-placed private school students must receive a service plan, similar to an IEP. *Id.* § 300.138. The student cannot, however, pursue a due process complaint to seek services. The student can only challenge a district's failure to provide generally equitable services. *Id.* §§ 300.151-.153. *See also* U.S. Dept. of Educ., The Individuals with Disabilities Education Act (IDEA): Provisions Related to Children with Disabilities Enrolled by Their Parents in Private Schools (Feb. 2008), *available at* http://www.rrfcnetwork.org/images/stories/FRC/IDEA/idea.pdf.

States are responsible for providing education to students with disabilities who are in correctional facilities. 34 C.F.R. § 300.2(b)(1)(iv) (2008); *see also* Peter Blanck, Keynote Address: Justice for All? Stories about Americans with Disabilities and Their Civil Rights, 8 J. Gender Race & Just. 1, 18-20 (2004) (discussing violations of this requirement). This obligation applies at all stages of incarceration, including pretrial detention. *E.g.*, Donnell C. v. Ill. State Bd. of Educ., 829 F.Supp. 1016, 1020 (N.D. Ill. 1993).

§ 23.3   Distance Learning

Likely an emerging issue in the law is that of the equal opportunities for students receiving IDEA services to participate in and benefit from distance learning (i.e., online or virtual) studies. Myhill and colleagues argue that students with disabilities "may have the most to gain from effective distance learning," in part, as it "may offer hope that an affordable choice or alternative is available to facilitate their academic, technical, or professional achievement necessary to live independent and self-determined lives." William N. Myhill et al., Distance Education Initiatives and Their Early 21st Century Role in the Lives of People with Disabilities, in Focus on Distance Education Developments 8 (2007)

(citations omitted) [hereinafter "Myhill, Distance Education Initiatives"].
Presently

- Hundreds of thousands of students with special needs attended the 10,793 (11.9%) public schools that failed to make adequate yearly progress for two consecutive years in 2005.

- IDEA mandated transition planning "frequently lacks relevance, is poorly implemented or is ineffective."

- In 2006, just 50% of all students IDEA services graduated from high school.

- "[F]ollowing high school graduation, 5.7% of students with disabilities attend a four-year college compared to 28.3% of their peers without disabilities."

- People with disabilities are "less than half as likely . . . to be employed" compared to those without disabilities.

Id. at 8-9 (citations omitted).

Yet, the technologies used for distance learning, even when purported to meet Section 508 or World Wide Web Consortium (W3C) accessibility standards, frequently pose barriers to students with varying impairments. *Id.* at 9. In a study of the cyberinfrastructure used for geographically distributed collaborations, Myhill and colleagues found

> persons with vision, hearing, fine motor, or cognitive impairments, and learning or attention difficulties experience the greatest barriers to effective communication when technologies demand multi-sensory interaction (e.g., unimpaired hearing, vision, attention, and fine motor skills), or permit limited forms of input/interaction (e.g., speech without closed captioning, or mouse without keyboard access).

William N. Myhill, et al., Developing Accessible Cyberinfrastructure-Enabled Knowledge Communities in the National Disability Community: Theory, Practice, and Policy, 20 Assistive Tech. 157, 166 (2008) (citation omitted).

For children receiving IDEA services, when a child's IEP includes a distance learning service, it may "run afoul of the FAPE mandate if inaccessibility impedes educational benefit or imposes costs on the family such as having to purchase assistive technologies, or if the services remove the student from the least restrictive or impose a more restrictive environment." Myhill, Distance Education Initiatives, *supra*, at 17.

As these issues have yet to be litigated, in avoiding litigation, best practices may include: (1) using universal design principles to guide the design of distance education services, (2) involving students with disabilities in the design and testing processes, (3) enhancing faculty understanding of the issues through laboratory demonstrations and hands-on training, and (4) training instructional designers in the issues and solutions of web accessibility. *Id.* at 28-29.

Chapter 24 PROCEDURAL SAFEGUARDS, EXHAUSTION AND REMEDIES

§ 24.1 Special Education Process

As discussed above, the centerpiece of the special education process is the Individualized Education Program (IEP). The requirements of the IEP are laid out in the IDEA. 20 U.S.C. § 1414 (2006). In addition to the requirements of the plan itself, the IDEA imposes specific deadlines and safeguards to ensure that parents have a meaningful opportunity to participate in determining the services to be provided to their children. These requirements arise from the constitutional due process principles enunciated in *Mills v. Board of Education of District of Columbia*, 348 F.Supp. 866, 875 (D.D.C. 1972).

A school district must provide written notice to a disabled child's parents whenever the school proposes to change the child's placement or refuses to change the placement. 20 U.S.C. § 1415(b)(3) (2006). The notice must be understandable and be in the parents' native language. *Id.* § 1415(b)(4). It must describe the proposed change, reasons for the change, assessments performed, and any other relevant factors. *Id.* § 1415(c). Parents must also be notified of their procedural rights. *Id.* § 1415(d).

Parents have the right to review the child's records. 34 C.F.R. § 300.501(a)(1) (2008). The parents must consent to the initial evaluation, the "[i]nitial provision of special education and related services," and reevaluation, before the school may take these actions. *Id.* § 300.300. Parents have a right to participate in IEP team meetings, contribute to the development of the IEP, and suggest and request changes. *Id.* § 300.501(a)(2). If the IEP Team cannot reach agreement on an assessment, placement, change of placement, or other service or component of the IEP, they may institute voluntary confidential mediation through a state-provided process using an impartial mediator. *Id.* § 300.506.

If mediation does not result in agreement, or if the parties do not pursue mediation, either the parents or school district may initiate an administrative due process hearing. *Id.* § 300.507. The hearing officer must be impartial. 34 C.F.R. § 300.511. Once a complaint has been filed with a hearing officer, the noncomplaining party has ten days to respond. *Id.* § 300.508. After a complaint is filed, the educational agency must convene a meeting of the parties within 15 days of receipt of the complaint. *Id.* § 300.510. If the complaint is not resolved within 30 days of receipt, the hearing may take place. *Id.* § 300.510(b). Parties may be accompanied by an attorney, submit evidence, examine and cross-examine witnesses, obtain a record of the proceeding, and obtain a written order. *Id.* § 300.512. The hearing decision must be issued within 45 days of the "resolution period." *Id.* § 300.515.

Filing an administrative complaint triggers the stay-put provision. 20 U.S.C. § 1415(j) (2006). The "stay-put" provision provides that unless the child's parent or guardian and the state or local school authorities agree otherwise, "the child shall remain in the then-current educational placement" during the pendency of any proceedings initiated under the Act. *Id.* Significantly, the provision prevents (1) a child from being placed in special education, (2) a child being placed in a manner inconsistent with the parents' wishes, and (3) a child's current placement in special education from changing during the administrative and/or judicial proceedings. *Id.* § 1415(j). Additionally, the provision "functions as an automatic preliminary injunction . . . without the traditional showing of irreparable harm." Ringwood Bd. of Educ. v. K.H.J., 469 F.Supp.2d 267, 269 (3d Cir. 2006) (citing Drinker v. Colonial Sch. Dist., 78 F.3d 859, 863 (3d Cir. 1996)).

Courts have differed in their interpretation of the pending proceedings that are entitled to application of the stay-put provision. Pending proceedings are accepted to include administrative hearings and claims before district courts. In *K.D. ex rel. C.L. v. Dep't of Educ., Hawaii*, 665 F.3d 1110, 1121 (9th Cir. 2011), the Ninth Circuit rejected the plaintiff's argument that a settlement agreement, which placed a child with a disability at a private school and required the state education agency to pay the child's tuition, established the private school as the child's "stay-put" school.

In *Andersen v. District of Columbia*, plaintiffs argued that any period in which there is a petition for certiorari to an appellate court, including the U.S. Supreme Court, constitutes a pending proceeding. Andersen v. District of Columbia, 877 F.2d 1018, 1023 (D.C. Cir. 1989). The Court of Appeals for the District of Columbia rejected this interpretation, indicating the then current language of § 20 U.S.C. § 1415(e)(2) as "speak[ing] of only three types of proceedings: due process hearings, state administrative review where available, and civil actions for review brought 'in any State court of competent jurisdiction or in a district court of the United States.'" *Id.* In contrast, the Third Circuit and the Washington Court of Appeals have held that the stay-put provision is applicable "throughout the *entire* process, including appeals." Ringwood Bd. of Educ., 469 F.Supp.2d at 270 (quoting N. Kitsap Sch. Dist. v. K.W., 123 P.3d 469, 483 (Wash. Ct. App. 2005)).

A two-year statute of limitations is provided for a due process complaint, unless the state has a shorter statute of limitations. 20 U.S.C. § 1415(f)(3)(c) (2006). Appeals of the hearing officer's decision must be filed within 90 days of the decision. *Id.* § 1415(i).

Only "parents" and public agencies have standing to pursue IDEA claims. 34 C.F.R. § 300.507 (2008). In *Idea Public Charter School v. District of Columbia*, 374 F.Supp.2d 158, 163 (D.D.C. June 21, 2005), the court addressed whether a school presently serving the child may "unilaterally request an impartial due process hearing" with the child's former school. The student had not been evaluated in timely manner for special education eligibility by the District of Columbia Public Schools district, in violation of the IDEA, when attending their schools. *Id.* at 160. After transferring to the Idea Public Charter School, the charter school performed the evaluations and requested an impartial due process hearing with the D.C. public school district seeking reimbursement of the costs for performing the evaluations. *Id.* The court concluded that impartial due process hearings under the Act "were contemplated only for the protection of parents and students, and not for disputes between [local education agencies]" and the Act "does not provide a private right of action for one LEA against another." *Id.* at 163, 168.

IDEA 2004 provides that

"The term 'parent' means:

(A) a natural, adoptive or foster parent of a child (unless a foster parent is prohibited by State law from serving as a parent);

(B) a guardian (but not the State if the child is a ward of the State);

(C) an individual acting in the place of a natural or adoptive parent (including a grandparent, stepparent, or other relative) with whom the child lives, or an individual who is legally responsible for the child's welfare; or

(D) ... an individual assigned ... to be a surrogate parent.

20 U.S.C. § 1401(23) (2006).

The IDEA does not specify which party bears the burden of proving whether an IEP meets the FAPE standard. Some courts and commentators argue that Congress intended the burden to fall on the school by virtue of the law's specific origins in *Mills* and *PARC*, in which both courts allocated the burden to the school districts. The Circuit Courts of Appeal split on the question for approximately twenty years. Blanck et al., Disability Civil Rights Law and Policy: Cases and Materials 1251, n.52 (2005). In 2005, the Supreme Court addressed this question.

SCHAFFER v. WEAST

Supreme Court of the United States, 2005
126 S.Ct. 528

Justice O'CONNOR delivered the opinion of the Court.

The Individuals with Disabilities Education Act (IDEA or Act) * * * is a Spending Clause statute that seeks to ensure that "all children with disabilities have available to them a free appropriate public education," § 1400(d)(1)(A). Under IDEA, school districts must create an "individualized education program" (IEP) for each disabled child. § 1414(d). If parents believe their child's IEP is inappropriate, they may request an "impartial due process hearing." § 1415(f). The Act is silent, however, as to which party bears the burden of persuasion at such a hearing. * * *

I

A

* * *

IDEA is "frequently described as a model of 'cooperative federalism.'" Little Rock School Dist. v. Mauney, 183 F. 3d 816, 830 (CA8 1999). It "leaves to the States the primary responsibility for developing and executing educational programs for handicapped children, [but] imposes significant requirements to be followed in the discharge of that responsibility." Board of Ed. of Hendrick Hudson Central School Dist., Westchester Cty. v. Rowley, 458 U.S. 176, 183 (1982). * * *

The core of the statute, however, is the cooperative process that it establishes between parents and schools. Rowley, supra, at 205-206 ("Congress placed every bit as much emphasis upon compliance with procedures giving parents and guardians a large measure of participation at every stage of the administrative process, . . . as it did upon the measurement of the resulting IEP against a substantive standard"). The central vehicle for this collaboration is the IEP process. * * *

Parents and guardians play a significant role in the IEP process. They must be informed about and consent to evaluations of their child under the Act. § 1414(c)(3). Parents are included as members of "IEP teams." § 1414(d)(1)(B). They have the right to examine any records relating to their child, and to obtain an "independent educational evaluation of the[ir] child." § 1415(b)(1). They must be given written prior notice of any changes in an IEP, § 1415(b)(3), and be notified in writing of the procedural safeguards available to them under the Act, § 1415(d)(1). If parents believe that an IEP is not appropriate, they may seek an administrative "impartial due process hearing." § 1415(f). School districts may also seek such hearings, as Congress clarified in the 2004 amendments. See S. Rep. No. 108-185, p. 37 (2003). They may do so, for example, if they wish to change an existing IEP but the parents do not consent, or if parents refuse to allow their child to be evaluated. As a practical matter, it appears that most hearing requests come from parents rather than schools. * * *

Although state authorities have limited discretion to determine who conducts the hearings, § 1415(f)(1)), and responsibility generally for establishing fair hearing procedures, § 1415(a), Congress has chosen to legislate the central components of due process hearings. It has imposed

727

minimal pleading standards, requiring parties to file complaints setting forth "a description of the nature of the problem," § 1415(b)(7)(B)(ii), and "a proposed resolution of the problem to the extent known and available . . . at the time," § 1415(b)(7)(B)(iii). At the hearing, all parties may be accompanied by counsel, and may "present evidence and confront, cross-examine, and compel the attendance of witnesses." §§ 1415(h)(1)-(2). After the hearing, any aggrieved party may bring a civil action in state or federal court. § 1415(i)(2). Prevailing parents may also recover attorney's fees. § 1415(i)(3)(B). Congress has never explicitly stated, however, which party should bear the burden of proof at IDEA hearings.

B

This case concerns the educational services that were due, under IDEA, to petitioner Brian Schaffer. Brian suffers from learning disabilities and speech-language impairments. From pre kindergarten through seventh grade he attended a private school and struggled academically. In 1997, school officials informed Brian's mother that he needed a school that could better accommodate his needs. Brian's parents contacted respondent Montgomery County Public Schools System (MCPS) seeking a placement for him for the following school year. MCPS evaluated Brian and convened an IEP team. The committee generated an initial IEP offering Brian a place in either of two MCPS middle schools. Brian's parents were not satisfied with the arrangement, believing that Brian needed smaller classes and more intensive services. The Schaffers thus enrolled Brian in another private school, and initiated a due process hearing challenging the IEP and seeking compensation for the cost of Brian's subsequent private education.

In Maryland, IEP hearings are conducted by [ALJs]. * * * After a 3-day hearing, the ALJ deemed the evidence close, held that the parents bore the burden of persuasion, and ruled in favor of the school district. The parents brought a civil action challenging the result. The United States District Court for the District of Maryland reversed and remanded, after concluding that the burden of persuasion is on the school district. Brian S. v. Vance, 86 F.Supp.2d 538 (2000). Around the same time, MCPS offered Brian a placement in a high school with a special learning center. Brian's parents accepted, and Brian was educated in that program until he graduated from high school. The suit remained alive, however, because the parents sought compensation for the private school tuition and related expenses.

Respondents appealed to the United States Court of Appeals for the Fourth Circuit. * * * On appeal, a divided panel of the Fourth Circuit reversed. Judge Michael, writing for the majority, concluded that petitioners offered no persuasive reason to "depart from the normal rule of allocating the burden to the party seeking relief." 377 F. 3d 449, 453 (2004). We granted certiorari, 543 U.S. 1145 (2005), to resolve the following question: At an administrative hearing assessing the appropriateness of an IEP, which party bears the burden of persuasion?

II

A

The term "burden of proof" is one of the "slipperiest member[s] of the family of legal terms." 2 J. Strong, McCormick on Evidence § 342, p. 433 (5th ed. 1999) (hereinafter McCormick).   Part of the confusion surrounding the term arises from the fact that historically, the concept encompassed two distinct burdens: the "burden of persuasion," i.e., which party loses if the evidence is closely balanced, and the "burden of production," i.e., which party bears the obligation to come forward with the evidence at different points in the proceeding.   Director, Office of Workers' Compensation Programs v. Greenwich Collieries, 512 U.S. 267, 272 (1994). We note at the outset that this case concerns only the burden of persuasion, as the parties agree, Brief for Respondents 14; Reply Brief for Petitioners 15, and when we speak of burden of proof in this opinion, it is this to which we refer.

When we are determining the burden of proof under a statutory cause of action, the touchstone of our inquiry is, of course, the statute. The plain text of IDEA is silent on the allocation of the burden of persuasion.   We therefore begin with the ordinary default rule that plaintiffs bear the risk of failing to prove their claims. McCormick § 337, at 412 ("The burdens of pleading and proof with regard to most facts have and should be assigned to the plaintiff who generally seeks to change the present state of affairs and who therefore naturally should be expected to bear the risk of failure or proof or persuasion"); C. Mueller & L. Kirkpatrick, Evidence §3.1, p. 104 (3d ed. 2003) ("Perhaps the broadest and most accepted idea is that the person who seeks court action should justify the request, which means that the plaintiffs bear the burdens on the elements in their claims").

Thus, we have usually assumed without comment that plaintiffs bear the burden of persuasion regarding the essential aspects of their claims. For example, Title VII of the Civil Rights Act of 1964, 42 U.S.C. §2000e-2 et seq., does not directly state that plaintiffs bear the "ultimate" burden of persuasion, but we have so concluded. St. Mary's Honor Center v. Hicks, 509 U.S. 502, 511 (1993); id., at 531 (SOUTER, J., dissenting). In numerous other areas, we have presumed or held that the default rule applies. See, e.g., Lujan v. Defenders of Wildlife, 504 U.S. 555, 561 (1992) (standing); Cleveland v. Policy Management Systems Corp., 526 U.S. 795, 806 (1999) (Americans with Disabilities Act); Hunt v. Cromartie, 526 U.S. 541, 553 (1999) (equal protection); Wharf (Holdings) Ltd. v. United Int'l Holdings, Inc., 532 U.S. 588, 593 (2001) (securities fraud); Doran v. Salem Inn, Inc., 422 U.S. 922, 931 (1975) (preliminary injunctions); Mt. Healthy City Bd. of Ed. v. Doyle, 429 U.S. 274, 287 (1977) (First Amendment). Congress also expressed its approval of the general rule when it chose to apply it to administrative proceedings under the Administrative Procedure Act, 5 U.S.C. §556(d) * * *

The ordinary default rule, of course, admits of exceptions. See McCormick § 337, at 412-415. For example, the burden of persuasion as to certain elements of a plaintiff's claim may be shifted to defendants, when such elements can fairly be characterized as affirmative defenses or exemptions. See, e.g., FTC v. Morton Salt Co., 334 U.S. 37, 44-45 (1948). Under some circumstances this Court has even placed the burden of persuasion over an entire claim on the defendant. See Alaska Dept. of Environmental Conservation v. EPA, 540 U.S. 461, 494 (2004). But while the normal default rule does not solve all cases, it certainly solves most of them. Decisions that place the entire burden of persuasion on the opposing party at the outset of a proceeding – as petitioners urge us to do here – are extremely rare. Absent some reason to believe that Congress intended otherwise, therefore, we will conclude that the burden of persuasion lies where it usually falls, upon the party seeking relief.

B

Petitioners contend first that a close reading of IDEA's text compels a conclusion in their favor. They urge that we should interpret the statutory words "due process" in light of their constitutional meaning, and apply the balancing test established by Mathews v. Eldridge, 424 U.S. 319 (1976). Even assuming that the Act incorporates constitutional due process doctrine, Eldridge is no help to petitioners, because "[o]utside the criminal law area, where special concerns attend, the locus of the burden of persuasion is normally not an issue of federal constitutional moment." Lavine v. Milne, 424 U.S. 577, 585 (1976). Petitioners next contend that we should take instruction from the lower court opinions of Mills v. Board of Education, 348 F.Supp. 866 (D.C. 1972), and Pennsylvania Association for Retarded Children v. Commonwealth, 334 F. Supp. 1257 (ED Pa. 1971) (hereinafter PARC). IDEA's drafters were admittedly guided "to a significant extent" by these two landmark cases. Rowley, 458 U.S., at 194. As the court below noted, however, the fact that Congress "took a number of the procedural safeguards from PARC and Mills and wrote them directly into the Act" does not allow us to "conclude . . . that Congress intended to adopt the ideas that it failed to write into the text of the statute." 377 F. 3d, at 455.

Petitioners also urge that putting the burden of persuasion on school districts will further IDEA's purposes because it will help ensure that children receive a free appropriate public education. In truth, however, very few cases will be in evidentiary equipoise. Assigning the burden of persuasion to school districts might encourage schools to put more resources into preparing IEPs and presenting their evidence. But IDEA is silent about whether marginal dollars should be allocated to litigation and administrative expenditures or to educational services. Moreover, there is reason to believe that a great deal is already spent on the administration of the Act. Litigating a due process complaint is an expensive affair, costing schools approximately $8,000-to-$12,000 per hearing. See Department of Education, J. Chambers, J. Harr, & A. Dhanani, What Are We Spending on Procedural Safeguards in Special Education 1999-2000, p. 8 (May 2003) * * * Congress has also repeatedly amended the Act in order to reduce its administrative and litigation-related costs. For example, in 1997 Congress mandated that States offer mediation for IDEA disputes. * * * In 2004, Congress added a mandatory "resolution session" prior to any due process hearing. * * * It also made new findings that "[p]arents and schools should be given expanded opportunities to resolve their disagreements in positive and constructive ways," and that "[t]eachers, schools, local educational agencies, and States should be relieved of irrelevant and unnecessary paperwork burdens that do not lead to improved educational outcomes." §§ 1400(c)(8)-(9).

Petitioners in effect ask this Court to assume that every IEP is invalid until the school district demonstrates that it is not. The Act does not support this conclusion. IDEA relies heavily upon the expertise of school districts to meet its goals. It also includes a so-called "stay-put" provision, which requires a child to remain in his or her "then current educational placement" during the pendency of an IDEA hearing. § 1415(j). Congress could have required that a child be given the educational placement that a parent requested during a dispute, but it did no such thing. Congress appears to have presumed instead that, if the Act's procedural requirements are respected, parents will prevail when they have legitimate grievances. See Rowley, supra, at 206 (noting the "legislative conviction that adequate compliance with the procedures prescribed would in most cases assure much if not all of what Congress wished in the way of substantive content in an IEP").

Petitioners' most plausible argument is that "[t]he ordinary rule, based on considerations of fairness, does not place the burden upon a litigant of establishing facts peculiarly within the knowledge of his adversary." United States v. New York, N. H. & H. R. Co., 355 U.S. 253, 256, n.5 (1957); * * * But this "rule is far from being universal, and has many qualifications upon its application." Greenleaf's Lessee v. Birth, 6 Pet. 302, 312 (1832); see also McCormick § 337, at 413 ("Very often one must plead and prove matters as to which his adversary has superior access to the proof"). School districts have a "natural advantage" in information and expertise, but Congress addressed this when it obliged schools to safeguard the procedural rights of parents and to share information with them. See School Comm. of Burlington v. Department of Ed. of Mass., 471 U.S. 359, 368 (1985). * * * The regulations clarify this entitlement by providing that a "parent has the right to an independent educational evaluation at public expense if the parent disagrees with an evaluation obtained by the public agency." 34 CFR § 300.502(b)(1) (2005). IDEA thus ensures parents access to an expert who can evaluate all the materials that the school must make available, and who can give an independent opinion. They are not left to challenge the government without a realistic opportunity to access the necessary evidence, or without an expert with the firepower to match the opposition.

Additionally, in 2004, Congress added provisions requiring school districts to answer the subject matter of a complaint in writing, and to provide parents with the reasoning behind the disputed action, details about the other options considered and rejected by the IEP team, and a description of all evaluations, reports, and other factors that the school used in coming to its decision. Pub. L. 108-446, § 615(c)(2)(B)(i)(I), 118 Stat. 2718, 20 U.S.C.A. § 1415(c)(2)(B)(i)(I) (Supp. 2006). Prior to a hearing, the parties must disclose evaluations and recommendations that they intend to rely upon. 20 U.S.C. §1415(f)(2). IDEA hearings are deliberately informal and intended to give ALJs the flexibility that they need to ensure that each side can fairly present its evidence. IDEA, in fact, requires state authorities to organize hearings in a way that guarantees parents and children the procedural protections of the Act. See § 1415(a). Finally, and perhaps most importantly, parents may recover attorney's fees if they prevail. § 1415(i)(3)(B). These protections ensure that the school bears no unique informational advantage.

III

Finally, respondents and several States urge us to decide that States may, if they wish, override the default rule and put the burden always on the school district. Several States have laws or regulations purporting to do so, at least under some circumstances. See, e.g., Minn. Stat. § 125A.091, subd. 16 (2004); Ala. Admin. Code Rule 290-8-9-.08(8)(c)(6) (Supp. 2004); Alaska Admin. Code tit. 4, § 52.550(e)(9) (2003); Del. Code Ann., Tit. 14, § 3140 (1999). Because no such law or regulation exists in Maryland, we need not decide this issue today. Justice BREYER contends that the allocation of the burden ought to be left entirely up to the States. But neither party made this argument before this Court or the courts below. We therefore decline to address it.

We hold no more than we must to resolve the case at hand: The burden of proof in an administrative hearing challenging an IEP is properly placed upon the party seeking relief. In this case, that party is Brian, as represented by his parents. But the rule applies with equal effect to school districts: If they seek to challenge an IEP, they will in turn bear the burden of persuasion before an ALJ. The judgment of the United States Court of Appeals for the Fourth Circuit is, therefore, affirmed.

It is so ordered.

The CHIEF JUSTICE took no part in the consideration or decision of this case.

Justice STEVENS, concurring.

[Omitted]

Justice GINSBERG, dissenting.

When the legislature is silent on the burden of proof, courts ordinarily allocate the burden to the party initiating the proceeding and seeking relief. As the Fourth Circuit recognized, however, "other factors," prime among them "policy considerations, convenience, and fairness," may warrant a different allocation. 377 F. 3d 449, 452 (2004) (citing 2 J. Strong, McCormick on Evidence § 337, p. 415 (5th ed. 1999) (allocation of proof burden "will depend upon the weight . . . given to any one or more of several factors, including: . . . special policy considerations . . .[,] convenience, . . . [and] fairness")); see also 9 J. Wigmore, Evidence § 2486, p. 291 (J. Chadbourn rev. ed. 1981) (assigning proof burden presents "a question of policy and fairness based on experience in the different situations"). The Court has followed the same counsel. See Alaska Dept. of Environmental Conservation v. EPA, 540 U.S. 461, 494, n.17 (2004) ("No 'single principle or rule . . . solve[s] all cases and afford[s] a general test for ascertaining the incidence' of proof burdens." (quoting Wigmore, supra, § 2486, p. 288; emphasis deleted)). For reasons well stated by Circuit Judge Luttig, dissenting in the Court of Appeals, 377 F. 3d, at 456–459, I am persuaded that "policy considerations, convenience, and fairness" call for assigning the burden of proof to the school district in this case.

The Individuals with Disabilities Education Act (IDEA), 20 U.S.C. § 1400 et seq., was designed to overcome the pattern of disregard and neglect disabled children historically encountered in seeking access to public education. * * * The IDEA is atypical in this respect: It casts an affirmative, beneficiary-specific obligation on providers of public education. School districts are charged with responsibility to offer to each disabled child an individualized education program (IEP) suitable to the child's special needs. 20 U.S.C. §§ 1400(d)(1), 1412(a)(4), 1414(d). The proponent of the IEP, it seems to me, is properly called upon to demonstrate its adequacy.

Familiar with the full range of education facilities in the area, and informed by "their experiences with other, similarly-disabled children," 377 F. 3d, at 458 (Luttig, J.,dissenting), "the school district is . . . in a far better position to demonstrate that it has fulfilled [its statutory] obligation than the disabled student's parents are in to show that the school district has failed to do so," id., at 457. Accord Oberti v. Board of Ed. of Borough of Clementon School Dist., 995 F. 2d 1204, 1219 (CA3 1993) ("In practical terms, the school has an advantage when a dispute arises under the Act: the school has better access to relevant information, greater control over the potentially more persuasive witnesses (those who have been directly involved with the child's education), and greater overall educational expertise than the parents."); Lascari v. Board of Ed. of Ramapo Indian

Hills Regional High School Dist., 116 N. J. 30, 45-46, 560 A. 2d 1180, 1188-1189 (1989) * * *[1]

Understandably, school districts striving to balance their budgets, if "[l]eft to [their] own devices," will favor educational options that enable them to conserve resources. Deal v. Hamilton County Bd. of Ed., 392 F. 3d 840, 864-865 (CA6 2004). Saddled with a proof burden in administrative "due process" hearings, parents are likely to find a district-proposed IEP "resistant to challenge." 377 F. 3d, at 459 (Luttig, J., dissenting). Placing the burden on the district to show that its plan measures up to the statutorily mandated "free appropriate public education," 20 U.S.C. § 1400(d)(1)(A), will strengthen school officials' resolve to choose a course genuinely tailored to the child's individual needs. * * *

The Court acknowledges that "[a]ssigning the burden of persuasion to school districts might encourage schools to put more resources into preparing IEPs." Ante, at 9. Curiously, the Court next suggests that resources spent on developing IEPs rank as "administrative expenditures" not as expenditures for "educational services." Ibid. Costs entailed in the preparation of suitable IEPs, however, are the very expenditures necessary to ensure each child covered by IDEA access to a free appropriate education. These outlays surely relate to "educational services." Indeed, a carefully designed IEP may ward off disputes productive of large administrative or litigation expenses.

This case is illustrative. Not until the District Court ruled that the school district had the burden of persuasion did the school design an IEP that met Brian Schaffer's special educational needs. See ante, at 5; Tr. of Oral Arg. 21-22 (Counsel for the Schaffers observed that "Montgomery County . . . gave [Brian] the kind of services he had sought from the beginning . . . once [the school district was] given the burden of proof."). Had the school district, in the first instance, offered Brian a public or private school placement equivalent to the one the district ultimately provided, this entire litigation and its attendant costs could have been avoided.

Notably, nine States, as friends of the Court, have urged that placement of the burden of persuasion on the school district best comports with IDEA's aim. See Brief for Virginia et al. as *Amici Curiae*. If

---

[1] The Court suggests that the IDEA's stay-put provision, 20 U.S.C. § 1415(j), supports placement of the burden of persuasion on the parents. Ante, at 536. The stay-put provision, however, merely preserves the status quo. It would work to the advantage of the child and the parents when the school seeks to cut services offered under a previously established IEP. True, Congress did not require that "a child be given the educational placement that a parent requested during a dispute." *Ibid.* But neither did Congress require that the IEP advanced by the school district go into effect during the pendency of a dispute.

allocating the burden to school districts would saddle school systems with inordinate costs, it is doubtful that these States would have filed in favor of petitioners. * * *

One can demur to the Fourth Circuit's observation that courts "do not automatically assign the burden of proof to the side with the bigger guns," 377 F. 3d, at 453, for no such reflexive action is at issue here. It bears emphasis that "the vast majority of parents whose children require the benefits and protections provided in the IDEA" lack "knowledg[e] about the educational resources available to their [child]" and the "sophisticat[ion]" to mount an effective case against a district-proposed IEP. Id., at 458 (Luttig, J., dissenting); cf. 20 U.S.C. § 1400(c)(7)-(10). See generally M. Wagner, C. Marder, J. Blackorby, & D. Cardoso, The Children We Serve: The Demographic Characteristics of Elementary and Middle School Students with Disabilities and their Households (Sept. 2002) * * * In this setting, "the party with the 'bigger guns' also has better access to information, greater expertise, and an affirmative obligation to provide the contested services." 377 F. 3d, at 458 (Luttig, J., dissenting). Policy considerations, convenience, and fairness, I think it plain, point in the same direction. Their collective weight warrants a rule requiring a school district, in "due process" hearings, to explain persuasively why its proposed IEP satisfies IDEA's standards. Ibid. I would therefore reverse the judgment of the Fourth Circuit.

Justice BREYER, dissenting.

As the majority points out, the [IDEA] * * * requires school districts to "identify and evaluate disabled children, . . . develop an [Individualized Education Program] for each one . . ., and review every IEP at least once a year." * * *

The Act also sets forth minimum procedures that the parties, the hearing officer, and the federal court must follow. * * * Despite this detailed procedural scheme, the Act is silent on the question of who bears the burden of persuasion at the state "due process" hearing.

The statute's silence suggests that Congress did not think about the matter of the burden of persuasion. It is, after all, a relatively minor issue that should not often arise. That is because the parties will ordinarily introduce considerable evidence (as in this case where the initial 3-day hearing included testimony from 10 witnesses, 6 qualified as experts, and more than 50 exhibits). And judges rarely hesitate to weigh evidence, even highly technical evidence, and to decide a matter on the merits, even when the case is a close one. Thus, cases in which an . . . ALJ[] finds the evidence in precise equipoise should be few and far between. Cf. O'Neal v. McAninch, 513 U.S. 432, 436-437 (1995). See also Individuals with Disabilities Education Improvement Act of 2004, Pub. L. 108-446, §§ 615(f)(3)(A)(ii)-(iv), 118 Stat. 2721, 20 U.S.C.A. §§ 1415(f)(3)(A)(ii)-(iv) (Supp. 2005) (requiring appointment of ALJ with technical capacity to understand Act).

Nonetheless, the hearing officer held that before him was that rara avis – a case of perfect evidentiary equipoise. Hence we must infer from Congress' silence (and from the rest of the statutory scheme) which party – the parents or the school district – bears the burden of persuasion.

One can reasonably argue, as the Court holds, that the risk of nonpersuasion should fall upon the "individual desiring change." That, after all, is the rule courts ordinarily apply when an individual complains about the lawfulness of a government action. * * * On the other hand, one can reasonably argue to the contrary, that, given the technical nature of the subject matter, its human importance, the school district's superior resources, and the district's superior access to relevant information, the risk of non-persuasion ought to fall upon the district. * * * My own view is that Congress took neither approach. It did not decide the "burden of persuasion" question; instead it left the matter to the States for decision.

The Act says that the "establish[ment]" of "procedures" is a matter for the "State" and its agencies. § 1415(a). It adds that the hearing in question, an administrative hearing, is to be conducted by the "State" or "local educational agency." 20 U.S.C.A. § 1415(f)(1)(A) (Supp. 2005). And the statute as a whole foresees state implementation of federal standards. § 1412(a); Cedar Rapids Community School Dist. v. Garret F., 526 U.S. 66, 68 (1999); Board of Ed. of Hendrick Hudson Central School Dist., Westchester Cty. v. Rowley, 458 U.S. 176, 208 (1982). The minimum federal procedural standards that the Act specifies are unrelated to the "burden of persuasion" question. And different States, consequently and not surprisingly, have resolved it in different ways. See, e.g., Alaska Admin. Code, tit. 4, § 52.550(e)(9) (2003) (school district bears burden); Ala. Admin. Code Rule 290-8-9.08(8)(c)(6)(ii)(I) (Supp. 2004); (same); Conn. Agencies Regs. § 10-76h-14 (2005) (same); Del. Code Ann., tit. 14, § 3140 (1999) (same); 1 D. C. Mun. Regs., tit. 5, § 3030.3 (2003) (same); W. Va. Code Rules § 126-16-8.1.11(c) (2005) (same); Ind. Admin. Code, tit. 511,7-30-3 (2003) (incorporating by reference Ind. Code § 4-21.5-3-14 (West 2002)) (moving party bears burden); 7 Ky. Admin. Regs., tit. 707, ch. 1:340, Section 7(4) (2004) (incorporating by reference Ky. Rev. Stat. Ann. § 13B.090(7) (Lexis 2003)) (same); Ga. Comp. Rules & Regs., Rule 160-4-7-.18(1)(g)(8) (2002) (burden varies depending upon remedy sought); Minn. Stat. Ann. § 125A.091, subd. 16 (West Supp. 2005) (same). There is no indication that this lack of uniformity has proved harmful.

Nothing in the Act suggests a need to fill every interstice of the Act's remedial scheme with a uniform federal rule. See Kamen v. Kemper Financial Services, Inc., 500 U.S. 90, 98 (1991) (citations omitted). And should some such need arise – i.e., if non-uniformity or a particular state approach were to prove problematic – the Federal Department of Education, expert in the area, might promulgate a uniform federal standard, thereby limiting state choice. 20 U.S.C.A. § 1406(a) (Supp. 2005); Irving Independent School Dist. v. Tatro, 468 U.S. 883, 891-893 (1984); see also Barnhart v. Walton, 535 U.S. 212, 217-218 (2002);

NationsBank of N. C., N. A. v. Variable Annuity Life Ins. Co., 513 U.S. 251, 256-257 (1995); Chevron U. S. A. Inc. v. Natural Resources Defense Council, Inc., 467 U.S. 837, 842-845 (1984).

Most importantly, Congress has made clear that the Act itself represents an exercise in "cooperative federalism." * * * Respecting the States' right to decide this procedural matter here, where education is at issue, where expertise matters, and where costs are shared, is consistent with that cooperative approach. See Wisconsin Dept. of Health and Family Servs. v. Blumer, 534 U.S. 473, 495 (2002) (when interpreting statutes "designed to advance cooperative federalism[,] . . . we have not been reluctant to leave a range of permissible choices to the States"). * * * And judicial respect for such congressional determinations is important. Indeed, in today's technologically and legally complex world, whether court decisions embody that kind of judicial respect may represent the true test of federalist principle. See AT&T Corp. v. Iowa Utilities Bd., 525 U.S. 366, 420 (1999) (BREYER, J., concurring in part and dissenting in part).

Maryland has no special state law or regulation setting forth a special IEP-related burden of persuasion standard. But it does have rules of state administrative procedure and a body of state administrative law. The state ALJ should determine how those rules, or other state law applies to this case. Cf., e.g., Ind. Admin. Code, tit. 511,7-30-3 (2003) (hearings under the Act conducted in accord with general state administrative law); 7 Ky. Admin. Regs., tit. 707, ch. 1:340, Section 7(4) (2004) (same). Because the state ALJ did not do this (i.e., he looked for a federal, not a state, burden of persuasion rule), I would remand this case.

Notes & Questions

1. Is it fair to place the burden of proving an IEP to be inappropriate on the parents, who may lack the educational expertise and knowledge of available services to properly assess the special education program? Would it be more appropriate to place the burden of proof on the party seeking to impose the more restrictive setting, in recognition of the IDEA's preference for integration?

2. Pursuant to statutory law, some jurisdictions assign the burden of proof to school districts. These include Alabama, Alaska, Connecticut, Delaware, Georgia, Kentucky, Minnesota, New Jersey, and New York. For example, in Connecticut, "[t]he party who filed for due process has the burden of going forward with the evidence. In all cases, however, the public agency has the burden of proving the appropriateness of the child's program or placement, or of the program or placement proposed by the public agency." Conn. Agencies Regs. § 10-76h-14 (West 2009); see also Ala. Admin. Code r. 290-8-9-.08(8)(c)(6)(ii)(I) (2008); Alaska Admin. Code tit. 4, § 52.550(e)(9) (2009); Del. Code Ann., tit. 14, § 3140 (Michie 2009); Ga. Comp. R. & Regs. r. 160-4-7.18(1)(g)(8) (2009); Ky. Rev. Stat. Ann. § 13B.090(7) (West 2008); Minn. Stat. § 125A.091(16) (West

2009); N.J. Stat. Ann. 18A:46-1.1 (West 2008); N.Y. Education Law § 4404(c) (McKinney 2007) (assigning the burden on school districts except in instances where a parent seeks tuition reimbursement for a unilateral parental placement).

3. Has *Schaffer* resolved the question once and for all? When might the *Schaffer* rule not apply? In *Vaughn G. v. Mayor & City Council of Baltimore*, No. MJG-84-1911, 2005 WL 1949688, at *1 (D.C. Md. Aug. 12, 2005), the court found that the school district's ongoing systemic inability to ensure the provision of IDEA mandated services, posed an educational emergency. In response, the state will direct an Intensive Management and Capacity Improvement Plan, which the court concluded "provides the only realistic chance that the [school system] can meet, or even approach meeting, its special education obligations" for the 2005-06 school year. *Id.* at *7. Myhill has argued that the presumption a school is providing FAPE should not fall on the family when the school repeatedly is unable to meet state substantive achievement standards. Myhill, No FAPE in MPCP, *supra*, at 1073-84. *Rowley* expressly includes meeting the standards of the state education agency in the provision of FAPE. Bd. of Educ. v. Rowley, 458 U.S. 176, 180-81 (1982). Do you agree?

4. After a series of appeals and remands, the district court weighed the parent's ability, given that they had the burden of proof to show Brian's eighth grade IEP was inadequate, to enter additional evidence. However, before the court could make a final decision, the parents moved to submit Brian's tenth grade IEP as evidence that his eighth grade IEP was inadequate. The district court reviewed this evidence but refused to give it weight, reasoning that an IEP two years after the fact should not reflect on how the earlier decision was made. On appeal, the Fourth Circuit upheld the lower court because a "hindsight-based review" conflicts with the "structure and purpose of the IDEA." Schaffer v. Bd. of Educ. of Montgomery County, 554 F.3d 470, 475 (4th Cir. 2009). The court reasoned, in part, that allowing the tenth grade IEP as evidence against the eighth grade IEP would create a disincentive for schools to reassess and update a student's IEP. Do you agree?

ॐ

§ 24.2   Exhaustion Of Administrative Remedies

The IDEA requires exhaustion of its administrative remedies before a civil action may be filed in state or federal court. 20 U.S.C. § 1415(l) (2006). *See* the description of the administrative process, *supra* § 30.1.

In some states, the state department of education can conduct a hearing and the losing party can immediately appeal to state or federal court. In other states, a hearing will be conducted by the school district, and then the losing party must appeal to the state department of education so as to exhaust all possible administrative remedies available.

Id. § 1415(g)(1). After all administrative remedies have been exhausted, then the "party aggrieved" has a right to bring a civil action "in any State court of competent jurisdiction or in a district court of the United States, without regard to the amount in controversy." *Id.* § 1415(i)(2)(A); 34 C.F.R. § 300.512(a) (2008).

Because parents do not always want to pursue the IDEA procedures, a number of cases have addressed whether, and when, parents may proceed directly to federal court to enforce disability rights in the educational context. In general, exhaustion is required unless the student alleges injuries that cannot be redressed by the IDEA's administrative procedures and remedies.

Therefore, students with injuries that can only be redressed with monetary compensation may not be required to exhaust IDEA remedies. *See* McCormick v. Waukegan Sch. Dist. No. 60, 374 F.3d 564, 569 (7th Cir. 2004) (damages for physical injuries – not required to exhaust); Robb v. Bethel Sch. Dist. No. 403, 308 F.3d 1047, 1054 (9th Cir. 2002) (lost educational opportunities and emotional damages based on inadequate education – must exhaust); Polera v. Bd. of Educ. of Newburgh, 288 F.3d 478, 490 (2d Cir. 2002) (lost educational opportunities and retroactive honor society recognition – must exhaust); Frazier v. Fairhaven Sch. Comm., 276 F.3d 52, 57-64 (1st Cir. 2002) (money damages for inappropriate discipline – must exhaust). *But see* Padilla v. Sch. Dist. No. 1, Denver, 233 F.3d 1268, 1274-75 (10th Cir. 2000) (damages for physical injuries – need not exhaust).

Exhaustion also has been excused when students are seeking relief from a blanket policy applicable to students with disabilities generally, under Title II of the ADA or § 504 of the Rehabilitation Act, and not resulting from any individual student's IEP process. Christopher S. v. Stanislaus County Office of Educ., 384 F.3d 1205, 1212 (9th Cir. 2004). However, even students with claims under the Americans with Disabilities Act (ADA) and Rehabilitation Act of 1973 must exhaust IDEA administrative remedies to the extent the relief sought is also available under the IDEA. 20 U.S.C. § 1415(l) (2006).

§ 24.3   Civil Action

Either party may file a civil action in federal court to challenge the findings of the hearing officer. 34 C.F.R. § 300.51d(a) (2008). The court "(1) receives the records of the administrative proceedings; (2) hears additional evidence at the request of a party; and (3) basing its decision on the preponderance of the evidence, grants the relief that the court determines to be appropriate." *Id.* § 300.516(c).

Many federal courts review administrative decisions *de novo*. M.L. v. Fed. Way Sch. Dist., 387 F.3d 1101, 1108 (9th Cir. 2004), *amended and superseded,* 394 F.3d 634 (9th Cir. 2005), *cert. denied,* 545 U.S. 1128, 125 S.Ct. 2941, 162 L.Ed.2d 867 (2005); Wexler v. Westfield Bd. of Educ.,

784 F.2d 176, 179-80 (3d Cir. 1986); Roncker v. Walter, 700 F.2d 1058, 1062 (6th Cir. 1983). Others apply a more deferential standard. *Town of Burlington v. Dep't of Educ. for Commonwealth of Mass.*, 736 F.2d 773, 792 (1st Cir. 1984), *affirmed on other grounds*, 471 U.S. 359 (1985) ("The court, in recognition of the expertise of the administrative agency, must consider the findings carefully and endeavor to respond to the hearing officer's resolution of each material issue. After such consideration, the court is free to accept or reject the findings in part or in whole.").

Notes & Questions

1. In reviewing an administrative decision, should a district court defer to the expertise of the administrative hearing officer? To the school district? To the experts? Is the IDEA provision allowing the acceptance of additional evidence consistent with the courts' tendency to defer to administrative hearing officers or school officials?

§ 24.4 *Pro Se* Representation In Federal Court

While the IDEA applies to children with disabilities, the ability to enforce the IDEA lies with the child's parents. In 2007, in *Winkelman v. Parma City School District*, 550 U.S. 516 (2007), the U.S. Supreme Court considered whether and on what basis parents may represent their child's interests and their own interests under the IDEA without an attorney.

WINKELMAN v. PARMA CITY SCHOOL DISTRICT

Supreme Court of the United States, 2007
550 U.S. 516

* * *

Justice KENNEDY delivered the opinion of the Court.

Some four years ago, Mr. and Mrs. Winkelman, parents of five children, became involved in lengthy administrative and legal proceedings. They had sought review related to concerns they had over whether their youngest child, 6-year-old Jacob, would progress well at Pleasant Valley Elementary School, which is part of the Parma City School District in Parma, Ohio.

Jacob has autism spectrum disorder and is covered by the Individuals with Disabilities Education Act (Act or IDEA) * * * as amended, 20 U.S.C. § 1400 *et seq.* His parents worked with the school district to develop an individualized education program (IEP), as required by the Act. All concede that Jacob's parents had the statutory right to contribute to this process and, when agreement could not be reached, to participate in administrative proceedings including what the Act refers to as an "impartial due process hearing." § 1415(f)(1)(A) (2000 ed., Supp. IV).

The disagreement at the center of the current dispute concerns the procedures to be followed when parents and their child, dissatisfied with the outcome of the due process hearing, seek further review in a United States District Court. The question is whether parents, either on their own behalf or as representatives of the child, may proceed in court unrepresented by counsel though they are not trained or licensed as attorneys. Resolution of this issue requires us to examine and explain the provisions of IDEA to determine if it accords to parents rights of their own that can be vindicated in court proceedings, or alternatively, whether the Act allows them, in their status as parents, to represent their child in court proceedings.

I

* * *

The school district proposed an IEP for the 2003-2004 school year that would have placed Jacob at a public elementary school. Regarding this IEP as deficient under IDEA, Jacob's nonlawyer parents availed themselves of the administrative review provided by IDEA. They filed a complaint alleging respondent had failed to provide Jacob with a free appropriate public education; they appealed the hearing officer's rejection of the claims in this complaint to a state-level review officer; and after losing that appeal they filed, on their own behalf and on behalf of Jacob, a complaint in the United States District Court for the Northern District of Ohio. In reliance upon 20 U.S.C. § 1415(i)(2) (2000 ed., Supp. IV) they challenged the administrative decision, alleging, among other matters: that Jacob had not been provided with a free appropriate public education; that his IEP was inadequate; and that the school district had failed to follow procedures mandated by IDEA. Pending the resolution of these challenges, the Winkelmans had enrolled Jacob in a private school at their own expense. They had also obtained counsel to assist them with certain aspects of the proceedings, although they filed their federal complaint, and later their appeal, without the aid of an attorney. The Winkelmans' complaint sought reversal of the administrative decision, reimbursement for private-school expenditures and attorney's fees already incurred, and, it appears, declaratory relief.

The District Court granted respondent's motion for judgment on the pleadings, finding it had provided Jacob with a free appropriate public education. Petitioners, proceeding without counsel, filed an appeal with the Court of Appeals for the Sixth Circuit. Relying on its recent decision in *Cavanaugh v. Cardinal Local School Dist.*, 409 F.3d 753 (2005), the Court of Appeals entered an order dismissing the Winkelmans' appeal unless they obtained counsel to represent Jacob. * * * In *Cavanaugh* the Court of Appeals had rejected the proposition that IDEA allows nonlawyer parents raising IDEA claims to proceed *pro se* in federal court. The court ruled that the right to a free appropriate public education "belongs to the child alone," 409 F.3d, at 757, not to both the parents and the child. It followed, the court held, that "any right on which the [parents] could proceed on their own behalf would be derivative" of the child's right, *ibid.*, so that parents bringing IDEA claims were not appearing on their own behalf, *ibid.* See also 28 U.S.C. § 1654 (allowing parties to prosecute their own claims *pro se*). As for the parents' alternative argument, the court held, nonlawyer parents cannot litigate IDEA claims on behalf of their child because IDEA does not abrogate the common-law rule prohibiting nonlawyer parents from representing minor children. 409 F.3d, at 756. As the court in *Cavanaugh* acknowledged, its decision brought the Sixth Circuit in direct conflict with the First Circuit, which had concluded, under a theory of "statutory joint rights," that the Act accords to parents the right to assert IDEA claims on their own behalf. See *Maroni v. Pemi-Baker Regional School Dist.*, 346 F.3d 247, 249, 250 (C.A.1 2003).

Petitioners sought review in this Court. In light of the disagreement among the Courts of Appeals as to whether a nonlawyer parent of a child with a disability may prosecute IDEA actions *pro se* in federal court, we granted certiorari. * * *

II

Our resolution of this case turns upon the significance of IDEA's interlocking statutory provisions. Petitioners' primary theory is that the Act makes parents real parties in interest to IDEA actions, not "mer[e] guardians of their children's rights." * * * If correct, this allows Mr. and Mrs. Winkelman back into court, for there is no question that a party may represent his or her own interests in federal court without the aid of counsel. See 28 U.S.C. § 1654 ("In all courts of the United States the parties may plead and conduct their own cases personally or by counsel . . ."). Petitioners cannot cite a specific provision in IDEA mandating in direct and explicit terms that parents have the status of real parties in interest. They instead base their argument on a comprehensive reading of IDEA. Taken as a whole, they contend, the Act leads to the necessary conclusion that parents have independent, enforceable rights. Brief for Petitioners 14 (citing *Koons Buick Pontiac GMC, Inc. v. Nigh*, 543 U.S. 50, 60, 125 S.Ct. 460, 160 L.Ed.2d 389 (2004)). Respondent, accusing petitioners of "knit[ting] together various provisions pulled from the crevices of the statute" to support these claims, Brief for Respondent 19, reads the text of IDEA to mean that any redressable rights under the Act belong only to children, *id.*, at 19-40.

* * *

A

The goals of IDEA include "ensur[ing] that all children with disabilities have available to them a free appropriate public education" and "ensur[ing] that the rights of children with disabilities and parents of such children are protected." 20 U.S.C. §§ 1400(d)(1)(A)-(B) (2000 ed., Supp. IV). To this end, the Act includes provisions governing four areas of particular relevance to the Winkelmans' claim: procedures to be followed when developing a child's IEP; criteria governing the sufficiency of an education provided to a child; mechanisms for review that must be made available when there are objections to the IEP or to other aspects of IDEA proceedings; and the requirement in certain circumstances that States reimburse parents for various expenses. See generally §§ 1412(a)(10), 1414, 1415. Although our discussion of these four areas does not identify all the illustrative provisions, we do take particular note of certain terms that mandate or otherwise describe parental involvement.

IDEA requires school districts to develop an IEP for each child with a disability, see §§ 1412(a)(4), 1414(d), with parents playing "a significant role" in this process, *Schaffer v. Weast,* 546 U.S. 49, 53, 126 S.Ct. 528, 163 L.Ed.2d 387 (2005). Parents serve as members of the team that develops the IEP. § 1414(d)(1)(B). The "concerns" parents have "for enhancing the education of their child" must be considered by the team. § 1414(d)(3)(A)(ii). IDEA accords parents additional protections that apply throughout the IEP process. See, *e.g.,* § 1414(d)(4)(A) (requiring the IEP Team to revise the IEP when appropriate to address certain information provided by the parents); § 1414(e) (requiring States to "ensure that the parents of [a child with a disability] are members of any group that makes decisions on the educational placement of their child"). The statute also sets up general procedural safeguards that protect the informed involvement of parents in the development of an education for their child. See, *e.g.,* § 1415(a) (requiring States to "establish and maintain procedures . . . to ensure that children with disabilities and their parents are guaranteed procedural safeguards with respect to the provision of a free appropriate public education"); § 1415(b)(1) (mandating that States provide an opportunity for parents to examine all relevant records). See generally §§ 1414, 1415. A central purpose of the parental protections is to facilitate the provision of a " 'free appropriate public education,' " § 1401(9), which must be made available to the child "in conformity with the [IEP]," § 1401(9)(D).

* * *

When a party objects to the adequacy of the education provided, * * *, IDEA provides procedural recourse: It requires that a State provide "[a]n opportunity for any party to present a complaint . . . with respect to any matter relating to the identification, evaluation, or educational placement of the child, or the provision of a free appropriate public education to such child." § 1415(b)(6). By presenting a complaint a party is able to pursue a process of review that, as relevant, begins with a preliminary meeting "where the parents of the child discuss their complaint" and the local educational agency "is provided the opportunity to [reach a resolution]." § 1415(f)(1)(B)(i)(IV). If the agency "has not resolved the complaint to the satisfaction of the parents within 30 days,"

§ 1415(f)(1)(B)(ii), the parents may request an "impartial due process hearing," § 1415(f)(1)(A), which must be conducted either by the local educational agency or by the state educational agency, *ibid.*, and where a hearing officer will resolve issues raised in the complaint, § 1415(f)(3).

IDEA sets standards the States must follow in conducting these hearings. Among other things, it indicates that the hearing officer's decision "shall be made on substantive grounds based on a determination of whether the child received a free appropriate public education," and that, "[i]n matters alleging a procedural violation," the officer may find a child "did not receive a free appropriate public education" only if the violation

> "(I) impeded the child's right to a free appropriate public education;
>
> "(II) significantly impeded the parents' opportunity to participate in the decisionmaking process regarding the provision of a free appropriate public education to the parents' child; or
>
> "(III) caused a deprivation of educational benefits." §§ 1415(f)(3)(E)(i)-(ii).

* * * "Any party aggrieved by the findings and decision made [by the hearing officer] shall have the right to bring a civil action with respect to the complaint." § 1415(i)(2)(A); see also § 1415(i)(1).

* * *

B

Petitioners construe these various provisions to accord parents independent, enforceable rights under IDEA. We agree. The parents enjoy enforceable rights at the administrative stage, and it would be inconsistent with the statutory scheme to bar them from continuing to assert these rights in federal court.

The statute sets forth procedures for resolving disputes in a manner that, in the Act's express terms, contemplates parents will be the parties bringing the administrative complaints. In addition to the provisions we have cited, we refer also to § 1415(b)(8) (requiring a state educational agency to "develop a model form to assist parents in filing a complaint"); § 1415(c)(2) (addressing the response an agency must provide to a "parent's due process complaint notice"); and § 1415(i)(3)(B)(i) (referring to "the parent's complaint"). A wide range of review is available: Administrative complaints may be brought with respect to "any matter relating to . . . the provision of a free appropriate public education." § 1415(b)(6)(A). Claims raised in these complaints are then resolved at impartial due process hearings, where, again, the statute makes clear that parents will be participating as parties. *See generally supra,* at 2001. *See also* § 1415(f)(3)(C) (indicating "[a] parent or agency shall request an impartial due process hearing" within a certain period of time); § 1415(e)(2)(A)(ii) (referring to "a parent's right to a due process hearing"). The statute then grants "[a]ny party aggrieved by the findings and decision made [by the hearing officer] . . . the right to bring a civil action with respect to the complaint." § 1415(i)(2)(A).

* * *

Respondent, resisting this line of analysis, asks us to read these provisions as contemplating parental involvement only to the extent parents represent their child's interests. In respondent's view IDEA accords parents nothing more than "collateral tools related to the child's underlying substantive rights-not freestanding or independently enforceable rights." Brief for Respondent 25.

This interpretation, though, is foreclosed by provisions of the statute. IDEA defines one of its purposes as seeking "to ensure that the rights of children with disabilities and parents of such children are protected." § 1400(d)(1)(B). The word "rights" in the quoted language refers to the rights of parents as well as the rights of the child; otherwise the grammatical structure would make no sense.

Further provisions confirm this view. IDEA mandates that educational agencies establish procedures "to ensure that children with disabilities and their parents are guaranteed procedural safeguards with respect to the provision of a free appropriate public education." § 1415(a). It presumes parents have rights of their own when it defines how States might provide for the transfer of the "rights accorded to parents" by IDEA, § 1415(m)(1)(B), and it prohibits the raising of certain challenges "[n]otwithstanding any other individual right of action that a parent or student may maintain under [the relevant provisions of IDEA]," §§ 1401(10)(E), 1412(a)(14)(E). To adopt respondent's reading of the statute would require an interpretation of these statutory provisions (and others) far too strained to be correct.

Defending its countertextual reading of the statute, respondent cites a decision by a Court of Appeals concluding that the Act's "references to parents are best understood as accommodations to the fact of the child's incapacity." *Doe v. Board of Ed. of Baltimore Cty.,* 165 F.3d 260, 263 (C.A.4 1998) * * * This, according to respondent, requires us to interpret all references to parents' rights as referring in implicit terms to the child's rights-which, under this view, are the only enforceable rights accorded by IDEA. Even if we were inclined to ignore the plain text of the statute in considering this theory, we disagree that the sole purpose driving IDEA's involvement of parents is to facilitate vindication of a child's rights. It is not a novel proposition to say that parents have a recognized legal interest in the education and upbringing of their child. See, *e.g., Pierce v. Society of Sisters,* 268 U.S. 510, 534-535, 45 S.Ct. 571, 69 L.Ed. 1070 (1925) (acknowledging "the liberty of parents and guardians to direct the upbringing and education of children under their control"); *Meyer v. Nebraska,* 262 U.S. 390, 399-401, 43 S.Ct. 625, 67 L.Ed. 1042 (1923). * * *

* * *

A variation on respondent's argument has persuaded some Courts of Appeals. The argument is that while a parent can be a "party aggrieved" for aspects of the hearing officer's findings and decision, he or she cannot be a "party aggrieved" with respect to all IDEA-based challenges. Under this view the causes of action available to a parent might relate, for example, to various procedural mandates, see, *e.g., Collinsgru,* 161 F.3d, at 233, and reimbursement demands, see, *e.g.,* § 1412(a)(10)(C)(ii). The argument supporting this conclusion proceeds as follows: Because a "party aggrieved" is, by definition, entitled to a remedy, and parents are, under IDEA, only entitled to certain procedures and reimbursements as remedies, a parent cannot be a "party aggrieved" with regard to any claim not implicating these limited matters.

This argument is contradicted by the statutory provisions we have recited. True, there are provisions in IDEA stating parents are entitled to certain procedural protections and reimbursements; but the statute prevents us from placing too much weight on the implications to be drawn when other entitlements are accorded in less clear language. We find little support for the inference that parents are excluded by implication whenever a child is mentioned, and vice versa. Compare, *e.g.,* § 1411(e)(3)(E) (barring States from using certain funds for costs associated with actions "brought on behalf of a child" but failing to acknowledge that actions might also be brought on behalf of a parent) with § 1415(i)(3)(B)(i) (allowing recovery of attorney's fees to a "prevailing party who is the parent of a child with a disability" but failing to acknowledge that a child might also be a prevailing party). * * *

We consider the statutory structure. The IEP proceedings entitle parents to participate not only in the implementation of IDEA's procedures but also in the substantive formulation of their child's educational program. * * *

The statute also empowers parents to bring challenges based on a broad range of issues. The parent may seek a hearing on "any matter relating to the identification, evaluation, or educational placement of the child, or the provision of a free appropriate public education to such child." § 1415(b)(6)(A). * * * When this hearing has been conducted by a local educational agency rather than a state educational agency, "any party aggrieved by the findings and decision rendered in such a hearing may appeal such findings and decision" to the state educational agency. § 1415(g)(1). Judicial review follows, authorized by a broadly worded provision phrased in the same terms used to describe the prior stage of review: "[a]ny party aggrieved" may bring "a civil action." § 1415(i)(2)(A).

These provisions confirm that IDEA, through its text and structure, creates in parents an independent stake not only in the procedures and costs implicated by this process but also in the substantive decisions to be made. We therefore conclude that IDEA does not differentiate, through isolated references to various procedures and remedies, between the rights accorded to children and the rights accorded to parents. As a consequence, a parent may be a "party aggrieved" for purposes of § 1415(i)(2) with regard to "any matter" implicating these rights. See § 1415(b)(6)(A). The status of parents as parties is not limited to matters that relate to procedure and cost recovery. To find otherwise would be inconsistent with the collaborative framework and expansive system of review established by the Act. Cf. *Cedar Rapids Community School Dist. v. Garret F.*, 526 U.S. 66, 73, 119 S.Ct. 992, 143 L.Ed.2d 154 (1999) (looking to IDEA's "overall statutory scheme" to interpret its provisions).

Our conclusion is confirmed by noting the incongruous results that would follow were we to accept the proposition that parents' IDEA rights are limited to certain nonsubstantive matters. The statute's procedural and reimbursement-related rights are intertwined with the substantive adequacy of the education provided to a child, see, *e.g.*, § 1415(f)(3)(E), see also § 1412(a)(10)(C)(ii), and it is difficult to disentangle the provisions in order to conclude that some rights adhere to both parent and child while others do not. Were we nevertheless to recognize a distinction of this sort it would impose upon parties a confusing and onerous legal regime, one worsened by the absence of any express guidance in IDEA concerning how a court might in practice differentiate between these matters. * * *

The bifurcated regime suggested by the courts that have employed it, moreover, leaves some parents without a remedy. The statute requires, in express terms, that States provide a child with a free appropriate public education "at public expense," § 1401(9)(A), including specially designed instruction "at no cost to parents," § 1401(29). Parents may seek to enforce this mandate through the federal courts, we conclude, because among the rights they enjoy is the right to a free appropriate public education for their child. Under the countervailing view, which would make a parent's ability to enforce IDEA dependant on certain procedural and reimbursement-related rights, a parent whose disabled child has not received a free appropriate public education would have recourse in the federal courts only under two circumstances: when the parent happens to have some claim related to the procedures employed; and when he or she is able to incur, and has in fact incurred, expenses creating a right to reimbursement. * * *

The potential for injustice in this result is apparent. What is more, we find nothing in the statute to indicate that when Congress required States to provide adequate instruction to a child "at no cost to parents," it intended that only some parents would be able to enforce that mandate. The statute instead takes pains to "ensure that the rights of children with disabilities and parents of such children are protected." * * *

We conclude IDEA grants parents independent, enforceable rights. These rights, which are not limited to certain procedural and reimbursement-related matters, encompass the entitlement to a free appropriate public education for the parents' child.

C

Respondent contends, though, that even under the reasoning we have now explained petitioners cannot prevail without overcoming a further difficulty. Citing our opinion in *Arlington Central School Dist. Bd. of Ed. v. Murphy,* 548 U.S. ----, 126 S.Ct. 2455, 165 L.Ed.2d 526 (2006), respondent argues that statutes passed pursuant to the Spending Clause, such as IDEA, must provide " 'clear notice' " before they can burden a State with some new condition, obligation, or liability. * * * Respondent contends that because IDEA is, at best, ambiguous as to whether it accords parents independent rights, it has failed to provide clear notice of this condition to the States. * * *

Respondent's reliance on *Arlington* is misplaced. In *Arlington* we addressed whether IDEA required States to reimburse experts' fees to prevailing parties in IDEA actions. "[W]hen Congress attaches conditions to a State's acceptance of federal funds," we explained, "the conditions must be set out 'unambiguously.' " 548 U.S., at ----, 126 S.Ct., at 2459 (quoting *Pennhurst State School and Hospital v. Halderman,* 451 U.S. 1, 17, 101 S.Ct. 1531, 67 L.Ed.2d 694 (1981)). The question to be answered in *Arlington,* therefore, was whether IDEA "furnishes clear notice regarding the liability at issue." 548 U.S., at ----, 126 S.Ct., at 2459. We found it did not.

The instant case presents a different issue, one that does not invoke the same rule. Our determination that IDEA grants to parents independent, enforceable rights does not impose any substantive condition or obligation on States they would not otherwise be required by law to observe. The basic measure of monetary recovery, moreover, is not expanded by recognizing that some rights repose in both the parent and the child. * * *

Respondent argues our ruling will, as a practical matter, increase costs borne by the States as they are forced to defend against suits unconstrained by attorneys trained in the law and the rules of ethics. Effects such as these do not suffice to invoke the concerns under the Spending Clause. Furthermore, IDEA does afford relief for the States in certain cases. The Act empowers courts to award attorney's fees to a prevailing educational agency whenever a parent has presented a "complaint or subsequent cause of action . . . for any improper purpose, such as to harass, to cause unnecessary delay, or to needlessly increase the cost of litigation." § 1415(i)(3)(B)(i)(III). This provision allows some relief when a party has proceeded in violation of these standards.

* * *

The judgment of the Court of Appeals is reversed, and the case is remanded for further proceedings consistent with this opinion.

It is so ordered.

Justice SCALIA, with whom Justice THOMAS joins, concurring in the judgment in part and dissenting in part.

* * *

Whether parents may bring suits under the IDEA without a lawyer depends upon the interaction between the IDEA and the general *pro se* provision in the Judiciary Act of 1789. The latter, codified at 28 U.S.C. § 1654, provides that "[i]n all courts of the United States *the parties* may plead and conduct their own cases personally or by counsel." (Emphasis added.) The IDEA's right-to-sue provision, 20 U.S.C. § 1415(i)(2)(A) (2000 ed., Supp. IV), provides that "[a]ny *party aggrieved* by the findings and decision [of a hearing officer] shall have the right to bring a civil action with respect to the [administrative] complaint." (Emphasis added.) Thus, when parents are "parties aggrieved" under the IDEA, they are "parties" within the meaning of 28 U.S.C. § 1654, entitled to sue on their own behalf.

As both parties agree; * * * "party aggrieved" means "[a] party entitled to a remedy; espy., a party whose personal, pecuniary, or property rights have been adversely affected by another person's actions or by a court's decree or judgment," Black's Law Dictionary 1154 (8th ed.2004); see also *ante,* at 2003-2004. This case thus turns on the rights that the IDEA accords to parents, and the concomitant remedies made available to them. Only with respect to such rights and remedies are parents properly viewed as "parties aggrieved," capable of filing their own cases in federal court.

A review of the statutory text makes clear that, as relevant here, the IDEA grants parents only two types of rights. First, under certain circumstances "a court or a hearing officer may require the [school district] to reimburse *the parents*" for private school expenditures "if the court or hearing officer finds that the [school district] had not made a free appropriate public education available to the child." 20 U.S.C. § 1412(a)(10)(C)(ii) (2000 ed., Supp. IV) (emphasis added). Second, parents are accorded a variety of procedural protections, both during the development of their child's individualized education program (IEP) * * *. It is clear that parents may object to procedural violations at the administrative due process hearing, see § 1415(b)(6)(A), and that a hearing officer may provide relief to parents for certain procedural infractions, see § 1415(f)(3)(E)(ii). Because the rights to reimbursement and to the various procedural protections are accorded to parents themselves, they are "parties aggrieved" when those rights are infringed, and may accordingly proceed *pro se* when seeking to vindicate them.

The Court goes further, however, concluding that parents may proceed *pro se* not only when they seek reimbursement or assert procedural violations, but also when they challenge the substantive adequacy of their child's FAPE-so that parents may act without a lawyer *in every IDEA case.* * * * In my view, this sweeps far more broadly than the text allows. Out of this sprawling statute the Court cannot identify even *a single* provision stating that parents have the substantive right to a FAPE. The reason for this is readily understandable: The right to a free appropriate public education obviously inheres in the child, for it is he who receives the education. As the IDEA instructs, participating States must provide a "free appropriate public education . . . to all children with disabilities . . . ." § 1412(a)(1)(A) (2000 ed., Supp. IV). The statute is replete with references to the fact that a FAPE belongs to the child. See, *e.g.,* § 1400(d)(1)(A) (IDEA designed "to ensure that all children with disabilities have available to them a free appropriate public education"); § 1408(a)(2)(C)(i) (referring to "the right of a child" to "receive a free appropriate public education"); § 1411(e)(3)(F)(i) (same); * * * But there is a difference between an *interest* and a statutory *right*. The text of the IDEA makes clear that parents have no *right* to the education itself.

The Court concedes, as it must, that while the IDEA gives parents the right to reimbursement and procedural protection in explicit terms, it does not do so for the supposed right to the education itself. *Ante,* at 2003-2004. The obvious inference to be drawn from the statute's clear and explicit conferral of discrete types of rights upon parents and children, respectively, is that it does not by accident confer the parent-designated rights upon children, or the children-designated rights upon parents. The Court believes, however, that "the statute prevents us from placing too much weight on [this] implicatio[n]." *Ibid.* That conclusion is in error. Nothing in "the statute," undermines the obvious "implication" of Congress's scheme. What the Court relies upon for its conclusion that parents have a substantive right to a FAPE is not the "statutory structure," *ante,* at 2004, but rather the myriad *procedural* guarantees accorded to parents in the administrative process, see *ibid.* But allowing parents, by means of these guarantees, to help shape the contours of their child's education is simply not the same as giving *them* the right to that education. * * * Parents thus have the power, at the administrative stage, to litigate *all* of the various rights under the statute since at that stage they are acting not only on their *own* behalf, but on behalf of *their child* as well. This tells us nothing whatever about *whose* rights they are. The Court's spraying statutory sections about like buckshot cannot create a substantive parental right to education where none exists.

Harkening back to its earlier discussion of the IDEA's "text and structure," * * * the Court announces the startling proposition that, in fact, the "IDEA does not differentiate . . . between the rights accorded to children and the rights accorded to parents." *Ante,* at 2004. If that were so, the Court could have spared us its painful effort to craft a distinctive parental right out of scattered procedural provisions. But of course it is not so. The IDEA quite clearly differentiates between the rights accorded to parents and their children. See *Emery v. Roanoke City School Bd.,* 432 F.3d 294, 299 (C.A.4 2005) ("[P]arents and children are distinct legal entities under the IDEA" (internal quotation marks omitted)). As even petitioners' *amici* agree, "Congress specifically indicated that parents have rights under the Act that are separate from and independent of their children's rights." Brief for Senator Edward M. Kennedy et al. as *Amici Curiae* 18. Does the Court seriously contend that a child has a right to reimbursement, when the statute most definitively provides that if *"the parents* of a child with a disability" enroll that child in private school, "a court . . . may require the [school district] to reimburse *the parents* for the cost of that enrollment"? § 1412(a)(10)(C)(ii) (2000 ed., Supp. IV) (emphasis added); see also Brief for Senator Edward M. Kennedy et al. as *Amici Curiae* 21 ("The right of reimbursement runs to the parents"). Does the Court believe that a child has a procedural right under §§ 1414(d)(1)(C)(i)-(iii) (2000 ed., Supp. IV), which gives *parents* the power to excuse an IEP team member from attending an IEP meeting? The IDEA does not remotely envision communal "family" rights.

The Court believes that because parents must prove the substantive inadequacy of a FAPE before obtaining reimbursement, § 1412(a)(10)(C)(ii) (2000 ed., Supp. IV), and because the suitability of a FAPE may also be at issue when procedural violations are alleged, § 1415(f)(3)(E)(ii), it is "out of accord with the statute's design" to "prevent [parents] from obtaining a judgment mandating that the school district provide their child" with a FAPE. *Ante,* at 2004-2005. That is a total non sequitur. That Congress has required parents to demonstrate the inadequacy of their child's FAPE in order to vindicate their own rights says nothing about whether parents possess an underlying right to education. The Court insists that the right to a FAPE is the right "most fundamental to the Act." *Ante,* at 2003-2004. Undoubtedly so, but that sheds no light upon whom the right belongs to, and hence upon who can sue in their own right. Congress has used the phrase "party aggrieved," and it is this Court's job to apply that language, not to run from it.

The Court further believes that a distinction between parental and child rights will prove difficult to administer. I fail to see why that is so. Before today, the majority of Federal Courts of Appeals to have considered the issue have allowed parents to sue *pro se* with respect to some claims, but not with respect to the denial of a FAPE. See *Mosely v. Board of Ed. of Chicago,* 434 F.3d 527, 532 (C.A.7 2006); *Collinsgru,* 161 F.3d, at 233; *Wenger v. Canastota Central School Dist.,* 146 F.3d 123, 126 (C.A.2 1998)*(per curiam); Devine v. Indian River Cty. School Bd.,* 121 F.3d 576, 581, n. 17 (C.A.11 1997). The Court points to no evidence suggesting that this majority rule has caused any confusion in practice. Nor do I see how it could, since the statute makes clear and easily administrable distinctions between parents' and children's legal entitlements.

Finally, the Court charges that the approach taken by the majority of Courts of Appeals would perpetuate an "injustice," *ante,* at 2005, since parents who do not seek reimbursement or allege procedural violations would be "without a remedy," *ante,* at 2004-2005. That, of course, is not true. They will have the same remedy as all parents who sue to vindicate their children's rights: the power to bring suit, represented by counsel. But even indulging the Court's perception that it is unfair to allow some but not all IDEA parents to proceed *pro se,* that complaint is properly addressed to Congress, which structured the rights as it has, and limited suit to "party aggrieved." And there are good reasons for it to have done so. *Pro se* cases impose unique burdens on lower courts-and on defendants, in this case the schools and school districts that must hire their own lawyers. Since *pro se* complaints are prosecuted essentially for free, without screening by knowledgeable attorneys, they are much more likely to be unmeritorious. * * * Actions seeking reimbursement are less likely to be frivolous, since not many parents will be willing to lay out the money for private education without some solid reason to believe the FAPE was inadequate. And actions alleging procedural violations can ordinarily be disposed of without the intensive record-review that characterizes suits challenging the suitability of a FAPE.

* * *

Notes & Questions

1. Following the *Winkelman* decision, does an attorney in an IDEA case represent the parent or the child? What if there is a conflict between the parent and the child? For example, what if a parent prefers a residential setting, not because of educational needs, but because the child has behavior problems at home? What if a parent prefers a residential setting for cultural, as opposed to educational, reasons (e.g., Deaf culture)?

2. On the issue of who else in the world of parents (e.g., divorced, custodial, adoptive, surrogate, natural/birth parents) may be able to initiate IDEA hearings or claims, *see Taylor v. Vermont Dep't of Educ.,* 313 F.d 768 (2d Cir. 2002).

ꕔ

§ 24.5   Remedies

The IDEA is a federal funding statute, meaning federal funding is conditioned on compliance and funding can be revoked by the federal government if noncompliance is found. However, students with disabilities also have a private right of action to enforce the IDEA through the special education process.

Parents who successfully challenge inadequate IEPs may be entitled to declaratory and injunctive relief directing the state to provide FAPE. They may be entitled to reimbursement for their out-of-pocket expenses, including private school tuition. Sch. Comm. of Town of Burlington v. Dept. of Educ., 471 U.S. 359, 369 (1985).

A student may also be entitled to compensatory educational services to remedy past failures to provide FAPE. *See, e.g.,* Lester H. v. Gilhool, 916 F.2d 865, 873 (3d Cir. 1990); Jefferson County Bd. of Educ. v. Breen, 853 F.2d 853, 857-58 (11th Cir. 1988); Miener v. State of Missouri, 800 F.2d 749, 753 (8th Cir. 1986); *see also* Barnett v. Memphis City Schs., No. 01-5050, 113 F. App'x 124, 128-29 (6th Cir. 2004) (24 year-old high school graduate entitled to compensatory education due to school's past denial of FAPE).

Most courts have found that tort-like monetary damages (for pain and suffering, emotional distress, lost parental wages, etc.) are unavailable under the IDEA. *See, e.g.,* Polera v. Bd. of Educ. of the Newburgh Enlarged City Sch. Dist., 288 F.3d 478, 486 (2d Cir. 2002). However, because the IDEA does not specify that monetary relief is unavailable, 42 U.S.C. § 1983 (2006) could arguably be used to seek monetary damages for violations of the IDEA. The circuits have split on the issue of whether such damages are available when using § 1983 to enforce IDEA rights. In 1984, the Supreme Court held that § 1983 could not be used to enforce rights under the IDEA. Smith v. Robinson, 468 U.S. 992, 1013 (1984). In response, in 1986, Congress enacted § 1415(l) of the IDEA, 20 U.S.C. § 1415(l), as amended, providing that

> Nothing in this chapter shall be construed to restrict or limit the rights, procedures, and remedies available under the Constitution, the Americans with Disabilities Act of 1990, title V of the Rehabilitation Act of 1973, or other Federal laws protecting the rights of children with disabilities, except that before the filing of a civil action under such laws seeking relief that is also available under this subchapter, the procedures under subsections (f) and (g) of this section shall be exhausted to the same extent as would be required had the action been brought under this subchapter.

Id. Therefore, all ADA, Rehabilitation Act, and constitutional claims for which relief is available under the IDEA must go through the IDEA administrative processes. However, this provision has not resolved the question of whether § 1983 may be used to recover monetary damages for IDEA violations.

Courts have rarely permitted recovery of monetary damages in individual special education cases, whether filed under the IDEA, § 1983, the ADA, or the Rehabilitation Act. In most cases, the question is not whether the law provides for damages in a civil suit, but whether the plaintiff has exhausted his administrative remedies. It is clear that a plaintiff cannot avoid the IDEA process simply by seeking damages, rather than reimbursement, compensatory education, or other equitable relief that is available through the IDEA process. *See, e.g.*, Charlie F. v. Bd. of Educ. Of Skokie Sch. Dist. 68, 98 F.3d 989, 992 (7th Cir. 1996) (We read "relief available" to mean relief for the events, condition, or consequences of which the person complains, not necessarily relief of the kind the person prefers.").

On the other hand, where a violation has already been pursued through the IDEA process and an additional remedy is needed that cannot be obtained through the IDEA process, § 1983 may be available. Quackenbush v. Johnson City Sch. Dist., 716 F.2d 141, 148 (2d Cir. 1983). However, the First, Third, Fourth, Sixth, Eighth, and Tenth, circuits have found damages unavailable through § 1983. Nieves-Marquez v. Puerto Rico, 353 F.3d 108, 124-25 (1st Cir. 2003); A.W. v. Jersey City Pub. Sch., 486 F.3d 791, 804 (3d. Cir. 2007); Sellers v. Sch. Bd. of City of Manassas, 141 F.3d 524, 529-32 (4th Cir. 1998); Crocker v. Tenn. Secondary Sch. Athletic Ass'n, 980 F.2d 382, 386-87 (6th Cir. 1992); Heidemann v. Rother, 84 F.3d 1021, 1033 (8th Cir. 1996); Padilla v. Sch. Dist. No. 1, 233 F.3d 1268, 1273 (10th Cir. 2000).

To the extent damages are permitted, sovereign immunity will limit the availability of damages from state governments. Bd. of Trs. of Univ. of Ala. v. Garrett, 531 U.S. 356, 368 (2001). Punitive damages are generally not available against government agencies. Barnes v. Gorman, 536 U.S. 181, 189 (2002).

Parents who prevail in an IDEA administrative or judicial proceeding are entitled to reasonable attorneys' fees, in the court's discretion. 20 U.S.C. § 1415(i)(3)(B) (2006). No multiplier of fees is permitted. *Id.* § 1415(i)(3)(C). Fees may not be awarded for attorney participation in IEP Team meetings. *Id.* § 1415(i)(3)(D)(ii).

In 2006, the Ninth Circuit Court of Appeals in *Ford v. Long Beach Unified School District,* held that parents or guardians who represent their children in IDEA actions are not entitled to attorneys' fees, regardless of whether the parent/guardian is an attorney. Ford v. Long Beach Unified Sch. Dist., 461 F.3d 1087, 1088 (9th Cir. 2006). Whitney and her father, Rodney Ford, filed a complaint in district court, seeking to recover attorneys' fees for two previous settlement agreements with the school district and the legal services provided by Whitney's mother and Rodney's wife, Tania Whiteleather. *Id.* at 1089. The settlement agreements arose out of disputes between the school district and Whitney's parents over the services that should be included in her IEP. *Id.*

The Ninth Circuit, reading the legislative history of the IDEA to indicate Congress likely intended the IDEA to be interpreted like 42 U.S.C. § 1988 (2006) and Title VII of the Civil Rights Act of 1964, followed the Supreme Court's decision in *Kay v. Ehrler*, 499 U.S. 432, 437 (1991). In *Kay*, an attorney appearing *pro se* in a § 1988 claim was not entitled to attorneys' fees. *Id.* In accord, the Ninth Circuit in *Ford* held that like an attorney appearing *pro se*, a child represented by his or her parent, regardless of whether that parent is an attorney, does not benefit from the skill and tact of an independent third party. *Ford*, 461 F.3d at 1091. Additionally, like in *Kay*, awarding attorneys' fees to parents who represent their children would create a disincentive to all parents who are faced with the opportunity to employ outside counsel. *Id.*

According to the 1997 amendments, attorneys' fees are not available to a prevailing school district. 20 U.S.C. § 1415(i)(3)(B) (2006) ("the court, in its discretion, may award reasonable attorneys' fees as part of the costs to the parents of a child with a disability who is the prevailing party"). However, as discussed below, the IDEA 2004 permits the court to grant attorney fees to prevailing school districts. *Id.* § 1415(3)(B)(i)(II)-(III).

In 2006, the Supreme Court heard *Arlington Central School District v. Murphy*, 402 F.3d 332 (2d Cir. 2005), 74 U.S.L.W. 3379 (U.S. Jan. 6, 2006) (No. 05-18), on the issue whether parents who prevail in special education cases may be reimbursed for the costs of their experts and/or educational consultants.

ം

ARLINGTON CENTRAL SCHOOL DISTRICT BOARD OF EDUCATION v. MURPHY

Supreme Court of the United States, 2006
548 U.S. 291

Justice ALITO delivered the opinion of the Court.

The Individuals with Disabilities Education Act (IDEA or Act) provides that a court "may award reasonable attorneys' fees as part of the costs" to parents who prevail in an action brought under the Act. 20 U.S.C. § 1415(i)(3)(B). We granted certiorari to decide whether this fee-shifting provision authorizes prevailing parents to recover fees for services rendered by experts in IDEA actions. * * *

I

Respondents Pearl and Theodore Murphy filed an action under the IDEA on behalf of their son, Joseph Murphy, seeking to require petitioner Arlington Central School District Board of Education to pay for their son's private school tuition for specified school years. Respondents prevailed in the District Court, 86 F.Supp.2d 354 (S.D.N.Y. 2000), and the Court of Appeals for the Second Circuit affirmed, 297 F. 3d 195 (2002).

As prevailing parents, respondents then sought $29,350 in fees for the services of an educational consultant, Marilyn Arons, who assisted respondents throughout the IDEA proceedings. The District Court granted respondents' request in part. It held that only the value of Arons' time spent between the hearing request and the ruling in respondents' favor could properly be considered charges incurred in an "action or proceeding brought" under the Act, see 20 U.S.C. § 1415(i)(3)(B). 2003 WL 21694398, *9 (S.D.N.Y. July 22, 2003). This reduced the maximum recovery to $8,650. The District Court also held that Arons, a nonlawyer, could be compensated only for time spent on expert consulting services, not for time spent on legal representation, *id.*, at *4, but it concluded that all the relevant time could be characterized as falling within the compensable category, and thus allowed compensation for the full $8,650, *id.*, at *10.

The Court of Appeals for the Second Circuit affirmed. 402 F. 3d 332 (2005). * * *

* * *

II

Our resolution of the question presented in this case is guided by the fact that Congress enacted the IDEA pursuant to the Spending Clause. U. S. Const., Art. I, § 8, cl. 1 * * * Like its statutory predecessor, the IDEA provides federal funds to assist state and local agencies in educating children with disabilities "and conditions such funding upon a State's compliance with extensive goals and procedures." *Board of Ed. of Hendrick Hudson Central School Dist., Westchester Cty. v. Rowley*, 458 U.S. 176, 179 (1982).

Congress has broad power to set the terms on which it disburses federal money to the States, see, *e.g.*, *South Dakota v. Dole*, 483 U.S. 203, 206-207 (1987), but when Congress attaches conditions to a State's acceptance of federal funds, the conditions must be set out "unambiguously," see *Pennhurst State School and Hospital v. Halderman*, 451 U.S. 1, 17 (1981); *Rowley, supra*, at 204, n.26. "[L]egislation enacted pursuant to the spending power is much in the nature of a contract," and therefore, to be bound by "federally imposed conditions," recipients of federal funds must accept them "voluntarily and knowingly." *Pennhurst*, 451 U.S., at 17. States cannot knowingly accept conditions of which they are "unaware" or which they are "unable to ascertain." *Ibid.* Thus, in the present case, we must view the IDEA from the perspective of a state official who is engaged in the process of deciding whether the State should accept IDEA funds and the obligations that go with those funds. We must ask whether such a state official would clearly understand that one of the obligations of the Act is the obligation to compensate prevailing parents for expert fees. In other words, we must ask whether the IDEA furnishes clear notice regarding the liability at issue in this case.

III

A

In considering whether the IDEA provides clear notice, we begin with the text. We have "stated time and again that courts must presume that a legislature says in a statute what it means and means in a statute what it says there." *Connecticut Nat. Bank v. Germain*, 503 U.S. 249, 253-254 (1992). * * *

The governing provision of the IDEA, 20 U.S.C. § 1415(i)(3)(B), provides that "[i]n any action or proceeding brought under this section, the court, in its discretion, may award reasonable attorneys' fees as part of the costs" to the parents of "a child with a disability" who is the "prevailing party." While this provision provides for an award of "reasonable attorneys' fees," this provision does not even hint that acceptance of IDEA funds makes a State responsible for reimbursing prevailing parents for services rendered by experts.

Respondents contend that we should interpret the term "costs" in accordance with its meaning in ordinary usage and that § 1415(i)(3)(B) should therefore be read to "authorize reimbursement of all costs parents incur in IDEA proceedings, including expert costs." * * *

This argument has multiple flaws. For one thing, as the Court of Appeals in this case acknowledged, " 'costs' is a term of art that generally does not include expert fees." 402 F. 3d, at 336. The use of this term of art, rather than a term such as "expenses," strongly suggests that § 1415(i)(3)(B) was not meant to be an open-ended provision that makes participating States liable for all expenses incurred by prevailing parents in connection with an IDEA case – for example, travel and lodging expenses or lost wages due to time taken off from work. Moreover, contrary to respondents' suggestion, § 1415(i)(3)(B) does not say that a court may award "costs" to prevailing parents; rather, it says that a court may award reasonable attorney's fees "as part of the costs" to prevailing parents. This language simply adds reasonable attorney's fees incurred by prevailing parents to the list of costs that prevailing parents are otherwise entitled to recover. * * * Thus, the text of 20 U.S.C. § 1415(i)(3)(B) does not authorize an award of any additional expert fees, and it certainly fails to provide the clear notice that is required under the Spending Clause.

Other provisions of the IDEA point strongly in the same direction. While authorizing the award of reasonable attorney's fees, the Act contains detailed provisions that are designed to ensure that such awards are indeed reasonable. See §§ 1415(i)(3)(C)-(G). The absence of any comparable provisions relating to expert fees strongly suggests that recovery of expert fees is not authorized. Moreover, the lack of any reference to expert fees in § 1415(d)(2) gives rise to a similar inference. This provision, which generally requires that parents receive "a full explanation of the procedural safeguards" available under § 1415 and refers expressly to "attorneys' fees," makes no mention of expert fees.

B

Respondents contend that their interpretation of § 1415(i)(3)(B) is supported by a provision of the Handicapped Children's Protection Act of 1986 that required the General Accounting Office (GAO) to collect certain data, § 4(b)(3), 100 Stat. 797 (hereinafter GAO study provision), but this provision is of little significance for present purposes. The GAO study provision directed the Comptroller General, acting through the GAO, to compile data on, among other things: "(A) the specific amount of attorneys' fees, costs, and expenses awarded to the prevailing party" in IDEA cases for a particular period of time, and (B) "the number of hours spent by personnel, including attorneys and consultants, involved in the action or proceeding, and expenses incurred by the parents and the State educational agency and local educational agency." *Id.*, at 797-798.

Subparagraph (A) would provide some support for respondents' position if it directed the GAO to compile data on awards to prevailing parties of the expense of hiring consultants, but that is not what subparagraph (A) says. Subparagraph (A) makes no mention of consultants or experts or their fees.[1]

Subparagraph (B) similarly does not help respondents. Subparagraph (B), which directs the GAO to study "the number of hours spent [in IDEA cases] by personnel, including ... consultants," says nothing about the award of fees to such consultants. Just because Congress directed the GAO to compile statistics on the hours spent by consultants in IDEA cases, it does not follow that Congress meant for

---

[1]   Because subparagraph (A) refers to both "costs" and "expenses" awarded to prevailing parties and because it is generally presumed that statutory language is not superfluous, it could be argued that this provision manifests the expectation that prevailing parties would be awarded certain "expenses" not included in the list of "costs" set out in 28 U.S.C. § 1920 and that expert fees were intended to be among these unenumerated "expenses." This argument fails because, whatever expectation this language might seem to evidence, the fact remains that neither 20 U.S.C. § 1415 nor any other provision of the IDEA authorizes the award of any "expenses" other than "costs." Recognizing this, respondents argue not that they are entitled to recover "expenses" that are not "costs," but that expert fees *are* recoverable "costs." As a result, the reference to awards of both "expenses" and "costs" does not support respondents' position. The reference to "expenses" may relate to IDEA actions brought in state court, § 1415(i)(2)(A), where "expenses" other than "costs" might be receivable. Or the reference may be surplusage. While it is generally presumed that statutes do not contain surplusage, instances of surplusage are not unknown.

States to compensate prevailing parties for the fees billed by these consultants.

Respondents maintain that "Congress' direction to the GAO would be inexplicable if Congress did not anticipate that the expenses for 'consultants' would be recoverable," * * * but this is incorrect. There are many reasons why Congress might have wanted the GAO to gather data on expenses that were not to be taxed as costs. Knowing the costs incurred by IDEA litigants might be useful in considering future procedural amendments (which might affect these costs) or a future amendment regarding fee shifting. And, in fact, it is apparent that the GAO study provision covered expenses that could not be taxed as costs. For example, the GAO was instructed to compile statistics on the hours spent by all attorneys involved in an IDEA action or proceeding, even though the Act did not provide for the recovery of attorney's fees by a prevailing state or local educational agency. * * * Similarly, the GAO was directed to compile data on "expenses incurred by the parents," not just those parents who prevail and are thus eligible to recover taxed costs.

In sum, the terms of the IDEA overwhelmingly support the conclusion that prevailing parents may not recover the costs of experts or consultants. Certainly the terms of the IDEA fail to provide the clear notice that would be needed to attach such a condition to a State's receipt of IDEA funds.

IV

Thus far, we have considered only the text of the IDEA, but perhaps the strongest support for our interpretation of the IDEA is supplied by our decisions and reasoning in *Crawford Fitting*, 482 U.S. 437, and *Casey*, 499 U.S. 83. In light of those decisions, we do not see how it can be said that the IDEA gives a State unambiguous notice regarding liability for expert fees.

In *Crawford Fitting*, the Court rejected an argument very similar to respondents' argument that the term "costs" in § 1415(i)(3)(B) should be construed as an open-ended reference to prevailing parents' expenses. It was argued in *Crawford Fitting* that Federal Rule of Civil Procedure 54(d), which provides for the award of "costs" to a prevailing party, authorizes the award of costs not listed in 28 U.S.C. § 1821. 482 U.S., at 439. The Court held, however, that Rule 54(d) does not give a district judge "discretion to tax whatever costs may seem appropriate"; rather, the term "costs" in Rule 54(d) is defined by the list set out in § 1920. *Id.*, at 441. Because the recovery of witness fees, see § 1920(3), is strictly limited by § 1821, the Court observed, a broader interpretation of Rule 54(d) would mean that the Rule implicitly effected a partial repeal of those provisions. *Id.*, at 442. But, the Court warned, "[w]e will not lightly infer that Congress has repealed §§ 1920 and 1821, either through Rule 54(d) or any other provision not referring explicitly to witness fees." *Id.*, at 445.

The reasoning of *Crawford Fitting* strongly supports the conclusion that the term "costs" in 20 U.S.C. § 1415(i)(3)(B), like the same term in Rule 54(d), is defined by the categories of expenses enumerated in 28 U.S.C. § 1920. This conclusion is buttressed by the principle, recognized in *Crawford Fitting*, that no statute will be construed as authorizing the taxation of witness fees as costs unless the statute "refer[s] explicitly to witness fees." 482 U.S., at 445 * * *.

Our decision in *Casey* confirms even more dramatically that the IDEA does not authorize an award of expert fees. In *Casey*, as noted above, we interpreted a fee-shifting provision, 42 U.S.C. § 1988, the relevant wording of which was virtually identical to the wording of 20 U.S.C. § 1415(i)(3)(B). * * * We held that § 1988 did not empower a district court to award expert fees to a prevailing party. *Casey, supra*, at 102. To decide in favor of respondents here, we would have to interpret the virtually identical language in 20 U.S.C. § 1415 as having exactly the opposite meaning. Indeed, we would have to go further and hold that the relevant language in the IDEA *unambiguously means* exactly the opposite of what the nearly identical language in 42 U.S.C. § 1988 was held to mean in *Casey*.

* * *

V

Respondents make several arguments that are not based on the text of the IDEA, but these arguments do not show that the IDEA provides clear notice regarding the award of expert fees.

Respondents argue that their interpretation of the IDEA furthers the Act's overarching goal of "ensur[ing] that all children with disabilities have available to them a free appropriate public education," 20 U.S.C. § 1400(d)(1)(A) as well as the goal of "safeguard[ing] the rights of parents to challenge school decisions that adversely affect their child." * * * These goals, however, are too general to provide much support for respondents' reading of the terms of the IDEA. The IDEA obviously does not seek to promote these goals at the expense of all other considerations, including fiscal considerations. Because the IDEA is not intended in all instances to further the broad goals identified by the respondents at the expense of fiscal considerations, the goals cited by respondents do little to bolster their argument on the narrow question presented here. * * *

Finally, respondents vigorously argue that Congress clearly intended for prevailing parents to be compensated for expert fees. They rely on the legislative history of § 1415 and in particular on the following statement * * * "The conferees intend that the term 'attorneys' fees as part of the costs' include reasonable expenses and fees of expert witnesses and the reasonable costs of any test or evaluation which is found to be necessary for the preparation of the . . . case." H. R. Conf. Rep. No. 99-687, at 5.

Whatever weight this legislative history would merit in another context, it is not sufficient here. Putting the legislative history aside, we see virtually no support for respondents' position. Under these circumstances, where everything other than the legislative history overwhelming suggests that expert fees may not be recovered, the legislative history is simply not enough. In a Spending Clause case, the key is not what a majority of the Members of both Houses intend but what the States are clearly told regarding the conditions that go along with the acceptance of those funds. Here, in the face of the unambiguous text of the IDEA and the reasoning in *Crawford Fitting* and *Casey*, we cannot say that the legislative history on which respondents rely is sufficient to provide the requisite fair notice.

* * *

We reverse the judgment of the Court of Appeals for the Second Circuit and remand the case for further proceedings consistent with this opinion.

It is so ordered.

Justice GINSBURG, concurring in part and concurring in the judgment.

I agree, in the main, with the Court's resolution of this case, but part ways with the Court's opinion in one respect. The Court extracts from *Pennhurst State School and Hospital v. Halderman*, 451 U.S. 1, 17 (1981), a "clear notice" requirement, and deems it applicable in this case because Congress enacted the Individuals with Disabilities Education Act (IDEA), as it did the legislation at issue in *Pennhurst*, pursuant to the Spending Clause. * * * That extraction, in my judgment, is unwarranted. *Pennhurst*'s "clear notice" requirement should not be unmoored from its context. The Court there confronted a plea to impose "an unexpected condition for compliance – a new [programmatic] obligation for participating States." *Bell v. New Jersey*, 461 U.S. 773, 790, n.17 (1983). The controversy here is lower key: It concerns not the educational programs IDEA directs school districts to provide, but "the remedies available against a noncomplying [district]." *Ibid*; see * * * (Breyer, J., dissenting).

The Court's repeated references to a Spending Clause derived "clear notice" requirement * * * are questionable on other grounds as well. For one thing, IDEA was enacted not only pursuant to Congress' Spending Clause authority, but also pursuant to § 5 of the Fourteenth Amendment. See *Smith v. Robinson*, 468 U.S. 992, 1009 (1984) (IDEA's predecessor, the Education of the Handicapped Act, was "set up by Congress to aid the States in complying with their constitutional obligations to provide public education for handicapped children."). Furthermore, no "clear notice" prop is needed in this case given the twin pillars on which the Court's judgment securely rests. First, as the Court explains, * * * the specific, attorneys'-

fees-oriented, provisions of IDEA, *i.e.*, 20 U.S.C. § 1415(i)(3)(B)-(G); § 1415(d)(2)(L), "overwhelmingly support the conclusion that prevailing parents may not recover the costs of experts or consultants[.]" * * * Second, as the Court develops, prior decisions closely in point "strongly suppor[t]," even "confir[m] . . . dramatically," today's holding that IDEA trains on attorneys' fees and does not authorize an award covering amounts paid or payable for the services of an educational consultant. * * * (citing *Crawford Fitting Co. v. J. T. Gibbons, Inc.*, 482 U.S. 437 (1987), and *West Virginia Univ. Hospitals, Inc. v. Casey*, 499 U.S. 83 (1991)).

* * *

Justice BREYER, with whom Justice STEVENS and Justice SOUTER join, dissenting.

* * * Unlike the Court, I believe that the word "costs" includes, and authorizes payment of, the costs of experts. The word "costs" does not define its own scope. Neither does the phrase "attorneys' fees as part of costs." But Members of Congress did make clear their intent by, among other things, approving a Conference Report that specified that "the term 'attorneys' fees as part of the costs' include[s] reasonable expenses of expert witnesses and reasonable costs of any test or evaluation which is found to be necessary for the preparation of the parent or guardian's case in the action or proceeding." H. R. Conf. Rep. No. 99-687, p. 5 (1986) * * *

There are two strong reasons for interpreting the statutory phrase to include the award of expert fees. First, that is what Congress said it intended by the phrase. Second, that interpretation furthers the IDEA's statutorily defined purposes.

A

Congress added the IDEA's cost-shifting provision when it enacted the Handicapped Children's Protection Act of 1986 (HCPA), 100 Stat. 796 * * *

[The dissent reviews House and Senate changing versions of the HCPA]

* * *

Members of the House and Senate (including all of the primary sponsors of the HCPA) then met in conference to work out certain differences. At the conclusion of those negotiations, they produced a Conference Report, which contained the text of the agreed-upon bill and a "Joint Explanatory Statement of the Committee of the Conference." See H. R. Conf. Rep. No. 99-687 (1986) * * *. The Conference * * * accepted (with minor changes) the cost-shifting provisions provided in both the Senate and House versions. The conferees explained:

"With slightly different wording, both the Senate bill and the House amendment provide for the awarding of attorneys' fees in addition to costs. The Senate recedes to the House and the House recedes to the Senate with an amendment clarifying that 'the court, in its discretion, may award reasonable attorneys' fees as part of the costs . . . .' This change in wording incorporates the Supreme Court['s] *Marek v. Chesny* decision [473 U. S 1 (1985)]. *The conferees intend that the term 'attorneys' fees as part of the costs' include reasonable expenses and fees of expert witnesses and the reasonable costs of any test or evaluation which is found to be necessary for the preparation of the parent or guardian's case in the action or proceeding, as well as traditional costs incurred in the course of litigating a case."* *Id.*, at 5 (emphasis added; citation omitted).

The Conference Report was returned to the Senate and the House. A motion was put to each to adopt the Conference Report, and both the Senate and the House agreed to the Conference Report by voice votes. * * * No objection was raised to the Conference Report's statement that the cost-shifting provision was intended to authorize expert costs. * * * And every Senator and Representative that took the floor preceding the votes voiced his strong support for the Conference Report. 132 Cong. Rec. 16823-16825 (1986) (Senate); *id.*, at 17607-17612 (House). The upshot is that Members of both Houses of Congress voted to adopt both the statutory text before us and the Conference Report that made clear that the statute's words include the expert costs here in question.

[Section B omitted, discussing the award of expert fees as furthering the IDEA's statutorily defined purposes]

* * *

II

The majority makes essentially three arguments against this interpretation. It says that the statute's purpose and "legislative history is simply not enough" to overcome: (1) the fact that this is a Spending Clause case; (2) the text of the statute; and (3) our prior cases which hold that the term "costs" does not include expert costs. * * * I do not find these arguments convincing.

A

At the outset the majority says that it "is guided by the fact that Congress enacted the IDEA pursuant to the Spending Clause." * * * "In a Spending Clause case," the majority adds, "the key is not what a majority of the Members of both Houses intend but what the States are clearly told regarding the conditions that go along with the acceptance of those funds." * * *

I agree that the statute on its face does not *clearly* tell the States that they must pay expert fees to prevailing parents. But I do not agree that the majority has posed the right question. For one thing, we have repeatedly examined the nature and extent of the financial burdens that the IDEA imposes without reference to the Spending Clause or any "clear-statement rule." See, *e.g.*, *Burlington*, *supra*, at 369 (private school fees); *Carter*, *supra*, at 13 (same); *Smith*, 468 U.S., at 1010-1011 (attorneys' fees); *Cedar Rapids Community School Dist. v. Garret F.*, 526 U.S. 66, 76-79 (1999) (continuous nursing service); but see *id.*, at 83 (Thomas, J., joined by Kennedy, J., dissenting). Those cases did not ask whether the statute "furnishes clear notice" to the affirmative obligation or liability at issue.

For another thing, neither Pennhurst nor any other case suggests that *every spending detail* of a Spending Clause statute must be spelled out with unusual clarity. To the contrary, we have held that *Pennhurst*'s requirement that Congress "unambiguously" set out "a condition on the grant of federal money" does *not* necessarily apply to legislation setting forth "*the remedies available against a noncomplying State*." *Bell v. New Jersey*, 461 U.S. 773, 790, n.17 (1983) (emphasis added) (rejecting *Pennhurst*-based argument that Elementary and Secondary Education Act of 1965 did not unambiguously provide that the Secretary could recover federal funds that are misused by a State). We have added that Pennhurst does not require Congress "specifically" to "identify" and "proscribe each condition in [Spending Clause] legislation." *Jackson v. Birmingham Bd. of Ed.*, 544 U.S. 167, 183 (2005) (rejecting argument that Pennhurst precluded interpreting Title IX's private cause of action to encompass retaliation (internal quotation marks and alterations omitted)); see also *Bennett v. Kentucky Dept. of Ed.*, 470 U.S. 656, 665-666 (1985). And we have denied any implication that "suits under Spending Clause legislation are suits in contract, or that contract-law principles apply to all issues that they raise." *Barnes v. Gorman*, 536 U.S. 181, 188-189, n.2 (2002) (emphasis added).

These statements and holdings are not surprising. After all, the basic objective of *Pennhurst*'s clear-statement requirement does not demand textual clarity in respect to every detail. That is because ambiguity about the precise nature of a statutory program's details – particularly where they are of a kind that States might have anticipated – is rarely relevant to the basic question: Would the States have accepted the Federal Government's funds *had they only known* the nature of the accompanying conditions? Often, the later filling-in of details through judicial interpretation will not lead one to wonder whether funding recipients would have agreed to enter the basic program at all. Given the nature of such details, it is clear that the States would have entered the program regardless. At the same time, to view each statutory detail of a highly complex federal/state program (involving say, transportation, schools, the environment) simply through the lens of linguistic clarity, rather than to assess its meanings in terms of basic legislative purpose, is to risk a set of judicial interpretations that can prevent the program, overall, from achieving its basic objectives or that might well reduce a program in its details to incoherence.

This case is about just such a detail. Permitting parents to recover expert fees will not lead to awards of "indeterminate magnitude, untethered to compensable harm" and consequently will not "pose a concern that recipients of federal funding could not reasonably have anticipated." *Barnes*, 536 U.S., at 191 (Souter, J., joined by O'Connor, J., concurring) (citation and internal quotation marks omitted). Unlike, say, punitive damages, an award of costs to expert parties is neither "unorthodox" nor "indeterminate," and thus does not throw into doubt whether the States would have entered into the program. *Id.*, at 188. If determinations as to whether the IDEA requires States to provide continuing nursing services, *Cedar Rapids*, *supra*, or reimbursement for private school tuition, *Burlington*, *supra*, do not call for linguistic clarity, then the precise content of recoverable "costs" does not call for such clarity here *a fortiori*.

B

If the Court believes that the statute's language is unambiguous, I must disagree. The provision at issue says that a court "may award reasonable attorneys' fees as part of the costs" to parents who prevail in an action brought under the Act. 20 U.S.C.A. § 1415(i)(3)(B) (Supp. 2006). The statute neither defines the word "costs" nor points to any other source of law for a definition. And the word "costs," alone, says nothing at all about which costs falls within its scope.

Neither does the statutory phrase – "as part of the costs to the parents of a child with a disability who is the prevailing party" – taken in its entirety unambiguously foreclose an award of expert fees. I agree that, read literally, that provision does not clearly grant authority to award any costs at all. And one might read it, as the Court does, as referencing another federal statute, 28 U.S.C. § 1920, which provides that authority. * * * But such a reading is not inevitable. The provision (indeed, the entire Act) says nothing about that other statute. And one can, consistent with the language, read the provision as both embodying a general authority to award costs while also specifying the inclusion of "reasonable attorneys' fees" as part of those costs (as saying, for example, that a court "may award reasonable attorneys' fees as part of [a] costs [award]").

* * *

C

The majority's most persuasive argument does not focus on either the Spending Clause or lack of statutory ambiguity. * * *

I am perfectly willing to assume that the majority is correct about the traditional scope of the word "costs." In two cases this Court has held that the word "costs" is limited to the list set forth in 28 U.S.C. § 1920 and does not include fees paid to experts. See *Crawford Fitting Co. v. J. T. Gibbons, Inc.*, 482 U.S. 437 (1987) (interpreting Fed. Rule Civ. Proc. 54(d)); *West Virginia Univ. Hospitals, Inc. v. Casey*, 499 U.S. 83 (1991) (interpreting 42 U.S.C. § 1988 (1988 ed.)). But Congress is free to redefine terms of art. See, *e.g.*, *Casey*, 499 U.S., at 88-90 (citing examples of statutes that shift " 'costs of litigation (including . . . expert witness fees)' "). And we have suggested that it might well do so through a statutory provision worded in a manner similar to the statute here * * *

Regardless, here the statute itself indicates that Congress did not intend to use the word "costs" as a term of art. The HCPA, which added the cost-shifting provision (in § 2) to the IDEA, also added another provision (in § 4) directing the GAO to "conduct a study of the impact of the amendments to the [IDEA] made by section 2" over a 3 year period following the Act's effective date. § 4(a), 100 Stat. 797. To determine the fiscal impact of § 2 (the cost-shifting provision), § 4 ordered the GAO to submit a report to Congress containing, among other things, the following information:

> "Data, for a geographically representative select sample of States, indicating (A) *the specific amount of attorneys' fees, costs, and expenses awarded to the prevailing party*, in each action and proceeding under [§ 2] from the date of the enactment of this Act through fiscal year 1988, *and* the range of such *fees, costs and expenses* awarded in the actions and proceedings under such section, categorized by type of complaint and (B) for the same sample as in (A) *the number of hours spent by personnel, including attorneys and consultants*, involved in the action or proceeding, and expenses incurred by the parents and the State educational agency and local educational agency." § 4(b)(3), *id.*, at 797-798 (emphasis added).

If Congress intended the word "costs" in § 2 to authorize an award of only those costs listed in the federal cost statute, why did it use the word "expenses" in § 4(b)(3)(A) as part of the "amount awarded to the prevailing party"? When used as a term of art, after all, "costs" does not cover expenses. Nor does the federal costs statute cover any expenses – at least not any that Congress could have wanted the GAO to study. Cf. 28 U.S.C. § 1920 (referring only once to "expenses," and doing so solely to refer to special interpretation services provided in actions initiated by the United States).

Further, why did Congress, when asking the GAO (in the statute itself) to study the "numbers of hours spent by personnel" include among those personnel both attorneys "*and consultants*"? Who but experts could those consultants be? Why would Congress want the GAO to study the hours that those experts "spent," unless it thought that it would help keep track of the "costs" that the statute imposed?

Of course, one might, through speculation, find other answers to these questions. One might, for example, imagine that Congress wanted the GAO to study the expenses that payment of expert fees engendered in state-court proceedings where state, but not federal, law requires that "'expenses' other than 'costs' might be receivable." * * * Or one might think that the word "expenses" is surplusage. *Ante*, at * * * n.1; but see *Duncan v. Walker*, 533 U.S. 167, 174 (2001) (expressing Court's "'reluctan[ce] to treat statutory terms as surplusage in any setting,'" but especially when they play "a pivotal role in the statutory scheme"). Or one might believe that Congress was interested in the hours these experts spent, but not in the fees they obtained. * * * But these answers are not necessarily consistent with the purpose of the GAO study provision, a purpose revealed by the language of the provision and its position in the statute. Its placement and its reference to § 2 indicate that Congress ordered the study to help it keep track of the magnitude of the reimbursements that an earlier part of the new statute (namely, § 2) mandated. * * * And the *only* reimbursement requirement that § 2 mandates is the payment of "costs."

* * *

For these reasons, I respectfully dissent.

Notes & Questions

1. During oral argument, Chief Justice Roberts expressed caution, noting that if the IDEA's use of the term "costs" is ambiguous (and the Court affirmed the ruling granting a prevailing party expert fees), a larger issue regarding the restrictive nature of the spending clause legislation (specifically, that statutes arising from the spending clause are narrowly construed) would be raised. Peter W.D. Wright, U.S. Supreme Court Hears Oral Arguments in *Arlington v. Murphy*, Wrightslaw, Apr. 24, 2006, http://www.wrightslaw.com/news/06/murphy.oral.argument.htm.

Ultimately, the majority invoked the Spending Clause to support its argument "when Congress attaches conditions to a State's acceptance of federal funds, the conditions must be set out 'unambiguously.'" Arlington Cent. Sch. Dist. Bd. of Educ. v. Murphy, 548 U.S. 291, 296 (2006). Do you agree? Is reimbursement of expert witness fees the type of "detail" that "must be spelled out with unusual clarity? Murphy, 548 U.S. at 317 (Breyer, J. dissenting). Is doing so necessary? *See id.* ("*Pennhurst* does not require Congress 'specifically' to 'identify' and 'proscribe *each* condition in [Spending Clause] legislation.") (citing Jackson v. Birmingham Bd. of Ed., 544 U. S. 167, 183 (2005)).

2. Was the IDEA's predecessor (The Education for All Handicapped Children Act) enacted more in contemplation of § 5 of the

Fourteenth Amendment? Murphy, 548 U.S. at 304-07 (Ginsburg, J. concurring).

3. Are what Congress contemplated as reimbursable "costs" clearly defined by the Act? As a term of art? Murphy, 548 U.S. at 296-300.

4. In the majority opinion does Justice Alito acknowledge that the legislative history of the IDEA supports a ruling that "costs" can include reimbursement for expert fees? H.R. Conf. Rep. No. 99-687 at 5.

5. See also Blackman v. District of Columbia, 633 F.3d 1088 (D.C. Cir. 2010) (awarding plaintiff's attorneys' fees under the IDEA in consolidated class actions against the District of Columbia, the court held that the $4000 fee cap under the 2006 District of Columbia Appropriations Act § 122 was not applicable because, inter alia, the "evident intent" of the statute was to address individual IDEA proceedings, rather than class actions).

Among the remedies for denial of appropriate services is compensatory services. 34 C.F.R. § 300.151(b)(1)(2012). Compensatory education is "an equitable remedy that the court may award in crafting appropriate relief." Friendship Edison Pub. Charter Sch. Collegiate Campus v. Nesbitt, 669 F.Supp.2d 80, 84 (D.D.C. 2009) (citing Parents of Student W. v. Puyallup Sch. Dist. No. 3, 31 F.3d 1489, 1497 (9th Cir. 1994)). In Friendship Edison, a plaintiff requested that additional time be added to the tutoring hours he had been awarded in compensatory education, and the defendant school district argued that the extra hours should be denied because the method for calculating the award was arbitrary. Id. The district court for the District of Columbia held that a formula-based method for calculating the amount of compensatory education to be awarded is appropriate if it incorporates a qualitative approach. Id. at 84-85. Such a calculation would be "reasonably calculated to provide the educational benefits that likely would have accrued from special education services the school district should have supplied in the first place." Id. (citing Reid v. District of Columbia, 401 F.3d 516 (D.C. Cir. 2005)).

Part 7

Discrimination In Housing
Analysis

Chapter 25 FAIR HOUSING ACT
§ 25.1 Overview
Chapter 26 COVERAGE
§ 26.1 Single-Family House And Living Quarters Exemption
§ 26.2 Maximum Occupancy Exemptions
Chapter 27 DISCRIMINATION
§ 27.1 Failure To Allow Reasonable Modifications To Premises Or To
Make Reasonable Accommodations To Rules, Policies, Practices,
Or Services
§ 27.2 Proving Discrimination
§ 27.3 Design And Construction Of Dwellings
Chapter 28 ENFORCEMENT AND REMEDIES

Chapter 25 FAIR HOUSING ACT

§ 25.1 Overview

Before 1988, the Fair Housing Act prevented discrimination on the basis of race, color, religion, or national origin. In 1988, Congress introduced a series of amendments to the Fair Housing Act, known as the "Fair Housing Amendments Act of 1988" (FHAA). The Fair Housing Amendments Act makes it unlawful to discriminate in the sale or rental of housing on the basis of disability.

The FHAA provides that it shall be unlawful:

(1)   To discriminate in the sale or rental, or to otherwise make unavailable or deny, a dwelling to any buyer or renter because of a handicap of –

    (A)   that buyer or renter,

    (B)   a person residing in or intending to reside in that dwelling after it is so sold, rented, or made available; or

    (C)   any person associated with that buyer or renter.

(2)   To discriminate against any person in the terms, conditions, or privileges of a sale or rental of a dwelling, or in the provision of services or facilities in connection with such dwelling, because of the handicap of –

    (A)   that person; or

(B)   a person residing in or intending to reside in that dwelling after it is so sold, rented, or made available; or

(C)   any person associated with that person.

42 U.S.C. § 3604(f) (2006).

Note at the outset there are two elements of the FHAA that create expansive coverage. First, it is not just discrimination against people with disabilities that is prohibited. Rather, it is also unlawful to discriminate against "any person associated" with a buyer or renter with a disability. Second, unlike most previous federal disability laws, the FHAA applies to private discrimination, as opposed to just discrimination in state, federal, and local housing.

Despite these two provisions (and in some cases because of them), courts have grappled with many substantive issues under the FHAA. This Part considers those issues in turn.

Chapter 26 COVERAGE

Generally, the Fair Housing Act, as amended, applies to a broad range of transactions and individuals relating to and affecting the housing and rental market, including rental and sale transactions, 42 U.S.C. § 3604(f) (2006), advertisements, *id.* § 3604(c), real-estate related and broker related services, *id.* § 3605, and zoning ordinances. City of Edmonds v. Oxford House, Inc., 514 U.S. 725 (1995).

The Act imposes obligations on most public and private housing providers, as well as agents, brokers, lenders, and others involved in the sale or rental of housing. *Id.* § 3605. But there are several important categorical exemptions to coverage under the FHAA.

§ 26.1 Single-Family House And Living Quarters Exemption

While the Fair Housing Act generally applies to individuals selling or renting housing, there are exceptions. The Fair Housing Act provides that, with the exception of the prohibition on discriminatory advertising, a single family home that is being sold or rented by an individual private owner is not covered:

> *Provided*, That such ... owner does not own more than three such single family houses at any one time: *Provided further,* That [if the owner is] not residing in [the] house at the time of such sale or ... was not the most recent resident of such house prior to such sale, the exemption ... shall apply only with respect to one such sale within any twenty-four month period: *Provided further*, That such ... owner does not own any interest in, ... proceeds from the sale or rental of, more than three such single-family houses at any one time: *Provided further,* That such house is sold or rented (A) without the use in any manner of the sales or rental facilities or ... services of any real estate broker, agent, or salesman, or of ... any person in the business of selling or renting dwellings, or of any employee or agent of any such broker, agent, salesman, or person and (B) without the publication, posting or mailing, after notice, of any advertisement or written notice in violation of section 3604(c) of this title . . . .

Id. § 3603(b)(1). Also exempted from coverage are:

> rooms or units in dwellings containing living quarters occupied or intended to be occupied by no more than four families living independently of each other, if the owner actually maintains and occupies one of such living quarters as his residence.

Id. § 3603(b)(2).

The following is an example of the application of this exception in a case involving alleged disability discrimination:

᪥

MICHIGAN PROTECTION & ADVOCACY SERVICE, INC. v. BABIN

United States Court of Appeals, Sixth Circuit, 1994
18 F.3d 337

BOGGS, Circuit Judge.

The plaintiffs filed several civil rights claims against the defendants, alleging that the defendants had denied and/or interfered with the plaintiffs' right to equal access to housing. The plaintiffs claim that their right to housing was violated when a house owner, who was negotiating with a state agency to rent the house as a group home for mentally disabled adults, sold the house at a profit to neighbors of the property. The plaintiffs allege that the seller's motivation for selling and the neighbors' motivation for buying the house were discriminatory. The plaintiffs brought suit against the seller, a real estate agency, and the group of neighbors who helped raise the money to purchase the property.

* * *

We hold that a proper interpretation of the text of the Fair Housing Amendments Act of 1988 does not reach the actions of the defendants in this case and we therefore affirm the district court's grant of summary judgment for the defendants.

I

In May 1988, the defendant Florence Hammonds was working as a real estate agent for Century 21 Town and Country Realty ("Century 21"). At that time, a couple listed their house ("24 Mile Road property" or "the house") with Century 21 and Hammonds marketed the property on their behalf. After eight months on the market, however, Hammonds had not sold the house.

In November 1988, while acting as the broker for the house, Hammonds contacted the Macomb-Oakland Regional Center ("MORC"), a state agency. Hammonds asked MORC if it would be interested in leasing the property as a group home for mentally disabled adults if she purchased it. MORC indicated that it was interested in leasing the property.

In early February 1989, Hammonds purchased the house for $95,000. She paid a broker's commission to Century 21 as the buyer, but recouped part of the commission as the real estate agent. Hammonds also took out a home equity loan and a mortgage to finance the purchase.

According to Hammonds, in March 1989 MORC indicated that it would execute a written lease and begin paying rent to Hammonds by the middle of May 1989. The leasing arrangements, however, did not progress as quickly as planned. In April 1989, MORC informed her that the lease could not be executed until July 15, 1989, because MORC was still waiting for various state agencies to approve the arrangement.

Meanwhile, on April 26, MORC officials sent out a letter to residents in the vicinity of the 24 Mile Road property to inform them that the house would be used as a group home. On April 28, 1989, Peggy Babin, a resident of the area, called Hammonds to arrange a meeting with her. On April 29, 1989, Babin and five other neighbors met with Hammonds at Hammonds's house to discuss the lease. At the meeting, Hammonds attempted to allay the neighbors' fears about having a group home in their neighborhood, but she also insisted on going through with her lease with MORC.

The neighbors then began a campaign to prevent the property from becoming a group home. Peggy Babin organized a petition drive to stop the group home, contacted several newspapers about the drive, and prepared a "mailing" about group homes. This mailing included 1) a newspaper article about a resident of a group home who had raped a nine-year old girl; 2) a list of addresses of people to write to express concern about the group home; 3) MORC's April 26 letter with a note indicating that MORC was talking about a group home such as the one discussed in the enclosed newspaper article; 4) a sheet entitled "Group Homes: Things You Should Know" that stated that the neighborhood would no longer be safe and property values would plummet if a group home was situated in the neighborhood; and 5) form letters to send to Century 21 and MORC to express concern about the group home.

After the neighbors began their petition drive, Hammonds initiated a conversation with John Kersten, the owner and sole shareholder of Century 21. Hammonds mentioned that she was concerned about the reaction of the neighbors to the proposed use of the 24 Mile Road property. Kersten indicated that Hammonds would have to handle the situation herself.

On the morning of May 12, Hammonds met with MORC representatives about hastening the leasing arrangement. According to Hammonds, the representatives promised to inquire about the delay in the approval of the lease and to call her that same day with an answer. They did not call her. Also, on May 12 a town meeting was held and approximately one hundred people showed up to express their concerns about the group home. Hammonds did not attend the meeting.

On May 13, Nosh Ivanovic offered Hammonds $100,000 for the house. On May 15, Hammonds made a counteroffer of $104,000. Ivanovic was unable to raise the additional cash, so Scott Babin provided the funds.

Scott Babin, with the help of Paul Hebert, then solicited funds from the neighbors to offset his donation to Ivanovic. Thomas Fortin donated $500.

The closing for the 24 Mile Road property took place on May 19. No one from Century 21 was at the closing and Hammonds did not pay a commission to the agency. Hammonds, however, used closing documents bearing the Century 21 logo, and the forms were pre-printed with Kersten's signature as the broker for the sale.

Based on these facts, the plaintiffs filed this suit against Hammonds, Kersten, Century 21, and the neighbors. The plaintiffs allege that each of the defendants violated, 42 U.S.C. § 3604(f)(1), which makes it illegal for a person to discriminate in the sale or rental, or to otherwise make unavailable or deny a dwelling to a person because of a disability.

* * *

III

* * *

A. Hammonds

The plaintiffs contend that Hammonds violated § 3604(f)(1) because she sold the house for financial gain knowing that the buyers were actively opposed to the group home. Whatever Hammonds's motivation, the transaction was exempt from § 3604.

Section 3603(b) exempts sales or rentals of single family homes by the owner if: (1) the owner does not own more than three such homes at any one time; (2) in the case of a sale of a dwelling where the owner was not occupying the residence at the time of the sale, or was not the most recent occupant of the dwelling, the owner has not made a similar sale within the past twenty-four months; (3) the owner does not have a beneficial interest in any part of the proceeds from the sale or rental of more than three such dwellings; and (4) the dwelling was sold (A) without the use "in any manner" of the sales or rental services or facilities of a real estate broker, agent, or sales person, and (B) the owner did not publish, post, or mail any advertisement or written notice that included discriminatory language. 42 U.S.C. § 3603(b). The statute also provides that "nothing in this proviso shall prohibit the use of attorneys, escrow agents, abstractors, title companies, and other such professional assistance as necessary to perfect or transfer the title. . . ." 42 U.S.C. § 3603(b).

The plaintiffs contend that Hammonds does not qualify for the exemption because she never lived in the house and her sole motive was to turn a quick profit on the real estate deal. The plaintiffs also argue that Hammonds does not fall within the § 3603(b) exemption because the sale of the property necessarily involved the use of a real estate agent since Hammonds is licensed as a real estate agent.

As the district court found, Hammonds's sale of the house falls squarely within § 3603(b). First, Hammonds only owned two dwellings, her principal place of residence and the 24 Mile Road property. Second, Hammonds had not made a similar sale in the past twenty-four months. Third, although Hammonds had earned commissions from the sales of other homes, this is not equivalent to owning an interest in the property, or having "title to or any right to all or a portion of the proceeds from the sale or rental of" more than three dwellings. We read this provision as excluding only those people who have some claim to proceeds of a sale because of their interest in the fee simple of the property. Since a contract for commissions does not affect the state of the property title, *see, e.g., Kelley v. Marlin,* 714 S.W.2d 303, 305 (Tex. 1986), Hammonds's occupation as a real estate agent does not disqualify her from the exemption.

Fourth, as the district court found, Hammonds did not "in any manner" use a real estate agency. The plaintiffs allege that Hammonds used the services of a real estate broker when she used a title company that Century 21 also used for its closings; used closing documents bearing the Century 21 logo and Kersten's pre-printed signature as the broker; and consulted Kersten about her problems with the neighbors.

Even though the statutory language, "in any manner," is very broad, Hammonds did not use the "facilities" or "services" of a real estate service or broker within the meaning of the FHAA. Although Hammonds used the Century 21 forms, she acquired the documents directly from Transamerica Title Company. Transamerica had these pre-printed forms in its possession because Century 21 frequently used the services of the title company. Transamerica, however, provided and assumed responsibility for the pre-printed forms. Finally, at the time of the sale, the 24 Mile Road property was not listed with Century 21, the Transamerica employees did not think that Kersten was involved in the sale, and Century 21 did not receive any commission from the sale. Consequently, the closing documents appear to be nothing more than form papers necessary to perfect title. As such, Hammonds's use of these documents does not vitiate the exemption provided by § 3603(b).

* * *

B. Kersten and Century 21

The plaintiffs argue that Kersten and Century 21 are liable under § 3604(f)(1) on a theory of direct and/or vicarious liability. For the plaintiffs to succeed on this claim, this court must find that either Century 21 was directly involved in the transaction or that Hammonds was a real estate agent within the meaning of § 3603(b) and acting within the scope of her employment. Restatement (Second) of Agency §§ 219, 220 (1957).

The plaintiffs rely on *Marr v. Rife, supra,* to support their argument. In *Marr,* we held that an owner of a real estate agency could be found liable for his agents' acts even if the owner did not approve of or direct the agents' actions. 503 F.2d at 742. In that case, the real estate agents were opposed to selling a house to the Marrs because they were African-American and the agents represented to the Marrs that the house was under contract when, in fact, it was not. Id. at 737.

Marr, however, is distinguishable from the present case. In Marr, the property was offered for sale by the real estate agency, the agents directly committed an illegal act, and the real estate business was liable under agency principles. Ibid. Here, there is no evidence that Century 21 listed the 24 Mile Road property while Hammonds was the owner. In her deposition, Hammonds stated that she considered the sale of the 24 Mile Road property a private transaction. Also, the closing documents indicate that Century 21 did not receive a commission from the sale. Moreover, Kersten testified that when Hammonds asked him for advice on the sale of the home, Kersten responded that Hammonds would have to handle it herself. This evidence indicates that Century 21 had no direct involvement in the transaction and that Hammonds was not acting as an agent for Century 21 during the sale of the 24 Mile Road property.

In response to this evidence, the plaintiffs rely on the pre-printed forms used during the closing. As noted above, this is merely a scintilla of evidence on the issue of Hammonds's agency status, and the defendants have presented evidence that rebuts any inference of agency on Hammonds's part. Consequently, the district court was correct to grant summary judgment for Kersten and Century 21 on the § 3604(f)(1) claim.

C. The Neighbors

The plaintiffs contend that the neighbors are liable under § 3604(f)(1) because they solicited and contributed money to support the Ivanovics' purchase of the house. According to the plaintiffs, the neighbors' actions fall within the "otherwise make unavailable" language of the statute.

We first note that Congress intended § 3604 to reach a broad range of activities that have the effect of denying housing opportunities to a member of a protected class. See, e.g., South-Suburban Hous. Ctr. v. Greater South-Suburban Bd. of Realtors, 935 F.2d 868, 882 (7th Cir. 1991), cert. denied, 502 U.S. 1074 (1992). When Congress amended § 3604(f) in 1988, it intended the section to reach not only actors who were directly involved in the real estate business, but also actors who directly affect the availability of housing, such as state or local governments. H.R.Rep. No. 711, 100th Cong., 2d Sess. 22 (1988), reprinted in 1988 U.S.C.C.A.N. 2173, 2183; cf. Marbrunak, Inc. v. City of Stow, 974 F.2d 43 (6th Cir. 1992).

The question presented by the plaintiffs' claim is to what extent the phrase "otherwise make unavailable" reaches out to make unlawful actions that are removed from the central event of purchasing or leasing a dwelling but nonetheless have some effect on a person's ability to acquire housing.

* * *

We agree with the Third Circuit that Congress's intent in enacting § 3604(f)(1) was to reach property owners and their agents who directly affect the availability of housing for a disabled individual. However, the scope of § 3604(f)(1) may extend further, to other actors who, though not owners or agents, are in a position directly to deny a member of a protected group housing rights. *Cf. Burrell v. City of Kankakee,* 815 F.2d 1127, 1130-31 (7th Cir. 1987) ("plaintiffs['] claims are not cognizable under the Fair Housing Act since defendants' conduct did not directly affect the availability of housing to minorities").

The crucial issue of interpretation with respect to § 3604(f)(1), as well as other sections of the act, is whether normal economic competition can constitute a violation under the act. In a certain semantic sense, every purchase or sale "directly affects" everyone else who may be in competition. Sometimes that effect is very small, as when one buys a highly fungible and readily available commodity, such as a gallon of gasoline or a pound of potatoes. However, if the commodity is artificially scarce or unique, the normal process of purchase and competition can have a much greater effect. If a motorist is in line for the last gallon of gasoline available under price regulations, that purchase will effectively make the commodity unavailable to the next person in line. If we secure the last good table at a fancy restaurant by bribing the maitre d', we may have effectively prevented another person, even a member of a protected class, from enjoying the public accommodation at that moment.

Real estate, of course, is the quintessential unique commodity. If we are able to purchase a house because we can offer more money, we have in one sense "denied" it to everyone else. But that is not generally the way the word is used. Only hyper-technical economists would normally say that we interfere with another person's rights when we purchase a house in fair economic competition, just as most people would not say that we "directly affect" a merchant's livelihood when we choose to patronize A, rather than B, no matter what the motive.

Given this general usage of the words, it would be a huge and unwarranted expansion of the act, with no hint of any congressional authority, to say that every purchaser or renter of property is liable under the act if his motives are found unworthy in such a purchase or rental transaction. The entire language of the act, as well as the evils the act is aimed at as described in hearings and debates, was designed to target those who owned or disposed of property, and those who, in practical effect, assisted in those transactions of ownership and disposition.

Consequently, however broad § 3604(f) may be, the scope of the statute cannot encompass the acts of the neighbors in this case. Their

777

action in collecting money to buy the house is not direct enough to fall within the terms of § 3604(f)(1). Under the plaintiffs' interpretation of the statute, *any* action that results in the unavailability of housing for protected classes is actionable, no matter how attenuated. We decline to extend the scope of § 3604(f)(1) to accommodate the plaintiffs' claims in this case.

* * *

We conclude that the district court was correct in granting summary judgment to all the defendants on the plaintiffs' § 3604(f)(1) claims.

Notes & Questions

1. What are the policy rationales for the single family house and living quarters exemptions? How are these rationales the same or different from the ADA's exemption for employers with less than 15 employees?

2. Compare the facts of this case with the facts of *City of Cleburne v. Cleburne Living Center*, 473 U.S. 432 (1985), discussed *supra* in Part 1, § 1.3. If the FHAA had been in effect at the time of the *Cleburne* case (1985), would the *Cleburne* plaintiffs have been any more successful? How do the facts in *Michigan Protection & Advocacy* and *City of Cleburne* demonstrate that disability discrimination does exist?

3. Are the single family house and living quarters exemptions a good balance between the types of disability prejudice shown in these cases, and the property rights and perhaps legitimate fears of individual landowners?

4. In a part of the case that has been edited out in this casebook, plaintiffs argued that all defendants violated 42 U.S.C. § 3617, which provides that

> [i]t shall be unlawful to coerce, intimidate, threaten, or interfere with any person in the exercise or enjoyment of, or on account of his having exercised or enjoyed, or on account of his having aided or encouraged any other person in the exercise or enjoyment of, any right granted or protected by [the Fair Housing Act].

Construct the plaintiff's argument. If you were the judge, how would you rule on it? The *Michigan Protection & Advocacy* court upheld the lower court's summary judgment dismissal of this claim. Michigan Protection and Advocacy, 18 F.3d at 348.

5. In *Hogar Agua y Vida en el Desierto, Inc. v. Suarez-Medina*, 36 F.3d 177 (1st Cir. 1993), a nonprofit organization negotiated to buy a residence to use as a group home for persons with HIV and AIDS, but the owner refused to execute the sale due to community opposition. The court

held that the owner was exempt from § 3604(f) because of the § 3604 single-family home exemption. *See also* Pulcinella v. Ridley Township, 822 F.Supp. 204 (E.D. Pa. 1993) (where a person with paraplegia and sister brought action under § 3604(f) against township for variance to add ramp to sister's house, court held that because plaintiffs could not compel sister to add ramp under § 3604(f) due to single family house exemption, it would be illogical to compel township under same theory) (case settled and vacated on July 26, 1993).

6. There is one additional categorical exception to the FHAA. 42 U.S.C. § 3607 (2006) allows religious organizations and private clubs to limit the rental or occupancy of its lodging to members of the same religion or club, and to give preferences to their members.

§ 26.2 Maximum Occupancy Exemptions

The FHAA does not apply to "any reasonable local, State, or Federal restrictions regarding the maximum number of occupants permitted to occupy a dwelling." *Id.* § 3607(b)(1). Consider the reasons for this exemption, as well as how courts have interpreted it, in the following case.

CITY OF EDMONDS v. OXFORD HOUSE, INC.

Supreme Court of the United States, 1995
514 U.S. 725

Justice GINSBURG delivered the opinion of the Court.

The Fair Housing Act (FHA or Act) prohibits discrimination in housing against, *inter alios,* persons with handicaps. Section 807(b)(1) of the Act entirely exempts from the FHA's compass "any reasonable local, State, or Federal restrictions regarding the maximum number of occupants permitted to occupy a dwelling." 42 U.S.C. § 3607(b)(1). This case presents the question whether a provision in petitioner City of Edmonds' zoning code qualifies for § 3607(b)(1)'s complete exemption from FHA scrutiny. The provision, governing areas zoned for single-family dwelling units, defines "family" as "persons [without regard to number] related by genetics, adoption, or marriage, or a group of five or fewer [unrelated] persons." Edmonds Community Development Code (ECDC) § 21.30.010 (1991).

The defining provision at issue describes who may compose a family unit; it does not prescribe "*the* maximum number of occupants" a dwelling unit may house. We hold that § 3607(b)(1) does not exempt prescriptions of the family-defining kind, *i.e.,* provisions designed to foster the family character of a neighborhood. Instead, § 3607(b)(1)'s absolute exemption removes from the FHA's scope only total occupancy limits, *i.e.,* numerical ceilings that serve to prevent overcrowding in living quarters.

I

In the summer of 1990, respondent Oxford House opened a group home in the City of Edmonds, Washington (City), for 10 to 12 adults recovering from alcoholism and drug addiction. The group home, called Oxford House-Edmonds, is located in a neighborhood zoned for single-family residences. Upon learning that Oxford House had leased and was operating a home in Edmonds, the City issued criminal citations to the owner and a resident of the house. The citations charged violation of the zoning code rule that defines who may live in single-family dwelling units. The occupants of such units must compose a "family," and family, under the City's defining rule, "means an individual or two or more persons related by genetics, adoption, or marriage, or a group of five or fewer persons who are not related by genetics, adoption, or marriage." ECDC § 21.30.010. Oxford House-Edmonds houses more than five unrelated persons, and therefore does not conform to the code.

Oxford House asserted reliance on the Fair Housing Act, which declares it unlawful "[t]o discriminate in the sale or rental, or to otherwise make unavailable or deny, a dwelling to any buyer or renter because of a handicap of . . . that buyer or renter." § 3604(f)(1)(A). The parties have stipulated, for purposes of this litigation, that the residents of Oxford House-Edmonds "are recovering alcoholics and drug addicts and are handicapped persons within the meaning" of the Act.

Oxford House asked Edmonds to make a "reasonable accommodation" by allowing it to remain in the single-family dwelling it had leased. Group homes for recovering substance abusers, Oxford urged, need 8 to 12 residents to be financially and therapeutically viable. Edmonds declined to permit Oxford House to stay in a single-family residential zone, but passed an ordinance listing group homes as permitted uses in multifamily and general commercial zones.

II

The sole question before the Court is whether Edmonds' family composition rule qualifies as a "restrictio[n] regarding the maximum number of occupants permitted to occupy a dwelling" within the meaning of the FHA's absolute exemption. 42 U.S.C. § 3607(b)(1). In answering this question, we are mindful of the Act's stated policy "to provide, within constitutional limitations, for fair housing throughout the United States." § 3601. We also note precedent recognizing the FHA's "broad and inclusive" compass, and therefore according a "generous construction" to the Act's complaint-filing provision. *Trafficante v. Metropolitan Life Ins. Co.,* 409 U.S. 205, 209, 212 (1972).

Turning specifically to the City's Community Development Code, we note that the provisions Edmonds invoked against Oxford House,

ECDC §§ 16.20.010 and 21.30.010, are classic examples of a use restriction and complementing family composition rule. These provisions do not cap the number of people who may live in a dwelling. In plain terms, they direct that dwellings be used only to house families. Captioned "USES," ECDC § 16.20.010 provides that the sole "Permitted Primary Us[e]" in a single-family residential zone is "[s]ingle-family dwelling units." Edmonds itself recognizes that this provision simply "defines those uses permitted in a single family residential zone."

Edmonds nevertheless argues that its family composition rule, ECDC § 21.30.010, falls within § 3607(b)(1), the FHA exemption for maximum occupancy restrictions, because the rule caps at five the number of unrelated persons allowed to occupy a single-family dwelling. But Edmonds' family composition rule surely does not answer the question: "What is the maximum number of occupants permitted to occupy a house?" So long as they are related "by genetics, adoption, or marriage," any number of people can live in a house. Ten siblings, their parents and grandparents, for example, could dwell in a house in Edmonds' single-family residential zone without offending Edmonds' family composition rule.

Family living, not living space per occupant, is what ECDC § 21.30.010 describes. Defining family primarily by biological and legal relationships, the provision also accommodates another group association: Five or fewer unrelated people are allowed to live together as though they were family. This accommodation is the peg on which Edmonds rests its plea for § 3607(b)(1) exemption. Had the City defined a family solely by biological and legal links, § 3607(b)(1) would not have been the ground on which Edmonds staked its case. It is curious reasoning indeed that converts a family values preserver into a maximum occupancy restriction once a town adds to a related person's prescription "and also two unrelated persons."

Edmonds additionally contends that subjecting single-family zoning to FHA scrutiny will "overturn Euclidian zoning" and "destroy the effectiveness and purpose of single-family zoning." This contention both ignores the limited scope of the issue before us and exaggerates the force of the FHA's antidiscrimination provisions. We address only whether Edmonds' family composition rule qualifies for § 3607(b)(1) exemption. Moreover, the FHA antidiscrimination provisions, when applicable, require only "reasonable" accommodations to afford persons with handicaps "equal opportunity to use and enjoy" housing. §§ 3604(f)(1)(A) and (f)(3)(B).

* * *

The parties have presented, and we have decided, only a threshold question: Edmonds' zoning code provision describing who may compose a "family" is not a maximum occupancy restriction exempt from the FHA under § 3607(b)(1). It remains for the lower courts to decide whether

Edmonds' actions against Oxford House violate the FHA's prohibitions against discrimination set out in §§ 3604(f)(1)(A) and (f)(3)(B). For the reasons stated, the judgment of the United States Court of Appeals for the Ninth Circuit is

AFFIRMED.

Notes & Questions

1. What is the purpose of the FHAA's exemption for maximum number restrictions? What was the purpose of Edmond's zoning policy? Were they in conflict?

2. In *City of Edmonds,* the Court notes that it recognizes the FHA's "broad and inclusive" compass, and therefore accords a "generous construction" to the Act's complaint-filing provision. Why? Is this similar to or different from the way that the Court has interpreted the ADA? If different, what justifies the difference?

3. That is not to say that courts are always deferential or take an expansive construction in FHAA cases. In *Chesler v. Conroy,* 2008 WL 4543031 (N.D. Ill. 2008), the plaintiffs' claims involved a landlord not maintaining a walkway to facilitate access for someone recovering from spinal surgery. The court viewed the legislative history behind FHAA as demonstrating that it was primarily intended to remedy discrimination in zoning and that Congress "did not enact the FHA to create a federal cause of action when a quarreling neighbor happens to become handicapped after the onset of a quarrel." *Id.* at *3.

4. Would it make a difference to the FHAA analysis if the reason Oxford House wanted to house more than five residents was for purely financial, rather than therapeutic, reasons? Would the accommodation being sought then be sufficiently disability-related?

5. There is one other threshold qualifier for FHAA coverage. Like the pre-1988 FHA provisions, FHAA only applies to "dwellings." The statute defines dwellings as "any building, structure, or portion thereof which is occupied as, or designed or intended for occupancy as, a residence by one or more families, and any vacant land which is offered for sale or lease for the construction or location thereon of any such building, structure, or portion thereof." 42 U.S.C. § 3602(b). In *Schwarz v. City of Treasure Island,* 544 F.3d 1201 (11th Cir. 2008), the court had to determine whether halfway houses for recovering substance abusers were dwellings. The City argued that they were not because the residents' stays were short and most of them intended to return to some other home upon completing treatment. The court rejected this argument, differentiating a halfway house, where someone intends to reside for a period of time, from a hotel, where someone typically does not.

Chapter 27 DISCRIMINATION

Discrimination on the basis of disability under the FHAA is divided into two main categories: failure to make reasonable accommodations to premises or rules and policies, and failure to design and construct accessible buildings.

The FHAA also provides that "nothing in this subsection requires that a dwelling be made available to an individual whose tenancy would constitute a direct threat to the health or safety of other individuals or whose tenancy would result in substantial physical damage to the property of others." 42 U.S.C. § 3604(f)(9) (2006).

§ 27.1 Failure To Allow Reasonable Modifications To Premises Or To Make Reasonable Accommodations To Rules, Policies, Practices, Or Services

Like the ADA, the FHAA defines discrimination in relation to the failure to make reasonable modifications and accommodations. The Act defines discrimination on the basis of disability as:

> (3)(A) A refusal to permit, at the expense of the handicapped person, reasonable modifications of existing premises occupied or to be occupied by such person if such modifications may be necessary to afford such person full enjoyment of the premises except that, in the case of a rental, the landlord may where it is reasonable to do so condition permission for a modification on the renter agreeing to restore the interior of the premises to the condition that existed before the modification, reasonable wear and tear excepted.
>
> (B) a refusal to make reasonable accommodations in rules, policies, practices, or services, when such accommodations may be necessary to afford such person equal opportunity to use and enjoy a dwelling . . . .

Id. § 3604(f)(3).

In terms of modifications to premises, the basic rule set forth by the statute is that tenants can make reasonable modifications to premises, at their own expense. But the Act is largely silent as to what differentiates a "reasonable" accommodation or modification from an unreasonable one. And, the Act is not clear as to who shoulders the burden for accommodations to "rules, policies, practices, or services" that have a financial cost.

Cognizant of these difficulties, the Department of Housing and Urban Development (HUD), the federal agency responsible for promulgating regulations pursuant to the FHAA, offered its own interpretation that major costs or administrative burdens should not be imposed on landlords or sellers:

> A number of commentators were concerned that this language [reasonable accommodation] could be interpreted as requiring that housing providers provide a broad range of services to persons with handicaps that a housing provider does not normally provide as part of its housing. The Department wishes to stress that a housing provider is not required to provide supportive services, e.g., counseling, medical, or social services that fall outside the scope of the services that the housing provider offers to residents. A housing provider is required to make modifications in order to enable a qualified applicant with handicaps to live in the housing, but is not required to offer housing of a fundamentally different nature. The test is whether, with appropriate modifications, the applicant can live in the housing that the housing provider offers; not whether the applicant could benefit from some other type of housing that the housing provider does not offer.

Implementation of Fair Housing Amendments of 1999, 54 Fed. Reg. 3231, 3249 (Jan. 23, 1989).

Nevertheless, courts have struggled with the line between reasonable and unreasonable accommodations and modifications. This first short case is a useful illustration of the difference between Part A's reasonable modifications to facilities, which a tenant undertakes at his or her own expense, and Part B's modification to rules, policies, practices, or services, on which the statute is silent as to who foots the bill.

RODRIGUEZ v. 551 WEST 157TH STREET OWNERS CORP.

United States District Court, Southern District of New York, 1998
992 F. Supp. 385

RAKOFF, District Judge

Plaintiffs, four mobility-impaired tenants of 551 West 157th Street, allege that the failure of the defendant landlord to install a ramp or lift that will make the building entrance accessible to wheelchairs constitutes a violation of the federal Fair Housing Act, 42 U.S.C. § 3601 *et seq.*, the New York State Human Rights Law, N.Y. Exec. Law § 290 *et seq.*, section 8-107(5) of the New York City Administrative Code, and the New York City Building Code, N.Y.Admin.Code, Title 27.

* * *

The relevant facts, taken most favorably to plaintiffs but largely undisputed, can be briefly summarized. The building located at 551 West

157th Street was constructed in 1910. *See* Affidavit of Frank Ferranti, dated October 16, 1997 ("Ferranti Aff."), Ex. C. Plaintiff Hector Rodriguez, who has resided at 551 West 157th Street for over forty years, is afflicted with cerebral palsy and is confined to a wheelchair, rendering him unable to enter and exit the building without assistance. Plaintiff Clara Tavarez is disabled and cannot enter and leave the building without assistance. Plaintiff Francisco Castillo has had two strokes during the past few years and as a result is unable to enter and exit the building without assistance. Finally, plaintiff Estella Toribio, who is seventy-three years old, and has lived in the building for over thirty years, suffers from diabetes, high blood pressure, and osteoporosis, which makes it difficult for her to walk and precludes her from entering or exiting the building without assistance. Id. ¶ 7. Plaintiffs, through their attorney, have demanded that defendant install a lift or ramp that will make the entrance of the building wheelchair-accessible, so that they can enter or exit on their own. Estimates for the cost of such a modification range from $25,000 to $55,000.

* * *

Specifically, the Complaint alleges that defendant's failure to provide an entrance lift or ramp constitutes discrimination in violation of Section 3604(f)(2) of the Fair Housing Act, which states that "discrimination includes . . . a refusal to make reasonable accommodations in rules, policies, practices, or services, when such accommodations may be necessary to afford such person equal opportunity to use and enjoy a dwelling." 42 U.S.C. § 3604(f)(3)(B).

Plaintiffs contend that defendant's refusal to make the building entrance accessible to wheelchairs constitutes a failure to make a "reasonable accommodation" in violation of the above-quoted provisions. However, the plain language of the statute defines this requirement in terms of reasonable accommodations in "rules, policies, practices, or services," 42 U.S.C. § 3604(f)(3)(B) and, by contrast with § 3604(f)(2), notably fails to mention "facilities." To undertake to construct an entirely new facility in an existing building does not, under these circumstances, qualify as an "accommodation" of a "rule, policy, practice or service," when the term "construction" is nowhere to be found and the term "facility" is excluded. *Cf. Shapiro v. Cadman Towers, Inc.,* 51 F.3d 328 (2d Cir. 1995) (affirming injunction requiring cooperative to abandon first come/first serve policy and to provide plaintiff with spot in its parking garage). Indeed, plaintiffs cite no case, and the Court is aware of none, interpreting section 3604(f) to require a landlord to undertake wholly new construction.

Moreover, even if one were to assume *arguendo* that section 3604(f) could in some circumstances be read to require a landlord to undertake new construction, such accommodation must still be "reasonable" and therefore not "pose an undue hardship or a substantial burden," *Shapiro,* 51 F.3d at 335; see also, e.g., *Salute v. Greens,* 918

F.Supp. 660, 667 (E.D.N.Y. 1996) ("[a]lthough the reasonable accommodation provision can and often will require a landlord to incur some expense, it does not require adjustments or modifications to existing programs that would be substantial, or would fundamentally alter the nature of the program, or pose an undue hardship or substantial burden"). Here, installation of an entrance ramp at a minimum cost of $25,000 would not constitute a "reasonable" accommodation, particularly in light of unrebutted evidence that defendant has incurred financial losses in the operation of the building over the last three years.

For these reasons, plaintiffs' Fair Housing Act claims must be dismissed.

SO ORDERED.

Notes & Questions

1. Clearly, the court here did not take up plaintiff's invitation to view a physical modification to premises as involving a rule, policy, practice, or service. But at least one other court has suggested otherwise. In *Oxford House, Inc. v. Township of Cherry Hill*, 799 F.Supp. 450, 462, n.25 (D.N.J. 1992), the court noted that "where everyone is provided with 'equal access' to a building in the form of a staircase, reasonable accommodation to those in wheelchairs may require building a ramp." In a portion of *Rodriguez* that has been omitted, the court characterized this as inapplicable dicta. *See* Rodriguez, 992 F.Supp. at 387, n.1.

2. Should tenants have to bear the cost of modifications to facilities? How is this different than an employer's obligation to make accommodations to physical facilities for an employee under Title I of the ADA, or the owner of a public accommodation's obligation under Title III of the ADA, to make physical modifications that are "readily achievable"?

3. Would it have made a difference in *Rodriguez* if the cost of building a ramp was negligible? Similarly, what would the landlord's obligations under the FHAA have been if the tenants had offered to build the ramp at their own expense? *See* United States v. Freer, 864 F.Supp. 324 (W.D.N.Y. 1994) (holding owners of trailer park in violation of FHAA where owners refused to allow renter to install desired wheelchair ramp at her own cost because such refusal had effect of denying renter equal opportunity to use and enjoy her home).

The next few cases explore the line between reasonable and unreasonable accommodations in rules, policies, practices, or services.

UNITED STATES v. CALIFORNIA
MOBILE HOME PARK MANAGEMENT CO.

United States Court of Appeals, Ninth Circuit, 1994
29 F.3d 1413

FRANK A. KAUFMAN, Senior District Judge.

Cohen-Strong alleges that the defendants discriminated in violation of the Fair Housing Amendments Act of 1988 ("FHAA"), by refusing to waive guest fees charged for her handicapped daughter's home health care aide. The principal issue in this appeal is whether the duty imposed under the FHAA to make "reasonable accommodations in rules" on behalf of handicapped persons may require a landlord to waive, in a given instance, fees generally applicable to all residents. Concluding that generally applicable fees are not immune from scrutiny for compliance with the FHAA's requirement of reasonable accommodation, we reverse the judgment of the district court and remand for further proceedings.

In 1989, plaintiff Cohen-Strong, and her infant daughter, were residing at a mobile home lot leased from defendant Costa Mesa Mobile Estates. Cohen-Strong's daughter had a respiratory disease which required her to be cared for by a home health care aide. The Management Company of Costa Mesa Estates demanded payment from Cohen-Strong for the presence of the home medical aide pursuant to its policy of charging residents a fee of $1.50 per day for the presence of long-term guests and $25.00 per month for guest parking. Cohen-Strong asked the Management Company to waive imposition of the fees on behalf of her daughter; however, that request was refused. As a result, Cohen-Strong paid $175 for the 2 1/4 months for which fees were assessed.

* * *

In granting defendants' motion to dismiss, the district court presumably concluded that the Fair Housing Act ("FHA"), 42 U.S.C. § 3601 *et seq.*, is never violated when a landlord refuses to waive generally applicable fees on behalf of a handicapped person. We disagree.

The FHA originally prohibited discrimination on the basis of race, color, religion, or national origin. The Supreme Court has ruled that the FHA must be given a "generous construction" in order to carry out a "'policy that Congress considered to be of the highest priority.'" *Trafficante v. Metropolitan Life Ins. Co.*, 409 U.S. 205, 211, 212 (1972). The generous spirit with which we are to interpret the FHA guides our analysis here.

Congress extended the FHA's protection to handicapped persons in the Fair Housing Amendments Act of 1988 ("FHAA"), Pub.L. 100-430, 102 Stat. 1619. Among the discriminatory practices proscribed by the amended Act is the "refusal to make reasonable accommodations in rules,

787

policies, practices, or services, when such accommodations may be necessary to afford [a handicapped] person equal opportunity to use and enjoy a dwelling." 42 U.S.C. § 3604(f)(3)(B). Cohen-Strong argues that a landlord's refusal to waive guest fees for a handicapped person's medical aide may constitute a refusal to make reasonable accommodations, in violation of § 3604(f)(3)(B).

As the language of § 3604(f)(3)(B) makes clear, the FHAA imposes an affirmative duty upon landlords reasonably to accommodate the needs of handicapped persons. Defendants assert, nonetheless, that this affirmative duty does not entail any requirement that landlords "financially subsidize" the handicapped. We find the effort to distinguish accommodations that have a financial cost from other accommodations unconvincing. Besides the fact that § 3604's reasonable accommodations requirement contains no exemption for financial costs to the landlord, the history of the FHAA clearly establishes that Congress anticipated that landlords would have to shoulder certain costs involved, so long as they are not unduly burdensome.

Congress based the FHAA's reasonable accommodations provision on the "regulations and caselaw dealing with discrimination on the basis of handicap" under section 504 of the Rehabilitation Act, 29 U.S.C. § 794, which prohibits discrimination against the handicapped in federally funded programs. The Supreme Court has held that, under the Rehabilitation Act, a proposed accommodation should not impose "undue financial . . . burdens" upon the accommodator, a rule that clearly contemplates *some* financial burden resulting from accommodation. *Southeastern Community College v. Davis,* 442 U.S. 397, 412 (1979). Therefore, in light of the legislative history of the FHAA and its incorporation of the Rehabilitation Act's standards regarding reasonable accommodations, we hold that § 3604(f)(3)(B) may require landlords to assume reasonable financial burdens in accommodating handicapped residents.

Although defendants argue that any fee which is generally applicable to all residents of a housing community cannot be discriminatory, the Act itself is concerned with facially neutral rules of all types. Congress recognized that "[a]nother method of making housing unavailable to people with disabilities has been the application or enforcement of otherwise neutral rules and regulations on health, safety and land-use in a manner which discriminates against people with disabilities. . . . These and similar practices would be prohibited." H.R. Rep. No. 100-711, at 24, *reprinted in* 1988 U.S.C.C.A.N. at 2185.

Finally, to exempt generally applicable fee rules from scrutiny under the FHAA would permit landlords to circumvent the Act's requirements simply by imposing fees for certain matters, rather than by imposing flat bans or other types of restrictive rules. For example, the regulations interpreting the FHAA provide that a landlord must waive a "no pets" rule for a blind tenant who requires a seeing-eye dog, and that a landlord must waive a "first come, first serve" rule for allocating parking spaces when a mobility-impaired tenant requires a parking space near her unit. 24 C.F.R. § 100.204(b) (1993). Under defendants' interpretation of the FHAA, a landlord might "allow" the blind tenant to have a dog, or the mobility-impaired tenant to have priority for a parking space, while imposing a high fee for exercising that right. In some extreme cases, such a fee could effectively prevent the handicapped tenant from obtaining the needed benefit.

In order to trigger review under § 3604(f)(3)(B), the challenged fee rule must, like the rules described above, have the potential to deny persons an "equal opportunity to use and enjoy a dwelling" because of their handicap. There are, of course, many types of residential fees that affect handicapped and non-handicapped residents equally; such fees are clearly proper. Fees that merit closer scrutiny are those with unequal impact, imposed in return for permission to engage in conduct that, under the FHAA, a landlord is required to permit.

Some generally applicable fees might be too small to have any exclusionary effect. Other fees might be sustained because to require their waiver would extend a preference to handicapped residents, as opposed to affording them equal opportunity. The waiver of others might impose an undue financial burden on the landlord. The reasonable accommodation inquiry is highly fact-specific, requiring case-by-case determination. In a case such as this one, a reviewing court should examine, among other things, the amount of fees imposed, the relationship between the amount of fees and the overall housing cost, the proportion of other tenants paying such fees, the importance of the fees to the landlord's overall revenues, and the importance of the fee waiver to the handicapped tenant.

We are not presently deciding that the fees in this case were improperly assessed. We hold only that such charges must be examined on a case-by-case basis to determine whether, in a given case, a waiver of the charge, in whole or at least in part, "may be necessary to afford [a handicapped] person equal opportunity to use and enjoy a dwelling," 42 U.S.C. § 3604(f)(3)(B), and whether such waiver would impose an undue burden on the landlord. Therefore, we reverse and remand to the district court for proceedings consistent with this opinion.

REVERSED AND REMANDED.

Notes & Questions

1. *California Mobile Home Park Management* clearly holds that landlords will have to bear some of the costs in making accommodations, so long as they are reasonable. Similarly, "neutral" rules can fall within the scope of the FHAA. How is this similar to the reasonable

accommodation mandate of the ADA? Is it fair to landlords and sellers of property?

2. The issue on remand in *California Mobile Home Park Management* is whether it is "reasonable" for the landlord to have to waive the guest fees. What facts would a judge need to know to decide the case? How would you argue the case for each side?

3. The implementing regulations to the FHAA speak directly to service animals as a reasonable accommodation. 24 C.F.R. § 100.204(b) (2007) provides that where a blind applicant for rental housing desires to live in a dwelling unit with a seeing-eye dog, but the building has a "no pets" policy, it is unlawful for the owner or manager of the apartment complex to refuse to permit the applicant to live in the apartment with a seeing-eye dog because, without the dog, the blind person will not have an equal opportunity to use and enjoy the dwelling.

4. Another frequently litigated reasonable accommodation request involves parking spaces. The next case considers this issue.

SHAPIRO v. CADMAN TOWERS, INC.

United States Court of Appeals, Second Circuit, 1995
51 F.3d 328

MINER, Circuit Judge:

Defendants-appellants Cadman Towers, Inc., a 400-unit city-aided cooperative apartment building in Brooklyn, and Sydelle Levy, the president of the cooperative's Board of Directors, appeal from an order entered on January 25, 1994 in the United States District Court for the Eastern District of New York (Sifton, J.) granting a preliminary injunction in favor of plaintiff-appellee Phyllis Shapiro, a Cadman Towers cooperative apartment owner who is afflicted with multiple sclerosis. The injunction, issued pursuant to the anti-discrimination provisions of the Fair Housing Amendments Act of 1988, 42 U.S.C. § 3604(f), requires Cadman Towers, Inc. and Levy (collectively "Cadman Towers") to provide Shapiro with a parking space on the ground floor of her building's parking garage. For the reasons that follow, we affirm the order of the district court.

BACKGROUND

In the late 1970s, plaintiff-appellee Phyllis Shapiro was diagnosed as suffering from multiple sclerosis ("MS"), a disease of the central nervous system. One of Shapiro's doctors, Lave Schainberg, describes the type of MS suffered by Shapiro as one that follows a "relapsing progressive course where the patient goes downhill in a stepwise fashion over many years and eventually, in 30 or 35 years, becomes totally confined to a wheelchair." While MS ordinarily is characterized by an "unpredictable course," the disease generally "manifest[s] itself by difficulty in walking, urinary problems, sensory problems, visual problems, and fatigue." Factors such as stress, cold temperatures, or infection tend to aggravate the symptoms. At times, Shapiro suffers physical weakness, difficulty in walking, loss of balance and coordination, fatigue, and severe headaches. During good periods, she can walk without assistance; at other times, she needs a cane or a wheelchair. Shapiro also suffers from severe bladder problems, resulting in incontinence. She presently catheterizes herself to relieve the buildup of urine.

In 1990, Shapiro moved into a two-bedroom apartment in Cadman Towers. During her first two years there, Shapiro used public transportation and private car services to commute to her job as a guidance counselor at a middle school and to various social events. However, each of these modes of transportation presented various difficulties to Shapiro because of her disease.

In early 1992, Shapiro acquired an automobile. Parking space in her Brooklyn Heights neighborhood, as in most parts of New York City, is extremely scarce. Initially, Shapiro parked her car on the street, taking advantage of a city-issued "handicapped" sticker that exempted her from normal parking rules and regulations. Even with that, however, it still was extremely difficult for her to find a parking spot, as many other persons who work or live in her neighborhood also have special parking privileges. Shapiro testified that the long delay in finding a parking space and walking to her building resulted in numerous urinary "accidents." When she used an indwelling catheter, this delay would cause the bag to fill up, resulting in pain and leakage.

The Cadman Towers apartment complex where Shapiro lives consists of two buildings and two parking garages. At 101 Clark Street, where Shapiro's apartment is located, there are 302 apartments and 66 indoor parking spaces. At 10 Clinton Street, there are 121 apartments and 136 parking spaces. The parking rate at either location is approximately $90 per month, considerably less than the $275 charged by the closest commercial garage.

Due to the disparity in numbers between apartments and parking spaces, Cadman Towers generally has adhered to a first-come/first-served policy when allocating parking spaces. Pursuant to this policy, an individual desiring a parking space makes a written request to have his or her name placed on a waiting list. An applicant first waits for a space at 10 Clinton, and, after being assigned one at that location, becomes eligible to await assignment of a space at 101 Clark. Parking-space users were required to live in Cadman Towers, and each apartment could be allocated only a single space. There were, however, exceptions to the building's usual policy. Six apartments had two parking spaces, apparently under a grandfathering arrangement, and at least one elderly resident was permitted to have her son, who works nearby, use her parking space. Also

791

exempted from the first-come/first-served policy are three spaces given without charge to certain building employees as part of their compensation.

In February of 1992, Shapiro requested that a parking spot in the 101 Clark Street garage be made available to her immediately on account of her disability. This request was denied by the cooperative's Board of Directors, and Shapiro was advised to place her name on the appropriate waiting list. Her present counsel and her brother, who also is an attorney, then wrote to the Board, requesting that Ms. Shapiro receive an immediate parking spot. After receiving these letters and consulting with counsel, Cadman Towers took the position that any duty under the Fair Housing Act to accommodate Shapiro's disability did not come into play until she was awarded a parking space in the normal course. Once Shapiro became entitled to a parking space, the building would then attempt reasonably to accommodate her disability, perhaps by assigning her a parking space near her apartment.

On June 11, 1992, Shapiro filed a complaint with the Department of Housing and Urban Development ("HUD"), alleging housing discrimination under the Fair Housing Amendments Act. After an investigation, HUD issued a charge of discrimination on November 29, 1993.

* * *

After conducting an evidentiary hearing, the district court granted Shapiro's motion for a preliminary injunction on January 21, 1994. The injunction prohibited Cadman Towers from refusing to provide Shapiro with an immediate parking space on the ground floor of the garage at 101 Clark Street. The district court found that Shapiro would suffer irreparable harm absent injunctive relief, because without a parking space she is subjected to continued risk of injury and humiliation from her inability to walk distances and her incontinence. The court also determined that Shapiro was likely to succeed on the merits of her claim, concluding that the concept of reasonable accommodation "will in all probability require modification of defendants' first come/first served policy." Id. at 127. The court also determined that Shapiro would be entitled to preliminary relief under the alternative test that requires plaintiff to show "sufficiently serious questions going to the merits to make them fair ground for litigation and a balance of hardships tipping decidedly toward the party requesting the preliminary relief." Id. at 127 n. 13. The court found that Cadman Towers would not suffer any significant harm in giving Shapiro a parking space for the duration of the litigation, because any of the three building employees could be relocated to a commercial garage at a *de minimis* cost. Id. The court also noted that the building could free up seven spaces simply by enforcing its own rules that each apartment should be allocated only one parking space and that spaces should only go to residents. Id.

DISCUSSION

* * *

Cadman Towers contends that the district court erred by failing to give sufficient weight to the testimony of other building occupants and the building staff regarding their observations of Shapiro's condition. These witnesses testified that, prior to the initiation of the proceedings giving rise to this appeal, Shapiro had always appeared to walk normally and that they had never observed her using a wheelchair. In discounting these observations by lay observers unfamiliar with Shapiro's disease or its symptoms, the district court relied instead on the testimony given by Shapiro's medical experts, including her treating physician. *Shapiro,* 844 F.Supp. at 123. The district court's reliance on medical evidence adduced at the evidentiary hearing unquestionably was proper and the findings based thereon cannot be said to be clearly erroneous. See *D'Amico v. New York State Bd. of Law Examiners,* 813 F.Supp. 217, 223 (W.D.N.Y. 1993) (treating physician's testimony ordinarily should be given "great weight" in determining reasonableness of requested accommodation); *accord Pushkin v. Regents of the Univ. of Colo.,* 658 F.2d 1372, 1390 (10th Cir. 1981). Moreover, any purported inconsistency between the lay witnesses' observations and the testimony of Shapiro's experts is, as the district court found, explainable by the fluctuating nature of Shapiro's symptoms.

Cadman Towers also takes issue with the district court's assessment of Shapiro's urinary difficulties, arguing that Shapiro's incontinence could be remedied by the permanent use of an indwelling catheter. While the district court did not make a specific finding with respect to this point, each party's expert testified that long-term use of an indwelling catheter was inadvisable due to the risk of serious complications, including recurring infections. It seems clear that the district court credited this testimony and found that the permanent use of an indwelling catheter was medically inadvisable for Shapiro. See *Shapiro,* 844 F.Supp. at 118. Inasmuch as this finding has substantial support in the record, it is not clearly erroneous.

* * *

Cadman Towers argues that Shapiro did not need a parking space in its garage, because she could park on the street in spaces set aside for handicapped persons or in a commercial parking garage. However, the district court found that parking spots on the street frequently were unavailable to Shapiro or were too far away, and this determination is supported by the record. Similarly, the record supports the district court's determination that, in view of the severity of the difficulties experienced by Shapiro, the closest commercial parking garage also is too far from her apartment.

In sum, we believe that the district court's factual findings with respect to Shapiro's medical condition and the associated hardships are well supported by the record and are not clearly erroneous. See *Anderson v. City of Bessemer,* 470 U.S. 564, 575 (1985). We therefore conclude that the district court did not err in determining that Shapiro would likely suffer irreparable physical and emotional harm absent issuance of the injunction.

* * *

Cadman Towers contends that the district court erred by failing to interpret the phrase "reasonable accommodation" used in 42 U.S.C. § 3604 in the same manner as the phrase has been interpreted under Title VII of the Civil Rights Act of 1964. Title VII requires an employer to "reasonably accommodate" an employee's religious observances or practices, provided that the requested accommodation would not work an "undue hardship" on the employer's business. 42 U.S.C. §§ 2000e(j), 2000e-2(a)(1). Cadman Towers contends that cases construing the term "reasonable accommodation" under Title VII consistently have held that the concept of "reasonable accommodation" requires only equal treatment and in no event extends to "affirmative action." See *Trans World Airlines, Inc. v. Hardison,* 432 U.S. 63, 76-77, 84 (1977) (Title VII's rule of "reasonable accommodation" did not require employer to compel a more senior worker to work a shift that the plaintiff could not work for religious reasons). Applying the Title VII standard for religious accommodation, Cadman Towers argues that, while Shapiro must be given an equal opportunity to use the building's parking garage, the court erred in granting her preferential treatment.

While Cadman Towers may be correct in its assertion that, under Title VII, any accommodation requiring more than a *de minimis* cost is an "undue hardship" and thus unreasonable, *see, e.g., Eversley v. Mbank Dallas,* 843 F.2d 172, 175 (5th Cir. 1988), its reliance on Title VII is misplaced. We believe that in enacting the anti-discrimination provisions of the FHAA, Congress relied on the standard of reasonable accommodation developed under section 504 of the Rehabilitation Act of 1973, codified at 29 U.S.C. § 794.

Section 504 prohibits federally-funded programs from discriminating on the basis of a handicap and requires such programs to reasonably accommodate an otherwise-qualified individual's handicaps. The legislative history of section 42 U.S.C. § 3604(f) plainly indicates that its drafters intended to draw on case law developed under section 504, a provision also specifically directed at eradicating discrimination against handicapped individuals. *See* House Report 711, 1988 U.S.C.C.A.N. at 2186 & n. 66, 2189-90 & n. 74 (citing *Southeastern Community College v. Davis,* 442 U.S. 397 (1979), a case construing section 504)); see also *United States v. California Mobile Home Park Mgmt. Co.,* 29 F.3d 1413, 1416-17 (9th Cir. 1994) (adopting same view).

The legislative history of section 3604(f) makes no reference to Title VII nor to the cases interpreting it. The absence of such a reference is highly significant, because the concept of reasonable accommodation under section 504 is different from that under Title VII. While the Supreme Court has held that section 504 was intended to provide for "evenhanded treatment of qualified handicapped persons" and that it does not "impose an affirmative-action obligation," *Davis,* 442 U.S. at 410-11, the Court explained in a later case that "the term 'affirmative action' referred to those 'changes,' 'adjustments,' or 'modifications' to existing programs that would be 'substantial' or that would constitute 'fundamental alteration[s] in the nature of a program' rather than those changes that would be reasonable accommodations," *Alexander v. Choate,* 469 U.S. 287, 300 n. 20 (1985) (citations and quotations omitted). Accordingly, "reasonable accommodation" under section 504 can and often will involve some costs. See *Dopico v. Goldschmidt,* 687 F.2d 644, 652 (2d Cir. 1982) ("[S]ection 504 does require at least 'modest, affirmative steps' to accommodate the handicapped. . . .").

In light of the legislative history of section 3604, which specifically indicates that the term "reasonable accommodation" was intended to draw on the case law under section 504 of the Rehabilitation Act, and the fact that both provisions are directed toward eliminating discrimination against handicapped individuals, we conclude that the district court correctly relied on the standards for "reasonable accommodations" developed under section 504, rather than the more restrictive standard of religious accommodation developed under Title VII. Thus, Cadman Towers can be required to incur reasonable costs to accommodate Shapiro's handicap, provided such accommodations do not pose an undue hardship or a substantial burden.

b. Duty to Accommodate Shapiro

Cadman Towers also argues that any duty to accommodate Shapiro has not yet arisen. In its view, only when Shapiro reaches the top of the parking garage's waiting list in the normal course will parking be a "service[ ] or facilit[y] . . . [offered] in connection" with the rental of her dwelling. 42 U.S.C. § 3604(f)(2). We disagree. Pursuant to section 3604(f)(3)(B), Cadman Towers is required to make reasonable accommodations in its rules and practices so as to enable Shapiro to "use and enjoy [her] dwelling." As discussed above, without a nearby parking space, Shapiro is subjected to a risk of injury, infection, and humiliation each time she leaves her dwelling and each time she returns home. We agree with the district court that, under these circumstances, nearby parking is a substantial factor in Shapiro's "use and enjoyment" of her dwelling.

Further support for this conclusion is found in 24 C.F.R. § 100.204(b), a regulation promulgated by HUD that provides an example of a "reasonable accommodation" under the FHAA. The example set forth in section 100.204(b) posits a building with 300 apartments and 450 parking spaces available on a first-come/first-served basis, and states that the duty to make "reasonable accommodations" obligates the building management to reserve a parking space for a mobility-impaired tenant near that tenant's apartment. It explains the reason for this as follows:

> Without a reserved space, [the tenant] might be unable to live in [the apartment] at all or, when he has to park in a space far from his unit, might have difficulty getting from his car to his apartment unit. The accommodation therefore is necessary to afford [the tenant] an equal opportunity *to use and enjoy a dwelling.*

Id. (emphasis added). Although the situation before us is different from the example, because at Cadman Towers there are fewer parking spaces than apartments, this regulation makes it clear that the use and enjoyment of a parking space cannot be considered in isolation from the tenant's ability to use and enjoy her dwelling place, a right specifically protected by the FHAA. We cannot say that this interpretation is unreasonable. See *Chevron U.S.A., Inc. v. Natural Resources Defense Counsel, Inc.,* 467 U.S. 837, 844 (1984) (agency regulations implementing a statute must be given "controlling weight" unless unreasonable).

Cadman Towers, however, attempts to use the example set forth in section 100.204(b) to support its position. It argues that HUD's inclusion of such an innocuous example of a reasonable accommodation must have been intended to demonstrate that only trivial burdens can be placed on property owners. This argument is without merit. "There is no suggestion in the regulations that [these examples] are intended to be exhaustive. . . ." *United States v. Village of Marshall,* 787 F.Supp. 872, 878 (W.D.Wis. 1991) (rejecting the same argument). Moreover, such a interpretation would be inconsistent with the Supreme Court's admonition that the Fair Housing Act be given a "generous construction," based on the importance of the anti-discrimination policies that it vindicates. *Trafficante v. Metropolitan Life Ins. Co.,* 409 U.S. 205, 211-12 (1972).

* * *

Cadman Towers also argues that a reasonable accommodation under the FHAA cannot include displacing tenants who already have parking spaces assigned to them or interfering with the expectancy of persons already on the waiting list. It bases this argument on lines of cases under section 504 and Title VII involving seniority rights in the workplace in which courts have held that displacing workers with seniority is not a reasonable accommodation. See *Hardison,* 432 U.S. at 82-83 (under Title VII); *Eversley,* 843 F.2d at 175-76 (under section 504). Cadman Towers analogizes its first-come/first-served allocation of parking spaces to a traditional seniority system in the workplace, typically implemented under a collective bargaining act.

The extent to which a "reasonable accommodation" for a handicapped individual can burden or take away rights or privileges enjoyed by non-handicapped persons is an important question of first impression in this Circuit, particularly in the non-workplace context. However, it would be premature for us to reach this issue now. The district court found that Shapiro could be accommodated without displacing any existing tenants, because three parking spots are reserved for building personnel and these workers could park in a commercial garage. Moreover, the court found that one parking space was used by a person that did not live in the building. These findings are well supported by the record and will not be disturbed on appeal. Accordingly, four parking spaces were available for handicapped individuals that would not impair the rights of other non-handicapped building tenants. We note, however, that the policies implicated in collective bargaining and labor-relations cases, see *Hardison,* 432 U.S. at 79, are different from the policies implicated in the assignment of a parking space to a handicapped person.

* * *

CONCLUSION

For the foregoing reasons, the order entered in the district court is AFFIRMED.

Notes & Questions

1. Is the *Shapiro* court correct in rejecting appellants' view that the FHAA's reasonable accommodation language should be interpreted in the same way as Title VII? Is Shapiro's requested accommodation a form of "affirmative action," as appellants suggest, or is it a way for Shapiro to enjoy her housing in the same way as other tenants? Can it be both?

2. What burden does immediately giving Shapiro a parking space put on appellants? Think both in terms of any financial cost and their business concerns in explaining the situation to other tenants, many of whom were clearly not amenable to Shapiro receiving her requested parking space.

3. In light of the U.S. Supreme Court's approach to reassignment under the ADA Title I in *Barnett,* finding that the expectations of more senior employees under a seniority system make reassignment of an employee with a disability to a vacant position unreasonable, how would the court today deal with the waiting list issue? Is the *Shapiro* court correct that "the policies implicated in collective bargaining and labor-relations cases . . . are different from the policies implicated in the assignment of a parking space to a handicapped person"?

4. In *Jankowski Lee & Associates v. Cisneros,* a tenant with multiple sclerosis requested an accommodation of either an increased number of handicapped parking spaces, or a space assigned to him. The record showed that even after the defendant added two spaces, there were only eight handicapped parking spaces and one van space for the 27

tenants registered to park at the apartment complex with handicapped stickers for their vehicles. The court held the defendant was in violation of the FHAA. *See also* Sporn v. Ocean Colony Condominium Ass'n, 173 F.Supp.2d 244 (D.N.J. 2001) (holding that condominium association's policy of requiring owners seeking handicapped parking to trade their deeded parking spaces for association-owned spaces closer to main entrance was reasonable accommodation under FHAA); Hubbard v. Samson Mgmt. Corp., 994 F.Supp. 187 (S.D.N.Y. 1998) (holding that landlord's proposal to designate fee-paid space for tenant, where complex offered fee-paid reserved parking and unreserved free parking, was not reasonable accommodation under FHAA); Trovato v. City of Manchester, N.H., 992 F.Supp. 493 (D.N.H. 1997) (holding city that denied zoning variance that would allow individuals with disabilities to build accessible parking spaces in front of their homes violated FHAA).

5. What about ordinances dealing with nuisance abatements? In *McGary v. City of Portland*, 386 F.3d 1259 (9th Cir. 2004), the City of Portland had an ordinance (as many cities do) regulating the amount of trash and debris in yards. The plaintiff, an individual with AIDS, was cited with violation of the ordinance, and he requested additional time to clean his yard in order to comply with the nuisance ordinance. The City refused. The district court dismissed the plaintiff's complaint, holding that plaintiff's accommodation was not necessary to afford him an equal opportunity to use and enjoy his home. The Ninth Circuit disagreed, and reversed.

6. In *Bentley v. Peace and Quiet Reality 2LLC,* 367 F.Supp.2d 341 (E.D. N.Y. 2005), the plaintiff argued that her landlord failed to accommodate her by refusing to allow her to move to a vacant lower-level unit in her rent stabilized apartment building at her current rent. The landlord argued that plaintiff's request, which would have kept the landlord from receiving maximum rent in the new unit, did not come within FHAA's concept of accommodation because (1) she sought to have her poverty rather than disability accommodated, and (2) offering the apartment at its maximum permissible legal rent under the state's disability neutral rent stabilization laws fulfilled the landlord's FHAA obligations. Plaintiff argued that if she vacated her current unit, the landlord could increase the rent of that unit to offset any financial burden to the defendants from the proposed accommodation. Holding that a request to transfer units within the same building falls within the scope of FHAA accommodations, the court set a hearing to assess the reasonableness of the accommodation

7. The reasonable accommodation request must be on the basis of disability, not some other trait, like poverty, that might correlate with disability. In *Sutton v. Piper*, 244 F. App'x 101, 103 (6th Cir. 2009), the court held that the FHAA did not require a defendant to modify its credit score requirements, finding that "a review of Sutton's credit report

confirms that his poor credit history resulted from his own financial mismanagement and not his disability."

The next case considers how far a landlord must go to accommodate a disruptive tenant, and discusses how the burdens of proof for reasonable accommodation are allocated.

GRONER v. GOLDEN GATE GARDENS APARTMENTS

United States Court of Appeals, Sixth Circuit, 2001
250 F.3d 1039

GILMAN, Circuit Judge.

Howard Groner and the Metropolitan Strategy Group, a nonprofit housing rights organization, brought suit against the owners and the manager of Golden Gate Gardens Apartments under the federal Fair Housing Act and Ohio's analogous anti-discrimination housing provisions. The dispute arose when Golden Gate threatened to evict Groner, a tenant with a known mental disability, following numerous complaints from another tenant about Groner's excessive noisemaking at all hours of the day and night. Groner alleges that Golden Gate's refusal to provide a reasonable accommodation that would have enabled him to remain in his apartment amounted to unlawful discrimination. The district court granted Golden Gate's motion for summary judgment, concluding that the defendants had attempted to reasonably accommodate Groner, albeit unsuccessfully. Groner now challenges that decision. For the reasons set forth below, we AFFIRM the judgment of the district court.

I. BACKGROUND

The Golden Gate apartment complex is located in Mayfield Heights, Ohio. Groner, who suffers from schizophrenia and depression, moved into one of the apartments in April of 1997. Golden Gate was aware of his mental disability, but Groner was able to live independently and had no special needs. He paid his rent in a timely manner and properly maintained the condition of his apartment.

Diane Arter had lived in the apartment located directly above Groner's since 1992. Approximately four months after Groner moved in, she registered her first complaint with the apartment manager, Kathleen Boyle. Arter reported that she was unable to sleep because Groner was screaming and slamming doors within his apartment throughout the night. In response to this complaint, Boyle contacted Ray Gonzalez, Groner's social worker, to inform him of the problem created by Groner's behavior. The disturbances persisted during the next month and a half, causing Arter to file a second complaint. Boyle again notified Gonzalez, who replied that he was working with Groner to resolve the issue. Shortly thereafter, with no noticeable improvement, Arter complained a third time. Gonzalez was once again contacted by Boyle. This time, he informed her that he had counseled Groner to "scream into the pillow" to muffle the noises at night.

By May of 1998, Arter had registered a total of four or five complaints concerning Groner's noisemaking. Because the situation remained unchanged when Groner's year-to-year lease expired that month, Golden Gate did not renew the annual lease. Groner became a month-to-month tenant, whose tenancy could be terminated on 30 days' notice to vacate the premises.

During the period in question, Golden Gate soundproofed the front door to Groner's apartment in an attempt to lessen the noise. This was done after Arter complained that Groner's door-slamming had caused a picture to fall off the wall in her apartment and break. Golden Gate also gave Arter the option of moving to a different apartment within the complex, or terminating her lease without penalty. Arter, however, refused the offer, saying that it would be unfair to expect her to move as the solution to a problem caused by Groner's behavior.

When Arter complained again in August of 1998 about Groner's yelling and door-slamming, Boyle notified Groner that his month-to-month tenancy was not being renewed, and that he would have to vacate his apartment by November 1. Groner relayed this information to Gonzalez, who then contacted Boyle to ascertain why Groner's tenancy was being terminated. Boyle informed him that Groner's noisemaking had continued and was disturbing Arter.

In a letter dated October 5, 1998, Gonzalez requested that Groner's lease be renewed as a reasonable accommodation in light of his disability. When Gonzalez had received no response by October 13, he faxed the letter along with a cover sheet that asked Boyle to call him to discuss the matter further. Boyle then sent Gonzalez a response by fax, agreeing to grant Groner a one-month extension that would provide additional time for Gonzalez to develop a strategy to resolve Groner's noisemaking. The letter cautioned, however, that the extension was conditioned on Boyle not receiving any further complaints about Groner. Otherwise, he would have to vacate his apartment.

In a reply dated October 16, 1998, Gonzalez wrote that he was continuing to work with Groner on a weekly basis in an attempt to modify Groner's behavior. Gonzalez again requested that Golden Gate make reasonable accommodations for Groner by (1) providing him a regular, twelve-month lease and (2) contacting Gonzalez immediately upon the receipt of any complaints about Groner. On October 21, 1998, Boyle called Gonzalez to inform him that Groner could remain in his apartment until at least November 30.

Less than two weeks later, Arter complained that Groner's noisemaking had persisted. Again Boyle notified Gonzalez, who consulted with Groner. Groner allegedly told Gonzalez that he was no longer making any noise. Despite Groner's purported denial to Gonzalez, Boyle notified Groner by letter dated November 21, 1998 that his month-to-month tenancy would not be renewed and that he should plan to vacate his apartment by December 31. Gonzalez then phoned Boyle on December 2 to urge her to reconsider. Boyle, however, refused, stating that previous delays had not helped to resolve the problem and that it would be too burdensome for Golden Gate to continue apprising Gonzalez each time Groner caused a disturbance. By this point, Arter had registered approximately ten to twelve complaints concerning Groner's excessive noisemaking.

In an attempt to extend Groner's tenancy, Gonzalez wrote Boyle on December 14, 1998 to request a face-to-face meeting and to reiterate the request for a reasonable accommodation. Gonzalez's affidavit states that when he did not hear from Boyle, he left her a phone message on December 23 and wrote yet another letter on December 28, restating his desire to discuss these matters in person. Boyle apparently never responded to these final inquiries made by Gonzalez. When Groner had not vacated his apartment by December 31, 1998, Golden Gate served him with an eviction notice to leave by January 5, 1999. Groner moved from his apartment at some point thereafter without awaiting the final outcome of this litigation.

* * *

II. ANALYSIS

* * *

The district court did not err in concluding that Golden Gate had met its burden in attempting to provide reasonable accommodations for Groner.

The Fair Housing Act makes it unlawful to discriminate against "any person in the terms, conditions, or privileges of sale or rental of a dwelling, or in the provision of services or facilities in connection with such dwelling," on the basis of that person's handicap. 42 U.S.C. § 3604(f)(2)(A). Discrimination prohibited by the Act includes the refusal to make reasonable accommodations in "rules, policies, practices, or services, when such accommodations may be necessary to afford [the handicapped individual an] equal opportunity to use and enjoy a dwelling." 42 U.S.C. § 3604(f)(3)(B). Moreover, the Act "imposes an affirmative duty upon landlords reasonably to accommodate the needs of handicapped persons." *United States v. California Mobile Home Park Mgmt. Co.,* 29 F.3d 1413, 1416 (9th Cir. 1994); see also H.R.Rep. No. 100-711 at 25 (1988), U.S. Code Cong. & Admin. News at 2173, 2186.

Accommodations required under the Act must be both reasonable and necessary to afford the handicapped individual an equal opportunity to use and enjoy a dwelling. See *Smith & Lee Assocs., Inc. v. City of Taylor,* 102 F.3d 781, 795-96 (6th Cir. 1996) (holding that the city had violated the Fair Housing Act by failing to allow adult foster care homes to operate in areas zoned for single-family neighborhoods). An accommodation is reasonable when it imposes no "fundamental alteration in the nature of a program" or "undue financial and administrative burdens." Id. at 795.

Whether a requested accommodation is required by law is "highly fact-specific, requiring case-by-case determination." *California Mobile Home Park,* 29 F.3d at 1418; *Hovsons, Inc. v. Township of Brick,* 89 F.3d 1096, 1104 (3d Cir. 1996) . Courts generally balance the burdens imposed on the defendant by the contemplated accommodation against the benefits to the plaintiff. See *Smith & Lee Assocs.,* 102 F.3d at 795. In determining whether the reasonableness requirement has been met, a court may consider the accommodation's functional and administrative aspects, as well as its costs. See *Bryant Woods Inn, Inc. v. Howard County,* 124 F.3d 597, 604 (4th Cir. 1997).

Groner argues that the district court erred when it placed on him the burden of showing that the requested accommodations were reasonable. For support of this contention, he points to the legal standard developed by the Third Circuit. There, "the burden of proving that a proposed accommodation is not reasonable rests with the defendant." *Hovsons, Inc.,* 89 F.3d at 1103. This particular question appears to be one of first impression in the Sixth Circuit. Nevertheless, this court in *Smith & Lee Associates* stated in a footnote that "[p]laintiffs bear the burden of demonstrating that the desired accommodation is necessary to afford equal opportunity." *Smith & Lee Assoc.,* 102 F.3d at 796 n. 11. Although *Smith & Lee Associates* limited its discussion to the *necessity* of an accommodation, it follows that the same analysis applies to our *reasonableness* determination.

Because the Fair Housing Act adopted the concept of a "reasonable accommodation" from § 504 of the Rehabilitation Act, 29 U.S.C. § 791, cases interpreting that term under the Rehabilitation Act also apply to claims under the Fair Housing Act. See *Smith & Lee Assocs.,* 102 F.3d at 795. Under the Rehabilitation Act, our circuit requires a plaintiff seeking an accommodation to show that it is reasonable. See *Monette v. Elec. Data Sys. Corp.,* 90 F.3d 1173, 1183 (6th Cir. 1996) ("[T]he disabled individual bears the initial burden of proposing an accommodation and showing that *that* accommodation is objectively reasonable.") (emphasis in original). The employer then has the burden of persuasion on whether the proposed accommodation would impose an undue hardship. See id. at 1183-84.

Moreover, the Fourth and Fifth Circuits require Fair Housing Act plaintiffs to bear the burden of proof on the question of reasonableness.

See *Bryant Woods Inn, Inc. v. Howard County,* 124 F.3d 597, 603-04 (4th Cir. 1997); *Elderhaven, Inc. v. City of Lubbock,* 98 F.3d 175, 178 (5th Cir. 1996).

* * *

Finally, other courts analyzing the issue under the Rehabilitation Act have concluded that the plaintiff has the burden of proof to establish reasonableness. See *Borkowski v. Valley Cent. Sch. Dist.,* 63 F.3d 131, 137-38 (2d Cir. 1995) (requiring a Rehabilitation Act plaintiff to show that she needed an accommodation to retain her employment and that such an accommodation existed); *Woodman v. Runyon,* 132 F.3d 1330, 1344 (10th Cir. 1997) (same). Based on this court's own precedents and the weight of other authorities, we conclude that the plaintiff in a Fair Housing Act case has the burden of proof to establish the reasonableness of a proposed accommodation.

Groner's interests should not be viewed lightly. He is, after all, suffering from a serious mental illness. Furthermore, both parties concede that his noisemaking was directly related to his handicap. Groner, however, has been unable to show that Golden Gate neglected to provide a reasonable accommodation that would have enabled Groner to remain in his apartment.

Initially, Groner requested two possible accommodations. The first suggested accommodation would have enabled Groner to remain in his apartment under the terms of a regular, twelve-month lease as he continued to seek counseling from Gonzalez in hopes of resolving his disturbing behavior. The second proposal would have involved contacting Gonzalez immediately upon the receipt of any complaints about Groner.

Groner was unable to demonstrate that either of these proposed accommodations was reasonable. Golden Gate had attempted to implement a limited version of both proposals when it granted Groner a number of extensions after its initial notice to vacate in October of 1998, and by advising Gonzalez of several disturbances. Gonzalez was aware of the problem since at least May of 1998, because at that time he had instructed Groner to scream into his pillow in an attempt to mute the noises. Moreover, Gonzalez's October 16, 1998 letter to Boyle states that he had "been working with Mr. Groner on a *weekly basis* regarding your concerns that he is making loud noises" (emphasis added). Yet Arter continued to register complaints about Groner's incessant "yelling, screaming, and slamming" of doors throughout this period.

In this appeal, Groner pursues a total of four accommodations that would have allowed him to remain a tenant at Golden Gate. (Although Groner's response to Golden Gate's motion for summary judgment included a fifth proposal that Arter report Groner to the police for each disturbance, he has abandoned that proposed accommodation on appeal.) The first proposal that he pursues on appeal is that Golden Gate could have moved Groner or Arter to another apartment within the complex. All Golden Gate apartments, however, were of the same two-story configuration, so that Groner would have likely disturbed whomever was the neighboring tenant. Groner has thus failed to show that this was a reasonable accommodation that Golden Gate neglected to implement. Furthermore, Golden Gate had given Arter the option of moving, and she had refused to do so. Golden Gate could not lawfully force Arter to vacate her apartment during her lease. "[A]s a matter of law, the [neighbor's] rights did not have to be sacrificed on the altar of reasonable accommodation." *Temple v. Gunsalus,* No. 95-3175, 1996 WL 536710, at *2 (6th Cir. Sept.20, 1996) (unpublished table decision) (internal quotation marks omitted) (holding that the Fair Housing Act did not require a landlord to evict a neighboring tenant in order to accommodate the plaintiff's multiple-chemical-sensitivity disorder). Groner, therefore, failed to show that moving either Arter or himself would have been a reasonable accommodation.

Second, Groner suggests that Arter could have been replaced by a "hard-of-hearing tenant" who would be a "perfect match" for Groner. In support of this assertion, Groner points to Boyle's deposition where she responded "probably" to a question about there being any hard-of-hearing tenants at Golden Gate. Groner ignores, however, the immediate follow-up question concerning her personal knowledge of such tenants. To this, Boyle responded: "I have no knowledge of anyone being hard-of-hearing." Groner was unable to produce evidence of any hard-of-hearing tenant within the apartment complex. Accordingly, this proposed accommodation was not shown to be feasible.

Third, Groner reiterates the suggestion that Gonzalez be contacted for his immediate intervention whenever a complaint was received. As discussed above, this proposed accommodation had proven to be ineffective in the past. Arter continued to complain of the noise even after Gonzalez's attempted intervention. Groner argues on appeal that Gonzalez had only been contacted three times during Groner's two-and-a-half-year tenancy at Golden Gate. The record shows, however, that Arter complained a total of ten to twelve times, and that Groner's screaming and slamming of doors occurred on a regular basis well after Gonzalez was made aware of the problem. Such an indefinite arrangement, moreover, would likely have imposed an undue administrative burden on the Golden Gate staff. Accordingly, Groner has failed to demonstrate that such an accommodation was reasonable.

Finally, Groner proposes that Golden Gate could have undertaken further soundproofing of his apartment. Although Golden Gate had soundproofed the front door to the apartment, Arter continued to be disturbed by his noisemaking. Golden Gate also raises legitimate safety concerns that could result from soundproofing an entire apartment, such as an increased fire hazard and an inability to communicate with the tenant in the event of an emergency. Moreover, such an undertaking would substantially alter Groner's apartment beyond his tenancy. Despite Groner's contention that he would have undertaken the expense under the Fair Housing Act, the Act does not require "changes, adjustments, or modifications . . . that would constitute fundamental alterations." *Bryant Woods Inn, Inc. v. Howard County,* 124 F.3d 597, 604 (4th Cir. 1997). Soundproofing the entire apartment would amount to such a fundamental change. As such, Groner has not shown that this would have been a reasonable accommodation.

Throughout this appeal, Groner also asserts that Golden Gate violated its duty to engage in a dialogue with Gonzalez in order to accommodate Groner's disability. Groner contends that the failure of Boyle to respond to Gonzalez's requests in December of 1998 for a face-to-face meeting to discuss possible accommodations is evidence of bad faith on the part of Golden Gate. By that point, however, Boyle had already been in close contact with Gonzalez for months, and previous efforts to accommodate Groner's disability had proven unsuccessful. We therefore agree with the district court's conclusion that such inaction did not establish bad faith on the part of Boyle, even though we do not condone her failure to respond to Gonzalez's eleventh-hour efforts. Moreover, while some courts have imposed an obligation on employers and employees to engage in an interactive process, there is no such language in the Fair Housing Act or in the relevant sections of the Department of Housing and Urban Development's implementing regulations that would impose such a duty on landlords and tenants. *See* 24 C.F.R. §§ 100.200-205.

Taking all of the circumstances into account, the balance of the equities in this case does not weigh in Groner's favor. All previous efforts to resolve the problem had failed. Groner's alternative proposed accommodations were not found to be reasonable. As the Seventh Circuit has recognized, a "reasonable accommodation does not entail an obligation to do everything humanly possible to accommodate a disabled person." *Bronk v. Ineichen,* 54 F.3d 425, 429 (7th Cir. 1995). Because Golden Gate has a legitimate interest in ensuring the quiet enjoyment of *all* its tenants, and because there has been no showing of a reasonable accommodation that would have enabled Groner to remain in his apartment without significantly disturbing another tenant, Groner has failed to raise a genuine issue of material fact as to a violation of his rights under either the Fair Housing Act or the equivalent laws of Ohio.

* * *

III. CONCLUSION

For all of the reasons set forth above, we AFFIRM the judgment of the district court.

Notes & Questions

1. As *Groner* notes, courts are split on who should bear the burden in a FHAA case to prove that the requested accommodation is reasonable. Some courts put the burden on the plaintiff. *See* Bryant Woods Inn, Inc. v. Howard County, 124 F.3d 597, 603-04 (4th Cir. 1997); Elderhaven, Inc. v. City of Lubbock, 98 F.3d 175, 178 (5th Cir. 1996). But other courts only place an initial burden on the plaintiff to show reasonableness, and then move the burden to the defendant to show that the accommodation is not reasonable. *See* Lapid-Laurel, LLC v. Zoning Bd. of Adjustment, 284 F.3d 442, 457 (3d Cir. 2002); Hovsons Inc. v. Township of Brick, 89 F.3d 1096, 1103 (3d Cir. 1996). Which approach is closer to the ADA burden shifting scheme? *See supra* Part 3, § 8.4. Which is preferable?

2. Do you agree with the *Groner* court that none of plaintiff's requested accommodations were reasonable? Can you think of an accommodation that would be reasonable? What if plaintiff had offered to completely soundproof his apartment, at his own expense?

3. The FHAA also provides that "nothing in this subsection requires that a dwelling be made available to an individual whose tenancy would constitute a direct threat to the health or safety of other individuals or whose tenancy would result in substantial physical damage to the property of others." 42 U.S.C. § 3604(f)(9) (2006). This must be proved with objective evidence that is sufficiently recent as to be credible, and not from unsubstantiated inferences. *See* Scoggins v. Lee's Crossing Homeowners Ass'n, 718 F.3d 262, 272 (2013) (rejecting plaintiff's request to use his all terrain vehicle on community's common driveways and roads); *see also* Corey v. HUD, 719 F.3d 322, 328 (4th Cir. 2013) (holding that unsubstantiated fears and stereotypes of people with autism did not make out direct threat defense); Howard v. City of Beavercreek, 108 F.Supp.2d 866, 875 (S.D. Ohio 2000) (holding that defendant was not required by FHAA to grant plaintiff permission to construct a six foot fence to alleviate the effects of post traumatic stress disorder, because fence posed a threat to pedestrian and vehicular traffic); Support Ministries for Persons with AIDS, Inc. v. Village of Waterford, N.Y., 808 F.Supp. 120 (N.D.N.Y. 1992) (holding that occupancy of proposed adult care facility by HIV-positive homeless persons would not constitute direct threat to health and safety of other individuals).

One last group of FHAA cases involves a fact pattern that you have already seen in *Cleburne, supra* Part 1, § 1.3, and *Michigan P & A*, in this Part. An organization or group of people with mental disabilities wants to set up a group home, and needs relief or an exemption from some type of zoning ordinance. A request is made to the city or local government for a "reasonable accommodation" in the form of an exception to the zoning ordinance or rule. The FHAA clearly applies to these types of laws. *See* 42 U.S.C. § 3615 (invalidating "any law of a State, a political subdivision, or other such jurisdiction that purports to require or permit any action that would be discriminatory housing practice under this subchapter").

The following two cases are examples of how courts deal with this issue. Note how the issue of burden allocation, discussed *supra*, Notes & Questions no. 1, affects the determination of whether any given accommodation is reasonable.

ॐ

OCONOMOWOC RESIDENTIAL PROGRAMS, INC. v.
CITY OF MILWAUKEE

United States Court of Appeals, Seventh Circuit, 2002
300 F.3d 775

ROVNER, Circuit Judge.

After the City of Milwaukee (City) denied Oconomowoc Residential Programs, Inc. (ORP) a zoning variance to operate a community living facility in the City, ORP sued the City for violations of the Fair Housing Amendments Act (FHAA) and the Americans with Disabilities Act (ADA). The district court granted Oconomowoc's and plaintiff-intervenors' motion for partial summary judgment and denied the City's motion for summary judgment. The City appeals, and we affirm.

I.

* * *

This controversy arose over plaintiff ORP's application to operate a community living facility for six adults impaired by traumatic brain injury or developmental disabilities or both. The City, through its Board of Zoning Appeals (BOZA), denied the request for a variance pursuant to a municipal ordinance restricting such homes from operating within 2,500 feet (approximately one half of a mile) of another community living arrangement.

ORP is a Wisconsin corporation licensed by the State to operate community-based residential programs. The Wisconsin Department of Health and Family Services (DHFS) regulates its operations. Homes for Independent Living (HIL), a division of ORP, operates approximately ninety-five group homes which provide residential and support services to persons with developmental disabilities, chronic mental illness, and traumatic brain injuries. Over 800 persons in ten southeastern Wisconsin counties receive services provided by HIL.

* * *

Aware of the need for community-based residential facilities for people with traumatic brain injury and developmental disabilities, ORP

807

staff worked for over a year with a local real estate agent to find a home that would be physically and financially appropriate for such a group home. On August 20, 1996, ORP applied for an occupancy permit for a community-based residential facility for six developmentally disabled or traumatically brain injured adults at 2850 North Menomonee River Parkway in Milwaukee. In September, 1996, ORP purchased the house for $280,000. During the application for an occupancy permit however, ORP ran into a stumbling block.

As part of its zoning code, Milwaukee restricts the placement of community living arrangements. Milwaukee permits community living arrangements for not more than eight persons in single residence districts, subject to certain special conditions. Milwaukee, Wi., Code of Ordinances § 295-112. Those conditions are as follows:

> Special Conditions. 1. GROUP LIVING FACILITIES. a. Small foster homes and community living arrangements shall not be located within 2,500 feet of each other and their cumulative capacities shall not exceed one percent of the population of an aldermanic district. * * *

Id. at § 295-14-1(a).

* * *

Relying on the Milwaukee ordinance regarding the 2,500-foot requirement, the City of Milwaukee Department of Building Inspection (DBI) refused to issue an occupancy permit to ORP. By letter dated November 4, 1996, DBI returned ORP's application stating that ORP could not operate a community-based residential facility at that site without violating § 25-14-1 of the Milwaukee ordinance, as there were already two other group homes operating within 2,500 feet of the proposed home, one of which was operating within 358 feet of the proposed home. In addition to its determination that the proposed home violated the spacing requirements, the DBI made several other observations in its letter. First, it noted that the proposed group home sits on the fringe of the flood plain of the Menomonee River. It then expressed concerns about the volume of traffic on the road during the summer months, and the fact that the road does not have sidewalks for pedestrian traffic. DBI informed ORP that it could seek a variance by appealing to BOZA. According to the Milwaukee municipal code, DBI has no authority to grant a permanent variance for the occupancy of any building if the intended use and plans do not conform with the City's ordinances. Id. at § 295-51-1(a).

By the time ORP received the letter from DBI, it had already applied to BOZA for a waiver of the 2,500-foot rule. In its application, filed on October 24, 1996, ORP submitted its plan of operation for a six-person home with non-live-in, round-the-clock staff. BOZA held a hearing on the variance request on January 16, 1997.

During the BOZA hearing, ORP's counsel argued that the variance was necessary as a reasonable accommodation under the FHAA. To support this claim, ORP presented evidence regarding the need in the City and County of Milwaukee for residential facilities for persons with traumatic brain injuries. Specifically, ORP presented evidence regarding the difficulties in locating resources and facilities to provide services to brain injured individuals in the least restrictive environment consistent with the needs of the disabled person as required by state statute. ORP presented detailed information about the needs of the individual plaintiffs Janet K. and Valerie D. At the time of the hearing, both plaintiffs were living in a nursing home, though each was the subject of a court order requiring them to be placed in a less restrictive environment, such as a community-based residential facility. Each of the plaintiffs' respective guardians desired that they be placed in the home at 2850 North Menomonee River Parkway. ORP and Milwaukee County had reviewed the placements of Janet K. and Valerie D and determined that they could be transferred to the proposed group home as soon as the facility could open.

ORP presented evidence that, due to limited state funding, community services for persons with disabilities are available to only a limited number of persons each year. Janet K. and Valerie D. were eligible for and received one of only a few specialized "brain injury waiver program" slots for 1996.

The prospective neighbors of the group home appeared at the hearing to lodge their concerns about the facility. Neighbors expressed concern that the brain injured patients might become violent and threaten the safety of residents of the community. One neighbor objecting to the proposed variance testified that his wife and the wife of another objecting neighbor were both psychologists and "could attest to the fact that brain injured patients can and do become violent." Another objecting neighbor testified that between 1942 and 1950 he had a brain injured uncle who lived with the family, but who had to be removed to a mental institution when he become violent. Other neighbors raised concerns about the amount of traffic on the parkway, parking restrictions that could constitute a hazard for the group home residents, the lack of sidewalks, particularly in relation to the amount and speed of the traffic on the parkway, and the potential for flooding. Some were concerned that the inclined driveway of the home could present a danger to residents as they entered and exited handicap-accessible vans. Lee Jensen, the Commissioner of DBI, testified at the hearing in opposition to the variance, not in his official capacity, but as a prospective neighbor of the facility.

As part of the proceedings, the Office of the City Engineer issued a report to BOZA that concluded that the proposed community-based residential facility would not have a "significant adverse impact" on traffic and parking conditions in the neighborhood.

An attorney for a number of neighbors opposing the variance presented evidence of ORP's history as a group home operator. The evidence included reports of various investigations by DHFS regarding allegations of errors, negligence, or wrongdoings by staff of ORP corporate affiliates. The history included reports that (1) one resident received a double dose of medication; (2) DHHS had determined that a staff member sexually assaulted a resident; (3) eight residents were left outside of a home without supervision for forty-five minutes; (4) one facility failed to report in a timely manner that a staff member had physically abused a resident; (5) another facility neglected a five-year-old basement flooding problem, and had rotting and mold problems as a result; (6) staff of a facility for developmentally disabled adults failed to control noise coming from the residents; (7) police officers were called to respond to physical outbursts by residents of a facility for the developmentally disabled; (8) police officers were called on numerous occasions to another group home to respond to reports of combative assaults by a particular resident; and (9) an elderly resident of a group home was found in the Menomonee River.

* * *

On February 6, 1997, BOZA voted to deny the request for a variance. On March 10, 1997, BOZA issued its written decision denying the request. The decision stated that the variance request was a "flagrant violation of the state's distance requirement," noting that there is another facility located 358 feet away, two others within 2,500 feet, and two more just slightly outside of the 2,500-foot boundary. BOZA's decision also expressed concern for the safety of the residents due to the high traffic and lack of sidewalks on the Menomonee River Parkway. The decision stated that, based on the allegations of problems emanating from other ORP facilities, the proposed facility could impose undue costs, expenses, or other burdens on the City. The decision went on to note that the City had done its fair share of providing community living arrangements and group homes, in part by granting thirty-nine variances to the spacing ordinance, and that the rest of Milwaukee County had many sites available.

* * *

II.

A. Reasonable Accommodation

The plaintiffs maintain that the City's refusal to grant them an exception to the 2,500-foot rule violates both the FHAA and the ADA. The Fair Housing Act (FHA) was enacted "to provide, within constitutional limitations, for fair housing throughout the United States." 42 U.S.C. § 3601. The amendments to the Fair Housing Act, contained in the FHAA, specifically prohibit discrimination in housing on the basis of disability. 42 U.S.C. § 3604(f).

* * *

Congress explicitly intended for the FHAA to apply to zoning ordinances and other laws that would restrict the placement of group homes. H.R.Rep. No. 100-711, at 24 (1988), *reprinted in* 1988 U.S.C.C.A.N. 2173, 2185 (stating that the amendments "would also apply to state or local land use and health and safety laws, regulations, practices or decisions which discriminate against individuals with handicaps").

* * *

The FHAA requires accommodation if such accommodation (1) is reasonable, and (2) necessary, (3) to afford a handicapped person the equal opportunity to use and enjoy a dwelling. 42 U.S.C. § 3604(f)(3)(B).

* * *

The burden is on the plaintiffs to show that the accommodation it seeks is reasonable on its face. *US Airways, Inc. v. Barnett,* 535 U.S. 391, 400 (2002). Once the plaintiffs have made this prima facie showing, the defendant must come forward to demonstrate unreasonableness or undue hardship in the particular circumstances. Id.; see also *Vande Zande v. Wisconsin Dep't of Admin.,* 44 F.3d 538, 543 (7th Cir. 1995).

The City argues that the plaintiffs bear the burden of proof with respect to the issue of reasonable accommodation, citing both the Fifth and Fourth circuits in *Bryant Woods Inn, Inc.,* 124 F.3d at 603-604 and *Elderhaven, Inc. v. City of Lubbock, Texas,* 98 F.3d 175, 178 (5th Cir. 1996). The City, however, offers no reason for choosing this regime over the method used by the Second, Third, Eighth, Ninth, and Tenth Circuits which require a plaintiff to make an initial showing that an accommodation is reasonable, but then places the burden on the defendant to show that the accommodation is unreasonable.

* * *

We begin by focusing on the definitions of the three key elements of a reasonable accommodation: "reasonable," "necessary," and "equal opportunity." Whether a requested accommodation is reasonable or not is a highly fact-specific inquiry and requires balancing the needs of the parties. *Dadian,* 269 F.3d at 838. An accommodation is reasonable if it is both efficacious and proportional to the costs to implement it. *Vande Zande,* 44 F.3d at 543. An accommodation is unreasonable if it imposes undue financial or administrative burdens or requires a fundamental alteration in the nature of the program. *Erdman,* 84 F.3d at 962 (internal citations omitted). In assessing costs, the court may look at both financial and administrative costs and burdens. *Bryant Woods Inn, Inc.,* 124 F.3d at 604. A zoning waiver is unreasonable if it is so "at odds with the purposes behind the rule that it would be a fundamental and unreasonable change." *Dadian,* 269 F.3d at 838-39.

"Whether the requested accommodation is necessary requires a 'showing that the desired accommodation will affirmatively enhance a disabled plaintiff's quality of life by ameliorating the effects of the disability.'" *Dadian,* 269 F.3d at 838 (citing *Bronk,* 54 F.3d at 429). In other words, the plaintiffs must show that without the required accommodation they will be denied the equal opportunity to live in a residential neighborhood.

In this context, "equal opportunity" means the opportunity to choose to live in a residential neighborhood. *Lapid-Laurel, L.L.C.,* 284 F.3d at 460; *Smith & Lee Assoc.,* 102 F.3d at 794. The FHAA "prohibits local governments from applying land use regulations in a manner that will ... give disabled people less opportunity to live in certain neighborhoods than people without disabilities." *Smith & Lee Assoc.,* 102 F.3d at 795 (internal citation omitted). Often, a community-based residential facility provides the only means by which disabled persons can live in a residential neighborhood, either because they need more supportive services, for financial reasons, or both. *Erdman,* 84 F.3d at 963; *Brandt v. Village of Chebanse, Illinois,* 82 F.3d 172, 174 (7th Cir. 1996); *Larkin,* 89 F.3d at 291; *Hovsons, Inc.,* 89 F.3d at 1105; *Smith & Lee Assoc.,* 102 F.3d at 795-96. When a zoning authority refuses to reasonably accommodate these small group living facilities, it denies disabled persons an equal opportunity to live in the community of their choice. *Erdman,* 84 F.3d at 963.

Turning to the facts in this case, the City argues that it reasonably accommodates group homes in two ways. First, it permits group homes in single family districts without qualification if they are not within 2,500 feet of one another. For those that are less than 2,500 feet from another group home, the ordinance allows the facility to apply for a waiver through BOZA's hearing process. Yet under no circumstances is BOZA required (or even encouraged) to grant a variance in favor of a group home. And the right to appeal to BOZA for a variance is not in and of itself an accommodation. As the district court pointed out, "merely because a group home will have the right to open in limited cases is not an accommodation, however, it is merely good fortune. It is just as likely, as in the present case, that the proposed home will fall within 2,500 feet of another group home rule and permit the municipality to veto the opening of the home in the first instance." *Oconomowoc Residential Programs, Inc. v. City of Milwaukee,* No. 97-C-251, slip op. at 13 (E.D.Wis. Mar. 16, 1999).

Since the City's current system does not provide a reasonable accommodation, we look to see whether the accommodation requested by the plaintiffs (1) is reasonable, and (2) necessary, (3) to allow them an equal opportunity to use and enjoy housing in the City.

The plaintiffs assert that the variance they request is a reasonable accommodation that would pose significant benefits to developmentally disabled and brain injured persons by allowing them to live together in a family setting in a residential community without imposing undue financial or administrative burdens on the City. The City counters that the variance requested by the plaintiffs would be unreasonable. As support for its proposition, the City focuses on ORP's history of problems operating other group homes, dangers emanating from the high volume of traffic along the Menomonee River Parkway during certain times of the day and year, the lack of sidewalks along the road, and the potential for the Menomonee River to flood. The City asserts that this evidence demonstrates that the home would impose undue financial and administrative burdens upon the City. Yet the City has failed to put forth evidence regarding the nature or quantity of these burdens.

For example, though the City describes many DHFS-written reports about ORP, describing individual instances of client over-medication, sexual abuse, neglect, physical abuse, client outbursts and fighting, police calls, and the drowning death of an elderly resident, it fails to link this laundry list of problems in other facilities with any financial or administrative burdens it might bear with this particular facility. Although any claim of abuse or neglect of disabled or elderly group residents is troubling, the state licensing authority has the burden of assuring the safety and security of group home residents through its licensing authority. The state has never refused, revoked, or suspended an ORP license to operate. The City argues that ORP's past errors "*tend to establish a burden*" and that "it *stands to reason* that the City of Milwaukee will have the *likelihood* of an increased burden with a group home operated by this particular provider." Reply brief at 7 (emphasis supplied). But this type of speculation fails to support the City's claim of unreasonableness.

The City did not put forth evidence that police calls from the group home will pose an undue burden. In its description of prior problems ORP has had at other homes, the City notes that the police were called to two other group homes on several occasions to respond to physical outbursts or combative behavior by residents. Again, the City did not demonstrate that the group home at issue in this case is any more likely to generate calls to the police than other area residents. There is simply no evidence anywhere in the record that group facilities impose on the City additional costs for emergency services. We are left to speculate that the police receive more complaints about group homes than they do about other neighborhood residences, that they respond to more requests from group homes, and that they would receive more calls from this particular group home.

As for the other alleged dangers, the majority of the evidence regarding the dangers imposed by the group home's geographic proximity to the river and the Menomonee River Parkway came from anecdotal testimony of various neighbors of the proposed facility, who also expressed concern about the potential for brain injured individuals to become violent and to threaten the safety of the neighborhood. The City cannot, however, rely on the anecdotal evidence of neighbors opposing the group home as evidence of unreasonableness. A denial of a variance due to public safety concerns or concerns for the safety of the residents themselves cannot be based on blanket stereotypes about disabled persons rather than particularized concerns about individual residents. *Bangerter v. Orem City Corp.*, 46 F.3d 1491, 1503-04 (10th Cir. 1995). The FHAA "repudiates the use of stereotypes and ignorance, and mandates that persons with handicaps be considered as individuals. Generalized perceptions about disabilities and unfounded speculations about threats to safety are specifically rejected as grounds to justify exclusion." Id. (quoting H.R.Rep. No. 100-711 at 18 (1988), 1988 U.S.C.C.A.N. 2173, 2179). The City has not presented any valid evidence that the residents who this group home seeks to serve will present a threat either to their own safety or the safety of others. On the other side of the traffic coin, the City's own engineer testified that the proposed group home would not have a significant adverse impact on traffic and therefore will not, in this fashion, impose any financial or administrative burdens on the City.

Similarly, the City made much of the potential for flooding near the group home, but again failed to provide any evidence that the group home would pose any higher burden on the City's emergency services than would any other residences in the flood-prone area. The one instance of flooding that the City cites in its brief took place four months after the BOZA hearing and after BOZA had already voted to deny the variance. The City's sole support of undue burden emanating from the flood zone comes from the affidavit of a firefighter who, while the Menomonee River had flooded, responded to a mistaken claim that gas was leaking in a group home for the elderly. The mere fact that residents of the proposed group home "will at times require the assistance of the local police and other emergency services does not rise to the level of imposing a cognizable administrative and financial burden upon the community." *Hovsons, Inc.*, 89 F.3d at 1105.

For the same reasons, the City's argument about the burden imposed by the clustering of group homes fails. The City asserts that over-concentration of group homes will result in disproportionate costs to emergency services for those facilities. Yet again, the City fails to explain how two group homes located close together will place a greater demand on emergency services than those same two homes placed 2,500 feet apart.

The plaintiffs, on the other hand, have met their burden of demonstrating that the variance was necessary to provide them with an equal opportunity to use and enjoy a dwelling. Janet K. and Valerie D.'s range of residential living choices is restricted by their disabilities. Both require a living arrangement where supportive services are available twenty-four hours a day. Janet K.'s home must be wheelchair accessible. Neither woman could afford to purchase a home on her own. The other disabled persons that ORP serves similarly are unable to live in residential communities without the resources of a group home facility.

The City argues that the plaintiffs needed to present evidence of the City's treatment of non-disabled renters, students, rooming home residents, or other individuals who are similarly situated in order to demonstrate that they were denied an equal opportunity to live in a residential neighborhood. The City, however, ignores the fact that group living arrangements can be essential for disabled persons who cannot live without the services such arrangements provide, and not similarly essential for the non-disabled.

Because the spacing ordinance draws a nearly half mile circle around each existing group home, it currently precludes new group homes from opening in most of the City of Milwaukee, thus preventing disabled adults who cannot live without some support from residing in almost all residential neighborhoods within the City. ORP presented evidence to BOZA regarding the shortage of facilities in the City for persons with traumatic brain injury. Furthermore, despite the fact that courts had ordered both Janet K. and Valerie D. into less restrictive community living arrangements, both remained in large institutions for some time until the ORP opened the home at 2850 North Menomonee River Parkway for them. A variance was absolutely essential for the plaintiffs to have the equal opportunity to live in a residential community.

The plaintiffs sufficiently established that the accommodation was reasonable and necessary to provide them with an equal opportunity to enjoy housing in a residential community in Milwaukee. The burden then shifted to the City to prove either that the accommodation was unreasonable or that it created an undue hardship. At this point, these two options merge, since in this case showing a lack of reasonableness or undue hardship amount to the same thing. See *Walton v. Mental Health Ass'n,* 168 F.3d 661, 670 (3d Cir. 1999). The City failed to carry its burden on either front.

* * *

III.

For the reasons stated above, we affirm the district court's grant of partial summary judgment in favor of the plaintiffs ORP, WCA, Janet K. and Valerie D., and its denial of summary judgment for the defendant, City of Milwaukee.

AFFIRMED.

ELDERHAVEN, INC. v. CITY OF LUBBOCK

United States Court of Appeals, Fifth Circuit, 1996
98 F.3d 175

PATRICK E. HIGGINBOTHAM, Circuit Judge:

Today we affirm a summary judgment granted to a Texas municipality dismissing claims of discrimination against handicapped persons under the Fair Housing Act. We are persuaded that the City in administering its zoning laws has reasonably accommodated the needs of the company complaining here.

I

In the late 1980s and early 1990s, Art and Mary Griffin founded Elderhaven, Inc., a corporation organized for the purpose of providing alternative living arrangements for elderly disabled persons. In November of 1990, Elderhaven bought a house with an address of 2510 Slide Road in a portion of the City of Lubbock zoned R-1. Elderhaven planned to establish a shared living residence for several elderly adults with mental or physical disabilities. Lubbock law at the time limited the use of land within the R-1 designation to single-family residences, and defined "family" as (i) any number of persons related by blood, marriage, or adoption, or (ii) any two unrelated persons living and cooking together as a unit. Because its proposed use was not in accordance with Lubbock zoning laws, Elderhaven began a dialogue with City officials regarding its plans for the Slide Road structure and regarding the City's duty to comply with the Fair Housing Act, 42 U.S.C. §§ 3601-31. This interaction included an application for a variance from the Lubbock Zoning Board of Adjustment, which was denied, and finally resulted in the 1991 passage of Lubbock Ordinance 9489.

Elderhaven's focus is upon Ordinance 9489. The parties agree that Ordinance 9489 amends the Code of Ordinances, City of Lubbock so as to provide the following regulatory scheme of uses within the R-1 zone. Any group of persons related by blood, marriage, or adoption, whether disabled or non-disabled, may live together as a single family in a residence. One or two persons, disabled or non-disabled, who are not related by blood, marriage, or adoption may live and cook together as a single family unit. Three or four persons disabled but not related by blood, adoption, or marriage, may live together in a residence so long as they first obtain a permit from the director of planning of the City of Lubbock. Groups of five or more disabled persons may apply for a special exception from the ZBA to the otherwise applicable limits on the use of plots of land within the R-1 zone. Lubbock law prohibits all other uses unless the landowner obtains a variance.

Ordinance 9489 outlines the requirements for a permit applicable to a group of three or four unrelated and disabled persons wishing to live together. An application for a permit must include a rudimentary site plan illustrating compliance with minimum square footage requirements for bedrooms. No bedroom may house more than two persons. The application must designate a person labeled a "care-provider," who will be responsible for compliance with the Ordinance, and the "care-provider" must have a "separate bedroom." The relevant City of Lubbock authorities must conduct a health inspection of the facility. A group living arrangement for the disabled may not be located within 600 feet of another group living arrangement already in place. This permitting process takes between 10 and 14 days to complete. Once issued, a permit may be renewed annually so long as the "care-provider" keeps the facility in compliance with the Ordinance.

Within its statutory context, the portion of the Ordinance requiring groups of five or more disabled individuals to request a special exception functions as follows. An application including a site plan is submitted; the relevant Lubbock authorities must conduct a health and fire inspection; all persons owning property within 200 feet of the structure at issue are given notice; and the ZBA holds a public hearing at which all persons may express an opinion before making a decision on whether to grant a special exemption. The Ordinance subjects a facility attempting to qualify for a special exemption to all the requirements of the permitting process described above except three: the minimum square footage per bedroom, the limit of two persons per bedroom, and the designation of a separate bedroom for the "care provider."

Late in 1991, as Ordinance 9489 took effect, Elderhaven applied for a special exemption allowing it to house up to 12 elderly disabled individuals at its Slide Road residence. In early 1992, Lubbock authorized Elderhaven to house 10 persons at Slide Road. Contending that Ordinance 9489 discriminated against persons with disabilities, Elderhaven sued the City in federal court seeking declaratory and injunctive relief.

* * *

II

42 U.S.C. § 3604(f)(1) makes unlawful discrimination against the disabled in housing. 42 U.S.C. § 3604(f)(3)(B) defines discrimination as "a refusal to make reasonable accommodations in rules, policies, practices, or services, when such accommodations may be necessary to afford such person equal opportunity to use and enjoy a dwelling." The question is thus whether Lubbock's ordinance, as it operates in the context of Lubbock's overall zoning law, constitutes a reasonable accommodation of the housing needs of the disabled.

Initially, we reject the suggestion of certain courts that a Fair Housing Act defendant bears the burden of proof on the question of reasonableness. See *Hovsons, Inc. v. Township of Brick,* 89 F.3d 1096, 1103 (3d Cir. 1996). The text of the Fair Housing Act provides no hint that Congress sought to change the normal rule that a plaintiff bears the burden of proving a violation of law by a preponderance of the evidence. Our case law under section 504 of the Rehabilitation Act, 29 U.S.C. § 794, supports the imposition of the burden of proof on Elderhaven. *McGregor v. Louisiana State University Board of Supervisors,* 3 F.3d 850, 859 n. 11 (5th Cir. 1993), *cert. denied,* 510 U.S. 1131 (1994).

Elderhaven has not borne its burden to raise a genuine issue of fact as to whether the City has applied Ordinance 9489 in a manner that fails to reasonably accommodate the needs of the disabled. We assume that the plaintiff is correct that a reasonable accommodation is one that does not place an undue burden upon the targeted government entity, despite its indeterminacy. We need not disagree with the plaintiff that the terms of Ordinance 9489, if applied rigidly and in a manner blind to the varying circumstances attending the needs of persons with disabilities, might constitute a violation of the Fair Housing Act. Plaintiff raises the hypothetical point that three or four deaf persons wishing to live together in an R-1 zone will be subject to the permitting requirement and thus to a health inspection. Even here, however, the fact that the residents are deaf may give the City a legitimate cause for concern in terms of safety, as, for instance, unmodified smoke alarms could not warn occupants of the danger of fire. We might also imagine a permitting process causing delays that inhibit the disabled from competing in Lubbock's tight rental market. Our task, however, is to decide concrete disputes. It is not to imagine.

The undisputed evidence in the record reflects the City's willingness to interpret its ordinance flexibly and in accordance with the circumstances of each case. Such flexibility may be an essential component of a process designed to provide reasonable accommodation and to operate in the marginal circumstances of the market. The record reflects, for instance, that the City no longer collects the permit application fee specifically required by the text of the ordinance.

We assume that plaintiffs are correct that a municipality may violate the Fair Housing Act by placing unduly burdensome conditions upon a proposed residence for the disabled. *See, e.g., Marbrunak, Inc. v. City of Stow,* 974 F.2d 43, 45 & n. 1 (6th Cir. 1992). The City's permitting process as it has functioned in the past is relatively rapid, and its inspections and building requirements are not unusually burdensome. The City's interest in these inspections and the permitting process in general is apparent from the face of the Ordinance's preamble, which states, "WHEREAS, it has been the experience of the City of Lubbock that unregulated and unlicensed homes for handicapped persons may not necessarily provide adequately for the health and safety of the residents."

Again, the permitting process and the inspections might be wholly inappropriate for certain situations, but the record illustrates the City's willingness to adjust under these circumstances.

The City has granted almost all of the permit and special exemption applications it has received. Elderhaven's arguments depend almost entirely on unrealized fear of possible application of the Ordinance. As yet, Elderhaven's only real concrete complaint is that it sought permission from the City to house 20 residents, and the City permitted only 18. We recognize that the economics of group living arrangements often require a critical mass of residents in order to make feasible the type of alternative living arrangements that the Fair Housing Act was designed to encourage. Elderhaven has never alleged, much less proven, that 20 is that critical number.

We iterate that our decision in this case is limited to the record before us, and we have relied on the City's past record of flexible interpretation and its current intention to continue this policy. In sum, our question is whether the City of Lubbock has reasonably accommodated handicapped persons in its zoning decisions. The ordinance sets a framework for decision-making, but is only part of a process. Whatever might have been, Elderhaven has failed to raise a genuine issue of material fact as to a violation of its rights under the Fair Housing Act.

AFFIRMED.

Notes & Questions

1. Can *Oconomowoc* and *Elderhaven* be reconciled? Clearly, the statutes take different positions on the plaintiff's burden to demonstrate the reasonableness of a requested accommodation. But is this difference determinative in these cases? Would the *Oconomowoc* plaintiffs have lost their case if the *Elderhaven* standard was applied; that is, if they needed to demonstrate that the City granting them an exception to the 2,500 foot rule was reasonable?

2. In *Oconomowoc*, the Seventh Circuit relied heavily on ADA cases in interpreting the FHAA. The Court states:

> The City, however, offers no reason for choosing this regime [giving plaintiff the burden of proof with respect to the issue of reasonable accommodation] over the method used by the Second, Third, Eight, Ninth, and Tenth Circuits which require a plaintiff to make an initial showing that an accommodation is reasonable, but then places the burden on the defendant to show that the accommodation is unreasonable.

Oconomowoc, 300 F.3d at 783. The court then cites a series of cases for this proposition. *Id.* at 784 (citing Lapid-Laurel, L.L.C., 284 F.3d at 457;

Vinson v. Thomas, No. CIV 97-00091 HG, 2000 WL 33313071 (D. Haw. Feb. 28, 2000); aff'd in part and rev'd in part, 288 F.3d 1145 (9th Cir. 2002); Jackan v. N.Y. State Dep't of Labor, 205 F.3d 562, 566 (2d Cir. 2000); Fjellestad v. Pizza Hut of Am., Inc., 188 F.3d 944, 950 (8th Cir. 1999); White v. York Int'l Corp., 45 F.3d 357, 361 (10th Cir. 1995)).

Although the court is discussing a burden-shifting scheme for the FHAA, with the exception of *Lapid-Laurel*, all the cases cited are ADA cases (although this is not noted). Is this "cross-pollinization" of statutes correct? Should the court at least be more up front about it?

3. How are the defendant's justifications in *Oconomowoc* similar to the defendants in *Cleburne*? How are they different? Would a constitutional theory have had any success?

4. What would the *Elderhaven* plaintiffs have needed to show to demonstrate an unreasonable application of the zoning ordinance? One denial? Two denials? Or some type of failure of process, whereby the zoning board did not adequately consider the statutory factors?

§ 27.2 Proving Discrimination

Like employment law, courts in FHAA cases have struggled with the concept of how a plaintiff proves discrimination. There are at least three ways to prove discrimination in a FHAA case: disparate treatment, disparate impact, and failure to reasonably accommodate.

The case of *Schwarz v. City of Treasure Island*, 544 F.3d 1201 (11th Cir. 2008), demonstrates all three. In this case, the owner of a company providing outpatient rehabilitative chemical dependency services in halfway houses for recovering substance abusers challenged a city's enforcement of occupancy-turnover rule. The purpose of the City's zoning ordinance was to create a community character in an area that was trending toward seasonal residents. Yet, when applied to halfway houses, the ordinance limited their ability to exist.

Plaintiffs alleged three theories of discrimination under FHAA: disparate treatment, disparate impact, and a failure to reasonably accommodate. Under a disparate treatment claim, a plaintiff must show that he has actually been treated differently than similarly situated people without disabilities. The court rejected this theory in *Schwartz*, noting that the plaintiffs had "utterly failed to establish that it was treated differently than anyone else. It cannot muster a single instance in which the City failed to enforce the occupancy-turnover rule against non-handicapped people . . . . Because [the plaintiff] was treated just like everyone else, it has no disparate treatment claim." *Id.* at 1216.

Because there was no history of different treatment, the court was untroubled that there were allegations that neighbors and city commissioners expressed the sentiment at community meetings that they did not want recovering substance abusers in their neighborhoods. *Id.* at 1216-17. The court distinguished this from a case where the plaintiffs might be claiming the city *adopted* an ordinance with a discriminatory intent; there were no such allegations in *Schwartz.*

Other courts have addressed the burden of proof in disparate treatment cases. In *Larkin v. Michigan Department of Social Services*, 89 F.3d 285 (6th Cir. 1996), the Sixth Circuit relied on case law under Title VII of the Civil Rights Act in the employment context. *Id.* at 289. In cases where the plaintiff can show that the statute is facially discriminatory, the burden shifts to the defendant to justify the challenged statutes. *Id.* at 290. It is clear that, to establish disparate treatment, the plaintiff does not need to show a discriminatory intent. *Id.*

However, courts have split on what the defendant must show to justify the challenged statute or practice. The Eighth Circuit has held that the defendant must meet rational basis scrutiny, as set forth in *City of Cleburne v. Cleburne Living Center*, 473 U.S. 432, 446 (1985). *See* Oxford House-C v. City of St. Louis, 77 F.3d 249, 252 (8th Cir. 1996).

Therefore, the defendant must show that the legislation, which distinguishes between people with disabilities and others, is "rationally related to a legitimate government purpose." The Sixth and Tenth Circuits require a defendant to meet a form of strict scrutiny by showing that the discriminatory statutes are either (1) justified by individualized safety concerns, or (2) really benefit, rather than discriminate against, persons with disabilities, and are not based on unsupported stereotypes. *See* Larkin, 89 F.3d at 291; Bangerter v. Orem City Corp., 46 F.3d 1491, 1503-4 (10th Cir. 1995).

Returning to *Schwartz*, plaintiffs next alleged a disparate impact theory of liability. A disparate impact claim typically involves claims that a statute, or defendant's policy, has an unnecessarily discriminatory effect on people with disabilities. The court held that a proper showing of disparate impact would have evidenced a statistically significant discrepancy between "recovering alcoholics and recovering drug abusers . . . and people who are neither recovering alcoholics nor recovering drug users." Schwartz, 544 F.3d at 1217 (internal citations omitted). The court held plaintiffs had not made such a showing, and thus could not proceed under a disparate impact theory. *See also* Quad Enters. Co., LLC v. Town of Southold, 369 F. App'x 202 (2010)(rejecting plaintiff's showing that the number of people with disabilities in town is larger than the number of accessible housing units as adequate evidence to prove disparate impact).

The case of *Cason v. Rochester Housing Authority*, 748 F.Supp. 1002 (W.D.N.Y 1990) demonstrates a more successful use of the disparate impact theory. There, plaintiffs showed that a housing authority denied housing, on the basis of inability to live independently, only to applicants with disabilities. The court held that the requisite discriminatory effect was proven by showing that no nondisabled persons were denied housing on the basis of inability to live independently, even though only 17 out of 276 applicants with disabilities were denied housing for that reason.

The third way of proving discrimination is the failure to make a reasonable accommodation. Most of the cases in this Part up until this point have used that theory. Returning to *Schwartz*, the plaintiffs argued that the City had violated FHAA's reasonable accommodation provision when it refused to relax and make an exception to its occupancy turnover rule. Tracking the statute, the plaintiffs argued that the inception was necessary to allow recovering substance abusers an equal opportunity to use and enjoy housing. The court held that there was a triable issue of fact on this issue.

Generally speaking, as discussed above, courts are split on the allocation of the burden of proof in reasonable accommodation cases. They have either placed the burden entirely on the plaintiff to prove reasonableness or provided that the plaintiff has the burden of proving the accommodation is necessary and generally reasonable, at which point the burden shifts to the defendant to prove unreasonableness or undue hardship.

§ 27.3 Design And Construction Of Dwellings

The FHAA also designates as "discriminatory" a failure to design and construct dwellings so that they are readily accessible and useable by people with disabilities. Specifically, the Act requires multi-family dwellings built for first occupancy after March 13, 1991 to be designed and constructed so that:

> (i) the public use and common portions of such dwellings are readily accessible to and usable by handicapped persons;

> (ii) all the doors designed to allow passage into and within all premises within such dwellings are sufficiently wide to allow passage by handicapped persons in wheelchairs; and

> (iii) all premises within such dwellings contain the following features of adaptive design:

> > (I) an accessible route into and through the dwelling;

> > (II) light switches, electrical outlets, thermostats, and other environmental controls in accessible locations;

> > (III) reinforcements in bathroom walls to allow later installation of grab bars; and

(IV) usable kitchens and bathrooms such that
an individual in a wheelchair can maneuver about the
space.

42 U.S.C. § 3604(f)(3)(C) (2006). A "covered multifamily dwelling" is defined as "buildings consisting of 4 or more units if such buildings have one or more elevators, and ground floor units in other buildings consisting of 4 or more units."

Consider how this statute, and the accompanying regulations promulgated by the Department of Housing and Urban Development (HUD) are interpreted in the following case.

&

UNITED STATES v. EDWARD ROSE & SONS

United States Court of Appeals, Sixth Circuit, 2004
384 F.3d 258

SILER, Circuit Judge.

This housing discrimination case turns on what doors must be accessible to the handicapped. At issue are two sets of apartment complexes, designed with an inaccessible front door, but an accessible back patio door. The district court granted the U.S. Justice Department ("government") a preliminary injunction halting the construction and occupancy of the buildings. The main defendant, the builder and owner, Edward Rose & Sons ("Rose"), appeals, arguing that court erred by misconstruing the requirements of the Fair Housing Act, 42 U.S.C. § 3601 *et seq.* ("FHA") * * *.

I. FACTUAL & PROCEDURAL BACKGROUND

Defendant Rose constructed and owns the nineteen apartment buildings, located in Michigan and Ohio, at issue. These buildings are at various stages of construction, but all have the same basic design. The ground floor apartments at issue have two exterior entrances – a front door and rear patio door. The front door is closer to the parking lot, but is handicapped inaccessible because it can only be reached by descending stairs. At the bottom of the stairs is a landing shared by two front doors leading into two different apartments. The rear patio entrance is accessible, but is located farther from the parking lot.

The government alleged that the apartments violated the disability portions of the FHA. The district court granted a preliminary injunction, adopting the government's position that the front door was the "primary entrance" used by the public and guests, and as such, it was a "public" or "common area" that the FHA mandates be accessible. *See* 42 U.S.C. 3604(f)(3)(C)(i). In reaching this conclusion, the court relied on the Housing and Urban Development ("HUD") regulations, guidelines, and design manual. The preliminary injunction halts construction on the "covered dwellings" and restrains the defendants from occupying "covered dwellings" not yet leased. In this case, "covered dwellings" means simply the ground floor. *See* 42 U.S.C. § 3604(f)(7) (stating if building has no elevator, only the ground floor is a covered dwelling subject to the FHA). Rose appeals.

* * *

III. ANALYSIS

* * *

The basic question of this litigation is whether the space outside the front door is a public or common use area that must be handicapped accessible. We are the first circuit to consider the issue.

* * *

The government asserts that because the landing at the bottom of the stairs is a "common area," § 3604(f)(3)(C)(i) mandates that the landing must be accessible. The landing in front of the entrances is not accessible because it can only be reached by the stairs. The government argues that this entrance is the "primary" door because it is in the front and closest to the parking lot. As such, it is the entrance most visitors will use, and thus the space or landing in front of the door is a public or common area. Additionally, the stair landing is shared by two entrances to two different apartment units, and thus a common area used by two tenants.

Rose correctly points out that neither the statute nor any possibly binding regulations make any reference or distinction between "primary," "front," or "back" doors. Rose argues that the government's interpretation requires almost every entrance to a unit be accessible. If the space in front of an entrance becomes a common use area, simply because people use the entrance, then the statute would require virtually every entrance to be accessible.

Rose asserts that if the space in front of virtually every entrance is a "common" or "public" area, § 3604(f)(3)(C)(iii)(I) becomes superfluous. Section 3604(f)(3)(C)(iii)(I) mandates all premises must have "*an* accessible route into and through the dwelling." (Emphasis added.) Rose contends that the indefinite article "an" indicates that the statute only requires one accessible route into each unit. As such, the space in front of every door to a private unit cannot be a common area, or all doors would have to be accessible, and there would be no need for § 3604(f)(3)(C)(iii)(I) to separately mandate "an accessible route" into the unit. Moreover, even if there were such a thing as a single "primary" entrance, whose anterior space must be accessible as a common area, there would still be no need for § 3604(f)(3)(C)(iii)(I) to redundantly mandate "*an* accessible route." An accessible route would already be mandated by the common area in front of the primary entrance of every unit.

We find that, in this particular case, the stair landing in front of the entrance is a common area that the statute mandates be accessible. The fact that two apartment units share the stair landing makes the space a common area. The plain meaning of "common use" unambiguously covers the entrance under dispute. At the time of the statute's enactment, dictionaries generally defined "common" as belonging to or shared by two or more individuals. See *The Oxford English Dictionary* 565 (J.A. Simpson & E.S.C. Weiner eds., Clarendon Press 2d ed. 1989) (defining common as "[b]elonging equally to more than one" and "possessed or shared alike by both or all."); *Webster's Third New International Dictionary* 458 (Philip Babcock Gove ed., Merriam-Webster 1986) ("held, enjoyed, experienced, or participated in equally by a number of individuals; possessed or manifested by more than one individual"); *Funk & Wagnalls New International Dictionary* (Publishers International Press Comprehensive ed. 1984) ("Pertaining to, connected with, or participated in by two or more persons or things; joint."). Here, the stair landing belongs to, and is shared by, two apartments, and exists for their "common use."

Our ruling is narrow; we simply hold in this case that because the two apartments share the stair landing, the stair landing qualifies as a "common area" that must be accessible. We express no opinion on what the FHA would require if the stairs only led to one apartment unit entrance and decline to delve into the parties' "primary entrance" arguments because we find them unnecessary for the resolution of this case. Assuming *arguendo* that, as Rose submits, not every entrance constitutes a "common area" because otherwise § 3604(f)(3)(C)(iii)(I)'s mandate that all premises have "*an* accessible route" is superfluous, we still would find that the shared landing is a common area. Section § 3604(f)(3)(C)(iii)(I) would not be superfluous because that section would ensure that apartment units that share no entrance with another apartment unit would still have "an accessible" entrance.

In sum, we find that the stair landing qualifies as a "common area" that the FHA mandates be accessible. Thus, the government's likelihood of success on the merits is strong.

Notes & Questions

1. In *Montana Fair Housing, Inc. v. American Capital Development, Inc.*, 81 F.Supp.2d 1057 (D. Mont. 1999), the Defendant argued that the term "adaptive design" was impermissibly ambiguous. The court rejected this argument, holding that it was a term of art in the construction industry, meaning design appropriate for use by persons of all abilities without modification.

2. HUD has promulgated regulations under Section 504 of the Rehabilitation Act requiring accessible housing for people with disabilities. *See* 24 C.F.R. §§ 8.20-33 (2007). When a public housing authority that receives federal funds constructs new housing or

substantially alters existing housing, these regulations require that five percent of the dwelling units in those facilities be fully accessible to persons with mobility impairments and two percent be accessible to persons with hearing or vision impairments. *See id.* §§ 8.22(a)-(b), 8.23(a).

When one or more dwelling units in an existing facility are altered, but the alternations do not rise to the level of substantial alterations, the units must be made accessible to the mobility impaired, until five percent of the units in the facility are accessible. *See id.* § 8.23(b)(1). In addition, accessible dwellings must, to the maximum extent feasible, be distributed throughout projects. *Id.* § 8.26. And, they must "be available in a sufficient range of sizes and amenities so that a qualified individual's choice of living arrangements is, as a whole, comparable to that of other persons eligible for housing assistance under the same program." *Id.* The requirement for fully accessible housing in federally funded developments expands upon the general FHAA requirement that all units be adaptable.

3. In *Three Rivers Center for Independent Living v. Housing Authority of the City of Pittsburgh*, 382 F.3d 412 (3d Cir. 2004), Three Rivers Center brought an action under these regulations challenging the Pittsburgh Housing Authority's failure to comply with the HUD regulations. The court found that the Housing Authority had failed to comply with the regulations, with the effect being that the demand for accessible public housing in Pittsburgh exceeded the supply. *Id.* at 417. The Housing Authority moved to dismiss plaintiff's complaint to the extent it sought relief for violations of the regulations, arguing that plaintiffs did not have a private right of action to enforce the regulations because the regulations were "too far removed from Congressional intent as reflected in § 504 to constitute 'federal rights' privately enforceable under § 504." *Id.* at 418. The court agreed with the Pittsburgh Housing Authority, holding that the HUD regulations did not construe or articulate personal rights created by § 504.

4. For a cogent discussion of barriers to accessible housing, *see* Robert G. Schwemm, Barriers to Accessible Housing: Enforcement Issues in "Design and Construction" Cases Under the Fair Housing Act, 40 U. Rich. L. Rev. 753 (2006). Under § 3604(f)(3)(C), virtually all new multi-family housing should be designed and constructed with certain accessibility features, yet many still are not. Professor Schwemm notes that "every noncompliant dwelling is not only a lawsuit waiting to happen, but also is a lawsuit that generally cannot be defended on the merits." *Id.* at 863.

౿

Under the design and construction provisions of the FHAA, builders and architects of dwellings, as well as owners and management, are potentially liable as defendants. It is not unusual at all for these various defendants to go after each other for contribution and indemnity.

See United States v. Gambone Bros. Dev. Co., No. 06-1386, 2008 WL 4410093 (E.D. Pa. Sept. 25, 2008).

How long does a potential FHAA plaintiff have to sue the various defendants? FHAA provides that "an aggrieved person may commence a civil action ... not later than 2 years after the occurrence or the termination of an alleged discrimination housing practice." 42 U.S.C. § 3613(a)(1)(A). The next case considers when the statute of limitations period starts to run in design and construction cases. This case grew out of several consolidated cases. In each case, the defendants claimed that the statute of limitations had run on plaintiffs' claims.

୶

GARCIA v. BROCKWAY

United States Court of Appeals, Ninth Circuit, 2008
526 F.3d 456

KOZINSKI, Chief Judge:

We consider when the statute of limitations begins to run in a design-and-construction claim under the Fair Housing Act (FHA).

* * *

The FHA prohibits the design and construction of multifamily dwellings that do not have certain listed accessibility features. ... The FHA provides that "[a]n aggrieved person may commence a civil action in an appropriate United States district court or State court not later than 2 years after the occurrence or the termination of an alleged discriminatory housing practice." 42 U.S.C. § 3613(a)(1)(A). In other words, an aggrieved person must bring the lawsuit within two years of either "the occurrence ... of an alleged discriminatory housing practice" or "the termination of an alleged discriminatory housing practice." Here, the practice is the "failure to design and construct" a multifamily dwelling according to FHA standards. *Id.* § 3604(f)(3)(C). The statute of limitations is thus triggered at the conclusion of the design-and-construction phase, which occurs on the date the last certificate of occupancy is issued. In both cases, this triggering event occurred long before plaintiffs brought suit.

Plaintiffs advance three theories that would extend the limitations period to cover their lawsuits. We address each in turn.

1. Plaintiffs contend that an FHA design-and-construction violation is a continuing one that does not terminate until the building defects are cured. The Supreme Court has held that "where a plaintiff, pursuant to the Fair Housing Act, challenges not just one incident of conduct violative of the Act, but an unlawful practice that continues into the limitations period, the complaint is timely when it is filed within [the statutory period, running from] the last asserted occurrence of that practice." *Havens Realty Corp. v. Coleman*, 455 U.S. 363, 380-81 (1982).

827

Congress has since codified this continuing violation doctrine by amending the FHA to include both "the occurrence [and] *the termination* of an alleged discriminatory housing practice" as events triggering the two-year statute of limitations. 42 U.S.C. § 3613(a)(1)(A) (emphasis added).

Plaintiffs claim Congress's insertion of "termination" would be meaningless if it weren't read as termination of the design-and-construction defect. HUD's *Fair Housing Act Design Manual* supports this reading: "With respect to the design and construction requirements, complaints could be filed at any time that the building continues to be in noncompliance, because the discriminatory housing practice-failure to design and construct the building in compliance-does not terminate." U.S. Dep't of Hous. & Urban Dev., *Fair Housing Act Design Manual: A Manual to Assist Designers and Builders in Meeting the Accessibility Requirements of the Fair Housing Act* 22.

Plaintiffs and HUD confuse a continuing violation with the continuing effects of a past violation. "Termination" refers to "the termination of an alleged discriminatory housing practice." The Supreme Court has "stressed the need to identify with care the specific [discriminatory] practice that is at issue." *Ledbetter v. Goodyear Tire & Rubber Co.,* 127 S.Ct. 2162, 2167, (2007). Here, the practice is "a failure to design and construct," which is not an indefinitely continuing practice, but a discrete instance of discrimination that terminates at the conclusion of the design-and-construction phase. This violation differs from the one Congress codified as "continuing" in light of *Havens,* where the claims were "based not solely on isolated incidents . . ., but a continuing violation manifested in *a number of incidents*-including at least one . . . that [wa]s asserted to have occurred within the [limitations] period." 455 U.S. at 381 (emphasis added).

Put differently, "[a] continuing violation is occasioned by continual unlawful acts, not by continual ill effects from an original violation." *Ward v. Caulk,* 650 F.2d 1144, 1147 (9th Cir.1981) (citing *Collins v. United Air Lines, Inc.,* 514 F.2d 594, 596 (9th Cir.1975)). The Supreme Court last Term reiterated the distinction between a continuing violation and continual effects when it held that "current effects alone cannot breathe life into prior, unchanged discrimination; as we held in *Evans,* such effects in themselves have 'no present legal consequences.'" *Ledbetter,* 127 S.Ct. at 2169. Although the ill effects of a failure to properly design and construct may continue to be felt decades after construction is complete, failing to design and construct is a single instance of unlawful conduct. Here, this occurred long before plaintiffs brought suit. Were we to now hold the contrary, the FHA's statute of limitations would provide little finality for developers, who would be required to repurchase and modify (or destroy) buildings containing inaccessible features in order to avoid design-and-construction liability for every aggrieved person who solicits tenancy from subsequent owners and managers. Indeed, now that we have recognized tester standing, an aggrieved person wouldn't even need to solicit tenancy, but merely observe the violation. This is not what Congress provided in erecting a two-year statute of limitations for FHA design-and-construction claims. If Congress wanted to leave developers on the hook years after they cease having any association with a building, it could have phrased the statute to say so explicitly.

* * *

2. Plaintiffs also argue that the statute of limitations should not begin to run until the aggrieved person *encounters* the design-and-construction defect.

There's some support for this "encounter" theory: "A damages action under the [FHA] sounds basically in tort-the statute merely defines a new legal duty, and authorizes the courts to compensate a plaintiff for the injury caused by the defendant's wrongful breach." *Curtis v. Loether,* 415 U.S. 189, 195 (1974). Because an FHA damages action "sounds basically in tort," plaintiffs claim the statute of limitations is not triggered until a disabled person is actually damaged by the practice. Plaintiffs contend that, upon completion of construction, no injury has yet occurred, and "the standard rule [for tort purposes is] that the limitations period commences when the plaintiff has a complete and present cause of action." *Bay Area Laundry & Dry Cleaning Pension Tr. Fund v. Ferbar Corp. of Cal.,* 522 U.S. 192, 201 (1997).

Plaintiffs make too much of the Supreme Court's observation that the FHA "sounds basically in tort." The Court was not dealing with the statute of limitations but with the very different question of whether FHA plaintiffs are entitled to a jury trial. This passing reference to tort law cannot be read to trump statutory provisions that deal expressly with the statute of limitations. The FHA's limitations period does not start when a particular disabled person is injured by a housing practice, but by "the occurrence or the termination of an alleged discriminatory housing practice." 42 U.S.C. § 3613(a)(1)(A). Under the FHA, the ability to privately enforce the "new legal duty" thus only lasts for two years from the time of the violation, and the violation here is "a failure to design and construct." Plaintiff's injury only comes into play in determining whether she has standing to bring suit. Some aggrieved persons may not encounter this violation until decades after the limitations period has run and thus will be unable to file a civil action, even though they have standing to raise the claim. However, "[i]t goes without saying that statutes of limitations often make it impossible to enforce what were otherwise perfectly valid claims. But that is their very purpose, and they remain as ubiquitous as the statutory rights or other rights to which they are attached or are applicable." *United States v. Kubrick,* 444 U.S. 111, 125 (1979).

* * *

3. [Plaintiff] argues that the limitations period does not begin to run until the aggrieved person *discovers* the design-and-construction defect. [Plaintiff] advances this theory as both the discovery rule and the equitable tolling doctrine, but neither helps him.

The discovery rule serves to extend the time from which the limitations period starts to run until "the plaintiff knows both the existence and the cause of his injury." *Kubrick,* 444 U.S. at 113. The discovery rule is strikingly similar to plaintiffs' encounter theory, and thus fails for the same reasons. Holding that each individual plaintiff has a claim until two years after he discovers the failure to design and construct would contradict the text of the FHA, as the statute of limitations for private civil actions begins to run when the discriminatory act occurs – not when it's encountered or discovered.

"Equitable tolling may be applied if, despite all due diligence, a plaintiff is unable to obtain vital information bearing on the existence of his claim." *Santa Maria v. Pac. Bell,* 202 F.3d 1170, 1178 (9th Cir. 2000). This doctrine "focuses on a plaintiff's excusable ignorance and lack of prejudice to the defendant." *Leong v. Potter,* 347 F.3d 1117, 1123 (9th Cir.2003). As Judge Posner has explained, "[e]quitable tolling is frequently confused . . . with the discovery rule. . . . It differs from the [discovery rule] in that the plaintiff is assumed to know that he has been injured, so that the statute of limitations has begun to run; but he cannot obtain information necessary to decide whether the injury is due to wrongdoing and, if so, wrongdoing by the defendant." *Cada v. Baxter Healthcare Corp.,* 920 F.2d 446, 451 (7th Cir.1990).

Here, [plaintiff] doesn't claim he was injured within the limitations period but was unable to obtain vital information concerning the existence of his claim until the period expired. Instead, he basically contends that it would be inequitable not to allow him to bring a civil lawsuit. Fairness, without more, is not sufficient justification to invoke equitable tolling, and the district court properly refused to apply it. In his plea for a fairer outcome, [plaintiff] fails to mention the extreme prejudice defendants would suffer if plaintiffs could indefinitely bring civil damages actions for buildings defendants no longer own and cannot fix without the cooperation of the current owners. This is hardly a situation where there is a "lack of prejudice to the defendant." *Leong,* 347 F.3d at 1123.

In sum, application of the discovery rule or the equitable tolling doctrine "would render the clear language of the statute meaningless and superfluous." Both doctrines would have the same effect as the continuing violation doctrine by tolling the statute of limitations indefinitely and thus stripping it of all meaning. Even if we thought this interpretation were more equitable, we don't have the authority to "interpret a provision in a manner that renders other provisions of the same statute inconsistent, meaningless or superfluous." *Boise Cascade,* 942 F.2d 1408, 1432 (9th Cir. 1991).

[A]n aggrieved person must bring a private civil action under the FHA for a failure to properly design and construct within two years of the completion of the construction phase, which concludes on the date that the last certificate of occupancy is issued. Because neither plaintiff brought a timely suit, their cases were properly dismissed.

PREGERSON and REINHARDT, Circuit Judges, dissenting:

We write ... to emphasize the extent to which the majority's holding perverts the purpose and intent of the statute. Indeed, the majority's decision well illustrates how statutes of limitations have been twisted by courts to limit the scope and thrust of civil rights laws.

The majority takes an Act that was designed to protect disabled persons by mandating that multifamily housing be made accessible to them and construes its statute of limitations in a way that solely benefits the housing construction industry and renders the statute of far less use to disabled individuals than Congress intended. The Fair Housing Act ("FHA") contains a 30 month grace period that gave developers building new multifamily housing clear notice of what was required to satisfy the statute's accessibility standards. There is no reason that a developer who fails to comply with these requirements should not be held accountable for such violations. Nevertheless, the majority holds that unless a disabled person happens to become aware of the developer's failure to comply within two years after the certificate of completion is issued, the developer is home-free-completely immune from suit. Thus, a disabled person who seeks to acquire an FHA non-compliant unit in a housing development more than two years after the development is certified for occupancy cannot sue the developer even if no person familiar with the needs of disabled persons had previously seen the property and no disabled person had been aware of or injured by the violation until the would-be plaintiff attempted to buy or lease the unit. It seems apparent to us that Congress intended the statute of limitations to have the opposite result: that the disabled person who is injured by the developer's violation of the FHA should be able to sue that developer if he institutes his action within two years of the injury. It did not intend to invite the developer to assume the risk of non-compliance, in order to save construction costs, by taking the chance that his violation of the law would remain undiscovered by the disabled community for a period of two years.

The purpose of the FHA's design and construction requirements was to protect an important civil right. It was to help provide disabled individuals equal access to multifamily housing and to eliminate the de facto segregation to which handicap-inaccessible housing gives rise. *See* H.R.Rep. No. 100-711, at 27-28 (1988), *reprinted in* 1988 U.S.C.C.A.N. 2173, 2188-89 ("The Committee believes that these basic features of adaptability are essential for equal access and to avoid future de facto exclusion of persons with handicaps, as well as being easy to incorporate in housing design and construction. Compliance with these minimal standards will eliminate many of the barriers which discriminate against persons with disabilities in their attempts to obtain equal housing opportunities."). The Act, including its statute of limitations provision, is to be construed in a manner that accomplishes this purpose. *See Trafficante v. Metropolitan Life Ins. Co.*, 409 U.S. 205, 209, (1972) (mandating a "generous construction" of the FHA's complaint-filing provisions to "give vitality to" the statute's "broad and inclusive" language). This the majority has not done. Instead, it construes the FHA's statute of limitations so as to offer the least benefit to disabled persons and the most to developers of multifamily housing. Because we cannot condone a construction so wholly at odds with the purpose of the statute, and the manner in which we are to construe it, we respectfully dissent.

Notes & Questions

1. Not every court has viewed the issue in exactly the same way as the Ninth Circuit. In *Fair Housing Council Inc. v. Village of Olde St. Andrews*, 210 F. App'x 469 (6th Cir. 2006), defendants argued that plaintiffs' design and construction claims were time barred because they were brought more than two years after the termination of the construction of the buildings. Unlike *Garcia*, the court disagreed, holding that "if the statute of limitations were to begin running immediately upon completion of the building, potential buyers may not even look at the property until after the statute of limitations has run. Such a result would run counter to the well established principle that in interpreting the Fair Housing Act, courts are to give effect to the broad remedial intent of Congress embodied in the Act." *Id.* at 480. The Court linked the "termination" of the discriminatory act with the sale of the specific unit, declining to go as far as plaintiff argued, which would have tolled the statute of limitations until the defect was found. *But see* Eve Hill & Peter Blanck, Future of Disability Rights: Part Three – Statutes of Limitations in Americans with Disabilities Act, "Design and Construct" Cases, 60 Syracuse L. Rev. 125, 126 (2009) (discussing application of the ADA's statute of limitations "to construction violations when the construction and the injury occur years apart" in *Frame v. City of Arlington*, 575 F.3d 432 (5th Cir. 2009). Ultimately, in a rehearing en banc, the Fifth Circuit held that the "action accrued when residents knew or should have known they were being denied benefits of newly built or altered sidewalks." Frame v. City of Arlington, 657 F.3d. 215, 238 (5th Cir. 2011).

2. The limitations periods for design and construction cases (like all FHA cases) are different depending on who brings the case and in what forum. Individual claims for damages were discussed in *Garcia* and *Fair Housing Council Inc.* For claims brought pursuant to the Housing and Urban Development (HUD) administrative complaint process, the statute of limitations is one year. *See* 42 U.S.C. 3610(a)(1)(A)(i). If the Attorney General seeks equitable relief alleging a pattern or practice of resistance

to FHA rights or invokes the public interest, there is no limitations period. *See* United States v. Inc. Vill. Of Island Park, 791 F.Supp. 354, 364-68 (E.D.N.Y. 1992). If the Attorney General seeks damages, there is a three year statute of limitations, *see* 42 U.S.C. 2415(b); if civil penalties are sought, the limitations period is five years. *Id.* at § 2462.

3. In *Garcia,* the Ninth Circuit notes that it recognizes tester standing in FHAA cases. But in *Equal Rights Ctr. v. Post Properties, Inc.,* 633 F.3d 1136 (D.C. Cir. 2011), the D.C. Circuit held that an organization that investigated a builder's alleged discriminatory design and construction practices did not have standing to bring an FHAA claim. The organization's diversion of resources to the investigation of, and resulting legal challenge to, the builder's alleged discriminatory practices was a "self-inflicted" injury. *Equal Rights Ctr.,* 633 F.3d at 1142. Citing other Circuits, a concurring Justice attempted to salvage tester standing in the D.C. Circuit: "[D.C. Circuit precedent] went too far in suggesting that 'testing' expenditures are necessarily self-inflicted injuries that cannot suffice to show injury in fact for purposes of constitutional standing." *Id.* at 1143 (Rogers, C.J., concurring).

Chapter 28 ENFORCEMENT AND REMEDIES

The FHAA may be enforced in several ways. First, an aggrieved individual can bring a direct complaint in federal district or state court. *See* 42 U.S.C. § 3613 (2006). There is no requirement that a plaintiff exhaust her administrative remedies prior to filing suit. The statue of limitations is two years. *Id.* The government's annual fair housing report shows that a record number of Americans are complaining about housing discrimination, with disability and race as the leading reasons for filing a complaint. *See* Ruth Mantel, Housing Discrimination Complaints Hit Record with Disability, Race as Leading Reasons, MarketWatch, Apr. 4, 2007.

Courts are authorized to appoint attorneys for persons alleging discriminatory housing practices (or persons against whom such a practice is alleged), or allow them to file a civil action without paying fees or costs, if, in the opinion of the court, such person is financially unable to bear the costs of such action. *Id.* at § 3613(b). Courts are authorized to award actual and punitive damages, and grant other relief as the court deems appropriate, including temporary inunctions, temporary restraining orders, or permanent orders. *Id.* at § 3613(c)(1).

It is worth noting that this is quite different from ADA Title III's remedial scheme, which makes no provision for compensatory or punitive damages. Under the FHA, it is within the court's discretion to award attorneys' fees to a prevailing plaintiff (except for the United States). *Id.* at § 3613(c)(2). The Attorney General may intervene in a private action. *Id.* at § 3613(e).

The FHAA also contemplates an administrative remedy scheme, through a complaint to HUD. *See* 42 U.S.C. § 3612. These actions have the advantage of expedited discovery and hearings. *Id.* § 3612(d). Attorneys' fees may be awarded, *id.* § 3612(p), and actual damages and civil penalties may be awarded up to $50,000. *Id.* § 3612(g)(3).

Finally, the Attorney General may bring action in cases where there appears to be a pattern or practice of resistance to compliance with the Act. 42 U.S.C. § 3614.

Part 8

Related Policy Issues: Employment, Welfare, Health Care, Technology And Tax

Analysis

Chapter 29 INTRODUCTION
§ 29.1 Overview
Chapter 30 DISABILITY AND EMPLOYMENT POLICY
§ 30.1 Workforce Investment Act (WIA)
    A.   Overview
    B.   Applicability Of The ADA To WIA
§ 30.2 Ticket To Work And Work Incentives Improvement Act (TWWIIA)
    A.   Overview
    B.   Applicability Of The ADA To TWWIIA's Employment Networks (ENs)
Chapter 31 DISABILITY AND WELFARE POLICY
§ 31.1 Social Security Disability Insurance (SSDI)
    A.   Overview
    B.   Interaction Of The ADA And SSDI
§ 31.2 Temporary Assistance For Needy Families (TANF) Programs
    A.   Overview
    B.   Applicability Of The ADA To TANF
Chapter 32 DISABILITY AND HEALTH CARE POLICY
§ 32.1 Medicare And Medicaid
    A.   Overview
    B.   Compliance And Litigation
§ 32.2 Patient Protection And Affordable Care Act (PPACA)
    A.   Provisions In Effect
    B.   Provisions Taking Effect 2013-14
§ 32.3 Genetic Discrimination
    A.   Genetic Information Nondiscrimination Act (GINA)
    B.   Asymptomatic Genetic Traits Under The ADA
Chapter 33 DISABILITY AND THE INTERNET
§ 33.1 Overview
§ 33.2 Internet Accessibility And Access To Data
§ 33.3 Applications Of The ADA: Title II
§ 33.4 Applications Of The ADA: Title III
    A.   The "Place" Requirement
    B.   Effective Communication
    C.   First Amendment Issues
§ 33.5 Applications Of Section 504 Of The Rehabilitation Act
§ 33.6 Applications Of Section 508 Of The Rehabilitation Act
§ 33.7 Twenty-First Century Communications And Video Accessibility Act Of 2010
§ 33.8 Other Policy Issues

§ 33.9 Commentary / Web Equality

Chapter 34 DISABILITY AND TAX POLICY

§ 34.1 Overview: Tax Policy And Persons With Disabilities

§ 34.2 Tax Policies And Economic Security For Americans With Disabilities

§ 34.3 Tax Policies And The ADA

    A. Disabled Access Credit

    B. Tax Deduction For Removal Of Architectural And Transportation Barriers

    C. Work Opportunity Credit

Chapter 29 INTRODUCTION

§ 29.1 Overview

The legal principles we have discussed so far in this casebook largely involve issues of antidiscrimination law and policy. The Americans with Disabilities Act of 1990 (ADA), taken at its highest level of generality, prohibits discrimination against people with disabilities. It prohibits certain actors – employers, public entities, and privately owned places of public accommodation – from taking actions against individuals on the basis of disability.

In this Part, we consider several different types of issues faced by people with disabilities. The first three – employment policy, welfare, and healthcare – involve governmental responses that are different from antidiscrimination law, which is not the policy tool the government has at its disposal. Indeed, in both the ADA and other contexts, some argue that antidiscrimination law is not particularly well suited to address the structural challenges that keep previously excluded groups on the margins of society. Samuel R. Bagenstos, The Structural Turn and the Limits of Antidiscrimination Law, 94 Cal. L. Rev. 1, 2 (2006). There are other, more direct policy tools that governments may use to improve the lives and the social, civic and economic participation of people with disabilities. Rather than providing negative rights (in that antidiscrimination law protects people with disabilities against negative actions taken against them), "social welfare" or "social support" programs may provide direct affirmative assistance to categories of people with disabilities. This may take the form of cash payments (as in the Social Security scheme), or providing people with disabilities access to needed support and services, like healthcare (as through Medicaid or Medicare).

First, we look at the federal government's policies that focus on the employment of people with disabilities. Programs like the Workforce Investment Act of 1998 (WIA) and the Ticket to Work and Work Incentives Improvement Act of 1999 (TWWIIA) work together with antidiscrimination law by attempting to increase labor force participation for qualified people with disabilities.

Next, we examine at the interaction of disability and welfare policy. Unfortunately, even today, often times social welfare programs are based on outdated assumptions about the inability of people with disabilities. Thus, they sometimes actually work against the empowering civil rights model embodied in the ADA. For instance, to qualify for Social Security Disability Income (SSDI), an individual (who otherwise may be capable of certain jobs, perhaps with workplace accommodation) must demonstrate a complete inability to work for a sustained period of time.

We then consider at disability and healthcare policy. The lack of universal coverage in the United States can place some people with disabilities in a difficult situation. They may be denied coverage in the private market and therefore directed toward government healthcare systems like Medicare and Medicaid. But these programs may contain significant work disincentives, and may not provide medical goods and therapies that support independent living and workforce participation.

We then turn to two final issues of disability policy, involving technology access issues and tax policy. Both are fast moving and crucial to the lives of people with disabilities. Technological advances offer opportunities for increased participation in society, yet also create challenges for making systems accessible, as in the case of the Internet. Tax policy can encourage asset accumulation for people with disabilities, a crucial step for financial independence and participation in all levels of society.

Chapter 30 DISABILITY AND EMPLOYMENT POLICY

While the U.S. Supreme Court and legal commentators have grappled over the reach of the ADA, there has been a parallel debate in the social sciences on how to assess the real-world impact of the ADA's Title I employment provisions. The central question is how to measure the law's impact on the employment prospects and economic independence of individuals with disabilities. Peter Blanck et al., Employment of People with Disabilities: Twenty-Five Years Back and Ahead, 25 Law & Ineq. 323 (2007)."

Much of the research attempting to determine the effects of Title I is not conclusive.   Early studies finding the employment levels of individuals with work disabilities declined in the early 1990s conclude that Title I is the likely cause. Sharona Hoffman, Settling the Matter: Does Title I of the ADA Work?, 59 Ala. L. Rev. 305, 329 (2008).

However, subsequent studies have not supported a causal link between employment rates of persons with longer-term disabilities and ADA implementation, and even suggest positive effects of the ADA. *See* Scott Burris & Kathryn Moss, The Employment Discrimination Provisions of the Americans with Disabilities Act: Implementation and Impact, 25 Hofstra Lab. & Emp. L.J. 1, 3 (2007).

Still, other studies find increased employment levels since the enactment of the ADA; however, these samples may not be representative of the population covered by the law.   H. Stephen Kaye, Improved Employment Opportunities for People with Disabilities 17-18 (Disability Statistics Report 17, 2003), *available at* http://dsc.ucsf.edu/pdf/report17.pdf (last visited Jan. 29, 2013); Douglas Kruse & Lisa Schur, Employment of People with Disabilities Following the ADA, 42 Indus. Relations 31, 50-51 (2003). Nevertheless, these studies show individuals with severe functional limitations that do not prevent them from working markedly improved their relative employment levels in the early 1990s.

A primary difference in the findings on employment outcomes hinges on how researchers define and measure disability. Burris & Moss, *supra*, at 7. Of course, how researchers (and lawyers and advocates) identify the group of individuals with disabilities is fundamental to whether their findings are informative as to the impact of the ADA. *See id* at 3.

In any case, there is little definitive evidence that American disability policies and laws have resulted in substantial increases in the numbers of persons with disabilities participating fully in American society. Even in periods of high employment, millions of persons with disabilities remained unemployed or underemployed.   Persons with disabilities are less likely to have full-time employment, and, even when employed, earn less income than their peers who do not have disabilities. Blanck, et al., *supra* at 325; *see also* United States Department of Labor,

Persons with a Disability: Labor Force Characteristics Summary (2011), http://www.bls.gov/news.release/disabl.nr0.htm; Nat'l Council on Disability, National Disability Policy: A Progress Report - October 2011 (2011), http://www.ncd.gov/progress_reports/Oct312011 #_Toc304437154.

As discussed in prior parts of this casebook, there are many reasons why individuals with disabilities are less likely to be employed, and, when they are employed, receive lower wages than workers without disabilities. Employment rates are suppressed by an inability to invest in training and education, workplace barriers that curtail productivity such as lack of workplace accommodations, and the inability to receive adequate health insurance. *See* Burris & Moss, *supra* at 9.

The existing evidence and studies lead to an important question: besides antidiscrimination law, what may be done to address these issues? Below we consider two policy tools that move beyond antidiscrimination law.

§ 30.1 Workforce Investment Act (WIA)

A. *Overview*

The Workforce Investment Act of 1998 (WIA) established state and local Workforce Investment Boards responsible for developing a "one-stop" delivery system of accessible, innovative, and comprehensive employment services. Workforce Investment Act Of 1998, PL 105-220, Aug. 7, 1998, 112 Stat. 939 (codified as amended at 29 U.S.C. § 2801 et seq. (2006). They partner with vocational rehabilitation agencies, businesses, and job training and education programs to assist local communities in increasing employment. *See, e.g.,* Positively Minn., Dep't of Emp. & Econ. Dev., Workforce Investment Act (WIA), http://www.positivelyminnesota.com/All_Programs_Services/Workforce_Investment_Act/index.aspx (last visited June 5, 2012).

Furthermore, the one-stop system provides assistance in job search activities, career planning, job skill assessments and training, and childcare resources. *See generally* Iowa Workforce Dev., http://www.iowaworkforce.org (last visited June 5, 2012); Tex. Workforce Comm'n, http://www.twc.state.tx.us/twc.html (last visited June 5, 2012). One-stops also provide resources for job and entrepreneurial training, transportation and housing assistance, and access to affordable health coverage. Allison Henig, Employment Aid for Youth Aging Out of Foster Care: Extending One-Stop Career Centers to Include A Division for Foster Care Youth, 47 Fam. Ct. Rev. 570, 579 (2009).

The Disability Program Navigator (DPN) demonstration project is a joint program of the Social Security Administration (SSA) and the U.S. Department of Labor (DOL). The primary goal of this project is to develop a comprehensive and seamless approach to enhancing employment opportunities for people with disabilities served by WIA's one-stop centers. To achieve this end, the DPN initiative is designed to increase employment and self-sufficiency for Social Security beneficiaries and others with disabilities, facilitate access to federal and state employment training programs and services, and enhance access to the private employer community. Additionally, DPNs assist youth with disabilities as they transition to working age to secure employment and maintain economic self-sufficiency.

DPNs conduct outreach to agencies and public and private organizations that serve people with disabilities. They serve as a resource on SSA's work incentive and employment support programs and the provision of services through Benefits Planning, Assistance and Outreach organizations. Although DPNs are not direct service staff, they work with people with disabilities to ensure partnership in the workforce system and elimination of system barriers for people with disabilities.

B. *Applicability Of The ADA To WIA*

WIA is designed to help individuals with disabilities achieve employment, economic independence, and inclusion into society. 29 U.S.C. § 701(b)(1) (2006). It is the federal funding vehicle for states to provide rehabilitation services and employment opportunities to people with disabilities. Martha F. Davis, Learning to Work: A Functional Approach to Welfare and Higher Education, 58 Buff. L. Rev. 147, 205 (2010).

The programs and services supported by WIA are covered by the antidiscrimination provisions of the ADA and Section 504 of the Rehabilitation Act of 1973. *See generally* Workforce Investment Act of 1998, PL 105–220, Aug. 7, 1998, 112 Stat. 939 (codified as amended at 29 U.S.C. § 2801 et seq. (2006). The antidiscrimination provisions apply to state and local agencies supported with WIA funds, state and local workforce boards, one-stop operators, and employment providers. 20 C.F.R. § 667.275(a)(1)-(3)(2012).

"Disability" is defined under WIA consistent with the regulations implementing the ADA. 29 C.F.R. § 37.4 (2012). Employees of private service providers are protected by Title I. State and local activities are covered under Title II. Title III's public accommodation provisions apply to private service providers receiving WIA funds from workforce boards.

A qualified person with a disability is entitled to effective benefits and services provided under WIA. One-stops, DPNs, and service providers must administer their programs in the most integrated setting possible and not impose criteria that screen out individuals with disabilities. *Id.* §§ 37.7(d) & (i). They must provide reasonable accommodations to qualified applicants, participants, and employees with disabilities, unless doing so causes undue hardship. *Id.* § 37.4. They also must make reasonable modifications to policies and practices to avoid discrimination. *Id.* § 37.8(a)-(b).

The U.S. Department of Labor publishes a "WIA Section 188 Checklist" for one-stop centers, workforce agencies, WIA grantees, and Job

Corps directors and contractors. The checklist provides policy and procedure guidance "to ensure nondiscrimination and equal opportunities for persons with disabilities." U.S. Dep't of Labor, WIA Section 188 Checklist, http://www.dol.gov/oasam/programs/crc/section188.htm (last visited Jan. 29, 2013). Examples of the antidiscrimination protections applicable to persons with disabilities in the employment provider context are provided in the following chapter on the applicability of the ADA to TWWIIA.

§ 30.2 Ticket To Work And Work Incentives Improvement Act (TWWIIA)

A. *Overview*

TWWIIA provides benefits to eligible individuals with disabilities who want to and are capable of working. 20 C.F.R § 411.125(a) (2012). One benefit allows working individuals with disabilities the option of maintaining Medicaid health insurance coverage. This promotes the ability of participants to return to work without the loss of essential health care benefits. Another benefit is providing "tickets" for persons with disabilities to choose, rather than be assigned to, service providers for employment training.

Historically, one of the barriers to work for persons with disabilities has been the inability to obtain health care coverage. Sara Rosenbaum & David Rousseau, Medicaid at Thirty-Five, 45 St. Louis U. L.J. 7, 40 (2001). Disability-based payments often diminish incentives to work, particularly when the attempt to work itself reduces eligibility for those health care benefits. Katherine Inge, et al., Survey Results from a National Survey of Community Rehabilitation Providers Holding Special Wage Certificates, Journal of Vocational Rehabilitation 30 (2009) 67-85, 83. Cash benefits, for instance under the SSI and SSDI programs, primarily have been available to individuals who could not engage in "substantial gainful activity." Stella L. Smetanka, The Disabled in Debt to Social Security: Can Fairness Be Guaranteed?, 35 Wm. Mitchell L. Rev. 1084, 1087 (2009).

TWWIIA allows states to permit qualified individuals with disabilities who have incomes above the poverty level the option of purchasing Medicaid health insurance or of maintaining their coverage throughout their employment. TWWIIA also covers people returning to work from SSDI (e.g., after being injured on the job) who may risk the loss of health insurance coverage. Incentives to Help You Return to Work, SSA Publication No. 05-10060, ICN 463261 (Aug. 2012), *available at* http://www.ssa.gov/pubs/10060.html#a0=1.

TWWIIA's Ticket to Work and Self-Sufficiency Program provides recipients of disability insurance with a "ticket" to purchase employment training services from qualified Employment Networks (ENs). *See* 20 C.F.R. § 411.300 (2012) (defining an EN's purpose). The goal is to encourage individuals with disabilities to seek employment rehabilitation services that aid in attaining employment and to reduce dependence on governmental benefit programs. The Ticket to Work and Self-Sufficiency Program, 66 Fed. Reg. 67,370, 67,370 (Dec. 28, 2001) (codified at 20 C.F.R.pt. 411 (2012)). Ticket program services include the provision of case management, workplace accommodations, peer mentoring, job training, and transportation assistance.

ENs receive payment from SSA when they succeed in placing the participant in employment. Public and private organizations may apply to be ENs, *id.* at 67,433 (codified at 20 C.F.R. pt. 411.305 (2012)), as may family and friends who meet the EN qualifications. *Id.* at 67,397 (codified at *id.*). To date, more than one-third of the states have implemented TWWIIA and others have passed legislation creating similar programs. Nat'l Council on Disability, Finding the Gaps: A Comparative Analysis of Disability Laws in the U.S. to the U.N. Convention on the Rights of Persons with Disabilities (May 12, 2008), http://www.ncd.gov/publications/ 2008/May122008. However, one study of the first four years of Ticket implementation indicated that only 1.1 percent of Ticket recipients assigned their Tickets to a provider, and of those, 90 percent assigned their Tickets to state VR agencies. Craig Thornton, et al., Mathematica Pol'y Res., Inc. & Cornell Univ. Inst. Pol'y Res., Evaluation of the Ticket to Work Program: Assessments of Post-Rollout Implementation and Early Impacts, Volume 1 at 158-77 (May 2007).

Trend analysis suggests the program will not reach Congressional expectations of exits from the rolls, unless there are major changes in beneficiary behavior. *Id.* at 249. Specifically, program participation would have to significantly increase and a larger number of recipients would have to surpass the earning amount that qualifies them for benefits. *Id.* Self-report data from Ticket users suggest that approximately 15% expect to exit the program within five years. *Id.* at 250. However, beneficiaries face challenges such as health declines and increased functional limitations, which may prevent these expected exits from occurring. *Id.*

The 2008 Ticket Regulations were meant to address many of these issues and trends, as well as to increase the number of EN providers. For instance, social security beneficiaries with disabilities ages 18 through 64 are eligible for a Ticket regardless of whether the beneficiary has passed a first Continuing Disability Review for determining ongoing disability status. Work World, Ticket to Work Regulation Changes – 2008, http://www.workworld.org/wwwebhelp/ticket_to_work_regulation_changes _2008.htm (last visited June 5, 2012). The new regulations recognize the need for and support an incremental return to work process. *Id.* Discussed below, the 2008 regulations also incentivize the creation of more ENs, in large part, by changing the manner and amounts of payments they may receive.

B. *Applicability Of The ADA To TWWIIA's Employment Networks (ENs)*

An individual with disability covered by TWWIIA is a person with a disability for purposes of SSI or SSDI, and may be considered a qualified individual with disability under the ADA. 42 U.S.C.A. §§ 12102(2) & 12131(2) (West 2009). The applicability of the ADA to ENs depends on the classification of the EN. ENs include individuals, cooperatives, and public and private rehabilitation providers.

Although Title I protects employees of an EN, the relationship between an EN and its Ticket participants is governed by Title II provisions for public entities or Title III provisions for private entities as places of public accommodation. *Id.* § 12181(7)(K). Public and private ENs receiving federal grants or contracts also are subject to the antidiscrimination provisions of Section 504 of the Rehabilitation Act of 1973. Nondiscrimination on the Basis of Disability by Public Accommodations and in Commercial Facilities, 56 Fed. Reg. 35544, 35552 (July 26, 1991).

Title II requires that ENs not exclude qualified individuals with disabilities from their services and programs. 42 U.S.C. § 12132 (2006). As such, these ENs must be physically and programmatically accessible. 20 C.F.R. § 411.315(a)(2) (2012).

State and local government ENs, covered under Title II, must ensure that their programs, when viewed in their entirety, are accessible. 28 C.F.R. §§ 35.149-150 (2012). Title III requires that privately-run ENs provide access to all persons with disabilities, not just those who are "qualified" for a particular program or service. 42 U.S.C. § 12182(a) (2006).

An individual, family member, or friend of a Ticket participant who owns, leases, or operates a place of public accommodation as an EN is subject to Title III. Privately-run ENs must remove barriers in existing buildings or provide services through alternative methods when "readily achievable." 42 U.S.C. § 12181(9) (2006); 28 C.F.R. § 36.304 (2012).

As ADA Title II or III entities, ENs must ensure effective communication with and physical and programmatic access to facilities and services for Ticket applicants, participants, their families, and the public. 42 U.S.C. § 12182(b)(2)(A)(iv) (2006).

ENs may not adopt program eligibility criteria that screen out people with certain disabilities (or individuals who have an association with people with disabilities) from programs or services, unless such criteria are necessary to program operation. 42 U.S.C. § 12182(b)(2)(A)(i) (2006). Public and private ENs must reasonably modify their policies, practices, and procedures when necessary to allow people with disabilities to participate, unless doing so would fundamentally alter the program. 28 C.F.R. §§ 35.130(b)(7), 36.202 (2012).

A program participant may assign her Ticket to a public or private EN willing and able to provide services. 20 C.F.R. § 411.140 (2008). The program encourages a range of service choices in which the participant and the EN choose their working partners. *Id.* §§ 411.145, 411.150. Likewise, a participant is able to choose her EN and deposit the Ticket to receive services from that EN or the state VR agency, and may choose to re-assign the Ticket to another EN. *Id.* § 411.150 (placing limitations on Ticket reassignment).

Program and service choice is a central theme in the new disability policy framework:

> The Ticket to Work program provides for a voluntary relationship between the beneficiary and the EN. While an EN may not discriminate in the provision of services based on a beneficiary's age, gender, race, color, creed, or national origin, *an EN may select the beneficiaries to whom it will offer services based on factors such as its assessment of the needs of the beneficiary and of its ability to help the individual.*

The Ticket to Work and Self-Sufficiency Program, 66 Fed. Reg. 67,370, 67,400 (Dec. 28, 2001) (emphasis added).

There are sound reasons why ENs specialize their services to particular groups of individuals. *Id.* at 67,399. Specialization may provide for greater efficiency and effectiveness in the delivery of services. Where an EN is not qualified to serve a particular individual, the ADA's undue burden provision does not require the EN to serve that Ticket holder. When accommodation is possible and reasonable, public or private ENs may not charge an individual to cover their costs. 28 C.F.R. §§ 36.301(c), 35.130(f) (2012).

However, questions remain about TWWIIA implementation. What is an EN's responsibility under the ADA to serve individuals with multiple disabilities? In the case of a Ticket participant who is deaf and blind, does an EN specializing in serving deaf Ticket holders violate the ADA's nondiscrimination provisions by not providing materials in Braille, effectively excluding the blind and deaf individual from services?

Addressing such issues under the ADA, one EN core obligation to Ticket holders is nondiscrimination in the provision of program access and services. An EN's decision not to provide service to a Ticket holder with multiple or secondary disabilities must be substantiated by evidence that such secondary disabilities require a service modification that would either fundamentally alter the program or pose an undue burden. Regardless, an EN must ensure physical and programmatic access to potential program participants, for instance, by providing alternative media formats and ensuring that data systems are fully accessible for independent use. 20 C.F.R. § 411.315(a)(2) (2012); Ticket to Work and

Work Incentives Advisory Panel, Testimony 35-37 (May 3, 2002) (statement of Peter Blanck) (transcript on file with authors).

Another prominent question related to Ticket implementation is whether the ADA prevents ENs from choosing to provide services only to the pool of participants who are the least disabled and "creamed." Disability advocates' concerns about program implementation reflect the emergence of two separate and perhaps unequal markets for EN services: one served by private specialized ENs and another by state VR providers. *Id.* at 26 (statement of Andrew Imparato, former president and CEO, American Association of People with Disabilities).

The economic incentives in the Ticket Program encourage ENs to serve participants who need the fewest and least costly services (e.g., workplace accommodations and job training), and those who are able to return to work for an extended period of time. Gina A. Livermore et al., Center for Studying Disability Policy, Mathematica Pol'y Res., Inc., Ticket to Work Participant Characteristics and Outcomes Under the Revised Regulations (Sept. 24, 2012), at 8. Subsequently, disability advocates are concerned that state VR agencies will bear a greater burden of serving individuals with more involved disabilities and costly service needs. Ticket to Work and Work Incentives Advisory Panel, supra, at 20-21 (statement of Ray Cebula, Senior Staff Attorney, Disability Law Ctr.).

Indeed, many ENs consider it financially risky to accept tickets. As of 2008, only 305 of the more than 1,200 organizations that had registered as ENs, had accepted tickets, and only 147 had accepted 5 or more. Livermore, et al., *supra*, at 4. There also continues to be an unfilled demand for employment services, and researchers have cited a difficulty in EN recruiting as a possible cause. Thornton, et al., *supra*, at 250.

SSA expected more ENs to participate in the Ticket to Work program following the July 21, 2008 implementation of SSA regulations that created a payment system based on attained levels of employment. Nat'l Consortium for Health Sys. Dev., At a Glance: The Final Ticket to Work Regulations 1 (June 1, 2009), http://www.nchsd.org/library/file.asp?id=300543 (last visited June 5, 2012). ENs will be able to reach payment milestones more quickly because they will be credited for services to beneficiaries at different points along the beneficiaries' paths to work. Work World, *supra*. Furthermore, the regulations foster collaboration amongst state VR agencies and private ENs via a new cost reimbursement system. Nat'l Consortium for Health Care, *supra*, at 1. The overall goal of these changes in the Ticket Program is to increase both EN participation and improve the rate of beneficiaries leaving the benefit roles due to employment. *Id.*

Education and outreach that explain the Ticket Program is vital for beneficiaries and service providers as well as for other stakeholders on the local, state, and federal levels. Research has concluded that outreach is most effective when targeted towards those with specific employment goals. *Id.* Such individuals tend to have two common characteristics: they are under the age of 55 and were recently employed. *Id.* This conclusion is supported by a report from the Social Security Advisory Board, which noted that individuals with a recent attachment to the work force are more likely to respond to these return to work initiatives. David Stapleton, Mathematica Pol'y Research, Ticket to Work at the Crossroads: A Solid Foundation with an Uncertain Future (Sept. 2008), 94, *available at* http://www.socialsecurity.gov/disabilityresearch/ttw4/TTW_Rpt4_508_vol1r.pdf. Moreover, Ticket participants must be knowledgeable about their rights and responsibilities under the program.

Information on the Ticket Program is crucial to assess questions such as: Who is being served and rejected? What is the nature of program access and accommodation for beneficiaries with multiple disabilities (and their families or representatives)? Will the ADA's antidiscrimination provisions and TWWIIA's reform of work incentives affect employers' and co-workers' attitudes about Ticket holders as job applicants and workers with disabilities? And, will the ADA and TWWIIA impact the attitudes of individuals with disabilities themselves with regard to their employment goals? Information is also necessary to shape program revisions and to expand the program's application. Gilbert W. Gimm, et al., Working with Disability: Who Are the Top Earners in the Medicaid Buy-In Program?, Working with Disability, No. 3, at 4 (Mar. 2007), *available at* http://www.chiip.org/pdf/Mathematica_topearners_issue_brief.pdf (last visited June 5, 2012).

Chapter 31 DISABILITY AND WELFARE POLICY

§ 31.1 Social Security Disability Insurance (SSDI)

A. *Overview*

SSDI is a federally-administered insurance program for long-term wage loss that provides a monthly income to individuals with physical or mental impairments that are expected to result in death or last one year or more. 42 U.S.C. §§ 423, 423(d)(1)(A) (2006). It is a federal cash benefit program, whereby benefits are paid to individuals who have a disability, defined as an "inability to engage in any substantial gainful activity by reason of any medically determinable physical or mental impairment which can be expected to result in death or which has lasted or can be expected to last for a continuous period of not less than twelve months." SSDI is limited to workers who have paid work experience of at least ten years and have paid payroll taxes into the Disability Insurance trust fund.

Social Security benefits serve different purposes from the ADA. While Social Security aims to provide persons who become disabled with income support, Title I of the ADA focuses on equal opportunity for workforce participation and the prevention of invidious discrimination. Marsha Rose Katz, et al., Aspects of Disability Decision Making: Data and Materials, 1 & 2 (Feb. 2012), *available at* http://ssab.gov/ Publications/Disability/GPO_Chartbook_FINAL_06122012.pdf.

B. *Interaction Of The ADA And SSDI*

In *Cleveland v. Policy Management Systems Corp.*, presented *supra* Part 2, § 5.3, the Supreme Court addressed the issue of whether an individual's SSDI eligibility precludes their cause of action under Title I of the ADA. The current Social Security definition of disability is based on an "inability to work" 42 U.S.C. § 423(d)(1) (2006); whereas, the ADA asserts that the goals of the legislation are "to assure equality of opportunity, full participation, independent living, and economic self-sufficiency for such individuals." 42 U.S.C. § 1210(a)(7) (2006). The Supreme Court in *Cleveland*, however, held that an ADA plaintiff must provide a sufficient explanation for the contradiction that she is a qualified person with a disability who is able to work with a reasonable accommodation, yet still satisfies the eligibility requirements of SSDI. Cleveland v. Policy Mgmt. Sys. Corp., 526 U.S. 795, 806 (1999).

Blanck served as a discussant before the Social Security Advisory Board (SSAB) on August 14, 2013 arguing:

> (1) The definitions of disability under the Social Security Act and under the Americans with Disabilities Act (ADA) serve different important, yet complementary, national policy goals.

> (2) To further the goals of a comprehensive national disability policy, additional study and dialogue on the

> Social Security disability programs should focus on supporting the economic security, stability, and productivity of people with disabilities.

Letter from Peter Blanck to SSAB, at 1 (Aug. 14, 2013), *available at* http://bbi.syr.edu/_assets/docs/news_events/Blanck_to_SSAB.pdf.

Blanck recommended that the SSAB "preserve cash assistance for current and future beneficiaries while continuing to expand the SSI/SSDI work incentives." *Id.* at 4. This might be done by "increasing the SGA level, simplifying the SSDI work incentives, and providing permanent eligibility for Medicare for individuals who no longer receive SSDI cash benefits." *Id.*

§ 31.2 Temporary Assistance For Needy Families (TANF) Programs

A. *Overview*

In 1996, the Personal Responsibility and Work Opportunity Reconciliation Act (PRWOR) created the Temporary Assistance for Needy Families (TANF) program. TANF replaced the Aid to Families with Dependent Children program as a shift away from long-term welfare services and toward the requirement of employment for welfare recipients. Janice Y. Law, Comment, Changing Welfare "As We Know It" One More Time: Assuring Basic Skills and Postsecondary Education Access for TANF Recipients, 48 Santa Clara L. Rev. 243, 249 & 252 (2008).

Among other goals, the TANF program strives to promote job preparation and employment to help reduce dependency on government welfare. 45 C.F.R. § 260.20(b) (2012). TANF's work requirements aim to encourage eligible recipients to seek employment and self-sufficiency. Recipients must begin working when the state determines they are ready for employment, or after twenty-four cumulative months of assistance. Yoanna X. Moisides, I Just Need Help . . . TANF, the Deficit Reduction Act, and the New "Work-Eligible Individual," 11 J. Gender Race & Just. 17, 22 (2007). Families receiving TANF benefits must participate in approved work activities for at least an average of twenty hours per week, with two-parent families required to work at least an average of thirty-five hours per week. *Id.* at 23. A state has the option to exempt single parents with a child under one year of age from these requirements. 42 U.S.C. § 607 (2012).

With a focus on reducing the number of welfare recipients, monetary benefits end "after a total of sixty months, regardless of whether an individual has found gainful employment." Moisides, *supra*, at 22. TANF agencies may reduce or terminate benefits if a recipient refuses to work. 42 U.S.C.A. § 607(e)(1) (West 2012). There are exceptions to the work term limit for personal hardship and situations involving family violence. *Id.* § 608(a)(7)(C)(iii).

TANF places requirements on the state administering agencies. The agency is responsible for developing an individual responsibility plan (IRP) for participants by assessing job skills, prior work experience, and prospects for employability. *See* Amir Paz-Fuchs, Behind the Contract for Welfare Reform: Antecedent Themes in Welfare to Work Programs, 29 Berkeley J. Emp. & Lab. L. 405, 452 (2008). The IRP is intended to help the individual achieve employment and to increase job responsibility over time. 42 U.S.C.A. § 608(b)(2)(A)(iii) (West 2012). States are subject to declines in federal assistance if they do not satisfy minimum participation rates, comply with work term time limits, or sanction recipients who refuse to work. 45 C.F.R. §§ 262.1(a)(4), (9), & (14) (2012).

In 2011, TANF services were provided to nearly two million families comprising over four million individuals. Over three million of the recipients were children. Office of Family Assistance, U.S. Dep't of Health & Hum. Servs. Caseload Data 2011 (Apr. 3. 2012), http://www.acf.hhs.gov/programs/ofa/resource/caseload2011 (last visited Oct. 17, 2012). Families typically end TANF services when they locate employment. Robert Wood, et al., Mathematica Pol'y Research, Inc., *Social Service Review*, Vol. 82, No. 1 (March 2008), pp. 3-28, http://www.jstor.org/stable/10.1086/525035. However, many families that have left the TANF program continue to rely on governmental programs such as Medicaid, Food Stamps, and housing subsidies. *Id.*

The TANF program is not directed specifically towards individuals with disabilities. Yet, "a substantially higher proportion of TANF recipients reported having physical or mental impairments than did adults in the non-TANF population." Nat'l Council on Disability, TANF and Disability – Importance of Supports for Families with Disabilities in Welfare Reform (Mar. 14, 2003) ("TANF Disability Position Paper"), http://www.ncd.gov/publications/2003/Mar52003. *See also* Wood, et al., *supra*, at 3-4. Many TANF families include a child with a disability or a member with an undiagnosed disability. Pamela Loprest and Elaine Maag, The Urban Institute, Disabilities Among TANF Recipients: Evidence from the NHIS (May 2009), http://aspe.hhs.gov/ hsp/09/disabilityamongtanf/index.shtml; Emily Sama Martin, et al., Creating TANF and Vocational Rehabilitation Agency Partneships, Mathematica Pol'y Research, Inc. (Feb. 2008), 4, *available at* http://www. mathematica-mpr.com/publications/PDFs/creatingTANF.pdf. Psychiatric disabilities and learning disabilities also are prevalent in the TANF population. *See id.*; Ladonna Pavetti, et al., Mathematica Pol'y Research, Inc., Conducting In-Depth Assessments (Feb. 2008), 8, *available at* http://www.mathematica-mpr.com/publications/PDFs/conductingindepth. pdf.

B.   *Applicability Of The ADA To TANF*

Programs and activities supported by TANF funds are subject to federal antidiscrimination laws such as the ADA, the Age Discrimination

Act of 1975, Section 504 of the Rehabilitation Act of 1973, and Title VI of the Civil Rights Act of 1964. 45 C.F.R. § 260.35 (2012). However, an individual with a physical or mental limitation receiving TANF benefits does not qualify automatically as an "individual with a disability" under the ADA. U.S. Dep't of Health and Human Servs. Office of Civil Rights, Summary of Policy Guidance, Prohibition Against Discrimination on the Basis of Disability in the Administration of TANF, *available at* http://www.hhs.gov/ocr/prohibition.html; Cary LaCheen, Using Title II of the Americans with Disabilities Act on Behalf of Clients in TANF Programs, 8 Geo. J. on Poverty L. & Pol'y 1, 89-90 (2001).

Many TANF recipients have undiagnosed disabilities, Jacqueline Kauff, Mathematica Pol'y Research, Inc., Assisting TANF Recipients Living with Disabilities to Obtain and Maintain Employment Final Report (Feb. 2008), 27, *available at* http://www.mathematica-mpr.com/publications/PDFs/assistingtanf.pdf, and their histories of disability do not establish a record of a substantially limiting impairment. LaCheen, *supra*, at 89. As TANF agencies develop and maintain recipient profiles and track their progress, more information about participants' records of disabilities may develop. *Id.*

Subject to restrictions, state TANF programs may establish exceptions to the mandatory work requirements. Sheila R. Zedlewski, et al., Hard-to-Employ Parents: A Review of Their Characteristics and the Programs Designed to Serve Their Needs (June 2007), 7, *available at* http://www.urban.org/UploadedPDF/411504_employ_parents.pdf. State programs have not ordinarily applied the ADA's definition of disability when defining exceptions from TANF program rules. *See* H.H.S., Policy Guidance Summary, *supra*. For instance, California's TANF program (CalWORKS) exempts from work requirements individuals with "a doctor's verification that the disability is expected to last at least 30 days and that it significantly impairs the recipient's ability to be regularly employed or participate in welfare-to-work activities." Cal. Welf. & Inst. Code § 11320.3(b)(3)(A) (2003). New York's program exempts individuals who are "disabled or incapacitated" based on a determination by the welfare agency or a private doctor referred by the agency. N.Y. Comp. Codes R. & Regs. tit. 12, § 1300.2(b)(4) (2002). New York also exempts those who are ill or injured and as a result unable to engage in work for up to three months. *Id.* § 1300.2(b)(1).

Professor LaCheen, *supra*, at 94, suggests several issues related to the applicability of ADA law to state TANF programs. For instance, if a claim of discrimination arises from lack of access to the application process, individuals with disabilities who are covered by the ADA need not qualify for TANF benefits to raise such a challenge. *Id.* However, where a job-training program requires participants to have a certain diploma to participate, and the applicant with a disability does not have such a diploma, the ineligibility requirement for program participation may properly preclude an ADA challenge. *Id.* at 95. Lastly, some states may argue that individuals who have not been compliant with TANF work requirements are not qualified individuals for purposes of an ADA challenge. *Id.*

TANF program work requirements may have an unfair impact on persons with disabilities. Studies consistently indicate higher rates of disabilities among TANF beneficiaries who are sanctioned for noncompliance with work requirements than among those who are not sanctioned. Ladonna Pavetti, *supra*, at 2. TANF recipients with disabilities also face more significant barriers to employment than recipients who are not disabled. H.H.S., Policy Guidance Summary, *supra*. To strengthen protections for persons with disabilities in TANF programs, the National Council on Disability (NCD) has recommended that states give assurances that participants with disabilities are screened with appropriate diagnostic tools, and that work activities include rehabilitation activities (e.g., as supported by TWWIIA) to help the individual attain work. *See* James Schmeling et al., The New Disability Law and Policy Framework: Implications for Case Managers 26 (2004), *available at* http://bbi.syr.edu/publications/blanck_docs/2003-2004/ch4 DisabilityLaw051704FINAL.pdf

In addition, states serving TANF recipients may train staff on issues related to disability to aid in access to Medicaid or other health coverage when recipients transition from welfare to work. Training may include periodic review to ensure that TANF programs comply with ADA and Section 504 requirements. H.H.S., Policy Guidance Summary, *supra*. For a review of the ADA's applicability to welfare programs, *see* Cary LaCheen, Welfare Law Ctr., Using the Americans with Disabilities Act to Protect the Rights of Individuals with Disabilities in TANF Programs: A Manual for Non-Litigation Advocacy (2004), *available at* http://www.nclej. org/pdf/manual/ ADA2004_manual_full.pdf (last visited June 5, 2012).

In *Aughe v. Shalala*, the court addresses whether an age nineteen eligibility limit for benefits under TANF's predecessor, Aid for Families with Dependent Children (AFDC), is an essential element of the program, or whether the requirement violates the Rehabilitation Act and the ADA.

ഔ

AUGHE V. SHALALA

United States District Court, Western District of Washington, 1995
885 F.Supp. 1428

DIMMICK, Chief Judge.

* * *

The plaintiffs in this case are Dallas Loghry and his mother Valarie Aughe. Loghry, who recently turned eighteen years of age, is a full-time student in the Everett School District. Loghry apparently suffers from a learning disability that has impaired his learning progress.

Aughe has received Aid for Families with Dependent Children ("AFDC"), 42 U.S.C. § 601 et seq., from Washington Department of Social and Health Services. When Loghry turned eighteen, DSHS terminated AFDC benefits because Loghry would not complete high school by his nineteenth birthday and was thus deemed ineligible for further benefits. See 42 U.S.C. § 606(a). Aughe appealed the termination of benefits, which was upheld by the administrative law judge.

* * *

III

AFDC, a welfare program for dependent children and their parent or relative who provides care, is jointly funded by the federal and state governments. See 42 U.S.C. § 601. Each state administers its own plan, which must meet federal guidelines and which must be approved by the Secretary of U.S. Department of Health and Human Services Department. See 42 U.S.C. § 602.

Section 606(a) of the AFDC defines a "dependent child" as a needy child who is deprived of parental support because of death, absence, or incapacity of one parent and who is living with the other parent or certain specified relatives and who meets an age requirement. To meet the age qualification, the child must be "(A) under the age of eighteen, or (B) at the option of the State, under the age of nineteen and a full-time student in a secondary school (or in the equivalent level of vocational or technical training), if, before he attains age nineteen, he may reasonably be expected to complete the program of such secondary school (or such training)." Id. § 606(a)(2). The Washington AFDC plan has opted for the second age requirement, and thus provides benefits for those "children" who are between eighteen and nineteen years of age and who are expected to finish secondary school (or a votech program) before their nineteenth birthday.

In this case, Aughe contends that Loghry could not finish his secondary school program by age nineteen because of a learning disability, and thus could not meet the age requirement. She asserts that that requirement is not essential or necessary to the AFDC program and that application of the requirement in this case violates both the ADA and the Rehabilitation Act. Even if the requirement is essential or necessary to the program, asserts Aughe, the ADA and the Rehabilitation Act still require reasonable modification. She asserts that waiving completion before nineteen would be a reasonable modification. Aughe also contends that the completion before nineteen creates an impermissible classification that does not serve a legitimate governmental interest, thereby violating equal protection guarantees.

The federal government contends that Loghry was not denied benefits because he was handicapped, but rather because he was not expected to finish his secondary education by age nineteen. Because he is not "otherwise qualified" for benefits, asserts the federal government, denial of such benefits does not violate the Rehabilitation Act. In addition, the federal government contends that the same result should obtain under the ADA because regulations governing that act are consistent with those governing the Rehabilitation Act. The federal government also asserts that even if the completion by age nineteen has a disparate impact on the handicapped, that fact alone does not establish a violation of the ADA. Finally, the federal government asserts that the age requirement is rationally related to a legitimate government interest – saving money and preserving AFDC funds for children and their families – and, thus, does not violate equal protection guarantees.

The state government argues that it must follow federal law defining "dependent child" or risk losing federal funding. The state government also contends that nothing in the ADA or the Rehabilitation Act is meant to repeal the AFDC's completion by age nineteen requirement. Finally, the state government asserts that the completion by age nineteen is rationally related to the government's interest in allocating finite resources and to the state government's interest in obtaining matching federal funds.

A

The first question presented is whether the AFDC as interpreted violated the Rehabilitation Act. * * *

While Aughe concedes that Loghry cannot meet the AFDC's "completion by age nineteen" requirement, she asserts that that requirement is not an essential one. Accordingly, she asserts that the requirement can be waived as a reasonable modification. She cites two cases to support this position: *University Interscholastic League v. Buchanan,* 848 S.W.2d 298 (Tex. Ct. App. 1993); and *Pottgen v. Missouri State High School Activities Ass'n,* 857 F.Supp. 654 (E.D. Mo. 1994). In each of those cases, the trial court found that an athletic association's rule barring participation of student athletes over nineteen violated the Rehabilitation Act when the athletes had been held back from school because of a prior learning disability. See *Buchanan,* 848 S.W.2d at 302; *Pottgen,* 857 F.Supp. at 664.

As the federal government argues, however, these cases are distinguishable because the rule in each case was an age eligibility policy promulgated by a voluntary athletic association, which could have been waived by the association. In contrast, the rule in this case is a federal statute that neither the state government nor Shalala can waive. Moreover, *Pottgen* has been reversed by the Eight Circuit Court of Appeals. See *Pottgen v. Missouri State High School Activities Ass'n,* 40 F.3d 926 (8th Cir. 1994).

In *Pottgen,* the Eight Circuit recognized that to be "otherwise qualified," an individual need not meet all requirements; rather, an individual must meet only those requirements that are necessary or essential. *Pottgen*, 40 F.3d at 929. The plaintiffs in the instant case advance the same argument that the Eighth Circuit rejected: That waiving the age requirement was a reasonable accommodation that made the plaintiff otherwise qualified. "The [trial] court framed the issue as not whether Pottgen meets all of the eligibility requirements, but rather whether reasonable accommodations existed. We disagree. A Rehabilitation Act analysis requires the court to determine both whether an individual meets all of the essential eligibility requirements *and* whether reasonable modifications exist." Id.

The Court then found that the *Pottgen* plaintiff could not meet the age requirements in spite of his handicap and that the age requirement was an essential portion of the program:

> An age limit helps reduce the competitive advantage flowing to teams using older athletes; protects younger athletes; protects younger athletes from harm; discourages student athletes from delaying their education to gain athletic maturity; and prevents over-zealous coaches from engaging in repeated red-shirting to gain a competitive advantage. These purposes are of immense importance in any interscholastic sports program. Id.

Here, as in *Pottgen,* the completion by age nineteen is an essential part of the program. The AFDC is designed to help children (i.e. those under eighteen years of age) and their families. By cutting off aid to those over eighteen the fiscal viability of the AFDC can be maintained.

The *Pottgen* court also recognized that even if the plaintiff could not meet the requirement, he could be "otherwise qualified" if "reasonable accommodations would enable him to meet the age limit." Id. "Reasonable accommodations do not require an institution 'to lower or to effect substantial modifications of standards to accommodate a handicapped person.' [*Southeastern Community College v. Davis,* 442 U.S. 397, 413, 99 S.Ct. 2361, 2371, 60 L.Ed.2d 980 (1979).] Accommodations are not reasonable if they impose 'undue financial and administrative burdens' or if they require a 'fundamental alteration in the nature of [the] program.' [*School Bd. of Nassau County v. Arline,* 480 U.S. 273, 287 n.17, 107 S.Ct. 1123, 1131 n.17, 94 L.Ed.2d 307 (1987).]" *Pottgen,* 40 F.3d at 930.

In *Pottgen,* the Court again rejected an argument made by Aughe – that waiving the age requirement is a reasonable modification:

> Waiving an essential eligibility standard would constitute a fundamental alteration in the nature of the baseball program. Other than waiving the age limit, no manner, method, or means is available which would permit Pottgen to satisfy the age limit. Consequently, no reasonable accommodations exist.

Since Pottgen can never meet the essential eligibility requirement, he is not an "otherwise qualified" individual. Section 504 was designed only to extend protection to those potentially able to meet the essential eligibility requirements of a program or activity. Id.

As in *Pottgen,* no modification short of waiving the "completion by nineteen" requirement could make Loghry into an "otherwise qualified individual." Because that would essentially rewrite the statute, it must be seen as a fundamental alteration in the nature of the program. In addition, such an alteration could impose an undue financial burden on the program. Accordingly, the completion by age nineteen requirement does not violate the Rehabilitation Act.

B

Aughe also argues that the completion by age nineteen requirement violates the ADA. * * * As Aughe recognizes, the requirements of the ADA and the Rehabilitation Act are governed by the same regulations and thus the analysis under both is similar. See *Pottgen,* 40 F.3d at 930.

The *Pottgen* court stated the analysis under the ADA as follows:

To determine whether Pottgen was a "qualified individual" for ADA purposes, the district court conducted an individualized inquiry into the necessity of the age limit in Pottgen's case. Such an individualized inquiry is inappropriate at this stage. Instead, to determine whether Pottgen is a "qualified individual" under the ADA, we must first determine whether the age limit is an essential eligibility requirement by reviewing the importance of the requirement to the interscholastic baseball program. If this requirement is essential, we then determine whether Pottgen meets this requirement with or without modification. It is at this later stage that the ADA requires an individualized inquiry. Id. at 930-31.

Relying on its Rehabilitation Act analysis, the *Pottgen* court concluded that the age limit was an essential requirement and that waiver of the age limit was not a reasonable modification. Id. at 931.

As was demonstrated in Section III A, supra, the "completion by age nineteen" requirement is an essential requirement of the AFDC program, which is designed to help dependent children. The only accommodation that could make Loghry eligible for AFDC is waiver of an essential element of the plan. Such waiver, which could impose an undue financial burden or which could fundamentally alter the nature of the program, is thus not required. See *Arline,* 480 U.S. at 287 n.17, 107 S.Ct. at 1131 n.17. Thus, the ADA does not require modification of the program.

In a "Submission of Supplemental Authority," Aughe brought a recent Vermont Supreme Court case to the Court's attention. In that case, *Howard v. Department of Social Welfare,* 655 A.2d 1102 (Vt. 1994), the Court applied the ADA to the Vermont version of the AFDC and held that the graduation by age nineteen requirement was not an essential element of that program and that accordingly plaintiffs were "qualified individuals" under the ADA.

As the state and federal governments argue, this Court is not bound by the *Howard* case, which made two critical errors in interpreting federal law. First, the court mistakenly determined that the graduation by nineteen requirement was not an essential element of the AFDC program. Compare *Howard,* 655 A.2d at 1108, with *Pottgen,* 40 F.3d at 930. Secondly, without extended discussion or analysis, the court erroneously found that the Health and Human Services Department would likely find that waiver of the completion by age nineteen requirement was a reasonable modification. See *Howard,* 655 A.2d at 1108 ("We see no reason that HHS would not consider the same modification to be reasonable when applied to a benefit program."). Finally, *Howard* is distinguishable in that it addressed a Vermont statute that extended benefits, if appropriated by the legislature, to full time students under the age of twenty one. See id.

In enacting the AFDC, Congress determined that the completion by age nineteen requirement was an essential element of that program. It may well be that a better social policy would extend benefits to those who are between eighteen and nineteen and who remain in school full time. That policy, however, is for Congress, and not this Court, to determine.

No genuine issues of material fact remain, and the federal and state governments are entitled to a judgment as a matter of law. Accordingly, summary judgment in their favor will be granted.

* * *

VII

In accordance with the forgoing, Aughe's motions for summary judgment * * * are all DENIED. The federal government's motion for summary judgment is GRANTED. In addition, the state government's motion for summary judgment is GRANTED. This case is DISMISSED, and the Clerk is directed to enter judgment in favor of defendants.

Notes & Questions

1. What are the applicable rules, though non-controlling, which the *Aughe* court discerns and relies upon from *Pottgen?*

2. Is fiscal viability alone a sufficient argument in support of the *Aughe* holding? Compare the factors identified in ADA Title II's "integration mandate" established by *Olmstead*, discussed in Part 4.

3. The Court in *Aughe* distinguished a Vermont case, *Howard v. Department of Social Welfare*, which held that under Vermont law implementing the AFDC, "the graduation by age nineteen requirement was not an essential element of that program . . . ." Aughe, 885 F.Supp at 1428. A California state court in *Fry v. Saenz*, 98 Cal.App.4th 256 (Cal. App. 2002), likewise addressed the age nineteen requirement of the CalWORKs program implementation of TANF. Examining the general purposes of the program, the court found that not only did the declared purposes of the program not require the age nineteen 'completion' rule as an eligibility condition to receive benefits, but also that such a requirement undermines the goals of reducing dependency and promoting rehabilitation. *Id*. at 264-66.

∾

Chapter 32 DISABILITY AND HEALTH CARE POLICY

The employment of persons with disabilities often is associated with a variety of complex issues, including the extent to which employees with disabilities have equal access to health care, as well as educational opportunities, transportation, assistive technology, support services, and career internships. Nat'l Council on Disability, Implementation of the Americans with Disabilities Act: Challenges, Best Practices, and New Opportunities for Success 26 (July 26, 2007), http://www.ncd.gov/publications/2007/July262007 (last visited June 5, 2012). Given the interconnected nature of these issues, health care policy has far-reaching effects.

One particular health care issue for many people with disabilities remains the extent to which employment and income affect benefits. A 2007 report from the NCD suggested that "the most important reason people with disabilities think they cannot strive for employment is that they fear they will lose certain essential government benefits, such as income support, health care coverage, personal assistance services, and affordable housing." *Id*. at 30.

Health care is often a significant cost to either the employer providing insurance, or the individual with a disability. *Id*. The NCD report indicated that some employers notice rising insurance premiums after a covered employee requires expensive care. *Id*. Although Title I of the ADA prohibits employers from discriminating against persons with disabilities, discrimination occurs at the hand of a variety of entities, based on the perception of a pending health or safety risk and often without evidentiary support. *Id*. at 73.

> Some insurance plans cap payments for durable medical equipment, which includes items such as wheelchairs, crutches, braces, and ventilators; in effect, making coverage for these items unavailable. Mental health services are limited by most policies, and frequently only prescription drugs that are included on an approved list are covered by a plan. Several disability community stakeholders pointed out that under these conditions, many working people with disabilities do not have access even to partial help to pay for life-sustaining assistive devices and prescription drugs, while limited mental health services can result in crises leading to job loss for people with psychiatric disabilities.

Nat'l Council on Disability, *supra*, at 73.

In addition to facing health care challenges in the course of employment, persons with disabilities may find obstacles in the medical sector. Some medical systems have failed to recognize the extensive need for physical and programmatic access to health facilities and services. *Id*. at 69. Individuals with disabilities attributed this problem, in part, to the possibility that health plans do not adequately compensate providers for all necessary services and products. The report noted that, "[o]verall, there is limited awareness of the issues and little interest or coordination among states, health plans, providers, and others responsible for finding solutions." *Id*.

In another 2007 report, the NCD concluded,

> Who receives health care services and how much service is obtained depends on one's health care coverage, or health insurance, which is, unfortunately for people with disabilities, intertwined with employment. Either an individual is able to work full-time at one employer long enough to qualify for employer-based health insurance (EBHI), or an individual must be assessed as totally unable to work, thereby qualifying for public health coverage. Those between these two extremes, where people with disabilities are likely to find themselves, have difficulty obtaining health coverage, threatening their access to health care, risking a deterioration of their health conditions, and further limiting their ability to work. Almost one of every five working age people with disabilities lacks health insurance. Even people with disabilities who are employed are less likely to have health insurance than workers without disabilities. Among fulltime employees, for example, 65 percent of those with disabilities had EBHI, compared to 74 percent of those without disabilities.

Nat'l Council on Disability, The Impact of the Americans with Disabilities Act: Assessing the Progress Toward Achieving the Goals of the ADA 85 (July 26, 2007) [hereinafter "NCD, Assessing the Progress"] (quoting Lisa A. Schur, Dead End Jobs or a Path to Economic Well-Being? The Consequences of Non-Standard Work Among People with Disabilities, 20 Behav. Scis. & L. 601, 601-620 (2002), *available at* http://www3. interscience.wiley.com/cgi-bin/fulltext/101520820/PDFST ART (last visited June 5, 2012).

§ 32.1 Medicare And Medicaid

A. *Overview*

The U.S. Department of Health and Human Services oversees the Medicare and Medicaid programs, which provide health care benefits to qualifying families and individuals. Medicare is a health insurance plan for people 65 and older, and also for people under 65 with certain disabilities or end-stage renal disease. Ctrs. for Medicare & Medicaid Servs., Medicare Program – General Information: Overview, http://www. cms.hhs.gov/MedicareGenInfo/ (last visited Nov. 10, 2013). Medicaid provides benefits to families and individuals who qualify in certain eligibility groups. *Id.* Medicaid eligibility is determined primarily by income and financial resources, while eligibility for Medicare is determined largely by age.

While Medicare is funded and administered by the federal government, Medicaid is administered and partially funded by the states. Medicaid eligibility varies between states. Soc. Sec. Admin., Annual Statistical Supplement to the Social Security Bulletin, 2011, at 56 (Feb. 2012), *available at* http://www.ssa.gov/policy/docs/statcomps/supplement/ 2011/supplement11.pdf (last visited October 12, 2012). States may determine eligibility based on having a disability, and consequently being medically needy, even if income might otherwise exclude them from Medicaid benefits. *Id.* at 2. It is possible to be eligible for both programs, and Medicaid recipients can use Medicaid to pay Medicare costs.

> NCD notes
>
> People with disabilities and people without disabilities are equally likely to be covered by some form of health insurance (88 percent – 91 percent). However, most of the people with disabilities covered (56 percent) are covered by Medicaid or Medicare, while most people without disabilities are covered by private insurance (78 percent). These differences in the sources of coverage are significant and may explain why people with disabilities are significantly more likely to go without needed medical care than people without disabilities (18 percent versus 7 percent).

NCD, Assessing the Progress, *supra*, at 85 (citation omitted).

Medicaid costs may be reduced by initiatives such as the Medicaid Buy-In program, which allows states to extend Medicaid coverage to working people with disabilities whose income might otherwise disqualify them from coverage. Buy-In participants are more likely to be male, white, and of prime working age (age 25-54) than are other Medicaid enrollees. Jody Schimmel, et al., How Do Buy-In Participants Compare with Other Medicaid Enrollees with Disabilities?, Working with Disability, No. 5 (June 2007), at 2, *available at* http://www.mathematica-mpr.com/publications/redirect_PubsDB.asp?strSite=PDFs/WWDcompare.p df (last visited June 6, 2012). Buy-In participants are more likely to receive treatment for psychiatric conditions and less likely to receive treatment for multiple conditions than are other Medicaid participants. *Id.* Data indicate that Medicaid expenditures per month per member are lower for Buy-In participants than they are for other Medicaid enrollees. *Id.* However, Schimmel and colleagues suggest program costs may rise if a Buy-In program attracts adults not previously enrolled in Medicaid. *Id.* at 4.

Data further indicate that participation in a Buy-In program often results in increased earnings; however, the extent to which earnings increase varies between states. Su Liu & Bob Weathers, Do Participants Increase Their Earnings After Enrolling in the Medicaid Buy-In Program?, Working with Disability, No. 4 (May 2007), at 1, *available at* http://www.chiip.org/pdf/Mathematica%20earnings%20increase%20issue%20brief%204.pdf (last visited June 6, 2012). Buy-In participants who increased their earnings were often younger than those who did not. *Id.* at 2. Participants who had earned at a higher earnings level before enrollment in the Buy-In program also saw increased earnings, suggesting that workers who earned at a lower level before participation may experience barriers to employment other than the threat of loss of health care benefits. *Id.* Variation between states occurred largely as a result of different program features. *Id.* at 3. For example, different income limits may allow earners in some states to increase their earnings to a greater extent than earners in other states. *See id.*

One criticism of the Medicaid Buy-In program is that eligibility is determined by the Social Security definition of disability. Jean P. Hall, Michael H. Fox, & Emily Fall, The Kansas Medicaid Buy-In: Factors Influencing Enrollment and Health Care Utilization, Disability & Health Journal, No. 3 (Apr. 2010), at 100, http://www.sciencedirect.com/science/article/pii/S1936657409000351# (last visited Oct. 24, 2012). The Social Security definition of disability is based on inability to work, yet Medicaid Buy-in participants must have at least some earned income verified through payroll or self-employment tax documentation. *Id.* However, under the Medicaid Buy-in states have the option to extend Medicaid benefits to individuals with disabilities who work. U.S. Gov't Accountability Office, GAO-10-812SP, Highlights of a Forum: Actions That Could Increase Work Participation for Adults with Disabilities 11 (July 2010), *available at* http://www.gao.gov/assets/210/204180.pdf (last visited Oct. 24, 2012).

On July 10, 2007, Andrew J. Imparato, then President and Chief Executive Officer of the American Association of People with Disabilities (AAPD) testified before the Senate Health, Education, Labor, and Pensions Committee, addressing the immediate need for Medicare and Medicaid reforms with respect to support and services for persons with disabilities. Imparato stressed the importance of long-term care for all Americans who may acquire a disability at birth, as they age, through accident, injury, and illness, or while serving their country. Community Support for Disabled and Elderly, Before the Senate Comm. on Health, Education, Labor & Pensions, 2007 WL 1986363 (F.D.C.H.) (July 10, 2007). He argued that such a diverse disability community demands investment in a long-term care system that provides choice and control to the population it serves. *Id.* The current Medicare and Medicaid systems continue to provide inadequate and inefficient services, perpetuating dependence, low expectations, unnecessary institutionalization, and civil rights violations. *Id.*

B.   *Compliance And Litigation*

Medicare and Medicaid contribute to the operation of nursing care facilities, where tension between the quantitative and qualitative need for care can be seen. Congressional investigators from the GAO reported that some nursing homes cycle through phases of compliance and noncompliance in quality of service, but remain in the Medicare and Medicaid programs with minimal negative consequences. Robert Pear, Oversight of Nursing Homes is Criticized, N.Y. Times, Apr. 22, 2007, at 1. The GAO noted that federal health officials hesitated to impose significant fines in part because of fear that higher fines might bankrupt nursing homes. Kathryn G. Allen, GAO, Nursing Homes: Efforts to Strengthen Federal Enforcement Have Not Deterred Some Homes from Repeatedly Harming Residents 24 (May 2007), *available at* http://www.gao.gov/ new.items/d07241pdf (last visited June 6, 2012).   Other facilities made temporary improvements to avoid serious repercussions, but later returned to noncompliance. *Id.* at 5.

Leslie V. Norwalk, administrator of the Centers for Medicare and Medicaid Services noted that fines may not be effective, especially if homes are forced to close when they lose Medicare and Medicaid payments.   Letter from Leslie V. Norwalk, Acting Administrator of the Centers for Medicare and Medicaid Services, to Kathryn G. Allen, G.A.O. Healthcare Director (Feb. 20, 2007), *reprinted in* Nursing Homes: Efforts to Strengthen Federal Enforcement Have Not Deterred Some Homes from Repeatedly Harming Residents 24 (May 2007), *available at* http://www.gao.gov/new.items/d07241.pdf.

The tension between quality and quantity of services may well be a recurring theme, as evidenced by a 2007 Supreme Court case.   A plaintiff filed suit alleging that her employer, *Long Island Care at Home*, failed to pay minimum and overtime wages to which the plaintiff was entitled under the Fair Labor Standards Act (FLSA). Long Island Care at Home v. Coke, 551 U.S. 158 (2007).   The central issue was whether companionship workers employed by a third party employer (other than the family or household using the employee's services) were exempt from FLSA wage standards, pursuant to a Department of Labor (DOL) regulation. *Id.* at 2344. In its regulation, the DOL distinguished between domestic service employees, who perform services in the home of the person by whom he or she is employed, and companionship workers, who are employed by a third party employer other than the household using the employee's services.   *Id.* at 2344-2345.   While domestic service employees are covered by FLSA wage standards, companionship workers are not. The Court found this exemption binding. *Id.* at 2346.

Coke represents an increasingly relevant issue.   A New York Times article noted that the number of home care attendants is expected to rise from 1.4 million to nearly two million by 2014, due to an aging population and government pressure to minimize institutionalization. Steven Greenhouse, Justices to Hear Case on Wages of Home Aides, N.Y. Times, Mar. 25, 2007, at 1. The Times noted that Ms. Coke and her supporters, including the Service Employees International Union and the AARP, argued that higher wages for home aides will provide a more consistent quality of care and prevent a shortage of home care workers. *Id.* Although they perform a critical function, the Times noted that many home care aides live in poverty, *id.*; Ms. Coke did not have health insurance through her employer.

However, Long Island Care at Home and its supporters argued that higher wages would have a substantial financial impact, which in turn could affect the ability to meet the need for in-home care. *Id.* The N.Y. Times reported that the Bloomberg administration filed an amicus brief on behalf of the defendant employer, arguing that requiring employers to pay overtime could increase Medicare and Medicaid costs, potentially stressing budgets to the point where many elderly could be left without home care, and leading to increased institutionalization. *Id.*

§ 32.2 Patient Protection And Affordable Care Act (PPACA)

Under the Patient Protection and Affordable Care Act (PPACA), insurers and employer-provided health plans must alter their health benefits to increase consumer coverage and choice. *See* Deborah Chollet & Jill Bernstein, How Will the ACA Affect Community Rehabilitation Programs?, Final Report, Mathematica Pol'y Res., Inc. (Apr. 2012), *available at* http://www.mathematica-mpr.com/publications/redirect_pub sdb.asp?strSite=pdfs/health/ACA_commrehab.pdf (last visited June 6, 2012). While portions of the Act are phasing in over time, several important provisions are already in place and are likely to impact people with disabilities. Others will be implemented between now and 2014 and are expected to have the greatest impact on people with disabilities.

A. *Provisions In Effect*

All individual and group policies that offer family coverage must allow adult children to remain on their parent's health care plan until they reach age 26, *id.*, including adult children with disabilities. Insurers may no longer deny coverage to children on the basis of a pre-existing medical condition. *Id.* Under this provision, children who are born with a disability cannot be denied health coverage solely on the basis of the disability. *See* Nat'l Council on Disability, National Disability Policy: A Progress Report - October 2011 [hereinafter NCD, October 2011 Progress Report], *available at* http://www.ncd.gov/rawmedia_repository/9f8821fb_ 3747_43d1_a5e3_197440aa7296?document.pdf (last visited June 6, 2012). Plans must cover certain preventive services with no deductibles or co-payments. *See* The Nat'l Spinal Cord Injury Ass'n, Impact of Health Care Reform on People with Disabilities 2 (Apr. 27, 2010) [hereinafter NSCIA,

Impact Report], *available at* http://www.unitedspinal.org/pdf/impact_
of_health_care_reform.pdf (last visited June 6, 2012).

Individual and group health plans are prohibited from placing
lifetime caps on coverage, and annual limits are currently being phased
out. *See* Chollet & Bernstein, *supra.* These provisions will end the
common practice of limiting the total dollar amount of insurance coverage
an individual can receive, which eventually cuts off coverage for many
people with disabilities and chronic illnesses. NSCIA, Impact Report,
supra at 2. Insurers may not retroactively cancel coverage except in cases
of fraud. *See* Chollet & Bernstein, *supra.* This provision will benefit
people who acquire disabilities and/or health conditions after enrolling in
an insurance plan and previously may have had their health insurance
rescinded before the PPACA took effect.

In addition, a provision benefits Medicare enrollees with
disabilities who receive coverage for prescription medications by closing
the "donut hole" – a gap in benefits requiring the recipient to pay full
prices when the recipient meets the cutoff threshold. NSCIA, Impact
Report, *supra* at 5. For example, Medicare may cover prescription cost
totals until $500. Between $501 through $1500, the enrollee will be
responsible for prescription costs. Medicare will start to cover costs at
$1501 and thereafter. Thus, the "donut hole" refers to the gap in coverage
from $501 through $1500. Enrollees received a $250 rebate in 2010 and
discounts on medications in 2011 to offset this cost until the prescription
gap is eventually closed. *Id.* The savings to Medicare enrollees is an
estimated $90 per person in 2011 and $160 in 2012. Enrollees in the
donut hole benefit even more: an estimated $631 per person in 2011 and
$735 in 2012. H.H.S., Medicare Beneficiary Savings and the Affordable
Care Act (Feb. 2012), http://www.aspe.hhs.gov/health/reports/2012/
MedicareBeneficiarySavings/ib.shtml (last visited June 7, 2012).

These savings are ultimately due to reduced Medicare spending,
which will be further reduced by fewer extra subsidies to Medicare
Advantage plans, a reduced rate of growth in provider payments, a more
efficient and quality-oriented program, and efforts to eliminate fraud and
abuse. *Id.* These savings in Medicare spending correspond with
beneficiary savings, including a slower increase rate in premiums for Part
B physicians as well as Part A and Part B co-payments and co-insurance,
due to the fact that the PPACA will slow the rate of growth of payments to
hospitals and health care providers. *Id.* In addition, closing the
prescription coverage gap saves beneficiaries thousands of out-of-pocket
dollars in payments, slowing the rate of growth of premiums. *Id.* Private
individual and group health plans must provide a summary of benefits
and coverage to all applicants and consumers so that they can compare
options. *See* Chollet & Bernstein, *supra.* This transparency will
especially benefit people with disabilities, who have traditionally been
disadvantaged by the insurance market.

The PPACA extends the Money Follows the Person program with an additional $450 million for each fiscal year from 2012 until 2016 to support transitioning individuals with disabilities from institutional to community settings. H.H.S., The Affordable Care Act for Americans with Disabilities, http://www.healthcare.gov/news/factsheets/2010/11/affordable -care-act-americans-disabilities.html (last visited June 6, 2012). The Act also creates the Community First Choice program for states to provide individuals with disabilities community living choices. *Id.*

B. *Provisions Taking Effect 2013-14*

In 2014, the majority of the PPACA provisions are scheduled to come into effect. In March 2012, the U.S. Supreme Court heard oral arguments in *Department of Health & Human Services v. Florida*, challenging the constitutionality of the Act. This case was decided on June 28, 2012, *Nat'l Fed'n of Indep. Bus. v. Sebelius*, 132 S. Ct. 2566, and focused on the constitutionality of two main provisions of the PPACA: (1) the mandate that all citizens have minimum essential health coverage, and (2) the expansion of Medicaid. American Public Health Association, The Supreme Court's ACA Decision & Its Implications for Medicaid 1 (July 27, 2012), *available at* http://www.apha.org/NR/rdonlyres/38837993-E528-4A49-8713-03AD6FEBE14A/0/ APHAFinalAnalysisFINAL8112.pdf.

The Supreme Court held that "the individual mandate is a valid exercise of Congress's taxing power." *Id.* at 3. Congress has this constitutional power under the Commerce Clause, the Necessary and Proper Clause, and the Taxing Clause. *Id.* The Court also held that the Medicaid Expansion is valid. However, the Court held that "Congress did not have the power under the Spending Clause to authorize termination of all existing federal Medicaid funding to States that refuse to expand Medicaid," as required by the PPACA. *Id.* at 6. While the PPACA has been upheld, as Justice Ginsburg notes in her opinion, "this invites future litigation about whether an Act of Congress, purporting to a law, is in reality not an amendment, but a new creation." Bazelon Center for Mental Health Law, The Supreme Court's Decision on the ACA, 2, *available at* http://www.bazelon.org/LinkClick.aspx?fileticket=IiolSKFo7 Uw%3D&tabid=40 (2012).

In the years ahead, States may have some ability to delay implementation of the Act. PPACA broadens the definition of the small-group market to include groups of 100 employees (currently 2-50 employees), and the Act will apply the present small-group market regulations to this larger group. However, states have the ability to defer this change until 2016. Chollet & Bernstein, *supra* at 2-3.

Assuming there are no substantial changes to PPACA, perhaps the biggest impact for Americans with disabilities is guaranteed health care coverage for all. After January 14, 2014, group plans may not exclude coverage for pre-existing conditions, a provision already in effect for children under the age of 19, which will affect 129 million Americans.

Id.; NCD, October 2011 Progress Report, *supra*. The PPACA also prohibits charging higher premiums, excluding benefits, and rescinding coverage on benefits based on pre-existing conditions. NSCIA, Impact Report, *supra* at 2. These provisions will benefit not only individuals born with disabilities but also those who acquire a disability or chronic illness after purchasing an insurance plan. *Id.*

Under PPACA, insurers may only vary premiums for individuals and small groups based upon age, geographical location, family composition, and tobacco use, and the law sets a limit of three times the lowest premium for the highest premium. Chollet & Bernstein, *supra* at 3. The Act also calls for accessibility standards for medical diagnostic equipment to be created by the Access Board — another step toward eliminating one of the largest barriers to health care access, inaccessible health care equipment. NCD, October 2011 Progress Report, *supra*. The Access Board began this process in 2012 by publishing the Proposed Accessibility Standards for Medical Diagnostic Equipment (Feb. 8, 2012), *available at* http://www.access-board.gov/attachments/article/664/nprm.pdf, for public comment.

In addition, PPACA increases choice for consumers by setting up state-based tiered exchanges to allow individuals and families to buy insurance: the American Health Benefits Exchange and SHOP for small employers. Chollet & Bernstein, *supra* at 3-4. The U.S. Department of Health and Human Services (HHS) has proposed requirements to ensure that Exchanges are accessible and understandable for people with disabilities, including website accessibility. NCD, October 2011 Progress Report, *supra*. This is expected to increase access for many individuals with disabilities, including those who rely on Internet access and related technology for vital services. *Id.*

Importantly, the Exchanges (as well as individual and small group plans) are required to provide "essential benefits." NSCIA, Impact Report, *supra* at 3. These include benefits for individuals with disabilities that insurers often do not include, such as mental health and substance use disorder services and rehabilitative and habilitative services and devices. *Id.* In addition, the law mandates Medicare coverage of anti-seizure, anti-anxiety, and smoking cessation drugs, formerly excluded under Medicare Part D, and other essential services including ambulatory patient services, emergency services, hospitalization, prescription drugs, and chronic disease management. *Id.* at 10.

Another essential provision for people with disabilities is the expansion of eligibility for Medicaid and the resulting impact on Medicare, since many people with disabilities have low incomes. *Id.* at 5; Chollet & Bernstein, *supra* at 5. By 2014, legal residents with a household income of less than 138% of the Federal Poverty Level will be eligible for Medicaid. Chollet & Bernstein, *supra* at 5. This does not affect Social Security Income beneficiaries, but Social Security Disability Beneficiaries will be eligible for Medicaid during the 24-month waiting period only if their household income is below 138% of the Federal Poverty Level. *Id.* People who are eligible for Medicaid because they are "blind or disabled" or who qualify for long-term Medicaid care or services will retain eligibility for full coverage, but people with disabilities who are newly eligible because of the low-income category may not receive the full support services. *Id.*

§ 32.3   Genetic Discrimination

In 1990, scientists began the Human Genome Project (HGP), a thirteen-year effort to sequence the human genome, coordinated and funded by the U.S. Department of Energy and the National Institutes of Health. Jessica L. Roberts, Preempting Discrimination: Lessons from the Genetic Information Nondiscrimination Act, 63 Vand. L. Rev. 439, 442 (2010). This chapter describes the dialogue on the interplay between the HGP and the employment provisions of ADA Title I.

The HGP, with over one thousand genetic tests available, has engendered a revolution in the diagnosis of human genetic conditions. *Id.* The rapid advances in genetic testing, therapy, and technology, however, have increased the possibility of stigmatization and discrimination against qualified individuals with current and possible future genetic disorders in the employment and health insurance contexts and in other areas of daily life. Peter Blanck et. al., Employment of People with Disabilities: Twenty-Five Years Back and Ahead, 25 Law & Ineq. 323, 344-45 (2007); William J. McDevitt, Esq., I Dream of GINA: Understanding the Employment Provisions of the Genetic Information Nondiscrimination Act of 2008, 54 Vill. L. Rev. 91, 95-96 (2009).

Myths and stereotypes in society contribute to the potential for genetic discrimination by employers, insurers, and the general public. Paul Steven Miller, Thinking About Discrimination in the Genetic Age, 35 J. L. Med. & Ethics 47, 49 (2007). Given the advances in the development of genetic tests, citizens are concerned about the misuse of this information in various areas of life including employment and insurance, particularly health insurance. Perry W. Payne, Jr., Genetic Information Nondiscrimination Act of 2008: The Federal Answer for Genetic Discrimination, 5 J. Health & Biomedical L. 33, 34 (2009).

A.   *Genetic Information Nondiscrimination Act (GINA)*

In 2008, Congress passed the Genetic Information Nondiscrimination Act (GINA), which aims to protect against discrimination in the employment context on the basis of one's genetic information. 42 U.S.C. §§ 2000ff-2000ff-11 et seq. (2006). Genetic information is defined as information about:

> (i)   An individual's genetic tests;
> (ii)   The genetic tests of that individual's family members;
> (iii) The manifestation of disease or disorder in family

members of the individual (family medical history); (iv) An individual's request for, or receipt of, genetic services, or the participation in clinical research that includes genetic services by the individual or a family member of the individual; or

(v) The genetic information of a fetus carried by an individual or by a pregnant woman who is a family member of the individual and the genetic information of any embryo legally held by the individual or family member using an assisted reproductive technology.

42 U.S.C § 2000ff(4) (2006).

The Act supersedes portions of other statutes, including the Employee Retirement Income Security Act of 1974, the Public Health Service Act, and Title XVIII of the Social Security Act among others. *See* Employee Retirement Income Security Act of 1974, 29 U.S.C.A § 1182 (West 2008); 42 U.S.C.A. §§ 300gg & 1355ss (West 2009). Title I of the Act applies specifically to insurers and health plans and prohibits discrimination in determining eligibility or cost of group health insurance premiums based on genetic information, such as increasing premiums for the group based on the results of one enrollee's genetic information or denying enrollment or coverage based on genetic information. 29 C.F.R. §§ 1635.4 & 1635.11 (2012). Similarly, it places restrictions on when insurers may request or collect genetic information.

Title II of the Act focuses on employers, employment agencies, labor agencies, and training programs. Mainly, it prohibits the use of genetic informational in the employment context, limits the acquisition of genetic information by the aforementioned entities, and expressly restricts the disclosure of such information. 42 U.S.C. § 2000ff et seq. (2006).

GINA does not prohibit the collection of genetic information in all circumstances. For instance, GINA provides that it will not be discrimination when: medical inquiries and information collection complies with the FMLA or similar state laws, "the employer conducts DNA analysis for law enforcement purposes," or "an employer inadvertently requests or requires family medical history of the employee or family member of the employee" among other exceptions. 42 U.S.C. § 2000ff-1(b)(6) (West 2012). GINA protections do not apply to employers with fifteen or fewer employees. 42 U.S.C. § 2000e(b) (2006). Further, GINA does not protect against discrimination from life insurance, disability insurance, long-term care insurance, or individual health insurance. 42 U.S.C.A. § 300gg-53 (2012).

The EEOC issued final regulations on November 10, 2010, which clarify the interplay between GINA and other statutes. Final Regulations Under the Genetic Information Nondiscrimination Act of 2008, 75 Fed. Reg. 68,912-68,939 (Nov. 9, 2010). The regulations note that Congress aimed to extend the protections of Title VII of the Civil Rights Act of 1964 to the area of genetic information. 75 Fed. Reg. 68,926 (explaining that the law incorporates by reference the definitions, remedies, and procedures of Title VII).

To pursue a claim under GINA, the plaintiff first must exhaust administrative remedies. Then, the plaintiff may file a private right of action under any of several different Acts: the Civil Rights Act of 1964, 42 U.S.C. §§ 2000e-4 & 2000e-16 (2006), the Age Discrimination in Employment Act, the Rehabilitation Act, or Title I of the ADA. 42 U.S.C. § 2000ff-6 (2006). Plaintiffs arguing violations of GINA in federal court have yet to state a claim. *See, e.g.,* Smith v. Donahoe, 917 F.Supp.2d 562, 570-71 (E.D. Va. 2013) (finding Plaintiff did not plead facts indicating "Defendants requested or obtained Plaintiff's 'genetic information' and discriminated against him on the basis of such 'genetic information.'"); Poore v. Peterbilt of Bristol, L.L.C., 852 F.Supp.2d 727, 731 (W.D. Va. 2012) (failing to state a claim because the information obtained by employer did not constitute "genetic information with respect to the employee"); Dumas v. Hurley Med. Ctr., 837 F.Supp.2d 655, 666 (E.D. Mich. 2011) (similar); Pulley v. United Health Group Inc., No. 4:11CV00634 KGB, ___ F.Supp.2d ___, 2013 WL 1947552, *10 (E.D. Ark. 2013) (similar).

ക

Notes & Questions

1. In May 2013, the EEOC filed a GINA class action against Founders Pavilion, Inc., a nursing and rehabilitation center, alleging Founders sought family medical history (protected genetic information during) during post-job offer, pre-employment medical exam process. *EEOC v. Founders Pavilion, Inc.,* 6:13-cv-06250 (W.D.N.Y. May 16, 2013), *available at* http://blog.hinshawlaw.com/hrlegalblog/wp-content/uploads/2013/05/EEOC-v.-Founders.pdf.

ക

B.   *Asymptomatic Genetic Traits Under The ADA*

The ADA prohibits covered entities from discriminating against a qualified person with a disability in employment, and in receipt of or access to public services and those of public accommodations. *See* Parts 3, 4 & 5 *supra.* What is less certain, however, is "whether individuals with presymptomatic genetic disorders or proclivities are protected by the ADA." Morse Hyun-Myung Tan, Advancing Civil Rights, the Next Generation: The Genetic Information Nondiscrimination Act of 2008 and Beyond, 19 Health Matrix 63, 80 (2009). If a medical examination reveals that a job applicant has the gene for Huntington's disease, for example, does Title I protect the applicant when the employer withdraws the offer because of his asymptomatic genetic trait? McDevitt, *supra* at 91-92.

Under *Bragdon v. Abbott*, 524 U.S. 624 (1998), to be covered as an actual disability, the defect must have some current physiological effect and that effect must limit a major life activity. Bragdon, 524 U.S. at 637-38. The *Bragdon* Court did not rely on the possible future effects of HIV in rendering its decision. However, the *Bragdon* Court relied on two findings in holding that HIV is a disability under the ADA even when the infection has not yet progressed to the symptomatic phase. First, HIV infection is a physiological disorder *"from the moment of infection,"* thereby satisfying the "definition of a physical impairment during every stage of the disease." Bragdon, 524 U.S. at 637 (emphasis added). Second, HIV infection places a substantial limitation on a woman's major life activity of reproduction. *Id.* at 639-40.

Some commentators suggest that the extension of *Bragdon* to asymptomatic genetic conditions is limited to similar circumstances. Abigail Lauren Perdue, Justifying GINA, 78 Tenn. L. Rev. 1051, 1082 (2011). More genetic conditions may qualify under the ADA as technology develops to identify new disorders and scientific advances improve our predictive ability to determine the probability that a disease will manifest itself. Daniel Schlein, New Frontiers for Genetic Privacy Law: The Genetic Information Nondiscrimination Act of 2008, 19 Geo. Mason U. Civ. Rts. L.J. 311, 325 (2009).

In addition, persons with genetic disabilities may be determined to be unqualified for a job if they pose a direct safety or health threat to themselves or others in the workplace. Chevron U.S.A. Inc. v. Echazabal, 536 U.S. 73, 76-85 (2002) (finding that an EEOC determination, permitting an employer to refuse hiring an individual whose own health would be endangered in the performance of the job, did not exceed EEOC authority under ADA); *see supra* Part 3, § 9.1.

As a result of the Supreme Court's analysis in *Chevron v. Echazabal*, 536 U.S. 73 (2002), it is not clear for purposes of ADA analysis whether an employer may refuse to hire a qualified individual, even though asymptomatic, if occupational exposure to certain substances is likely to increase the employee's known genetic susceptibility to disease, even with the provision of reasonable accommodations. *See* Muller v. Costello, No. 94-CV-842 (FJS), 1996 WL 191977, at *5 & *8 (N.D.N.Y. Apr. 16, 1996) (holding that corrections officer with asthma, triggered by exposure to secondhand smoke on the job, may proceed with his claims alleging ADA violations); *see also* Occupational Safety & Health Admin., U.S. Dep't of Labor, Recommendations for Workplace Violence Prevention Programs in Late-Night Retail Establishments OSHA 3153-12R-2009 6 (2009) (stating that the management commitment should include "organizational concern for employee emotional and physical safety and health"), *available at* http://www.osha.gov/Publications/osha3153.pdf (last visited Oct. 24, 2012). For a detailed discussion of *Echazabal, see* Part 3, § 9.1 *supra*. However, few instances of genetic conditions that require differential treatment in the workplace have been documented or studied systematically. Marvin R. Natowicz et al., Genetic Discrimination and the Law, 50 Am. J. Hum. Genetics 465, 467 (1992).

The EEOC specifies that blood tests to detect genetic markers or diseases are medical examinations for purposes of the ADA. Laurie A. Vasichek, Genetic Discrimination in the Workplace: Lessons from the Past and Concerns for the Future, 3 St. Louis U.J. Health L. & Pol'y 13, 39 (2009). Vasichek argues that post-ADAAA it will be easier for "individuals whose genetic conditions have manifested . . . to argue that their conditions have affected a major life activity," due to the addition of "major bodily functions" in the EEOC regulations. *Id*. at 27.

Employees may be subjected legitimately to urine and blood tests to screen for alcohol or substance use. *See* Patricia A. Montgomery, Workplace Drug Testing: Are There Limits?, Tenn. Bar J., Mar./Apr. 1996, at 21 (discussing employers that use random employee drug testing and Tennessee law which denies employment compensation to employees that leave their jobs to avoid testing). However, in one case settled with the EEOC, the Burlington Northern and Santa Fe Railway Company (BNSF) required that certain employees who had filed claims of work-related carpal tunnel syndrome injuries against the company submit blood samples for genetic screening. Press Release, Equal Emp. Opportunity Comm'n, EEOC and BNSF Settle Genetic Testing Case Under Americans with Disabilities Act (May 8, 2002), http://www.eeoc.gov/press/5-8-02.html (last visited June 6, 2012). BNSF required the genetic tests without the employees' knowledge or consent. *Id*. As a result of a mediated settlement, BNSF agreed to pay $2.2 million to thirty-six employees who were ordered to submit to the testing. *Id. But see* EEOC v. Woodbridge Corp, 263 F.3d 812 (8th Cir. 2001) (holding that company did not violate the ADA when excluding applicants from employment on a manufacturing line, based on test results that indicated they may be susceptible to injuries from repetitive motion; plaintiffs held not to be covered as persons with disabilities under the ADA).

In addition to direct testing, employers often obtain the results of genetic testing conducted in other contexts and may potentially use that information to restrict the employment opportunities of qualified applicants and employees. Mark A. Rothstein, Genetic Discrimination in Employment and the Americans with Disabilities Act, 29 Hous. L. Rev. 23, 62-68 (1992). This information may be obtained through releases by employees, health insurance claims, or voluntary medical examinations and wellness programs. *Id.*; *see also* Nat'l P'ship for Women & Families, Faces of Genetic Discrimination: How Genetic Discrimination Affects Real People 3-12 (2004), *available at* http://www.geneticalliance.org/ksc_assets/documents/facesofgeneticdiscrimination.pdf (profiling examples of individuals denied employment and health insurance coverage and fired from their jobs, based on lawfully and unlawfully acquired genetic information, and other individuals purposefully avoiding genetic testing for fear of losing their jobs, despite likely, hereditary risks for serious illnesses).

However, individuals may find additional privacy protection in the state common-law duty of confidentiality, which limits physicians' disclosure of their patients' medical records to employers. Lawrence O. Gostin, Health Information Privacy, 80 Cornell L. Rev. 451, 508 (1995). Further, twenty-eight states had enacted laws that limit the ability of employers to collect, use, and disclose genetic information. Sonia M. Suter, The Allure and Peril of Genetics Exceptionalism: Do We Need Special Genetics Legislation? 79 Wash. U. L.Q. 669, 692 (2001). Washington State legislation went into effect in June 2004, prohibiting genetic testing as a condition of obtaining or continuing employment. Wash. Rev. Code § 49.44.180 (West 2004). Additionally, all fifty states and the District of Columbia had enacted genetic privacy laws as of 2011 in the context of healthcare services. Scott Smith et al., Genetic Privacy Laws: 50 State Survey, 5 J. Health & Life Scis. L. 75 (2011).

Although an employer cannot use the results of genetic screening conducted as part of a post-offer medical examination to withdraw an offer of employment to a qualified applicant, the results may be used to modify health care coverage provided through the employer's self-funded benefits plan. The ADA does not prohibit insurance companies from underwriting and classifying medical health risks, if the classifications are consistent with state law practices. 29 C.F.R. § 1630.16(f) (2012). Third party insurers or employers self-funding their insurance plans may classify employees with regard to health insurance coverage on the basis of their medical and health histories. Because the ADA's legislative history only addresses health insurance, it is uncertain whether employees may be denied life and disability insurance provided by employers. S. Rep. No. 101-116, at 29 (1989); Natowicz et al., *supra*, at 471. Limitations on health insurance coverage or exclusions of certain genetic conditions from coverage are permitted under the ADA when not a "subterfuge" for disability-based discrimination. *Id.* For example, a self-funded employer may offer a health insurance policy to all employees that does not cover experimental treatment for Huntington's disease. However, under the ADA, a self-insured employer with an employee whose child develops cystic fibrosis may not withdraw dependent coverage for that particular employee on the basis of that disability.

Several states have enacted legislative protections against health insurance denial based solely on genetic status. Roberts, *supra* at 446. State laws, however, often do not provide protection for those who obtain their health insurance coverage through employer-based plans, because the federal Employee Retirement Income Security Act (ERISA) exempts self-funded plans from state oversight. 29 U.S.C. § 1144(a) (2006); *see also* Roberts, *supra* at 446-447.

Prior to enactment of GINA, the EEOC issued guidance extending protections to qualified federal employees who experience employment discrimination on the basis of their genetic profiles. EEOC Policy Guidance on Executive Order 13145: To Prohibit Discrimination in Federal Employment Based on Genetic Information (July 26, 2000). As of November 21, 2009, however, Title II of GINA supersedes the EEOC Policy Guidance, and protects federal applicants and employees (as well as applicants and employees of other covered entities) from discrimination based on genetic information. Federal applicants and employees should use the Federal complaint process to file complaints of discrimination on the basis of genetic information. EEOC, Genetic Information Discrimination, *available at* www.eeoc.gov/laws/types/genetic.cfm (last visited Jan. 29, 2013).

The ADA Amendments Act (ADAAA) did not mention genetic discrimination. Experts suggest that the drafters of the ADAAA did not believe it was necessary to consider these matters in light of the enactment of GINA in May 2008. Mark A. Rothstein, GINA, the ADA, and Genetic Discrimination in Employment, 36 J.L. Med. & Ethics 837, 838 (2008).

Chapter 33   DISABILITY AND THE INTERNET

§ 33.1   Overview

The rise of the disability civil rights movement, bolstered by passage of federal and state antidiscrimination laws, coincided with technological advances that began to enhance the inclusion and equal participation of persons with disabilities in society. David Klein et al., Electronic Doors to Education: Study of High School Website Accessibility in Iowa, 21 Behav. Sci. & L. 27, 42 (2003) (citations omitted). Emblematic of the wave of technological advances is the development and use of the Internet. This spread of technology offers increased connectivity between persons with disabilities and both the community and the workforce. Paul M.A. Baker et al., Municipal WiFi and Policy Implications for People with Disabilities 1, 2 (2008), *available at* http://dl.acm.org/ft_gateway.cfm?id=1367870&type=pdf (last visited June 6, 2012).

The Internet has the potential to make products and services available to people with disabilities who were previously excluded because of inaccessible facilities and materials.   However, many of these technologies have created new barriers to participation for people with disabilities. William N. Myhill, et al., Developing Accessible Cyberinfrastructure-enabled Knowledge Communities in the National Disability Community: Theory, Practice, and Policy, 20 Assistive Tech. J. 158 (2008) [hereinafter Myhill, et al., Developing Accessible Cyber-infrastructure]. Equal access to the Internet by persons with disabilities is a prominent topic of discussion in disability law and policy.

The drafters of the ADA could not contemplate the significance of the Internet and the World Wide Web (WWW). Nonetheless, issues of Internet accessibility for persons with disabilities are implicated by the public accommodations language of Title III and by state and local governmental activities covered by Title II. William N. Myhill, Law and Policy Challenges for Achieving an Accessible eSociety: Lessons from the United States, in 2 Euro. Yrbk. of Disability Law, at 109 (2010) [hereinafter Myhill, Achieving an Accessible eSociety].   In addition, Section 504 of the Rehabilitation Act of 1973 imposes accessibility requirements on recipients of federal funds.   29 U.S.C. § 794 (2006). Section 508 of the Rehabilitation Act requires federal government agencies to purchase accessible technology.

Parallel to the Internet, since passage of the ADA, computers and assistive technologies (AT) have come to play a central role in the lives of individuals with disabilities. The importance of AT in the workplace has broad implications for the employment of people with disabilities. *See generally*, Jonathan Stead, Toward True Equality of Educational Opportunity: Unlocking the Potential of Assistive Technology Through Professional Development, 35 Rutgers Computer & Tech. L.J. 224 (2009). For instance, "computer technologies help compensate for the physical limitations inherent in some disabilities . . . [T]hose without finger dexterity use voice-recognition software to run a computer, and those with severe speech impediments use special software to 'speak' through the computer." Peter Blanck et al., Calibrating the Impact of the ADA's Employment Provisions, 14 Stan. L. & Pol'y Rev. 267, 283-84 (2003) (citation omitted). Video over Internet Protocol allows deaf individuals to communicate using American Sign Language, and text and instant messaging facilitates communication by individuals with speech impairments. William N. Myhill, et al., Distance Education Initiatives and Their 21st Century Role in the Lives of People with Disabilities, in Focus on Distance Education Developments 23 (E.P. Bailey, ed., 2007) [hereinafter Myhill, et al., Distance Education Initiatives].

The Internet has transformed the nature of access to information. Studies have shown that societal participation increasingly depends on the ability to use information technology and to access computers and the Internet. Baker et al., *supra,* Municipal WiFi Implementation and Policy Implications for People with Disabilities 1, 2 (2008). For example, library card catalog systems have lost practical use, in large part due to the difficulty of maintaining them as compared to the efficiency of technology to constantly update and search the vast electronic catalogs. However, even when a public library uses accessible software to search these databases, persons with disabilities often encounter barriers posed by inaccessible website design. William N. Myhill et al., Developing the Capacity of Teacher-Librarians to Meet the Diverse Needs of All School Children: Project ENABLE, J. Research Spec. Educ'l Needs, 12, 201 (2012) (presenting objectives of librarian training program including web and information technology accessibility). Much of the Internet remains inaccessible for individuals with vision, print, and hearing impairments. Ali Abrar & Kerry J. Dingle, From Madness to Method: The Americans with Disabilities Act Meets the Internet, 44 Harv. C.R.-C.L. L. Rev. 133, 134 (2009) (citations omitted).

Despite the positive effects of AT and the Internet on the employment and earnings potential of people with disabilities, research shows that people with disabilities generally are less likely to be computer users. A 2007 study found 51% of the population with a "disability, handicap, or chronic disease" uses the Internet compared to 74% of those without reported disabilities. Susannah Fox, E-patients with a Disability or Chronic Disease (Oct. 9, 2007), http://pewresearch.org/pubs/608/e-patients (last visited June 6, 2012).

The next chapter addresses issues related to the applicability of the ADA and other disability antidiscrimination laws to Internet and technological accessibility in workplaces, homes, and schools.

§ 33.2 Internet Accessibility And Access To Data

The issue of Internet accessibility has received national attention. *See* Carla J. Rozycki & David K. Haase, Do WebSites Need to be Accessible to the Blind?, Law.com (Jan. 10, 2007), http://www.law.com/jsp/

article.jsp?id=1168336938732 (last visited June 6, 2012). In 1999, the National Federation of the Blind (NFB) began filing class action lawsuits against online service providers and businesses, the first of which was against American Online, Inc (AOL). Nat'l Fed'n of the Blind v. Am. Online, Inc., No. 99CV12303EFH (D. Mass. filed Nov. 4, 1999), reprinted in 6 Am. Disabilities Pract. & Compliance Man. § 6:59 (West 2004).

NFB alleged that AOL's proprietary Internet browser and services were not accessible to blind users as they interfered with the use of screen reader software, and thus did not comply with the accessibility requirements of ADA Title III. Robert L. Burgdorf Jr., Restoring the ADA and Beyond: Disability in the 21st Century, 13 Tex. J. C.L. & C.R. 241, 275 (2008). The plaintiffs claimed that AOL's online service sign-up form, welcome screens, and chat rooms were not accessible because screen readers[1] could not read text hidden within graphic displays. People with significant impairments affecting their manual dexterity (e.g., cerebral palsy or quadriplegia) who cannot use a computer mouse, also benefit from accessible formats that allow the user to use other commands (e.g., arrows or tabs) for Internet navigation.

In 2000, the AOL lawsuit and the applicability of the ADA to private internet sites were the subject of Congressional hearings. Applicability of the Americans with Disabilities Act (ADA) to Private Internet Sites: Hearing Before the Subcomm. on the Constitution of the House Judiciary Comm., 106th Cong. (2000) (hereinafter "Private Internet Site Hearing"), http://commdocs.house.gov/committees/judiciary/hju65010. 000/hju65010_0f.htm (last visited June 6, 2012). Testimony was presented by persons with disabilities, technology specialists, industry executives, and legal analysts. Later that year, the parties to the AOL litigation announced they had reached a settlement. AOL agreed to make its Internet browsing software compatible with screen reader technology, to ensure AOL software was accessible to blind users. It also agreed to make the existing and future content of AOL services accessible to blind users, and to publish an Accessibility Policy and post it on its website. Agreement Between Complainants and AOL (July 26, 2000), http://www.nfbcal.org/nfb-rd/1633.html (last visited Oct. 18, 2012).

In March 2007, the NFB and Amazon.com announced that they agreed to work together to promote and improve technology that enables blind people to use and access the Internet. The goal of the collaboration was to make improvements for both sighted customers and customers who

---

[1] "Screen readers" use an artificial voice to read aloud text appearing on the computer monitor. People who are blind or deaf-blind use "refreshable Braille" computer displays that move pins to form Braille letters, which a user can then read. Screen readers and Braille displays cannot be used with non-accessible web-based formats (e.g., with certain graphic images).

use screen reading software to shop on the Internet. Press Release, Nat'l Fed'n of the Blind, Amazon.com and National Federation of the Blind Join Forces to Develop and Promote Web Accessibility (Mar. 28, 2007), http://nfb.org/node/1195 (last visited Oct. 18,, 2012). In January 2013, NFB, the Massachusetts Attorney General's office and Moster.com announced an agreement to "provide job seekers who are blind with full and equal access to all of its products and services including mobile applications." Press Release, Attorney Gen. of Mass., Monster.com First in Industry to make Website Accessible to Blind Users (Jan. 30, 2013), http://www.mass.gov/ago/news-and-updates/press-releases/2013/2013-01-30-monster-agreement.html.

In June 2012, a Massachusetts District Court found in favor of the plaintiffs in a Title III case against Netflix. *Nat'l Ass'n of the Deaf v. Netflix, Inc.*, 869 F.Supp.2d 196 (D. Mass. 2012). The Court found "that the Watch Instantly website falls within at least one, if not more, of the enumerated ADA categories" to qualify as a place of public accommodation. *Id.* at 201. However, it is necessary to note that this case was not fully litigated – it only survived a motion for judgment on the pleadings.

The following chapters examine the particular application of the ADA's accessibility requirements to private and public Internet websites and services.

§ 33.3 Applications Of The ADA: Title II

ADA Title II prohibits discrimination against persons with disabilities by public entities, including state and local governmental programs and services. 42 U.S.C. §§ 12131-12132 (2006). The U.S. Department of Justice holds the position that Titles II and III to apply to the Internet. U.S. Dep't of Justice, Nondiscrimination on the Basis of Disability in State and Local Government Services, 178 (Sep. 15, 2010), *available at* http://www.lexisnexis.com/lawschool/study/texts/pdf/2011 StatutesRegsPart3TitleIIRegs3036.pdf (last visited Oct. 25, 2012); Peter Blanck et al., Legal Rights of Persons with Disabilities: An Analysis of Federal Law 8:13 (2d ed. 2013),. This position arises from the ADA mandate that public entities ensure effective communication with individuals with disabilities. 28 C.F.R. § 35.160(a) (2012). Unlike Title III, Title II does not include a "place" requirement to limit its application to Internet sites.

MARTIN v. METRO. ATLANTA RAPID TRANSIT AUTHORITY

United States District Court, Northern District of Georgia, 2002
225 F.Supp.2d 1362

Opinion

THRASH, District Judge:

* * *

I. Background

Plaintiffs have brought this action for injunctive and declaratory relief on behalf of themselves and all other similarly situated individuals with disabilities alleging that there is a system-wide pattern and practice of discrimination against people with disabilities by Defendants. * * *

Plaintiffs allege that they have suffered and continue to suffer immediate and irreparable injury due to MARTA's continuous violations of both the ADA and the Rehabilitation Act in the operations of its mass transit system. Plaintiffs have profound physical impairments. Plaintiffs Martin, Thomas and Reynolds are blind or visually impaired. Plaintiff Baker has cerebral palsy and requires a wheelchair for mobility. Plaintiffs Davis and Hasan Amin are quadraplegics and require wheelchairs for mobility. The Plaintiffs contend that they are dependent upon MARTA to provide them with their daily transportation needs.

* * *

II. Injunctive Relief Standard

"A preliminary injunction is an extraordinary and drastic remedy not to be granted until the movant clearly carries the burden of persuasion as to the four prerequisites." *Northeastern Fla. Chapter of Ass'n of General Contractors of America v. Jacksonville, Fla.,* 896 F.2d 1283, 1285 (11th Cir. 1990). In order to obtain a preliminary injunction, the movant must demonstrate: "(1) a substantial likelihood that he will ultimately prevail on the merits; (2) that he will suffer irreparable injury unless the injunction issues; (3) that the threatened injury to the movant outweighs whatever damage the proposed injunction may cause the opposing party; and (4) that the injunction, if issued, would not be adverse to the public interest." *Zardui-Quintana v. Richard,* 768 F.2d 1213, 1216 (11th Cir. 1985); *Gold Coast Publications, Inc. v. Corrigan,* 42 F.3d 1336, 1343 (11th Cir. 1994).

Moreover, when a party seeks to enjoin a government agency, "his case must contend with the well-established rule that the Government has traditionally been granted the widest latitude in the dispatch of its own affairs." *Rizzo v. Goode,* 423 U.S. 362, 378-79, 96 S.Ct. 598, 46 L.Ed.2d 561 (1976). "This 'well-established' rule bars federal courts from

878

interfering with non-federal government operations in the absence of facts showing an immediate threat of substantial injury." *Midgett v. Tri-County Metropolitan District of Oregon,* 74 F.Supp.2d 1008, 1012 (D.Or. 1999), *aff'd* 254 F.3d 846 (9th Cir. 2001). * * * Therefore, any injunction against a state agency must be narrowly tailored to "fit the nature and extent" of the established constitutional or statutory violation. *See Gibson v. Firestone,* 741 F.2d 1268, 1273 (11th Cir. 1984). Greater caution or care should be exercised where a government subdivision is involved, particularly where the injunction will require "detailed and continuous supervision" over the conduct of that subdivision. *Brown,* 187 F.2d at 24. Thus, Plaintiffs must show an even stronger likelihood of success when they request mandatory injunctive relief rather than prohibitory injunctive relief against a government entity. See *Harris v. Wilters,* 596 F.2d 678, 680 (5th Cir. 1979).

III. Discussion

A. Legal Framework

* * *

In 1990, Congress passed the ADA. * * * Part B of Title II describes certain actions by public entities in the area of public transportation that are considered discriminatory. 42 U.S.C. § 12141 et seq.

* * *

MARTA is a public transportation provider subject to Title II of the ADA. As a public entity, it is subject to all of Title II, not simply the transportation provisions found in Part B of the Title. *Burkhart v. Washington Metropolitan Area Transit Authority,* 112 F.3d 1207, 1210 (D.C. Cir. 1997). MARTA also receives federal financial assistance making it subject to § 504 of the Rehabilitation Act.

Title II of the ADA and § 504 of the Rehabilitation Act define discrimination broadly as (1) the exclusive [sic] from participation in the services, programs or activities of a public entity because of a disability; (2) the denial of the benefits of the services, programs or activities of a public entity because of a disability; or (3) being subjected to discrimination by any public entity. 42 U.S.C. § 12132; 29 U.S.C. § 794. Title II also contains specific provisions that define discrimination in the transportation context. See 42 U.S.C. §§ 12142-12144, 12146-12148. These specific transportation provisions also define discrimination for purposes of the Rehabilitation Act. Id.

There are a number of regulations adopted by the Secretary of Transportation that are relevant to the Plaintiffs' claims. * * * "Public and private entities providing transportation services shall maintain in operative condition those features of facilities and vehicles that are required to make the vehicles and facilities readily accessible to and usable by individuals with disabilities." 49 C.F.R. § 37.161(a). "These features include, but are not limited to, lifts and other means of access to vehicles, securement devices, elevators, signage and systems to facilitate communications with persons with impaired vision or hearing." Id. "Accessibility features shall be repaired promptly if they are damaged or out of order. When an accessibility feature is out of order, the entity shall take reasonable steps to accommodate individuals with disabilities who would otherwise use the feature." 49 C.F.R. § 37.161(b). This regulation "does not prohibit isolated or temporary interruptions in service or access due to maintenance or repairs." 49 C.F.R. § 37.161(c).

* * *

On fixed route systems a public entity providing transportation services * * * "shall make available to individuals with disabilities adequate information concerning transportation services. This obligation includes making adequate communications capacity available, through accessible formats and technology, to enable users to obtain information and schedule service." 49 C.F.R. § 37.167(f).

* * *

B. Injunctive Relief

1. Substantial Likelihood of Success on the Merits

Generally, to establish a violation of the ADA and Rehabilitation Act, the Plaintiffs must prove: (1) that they have disabilities; (2) that they were otherwise qualified for the benefit or service in question; and (3) that they were subjected to unlawful discrimination because of their disabilities. *Holbrook v. City of Alpharetta,* 112 F.3d 1522, 1526 (11th Cir. 1997). Plaintiffs can clearly satisfy the first and second elements to establish violations of the ADA and the Rehabilitation Act. * * *

* * *

The third element presents the crucial issue of whether the Plaintiffs were subjected to unlawful discrimination because of their disabilities. In order to succeed on their claims, it is not necessary that Plaintiffs show intentional discrimination. The Supreme Court has recognized that discrimination against the disabled is typically due to "apathetic attitudes rather than affirmative animus." *Alexander v. Choate,* 469 U.S. 287, 296, 105 S.Ct. 712, 83 L.Ed.2d 661 (1985). The ADA is intended to combat not only intentional discrimination, but also benign neglect, apathy and indifference so that qualified individuals receive transportation services in a manner consistent with basic human dignity. *Helen L.,* 46 F.3d at 335. Plaintiffs' Complaint alleges numerous discriminatory acts in violation of Title II of the ADA and § 504 of the Rehabilitation Act. See Complaint §§ 53, 54, 59, 60. This Court finds that Plaintiffs have shown sufficient likelihood of success on the merits in several of their claims against Defendant MARTA.

a. Information in Accessible Formats

MARTA makes schedule and route information freely available to the general public. This information is contained in maps and brochures available at MARTA stations. The information is also accessible to the general public on MARTA's web site. The information is not equally accessible to disabled persons, particularly the visually impaired. Although particular route and schedule information is available by telephone, this is not the equivalent to what MARTA provides to the general public. MARTA can do a better job of making information available in accessible formats to the visually impaired. This Court holds that the Plaintiffs have met their burden to show a likelihood of success on the merits for Defendants' failure to make available to individuals with disabilities adequate information concerning transportation services through accessible formats and technology to enable users to obtain information and schedule service. 49 C.F.R. § 37.167(f); 28 C.F.R. § 35.160. A disabled transit user cannot adequately use the bus system if schedule and route information is not available in a form he or she can use. 49 C.F.R. § 37.167.

The Court accepts the testimony from MARTA that it will provide individual schedules in Braille as requested, but that it is not feasible, practical or cost effective to provide the entire 190 route bus service schedule in Braille. It appears from the evidence presented that disabled individuals can either use MARTA's information telephone number to receive scheduling information or request information in alternative formats through MARTA's Customer Service department. These procedures, if implemented properly, would follow the guidelines set forth in the ADA. Where MARTA seems to fall short is in the implementation of both of these procedures. Here, as elsewhere, it must deliver on its promises. There should not be a lengthy wait time when you call MARTA's information telephone number; you should be able to receive comprehensive information from a representative and it should not take months to receive a requested Braille schedule. MARTA representatives also concede that the system's web page is not formatted in such a way that it can be read by persons who are blind but who are capable of using text reader computer software for the visually impaired. * * * However, it now appears that MARTA is attempting to correct this problem. Until these deficiencies are corrected, Marta is violating the ADA mandate of "making adequate communications capacity available, through accessible formats and technology, to enable users to obtain information and schedule service." 49 C.F.R. § 37.167(f).

* * *

2. Substantial Threat of Irreparable Injury

A plaintiff seeking an injunction against a local or state government must present facts showing a threat of immediate, irreparable harm before a federal court will intervene. *Rizzo v. Goode,* 423 U.S. 362,

378-79, 96 S.Ct. 598, 46 L.Ed.2d 561 (1976). The Defendants argue that Plaintiffs' testimony shows only that disabled individuals are sometimes inconvenienced by occasional equipment malfunctions or an uncooperative driver. They argue that this is insufficient to show irreparable injury. * * *

* * *

* * * In this case, * * * the Plaintiffs have established a strong factual record of more than isolated incidents of poor service. Their complaints are corroborated by the findings of the FTA that MARTA's paratransit operation is not in compliance with the ADA. * * *

MARTA also contends that it has improved its service in recent months and that the problems identified by the Plaintiffs have been rectified. Voluntary cessation of illegal conduct does not render a challenge to that conduct moot unless (1) there is no reasonable expectation that the wrong will be repeated, and (2) interim relief or events have completely and irrevocably eradicated the effects of the alleged violation. *Los Angeles County v. Davis,* 440 U.S. 625, 631, 99 S.Ct. 1379, 59 L.Ed.2d 642 (1979); * * *. Improvements in service will not preclude injunctive relief where there has been a clearly established pattern of failing to provide an acceptable level of service to the disabled. *Cupolo v. Bay Area Rapid Transit,* 5 F.Supp.2d 1078, 1084 (N.D. Cal. 1997). The testimony presented at the evidentiary hearing corroborated by the FTA assessment is sufficient to establish such a pattern. It appears to the Court that MARTA did not seriously address these issues until forced to do so by the FTA Assessment and the threat of this litigation. The Court is not persuaded that recent improvements in service to the disabled make an injunction unnecessary.

The goal of the ADA is "to assure equality of opportunity, full participation, independent living, and economic self-sufficiency" for the disabled. 42 U.S.C. § 12101. At the evidentiary hearing, the Court was impressed by the heroic efforts of Plaintiffs to overcome the daily obstacles they face in their quest to achieve independent living and economic self-sufficiency. In this case, Plaintiffs will be irreparably injured in the absence of a preliminary injunction, as a result of MARTA's continued failure to accommodate their disabilities and to provide them full and equal access to public transportation.

3. Balancing the Harms

The implementing regulations of Title II of the ADA lay out very specific requirements for the operation of public transportation services. Defendants have failed to comply with several of these requirements. The balance of harms in this case tips sharply in the favor of issuing a preliminary injunction because the Defendant has not shown any cognizable injury that would result. An injunction is an appropriate mechanism to ensure that competing priorities do not overwhelm

MARTA's obligation to comply with the ADA. *Cupolo v. Bay Area Rapid Transit,* 5 F.Supp.2d 1078, 1085 (N.D. Cal. 1997). In the particular facts of this case, an injunction is an appropriate means of guaranteeing that recent improvements in service and plans for added personnel are carried through and do not once again become victims of competing priorities.

4. The Public Interest

Congress stated in the enactment of the ADA that it is in the public interest to eliminate discrimination against individuals with disabilities. See 42 U.S.C. § 12101. Granting the preliminary injunction would serve that public interest in providing accessible public transportation to individuals with disabilities throughout metropolitan Atlanta. The public has an interest in the full participation of the disabled in the economic, social and recreational life of the community. *Tugg v. Towey,* 864 F.Supp. 1201, 1211 (S.D. Fla. 1994). Unreliable transportation affects not only the disabled. Their relatives, friends, employers and physicians, among others, are all affected. * * *

III. Conclusion

Plaintiffs are among an estimated 24 million * * * disabled Americans who are dependent upon public transportation. Plaintiffs and other members of the disabled community who attended the June and August hearings are making heroic efforts to overcome the daily obstacles they encounter in their quest for independent living and economic self-sufficiency. They must rely upon MARTA for their daily transportation needs if they are to live active lives in the community, to work and pay taxes and avoid complete dependency upon the public dole or private charity. The ADA embodies a national policy that encourages self-reliance and self-sufficiency. Pursuant to the ADA, Plaintiffs are entitled to receive a level of service which is comparable to that MARTA provides to the non-disabled. Plaintiffs have convinced this Court that MARTA is not providing that level of service to the disabled. It should do better.

For the reasons set forth above, Plaintiffs' Motion for a Preliminary Injunction against Metropolitan Atlanta Rapid Transit Authority (MARTA) [Doc. 15 & 25] is GRANTED IN PART AND DENIED IN PART as to liability. The parties are directed to confer in a good faith attempt to agree upon an appropriate remedies Order that is narrowly tailored to address the violations of the ADA outlined in this Order. * * *

So Ordered.

If a public entity selects software and hardware that is not accessible to people with disabilities, the subsequent cost of making them accessible will generally not be considered an undue burden, when the cost could have been avoided or reduced by considering accessibility at the time of selection. Letter to Dr. James Rosser, President of Cal. St. Univ.

at L.A., from Adriana Cardenas, Team Leader, Office for Civil Rights, U.S. Dept. of Educ. (April 7, 1997), http://people.rit.edu/easi/law/csula.htm (last visited June 6, 2012); Peter Blanck et al., Disability Civil Rights Law and Policy: Accessible Courtroom Technology, 12 Wm. & Mary Bill Rts. J. 825, 828-38 (2004) (discussing the requirements of courtrooms as Title II entities in ensuring technological access).

Although a government entity may meet its effective communication obligation by providing web-based information and services in alternate formats (with the same hours of availability and response times), generally, making the online services and websites themselves accessible is more effective and economical. ADA Best Practices Tool Kit for State and Local Governments, Chapter 5, "Website Accessibility Under Title II of the ADA," http://www.ada.gov/pca toolkit/chap5toolkit.htm (last visited Oct. 18, 2012).

In accord, city governments across the United States have entered into settlement agreements with the U.S. Department of Justice (DOJ) following investigations that found widespread inaccessibility. *See* Settlement Agreement between U.S. and City of Shreveport, Louisiana, http://www.ada.gov/shreveportlasa.htm (Oct. 24, 2006); U.S. Dep't of Justice, Project Civic Access, http://www.ada.gov/civicac.htm (last modified Feb. 8, 2012) (last visited Oct. 18, 2012). For instance, the city of Davenport, Iowa, agreed to implement, *inter alia*, the following remedial actions:

> Within six months of the effective date of this Agreement, and on subsequent anniversaries of the effective date of this Agreement, the City will distribute to all persons – employees and contractors – who design, develop, maintain, or otherwise have responsibility for content and format of its website(s) or third party websites used by the City (Internet Personnel) the technical assistance document, "Accessibility of State and Local Government Websites to People with Disabilities," ... *available at* www.ada. gov/websites2.htm (last visited June 6, 2012).

> Within six months of the effective date of this Agreement, and throughout the life of the Agreement, the City will do the following:

> A. Establish, implement, and post online a policy that its web pages will be accessible and create a process for implementation;

> B. Ensure that all new and modified web pages and content are accessible;

> C. Develop and implement a plan for making existing web content more accessible;

D. Provide a way for online visitors to request accessible information or services by posting a telephone number or e-mail address on its home page; and

E. Periodically (at least annually) enlist people with disabilities to test its pages for ease of use.

Settlement Agreement Between the United States and the City of Davenport, Iowa Under the Americans with Disabilities Act DJ 204-28-57 (Aug. 5, 2004), http://www.usdoj.gov/crt/ada/DavenportSA.htm (last visited Oct. 25, 2012).

Website accessibility standards vary by state, but they tend to be drawn from Section 508 standards and the World Wide Web Consortium's (W3C) Web Content Accessibility Guidelines (WCAG). *Id.* Nevertheless, to the extent that public websites remain inaccessible to persons with disabilities, concurrent reductions in traditional communications due to cost or other reasons may impede the availability of programs and services. Nat'l Council on Disability, Over the Horizon: Potential Impact of Emerging Trends in Information and Communication Technology on Disability Policy and Practice, 21-24 (Dec. 26, 2006) [hereinafter "NCD, Over the Horizon"], *available at* http://www.ncd.gov/rawmedia_repository/8dd0faca_3585_4381_89cf_3cb635b3c76d?document.pdf (last visited Oct. 25, 2012).

§ 33.4   Applications Of The ADA: Title III

One of the ADA's major goals is removing architectural and communication barriers faced by people with disabilities. Congress was careful in drafting the ADA's accessibility provisions to balance the needs of people with disabilities and the legitimate concerns of entities covered by the law, such as businesses, non-profit organizations, and state and local governments.

As discussed *supra* in Part 5 of this casebook, Title III prohibits discrimination against persons with disabilities in the "equal enjoyment of . . . places of public accommodation." 42 U.S.C. § 12182(a) (2006). A place of public accommodation generally is a private entity in one of twelve categories that offers goods and services to the public. *Id.* § 12181(7). The following sections will address how Title III applies to the Internet and online accessibility, as well as emerging issues in technology policy under this Title.

A.   *The "Place" Requirement*

Federal circuit courts are split on the issue whether Title III covers only physical "places" of public accommodation. *See supra* § 15.1. The Third Circuit, in *Ford v. Schering-Plough Corp.*, 145 F.3d 601, 612-13 (3d Cir. 1998), and the Sixth Circuit in *Parker v. Metropolitan Life Insurance Co.*, 121 F.3d 1006, 1014 (6th Cir. 1997), have held that public accommodations are limited to physical places. The First, Second and

Seventh circuits have held otherwise. Pallozzi v. Allstate Life Ins. Co., 198 F.3d 28, 32-33 (2d Cir. 2000) (ADA guarantees "more than mere physical access"); Doe v. Mut. of Omaha Ins. Co., 179 F.3d 557, 560 (7th Cir. 1999); Carparts Distr. Ctr., Inc. v. Automotive Wholesaler's Ass'n of New England, Inc., 37 F.3d 12 (1st Cir. 1994).

The First Circuit in *Carparts Distribution Center, Inc.* reasoned that the term "place of public accommodation" is not limited to actual physical structures. *Id.* at 20. Title III's definition of "public accommodation" includes business entities such as banks, travel services, pharmacies, and insurance offices. 42 U.S.C. § 12181(7)(F) (2006). By including travel services among the list of Title III public accommodations, the First Circuit concluded that service establishments, including providers of services that do not require a person to enter an actual physical structure, should be covered by Title III. Carparts Distribution Ctr., 37 F.3d at 20. The court based this conclusion on the fact that travel agencies conduct business by telephone and email and do not require customers to enter an office. *Id.* at 19.

As the First Circuit stated in *Carparts*:

> [O]ne can easily imagine the existence of other service establishments conducting business by mail and phone without providing facilities for their customers to enter in order to utilize their services. It would be irrational to conclude that persons who enter an office to purchase services are protected by the ADA, but persons who purchase the same services over the telephone or by mail are not.

Id. Following the logic of the First Circuit, web-based commercial services are subject to the Title III provisions. *See* Nat'l Ass'n of the Deaf v. Netflix, Inc., 869 F.Supp.2d 196 (D. Mass. 2012) (finding purely virtual services to be public accommodations).

In *Pallozzi v. Allstate Life Insurance Co.*, the Second Circuit held that "Title III's mandate that the disabled be accorded 'full and equal enjoyment of the goods, [and] services . . . of any place of public accommodation,' . . . suggests to us that the statute was meant to guarantee them more than mere physical access." Pallozzi, 198 F.3d at 32 (citing Carparts Distribution Ctr., 37 F.3d at 20). Likewise, in *Doe v. Mutual of Omaha Insurance Co.*, the Seventh Circuit concluded that the plain meaning of ADA Title III mandates that the owner or operator of a public website "cannot exclude disabled persons from entering the facility and, once in, from using the facility in the same way that the nondisabled do." Doe, 179 F.3d at 559. The Eleventh Circuit would require at least a nexus with a physical place, although the discrimination need not occur at the place. Rendon v. Valleycrest Prods., Ltd., 294 F.3d 1279, 1284 n.8 (11th Cir. 2002).

RENDON v. VALLEYCREST PRODUCTIONS, LTD.

United States Court of Appeals, Eleventh Circuit, 2002
294 F.3d 1279

Opinion

BARKETT, Circuit Judge:

* * *

Background

ABC and Valleycrest produce the television quiz show Millionaire. The program is filmed at ABC's New York City production studio, and contestants are selected for appearance on the program via an automated telephone answering system. Aspiring contestants call a toll-free number on which a recorded message prompts them to answer a series of questions. Callers record their answers to these questions by pressing the appropriate keys on their telephone keypads. Callers who answer all of the questions correctly in the first round of the competition (the "fast finger process") are then subject to a random drawing to narrow the contestant field, and the selected individuals proceed to the second round, in which they are required to answer additional trivia questions. Of the approximately 240,000 persons who call the contestant hotline each day to compete on Millionaire, only 6% proceed to the second round.

In this case, the named plaintiffs are persons with hearing and upper-body mobility impairments who sought selection to compete on Millionaire by calling the automated hotline, but who could not register their entries, either because they were deaf and could not hear the questions on the automated system, or because they could not move their fingers rapidly enough to record their answers on their telephone key pads. Specifically, Rendon, Leon and Norris suffer from a condition that limits their finger mobility. Jebian could not record his answers because he could not hear the pre-recorded questions and no Telecommunications Devices for the Deaf services[1] ("TDD services") were made available. Kelly Greene, the last named plaintiff, is the Director of the Center for Independent Living, and seeks relief on behalf of his disabled clients who had attempted to compete for the game on the hotline.

---

[1] A TDD machine allows a deaf person to conduct a telephone conversation with another person by typing comments into a "relay" device. * * * Since 1990, the ADA has required telecommunication carriers nationwide to provide TDD relay operators to their customers as a standard service, thereby providing the necessary intermediaries for communication between deaf and hearing telephone users. *See* 47 U.S.C. § 225(a)(2).

Plaintiffs filed a class action complaint alleging that Valleycrest and ABC were in violation of the ADA because the telephone contestant selection process for Millionaire tended to screen out hearing-impaired or upper-body mobility-impaired persons. Plaintiffs allege that they can be reasonably accommodated through the use of several well established technological devices, such as TDD services, which would permit them to participate in the existing fast finger competition.

Defendants moved to dismiss Plaintiffs' complaint, arguing that the Title III requirements did not apply to the contestant hotline because the protections of Title III are limited to physical locations; that is, they guarantee the disabled fair access only to privileges and services that are offered from a physical "public accommodation."

The district court granted the motion to dismiss, holding that Title III is inapplicable to the defendants' automated telephone system of selecting contestants to participate on the Show because the system is not administered at a palpable public accommodation. This appeal followed, with the Department of Justice intervening and joining Plaintiffs' argument that Title III precludes the sort of screening mechanism used to select Millionaire contestants. * * *

Discussion

* * *

42 U.S.C. § 12182(a) outlines Title III's purpose in general terms, providing that

> [n]o individual shall be discriminated against on the basis of disability in the full and equal enjoyment of the goods, services, facilities, privileges, advantages, or accommodations of any place of public accommodation by any person who owns, leases (or leases to), or operates a place of public accommodation.

The statute in turn lists those entities regulated under the statute as places of "public accommodation," explaining that an entity is covered if its operations "affect commerce," and it falls within one of twelve enumerated categories. 42 U.S.C. § 12181(7)(A)-(L).[3] The categories of covered entities include, *inter alia,* "a motion picture house, theater, concert hall, stadium, or other place of exhibition or entertainment." 42 U.S.C. § 12181(7)(C).

---

[3]   28 C.F.R. § 36.104 further explains the class of "public accommodations" covered under Title III, defining a public accommodation as a "place" or "a facility, operated by a private entity, whose operations affect commerce" and which falls under one of the twelve public accommodation categories listed under § 12181(7).

The ADA also precisely defines the term "discrimination" in § 12182(b)(2)(A)(i), which, *inter alia,* prohibits

> the imposition or application of eligibility criteria that screen out or tend to screen out an individual with a disability or any class of individuals with disabilities from fully and equally enjoying any goods, services, facilities, privileges, advantages, or accommodations, unless such criteria can be shown to be necessary for the provision of the goods, services, facilities, privileges, advantages, or accommodations being offered * * *.[4]

* * * At this juncture, on the record before us, this case does not involve issues regarding the reasonableness of any proposed accommodations, or require us to resolve whether any proposed accommodations or auxiliary services would constitute an "undue burden" to the Millionaire program. See 42 U.S.C. § 12182(b)(2)(A)(iii). Rather, this appeal involves only the question of whether Title III encompasses a claim involving telephonic procedures that, in this case, tend to screen out disabled persons from participation in a competition held in a tangible public accommodation. Under a plain reading of the foregoing provisions, then, in order to state a valid claim, Plaintiffs must allege that they suffer from disabilities, and that Defendants' imposition or application of unnecessary eligibility criteria has screened them out or tended to screen them out from accessing a privilege or advantage of Defendants' public accommodation.

---

[4]   Subsections (ii) and (iii) further prohibit:

> (ii) a failure to make reasonable modifications in policies, practices, or procedures, when such modifications are necessary to afford such goods, services, facilities, privileges, advantages, or accommodations to individuals with disabilities, unless the entity can demonstrate that making such modifications would fundamentally alter the nature of such goods, services, facilities, privileges, advantages, or accommodations.

> (iii) a failure to take such steps as may be necessary to ensure that no individual with a disability is excluded, denied services, segregated or otherwise treated differently than other individuals because of the absence of auxiliary aids and services, unless the entity can demonstrate that taking such steps would fundamentally alter the nature of the good, service, facility, privilege, advantage or accommodation being offered or would result in an undue burden.

42 U.S.C. § 12182(b)(2)(A)(ii)-(iii).

Plaintiffs' complaint clearly makes the requisite allegations, * * * and moreover, a number of the assertions are uncontested for the purposes of the motion to dismiss now on appeal in this case. Defendants concede that Plaintiffs are disabled as defined by the ADA. Defendants also concede, and we agree, that the Millionaire show takes place at a public accommodation (a studio) within the meaning of 42 U.S.C. § 12181(7)(C) (covering theaters and other places of entertainment), and that the automatic process used to select contestants tends to "screen out" many disabled individuals as described in § 12182(b)(2)(A)(i). Lastly, Defendants concede that the opportunity to appear on Millionaire and compete for one million dollars is a privilege or advantage as those terms are defined by the ADA (although they specifically refer to the Show as a "good or service" of the studio, rather than as a privilege or advantage thereof).

Having conceded nearly all of the requisite elements of a valid Title III claim, Defendants nonetheless contend that they are entitled to dismissal because Plaintiffs have failed to assert that Defendants erected "barriers to the entry of disabled persons into the auditoriums or studios in which the Show is recorded." * * * As we understand their contention, Defendants argue that the Millionaire contestant hotline may not serve as the basis for a Title III claim because it is not itself a public accommodation or a physical barrier to entry erected at a public accommodation.

We find this argument entirely unpersuasive. A reading of the plain and unambiguous * * * statutory language at issue reveals that the definition of discrimination provided in Title III covers both tangible barriers, that is, physical and architectural barriers that would prevent a disabled person from entering an accommodation's facilities and accessing its goods, services and privileges, see 42 U.S.C. § 12182(b)(2)(A)(iv), and intangible barriers, such as eligibility requirements and screening rules or discriminatory policies and procedures that restrict a disabled person's ability to enjoy the defendant entity's goods, services and privileges, see 42 U.S.C. § 12182(b)(2)(A)(i)-(ii). * * * There is nothing in the text of the statute to suggest that discrimination via an imposition of screening or eligibility requirements must occur on site to offend the ADA.

In support of their assertion to the contrary, Defendants rely primarily on *Stoutenborough v. Nat'l Football League, Inc.,* 59 F.3d 580 (6th Cir. 1995) , in which a group of hearing-impaired plaintiffs sued the NFL and the Cleveland Browns football team seeking to eliminate a so-called "blackout rule" that prohibited live video broadcasts of football games that were not sold out. The *Stoutenborough* plaintiffs argued that, because they were unable to hear the broadcasts of the games offered on the radio, the "blackout rule" effectively deprived them of the opportunity to enjoy a live broadcast of the games, while hearing persons could enjoy them. The plaintiffs sought a court order to compel the NFL and the Browns to broadcast all live games on television.

The Sixth Circuit upheld the district court's dismissal of the suit, citing two reasons. First, the Court determined that the blackout rule was not discriminatory, because it applied equally to the hearing and the hearing-impaired; both groups were precluded from viewing blacked-out home football games. Id. at 582. The mere fact that hearing persons could listen to the games on the radio was insignificant, since the rule did not attempt to regulate radio broadcast. Id. Second, the Court held that the televised broadcast of football games was not offered by the defendants as a service of a public accommodation. The Court observed that, although the defendants were in fact lessors of a stadium (a public accommodation), the broadcasts at issue were not services of that public accommodation. Id. at 583. Because the NFL, member clubs and media defendants did not otherwise fall within any of the twelve "public accommodation" categories identified in 42 U.S.C. § 12181(7), the plaintiffs had failed to state a Title III claim. Id.

Stoutenborough is not analogous to the present case. Defendants rely on language in *Stoutenborough* that suggests video broadcasts are not covered under Title III because they are not a "service" that defendant entities operate from a "place" of "public accommodation," id. at 583, but this language is irrelevant to the question we face here. The *Stoutenborough* court held as it did because it found that the broadcast of games was not a service of the football stadium – the only identifiable "public accommodation" under the ADA in that suit. Plaintiffs in the present case, however, are not suing merely to observe a television show; rather, they seek the privilege of competing in a contest held in a concrete space, a contest they have been screened out of because of their disabilities. * * *

Defendants urge us to hold, in effect, that so long as discrimination occurs off site, it does not offend Title III. We do not believe this is a tenable reading of Title III; indeed, off-site screening appears to be the paradigmatic example contemplated in the statute's prohibition of "the imposition or application of eligibility criteria that screen out or tend to screen out an individual with a disability." 42 U.S.C. § 12182(b)(2)(A)(i). There would be little question that it would violate the ADA for the Defendants to screen potential contestants just outside the studio by refusing otherwise qualified persons because they were deaf or suffered from diabetes or HIV.

To contend that Title III allows discriminatory screening as long as it is off site requires not only misreading the relevant statutory language, but also contradicting numerous judicial opinions that have considered comparable suits dealing with discrimination perpetrated "at a distance." For cases arising under the ADA, see, e.g., *Ferguson v. City of Phoenix,* 157 F.3d 668 (9th Cir. 1998) (hearing-disabled plaintiffs' ADA Title II challenge to 9-1-1 emergency response system that lacked TDD capacity * * *; *Bartlett v. N.Y. State Bd. of Law Examiners,* 226 F.3d 69

(2d Cir. 2000) (dyslexic bar exam taker entitled to reasonable accommodations under Title II of ADA). * * *

Furthermore, the fact that the plaintiffs in this suit were screened out by an automated telephone system, rather than by an admission policy administered at the studio door, is of no consequence under the statute; eligibility criteria are frequently implemented off site – for example, through the mail or over the telephone. Indeed, Congress specifically noted in the ADA's "findings of fact" that "individuals with disabilities continually encounter various forms of discrimination, including outright intentional exclusion, the discriminatory effects of architectural, transportation, and *communication barriers,*" the very sorts of discrimination the statute seeks to redress. 42 U.S.C. § 12101(a)(5) (emphasis added) * * *

In light of the foregoing, we conclude that Plaintiffs have stated a valid claim under Title III by alleging that the fast finger telephone selection process is a discriminatory screening mechanism, policy or procedure, which deprives them of the opportunity to compete for the privilege of being a contestant on the Millionaire program. Therefore, we REVERSE the district court and remand for further proceedings consistent with this opinion.

Notes & Questions

1. To what extent does the Eleventh Circuit agree with the First Circuit in *Carparts*?

2. How necessary is it that the plaintiffs demonstrate a nexus between the alleged discrimination and a physical place?

3. For further discussion, *see* Richard E. Moberly, The Americans with Disabilities Act in Cyberspace: Applying the "Nexus" Approach to Private Internet Websites, 55 Mercer L. Rev. 963 (2004); Katherine Rengel, The Americans with Disabilities Act and Internet Accessibility for the Blind, 25 J. Marshall J. Computer & Info. L. 543, 572 (2008) (arguing the arbitrariness of the "nexus requirement" by noting that "[a]s more and more businesses go online, courts will become bogged down with arbitrary decisions over what constitutes a nexus connection, rather than important decisions like balancing the burdens and the benefits of Web site modifications.").

Read *Access Now, Inc. v. Southwest Airlines, Co.* in Part 5, § 15.1.D, *supra.*

1. In a footnote, the *Access Now* court concluded that "no well-defined, generally accepted standards exist for programming assistive software and websites so as to make them uniformly compatible . . . ." 227 F. Supp 2d 1312, 1315 n.1. This was in spite of the fact that the plaintiffs presented a copy of W3C's Web Content Accessibility Guidelines (WCAG) 1.0 to the court. *Id. See generally*, W3C, Web Content Accessibility Guidelines 1.0 (May 5, 1999), http://www.w3.org/TR/WAI-WEBCONTENT/ (last visited Oct. 25 2012). The W3C has since updated these standards to WCAG 2.0, http://www.w3.org/TR/WCAG20/ (last visited Oct. 25 2012).

2. Did the court overstate the Eleventh Circuit's position regarding a nexus with a physical place? Recall that, citing *Rendon*, the court stated, "the Eleventh Circuit has recognized Congress' clear intent that Title III of the ADA governs solely access to physical, concrete places of public accommodation." Access Now, 227 F. Supp.2d at 1318.

3. On appeal, the Eleventh Circuit in *Access Now* affirmed the district court's dismissal of the case and found no justification for permitting new claims on appeal. Access Now, Inc. v. Southwest Airlines Co., 385 F.3d 1324 (11th Cir. 2004).

Other complaints have been filed challenging the inaccessibility of online places of public accommodation. *National Federation of the Blind v. Target Corp.* is the first major case to address inaccessibility of a physical place of public accommodation that also offers its services via a website.

NATIONAL FEDERATION OF THE BLIND V. TARGET CORP.

United States District Court, Northern District of California, 2007
582 F.Supp.2d 1185

Memorandum & Order

PATEL, District Judge:

Plaintiffs National Federation of the Blind ("NFB"), National Federation of the Blind of California ("NFB-CA"), Bruce Sexton, and all those similarly situated, filed this action against Target Corporation ("Target"), seeking declaratory, injunctive and monetary relief. Plaintiffs claim that Target.com is inaccessible to the blind, and thereby violates federal and state laws prohibiting discrimination against the disabled. Now before the court is plaintiffs' motion for class certification and motion for bifurcation; defendant's motion for summary judgment and the parties' supplemental briefing on the state law claims. Having considered the parties' arguments and submissions, and for the reasons set forth below, the court enters the following memorandum and order.

* * *

I. Parties

Plaintiffs NFB and NFB-CA are non-profit organizations. NFB is a nationwide organization with a 50,000 strong membership, composed primarily of blind individuals. NFB-CA is the California affiliate of NFB. The purpose of NFB is to promote the general welfare of the blind by (1) assisting the blind in their efforts to integrate themselves into society on terms of equality and (2) removing barriers and changing social attitudes, stereotypes and mistaken beliefs that sighted and blind persons hold concerning the limitations created by blindness and that result in the denial of opportunity to blind persons in virtually every sphere of life. These organizations have brought suit on their own behalf and on behalf of their members.

Plaintiff Sexton is a member of the NFB and the NFB of California. He is legally blind and uses JAWS screen reading software to access the internet. Sexton Apr. 12, 2006 Dec. ¶¶ 2, 13. Sexton relies on the internet for a variety of functions and frequently uses the internet in order to "research products, compare prices, and make decisions about purchasing goods in the stores' physical locations." *Id.* ¶ 16. He has attempted to use Target.com with his screen reader on "numerous occasions" but has been unable to access certain features of the website. *Id.* at ¶ 32.

Defendant Target operates approximately 1,400 retail stores nationwide, including 205 stores in California. Target.com is a website owned and operated by Target. By visiting Target.com, customers can purchase many of the items available in Target stores. Target.com also allows a customer to perform functions related to Target stores. For example, through Target.com, a customer can access information on store locations and hours, refill a prescription or order photo prints for pick-up at a store, and print coupons to redeem at a store.

II. Background

Plaintiffs allege that Target.com is not accessible to blind individuals. According to plaintiffs, designing a website to be accessible to the blind is technologically simple and not economically prohibitive. Protocols for designing an accessible internet site rely heavily on "alternative text": invisible code embedded beneath graphics. A blind individual can use screen reader software, which vocalizes the alternative text and describes the content of the webpage. Similarly, if the screen reader can read the navigation links, then a blind individual can navigate the site with a keyboard instead of a mouse. Plaintiffs allege that Target.com lacks these features that would enable the blind to use

Target.com. Since the blind cannot use Target.com, they are denied full and equal access to Target stores, according to plaintiffs.

III. Procedural History

On February 7, 2006 plaintiffs filed this action in Superior Court of California for the County of Alameda. On March 9, 2006 defendant removed the case to federal court and subsequently filed a motion to dismiss the complaint for failure to state a claim. In its motion, defendant claimed that each of the anti-discrimination laws protecting the disabled – the Americans with Disabilities Act, 42 U.S.C. section 12182 ("ADA"), Unruh Civil Rights Act, Cal. Civ.Code section 51 ("Unruh Act"), and the Disabled Persons Act, Cal. Civ.Code section 54.1 ("DPA") – cover access to physical spaces only. Since Target.com is not a physical space, defendant asserted that the complaint does not state a claim under these laws. On September 5, 2006 the court granted in part and denied in part defendant's motion to dismiss. The court reasoned that the inaccessibility of Target.com impeded full and equal enjoyment of goods and services offered in Target stores pursuant to the ADA. Thus, the court dismissed plaintiffs' claims to the extent that they are based on Target.com features that are unconnected to the stores. The court also denied the motion to dismiss plaintiffs' state law claims. At the same time, the court denied plaintiffs' request for a preliminary injunction as premature.

Plaintiffs filed the instant motion for class certification on February 1, 2007. On March 8, 2007 defendant filed a motion for summary judgment on the grounds that plaintiff Sexton has not suffered a cognizable injury under the ADA. The court held an initial hearing on these matters on April 12, 2007. At the hearing, the court requested supplemental briefing on the reach of the relevant state statutes before ruling on the class certification motion as it related to the California subclass. Following the hearing, the court issued an order on the motion for class certification on April 25, 2007. In its order, the court narrowed the proposed class definition for the nationwide class to include the nexus requirement from its earlier order. Accordingly, the nationwide class consists of all legally blind individuals in the United States who have attempted to access Target.com and as a result have been denied access to the enjoyment of goods and services offered in Target stores. Subsequently, the parties submitted supplemental briefing on whether the DPA and the Unruh Act apply to websites. Plaintiffs also submitted supplemental declarations of class members in accordance with the court's April 25, 2007 order. Both parties submitted additional briefing on the class certification issues.

IV. Recent Modifications to Target.com

After the filing of the present complaint, Target undertook certain modifications of its website to make it more accessible to the blind. In response to this litigation, Target began drafting Online Assistive

Technology Guidelines based on plaintiffs' expert report. Nemoir Dep. at 21:18-22:5.

LEGAL STANDARD

I. Motion for Class Certification

* * *

IV. Motion for Summary Judgment

Shortly after plaintiffs filed their motion for class certification, Target filed a motion for summary judgment arguing that plaintiff Sexton had suffered no legally cognizable injury. Specifically, Target argues that Sexton had failed to meet the nexus requirement for the purposes of his ADA claim. Because his state law claims were dependent on his ADA claim, those too must fail according to Target.

A. ADA claim

The court agrees that Sexton has not demonstrated that his inability to access Target.com renders him unable to access the goods and services of Target stores. Sexton has submitted at least four declarations over the course of this litigation. *See* App. of Supp. Dec., Exh. 14 (compiling declarations). His most recent one, submitted May 25, 2007, describes how Sexton frequently pre-shops on several stores' websites before shopping. Sexton May 25, 2007 Dec. ¶ 4. It further describes the cost and time incurred when he is unable to pre-shop. *Id.* ¶ 5. However, Sexton's declarations do not establish how his difficulties with the Target.com website have impeded his access to the goods and services in the store. He states only that he has been "unable to use Target.com for th[e] purpose" of pre-shopping and that he has been unable to use the weekly advertisements on Target.com for use in the stores. *Id.* ¶ 6-7. The only specific incident described in his declarations involves his purchase of towels for his dorm room. Sexton Apr. 12 2006 Dec. ¶ 33. While he was unable to access information about the towels online, he was ultimately successful in purchasing them in the store after hiring a driver and coordinating a trip with a companion. *Id.* While Sexton's experience may qualify under the class definition if he incurred increased expense and time from the inability to access the website, nonetheless his declaration does not suggest that hiring the driver and arranging for the companion were necessary only because he could not pre-shop. Accordingly, the court will grant defendant's motion for summary judgment on Sexton's ADA claim, but allow substitution of another plaintiff or plaintiffs on this claim.[4]

---

[4] Anticipating that plaintiffs may attempt another declaration by Mr. Sexton, the court instructs that this avenue has been exhausted and it will not entertain any further declarations from Mr. Sexton or other plaintiffs. Plaintiffs may substitute another named plaintiff who does not

B. State law claims

While Target contends that plaintiffs' state law claims rest entirely on their ADA claims, plaintiffs have stated independent bases for their claims under the Unruh Act and the DPA. *See* FAC ¶¶ 42, 50. Therefore, Sexton's failure to meet the nexus requirement does not necessarily defeat his state law claims. Having determined that the DPA and the Unruh Act apply to Target.com without a nexus requirement, Sexton's state law claims may survive.

1. Unruh Act

The Unruh Act, California Civil Code section 51, *et seq.* provides in relevant part:

> (b) All persons within the jurisdiction of this state are free and equal, and no matter what their sex, race, color, religion, ancestry, national origin, disability, medical condition, marital status, or sexual orientation are entitled to the full and equal accommodations, advantages, facilities, privileges, or services in all business establishments of every kind whatsoever.

> (d) Nothing in this section shall be construed to require any construction, alteration, repair, structural or otherwise, or modification of any sort whatsoever, beyond that construction, alteration, repair, or modification that is otherwise required by other provisions of law, to any new or existing establishment, facility, building, improvement, or any other structure, nor shall anything in this section be construed to augment, restrict, or alter in any way the authority of the State Architect to require construction, alteration, repair, or modifications that the State Architect otherwise possesses pursuant to other laws.

With respect to the Unruh Act claim, Target notes that there are only a few contexts in which an Unruh Act claim can exist independent of an ADA claim. It contends that the facts presented here are not one of those contexts. *Compare Chabner v. United of Omaha Life Ins. Co.,* 225 F.3d 1042, 1047 (9th Cir.2000) (holding that insurance policy that discriminated against the disabled did not violate the ADA but did independently violate the Unruh Act) *with Molski v. M.J. Cable, Inc.,* 481 F.3d 724, 731 (9th Cir.2007) ("In the disability context, California's Unruh Civil Rights Act operates virtually identically to the ADA."). The distinguishing factor, according to Target, is that an independent cause of action under the Unruh Act involves a discriminatory policy. That

---

have the shortcomings of Mr. Sexton as described above and set forth in the amended complaint the basis on which the newly named plaintiff satisfies the standing requirements.

argument is easily set aside. Nothing in the text of the Unruh Act suggests that a discriminatory policy is required for a claim independent of an ADA claim, nor does Target cite any case law to support that position.

Target notes that section 51(c) limits Unruh Act claims to those that do not require any "modification or alterations" beyond that required by other provisions of law. Cal. Civ.Code § 51(c). It is premature, at this stage, to determine whether the ADA or the DPA would require modifications of the Target.com website. The court sees no reason why the Unruh Act's reference to other provisions of law would not refer to either the ADA or the state statute. *Id.* Moreover, plaintiffs argue that the modification language refers to physical modification or construction and, therefore, would not restrict remedies in the instant action, which require only modification of a website.

Second, Target argues that Sexton has failed to make the requisite intent showing. *Harris v. Capital Growth Investors XIV,* 52 Cal.3d 1142, 1175, 278 Cal.Rptr. 614, 805 P.2d 873 (1991) ("[T]he language and history of the Unruh Act indicate that the legislative object was to prohibit intentional discrimination in access to public accommodations."). Under Ninth Circuit law, intentional discrimination is not required for an Unruh Act claim predicated on an ADA claim. *See Lentini v. Cal. Ctr. for the Arts,* 370 F.3d 837, 846-47 (9th Cir.2004) ("We find that, regardless of whether *Harris* may continue to have relevance to other Unruh Act suits, no showing of intentional discrimination is required where the Unruh Act violation is premised on an ADA violation."). Having determined that Sexton has failed to establish his ADA claims, *Lentini* does not absolve him of his duty to prove intent for his independent claim under the Unruh Act.

Whether intent is required for an independent disability claim under the Unruh Act has not been addressed by the Ninth Circuit. *Harris* held that disparate impact theories for gender discrimination were not actionable under the Unruh Act. 52 Cal.3d at 1175, 278 Cal.Rptr. 614, 805 P.2d 873. However, the legislative history of the Act and its subsequent construction tilts in favor of plaintiffs' preferred reading. The 1992 amendments to the Unruh Act included a provision to make a violation of the ADA a per se violation of the Unruh Act. In doing so, the legislature noted its intent "to strengthen California law in areas where it is weaker than the Americans with Disabilities Act of 1990, and to retain California law when it provides more protection for individuals with disabilities. . . ." 1992 Cal. Stats. 4282. This statement of legislative intent, issued after *Harris,* suggests that *Harris'* proclamations on the legislature's intent may no longer be applicable, particularly in disability cases. *But see Gunther v. Lin,* 144 Cal.App.4th 223, 50 Cal.Rptr.3d 317 (2007) (relying on *Harris* to conclude that a plaintiff must prove intent for a damages claim, but not for injunctive relief, under the Unruh Act).

Plaintiffs argue that the unique nature of discrimination on the basis of disability makes the reasoning in *Harris* inapposite. Disability discrimination, they contend, is characterized by inaction and the appropriate remedy for this type of discrimination is modification of otherwise neutral policies or practices. *Presta v. Peninsula Corridor Joint Powers Bd.,* 16 F.Supp.2d 1134, 1136 (N.D.Cal.1998) (Henderson, J.) ("[D]iscrimination against persons with disabilities differs from discrimination on the basis of, for example, gender, or race. Discrimination in the latter instances has been judicially defined as disparate treatment on the basis of a certain characteristic that identifies an individual as a member of a protected class. However, a person with a disability may be the victim of discrimination precisely because she did not receive disparate treatment when she needed accommodation."). The ADA thus departs from other anti-discrimination statutes in requiring that places of public accommodation take affirmative steps to accommodate the disabled. H .R. Rep. No. 101-485, pt.2, at 104 (1990); 42 U.S.C. § 12182(b)(2) (A) (ii-iv). The court is not persuaded that the California Court of Appeals properly acknowledged the unique nature of disability discrimination in applying *Harris* to disability claims for damages. *Gunther,* 144 Cal.App.4th at 223, 50 Cal.Rptr.3d 317. At least one other district court has reached this conclusion. *See Wilson v. Haria and Gogri Corp.,* 479 F.Supp.2d 1127, 1141 (E.D.Cal.2007) (rejecting *Gunther* where Unruh claim depended on violations of the ADA).

Plaintiffs have alleged intentional discrimination in their complaint. FAC ¶ 41. Target argues that they have not established intent nor can they for four reasons: 1) Target did not engage in any discriminatory personal contact with Sexton; 2) Target has not engaged in any willful, affirmative misconduct; 3) Discriminatory intent cannot be inferred from the effect on the class; 4) Discriminatory intent cannot be inferred from Target's refusal to modify its website. Plaintiffs, in their supplementary brief on state law issues, set out their evidentiary proffer of intent for a later stage of litigation, namely that Target's knowing failure and refusal to adopt certain accessibility features in Target.com constitute the requisite intent. They cite *Hankins v. El Torito Restaurants, Inc.,* 63 Cal.App.4th 510, 518, 74 Cal.Rptr.2d 684 (1998) for the proposition that such a knowing failure establishes the requisite intent. That case is far from clear on the nature of the intent showing required by the Unruh Act.

2. DPA

The DPA provides in relevant part:

> § 54(a) Individuals with disabilities or medical conditions have the same right as the general public to the full and free use of the streets, highways, sidewalks, walkways, public buildings, medical facilities, including hospitals,

clinics, and physicians' offices, public facilities, and other public places.

...

(c)   A violation of the right of an individual under the Americans with Disabilities Act of 1990 (Public Law 101-336) also constitutes a violation of this section.

§ 54.1(a) (1) Individuals with disabilities shall be entitled to full and equal access, as other members of the general public, to accommodations, advantages, facilities, medical facilities, including hospitals, clinics, and physicians' offices, and privileges of all common carriers, airplanes, motor vehicles, railroad trains, motorbuses, streetcars, boats, or any other public conveyances or modes of transportation (whether private, public, franchised, licensed, contracted, or otherwise provided), telephone facilities, adoption agencies, private schools, hotels, lodging places, places of public accommodation, amusement, or resort, and other places to which the general public is invited, subject only to the conditions and limitations established by law, or state or federal regulation, and applicable alike to all persons.

...

(3) "Full and equal access," for purposes of this section in its application to transportation, means access that meets the standards of Titles II and III of the Americans with Disabilities Act of 1990 (Public Law 101-336) and federal regulations adopted pursuant thereto, except that, if the laws of this state prescribe higher standards, it shall mean access that meets those higher standards.

Cal. Civ.Code § 54 *et seq.*

Target argues that Sexton's DPA claim must fail because the DPA requires an ADA violation or a building code violation. Under this view, because Sexton has not suffered an injury under the ADA and has provided no evidence of a building code violation, his DPA claim must also fail. Target relies on two cases for the proposition that the DPA requires a violation of the ADA or a building code violation. The first, *Mannick v. Kaiser Foundation Health Plan, Inc.,* No. 03-5905, 2006 WL 2168877, at *16 (N.D.Cal. July 31, 2006) (Hamilton, J.), involved a DPA claim that was based solely on the plaintiff's claims under the ADA. Here, plaintiffs have alleged an independent DPA claim from the alleged ADA violations. Like *Mannick,* the second case, *Arnold v. United Artists Theatre Cir., Inc.,* also involved building code violations and thus the court referred to those as the appropriate state law for the purposes of determining what "full and equal access" meant in that context. *See* Cal Civ.Code § 54.1(a)(3)

("Full and equal access," for purposes of this section in its application to transportation, means access that meets the standards [of the ADA] . . . except that, if the laws of this state prescribe higher standards, it shall mean access that meets those higher standards."). Nothing in the language of the DPA suggests that it is limited to building code violations; rather the statutory language refers to the higher standards of state law. *Id.* In *Arnold* and in *Mannick,* the relevant higher standard of state law was the building code because the disputes concerned building accessibility.[5] Here, if state law requires higher standards of website accessibility than the ADA, those standards are the relevant ones for the purposes of the DPA. Accordingly, the applicable standards of "full and equal access" under state law is still an open question. The court declines to adopt Target's cramped reading of the DPA.

* * *

CONCLUSION

Based upon the foregoing, IT IS HEREBY ORDERED that:

1)   Plaintiffs' motion to certify a class is GRANTED.

2)   The nationwide class consists of all legally blind individuals in the United States who have attempted to access Target.com and as a result have been denied access to the enjoyment of goods and services offered in Target stores. The California subclass includes all legally blind individuals in California who have attempted to access Target.com, for plaintiffs' claims arising under the California Unruh Civil Rights Act, California Civil Code §§ 51 *et seq.* and the Disabled Persons Act, California Civil Code §§ 54 *et seq.*

3)   Plaintiffs are ordered to substitute a new class representative with respect to the ADA claims consistent with this order within thirty (30) days of the date of this order.

4)   The counsel of named plaintiff shall serve as counsel for the class.

5)   Defendant's motion to strike Taylor's supplementary declaration is GRANTED.

6)   Plaintiffs' motion for bifurcation of trial is GRANTED.

---

[5]   Target also cites to Urhausen v. Longs Drug Stores of Ca., Inc., No. A113937, 2007 WL 2092927 (Cal. Ct. App. Sept. 18, 2007). *Urhausen,* however, provides further support for the court's holding since it defines "full and equal access" as access that complies with the ADA, or complies with state statutes, if the latter impose a higher standard. *Id.* at *3. Specifically, the court declines to limit the definition of access "only to entry into a building." *Id.*

7)   Defendant's motion for summary judgment is DENIED subject to the provisions of this order.

* * *

Notes & Questions

1.   In August of 2008, Target Corporation reached a settlement agreement with the NFB. In the three-year agreement, Target promised to ensure that its website met online accessibility guidelines. NFB agreed to confer to discuss periodic updates, as well as monitor the results of quarterly and annual user accessibility tests. Target stipulated that its Target.com coding employees would attend periodic training to ensure website accessibility. Guest feedback was also a portion of the settlement, where users of screen-reading technology would test the site and report both to a compliance individual and to the NFB. Included in the agreement were monetary damages in the amount of six million dollars, to be paid to the Californian settlement class. Nat'l Fed. of the Blind v. Target Corp., No.: C 06-01802 MHP, http://www.nfbtargetlawsuit.com/final-settlement-and-commerce-clause (last visited Nov. 1, 2012).

ക

B.   *Effective Communication*

The issue in *Access Now, Inc. v. Southwest Airlines* was whether plaintiffs were excluded in violation of Title III from the services offered by the airline. Discrimination under Title III would include the failure of a place of public accommodation to provide appropriate auxiliary aids or services (e.g., sign-language interpreters, assistive listening devices, Braille, or audiocassettes for individuals with sensory impairments) to ensure effective communication with customers with disabilities. 28 C.F.R. § 36.303 (2012). As mentioned, such accommodation is mandated unless it would fundamentally alter the nature of the services provided or result in an undue burden to the public accommodation. 42 U.S.C. § 12182(b)(2)(A)(ii) (2006).

In an early policy letter concerning website accessibility, the U.S. Department of Justice (DOJ) concluded that, pursuant to Titles II and III, state and local governments and the business sector must provide "effective communication" whenever they convey information, through the Internet or otherwise, regarding their programs, goods, or services. Letter from Deval Patrick, Assistant Attorney General, Civil Rights Division, U.S. Dep't Justice, to Tom Harkin, U.S. Senate (Sept. 9, 1996) www.justice.gov/crt/foia/readingroom/frequent_requests/ada_tal/tal712.txt (last visited June 6, 2012); *see also* Cynthia D. Waddell, The Growing Digital Divide in Access for People with Disabilities: Overcoming Barriers to Participation in the Digital Economy, Remarks at Understanding the Digital Economy Conference, Washington, D.C. (May 25-26, 1999), http://www.icdri.org/CynthiaW/the_digital_divide.htm (last visited June 6, 2012).

The U.S. Department of Education, Office of Civil Rights (OCR), defines "effective communication" in the context of Title II as the transfer of information with three basic components: accuracy, timeliness and appropriate medium and manner. Lex Frieden, When the Americans with Disabilities Act Goes Online: Application of the Americans with Disabilities Act to the Internet and Worldwide Web (July 10, 2003), (citation omitted), *available at* http://www.ncd.gov/publications/2003/July102003 (last visited Dec. 5, 2013) (noting that "[i]n determining the effectiveness of communication strategies and the adequacy of the "auxiliary aids and services" used to do the communicating, the OCR decisions set forth a three-prong test: accuracy, timeliness and appropriateness.").

From a technological standpoint, accessible web design is a more effective and efficient way of ensuring access than other auxiliary aids. Accessible web design reduces or eliminates the need for translation into Braille, thereby avoiding the introduction of inaccuracies. In addition, it enables the "timeliness of delivery" requirement to be satisfied in cost-effective and technologically efficient ways that do not require entities to engage in case-by-case accommodations for individuals needing accessibility. *But see* Private Internet Site Hearing, *supra*, at 114 (statement of Walter Olson, Fellow at the Manhattan Institute) (discussing "the ADA's application [to the Internet] as a serious threat to the freedom, spontaneity and continued growth of the Web"). Accessible web design further allows communication to take place in a manner and medium appropriate for all individuals without case-by-case judgments of the significance of the message and the abilities of the individual.

Still, courts have been hesitant to require website modifications that might "jeopardize the overall viability" or solvency of public accommodations. Emery v. Caravan of Dreams, Inc., 879 F. Supp. 640, 643 (N.D. Tex. 1995) (citing N.M. Ass'n for Retarded Citizens v. New Mexico, 678 F.2d 847 (10th Cir. 1982)). However, this threat appears exaggerated because the Title III effective communication requirement does not require a public accommodation to undertake an undue burden. *See* 28 C.F.R. § 36.303(c) (2012) (providing that a public accommodation must "furnish appropriate auxiliary aids and services where necessary to ensure effective communication").

As an alternative to providing accessibility through the Internet, Title III entities may offer their services in other effective formats. A public accommodation may choose to make its services available through a telephone help-line or offer print catalogues in Braille format. The help-line – which Title III would require to be staffed in a fashion equal to the services provided to customers who do not have disabilities via their website (e.g., presumably 24 hours a day) – would be costly relative to website access. Likewise, producing an updated print catalogue in Braille is costly relative to placing the information online in a format accessible to screen readers and refreshable Braille.

Notes & Questions

1. Eleanor, an administrative assistant with an insurance company, seeks job advancement in her company. She would like to develop auditing, business writing, and client interviewing skills to be eligible for a claims adjuster position. Eleanor has limited vision and cannot differentiate faces and words, though she is very successful at her job using screen reader software, a headset, and a standard keyboard.

Stellar Learning, Inc. provides online distance courses that can meet Eleanor's skill advancement needs. Stellar engages in substantial interstate commerce. Stellar's web based courses are self-paced and require, in part, extensive reading of online material and taking online tests. Stellar staff support is available via email and instant messaging.

What obligations does Stellar have for providing Eleanor with effective online communications and full and equal enjoyment of its services? *See* Myhill, et al., Distance Education Initiatives, *supra*, at 27-28.

C. *First Amendment Issues*

It is likely that the application of Title III to private Internet sites and services does not violate the First Amendment, which guarantees private parties the right to engage in expressive activities without governmental interference. Title III does not require a covered entity to change the subject matter or content of websites and services, but only to address the manner by which information is presented. *See* Paul Taylor, The Americans with Disabilities Act and the Internet, 7 B.U. J. Sci. & Tech. L. 26, 45 (2001) (stating that requiring websites to "mirror" content in an accessible form is not "forced speech").

Furthermore, Title III does not target speech or any group of speakers, but applies equally to all entities covered by the law. Private Internet Site Hearing, *supra*, at 121-22 (statement of Charles J. Cooper) (arguing that the "fact that the cost of compliance with a statute would divert some of an organization's funds away from its speech activities [or toward accessibility requirements] does not implicate the first amendment"). However, recent commenters have expressed concern that applying Title III to the Internet could chill free speech and must take care not to. Michael P. Anderson, Ensuring Equal Access to the Internet for the Elderly: The Need to Amend Title III of the ADA, 19 Elder L.J. 159, 182 (2011); *see also*, Abrar & Dingle, *supra*, at 168 (arguing that Title III "[l]egislation that is closely tailored to increasing Internet accessibility . . . and that does not risk chilling significant amounts of Internet content is less likely to trigger First Amendment concerns").

Given Title III's undue hardship defense, accessibility is unlikely to impose conditions that stifle speech. Rather, information technology has the potential to transform the limitations of print media by enabling the message to be communicated in multiple modes effectively and in ways that separate style from content.

Nonetheless, responding to a lawsuit brought by the Greater Los Angeles Council on Deafness alleging Cable News Network (CNN) violated the civil rights of deaf Californians by failing to provide close captions for its online news videos, CNN argued being required to caption these videos interferes with its rights to free speech. Brief for Defendant-Appellant, Greater Los Angeles Agency of Deafness, Inc. v. Cable News Network, Inc. (9th Cir. Sept. 12, 2012), *available at* http://www.courthousenews.com/2013/03/12/cnnbrief.pdf.

§ 33.5 Applications Of Section 504 Of The Rehabilitation Act

In addition to the ADA, Section 504 of the Rehabilitation Act prohibits disability discrimination by state and private entities receiving federal funding. Section 504 is applicable to title II institutions of higher education for their receipt of Federal student aide and research grants. Miller v. Abilene Christian Univ. of Dallas, 517 F.Supp. 437, 439-40 (D.C. Tex. 1981); Tyndall v. Nat'l Educ. Ctrs., Inc., 31 F.3d 209 (4th Cir. 1994). Likewise, § 504 is applicable to the programs and services of public schools as a recipient of Federal Individuals with Disabilities Education Act (IDEA) funds. Sandison v. Michigan High School Athletic Association, Inc., 863 F. Supp. 483, 487 (D. Mich. 1994), rev'd in part, appeal dismissed in part, 64 F.3d 1026 (1995). In public schools, for instance, students with disabilities are entitled to services that are equal to and as effective as those provided for other students. 34 C.F.R. § 104.4(b)(ii)-(iv) (2012). When Internet access is required for successful completion of homework assignments or a program is only available via the Web (e.g., a distance-learning course), inaccessible technologies that prevent access by students with disabilities may violate Section 504. Myhill, et al., Distance Education Initiatives, *supra*, at 15, 26-27.

In contrast with a Title II claim that technology is inaccessible, the § 504 claim may permit a private lawsuit without having to exhaust administrative remedies. *See* Freed v. Consolidated Rail Corp., 201 F.3d 188, 192-93 (3d Cir. 2000) ("plaintiffs suing private recipients of federal funds under section 504 do not need to exhaust"); Gary B. v. Cronin, 542 F.Supp. 102, 114-15 (N.D. Ill. 1980) (holding exhaustion is not required of plaintiff suing public school under 504 when "regulations do not provide [a] meaningful enforcement mechanism"). For allegations of discrimination under § 504 and 508, the Department of Justices "may seek individual relief for the victim(s), in addition to changes in the policies and procedures of the law enforcement agency." U.S. Dep't of Justice,

Addressing Police Misconduct, *available at* http://www.justice.gov/crt/about/cor/Pubs/polmis.pdf (last visited Oct. 25, 2012).

Notes & Questions

1. Raymond, who is deaf, uses American Sign Language (ASL) for daily communications. The quality and clarity of his speech is notably lacking. Raymond is a qualified individual with a disability and meets the essential eligibility requirements for the library sciences program at City College. The college receives federal funding. As Raymond works full-time, he will take the College's online courses towards the library science degree from home in the evenings and on weekends. However, each of Raymond's classes requires one meeting per week via web conference, where the students can ask questions and discuss the course material with the instructor. This also provides students an important opportunity to meet and form study groups.

2. What obligation does City College have to ensure its web conference class meetings provide Raymond with communications that are as effective for him as for his classmates? *See* Myhill, et al., Developing Accessible Cyberinfrastructure, *supra*, at 26-27.

3. For a discussion of the legal obligations of state and local education agencies providing online distance learning for children receiving special education services, *see* Part 6, § 23.3. For further discussion of the application of § 504 to technology and information technology, *see generally* Myhill, et al., Developing Accessible Cyber-infrastructure, *supra*.

§ 33.6 Applications Of Section 508 Of The Rehabilitation Act

The implementation of Section 508 of the Rehabilitation Act was designed to spur innovation throughout the e-commerce industry. Enacted as part of the Workforce Investment Act of 1998 (WIA), Pub. L. No. 105-220, 112 Stat. 936 (1998), Section 508 requires that electronic and information technology (EIT) purchased by the federal government, such as federal websites, telecommunications, software, and information kiosks, be usable by persons with disabilities. 29 U.S.C. § 794(a)(1) (2006). Federal agencies may not purchase, maintain, or use EIT that is not accessible to persons with disabilities, unless accessibility poses an undue burden.

The Architectural and Transportation Barriers Compliance Board developed the Electronic and Information Technology Accessibility Standards (EITAS), finalized on December 21, 2000, which detail the requirements for federal entities. Architectural and Transp. Barriers

Compliance Bd., Electronic and Information Technology Accessibility Standards, 36 C.F.R. pt. 1194 (2012), http://www.access-board.gov/ sec508/standards.htm (last visited Oct. 26, 2012). The EITAS provides accessibility guidelines for federal agencies in areas related to hardware and software products, technical criteria and performance-based requirements, web-based information and applications, telecommunications, video and multi-media, and compatibility with the adaptive equipment used by persons with disabilities for information and communication access. *Id.* To keep pace with technological advances, the Access Board is required to periodically update the EITAS. 29 U.S.C. § 794d(a)(2)(B) (2006).

Section 508 does not require private companies that market technologies to the federal government to modify the EIT products used by company employees, or to make their Internet sites accessible to people with disabilities. Peter Blanck, Flattening the (Inaccessible) Cyberworld for People with Disabilities, 20 Assistive Technology: The Official Journal of RESNA 50, 51 (2008).

Although the Section 508 standards do not apply specifically to the states' use and procurement of technology, most states are implementing policies, and in some cases enacting statutes, imposing accessibility standards, in part to comply with their obligations under ADA Title II. Myhill et al., Distance Education Initiatives, *supra*, at 16. These laws frequently parallel Section 508 with regard to state governmental services, purchase of IT products, website design, and hardware. In addition, the U.S. Department of Education has interpreted Section 508 to apply to states that receive federal funds under the Assistive Technology Act of 1998. Assistive Technology Act of 1998, Pub. L. No. 105-394, 112 Stat. 3627 (codified in scattered sections of Titles 15 and 29 U.S.C.); Constance S. Hawke & Anne L. Jannarone, Emerging Issues of Web Accessibility: Implications for Higher Education, 160 Educ. L. Rep. 715, 719 (2002).

The enforcement provisions of § 508 permit any person with a disability to file a complaint for injunctive relief with the applicable Federal department (or agency) alleging a violation of § 508 in an ICT product or service. Myhill, Achieving an Accessible eSociety, supra, at 117 (discussing remedies for violations of federal ICT accessibility requirements. The department receiving the complaint applies its internal complaint procedures used for resolving § 504 allegations of discrimination. 29 U.S.C. § 794d(f)(1)-(3) (2006)); U.S. Dep't of Justice, Administrative Complaints (June 14, 2004), http://www.usdoj.gov/crt/ 508/report2/complaints.htm (last visited June 6, 2012). Injunctive relief may include removal of a barrier to using technology, or providing an accommodation or assistive technology device to permit the employee equal use of the tool.

Additionally, the aggrieved party has a private right of action against the agency. M. Christine Fotopulos, Civil Rights Across Borders: Extraterritorial Application of Information Technology Requirements Under Section 508 of the Rehabilitation Act, 36 Pub. Contract L. J. 95, 113-14 (2006) (citing 29 U.S.C. § 794d(f)). In *Pantazes v. Jackson*, 366 F.Supp.2d 57 (D.D.C. 2005), a federal employee with a vision impairment and diminished short-term memory sued his employer, the U.S. Department of Housing and Urban Development (HUD), alleging in part the department failed to provide a reasonable accommodation and accessible technology. The federal district court found that a jury could conclude the software magnifying tool HUD provided as an accommodation did not satisfy its duty to provide a reasonable accommodation. The employee was unable to view the text of an entire screen using the magnification program provided, "significantly imped[ing] his ability to perform essential work tasks," because unlike a comparable product "Zoomtext," the one provided increased text-size in inefficient increments. *Id.* at 69.

Since 2004, federal website accessibility has continued to improve. Section 53.1 of the Office of Management and Budget's 2006 OMB Circular No. A-11, addressing "Information Technology and E-Government" explains to federal agencies they must report to OMB, in part, how their IT spending "supports agency compliance with the requirements of Section 508 . . . and Section 504 of the Rehabilitation Act of 1973 (Reasonable Accommodation)." U.S. Office of Mgmt. & Budget, OMB Circular No. A-11, at § 53, p. 2 (June 2006), *available at* http://www.whitehouse.gov/omb/circulars/a11/current_year/s53.pdf (last visited June 6, 2012). Critics of Section 508, however, suggest that the implementing regulations "are fantastically complex," and that in avoiding a divisive debate, Congress failed to decide whether the statute would have an extra-remedial reach and upon whom liability, responsibility, and costs would fall. Christopher R. Yukins, Making Federal Information Technology Accessible: A Case Study in Social Policy and Procurement, 33 Pub. Cont. L.J. 667, 669-70 (2004).

On September 12, 2012, the Justice Department released a report regarding accessibility of governmental data. U.S. Dep't of Justice. Justice Department Releases a Report on Accessibility of Federal Government Electronic and Information Technology, http://www.justice.gov/opa/pr/2012/September/12-crt-1103.html (2012). This report discusses Section 508 of the Rehabilitation Act and a study on the implementation of the EIT accessibility requirements by federal agencies. *Id.* While the study found that "most agency components have general Section 508 policies (over 50 percent)," the report recommends that federal agencies "establish more Section 508 programs, provide more Section 508 training to personnel, . . . establish specific Section 508 complaint processes, . . . and improve inter-agency coordination on Section 508 compliance." *Id.*

Other shifts in law and policy benefit technology innovation and induce market activity for accessible Internet sites, goods, and services. Heidi M. Berven & Peter Blanck, The Economics of the Americans with Disabilities Act Part II – Patents and Innovations in Assistive Technology, 12 Notre Dame J.L. Ethics & Pub. Pol'y 9, 18-19 (1998) (hereinafter "Berven & Blanck, Economics of the ADA").

Review of economic activity in the assistive technology market illustrates that laws like the ADA and Section 508 foster technological innovation and economic activity in the Internet-based service industry in ways unanticipated at the time these laws were passed. *See generally* Heidi M. Berven & Peter Blanck, The Economics of the Americans with Disabilities Act Part II – Patents and Innovations in Assistive Technology, 12 Notre Dame J.L. Ethics & Pub. Pol'y 9 (1998) (hereinafter "Berven & Blanck, Economics of the ADA"); Heidi M. Berven & Peter Blanck, Assistive Technology Patenting Trends and the Americans with Disabilities Act, 17 Behav. Sci. & L. 47 (1999) (hereinafter "Berven & Blanck, AT Patenting Trends") (discussing this line of research). This "push-pull" of disability policy is fostering research initiatives of individual and corporate inventors. The regulatory "push," introduced by the ADA and furthered by Section 508, expanded the market for accessible technology to include a range of consumer groups, including persons with disabilities; the elderly; employers; and public, municipal, and governmental entities.

Financial incentives and investment (the "pull") provide research and development opportunities to Internet inventors and e-commerce companies. *See* Leonard A. Sandler & Peter Blanck, The Quest to Make Accessibility a Corporate Article of Faith at Microsoft: Case Study of Corporate Culture and Human Resource Dimensions, 23 Behav. Sci. & L. 39 (2005) (examining the relation among corporate culture, technological innovation, and disability).

These incentives are important in light of studies showing that web accessibility solutions are inexpensive and reflect effective web design strategies. *See* Private Internet Site Hearing, *supra*, at 48-50 (statement of Judy Brewer, Dir. of Web Accessibility Initiative International Program Office, World Wide Web Consortium (W3C)) (discussing technological aspects of accessible web design). In addition, a tax credit is available to small businesses to offset expenses in complying with the ADA, such as website accessibility improvements. Steven Mendelsohn et al., Tax Subsidization of Personal Assistance Services, Disability & Health J., 5, 75, 79 (2012).

§ 33.7 Twenty-First Century Communications And Video Accessibility Act Of 2010

The Twenty-First Century Communications and Video Accessibility Act of 2010 (CVAA) mandated accessibility for a number of key communications technology issues. The CVAA requires customer premises equipment to ensure there is an internal means for effective use with hearing aids that are compatible with telephones. 47 USC § 610(b)(1) (West 20112). Customer premises equipment are those "equipment employed on the premises of a person (other than a carrier) to originate, route, or terminate telecommunications," § 153(16), and include, in part: essential telephones, all telephones made in the United States for domestic use, and customer premises equipment used with advanced communications services and designed for 2-way voice communication in a manner that is functionally equivalent to using a telephone. § 610(b)(1)(B)-(C).

The CVAA requires the FCC to implement a National Deaf-Blind Equipment Distribution Program (NDBED) that will be responsible for distributing "specialized customer premises equipment" designed to be accessible by low-income persons who are deaf-blind, including telecommunications, Internet, interexchange, advanced telecommunications and information services. § 620(a). Beginning in October 2011, Voice-Over I.P. or VoIP service providers, who offer the sending and receiving of calls over high speed internet, were required to "participate in and contribute to the Telecommunications Relay Services Fund . . . ." § 616. The CVAA established the Emergency Access Advisory Committee to ensure individuals with disabilities can rely on real-time text communication to access internet protocol (IP) enabled emergency services. § 615c(a).

Manufacturers and providers of mobile phones must ensure that internet browsers functions "are accessible to and usable by individuals who are blind or have a visual impairment . . . ." § 619(a). They may not require the consumer to use assistive devices in order to have accessibility. § 619(b)(1)-(2). Manufacturer and providers are not responsible for the accessibility of Internet content, applications, or services provided by third parties. § 619(a)(2). Manufacturers of "advanced communications services" (ACS) equipment and ACS providers also must ensure that their equipment, services and software operating in interstate commerce is "accessible to and usable by individuals with disabilities." § 617(a)(1) & (b)(1). ACS are defined to include: (1) interconnected VoIP service, (2) non-interconnected VoIP service, (3) electronic messaging service, and (4) interoperable video conferencing service. § 153(1).

The CVAA requires that persons alleging a violation of the Act file a complaint with the FCC, which in turn obligates the Commission to investigate, § 618(a)(3)(A) & (a)(1), and issue an order determining whether a violation has occurred within 180 days. § 618(a)(3)(B). The party who is alleged to have violated the CVAA is entitled a reasonable opportunity to respond to the complaint before the order and decision are finalized. § 618(a)(4). When a violation is found, the Commission is authorized to direct the manufacturer or provider to comply "within a reasonable time established by the Commission in its order." § 618(a)(3)(B)(i).

The Commission adopted rules to implement these provisions that took effect June 24, 2013. Accessibility Requirements for Internet Browsers, 78 Fed. Reg. 30,226-01, 31,226 (May 22, 2013). The central feature of these rules is to specify "[o]bligations with respect to internet browsers built into mobile phones." 78 Fed. Reg. 31,226 (to be codified at 47 C.F.R. § 1461). Manufacturers of such phones, as well as providers of mobile services that arrange for the inclusion of an internet browser in the telephones that the provider sells, "shall ensure that the functions of the included browser (including the ability to launch the browser) are accessible to and usable by individuals who are blind or have a visual impairment, unless doing so is not achievable. . . ." 78 Fed. Reg. 31,226 (to be codified at 47 C.F.R. § 1461(a)). Manufacturers and providers can satisfy these requirements by ensuring browsers are "accessible to and usable by individuals with disabilities without the use of third party applications, peripheral devices, software, hardware, or customer premises equipment" or by using such third party software and hardware "that is available to the consumer at nominal cost and that individuals with disabilities can access." 78 Fed. Reg. 31,226 (to be codified at 47 C.F.R. § 1461(b)(1)-(2)).

§ 33.8   Other Policy Issues

Prior to the CVAAA, the government helped provide the catalyst for change.   For instance, the NFB and the Connecticut Attorney General's office reached an agreement with HDVest, Intuit, H & R Block, and Gilman and Ciocia to provide accessible on-line tax filing services. Press Release, Conn. Attorney General's Office, National Federation of Blind Applaud On-Line Tax Filing Services for Agreeing to Make Sites Blind-Accessible for 2000 Tax Season (Apr. 17, 2000), http://lists. w3.org/Archives/Public/w3c-wai-ig/2000AprJun/0194.html (last visited June 6, 2012).   The Internal Revenue Service had listed these companies on its site as partners for e-filing, but users with screen readers could not file returns on those sites. *Id.; see supra* § 33.2, n.1 (describing screen readers). Here, the accessibility laws helped promote innovative solutions.

Furthermore, President Bush signed the Assistive Technology Act of 2004 into law on Oct. 26, 2004. Joy Relton, The Assistive Technology Act of 2004, Access World, 6(1), http://www.afb.org/afbpress/pub.asp? DocID=aw060109 (last visited June 12, 2012). The Act was designed to extend the AT Act of 1998 and enhance the availability of, and access to, necessary AT for persons with disabilities for greater independence at school, work, and in the home. *Id.*; Assistive Technology Act of 2004, Pub. L. No. 108-364, 118 Stat. 1707 (codified as amended at 29 U.S.C.A. § 3001 (West 2004), § 3002 (West 2008), §§ 3003-3004 (West 2004), § 3005 (West 2007), §§ 3006-3007 (West 2004)). For instance, the Act requires states to use the majority of grant funds on direct service and aid programs, such as AT device reutilization programs, alternative financing programs, device loan programs, and AT demonstration programs. *Id.* § 3003(e)(2).

911

Key provisions of the Act include:

- Strengthening existing successful state AT programs.

- Authorizing additional financial resources.

- Making certain "that technology will be available where people need it."

- Requiring that states "focus on two populations: students with disabilities receiving transition services and adults with disabilities maintaining or transitioning to community living. This aligns the Act with recent federal priorities, including the Individuals with Disabilities Education Act and the Americans with Disabilities integration mandate in the *Olmstead* decision."

- Improving public Internet sites, technical assistance, and data collection.

Nat'l Conference of State Legislatures: Ass'n of Assistive Tech. Act Programs, Summary of Assistive Technology Act of 1998, As Amended Public Law 108-364, http://www.ataporg.org/summaryact.html (last visited Nov. 10, 2013).

However, emerging technological trends pose significant barriers to people with disabilities. Smaller and smaller devices pose barriers for people with vision and manual dexterity disabilities; more complex devices make access difficult for people with intellectual disabilities; digital controls (such as touch screens) create barriers for people with vision disabilities; digital security mechanisms and digital rights management arrangements limit access for people who use assistive technology (such as screen readers); increasing use of inaccessible automated systems and the corresponding decrease in staff assistance make inaccessibility an absolute barrier. NCD, Over the Horizon, *supra*, at 21-31.

The fast pace of technological advances threatens to outstrip the ability of assistive technology to keep pace and has exceeded the progress of disability law and policy. *Id.* The drafters of the ADA in 1990 focused on the existing technologies (e.g., TTYs), rather than on the underlying functions, and did not foresee the development of the new technologies (e.g., videophones and instant messaging) that threaten to make them obsolete. *Id.*

It is essential to analyze the relation among Internet technologies and services and federal and state disability policies. Nat'l Council on Disability, When the Americans with Disabilities Act Goes Online: Application of the ADA to the Internet and the Worldwide Web (July 10, 2003), *available at* http://www.ncd.gov/rawmedia_repository/960de0db_0548_4c4c_b000_6f1eabb0f84a?document.pdf (last visited June 6, 2012). Examination of the application of disability statutes to Internet services and sites is needed, not only for people with disabilities, but for all underrepresented individuals in society – the poor and isolated, and the vulnerable. *See* Paul M.A. Baker et al., The Promise of Municipal WiFi and Failed Policies of Inclusion: The Disability Divide, 14 Info. Polity (forthcoming 2009) (analyzing the "disability divide" for persons with disabilities and the greater disparity for those living in remote locations).

§ 33.9 Commentary / Web Equality

Professor Peter Blanck analyzes whether there is a right to web equality for people with disabilities in his forthcoming book, eQuality: Web Rights, Human Flourishing and Persons with Cognitive Disabilities (forthcoming 2014).

> If there is a "right" to the full and equal enjoyment of online information, what is it? How may it be used by people with visual, hearing and cognitive disabilities? Against what standards is such a right to web content to be measured? And, if a right to the Internet's World Wide Web ("web") may be realized, how may it further economic, civic and social participation of people with disabilities, and at the same time be feasible to implement by online service providers and by their content developers and designers?

> Online service providers are those public and private enterprises that use software systems to provide web content, for instance, to offer governmental amenities, commercial services and goods, and social media, entertainment, and gaming platforms. But more broadly, today the web is the principal way to spur collective action in democracy and to foster the participatory rights of people with cognitive and other disabilities.

> The accessibility and usability of web content by people with disabilities has been examined in groundbreaking U.S. legal cases, some of which have been discussed, such as NFB v. Target, supra, and elsewhere NAD v. Netflix, 869 F.Supp.2d 196 (D. Mass., 2012). In *Netflix*, for the first time a U.S. federal court interpreted title III to cover exclusively online commercial establishments (in this case the right under ADA title III to web captioning). These cases established the basic right for persons with visual and hearing impairments to the full and equal enjoyment of web content under the ADA.

> Of course, the web and its interactive and responsive design is evolving at a fast pace. The legal right to the web for people with disabilities must be sensitive to the dynamic nature of the web, its design and development, its software and hardware infrastructures and product life cycles, and all of this in interaction with human development and

across context. Activities at the forefront of these developments include those involving the Human Computer Interface (HCI) and Artificial Intelligence (AI), infrastructure design, development, and distribution, and computer coding and markup languages.

eQuality examines the extent to which the right to equal access to web content may be grounded in U.S. and other civil rights laws. This examination necessarily leads to questions such as the nature of "web content" and who controls it? To be able to fully and freely use web content within reasonable bounds is to participate in society. It is not to be denied this right by societal barriers on the basis of disability. This may require the opportunity for appropriate content adjustments to promote simplicity and enhance its ease of use. It also may require the reasonable opportunity to be presented with web content that is usable with assistive technologies (such as screen reader software), regardless of disability. The measure of the right is comparable enjoyment of all that the web has to offer, and which online service providers have chosen to offer to the public. This principle is as appropriate in regard to access to online information for blind individuals who use screen readers to translate visual information as it is for deaf individuals who use caption text to convert audio information. For individuals with cognitive disabilities – intellectual and developmental disabilities, autism, or with traumatic or acquired brain injuries – it is similarly appropriate to comprehend web content.

The pursuit of the right to the web is crucial in the age of global and ubiquitous connectivity. At its best, the right to the web fosters self-determination and the choice to be included meaningfully in society, to be heard and belong, and to participate in one's community. Never before in modern history has the civil rights of people with disabilities aligned so well with fast-moving developments in online technology. The web has opened up unprecedented opportunities for active participation in democratic society; indeed, it has changed the basic ways in which we interact as humans and with machines.

The ADA is helping to ensure that the physical and online worlds are inclusive of people with disabilities and their families. Building on the efforts of many others and prior case law, Professor Blanck expresses the right to the web as:

Full and equal enjoyment of the web under the ADA is to have the meaningful and reasonably objective opportunity to enjoy – access and use – web content, and to not be excluded from that prospect on the basis of disability, either by individuals or through the design of web technology.

This means comparable opportunity among persons with and without disabilities to use the web, and in ways that are reasonable under the particular circumstances. *See, e.g.,* Wash. State Communication Access Project v. Regal Cinemas, 293 P.3d 413, 422 (Wash Ct. App., Jan. 28, 2013) ("question for places of public accommodation is not whether the steps they are required to take for their disabled patrons are different from those taken for the non-disabled. Instead, . . . it is whether those steps create a comparable opportunity, reasonable under the circumstances, between the disabled and others. A place of public accommodation is not required to provide extra services to persons with disabilities, but it may not deny full access to services already provided."). The right to equal and inclusive web enjoyment, thus, is full access to and use of the content offered to the public by ADA covered entities (under titles I, II and III). But questions remain to be decided such as: is the web to be treated similar to a physical "place" and thereby covered by ADA title III? How is equivalent web access and use defined for people across the spectrum of disabilities, such as those with cognitive and print-related disabilities, and across different websites and within the pages and services of those websites?

Other issues to consider include: How will the U.S. Department of Justice (DOJ) proposed ADA title III regulations for nondiscrimination in web use apply to persons with different disabilities? The DOJ is charged by Congress to enforce ADA title III and to issue guidance and regulations regarding its accessibility provisions. 42 U.S.C. § 12186(b). What will be the impact of the Web Accessibility Initiative's (WAI) Web Content Accessibility Guidelines (WCAG 2.0) for users with different disabilities, which was developed for web browsers? Is a comparable standard possible for mobile devices, which are constantly changing? How do existing web technical standards and performance criteria further equal online enjoyment for persons with disabilities?

Finally, given its global nature, may there found be a universal right to the web, for instance, as suggested by the

United Nations Convention on the Rights of Persons with Disabilities? Such a right may be embedded in the more general right to full and equal inclusion and participation in society. U.S. courts and the courts of other countries have yet to address the boundaries of this right. However, the right to the web may come to mean that those individuals who choose to engage with it have the prospect for reasonably equivalent and objective comparable use of its content, as do others without disabilities in the same situation.

Excerpt from Peter Blanck, eQuality, *supra.*

The title of Professor Blanck's book, "eQuality," thus has a double meaning. The first is of "equality" or justice under law, annotated as "3.0" for the third frontier of ADA title III advocacy. The second meaning is of "electronic quality," which is to signify the meaningful and objective opportunity for comparable use of web content by persons with disabilities. These dual meanings of eQuality ultimately are grounded in a civil and human rights perspective.

Chapter 34 DISABILITY AND TAX POLICY

§ 34.1 Overview: Tax Policy And Persons With Disabilities

The purposes of the ADA are intended to be supported by tax policy that provides incentives and financial subsidies for accessibility improvements. Just as nondiscrimination requirements support employment, social participation, and financial security of people with disabilities (and other groups), employment, social participation, and financial security reduce discrimination. Just as tax policy is used to influence behaviors in other arenas (e.g., tax deductions encourage home ownership), tax policy can influence both discriminatory behaviors among employers, businesses, and employment, and behaviors among people with disabilities.

American tax policy on an individual or corporate level ideally spurs accessibility, asset accumulation, economic independence and social empowerment. For many who advocate for inclusion of Americans with disabilities in the economic mainstream, however, the subject of tax policy is unfamiliar. Theodore P. Seto & Sande L. Buhai, Tax and Disability: Ability to Pay and the Taxation of Difference, 154 U. Pa. L. Rev. 1053, 1053 (2006); Steve Mendelsohn, Steven, Federal Income Tax Law: A Tool for Increasing Employment Opportunities for Americans with Disabilities, Report to the Presidential Task Force on Employment of Adults with Disabilities (2002) (on file with authors).

Tax policy can have effects on two levels – assisting individuals with disabilities, themselves, to escape or avoid poverty, and assisting businesses and employers to increase access and employment of people with disabilities. However, current American tax policy has not succeeded on either front. See Nat'l Council on Disability, The State of 21st Century Financial Incentives for Americans with Disabilities 105, 138-39 (Aug. 8, 2008) (hereinafter "NCD, 21st Century"), *available at* http://www. ncd.gov/rawmedia_repository/c6532f97_fbb7_42dd_a2e9_e361967b5c76?do cument.pdf (last visited June 6, 2012).

The following chapter examines the applicability of federal tax policies to the employment of persons with disabilities, for instance, through federal provisions such as the "disabled access credit" and the small business tax deduction for expenses incurred making workplaces accessible. As such, the tax laws provide opportunities for persons with disabilities to attain and retain employment, and thereby accumulate assets.

§ 34.2 Tax Policies And Economic Security For Americans With Disabilities

Individuals with disabilities face greater "gateway costs" of health care, personal assistance services (PAS), transportation, housing, education, and assistive technology than people without disabilities. *Id.* at 14. *See also* Mendelsohn, "Role of the Tax Code in Asset Development for People with Disabilities," 26 Disability Studies Quarterly 1 (Winter 2006), http://dsq-sds.org/article/view/653/830 (last visited June 7, 2012). People with disabilities, therefore, face larger obstacles to escaping or avoiding poverty. Current tax policy attempts to address some of these greater gateway costs, but, according to experts, is not sufficient to equalize opportunity for people with disabilities to engage in work.

The Internal Revenue Code provides the Impairment-Related Work Expense (IRWE) exemption for certain expenses incurred "in connection with the place of employment." Internal Revenue Code, 26 U.S.C. § 67 (2006). This provision exempts disability-related employment expenses from the general 2% floor for miscellaneous deductions, thus allowing deduction of disability-related employment expenses that constitute less than 2% of adjusted gross income. Seto and Buhai, *supra* at 1128-29. According to NCD, there are few interpretations of this provision, which is intended to cover costs of attendant services at work but which has been applied more broadly to cover any reasonable expense incurred for the purpose of employment. NCD, 21st Century, *supra* at 139-40. NCD recommends that the covered expenses should include home-based PAS when used to prepare for and go to work and add-on costs of accessible transportation attributable to disability. *Id.* at 140.

The effectiveness of the IRWE is limited by the fact that it is a deduction that can only be claimed if the individual with a disability itemizes their deductions. Because fewer than 40% of taxpayers itemize, and because disability-related expenses are likely to be greatest at the beginning of employment, when income is lowest, NCD recommends that the deduction be changed to an above-the-line deduction subject to carry-over beyond the first year. *Id.*

The Internal Revenue Code also provides a deduction for medical expenses, which covers many disability-related costs, including those related to employment. 26 U.S.C. § 213 (2006). Much assistive technology, service animals, and other costs qualify for this deduction. There is case law interpreting this deduction broadly to cover many items. However, the deduction is difficult to claim for several reasons. First, the deduction is available only if the taxpayer itemizes deductions. Second, the deduction is available only if the expenses exceed 7.5% of the taxpayer's adjusted gross income. NCD recommends that the deduction be converted to an above-the-line deduction and that the threshold requirement be waived for disability-related costs. NCD, 21st Century, *supra* at 140-41.

In a recent study, Mendelsohn, Myhill and Morris identified and examined eight federal tax provisions, including tax credits and waivers, itemized deductions, and excludable income that are available to subsidize the costs of PAS incurred by families and individuals with disabilities.

Steven Mendelsohn et al., Tax Subsidization of Personal Assistance Services, 5 Disability & Health J. 75, 77 (2012). PAS are particularly important to the disability community as they are central to supporting many individuals live in the communities of their choice rather than in institutions, but often are costly services. *Id.* at 75-76. PAS will become more important as the Baby Boom generation retires. *Id.* at 76. The tax provisions analyzed include the: household and dependent care credit, disabled access credit, waiver of premature withdrawal penalty, itemization of medical expenses and IRWE, and income exclusions for dependent care assistance, long-term care insurance, and flexible spending accounts. For a complete analysis, *see id.* at 77-84.

American tax policy seeks to encourage advancement of children through tax-advantaged savings mechanisms ("Section 529 savings accounts") for post-secondary education. 26 U.S.C.A. § 529 (West 2009). Children with disabilities who may not be able to pursue higher education, could benefit from these mechanisms and achieve a better economic future if Section 529 were modified to allow families of children with disabilities to save to start small businesses, purchase assistive technology or transportation, or pursue non-degree education and training. NCD, 21st Century Financial Incentives, *supra* at 141.

Some American tax policies actually encourage reliance on government benefits, rather than employment. Social Security Disability Insurance benefits are excluded from taxation only if 50% of the taxpayer's total income (including SSDI benefits) is less than $25,000 for an individual or $32,000 for a couple. IRS Publication 915, "Social Security and Equivalent Railroad Retirement Benefits" (2008), *available at* http://www.irs.gov/pub/irs-pdf/p915.pdf (last visited June 6, 2012).

Some tax policies do assist members of specific disability groups – mainly those who are blind. An additional standard deduction for blind taxpayers recognizes the larger gateway costs of individuals who are blind. However, they do not apply to members of other disability groups. Internal Revenue Code, 26 U.S.C.A. § 63(f) (West 2009).

Professors Seto and Buhai propose a greater restructuring of tax policy regarding individuals with disabilities, noting that, consistent with the "human variation" paradigm, "society should be structured affirmatively to take differences into account, with the goal of allowing equal participation by all, despite those differences, to the greatest extent possible." Seto & Buhai, *supra*, at 1057. In contrast, the widely accepted comprehensive tax base theory "ignores differences – other than differences in 'income' – in the ability of taxpayers to pay taxes." *Id.* For instance, "[a] tax system structured to take into account only the needs and abilities of the 'normal' majority is no more fair or just than a courthouse or other public facility built solely to accommodate the physical needs and abilities of that majority." *Id.* at 1138. They propose an "ability-to-pay theory." *Id.* at 1139-43.

§ 34.3 Tax Policies And The ADA

The ADA places a burden on private businesses to eliminate some of the societal barriers traditionally excluding people with disabilities. To offset some of that burden, the federal government has provided tax incentives for compliance with the law. When businesses make use of the tax advantages of ADA compliance, the benefits and burdens of compliance are shared between the business and the federal government.

However, studies indicate that the tax incentives are not fulfilling their potential. According to NCD, "[a] [General Accounting Office] study completed in late 2002 concludes that the three major Internal Revenue Code provisions aimed at enhancing the employment of persons with disabilities *cannot be demonstrated to have had significant effect.*" Nat'l Council on Disability, National Disability Policy: A Progress Report December 2001-December 2002, at 101 (July 26, 2003) (emphasis added) (citation omitted), *available at* http://www.ncd.gov/rawmedia_repository/ 2f391721_fcb8_4d5e_8358_351273fe6c6d?document.pdf (last visited June 6, 2012); U.S. General Accounting Office, "Business Tax Incentives: Incentives to Employ Workers with Disabilities Receive Limited Use and Have an Uncertain Impact GAO-03-39 (Dec. 2002), *available at* http://www.gao.gov/new.items/d0339.pdf (last visited June 6, 2012).

There are several federal tax provisions set out in the Internal Revenue Code available to business to foster ADA implementation and compliance. For a review, *see* Office of the Attorney Gen., Tax Incentives Packet on the Americans with Disabilities Act, http://www.ada.gov/ archive/taxpack.htm (Sept. 4, 1998) (last visited June 6, 2012) (hereinafter "Tax Incentives Packet"). *See* Internal Revenue Code, 26 U.S.C. §§ 44 & 190 (2006), 51 (2011). There is a "disabled access credit" available for small businesses, 26 U.S.C. § 44, a tax deduction available to any business when improving accessibility for customers and employees with disabilities, 26 U.S.C. § 190, and a tax credit available to any employer for a percentage of the first and second year wages of a new employee with a disability. 26 U.S.C. § 51. *See* Tax Incentives Packet, *supra*. In addition, there are state tax code provisions applicable to small businesses to foster the hiring and retention of employees with disabilities. *Id.*

A.   *Disabled Access Credit*

The Internal Revenue Code provides a small business disabled tax credit for architectural adaptations (but not new construction), equipment acquisitions such as assistive technology (AT), and services such as sign language interpreters. 26 U.S.C. § 44(c)(2) (2006). Small businesses, including service firms such as law firms and physician practice groups, may be eligible for the credit, for instance to defray the cost of accommodations for interpreters for client meetings. *See, e.g.*, Beth Gallie & Deirdre M. Smith, Representing Deaf Clients: What Every Lawyer Should Know, 15 Me. B.J. 128, 130 n.18 (Apr. 2000).

The tax credit is subtracted from tax liability after the calculation of taxes owed. Businesses with revenues of $1,000,000 or less or with fewer than 31 full-time workers may use the credit. 26 U.S.C. § 44(a). The tax credit may equal up to 50% of the eligible access expenditures in a year, to a maximum expenditure of $10,250. *Id.* There is no credit for the first $250 of expenditures; therefore, the maximum tax credit is $5,000 annually.

℘

HUBBARD v. COMMISSIONER

United States Tax Court, 2003
86 T.C.M. (CCH) 276

Memorandum Findings of Fact and Opinion

SWIFT, Judge:

Respondent determined a deficiency in petitioners' Federal income tax for 1997 in the amount of $5,814. * * * The issue for decision is whether the cost of certain equipment purchased by petitioner for use in his optometric practice qualifies under [26 U.S.C.] § 44 for the "disabled access" Federal income tax credit.

Findings of Fact

* * * At the time the petition was filed, petitioners resided in Reno, Nevada. * * * From 1977 through 2000, petitioner, was an optometrist and owned and operated his own optometric practice in Winnemucca, Nevada. During those 23 years, the only optometric practice located in a three-county area (namely, Humboldt County, Pershing County, and Lander County, Nevada), was petitioner's. The optometric practice located closest to petitioner's practice was in Elko, Nevada, approximately 120 miles from Winnemucca.

As an optometrist, petitioner diagnosed and treated certain eye diseases, tested vision problems, prescribed corrective lenses, and sold eyeglasses and contact lenses. Generally, prior to 1997, to test the vision of his patients and to prescribe corrective lenses, petitioner determined his patients' "refractive error" by performing subjective refractions using a manual refractor. To perform subjective refractions, petitioner would have his patients sit in an examination chair behind a manual refractor, view various charts through lenses in the manual refractor, and answer a series of questions that petitioner would ask them. Subjective refractions of patients would take approximately 5 to 10 minutes each.

On disabled patients, however, petitioner occasionally was not able to perform subjective refractions. For example, some mentally handicapped patients and hearing impaired patients were unable to understand and answer questions asked during subjective refractions, and some physically disabled patients could not be moved from their wheelchairs into petitioner's examination chair behind the manual refractor.

Although petitioner and hearing impaired patients could write notes to each other during subjective refractions, it was difficult for hearing impaired patients to look through the manual refractor while reading notes from and writing notes to petitioner, thereby affecting the accuracy of the subjective refractions.

Prior to 1997, as a result of the above difficulties in diagnosis, petitioner was not able to treat a number of disabled patients, and petitioner referred those disabled patients to other optometrists located in distant communities. In 1996, due to petitioner's inability to treat them, approximately 30 disabled patients were referred by petitioner to other optometrists.

In 1997, in order to increase petitioner's ability to treat disabled patients, petitioner purchased for $12,950 a Humphrey Instruments automatic refractor/keratometer (automatic refractor). Also in 1997, petitioner purchased for $4,495 a Rush Ophthalmics height-adjustable rotary instrument stand on which to place the automatic refractor. This rotary instrument stand made the automatic refractor accessible to wheelchair patients.

Using the automatic refractor and the rotary instrument stand together petitioner was able to perform "objective" refractions on all of his patients in order to test their vision and in order to prescribe corrective lenses without the patients having to be seated in an examination chair behind a manual refractor and without having to engage in a series of written questions and answers.

* * *

Using the automatic refractor, petitioner was able to test the vision of some disabled patients whom petitioner would not have been able to test using a manual refractor. In 1997, petitioner's optometric practice realized gross receipts of $586,649.

Petitioners timely filed their 1997 joint Federal income tax return, with a Form 8826, Disabled Access Credit, on which petitioners claimed under § 44 a disabled access tax credit in the amount of $5,000 relating to petitioner's costs of purchasing the automatic refractor and the rotary instrument stand. In a notice of deficiency, respondent disallowed petitioners' claimed $5,000 disabled access tax credit.

Opinion

The Americans with Disabilities Act of 1990 (ADA) * * * prohibits discrimination against disabled individuals in the full and equal enjoyment of goods, services, facilities, privileges, advantages, and accommodations by any "place of public accommodation." For purposes of ADA, professional offices of health care providers, such as petitioner's

922

optometric practice, are included within the definition of places of public accommodation. 42 U.S.C. § 12181(7)(F).

With regard particularly to disabled individuals, ADA regulations provide as follows:

> A health care provider may refer an individual with a disability to another [health care] provider, if that individual is seeking, or requires, treatment or services outside of the referring provider's area of specialization, and if the referring provider would make a similar referral for an individual without a disability who seeks or requires the same treatment or services. A physician who specializes in treating only a particular condition *cannot refuse to treat an individual with a disability* for that condition * * *. [28 C.F.R. § 36.302(b)(2) (2008); emphasis added.]

In order to comply with the above general ADA prohibition of discrimination against individuals with disabilities, places of public accommodation such as petitioner's optometric practice are required to make reasonable modifications to their facilities and procedures that are necessary in order to provide services to individuals with disabilities. 42 U.S.C. § 12182(b)(2)(A)(ii); 28 C.F.R. § 36.302(a). Places of public accommodation are required to remove any physical barriers including communication barriers that are structural in nature, where such removal is "readily achievable." 42 U.S.C. § 12182(b)(2)(A)(iv); 28 C.F.R. § 36.304(a). "Readily achievable" is defined by ADA as being "easily accomplishable and able to be carried out without much difficulty or expense." 42 U.S.C. § 12181(9).

Factors to be considered include the following: (1) The nature and cost of the action to be taken; (2) The financial resources of the place of public accommodation, and the effect of the action on its expenses and resources; and (3) The type of operations of the place of public accommodation, and the impact of the action on its operations. Id.

Cases discussing * * * 42 U.S.C. § 12182(b)(2)(A)(ii), make it clear that determining whether expenditures and modifications by service providers would be reasonable * * *

> * * * involves a fact-specific, case-by-case inquiry that considers, among other factors, the effectiveness of the modification in light of the nature of the disability in question and the cost to the organization that would implement it. [Citations omitted.]

Section 44(a) provides "eligible small businesses" with a Federal income tax credit equal to 50 percent of "eligible access expenditures" exceeding $250 and up to $10,250 (with a maximum credit of $5,000) which enable the businesses to comply with ADA. "Eligible small businesses" are defined as businesses with gross receipts less than $1 million or with less than 30 employees (and which elect to be treated as such by filing a Form 8826). § 44(b).

"Eligible access expenditures" are defined as amounts paid or incurred by eligible small businesses for the purpose of complying with ADA, including the following: (1) Expenditures to remove architectural, communication, physical, or transportation barriers preventing the business from being accessible to, or usable by, individuals with disabilities; and (2) expenditures to acquire or modify equipment for use by or to benefit individuals with disabilities. § 44(c)(2)(A), (D). Also, to qualify as eligible access expenditures the expenditures must be reasonable and necessary. § 44(c)(3).

* * *

In *Fan* [v. Commissioner, 117 T.C. 32 (T.C. 2001)], because, prior to purchasing the intraoral camera system, the dentist was already in compliance with ADA through the use of handwritten notes to communicate with hearing impaired patients and because the dentist had always been able to treat disabled patients, we disallowed the claimed disabled access credit. Id. at 37-39. We also noted that the intraoral camera system had a general applicability and usefulness to all of the dentist's patients. Id. at 34.

Relying on *Fan,* respondent argues that prior to purchasing the automatic refractor and the instrument stand at issue in this case petitioner already was in compliance with ADA and that because the automatic refractor and instrument stand had general applicability and usefulness in treating all of petitioner's patients, petitioner should not be entitled to the § 44 disabled access tax credit relating to the cost of purchasing the equipment. Respondent also alleges that the automatic refractor and the instrument stand did not represent reasonable and necessary expenses of petitioner's optometric practice.

Petitioner argues that because the automatic refractor and the instrument stand enabled him to provide vision testing to disabled patients for whom petitioner previously had not been able to provide treatment and whom petitioner previously had referred elsewhere, petitioner's purchase of the automatic refractor and the instrument stand enabled petitioner to comply with the requirements of ADA, and he should be entitled to the § 44 disabled access tax credit with respect to the total $17,445 cost of the equipment, subject to the annual credit limit of $5,000.

In distinction to the facts involved in *Fan v. Commissioner,* * * * prior to purchasing the automatic refractor and the instrument stand, petitioner herein was not able to provide vision testing services to some disabled patients. Petitioner's testimony was credible on this point. During 1997, petitioner's optometric practice was the only optometric practice located in a three-county area in Nevada.

The fact that the automatic refractor was also used by petitioner to treat nondisabled patients is not fatal to petitioner's entitlement to the disabled access tax credit. We find no exclusive use or benefit test in § 44(a). Certainly, a wheelchair ramp into a restaurant for disabled access will be used by nondisabled customers of the restaurant, and nothing in § 44 or the regulations would deprive the restaurant owner of the disabled access tax credit with regard thereto. See 28 C.F.R. § 36.304(b)(1) (2008).

We conclude that petitioner purchased the automatic refractor and the instrument stand in order to treat disabled patients and to comply with ADA's prohibition of discrimination against disabled individuals. We also conclude – in light of the size of petitioner's practice compared to the cost of the equipment, the benefit to his practice, and the benefit to the community – that petitioner's purchase of the automatic refractor and of the instrument stand was reasonable and necessary. Petitioner's costs of the equipment constitute eligible access expenditures. See § 44(c); 42 U.S.C. § 12182(a) and (b)(2)(A)(iii).

Petitioners are entitled to the claimed $5,000 § 44 disabled access tax credit. * * *

FAN v. COMMISSIONER

United States Tax Court (2001)
117 T.C. 32

Opinion by Judge DAWSON

Opinion of the Special Trial Judge by Judge CARLUZZO.

Opinion

DAWSON, Judge:

In 1995, petitioner purchased an intraoral camera system (the system) for use in his dental practice. The system has general applicability and usefulness to all dental patients. It reduces the time necessary for a dentist to explain diagnoses, "procedures" and recommended treatment with patients. Petitioner considered the system to be a more effective and efficient way to communicate with hearing-impaired patients. On their 1995 Federal income tax return, Petitioners claimed a disabled access credit for the cost of the system. * * * Respondent determined that the system was not an "eligible access expenditure" for purposes of [26 U.S.C.] § 44(c), I.R.C., and disallowed the credit.

* * *

This case was assigned to Special Trial Judge Lewis R. Carluzzo pursuant to § 7443A(b)(3) and Rules 180, 181, and 182 * * *. The Court

the use of a VCR and television set. None of his hearing-impaired patients complained to petitioner about this method of communication. Nevertheless, petitioner found communicating in this manner to be cumbersome and time consuming. According to petitioner, the use of handwritten notes generally added about 20 minutes to an examination. Furthermore, after each examination, the pens, pencils, and notepads had to be disinfected or disposed of due to health requirements. Petitioner also found use of the VCR and television to be inconvenient because the equipment had to be brought into and removed from the examination room during the examination.

Prior to purchasing the system, petitioner did not refuse treatment to a prospective patient because the patient had a hearing impairment. He did not purchase the system at the suggestion or recommendation of one of his hearing-impaired patients, and during the years in issue he did not limit the use of the system to his hearing-impaired patients. Nevertheless, when compared to handwritten notes, he considers the system to be a more effective and efficient way to communicate with his hearing-impaired patients. When used in the examination of a hearing-impaired patient, the system, in some instances, reduced the need for petitioner to communicate with the patient by handwritten notes. Petitioner further found that if he used the system during the examination of a hearing-impaired patient, the patient was more likely to understand and agree to any recommended treatment. According to promotional materials, "studies show case acceptance increases by approximately 30 percent with an intraoral camera system."

Petitioners filed a timely 1995 Federal income tax return. On a Form 8826, Disabled Access Credit, included with that return, they reported a $4,879 current year disabled access credit attributable to the purchase of the system. After taking into account applicable limitations, the current year disabled access credit resulted in a claimed general business credit of $2,969. * * * The balance of the 1995 credit ($1,910) was treated as a carryforward general business credit on a Form 3800, General Business Credit, included with petitioners' 1996 Federal income tax return. Taking into account applicable limitations, they claimed a general business credit of $1,114 for that year, all of which is attributable to the purchase of the system in 1995.

In the notice of deficiency, respondent disallowed the disabled access credit for 1995 and the associated carry-forward to 1996; instead respondent treated the entire cost of the intraoral camera system as a deductible business expense under section 179. According to the explanation contained in the notice of deficiency, the disabled access credits attributable to the system were disallowed because the system "does not permit patients to be treated who were excluded from services before the purchase of the camera."

Discussion

* * * The parties agree that petitioner qualifies as an "eligible small business" for the years in issue, § 44(b); their disagreement focuses on whether the cost of the system qualifies as an "eligible access expenditure," § 44(c).

To qualify as an eligible access expenditure within the meaning of section 44, the expenditure must be "paid or incurred by an eligible small business for the purpose of enabling such eligible small business to comply with applicable requirements under the Americans With Disabilities Act of 1990" (ADA). § 44(c)(1).

* * * Petitioner's dental office is a place of public accommodation within the meaning of the ADA. * * * Consequently, we focus our attention on Title III of the ADA. 42 U.S.C. §§ 12181-12189.

* * * Relevant for our purposes, Title III specifically defines discrimination to include a failure to take necessary steps to ensure that no individual with a disability is denied services because of the absence of auxiliary aids and services. 42 U.S.C. § 12182(b)(2)(A)(iii). The term "auxiliary aids and services" includes:

> (A) qualified interpreters or other effective methods of making aurally delivered materials available to individuals with hearing impairments;
> (B) qualified readers, taped texts, or other effective methods of making visually delivered materials available to individuals with visual impairments;
> (C) acquisition or modification of equipment or devices; and
> (D) other similar services and actions.

42 U.S.C. § 12102(1).

* * * The final regulations implementing the ADA include examples of auxiliary aids and services required to be furnished to ensure effective communication. 28 C.F.R. § 36.303(b). With respect to individuals with hearing impairments, the examples given include: Qualified interpreters, notetakers, computer-aided transcription services, written materials, telephone handset amplifiers, assistive listening devices, assistive listening systems, telephones compatible with hearing aids, closed caption decoders, open and closed captioning, telecommunications devices for deaf persons (TDD's), videotext displays, or other effective methods of making aurally delivered materials available to individuals with hearing impairments. 28 C.F.R. § 36.303(b)(1).

The ADA requires businesses to ensure effective communication through the use of auxiliary aids and services. Costs associated with complying with this requirement are "eligible access expenditures" for purposes of the disabled access credit. § 44(c)(2). Petitioner argues that the purchase of the system enables his business to meet this requirement with respect to hearing impaired individuals and, therefore, the cost of the system qualifies as an eligible access expenditure. For the following reasons, we disagree.

At the outset, we note that petitioner was already in compliance with the ADA at the time that he purchased the system. Petitioner did not discriminate against, or refuse to treat, hearing impaired individuals "on the basis of disability." 42 U.S.C. § 12182(a). Nor did he fail to take necessary steps to ensure that no individual with a disability is denied services because of the absence of auxiliary aids and services. See 42 U.S.C. § 12182(b)(2)(A)(iii). He effectively communicated with his hearing- impaired patients through the use of handwritten notes, which is an acceptable "auxiliary aid" or service under the ADA.

More importantly, the system is not a replacement for, or acceptable alternative to, handwritten notes for purposes of the § 44 credit. The system itself was not designed or marketed as a communication device for hearing impaired individuals, and petitioner did not limit the use of the system to his hearing-impaired patients. We accept his claim that, by permitting a patient to view a video image of a particular dental condition, the system might have allowed a patient to better understand the nature of his or her dental condition and the recommended treatment, but it does not eliminate the need for the dentist and the patient to communicate with each other. See 28 C.F.R. § 36.303, Appendix B (2008) (noting that communications involving areas such as health, legal matters, and finances may require the use of notes or interpreters, or an effective alternative such as the use of a computer terminal upon which the customer can exchange typewritten messages). As a result, we fail to see how the system constitutes an effective method "of making aurally delivered materials available to individuals with hearing impairments." 42 U.S.C. § 12102(1)(A). * * *

It is our view that petitioner did not purchase the system, in lieu of using handwritten notes, so as to be in compliance with the ADA. Section 44 was enacted as part of the Omnibus Budget Reconciliation Act of 1990, Pub. L. 101-508, § 11611(a), 104 Stat. 1388-501, and is intended to complement the ADA by providing "relief to small businesses making the accommodations required by the ADA." 136 Cong. Rec. S12852 (daily ed. Sept. 12, 1990) (statement by Senator Kohl). The legislative history indicates that the Congress was concerned that the requirements contained in the ADA may impose a severe financial burden on certain small businesses. See H. Conf. Rept. 101-964, at 1138-1140 (1990). To alleviate the burden, the Congress provided small businesses with a tax credit for a portion of the costs incurred in complying with the ADA. See id. If the expenditure was not made to enable compliance with the ADA, then the expenditure does not qualify for credit under § 44.

In this case, petitioner's acquisition of the system did not enable him to comply with the ADA – he was already in compliance with the ADA through the use of handwritten notes to communicate with his hearing-impaired patients. Furthermore, the system is not a replacement or substitute for the use of handwritten notes. It follows that cost of the system is not an eligible access expenditure within the meaning of § 44(c), and, consequently, the system does not qualify for the disabled access credit. Respondent's determination in this regard is therefore sustained.

To reflect the foregoing,

Decision will be entered for respondent.

Notes & Questions

1. Courts have applied the disabled access credit to be strictly a credit for expenses necessary for compliance with the ADA. In *Svoboda v. Commissioner*, No. 3176-04, 2006 WL 12952 (Tax Ct. Jan. 3, 2006), petitioner Svoboda provided customers telecommunications relay service (TRS) access in compliance with ADA Title IV, and subscribed to an additional service improving their compliance. The taxpayers claimed the disabled access credit but the IRS determined a corresponding deficiency in their federal income tax for 2001. The Tax Court held that the taxpayers' subscription to the alternative program did not enable them to comply with the ADA because they already were in compliance through their use of the TRS. Therefore, they were ineligible to take the disabled access credit. *See also* Galyen v. Commissioner, 2006 WL 416404 (Tax Ct. 2006). By not permitting credit for access expenditures that go beyond the minimum required for ADA compliance, has the court limited the effectiveness of the credit to incentivize accessibility? While the ADA in 1990 relied on telephone relay services as a means of providing communication access to people who are hearing impaired, communications technology has evolved to offer videophone, video relay services, and text communications, which are substantial improvements over the TTY. Would a small business that purchased equipment or services to permit access through these improved methods be entitled to the disabled access credit?

2. An in-depth discussion of the disabled access credit can be found in Anne M. Esteves & Beth S. Joseph, Public Accommodations Under The Americans With Disabilities Act Compliance and Litigation Manual, ch. 13, sect. 13.1 (2006).

B.   *Tax Deduction For Removal Of Architectural And Transportation Barriers*

A tax deduction can be used for architectural or transportation adaptations under the Internal Revenue Code. 26 U.S.C. § 190 (2006).

The tax deduction is subtracted from total income before taxes, to establish the taxable income rate. *Id.*

The tax deduction is a maximum of $15,000 per year. *Id.* § 190(c). Businesses of any size (including active owners of an apartment building) may use the deduction for the removal of architectural and transportation barriers. *Id.* § 190(b)(1). Small businesses may use the Section 190 tax deduction and the Section 44 disabled tax credit in combination. However, if a business spends more than can be claimed in a single year, it cannot carry the deduction over into subsequent years.

C.   *Work Opportunity Credit*

The Work Opportunity Credit provides businesses with an incentive to hire individuals from targeted groups with historically high unemployment rates. Individuals with disabilities qualify if they are referred by Vocational Rehabilitation, if they receive Social Security Insurance benefits, or if they are veterans with disabilities. The Small Business and Work Opportunity Tax Act of 2007, Pub. L. No. 110-28, 121 Stat. 190, enacted on May 25, 2007, extended the Work Opportunity Tax Credit, August 31, 2011. A business can claim the credit for 40 percent of the first $6,000 of first-year wages (or $2,400) of a new eligible employee if the employee works 400 or more hours. The business can claim 25% if the employee works 120-399 hours. For disabled veterans, the business can claim up to $4,800. U.S. Dep't of Labor/Employment & Training Admin., Work Opportunity Tax Credit, http://www.doleta.gov/business/Incentives/opptax/ (last updated Apr. 20, 2012) (last visited June 8, 2012).

Part 9

Introduction To Comparative And International Disability Rights Law
Analysis

Chapter 35 OVERVIEW
§ 35.1 Statistics On People With Disabilities
§ 35.2 Legal Approaches Toward Disability Issues
**Chapter 36 OTHER STATES' APPROACHES TO DISABILITY
RIGHTS**
§ 36.1 Welfare/Medical Model Versus Rights-Based Social Model
§ 36.2 States Following A Rights Model
    A. Canada
    B. South Africa
§ 36.3 States Following A Welfare/Medical Model: France
Chapter 37 INTERNATIONAL HUMAN RIGHTS LAW BASICS
Chapter 38 UNITED NATIONS
§ 38.1 United Nations Initiatives Prior To 2001
§ 38.2 Convention On The Rights Of Persons With Disabilities
    A. Background
    B. The Convention
    C. Impact

Chapter 35 OVERVIEW

It is not possible to look at disability rights through a parochial, United States periscope. Other states – as countries are referred to in international discourse – face the same issues and challenges to dealing with them that the United States faces. They have dealt in their own ways with those issues. Some, especially in Europe, have been dealing with them since before "disability rights" became a recognized branch of law. Many states have been developing legal regimes in parallel with the United States; many others are now beginning to address disability in their legal systems. Cultural and economic differences affect their responses.

What has opened the lens is potentially the most significant legal development in the disability rights arena in the last five years: the entry into force, on May 3, 2008, of the United Nations Convention on the Rights of Persons with Disabilities, http://www.un.org/disabilities/default.asp? id=259 (CRPD). We will discuss that treaty in detail. We begin, however, by setting the stage with some statistical data. We then move through alternative legal models used by other states. We next canvass international human rights law as a prelude to the CRPD.

There is another level of regulation of disability issues – between the level of individual states and the United Nations, regional groups of states can establish policies keyed to the abilities of states in the region to respond. By the 1990s, these regional initiatives – including the Organization of American States, European Union, and the African Union have been important forums to establish and vindicate disability rights. Only space prevents us from discussing them here. For excellent accounts, *see, e.g.,* Aspects of Disability Law in Africa (Pretoria University Press 2012); Lisa Waddington, Future Prospects for EU Equality Law. Lessons to be Learnt from the Proposed Equal Treatment Directive, 36 Euro. L. Rev. 163 (2011); Lisa Waddington, The European Union and the United Nations Convention on the Rights of Persons with Disabilities: A Story of Exclusive and Shared Competences, 18 Maastricht J. Euro. & Comp. L. 431 (2011).

Although states and international organizations have developed varying philosophies of human rights in general and disability rights in particular, the question at the end of the day is the effectiveness of the statutory or treaty scheme. Are more children with disabilities receiving a sound education? Are more adults with disabilities employed to their potentials? Is the infrastructure of society – concert halls, lawyers' offices, bistros – accessible to people with disabilities? Also, if the statutes or international agreements require expenditures, are those expenditures being made?

The efficacy questions should be at the heart of any discussion of disability rights. The legal instruments chosen are only part of the equation. The other is the abilities of various states to fulfill their obligations.

§ 35.1 Statistics On People With Disabilities

It is difficult to estimate the total number of people with disabilities throughout the world. The count depends on definitional issues, such as the meaning of disability. *E.g.,* International Disability Rights Monitor, Regional Report on Europe, Executive Summary x-xii (2007). *See generally*, UN, Washington Group on Disability Statistics (Mar. 5, 2013), http://unstats.un.org/unsd/methods/citygroup/washington. htm. Mitchell E. Loeb, et al., Approaching the Measurement of Disability Prevalence: The Case of Zambia, 2 Euro. J. Disability Research 32 (2008), *available at* siteresources.worldbank.org/DISABILITY/Resources/Data/ ApprchngMeasureZambia.pdf.[1]

---

[1] For data going back to the early 1990s and prior see UN, United Nations Disability Statistics Database [DISTAT], http://unstats.un.org/ unsd/demographic/sconcerns/disability/disab2.asp (last visited Nov. 26, 2013).

Cultural differences come into play in the definitional process. *See* Ann Elwan, Poverty and Disability – A Survey of the Literature No. 9932, at 9-10 (Soc. Protection Unit, World Bank Dec. 1999) (gender distinctions in some states may affect estimates of people with disabilities). Moreover, many states lack an ability to survey their populations, *id.* at iii-iv, and sampling techniques vary. Even in the United States, the 43 million estimate of the number of people with disabilities used in the ADA is subject to interpretation. But, with all those caveats, the estimates remain substantial.

In 1981, the World Health Organization stated that the percentage could not be estimated more accurately than 10%. World Health Org., Disability Prevention and Rehabilitation, Technical Report Series No. 668 (1981), cited in report by Leandro Despouy, Human Rights and Disabled Persons, Human Rights Series No. 6 (1988). A later UN study of 55 states found a range of 0.2% to 20.9%. Dep't of Int'l Econ. & Soc. Affairs, United Nations Disability Statistics Compendium, Statistics on Special Population Groups, Series Y, No. 4, 25-26, Figure II.1 (1990) [hereinafter "UN Compendium"]. Another UN agency has conservatively estimated that about five percent of the people in developing countries are moderately to severely disabled. Social Development Division, United Nations, Hidden Sisters: Women and Girls with Disabilities in the Asian and Pacific Region, UN Doc. ST/ESCAP/1548 (1995) [hereinafter "Hidden Sisters"] (citing Einer Helander, Prejudice and Dignity: An Introduction to Community-Based Rehabilitation (U.N. Dev. Programme Report 1992)).

The International Disability Rights Monitor (IDRM), using estimates from governmental and non-governmental sources, has reported rates among a group of European states ranging from 3.3% (Bulgaria) to 18.2% (UK). IDRM Europe Report, *supra*, Executive Summary xiii. It is likely that the measured rates in developing countries are higher than in developed countries – 10% to 25% of children under 15 are disabled in developing states versus 4% in Austria to 11% in Canada. Elwan, *supra*, at 8.

The 2011 World Report on Disability (conducted by the World Health Organization and the World Bank) estimated that more than a billion people live with some form of disability (about 15% of the world's population). World Health Organization & World Bank, Summary 2011 World Report on Disability 7 (2011) [hereinafter "2011 World Report"], *available at* http://whqlibdoc.who.int/hq/2011/WHO_NMH_VIP_11.01_eng.pdf. Looking at various surveys, the 2011 World Report finds that between 2.2% and 3.8% of the world's population have very significant disabilities. *Id.* at 8. The 2011 World Report also finds that the number of people with disabilities is growing, that that disability affects vulnerable populations. *Id.*

Disability has a significant impact on social and economic indicators, and particularly so in developing countries. There has been substantial concern about the adequacy of statistical measures linking disability with measures of economic or educational achievement. *E.g.*, Jeanine Breathwaite & Daniel Mott, Disability and Poverty: A Survey of World Bank Poverty Assessments and Implications (Feb. 2008), *available at* http://siteresources.worldbank.org/DISABILITY/Resources/280658-1172 608138489/WBPovertyAssessments.pdf. *See also* Global Partnership for Disability and Development (GPDD) (2009), http://www.gpdd-online.org/ (last visited Nov. 26, 2013), sponsored by the World Bank and hosted by the Burton Blatt Institute, which is a new initiative to accelerate inclusion of people with disabilities and their families into development policies and practices.

Nonetheless, existing evidence suggests that people with disabilities are severely disadvantaged relative to people without disabilities. The 2011 World Report finds that people with disabilities have experience poorer levels of health than the general population, that children with disabilities are less likely to start school than their peers without disabilities, and have lower rates of staying and being promoted in schools, are more likely to be unemployed and generally earn less even when employed, and experience higher rates of poverty. 2011 World Report at 10-11.

To look at state-level data of a few of these, people with disabilities receive less education than others.

- Argentina: In 2000, only 0.69% of children in school reported having a disability versus 10% of the population believed to have a disability. International Disability Rights Monitor, Report on the Americas 36 (2004) ("IDRM Americas Rep.").

- Bahrain: In the 1981 census, 27% of all persons aged ten and over were illiterate, but in the same age group of the disabled population, the proportion was 77%. UN Compendium, *supra*, at tbl.6.

- Canada: A 1983-84 survey showed that about 6% of the total population aged 15-24 had attended only eight years of schooling or less, while the proportion in the disabled group was 17%. *Id.*

- Hong Kong: In 1981, 2% of the general population of 15-24 year olds had received no formal schooling versus 25% of those with disabilities. *Id.*

- Vietnam: "[T]he enrollment rate of primary education is 91 per cent, and 61 per cent of children aged 6 to 15 years completed their primary education. However, a UNICEF survey in 1998 estimated that only 3-5 per cent of children with disabilities attended school in Viet Nam." Yutaka Takamine, Disability Issues in East Asia: Review and Ways Forward 22 (July 2003), *available at* http://siteresources.

worldbank.org/DISABILITY/Resources/Regions/East-Asia-
Pacific/DisIssuesTakamine.pdf

Likewise, people with disabilities participate in the economy far
less than people without disabilities.

- Argentina: In 2004, it was estimated that the unemployment
rate of people with disabilities 61%, approximately four times
that of people without disabilities. IDRM Americas Rep. at 40.

- Australia: A 1981 survey showed the proportion of disabled
people not in the labor force was around 60%, twice as high as
the proportion for the total population (30%). UN
Compendium, *supra*, at tbl.7. In 1993, 46.5% of the disabled
population participated in the labor force, compared with
73.6% for the general population. Disability and Self-Directed
Employment: Business Development Models 173 (Alfred H.
Neufeldt & Alison L. Albright, eds. 1998) (citing Australian
Bureau of Statistics (1993)) (figures given for illustration of
orders of magnitude only; without further review, the 1981
and 1993 figures should not be compared).

- Canada: In a 1983/84 survey, 41% of the disabled population
aged 15-64 was employed, compared to 65% of the total
population in the same age range. UN Compendium, *supra*, at
tbl.7. Again, only a few tables present comparables for the
total population. In 1991, 44% of disabled people were not in
the labor force, compared to 19% of non-disabled people.
Neufeldt & Albright, *supra*, at 186 (citing the Health Activity
Limitation Survey in Canada (figures for illustration only; the
1983/4 and 1991 figures may not be comparable)).

- United Kingdom: In 1981, 16% of registered disabled people
were unemployed – twice as many as in the workforce as a
whole. Caroline Glendinning & Sally Baldwin, The Costs of
Disability, in Money Matters, Income, Wealth and Financial
Welfare 63-80 (Robert Walker & Gillian Parker, eds. 1988)
(citing Peter Townsend, Employment and Disability, in
Disability in Britain: A Manifesto of Rights (Alan Walker &
Peter Townsend, eds. 1981)).

- A 1984 study of the United States and several European
countries found that, in terms of labor market participation,
persons with disabilities were less likely to work, and when
they did work, it was more likely to be part-time. Neufeldt &
Albright, *supra*, at 8-9 (citing Robert H. Haveman et al., Public
Policy Toward Disabled Workers: Cross-National Analyses of
Economic Impacts (1984)); R. L. Metts & T. Oleson, Assisting
Disabled Entrepreneurs in Kenya: Implications for Developed
Countries, in Partners for Independence: Models that Work

313-22, Proceedings Before the N. Am. Reg'l Conference of Rehab. Int'l (1993).

- The Swedish International Development Authority reports that only 16% of the disabled population in Mauritius is engaged in economic activities compared to 53% of the total population; and that in Botswana, the figures are 34% and 51%, respectively. Swedish Int'l. Dev. Auth., Poverty and Disability: A Position Paper 2 (Apr. 1995).

The consequences are ineluctable – lower income levels among people with disabilities even in states with generous social welfare systems, lower assets, including home ownership, and higher poverty levels. Elwan, *supra*, at 13.

Lack of access to resources diminishes the ability of people with disabilities to protect themselves. In Japan, between 1946 and 1992, over 16,000 women with disabilities were sterilized without their consent. Bureau of Democracy, Human Rights, & Lab., U.S. Dep't of State, Country Reports on Human Rights Practices for 1999 (Feb. 2, 2000), http://www. state.gov/g/drl/rls/hrrpt/1999/index.htm (last visited Nov. 26, 2013).

There is also substantial literature demonstrating that when disability is coupled with being a woman, the discriminatory effects are multiplied. Hidden Sisters, *supra*, at 11. Likewise, people with disabilities are unable to fight against inhumane conditions in mental institutions. *See, e.g.*, Mental Disability Rights Int'l, Publications, http:// www.mdri.org/publications/index.htm (last visited Feb. 16, 2005) (reporting on conditions in Mexico, Kosovo, Hungary, Uruguay and Russia).

The data confirm that historically, disability was overlooked as a civil or human rights issue. Part of the problem no doubt lay in the economic conditions of many states. Ameliorating disability discrimination via modification of the physical environment uses more resources than requiring employers to treat the genders equally. Part of the problem also sprang from a misunderstanding of the nature of disability that leads to a diminished appreciation for the abilities of people with disabilities. Indeed, that may have flowed from the medical model of disability, which still permeates the thinking in many states. Over the past few decades, states have moved, first tentatively and now more aggressively, to attack the conditions illustrated by those statistics. A number have either added to their constitutions or enacted domestic legislation dealing with disability rights. They have begun to consider international agreements that establish rights.

§ 35.2　Legal Approaches Toward Disability Issues

Societies that elect to address disability issues respond to them at every political level, in ways that are most congenial to background historical and cultural patterns. *See* Jerome Bickenbach, Disability

Human Rights. Law, and Policy, in Handbook of Disability Studies 568 (2001), (offering four basic types of legal expression of human rights for people with disabilities: enforceable antidiscrimination legislation, constitutional guarantees of equality, specific entitlement programs, and voluntary human rights manifestos). As discussed in Section 36.3, some, such as France, have followed a medical or welfare model, which emphasizes providing specific, albeit circumscribed, benefits to people with disabilities. Others follow a model like that in the United States, which depends crucially on removing barriers to the exercise of the same rights others enjoy. The demarcation between rights models (including the ADA) and welfare models (such as France's) also may have practical consequences. The statistics in employment, for example, raise the question whether the rights model leads to better outcomes.

Increasingly, the rights of people with disabilities have been assumed to be among those groups that merit protection at the international level. As states developed their responses, at the behest of advocates, regional international organizations, such as the Council of Europe and the Organization of American States, developed their own strategies and legal regimes.

But little happened linearly. The Council of Europe enacted a series of measures from 1992 to 2003 and is currently in the midst of its of its Disability Action Plan 2006-2015. *See generally* Thorsten Afflerbach & Angela Garabagiu, Council of Europe Actions to Promote Human Rights and Full Participation of People with Disabilities: Improving the Quality of Life of People with Disabilities in Europe, 34 Syracuse J. Int'l Law & Comm. 463, 464-5 (2007). The path that culminated in the United Nations CRPD was even longer, beginning in 1971, with the Declaration of the Rights of Mentally Retarded Persons, G.A. Res. 2027, U.N. GAOR, 26th Sess., U.N. Doc. 20.7.1 (i)-(vi) (1971). *See generally* Charles Siegal, Fifty Years of Disability Law: The Relevance of the Universal Declaration, 5 ILSA J. Int'l & Comp. L. 267 (1999).

Chapter 36   OTHER STATES' APPROACHES TO DISABILITY RIGHTS

States have developed a range of approaches toward people with disabilities. A state might address disability discrimination as a civil or human rights issue, attempting to ensure that people with disabilities enjoy the same rights as others. The rights can be constitutional or statutory. If people are given rights, they also can be given causes of action to enforce them or there can be administrative enforcement bodies. Or, the state might decree that specific areas, such as employment, must encompass some people with disabilities, enforcing quotas through criminal penalties. Alternatively, the issues may be dealt with as part of the welfare program of the state, requiring public and private employers to set aside a fixed percentage of positions for people with disabilities, supporting their income and providing protected work environments for those who cannot work in the private sector.

We describe the legal regimes of other states with some diffidence. We have given several hundred pages to the ADA, but will give only small fractions of that to other models, which have equally venerable and complex systems.

§ 36.1   Welfare/Medical Model Versus Rights-Based Social Model

We discussed in Part 1 the models that governed societies' understanding of disabilities. Often, the models are only implicit; no one thinks she is imposing a particular concept on a set of facts until someone else looks at the same facts and suggests an alternate way to understand them. Only then does one realize that the implicit model may not only define what the "problem" is, but also determine the set of acceptable solutions.

In the classic example, if the problem is defined as "certain people are unable to climb stairs," one set of solutions may be appropriate. On the other hand, defining the problem as "most buildings are constructed in a way that prevents a substantial number of people from entering them," suggests another solution set. Many countries developed programs to deal with disabilities using the former model, but are now reorienting their thinking and switching to the latter.

The long silence of the international community on disability issues is, in part, explained by the paradigm applied to disabilities. The controlling model that views disability as primarily a medical problem attempts to relieve the symptoms of the medical condition. Once those are dealt with – to the extent medically possible – the only question is whether the state should provide support to the individual. Assuming that the state feels a need to do so, the remaining question is the level of support. The welfare state systems of post-World War II Europe accommodated well to that approach. Their disability laws, to the extent they existed, treated people with disabilities according to that model.

European states had begun addressing disability prior the World War II. As early as the end of World War I, in view of the huge increase of people who suffered disabling injuries in combat, a number of European states adopted programs to assist people with disabilities. Eric Besner, Employment Legislation for Disabled Individuals: What Can France Learn from the Americans with Disabilities Act? 16 Comp. Lab. L.J. 399, 401-02 (1995); Lisa Waddington, Reassessing the Employment of People with Disabilities in Europe: From Quotas to Anti-Discrimination Laws, 18 Comp. Lab. L.J. 62, 63-64 (1996). Most often those took the form of quotas for the number of disabled employees entities had to hire. The quota approach to jobs endures in much of Western Europe. Waddington, *supra*, at 64. In some states, compliance was voluntary; in others, governments tried to impose systems of penalties for non-compliance. *Id.* at 64-69. In some, for example, France, the government undertakes part of the cost. *See infra* § 36.3. Whatever the chosen means, access to employment, including quotas, has been at the center of governmental efforts. However, the effectiveness of quotas appears to be limited. *Id.* at 69. Moreover, simply imposing quotas avoids recognizing the particular attributes of disability discrimination. Perhaps worst, the quotas stigmatize, by implying that workers with disabilities could not compete for equivalent jobs absent the mandate.

If one sees the issues through a "rights" lens, the questions and the set of potential answers morph. Rosemary Kayess & Phillip French, Out of Darkness into Light? Introducing the Convention on the Rights of Persons with Disabilities, 8 Hum. Rts. L. Rev. 1 (2008); Oliver Lewis, The Expressive, Educational and Proactive Roles of Human Rights: An Analysis of the United Nations Convention on the Rights of Persons with Disabililties, in Rethinking Rights-based Mental Health Laws 97 (Bernadette McSherry & Penelope Weller eds., 2010),; Janet E. Lord & Michael Ashley Stein, The Domestic Incorporation of Human Rights Law and the United Nations Convention on the Rights of Persons with Disabilities, 83 U. Wash. L. Rev. 449, 456 (2008); Michael Ashley Stein, Disability Human Rights, 95 Cal. L. Rev. 75, 83 (2007); Gerard Quinn, Resisting the 'Temptation of Elegance': Can the Convention on the Rights of Persons with Disabilities Socialise States in Rights Behaviour?, in The UN Convention on the Rights of Persons with Disabilities: European and Scandinavian Perspectives 215, 224-29 (Oddný Mjöll Arnardóttir & Gerard Quinn eds., 2009); Theresia Degener & Gerard Quinn, A Survey of International, Comparative and Regional Disability Law Reform, pt. 1.A. (paper delivered at the Expert Group Meeting on the Comprehensive and Integral International Convention to Promote and Protect the Rights and Dignity of Persons with Disabilities, Oct. 22-26, 2000). People have equal rights to certain facets of societies. Equal rights must, of course, be given content. As Degener and Quinn point out, this can mean "(1) formal or juridical equality, (2) equality of results, and (3) equal opportunity or structural equality." Degener & Quinn, *supra*, at pt. 1.A.2. Formal equality requires the law treat all people equally and, for example, does nothing to assist people who have the same formal "right" to vote, but who cannot see the ballot. Arguably, it is an illusory benefit.

Assuring the equality of results might be appropriate in the voting case, but generally pursuing it raises distributive justice issues in other cases. For example, it might be expensive for employers and disturbing to people without disabilities to guarantee people with disabilities that they will have jobs for which they are not otherwise qualified. In addition, equalizing results may present problems from the perspective of a person with a disability:

> Segregated education for disabled students, for example, might be deemed legitimate if special schools for disabled students provide the same educational opportunities and degrees as regular schools. To put it bluntly, if we accept equality of results as the sole way of understanding equality, the mainstreaming of disabled students into regular schools could be viewed as an illegitimate goal.

Id.

More typically, in the United States certainly, laws try to assure equality of opportunity. The ADA addresses this by requiring "reasonable" accommodations in its employment provisions and similar limiting devices in its other commands.[1] That accords with the dominant free market economic gestalt: people with disabilities are given the right to compete in a setting where their disabilities must be ignored if they are not relevant to the job or the societal benefit.

But, in other states, even reasonable requirements for accommodations and other benefits may be problematic. In the first place, there is a question of who pays. In the employment context, in the United States, burdening private employers (especially in view of some tax incentives) does not place an insurmountable barrier in the way of equal opportunity. In other states, with substantially fewer economic resources, it is not clear that choice will work. In many states, moreover, it will not be feasible to have the government pay.

In the second place, any regime based on a reasonableness standard will generate disputes, which necessitates a functioning judicial or administrative dispute resolution structure. These kinds of institutions

---

[1] The term "adjustments" replaces "accommodations" in the UK's Disability Discrimination Act. Disability Discrimination Act, 1995, c. 50 (Eng.) § 6 [hereinafter "DDA"], *available at* http://www.opsi.gov.uk/acts/ acts1995/ ukpga_19950050_en_2 (last visited Nov. 26, 2013).

do not exist in all states and where they do, a complex ADA-like statute will impose additional burdens.

Despite those impediments, for the past decade, now spurred on by the CRPD, the trend in disability legislation has been to adopt a rights paradigm. *See, e.g.*, Rodrigo Jimenez, The Americans with Disabilities Act and Its Impact on International and Latin American Law, 52 Ala. L. Rev. 419, 420-22 (2000) (discussing Latin American statutes adopting the rights-based model and, in particular, Costa Rican cases). The trend is not universal, however, and we have no evidence of whether such laws and other provisions as do exist are being enforced.

As an added complication, even among those states following a rights model, approaches vary. The United States, the United Kingdom, and New Zealand have extensive disability rights laws, but the laws are essentially stand-alone pieces of legislation. In Canada, *see infra* § 36.2.A, disability rights are placed in the matrix of anti-discrimination legislation, including race and gender.

The disparate approaches among states following flavors of a "rights" model flow from a conceptual distinction. Following World War II, broad conceptions of human rights have developed at national and international levels. Disability rights have developed in parallel with – albeit often later than – those conceptions and have sometimes been nurtured by them.

In contrast, much of United States disability rights legislation is rooted in more stratified notions of injustice, which establish tiers of protection depending on the "classification" challenged because it harms the claimant, with the highest level of protection going to racial classifications, and less protection going to other groups. *See, e.g.*, Frontiero v. Richardson, 411 U.S. 677, 686-87 (1973) (sex discrimination subject to heightened standard of review) (plurality opinion); City of Cleburne v. Cleburne Living Ctr., 473 U.S. 432 (1985) (discussed *supra* Part 1, § 1.3; disability discrimination subject only to rational basis protection).

໖

Notes & Questions

1. What are the merits of a medical/welfare approach? Should the state provide some level of support for people with disabilities in the job market, by requiring quotas? Isn't this just an indirect tax? Who should pay it? Should the government just set up workshops to employ people with disabilities?

2. In a quota system, how can one insure people are qualified?

3. The UK's Disability Discrimination Act, 1995, c. 50 (Eng.) reflects a good deal of the ADA. The DDA expressly addresses a number of areas. It forbids discrimination in employment (Part II), "goods,

facilities and services" and "premises" (Part III), education (Part IV) and "public transport" (Part V). *See* Ross v. Ryanair Ltd., 1 W.L.R. 2447 (C.A. 2005) (airport and airline both liable for failing to provide free wheelchair service to traveler who did not have own wheelchair), available at 2004 WL 2932907. Employers have an obligation to make "reasonable adjustments." "(1) Where – (a) any arrangements made by or on behalf of an employer, or (b) any physical feature of premises occupied by the employer, place the disabled person concerned at a substantial disadvantage in comparison with persons who are not disabled, it is the duty of the employer to take such steps as it is reasonable, in all the circumstances of the case, for him to have to take in order to prevent the arrangements or feature having that effect." DDA at (Part II) § 6(1). Sections 5(3) and 5(4) of the DDA provide:

> (3) Subject to subsection (5), for the purposes of subsection (1) treatment is justified if, but only if, the reason for it is both material to the circumstances of the particular case and substantial. . . . . (4) For the purposes of subsection (2), failure to comply with a section 6 duty is justified if, but only if, the reason for the failure is both material to the circumstances of the particular case and substantial.

For a comparison of United Kingdom and United States disability discrimination statutes, *see* Suzanne Bruyère, A Comparison of the Implementation of the Employment Provisions of the Americans with Disabilities Act of 1990 (ADA) in the United States and the Disability Discrimination Act 1995 (DDA) in the United Kingdom (Cornell Univ. Program on Emp. & Disability Sch. of Indus. & Lab. Relations 1999). For a critique of the English courts' treatment of the justification defense, *see* Jackie Davies, A Cuckoo in the Nest? A 'Range of Reasonable Responses', Justification and the Disability Discrimination Act 1995, 32 Indus. L.J. 164 (2003).

On the other hand, in 1998, the United Kingdom adopted Human Rights Act of 1998, 1998 Chapter 42, which came into force in 2000. That statute requires the United Kingdom to follow the European Convention on Human Rights. *See* Caroline Gooding, The Application of the ECHR in British Courts in Relation to Disability Issues (DRC, 2003).

New Zealand follows a similar model. Human Rights Act, 1993 (N.Z.) [HRA], http://www.legislation.govt.nz/act/public/1993/0082/latest/DLM304212.html (last visited Nov. 26, 2013). The HRA prohibits discrimination generally and then in specific areas, such as employment, education, provision of goods and services, and provision of "land, housing and other accommodations." *Id.* §§ 21, 22, 42, 44, 53 & 57. It then creates certain circumscribed exceptions, among them exceptions related to disability. *See* § 21(h) (prohibiting discrimination on the basis of disability); § 29(a) (exception to § 22 requirement of non-discrimination in employment where "[t]he position is such that the person could perform the duties of the position satisfactorily only with the aid of special services or facilities and it is not reasonable to expect the employer to provide those services or facilities"); § 43(2) (excepting from public access requirement of § 42 cases in which, "by reason of the disability of that person, special services or special facilities to enable any such person to gain access to or use any place or vehicle when it would not be reasonable to require the provision of such special services or facilities"); § 43(4) (excepting from public access requirement of § 42 cases in which "the disability of a person is such that there would be a risk of harm to that person or to others, including the risk of infecting others with an illness, if that person were to have access to or use of any place or vehicle and it is not reasonable to take that risk"); § 60 (dealing with exceptions to non-discrimination requirements for educational institutions).

5.   Do you think a directed approach, such as the ADA or the DDA, will show better results than a more explicitly "human rights" approach, such as Canada's? How do you define "better"?

§ 36.2   States Following A Rights Model

A. *Canada*

Certain states create wholly new apparatuses for disability rights, such as the United States and the United Kingdom. Others place disability rights among their general equality protections, although they must have some specific legislation to deal with the differences between disability and other protected statuses, such as race and gender. One might ask whether situating disability rights among other human rights laws does not conduce a broader conception of disability rights.

At the federal level, Canada has placed its disability discrimination guarantee squarely within its apparatus for dealing with all forms of discrimination. It substantially amended its Constitution in 1982, including its Charter of Rights and Freedoms. Article 15 of the Charter expressly prohibits discrimination on the basis of mental or physical disability:

> (1)   Every individual is equal before and under the law and has the right to the equal protection and equal benefit of the law without discrimination and, in particular, without discrimination based on race, national or ethnic origin, colour, religion, sex, age or mental or physical disability.
>
> (2)   Subsection (1) does not preclude any law, program or activity that has as its object the amelioration of conditions of disadvantaged individuals or groups including those that are disadvantaged because of race, national or ethnic origin, colour, religion, sex, age or mental or physical disability.

Constitution Act (1982), art. 15 (enacted as part of Schedule B to Canada Act 1982 (UK), 1982, c. 11), http://www.solon.org/Constitutions/Canada/English/ca_1982.html (last visited Jan. 12, 2005). Note that Canada finesses anti-affirmative action attacks on the Constitution by specifically allowing affirmative action as a matter of constitutional law.

In addition to the inclusion of disability within the Charter, Canada has human rights laws and commissions at the federal and provincial levels. The Canadian courts have used each set of laws to inform the interpretation of the other. Dianne Pothier, Appendix: Legal Developments in the Supreme Court of Canada Regarding Disability, in Dianne Pothier & Richard Devlin, Critical Disability Theory 305 (2007). The 1985 Canadian Human Rights Act prohibits discrimination on the basis of "race, national or ethnic origin, colour, religion, age, sex, sexual orientation, marital status, family status, disability and conviction for which a pardon has been granted." Canadian Human Rights Act, R.S.C., c. H-6, § 3 (1985) (Can.). This statute applies to the Canadian federal government and businesses regulated by the federal government, such as banks, and reaches employment, as well as government, services. Employment Equity Act, S.C., c. 44, § 4 (1995) (Can.) 42-43-44 Eliz. II, 1994-95, *available at* http://laws-lois.justice.gc.ca/PDF/E-5.401.pdf (last visited Nov. 26, 2013) (Section 4 addresses private and public sector employers). In addition, the Employment Equity Act, passed in 1995, specifically extends protection for people with disabilities and other classes to private employment. The Employment Equity Act defines persons with disabilities as:

> persons who have a long-term or recurring physical, mental, sensory, psychiatric or learning impairment and who
>
> (a) consider themselves to be disadvantaged in employment by reason of that impairment, or
>
> (b) believe that an employer or potential employer is likely to consider them to be disadvantaged in employment by reason of that impairment,
>
> and includes persons whose functional limitations owing to their impairment have been accommodated in their current job or workplace . . . .

Id. § 3. Note that the disabling characteristic is viewed from the perspective of the person with the disability.

In addition to the federal statute, each province and territory has its own disability rights legislation as part of the provincial human rights act or code. *See, e.g.,* Human Rights Act, R.S.N.B. 1973, c. H-11, s. 3 (New Brunswick). The Supreme Court of Canada may render decisions on provincial statutes. *E.g.,* Québec (Commission des Droits de la Personne & des Droits de la Jeunesse) v. Montréal (Ville), [2000] 1 S.C.R. 665, 185

D.L.R. (4th) 385, 2000 CarswellQue 650 (2000) ("Québec v. Montreal"). As one might expect, their approaches differ slightly. For example, New Brunswick defines "mental disability" as:

> (a) any condition of mental retardation or impairment,
>
> (b) any learning disability, or dysfunction in one or more of the mental processes involved in the comprehension or use of symbols or spoken language, or
>
> (c) any mental disorder

and physical disability as

> any degree of disability, infirmity, malformation or disfigurement of a physical nature caused by bodily injury, illness or birth defect and, without limiting the generality of the foregoing, includes any disability resulting from any degree of paralysis or from diabetes mellitus, epilepsy, amputation, lack of physical co-ordination, blindness or visual impediment, deafness or hearing impediment, muteness or speech impediment, or physical reliance on a guide dog or on a wheelchair, cane, crutch or other remedial device or appliance.

R.S.N.B. 1973, c. H-11, s. 2.

Nova Scotia, on the other hand, defines both together and expands the definition explicitly to cover learning disabilities:

> (l) "physical disability or mental disability" means an actual or perceived
>
> (i) loss or abnormality of psychological, physiological or anatomical structure or function,
>
> (ii) restriction or lack of ability to perform an activity,
>
> (iii) physical disability, infirmity, malformation or disfigurement, including, but not limited to, epilepsy and any degree of paralysis, amputation, lack of physical coordination, deafness, hardness of hearing or hearing impediment, blindness or visual impediment, speech impairment or impediment or reliance on a hearing-ear dog, a guide dog, a wheelchair or a remedial appliance or device,
>
> (iv) learning disability or a dysfunction in one or more of the processes involved in understanding or using symbols or spoken language,
>
> (v) condition of being mentally handicapped or impaired,
>
> (vi) mental disorder, or

(vii)   previous dependency on drugs or alcohol.

Human Rights Act, R.S.N.S. 1989, c. 214, s. 3 (Nova Scotia).

As in the Canadian federal context, provincial legislation may strike out beyond the ADA. In both definitions, for example, analogous to the federal statute, reliance on a remedial device is an indicium of disability, not a way to find there is no disability, as the United States Supreme Court did in *Sutton*. *See* discussion *supra* Part 2, § 3.2.B. (*Sutton* has, of course, been legislatively overruled in the 2008 ADAAA.) The Canadian Supreme Court recognized this distinction between the ADA and the Canadian statute in *Granovsky v. Minister of Employment and Immigration*, [2000] 1 S.C.R. 703, ¶ 36.

One might contrast the Canadian and United States interpretive schemes. Early on, applying tiered levels of scrutiny, the United States Supreme Court held that disability is not a "suspect class," entitled to the same degree of protection as race, or even as gender. City of Cleburne v. Cleburne Living Ctr., 473 U.S. 432, 440-47 (1985).   The more comprehensive approach of Canadian statutes places disabilities with other protected criteria and provides broader protection.   Eldridge v. British Columbia, [1997] 151 D.L.R. (4th) 577, 3 S.C.R. 624 (hospital funded by province required by Constitution to provide sign language interpreter to hearing impaired patient).

Canadian law also must face the issue of how to accommodate individuals with disabilities.   It employs a variant of the reasonable accommodation approach. Section 15(1) of the Human Rights Act defines "exceptions" to human rights requirements. The first is:

> (a)   any refusal, exclusion, expulsion, suspension, limitation, specification or preference in relation to any employment is established by an employer to be based on a *bona fide* occupational requirement; . . .

> (g)   in the circumstances described in section 5 or 6, an individual is denied any goods, services, facilities or accommodation or access thereto or occupancy of any commercial premises or residential accommodation or is a victim of any adverse differentiation and there is *bona fide* justification for that denial or differentiation.

The Human Rights Act goes on to say:

> For any practice mentioned in paragraph (1)(a) to be considered to be based on a *bona fide* occupational requirement and for any practice mentioned in paragraph (1)(g) to be considered to have a *bona fide* justification, it must be established that accommodation of the needs of an individual or a class of individuals affected would impose undue hardship on the person who would have to

accommodate those needs, considering health, safety and cost.

Canadian Human Rights Act, R.S., c. H-6, § 15(2) (1985) (Can.), *available at* http://laws-lois.justice.gc.ca/PDF/H-6.pdf.

Canadian courts have developed a test for appropriate accommodations in the sex discrimination area. In *British Columbia (Public Service Employee Relations Commission) v. B.C.G.E.U.*, [1999] 3 S.C.R. 3 Can. (*"Meiorin"*), http://scc-csc.lexum.com/decisia-scc-csc/scc-csc/scc-csc/en/item/1724/index.do (last visited Nov. 26, 2013), a gender discrimination case brought under a British Columbia statute worded the same way as section 15 of the Human Rights Act, the Canadian Supreme Court rejected its prior distinction between direct discrimination and adverse effect discrimination. The court noted that section 15 of the Human Rights Act does not support such a distinction, stating that

> [w]hile it is well established that it is open to a s. 15(1) claimant to establish discrimination by demonstrating a discriminatory legislative purpose, proof of legislative intent is not required in order to found a s. 15(1) claim: . . . . What is required is that the claimant establish that either the purpose or the effect of the legislation infringes s. 15(1), such that the onus may be satisfied by showing only a discriminatory effect.

Id. at ¶ 47 (citation omitted). It held that to constitute a bona fide occupational requirement ("BFOR"):

> An employer may justify the impugned standard by establishing on the balance of probabilities:
>
> (1)   that the employer adopted the standard for a purpose rationally connected to the performance of the job;
>
> (2)   that the employer adopted the particular standard in an honest and good faith belief that it was necessary to the fulfillment of that legitimate work-related purpose; and
>
> (3)   that the standard is reasonably necessary to the accomplishment of that legitimate work-related purpose. To show that the standard is reasonably necessary, it must be demonstrated that it is impossible to accommodate individual employees sharing the characteristics of the claimant without imposing undue hardship upon the employer.

Id. at ¶ 54.

B. *South Africa*

Determining the legal situation of disability rights in developing states is complicated by the lack of transparency. South Africa presents a good example. The Constitution of 1996, widely hailed as a model, expressly outlaws discrimination based upon disability:

> 9. (1) Everyone is equal before the law and has the right to equal protection and benefit of the law.
>
> (2) Equality includes the full and equal enjoyment of all rights and freedoms. To promote the achievement of equality, legislative and other measures designed to protect or advance persons, or categories of persons, disadvantaged by unfair discrimination may be taken.
>
> (3) The state may not unfairly discriminate directly or indirectly against anyone on one or more grounds, including race, gender, sex, pregnancy, marital status, ethnic or social origin, colour, sexual orientation, age, disability, religion, conscience, belief, culture, language and birth.
>
> (4) No person may unfairly discriminate directly or indirectly against anyone on one or more grounds in terms of subsection (3). National legislation must be enacted to prevent or prohibit unfair discrimination.
>
> (5) Discrimination on one or more of the grounds listed in subsection (3) is unfair unless it is established that the discrimination is fair.

Constitution of the Republic of South Africa Act 108 of 1996, Chap. 2, § 9, *available at* http://www.info.gov.za/documents/constitution/1996/a108-96.pdf.

South Africa has also enacted an Employment Equity Act, which provides:

> (1) No person may unfairly discriminate, directly or indirectly, against an employee, in any employment policy or practice, on one or more grounds, including race, gender, sex, pregnancy, marital status, family responsibility, ethnic or social origin, colour, sexual orientation, age, disability, religion, HIV status, conscience, belief, political opinion, culture, language and birth.
>
> (2) It is not unfair discrimination to –
>
> > (a) take affirmative action measures consistent with the purpose of this Act; or
> >
> > (b) distinguish, exclude or prefer any person on the basis of an inherent requirement of a job.

Employment Equity Act 55 of 1998, Chap. 2, § 6, *available at* http://www.labour.gov.za/DOL/downloads/legislation/acts/employment-equity/Act%20-%20Employment%20Equity.pdf.

Affirmative action measures include: "making reasonable accommodation for people from designated groups in order to ensure that they enjoy equal opportunities and are equitably represented in the workforce of a designated employer." Employment Equity Act 55 of 1998, Chap. 3, § 15(2)(c). In addition, the act limits medical and psychometric testing. Sections 7 and 8 of the act read:

> 7.   Medical testing. – (1) Medical testing of an employee is prohibited, unless –
>
>> a.   legislation permits or requires the testing; or
>>
>> b.   it is justifiable in the light of medical facts, employment conditions, social policy, the fair distribution of employee benefits or the inherent requirements of a job.
>
> (2)   Testing of an employee to determine that employee's HIV status is prohibited unless such testing is determined justifiable by the Labour Court in terms of section 50 (4) of this Act.
>
> 8.   Psychometric testing. – Psychometric testing and other similar assessments of an employee are prohibited unless the test or assessment being used –
>
>> a.   has been scientifically shown to be valid and reliable;
>>
>> b.   can be applied fairly to employees; and
>>
>> c.   is not biased against any employee or group.

Complaints under the Employment Equity Act may be brought to a governmental labour inspector, the Commission for Employment Equity established under the act, or the Director-General of the Department of Labour. *Id.* § 34. The employer may object to any proposed compliance order. If the Director-General issues an order, an aggrieved employer may appeal to the Labour Court. *Id.* § 40.

The act is implemented by a Code of Good Practice, which came into effect in August 2002 and sets forth detailed rules for dealing with employees with disabilities. Ministry of Lab., Code of Good Practice on Key Aspects of Disability in the Workplace (Aug. 2002)), *available at* http://www.workinfo.com/free/sub_for_legres/data/equity/dicibili.pdf. The Code represents South Africa's attempt to address many of the issues that have bedeviled ADA interpretation. For example:

- It defines a long-term impairment, as one that "has lasted or is likely to persist for at least twelve months." A short-term or temporary illness or injury is not an impairment which gives rise to a disability. *Id.* § 5.1.1(i).

- With respect to "substantially-limiting," it states: "Some impairments are so easily controlled, corrected or lessened, that they have no limiting effects. For example, a person who wears spectacles or contact lenses does not have a disability unless even with spectacles or contact lenses the person's vision is substantially impaired." *Id.* § 5.1.3(ii).

- On public policy grounds, it excludes, among other things "compulsive gambling, tendency to steal or light fires; [and] disorders that affect a person's mental or physical state if they are caused by current use of illegal drugs or alcohol, unless the affected person is participating in a recognised programme of treatment." *Id.* § 5.1.3(iv).

- It requires reasonable accommodations, but provides: "The employer need not accommodate a qualified applicant or an employee with a disability if this would impose an unjustifiable hardship on the business of the employer."

- "Unjustifiable hardship is action that requires significant or considerable difficulty or expense and that would substantially harm the viability of the enterprise. This involves considering the effectiveness of the accommodation and the extent to which it would seriously disrupt the operation of the business."

- "An accommodation that imposes an unjustifiable hardship for one employer at a specific time may not be so for another or for the same employer at a different time." *Id.* §§ 6.11-6.13.

- Its requirements for testing and interviewing are very much like the ADA's. *Id.* § 8; Employment Equity Act 55 of 1998, §§ 7-8.

Awareness of disability issues appears high in South Africa. But it is difficult to gauge the effect of the legislation. According to the United States Department of State's 2002 Human Rights Report on South Africa, in practice discrimination against people with disabilities continues to exist. U.S. Dep't of State, Country Reports on Human Rights Practices: South Africa (Mar. 31, 2003), http://www.state.gov/g/drl/rls/hrrpt/2002/18227.htm (last visited Nov. 26, 2013). It also wrote, "The law mandates access to buildings for persons with disabilities; however, such regulations rarely were enforced, and public awareness of them remained minimal." *Id.* The African Disability Rights Yearbook of 2013 confirms that like other countries, in South Africa there is a gap between law as written and implemented. *See* African Disability Rights Yearbook of 2013, 338 (detailing gaps in participation in political life for people with disabilities in South Africa), *available at* http://www.pulp.up.ac.za/pdf/2013_07/2013_07.pdf.

Statistically, in 2001, only 0.2% of the public sector workforce was disabled, although people with disabilities constituted 5.9% of the population. But the statistics must be judged against South Africa's other problems. A disability rights activist in South Africa's Parliament was quoted in 2001:

> The Employment Equity Act is having an effect. It is slow and there have been problems, but its demands are gradually being realized. . . .
>
> But, bit by bit, some of the fruits of the disabled's struggle for their place in the sun are ripening. There is still stereotyping. Blind people are mostly employed as switchboard operators, but the equity plans presently being submitted to the Department of Labour are going to show that real progress has been made.

Peta Thornycroft, Beating the Drum, Johannesburg Mail and Guardian, July 27, 2001 (quoting Hendrietta Bogopane), reprinted in Peta Thornycroft, Disabled Take Struggle to Parliament, The Braille Monitor, Dec. 2001, http://www.nfb.org/Images/nfb/Publications/bm/bm01/bm0112/bm011208.htm (last visited Nov. 25, 2013).

§ 36.3 States Following A Welfare/Medical Model: France

Another approach to disability rights is to provide special treatment and programs for people with disabilities, rather than to attempt to situate them in mainstream settings by providing them equalizing assistance. The system either mandates quotas – an epithet in the United States – or gives people with disabilities a priority. For example, Germany, Japan and Greece require quotas. *See* Katharina C. Heyer, The ADA on the Road: Disability Rights in Germany, 27 Law & Soc. Inquiry 723, 728-31 (2002); Katharina Heyer, From Special Needs to Equal Rights: Japanese Disability Law, 1 Asian-Pac. L. & Pol'y J. 7 (2000); Org. for Econ. Co-Operation & Dev., Labour Market and Social Policy, Occasional Papers, Employment Policies for People with Disabilities, Occasional Papers No. 8, OCDE/GD(92)7 at ¶ 123 (1992); Koula Labropoulou & Eva Suomeli, Workers with Disabilities: Law, Bargaining and the Social Partners (2001), http://www.eurofound.europa.eu/eiro/2001/02/study/tn0102201s.htm (last visited Nov. 26, 2013).

Perhaps the best example of the attitudinal difference is this quote from the French Senate's website describing various states' approaches to placing people with disabilities in jobs: "La loi de 1990 [the ADA] ne crée aucune obligation d'emploi des handicapés." ["The law of 1990 does not establish any duty to employ handicapped people."] Sénat, L'Insertion des Handicapes dans L'Entreprise: Les États-Unis at 1(a), http://www.senat.fr/lc/lc116/lc1167.html (last visited Nov. 26, 2013). The French would not leave it to private employers to apply non-discriminatory criteria, but would rely on the government to mandate employment.

That approach keeps alive the focus on disabilities as factors that set people apart, in place of a focus on the environment as excluding people who are differently-abled. It also entails substantial and often complex state intervention. However, given the mixed evidence on the success of the rights model, in theory application of aspects of the welfare model could be beneficial. *See* Mark C. Weber, Reciprocal Lessons of the ADA and European Disability Law, 93 Am. Soc'y Int'l L. Proc. 338, 339-41 (1999) (arguing in favor of such welfare programs as job set-asides, though presenting no data on the benefits of those programs); Mark C. Weber, Beyond the Americans with Disabilities Act: A National Employment Policy for People with Disabilities, 46 Buff. L. Rev. 123, 166-74 (1998) (same). On the other hand, even states that follow this model are adopting some aspects of the rights model. *E.g., see* the Decree "Relatif à l'Accessibilité aux Personnes Handicapées des Locaux d'Habitation, des Établissements et Installations Recevant du Public, Modifiant et Complétant le Code de la Construction et de l'Habitation et la Code de l'Urbanisme." Décret No. 94-86, Jan. 26, 1994, Journal Official [J.O.] Jan. 28, 1994, 1585, http://www.legifrance.gouv.fr/affichTexte.do?cidTexte= JORFTEXT000000545546&fastPos=1&fastReqId=1564636486&categorie Lien=cid&oldAction=rechTexte (last visited Nov. 26, 2013). This decree changes building codes to require that all buildings must make known to people with disabilities that they can enter, move about, exit and avail themselves of all the benefits the establishment offers to the public. *Id.*

France exemplifies the welfare model. *See generally* Le Service Public de la Diffusion du Droit, Legifrance (providing access to French laws), http://www.legifrance.gouv.fr/ (last visited Nov. 26, 2013). In 1987, in debates about the need for a United Nations convention, the French delegate stated, "the issue of the disabled was one of national solidarity . . . was not a human rights issue warranting the drafting of further legal instruments." Osamu Nagase, Difference, Equality and Disabled People: Disability Rights and Disability Culture (1995) (quoting U.N. Doc. A/C.3/42/SR.18, 4 (1987) (statement of the French delegation)), http:// www.arsvi.com/0w/no01/1995.txt (last visited Nov. 26, 2013).

France's disability laws date to the post-World War I period, when it had to deal with large numbers of disabled veterans. Eric A. Besner, Employment Legislation for Disabled Individuals: What Can France Learn from the Americans with Disabilities Act? 16 Comp. Lab. L.J. 399, 401 (1995). Over the next 65 years, the law was expanded from veterans, military widows and orphans to all those designated as disabled by the Commission Technique d'Orientation et de Reclassement Professionnel (COTOREP), a French government commission. *Id.* at 401-02. The original 1924 law applied to any enterprise employing more than 10 workers and required such employers to have 10% of their workforce be disabled veterans. Patricia Thornton & Neil Lunt, Employment Policies for Disabled People in Eighteen Countries: A Review 90-91 (1997). In

1955, the law was extended to people who had suffered workplace injuries, but the quota was only 3%.

A law of November 23, 1957 required private employers to hire people with disabilities on a priority basis. Law No. 57-1223, Nov. 23, 1957, J.O., Nov. 24, 1957, p. 10,858, 1957 D.L. 346 (codified at Code du Travail, art. L. 323-9 et seq.). Département level committees classified workers into various categories and skill levels. Thornton & Lunt, *supra*, at 91.

> The 1957 act laid the foundations for compulsory employment, a quota system for the private and public sectors, and reserved employment for particular categories of workers in certain occupational activities. There were no penalties for non-compliance. Employers were expected to conform to a laid-down procedure for notifying to the employment offices vacancies in reserved jobs or where the quota had not been obtained. If the employment office could not produce a candidate within eight days (later 15 days), the employer was free to engage any worker. In calculating whether the quota had been met, a weighting was attached to workers classified in different categories by the committee for vocational guidance.

Id.

The 1957 law also permitted people who could not work in normal environments to work in sheltered workshops ("ateliers protégés"), "centres d'aide par le travail" ("CATs"), or home-work distribution centers ("centres de distribution de travail à domicile"). *Id.* However, it failed to meet expectations of employing people in ordinary jobs, largely due to its "ponderous and complex" structure. *See* Marie-Louise Cros-Courtial, Les Obligations Patronales à l'Égard des Handicapés Après la Loi du 10 Juillet 1987 [Protective Obligations Toward Handicapped People Following the Law of July 10, 1987], Droit Social 598 (Juillet-Août 1988).

In 1975, France enacted a law establishing a broad charter of rights for people with disabilities, young and old, including education, training and social integration. Law No. 75-534 of July 1, 1975, J.O., No. 150, July 1, 1975, p. 6596, 975 D.S.L. 207 (codified at Code du Travail, art. L. 323-9 et seq.). *See* Cros-Courtial, *supra*, at 598. It was intended comprehensively to deal with disability issues. But, in the employment area it generally built on existing – dysfunctional – laws.

Still, as with earlier laws, the 1975 law lacked any effective mechanism for moving people into the labor force. It exempted employers who entered a contract with a CAT or a sheltered workshop. By the mid-1980s, it was evident that the law was not working:

- The percentage of people with disabilities in the population was about 5%, but only about 0.6% of private sector employees and 1% of public sector employees ("according to the most optimistic statistics") were "handicapés."

- Fifty-five percent of workers recognized by COTOREP as disabled were unemployed and their periods of unemployment averaged twice as long as non-disabled workers in 1985.

- Although the number of people with disabilities employed in regular business had increased from 20,000 in 1965 to 75,000 in 1987, the number of people in "protected" work had increased from 3,000 to 69,000.

Cros-Courtial, *supra*, at 598.

France confronted issues of disabilities in employment in the law of July 10, 1987, which, like its predecessors, is codified in the Code du Travail (Labor Code). Law No. 87-517, July 10, 1987, J.O., No. 160, July 12, 1987, p. 7822, 1987 D.S.L. 282 (codified at Code du Travail, art. L. 323-1 et seq.). It imposes an enforceable obligation on public sector employers and on private sector employers with 20 or more employees to meet a fixed quota, which increased from 3% in 1988 to 6% in 1991, with employees hired weighted according to their disability. It also encouraged employers and employees' organizations to adopt joint plans to assist workers with disabilities to integrate in the workforce. Moreover, if an employee is referred by COTOREP, the employer cannot refuse to hire her. However, the employer can pay a smaller wage, the difference being made up by the state.

Although the 1987 law retains a number of features of earlier legislation,[2] it does depart from them. First, it imposes a duty on employers before particular potential employees are identified. Second, it focuses, not primarily on those injured in war, to whom the country owes a debt, but "handicapped workers." Thus, more than earlier legislation, it stresses the obligation to improve the conditions of all people with disabilities. In 1990, France added a statute that increased the penalties

---

[2] They include:

obligations to war-disabled workers; the recognition of disability by a commission, the weighting of categories of disability; compulsory employment with a percentage of workforce quota; scope to meet part of the quota obligation by contracting with sheltered workshops; [and] the right to a minimum working wage in open and sheltered employment.

Thornton & Lunt, *supra*, at 91.

for refusing to hire people with disabilities. Law No. 90-602, July 12, 1990, J.O., No. 162, July 12, 1990, p. 8272, 1990 D.S.L. 321 (vol. 2) (codified in part at Code du Travail, art. L. 122-45).

The 1987 law, however, resulted from a political compromise. One of its authors noted that "it is neither possible nor desirable to impose [the direct hiring of persons with disabilities] on a business which does not want to employ its quota of disabled workers or even an amount under quota." Philippe Auvergnon, L'Obligation d'Emploi des Handicapes [The Obligation to Employ Persons with Disabilities], Droit Social 596, 602 (Juillet-Août 1991) (quoting D. Jacquart, Rapport du Projet de Loi au Nom de la Commission des Affaires Culturelles, Familiales et Sociales de l'Assemblée Nationale [Report of the Legal Project in the Name of the Commission of Cultural, Domestic, and Social Affairs of the National Assembly] 30 (1987)). A French commentator, Marie-Louise Cros-Courtial, has said that the way the law takes "economic réalisme" into account results in a law that seems like a retreat. Cros-Courtial, *supra*, at 603.

This attitude no doubt underlies provisions that blunt the law's effect. In the first place, the beneficiaries of the act include not those recognized by COTOREP as "handicaps," but eight other categories, including those who suffered at least 10% permanent incapacity due to workplace injuries, holders of social security pensions, and war widows and orphans under 21. Code du Travail, art. L. 323-3. An employer can meet his quota by hiring the "socially handicapped," not losing any perceived efficiency and not employing people with disabilities.

In addition to the implicit loophole, the law contains three alternatives to regular employment, each of which meets the quota requirements. *Id*. art. L. 323-4.

1. Employers may meet up to half their quota by establishing protected workshops, home work distribution centers or CATs. *Id*. art. L. 323-8.

2. Employers can enter into "enterprise accords," approved by Departmental Commission of Handicapped Workers, War-Mutilated, and the Equivalent (CDTHMGA), in which they agree to implement one or more of a hiring program, a training program, technological adaptive measures or a program for maintaining people with disabilities in times of cutbacks. *Id*. art. L. 323-8-1. This provision applies only to people with disabilities recognized by COTOREP. However, it has no enforcement mechanism and requires only a plan, not action.

3. Employers may make an annual contribution for each person they would have employed to a fund overseen by the Association de gestion du fonds de développement pour

l'insertion professionnelle des handicapeés (AGEFIPH), an organization of people with disabilities, employers and others created by the Code du Travail. *Id*. art. L. 323-8-2.

The availability of those avoidance devices, inter alia, led Cros-Courtial to predict that the 1987 law would not open many doors to employment for people with disabilities and that the hopes pinned on it could lead to disillusion. Cros-Courtial, *supra*, at 609. Statistics from the early years of the law seem to validate those concerns. The percentage of people with disabilities employed stayed almost constant at 3% from 1988 to 1994; even accounting for the severity of the disability, it rose to only 4.11%.

While the statistics on employment of people with disabilities in France indicate that the 1987 law, including its amendments, have not reversed the trend of gross under-employment, they do not present a picture so different from the United States statistics, so that one cannot say from an outcome point of view that one system is obviously superior. That suggests that some combination of the welfare model and the rights model may be superior to either.

Like many other states, France has enacted legislation in areas other than employment. For example, French law provides:

> 1.   Education is a right "secured to all." Code de L'Éducation, art L.111-1. Since 1975, French law has made schooling compulsory for children with disabilities. *Id*., at art. L.112-1, codifying Act 75/534 of June 30, 1975. The law encourages integration, *id*., at art. L.112-2, but also provides for special education. *Id*., at art. L.112-3. Children with disabilities are first to be taught in mainstream classes. *Id*., at art. L. 351-1.
>
> 2.   Transportation for "gravely disabled" students must be provided. *Id*. at art. L. 213-11.
>
> 3.   Buildings must be made accessible. Law Number 91-663 of July 13, 1991, recognized that the 1975 law had not been fully complied with. The 1991 law extended accessibility requirements to multifamily apartments. Notably, it also provided that advocacy groups could bring cases if accessibility standards were not complied with.

France has adopted more sweeping legislation protecting the rights of individuals with disabilities. *See* La Loi n°2005-102 du 11 février 2005 pour l'égalité des droits et des chances, la participation et la citoyenneté des personnes handicapée (Feb. 11, 2005) (describing the new provisions in place), http://legifrance.gouv.fr/affichTexte.do?cid Texte= JORFTEXT000000809647&dateTexte (last visited Nov. 26, 2013). The law, inter alia:

- Recognizes the right of every child with disabilities to attend, in the normal environment, the school closest to his or her home. *Id.* art. 19.

- Sets deadlines of 3 to 10 years for the accessibility of housing, public spaces and transport. *Id.* ch. III.

- Creates a new social security division for people with disabilities, the Caisse Nationale de Solidarité pour l'Autonomie (National Independent Living Support Fund) which guarantees compensation for all individuals with disabilities regardless of age, personal circumstance, and the source or nature of the disability. *Id.* art. 55.

- Increases fines for those companies not in accordance with the law of July 10, 1987. *Id.* art. 43.

- Creates resource centers in each French *department* to assist persons with disabilities to receive social service support and employment assistance. *Id.* art. 64.

In October 2007, the French Secretary of State for Solidarity announced the formation of a committee to study the effects of the Law of February 11, 2005 in six areas, including accessibility, education, compensation, the functioning of the departmental offices dealing with persons with disabilities, and employment. Ministère du Travail, des Relations Sociales, de la Famille, de la Solidarité et de la Ville, *available at* http://www.sante.gouv.fr/IMG/pdf/sts_20090006_0001_p000.pdf. In summary, France has explored and continues to explore a number of possibilities to bring people with disabilities into the mainstream. As in all countries, there remain questions of the success of the approaches.

Chapter 37   INTERNATIONAL HUMAN RIGHTS LAW BASICS

One can view the development of disability rights law in the United States and elsewhere as a more general expression of human rights law. Since the end of World War II, nations have signed a range of documents that aim to improve the international protection of human rights. International human rights is distinct from International Humanitarian Law, which deals with the treatment of individuals in situations of armed conflict, commonly known as the law of war.

"Human rights" encompass civil and political rights, such as the rights to free speech and assembly, the right to vote, and due process rights in civil and criminal proceedings. They include economic and social rights, such as the right of workers to organize. They include the right to be free from torture and heightened protection for at-risk groups, such as women and children. Those at-risk groups now include people with disabilities.

The United Nations began developing a series of human rights instruments with the Universal Declaration on Human Rights in 1948. G.A. Res. 217A (III), at 71, U.N. Doc. A/180 (1948), *available at* http:// http://www.un.org/en/documents/udhr/index.shtml (last visited Nov. 26, 2013). Although the Universal Declaration, at least in the view of the United States, is not a legally binding document, it set the stage for later human rights treaties.

Over the course of the next eighteen years, United Nations members negotiated the two principal human rights documents that have the force of law, the International Covenant on Civil and Political Rights, G.A. Res. 2200A, 21 U.N. GAOR, Supp. No. 16, at 52, U.N. Doc. A/6316 (1966) [hereinafter "ICCPR"], *available at* http://www1.umn.edu/ humanrts/instree/b3ccpr.htm (last visited Nov. 26, 2013), and the International Covenant on Economic, Social and Cultural Rights. G.A. Res. 2200A, 21 U.N. GAOR, Supp. No. 16, at 49, U.N. Doc. A/6316 (1966) [hereinafter "ICESCR"], *available at* http://www1.umn.edu/ humanrts/instree/b2esc.htm (last visited Nov. 26, 2013). Together, these instruments establish a series of rights that apply to all people, "without distinction of any kind, such as race, colour, sex, language, religion, political or other opinion, national or social origin, property, birth or other status" – but not disability. ICCPR, art. 2(1); ICESCR, art. 2(2). They require those who have acceded to the conventions – "States Parties" – to take action to ensure the rights established by the documents. ICESCR, art. 2(1).

They also establish monitoring mechanisms. The ICCPR establishes a Human Rights Committee to which States Parties are to provide "reports on the measures they have adopted which give effect to the rights recognized herein and on the progress made in the enjoyment of those rights." ICCPR, art. 40(1). States Parties to the ICESCR commit to provide reports to the United Nations' Economic and Social Council on the "measures which they have adopted and the progress made in achieving the observance of the rights recognized" in the ICESCR. ICESCR, art. 16(1).

The two overarching agreements have been followed by a legion of specific ones. *E.g.*, International Convention on the Elimination of All Forms of Racial Discrimination, G.A. Res. 2106 (1965); Convention on the Elimination of All Forms of Discrimination Against Women, G.A. Res. 34/180 (1979); The Convention on the Rights of a Child, G.A. Res. 44/25 (1989). The various oversight mechanisms make clear what is implicit in human rights treaties – the obligations must be enforced locally to have a significant impact on the lives of people. However, this structure of agreements ignored disability as a protected class.

The Universal Declaration mentions disability in Article 25:

> Everyone has the right to a standard of living adequate for the health and well-being of himself and of his family, including food, clothing, housing, and medical care and necessary social services, and the right to security in the event of unemployment, sickness, disability, widowhood, old age, or other lack of livelihood in circumstances beyond his control.

But disability is not recognized as a protected classification, like race, religion, or gender. The Universal Declaration says nothing about employment, training or even treatment. Certainly, it says nothing about access. The ICESCR, where one might expect a reference, is silent, as is the ICCPR. *See generally* Charles Siegal, Fifty Years of Disability Law: The Relevance of the Universal Declaration, 5 ILSA J. Int'l & Comp. L. 267 (1999).

Chapter 38 UNITED NATIONS

The United Nations (UN),[1] founded in 1945 with 51 member states, presently has 193 member states. United Nations, Growth in United Nations Memberships, 1945-Present, http://www.un.org/Overview/ growth.htm (last visited Nov. 26, 2013). The trajectory of disability issues on the UN's radar screen reprises the development of those issues in individual states – beginning with complete ignorance, moving to advisory, rather than legally binding, measures in selected areas, such as mental health and employment, and, to a broad legally-binding document, a treaty.

The history of disability rights at the UN displays all the crosscurrents that have made the passage of domestic legislation difficult, from philosophical uncertainty about overall approaches to the disparate economic abilities among states beset with many competing needs. *See generally* Theresia Degener & Gerard Quinn, The Current Use and Future Potential of United Nations Human Rights Instruments in the Context of Disability (2002). We will not attempt to cover it in detail, but will sketch its outlines.

§ 38.1   United Nations Initiatives Prior To 2001

Disability issues hardly reached the international agenda until the 1970s and, even then, the efforts were tentative.[2] The seminal human rights text, the 1948 UN General Assembly Universal Declaration of Human Rights, mentions disability once, to say that people have a right to an adequate standard of living, even if they are disabled. Adopted by the General Assembly at its 3d session, New York, 10 Dec. 1948, GA Res. 217A (III), U.N. Doc A/810 at 71 (1948) ("Universal Declaration"). Article 25 of the Universal Declaration states that:

---

[1]   *See generally* United Nations at http://www.un.org.

[2]   In international human rights matters, much of the impetus for legal change comes from non-governmental organizations – NGOs. Among the principal ones in this area are Disabled Peoples International, http://www.dpi.org (last visited Nov. 26, 2013); Inclusion International, http://www.inclusion-international.org/ (last visited Nov. 26, 2013); Rehabilitation International, http://www.rehab-international.org (last visited Nov. 26, 2013); World Blind Union, http://www.worldblind union.org/English/Pages/default.aspx (last visited Nov. 26, 2013); World Federation of the Deaf, http://www.wfdeaf.org/ (last visited Nov. 26, 2013); Survivors Corps, http://www.survivorcorps.org/ (last visited Nov. 26, 2013); International Center for Disability Resources on the Internet, http://www.icdri.org/ (last visited A Nov. 26, 2013); and Disability Rights Education & Defense Fund, http://www.dredf.org/ (last visited Nov. 26, 2013).

[e]veryone has the right to a standard of living adequate for the health and well-being of himself and of his family, including food, clothing, housing and medical care and necessary social services, and the right to security in the event of unemployment, sickness, disability, widowhood, old age or other lack of livelihood in circumstances beyond his control.

One of the first overt efforts of the international community was the 1971 Declaration of the Rights of Mentally Retarded Persons. Adopted by the General Assembly at its 26th session, 2027th plenary meeting, New York, 20 Dec. 1971, G.A. Res. 2856 (XXVI), 26 U.N. GAOR Supp. (No. 29) at 93, U.N. Doc. A/8429 (1971). Although broadly phrased, it was a substantial jump. Article 3 reads:

> The mentally retarded person has a right to economic security and to a decent standard of living. He has a right to perform productive work or to engage in any other meaningful occupation to the fullest possible extent of his capabilities.

It emphasized integration, promising employment to the fullest extent of "his" capabilities. However, the 1971 Declaration was hortatory; it established no legal obligations.

The 1975 Declaration on the Rights of Disabled Persons was the first detailed attempt at the UN to articulate rights of people with disabilities generally. Adopted by the General Assembly at its 30th session, 2433rd plenary meeting, New York, 9 Dec. 1975, G.A. Res. 3447 (XXX), 30 U.N. GAOR Supp. (No. 34) at 88, U.N. Doc. A/10034 (1975). It represents a major doctrinal step beyond the 1971 Declaration. In a sense, the 1975 Declaration added "disability" as a protected class. Still, note the silence on exactly how the entitlement will be realized. The 1975 Declaration provides no guidance. Nor does it establish any legally binding duties. Thus, as of the mid-1970s, the UN had not addressed disability rights in a juridical framework. In context, however, that is not startling: the United States had just enacted the Rehabilitation Act two years earlier; Canada would wait seven years to add disability to its Charter of Rights and Freedoms; the United States would wait 15 years to pass the ADA (although many of the United States would by then have disability legislation).

During the 1980s, the UN and various of its subsidiary bodies began to view disability issues in a range of contexts. Those appear to have promoted a consensus on the significance of disability issues, although they left open the modalities for dealing with them.

- 1980 – The World Health Organization published the International Classification of Impairments, Disabilities and Handicaps.

- 1981 – UN International Year of Disabled Persons. Adopted by the General Assembly at its 31st session, New York, 16 Dec. 1976, GA Res. 123 (XXXI) (1976). The UN set out to define the rights of people with disabilities, increase public awareness, and encourage the formation of advocacy organizations.

- 1983 – World Programme of Action Concerning Disabled Persons. Adopted by the General Assembly at its 37th session GA Res. 37/52, UN Doc. A/RES/37/52, GAOR, 37th session (1982). The UN incorporated the lessons from the International Year of Disabled Persons into the World Programme of Action. Beyond prevention and rehabilitation, it stressed "equalization of opportunities."[3] It linked national legislation, as part of member states' human rights efforts, to ensuring equal opportunities. This linkage expressed the growing view that the task of the disability rights agenda was to develop ways to put people with disabilities on an equal footing, rather than find them isolated but protected social niches.

- 1983 – International Labor Organisation (ILO) Convention No. 159, Vocational Rehabilitation and Employment (Disabled Persons) Convention entered into force June 20, 1983. Int'l Labour Office, C159 Vocational Rehabilitation and Employment (Disabled Persons) Convention, 1983 (No. 159), http://www.ilo.org/dyn/normlex/en/f?p=NORMLEXP UB:12100:0::NO:12100:P12100_INSTRUMENT_ID:3 12304:NO (last visited Nov. 26, 2013). Here, the signatories agreed to provide equal vocational rehabilitation opportunities to people with and without disabilities. The convention evinces the

---

[3] The UN Department of Economic and Social Affairs explains:

'Equalization of opportunities' is a central theme of the WPA and its guiding philosophy for the achievement of full participation of persons with disabilities in all aspects of social and economic life. An important principle underlying this theme is that issues concerning persons with disabilities should not be treated in isolation, but within the context of normal community services.

Dep't of Econ. & Soc. Affairs, United Nations, World Programme of Action Concerning Disabled Persons, http://www.un.org/esa/socdev/enable/ diswpa00. htm (last visited Nov. 26, 2013).

duality in disability rights: strict equality may be ineffective. "The said policy shall be based on the principle of equal opportunity between disabled workers and workers generally. Equality of opportunity and treatment for disabled men and women workers shall be respected. Special positive measures aimed at effective equality of opportunity and treatment between disabled workers and other workers shall not be regarded as discriminating against other workers." *Id.* at art. 14.

- 1983-1992 – UN Decade of Disabled Persons. Adopted at the 90th plenary meeting, 3 Dec. 1982, GA Res. 37/53, UN Doc. A/RES/37/53 (1982). The UN proclaimed a decade of disabled persons, which began a significant effort directed to a range of projects to implement the World Programme of Action.

- 1984 – The UN Sub-Commission on Prevention of Discrimination and Protection of Minorities[4] appointed a Special Rapporteur, Leandro Despouy, to conduct a comprehensive study on the relationship between human rights and disability. *See* Leandro Despouy, Human Rights and Disabled Persons, Human Rights Study Series No. 6, *available at* http://www.un.org/esa/socdev/enable/dis paperdes0.htm (last visited Nov. 26, 2013).

- 1987 – UN rejected a proposed Convention on the Elimination of All Forms of Discrimination Against Disabled Persons. *See generally* Theresia Degener, Disabled Persons and Human Rights: The Legal Framework, in Human Rights and Disabled Persons 12 (Theresia Degener & Yolan Koster-Dreese, eds. 1995).

- 1989 – Convention on the Rights of the Child. G.A. Res. 44/25, annex, 44 U.N. GAOR Supp. (No. 49) at 167, U.N. Doc. A/44/49 (1989), http://www.un.org/ documents/ga/res/44/a44r025.htm (last visited Nov. 26, 2013), entered into force 2 September 1990. This was the first time, albeit in a limited context, the UN tried to put into law programs necessary to achieve equality. Art. 23(1) reads:

---

[4]   Sub-Commission on Prevention of Discrimination and Protection of Minorities resolution 1984/20.

States Parties recognize that a mentally or physically disabled child should enjoy a full and decent life, in conditions which ensure dignity, promote self-reliance and facilitate the child's active participation in the community.

Article 23(3) requires that assistance provided to children with disabilities:

shall be designed to ensure that the disabled child has effective access to and receives education, training, health care services, rehabilitation services, preparation for employment and recreation opportunities in a manner conducive to the child's achieving the fullest possible social integration and individual development, including his or her cultural and spiritual development.

The problem is that the Convention does not commit the parties to provide any assistance.

- 1989 – Tallinn Guidelines for Action on Human Resources Development in the Field of Disability. Adopted by the General Assembly in its 78th plenary meeting, 8 Dec. 1989, G.A. Res. 44/70, UN Doc. A/RES/44/70 (1989), http://www.un.org/documents/ga/res/44/a44r070.htm (last visited Nov. 26, 2013). These urged governments to adopt certain measures to promote the full participation of people with disabilities in society. Among other things, Article 11 recommended that information be provided in formats, such as Braille, that gave people with disabilities access to it, and Article 12 recommended that governments "adopt, enforce and fund" access standards for buildings and transportation.

- 1991 – General Assembly adopted the Principles for the Protection of Persons with Mental Illness and for the Improvement of Mental Health Care. Adopted by the General Assembly at the 75th plenary meeting, 46th session, 17 Dec. 1991, G.A. Res. 46/119 and Annex: Principles for the Protection of Persons with Mental Illness and for the Improvement of Mental Health Care U.N. Doc. A/RES/46/119 (1991), http://www.un.org/documents/ga/res/46/a46r119.htm (last visited Nov. 26, 2013). These principles are a broad set of rights for people with mental illnesses or disabilities, including, *inter alia*, rights to treatment, civil and political rights, the right to live in the community and the right to confidentiality. Like the other resolutions, this is non-binding, but the General Assembly here recognized a panoply of civil rights, which, if they attain the status of customary international law, would bind states.

With the foregoing as prologue, in 1994, the United Nations adopted the Standard Rules on the Equalization of Opportunities for Persons with Disabilities. Adopted by the General Assembly at the 85th plenary meeting, 48th session, 20 Dec. 1993, GA Res. 48/96, annex, UN Doc. A/RES/48/96 (1993) [hereinafter "Standard Rules"], http://www.un. org/esa/socdev/enable/dissre00.htm (last visited Nov. 26, 2013). While explicitly recognizing that they are not "compulsory, they can become international customary rules when they are applied by a great number of States with the intention of respecting a rule in international law." The Rules address the "preconditions," such as consciousness raising and rehabilitation services, the "target areas" in which equality must be established (accessibility, both to the physical environment and information, education, employment, income maintenance and social security, family life and personal integrity, culture, recreation and sports, and religion), and a range of "implementation measures," such as legislation, "policy and planning," "work coordination" and "technical and economic cooperation."

One of the more interesting things the Rules do is create a monitoring mechanism, much as other UN human rights treaties have monitors. The monitoring, under the direction of a Special Rapporteur, who was appointed in March 1994, *see* Despouy, *supra*, at 8, was designed to "assist each State in assessing its level of implementation of the Rules and in "measuring its progress" under them. Standard Rules, *supra*, at IV. As part of that effort, the Special Rapporteur surveys states, UN organizations and NGOs.

The Special Rapporteur's original three-year mandate has now been extended several times, and he or she has produced multiple periodic reports on whether states follow the individual rules. *See* Special Rapporteur on Disability of the Commission for Social Development (collecting reports), http://www.un.org/disabilities/default.asp?id=183(last visited Nov. 26, 2013).

In addition, the World Health Organization (WHO) has conducted a survey of three of the Rules that relate to health issues. World Health Organization, Monitoring of United Nations Standard Rules on the Equalization of Opportunities for Persons with Disabilities: Government Responses to the Implementation of the Rules on Medical Care, Rehabilitation, Support Services and Personnel Training: Summary, vol. I (WHO/DAR/01.1) (2001) and Main Report, vol. II (WHO/DAR/01.2) (2001), *available at* http://www.who.int/disabilities/policies/monitoring/en/ (last visited Nov. 26, 2013).[5] In the Special Rapporteur's Third Report, he proposed a Supplement to the Standard Rules to focus on specific problems of the most disadvantaged people with disabilities. Report of the Special Rapporteur-Third, *supra*, at Annex: Reaching the most vulnerable; proposed supplement to the Standard Rules on the Equalization of Opportunities for Persons with Disabilities.

§ 38.2   Convention On The Rights Of Persons With Disabilities

A. *Background*

The notion of a convention was raised as early as the mid 1980's. NGOs promoted the idea. In 1998, the United Nations convened the Consultative Expert Group and Meeting on International Norms and Standards Relating to Disability, which discussed a new international convention. *See* Dep't of Econ. & Soc. Affairs, United Nations, Enable: Report of the U.N. Consultative Expert Group Meeting on International Norms and Standards Relating to Disability (2003-2004), http://www.un.org/esa/socdev/enable/disberk0.htm (last visited Nov. 26, 2013). The report of the Expert Group Meeting recognized the arguments for and against a convention, including the possibility that by establishing a separate convention, disability issues would become marginalized from mainstream human rights issues. Nonetheless, momentum toward a convention continued.

The Government of Mexico promoted such a convention as a major policy initiative at the United Nations. Through its efforts, the Program of Action adopted by the World Conference against Racism, Racial Discrimination, Xenophobia and Related Intolerance included a paragraph inviting the "United Nations General Assembly to consider elaborating an integral and comprehensive international convention to protect and promote the rights and dignity of disabled people." World Conference Against Racism, Racial Discrimination, Xenophobia and Related Intolerance, Durban, South Africa, 31 August-8 September 2001, UN Doc. A/CONF. 189/12, Chapter 1, ¶ 180, *available at* http://www.un.org/WCAR/durban.pdf (last visited Nov. 26, 2013).

---

[5]   WHO also broke its work into various regional reports, addressing the nations of Africa, North and South America, the Middle East, South Pacific, Asia and Southeast Asia. World Health Organization, Monitoring of United Nations Standard Rules on the Equalization of Opportunities for Persons with Disabilities (2001-02), http://www.who.int/disabilities/policies/monitoring/en/ (last visited Nov. 26, 2013)); *see also* Dimitris Michailakis, Government Action on Disability Policy: A Global Survey (1997), *available at* http://www.independentliving.org/standardrules/UN_Answers/UN.pdf, which assembles the data from the first surveys.

Largely as a result of these efforts, at the end of 2001, the General Assembly adopted a resolution creating an Ad Hoc Committee to consider proposals for a Convention "based on the holistic approach in the work done in the fields of social development, human rights and non-discrimination." Adopted by the General Assembly 19 December 2001 GA Res. 56/168, UN Doc. A/RES/56/168 (2001), *available at* http://www.un.org/esa/socdev/enable/disA56168e1.htm (last visited Nov. 26, 2013). It also called for states to hold regional conferences on such a proposal.

In 2002, the Ad Hoc Committee met in New York. *See* Ad Hoc Comm., United Nations, Enable, Meeting of the Ad Hoc Committee 29 July-9 August 2002 United Nations, New York (on file with authors). The Report also called for Regional Meetings; the American regional meeting took place in Quito in April 2003 and other regional meetings were scheduled for Johannesburg in early May 2003, Beirut in late May 2003 and Bangkok in June 2003. Links to those meetings can be found at Ad Hoc Comm., United Nations, Enable, Regional and Interregional Workshops and Seminars Organized in Relation to the Proposed Convention (2003-2004), http://www.un.org/esa/socdev/enable/rights/adhoc regional.htm (last visited Nov. 26, 2013).

The second session of the Ad Hoc Committee took place mid June 2003 at the United Nations Headquarters in New York. *See* Report of the Ad Hoc Committee on a Comprehensive and Integral International Convention on Protection and Promotion of the Rights and Dignity of Persons with Disabilities, U.N. Doc. A/58/118, 3 July 2003, http://www.un.org/esa/socdev/enable/rights/a_58_118_e.htm (last visited Nov. 26, 2013). In 2004, the Ad Hoc Committee met twice, in June and in August. *See* Ad Hoc Comm., United Nations, Ad Hoc Committee Documents (2003-2004), http://www.un.org/esa/socdev/enable/rights/adhoc docs.htm (last visited Nov. 26, 2013).

B. *The Convention*

On December 13, 2006, the UN General Assembly adopted by consensus the draft Convention on the Rights of Persons with Disabilities (CRPD) and the Optional Protocol. *See generally*, *available at* http://www.un.org/disabilities/documents/convention/convoptprot-e.pdf. The CRPD and the Optional Protocol were opened for signature on March 30, 2007 and entered into force for the parties that had ratified it on May 3, 2008, thirty days after the 20th state had ratified it. The United States signed the CRPD in July 2009, but has not ratified it. As of April 2012, 112 states had ratified the CRPD and 67 had ratified the Optional Protocol.

The CRPD not only sets forth a range of rights for people with disabilities, it also establishes an organizational structure at the United Nations to implement the CRPD. The Optional Protocol provides a mechanism by with individuals or groups may file complaints asserting violations of the CRPD with the United Nations Committee on the Rights of Persons with Disabilities.

In the following, we will discuss several provisions of the CRPD. At this point, there is little law on its implementation, although many states have laws or judicial decisions that may conform to various provisions of the CRPD. The CRPD begins with a 25 paragraph preamble that refers to the United Nations Charter, the Universal Declaration of Human Rights and the prior international human rights documents, such as the International Covenant on Economic, Social and Cultural Rights and the International Covenant on Civil and Political Rights. It also recognizes the importance of "principals and policy guidelines contained in the World Programme of Action Concerning Disabled Persons and on the Standard Rules on the Equalization of Opportunities for Persons with Disabilities." Most significantly, perhaps, it recognizes that

> Disability is an evolving concept and that disability results from the interaction between persons with impairments and attitudinal and environmental barriers that hinders [sic] their full and effective participation in society on an equal basis with others.

CRPD, preamble, ¶ 6. That, of course, is perhaps the central practical insight or mantra of the disability rights movement – that disability is an interaction between a person with an impairment and the physical world and society into which the person must fit.

In keeping with that, it recognizes the "importance of accessibility to the physical, social, economic and cultural environment, to health and education and to information and communication, in enabling persons with disabilities to fully enjoy all human rights and fundamental freedoms." *Id.*, ¶ 22. The preamble then touches on a range of aspects of disability discrimination, including the multiple forms of discrimination a person with a disability who is a woman, or someone who would be otherwise subject to racial, language, religious, or political discrimination might suffer in addition to disability discrimination. *Id.*, ¶ 16-18. From these starting points, the CRPD purports to impose a broad range of obligations on ratifying states.

The convention begins, after an article on purpose, with a set of definitions. Significantly, "disability" is, famously,[6] not defined. "Discrimination on the basis of disability" is, on the other hand, defined quite broadly. It is "any distinction, exclusion or restriction on the basis of disability which has the purpose or effect of impairing or nullifying the recognition, enjoyment or exercise, on an equal basis with others, of all human rights and fundamental freedoms in the political, economic, social, cultural, civil or any other field." Presumably, "all human rights and fundamental freedoms" are defined sufficiently broadly so that nothing of

---

[6]   E.g., Anna Lawson, The United Nations Convention on the Rights of Persons with Disabilities: New Era or False Dawn, 34 Syr. J. Int'l L. & Com. 563, 593-95 (2007),.

significance that a person would want or need to do is omitted. In theory, that approach, coupled with the general obligations, set forth in Article 4, which include an undertaking "to adopt all appropriate legislative, administrative and other measures for the implementation of the rights recognized in the present Convention" and to "take all appropriate measures, including legislation to modify or abolish existing laws, regulations . . . against persons with disabilities" has a broader reach than, for example, the ADA. The latter limits its scope to its four sections, employment, public services, public accommodation by private entities and telecommunications. However, one might ask whether the practical reach of the two regimes substantially differ, putting aside the slightly restricted definition of an employer (15 or more employees for 20 weeks of the year) and other similar restrictions.

The drafters of the CRPD intended, to some extent, that it particularize rights in preceding conventions to people with disabilities. The substantive provisions of the CRPD run from article 9 to article 30.[7] Of those articles, some are unique to disability. For example, article 9 on accessibility and article 13 on access to justice deal with issues that the more general documents do not reach. Most sections, however, echo either the first generation rights of the International Covenant on Civil and Political Rights or the second generation rights of the International Covenant on Economic, Social and Cultural Rights. Articles 10, 12, 14, 15, 18, 21, 22 and 23 address rights recognized in the ICCPR. Articles 16, 24-25, 27-28 and 30 reflect the ICESCR. In each of those cases, the CRPD tailors its language to the particular context of disability.

Article 6.1 of the ICCPR reads: "Every human being has the inherent right to life. This right shall be protected by law. No one shall be arbitrarily deprived of his life." Article 10 of the CRPD reads:

> States Parties reaffirm that every human being has the
> inherent right to life and shall take all necessary measures
> to ensure its effective enjoyment by persons with
> disabilities on an equal basis with others.

Thus, article 10 of the CRPD requires affirmative steps, not contemplated by the ICCPR, to ensure that people with disabilities "effectiv[ely] enjoy" the right to life. But what does that mean? It could entail huge expenditures by the state. Is that what the drafters intended? Does it require states to provide medical care to people independent of their "quality of life?" Does it preclude euthanasia? What effect does it have on the "when-life-begins" debate? For a detailed discussion of these issues in Australia, *see* Phillip French & Rosemary Kayess, Deadly Currents Beneath Calm Waters: Persons with Disability and the Right to Life in Australia, University of New South Wales Faculty of Law Research Series,

---

[7] For discussions of the individual articles, *see* Lawson, *supra* note 6.

Paper 34 (2008). http://law.bepress.com/cgi/viewcontent.cgi? article=1109 &context=unswwps-flrps08.

French and Kayess demonstrate the ambivalence that attends central legal issues relating to disability. They describe two criminal cases in which parents murdered their severely disabled children and the courts essentially treated the trauma caused the parent by the child's disability as a mitigating factor. *Id.* at 17-24. As French and Kayess write:

> Both at first instance and on appeal, the courts appear to focus on Jason's victim characteristics not as matters aggravating the seriousness of the offence, even though the relevant provisions are formally adverted to, but as matters mitigating its seriousness. Neither court does so in any explicit way, but their detailed interrogation of Jason's impairment and disability-related characteristics and behaviour, and the impact of this on Ms Dawes, her husband and daughter, can lead to no other conclusion.

Id. at 20 (footnotes omitted). While, this case predated the CRPD, it illustrates underlying attitudinal barriers to article 10's efficacy.

In a similar way, Article 14 of the CRPD simply makes clear that an existing right applies to persons with disabilities. That Article reads:

> 1. States Parties shall ensure that persons with disabilities, on an equal basis with others:
>   1. Enjoy the right to liberty and security of person;
>   2. Are not deprived of their liberty unlawfully or arbitrarily, and that any deprivation of liberty is in conformity with the law, and that the existence of a disability shall in no case justify a deprivation of liberty.

That language differs slightly from the analogous Article 9.1 of the ICCPR:

> Everyone has the right to liberty and security of person. No one shall be subjected to arbitrary arrest or detention. No one shall be deprived of his liberty except on such grounds and in accordance with such procedure as are established by law.

The situation addressed here is that in which people with mental disabilities are forced to live in group homes or are prevented from living in the community.

Some provisions of the CRPD, however, expand on prior recognition of rights in ways particular to the disabilities community. Thus, Article 16 of the ICCPR states, "Everyone shall have the right to recognition everywhere as a person before the law." That is the entirety of the Article. Article 12 of the CRPD begins in paragraph 1, "States Parties reaffirm that persons with disabilities have the right to recognition everywhere as persons before the law." However, in the remaining paragraphs of Article 12, the CRPD goes on to deal in detail with the capacity issue, a major issue in the drafting of the CRPD. Amita Dhanda, Legal Capacity in the Disability Rights Convention: Stranglehold of the Past or Lodestar for the Future? 34 Syr. J. of Int'l L. & Com. 429 (2007). Thus, the CRPD goes beyond prior recognitions of rights in order to address particular disability issues.

Perhaps because they address more specifically areas in which people with disabilities need assistance, the provisions that nominally echo the ICESCR do not display a similar pattern. Those rights require that states take measures to meet the specific needs of people with disabilities to exercise rights guaranteed by the ICESCR.

As an example, article 6 of the ICESCR deals with the right to work:

> 1.   The States Parties to the present Covenant recognize the right to work, which includes the right of everyone to the opportunity to gain his living by work which he freely chooses or accepts, and will take appropriate steps to safeguard this right.
>
> 2.   The steps to be taken by a State Party to the present Covenant to achieve the full realization of this right shall include technical and vocational guidance and training programmes, policies and techniques to achieve steady economic, social and cultural development and full and productive employment under conditions safeguarding fundamental political and economic freedoms to the individual.

The drafters of the CRPD understood that more detail was necessary to give life to a right to work for people with disabilities. They prepared an article on work that codifies a range of steps needed to make the work environment hospitable to those people. Article 27 on education requires, inter alia:

> 1. ... States Parties shall safeguard and promote the realization of the right to work, including for those who acquire a disability during the course of employment, by taking appropriate steps, including through legislation, to, inter alia:
>
> a) Prohibit discrimination on the basis of disability with regard to all matters concerning all forms of employment, including conditions of recruitment, hiring and employment, continuance of employment, career advancement and safe and healthy working conditions;

b) Protect the rights of persons with disabilities, on an equal basis with others, to just and favourable conditions of work, including equal opportunities and equal remuneration for work of equal value, safe and healthy working conditions, including protection from harassment, and the redress of grievances; . . .

d) Enable persons with disabilities to have effective access to general technical and vocational guidance programmes, placement services and vocational and continuing training; . . .

f) Promote opportunities for self-employment, entrepreneurship, the development of cooperatives and starting one's own business;

g) Employ persons with disabilities in the public sector;

h) Promote the employment of persons with disabilities in the private sector through appropriate policies and measures, which may include affirmative action programmes, incentives and other measures;

i) Ensure that reasonable accommodation is provided to persons with disabilities in the workplace;

j) Promote the acquisition by persons with disabilities of work experience in the open labour market;

k) Promote vocational and professional rehabilitation, job retention and return-to-work programmes for persons with disabilities. . . .

Of particular significance is paragraph 2: "States Parties shall ensure that persons with disabilities are not held in slavery or in servitude, and are protected, on an equal basis with others, from forced or compulsory labour." A comparison between the provisions of the ICESCR and the CRPD dealing with education (article 13 and article 24, respectively) evince a similar pattern. The latter contains the following:

2. . . . c) Reasonable accommodation of the individual's requirements is provided;

d) Persons with disabilities receive the support required, within the general education system, to facilitate their effective education;

e) Effective individualized support measures are provided in environments that maximize academic and social development, consistent with the goal of full inclusion.

3. . . . a) Facilitating the learning of Braille, alternative script, augmentative and alternative modes, means and formats of communication and orientation and mobility skills, and facilitating peer support and mentoring;

b) Facilitating the learning of sign language and the promotion of the linguistic identity of the deaf community;

c) Ensuring that the education of persons, and in particular children, who are blind, deaf or deafblind, is delivered in the most appropriate languages and modes and means of communication for the individual, and in environments which maximize academic and social development.

4. In order to help ensure the realization of this right, States Parties shall take appropriate measures to employ teachers, including teachers with disabilities, who are qualified in sign language and/or Braille, and to train professionals and staff who work at all levels of education. . . .

This trend continues through other articles of the CRPD – setting ambitious, but ill-defined, goals for parties to implement legislatively. The key question, of course, is how well they will do. As pointed out above, states will need to take significant steps to meet the CRPD's requirements. *See* French & Kayess, *supra*; Sandor Gurbai, Case Study from Hungary – Systematic Revision of Legislation in Contradiction. The EU has assembled a High Level Group on Disability, which has issued four reports to date. *See* Fourth Disability High Level Group Report on the Implementation of the UN Convention on the Rights of Persons With Disabilities (May 2011), *available at* http://ec.europa.eu/justice/ discrimination/files/dhlg_4th_report_en.pdf. The reports show that most EU states still have a substantial distance to go before full compliance.

While the United States has not yet ratified the CRPD, the National Council on Disability, a United States government agency, has analyzed the conformity of United States legislation with the Convention. NCD, Finding the Gaps: A Comparative Analysis of Disability Laws in the United States to the United Nations Convention on the Rights of Persons with Disabilities (CRPD) (May 12, 2008), *available at* http://www.ncd.gov/rawmedia_repository/bbae6ede_8719_48b8_b40f_3393 8b9a2189?document.pdf. The Executive Summary of the NCD analysis concluded:

The paper finds that, as a general matter, the aims of the CRPD are consistent with U.S. disability law. For the majority of articles, U.S. law can be viewed as either being of a level with the mandates of the Convention or capable of reaching those levels either through more rigorous implementation and/or additional actions by Congress. However, this paper also identifies several CRPD Articles that illustrate significant gaps between United States disability laws and the Convention (p. 1).

The three thrusts of the CRPD, specific disability provisions and provisions that build on the ICCPR and the ICESCR, are, in a sense, unified. That is, to ensure that the roles of people with disabilities in society are maximized, the negative rights must be melded with the positive ones. That is the essence of the right to development:

> The right to development is an inalienable human right by virtue of which every human person and all peoples are entitled to participate in and contribute to and enjoy economic, social, cultural, and political development in which all human rights and fundamental freedoms can be fully realized.

Declaration on the Right to Development, General Assembly Resolution 4/128, art. 1 (Dec. 4, 1986), http://www.unhchr.ch/html/menu3/b/74.htm. *See generally* Arjun Sengupta, The Right to Development as a Human Right (2000). *See also* Stein, *supra*, at 95 n. 103 (citing Anne Orford, Globalization and the Right to Development, in People's Rights 127 (Philip Alston ed., 2001); Philip Alston, Making Space for New Human Rights: The Case of the Right to Development, 1 Harv. Hum. Rts. Y.B. 3 (1988); James C. N. Paul, The Human Right to Development: Its Meaning and Importance, 25 J. Marshall L. Rev. 235 (1992); Henry J. Steiner, Social Rights and Economic Development: Converging Discourses?, 4 Buff. Hum. Rts. L. Rev. 25 (1998).

Acknowledgement of the question whether negative rights may be achieved without positive rights poses the next question – whether one is serious about the former unless one admits a conjunction of them – a right to development. Although this might be seen as the core question for one in the United States, which has a system based mainly on negative rights, arguably the theoretical question has been answered in the ADA. That statute requires reasonable accommodations, an obvious foray into the second generation. That step implies that, if one is serious about making certain that people with disabilities are to benefit from legislation removing barriers, the legislation must remove not only the paper ones, but the concrete ones as well. The only remaining question is how far one is willing to dedicate social resources.[8]

---

[8]   Professor Stein argues that the logic that justifies the right to development for people with disabilities extends to other disadvantaged groups. Stein, *supra*, at 113-120.

C. *Impact*

Any attempt to evaluate the impact of the CRPD since it went into effect in 2008 must be highly preliminary. The self-reporting process required by the CRPD provides some insight into how states have begun responding to the Convention.[9] For a general discussion *see* Michael A. Stein & Janet E. Lord, Monitoring the Committee on the Rights of Persons with Disabilities: Innovations, Lost Opportunities, and Future Potential' 31 Human Rights Q. 689 (2010); *see also* National Council on Disability, Towards the Full Inclusion of People with Disabilities: Examining the Accessibility of Overseas Facilities and Programs (2013), http://www. ncd.gov/rawmedia_repository/91eefd87_5f67_49cb_9c5e_e8fb86ccf5a4?doc ument.pdf. Article 35 requires each state party to submit a "comprehensive report" to the Committee on the Rights of Persons with Disabilities describing measures taken to implement the Convention and the status of compliance. The initial report is to be submitted within two years after the state becomes a party to the Convention, with subsequent reports to be provided at least once every four years. *Id.* The Committee considers the reports and provides recommendations or requests further information as appropriate. Art. 36. Members of civil society, such as NGOs, are also permitted to submit parallel reports or otherwise contribute information to the review process. *See* Working Methods of the Committee on the Rights of Persons with Disabilities Adopted at its Fifth Session (11-15 April 2011) ¶¶ 41-53, *available at* http://www.ohchr.org/ Documents/HRBodies/CRPD/CRPD-C-5-4_en.doc.

To date about 25 states parties have submitted their initial reports, which are collected at Committee on the Rights of Persons with Disabilities – Sessions, http://www.ohchr.org/EN/HRBodies/CRPD/Pages/ Sessions.aspx (last visited Apr. 22, 2012). The Committee has considered about five of these reports. *See id.*

The Committee's consideration of Spain's report will provide an illustration of the review process. Spain submitted its initial report on May 3, 2010. *See* Initial reports submitted by States parties in accordance with article 35 of the Convention – Spain (May 3, 2010) [hereinafter "Spain's Initial Report"], *available at* http://www2.ohchr.org/SPdocs/ CRPD/5thsession/CRPD.C.ESP.1_en.doc . The report is broken into three primary components. The first describes the status of Spain's compliance with the general provisions of the Convention (articles 1 to 4), such as the extent to which national legislation defines key concepts consistent with the Convention. The last component describes Spain's compliance with

---

[9] The parties to the Convention also meet annually at a Conference of States Parties to discuss implementation challenges and best practices. *See* Art. 40. Agendas, background papers, and reports from each conference are collected at http://www.un.org/disabilities/default.asp? id=1535 (last visited Nov. 26, 2013).

the specific obligations to collect data, cooperate internationally, and promote and monitor implementation nationally (articles 31 to 33).

The middle section, constituting the bulk of the report, describes Spain's efforts to implement each specific right enumerated in articles 5 through 30. Here, for example, is an excerpt addressing the affirmative action measures Spain has taken to promote the employment of persons with disabilities:

> 180. The general legislation on training, employment and engagement is applicable to the specific group consisting of workers with disabilities. Consequently these workers may enter into contracts of any of the types regulated by Spanish law.
>
> 181. The law also establishes reserved quotas whereby small and medium-sized public and private enterprises employing 50 or more workers are required to ensure that workers with disabilities make up at least 2 per cent of their workforce. Exemptions from this obligation are permitted in exceptional circumstances or where alternative arrangements are in place, such as the conclusion of a commercial or civil contract with a special employment centre or a self-employed worker with a disability, or the creation of a labour enclave established to promote sheltered employment for persons with disabilities and facilitate their transition to ordinary employment.
>
> 182. Incentives are also provided to any enterprise or associated cooperative engaging workers with disabilities equal to or exceeding 33 per cent.
>
> 183. Contracts may be of indeterminate or temporary duration, full-time or part-time. The incentives offered include subsidies for indeterminate contracts in the form of a lump sum of €3,900 for each indeterminate contract concluded, social security contribution rebates of amounts fixed in the annual employment promotion plan and varying between €3,500 and €6,300 according to the type of contract (indeterminate or temporary), the degree of disability and the sex of the worker, grants of up to €900 for job adaptation, subsidies for the training of disabled workers and company tax rebates.

184. Enterprises offering induction training contracts for workers with disabilities (either formal or on-the-job training, full-time or part-time) are entitled to a 50 per cent reduction of employer social security contributions for the entire period of the contract in addition to the subsidy of up to €900 for job adaptation.

Id.

At its April 2011 session, the Committee submitted a list of 38 questions to Spain. With respect to employment matters, for example, the Committee made the following requests:

27. Please provide data on the level and type of employment and average income of men and women with disabilities in open employment in comparison with other workers over the past three years.

28. Please provide information on the unemployment rate of men and women with disabilities. Please also provide data on the numbers of persons with disabilities working in sheltered employment and labour enclaves as compared to the open labour market.

List of issues to be taken up in connection with the consideration of the initial report of Spain (CRPD/C/ESP/1), concerning articles 1 to 33 of the Convention on the Rights of Persons with Disabilities, *available at* http://www2.ohchr.org/SPdocs/CRPD/5thsession/CRPD.C.ESP.Q.1_en.doc (last visited Apr. 29, 2012). Spain submitted its 35-page reply several months later.[10]

An umbrella organization called the Comitê Español de Representantes de Personas con Discapacidad (CERMI) submitted a parallel report. *See* CERMI, Human Rights and Disability: Alternative Report Spain 2010, *available at* http://www2.ohchr.org/SPdocs/CRPD/5th session/CERMI_Spain_5thSession_en.doc [hereinafter "CERMI Report"]. CERMI, which comprises about 5,500 constituent associations representing about 4 million persons with disabilities, was appointed by the Spain government to serve as the independent monitoring body required by Article 33 of the CRPD. *See id.* at ¶ 4. Addressing the employment quota described above, the CERMI Report notes that little actual progress has been made in raising awareness of this quota and requiring compliance by employers. *See id.* at ¶ 131. The CERMI Report also identifies gaps on the ground overlooked in Spain's Initial Report, such as the fact that the jobs to which many persons with disabilities have access offer low salaries. *See id.* at ¶ 124.

---

[10] An advance, unedited version of Spain's reply is available. *See* Respuestas de España. (July 4, 2011) (in Spanish), http://www2.ohchr. org/SPdocs/CRPD/6thsession/CRPD.C.ESP.Q.1.Add.1_sp.doc.

The Committee issued its concluding observations to Spain at the September 2011 session. *See* Concluding Observations of the Committee on the Rights of Persons with Disabilities, Sixth Session – Spain (Oct. 19, 2011), *available at* http://www.ohchr.org/Documents/HRBodies/CRPD/6th session/CRPD.C.ESP.CO.1_en.doc. The concluding observations include both "positive aspects," in which the Committee commends Spain for successful steps taken, and "principal areas of concern and recommendations." As to the latter, it is unclear whether the Committee's recommendations are sufficiently specific to be effective. For example, the Committee stated only the following regarding Spain's efforts in employment:

> 45. Despite a number of enabling provisions to keep persons with disabilities in employment, the Committee is concerned with the overall low rate of employment of persons with disabilities.
>
> 46. The Committee recommends that the State party develop open and advanced programmes to increase employment opportunities for women and men with disabilities.

Id. Thus, while the mere act of reporting and engaging with the Committee is likely to have some effect on states' practices, it remains to be seen whether the Committee will undertake a more robust role in fostering compliance.

Apart from the self-reporting process, some independent assessments of the Convention's impact have been undertaken. The most comprehensive such study is Michael Fembek et al., Zero Project Report 2012: International Study on the Implementation of the UN Convention on the Rights of Persons with Disabilities (Nov. 2011), *available at* http://www.zeroproject.org/wp-content/uploads/2011/11/Zero-Project-Report-2012.pdf. The report compiles survey data on 36 states based on 21 social indicators, such as accessibility of new buildings, workplace accommodations, and access to voting. The report also highlights good practices and policies. For example, the report describes how Austria's use of peer-counseling education takes advantage of the fact that persons with disabilities are themselves the most effective trainers for others in similar circumstances, and they can serve as key role models. *Id.* at 116. For a good policy example, the United Kingdom's Equality Act 2010, which consolidated 116 separate pieces of legislation, is described as "the most comprehensive and detailed anti-discrimination legislation in Europe." *Id.* at 158.

The CRPD was widely seen as an important milestone in the advancement of the rights model over the welfare model, and the inclusive manner in which it was drafted gave many optimism that it would achieve positive results on the ground. *See* Rosemary Kayess & Phillip French, Out of Darkness Into Light? Introducing the Convention on the Rights of

Persons With Disabilities, 8 Hum. Rts. L. Rev. 1, 3-4 (2008) (describing the CRPD negotiations as "reputed to have involved the highest level of participation by representatives of civil society, overwhelmingly that of persons with disability and disabled persons organisations, of any human rights convention in history"). Resource constraints and entrenched attitudes will ensure that progress is gradual, but the initial accounts suggest that the Convention is starting to have an impact.